AF753415

FREELANDER

WORKSHOP MANUAL

This manual covers all vehicles from
1998-2000 MY

The following overhaul manuals can be found at the back of this publication.

LRL 0157 'L' Series Engine
LRL 0158 'K' Series Engine
LRL 0159 PG1 Manual Gearbox

Publication Part No. LRL 0144ENG (5thEdition)

INTRODUCTION
GENERAL INFORMATION
INFORMATION

MAINTENANCE

ENGINE - 'K' SERIES
ENGINE - 'L' SERIES

EMISSION CONTROL
ENGINE MANAGEMENT SYSTEM:
- MEMS
- EDC
FUEL DELIVERY SYSTEM

COOLING SYSTEM - 'K' SERIES
COOLING SYSTEM - 'L' SERIES

MANIFOLD & EXHAUST SYSTEMS

CLUTCH

MANUAL GEARBOX - 'PG1'
TRANSFER BOX - 'IRD'

DRIVE SHAFTS
REAR AXLE AND FINAL DRIVE

STEERING

FRONT SUSPENSION
REAR SUSPENSION

BRAKES

RESTRAINT SYSTEMS
BODY

HEATING & VENTILATION
AIR CONDITIONING

WIPERS & WASHERS
ELECTRICAL
INSTRUMENTS

This Workshop Manual covers all Freelander models from 1998
up to the end of the 2000 model year.
Engines covered include the 'K' Series 1.8 petrol
and the 'L' Series 2.0 diesel.

The following Overhaul Manuals have been included at the
back of this book for easy reference.

LRL 0157 - 'L' Series Diesel Engine
LRL 0158 - 'K' Series Petrol Engine
LRL 0159 - PG1 Manual Gearbox

CONTENTS

Page

INTRODUCTION

INTRODUCTION

How to use this Manual

For ease of use, this Manual is structured to display the section title at the top of each page and the relevant sub-section at the bottom of each page. In addition, a section icon is displayed at the top outer corner of right-hand pages.

Each major section is preceded by a contents page, which lists titles of the topics and procedures contained in the relevant sub-sections.

Technical data is subject to change; to facilitate the periodic revision of technical information, each sub-section is numbered from page 1 so that revised sub-sections can be replaced if required.

Repair operations are to be performed in the sequence and manner described. Item numbers annotated in the illustration are referred to in the accompanying text.

Adjustment and repair operations may include reference to service tool numbers and the associated illustration depicts the tool. Where usage is not obvious the tool is shown in use. Adjustment and repair operations also include reference to wear limits, relevant data, torque figures, specialist information and useful assembly details. Each adjustment or repair operation is given its Scheduled Repair Operation number.

WARNINGS, CAUTIONS and **NOTES** have the following meanings:

WARNING: Procedures which must be followed precisely to avoid the possibility of injury.

CAUTION: Calls attention to procedures which must be followed to avoid damage to components.

NOTE: Gives helpful information.

References

References to the LH or RH side given in this Manual are made when viewing the vehicle from the normal driving position. With the engine and gearbox assembly removed, the crankshaft pulley end of the engine is referred to as the front.

Operations covered in this Manual do not include instructions for testing the vehicle after repair. It is essential that work is inspected and tested after completion and if necessary a road test of the vehicle should be conducted.

WARNING: It is particularly important to test a vehicle after repairs to safety related items have been performed.

Dimensions

The dimensions quoted are to design engineering specification with service limits where applicable.

Electrical Reference Library (ERL) and Circuit Diagrams

The Electrical Reference Library (ERL) and Circuit Diagrams are separate publications intended for use by trained Land Rover technicians and should be referred to when attempting to diagnose electrically related concerns.

The ERL contains descriptions of how the circuits operate, fuse details, earth point locations, and a definitive guide to the attributes and location of every connector on the vehicle.

The ERL is used in conjunction with the Circuit Diagrams. Both publications are designed to support all aspects of electrical fault diagnosis.

TESTBOOK (Fault Diagnostic Equipment)

Freelander is equipped with a number of electronic control systems to provide the optimum performance of the vehicle's systems.

Diagnostic equipment (TESTBOOK) is available to assist with the fault diagnostic abilities of the dealer workshop. This repair manual is produced as a reference source to supplement Testbook. When available, Testbook should be used as the primary means of fault diagnosis on electronically controlled systems.

Features of Testbook include :-

- Fully upgradable support for the technician.
- Structured diagnostics to accommodate all skill levels.
- Touch screen operation.
- Direct print out of screen information and test results.

J5408M

REPAIRS AND REPLACEMENTS

When replacement parts are required it is essential that only Land Rover recommended parts are used.

The following points concerning repairs and the fitting of replacement parts and accessories is emphasised:

- Safety features and corrosion prevention treatments embodied in the vehicle may be impaired if other than Land Rover recommended parts are fitted.
- In certain territories, legislation prohibits the fitting of parts which are not compliant with the manufacturer's specification.
- Torque figures shown in this Manual should be used where specified.
- Locking devices (circlips, split pins etc.) must be fitted where specified.
- If a locking device is damaged during removal, or its efficiency is impaired, it must be renewed.
- Owners purchasing accessories while travelling abroad should ensure that the accessory and its installation or application conform to the legal requirements of the territory.
- The Terms of the vehicle Warranty may be invalidated by the fitting of other than Land Rover recommended parts.
- All Land Rover recommended parts are covered under the terms of the vehicle Warranty.
- Land Rover Dealers are obliged to supply only Land Rover recommended parts.

SPECIFICATION

Land Rover are constantly seeking to improve the specification, design and production of their vehicles and alterations take place accordingly. While every effort has been made to ensure the accuracy of this Manual, it should not be regarded as an infallible guide to current specifications of any particular vehicle.

This Manual does not constitute an offer for sale of any particular vehicle. Land Rover Dealers are not agents of Land Rover and have no authority to bind the manufacturer by any expressed or implied undertaking or representation.

ABBREVIATIONS AND SYMBOLS

ABDC	After Bottom Dead Centre
ATDC	After Top Dead Centre
A/C	Air conditioning
AFR	Air Fuel Ratio
ac	Alternating current
A	Amperes
ABS	Anti-lock Brake System
BBDC	Before Bottom Dead Centre
BBUS	Battery Backed-Up Sounder
BCU	Body Control Unit
BDC	Bottom Dead Centre
BTDC	Before Top Dead Centre
BS	British Standards
CO	Carbon monoxide
CAT	Catalytic converter
C	Celsius (Centigrade)
cm	Centimetre
CCU	Central Control Unit
CDL	Central Door Locking
CFCs	Chlorofluorocarbons
CHMSL	Centre High Mounted Stop Lamp
CKP	Crankshaft Position
cm^3	Cubic centimetres
deg. or °	Degree (angle)
deg. or °	Degree (temperature)
DCU	Diagnostic Control Unit
DTI	Dial Test Indicator
dia.	Diameter
dc	Direct current
DOHC	Double Overhead Camshaft
ECM	Engine Control Module
ECT	Engine Coolant Temperature
ECU	Electronic Control Unit
EDC	Electronic Diesel Control
EGR	Exhaust Gas Recirculation
EKA	Emergency Key Access
ELR	Emergency Locking Retractor
EMS	Engine Management System
ETC	Electronic Traction Control
ETM	Electrical Troubleshooting Manual
FIP	Fuel Injection Pump
g	Gramme (mass)
HRW	Heated rear window
HO2S	Heated oxygen sensor
Hz	Hertz
hc	High compression
h.t.	High tension
HDC	Hill Descent Control
h	Hour
in.	Inches
IACV	Idle air control valve
IAT	Intake air temperature
IFS	Independent Front Suspension
IRD	Intermediate Reduction Drive
i.dia.	Internal diameter
ISO	International Organisation for Standardization
km	kilometre
km/h	kilometres per hour
kg	kilogramme
kPa	kilo Pascal
LH	Left-hand
LHD	Left-hand drive
LED	Light emitting diode
l	Litre
lc	Low Compression
MAP	Manifold Absolute Pressure
MAF	Mass Air Flow
MEMS	Modular Engine Management System
MIL	Malfunction Indicator Lamp
Hg	Mercury
m	Metre
mph	Miles per hour
mm	Millimetre
min	Minimum
-	Minus (of tolerance)
'	Minute (angle)
MY	Model Year
MFU	Multi-function unit
MPi	Multi-point injection
(-)	Negative (electrical)
Nm	Newton metre
No.	Number
o.dia.	Outside diameter

%	Percentage
±	Plus or minus
+	Plus (tolerance)
+	Positive (electrical)
PCV	Positive crankcase ventilation
psi	pounds/square inch
PTC	Positive temperature coefficient
PAS	Power assisted steering
PCRV	Pressure Conscious Reducing Valve
RF	Radio Frequency
r	Radius
:	Ratio
ref	Reference
rev	Revolution
rev/min	Revolutions per minute
RH	Right-hand
RHD	Right-hand drive
RES	Rover Engineering Standards
"	Second (angle)
SOHC	Single overhead camshaft
sp.gr	Specific gravity
cm^2	Square centimetres
std.	Standard
SRS	Supplementary Restraint System
synchro	Synchronizer/synchromesh
k	Thousand
TDC	Top dead centre
TP	Throttle position
UK	United Kingdom
US	United States
VIN	Vehicle identification number
V	Volt
VSS	Vehicle speed sensor
W	Watt

CONTENTS

GENERAL PRECAUTIONS

Dangerous substances

WARNING: Many liquids and other substances used in motor vehicles are poisonous and should not be consumed under any circumstances.

As far as possible, try to prevent skin contact with any potentially harmful materials.
Substances to be treated with particular caution include (but is not limited to): acid, anti-freeze, asbestos, brake fluid, fuel, windscreen washer additives, lubricants, refrigerant and various adhesives.

Always read the instructions printed on labels or stamped on components carefully.
Such instructions should be strictly complied with; they are included to ensure your health and personal safety is not compromised through the incorrect use of the materials to which they relate.

Synthetic rubber

WARNING: Many 'O' rings, seals, hoses, flexible pipes and other similar items which appear to be natural rubber, are in fact, made of synthetic materials called Fluoroelastomers.
Under normal operating conditions this material is safe and does not present a health hazard. However, if the material is damaged by fire or excessive heating, it can break down and produce highly corrosive Hydrofluoric acid which can cause serious burns on contact with skin.

If skin contact does occur:
- Remove any contaminated clothing immediately.
- Irrigate effected area of skin with a copious amount of cold water or limewater for 15 to 60 minutes.
- Obtain medical assistance immediately

Should any material be in a burnt or over-heated condition, handle with extreme caution and wear protective clothing (seamless industrial gloves, protective apron etc.).
Decontaminate and dispose of gloves immediately after use.

Engine oils

WARNING: Prolonged and repeated contact with mineral oil can result in the removal of natural fats from the skin; this may cause dryness, irritation and dermatitis.

In particular, used engine oil contains potentially harmful carcinogenic contaminants. Adequate means of skin protection (barrier creams etc.) and washing facilities must be provided.

Avoid excessive skin contact with used engine oils and always adhere to the following health protection recommendations:

Health Protection Precautions

- **Avoid prolonged and repeated contact with oils, particularly used engine oils.**
- **Wear protective clothing, including impervious gloves where practicable.**
- **Do not put oily rags in pockets.**
- **Avoid contaminating clothes (particularly underpants) with oil.**
- **Overalls must be cleaned regularly. Discard heavily soiled clothing and oil impregnated footwear.**
- **First aid treatment should be obtained immediately for open cuts and wounds.**
- **Use barrier creams: apply before each work period to help removal of engine oil from the skin.**
- **Wash with soap and water to ensure all oil is removed (propriety skin cleansers and nail brushes will help).**
- **Use moisturisers after cleaning; preparations containing lanolin help replace the skin's natural oils which have been removed.**
- **Do not use petrol, kerosene, diesel fuel, gas, oil, thinners or solvents for cleaning skin.**
- **If skin disorders develop, obtain medical advice without delay.**
- **Where practicable, degrease components prior to handling.**
- **Wear eye protection (e.g. goggles or face shield) if there is a risk of eye contamination. Eye wash facilities should be provided in the close vicinity of the work area.**

Environmental Protection Precautions

It is illegal to pour used oil on to the ground, down sewers or drains, or into water courses.

Burning of used engine oil in small space heaters or boilers should only be considered for units of approved design and in compliance with the equipment manufacturer's recommendations. The heating system must meet the regulatory standards of HMIP for small burners of less than 0.4 MW. If in doubt check with the appropriate local authority and/or manufacturer of the approved appliance.

Dispose of used oil and filters through authorised waste disposal contractors and licensed waste disposal sites, or through the waste oil reclamation trade. If in doubt, contact the Local Authority for advice on disposal facilities.

Precautions against damage

CAUTION: Always fit wing and seat covers before commencing work. Avoid spilling brake fluid or battery acid on paintwork; immediately wash off with water if this occurs.

CAUTION: Disconnect the battery earth lead before starting work, see ELECTRICAL PRECAUTIONS.

CAUTION: Always use the recommended service tool or a satisfactory equivalent where specified.

CAUTION: Protect exposed bearing surfaces, sealing surfaces and screw threads from damage.

SAFETY INSTRUCTIONS

Whenever possible, use a lift or pit when working beneath vehicle, in preference to jacking. Chock wheels as well as applying parking brake.

Jacking

The recommended jacking points are shown in the **LIFTING AND TOWING** sub-section of the INFORMATION section.
Always ensure that any lifting apparatus has sufficient load capacity for the weight to be lifted.

Ensure the vehicle is standing on level ground prior to lifting or jacking.

Apply the handbrake and chock the wheels.

WARNING: Never rely on a jack as the sole means of support when working beneath the vehicle. Use additional safety supports beneath the vehicle.

Do not leave tools, lifting equipment, spilt oil, etc., around or on the work bench area. Always keep a clean and tidy work area.

Brake shoes and pads

WARNING: Always fit the correct grade and specification of brake linings. When renewing brake pads and brake shoes always replace as complete axle sets only.

Brake hydraulics

WARNING: It is imperative that the correct brake fittings are used and that threads of components are compatible.

- Always use two spanners when loosening or tightening brake pipe or hose connections.
- Ensure that hoses run in a natural curve and are not kinked or twisted.
- Fit brake pipes securely in their retaining clips and ensure that the pipe run cannot contact a potential chafing point.
- Containers used for hydraulic fluid must be kept absolutely clean.
- Do not store hydraulic fluid in an unsealed container, it will absorb water and in this condition would be dangerous to use due to a lowering of its boiling point.
- Do not allow hydraulic fluid to be contaminated with mineral oil, or use a container which has previously contained mineral oil.
- Do not re-use fluid from the system.
- Always use clean brake fluid or a recommended alternative to clean hydraulic components.
- Fit a blanking cap to an hydraulic union and a plug to its socket after removal to prevent the ingress of dirt.

CAUTION: Absolute cleanliness must be observed with hydraulic components.

Engine coolant caps and plugs

WARNING: Extreme care is necessary when removing engine coolant caps and plugs when the engine is hot and especially if it is overheated. To avoid the possibility of scalding allow the engine to cool before attempting coolant cap or plug removal.

GENERAL FITTING INSTRUCTIONS

Component removal

Whenever possible, clean components and surrounding area before removal.

- Blank off openings exposed by component removal.
- Immediately seal fuel, oil or hydraulic lines when apertures are exposed; use plastic caps or plugs to prevent loss of fluid and ingress of dirt.
- Close open ends of oilways exposed by component removal with tapered hardwood plugs or conspicuous plastic plugs.
- Immediately a component is removed, place it in a suitable container; use a separate container for each component and its associated parts.
- Clean bench and provide marking materials, labels, containers and locking wire before dismantling a component.

Dismantling

Observe scrupulous cleanliness when dismantling components, particularly when brake, fuel or hydraulic system parts are being worked on.

CAUTION: A particle of dirt or a cloth fragment could cause a serious malfunction if trapped in these systems.

- Blow out all tapped holes, crevices, oilways and fluid passages with an air line. Ensure that any O-rings used for sealing are correctly replaced or renewed, if disturbed during the process.
- Use marking ink to identify mating parts and ensure correct reassembly. Do not use a centre punch or scriber to mark parts, they could initiate cracks or distortion in marked components.
- Wire together mating parts where necessary to prevent accidental interchange (e.g. roller bearing components).
- Wire labels on to all parts which are to be renewed, and to parts requiring further inspection before being passed for reassembly; place these parts in separate containers from those containing parts for rebuild.
- Do not discard a part due for renewal until after comparing it with a new part, to ensure that its correct replacement has been obtained.

Cleaning components

Always use the recommended cleaning agent or equivalent.

WARNING: Ensure that adequate ventilation is provided when volatile degreasing agents are being used.

CAUTION: Do not use degreasing equipment for components containing items which could be damaged by the use of this process.

General Inspection

- Never inspect a component for wear or dimensional check unless it is absolutely clean; a slight smear of grease can conceal an incipient failure.
- When a component is to be checked dimensionally against recommended values, use the appropriate measuring equipment (surface plates, micrometers, dial guages etc.). Ensure the measuring equipment is calibrated and in good serviceable condition.
- Reject a component if its dimensions are outside the specified tolerances, or if it appears to be damaged. A part may be refitted if its critcal dimension is exactly to its tolerance limit and it appers to be in satisfactory condition.
- Use 'Plastigauge' 12 Type PG-1 for checking bearing surface clearances.

WARNING: When washing under bonnet, never direct water onto ECM as water ingress may occur resulting in damage to electrical components inside.

BALL AND ROLLER BEARINGS

⚠ **CAUTION: Never refit a ball or roller bearing without first ensuring that it is in a fully serviceable condition.**

⚠ **CAUTION: When hub bearings are removed or displaced, NEW bearings must be fitted; do not attempt to refit the old hub bearings.**

- Remove all traces of lubricant from bearing under inspection by cleaning with a suitable degreaser; maintain absolute cleanliness throughout operations.
- Conduct a visual inspection for markings on rolling elements, raceways, outer surface of outer rings or inner surface of inner rings. Reject any bearings found to be marked, since marking in these areas indicates onset of wear.
- Hold inner race of bearing between finger and thumb of one hand and spin outer race to check that it revolves absolutely smoothly. Repeat, holding outer race and spinning inner race.
- Rotate outer ring gently with a reciprocating motion, while holding inner ring; feel for any check or obstruction to rotation. Reject bearing if action is not perfectly smooth.
- Lubricate bearing with generous amounts of lubricant appropriate to installation.
- Inspect shaft and bearing housing for discoloration or other markings which indicate movement between bearing and seatings.
- Ensure that shaft and housing are clean and free from burrs before fitting bearing.
- If one bearing of a pair shows an imperfection, it is advisable to replace both with new bearings; an exception could be if the faulty bearing had covered a low mileage, and it can be established that damage is confined to only one bearing.

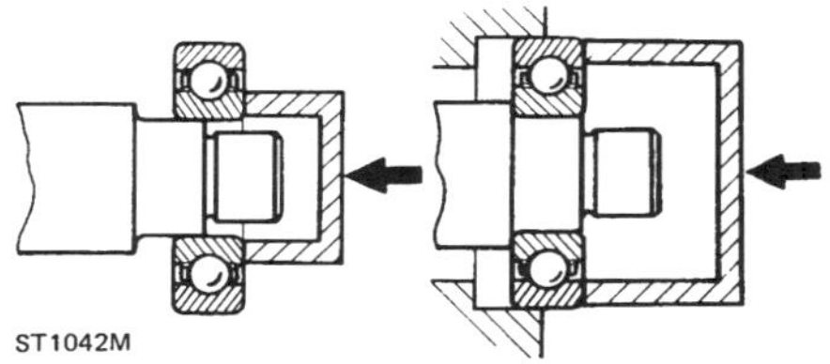

ST1042M

- When fitting a bearing to a shaft, only apply force to the inner ring of the bearing. When fitting a bearing into a housing, only apply force to the outer ring of the bearing.
- In the case of grease lubricated bearings (e.g. hub bearings) fill the space between bearing and outer seal with the recommended grade of grease before fitting seal.
- Always mark components of separable bearings (e.g. taper roller bearings) when dismantling, to ensure correct reassembly. Never fit new rollers in a used outer ring; always fit a complete new bearing assembly.

OIL SEALS

Always renew oil seals which have been removed from their working location (whether as an individual component or as part of an assembly).

- Carefully examine seal before fitting to ensure that it is clean and undamaged.
- Ensure the surface on which the new seal is to run is free of burrs or scratches. Renew the component if the original sealing surface cannot be completely restored.
- Protect the seal from any surface which it has to pass when being fitted. Use a protective sleeve or tape to cover the relevant surface.
- Certain oil seals are coated with a protective wax and must be fitted dry unless stated otherwise. Where an oil seal needs to be lubricated prior to fitment, lubricate the sealing lips with a recommended lubricant before use to prevent damage during initial use. On dual lipped seals, smear the area between the lips with grease.
- If a seal spring is provided, ensure that it is fitted correctly.
- Place lip of seal towards fluid to be sealed and slide into position on shaft. Use fitting sleeve where possible to protect sealing lip from damage by sharp corners, threads or splines. If a fitting sleeve is not available, use plastic tube or tape to prevent damage to the sealing lip.

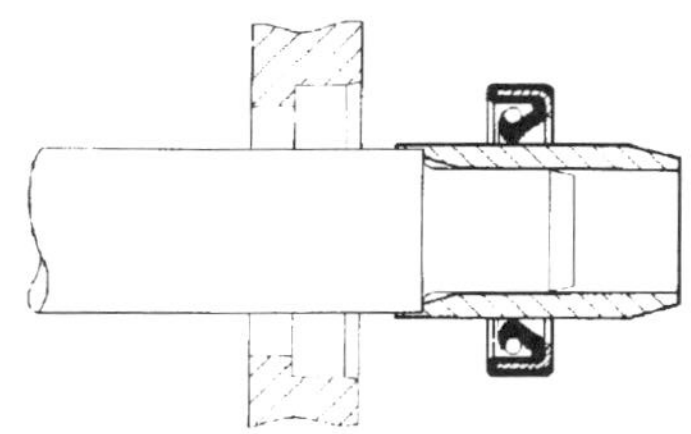

1M0072

- Grease outside diameter of seal, place square to housing recess and press into position using great care, and if possible a 'bell piece' to ensure that seal is not tilted. Never let weight of unsupported shaft rest in seal.

△ NOTE: In some cases it may be preferable to fit seal to housing before fitting to shaft.

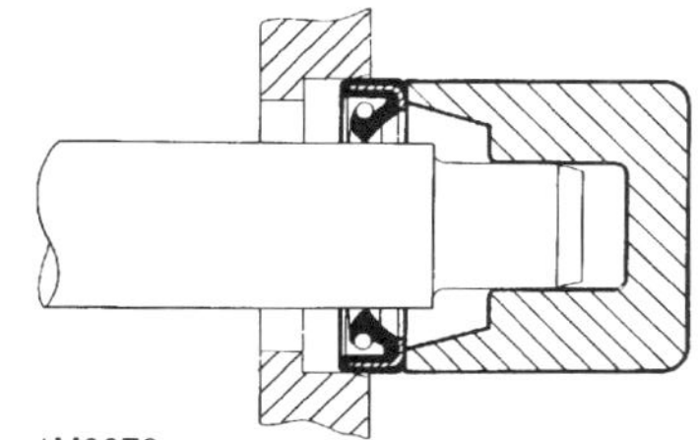

1M0073

- Use the recommended service tool to fit an oil seal. If the correct service tool is not available, use a suitable tube approximately 0.4 mm (0.015 in.) smaller than the outside diameter of the seal. Use an hammer **VERY GENTLY** on drift if a suitable press is not available.
- Press or drift the seal in to the depth of its housing with the sealing lip facing the lubricant to be retained if the housing is shouldered, or flush with the face of the housing where no shoulder is provided. Ensure that the seal does not enter the housing in a tilted position.

△ NOTE: Most cases of failure or leakage of oil seals are due to poor fitting, which can result in damage to both seals and sealing surfaces. NEVER use a seal which has been improperly stored or handled, such as hung on a hook or nail.

JOINTS AND JOINT FACES

Fit joints dry unless specified otherwise.

- Always use the correct gaskets as specified.
- When jointing compound is used, apply in a thin uniform film to metal surfaces; take care to prevent jointing compound from entering oilways, pipes or blind tapped holes.
- If gaskets and/or jointing compound is recommended for use; remove all traces of old jointing material prior to reassembly. Do not use a tool which will damage the joint faces and smooth out any scratches or burrs using an oil stone. Do not allow dirt or jointing material to enter any tapped holes or enclosed parts.
- Prior to reassembly, blow through any pipes, channels or crevices with compressed air.

LOCKING DEVICES

Tab Washers

CAUTION: Always release locking tabs and fit new locking washers, do not re-use locking tabs. Ensure the new tab washer is the same design as that replaced.

Locking Nuts

Always use a backing spanner when slackening or tightening brake and fuel pipe unions.

Roll Pins

Always fit new roll pins of an interference fit in the hole.

Circlips

Always fit new circlips of the correct size for the groove.

Locking wire

Always fit locking wire of the correct type. Arrange wire so that its tension tends to tighten the bolt heads or nuts to which it is fitted.

Keys and Keyways

- Remove burrs from edges of keyways with a fine file and clean thoroughly before attempting to refit key.
- Clean and inspect key closely; keys are suitable for refitting only if indistinguishable from new, as any indentation may indicate the onset of wear.

Fitting a split pin

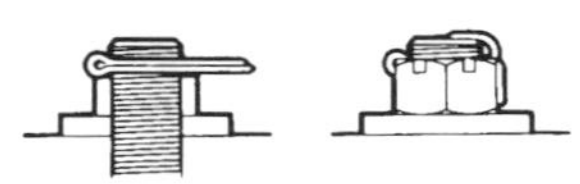

1M0057

CAUTION: Always fit new split-pins of the correct size for the hole in the bolt or stud. Do not slacken nut to enter split-pin.

SCREW THREADS

Metric threads to ISO standards are used.

Damaged nuts, bolts and screws must always be discarded.

NOTE: Cleaning damaged threads with a die or tap impairs the strength and closeness of fit of the threads and is not recommended.

CAUTION: Always ensure that replacement bolts are at least equal in strength to those replaced.

Castellated nuts must not be slackened to accept a split-pin, except in recommended cases when this forms part of an adjustment.

Do not allow oil or grease to enter blind threaded holes. The hydraulic action on screwing in the bolt or stud could split the housing.

Always tighten a nut or bolt to the recommended torque figure. Damaged or corroded threads can affect the torque reading.

To check or re-tighten a bolt or screw to a specified torque figure, first slacken a quarter of a turn, then retighten to the correct torque figure.

Oil thread lightly before tightening to ensure a free running thread, except in the case of threads treated with sealant / lubricant, and self-locking nuts.

BOLT IDENTIFICATION

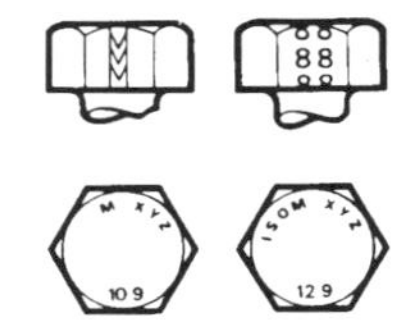

1M0055

An ISO metric bolt or screw made of steel and larger than 6 mm in diameter can be identified by either of the symbols ISO M or M embossed or indented on top of the bolt head.

In addition to marks identifying the manufacturer, the top of the bolt head is also marked with symbols indicating the strength grade, e.g. 8.8; 10.9; 12.9; 14.9. As an alternative, some bolts and screws have the M and strength grade symbol stamped on the flats of the hexagon.

Encapsulated bolts and screws

1M0062

Encapsulated bolts and screws have a micro-encapsulated locking agent pre-applied to the thread. They are identified by a coloured section which extends 360° around the thread. The locking agent is released and activated by the assembly process and is then chemically cured to provide the locking action.

Unless a specific repair procedure states otherwise, encapsulated bolts may be re-used providing the threads are undamaged and the following procedure is adopted:

- Remove loose adhesive from the bolt and housing threads.
- Ensure threads are clean and free of oil and grease.
- Apply an approved locking agent.

NOTE: Always fit a new encapsulated bolt when replacing; or if not available, a bolt of equivalent specification treated with an approved locking agent.

Self-locking bolts and screws

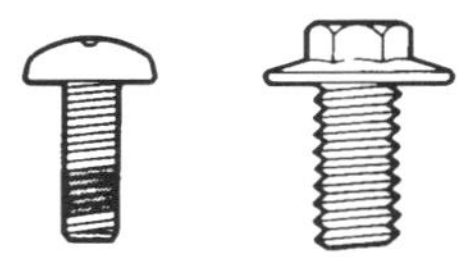

1M0059

Self-locking bolts and screws, i.e. nylon patched or trilobular thread can be re-used providing resistance can be felt when the locking portion enters the female thread.

Nylon patched bolts and screws have a locking agent pre-applied to the threads. They are identified by the presence of a coloured section of thread which extends for up to 180° around the thread.

Trilobular bolts (i.e. Powerlok) have a special thread form which creates a slight interference in the tapped hole or threads of the nut into which it is screwed.

CAUTION: DO NOT re-use self-locking fasteners in critical locations (e.g. engine bearings, flywheel). Always use the correct replacement self-locking nut, bolt or screw.

CAUTION: DO NOT fit non self-locking fasteners in applications where a self-locking nut, bolt or screw is specified.

NUT IDENTIFICATION

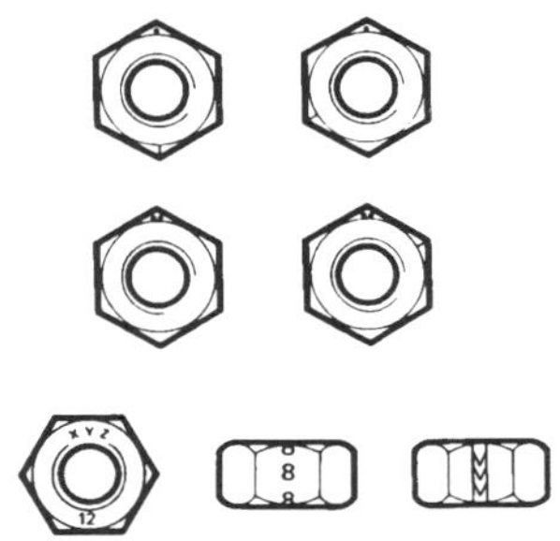

1M0056

A nut with an ISO metric thread is marked on one face or on one of the flats of the hexagon with the strength grade symbol 8, 12, or 14. Some nuts with a strength grade 4, 5 or 6 are also marked and some have the metric symbol M on the flat opposite the strength grade marking.

A clock face system is sometimes used as an alternative method of indicating the strength grade. The external chamfers or a face of the nut is marked in a position relative to the appropriate hour mark on a clock face to indicate the strength grade.

A dot is used to locate the 12 o'clock position and a dash to indicate the strength grade. If the grade is above 12, two dots identify the 12 o'clock position.

Self-locking nuts

1M0058

Self-locking nuts, i.e. nylon insert or deferred thread nuts can be re-used providing resistance can be felt when the locking portion of the nut passes over the thread of the bolt or stud.

CAUTION: Do not apply heat in an attempt to free deferred thread nuts or fittings; as well as causing damage to protective coatings, there is a risk of damage to electronic equipment and brake linings from stray heat.

When tightening a slotted or castellated nut, never loosen it to insert a split pin or locking wire except where recommended as part of an adjustment. If difficulty is experienced, alternative washers or nuts should be selected, or the washer thickness reduced.

Where self-locking nuts have been removed, it is advisable to replace them with new ones of the same type.

NOTE: Where bearing pre-load is involved nuts should be tightened in accordance with special instructions.

FLEXIBLE HYDRAULIC PIPES AND HOSES

WARNING: Do not disconnect any pipes in an air conditioning refrigeration system unless trained and instructed to do so. A refrigerant is used which can cause blindness if allowed to contact eyes.

- Before removing any brake or power steering hose, clean end fittings and area surrounding them as thoroughly as possible.
- Obtain appropriate plugs or caps before detaching hose end fittings, so that the ports can be immediately covered to prevent the ingress of dirt.
- Clean hose externally and blow through with airline. Examine carefully for cracks, separation of plies, security of end fittings and external damage. Reject any faulty hoses.
- When refitting a hose, ensure that no unnecessary bends are introduced, and that hose is not twisted before or during tightening of union nuts.
- Fit a cap to seal a hydraulic union and a plug to its socket after removal to prevent ingress of dirt.
- Absolute cleanliness must be observed with hydraulic components at all times.
- After any work on hydraulic systems, carefully inspect for leaks underneath the vehicle while a second operator applies maximum brake pressure to the brakes (engine running) and operates the steering.

Fuel System Hoses

CAUTION: All fuel hoses are made up of two laminations, an armoured rubber outer sleeve and an inner viton core. If any of the fuel system hoses have been disconnected, it is imperative that the internal bore is inspected to ensure that the viton lining has not become separated from the armoured outer sleeve. A new hose must be fitted if separation is evident.

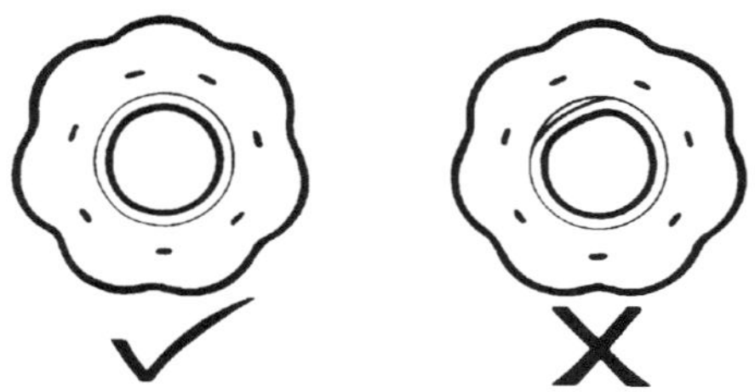

RR2302M

COOLING SYSTEM HOSES

CAUTION: The following precautions MUST be followed to ensure that integrity of cooling hoses and their connections to system components are maintained.

Hose orientation and connection

1. Correct orientation of cooling hoses is important in ensuring that the hose does not become fatigued or damaged through contact with adjacent components.
2. Where 'timing' marks are provided on the hose and corresponding connection, these must be used to ensure correct orientation.
3. Hoses must be pushed fully onto their connection points. Usually, a moulded form on the stub pipe provides a positive indicator.

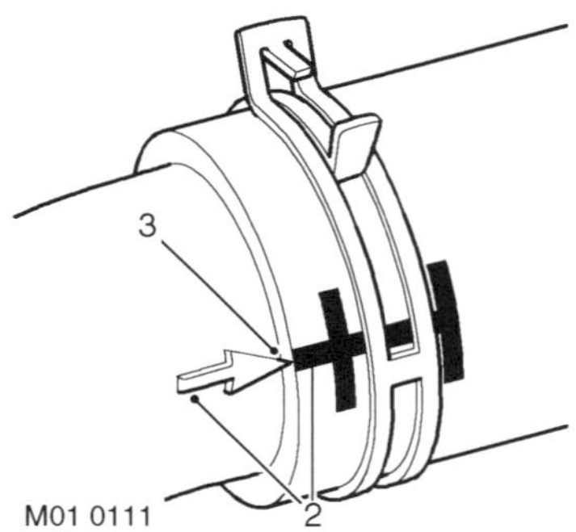

M01 0111

Hose clips

1. Markings are usually provided on the hose to indicate the the correct clip position. If no markings are provided, position the clip directly behind the retaining lip at the end of the stub as shown.
2. Worm drive clips should be oriented with the crimped side of the drive housing facing towards the end of the hose, or the hose may become pinched between the clip and the stub pipe retaining lip.

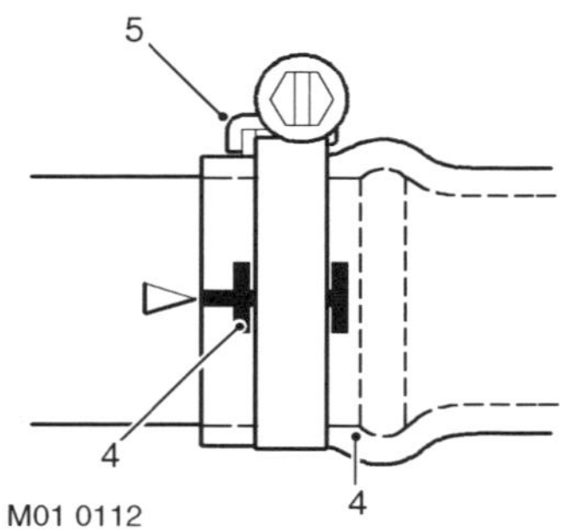

M01 0112

3. Worm drive clips should be tightened to 3Nm (2 lbf.ft) unless otherwise stated.

CAUTION: Ensure that hose clips do not foul adjacent components.

Heat protection

1. Always ensure that heatshields and protective sheathing are in good condition. Replace if damage is evident.
2. Particular care must be taken when routing hoses close to hot engine components, such as the exhaust manifold and the Exhaust Gas Recirculation (EGR) pipe.

CAUTION: Hoses will relax and deflect slightly when hot; ensure this movement is taken into account when routing and securing hoses.

SERVICE TOOLS AND GARAGE EQUIPMENT

Special service tools have been developed to facilitate removal, dismantling and assembly of mechanical components in a cost effective and time efficient manner. The use of such special tools also helps prevent the potential for damage to components.
Some operations described in this Manual cannot be carried out properly without the aid of the relevant service tools.

Where specific garage equipment is required for diagnosis and repair, reference should be made to the Service Tools and Equipment Programme where details of the equipment recommended by Land Rover Service may be found.

DYNAMOMETER TESTING - NON ANTI-LOCK BRAKE VEHICLES

The front and rear wheels cannot be driven independently due to the viscous coupling. This eliminates the need for differential lock by progressively applying more torque to the rear wheels if the front wheels start to slip.

WARNING: DO NOT attempt to drive individual wheels with vehicle supported on floor jacks or stands.

Four wheel dynamometers

Provided that front and rear dynamometer rollers are rotating at identical speeds and that normal workshop safety standards are applied, there is no speed restriction during testing, except any that may apply to the tyres.

Two wheel dynamometers

IMPORTANT: Use a four wheel dynamometer for brake testing if possible.

If brake testing on a single rig is necessary, the following procedures should be ensured:

- propeller shaft to the rear axle is removed
- neutral selected in gearbox
- hill descent control not selected.

When checking brakes, run engine at idle speed to maintain servo vacuum.

DYNAMOMETER TESTING - VEHICLES WITH ANTI-LOCK BRAKES (ABS)

WARNING: Do not attempt to test ABS function on a dynamometer

Four wheel dynamometers

NOTE: Before testing a vehicle on a four wheel dynamometer disconnect the ABS valve relay. The ABS function will not work, the ABS warning light will illuminate. Normal braking will be available.

Provided that front and rear rollers are rotating at identical speeds and that normal workshop safety standards are applied, there is no speed restriction during testing except any that may apply to the tyres.

Two wheel dynamometers

IMPORTANT: Use a four wheel dynamometer for brake testing if possible.

NOTE: ABS will not function on a two wheel dynamometer. The ABS light will illuminate during testing. Normal braking will be available.

If brake testing on a single rig is necessary, the following procedures should be ensured:

- propeller shaft to the rear axle is removed
- neutral selected in gearbox
- hill descent control not selected

If checking engine performance, ensure hill descent control is not selected and drive shaft to rear differential is disconnected.

FUEL HANDLING PRECAUTIONS

General

The following information provides basic precautions which must be observed if petrol (gasoline) is to be handled safely. It also outlines other areas of risk which must not be ignored. This information is issued for basic guidance only, if in doubt consult your local Fire Officer.

Petrol - Gasoline

Petrol/gasoline vapour is highly flammable and in confined spaces is also explosive and toxic.

When petrol/gasoline evaporates it produces 150 times its own volume in vapour, which when diluted with air becomes a readily ignitable mixture. The vapour is heavier than air and will always fall to the lowest level. The vapour can be easily distributed throughout a workshop by air currents; consequently, even a small spillage of petrol/gasoline is potentially very dangerous.

WARNING: Do not use a pit when removing fuel system components.

Always have a fire extinguisher containing FOAM, CO_2, GAS or POWDER close at hand when handling or draining fuel or when dismantling fuel systems. Fire extinguishers should also be located in areas where fuel containers are stored.

Always disconnect the vehicle battery before carrying out dismantling or draining work on a fuel system.

Whenever petrol/gasoline is being handled, drained or stored, or when fuel systems are being dismantled, all forms of ignition must be extinguished or removed; any leadlamps must be flameproof and kept clear of spillage.

WARNING: No one should be permitted to repair components associated with petrol/gasoline without first having specialist training.

Fuel tank drainage

WARNING: Petrol/gasoline must not be extracted or drained from any vehicle whilst it is standing over a pit.
Draining or extraction of petrol/gasoline from a vehicle fuel tank must be carried out in a well ventilated area.
The receptacle used to contain the petrol/gasoline must be more than adequate for the full amount of fuel to be extracted or drained. The receptacle should be clearly marked with its contents, and placed in a safe storage area which meets the requirements of local authority regulations.

WARNING: When petrol/gasoline has been extracted or drained from a fuel tank the precautions governing naked lights and ignition sources should be maintained.

Fuel tank removal

When the fuel line is secured to the fuel tank outlet by a spring steel clip, the clip must be released before the fuel line is disconnected or the fuel tank is removed. This procedure will avoid the possibility of residual petrol fumes in the fuel tank being ignited when the clip is released.

As an added precaution fuel tanks should have a 'PETROL (GASOLINE) VAPOUR' warning label attached to them as soon as they are removed from the vehicle.

Fuel tank repairs

Under no circumstances should a repair to any fuel tank be carried out without first rendering the tank SAFE, by using one of the following methods:

a. STEAMING: With the filler cap and tank unit removed, empty the tank. Steam the tank for at least two hours with low pressure steam. Position the tank so that condensation can drain away freely, ensuring that any sediment and sludge not volatized by the steam is washed out during the steaming process.

b. BOILING: With the filler cap and tank unit removed, empty the tank. Immerse the tank completely in boiling water containing an effective alkaline degreasing agent or a detergent, with the water filling and also surrounding, the tank for at least two hours.

After steaming or boiling, a signed and dated label to this effect should be attached to the tank.

Body repairs

WARNING: When body repairs involve the use of heat, all fuel pipes which run in the vicinity of the repair area must be removed, and the tank outlet plugged, BEFORE HEAT IS APPLIED. If the repair is in the vicinity of the fuel tank, the tank must be removed.

Plastic fuel pipes are particularly susceptible to heat, even at relatively low temperature, and can be melted by heat conducted from some distance away.

Fuel lines or tanks must not be removed whilst the vehicle is over an inspection pit.

ELECTRICAL PRECAUTIONS

General

The following guidelines are intended to ensure the safety of the operator whilst preventing damage to the electrical and electronic components fitted to the vehicle. Where necessary, specific precautions are detailed in the relevant sections of this Manual which should be referred to prior to commencing repair operations.

Equipment

Prior to commencing any test procedure on the vehicle ensure that the relevant test equipment is working correctly and any harness or connectors are in good condition. It is particularly important to ensure the propriety of the lead and plugs of mains operated equipment.

Polarity

Never reverse connect the vehicle battery and always ensure the correct polarity when connecting test equipment.

High Voltage Circuits

Whenever disconnecting live ht-circuits always use insulated pliers and never allow the open end of the ht-lead to contact other components - particularly ECU's.

CAUTION: Exercise caution when measuring the voltage on the coil terminals while the engine is running, high voltage spikes can occur on these terminals.

Connectors and Harnesses

The engine compartment of a vehicle is a particularly hostile environment for electrical components and connectors. Always ensure electrically related items are dry and oil free before disconnecting and connecting test equipment.

CAUTION: Ensure disconnected multiplugs and sensors are protected from being contaminated with oil, coolant or other solutions. Contamination could impair performance or result in catastrophic failure.

Never force connectors apart using tools to prise apart or by pulling on the wiring harness.

Always ensure locking tabs are disengaged before disconnection, and match orientation to enable correct reconnection.

Ensure that any protection (covers, insulation etc.) is replaced if disturbed.

Having confirmed a component to be faulty:

- switch off the ignition and disconnect the battery.
- remove the component and support the disconnected harness.
- when replacing the component keep oily hands away from electrical connection areas and push connectors home until any locking tabs fully engage.

Battery disconnection

Before disconnecting the battery, disable the alarm system and switch off all electrical equipment. If the radio is to be serviced, ensure the security code has been deactivated.

CAUTION: To prevent damage to electrical components ALWAYS disconnect the battery when working on the vehicle electrical system. The earth lead must be disconnected first and reconnected last. Always ensure that battery leads are routed correctly and are not close to any potential chafing points.

Battery charging

Only recharge the battery with it removed from the vehicle.

Always ensure any battery charging area is well ventilated and that every precaution is taken to avoid naked flames and sparks.

Ignition system safety precautions

WARNING: Before commencing work on an ignition system, all high tension terminals, adapters and diagnostic equipment should be inspected.

Ensure all cables, connectors and components are adequately insulated and shielded. Accidental contact with a poorly insulated ignition system component could result in a severe electrical shock.

Wearers of surgically implanted pacemaker devices should not be in close proximity to ignition circuits or diagnostic equipment.

Disciplines

Switch off the ignition prior to making any connection or disconnection in the system to prevent electrical surges caused by disconnecting 'live' connections damaging electronic components.

Ensure hands and work surfaces are clean and free of grease, swarf, etc. Grease collects dirt which can cause electrical tracking (short-circuits) or high-resistance contacts.

When handling printed circuit boards, treat with care and hold by the edges only; note that some electronic components are susceptible to body static.

Connectors should never be subjected to forced removal or refit, especially inter-board connectors. Damaged contacts can cause short-circuit and open-circuit fault conditions.

Prior to commencing test, and periodically during a test, touch a good vehicle body earth to discharge static charge. Some electronic components are vulnerable to the static electricity that may be generated by the operator.

Grease for electrical connectors

Some under bonnet and under body connectors may be protected against corrosion by the application of a special grease during vehicle production. Should connectors be disturbed in service, or repaired or replaced, additional grease should be re-applied: Part No. BAU 5811, available in 150 gm tubs.

NOTE: The use of greases other than BAU 5811 must be avoided as they can migrate into relays, switches etc. contaminating the contacts and leading to intermittent operation or failure.

SUPPLEMENTARY RESTRAINT SYSTEM PRECAUTIONS

General

The Supplementary Restraint System (SRS) provides active protection for vehicle occupants in the event of a serious collision. The system components include airbags and pre-tensioner seatbelts which are automatically deployed when a severe frontal crash condition is detected.

WARNING: Do not use rear facing child seats in the front passenger seat if the vehicle is fitted with a passenger airbag.

In order to assure system integrity, it is essential that the SRS system is regularly checked and maintained so that it is ready for operation in the event of an accident.

The SRS system contains components which could be potentially hazardous to the service engineer if not serviced and handled correctly. The following guidelines are intended to alert the service engineer to potential sources of danger and emphasise the importance of ensuring integrity of the SRS components fitted to the vehicle.

Where necessary, additional specific precautions are detailed in the relevant sections of this Manual which should be referred to prior to commencing repair operations.

It should be noted that these precautions are not restricted to operations performed when servicing the SRS system, the same care should be exercised when working on ancilliary systems and components located in the vicinity of SRS components; these include but are not limited to steering system (steering wheel airbag), body and trim components (passenger airbag and seat belt pre-tensioners) and electrical system components (SRS harnesses etc.).

WARNING: Always follow the Safety Guidelines and correct procedures for working on SRS components.

NOTE: Airbag modules should be replaced every ten years.

Preliminary Procedures

WARNING: Always remove the ignition key from the starter switch, disconnect the vehicle battery and wait 10 minutes before commencing work on the SRS system.

The SRS system uses energy reserve capacitors that keep the system active in the event of electrical supply failure under crash conditions. It is necessary to allow the capacitor sufficient time to discharge (10 minutes) in order to avoid the risk of accidental deployment.

WARNING: Always disconnect both battery leads before beginning work on the SRS system. Disconnect the negative battery lead first. Never reverse connect the vehicle battery.

CAUTION: Always disconnect the vehicle battery before carrying out any electric welding on a vehicle fitted with an SRS system.

CAUTION: Do not expose an airbag module or seat belt pre-tensioner to heat exceeding 85°C (185°F).

WARNING: Carefully inspect any SRS component before installation. Do not install any SRS component that shows signs of damage such as dents, cracks or deformity.

CAUTION: Ensure SRS components are not contaminated with oil, grease, detergent or water.

CAUTION: Prior to commencing any test procedure on the vehicle, ensure that only test equipment approved for the purpose is being utilised and that it is in good working order. Ensure any harness or connectors are in good condition and any warning lamps are functional.

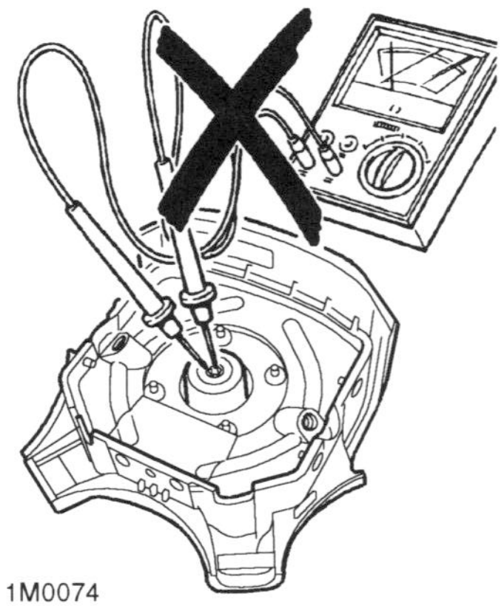

1M0074

WARNING: Never use multimeters or other general purpose test equipment on SRS system components or connectors. System faults should be diagnosed through the use of recommended test equipment only.

Component handling

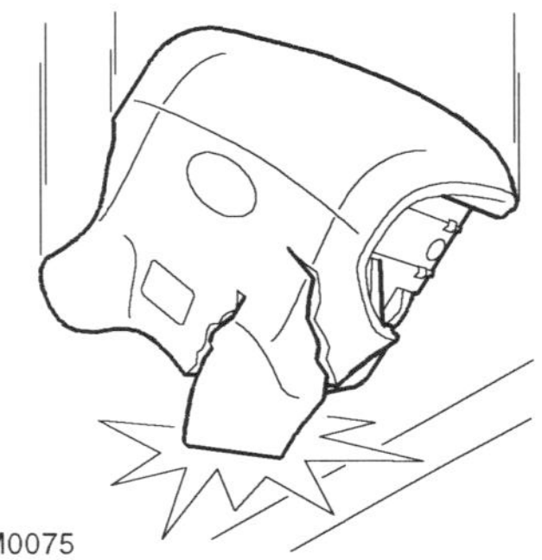

1M0075

WARNING: The SRS components are sensitive and potentially hazardous if not handled correctly; always comply with the following handling precautions:

- Never drop an SRS component. The airbag diagnostic control unit is a particularly shock sensitive device and must be handled with extreme care. Airbag modules and seat belt pre-tensioner units could deploy if subjected to a strong shock.
- Never wrap your arms around an airbag module. If an airbag module has to be carried, hold it by the cover, with the cover uppermost and the base away from your body.
- Never transport airbag modules or seat belt pre-tensioners in the cabin of a vehicle. Always use the luggage compartment of the vehicle for carrying airbag modules and seat belt pre-tensioner units.

Storage

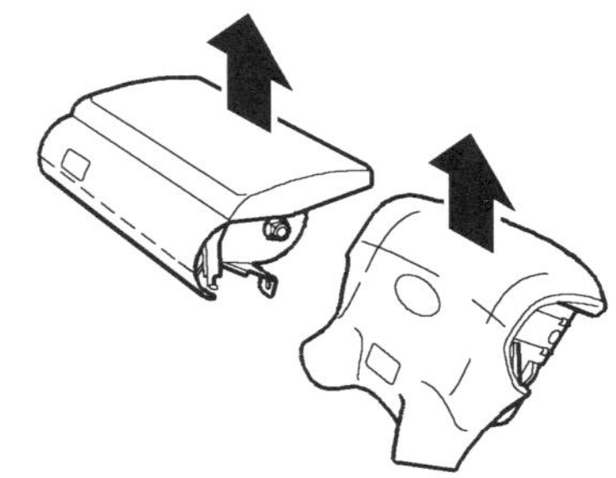

1M0076

WARNING: Always store airbag modules with the cover face up. If the airbag module is stored face down, accidental deployment could propel the unit with enough force to cause serious injury.

WARNING: Airbag modules and seat belt pre-tensioners are classed as explosive devices. For overnight and longer term storage, they must be stored in a secure steel cabinet which has been approved as suitable for the purpose and has been registered by the local authority.

CAUTION: For the temporary storage of an airbag module or seat belt pre-tensioner during service, place in a designated storage area. If there is no designated storage area available, store in the luggage compartment of the vehicle and inform the workshop supervisor.

CAUTION: Always observe the following precautions when temporarily storing an airbag module:

- **Ensure the cover is facing upwards and the luggage compartment is secured.**
- **Always keep components cool, dry and free from contamination.**
- **Do not allow anything to rest on the airbag module.**
- **Store any removed airbag assembly on a secure flat surface away from electrical equipment and heat sources (exceeding 85°C (185°F).**

Installation and Testing Precautions

WARNING: The integrity of SRS system components are critical for safety reasons. Ensure the following precautions are always adhered to:

- Never install used SRS components from another vehicle or attempt to repair an SRS component.
- When repairing an SRS system only use genuine new parts.
- Never apply electrical power to an SRS component unless instructed to do so as part of an approved test procedure.
- Special Torx bolts are necessary for installing the airbag assembly - do not use other bolts. Ensure bolts are tightened to the specified torque (refer to SRS section).
- Ensure that SRS component fixings are correctly positioned and torqued during service and repair.
- Always use new fixings when replacing an SRS component.
- Ensure the SRS Diagnostic Control Unit (DCU) is always installed correctly. There must not be any gap between the DCU and the bracket to which it is mounted. An incorrectly mounted unit could cause the system to malfunction.
- The SRS Diagnostic Control Unit is a non-serviceable component and no attempt should be made to repair or modify the unit.
- Do not try to disassemble the airbag assembly. It has no serviceable parts. Once an airbag has been deployed, it cannot be repaired or reused.
- If you suspect an airbag assembly could be defective, install a new unit and dispose of the old unit. Manually deploy the old unit before disposal. *See SRS Precautions.*

WARNING: When removing, testing or installing an airbag module do not lean directly over it.

SRS Harnesses and Connectors

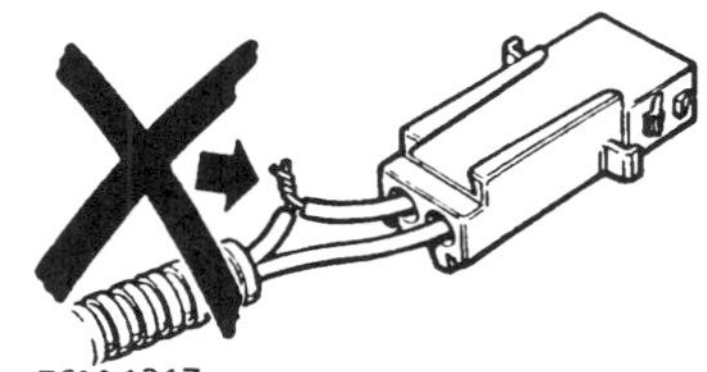

76M 1317

CAUTION: Always observe the following precautions with regards to SRS systems:

Never attempt to modify, splice or repair SRS wiring.

- Never install electronic equipment (such as a mobile telephone, two way radio or in-car entertainment system) in such a way that it could generate electrical interference in the airbag harness. Seek specialist advice when installing such equipment.

NOTE: SRS wiring can be identified by a special yellow outer protective covering (black with yellow stripe protective coverings are sometimes used).

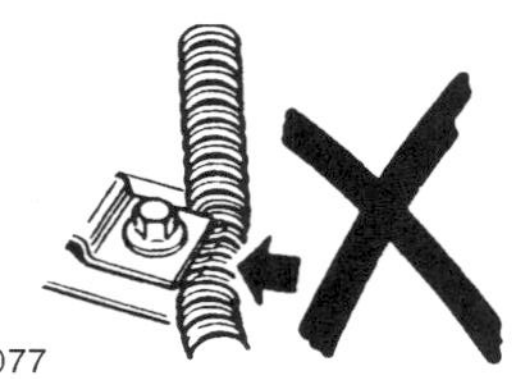

1M0077

CAUTION: Always ensure SRS harnesses are routed correctly. Be careful to avoid trapping or pinching the SRS harness. Route the harness to avoid possible points of chafing.

- Always use specified earth fixings tightened to the correct torque. Poor earthing can cause intermittent problems that are difficult to diagnose.

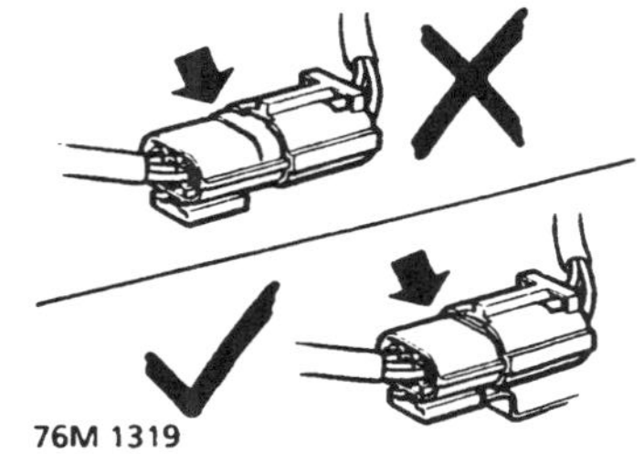

76M 1319

CAUTION: Ensure all airbag harness connectors are mated correctly and securely fastened. Do not leave the connectors hanging loose.

- Do not allow SRS components to hang from their harnesses.

Rotary Coupler

CAUTION: Always follow the procedure for fitting and checking the rotary coupler as instructed in the SRS section of this manual. Comply with all safety and installation procedures to ensure the system functions correctly. Observe the following precautions:

- **Do not install a rotary coupler if it is suspected to be defective.**
- **Do not attempt to service, modify or repair a rotary coupler.**
- **Do not cut, splice or modify the wires attached to yellow SRS connector and lead.**
- **Always ensure the rotary coupler connectors are mated correctly and securely fastened.**
- **Always ensure the battery is disconnected before working on the rotary coupler.**
- **Always ensure the rotary coupler is removed and installed in its centered position and with the front road wheels in the straight ahead position - refer to the SRS section of this manual for the full correct removal and installation procedure.**
- **If a new rotary coupler is being installed, ensure the locking tab holding the coupler's rotational position is not broken; units with a broken locking tab should not be used.**

Warning Labels

Warning symbols are displayed at various positions in the vehicle (either in a suitable prominent position such as driver and passenger side glass, or attached to the component itself) to indicateSRS items which must be treated with particular care. These include:

A - The need for caution when working in close proximity to SRS components.

B - Refer to the publication where the procedures, instructions and advice can be found (usually Workshop Manual or Owner's Handbook) for working on the SRS system.

C - Do not use rear facing child seats in the front passenger seat if the vehicle is fitted with a passenger airbag.

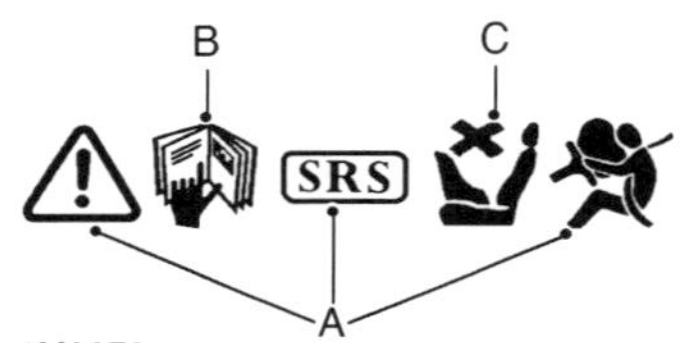

1M0078

Driver and Passenger side windows

1M0079

NOTE: It is imperative that the appropriate publication is read thoroughly prior to any work being undertaken on the SRS system.

NOTE: Exact positions of SRS warning labels may vary dependent on legislation and market trends.
Refer to the Owner's Handbook for additional information regarding the SRS system.

Rotary coupler

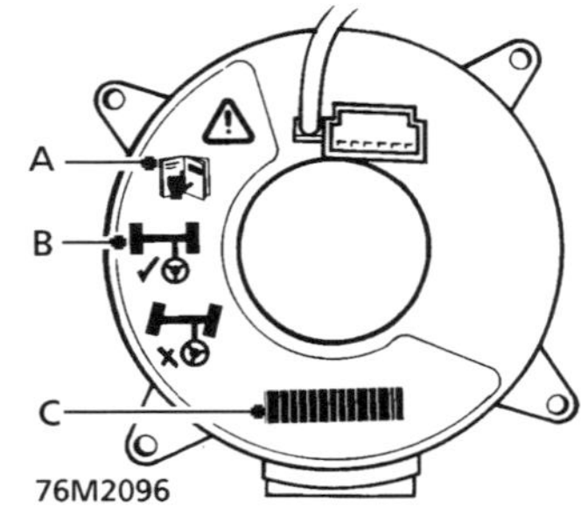

76M2096

A - Refer to the Workshop Manual for detailed instructions.
B - Ensure wheels are in the straight ahead position before removal and refitting.
C - LAND ROVER Part Number/Bar code - The code must be recorded and quoted for ordering purposes.

End of Fascia

Label warning the owner not to use rear facing child seats in the front passenger seat in vehicles fitted with a passenger side airbag.

AIRBAG AND PRE-TENSIONER MANUAL DEPLOYMENT

WARNING: Only personnel who have undergone the appropriate training should undertake deployment of airbag and pre-tensioner modules.

WARNING: A deployed airbag is very hot, DO NOT return to a deployed airbag module until at least 30 minutes have elapsed since deployment.

WARNING: Deployment procedures and precautions as detailed in this service manual should be strictly adhered to. The following precautions must be complied with:

- Only use deployment equipment approved for the intended purpose.
- Before beginning deployment procedure, ensure deployment tool functions properly by performing the self test procedure. *See SRS Precautions.*
- *Deployment of airbag / pre-tensioner modules should be performed in a well ventilated area which has been designated for the purpose.*
- *Ensure airbag / pre-tensioner modules are not damaged or ruptured before attempting to deploy.*
- *Notify the relevant authorities of intention to deploy airbag and pre-tensioner units.*
- *When deploying airbag pre-tensioner units, ensure that all personnel are at least 15 metres away from the deployment zone.*
- *Ensure deployment tool is connected correctly, in compliance with the instructions detailed in the SRS section of this manual. In particular, ensure deployment tool is NOT connected to battery supply before connecting to airbag module connector.*
- *When deploying seat belt pre-tensioners, ensure pre-tensioner unit is secured correctly to seat.*
- *When removing deployed airbag modules and pre-tensioner units, wear protective clothing. Use gloves and seal deployed units in a plastic bag.*
- *Following deployment of any component of the SRS system within the vehicle, all SRS components must be replaced. DO NOT re-use or salvage any parts of the SRS system.*
- *Do not lean over airbag module when connecting deployment equipment.*

WARNING: If a vehicle is to be scrapped, undeployed airbag modules and pre-tensioner units must be manually deployed. Deleted end of paragraph.

NOTE: Passenger airbag and pre-tensioners are deployed before removal from the vehicle.

Before the manual deployment procedure is started, perform the deployment tool self test procedure.

Deployment tool SMD 4082/1 self test procedure

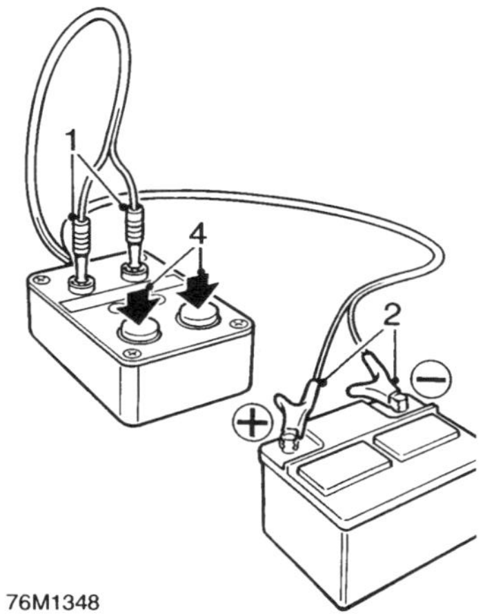

76M1348

1. Insert blue and yellow connectors of tool lead into corresponding sockets on face of tool.
2. Connect crocodile clips of second tool lead to battery, red to positive and black to negative.
3. Red "READY" light should illuminate.
4. Press and hold both operating buttons.
5. Green "DEFECTIVE" light should illuminate.
6. Release both operating buttons.
7. Red "READY" light should illuminate.
8. Disconnect tool from battery.
9. Disconnect blue and yellow connectors from tool face sockets.

Deployment of pre-tensioner

These guidelines are written to aid authorised personnel carry out the safe disposal of the pretensioner.

WARNING:

- **Only use the approved deployment equipment.**
- **Deploy pre-tensioner in a designated area.**
- **Ensure pre-tensioner is not damaged or ruptured before deploying.**
- **Notify relevant authorities.**

1. Carry out deployment tool self test.
2. Slide seat fully rearwards to access pre-tensioner harness connector.

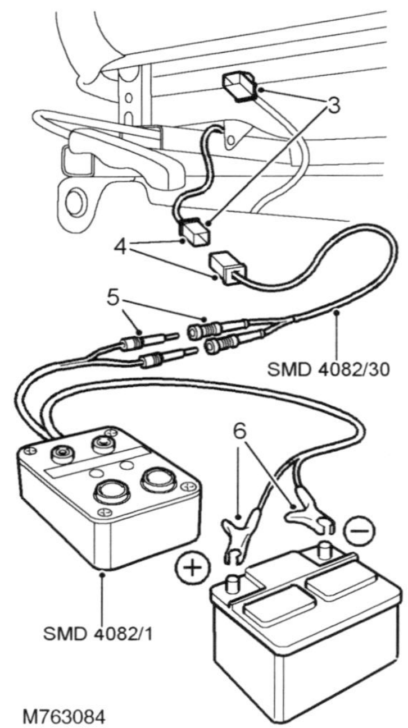

M763084

3. Disconnect pre-tensioner harness connector.

WARNING: Ensure deployment tool SMD 4082/1 is not connected to battery.

4. Connect flylead **SMD 4082/30** to pre-tensioner connector.
5. Connect flylead **SMD 4082/30** to tool **SMD 4082/1.**

WARNING: Do not lean over pretensioner whilst connecting.

WARNING: Ensure pre-tensioner is secured tightly to seat.

WARNING: Ensure all personnel are standing at least 15 metres away from vehicle.

6. Connect tool **SMD 4082/1** to battery.

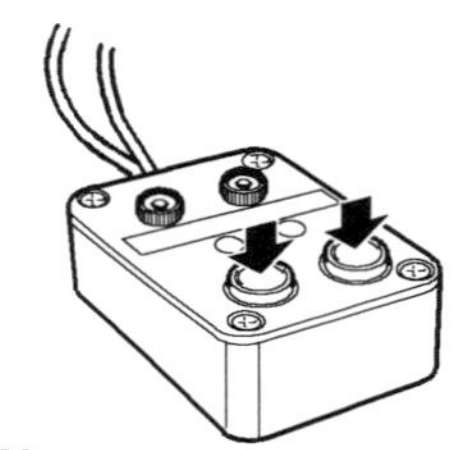

M763086

7. Press both operating buttons to deploy pre-tensioner.
8. Wearing gloves, disconnect flylead **SMD 4082/30** from pre-tensioner connector and remove pre-tensioner from seat. Place pre-tensioner in plastic bag and seal bag.
9. Transport deployed pre-tensioner to designated area for incineration.

NOTE: DO NOT transport pre-tensioner in the vehicle passenger compartment.

10. If the vehicle is being scrapped, scrap all remaining parts of airbag system. **DO NOT** re-use or salvage any parts of the airbag system.

Deployment of driver airbag module

These guidelines are written to aid authorised personnel carry out the safe disposal of the passenger airbag module.

WARNING:

- **Only use the approved deployment equipment.**
- **Deploy airbag modules in a well ventilated designated area.**
- **Ensure airbag module is not damaged or ruptured before deploying.**
- **Notify relevant authorities.**

1. Carry out deployment tool self test.
2. Remove airbag module from steering wheel. ***See RESTRAINT SYSTEMS, Repairs.***

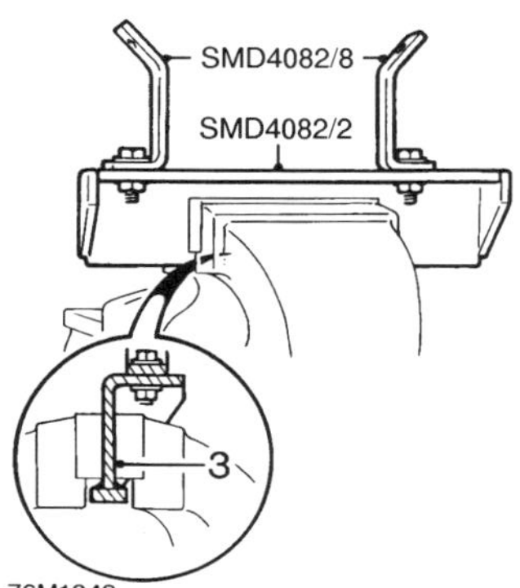

76M1349

3. Position tool **SMD 4082/2** in vice, ensuring that vice jaws grip tool above bottom flange to prevent possibility of tool being forced upwards from vice. Tighten vice.

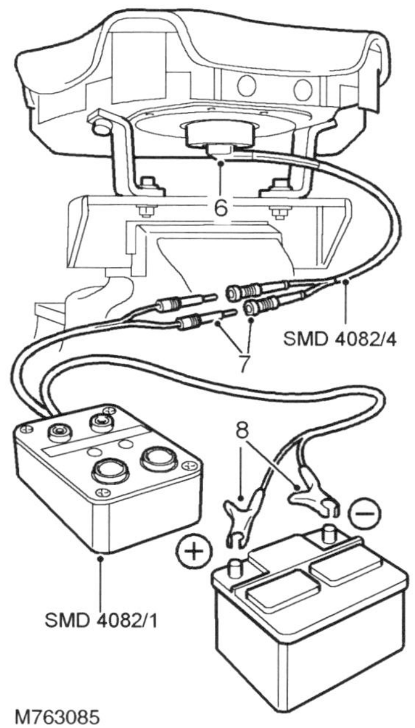

M763085

4. Secure airbag module to tool **SMD 4082/2.** Ensure module is correctly secured using both fixings.
5. Ensure airbag module mounting brackets are secure.

WARNING: Ensure deployment tool SMD 4082/1 is not connected to battery.

6. Connect flylead **SMD 4082/4** to airbag module.
7. Connect flylead **SMD 4082/4** to tool **SMD 4082/1.**

WARNING: Do not lean over airbag module whilst connecting.

8. Connect tool **SMD 4082/1** to battery.

WARNING: Ensure all personnel are standing at least 15 metres away from module.

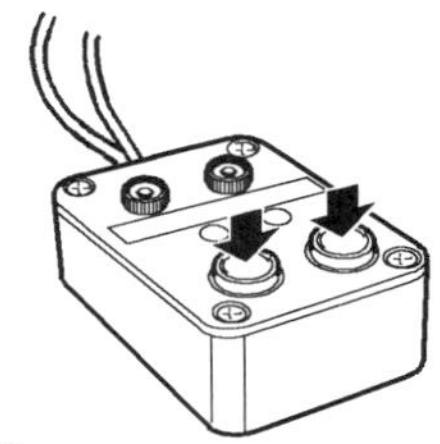

M763086

9. Press both operating buttons to deploy airbag module.
10. **DO NOT** return to airbag module for 30 minutes.
11. Wearing gloves and face mask, disconnect flylead **SMD 4082/4** from airbag module and remove airbag module from tool. Place airbag module in plastic bag and seal bag.
12. Wipe down tool with damp cloth.
13. Transport deployed airbag module to designated area for incineration.

NOTE: DO NOT transport airbag module in the vehicle passenger compartment.

14. If the vehicle is being scrapped, scrap all remaining parts of airbag system. **DO NOT** re-use or salvage any parts of the airbag system.

Deployment of passenger airbag module

WARNING:

- **Only use the approved deployment equipment.**
- **Deploy airbag modules in a well ventilated designated area.**
- **Ensure airbag module is not damaged or ruptured before deploying.**
- **Notify relevant authorities.**

1. Release passenger airbag module from fascia. ***See BODY, Repairs.***
2. Connect **SMD 4082/4** to passenger airbag module.
3. Refit passenger airbag module, ensuring that **SMD 4082/4** is routed to accessible area beneath fascia.
4. Tighten passenger airbag fixings to 9Nm.
5. Carry out deployment tool self test. ***See SRS Precautions.***

WARNING: Ensure tool SMD 4082/1 is not connected to battery.

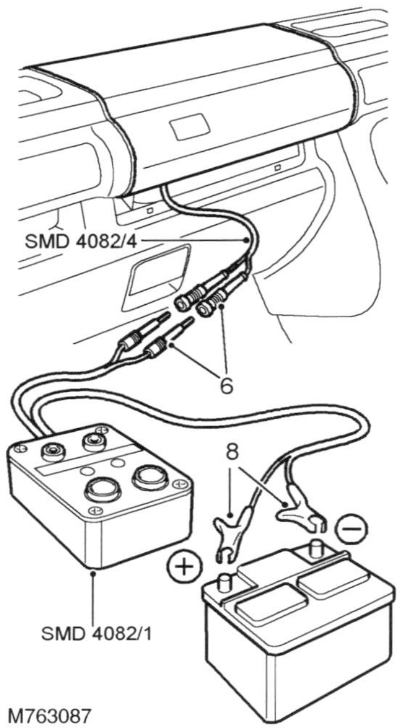

M763087

WARNING: Do not lean over airbag module whilst connecting.

6. Connect flylead **SMD 4082/4** to tool **SMD 4082/1.**
7. Ensure all vehicle doors are open.

WARNING: Ensure all personnel are standing at least 15 metres away from vehicle.

8. Connect tool **SMD 4082/1** to battery.

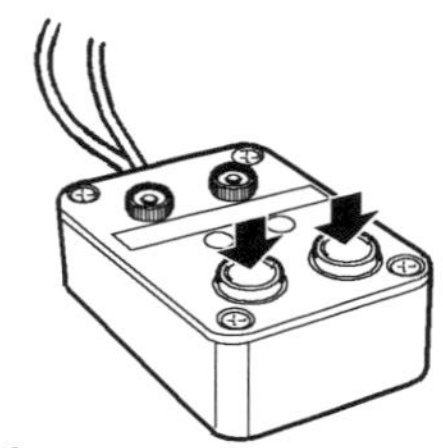
M763086

9. Press both operating buttons to deploy airbag module.
10. **DO NOT** return to vehicle for 30 minutes.
11. Wearing gloves and face mask, release passenger airbag module and disconnect **SMD 4082/4** . Remove airbag module from vehicle. Place airbag module in plastic bag and seal bag.
12. Transport deployed airbag module to designated area for incineration.

NOTE: DO NOT transport airbag module in the vehicle passenger compartment.

13. If the vehicle is being scrapped, scrap all remaining parts of airbag system. **DO NOT** re-use or salvage any parts of the airbag system.

CAUTION: If vehicle is not being scrapped, ensure all dust/particle by-products of airbag deployment are removed from vehicle interior; vacuum all fabric surfaces and wipe all other surfaces with damp cloth.

COMPONENT REPLACEMENT POLICY

IMPACTS WHICH DO NOT DEPLOY AIRBAGS

CAUTION: Check for structural damage in the area of the impact, paying particular attention to bumper armatures, longitudinals, crash cans and bracketry.

IMPACTS WHICH DEPLOY AIRBAGS

CAUTION: Renew the following components:

- Airbag ECU.
- Airbag module(s).
- SRS Wiring.
- Pretensioners.
- Rotary coupler.

AIR CONDITIONING SYSTEM PRECAUTIONS

General

The air conditioning system contains fluids and components which could be potentially hazardous to the service engineer or the environment if not serviced and handled correctly. The following guidelines are intended to alert the service engineer to potential sources of danger and emphasise the importance of ensuring the integrity of the Air Conditioning operating conditions and components fitted to the vehicle.

Where necessary, additional specific precautions are detailed in the relevant sections of this Manual which should be referred to prior to commencing repair operations.

The refrigerant used in the air conditioning system is HFC-134a (Hydrofluorocarbon) R134a.

WARNING: The air conditioning system is charged with a high pressure, potentially toxic refrigerant. Repairs or servicing must only be carried out by a trained operator familiar with both the vehicle system and the charging and testing equipment.

WARNING: All operations pertaining to the air conditioning system must be carried out in a well ventilated area. Always observe the following precautions:

- **R134a is odourless and colourless. Do not handle or discharge in an enclosed area, or any area where the vapour and liquid can come into contact with a naked flame or hot metal. R134a is not flammable, but it can cause a highly toxic gas.**
- **Do not smoke or weld in areas where R134a is in use.**
- **Inhalation of concentrations of vapour can cause dizziness, disorientation, incoordination, narcosis, nausea or vomiting.**
- **Refrigerant R134a from domestic and commercial sources must not be used in motor vehicle air conditioning systems.**

WARNING: HFC-134a (R134a) is a hazardous liquid which if handled incorrectly can cause serious injury. The following precautions should be adhered to at all times when working on an air conditioning system:

- **Suitable protective clothing must be worn when carrying out service operations on the air conditioning system.**
- **Air conditioning connections should be opened carefully to allow any liquid or pressure to bleed off slowly.**
- **Do not allow a refrigerant container to be heated by direct flame or to be placed near any heating appliance. A refrigerant container must not be heated above 50 C.**
- **Do not leave a refrigerant container without its cap fitted.**
- **Do not transport a refrigerant container that is unrestrained (especially in the luggage compartment of a car).**
- **Do not allow fluids, other than R134a or compressor lubricant, to enter the air conditioning system; spontaneous combustion could occur.**
- **R134a splashed onto exposed skin will cause immediate freezing of that area.**
- **Refrigerant cylinders and replenishment trolleys can become cooled when discharging, this could cause skin to become frozen to them if contact is made.**
- **The refrigerant used in an air conditioning system must be reclaimed in accordance with the recommendations stipulated by a Refrigerant Recovery, Recycling & Recharging Station.**

Protective Clothing

NOTE: Suitable protective clothing comprises:

- Wrap round safety glasses or helmet
- Heat proof gloves
- Rubber apron, or waterproof overalls
- Rubber boots.

REMEDIAL ACTIONS

If an accident involving R134a should occur, conduct the following remedial actions:

- If liquid R134a enters the eye, do not rub it. Gently run large quantities of eye wash over affected eye to raise the temperature. If an eye wash is not available, cool, clean water may be used to flush the eye. After rinsing, cover the eye with a clean pad and seek immediate medical attention.
- If liquid R134a is splashed onto the skin, run large quantities of water over the affected area to raise the temperature. Implement the same action if the skin comes in contact with discharging cylinders. Wrap the contaminated body parts in blankets (or similar materials) and seek immediate medical attention.
- If the debilitating effects of inhalation of R134a vapour is suspected, seek fresh air. If the affected person is unconscious, move them away from the contaminated area to fresh air and apply artificial respiration and/or oxygen and seek immediate medical attention.

WARNING: Due to its low evaporating temperature of -30°C, R134a should be handled with extreme care.

SERVICE PRECAUTIONS

CAUTION: Observe the following precautions when handling components used in the air conditioning system:

- **Air conditioning units must not be lifted by their hoses, pipes or capillary lines.**
- **Hoses and lines must not be subjected to any twist or stress - the efficiency of the system will be impaired by kinks or restrictions. Ensure that hoses are correctly positioned before tightening couplings, and ensure that all clips and supports are utilised.**
- **Flexible hoses should not be postioned close to the exhaust manifold (less than 100mm) unless protected by heat shielding.**
- **Completed assemblies must be checked for refrigeration lines touching metal panels. Any direct contact of components and panels may transmit noise and so must be eliminated.**
- **The appropriate torque wrench must be used when tightening refrigerant connections to the stipulated value. An additional spanner must be used to hold the union to prevent twisting of the pipe when tightening connections.**
- **Before connecting any hose or pipe, ensure that refrigerant oil is applied to the seat of the new 'O' ring seals, BUT NOT to the threads of the connection.**
- **All protective plugs must remain in place to seal the component until immediately prior to connection.**
- **Ensure components are at room temperature before uncapping, to prevent condensation of moisture from the air that enters it.**
- **Components must not remain uncapped for longer than 15 minutes. In the event of a delay, the caps must be fitted.**
- **When disconnecting, immediately cap all air conditioning pipes to prevent ingress of dirt and moisture into the system.**
- **The receiver/dryer contains desiccant which absorbs moisture. It must be positively sealed at all times. A receiver/drier that has been left uncapped must not be used, fit a new unit.**
- **The receiver/drier should be the last component connected to the system to ensure optimum dehydration and maximum moisture protection of the system.**
- **Whenever the refrigerant system is opened, the receiver/dryer must be renewed immediately before evacuating and recharging the system.**
- **Use alcohol and a clean lint-free cloth to clean dirty connections.**
- **Ensure that all new parts fitted are marked for use with R134a.**
- **When a major repair has been completed, a leak test should be conducted; refer to the air conditioning section of this manual for the correct procedure.**

Refrigerant oil

Use an approved refrigerant lubricating oil:

ND Oil 8

⚠ **CAUTION: Do not use any other type of refrigerant oil.**

⚠ **CAUTION: Refrigerant oil easily absorbs water and must not be stored for long periods. Do not pour unused oil back into the container.**

When renewing system components, add the quantities of refrigerant oil recommended in the Air Conditioning section of this manual.

Compressor

A new compressor is sealed and pressurised with Nitrogen gas. When fitting a new compressor, slowly release the sealing cap; gas pressure should be heard to vent as the seal is broken.

⚠ **CAUTION: A new compressor should always have its sealing cap in place and must not be removed until immediately prior to fitting the compressor air conditioning pipes.**

Rapid refrigerant discharge

⚠ **CAUTION: If the air conditioning system is involved in accident damage and the system is punctured, the refrigerant will discharge rapidly. The rapid discharge of refrigerant will also result in the loss of most of the oil from the system. The compressor must be removed and all the remaining oil in the compressor drained and refilled as instructed in the air conditioning section of this manual.**

GENERAL INFORMATION

PRECAUTIONS FOR REFRIGERANT RECOVERY, RECYCLING AND RECHARGING

⚠ WARNING: Refrigerant must always be recycled before reuse to ensure that the purity of the refrigerant is high enough for safe use in the air conditioning system.

⚠ WARNING: Recycling should always be carried out with equipment which is design certified by Underwriter Laboratory Inc. for compliance with SAE-J1991. Other equipment may not recycle refrigerant to the required level of purity.

A R134a Refrigerant, Recovery, Recycling and Recharging Station must not be used with any other type of refrigerant.

⚠ **CAUTION: When using an air conditioning portable Refrigerant, Recovery, Recycling and Recharging Station the operator must adhere to the equipment manufacturer's instructions.**

⚠ **CAUTION: The system must be evacuated immediately before recharging commences. Delay between evacuation and recharging must not be permitted.**

⚠ **CAUTION: Overcharging the air conditioning system will cause excessive head pressure.**

VEHICLE IDENTIFICATION NUMBER

Location

The Vehicle Identification Number (VIN) plate is attached to the LH 'B' post.
The VIN is also stamped in the following locations:

- At the centre top of the engine bulkhead.
- On a plate behind the LH lower corner of the windscreen.

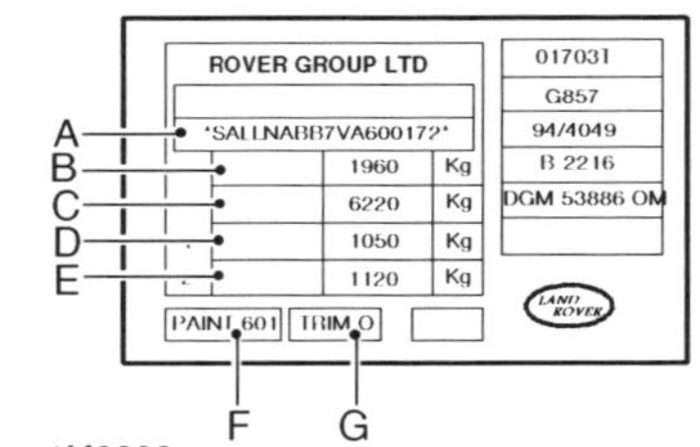

1M0080

A - Vehicle Identification Number (VIN)
B - Gross vehicle weight
C - Gross train weight
D - Maximum front axle load
E - Maximum rear axle load
F - Paint Code
G - Trim Code

Vehicle identification number

Example: **SALLNABB7VA600172**

S = Geographic area (S = Europe)
A = Country (A = UK)
L = Manufacturer (L = Land Rover)
LN = Marque/Model (LN = Freelander)
A = Trim Level (A = Trim Level 1)
B = Body
- A = 3 door models
- B = 5 door models

B = Engine
- A = K16 Petrol engine models
- B = TCIE Diesel engine models

7 = Transmission and Steering
- 7 = RHD manual steering
- 8 = LHD manual steering

V = Model change (V = 1997 Model year)
A = Assembly plant (A = Solihull)
6 figures = Serial number

Paint and Trim colour codes:

Paint Code (F) - 3-digit code identifying the original Paint colour is stamped on the VIN plate:

Example: **601**

601 = Rioja Red
507 = Caledonian Blue
603 = Chawton White
624 = Cobar Blue
618 = White Gold
622 = Venetian Mauve
587 = Altai Silver
610 = Charleston Green
961 = Epson Green
416 = Beluga Black

Refer to Parts Catalogue for full list of colour codes.

Trim (G) - a code identifying the original trim type and colour is stamped on the VIN plate, refer to the relevant Parts Catalogue for coding details:

IDENTIFICATION NUMBER LOCATIONS

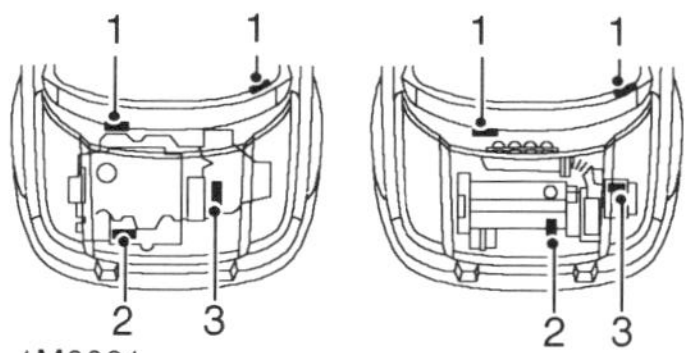

1M0081

1. Vehicle identification number
2. Engine number
3. Gearbox number

Vehicle Identification Number

The VIN is displayed at the centre top of the engine bulkhead and on a plate behind the LH lower corner of the windscreen.

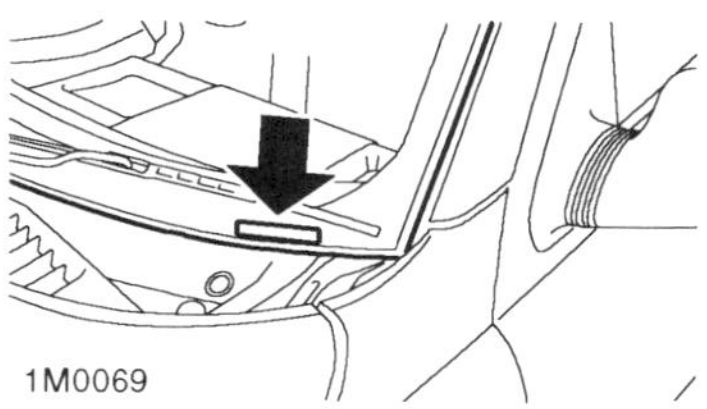

1M0069

Engine number

1.8 'K' Series Engine: Stamped on the front face of the cylinder block adjacent to the gearbox.

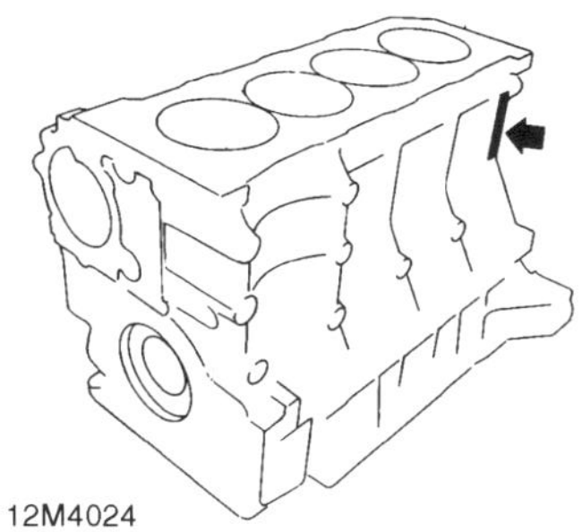

12M4024

2.0 'L' Series Engine: Stamped on the front face of the cylinder block at top centre.

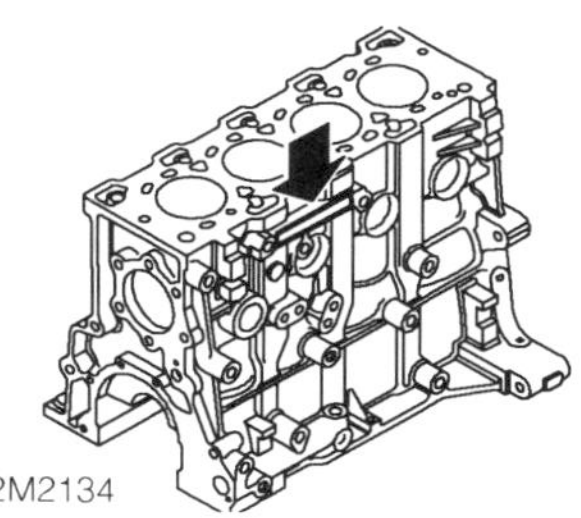

12M2134

Gearbox number (3)

Manual Gearbox - PG1: Stamped on a label attached to the front face of the clutch housing.

CONTENTS

CONTENTS

JACKING

The following instructions must be carried out before raising the vehicle off the ground:

- Use a solid level surface.
- Apply parking brake.
- Select 1st. gear in main gearbox and ensure HDC is not selected.

CAUTION: To avoid damage to under body components of the vehicle, adhere to the following jacking procedures:

DO NOT POSITION JACKS OR AXLE STANDS UNDER THE FOLLOWING COMPONENTS:

- **Bumpers**
- **Brake or Fuel lines**
- **Exhaust pipe**
- **Suspension components**
- **Steering rack and linkages**
- **Fuel tank**
- **Engine sump**
- **Gearbox**

Jack or support vehicle only on approved jacking points as detailed in the illustration below:

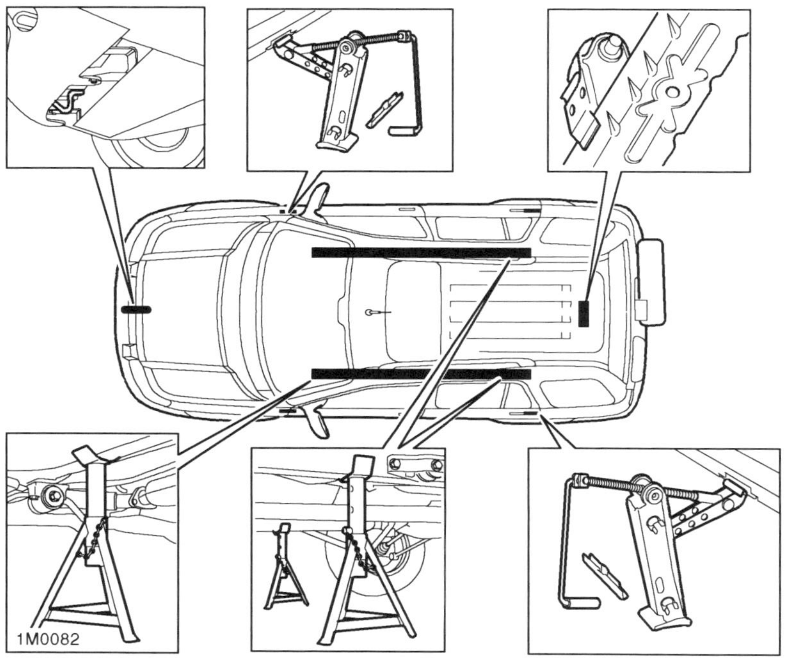

Vehicle jack

The jack provided with the vehicle is only intended to be used in an emergency, for changing a tyre. Do **NOT** use the jack for any other purpose. Refer to the Owner's Handbook for vehicle jack location points and procedure. Never work under a vehicle only supported by the vehicle jack.

Hydraulic jack

A hydraulic jack with a minimum 1500 kg (3,300 lbs) load capacity must be used.

WARNING: Do not work on the underside of a vehicle until suitable stands have been positioned.

Raising the front of a vehicle

Position the cup of the hydraulic arm under the centre of the front body crossmember assembly.

Use jack to raise front road wheels to enable safety stands to be installed under the front end of each longitudinal member as shown.
Carefully lower jack until vehicle sits securely on both safety stands. Remove trolley jack.

Before working on the underside of a vehicle re-check the stability of the vehicle on the stands.

Use the reverse procedure when removing a vehicle from stands.

NOTE: For some repair operations it may be necessary to use a jack to support the engine under the sump. In this case, a block of wood should be used on the jack to protect the sump.

Raising the rear of a vehicle

Position cup of hydraulic arm under the centre of the rear subframe crossmember at the position identified by the embossed arrows.

Use jack to raise rear road wheels to enable safety stands to be installed under the rear ends of the body longitidinal members as shown.
Carefully lower jack until vehicle sits securely on both safety stands. Remove trolley jack.

Before working on the underside of a vehicle, re-check the stability of the vehicle on the stands.

Use the reverse procedure when removing a vehicle from stands.

Wheel-free lift

Locate the lifting pads under the ends of the body longitudinal members shown. Raise the ramp to support the weight of the vehicle, ensure the vehicle is secure on the lifting pads, then raise the ramp to the required height.

TOWING

CAUTION: The vehicle has permanent four-wheel drive. The following towing instructions must be adhered to:

Towing the vehicle on all four wheels with driver operating steering and brakes.

1M0083

- Turn ignition key turn to position '1' to release steering lock and then to position 'II' to enable the brake lights, wipers and direction indicators to be operated, if necessary.
- Select neutral in gearbox and ensure HDC (hill descent control) is deselected.
- Secure tow rope, chain or cable to towing eye.
- Release the parking brake.

CAUTION: The brake servo and power assisted steering system will not be functional without the engine running. Greater pedal pressure will be required to apply the brakes and the steering system will require greater effort to turn the front road wheels. The vehicle tow connection should only be used under normal road conditions, 'snatch' recovery should be avoided.

Suspended tow by breakdown vehicle

CAUTION: To prevent vehicle damage, rear propeller shaft MUST BE removed.

Mark propeller shaft drive flanges and mating flanges with identification lines to enable the propeller shaft to be refitted in its original position.

Remove the propeller shaft fixings then remove the shaft from the vehicle.

If the front of the vehicle is to be trailed, turn ignition key to position 'I' to release steering lock.

CAUTION: If it is considered unsafe to turn the starter switch to position 'I' due to accident damage or an electrical fault; disconnect the battery before turning the ignition switch.

WARNING: Do not turn the starter switch to position '0' or remove the ignition key while the vehicle is being towed.

CAUTION: The steering wheel and/or linkage must be secured in a straight ahead position. DO NOT use the steering lock mechanism for this purpose.

CAUTION: Under no circumstances should the vehicle be towed or recovered by means of lashing to the rear subframe. Serious damage to the subframe and body could result.

CAUTION: Only use the rear towing eye for towing another vehicle.

TRANSPORTING THE VEHICLE BY TRAILER

Lashing rings are provided at the front and rear of the body to facilitate the securing of the vehicle to a trailer or other means of transportation.

CAUTION: Underbody components must not be used as lashing points. The lashing rings must not be used for towing.

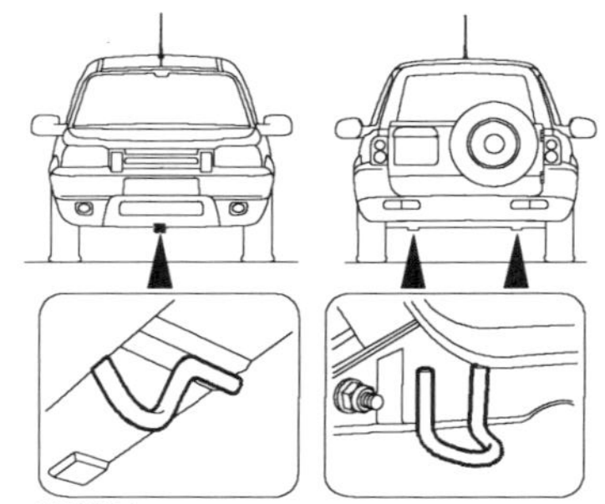

1M0084

Install the vehicle on trailer and apply the parking brake. Select neutral.

EMERGENCY STARTING

WARNING: Hydrogen and oxygen gases are produced during normal battery operation. This gas mixture can explode if sources of combustion (e.g. flames, sparks or lighted tobacco etc.) are brought near the battery. When charging or using a battery in an enclosed space, always ensure ventilation and wear eye protection (goggles etc.).

WARNING: Keep dangerous substances out of the reach of children.
Batteries contain sulphuric acid; avoid contact with skin, eyes, or clothing.
If handling batteries, wear a protective industrial apron and gloves and wear safety goggles to protect against possible splashing of acid solution.
In case of acid contacting with skin, eyes, or clothing; flush immediately with water for a minimum of fifteen minutes.
If acid is swallowed, drink large quantities of milk or water, followed by milk of magnesia, a beaten egg, or vegetable oil.

SEEK MEDICAL AID IMMEDIATELY.

To Jump Start - Negative Ground Battery

WARNING: To avoid any possibility of injury use particular care when connecting a booster battery to a discharged battery.

Position vehicles so that jump leads will reach, ensuring that vehicles **DO NOT TOUCH,** alternatively a fully charged slave battery may be positioned on the floor adjacent to the vehicle.

Ensure that:

- the ignition and all electrical accessories are switched off
- the parking brake is applied and neutral is selected on gearbox

Connect the jump leads as follows:

WARNING: Making final cable connection could cause an electrical arc which if made near battery could cause an explosion.

A. Connect one end of first jumper cable to positive (+) terminal of booster battery.

B. Connect other end of first jumper cable to positive (+) terminal of discharged battery.

C. Connect one end of second jumper cable to negative terminal of booster battery.

D. Connect other end of second jumper cable to a good earth point on the engine, **NOT TO NEGATIVE TERMINAL OF DISCHARGED BATTERY.**

CAUTION: Keep jumper leads away from moving parts, pulleys, drive belts and fan blade assembly.

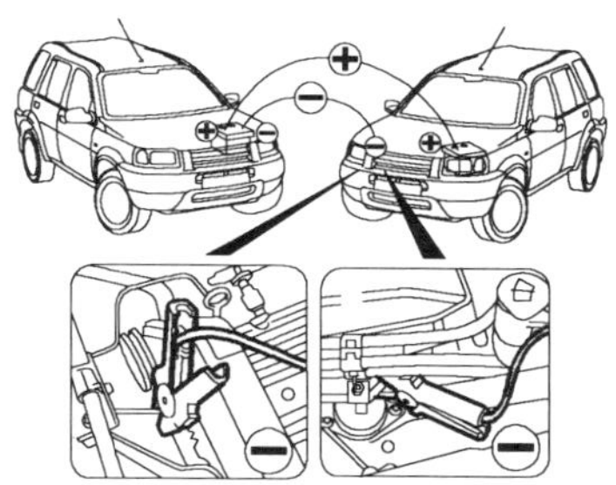

1M0085

If the booster battery is installed in another vehicle, start engine and allow to idle.

Start engine of vehicle with discharged battery, following starting procedure in Owners' Handbook.

CAUTION: If vehicle fails to start within a maximum time of 12 seconds, switch ignition off and investigate cause. Failure to follow this instruction could result in irreparable damage to catalyst.

To disconnect:

- Remove negative (-) jumper cable from the engine and then terminal of booster battery.
- Remove positive (+) jumper cable from positive terminals of booster battery and discharged battery.

ENGINE - 'K' SERIES

Type	16 valve DOHC
Cylinder arrangement	4 in line - transverse
Bore	80.00 mm
Stroke	89.30 mm
Capacity	1796 cm^3
Compression ratio (nominal)	10.5 : 1
Firing order	1 - 3 - 4 - 2
Height (nominal)	615 mm
Width (nominal)	600 mm
Length (nominal)	654 mm
Rotation	Clockwise, viewed from front of engine
Valve operation	Self-adjusting hydraulic tappets
Cylinder head warp - maximum	0.05 mm
Emissions Standard	ECD2 (EU2)
Maximum Power	88kW (118 bhp) @ 5550 rpm
Maximum torque	165Nm (223.7 lbf.ft) @ 2750 rpm

Cylinder head

Cylinder head height:	
New	118.95 to 119.05 mm
Reface limit	0.20 mm

Cylinder block

Cylinder liner bore:	
RED grade A	80.000 to 80.015 mm
BLUE grade B	80.016 to 80.030 mm

Crankshaft

Crankshaft end-float	0.10 to 0.25 mm
Service limit	0.34 mm
Thrust washer halves thickness	2.61 to 2.65 mm
Main journal diameter	47.979 to 48.000 mm
Maximum out of round	0.010 mm
Main journal tolerance:	
Grade 1	47.993 to 48.000 mm
Grade 2	47.986 to 47.993 mm
Grade 3	47.979 to 47.986 mm
Clearance in bearings	0.02 to 0.05 mm
Big-end journal diameter	47.986 to 48.007 mm
Maximum out of round	0.010 mm
Big end journal tolerance:	
Grade A	48.000 to 48.007 mm
Grade B	47.993 to 48.000 mm
Grade C	47.986 to 47.993 mm
Clearance in bearings	0.021 to 0.049 mm
Big-end end-float	0.10 to 0.25 mm

Continued.....

Pistons
Piston diameter:
Grade A .... 79.975 to 79.990 mm
Grade B .... 79.991 to 80.005 mm
Clearance in bore .... 0.01 to 0.04 mm
Maximum ovality .... 0.30 mm

Piston rings
New ring to groove clearance:
Top compression .... 0.040 to 0.072 mm
2nd compression .... 0.030 to 0.062 mm
Oil control .... 0.010 to 0.180 mm

Ring fitted gap 20 mm from top of bore:
Top compression .... 0.20 to 0.35 mm
2nd compression .... 0.28 to 0.48 mm
Oil control .... 0.15 to 0.40 mm

Camshaft
Camshaft end-float .... 0.06 to 0.19 mm
Service limit .... 0.30 mm
Bearing clearance .... 0.060 to 0.094 mm
Service limit .... 0.15 mm

Tappets
Tappet outside diameter .... 32.959 to 32.975 mm

Valve springs
Free length .... 50.0 mm
Fitted length .... 37.0 mm
Load at fitted length .... 250 ± 12 N
Load at valve open length .... 450 ± 18 N

Valves
Valve stem diameter:
Inlet .... 5.952 to 5.967 mm
Exhaust .... 5.947 to 5.962 mm
Valve stem to guide clearance:
Inlet .... 0.033 to 0.063 mm
Service limit .... 0.07 mm
Exhaust .... 0.038 to 0.078 mm
Service limit .... 0.11 mm

Valve stem fitted height:
New .... 38.93 to 39.84 mm
Service limit .... 40.10 mm

Valves
Valve stem diameter:
Fitted height .... 6.00 mm

Continued.....

Valve seats
Valve seat angle - Inlet and Exhaust .... 45°
Valve seat width - Inlet and Exhaust .... 1.5 mm
Valve face angle - inlet and Exhaust .... 45°

Lubrication
System Type .... Cast aluminium wet sump; crankshaft driven eccentric rotor oil pump

Oil pump:
Outer rotor to housing clearance .... 0.28 to 0.36 mm
Inner rotor tip clearance .... 0.05 to 0.13 mm
Rotor end float .... 0.02 to 0.06 mm
Relief valve spring free length .... 38.90 mm
Minimum oil pressure at idle .... 100 kPa (14.5 $lbf.in^2$)
Relief valve opening pressure .... 410 kPa (59.5 $lbf.in^2$)
Oil pressure warning lamp switch pressure .... 20 to 58 kPa (3.0 to 8.5 $lbf.in^2$)
Oil filter .... Full flow disposable screw-on canister

ENGINE - 'L' SERIES

Type	8 valve SOHC, turbocharged, intercooled
Cylinder arrangement	4 in line - transverse
Bore	84.50 mm
Stroke	88.90 mm
Capacity	1994 cm^3
Compression ratio (nominal)	19.5 : 1
Firing order	1 - 3 - 4 - 2
Rotation	Clockwise, viewed from the front of the engine
Cylinder head warp - maximum	0.010 mm
Valve operation	Self-adjusting hydraulic tappets
Emissions Standard	ECD2 (EU2)
Maximum Power	88kW (118 bhp) @ 4200 rpm
Maximum torque	210Nm (284 lbf.ft) @ 2000 rpm
Turbocharger	Garrett GT 1549

Cylinder head

Cylinder head bolt length	243.41 mm

Cylinder block

Cylinder bore diameter[2]	84.442 to 84.460 mm

Crankshaft

Crankshaft end-float	0.03 to 0.26 mm
Crankshaft end thrust	Single size thrust washers at centre main bearing (No.3)
Thrust washer halves thickness	2.31 to 2.36 mm
Main bearings:	
Quantity	5
Type	Grooved shells in cylinder block, plain shells in main bearing caps
Main journal diameter	60.703 to 60.719 mm
Clearance in bearings	± 0.005 mm
Big-end journal diameter	57.683 to 57.696 mm
Clearance in bearings	± 0.005 mm

Gudgeon pins

Type	Fully floating, offset towards thrust side of piston
Diameter	29.995 to 30.000 mm

Pistons

Type	Aluminium alloy, graphite coated; combustion chamber in domed crown
Piston diameter[1]	84.262 mm
Clearance in bore	0.18 to 0.20 mm

[1]measured at right angles to gudgeon pin hole and 44 mm from bottom of skirt
[2]measured 70mm from top of skirt

Continued.....

Piston rings

New ring to groove clearance:	
Top compression	0.115 to 0.135 mm
2nd compression	0.050 to 0.082 mm
Oil control	0.050 to 0.082 mm
Ring fitted gap on piston:	
Top compression	0.30 to 0.50 mm
2nd compression	0.40 to 0.60 mm
Oil control	0.25 to 0.50 mm
Ring fitted gap 30mm from top of cylinder bore:	
Top compression	0.25 to 0.27 mm
2nd compression	0.40 to 0.42 mm
Oil control	0.30 to 0.32 mm

Camshaft

Drive	via toothed belt from gear on crankshaft
Number of bearings	5
Camshaft maximum end-float	0.51 mm
Bearing clearance	0.043 to 0.094 mm
Camshaft timing belt tensioner spring free length	65 mm

Tappets

Tappet outside diameter	34.959 to 34.975 mm

Valve springs

Free length	37.00 mm

Valves

Valve stem diameter:	
Inlet	6.907 to 6.923 mm
Exhaust	6.897 to 6.913 mm
Valve stem to guide clearance:	
Inlet	0.56 mm
Exhaust	0.066 mm
Valve face angle	45° to 45°30'
Valve head stand down:	
Inlet	1.45 mm
Exhaust	1.35 mm

Valve guides:

Inside diameter after reaming	6.950 to 6.963 mm
Fitted length above cylinder head	61.1 to 61.7 mm

Valve seat inserts

Seat angle:	
Inlet	60°
Exhaust	58° to 62°
Insert diameter:	
Inlet	35.697 mm
Exhaust	31.05 to 31.55 mm

Continued.....

Lubrication

System Type	Cast iron wet sump, crankshaft driven eccentric rotor oil pump
Oil pump:	
Type	Rotor
Drive	Front of crankshaft
Outer rotor to body clearance	0.05 to 0.10 mm
Rotor lobe clearance	0.025 to 0.120 mm
Outer rotor end float	0.03 to 0.08 mm
Relief valve spring free length	38.90 mm
Minimum pressure at idle	70 kPa (10 $lbf.in^2$)
Maximum pressure at 3000 rpm (hot)	380 kPa (55 $lbf.in^2$)
Relief valve opening pressure	450 kPa (65 $lbf.in^2$)
Oil pressure warning lamp switch pressure	20 to 58 kPa (3.0 to 8.5 $lbf.in^2$)
Oil filter	Full flow with disposable canister
Engine oil cooler	Connected to vehicle cooling system

FUEL SYSTEM - 'K' SERIES

System	Returnless Multipoint Fuel Injection, electronically controlled with electro-mechanical fuel injectors.
Fuel Pump	Continuous flow electrically driven roller vane pump submerged in fuel tank.
Fuel pressures	350 ± 20 kPa (50.7 ± 2.9 $lbf.in^2$), controlled by in-tank pressure regulator
Fuel pump delivery	39 litres @ 300 kPa (43.5 $lbf.in^2$)
Fuel filter	Mesh area 584 cm^2; Mesh size 8 to 10 microns
Air cleaner	Paper element type

FUEL SYSTEM - 'L' SERIES

System	Electronic Bosch fuelling system
Fuel injection pump	Electronic, VP37 High pressure
Fuel pump drive	Via belt from rear end of camshaft
Fuel filter	In-line canister type
Fuel line	In-line hand operated primer
Fuel cooler	in return line from pump to fuel tank
Heater plugs	*Refer to Engine Management System - EDC for Glow Plug operation times*
Air cleaner	Paper element type
Fuel injectors	*Bosch two spring, needle lift sensing on number one injector*
Turbocharger	Garrett GT 1549

COOLING SYSTEM - 'K' SERIES

System	By-pass type also cooling Intermediate Reduction Drive (IRD)
Expansion tank cap relief valve setting	89.5 to 120.5 kPa (13 to 17.5 $lbf.in^2$)
Thermostat starts to open	88°C
Thermostat fully open	102°C
Thermostat type	Wax element
Coolant Pump	
Type	Centrifugal impeller driven from engine cam belt
Drive Ratio	1 : 1 with crankshaft
Flow Rate	6 litre/min (1.4 gal./min.) around by-pass @ 1000rpm with thermostat closed
Coolant	
Initial fill	70% clean water, 30% antifreeze
Recommended service re-fill	50% clean water, 50% antifreeze

Cooling fan switching temperatures

Without air conditioning	On: 102°C, Off: 96°C
With air conditioning:	
Slow speed	On: 106°C, Off: 100°C
Fast speed	On: 112°C, Off: 106°C

COOLING SYSTEM - 'L' SERIES

System	By-pass type circulating engine and heater circuit; also cooling engine oil, IRD and EGR cooler
Expansion tank cap relief valve setting	89.5 to 120.5 kPa (13 to 17.5 $lbf.in^2$)
Thermostat starts to open	80 to 84°C
Thermostat fully open	96°C
Thermostat type	Wax element
Coolant Pump	
Type	Rotor type on rear face of PAS pump - belt driven
Coolant	
Initial fill	60% clean water, 40% antifreeze
Recommended service re-fill	50% clean water, 50% antifreeze

Cooling fan switching temperatures

Without air conditioning	On: 106°C, Off: 99°C
With air conditioning:	
Slow speed	On: 106°C, Off: 100°C
Fast speed	On: 112°C, Off: 106°C

IRD cooler thermostatic restrictor:

Starts to open	80° to 84°C
Fully open	96°C

CLUTCH

Type	Maintenance free hydraulic system
Pressure plate diameter	228 mm
Clutch drive plate diameter	
1.8 'K' series	215 mm
2.0 'L' series	228 mm
Facing material	APTEC T385
Diaphragm finger height	
New	32.10 to 37.50 mm
Service limit	42.75 mm
Diaphragm finger clearance (service limit)	1.00 mm
Clutch plate thickness	
New	6.90 to 7.40 mm
Service limit	5.60 mm
Rivet depth	
New	1.00 mm
Service limit	0.20 mm
Clutch plate run-out	
New	0.80 mm
Service limit	1.00 mm
Pressure plate warpage (Service limit)	0.15 mm

MANUAL GEARBOX - PG1

Gear ratios:	**1.8 'K'**	**2.0 'L'**
Fifth	0.649 : 1 (overall 3.974)	0.649 : 1 (overall 3.446)
Fourth	0.848 : 1 (overall 5.019)	0.848 : 1 (overall 4.509)
Third	1.222 : 1 (overall 7.483)	1.222 : 1 (overall 6.498)
Second	1.894 : 1 (overall 11.598)	1.894 : 1 (overall 10.071)
First	3.250 : 1 (overall 19.902)	3.250 : 1 (overall 17.281)
Reverse	3.000 : 1	3.000 : 1

Reverse idler gear to selector fork clearance	0.5 to 1.1 mm
Selector fork prong width	13.0 to 13.3 mm
Selector fork groove to pin clearance:	
Standard	0.05 to 0.35 mm
Service limit	0.50 mm
Selector fork groove width	7.05 to 7.25 mm
Gearshift arm to guide clearance:	
Standard	0.20 to 0.30 mm
Service limit	0.55 mm
Interlock shift guide groove width	8.10 to 8.20 mm
Synchro ring to gear clearance:	
Standard	0.85 to 1.10 mm
Service limit (minimum clearance)	0.40 mm
Selector shaft forks in synchro sleeve grooves clearance:	
Standard	0.45 to 0.65 mm
Service limit	1.00 mm
Gearshift arm guide to selector fork clearance:	
Standard	0.20 to 0.50 mm
Service limit	0.80 mm
Gearshift arm guide tongue width	11.90 to 12.00 mm
Gearshift arm guide to interlock assembly clearance:	
Standard	0.05 to 0.35 mm
Service limit	0.60 mm
Gearshift arm guide groove width	13.05 to 13.25 mm
Interlock ball to gearshift arm guide clearance:	
Standard	0.05 to 0.25 mm
Service limit	0.50 mm
Interlock ball outside diameter	12.05 to 12.15 mm

Continued.....

2nd to 3rd gear clearance:	
Standard	0.06 to 0.21 mm
Service limit	0.30 mm
3rd gear thickness:	
Standard	35.42 to 35.47 mm
Service limit	35.30 mm
4th to 5th gear clearance:	
Standard	0.06 to 0.21 mm
Service limit	0.30 mm
Spacer collar length:	
Standard	26.03 to 26.08 mm
Service limit	26.01 mm
4th gear thickness:	
Standard	30.92 to 30.97 mm
Service limit	30.80 mm
5th gear thickness	
Standard	30.42 to 30.47 mm
Service limit	30.30 mm
1st gear to thrust washer clearance:	
Standard	0.03 to 0.08 mm
Service limit	0.18 mm
2nd to 3rd gear clearance	0.03 to 0.10 mm
Input shaft end thrust	0.14 to 0.21 mm

FINAL DRIVE

Ratios:		
1.8 'K' series with MPi	4.200 : 1	
2.0 'L' series	3.647 : 1	
Road speed at 1000 rev/min in top gear:		
1.8 'K' series with MPi	31.7 km/h	19.7 mph
2.0 'L' series	36.5 km/h	22.7 mph
HDC speeds:		
Minimum forward	9.6 km/h	6.0 mph
Minimum reverse	6.5 km/h	4.0 mph

INTERMEDIATE REDUCTION DRIVE

Ratios:	
IRD input shaft to IRD countershaft	0.828 : 1
IRD countershaft to Front driveshaft	1.762 : 1
IRD countershaft to Propeller shaft	0.553 : 1
IRD ratio	1.458 : 1
Oil cooler	Connected to vehicle cooling system

REAR AXLE

Type	Hypoid gear, centreline of drive pinion below centre of ring gear
Differential carrier material	Aluminium
Ring gear to Pinion Gear:	
Backlash tolerance	0.13 to 0.20 mm
Ratios:	
Propeller shaft to rear driveshaft	3.214 : 1

VISCOUS COUPLING

Rating:	
Max	440 Nm (325 lbf.ft) @75 rpm
Min	360 Nm (265 lbf.ft) @75 rpm

STEERING

Type	Power assisted rack and pinion
Steering column	Height adjustable by 3.5° or 30 mm vertical movement of steering wheel
Turns - lock to lock:	3.16
Turning circle	11.6 m (38.1 ft) kerb to kerb

NOTE: The following steering geometry settings are given in degrees and minutes, decimal parts of a degree and millimetres. Steering and suspension geometry settings are for a vehicle at unladen weight.

Wheel alignment

Front:		
Camber angle - negative	0° 15' ±0° 45'	0.25° ±0.75°
$5^1/_2$ J x 15 wheel	1.710 mm ±5.11 mm	
6J x 16 wheel	1.811 mm ±5.323 mm	
Castor angle	3° 30' ±1°	3.5° ±1.0°
$5^1/_2$ J x 15 wheel	21.322 mm ±6.71 mm	
6J x 16 wheel	24.872 mm ±7.11 mm	
King pin inclination	12° 18'	12.3°
$5^1/_2$ J x 15 wheel	83.05 mm	
6J x 16 wheel	88.61 mm	
Front wheel alignment - toe-out - total	0° 20' ±0° 15'	0.3° ±0.25°
$5^1/_2$ J x 15 wheel	2.211 mm ±0.710 mm	
6J x 16 wheel	2.360 mm ±1.811 mm	
Rear:		
Camber angle - negative	0° 30' ±0° 45'	0.5° ±0.75°
$5^1/_2$ J x 15 wheel	3.314 mm ±1.710 mm	
6J x 16 wheel	3.551 ±1.811 mm	
Thrust angle	0° 0' ±0° 5'	0° ±0.08°
$5^1/_2$ J x 15 wheel	0 mm ±0.601 mm	
6J x 16 wheel	0 mm ±0.611 mm	
Rear wheel alignment - toe-in - total	0° 20' ±0° 15'	0.3° ±0.25°
$5^1/_2$ J x 15 wheel	2.211 mm ±1.710 mm	
6J x 16 wheel	2.360 mm ±1.811 mm	

Power Assistance System

Maximum Operating Pressure	9203 - 300 kPa (1334 -43.5 lbf.in^2), limited by pressure relief valve in pump
Maximum flow	5.5 -0.5 litres/min. (1.45 -0.13 US gal/min), limited by flow control valve in pump
Displacement	
1.8 'K' Series	8.2 cm^3/rev (0.50 in^3/rev)
2.0 'L' Series	9.5 cm^3/rev (0.58 in^3/rev)

SUSPENSION

Front

Type	Independent: MacPherson struts with coil springs, lower "L" shaped arms and anti-roll bar
Nominal height to wheel arch from hub centre*	453 mm
Road spring identification (colour code):	
1.8 'K' series without air conditioning	GREEN & BLUE
1.8 'K' series with air conditioning	GREEN & WHITE
2.0 'L' series without air conditioning	BROWN or BROWN and GREEN
2.0 'L' series with air conditioning	YELLOW or YELLOW and GREEN
Anti-roll bar diameter	20.5 mm

Rear

Type	Independent: MacPherson struts with coil springs and lower "trapezoidal links"
Nominal height to wheel arch from hub centre*	470 mm
Road spring identification (colour code	PINK

* At unladen weight

WHEELS

Wheel type and size:

Standard	5.5J x 15" steel
Option	5.5J x 15" alloy
Option	6.0J x 16" alloy

TYRE SIZES

1.8 'K' series and 2.0 'L' series

5.5J x 15" Wheels	195/80 R15
6J x 16" Wheels	215/65 R16

TYRE PRESSURES

All driving conditions

Front and rear	206 kPa (30 lbf.in^2)

BRAKES

Front disc brakes

Disc diameter:	262 mm
Disc thickness	
New	14.00 mm
Service limit	11.00 mm
Disc run out (maximum)	0.040 mm, with wheel on
Pad minimum thickness	3.00 mm

Rear drum brakes

Drum inside diameter	254 mm
Drum wear limit	255.50 mm, discard drum
Lining minimum thickness	2.00 mm
Drum ovality limit	0.012 mm
Parking brake	Mechanically operated via twin cables on rear drum brakes

Master cylinder

Bore diameter	23.80 mm

Brake servo

Servo boost ratio:	4.5 : 1

Anti-lock braking system

System type	4-channel

AIR CONDITIONING

System	CFC free, sealed, closed-loop system
Refrigerant	R134a
Compressor	
Displacement	177.7 cm^3/rev
Relief valve operation pressure	3432 kPa (498 $lbf.in^2$)
Lubricating oil	Nippon Denso ND-8
Oil fill quantity (new)	150 ± 20 cm^3

Thermostat

Opens	- 1°C
Closes	+ 1°C

Trinary switch operating pressures:

Low	
Closing pressure	140 kPa (20.3 $lbf.in^2$)
Opening pressure	100 kPa (14.5 $lbf.in^2$)
Normal	
Closing pressure	1650 kPa (239 $lbf.in^2$)
Opening pressure	2150 kPa (319 $lbf.in^2$)
High	
Opening pressure	2850 kPa (413 $lbf.in^2$)
Closing pressure	2250 kPa (326 $lbf.in^2$)

Engine overheat protection

Petrol	
A/C off	118°C
A/C on	114°C
Diesel	
A/C off	117.5°C
A/C on	115°C

ELECTRICAL - 'K' SERIES

System	12 volt, negative earth

Battery

Type	"Delco freedom" - 011, maintenance free
Capacity	55 ampere hour

Alternator

Type	Denso 12V
Maximum output	
Without air conditioning	90 amperes
With air conditioning	105 amperes
Drive method	5 groove poly Vee belt
Drive Ratio	2.63 : 1

Starter motor

Type	Denso P1.0
Power	1.0 kW pre-engaged type

ELECTRICAL - 'L' SERIES

System	12 volt, negative earth

Battery

Type	Delphi 096
Capacity	75 ampere hour

Alternator

Type	Nippon Denso
Maximum output:	
Without air conditioning	80 amperes
With air conditioning	105 amperes

Starter motor

Type	Nippon Denso
Power	1.8 kW

DIMENSIONS

Overall length (inc. spare)	4.382 m
Overall width:	
Including mirrors	2.074 m
Excluding mirrors	1.805 m
Overall height (including roof rails)*	1.757 m
Ground clearance *:	
Front	186 mm
Running	220 mm
Rear	214 mm
Wheelbase	2.555 m
Overhang:	
Front	836 mm
Rear (inc. spare wheel)	989 mm
Track:	
Front	1534 mm
Rear	1545 mm

* At unladen weight

WEIGHTS

Unladen weight (no options):		
Petrol models	1380 - 1425 kg	3045 - 3140 lb
Diesel models	1480 -1525 kg	3265 - 3365 lb
Unladen weight (all options):		
Petrol models	1449 - 1484 kg	3195 - 3270 lb
Diesel models	1545 -1580 kg	3405 - 3485 lb
Maximum gross vehicle weight:		
Petrol models	1960 kg	4322 lb
Diesel models	2050 kg	4520 lb
Maximum front axle weight	1050 kg	2315 lb
Maximum rear axle load (must NOT be exceeded)	1120 kg	2470 lb
Maximum braked trailer weight	1800 kg	3970 lb
Maximum Gross Towing Weight		
Petrol models	3760 kg	8291 lb
Diesel models	3850 kg	8489 lb
Towing hitch downward load (nose weight)	140 kg	309 lb
Maximum roof rack load (includes weight of rack)	75 kg	165 lb

MODEL: 1.8 - 'K' SERIES

Engine	
Type/capacity:	1.8 K16 / 1796 cm^3
Firing order	1-3-4-2
Compression ratio	10.5 : 1
Idle speed	775 ± 50 rev/min
Engine Management System	
Type	Fully mapped, electronic with breakerless ignition and indirect multi-port fuel injection
Igniton Coil	
Type	Denso Dry coil - single output
Primary resistance at 20° C	0.71 to 0.81 ohm
Spark plug	
Type	Champion RC8PYP double platinum
Gap	0.85 ± 0.1 mm
Fuel	
Grade	95 RON minimum - **UNLEADED**

⚠ **CAUTION: Serious damage to the engine may occur if a fuel with a lower octane number than that recommended is used. Serious damage to the catalyst will occur if LEADED fuel is used.**

2.0 - 'L' SERIES

Engine	
Capacity:	1994 cm^3
Firing order	1 - 3 - 4 - 2
Compression ratio	19.5 : 1
Idle speed:	
Without A/C and A/C off	805 ± 50 rev/min
With A/C on	875 ± 50 rev/min
Maximum no load engine speed:	5300 rev/min

Refer to appropriate section heading for component torque figures, e.g.
Road wheel nuts - refer to **SUSPENSION,**
Exhaust front pipe to manifold - refer to **MANIFOLD AND EXHAUST**

GENERAL

Bolt M5	6 Nm
Bolt M6	10 Nm
Bolt M8	25 Nm
Bolt M10	45 Nm
Bolt M12	80 Nm

ENGINE - 'K' SERIES

Engine - internal & timing

Camshaft cover to carrier bolts +	10 Nm
Camshaft carrier to cylinder head bolts	10 Nm
Timing belt rear cover to cylinder head bolts	9 Nm
Tensioner pulley backplate bolt - Manual timing belt tensioner	10 Nm
Timing belt tensioner pulley Allen bolt - Manual timing belt tensioner	45 Nm
Timing belt tensioner bolt - Automatic timing belt tensioner *	25 Nm
Camshaft gear bolts	65 Nm
Camshaft timing belt lower front cover bolts	9 Nm
Camshaft timing belt upper front cover bolts	9 Nm
Crankshaft pulley bolt	205 Nm
Cylinder head bolts, tighten progressively:	
1st stage +	20 Nm
2nd stage +	a further 180°
3rd stage +	a final 180°
Oil pressure switch	12 Nm
Alternator top mounting bracket nut/bolt	10 Nm
Spark plug cover screws	10 Nm
Engine lifting bracket bolts	9 Nm
Flywheel to crankshaft new bolts + *	78 Nm
Dipstick tube to block	9 Nm
Dipstick tube bracket to thermostat housing bolt	10 Nm
Oil pump to block bolts + *	10 Nm
Sump to gearbox bolts +	45 Nm
Sump to engine bearing ladder bolts	25 Nm
Engine sump drain plug:	25 Nm

Engine mountings

Engine RH mount to body bolts	45 Nm
Engine RH mounting/PAS pipe bracket nut	80 Nm
Engine RH mounting bracket to bolts	170 Nm
Engine RH mounting bracket to upper tie-rod bolt	80 Nm
Upper tie-rod to body bolt	80 Nm
Tie-rod bracket to body bolts	80 Nm
Engine lower tie rod to bracket bolt	80 Nm
Engine lower tie rod to subframe bolt	80 Nm
Lower tie rod bracket to sump bolts	45 Nm
Engine LH mounting to body bolts	45 Nm
Engine LH mounting to gearbox bolts	65 Nm
Engine LH gearbox mounting bracket through bolt	80 Nm
Strut to LH engine mounting bolt	80 Nm

+ Tighten in sequence
* New Patchlok bolt must be fitted

ENGINE - 'L' SERIES

Engine cover screw	4 Nm
Camshaft cover bolts +	12 Nm
Camshaft timing belt gear centre bolt	20 Nm then further 90°
Idler pulley stud	12 Nm
FIP timing belt gear hub bolts	25 Nm
FIP timing belt gear centre bolt	20 Nm then further 90°
FIP drive belt backplate screws	8 Nm
FIP timing belt tensioner Allen bolt	44 Nm
FIP timing belt cover bolts	5 Nm
Camshaft timing belt upper rear cover bolts	8 Nm
Camshaft timing belt lower rear cover bolts	8 Nm
Camshaft timing belt upper front cover bolts	5 Nm
Camshaft timing belt lower front cover bolts	5 Nm
Camshaft timing belt tensioner pulley Allen bolt	55 Nm
Camshaft timing belt tensioner bolt	45 Nm
Camshaft timing belt idler pulley nut	45 Nm
Camshaft carrier to cylinder head bolts	11 Nm
Camshaft gear damper Torx screws *	10 Nm
Crankshaft pulley bolt	63 Nm then a further 90°
Crankshaft main bearing cap bolts	112 Nm
Crankshaft rear oil seal housing bolts +	10 Nm
Cylinder head bolts	
First stage +	30 Nm
Second stage +	65 Nm
Third stage +	a further 90°
Fourth stage +	a final 90°
Connecting rod cap bolts	20 Nm then a further 85°
EGR recirculation pipe bolts	10 Nm

Continued.....

Engine mountings

Engine front mounting cover plate bolts	45 Nm
Engine front mounting cover plate nuts	35 Nm
Engine RH mounting/PAS pipe bracket nut	80 Nm
Engine LH mounting to body bolts	45 Nm
Engine LH mounting to gearbox bolts	65 Nm
Engine LH gearbox mounting bracket through bolt	80 Nm
Strut to LH engine mounting bolts	80 Nm
Strut to starter motor bolt	80 Nm
Engine RH mounting to body bolts	45 Nm
Engine RH mounting bracket to engine bolts	120 Nm
Engine RH mounting bracket to upper tie-rod bolt	80 Nm
Upper tie-rod to body bolt	80 Nm
Upper tie-rod bracket to body bolts	80 Nm
Lower tie rod bolts	80 Nm
Lower tie rod bracket to sump bolts	45 Nm
Upper tie rod to engine mounting bracket	80 Nm
RH engine mounting plate to engine bolts and nuts	30 Nm + 120°
Oil pump to block:	
M10 bolts +	45 Nm
M6 bolts +	10 Nm
Oil pump diverter plug	35 Nm
Oil pick-up pipe bolts (Patchlok)	8 Nm
Oil squirt jet banjo bolts	12 Nm
Oil pipe to oil pipe union	10 Nm
Oil pipes to pump	25 Nm
Oil strainer to cylinder block bolts	8 Nm
Sump bolts +	25 Nm
Sump drain plug	25 Nm
Sump to gearbox support bracket	25 Nm
Main oil gallery plug	12 Nm
Oil filter	17 Nm; Hand tighten then further 1/2 turn
Dipstick tube bracket bolt	25 Nm
Oil pressure switch	15 Nm
Oil cooler to block:	
M10 bolts	45 Nm
M8 bolts	25 Nm
Oil cooler pipe unions	25 Nm
Fuel injection pipe union nuts	28 Nm
Spill return pipes to injectors	10 Nm
Flywheel to crankshaft NEW (Patchlok) bolts +	15 Nm then further 90°
Turbocharger:	
Oil drain pipe bolts	8 Nm
Oil feed pipe banjo bolt	20 Nm
Vacuum pipe banjo bolt	25 Nm
Oil pipe union - pump to turbocharger feed pipe	25 Nm

+ Tighten in sequence
* New Torx screws must be fitted

ENGINE MANAGEMENT SYSTEM - MEMS

Air cleaner to battery tray bolts	9 Nm
Intake resonator to body bolts	9 Nm
Throttle housing to inlet manifold bolts	7 Nm
Spark plugs to cylinder head	27 Nm
h.t. lead cover bolts	10 Nm
Rotor arm to camshaft, NEW patchlock screw	8 Nm
Ignition coil to bracket screws	9 Nm
Ignition coil bracket to cylinder head bolts	25 Nm
ECM to bracket nut & bolt	9 Nm
Idle air control valve to manifold Torx screws	1.5 Nm
Intake air temperature sensor to manifold	7 Nm
Engine coolant temperature sensor to housing	15 Nm
Crankshaft position sensor to housing bolt	6 Nm
Throttle position sensor to housing Torx screws	1.5 Nm
Oxygen sensor to exhaust manifold	50 Nm
Fuel cut-off inertia switch nuts	2 Nm
Fuel rail to inlet manifold bolts	10 Nm

ENGINE MANAGEMENT SYSTEM - EDC

Air cleaner to battery tray bolts	9 Nm
Intake resonator to body bolts	9 Nm
Crankshaft position sensor (CKP) to adapter plate bolt	6 Nm
Engine breather hose clamp screws	2.5 Nm
ECM to bracket nuts	9 Nm
Exhaust gas recirculation:	
EGR pipe to plenum chamber	9 Nm
EGR valve to manifold	25 Nm
EGR valve to recirculation pipe	25 Nm
EGR modulator to bulkhead nuts	5 Nm
Glow plug	20 Nm
Glow plug lead terminal nut	2.5 Nm
Intake air temperature (IAT) sensor to intake manifold	12 Nm
Manifold atmospheric pressure (MAP) sensor nut	5 Nm
Injector clamp plate bolt	25 Nm
Coolant temperature sensor (ECT)	5 Nm
Throttle position (TP) sensor to bracket nuts	4 Nm
Injection pump gear nut	60 Nm
Injection pump spacer bolt	10 Nm
Injection pump adaptor bracket bolts	10 Nm
Injection pump feed/return pipe banjo bolt	25 Nm
Injector pipe union nuts	20 Nm
Injector clamp plate bolts	25 Nm
Spill return hose banjo to injector bolts	9 Nm
Fuel cut-off solenoid to fuel injection pump	20 Nm
Fuel cut-off solenoid lead stud nut	2.5 Nm
Exhaust manifold elbow to turbocharger bolts	25 Nm
Turbocharger to manifold nuts	10 Nm
Exhaust manifold to mounting bracket bolts	25 Nm
Oil drain tube to turbocharger nuts	10 Nm
Oil feed/return pipe to turbocharger nuts	20 Nm
Turbocharger air pipe to cylinder head bolts	10 Nm
Intercooler to radiator bolts	7 Nm

FUEL DELIVERY SYSTEM

Filler neck to body screws	9 Nm
Breather/separator to body screws	9 Nm
Fuel tank cradle bolts	45 Nm
Fuel pump aperture cover screws	1.25 Nm
'K' Series	
Inertia fuel shut-off switch	2 Nm
Fuel pump/sender unit to tank locking ring	45 Nm
'L' Series	
Fuel cooler bracket bolts	9 Nm
Injector pipes	20 Nm
Plenum chamber to camshaft cover bolt	9 Nm
Plenum chamber to inlet manifold	9 Nm
Fuel pick-up/sender unit to tank locking ring	45 Nm

COOLING

'K' Series	
Cooling fan to housing bolts	6 Nm
Cooling fan housing to radiator	6 Nm
Thermostat housing cover bolts	9 Nm
Thermostat housing to block bolts	9 Nm
Coolant rail to cylinder block bolts	9 Nm
Coolant rail bleed screw	9 Nm
Coolant pump to cylinder block bolts[1]	10 Nm
Coolant pump cover bolts	10 Nm
'L' Series	
Intercooler hose connecting clips	6.25 Nm
Coolant outlet elbow to cylinder head nuts	25 Nm
Coolant pump/cover to bracket bolts	10 Nm
Support bracket to pump	25 Nm
Cooling fan to housing	6 Nm
Cooling fan housing to radiator bolts	6 Nm
Thermostat housing to oil cooler bolts	9 Nm

[1]Tighten in diagonal sequence

MANIFOLD AND EXHAUST

Exhaust front pipe to catalytic converter nuts	60 Nm
Catalytic converter to intermediate pipe nuts	60 Nm
Intermediate pipe to tail pipe clamp nut	55 Nm
'K' Series	
Inlet manifold to cylinder head nut and bolts[1]	17 Nm
Exhaust manifold to cylinder head nuts[1]	45 Nm
Exhaust front pipe to manifold nuts	45 Nm
Exhaust front pipe to sump bolts	25 Nm
Exhaust front pipe support bracket to IRD nuts	25 Nm
'L' Series	
Inlet manifold to plenum chamber	9 Nm
Inlet manifold to cylinder head bolts[1]	25 Nm
Exhaust front pipe to manifold	45 Nm
Exhaust manifold to cylinder head:	
Nuts[1]	25 Nm
Bolts[1]	33 Nm
Exhaust front pipe to gearbox support bracket bolts	25 Nm
Exhaust manifold support bracket bolt	25 Nm
Turbocharger to exhaust manifold nuts	25 Nm
Turbocharger pipe to cylinder head bolts	10 Nm

[1]Tighten in diagonal sequence

CLUTCH

'K' Series	
Pressure plate to flywheel Torx bolts:[1]	25 Nm
Clutch slave cylinder bracket to gearbox bolts	45 Nm
'L' Series	
Pressure plate to flywheel Torx bolts[1]	25 Nm
Clutch release fork to shaft	29 Nm
Clutch slave cylinder bracket to gearbox bolts	45 Nm

[1]Tighten in diagonal sequence

MANUAL GEARBOX - PG1

First gear switch	25 Nm
Reverse light switch	25 Nm
Drain plug	35 Nm
Filler/level plug	45 Nm
Gearbox lifting eye bolt	27 Nm
Gearbox mounting bracket bolts	45 Nm
LH mounting to body bracket bolts	83 Nm
LH engine mounting to gearbox bolts	65 Nm
Gear change mechanism to gearbox nut and bolt	22 Nm
Gear change mechanism to body bolt	22 Nm
Gear change boot holder to underbody nuts	9 Nm
Gear change steady rod to gearbox bolt	25 Nm
Final drive gear to carrier bolts	110 Nm
Output shaft nut (LH thread)	110 Nm
Reverse idler shaft bolt	67 Nm
Gear case to clutch housing bolts[1]	45 Nm
Shaft bearing retaining plate bolts	8 Nm
Selector shaft guide to selector shaft bolt	28 Nm
Clutch release shaft pivot bolt	29 Nm
Cap bolt - detent ball and spring	22 Nm
Speedometer drive pinion retining plate bolt	5 Nm
Support bracket to gearbox bolt	80 Nm
Support bracket to sump bolt	45 Nm
Gearbox to adaptor plate/engine bolts	80 Nm
IRD to gearbox bolts	80 Nm

'K' Series

Flywheel front cover top bolt and nut	10 Nm

[1]Tighten in sequence

INTERMEDIATE REDUCTION DRIVE

Filler/level plug	35 Nm
Lower tie bar bracket to sump - Diesel	90 Nm
IRD support bracket to sump - Petrol	90 Nm
IRD support bracket to PAS pump bracket - Petrol	50 Nm
Lower tie bar bolts	80 Nm
Support bracket to IRD bolts	50 Nm
IRD adapter plate to gearbox	80 Nm

DRIVE SHAFTS

Front propeller shaft to IRD unit bolts and nuts	40 Nm
Propeller shaft to viscous coupling bolt	36 Nm
Mass damper to viscous coupling bolts	90 Nm
Rear propeller shaft to axle bolts and nuts	65 Nm
Rear differential flange nut:	
Initial tightening	176 Nm
Maximum	542 Nm
Rear differential front mounting bracket bolt	120 Nm
Rear differential front mounting bracket screws	45 Nm
Rear differential rear mounting bracket bolt	120 Nm
Rear differential rear mounting bracket screws	65 Nm
Rear differential oil plug	27 Nm
Viscous coupling support bearing bolts	25 Nm

STEERING

Steering wheel nut	18 Nm
Steering column adjuster nut	10.5 Nm
Steering column lower cowl screws	2 Nm
Steering column lock bolt	SHEAR
Steering column bracket (Nyloc) nuts	14 Nm
Steering column to PAS rack pinion clamp pinch bolt	32 Nm
Steering column bracket side support bolt	10 Nm
Steering column switchgear screws	2.25 Nm
Track-rod ball pin Nyloc nut	55 Nm
Track-rod pinch bolt	28 Nm
Track-rod to rack bolts	100 Nm
Track-rod end pinch bolt	28 Nm
PAS reservoir bracket bolts	10 Nm
PAS rack mounting bolts	45 Nm
PAS rack clamp bolts	45 Nm
Ram feed pipe union nuts:	
Small (6 mm) diameter	18 Nm
Large (10 mm) diameter	24 Nm
PAS rack to fluid cooler pipe union nut	22 Nm
PAS pipe mounting bracket to body & rack bolts	10 Nm
PAS hose clamp to engine mounting bracket nut and bolt	10 Nm
PAS fluid cooler clamps to front crossmember bolts	10 Nm
PAS rack feed pipe union nut	18 Nm

'K' Series

PAS pump to mounting bracket bolts	25 Nm
PAS pump pulley bolts	9 Nm
High pressure hose union to PAS pump	25 Nm
High pressure hose bracket to pump bolt	10 Nm

'L' Series

High pressure hose union to PAS pump	25 Nm
PAS pump pulley screws	9 Nm
PAS pump/coolant pump support bracket bolts	25 Nm

SUSPENSION AND SUBFRAME

Road wheel nuts[1]	115 Nm

Front Suspension

Anti-roll bar link to strut bolt	45 Nm
Anti-roll bar to link nut	55 Nm
Anti-roll bar clamp to subframe bolts	23 Nm
Damper shaft locking nut	57 Nm
Strut assembly to body top mounting nuts[2]	45 Nm
Strut to hub nuts & bolts[2]	205 Nm
Lower arm ball joint nut	65 Nm
Lower arm to rear bush housing nut[2]	140 Nm
Lower arm front bush to subframe bolt[2]	190 Nm
Lower arm rear bush housing bolts to body[2]	105 Nm
Hub shaft nut[3]	400 Nm

Rear Suspension

Damper shaft self locking nut	57 Nm
Strut mounting plate nuts	45 Nm
Strut to hub nuts & bolts[2]	205 Nm
Hub shaft nut[3]	400 Nm
Trailing link to body bracket bolt	120 Nm
Trailing link to hub knuckle nut and bolt	120 Nm
Trailing link bracket to body bolts	120 Nm
Adjustable Transverse link locknuts	90 Nm
Transverse link to subframe nuts and bolts:	
Adjustable	120 Nm
Fixed	120 Nm
Transverse link to hub nut and bolt:	105 Nm

Front Subframe

Front subframe to body front bolts	190 Nm
Front subframe to body rear bolts	105 Nm

Rear Subframe

Rear subframe to body bolts	190 Nm

[1]Tighten in diagonal sequence
[2]Tighten with weight of vehicle on suspension.
[3]Use NEW nuts

BRAKES

ABS ECU to bracket screws	4 Nm
ABS ECU bracket to body nuts	6 Nm
ABS ECU cover to bracket screw	4 Nm
ABS ECU pipe unions	14 Nm
ABS modulator bell cup nut	9 Nm
ABS modulator mounting bracket nuts	13 Nm
Pressure conscious reducing valve bracket nuts	9 Nm
Pressure conscious reducing valve pipe unions	14 Nm
Handbrake cable brackets bolts	23 Nm
Handbrake cable retaining plate to back plate bolts	22 Nm
Handbrake lever to body bolts	23 Nm
Brake servo to bulkhead nuts	22 Nm
Master cylinder to servo nuts	14 Nm
Primary and secondary brake pipe union nuts	14 Nm

'L' Series:

Vacuum pump to alternator	8 Nm

Front disc brakes

Bleed screw - calipers	10 Nm
Front caliper mounting bolts	83 Nm
Front disc to drive flange screws	5 Nm
Front disc shield to hub screw	8.5 Nm
Front caliper guide pin bolts	27 Nm
Front caliper brake hose banjo bolt	28 Nm

Rear drum brakes

Bleed screw - rear wheel cylinder	7 Nm
Rear brake drum to hub screws	5 Nm
Rear wheel cylinder to backplate bolts	8 Nm
Rear wheel cylinder pipe union nut	14 Nm
Back plate to hub bolts	45 Nm

SUPPLEMENTARY RESTRAINT SYSTEMS

Airbag ECU fixing bolts	9 Nm
Driver's airbag module Torx screws	9 Nm
Passenger's airbag module to fascia screws	9 Nm
Passenger airbag module finisher fixing screws	1.5 Nm

BODY

Doors

Front door glass regulator to door screws	8 Nm
Rear door glass regulator clamp nuts	8 Nm
Rear door glass regulator to door screws	9 Nm
Tail door glass regulator to door screws	9 Nm
Tail door glass regulator lock nuts	14 Nm
Door stiffener plate screws	8 Nm
Door lock striker to body screws	25 Nm
Door lock to outside handle screws	4 Nm
Door interior handle screws	2.5 Nm
Door latch to door screws	6 Nm
Door interior casing screws	2.5 Nm
Tail door latch, male dovetail screws	9 Nm
Tail door latch actuator to body screws	9 Nm
Tail door hinges to body bolts	30 Nm

Exterior Fitting

Exterior mirror to door Torx screws	4 Nm
Door mirror cheater screws	2 Nm
Bonnet hinge, bolts	22 Nm
Bonnet lock and striker to body bolts	20 Nm
Spare wheel mounting bracket:	
Bolts	13 Nm
Nuts	25 Nm
Centre high mounted stop lamp cover plate screws	6 Nm
Spare wheel to spare wheel bracket retention nuts	45 Nm
Towbar to body bolts:	
M12	120 Nm
M10	45 Nm
Front recovery loop bolt	85 Nm
Rear recovery loop bolts	65 Nm
Mudflap to body screws	4 Nm
Wheel arch liner to body screws	4 Nm
Underbelly panel to body bolts	45 Nm
Underbelly panel to body rear screws	9 Nm
Front bumper to underbelly panel screws	4 Nm
Front bumper fixing screws	4 Nm
Front bumper support bracket screws	3 Nm
Front bumper to body studs and nuts	12 Nm
Front bumper armature bolts	25 Nm
Rear bumper screws	30 Nm
Rear bumper scrivets	4 Nm
Engine splash shield to body screws	10 Nm
Roof rack rail bung screws	11 Nm

Continued.....

3 door vehicles

Roof rack side rail bolts	22 Nm
Hood release mechanism 'E' post recetacle clamp screws	7 Nm
'D' post hood finisher screws	4 Nm
Hood to rear finisher screws	4 Nm
Hood to roof finisher screws	2 Nm
Soft top bracket screws	25 Nm
Roof rack adapter to 'E' post screws	8 Nm
Roof rack Assembly screws	22 Nm

5 door vehicles

Roof rack side rail bolts	22 Nm

Vehicle controls

Brake/accelerator pedal bracket to body nuts	23 Nm
Clutch pedal bracket to body nuts	23 Nm

Alarm system

Alarm bonnet switch bracket screws	4 Nm
Volumetric sensor bracket screws	1.5 Nm

Interior Trim Components

Fascia mounting screws	4 Nm
Upper fascia mounting bracket screws	4 Nm
Lower fascia mounting bracket screws	9 Nm
Clock/radio remote display fixing screws	1.25 Nm
Glovebox inner screws	1.5 Nm
Instrument pack cover screws	1.5 Nm
Instrument pack finisher screws	1.5 Nm
Front console screws	1.5 Nm
Rear console screws	1.5 Nm
Sun visor screws	2.5 Nm
Sun visor clip screw	2.5 Nm
Luggage tie-down loop screw	22 Nm
Loadspace cover bracket (3-door) screws	2.5 Nm
Rear end door treadplate screws	1.6 Nm
Front sill finisher screws	1.6 Nm
Rear sill finisher (5-door) screws	1.6 Nm
Rear sill finisher (3-door) screws	2.2 Nm
'B/C' post lower finisher (5-door) screws	1.6 Nm
'D' post upper trim (5-door) screws	1.25 Nm
Rear quarter casing (3-door) screws	2.5 Nm
Head lining support bracket screws	5 Nm
Headlining (3-door) screws	2.5 Nm
Bonnet release handle screws	9 Nm
HDC Gearknob bolt	5 Nm

Non passenger side airbag vehicles

Grab handle	4 Nm
Facia stowage bin screws	2.5 Nm

Continued.....

Seats

Front seat runner to body bolts	45 Nm
Front seat slide finisher screws	1.6 Nm
Front seat squab to seat frame Torx bolts	45 Nm
Front seat valance fixing screws	1.6 Nm
Rear seat retaining bar bolts	45 Nm
Rear seat squab to seat frame Torx bolts	45 Nm
Rear bench seat to body bolts	25 Nm
Rear split seats to body bolts	25 Nm
Rear seat striker loop bolts	25 Nm

5-door seat belts

Seat belt pretensioner to seat bolt	32 Nm
Seat belt height adjuster bolts	26 Nm
Front seat belt loop to adjuster nut	31 Nm
Front seat belt reel bolt	31 Nm
Front seat belt lower anchor plate to B/C post bolt	40 Nm
Rear side seat belt upper mounting bolt	32 Nm
Rear side seat belt reel bolt	50 Nm
Rear side seat belt lower fixing bolt	40 Nm
Rear centre seat belt reel fixing nut	32 Nm
Rear centre seat belt lower fixing bolt	40 Nm
Rear seat belt buckle bolts	32 Nm

3-door seat belts

Seat belt pretensioner to seat bolt	32 Nm
Front seat belt reel bolt	31 Nm
Front seat belt loop to 'B' post bolt	31 Nm
Front seat belt slider bar bolts	40 Nm
Rear seat belt upper mounting bolt	32 Nm
Rear seat belt reel bolt	49 Nm
Rear seat belt lower fixing bolt	50 Nm
Rear seat belt anchor plate bolts	40 Nm

Screens

Quarter light bracket fixing screws	4 Nm
Backlight finisher screws	3 Nm
Sun roof mountings screws	6 Nm
Sun roof to body bolts	8.5 Nm

HEATING AND VENTILATION

Air intake assembly fixing nuts	9 Nm
Fascia duct bolts	4 Nm
Left hand demister duct fixing screw	9 Nm
Heater control panel screws	1.5 Nm
Heater unit to bulkhead	9 Nm
Blower motor screws	9 Nm

AIR CONDITIONING

Condenser bracket to bonnet locking platform bolts	9 Nm
Condenser to bracket bolts	9 Nm
Trinary switch	12 Nm
Receiver/drier to body bolts	9 Nm
Pipes to receiver/drier bolts	9 Nm
A/C pipes to condenser bolts	9 Nm
Pipe to component union bolts	9 Nm
Evaporator unit assembly bolts	9 Nm
Pipe flange to evaporator bolt	9 Nm

'K' Series

Compressor to mounting bracket bolts	45 Nm
Evaporator pipe to compressor	9 Nm
Condenser pipe to compressor	9 Nm
Engine overheat sensor	15 Nm

'L' Series

Compressor mounting bolts	45 Nm
Engine overheat sensor	15 Nm

WIPERS AND WASHERS

Windscreen wiper motor linkage bolts	7 Nm
Windscreen wiper motor bolts	5 Nm
Windscreen wiper arm nut	18 Nm
Rear wiper arm nut	13 Nm
Rear wiper motor bolts	5 Nm
Rear wiper motor spindle nut	5 Nm
Washer bottle mounting bolt	5 Nm
Washer bottle filler neck	4 Nm

ELECTRICAL

Aerial base mounting nuts	2 Nm
Battery tray to body bolts	9 Nm
Battery clamp bolts	10 Nm
Battery connection nuts	7 Nm
Battery positive fly lead to fusebox screw	2.75 Nm
Earth fly lead to body bolt	7 Nm
Earth header block screws	7 Nm
Headlamp to body bolts	4 Nm
Rear fender lamp cover screws	1.5 Nm
Rear bumper lamp cover screws	1.5 Nm
Centre high mounted stop lamp cover nut and screw	1.5 Nm
Horn bracket to body screw	22 Nm
Inertia switch mounting nut	2 Nm
Engine compartment fusebox to body bolts	4 Nm
Passenger compartment fusebox bracket to body bolts	9 Nm
Passenger compartment fusebox to bracket bolts	5 Nm
Main harness to body harness connector mounting bracket nuts	6 Nm
Door speaker to door mounting screws	1.3 Nm
Interior light (3-door) fixing nuts	2.5 Nm
Volumetric sensor to bracket screws	1.2 Nm

'K' Series

Battery cable to alternator fixing nut	4 Nm
Starter motor to engine bolts	85 Nm
Battery cable to starter solenoid nut	4 Nm

Non A/C models:

Alternator drive belt tensioner bolt	25 Nm
Alternator mounting bolts	45 Nm

A/C models:

Alternator mounting bolt to adjustment bracket	25 Nm
Alternator top mounting nut/bolt	45 Nm

'L' Series

Alternator lower fixing bolt/nut	45 Nm
Alternator upper fixing bolt	25 Nm
Battery cable to alternator fixing nut	4 Nm
Battery cable to starter solenoid nut	4 Nm
Starter motor to engine bolts	85 Nm

INSTRUMENTS

Instrument pack fixing screws	1.5 Nm
Engine coolant temperature gauge sensor	10 Nm
Speedometer transducer to gearbox	4 Nm

CAPACITIES

Fuel tank	59 litres (13 gallons)
Engine oil refill and filter change:	
1.8 'K' Series	4.5 litres (7.9 imp. pints)
2.0 'L' Series	4.9 litres (8.6 imp. pints)
Engine oil refill from dry:	
1.8 'K' Series	4.8 litres (8.4 imp. pints)
2.0 'L' Series	5.3 litres (9.3 imp. pints)
Manual gearbox - PG1	
Refill	2.0 litres
From dry	2.2 litres (3.875 imp. pints)
Intermediate Reduction Drive	1.1 litres (2 imp. pints)
Rear differential	
Maximum	830 ml (29.2 Imp. fl. oz.)
Minimum	750 ml (26.4 Imp. fl. oz.)
Power steering reservoir	335 cc
Cooling system from dry (with reservoir tank): *	
1.8 'K' Series	5.5 litres (9.6 imp. pints)
2.0 'L' Series	7.2 litres (12.6 imp. pints)
Reservoir tank	
maximum fill	0.44 litres (0.75 imp. pints)
expansion tank volume	1.2 litres (2.125 imp. pints)
gross expansion capacity	0.72 litres (1.27 imp. pints)
Air conditioning compressor	150 ± 20cc
Washer reservoir	4.0 litres (7 imp. pints)

Refill capacity is approx. 0.7 litre less than the from dry figures.

FLUIDS

Brake Fluid

Use only AP New Premium Super DOT 4 brake fluid or Castrol Girling Universal DOT 4 brake/clutch fluid. DO NOT use any other type of fluid.

Anti-freeze solutions

The overall anti-freeze concentration should not fall, by volume, below 50% to ensure that the anti-corrosion properties of the coolant are maintained. Anti-freeze concentrations greater than 60% are not recommended as cooling efficiency will be impaired.

Use **Land Rover Parts RTC5779A antifreeze and Summer Coolant** to protect the cooling system.

The cooling system should be drained, flushed and refilled with the correct amount of anti-freeze solution at the intervals given on the Service Maintenance Check Sheet.

CAUTION: No other 'universal' anti-freeze should be used with UNIPART Superplus 3 Anti-freeze and Summer Coolant. If Land Rover Parts RTC5779A antifreeze and Summer Coolant is not available, use an ethylene glycol based anti-freeze containing no methanol with non-phosphate corrosion inhibitors which meet specifications BS6580 and BS5117 suitable for use in mixed metal engines. To ensure the protection of the cooling system against corrosion, these anti-freezes must be renewed every 24 months (or every 36 months for Land Rover Parts RTC5779A).

After filling with anti-freeze solution, attach a warning label to a prominent position on the vehicle stating the type of anti-freeze contained in the cooling system to ensure that the correct type is used for topping-up.

The recommended quantities of anti-freeze for different degrees of frost protection are:

Solution	Amount of anti-freeze	Commences freezing		Frozen solid	
50%	Litres	°C	°F	°C	°F
1.8 'K' Series models	2.7	-36	-33	-48	-53
2.0 'L' Series models	3.5	-36	-33	-48	-53

LUBRICATION

The engine and other lubricating systems are filled with high- performance lubricants giving prolonged life.

CAUTION: You should always use a high quality oil of the correct viscosity range in the engine and gearbox during maintenance and when topping-up. The use of oil not to the correct specification can lead to high oil and fuel consumption and ultimately to damaged components.

Oil to the correct specification contains additives which disperse the corrosive acids formed by combustion and prevent the formation of sludge which can block the oil ways. Additional oil additives should not be used.
Always adhere to the recommended servicing intervals.

Engine oil

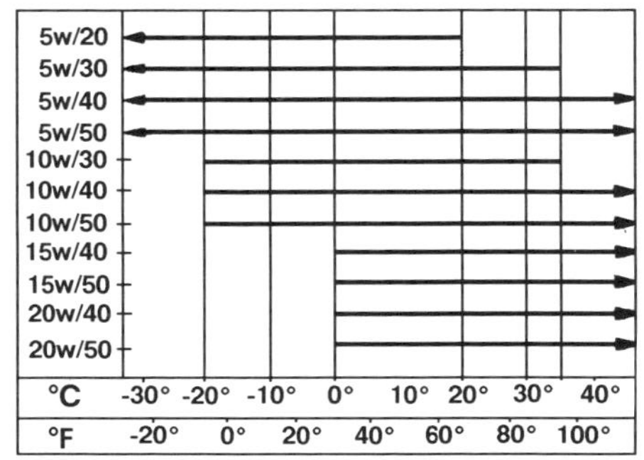

1M0060A

Petrol vehicles

Use oil meeting ACEA A2 specification and having a viscosity band recommended for the temperature range of your locality.
Where oils to these Land Rover and European specifications are not available, well known brands of oils meeting API SH quality should be used.

Diesel vehicles

Use oil meeting specification ACEA B2 and having a viscosity band recommended for the temperature range of your locality.
Where oils to these Land Rover and European specifications are not available, well known brands of oils meeting API SG,SN or SG/Cd quality should be used.

Manual gearbox - PG1

Use the following oils for refill or topping-up:

TEXACO MTF 94

The following oils may be used for topping-up only:
Use oil meeting the requirments of ACEA A2 and a viscosity of 10W/40.
Fill level to plug.

Intermediate Reduction Drive

Factory Fill: Texaco S5 75W90
Specification: API GL5

Rear Differential

Factory Fill: Texaco Multigear 80W-90 ETL 7441
Specification: API GL5

Power Steering

TOPPING-UP: Use Dexron IIde & III or equivalent

Gear linkage - Manual

Use grease Part No. AFU 1500 containing 3% Molybdenum Disulphide.

General Greasing

Use Multipurpose Lithium Base Grease N.L.G.I. consistency No. 2.

Bonnet latch

Lubricate cable and latch with oil.

Locks, Latches and Hinges

Use Door Lock and Latch Lubricant, Part No. VWN 10075.

CONTENTS

Page

VEHICLE INTERIOR

Check condition and security of seats and seat belts.

1. Check seat frames are secured to floor and show no signs of movement.
2. Check operation of seat slide and tilt mechanisms, ensuring there is no excessive play between seat cushion and seat back.
3. Check tightness of accessible seat fixings.
4. Fully extract seat belt and allow it to return under its own recoil mechanism.
5. Check entire length of seat belt webbing for signs of fraying or damage. Repeat for all belts.
6. Check security of seat belt upper mountings.
7. Check for correct operation of seat belt height adjusters.
8. Check security of seat belt buckle mountings.
9. Connect each belt to the correct buckle, check seat belt buckle and tongue are secure. Release seat belt buckle and check for correct operation.
10. Check tightness of accessible seat belt mountings

Check operation of all lamps, horns and warning indicators.

1. Switch on side, head and tail lights and check operation.
2. Check headlamp dim/dip operation.
3. Check headlamp levelling operation.
4. Check turn signals and hazard warning lights operation.
5. Press brake pedal and check operation of brake lights.
6. Check all exterior lamp lenses for clarity and condition. Pay particular attention to head lamp lenses for signs of stone chips or damage.
7. Check horn for loud clear sound.
8. Check operation of all instrument pack warning and indicator lights.
9. Check for correct operation of interior courtesy lights.
10. Switch on headlamps (with ignition switch at 'O' position) and check light reminder warning operates when door is opened.

Check operation of front/rear wipers and washers and condition of wiper blades.

10M0508

1. Operate screen washer and switch on wipers. Check washer jets are correctly aimed and check for smooth smearless operation across screen of wiper blades at all speeds, including intermittent.
2. Repeat operation for rear screen wipers/washers.
3. Check all wiper blades for condition and signs of splits or damage.
4. Check security of wiper arms.

Check operation of handbrake.

1. With the vehicle stationary, apply handbrake and check for correct operation. ***See BRAKES, Adjustments.***
2. Release handbrake and check for correct operation.

NOTE: Any adjustment required as a result of the checking process will be subject to additional labour and/or material cost and should not be carried out without the authorisation of the customer.

Adjust handbrake (First 12,000 miles/12 months only

1. Adjust handbrake cable. ***See BRAKES, Adjustments.***

NOTE: Additional time is built into the first 12,000/12 months service time to allow for handbrake cable adjustment.

VEHICLE EXTERIOR

Remove road wheels

1. Loosen wheel nuts. Raise vehicle for wheel free condition and remove the wheel nuts.
2. Mark the wheel to stud relationship to ensure that the wheels are refitted in the same orientation.

Refit road wheels to original hub position

1. Apply a thin coat of anti-seize compound to wheel hub centre.
2. Refit wheels to original hub position.

NOTE: When refitting road wheel nuts do not overtighten using powered tools. Ensure the wheel nuts are correctly torqued in the correct sequence.

3. Tighten wheel nuts to 115 Nm.

Check tyre pressures, condition and tread depth (mm)

1. Check for any apparent damage to tyres, paying particular attention to side walls.
2. Look at tyre treads and check for any unusual wear patterns which may indicate out of specification adjustment of steering or suspension.

NOTE: Any adjustments to steering or suspension will be subject to additional labour and/or material cost and should not be carried out without the authorisation of the customer.

3. Measure the tread depth across the width of the tyre and around the circumference. Annotate the maintenance check sheet with the lowest figure obtained from each tyre.

NOTE: Any requirement to replace tyres should be advised to the customer before any remedial work is carried out. This will be subject to additional labour and/or material cost and should not be carried out without the authorisation of the customer.

CAUTION: If new tyres are to be fitted, ensure that they are fitted to the rear axle only or to both front and rear axles. DO NOT fit new tyres to front axle only.

Inspect brake pads for wear, calipers for leaks and discs for condition.

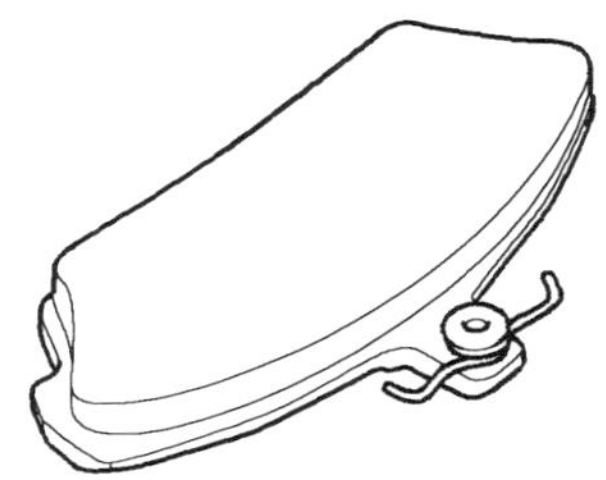

10M0511

1. With front road wheels removed, check brake pad thickness and ensure that both pads are wearing evenly.
2. Check brake discs for signs of cracking, excessive scoring or oil contamination.

NOTE: Any requirement to replace brake pads or brake disc should be advised to the customer as this will incur additional labour and/or material cost and should not be carried out without the authorisation of the customer.

3. Check for any signs of brake fluid leakage from caliper seals, hoses or unions.
4. Using brake cleaner, remove excessive deposits of brake dust from pads, calipers and disc shields.

Inspect rear brake shoes via back plate inspection point.

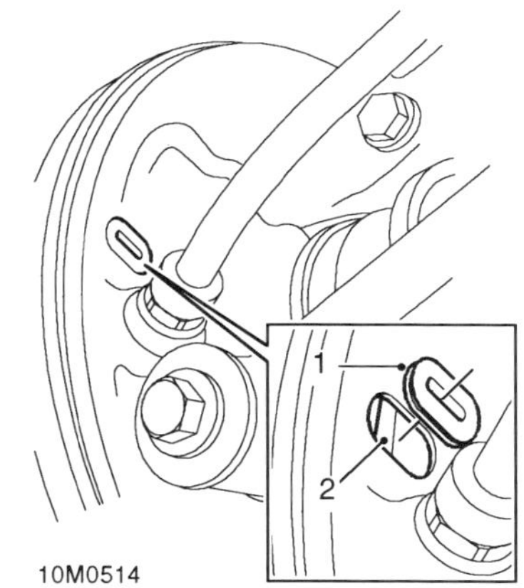

10M0514

1. With the vehicle at a convenient working height, remove the rubber plugs from the rear of the back plate.
2. Using a lamp, inspect thickness of rear brake shoes.

NOTE: Any requirement to replace brake shoes should be advised to the customer as this will incur additional labour and/or material cost and should not be carried out without the authorisation of the customer.

3. Check for any signs of brake fluid contamination on brake shoes, or evidence of brake fluid leakage from drum/backplate.
4. Ensure that rubber plug is correctly fitted into back plate upon completion of check.

Remove brake drums, inspect shoes for wear and drums fo condition.

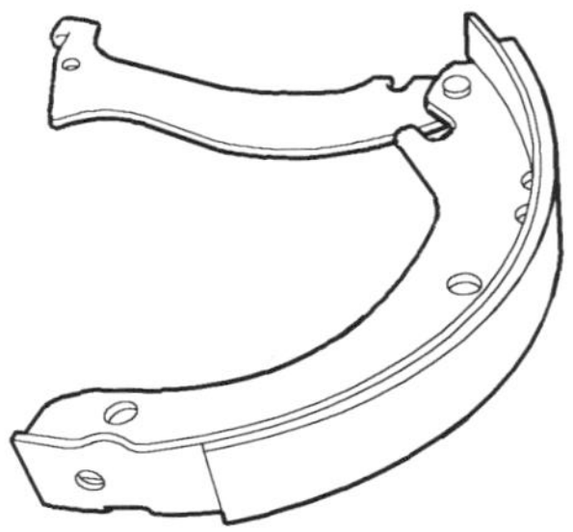

10M0509

1. With vehicle at a convenient working height and the wheels removed, remove the rear brake drums. ***See BRAKES, Repairs.***
2. Check brake shoe thickness, and for any evidence of brake shoe contamination from brake fluid.
3. Check brake drum for signs of cracking, excessive scoring or oil contamination.

NOTE: Any requirement to replace brake shoes, wheel cylinders or brake drums should be advised to the customer as this will incur additional labour and/or material cost and should not be carried out without the authorisation of the customer.

4. Using brake cleaner, remove excessive deposits of brake dust from drums, shoes and back plate.
5. Refit drums. ***See BRAKES, Repairs.***

Renew fuel filter - Petrol

1. Renew fuel filter. ***See FUEL DELIVERY SYSTEM, Repairs.***

Lubricate door locks, hinges, check straps and bonnet catch.

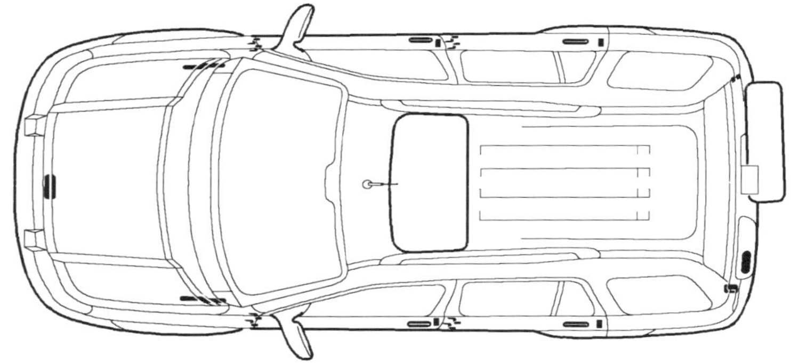

10M0507

Front and rear doors

1. Open each door in turn and lubricate door hinges and check strap using recommended lubricant.
2. Lubricate door lock, striker and private lock using PTFE lubricant. Remove excessive lubricant, particularly from door striker area, to avoid customer complaint.
3. Check tightness of accessible door lock and striker fixings
4. Open and close door to check for smooth, noise-free operation. Ensure door closes securely.
5. Check for smooth operation of private lock.

Tail door

6. Open tail door and lubricate hinges using recommended lubricant.
7. Grease tail door check slide.
8. Lubricate rear door lock and striker using PTFE lubricant. Remove excessive lubricant to avoid customer complaint, particularly from door striker area.
9. Check tightness of accessible tail door lock and striker fixings.

Bonnet

10. With bonnet open, lubricate hinges, striker, lock and safety catch using a suitable lubricant.

Lubricate sunroof guide rails, slides and seal.

1. With sunroof open, lubricate accessible guide rails, slides and seals. Remove any excess lubricant to avoid contaminating roof lining and trim.
2. Ensure sunroof closes correctly.

Clean sunroof drain tubes and channels.

1. Remove any debris from sunroof tray.
2. Ensure that all accessible sunroof drain tubes are clear using a low pressure air line.

UNDER BONNET

Check cooling system and intercooler

1. Check for any obstructions in the radiator matrix and remove debris as necessary.
2. Check condition of all coolant hoses. Check for any signs of leakage or chafing.
3. Check tightness of accessible hose clips
4. Check for any obstructions in the intercooler matrix and remove debris as necessary. **Diesel only.**
5. Check intercooler hoses for security and condition.
6. Check security of radiator and intercooler mountings.

Check coolant level

1. Check coolant level and top up if necessary.

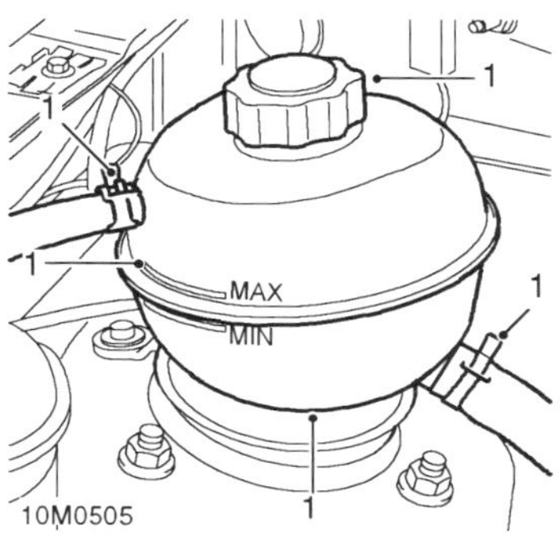

Renew spark plugs

1. Renew spark plugs. ***See ENGINE MANAGEMENT SYSTEM - MEMS, Repairs.***

Renew fuel filter - Diesel

1. Renew fuel filter. ***See ENGINE MANAGEMENT SYSTEM - EDC, Repairs.***

Check condition of auxilliary drive belt.

1. Check auxilliary drive belts for tension, signs of fraying, damage and for any oil contamination.

NOTE: Any requirement to replace or adjust the auxilliary drive belt should be advised to the customer, as this will incur additional labour and/or material cost and should not be carried out without the authorisation of the customer.

Renew auxilliary drive belt (Diesel only)

1. Renew alternator drive belt. ***See ELECTRICAL, Repairs.***

Replace camshaft drive belt

1. Renew camshaft drive belt. ***See ENGINE - 'K' SERIES, Repairs.***
2. Renew camshaft drive belt. ***See ENGINE - 'L' SERIES, Repairs.***

Replace rear fuel injection pump drive belt (Diesel only)

1. Renew Fuel Injection Pump (F.I.P) drive belt ***See ENGINE - 'L' SERIES, Repairs.***

Check PAS fluid level

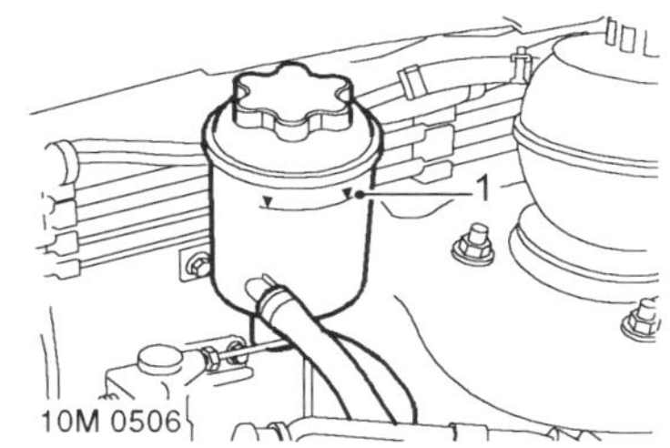

1. Check Power Assisted Steering (PAS) fluid level. Before topping up PAS fluid level, ensure there are no leaks from the pump, hoses, unions or steering rack.

Check clutch fluid level

1. Check and top up clutch fluid level. Check system for leaks before topping up.

Check brake fluid level

1. Check brake fluid level, take into account any brake friction material wear before topping up. Check remainder of system for leaks before topping up.

Check and top up intermediate reduction drive, gearbox and rear axle oil

Intermediate reduction drive

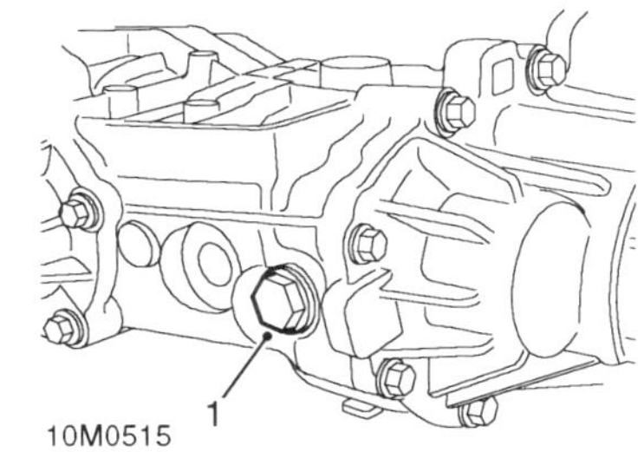

1. With vehicle on a ramp at a convenient working height, carefully remove IRD level plug and collect sealing washer.
2. Check oil level. Before topping up oil level, check for visible signs of leakage. Pay particular attention to drive shaft and prop shaft oil seals.
3. Refit level plug to IRD unit using a new sealing washer.

Gearbox

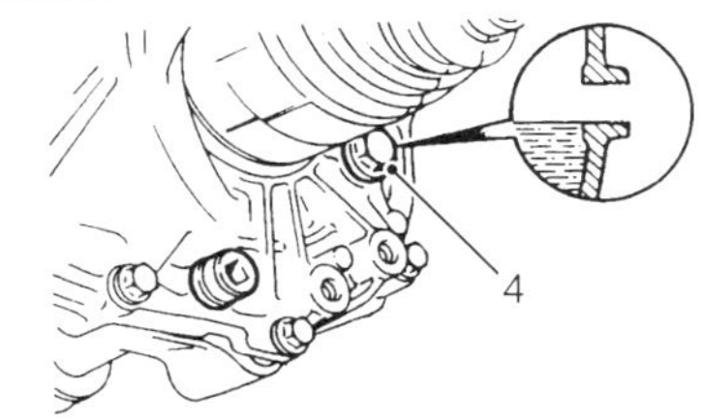

4. With vehicle on a ramp at a convenient working height, carefully remove gearbox level plug and collect sealing washer.
5. Check oil level. Before topping up oil level, check for visible signs of leakage. Pay particular attention to drive shaft oil seal.
6. Refit level plug to gearbox using a new sealing washer.

Rear axle

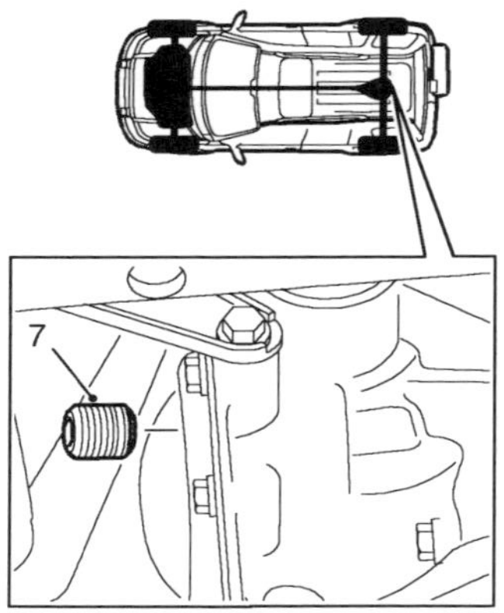

10M0516

7. With vehicle on a ramp at a convenient working height, carefully remove rear differential level plug.
8. Check oil level. Before topping up oil level, check for visible signs of leakage. Pay particular attention to drive shaft oil seals, differential pinion oil seal and backplate gasket.
9. Refit level plug to rear differential.

Check clutch pipes and unions for chafing, leaks and corrosion.

1. Check route of clutch pipe from master cylinder to slave cylinder. Ensure that pipe is correctly retained and shows no signs of fluid leakage or chafing.
2. Check unions for signs of fluid leakage.

Check and top-up windscreen and rear washer reservoir.

1. Release cap from washer reservoir and fill with the correct concentration of screen washer fluid.
2. Refit cap ensuring it is securely fastened.

Check battery condition and clean/grease terminals

1. Check battery condition indicator.
   Green = OK.
   Black = Battery requires charging.
   Clear/white = New battery required.

NOTE: Any requirement to replace or charge the battery should be advised to the customer as this will incur additional labour and/or material cost and should not be carried out without the authorisation of the customer.

2. Clean and check security of battery terminals. Smear with petroleum jelly.

Check intercooler and radiator for external obstructions.

1. Using lead lamp, view condition of radiator and intercooler through radiator grill. Ensure cooling fins are in good condition and are clear of any obstructions.

NOTE: Any remedial work required to remove obstructions should be advised to the customer as this will incur additional labour and/or material cost and should not be carried out without the authorisation of the customer.

Renew engine oil and filter

Drain

1. With the vehicle at a convenient working height, remove the underbelly panel. ***See BODY, Repairs.***

NOTE: The oil should be drained when engine is warm.

NOTE: The oil filter can be renewed while oil is being drained.

WARNING: Observe due care when draining as the oil can be extremely hot. Prolonged and repeated contact with used engine oil may cause serious skin disorders, wash thoroughly after contact. Keep out of reach of children.

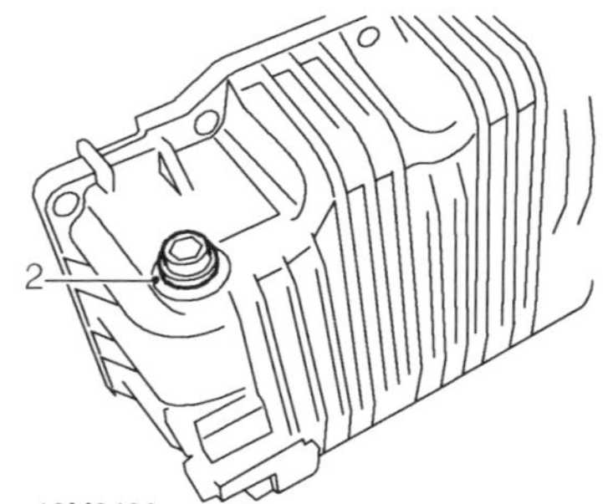

10M0400

2. Place a container beneath engine sump, remove drain plug and discard sealing washer. Allow oil to drain.
3. Remove oil filter. ***See ENGINE, Repairs.***

Refill

4. Fit new oil filter. ***See ENGINE, Repairs.***
5. Clean drain plug, fit NEW sealing washer and tighten drain plug to the torque specified in the Information section.
6. Remove oil filler cap, refill engine with oil to correct level.
7. Fit oil filler cap.

Fuel hoses and pipes

Petrol engines

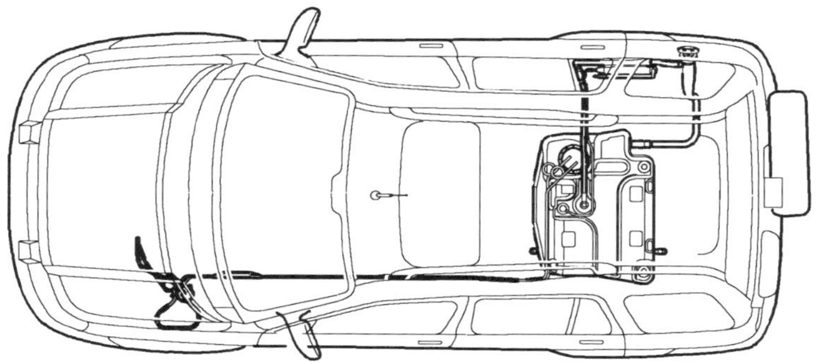

10M0498

Diesel engines

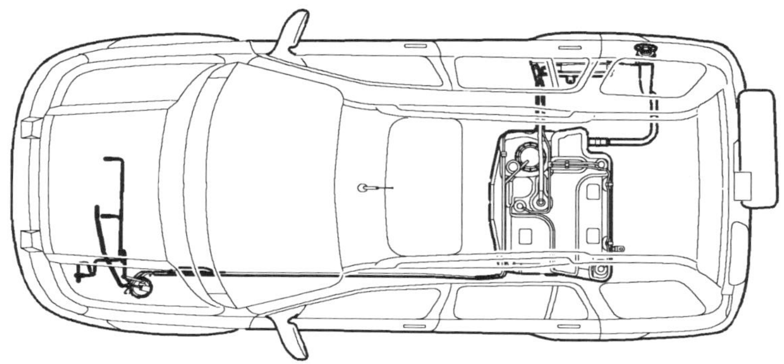

10M0497

8. Check security of all fuel hoses paying particular attention to those running under the vehicle. Check all hoses and pipes are correctly routed and secured. Check for signs of leakage or damage.

Check brake and fuel hoses, pipes and unions

Brake hoses and pipes

1. Visually check condition of all brake hoses. Look for any sign of damage or chafing. Check for any signs of fluid leakage.
2. Check brake pipes for signs of leakage or corrosion. Pay particular attention to pipe unions and joints. Ensure all pipes and hoses are correctly routed and secured.

Check exhaust system

1. Visually check condition of exhaust system for signs of damage. Extra care should be taken to ensure the catalyst is in good condition and shows no signs of damage. Check condition of exhaust heat shields.
2. Check exhaust system is firmly secured and check condition of exhaust mounting rubbers, clamps and brackets.

Check suspension and steering

Suspension.

Front suspension

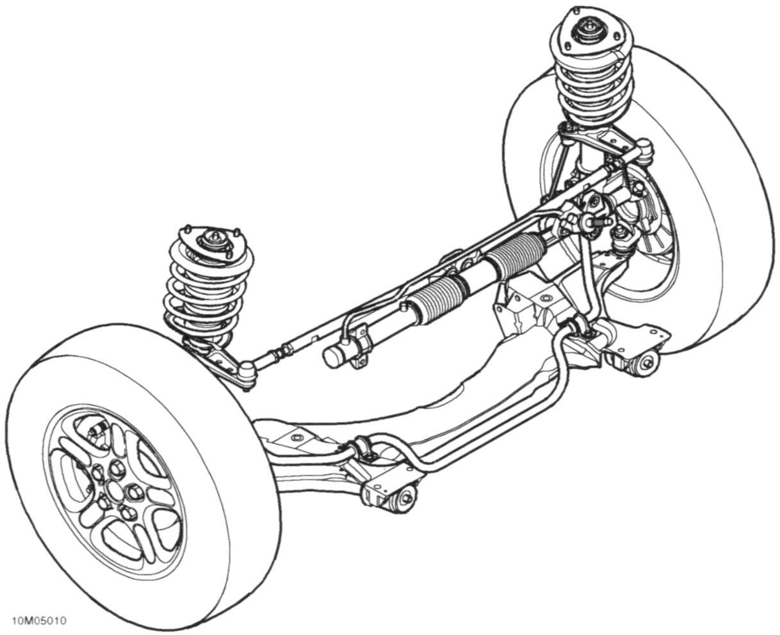

10M05010

1. Check condition of all ball joint dust covers, including anti-roll bar links.
2. Check tightness of all accessible suspension fixings including tie rods.
3. Check wheel bearings and suspension struts for signs of excessive play or wear
4. Check for signs of leakage from suspension dampers.

Rear suspension

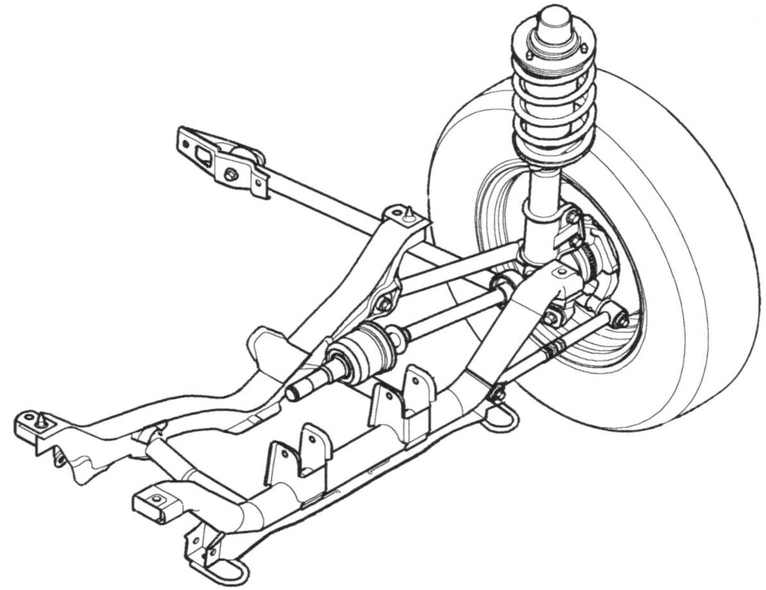

10M0499

5. Check tightness of all accessible suspension fixings including transverse links.
6. Check wheel bearings and suspension struts for signs of excessive play or wear.
7. Check for signs of leakage from suspension dampers.

Steering

8. Check for excessive play from steering joints.
9. Check condition of steering ball joints paying particular attention to dust covers.
10. Check steering rack bellows for any signs of leakage.

Check PAS system

1. Check for signs of leakage from PAS pump, hoses, and hose unions.

Check road wheel speed sensor electrical harness

1. Check harness is correctly routed and secured. Ensure harness shows no signs of damage or chafing.
2. Check speed sensor is fully inserted to the correct position. Check reluctor ring condition and that it is free of any debris.

Replace brake fluid

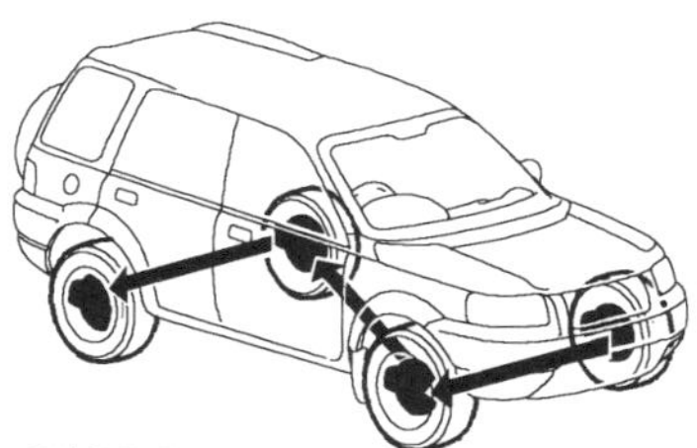

70M0745

NOTE: Bleed brakes in the sequence shown.

1. Renew brake fluid ***See BRAKES, Adjustments.***

Road test

There are two purposes for conducting a road test. Firstly, to ensure the work completed within the dealership meets the standards required as layed down by dealership processes. Secondly, for a skilled technician to assess the general condition of the vehicle and report any conditions that the customer should be made aware of.

CAUTION: Two wheel roller tests must not be carried out. Four wheel roller tests must be restricted to 3 mph (5 kph).

1. Check for correct operation of starter switch. Ensure the engine starts in a correct manner. Leave the engine running.
2. With vehicle stationary, turn steering from lock to lock. Check for smooth operation and ensure there is no undue noise from the power steering pump or drive belt.
3. Depress clutch and select all gears in turn. Check for smooth notch free engagement.
4. Drive vehicle on a short road test. Check all vehicle systems for correct operation. Pay particular attention to:
   - Engine noise
   - Gearbox noise
   - Suspension noise
   - Body noise
   - Braking system operation
   - Gear selection
   - Engine performance
5. Check for correct operation of all instruments and warning devices where practical.
6. Where possible, check for correct operation of Hill Descent Control (HDC) system. This should not be carried out if excessive journey time is required.
7. After road test, carry out a final inspection of the vehicle on vehicle ramps.
8. Check all underbonnet fluid levels and top-up if necessary.

Endorse service record

1. Insert date and mileage of next service.
2. Insert current mileage.
3. Tick one of the boxes on the brake fluid replacement indicator.
4. Tick one of the boxes on the camshaft drive belt indicator.
5. Endorse service record with dealer stamp.
6. Sign and date the service record.
7. Sign and date the maintenance check sheet.

Report any unusual features

1. Produce a written report detailing additional work necessary, or items which may require attention prior to the next service.

CONTENTS

Page

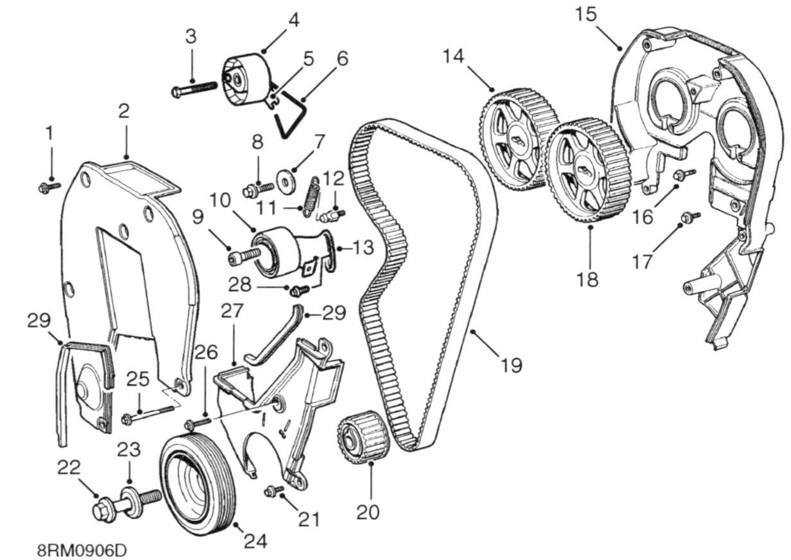

8RM0906D

TIMING BELT COMPONENTS

1. Screw - M6 - timing belt upper front cover
2. Timing belt upper front cover
3. Bolt - Patchlok - automatic timing belt tensioner
4. Automatic timing belt tensioner
5. Pointer
6. Index wire
7. Plain washer
8. Camshaft gear bolt
9. Allen screw - manual timing belt tensioner
10. Pulley - manual timing belt tensioner
11. Tensioner spring - manual timing belt tensioner
12. Pillar bolt - manual timing belt tensioner
13. Backplate - manual timing belt tensioner
14. Inlet camshaft gear
15. Timing belt rear cover
16. Screw - rear cover to cylinder head
17. Screw - rear cover to cylinder head
18. Exhaust camshaft gear
19. Camshaft timing belt
20. Crankshaft timing gear
21. Screw - timing belt lower cover
22. Crankshaft pulley bolt
23. Special washer - crankshaft pulley bolt
24. Crankshaft pulley
25. Bolt - M6 x 90 - upper front and lower covers
26. Screw - lower cover
27. Timing belt lower cover
28. Bolt - manual timing belt tensioner backplate
29. Sealing strips - upper front and lower covers

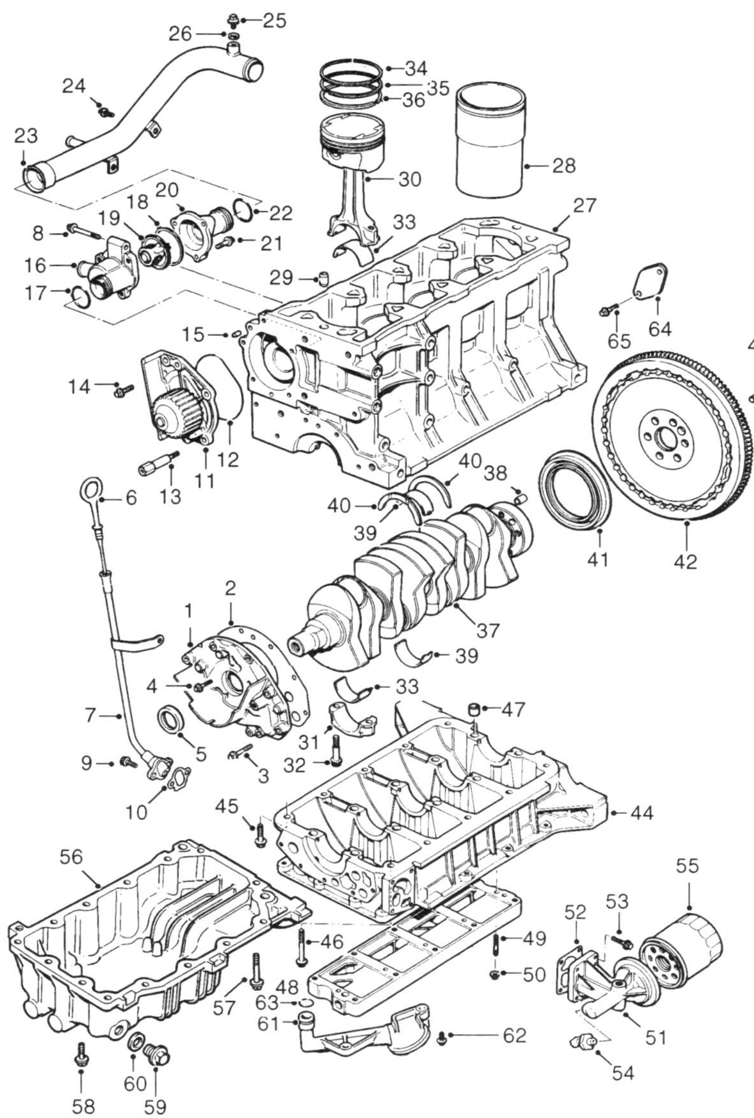

12M3938

CYLINDER BLOCK COMPONENTS

1. Oil pump assembly
2. Gasket - oil pump
3. Screw - M6 x 30 - oil pump
4. Screw M6 x 20 - oil pump
5. Crankshaft front oil seal
6. Dipstick
7. Dipstick tube
8. Screw - dipstick tube and thermostat housing
9. Screw - dipstick tube
10. Gasket
11. Coolant pump
12. 'O' ring - coolant pump
13. Pillar bolt
14. Bolt - coolant pump
15. Locating dowel
16. Thermostat housing - plastic
17. 'O' ring
18. Seal - thermostat
19. Thermostat
20. Cover - plastic
21. Screw
22. 'O' ring
23. Coolant pipe
24. Screw - coolant pipe
25. Vent screw - if fitted
26. Sealing washer
27. Cylinder block
28. Cylinder liner
29. Ring dowel
30. Piston and connecting rod assembly
31. Big-end bearing cap
32. Connecting rod bolt
33. Big-end bearing shells
34. Top compression ring
35. 2nd compression ring
36. Oil control ring
37. Crankshaft
38. Ring dowel
39. Main bearing shells
    Plain in block Nos.1 and 5
    Grooved in block Nos. 2, 3 and 4
    Plain in bearing ladder
40. Thrust washers
41. Crankshaft rear oil seal
42. Flywheel assembly
43. Flywheel bolt - Patchlok
44. Bearing ladder
45. Bolt - bearing ladder
46. Bolt - oil rail
47. Ring dowel
48. Oil rail
49. Stud
50. Nut
51. Oil filter adapter
52. Gasket
53. Bolt
54. Oil pressure switch
55. Oil filter element
56. Alloy sump
57. Sump bolt - M8 x 20
58. Sump bolt - M8
59. Drain plug
60. Sealing washer
61. Oil pick-up pipe
62. Screw - pick-up pipe
63. 'O' ring
64. Blanking plate
65. Screw - blanking plate

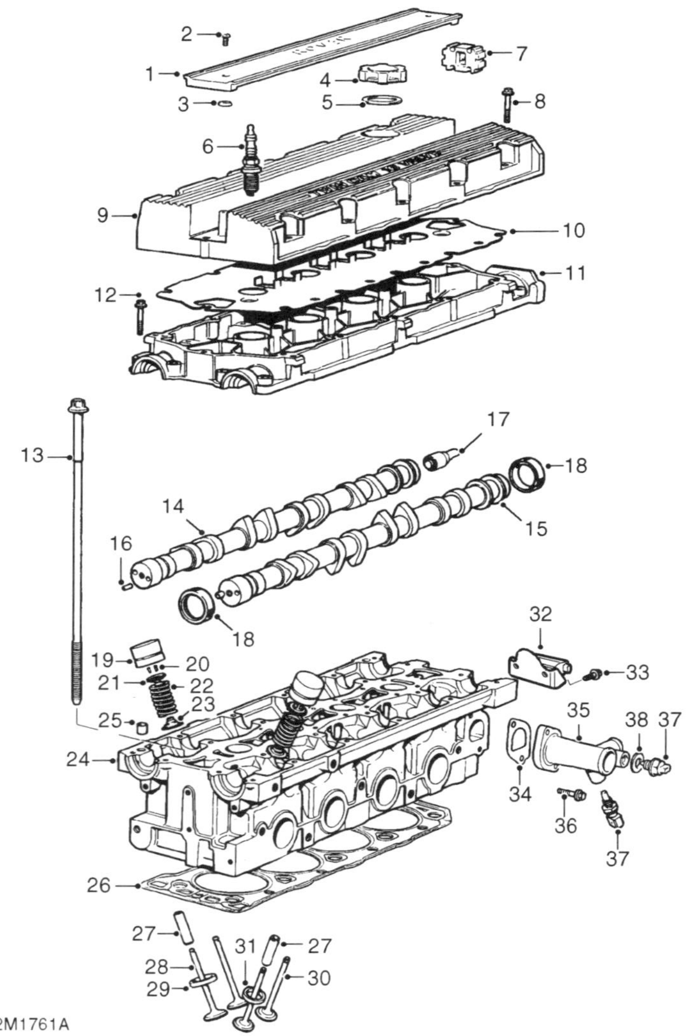

12M1761A

CYLINDER HEAD COMPONENTS

1. Spark plug cover
2. Screw M4 - cover
3. Screw retaining washer
4. Engine oil filler cap
5. Filler cap seal
6. Spark plug
7. Clip - HT leads
8. Bolt M6 - camshaft cover
9. Camshaft cover
10. Camshaft cover gasket
11. Camshaft carrier
12. Bolt M6 - camshaft carrier
13. Cylinder head bolt
14. Camshaft - inlet
15. Camshaft - exhaust
16. Drive pin - camshaft gear
17. Drive spindle - rotor arm
18. Camshaft oil seal
19. Hydraulic tappet
20. Collets - cap
21. Valve spring cap
22. Valve spring
23. Valve stem oil seal
24. Cylinder head
25. Ring dowel - cylinder head to camshaft carrier
26. Cylinder head gasket
27. Valve guide
28. Inlet valve
29. Valve seat insert - inlet
30. Exhaust valve
31. Valve seat insert - exhaust
32. Coil mounting bracket
33. Screw M6
34. Gasket - coolant outlet elbow
35. Coolant outlet elbow
36. Screw M6 - coolant outlet elbow
37. Coolant temperature sensors
38. Sealing washer

OPERATION

The K Series engine is built up from aluminium castings bolted together. These consist of three major castings; the cylinder head, cylinder block and a bearing ladder which is line bored to provide the main bearing bores. Attached to these are three minor castings; above the cylinder head, the camshaft carrier and the camshaft cover. Below the bearing ladder is an oil rail.

Each of the ten cylinder head bolts passes through the cylinder head, cylinder block and bearing ladder to screw into the oil rail. This puts the cylinder head, cylinder block and bearing ladder into compression with all the tensile loads being carried by the cylinder head bolts.

When the cylinder head bolts are removed; additional fixings are used to retain the bearing ladder to the cylinder block and the oil rail to the bearing ladder.

The cross flow cylinder head is based on a four valve, central spark plug, combustion chamber with the inlet ports designed to induce swirl and control the speed of the induction charge. This serves to improve combustion and hence fuel economy, performance and exhaust emissions. The camshafts are retained by the camshaft carrier, which is line bored with the cylinder head.

Self adjusting hydraulic tappets are fitted on top of each valve and are operated directly by the camshaft. The valve stem oil seals are moulded onto a metal base which also act as the valve spring seat on the cylinder head.

Exhaust valves are of the carbon break type. A machined profile on the valve stem removes any build up of carbon in the combustion chamber end of the valve guide thereby preventing valves from sticking.

The stainless steel cylinder head gasket has moulded seals around all coolant, breather and oil apertures and has steel cylinder bore eyelets. Compression of the gasket is controlled by limiters at each end of the gasket.

The cylinder block is fitted with 'damp' cylinder liners, the lower part of the 'damp liner' is stepped and is a sliding fit into the cylinder block. The liners are sealed in the block with a bead of sealant applied around the stepped portion of the liner. The seal at the cylinder head is effected by the cylinder head gasket with the liner top acting as a break between the combustion chamber and gasket.

The aluminium alloy, thermal expansion pistons have a semi- floating gudgeon pin which is offset towards the thrust side and has an interference fit in the small end of the connecting rod. Pistons and cylinder liners are supplied in two grades. Big-end bearing diametric clearance is controlled by three grades of selective shell bearings.

The five bearing, eight balance weight crankshaft has its end-float controlled by thrust washer halves at the top of the central main bearing. Bearing diametric clearance is controlled by three grades of selective shell bearing. Oil grooves are provided in the upper halves of main bearings No. 2, 3 and 4 to supply oil, via drillings in the crankshaft, to the connecting rod big-end bearings.

Engine lubrication system

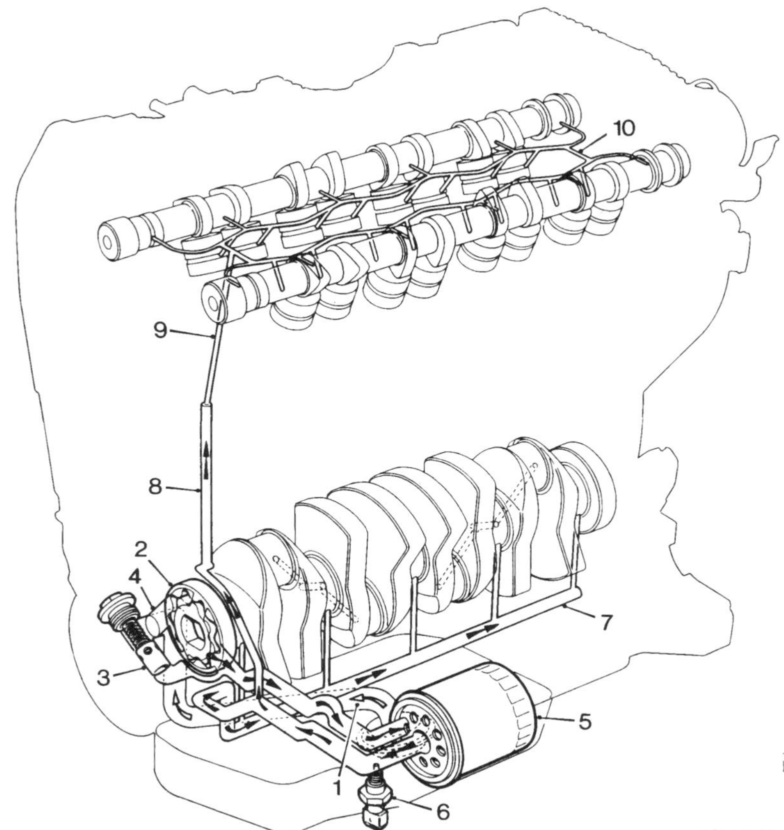

12M1758

Lubrication

The lubrication system is of the full-flow filtration, forced fed type. The oil sump is manufactured from aluminium alloy and is sealed to the bearing ladder with a bead of liquid sealant applied to the sump flange.

Oil is drawn, via a strainer and suction pipe (1) in the sump, into the crankshaft driven oil pump (2) of the trochoid type which has an integral pressure relief valve (3), excess oil is diverted into the intake (4) of the oil pump. Oil is pumped through the full-flow cartridge type oil filter (5), mounted on an adapter attached to the oil pump housing. The low oil pressure sensor (6) is also screwed into the adapter and registers the oil pressure in the main oil gallery on the outflow side of the filter.

The main oil gallery (7) is fed through the oil rail below the main bearing ladder in which drillings direct the oil to the main bearings. Cross drillings in the crankshaft from No. 2 and 4 main bearings carry the oil to the big-end bearings. A passage in the oil pump housing connects to a drilling (8) in the cylinder block to oilways (9) in the cylinder head.

Oil is fed through the cylinder head to twin full length oilways (10) in the camshaft carrier to supply oil to each hydraulic tappet and camshaft bearing.

Crankcase ventilation

A positive crankcase ventilation system is used to vent blow-by gas from the crankcase to the air intake system.

Crankcase gas is drawn through a gauze oil separator in the camshaft cover and passes via hoses into the throttle housing.

ENGINE NUMBER LOCATION

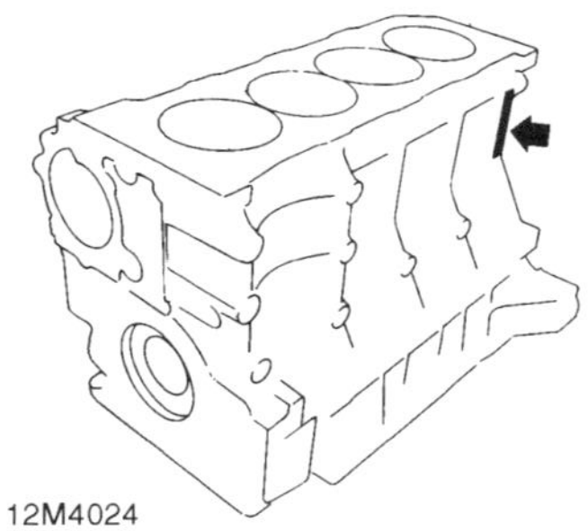

12M4024

The engine number can be found stamped on the rear LH side of the block.

ENGINE OIL PRESSURE CHECK

Service repair no - 12.90.09/01

Remove

1. Remove oil pressure switch. ***See Repairs.***

Check

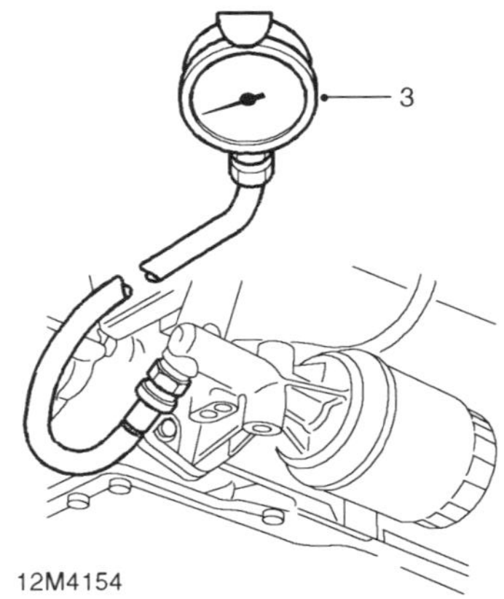

12M4154

2. Top up engine oil if necessary. ***See MAINTENANCE.***
3. Use pressure check kit **LRT-12-052B** fit adaptor and gauge to oil pump.
4. Run engine at idle speed and check for correct oil pressure. ***See INFORMATION, General data.***
5. Switch off ignition.
6. Remove pressure gauge and adaptor.
7. Clean oil spillage.

Refit

1. Fit oil pressure switch. ***See Repairs.***

SEAL - FRONT - INLET AND EXHAUST CAMSHAFT

Service repair no - 12.13.07 - seal - exhaust camshaft
Service repair no - 12.13.09 - seal - inlet camshaft

Remove

1. Disconnect battery earth lead.
2. Remove and discard camshaft timing belt. ***See this section.***

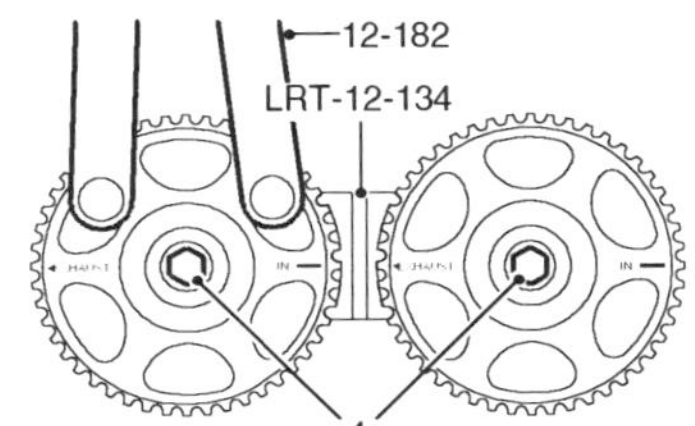

12M 3983B

3. Restrain camshaft gear with holding tool **12-182.**
4. Remove bolt and washer securing camshaft gear to camshaft.

NOTE: Only remove gear from camshaft which is to have oil seal replaced.

5. Remove camshaft gear alignment tool. **LRT-12-134.**
6. Remove camshaft gear.

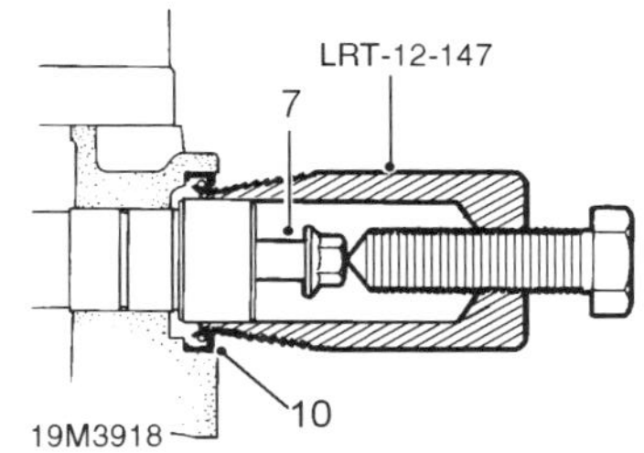

19M3918

7. Fit camshaft gear retaining bolt to camshaft.
8. Screw oil seal removal tool **LRT-12-147** into camshaft oil seal.
9. Remove oil seal by tightening centre bolt of tool **LRT-12-147.**
10. Discard camshaft oil seal.
11. Remove bolt from camshaft.

Refit

1. Clean seal area of cylinder head and camshaft carrier, ensuring all traces of rubber are removed. DO NOT use a scraper as this may damage sealing surfaces.

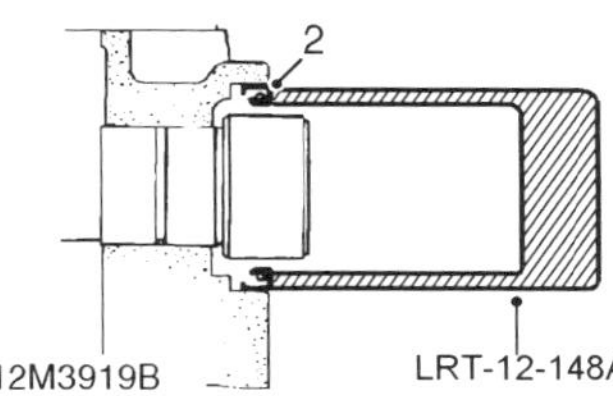

12M3919B

2. Using tool **LRT-12-148A,** fit new camshaft oil seal.

NOTE: This oil seal is coloured BLACK.

CAUTION: Oil seal must be fitted dry. Do not use tool LRT-12-148.

3. Clean camshaft gear.

⚠ **CAUTION: If the sintered gears have been subjected to prolonged oil contamination, they must be soaked in a solvent bath and thoroughly washed in clean solvent before refitment. Because of the porous construction of sintered material, oil impregnated in the gear will emerge and contaminate a new timing belt.**

4. Fit bolt and washer securing camshaft gear to camshaft, fit camshaft gear.
5. Use holding tool **12-182** to restrain camshaft gear.
6. Fit bolt securing camshaft gear and tighten to 65 Nm.
7. Align camshaft gear timing marks.
8. Fit camshaft gear alignment tool. **LRT-12-134.**
9. Fit NEW camshaft timing belt. ***See this section.***
10. Connect battery earth lead.

SEAL - REAR - EXHAUST CAMSHAFT

Service repair no - 12.13.08

Remove

1. Disconnect battery earth lead.
2. Remove air cleaner assembly, ***See ENGINE MANAGEMENT SYSTEM - MEMS, Repairs.***
3. Remove 2 bolts securing coil bracket, release coil and position aside.

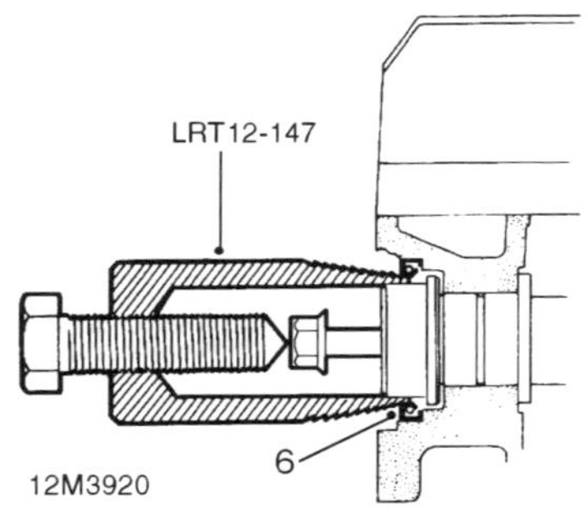

12M3920

4. Screw tool **LRT-12-147** into camshaft rear oil seal.
5. Remove oil seal by tightening centre bolt of tool **LRT-12-147.**
6. Discard camshaft oil seal.

Refit

1. Clean seal area of cylinder head and camshaft carrier, ensuring all traces of rubber are removed. DO NOT use a scraper as this may damage sealing surfaces.

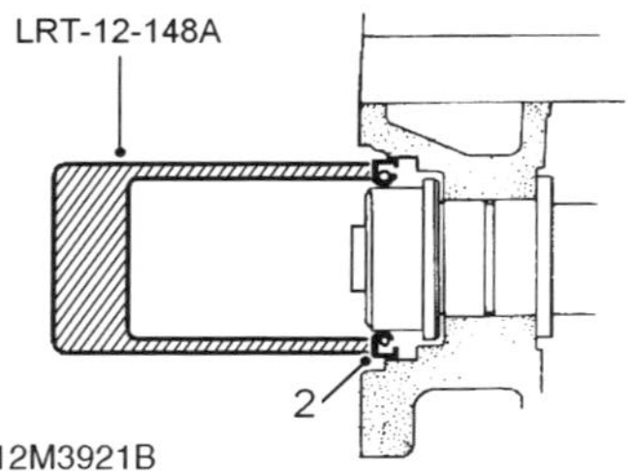

12M3921B

2. Using tool **LRT-12-148A** fit new camshaft oil seal.

△ NOTE: This oil seal is coloured RED.

⚠ **CAUTION: Oil seal must be fitted dry. Do not use tool LRT-12-148.**

3. Position coil bracket, fit and tighten bolts to 25 Nm
4. Fit air cleaner assembly. ***See ENGINE MANAGEMENT SYSTEM - MEMS, Repairs.***
5. Connect battery earth lead.

SEAL - REAR - INLET CAMSHAFT

Service repair no - 12.13.10

Remove

1. Disconnect battery earth lead.
2. Remove air cleaner assembly. ***See ENGINE MANAGEMENT SYSTEM - MEMS, Repairs.***
3. Remove distributor cap, rotor arm and anti-flash shield. ***See ENGINE MANAGEMENT SYSTEM - MEMS, Repairs.***

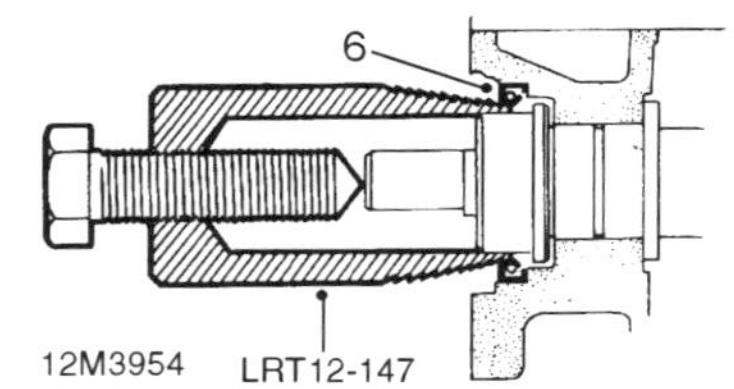

12M3954

4. Screw tool **LRT-12-147** into camshaft rear oil seal.
5. Remove seal by tightening centre bolt of **LRT-12-147.**
6. Remove and discard camshaft oil seal.

Refit

1. Clean sealing area of cylinder head and camshaft carrier, ensuring all traces of rubber are removed. DO NOT use a scraper as this may damage sealing surfaces.

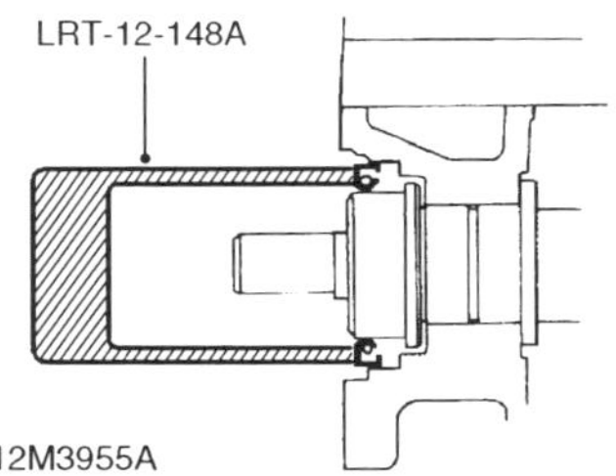

12M3955A

2. Using tool **LRT-12-148A** fit new camshaft oil seal.

NOTE: This oil seal is coloured RED.

CAUTION: Oil seal must be fitted dry. Do not use tool LRT-12-148.

3. Fit rotor arm, anti-flash shield and distributor cap. ***See ENGINE MANAGEMENT SYSTEM - MEMS, Repairs.***
4. Fit air cleaner assembly, ***See ENGINE MANAGEMENT SYSTEM - MEMS, Repairs.***
5. Connect battery earth lead.

HOUSING - CAMSHAFT - RESEAL AND RENEW OIL SEALS

Service repair no - 12.13.22

1. Remove camshaft timing belt. ***See this section.***

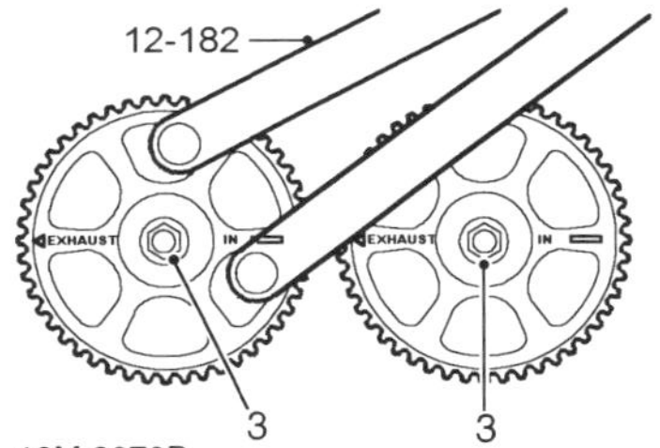

12M 3979B

2. Restrain camshaft gears using **12-182.**
3. Remove bolts and plain washers securing gears to camshaft.

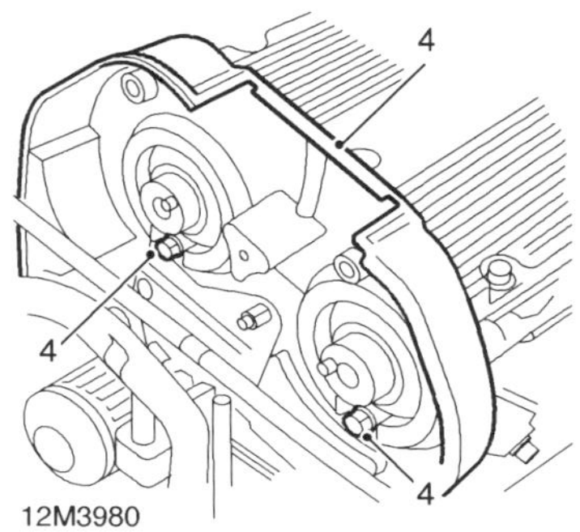

12M3980

4. Remove 2 bolts securing camshaft timing belt rear cover to cylinder head.
5. Remove distributor cap and rotor arm. ***See ENGINE MANAGEMENT SYSTEM - MEMS, Repairs.***

ENGINE - 'K' SERIES

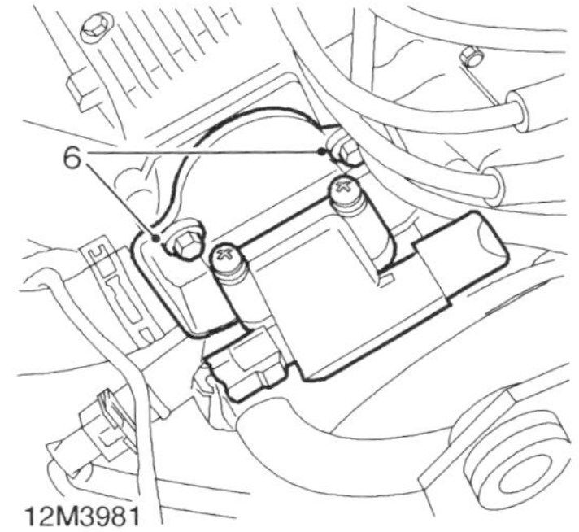

12M3981

6. Remove 2 bolts securing coil bracket to cylinder head and position aside.
7. Remove camshaft cover. ***See this section.***

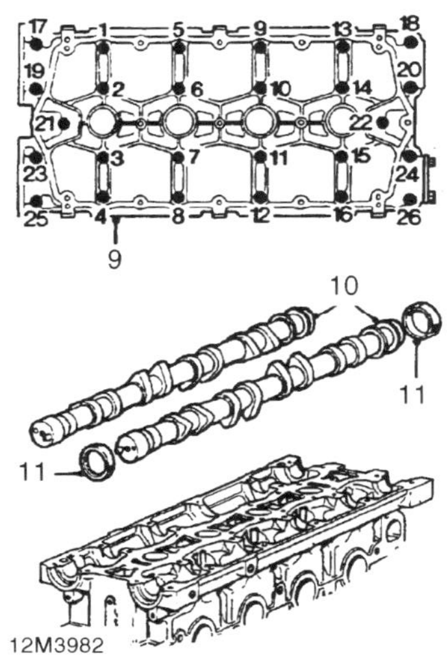

12M3982

8. Using the sequence shown, progressively loosen 26 bolts securing camshaft carrier to cylinder head, until valve spring pressure is no longer acting on camshafts.
9. Remove camshaft carrier.
10. Remove both camshafts.
11. Remove and discard oil seals from camshafts.

Refit

1. Clean camshafts.
2. Clean mating faces of cylinder head and camshaft carrier.
3. Clean camshaft carrier bolt holes and dowels.
4. Blow out oil ways and lubricate camshaft journals.
5. Fit camshafts and position inlet drive pin at 4 o'clock and exhaust camshaft drive pin at 8 o'clock.
6. Apply continuous thin beads of sealant, Part No. GUG 705963GM to paths on camshaft carrier then spread to an even film using a roller or brush.
7. Fit camshaft carrier to cylinder head.
8. Fit and progressively tighten bolts securing camshaft carrier to cylinder head to 10 Nm.
9. Clean camshaft seal locations and running surfaces.

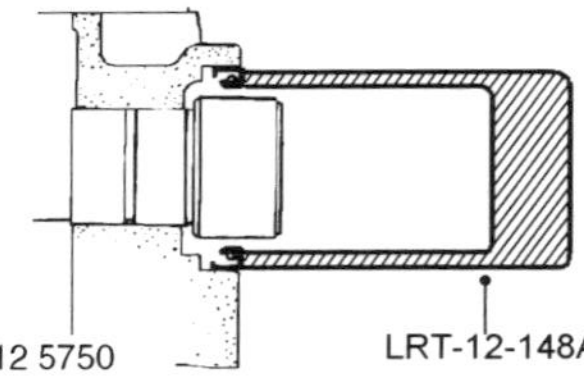

M12 5750

Front oil seal

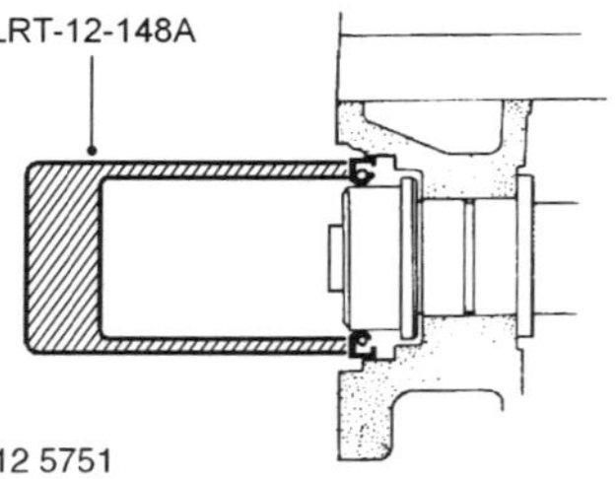

M12 5751

Rear oil seal

NOTE: Front oil seals are coloured BLACK, rear oil seals are coloured RED.

10. Fit new oil seals using tool **LRT-12-148A.**

CAUTION: Oil seals must be fitted dry. Do not use tool LRT-12-148.

11. Fit camshaft cover. ***See this section.***
12. Position coil bracket, fit and tighten bolts to 25 Nm.
13. Fit distributor cap and rotor arm. ***See ENGINE MANAGEMENT SYSTEM - MEMS, Repairs.***
14. Fit and tighten 2 bolts securing camshaft timing belt rear cover to cylinder head.
15. Restrain camshaft gears using tool **12-182** fit bolts and plain washers, tighten bolts to 65 Nm.
16. Fit timing belt. ***See this section.***

PULLEY - CRANKSHAFT - 'K' SERIES

Service repair no - 12.21.01

Remove

1. Disconnect battery earth lead.
2. Remove alternator drive belt. ***See ELECTRICAL, Repairs.***
3. Remove starter motor, ***See ELECTRICAL, Repairs.***

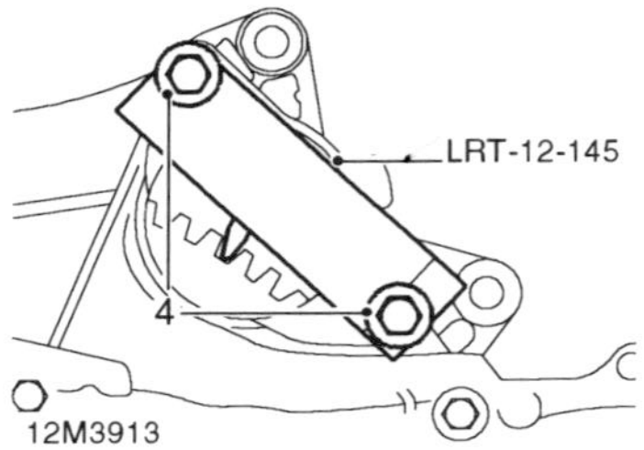

12M3913

4. Fit flywheel locking tool **LRT-12-145** to flywheel housing and secure with 2 bolts.

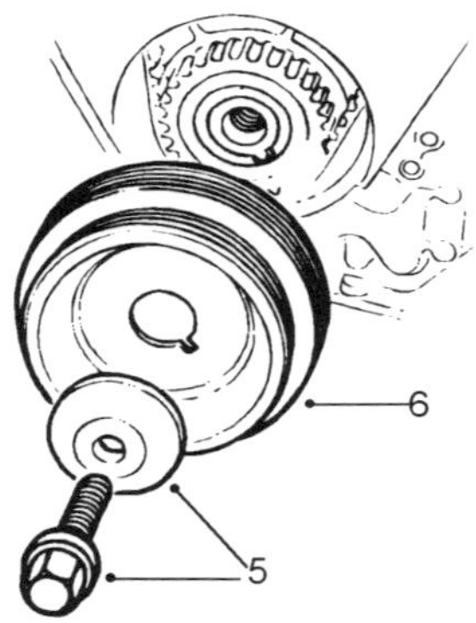

12M3914

5. Remove bolt securing pulley to crankshaft and collect washer.
6. Remove crankshaft pulley.

Refit

1. Clean crankshaft pulley and gear.

12M3915

2. Fit crankshaft pulley to crankshaft gear ensuring that indent on pulley locates over lug on gear (arrowed in illustration).
3. Fit washer and bolt securing crankshaft pulley to crankshaft and tighten to 205 Nm.
4. Remove 2 bolts securing tool **LRT-12-145** to flywheel housing and remove tool.
5. Fit starter motor. ***See ELECTRICAL, Repairs.***
6. Fit alternator drive belt. ***See ELECTRICAL, Repairs.***

SEAL - FRONT - CRANKSHAFT

Service repair no - 12.21.14

Remove

1. Remove camshaft timing belt. ***See this section.***

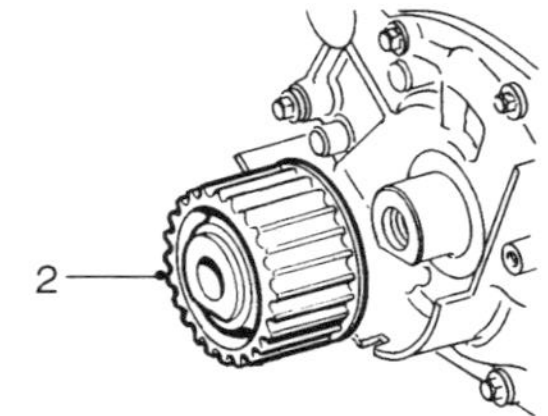

12M1636

2. Remove crankshaft gear.

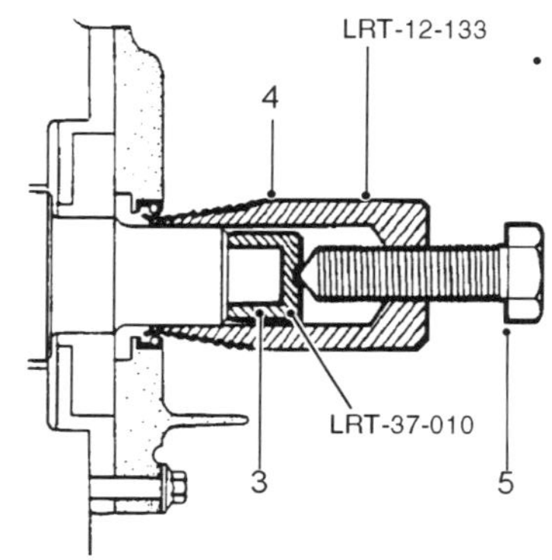

19M3916

3. Fit thrust button, tool **LRT-37-010** to end of crankshaft.
4. Ensure bore of tool **LRT-12-133** is free from burrs.
5. Screw tool **LRT-12-133** into crankshaft front oil seal.

6. Tighten centre bolt of tool **LRT-12- 133** to remove seal.
7. Discard crankshaft front oil seal.
8. Remove thrust button from crankshaft.

Refit

1. Using a lint free cloth, throughly clean oil seal recess in oil pump and running surface on crankshaft.

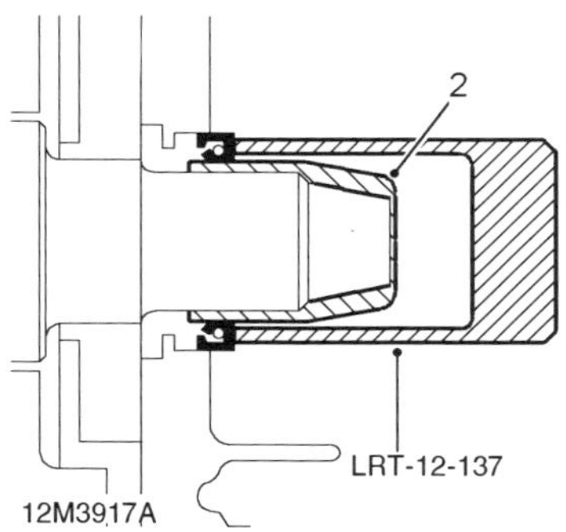

12M3917A

2. Fit oil seal guide, from seal kit, over end of crankshaft, against the oil pump housing. Drift new seal into place using tool **LRT-12-137.**

CAUTION: Oil seal must be fitted dry.

3. Remove tool and oil seal guide.
4. Clean crankshaft gear.
5. Fit crankshaft gear to crankshaft.
6. Fit camshaft timing belt. ***See this section.***
7. Connect battery earth lead.

CRANKSHAFT REAR OIL SEAL - 'K'SERIES

Service repair no - 12.21.20

Remove

1. Remove engine flywheel. ***See this section.***

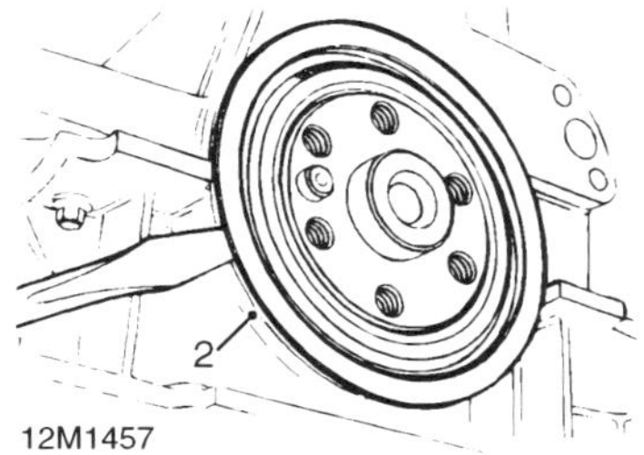

12M1457

2. Using a burr free flat ended screwdriver, ease crankshaft rear oil seal from cylinder block and discard seal.

CAUTION: Do not mark sealing surface on crankshaft or seal housing surfaces.

Refit

1. Remove all traces of oil and sealant from cylinder block, oil seal recess and running surface on crankshaft.

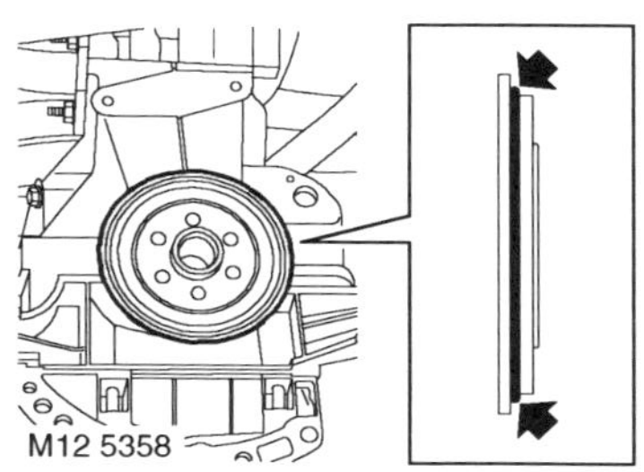
M12 5358

2. Apply a 1.5 mm thick bead of sealant, Part No. GAC 8000 to replacement oil seal as shown.

CAUTION: Do not apply oil or grease to any part of oil seal or running surface of crankshaft. Seal must be fitted immediately after applying sealant.

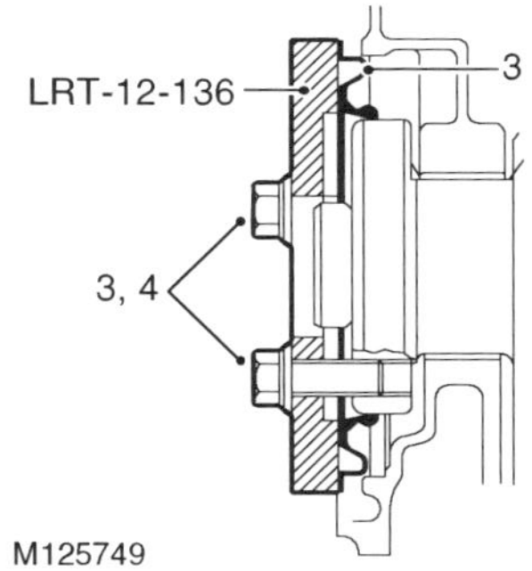

M125749

3. Position oil seal to cylinder block and fit oil seal replacer tool **LRT-12-136,** retain tool using 3 slave bolts.
4. Evenly tighten oil seal replacer bolts to press oil seal squarely into cylinder block.
5. Leave oil seal replacer tool in clamped position for one minute.
6. Remove oil seal replacer tool **LRT-12-136.**
7. Allow sealant to cure for a minimum of 30 minutes before topping-up engine oil or rotating crankshaft.
8. Fit engine flywheel. ***See this section.***
9. Top-up engine oil. ***See MAINTENANCE.***

GASKET - CYLINDER HEAD - 'K' SERIES

Service repair no - 12.29.02

Remove

1. Disconnect battery earth lead.
2. Raise front of vehicle.

WARNING: Support on safety stands.

3. Remove and discard camshaft timing belt. ***See this section.***
4. Drain cooling system. ***See COOLING SYSTEM, Adjustments.***

Engines fitted with manual timing belt tensioner

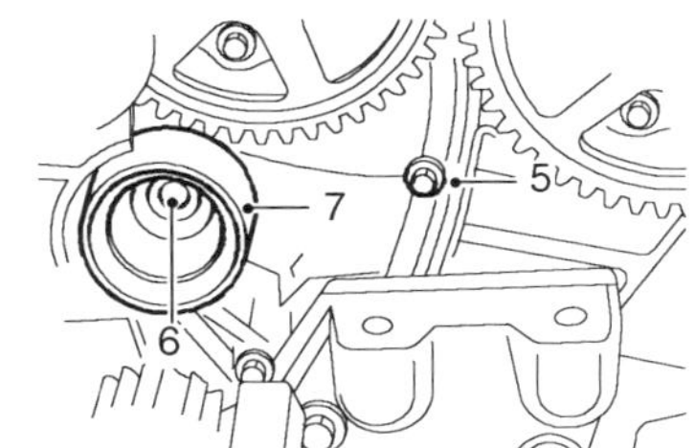

12M3956A

5. Remove bolt securing camshaft timing belt tensioner backplate to cylinder head.
6. Remove Allen bolt securing camshaft timing belt tensioner pulley to cylinder head using a socket mounted Allen key.
7. Remove camshaft timing belt tensioner.

All engines

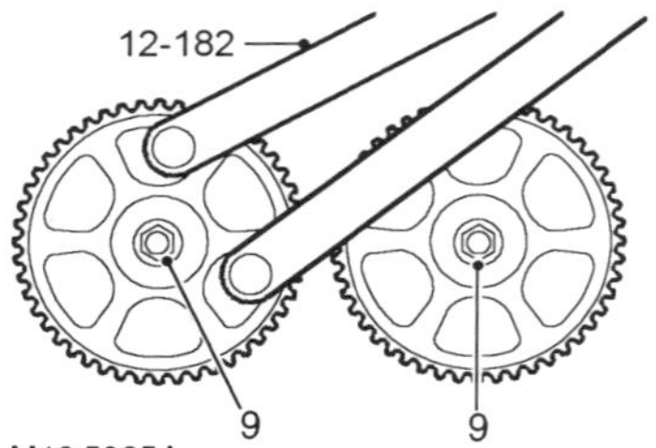

M12 5025A

8. Restrain camshaft gears using **12-182.**
9. Remove bolts and plain washers securing camshaft gears to camshafts.
10. Remove camshaft gear alignment tool **LRT-12-134.**
11. Mark camshaft gears for identification when refitting.
12. Remove 2 camshaft gears.

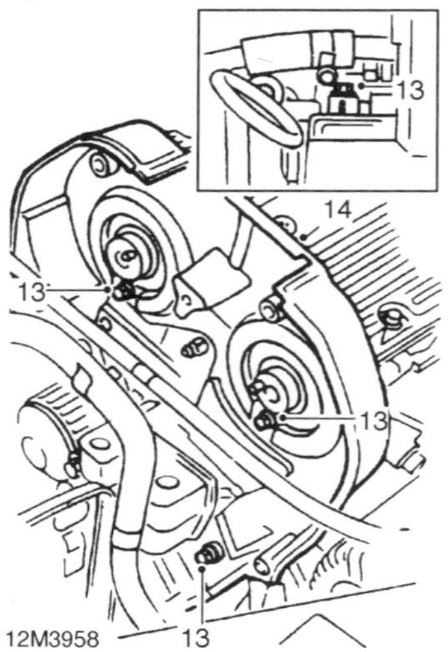

12M3958

13. Remove 4 bolts securing camshaft timing belt rear cover to cylinder head and block.
14. Remove camshaft timing belt rear cover.

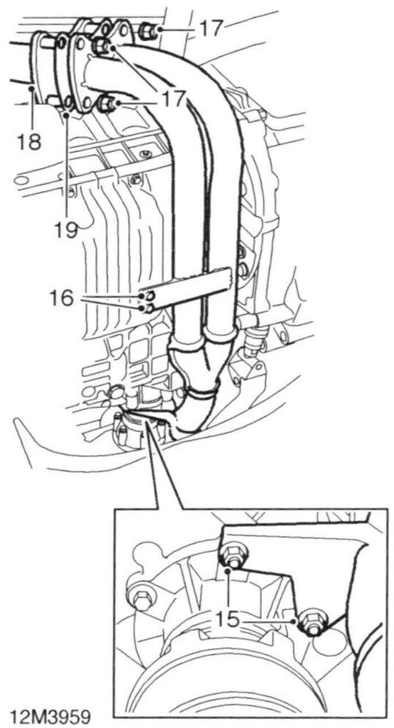

12M3959

15. Remove 2 nuts securing exhaust front pipe to mounting bracket on IRD unit housing.
16. Remove 2 bolts securing exhaust front pipe to sump.
17. Remove 4 nuts securing exhaust front pipe to exhaust manifold.
18. Release exhaust front pipe from exhaust manifold.
19. Remove and discard exhaust manifold flange gasket.

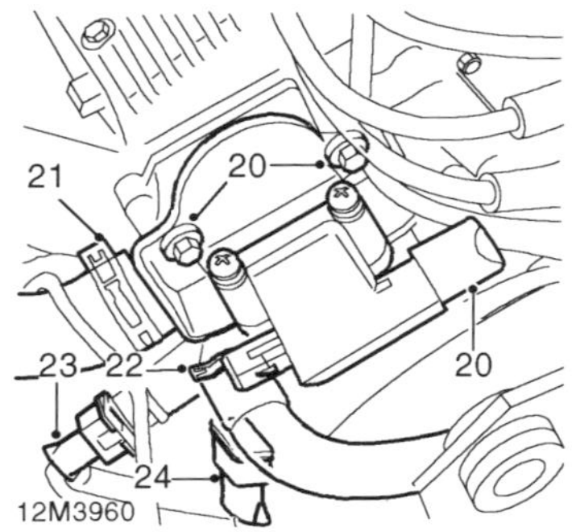

12M3960

20. Remove 2 bolts securing coil bracket to cylinder head, disconnect coil HT lead and position coil aside.
21. Release clip and disconnect radiator top hose from coolant outlet elbow.
22. Release clip and disconnect coolant hose from coolant outlet elbow.
23. Disconnect multiplug from engine coolant temperature sensor.
24. Disconnect multiplug from engine coolant temperature gauge sensor.

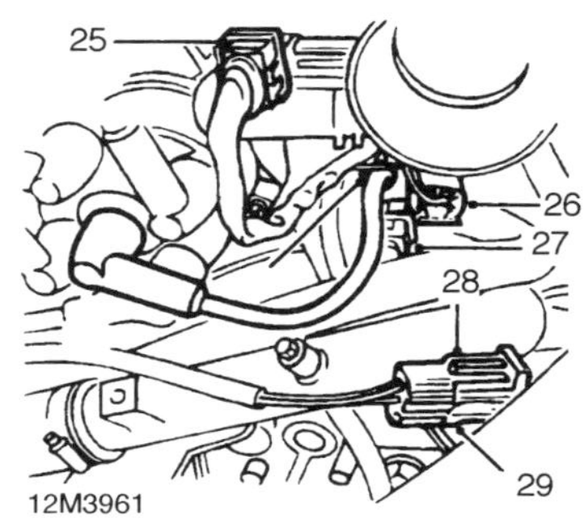

12M3961

25. Disconnect multiplug from throttle position sensor.
26. Disconnect multiplug from injector harness.
27. Disconnect multiplug from intake air temperature sensor.
28. Disconnect heated oxygen sensor multiplug from engine harness.
29. Release heated oxygen sensor multiplug from clip on bracket.

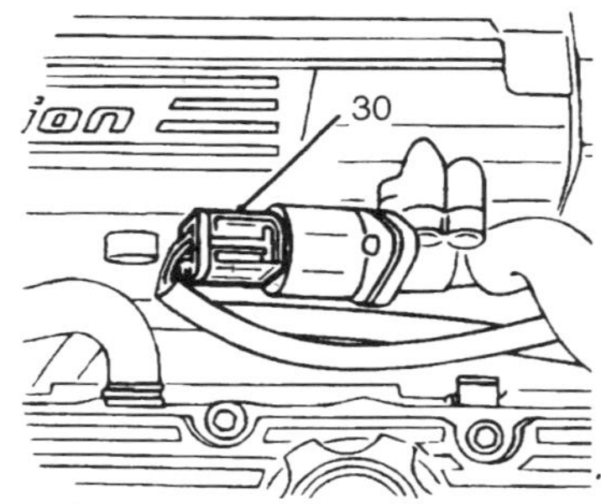

12M3962

30. Disconnect multiplug from idle air control valve.

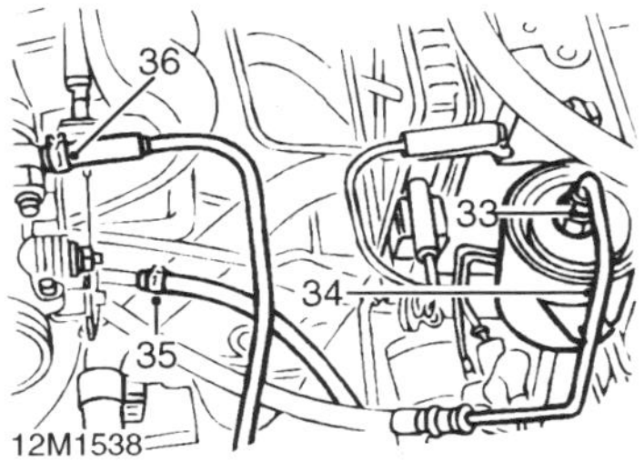

12M1538

31. Position absorbent cloth around fuel feed pipe connection to collect spillage.

WARNING: Fuel pressure of up to 3.5 bar will be present in the system of petrol vehicles, even if the engine has not been run for some time. Always depressurise the system before disconnecting any components in the fuel feed line (between the fuel pump and the fuel rail). The spilling of fuel is unavoidable during this operation. Ensure that all necessary precautions are taken to prevent fire and explosion.

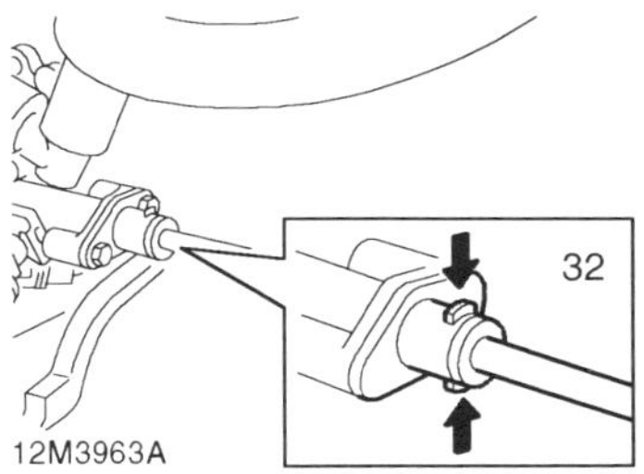

12M3963A

32. Depress plastic collar on feed pipe and release feed pipe from manifold.

CAUTION: Plug fuel system hoses and connections.

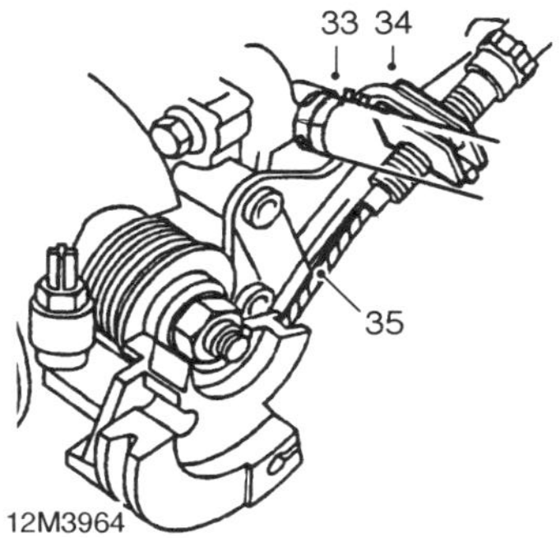

12M3964

33. Release clip and disconnect purge hose from throttle housing.
34. Release throttle cable adjusting nut from abutment bracket.
35. Release throttle cable from throttle cam.

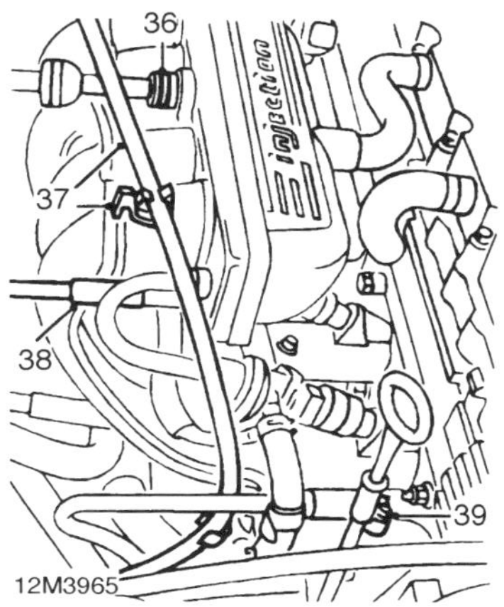

12M3965

36. Depress plastic collar on quick release connector and disconnect brake servo vacuum hose from inlet manifold.
37. Release throttle cable from clip on inlet manifold.
38. Disconnect vacuum hose from inlet manifold.
39. Release clip and disconnect expansion tank hose from inlet manifold.

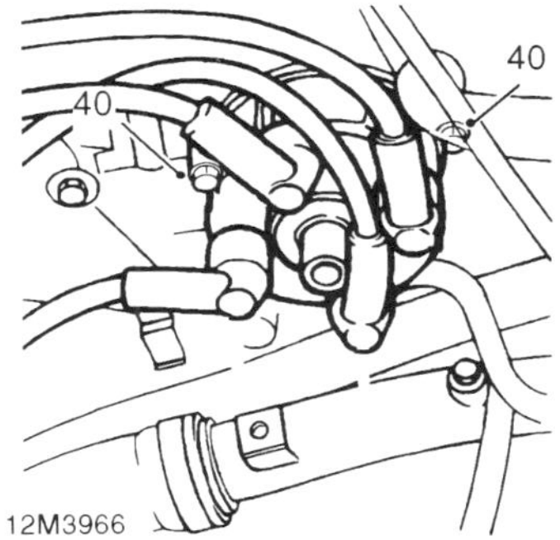

12M3966

40. Remove 2 screws securing distributor cap and remove distributor cap.
41. Remove camshaft cover, ***See this section.***

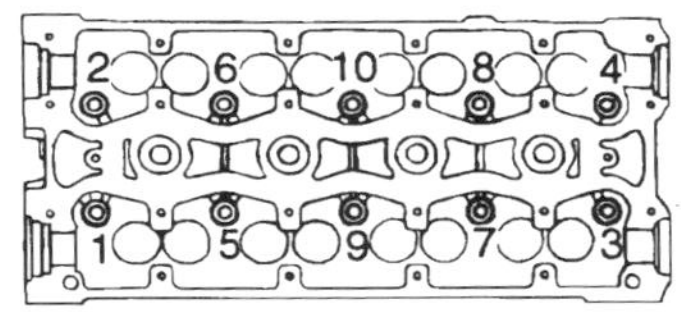

12M3967

42. Working in the sequence shown, loosen 10 cylinder head to oil rail bolts.
43. Remove cylinder head bolts and store in fitted order.
44. Using assistance, remove cylinder head assembly from cylinder block.

CAUTION: Take care not to damage heated oxygen sensor when removing cylinder head.

CAUTION: Cylinder head is dowel located; do not tap it sideways to free it from cylinder block. Place cylinder head on wooden blocks to prevent damage to valves.

CAUTION: Removal of cylinder head bolts will result in a 'tightening up' of the crankshaft. Rotation of the crankshaft must, therefore, be kept to a minimum. Do not rotate until cylinder liner clamps LRT-12-144 are fitted.

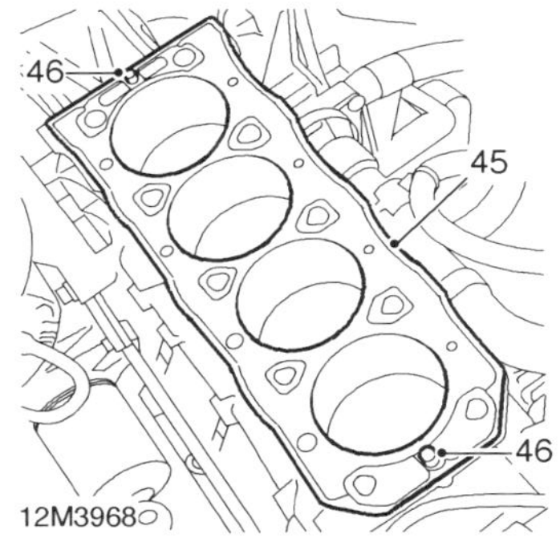

12M3968

45. Remove and discard cylinder head gasket from cylinder block.
46. Remove 2 location dowels from cylinder block.

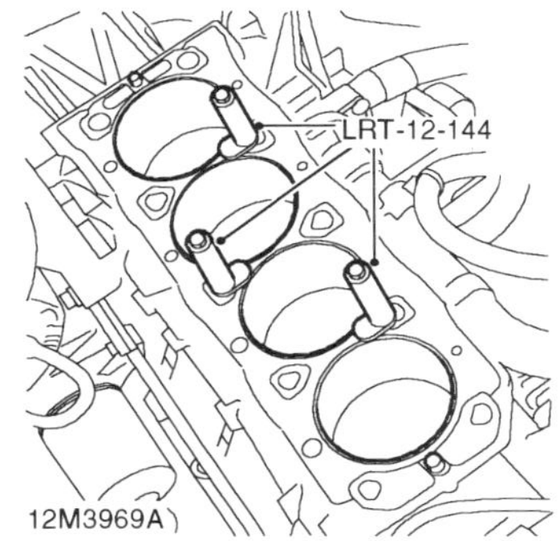

12M3969A

47. Fit cylinder liner clamps **LRT-12- 144** to cylinder block and secure with cylinder head bolts.

CAUTION: Do not rotate crankshaft with cylinder head removed.

Refit

1. Remove bolts securing cylinder liner clamps to cylinder block and remove clamps.
2. Clean joint surfaces of cylinder head and cylinder block.
   Clean oil and coolant passages.
   Clean mating face of exhaust manifold and exhaust front pipe.
   If necessary, de-carbonise piston crowns and cylinder head.
3. Clean cylinder head bolts with a wire brush. Inspect cylinder head bolts for signs of damage. ***See this section.***
4. Wash cylinder head bolts and wipe dry. Apply a light film of oil to bolt threads and underside of bolt heads.
5. Clean location dowels and fit to cylinder block.
6. Fit NEW cylinder head gasket, dry, to cylinder block.
7. Using assistance, fit cylinder head onto cylinder block carefully locating on dowels.

CAUTION: Never shuffle head from side to side to align dowels. If necessary, lift head off and try again.

CAUTION: Take care not to damage heated oxygen sensor when refitting cylinder head.

8. Carefully enter cylinder head bolts, DO NOT DROP. Screw bolts into place by hand.

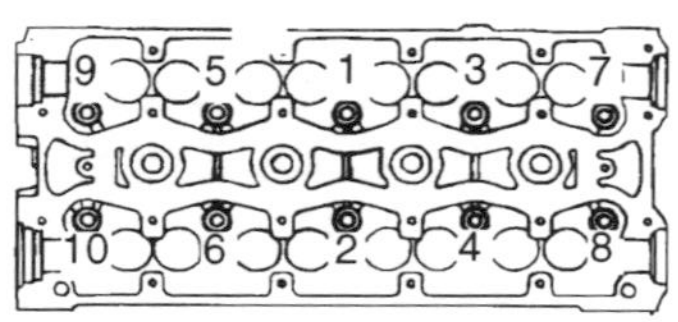

12M3970

9. Working in the sequence shown, progressively tighten the cylinder head bolts using the following procedure.
   i. All bolts to 20 Nm. Use a felt tip pen and mark position of radial mark on each bolt head.
   ii. Turn all bolts through 180°.
   iii. Turn all bolts through another 180° and align radial mark.

CAUTION: If bolt is overtightened, back off 90° then re-align radial marks.

10. Fit camshaft cover. ***See this section.***
11. Position distributor cap, fit and tighten screws.
12. Connect expansion tank hose to inlet manifold and secure clip.
13. Connect vacuum hose to inlet manifold.
14. Secure throttle cable to clip on inlet manifold, ensure throttle cable is correctly routed.
15. Connect brake servo vacuum hose to inlet manifold.
16. Connect throttle cable to throttle cam.
17. Locate throttle cable adjusting nut in abutment bracket.
18. Connect purge hose to throttle housing and secure with clip.
19. Remove plug from fuel system hose.
20. Connect fuel feed pipe to manifold.
21. Connect multiplug to idle air control valve.
22. Connect heated oxygen sensor multiplug to engine harness and secure to clip on bracket.
23. Connect multiplug to intake air temperature sensor.
24. Connect multiplug to injector harness.
25. Connect multiplug to throttle position sensor.
26. Connect multiplugs to engine coolant temperature sensors.
27. Connect coolant hose to coolant outlet elbow and secure clip.
28. Connect radiator top hose to coolant outlet elbow and secure clip.
29. Position coil bracket, fit and tighten bolts to 25 Nm.
30. Connect coil HT lead to distributor.
31. Fit NEW gasket to exhaust manifold flange and connect exhaust front pipe.
32. Fit 4 nuts securing exhaust front pipe to exhaust manifold and tighten to 45 Nm.
33. Fit 2 bolts securing exhaust front pipe to sump and tighten to 25 Nm.
34. Fit 2 nuts securing exhaust front pipe to IRD housing and tighten to 25 Nm.
35. Fit camshaft timing belt rear cover to cylinder head and cylinder block.
36. Fit 4 bolts securing camshaft timing belt rear cover to cylinder head and tighten bolts to 9 Nm.
37. Fit 2 camshaft gears to their respective camshafts.

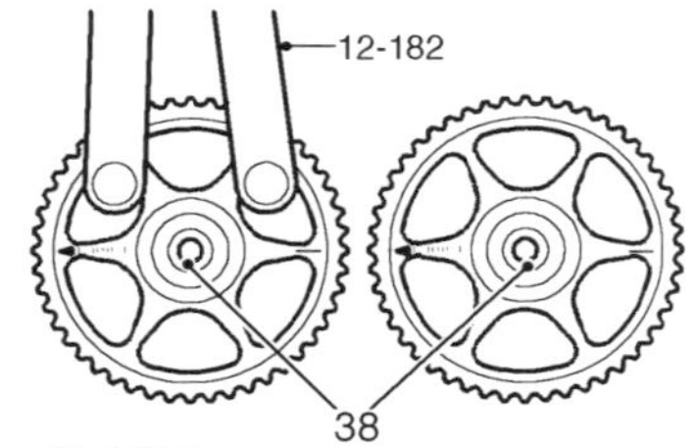

12M3971B

38. Fit bolts and plain washers securing camshaft gears to camshafts. Using tool **12-182,** restrain camshaft gears and tighten bolts to 65 Nm.
39. Using tool **12-182,** align camshaft gear timing marks and fit camshaft gear alignment tool **LRT-12-134.**

Engines fitted with manual timing belt tensioner

40. Fit camshaft timing belt tensioner to cylinder head.
41. Fit tensioner pulley Allen bolt.
42. Fit pillar bolt and spring supplied with replacement timing belt.

NOTE: This spring is not fitted with a sleeve.

43. Connect tensioner spring to pillar bolt on cylinder head.
44. Connect spring to tensioner.
45. Push tensioner pulley down to fully OFF position, fit and tighten backplate bolt to 10 Nm.

All engines

46. Fit new camshaft timing belt. ***See this section.***
47. Remove stand(s) and lower vehicle.
48. Refill cooling system. ***See COOLING SYSTEM, Adjustments.***
49. Connect battery earth lead.
50. Adjust throttle cable. ***See ENGINE MANAGEMENT SYSTEM - MEMS, Adjustments.***

TAPPETS

Service repair no - 12.29.57

Remove

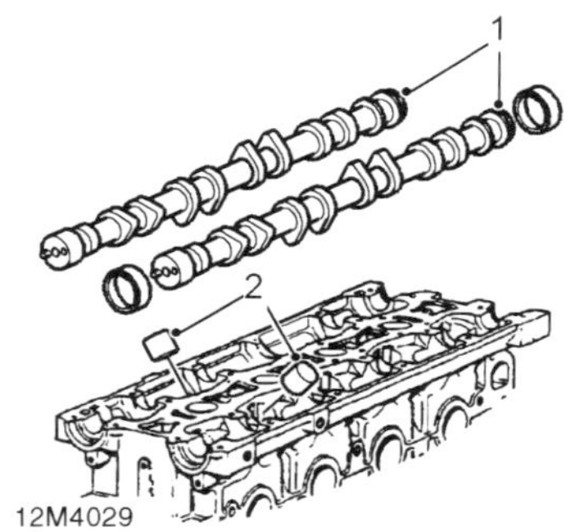

12M4029

1. Remove camshafts. ***See this section.***
2. Remove tappets

Refit

1. Clean tappets.
2. Lubricate tappets with clean engine oil.
3. Fit tappets.
4. Fit camshafts. ***See this section.***

VALVE STEM OIL SEAL - ENGINE SET

Service repair no - 12.30.27

Remove

1. Disconnect battery earth lead.
2. Remove inlet and exhaust camshafts. See **'K' Series Engine Overhaul Manual - Overhaul.**

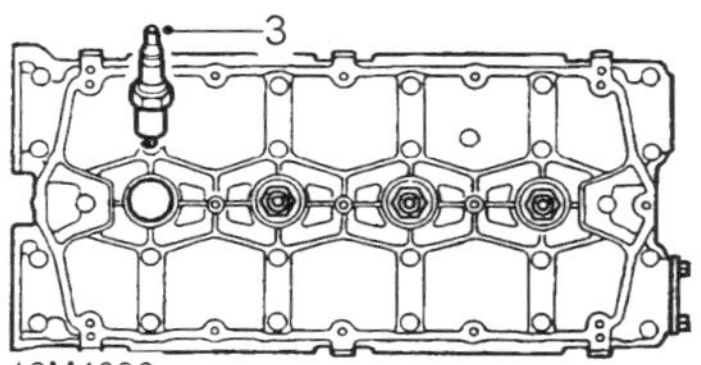

12M4086

3. Using a 16 mm spark plug socket, remove 4 spark plugs.

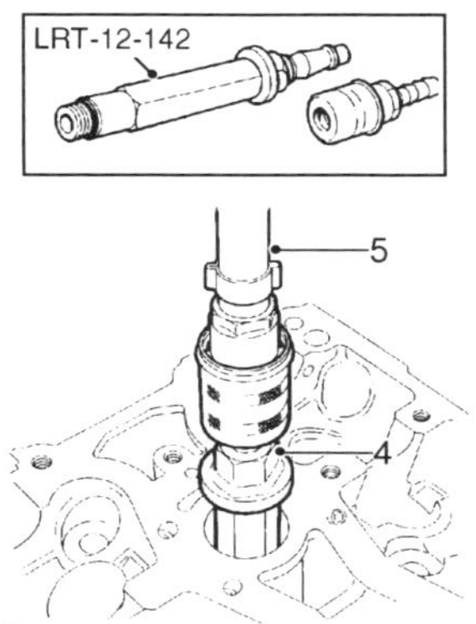

12M4124

4. Fit and tighten air line adaptor tool **LRT-12-142** into spark plug hole.
5. Connect an airline to adaptor and apply air pressure.
6. Remove hydraulic tappet from each valve.

⚠ **CAUTION: Retain tappets in fitted order and store inverted to prevent oil loss.**

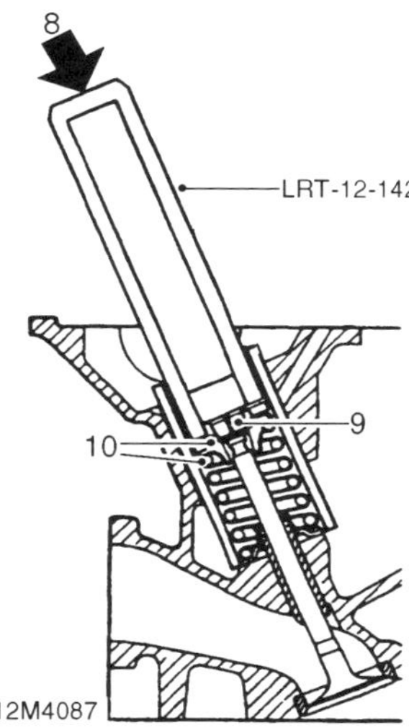

12M4087

7. Fit tool **LRT-12-142** to valve spring cap.
8. Strike head of tool firmly with hammer to release valve spring collets.
9. Remove collets from magnetic end of tool.
10. Remove valve spring cap and spring.

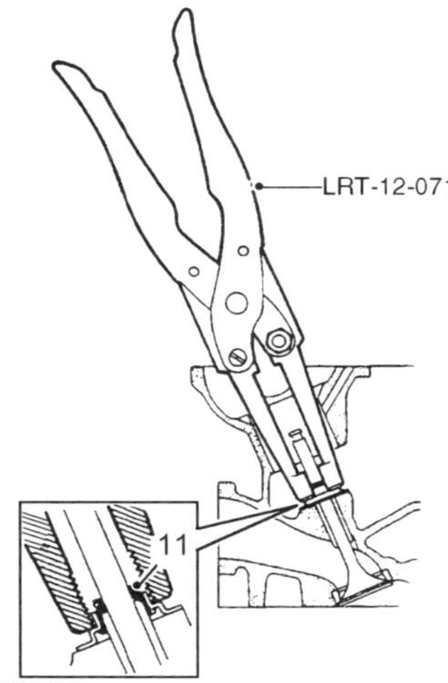

12M4088

11. Use tool **LRT-12-071** to remove valve stem oil seal.
12. Repeat operations to remove other valve oil seals.

Refit

1. Lubricate NEW valve stem oil seal with engine oil.
2. Use **LRT-12-071** to fit oil seals.
3. Fit valve spring and spring cap to each valve.

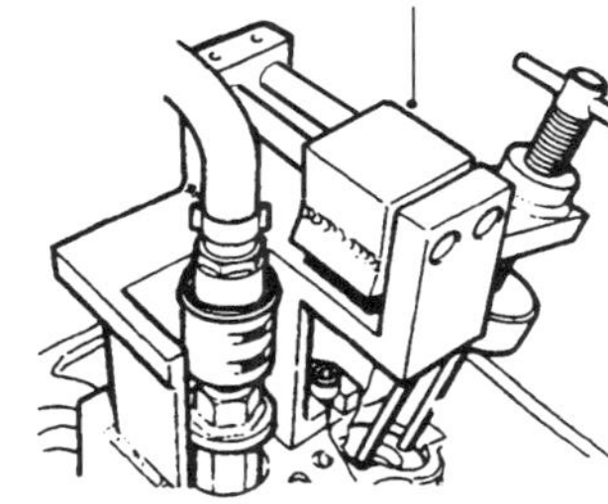

12M4089

4. Assemble tool **LRT-12-139** over exhaust valve.
5. Locate valve spring cap with compressor tool **LRT-12-139**
6. Screw down valve spring compressor until valve stem collet groove is level with top face of spring cap.
7. Attach collets to end of a small flat screwdriver with grease and locate collets in valve stem groove.
8. Unscrew valve spring compressor ensuring collets are correctly located in valve spring cap.
9. Slide head of **LRT-12-139** along to second exhaust valve position.
10. Repeat refit operations on second valve.
11. Remove **LRT-12-139.**
12. Lubricate tappets with clean engine oil and refit in original positions.
13. Disconnect air line from **LRT-12-142.**
14. Remove **LRT-12-142.**
15. Clean spark plugs and set gaps to 0.85mm.
16. Fit inlet and exhaust camshafts. See **'K' Series Engine Overhaul Manual - Overhaul.**
17. Connect battery earth lead.

ENGINE ASSEMBLY - REMOVE/REFIT - 'K' SERIES

Service repair no - 12.37.01/99

Remove

1. Remove bonnet. ***See BODY, Repairs.***
2. Drain cooling system. ***See COOLING SYSTEM - 'K' SERIES, Adjustments.***
3. Drain gear box oil. ***See MANUAL GEARBOX, Adjustments.***
4. Drain IRD unit. ***See MANUAL GEARBOX, Adjustments.***
5. *If required:* Drain engine oil. ***See MAINTENANCE.***
6. Remove both front drive shafts. ***See DRIVE SHAFTS, Repairs.***
7. Remove exhaust front pipe. ***See MANIFOLD & EXHAUST SYSTEMS, Repairs.***

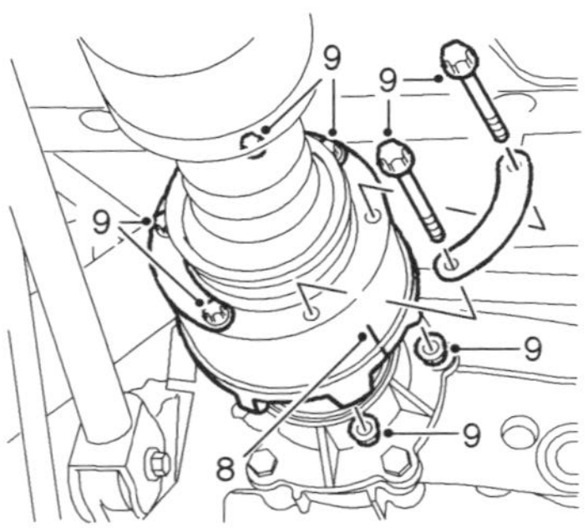

12M3996

8. Reference mark propeller shaft and IRD unit flanges to aid reassembly.
9. Remove 6 nuts and bolts securing propeller shaft to IRD unit, release propeller shaft and position aside.

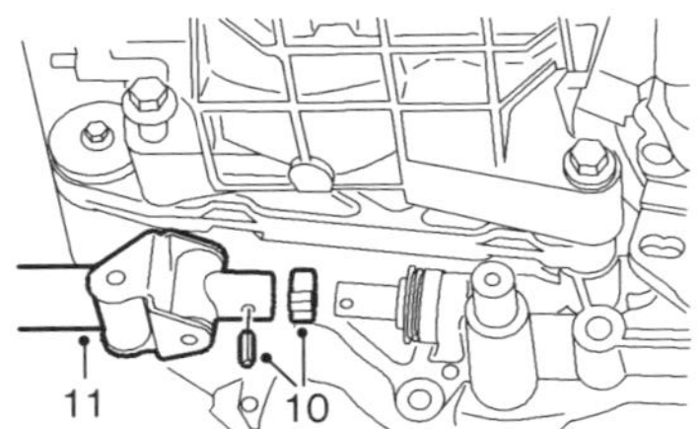

12M3997

10. Release gear change rod roll pin cover, remove and discard roll pin.
11. Release gear change rod from gear box.

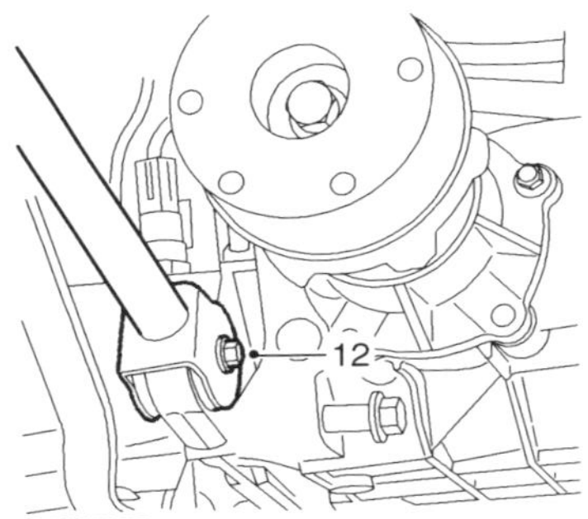

12M3998

12. Remove bolt securing gear change steady rod to gearbox.

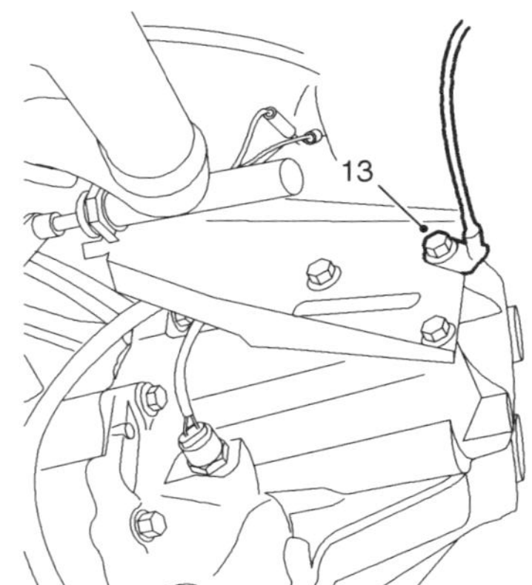

12M3999

13. Remove bolt securing engine earth lead to gearbox and position earth lead aside.

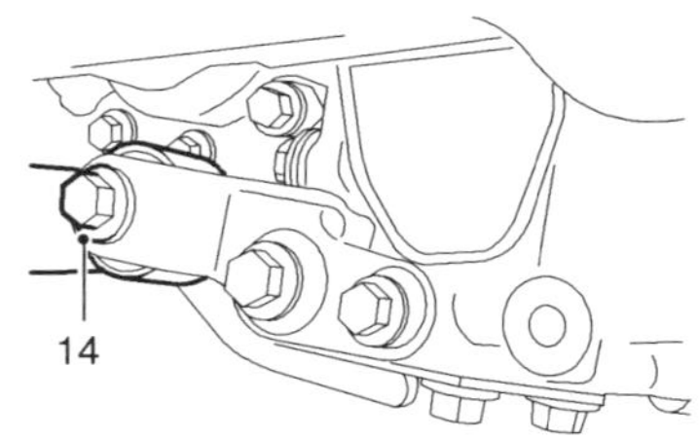

12M4000

14. Remove bolt securing engine lower tie rod to engine, loosen rear bolt and release tie rod.
15. Remove battery carrier. ***See ELECTRICAL, Repairs.***

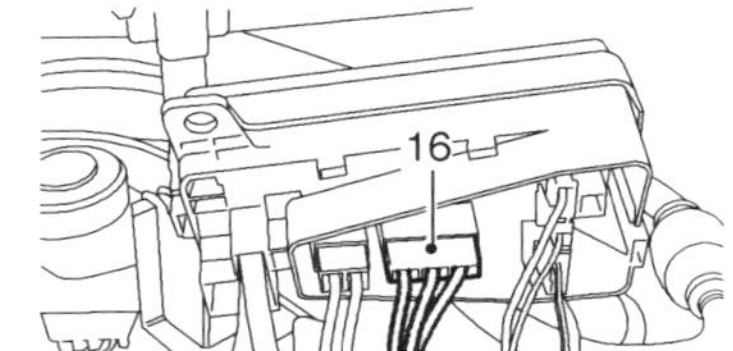

12M4001

16. Disconnect engine harness multiplug from fuse box.

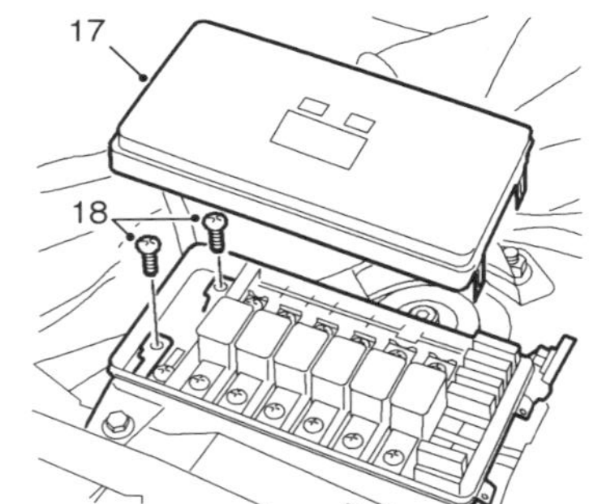

12M4002

17. Remove fuse box cover.
18. Remove 2 screws securing positive leads and release positive leads from fuse box.

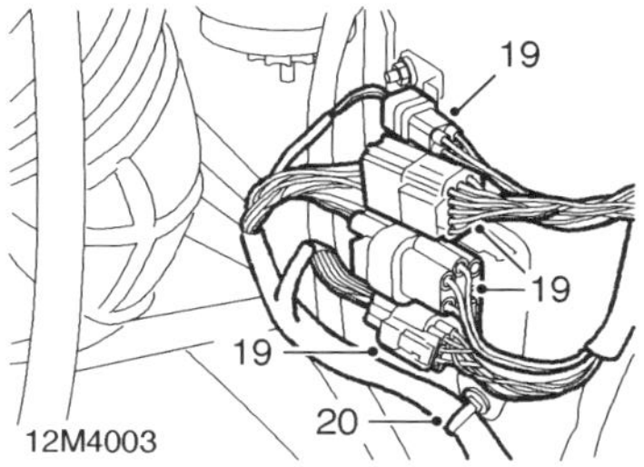

12M4003

19. Disconnect and release engine harness to main harness multiplugs.
20. Release harness from securing clip.

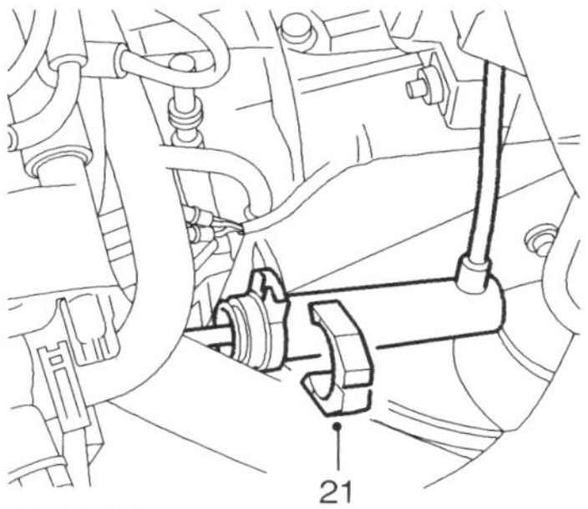

12M4004

21. Remove 'C' clip securing clutch slave cylinder, release cylinder and position aside.

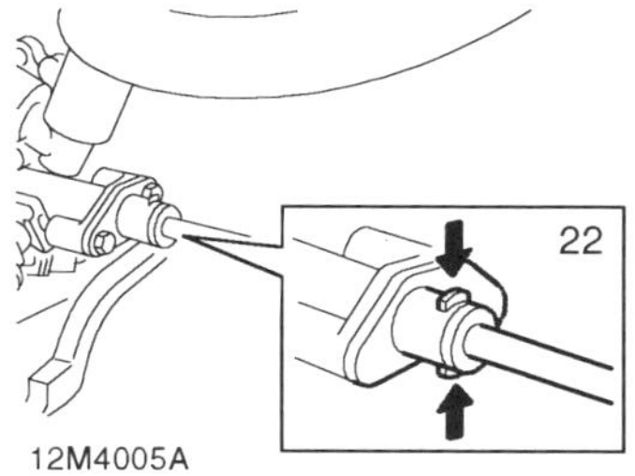

12M4005A

22. Disconnect fuel feed pipe from manifold.

⚠ **CAUTION: Plug the connections.**

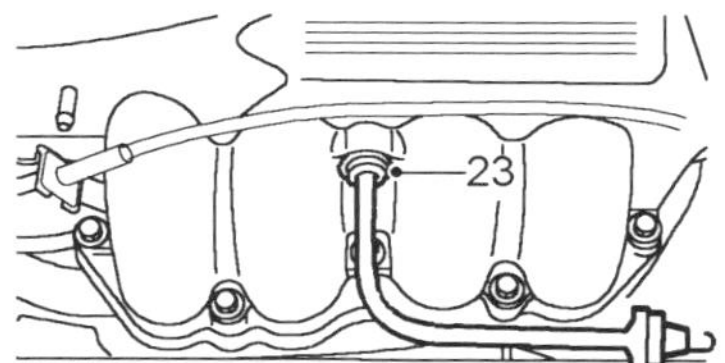

12M4006

23. Disconnect vacuum pipe from manifold.

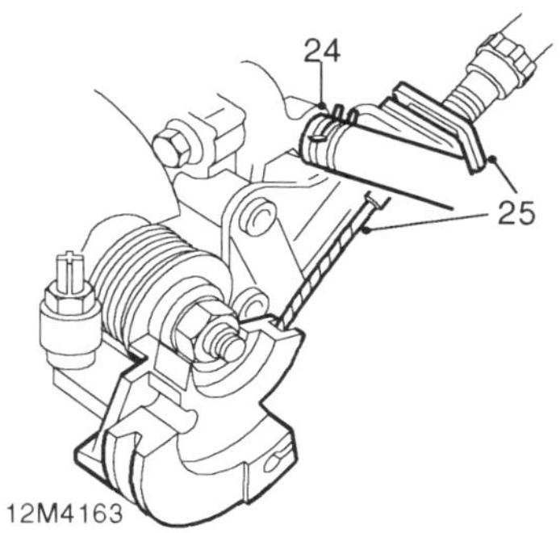

12M4163

24. Disconnect purge valve pipe from manifold.
25. Disconnect throttle cable from cam and abutment bracket.
26. Release cable from clip and position aside.

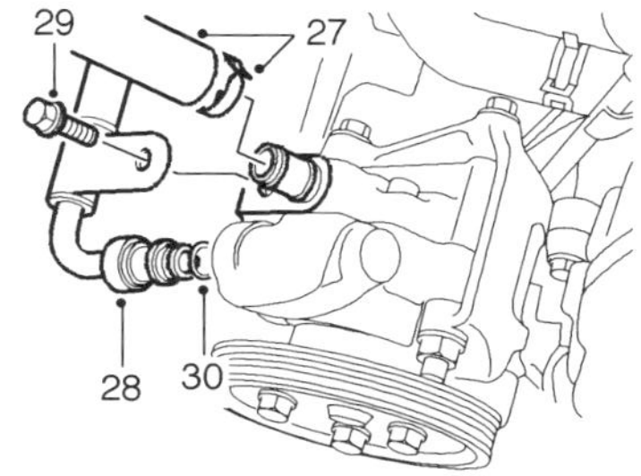

12M4007

27. Remove clip securing low pressure pipe to PAS pump and release pipe.
28. Unscrew union securing high pressure pipe to PAS pump.
29. Remove bolt securing pipe to bracket and release pipe.
30. Collect 'O' ring.

⚠ **CAUTION: Plug the connections.**

31. Release clips, disconnect and remove top hose.
32. Release clip and disconnect bottom hose from coolant rail.
33. Release clip and disconnect heater hose from water outlet elbow.

34. Release clip and disconnect heater hose from coolant rail.
35. Release clip and disconnect expansion tank hose from coolant rail.
36. Release clip and disconnect expansion tank vent hose from engine.
37. Release clips and disconnect IRD coolant hoses from IRD unit.

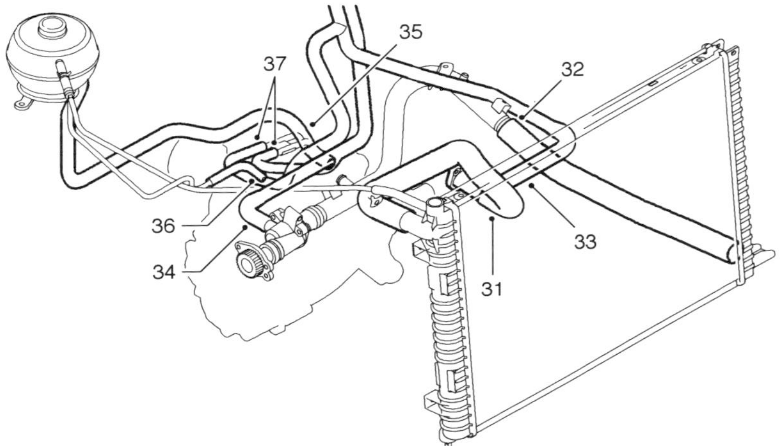

12M4008

Vehicle with air conditioning

38. Remove alternator. ***See ELECTRICAL, Repairs.***

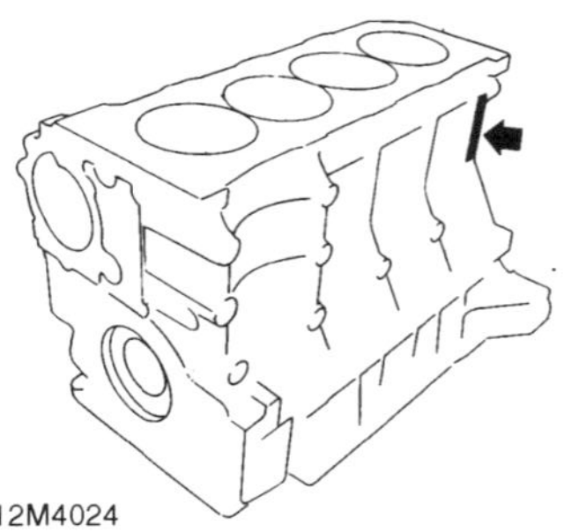

12M4024

39. Remove 4 bolts, release compressor and tie aside.

All models

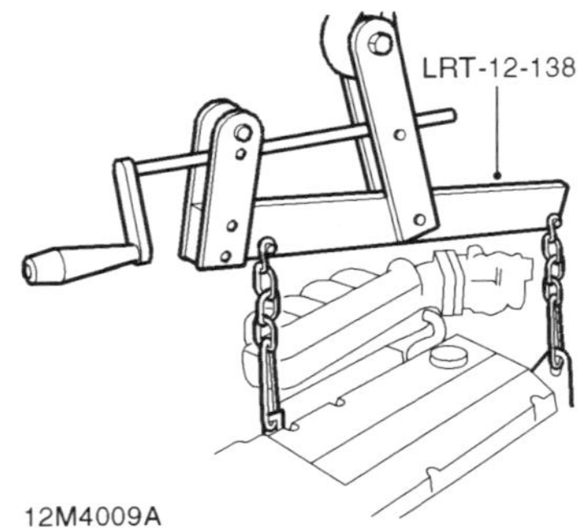

12M4009A

40. Attach suitable lifting eyes to engine.
41. Attach lifting cradle to chains and lifting eyes.
42. Take weight of engine on lifting chains.

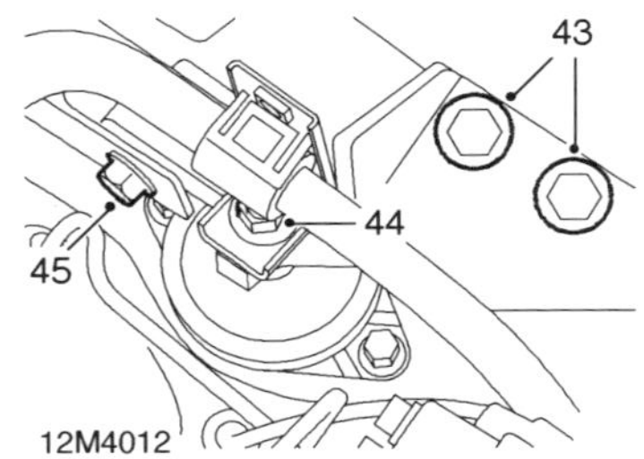

12M4012

43. Remove 2 bolts securing engine mounting bracket to engine.
44. Remove nut securing PAS pipes, release PAS pipes and position aside.
45. Remove bolt securing mounting bracket to tie rod and remove mounting bracket.

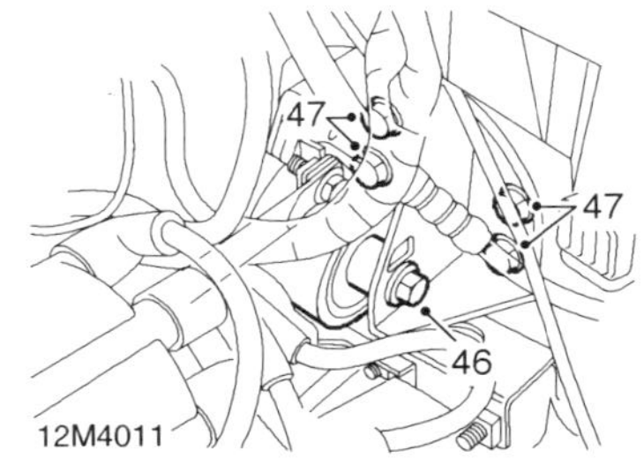

12M4011

46. Remove through bolt from gear box mounting.
47. Remove 4 bolts securing gear box mounting bracket and remove bracket.
48. With assistance remove engine and gearbox from vehicle.

Refit

1. With assistance position engine and gearbox in vehicle.
2. Position gear box mounting bracket, fit and tighten bolts to 45 Nm.
3. Align engine to LH mounting, fit and tighten through bolt to 80 Nm.
4. Position RH engine mounting bracket, fit and tighten bolt securing bracket to tie rod to 80 Nm.
5. Position PAS pipes, fit and tighten nut to 80 Nm.
6. Fit bolts securing engine mounting bracket to engine, tighten to 170 Nm.
7. Release lifting chains and remove cradle.
8. Remove lifting eyes.

Vehicle with air conditioning

9. Position compressor, fit and tighten bolts to 25 Nm.
10. Fit alternator. ***See ELECTRICAL, Repairs.***

All models

11. Connect IRD coolant hoses and secure clips.
12. Connect expansion tank vent hose and secure clip.
13. Connect expansion tank hose to coolant rail and secure clip.

14. Connect heater hose to coolant rail and secure clip.
15. Connect heater hose to water outlet elbow and secure clip.
16. Connect bottom hose to coolant rail and secure clip.
17. Fit top hose and secure clips.
18. Connect high pressure pipe to PAS pump, fit and tighten bracket bolt to 10 Nm.
19. Tighten PAS pipe union to 25 Nm.
20. Connect low pressure pipe to PAS pump and secure clip.
21. Position throttle cable in clip, locate in cam and abutment bracket.
22. Connect purge valve pipe to manifold.
23. Connect vacuum pipe to manifold.
24. Connect fuel feed pipe to manifold.
25. Position slave cylinder and secure with 'C' clip.
26. Secure harness clip, connect and secure multiplugs to main harness.
27. Position positive leads to fuse box fit and tighten screws.
28. Fit fuse box cover.
29. Connect engine harness multiplug to fuse box.
30. Fit battery carrier. ***See ELECTRICAL, Repairs.***
31. Align lower tie rod to bracket, fit and tighten bolt to 80 Nm.
32. Fit lower tie rod to subframe bolt, tighten to 80 Nm.
33. Position engine earth lead to gearbox, fit and tighten bolt to 45 Nm.
34. Fit bolt to gear change steady rod and tighten to 25 Nm.
35. Fit NEW roll pin to gear change and secure cover.
36. Position propeller shaft, align reference marks, fit and tighten bolts to 40 Nm.
37. Fit exhaust front pipe. ***See MANIFOLD & EXHAUST SYSTEMS, Repairs.***
38. Fit front drive shafts. ***See DRIVE SHAFTS, Repairs.***
39. If required refill engine with oil. ***See MAINTENANCE.***
40. Refill IRD unit with oil. ***See MANUAL GEARBOX, Adjustments.***
41. Refill gear box with oil. ***See MANUAL GEARBOX, Adjustments.***
42. Refill cooling system with coolant. ***See COOLING SYSTEM - 'K' SERIES, Adjustments.***
43. Fit bonnet. ***See BODY, Repairs.***

GASKET - CAMSHAFT COVER - 'K' SERIES

Service repair no - 12.29.40

NOTE: In the event of slight weepage from the camshaft cover gasket, first check torque of cover fixings before replacing gasket. Retighten fixings to 10 Nm if necessary.

1. Disconnect battery earth lead.

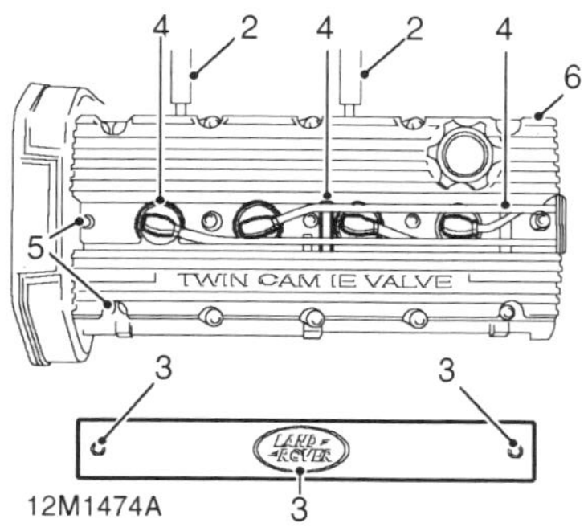

12M1474A

2. Release 2 clips and disconnect 2 breather hoses from camshaft cover.
3. Remove 2 screws securing spark plug cover and remove cover.
4. Disconnect h.t. leads from spark plugs, release lead mounting rubbers and place leads aside.
5. Progressively loosen and remove 15 bolts securing camshaft cover.
6. Remove camshaft cover.

NOTE: The gasket is re-usable and should remain attached to camshaft cover.

7. Check condition of sealing path. It should be complete and attached to gasket. Remove gasket from camshaft cover only if sealing path is damaged or detached from gasket.

Refit

1. Clean mating surfaces of camshaft cover and carrier.
2. Clean inside of camshaft cover. If necessary, wash oil separator elements in solvent and blow dry.

CAUTION: If camshaft cover gasket is to be renewed, fit new gasket with 'EXHAUST MAN SIDE' mark towards exhaust manifold.

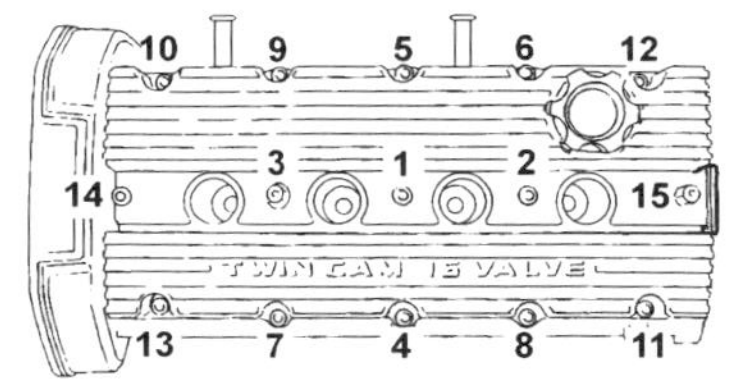

12M1475

3. Fit camshaft cover to camshaft carrier. Fit bolts and working in sequence illustrated, tighten progressively to 10 Nm.
4. Connect HT leads to plugs and secure mounting rubbers in camshaft cover.
5. Connect breather hoses and secure with clips.
6. Connect battery earth lead.
7. Start engine and run to normal operating temperature is reached.
8. Retorque cover fixings to 10 Nm.
9. Fit spark plug cover, fit screws and tighten to 2 Nm.

MOUNTING - ENGINE - LH - 'K' SERIES

Service repair no - 12.45.11

Remove

1. Remove underbelly panel. ***See BODY, Exterior fittings.***
2. Remove air cleaner assembly ***See ENGINE MANAGEMENT SYSTEM - MEMS, Repairs.***
3. Remove LH front wheel.

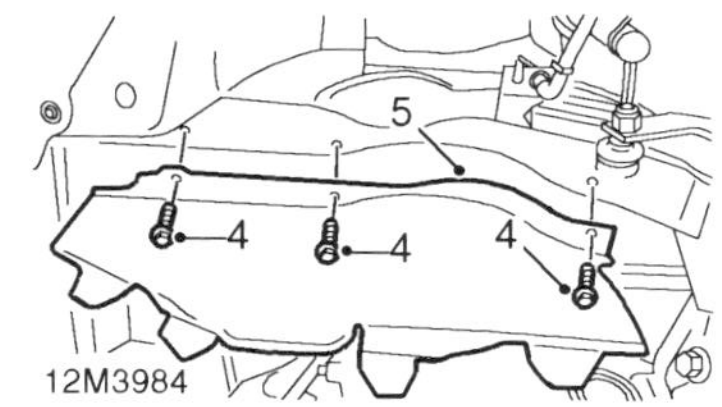

12M3984

4. Remove 3 bolts securing LH splash shield.
5. Remove LH splash shield.

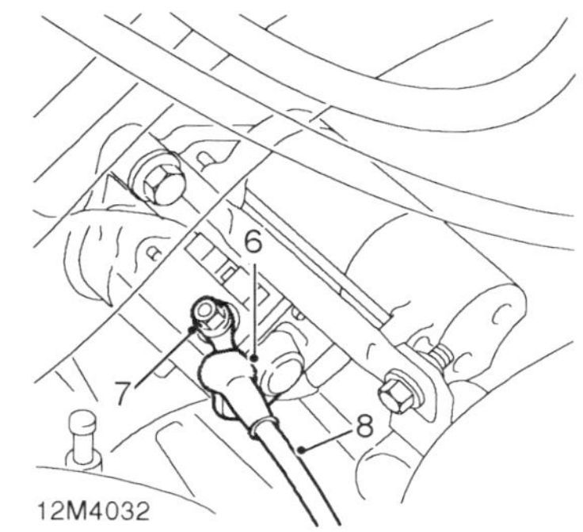

12M4032

6. Release cover from battery lead terminal on starter motor.
7. Remove nut securing battery lead to starter motor terminal.
8. Release battery lead from starter motor terminal.

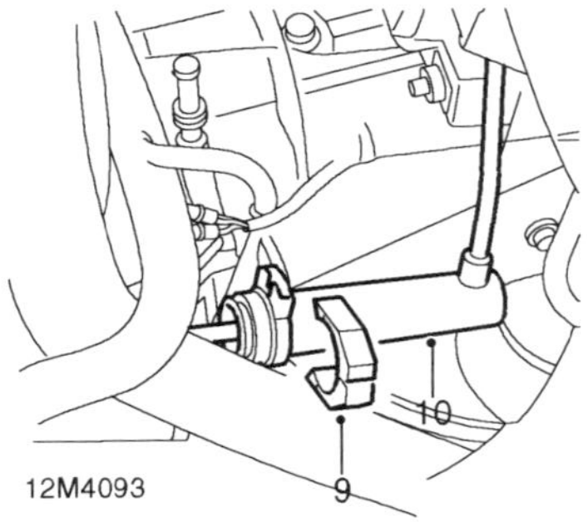

12M4093

9. Remove clip securing clutch slave cylinder to bracket.
10. Move slave cylinder aside.

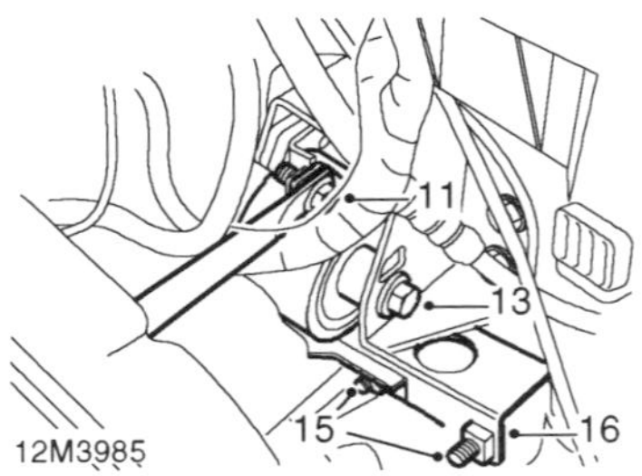

12M3985

11. Remove bolt securing support strut to LH engine mounting.
12. Support engine on a jack.

⚠ **CAUTION: Fit a suitable block of wood on jack to protect engine.**

13. Remove bolt securing LH engine mounting to bracket on body.
14. Lower engine sufficiently only for access to engine mounting bolts.
15. Remove 2 bolts securing engine mounting to gearbox.
16. Remove LH engine mounting.

Refit

1. Fit LH engine mounting to gearbox and tighten bolts to 65 Nm.
2. Raise engine to align LH engine mounting to bracket on body.
3. Fit bolt securing LH engine mounting to bracket on body and tighten to 80 Nm.
4. Remove jack.
5. Fit bolt securing strut to LH engine mounting and tighten to 60 Nm.
6. Fit clutch slave cylinder to bracket, ensure push rod is engaged with lever and fit clip to secure cylinder to bracket.
7. Fit battery lead to starter motor terminal and secure with nut.
8. Fit terminal cover.
9. Fit LH splash shield and secure with bolts.
10. Fit road wheel(s) and tighten nuts to correct torque. ***See INFORMATION, Torque wrench settings.***
11. Fit air cleaner assembly. ***See ENGINE MANAGEMENT SYSTEM - MEMS, Repairs.***
12. Fit underbelly panel. ***See BODY, Exterior fittings.***

MOUNTING - ENGINE - RH - 'K' SERIES

Service repair no - 12.45.12

Remove

1. Disconnect battery earth lead.
2. Remove underbelly panel. ***See BODY, Exterior fittings.***

Models with air conditioning.

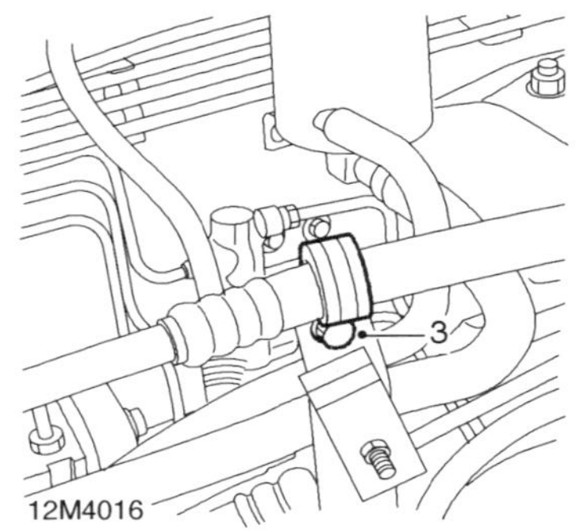

12M4016

3. Remove bolt securing air conditioning hose clip to PAS hose support bracket.

All models

4. Use a jack to support engine under sump.

⚠ **CAUTION: Use a block of wood on jack to protect the sump.**

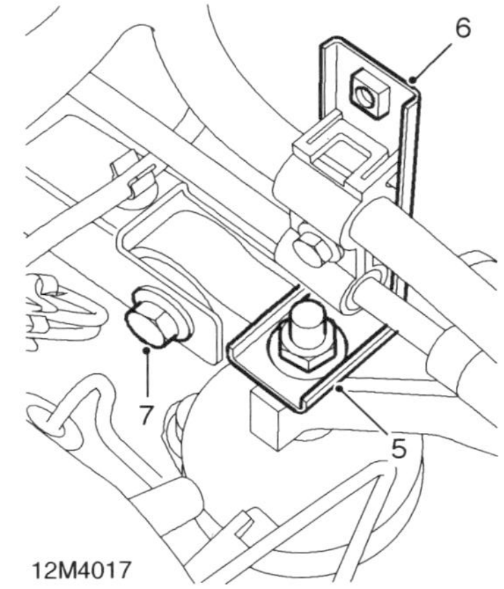

12M4017

5. Remove nut securing PAS hose support bracket to engine mounting stud.
6. Release PAS hose bracket from mounting stud.
7. Remove bolt securing engine upper tie bar to engine mounting bracket.

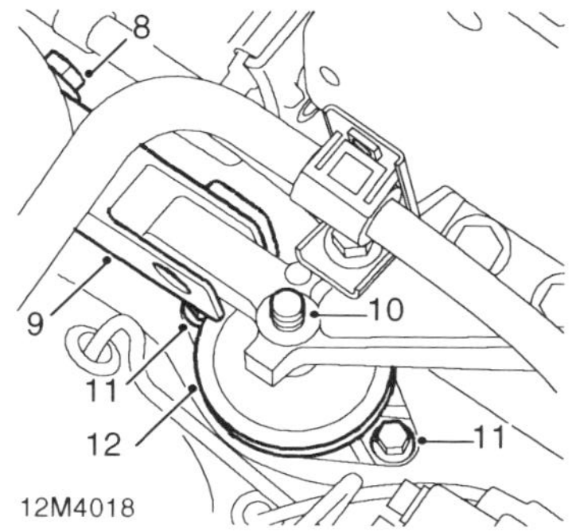

12M4018

8. Loosen bolt securing engine upper tie bar to bracket on body.
9. Raise upper tie bar to clear engine mounting bracket.
10. Raise RH side of engine on jack sufficiently only to clear RH engine mounting stud.
11. Remove 2 bolts securing RH engine mounting to wing valance.
12. Remove RH engine mounting.

Refit

1. Connect battery earth lead.
2. Fit RH engine mounting to wing valence and tighten bolts to 45 Nm.
3. Lower engine onto RH mounting.
4. Fit upper tie bar to engine mounting bracket and tighten both bolts securing tie bar to 80 Nm.
5. Remove jack from under engine.
6. Fit PAS hose bracket to engine mounting stud and tighten nut to 80 Nm.

Models with air conditioning

7. Fit air conditioning hose clip to PAS hose support bracket and secure with bolt.

All models

8. Fit underbelly panel. ***See BODY, Exterior fittings.***

FLYWHEEL

Service repair no - 12.53.07

Remove

1. Remove clutch assembly. ***See CLUTCH, Repairs.***
2. Fit flywheel locking tool **LRT-12-145** to cylinder head and secure with bolts.
3. Remove CKP sensor. ***See ENGINE MANAGEMENT SYSTEM - MEMS, Repairs.***

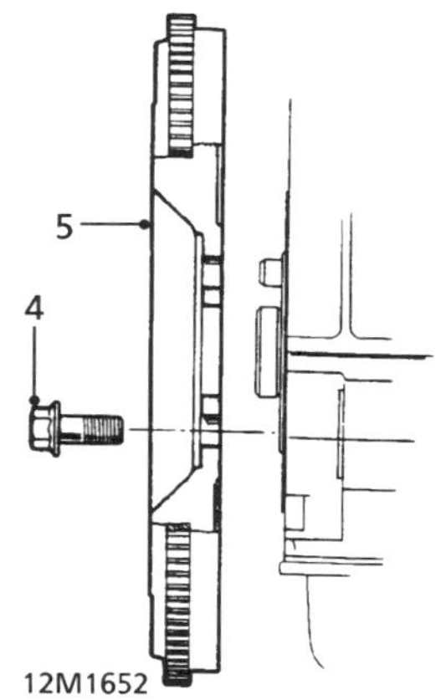

12M1652

4. Remove and discard 6 bolts securing flywheel to crankshaft.
5. Remove flywheel from crankshaft.

Refit

1. Clean adhesive from threads of flywheel bolt holes in crankshaft.

NOTE: Do not use a tap to clean threads.

2. Clean flywheel and mating face of crankshaft.
3. Fit flywheel to crankshaft.
4. Fit NEW Patchlok bolts securing flywheel to crankshaft and working in a diagonal sequence tighten bolts to 85 Nm.
5. Fit CKP sensor. ***See ENGINE MANAGEMENT SYSTEM - MEMS, Repairs.***
6. Remove bolts securing locking tool **LRT-12-145** , remove tool.
7. Fit clutch assembly. ***See CLUTCH, Repairs.***

FILTER - ENGINE OIL

Service repair no - 12.60.04

Remove

1. Remove underbelly panel. ***See BODY, Exterior fittings.***
2. Clean area around filter head and place a container beneath engine

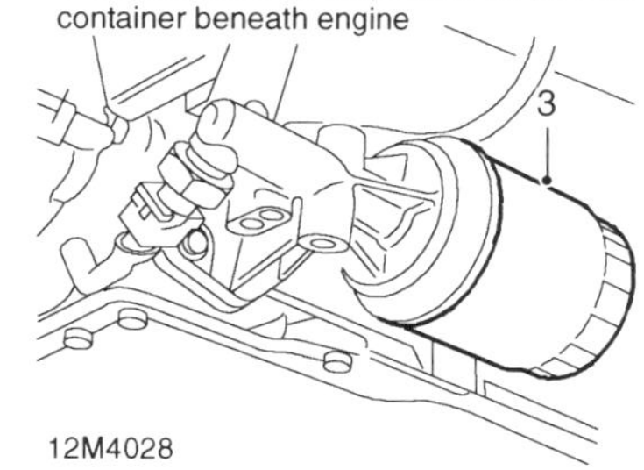

12M4028

3. Using a strap wrench, unscrew and discard filter.

Refit

1. Clean mating face of filter head.
2. Lubricate sealing ring of NEW filter with clean engine oil.
3. Fit filter and tighten by hand until it seats then tighten a further half to three quarters of a turn.
4. Top up engine oil. ***See MAINTENANCE.***
5. Start and run engine and check for leaks.
6. Stop engine, wait a few minutes, then check oil level. Top up if necessary.
7. Fit underbelly panel. ***See BODY, Exterior fittings.***

PUMP - ENGINE OIL

Service repair no - 12.60.26

Remove

1. Remove camshaft timing belt. ***See this section.***
2. Remove crankshaft gear.
3. Remove PAS drive belt auto tensioner.

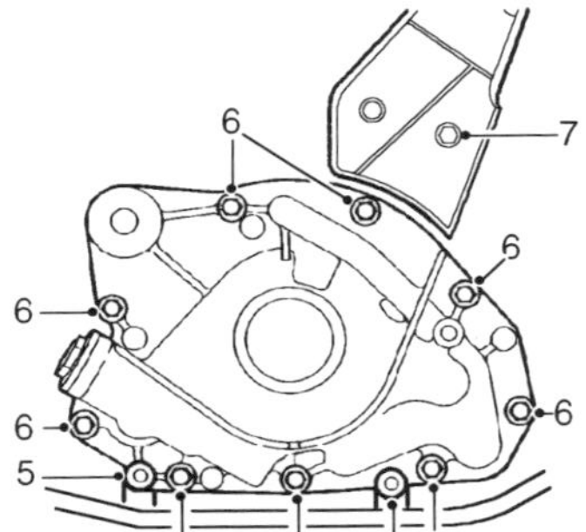

12M4022

4. Remove 2 bolts securing engine harness to oil pump and release harness.
5. Remove and discard bolts securing oil pump to cylinder block.
6. Remove lower bolt from timing belt rear cover.
7. Release rear cover to facilitate oil pump removal
8. Remove oil pump and gasket.

Refit

1. Clean oil pump bolt holes in cylinder block.
2. Clean oil pump and mating face.
3. Clean oil seal running surface on crankshaft.
4. Fit new oil pump gasket, align and fit oil pump.

CAUTION: Do not lubricate front oil seal or running surface on crankshaft.

5. Release rear cover to facilitate oil pump fitting.

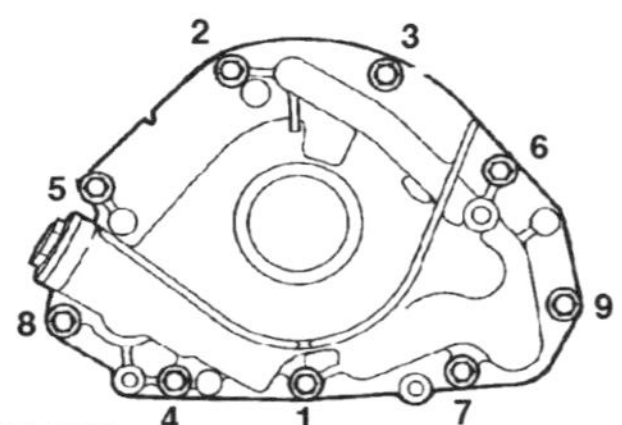

12M1769

6. Fit new Patchlok bolts and tighten in sequence shown to 10 Nm.
7. Position engine harness, fit and tighten bolts to 10 Nm.
8. Fit and tighten lower bolt on timing belt rear cover to 9 Nm.
9. Fit PAS auto tensioner and tighten bolts to 25 Nm.
10. Clean crankshaft timing gear. Fit crankshaft gear.
11. Fit camshaft timing belt. ***See this section.***

OIL SUMP - 'K' SERIES

Service repair no - 12.60.44

Remove

1. Remove exhaust front pipe. ***See MANIFOLD & EXHAUST SYSTEMS, Repairs.***
2. Drain engine oil. ***See MAINTENANCE.***

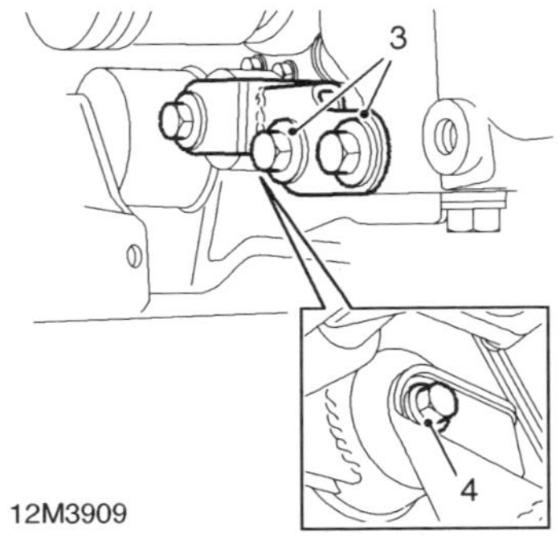

12M3909

3. Remove 2 bolts securing front of engine tie bar.
4. Loosen rear bolt on engine tie bar and lower tie bar.

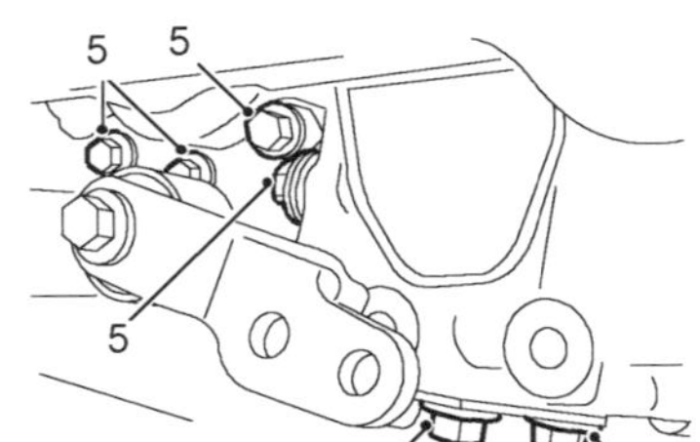

12M3910

5. Remove 6 bolts securing IRD lower support bracket and remove bracket.

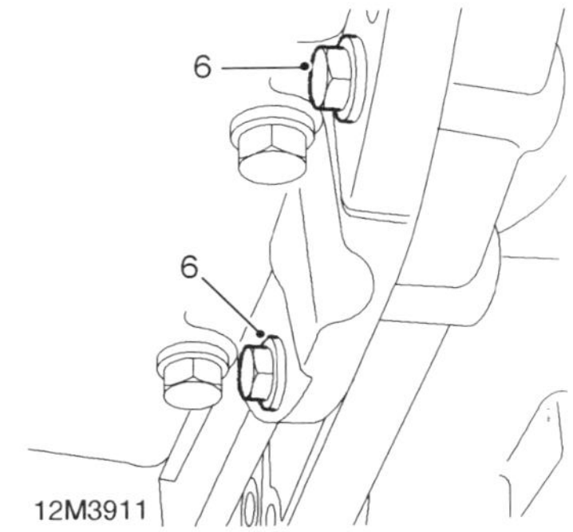

12M3911

6. Remove 2 bolts securing sump to gearbox.

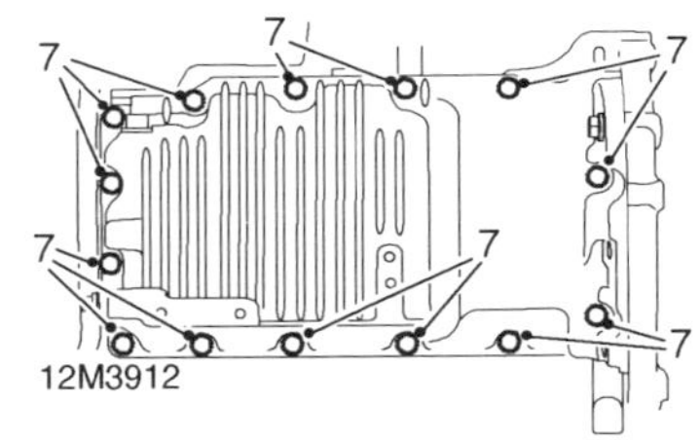

12M3912

7. Noting fitted positions of 2 longest bolts, remove 14 bolts securing sump to engine.
8. Gently tap sump sideways to break sealant bond; remove sump.

CAUTION: Do not lever between sump and bearing ladder.

Refit

1. Clean inside of sump. Remove all traces of sealant using a suitable solvent.
2. Apply sealant, Part No. GUG 705963GM to sump face and spread to an even film using a brush or roller.

CAUTION: To avoid contamination, assembly must be completed immediately after applying sealant. Do not use any sealant other than that specified.

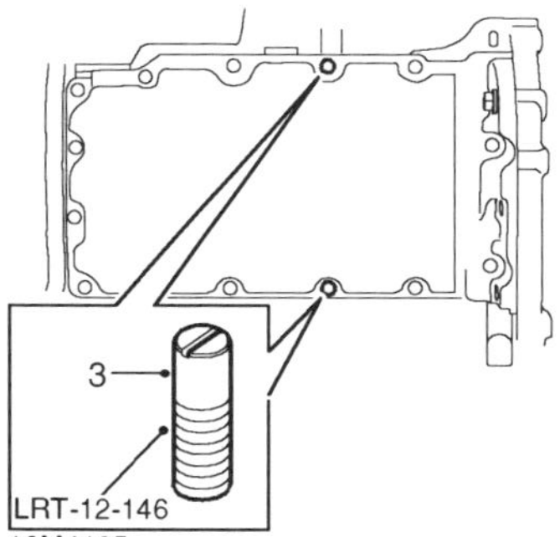

12M4165

3. Fit alignment pins **LRT-12-146** to holes as shown.

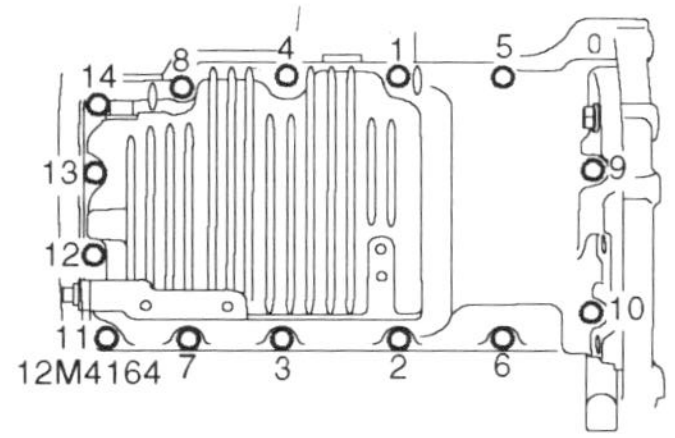

12M4164

4. Position sump to engine, fit 2 bolts at positions 5 and 6 and tighten to 4 Nm.
5. Fit 10 bolts into remaining holes ensuring that 2 longest bolts are in original fitted positions, finger tighten bolts.
6. Remove alignment pins **LRT-12-146,** fit and finger tighten remaining 2 bolts.
7. Progressively tighten sump bolts to 25 Nm in the sequence shown.
8. Fit sump to gearbox bolts and tighten to 45 Nm.
9. Position IRD lower support bracket, fit bolts and tighten to 45 Nm.
10. Position engine lower tie bar, fit front bolts and tighten to 80 Nm.
11. Tighten rear bolt on engine lower tie bar to 80 Nm.
12. Fit exhaust front pipe. ***See MANIFOLD & EXHAUST SYSTEMS, Repairs.***
13. Fill engine with oil. ***See MAINTENANCE.***

SWITCH - OIL PRESSURE - 'K' SERIES

Service repair no - 12.60.50

Remove

1. Disconnect battery earth lead.
2. Raise front of vehicle, RH side.

WARNING: Support on safety stands.

3. Turn steering wheel to full RH lock.

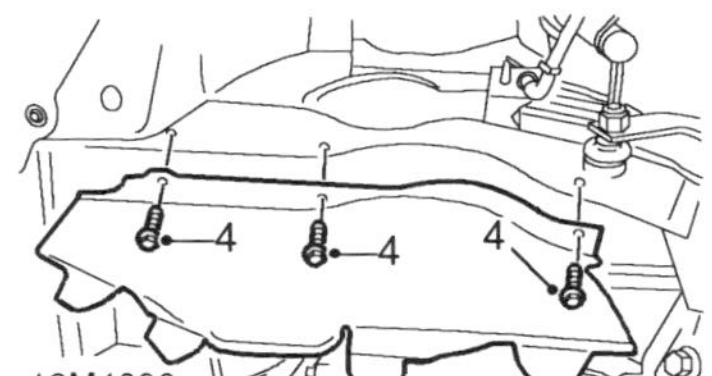

12M4036

4. Remove 3 bolts securing RH splash shield and remove guard.

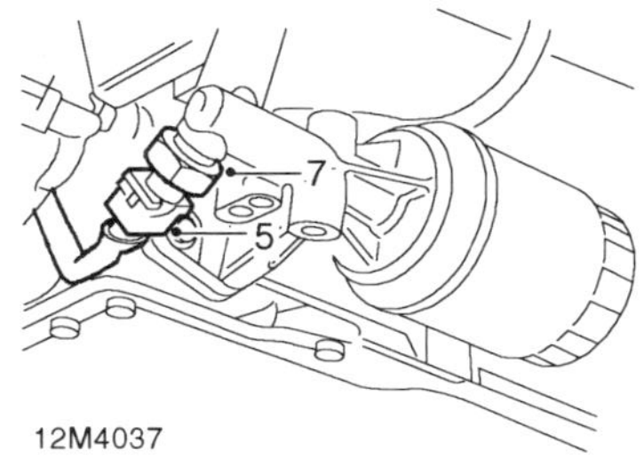

12M4037

5. Disconnect multiplug from oil pressure switch.
6. Position drain tin below switch to catch spillage.
7. Remove oil pressure switch.

Refit

1. Clean oil pressure switch threads.
2. Fit oil pressure switch and tighten to 12 Nm.
3. Connect multiplug to oil pressure switch.
4. Position splash shield, fit and tighten bolts to 10 Nm.
5. Position steering wheel straight ahead.
6. Remove stand(s) and lower vehicle.
7. Top-up engine oil. ***See MAINTENANCE.***

TIMING BELT - CAMSHAFT - 'K' SERIES

Service repair no - 12.65.18

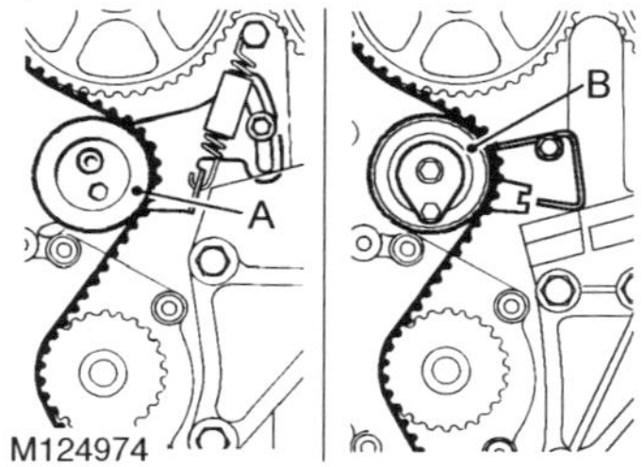

M124974

NOTE: Two types of timing belt tensioner are fitted, type A is a manual tensioner, type B is an automatic tensioner. The tensioners and their timing belts are not interchangeable.

CAUTION: Timing belt must be replaced if cylinder head is to be removed or new timing gears, tensioner or coolant pump are to be fitted.
Timing belts must be stored and handled with care.
Always store a timing belt on its edge with a bend radius greater than 50 mm.
Do not use a timing belt that has been twisted or bent double as this will damage the reinforcing fibres.
Do not use a timing belt if debris other than belt dust is found in timing cover.
Do not use a timing belt if partial engine seizure has occurred.
Do not use a timing belt if belt mileage exceeds 48,000 miles (77,000 km).
Do not use an oil or coolant contaminated belt.

NOTE: The cause of contamination MUST be rectified.

Remove - Engines fitted with manual timing belt tensioner

1. Disconnect battery earth lead.
2. Raise front of vehicle.

WARNING: Support on safety stands.

3. Remove RH road wheel.
4. Remove underbelly panel, ***See BODY, Repairs.***

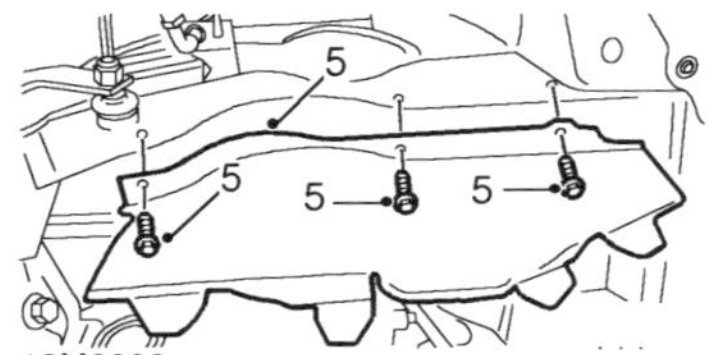

12M3989

5. Remove 3 bolts securing RH splash shield and remove splash shield.
6. Remove timing belt upper cover. ***See this section.***

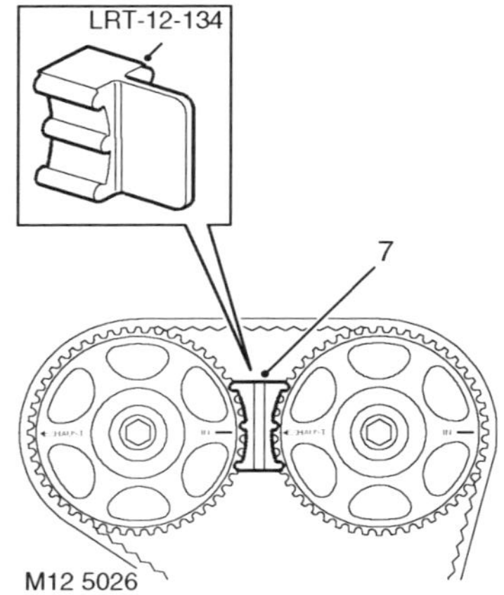

M12 5026

7. Using a socket on the crankshaft pulley bolt, rotate crankshaft clockwise to align the camshaft gear timing marks with mark on backplate.

CAUTION: Never use the camshaft gear, gear retaining bolts or timing belt to rotate the engine.

8. Fit camshaft gear alignment tool **LRT-12-134.**
9. Fit wooden block to jack and position jack to support engine.

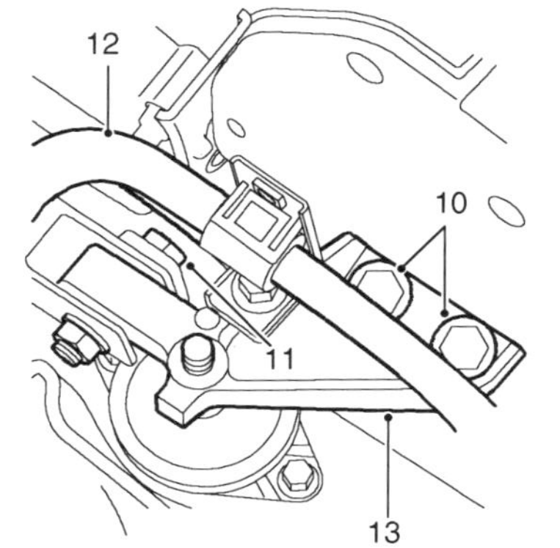

12M3993A

10. Remove 2 bolts securing engine RH mounting bracket to engine.
11. Remove through bolt and nut securing RH mounting bracket to upper tie rod.
12. Release PAS cooling pipes and position aside.
13. Remove engine RH mounting bracket.
14. Remove camshaft timing belt lower cover. ***See this section.***

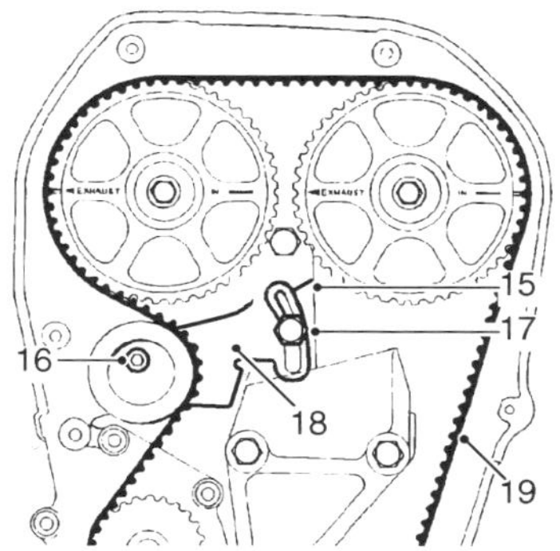

12M3995B

15. If camshaft timing belt is to be re-used, mark position of tensioner backplate to cylinder head for belt tensioning reference. Mark direction of rotation on belt using chalk.
16. Loosen tensioner pulley Allen bolt 1/2 turn.
17. Loosen tensioner backplate bolt 1/2 turn.
18. Push tensioner pulley down to fully OFF position and tighten backplate bolt to 10 Nm.
19. Remove camshaft timing belt.

CAUTION: Ease timing belt off timing gears using fingers only. Metal levers may damage the belt and gears.
Do not rotate the crankshaft with the timing belt removed and the cylinder head fitted.

Refit - Engines fitted with manual timing belt tensioner

1. Clean crankshaft pulley, timing belt gears, coolant pump drive gear and tensioner pulley.

CAUTION: If the sintered gears have been subjected to prolonged oil contamination, they must be soaked in a solvent bath and then thoroughly washed in clean solvent before refitting. Because of the porous construction of sintered material, oil impregnated in the gears will emerge and contaminate the belt.

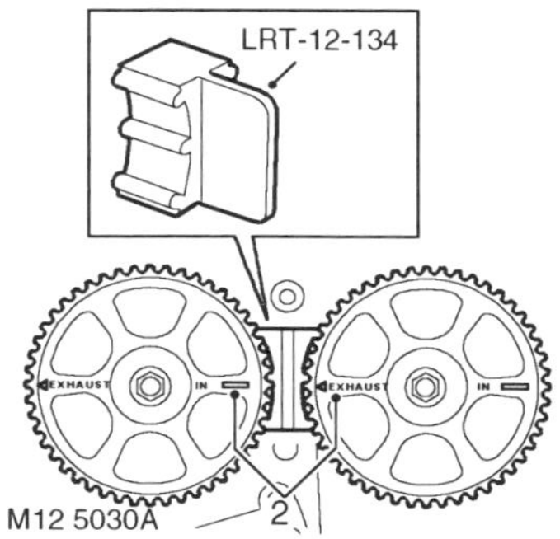

M12 5030A

2. Check correct alignment of camshaft timing marks for 90° BTDC and that tool **LRT-12-134** is locking camshaft gears.

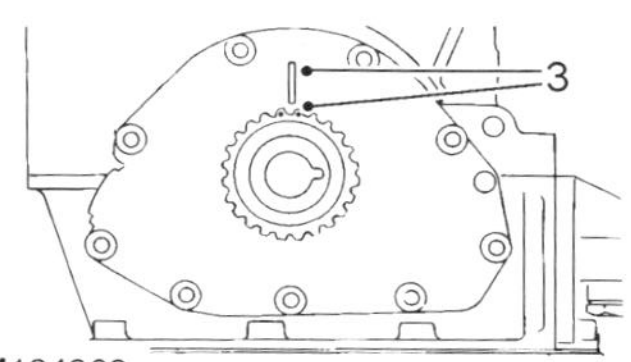

M124962

3. Ensure dots on crankshaft gear are aligned with flange on oil pump and that tool **LRT-12-145** is locking flywheel.

Replacement timing belt

4. Fit pillar bolt supplied with replacement timing belt to cylinder head.
5. Fit spring supplied with replacement timing belt to tensioner and pillar bolt.

NOTE: This spring is not fitted with a sleeve.

All timing belts

6. Push tensioner down to OFF position and tighten backplate bolt to 10 Nm.
7. Using fingers only, fit timing belt, ensure belt run between the crankshaft gear and the camshaft gears is kept taut during the fitting procedure.

CAUTION: If the original belt is to be refitted, ensure the direction of rotation mark is facing the correct way.

8. Check that timing belt is positioned centrally around all gears and tensioner pulley.
9. Fit timing belt lower cover. ***See this section.***

NOTE: Do not fit timing belt upper cover at this stage.

10. Fit RH engine mounting bracket, position PAS cooling pipes.
11. Fit through bolt and nut securing bracket to body but do not tighten at this stage.
12. Fit bolts securing bracket to engine and tighten to 170 Nm.
13. Fit through bolt and nut to RH engine mounting bracket and upper tie rod and tighten to 80 Nm.
14. Lower jack supporting engine and remove from vehicle.
15. Remove camshaft gear alignment tool **LRT-12-134.**

Tensioning existing timing belt

16. Loosen tensioner backplate bolt.
17. Position tensioner to align mark on backplate with mark on cylinder head.
18. Tighten tensioner backplate bolt to 10 Nm.
19. Tighten tensioner pulley Allen bolt to 45 Nm.

Tensioning replacement timing belt

20. Loosen tensioner pulley backplate bolt and ensure that tensioner moves freely through its adjustment range and returns under spring tension.
21. Tension timing belt by applying finger pressure to backplate and pushing tensioner pulley against belt.
22. Hold tensioner in this position and tighten backplate bolt to 10 Nm.
23. Rotate crankshaft clockwise 2 complete revolutions and align camshaft timing gear marks.

CAUTION: Do not use camshaft gears, gear retaining bolts or timing belt to rotate crankshaft.

24. Loosen backplate bolt and check that belt tension is being applied by tensioner spring.
25. Tighten tensioner backplate bolt to 10 Nm.
26. Tighten tensioner pulley Allen bolt to 45 Nm.
27. Remove and discard pillar bolt and tensioner spring.

All timing belts

28. Fit timing belt upper cover. ***See this section.***
29. Position RH splash shield, fit and tighten bolts to 10 Nm.
30. Fit underbelly panel. ***See BODY, Repairs.***
31. Fit road wheel(s) and tighten nuts to correct torque. ***See INFORMATION, Torque wrench settings.***
32. Connect battery earth lead.
33. Remove stand(s) and lower vehicle.

Remove - Engines fitted with automatic timing belt tensioner

1. Disconnect battery earth lead.
2. Raise front of vehicle.

WARNING: Support on safety stands.

3. Remove RH road wheel.
4. Remove underbelly panel. ***See BODY, Repairs.***

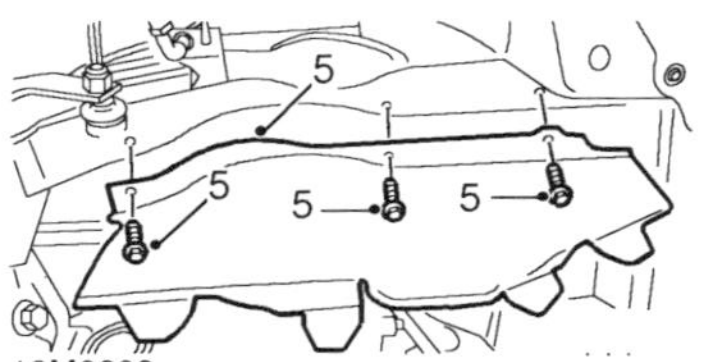

12M3989

5. Remove 3 bolts securing RH splash shield and remove splash shield.
6. Remove timing belt upper cover. ***See this section.***

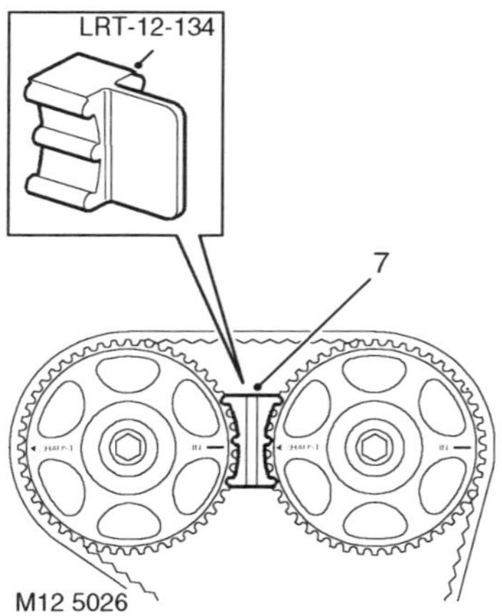

M12 5026

7. Using a socket and extension bar on the crankshaft pulley bolt, rotate crankshaft clockwise to align camshaft gear timing marks with mark on backplate - 90° BTDC.

CAUTION: Never use camshaft gears, gear retaining bolts or timing belt to rotate crankshaft.

8. Fit camshaft gear alignment tool **LRT-12-134.**
9. Fit wooden block to jack and position jack to support engine.

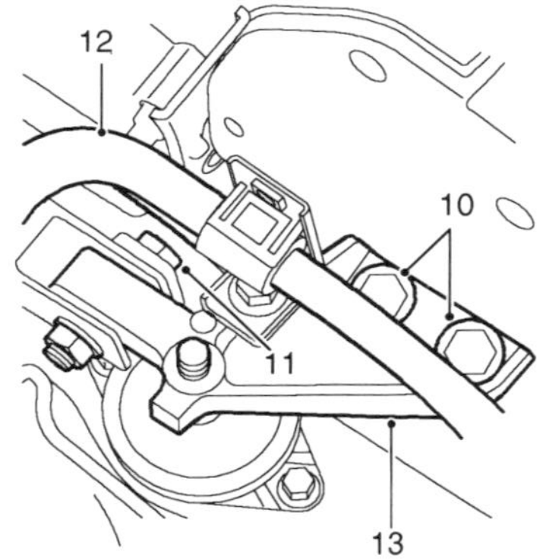

12M3993A

10. Remove 2 bolts securing engine RH mounting bracket to engine.
11. Remove through bolt and nut securing RH mounting bracket to upper tie rod.
12. Release PAS cooling pipes and position aside.
13. Remove engine RH mounting bracket.

14. Remove camshaft timing belt lower cover. ***See this section.***

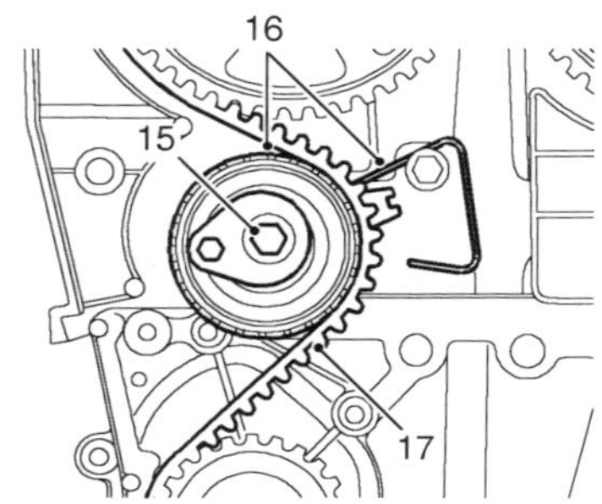

M12 5027

15. Remove and discard timing belt tensioner bolt.
16. Disengage index wire from its fitted position whilst at the same time removing the timing belt tensioner.
17. If camshaft timing belt is to be re-used, mark direction of belt rotation using chalk, remove camshaft timing belt.

CAUTION: Ease timing belt off timing gears using fingers only. Metal levers may damage the belt and gears.
Do not rotate the crankshaft with the timing belt removed and the cylinder head fitted.

Refit - Engines fitted with automatic timing belt tensioner

1. Clean crankshaft pulley, timing belt gears, coolant pump drive gear and tensioner pulley.

CAUTION: If the sintered gears have been subjected to prolonged oil contamination, they must be soaked in a solvent bath and then thoroughly washed in clean solvent before refitting. Because of the porous construction of sintered material, oil impregnated in the gears will emerge and contaminate the belt.

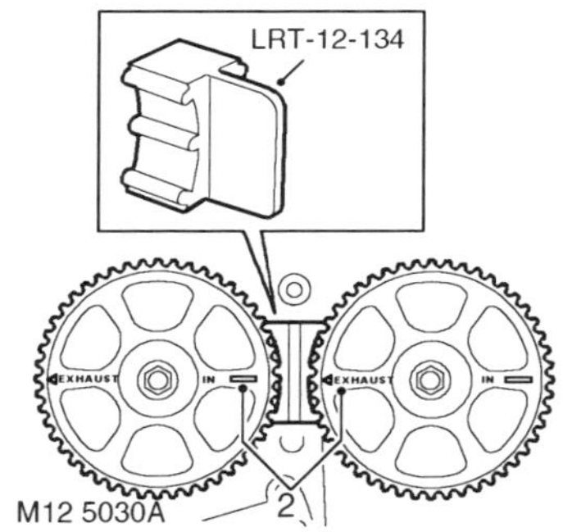

M12 5030A

2. Check correct alignment of camshaft timing marks for 90° BTDC and that tool **LRT-12-134** is locking camshaft gears.

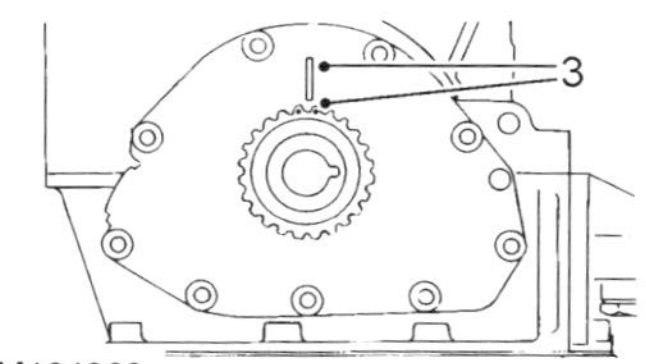

M124962

3. Ensure dots on crankshaft gear are aligned with flange on oil pump and that tool **LRT-12-145** is locking flywheel.

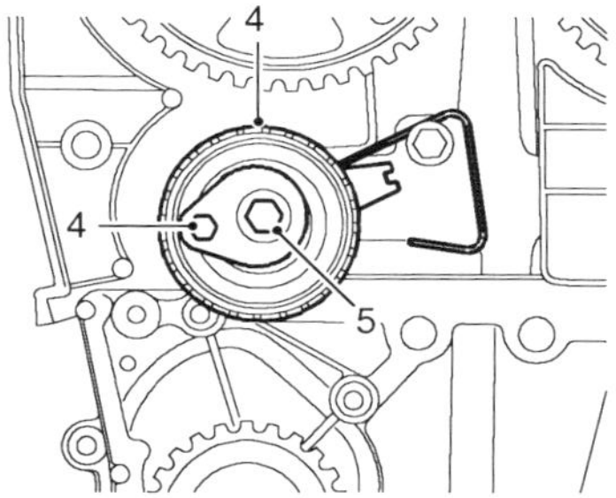

M12 4956

4. Fit timing belt tensioner ensuring that index wire is positioned over pillar bolt and that tensioner lever is at 9 o'clock position.
5. Fit a new tensioner Patchlok bolt and tighten bolt until it is just possible to move tensioner lever.
6. Using the fingers only, fit the timing belt over crankshaft timing gear, then over camshaft gears, coolant pump drive gear and tensioner pulley ensuring that the belt run is kept taut between the crankshaft timing gear and exhaust camshaft gear.

CAUTION: If original belt is being refitted, ensure that direction of rotation mark is facing correct way.

7. Check that timing belt is positioned centrally around all gears and tensioner pulley.
8. Fit timing belt lower cover. ***See this section.***

NOTE: Do not fit timing belt upper cover at this stage.

9. Fit RH engine mounting bracket, position PAS cooling pipes.
10. Fit through bolt and nut securing bracket to body but do not tighten at this stage.
11. Fit bolts securing bracket to engine and tighten to 170 Nm.
12. Fit through bolt and nut to RH engine mounting bracket and upper tie rod and tighten to 80 Nm.
13. Lower jack supporting power unit and remove jack from beneath vehicle.
14. Remove camshaft gear alignment tool **LRT-12-134.**

Tensioning timing belt

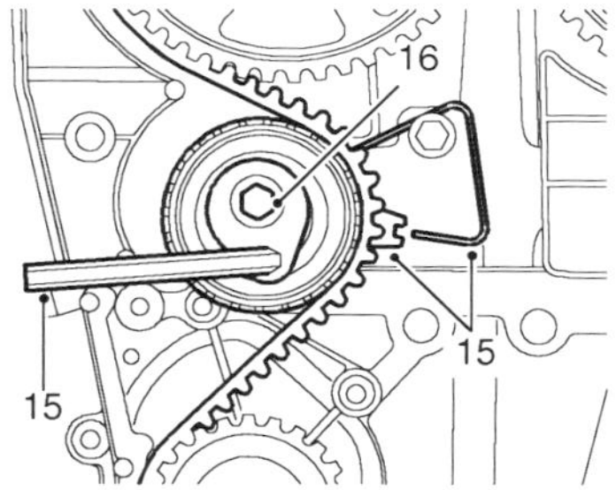

M12 5028

15. Using a 6 mm Allen key, rotate tensioner anti-clockwise and align the tensioner pointer to the index wire.

NOTE: If original belt is being refitted, align index wire to lower land of pointer.

CAUTION: Ensure that pointer approaches the index wire from above. Should pointer go past index wire, release tension completely and repeat tensioning procedure.

16. Ensuring that pointer maintains correct position, tighten tensioner bolt to 25 Nm.

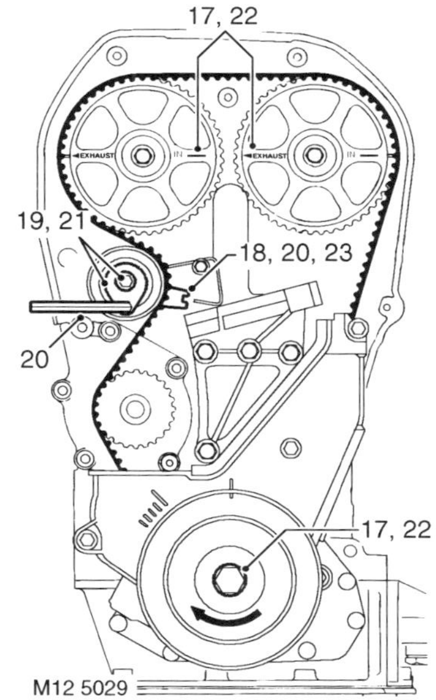

M12 5029

17. Using crankshaft pulley bolt, rotate crankshaft 2 turns clockwise and align camshaft gear timing marks.

CAUTION: Do not use camshaft gears, gear retaining bolts or timing belt to rotate crankshaft.

18. Check that pointer is still correctly aligned with index wire.

CAUTION: If pointer is not correctly aligned, carry out the following procedure.

19. Slacken tensioner bolt until it is just possible to move the tensioner lever.
20. Using a 6 mm Allen key, rotate tensioner lever clockwise until pointer is just above the index wire then rotate the lever anti-clockwise until pointer is correctly aligned with index wire.
21. Ensuring that pointer maintains correct position, tighten tensioner bolt to 25 Nm.
22. Using crankshaft pulley bolt, rotate crankshaft 2 turns clockwise and align camshaft gear timing marks.
23. Check that pointer is still correctly aligned with index wire.
24. Fit timing belt upper cover. ***See this section.***
25. Position RH splash shield, fit and tighten bolts to 10 Nm.
26. Fit underbelly panel. ***See BODY, Repairs.***
27. Fit road wheel(s) and tighten nuts to correct torque. ***See INFORMATION, Torque wrench settings.***
28. Connect battery earth lead.
29. Remove stand(s) and lower vehicle.

MANUAL TENSIONER - CAMSHAFT - TIMING BELT

Service repair no - 12.65.19

Remove

> ⚠ NOTE: Automatic timing belt tensioner is removed and refitted during camshaft timing belt remove and refit.

1. Disconnect battery earth lead.
2. Remove and discard camshaft timing belt. ***See this section.***

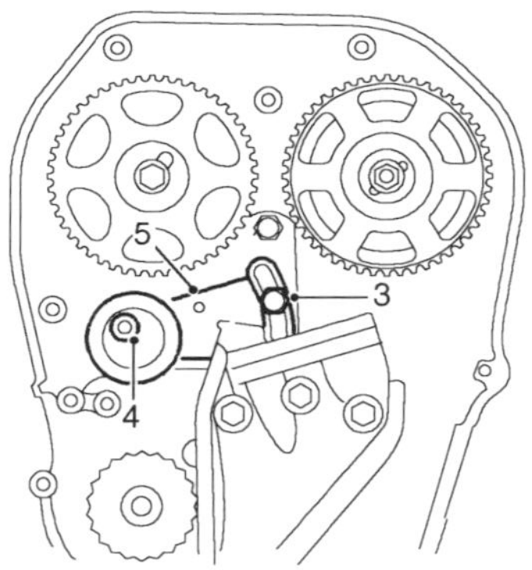

12M4020A

3. Remove tensioner backplate screw.
4. Remove tensioner pulley Allen bolt.
5. Remove timing belt tensioner.

Refit

1. Position timing belt tensioner and fit but do not tighten tensioner pulley Allen bolt.
2. Fit tensioner backplate screw but do not tighten at this stage.
3. Fit new camshaft timing belt. ***See this section.***
4. Connect battery earth lead.

COVER - TIMING BELT - FRONT UPPER - 'K' SERIES

Service repair no - 12.65.41

Remove

1. Disconnect battery earth lead.

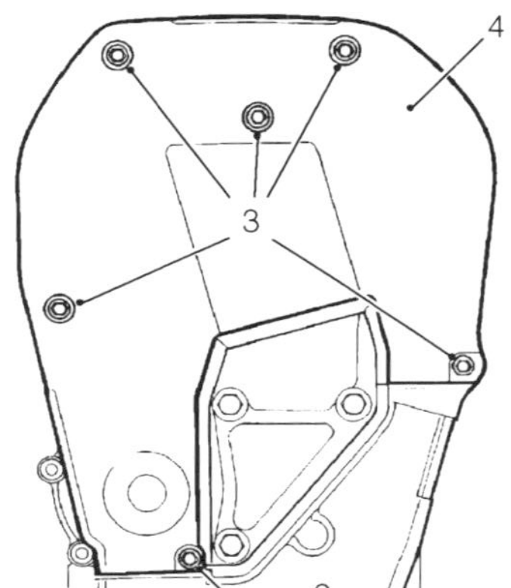

12M1433

2. Loosen lower bolt securing camshaft timing belt lower cover to engine.
3. Remove 5 bolts securing camshaft timing belt upper cover to rear cover.
4. Remove camshaft timing belt upper cover and rubber seal.

Refit

1. Clean timing belt upper cover.
2. Fit timing belt upper cover, ensuring correct position of upper cover.
3. Fit 5 bolts securing camshaft upper cover and tighten to 5 Nm.
4. Tighten bolt securing camshaft timing belt top cover to engine, to 5 Nm .
5. Connect battery earth lead.

COVER - INNER - TIMING BELT

Service repair no - 12.65.42

Remove

1. Remove camshaft timing belt. ***See this section.***

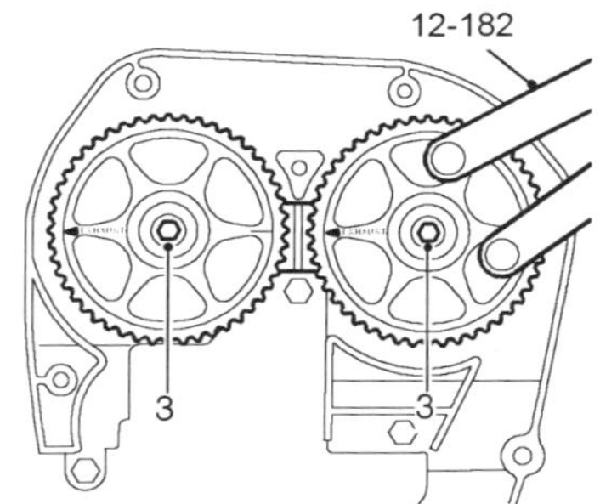

12M3976B

2. Restrain gears using camshaft gear holding tool **12-182.**
3. Remove 2 bolts and washers securing camshaft gears to camshaft.

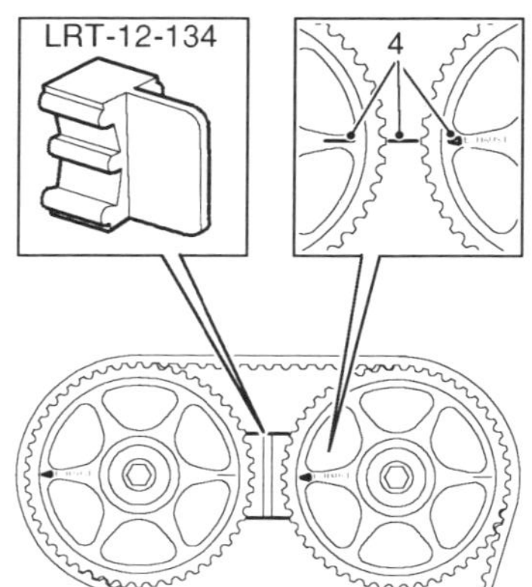

12M3977A

4. Check valve timing marks and remove camshaft gear alignment tool **LRT-12-134.**
5. Remove camshaft gears.

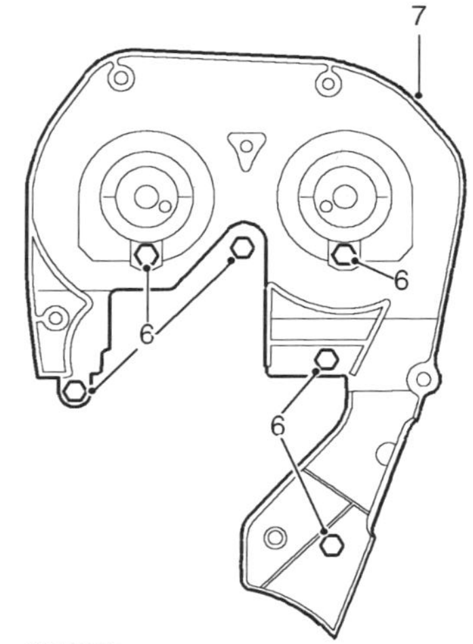

12M3978

6. Remove bolts securing timing belt rear cover to cylinder block.
7. Remove rear cover.

Refit

1. Position timing belt rear cover to cylinder block.
2. Fit and tighten bolts securing rear cover to cylinder block to 9 Nm.
3. Clean camshaft timing gears.
4. Fit 2 camshaft gears to their respective camshafts.
5. Fit bolts and washers securing camshaft gears to camshafts. Using **12-182,** restrain camshaft gears and tighten bolts to 65 Nm.
6. Align camshaft gear timing marks.
7. Fit camshaft gear locking tool **LRT -12- 134.**
8. Fit camshaft timing belt. ***See this section.***

COVER - TIMING BELT - FRONT LOWER

Service repair no - 12.65.43

Remove

1. Disconnect battery earth lead.
2. Remove underbelly panel. ***See BODY, Exterior fittings.***
3. Remove starter motor. ***See ELECTRICAL, Repairs.***

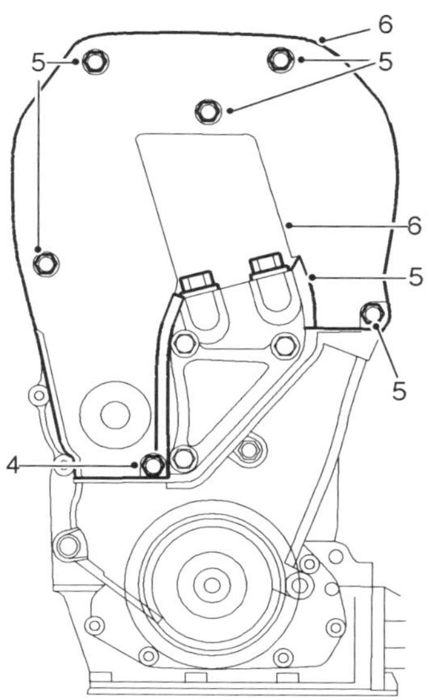

12M3972

4. Loosen lower bolt securing camshaft timing belt top cover to engine.
5. Remove 5 bolts securing camshaft timing belt top cover to rear cover.
6. Remove camshaft timing belt top cover and rubber seal.

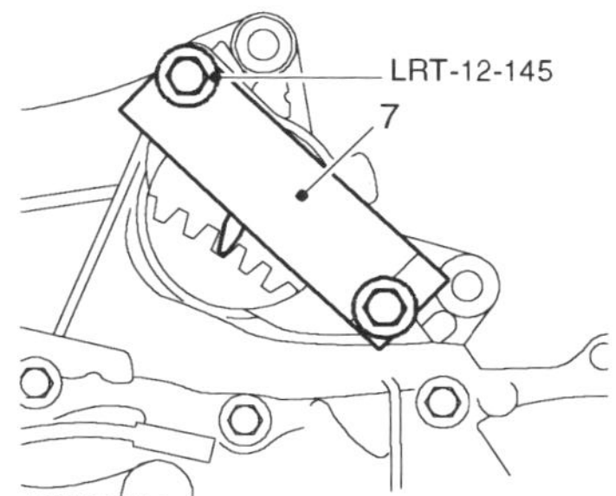

12M3973A

7. Fit flywheel locking tool **LRT-12-145** to flywheel housing and secure with 2 bolts.
8. Remove alternator drive belt. ***See ELECTRICAL, Repairs.***

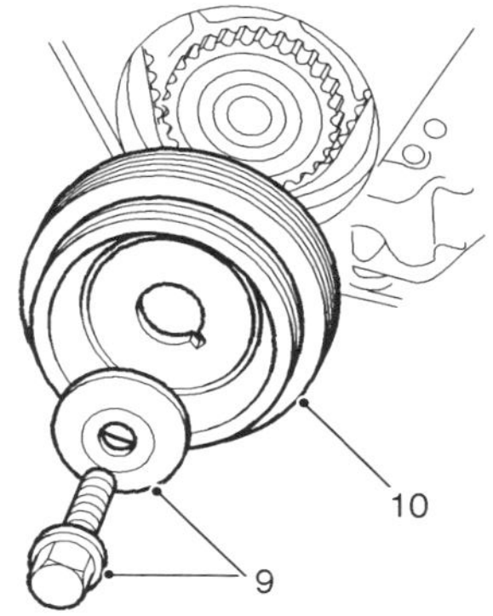

12M3974

9. Remove bolt securing pulley to crankshaft and collect washer.
10. Remove crankshaft pulley.

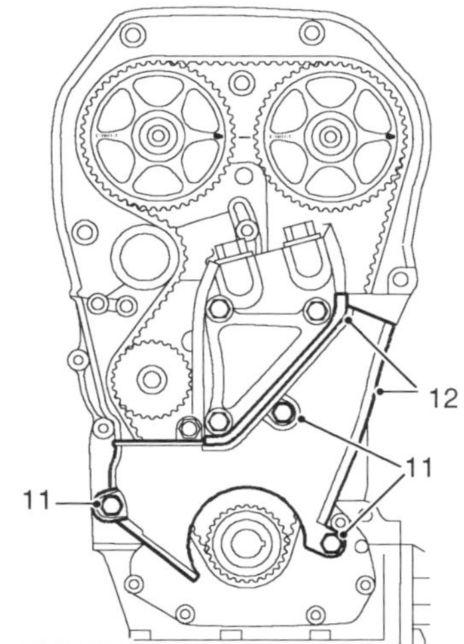

12M3975A

11. Remove 3 bolts securing camshaft timing belt lower cover to engine.
12. Remove camshaft timing belt lower cover and rubber seal.

Refit

1. Clean crankshaft pulley.
2. Clean timing belt lower cover.
3. Fit timing belt lower cover ensuring correct position of rubber seal.
4. Fit bolts securing timing belt lower cover to engine and tighten to 9 Nm .
5. Fit crankshaft pulley to crankshaft gear ensuring that indent on pulley locates over lug on gear.
6. Fit washer and bolt securing crankshaft pulley to crankshaft and tighten to 205 Nm.
7. Fit alternator drive belt. ***See ELECTRICAL, Repairs.***
8. Remove 2 bolts securing tool **LRT-12-145** to flywheel housing and remove tool.
9. Position camshaft timing belt top cover ensuring correct position of rubber seal.
10. Fit 5 bolts securing camshaft timing top cover to rear cover and tighten to 5 Nm.
11. Tighten bolt securing camshaft timing belt top cover to engine, to 5 Nm.
12. Fit starter motor. ***See ELECTRICAL, Repairs.***
13. Fit underbelly panel. ***See BODY, Exterior fittings.***

CONTENTS

Page

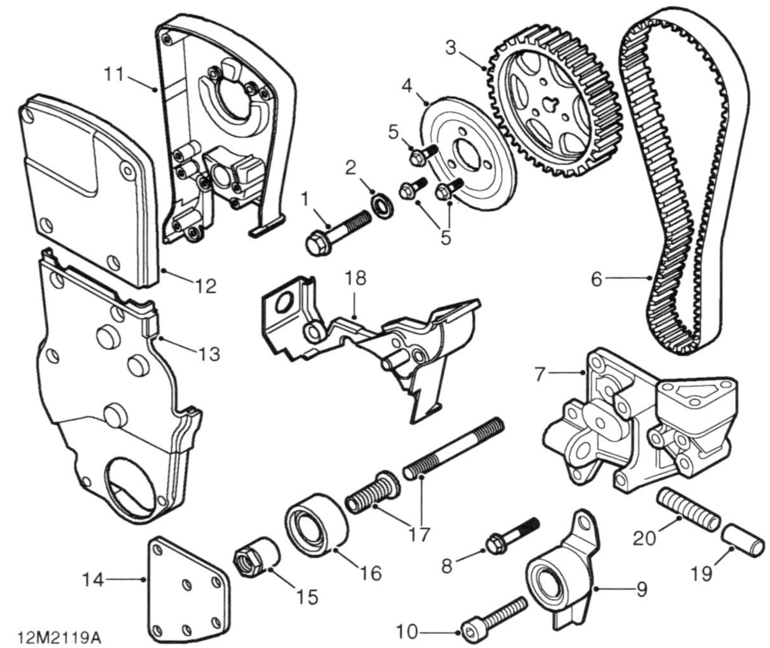

12M2119A

CAMSHAFT TIMING BELT COMPONENTS

1. Bolt - timing belt gear
2. Washer
3. Timing belt gear
4. Timing belt gear - damper
5. Torx screws - damper to timing gear
6. Camshaft timing belt
7. Tensioner housing
8. Bolt - tensioner pulley
9. Tensioner pulley
10. Allen screw - tensioner pulley
11. Timing belt upper rear cover
12. Timing belt upper front cover
13. Timing belt lower front cover
14. Engine front mounting cover plate
15. Nut - idler pulley
16. Idler pulley
17. Stud and adaptor - idler pulley
18. Timing belt lower rear cover
19. Tensioner plunger
20. Tensioner spring

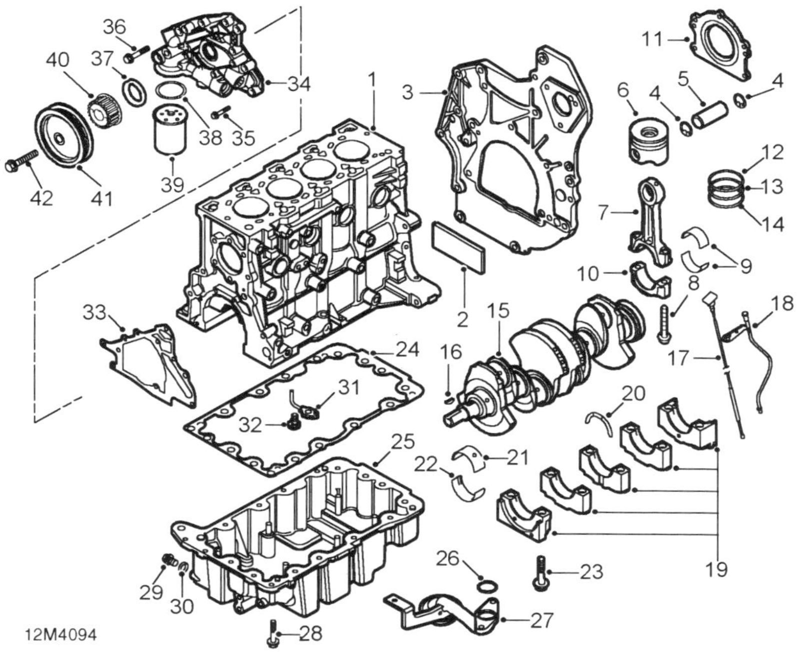

12M4094

CYLINDER BLOCK COMPONENTS

1. Cylinder block
2. Foam pad
3. Gearbox adaptor plate
4. Circlip - gudgeon pin
5. Gudgeon pin
6. Piston
7. Connecting rod
8. Bolt - connecting rod
9. Big-end bearing shells
10. Big-end bearing cap
11. Crankshaft rear oil seal and housing
12. Top compression ring
13. 2nd compression ring
14. Oil control ring
15. Crankshaft
16. Woodruff key
17. Dipstick
18. Dipstick tube
19. Main bearing cap
20. Thrust washer
21. Upper main bearing shell - grooved
22. Lower main bearing shell - plain
23. Bolt - main bearing cap
24. Gasket - sump
25. Sump
26. 'O' ring
27. Oil strainer and pick-up pipe
28. Bolt - sump
29. Drain plug
30. Sealing washer
31. Oil squirt jet
32. Banjo bolt
33. Gasket - oil pump
34. Oil pump
35. Bolt - M6
36. Bolt - M10
37. Crankshaft front oil seal
38. Sealing ring
39. Oil filter element
40. Timing gear
41. Crankshaft pulley
42. Bolt - crankshaft pulley

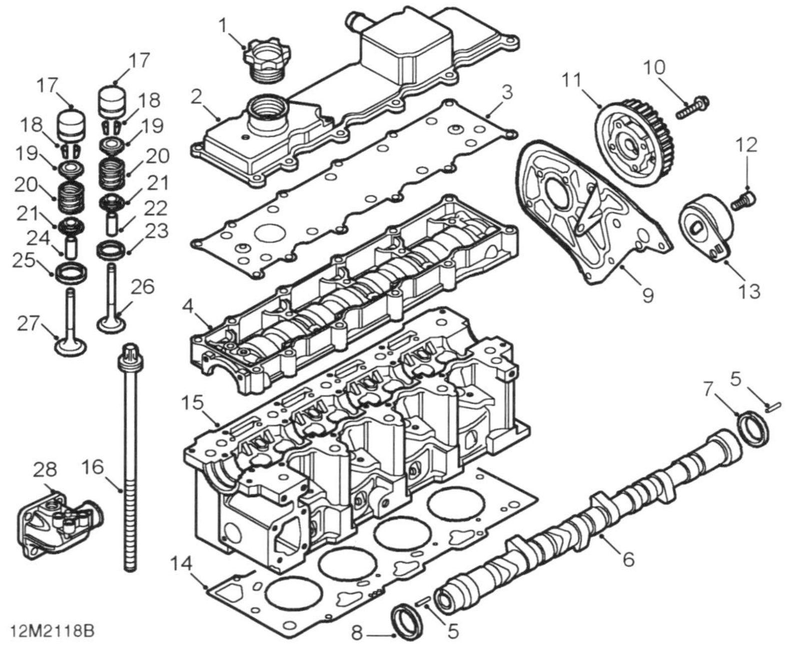

12M2118B

CYLINDER HEAD COMPONENTS

1. Oil filler cap
2. Camshaft cover
3. Gasket - camshaft cover
4. Camshaft carrier
5. Drive pin
6. Camshaft
7. Camshaft rear oil seal
8. Camshaft front oil seal
9. Fuel injection pump drive belt rear cover
10. Bolt - fuel injection pump drive gear
11. Fuel injection pump drive gear
12. Allen screw
13. Fuel injection pump drive belt tensioner
14. Gasket - cylinder head
15. Cylinder head
16. Bolt - cylinder head
17. Tappet
18. Collets
19. Spring cap
20. Valve spring
21. Spring seat and valve stem oil seal
22. Valve guide - exhaust
23. Valve seat insert - exhaust
24. Valve guide - inlet
25. Valve seat insert - inlet
26. Exhaust valve
27. Inlet valve
28. Coolant outlet elbow

DESCRIPTION

The ' L' Series 2.0 litre engine is a 4 cylinder, in-line, direct diesel engine having 2 valves per cylinder operated by a single overhead camshaft.
A cast iron cylinder block incorporates direct bored cylinders, each pair of cylinders being strategicly positioned in the cylinder block to reduce engine length and give good structural rigidity.

An alloy camshaft carrier is bolted directly to the alloy cylinder head, the camshaft bearing journals are line bored between the two components. The camshaft operates the valves via hydraulic tappets, the camshaft gear, which incorporates a tortional damper, is driven by an internally toothed drive belt by a gear on the front of the crankshaft. Belt tension is achieved by means of a semi-automatic tensioner and an idler pulley is also fitted. A gear on the rear end of the camshaft drives the fuel injection pump belt.

A single spring is fitted to each valve, the valve stem oil seals are moulded onto a metal base which also forms the valve spring seat on the cylinder head. The valve stems run in guides pressed into the cylinder head.

The aluminium alloy, graphite coated pistons are fitted with two compression and an oil control ring, the top ring is located in a steel insert which helps to provide a minimal reaction to compression forces. The piston crowns are domed in the centre, the combustion chamber being formed in a bowl around the dome. Fully floating gudgeon pins retain the pistons to the connecting rods, the pins are offset towards the thrust side of the pistons and are secured in the pistons by circlips.

Oil squirt jets, located in the cylinder block provide additional piston cooling and gudgeon pin lubrication. Plain big-end bearing shells without location tags are fitted, with the connecting rod bearing caps being retained by flange headed bolts to the connecting rods. The big-end has a 'Fracture Split' joint between the connecting rod and bearing cap. The connecting rod to bearing cap has no identification marks, therefore, to prevent incorrect fitment of the bearing cap to connecting rod, the bolts are off-set by 1mm.

The crankshaft runs in 5 main bearings, grooved bearing shells are fitted in the cylinder block with plain bearing shells in each main bearing cap. Positive location of each main bearing cap is by means of hollow dowels. Crankshaft end-float is controlled by single size thrust washers, located each side of the centre - (Number 3) main bearing in the cylinder block. The crankshaft front oil seal is located in the oil pump body whilst the rear oil seal is integral with a housing bolted to the rear of the cylinder block. Additional oil sealing is provided by RTV sealant injected into grooves and along the joint lines of the front main - (Number 1) bearing cap and the crankshaft rear oil seal.

A rotor type oil pump is driven from the front of the crankshaft, the pump is sealed to the cylinder block with a gasket.

The cast alloy sump is bolted to the cylinder block and rear main bearing cap and is sealed to the block with a rubber gasket which incorporates location lugs for the block and sump. Compression limiters in the bolt holes prevent distortion of the gasket.

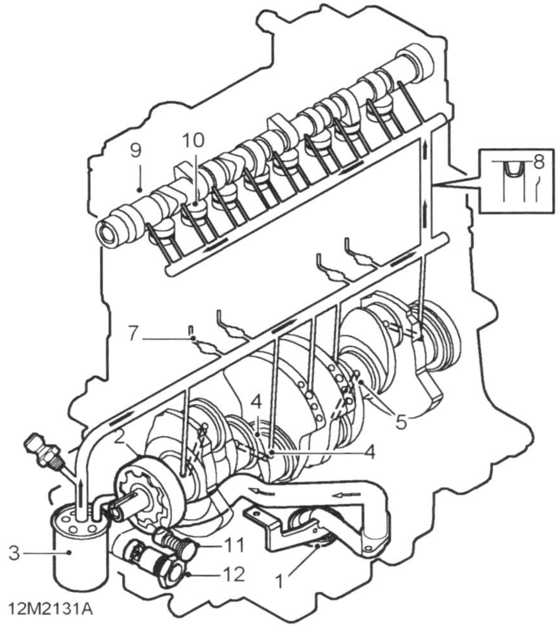

12M2131A

Lubrication

Oil is drawn through a gauze strainer (1) and through a passage in the cylinder block to the oil pump (2). Pressurised oil flows via the full flow filter (3) to the main oil gallery in the cylinder block. Drillings from the main oil gallery direct oil to the crankshaft main bearings (4) and cross drillings in the crankshaft direct oil to the big-end bearings (5). Additional drillings in the cylinder block supply oil at reduced pressure to the oil squirt jets (7) for piston cooling and gudgeon pin lubrication and via a restrictor (8) in the top of the cylinder block to the rear of the cylinder head. A full length drilling in the cylinder head directs oil to the camshaft journals (9) and tappets (10).

An oil pressure relief valve (11) is located in the oil pump body which also carries the oil filter adapter and the return union for the externally mounted oil cooler.

A thermostatic valve (12), comprising a valve, spring and diverter plug is located in the oil pump body. The oil flow union to the oil cooler is screwed into the end of the diverter plug. The valve is closed during engine warm-up thereby preventing oil flow to the oil cooler. As soon as the oil reaches a pre-determined temperature, the valve opens and allows oil to flow to the cooler.

Crankcase ventilation

A positive crankcase ventilation system is used to vent crankcase gases to the air induction system.

The gases are drawn from the camshaft cover, through a depression limiting valve and into the turbocharger intake.

As engine speed increases, the depression limiting valve progressively closes thereby limiting the depression in the crankcase.

Engine number location

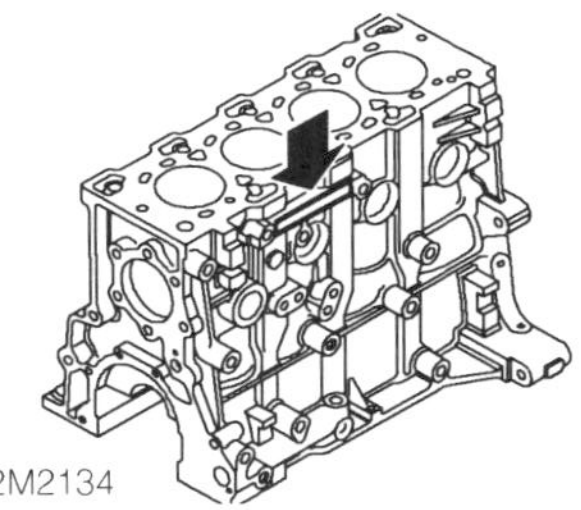
12M2134

The engine number will be found on the side of the cylinder block adjacent to Number 2 cylinder.

ENGINE OIL PRESSURE CHECK

Service repair no - 12.90.09/01

Remove

1. Remove oil pressure switch. ***See Repairs.***

Check

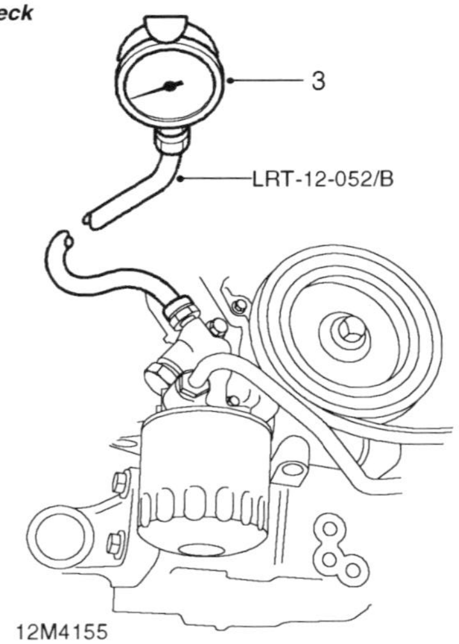

12M4155

2. Top up engine oil if necessary. ***See MAINTENANCE.***
3. Use pressure check kit **LRT-12-052B** fit adaptor and gauge to oil pump.
4. Run engine at idle speed and check for correct oil pressure. ***See INFORMATION, General data.***
5. Switch off ignition.
6. Remove pressure gauge and adaptor.
7. Clean oil spillage.

Refit

1. Fit oil pressure switch. ***See Repairs.***

SEAL - CAMSHAFT - FRONT

Service repair no - 12.13.05

Remove

1. Remove camshaft timing gear upper cover. ***See this section.***
2. Raise RH side of engine on jack. Sufficiently only to give access to camshaft gear retaining bolt.

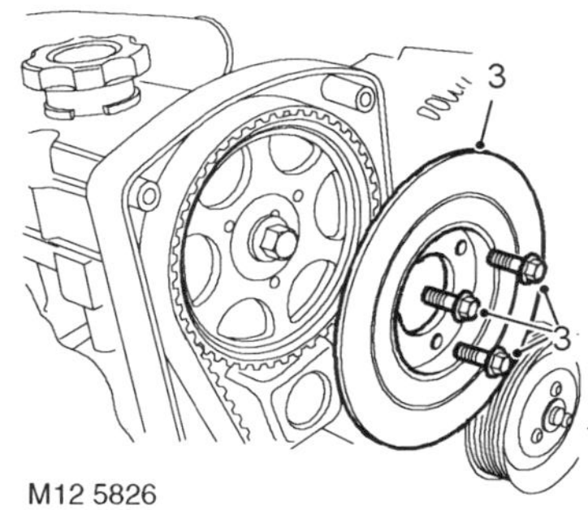

M12 5826

3. Remove and discard 3 Torx screws securing damper to camshaft gear, remove damper.

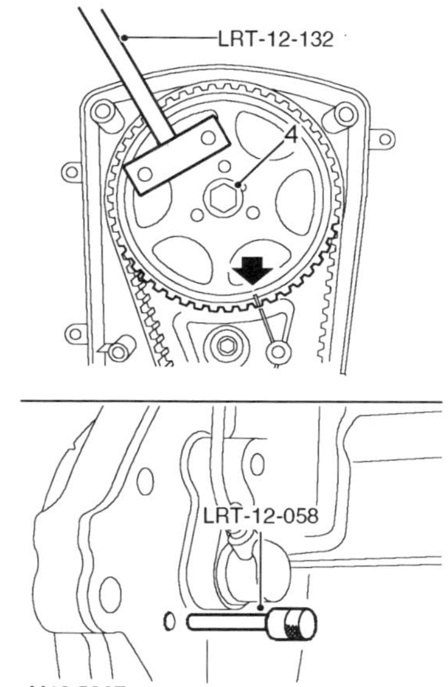

M12 5827

4. Restrain camshaft gear using tool **LRT-12-132** and loosen but do not remove camshaft gear bolt.
5. Insert timing pin **LRT-12-058** through hole in gearbox mounting plate.
6. Hold pin in contact with flywheel.
7. Using assistance, rotate crankshaft clockwise until timing pin **LRT-12-058** can be felt to enter hole in flywheel.

⚠ **CAUTION: Do not use camshaft gear, gear retaining bolt or timing belt to rotate crankshaft.**

8. Check that timing marks on camshaft gear and back cover are aligned.

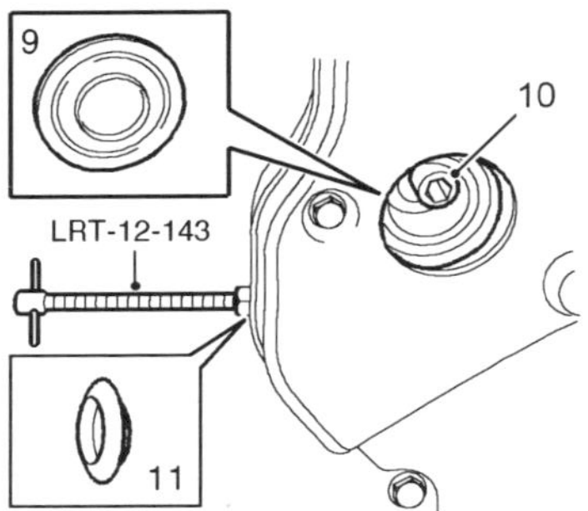

12M4125A

9. Remove timing belt tensioner access plug from timing gear lower cover.
10. Loosen Allen bolt securing belt tensioner pulley.
11. Remove tensioner access plug from back cover.
12. Screw timing belt tensioner retractor tool **LRT-12-143** into timing belt tensioner plunger.
13. Tighten nut on tool **LRT-12-143** until timing belt tension is released.
14. Tighten tensioner pulley Allen bolt.

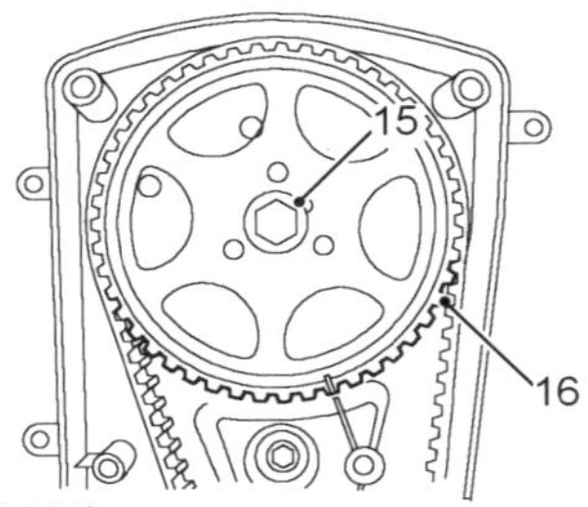

M12 5828

15. Remove and retain camshaft gear retaining bolt.
16. Release camshaft gear from camshaft and remove from belt.

⚠ **CAUTION: Do not rotate camshaft or crankshaft with timing belt removed. If the sintered gears have been subjected to prolonged oil contamination, they must be soaked in a solvent bath and thoroughly washed with solvent before refitment. Because of the porous construction of the sintered material, oil impregnated in the gear will emerge and contaminate a new belt. If camshaft timing belt shows any sign of oil or coolant contamination renew camshaft timing belt.** ***See this section.*** **Cause of contamination must be rectified.**

17. Fit but do not tighten the old camshaft gear retaining bolt.

⚠ **CAUTION: Ensure camshaft does not rotate.**

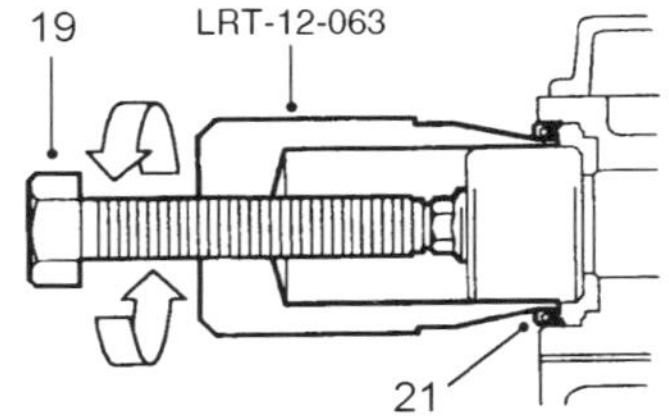

12M4127A

18. Fit and tighten seal remover tool **LRT-12-063** to camshaft seal.
19. Tighten seal remover centre screw to remove camshaft seal.
20. Remove seal remover **LRT-12-063.**
21. Remove and discard seal from seal remover tool.
22. Remove and discard camshaft gear retaining bolt.

Refit

1. Clean seal recess and camshaft.

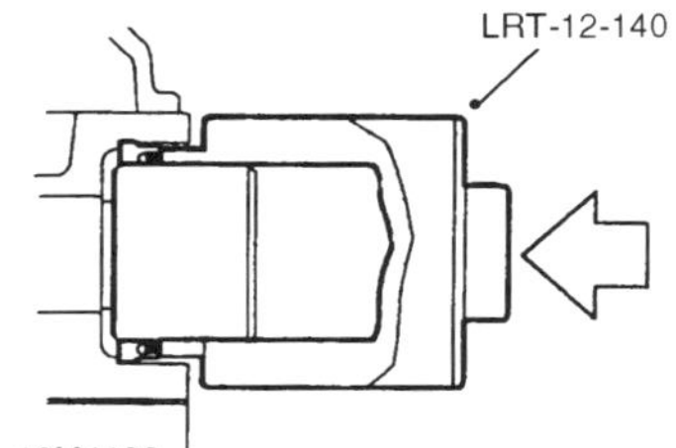

12M4128

2. Ensure seal fitting tool **LRT-12-140** is clean.
3. Fit camshaft oil seal using tool **LRT-12- 140.**

⚠ **CAUTION: Oil seal must be fitted dry.**

4. Remove tool **LRT-12-140.**
5. Clean camshaft gear and mating face.
6. Fit camshaft gear to belt and position gear to camshaft.

⚠ **CAUTION: Ensure timing marks on camshaft gear and rear cover are aligned.**

7. Apply clean engine oil to threads of new camshaft gear retaining bolt.
8. Fit camshaft gear bolt but do not tighten at this stage.

⚠ **CAUTION: Ensure camshaft does not rotate.**

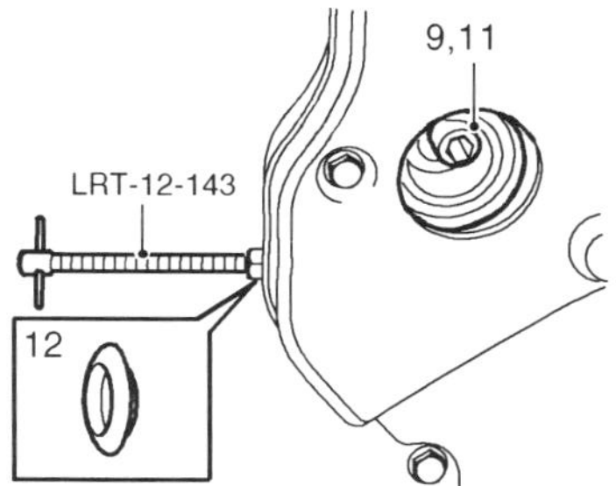

M12 5829

9. Loosen tensioner pulley Allen bolt until tensioner moves easily without tipping.
10. Release camshaft timing belt tensioner plunger using tool **LRT-12-143.**
11. Remove tool **LRT-12-143** from camshaft timing belt tensioner and tighten Allen bolt to 55 Nm.
12. Fit access plug to back cover.
13. Remove timing pin **LRT-12-058** from flywheel.
14. Using a socket and extension bar on crankshaft pulley bolt, rotate crankshaft 2 turns clockwise and fit timing pin **LRT-12-058** into flywheel ensuring pin is fully inserted in hole in flywheel.
15. Check camshaft gear timing mark is aligned with mark on back cover.
16. Slacken Allen bolt securing belt tensioner pulley, allow pulley to react and tighten Allen bolt to 55 Nm.

CAUTION: Do not exceed specified torque figure.

17. Fit access plug to timing gear lower cover.
18. Remove timing pin **LRT-12-058.**

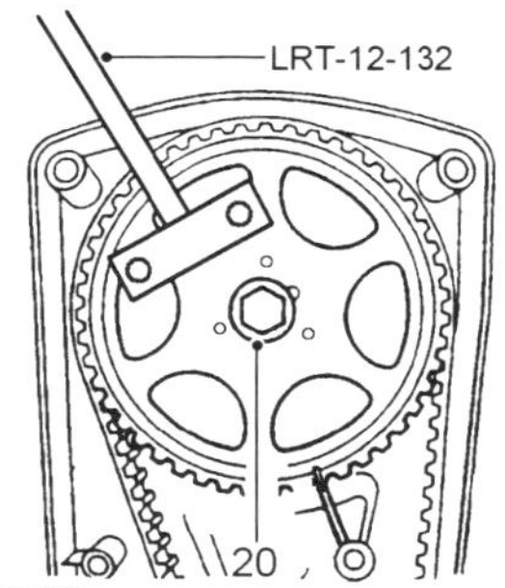

M12 5830

19. Restrain camshaft gear using tool **LRT-12-132.**
20. Tighten camshaft gear retaining bolt to 20 Nm + 90° .
21. Fit camshaft gear damper and align timing mark with camshaft gear. Secure with new Torx screws. Tighten screws to 10 Nm.
22. Lower RH side of engine to body.
23. Fit timing gear upper cover. ***See this section.***

SEAL - CAMSHAFT - REAR

Service repair no - 12.13.06

Remove

1. Remove FIP timing belt cover. ***See this section.***
2. Remove camshaft timing gear upper cover. ***See this section.***

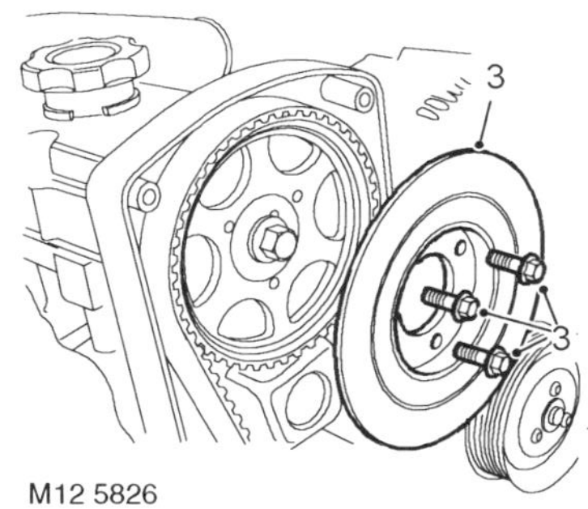

M12 5826

3. Remove and discard 3 Torx screws securing damper to camshaft gear, remove damper.

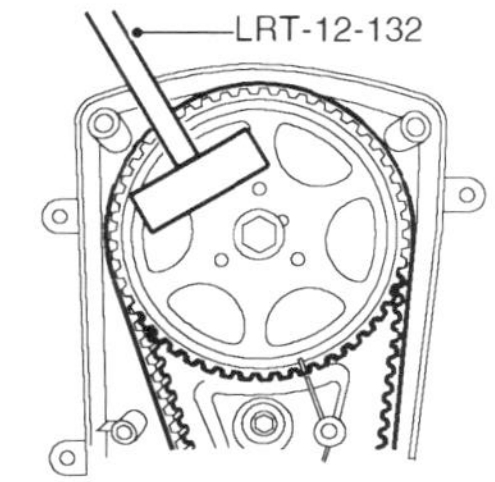

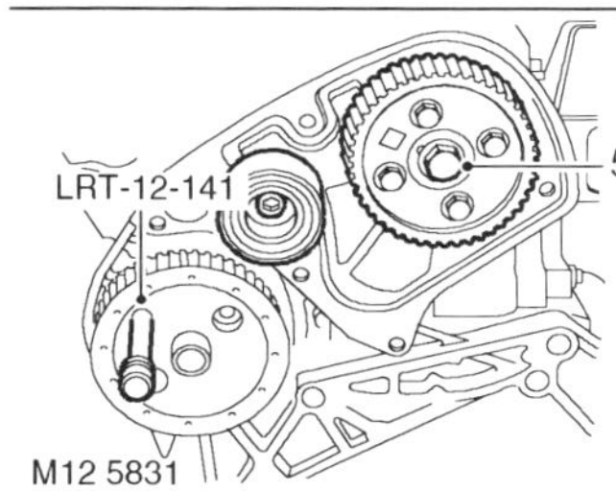

M12 5831

4. Restrain camshaft gear using tool **LRT-12-132.**
5. Loosen but do not remove FIP belt drive gear bolt.
6. Remove FIP belt. ***See this section.***

CAUTION: Do not rotate crankshaft or FIP with timing belt removed. Do not remove locking pin inserted during FIP belt removal from FIP gear.

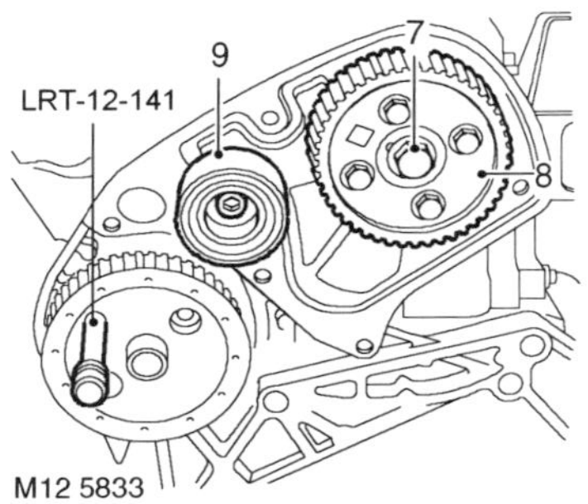

M12 5833

7. Remove but do not discard bolt securing FIP belt drive gear.
8. Remove FIP belt drive gear.
9. Remove Allen bolt securing FIP drive belt tensioner and remove tensioner.

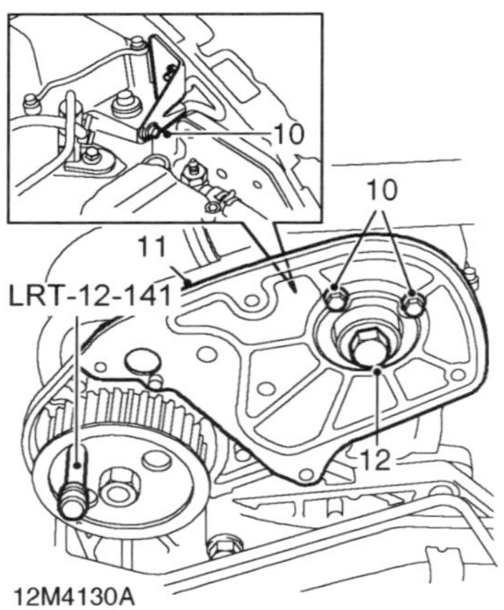

12M4130A

10. Remove 3 bolts securing FIP drive belt rear cover.
11. Remove rear cover.
12. Fit but do not tighten the old FIP gear retaining bolt.

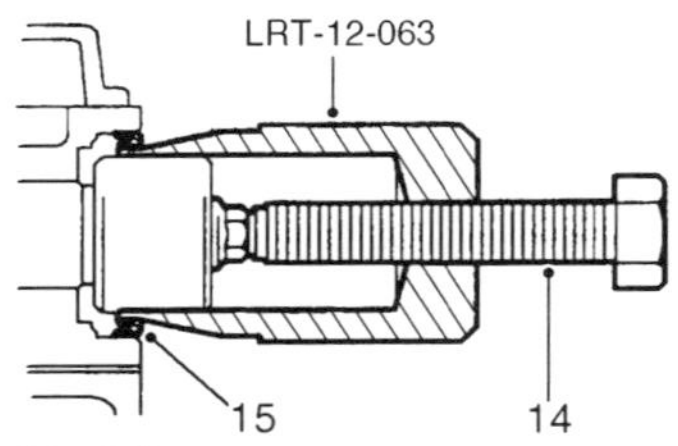

12M4131A

13. Fit and tighten seal remover tool **LRT-12-063** to camshaft seal.
14. Tighten seal remover centre screw to remove camshaft seal.
15. Remove seal remover **LRT-12-063,** remove and discard seal from seal remover tool.
16. Remove and discard FIP gear retaining bolt.

Refit

1. Clean seal recess and camshaft.

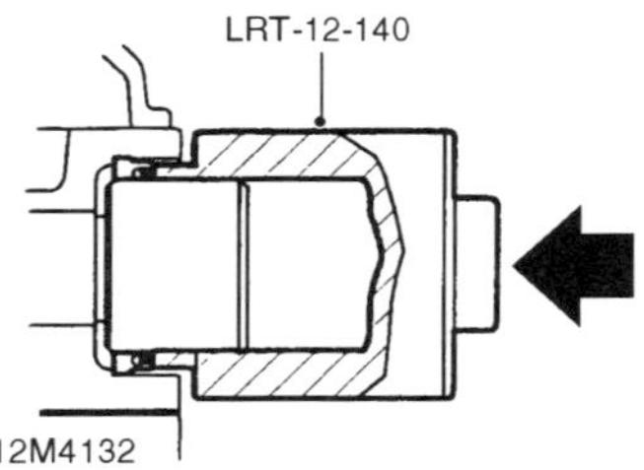

12M4132

2. Ensure seal fitting tool **LRT-12-140** is clean.
3. Fit camshaft oil seal using **LRT-12- 140.**

CAUTION: Oil seal must be fitted dry.

4. Fit FIP drive belt rear cover.
5. Fit bolts securing FIP drive belt rear cover, tighten bolts to 8 Nm.
6. Fit drive belt tensioner, fit but do not tighten Allen bolt.
7. Clean camshaft gear and mating face.
8. Fit FIP gear to camshaft.

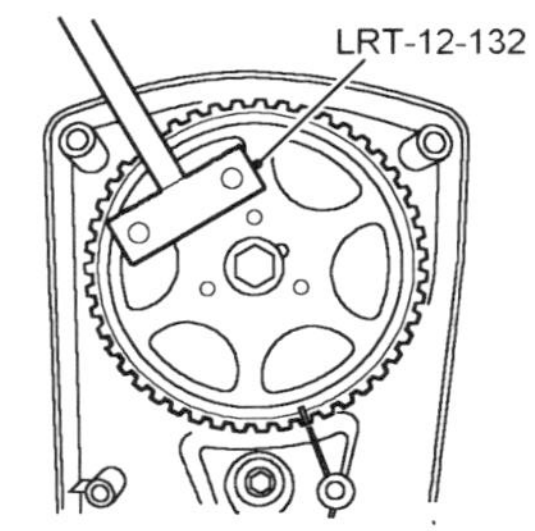

12M4622

9. Restrain camshaft gear using tool **LRT-12-132.**
10. Apply clean engine oil to threads of new bolt. Fit FIP gear bolt and tighten to 20 Nm. + 90°

CAUTION: Ensure camshaft does not rotate.

11. Fit FIP timing belt. ***See this section.***
12. Fit FIP timing belt cover. ***See this section.***
13. Fit damper to camshaft gear ensuring marks are aligned, fit new Torx screws and tighten to 10 Nm.
14. Fit camshaft timing gear upper cover. ***See this section.***

CRANKSHAFT PULLEY

Service repair no - 12.21.01

Remove

1. Remove auxiliary drive belt. ***See ELECTRICAL, Repairs.***
2. Remove RH front road wheel.

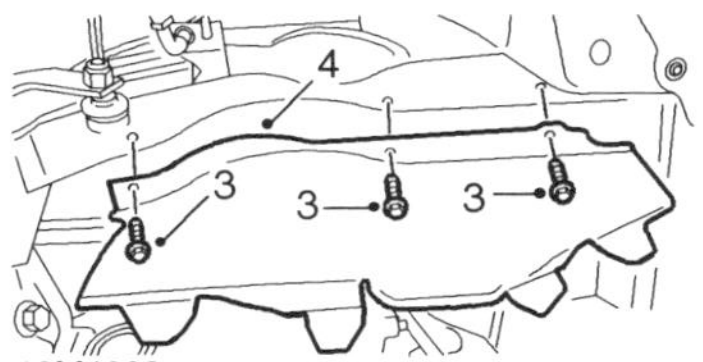

12M4038

3. Remove 3 bolts securing RH splash shield.
4. Remove splash shield.
5. Remove camshaft timing gear upper cover. ***See this section.***

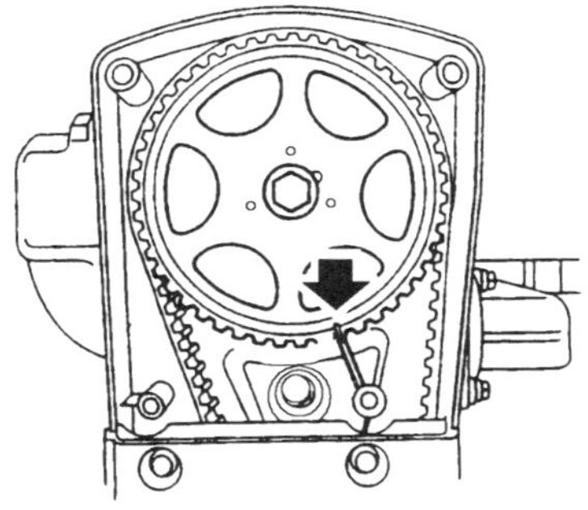

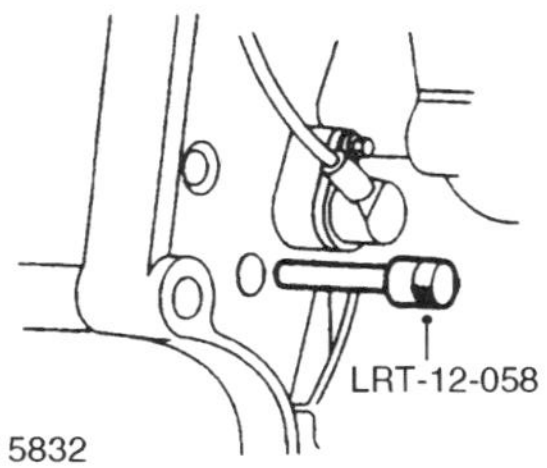

M12 5832

6. Insert timing pin **LRT-12-058** through hole in gearbox mounting plate, hold pin in contact with flywheel and using assistance, rotate crankshaft clockwise until pin can be felt to enter hole in flywheel.

CAUTION: Never use the camshaft timing gear, gear retaining bolt, or timing belt to rotate the engine.

7. Check that timing marks on camshaft gear and back cover are aligned.

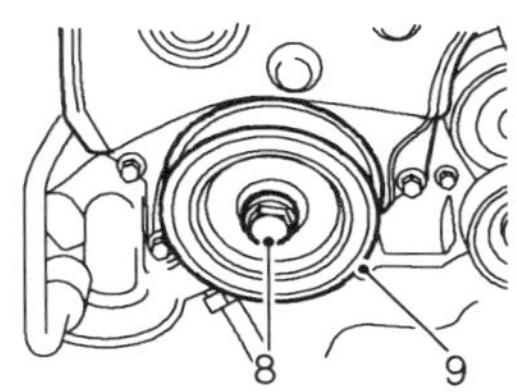

12M4568

8. Remove bolt securing crankshaft pulley.
9. Remove crankshaft pulley.

Refit

1. Clean crankshaft pulley.
2. Position pulley on crankshaft, fit bolt and tighten to 63 Nm + 90° .
3. Remove FIP timing belt cover. ***See this section.***

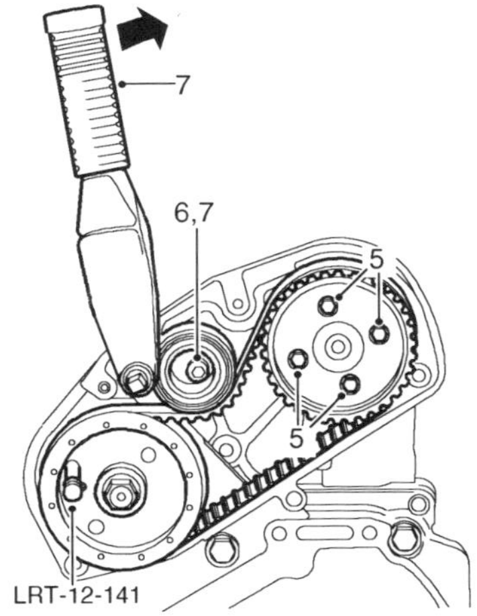

M12 5834

4. Insert locking pin **LRT-12-141** through FIP gear and into hole in adapter plate. Locking pin must be a sliding fit. If pin is a tight fit, proceed as follows:
5. Loosen 4 bolts securing FIP timing belt drive gear to hub.
6. Loosen timing belt tensioner Allen bolt.
7. Using a torque wrench fitted to tensioner pulley backplate, apply a **clockwise** as viewed from rear of engine, torque loading of 6 Nm to drive belt. Maintain loading and tighten tensioner pulley Allen bolt to 44 Nm.

CAUTION: Do not exceed specified torque figure.

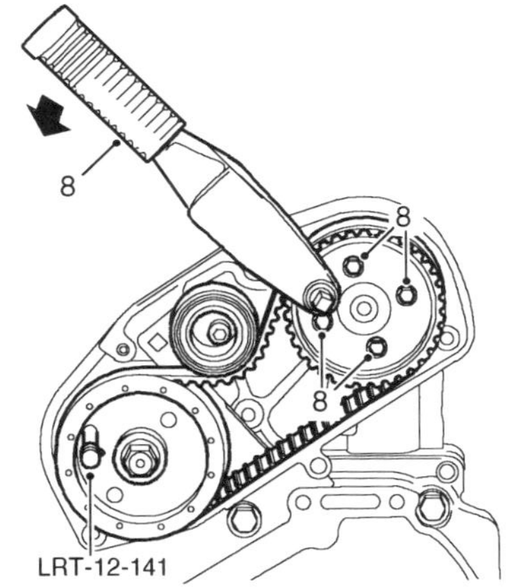

M12 5835

8. Fit torque wrench to square hole in FIP timing belt drive gear as shown and apply an **anti-clockwise,** as viewed from rear of engine torque loading of 25 Nm. Maintain loading and tighten 4 bolts securing gear to 25 Nm.
9. Remove FIP drive gear locking pin **LRT-12-141** and timing pin **LRT-12-058.**

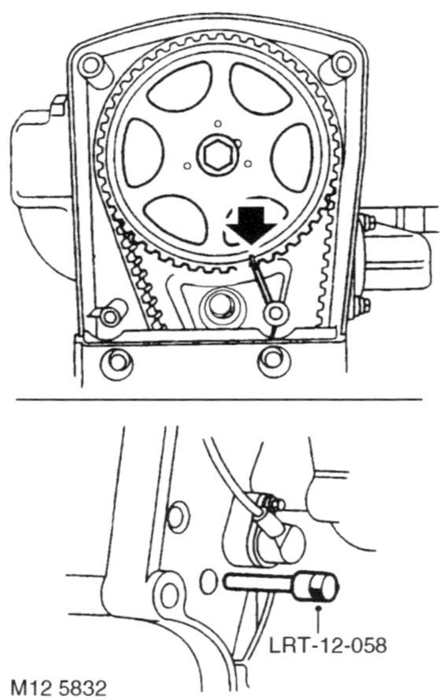

M12 5832

10. Rotate crankshaft 2 revolutions clockwise and fit timing pin **LRT-12-058.**

⚠ **CAUTION: Ensure pin is fully inserted into hole in flywheel.**

11. Check that camshaft gear timing mark is aligned with mark on back cover.

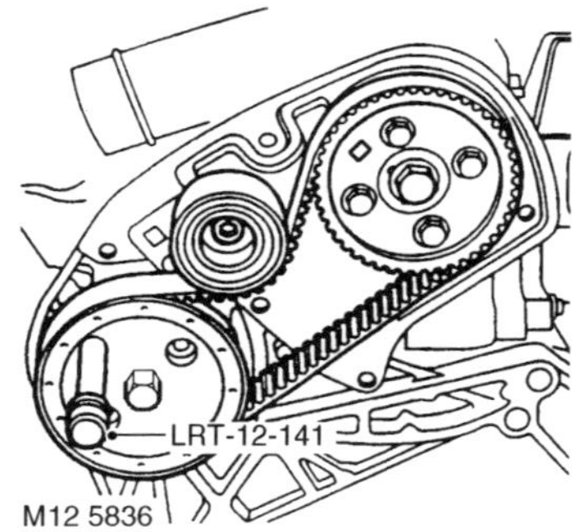

M12 5836

12. Insert locking pin **LRT-12-141** through FIP drive gear and into hole in adapter plate.

⚠ **CAUTION: To ensure FIP timing is correct, locking pin must be a sliding fit. If pin is a tight fit, drive belt adjustment procedure must be repeated.**

13. On completion, remove timing pin **LRT-12-058** and locking pin **LRT-12-141.**
14. Fit camshaft timing gear upper cover. ***See this section.***
15. Fit FIP timing belt cover. ***See this section.***
16. Fit auxiliary drive belt. ***See ELECTRICAL, Repairs.***
17. Fit RH splash shield and secure with bolts.
18. Fit road wheel(s) and tighten nuts to correct torque. ***See INFORMATION, Torque wrench settings.***
19. Remove stand(s) and lower vehicle.

SEAL - CRANKSHAFT - FRONT

Service repair no - 12.21.14

Remove

1. Remove camshaft timing belt. ***See this section.***

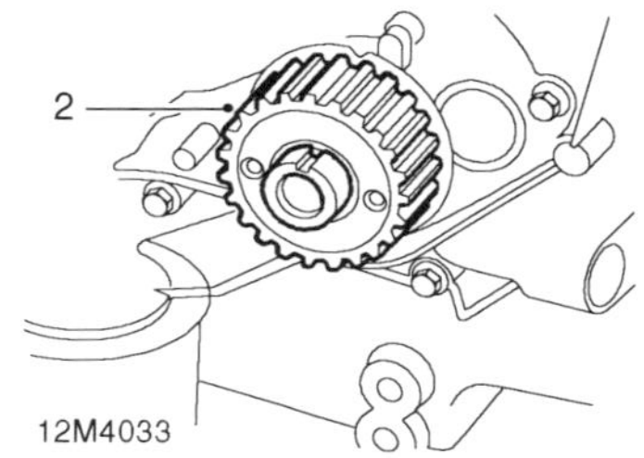

12M4033

2. Remove timing gear from crankshaft.

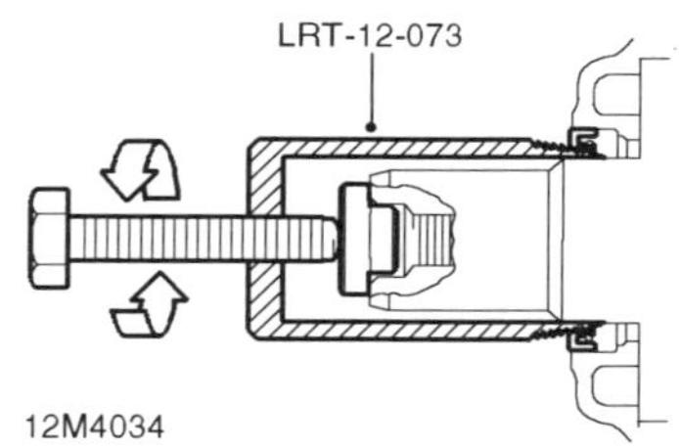

12M4034

3. Ensure bore of **LRT-12-073** is burr free, screw tool into crankshaft front oil seal.
4. Remove oil seal by tightening centre bolt of tool.

Refit

1. Use lint free cloth and thoroughly clean seal recess in oil pump and running surface on crankshaft.
2. Fit guide tools **LRT-12-070** and **LRT-12-130** onto crankshaft.
3. Using guide tools position new oil seal on crankshaft journal and against oil pump, drift into place using tool **LRT-12-069.**

⚠ **CAUTION: Oil seal must be fitted dry.**

4. Remove guide tools from crankshaft.
5. Clean crankshaft timing gear and fit onto crankshaft.
6. Fit camshaft timing belt. ***See this section.***

SEAL - CRANKSHAFT - REAR

Service repair no - 12.21.20

Remove

1. Remove flywheel. ***See this section.***
2. Remove sump. ***See this section.***

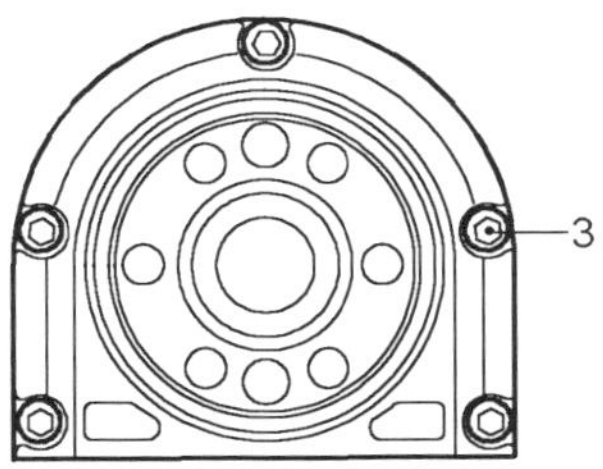

12M3555

3. Remove 5 bolts securing oil seal housing, remove and discard oil seal and housing.

Refit

1. Ensure oil seal running surface on crankshaft and oil seal housing mating surfaces on cylinder block are clean and oil free and that bolt and dowel holes are clean and dry.

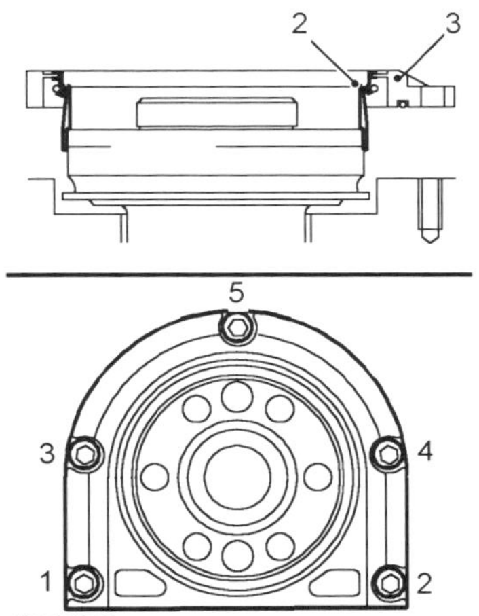

12M3556

CAUTION: Do not lubricate oil seal or running surfaces on crankshaft. Do not separate protector sleeve from oil seal and do not touch lip of oil seal. If seal is inadvertently handled it must not be fitted as the coating applied to the seal during manufacture will be destroyed and oil leakage can result.

2. Slide oil seal protector sleeve, oil seal and housing over end of crankshaft.
3. Position oil seal and housing on cylinder block.

NOTE: Oil seal protector sleeve will be displaced as seal and housing are fitted.

4. Fit bolts and working in sequence shown, tighten to 8 Nm.
5. Fit sump. ***See this section.***
6. Fit flywheel. ***See this section.***
7. Fill engine with oil. ***See MAINTENANCE.***

GASKET - CYLINDER HEAD

Service repair no - 12.29.02

Remove

1. Drain cooling system. ***See COOLING SYSTEM - 'L' SERIES, Adjustments.***
2. Remove camshaft timing belt. ***See this section.***
3. Remove FIP timing belt. ***See this section.***
4. Remove fuel injection pipes. ***See ENGINE MANAGEMENT SYSTEM - EDC, Repairs.***
5. Remove inlet and exhaust manifold gasket. ***See MANIFOLD & EXHAUST SYSTEMS - 'L' SERIES, Repairs.***
6. Place a suitable support beneath the engine and gearbox and disconnect the chains.

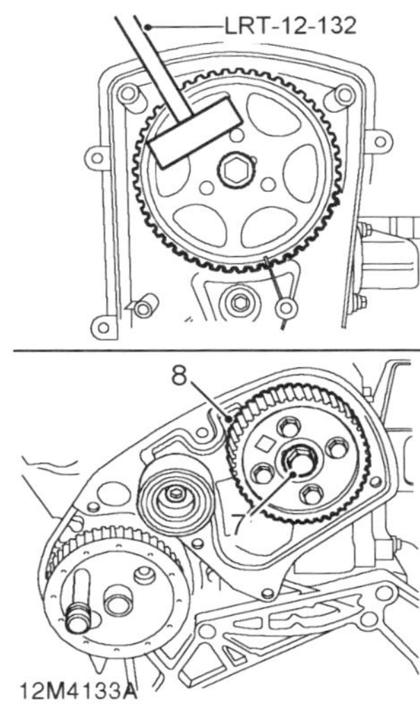

12M4133A

7. Use **LRT-12-132** to hold camshaft drive gear, remove and discard FIP belt drive gear bolt.
8. Remove FIP belt drive gear.

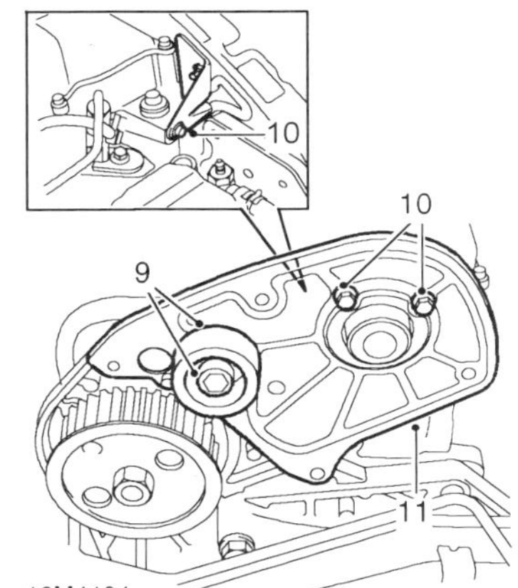

12M4134

9. Remove Allen bolt securing FIP drive belt tensioner and remove tensioner.
10. Remove 3 bolts securing FIP drive belt rear cover.
11. Remove rear cover.

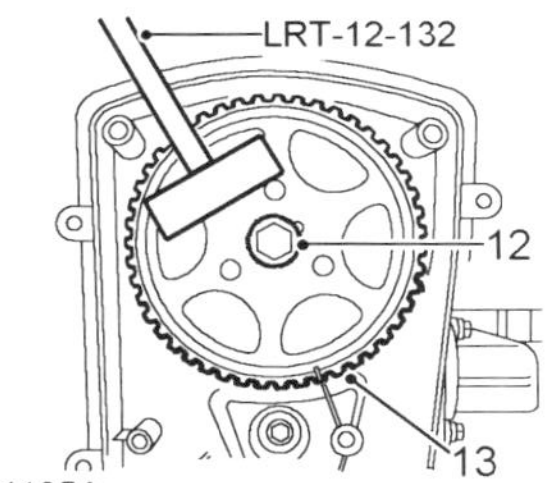

12M4135A

12. Use **LRT-12-132** to hold camshaft drive gear, remove and discard retaining bolt.
13. Remove camshaft drive gear.

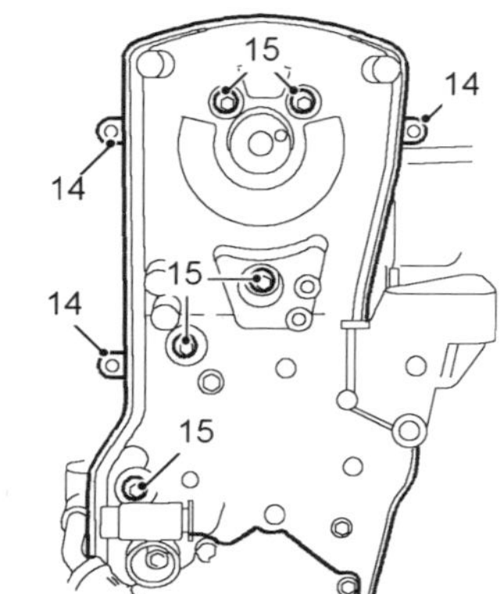

12M4136

14. Release engine harness clips from camshaft drive belt rear cover.
15. Remove 5 bolts and remove camshaft timing belt rear cover.

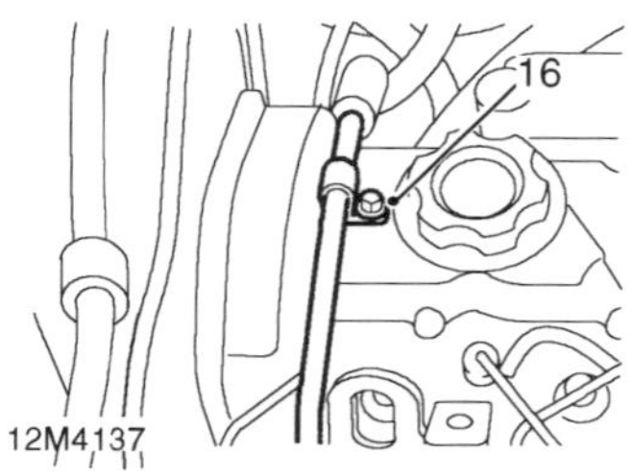

12M4137

16. Remove bolt securing brake servo vacuum pipe to camshaft cover.

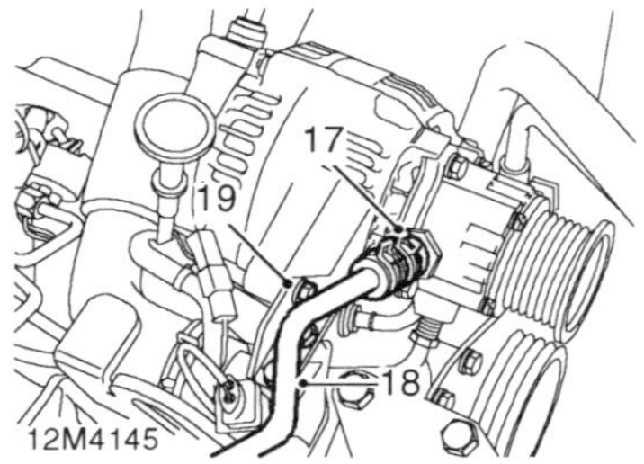

12M4145

17. Release clip and disconnect brake servo vacuum hose from vacuum pump.

CAUTION: Plug hose and pump.

18. Move vacuum pipe aside.

Models with air conditioning

19. Remove alternator upper fixing bolt.

All models

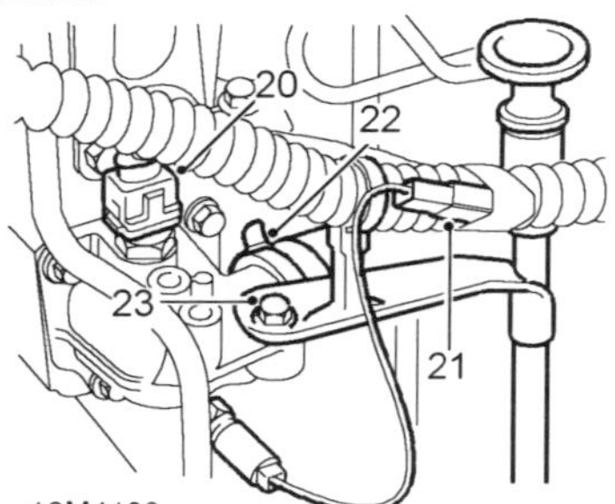

12M4138

20. Disconnect multiplug from coolant temperature sensor.
21. Disconnect coolant temperature transmitter lead from engine harness.
22. Release top hose clip and disconnect hose from engine.
23. Remove bolt securing dip stick tube to coolant outlet elbow.

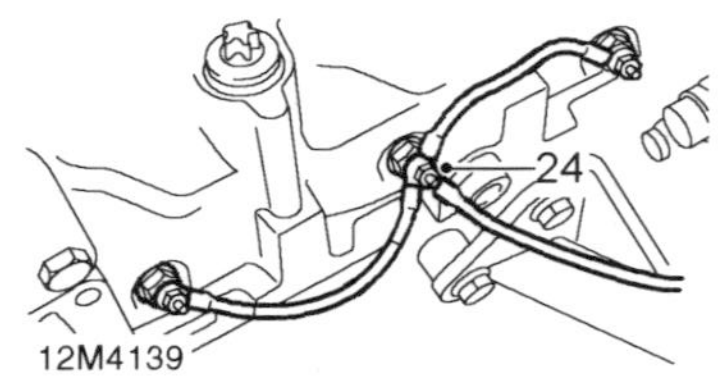

12M4139

24. Remove nut and disconnect feed lead from glow plug.

NOTE: 4 glow plugs fitted to later engines.

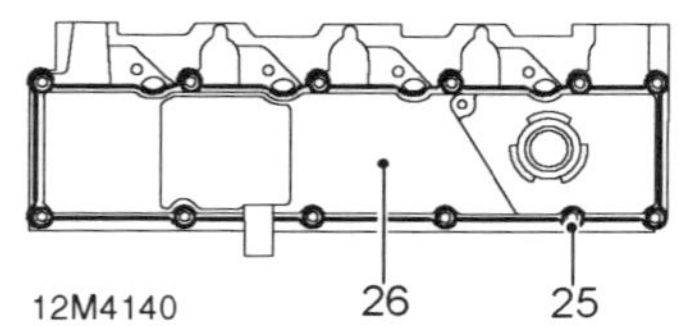

12M4140

25. Remove 12 bolts securing camshaft cover.
26. Remove camshaft cover and gasket.

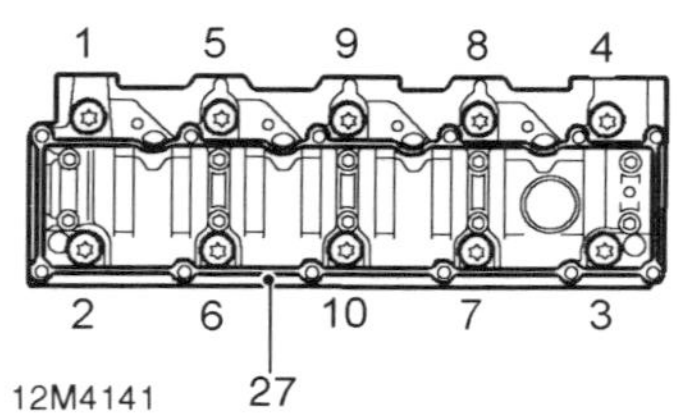

12M4141

27. Working in the sequence shown, progressively loosen and remove 10 cylinder head bolts.

NOTE: Store cylinder head bolts in their original positions for refitment.

28. Remove cylinder head assembly and place on wooden blocks or stands.

CAUTION: The tips of the injectors and glow plugs protrude below the face of the cylinder head and could be damaged if the cylinder head is placed face down on a work bench.

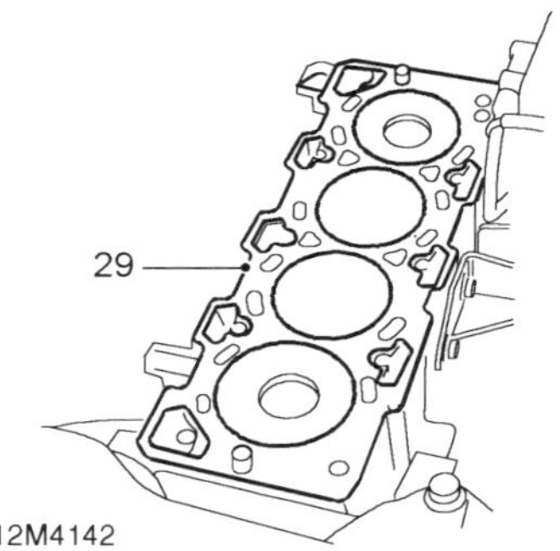

12M4142

29. Remove cylinder head gasket.

CAUTION: Note the gasket thickness indicator and ensure the same thickness gasket is used on refitment of cylinder head.

Refit

1. Clean mating faces of cylinder head and block.
2. Ensure oil and coolant passages are clean, clean dowels and dowel holes.

12M3559

3. Check that oil feed restrictor in cylinder block is clear and fitted below cylinder block top face.
4. Clean and dry cylinder head bolts.
5. Measure length of cylinder head bolts. If any bolt exceeds the maximum length of 243.41 mm. then all bolts must be renewed.
6. Ensure dowels are fitted to cylinder block and fit NEW cylinder head gasket, dry, over the dowels.

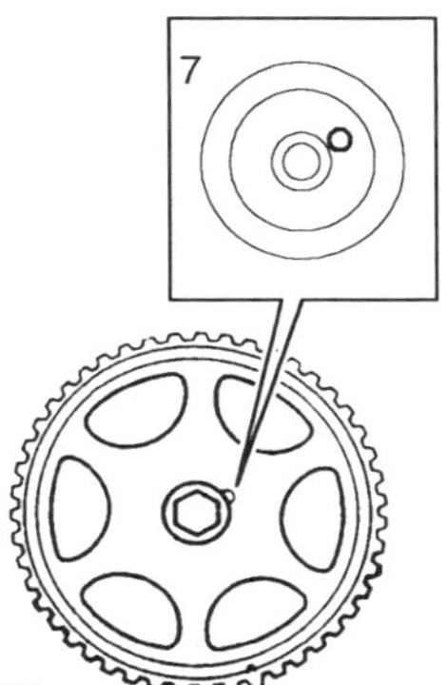

M12 5285

7. Check that camshaft timing gear drive pin is at 2 o'clock position. If necessary, temporarily fit camshaft gear and rotate camshaft until pin is positioned. Remove camshaft gear.
8. Temporarily fit crankshaft pulley bolt, remove timing pin **LRT-12-058** and using crankshaft pulley bolt, rotate crankshaft anti-clockwise until numbers 1 and 4 pistons are approximately 25 mm below cylinder block top face. Do not remove pulley bolt at this stage.
9. Fit cylinder head onto cylinder block, carefully locating onto dowels.
10. Use clean engine oil to lubricate the thread and under side of each cylinder head bolt head

⚠ **CAUTION: Do not lubricate under side of washers.**

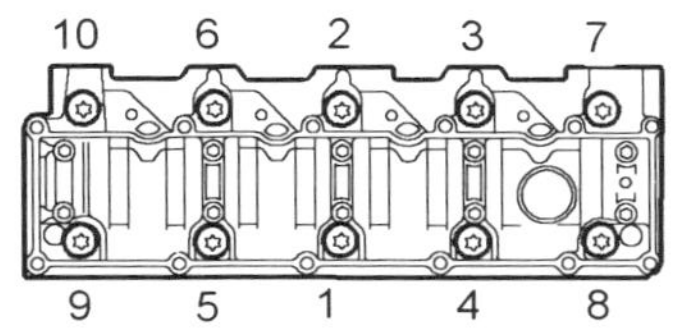

12M4143

11. Fit and tighten the cylinder head bolts progressively in the sequence shown, using the following procedure.
    1. Tighten all bolts to 30 Nm.
    2. Tighten all bolts to 65 Nm.
    3. Tighten each bolt through 90.°
    4. Tighten each bolt through a further 90°

⚠ **CAUTION: Ensure correct sequence is followed for all 4 stages. Do not tighten bolts 180° in one operation.**

12. Clean camshaft cover and mating face on camshaft carrier.
13. Fit NEW gasket to camshaft cover.

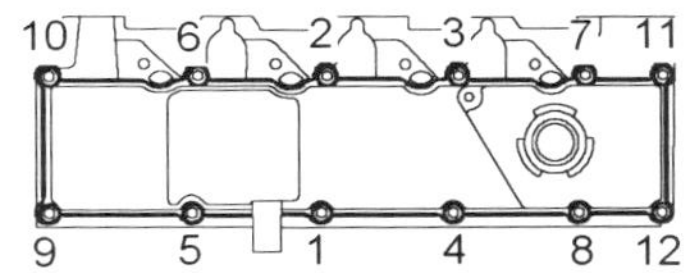

12M4144

14. Fit camshaft cover and tighten bolts in sequence shown to 9 Nm.
15. Connect glow plug feed lead and tighten nut to 2.5 Nm.
16. Connect top hose to engine and tighten hose clip.

Models with air conditioning

17. Fit alternator upper fixing bolt and tighten to 25 Nm.

All models

18. Connect multiplug to coolant temperature sensor and coolant temperature transmitter lead to engine harness.
19. Connect brake servo vacuum hose to vacuum pump and secure with clip.
20. Align brake servo vacuum pipe to camshaft cover and secure with bolt.
21. Fit FIP drive belt rear cover and tighten bolts.
22. Clean FIP drive belt tensioner.
23. Hold tensioner off and fit Allen bolt.
24. Fit camshaft drive belt rear cover and secure with bolts.
25. Align engine harness to belt cover and secure with clips.
26. Clean camshaft drive gear and mating face.
27. Fit camshaft drive gear and fit new bolt; do not tighten bolt at this stage.
28. Clean FIP belt drive gear and mating face.
29. Fit FIP belt drive gear and fit new bolt.
30. Restrain camshaft drive gear using tool **LRT-12-132** and tighten camshaft and FIP drive gear bolts to 20 Nm + 90°.

⚠ **CAUTION: Ensure camshaft does not rotate.**

31. Fit inlet and exhaust manifold. ***See MANIFOLD & EXHAUST SYSTEMS - 'L' SERIES, Repairs.***
32. Fit injector pipes. ***See ENGINE MANAGEMENT SYSTEM - EDC, Repairs.***

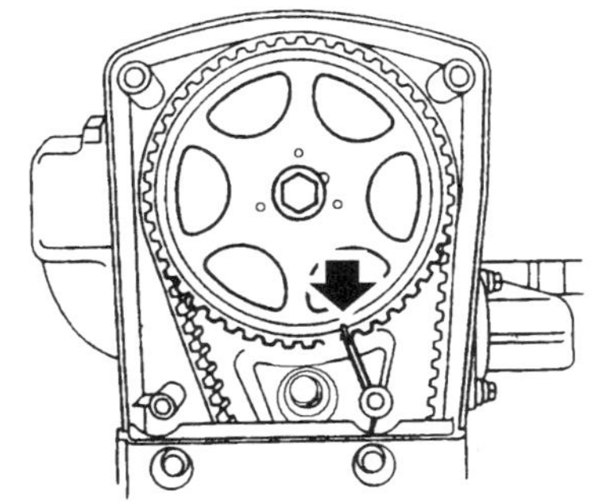

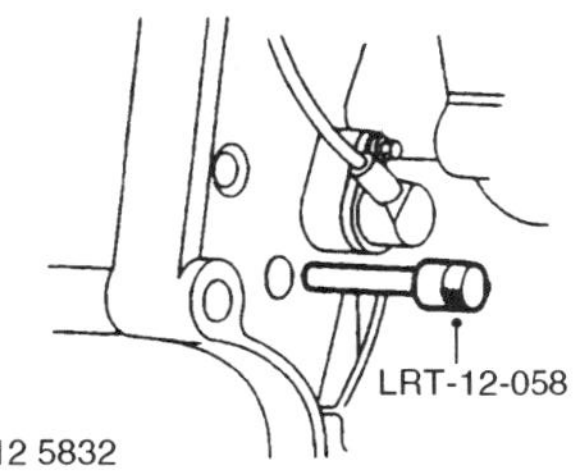

M12 5832

33. Align camshaft gear timing mark with mark on back cover.
34. Insert timing pin **LRT-12-058** through hole in gearbox mounting plate. Hold pin in contact with flywheel and using assistance, carefully rotate crankshaft clockwise until timing pin can be felt to enter hole in flywheel.

⚠ **CAUTION: Do not rotate crankshaft too far, pistons may contact valves.**

35. Remove crankshaft pulley bolt.

36. Fit camshaft drive belt. ***See this section.***
37. Fit FIP drive belt. ***See this section.***
38. Connect battery earth lead.
39. Refill cooling system. ***See COOLING SYSTEM - 'L' SERIES, Adjustments.***

GASKET - CAMSHAFT COVER

Service repair no - 12.29.40

Remove

1. Remove plenum chamber. ***See ENGINE MANAGEMENT SYSTEM - EDC, Repairs.***

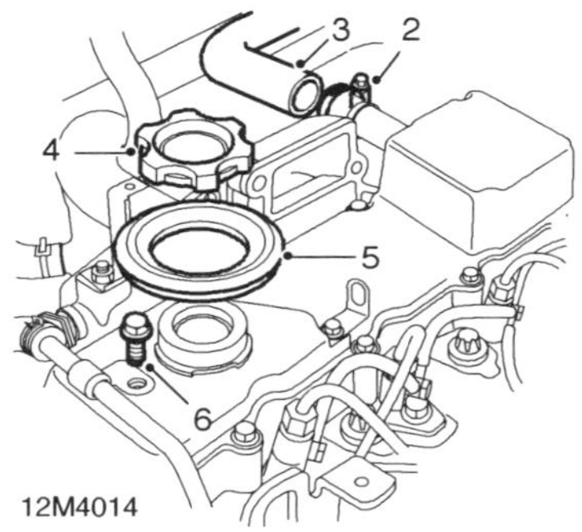

12M4014

2. Slacken clip securing engine breather hose to camshaft cover.
3. Disconnect engine breather hose from camshaft cover.
4. Remove oil filler cap from camshaft cover.
5. Remove seal from oil filler neck.
6. Remove bolt securing brake servo vacuum pipe to camshaft cover.

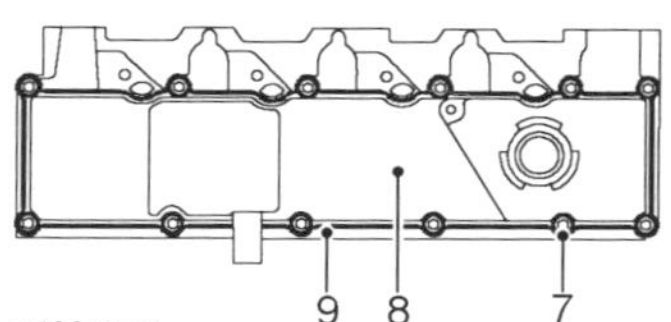

12M4015

7. Remove 12 bolts securing camshaft cover.
8. Remove camshaft cover.
9. Remove and discard camshaft cover gasket.

Refit

1. Clean camshaft cover and mating face on camshaft carrier.
2. Fit NEW gasket to camshaft cover.

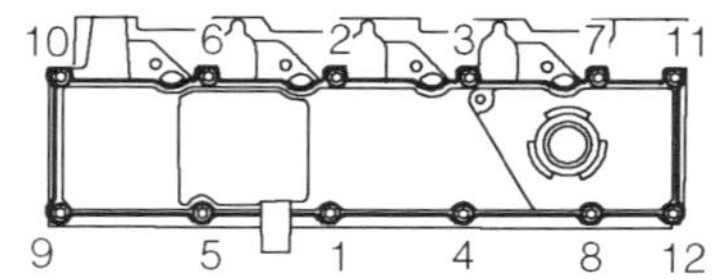

12M2412

3. Fit camshaft cover and tighten bolts in sequence shown to 9 Nm.
4. Align brake servo vacuum pipe to camshaft cover and secure with bolt.
5. Fit seal to oil filler neck.
6. Fit oil filler cap.
7. Connect engine breather hose to camshaft cover and tighten clip.
8. Fit plenum chamber. ***See ENGINE MANAGEMENT SYSTEM - EDC, Repairs.***

COVER - ENGINE ACOUSTIC

Service repair no - 12.30.50

Remove

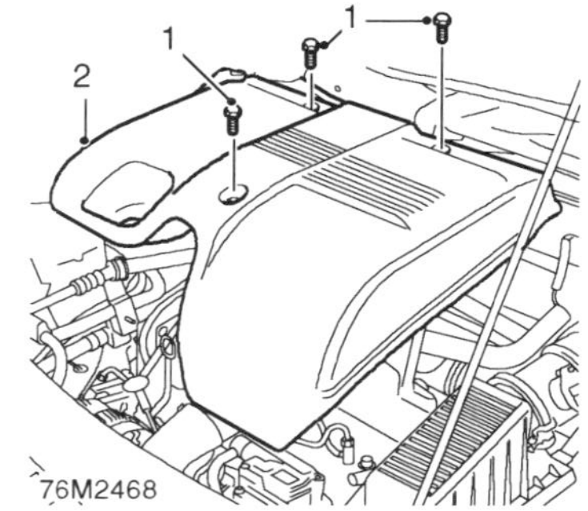

76M2468

1. Remove 3 bolts securing acoustic cover to engine.
2. Remove engine acoustic cover.

Refit

1. Fit acoustic cover.
2. Fit and tighten bolts.

ENGINE AND GEARBOX

Service repair no - 12.37.01/99

Remove

1. Remove bonnet. ***See BODY, Repairs.***
2. Drain cooling system. ***See COOLING SYSTEM - 'L' SERIES, Adjustments.***
3. Drain gear box oil. ***See MANUAL GEARBOX, Adjustments.***
4. Drain IRD unit. ***See MANUAL GEARBOX, Adjustments.***
5. *If required:* Drain engine oil. ***See MAINTENANCE.***
6. Remove both front drive shafts. ***See DRIVE SHAFTS, Repairs.***

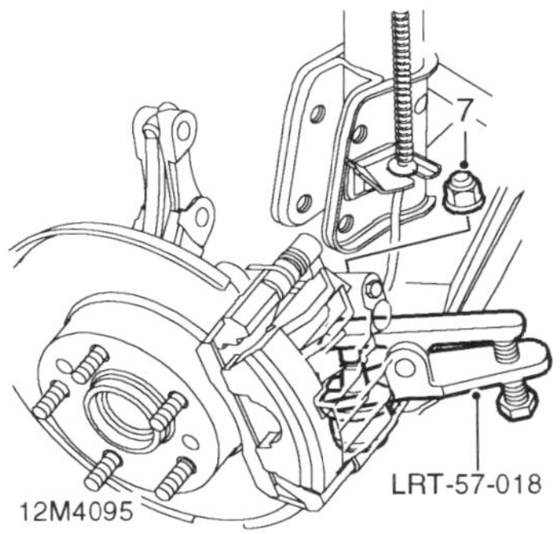

12M4095

7. Remove 2 nuts securing lower arm ball joints to hubs.
8. Break lower arm joint tapers using **LRT 57-018** and disconnect arms from hubs.

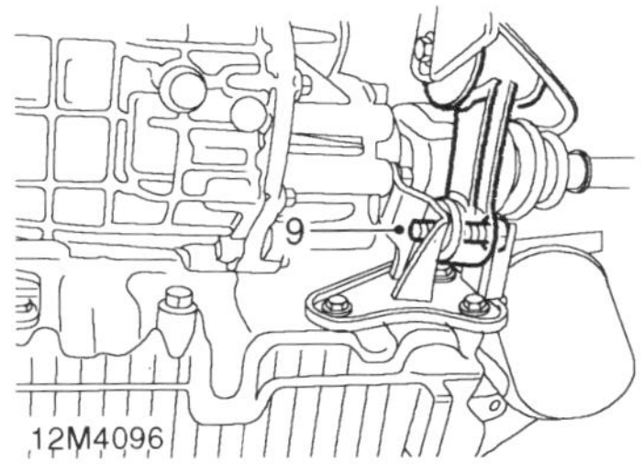

12M4096

9. Remove bolt securing engine lower tie bar to bracket on engine.

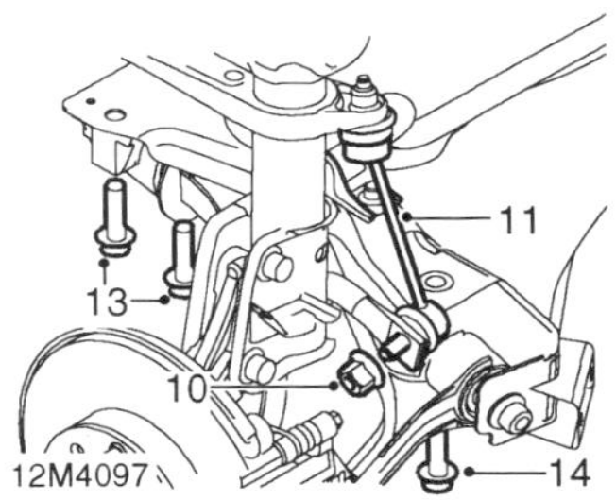

12M4097

10. Remove 2 nuts securing anti roll bar to links.
11. Remove links from anti roll bar.
12. Position a transmission jack under rear beam.
13. Remove 4 bolts securing lower arm rear mountings and rear of beam to body.
14. Remove 2 remaining bolts securing beam to body.
15. With assistance, lower beam assembly and remove from under vehicle.
16. Remove exhaust front pipe. ***See MANIFOLD & EXHAUST SYSTEMS, Repairs.***

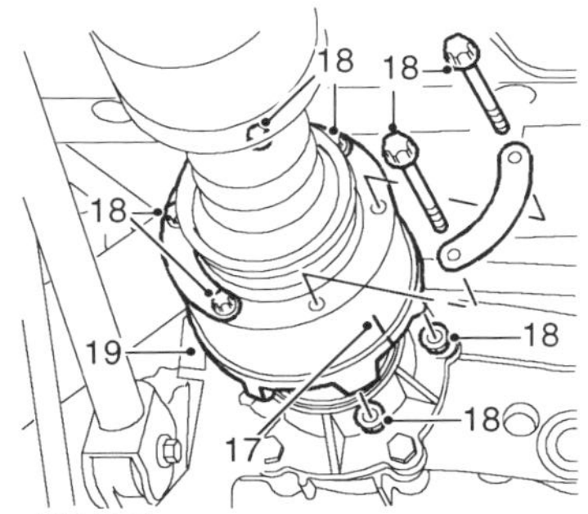

12M4098

17. Reference mark propeller shaft and IRD unit flanges to aid reassembly.
18. Remove 6 nuts and bolts securing propeller shaft to IRD unit, release
19. Release propeller shaft from IRD and tie aside.

CAUTION: Care must be taken to support the Tripode joint when removed from the IRD unit. The joint must not be allowed to fully extend or be dropped as this could damage the joint and reduce its service life.

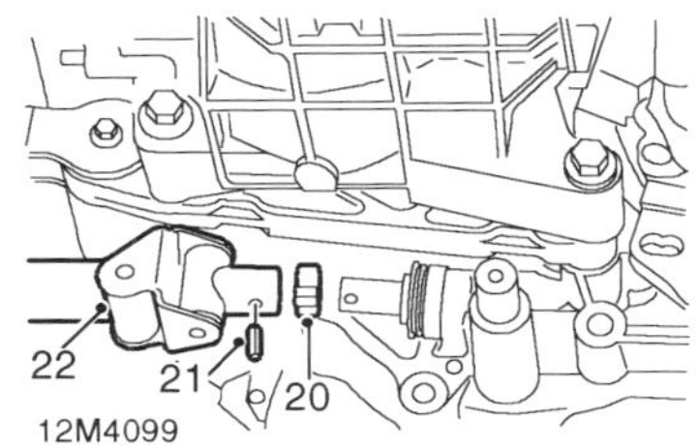

12M4099

20. Remove retainer from gear selector rod roll pin.
21. Remove and discard gear selector rod roll pin.
22. Release gear selector rod from gear box.

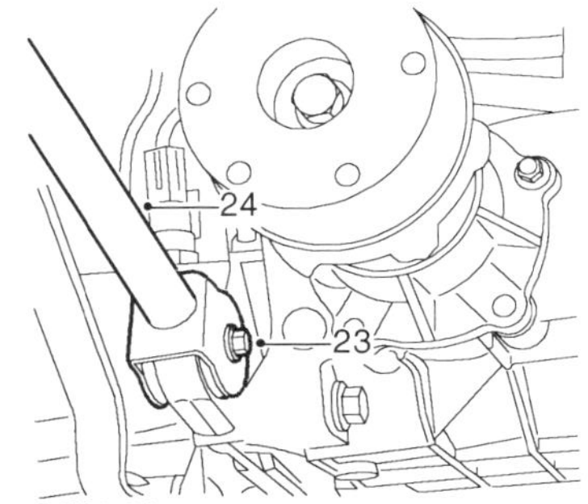

12M4100

23. Remove bolt securing gear change steady rod to IRD adaptor plate.
24. Release steady rod from adaptor plate.
25. Tie selector and steady rods aside.

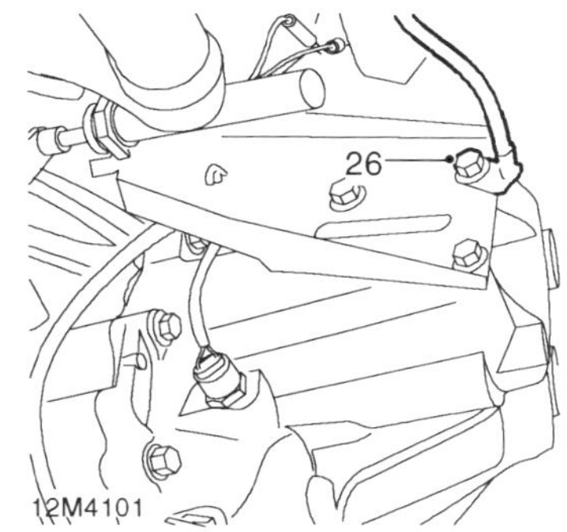

12M4101

26. Remove bolt securing engine earth lead to gearbox and position earth lead aside.

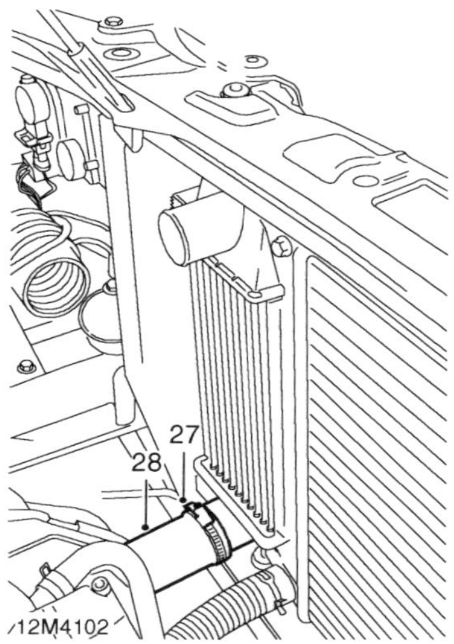

12M4102

27. Loosen clip securing turbocharger hose to intercooler.
28. Disconnect hose from intercooler.

Models fitted with air conditioning.

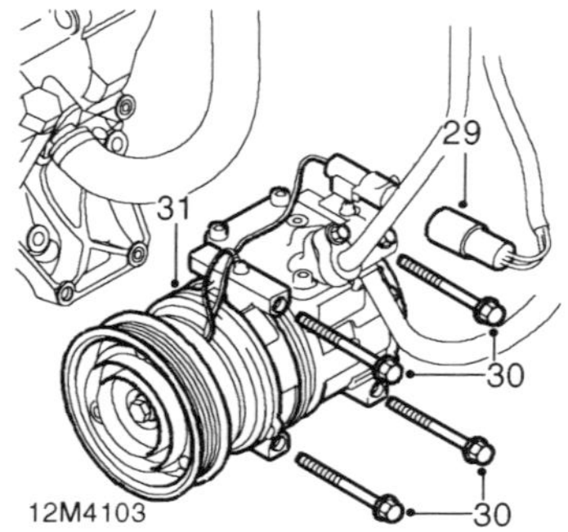

12M4103

29. Disconnect multiplug from compressor.
30. Remove 4 bolts securing compressor to water pump housing.
31. Release compressor from dowels and tie aside.

All models.

32. Remove battery carrier. ***See ELECTRICAL, Repairs.***

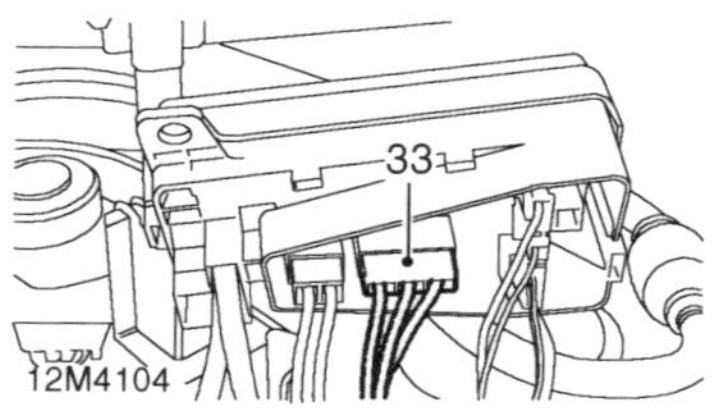

12M4104

33. Disconnect engine harness multiplug from fuse box.

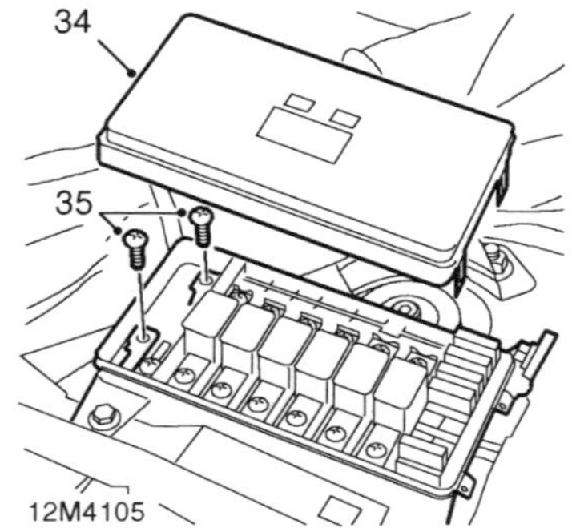

12M4105

34. Remove fuse box cover.
35. Remove 2 screws securing positive leads and release positive leads from fuse box.

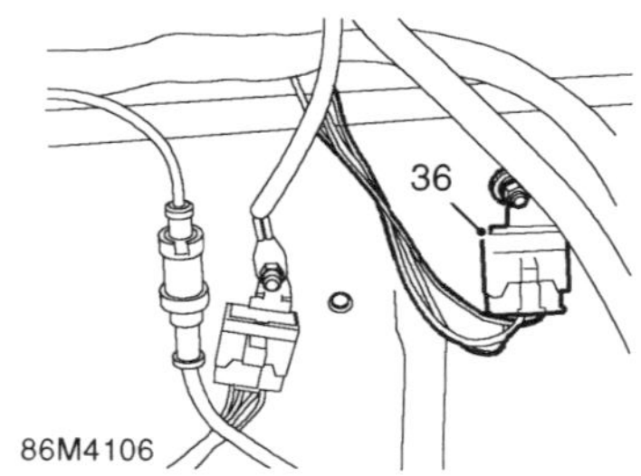

86M4106

36. Disconnect multiplug from earth lead header.

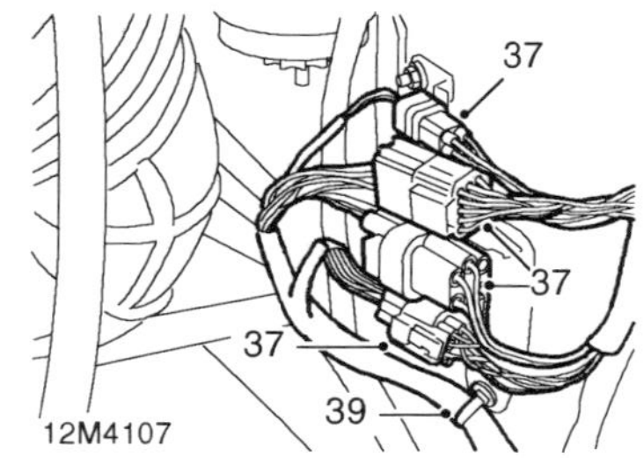

12M4107

37. Disconnect 4 engine harness multiplugs from main harness.
38. Release engine harness multiplug from bracket.
39. Release harness securing clip from bracket.

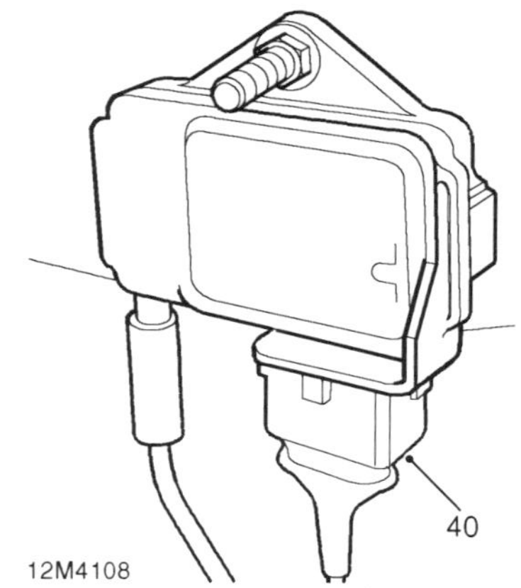

12M4108

40. Disconnect multiplug from MAP sensor.

12M4109

41. Disconnect multiplug from EGR modulator valve.

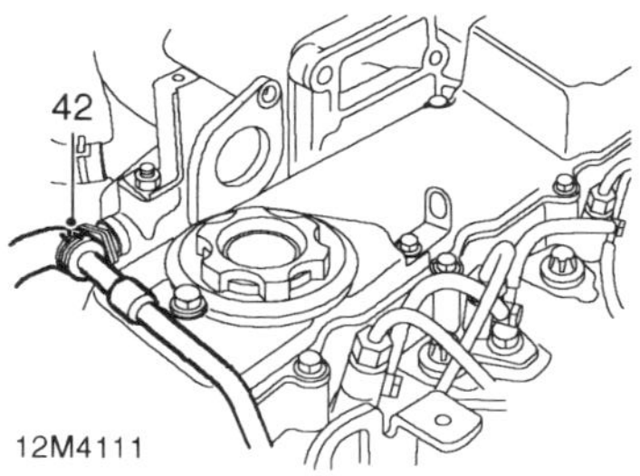

12M4111

42. Release clip and disconnect brake servo hose from pipe at camshaft cover.

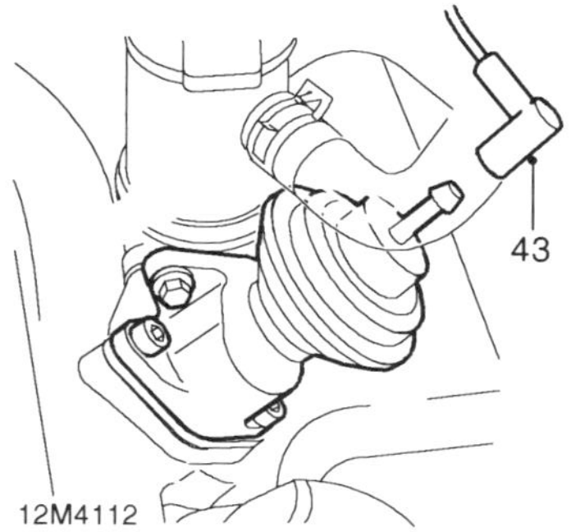

12M4112

43. Disconnect vacuum pipe from EGR valve.

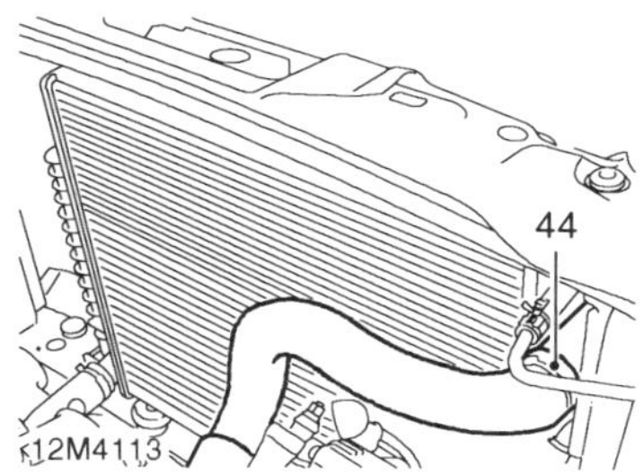

12M4113

44. Release clip and disconnect coolant top hose from radiator.

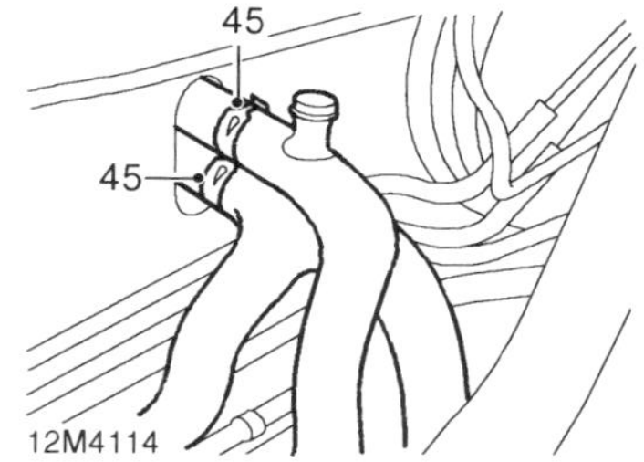

12M4114

45. Release clip and disconnect 2 coolant hoses from heater matrix.

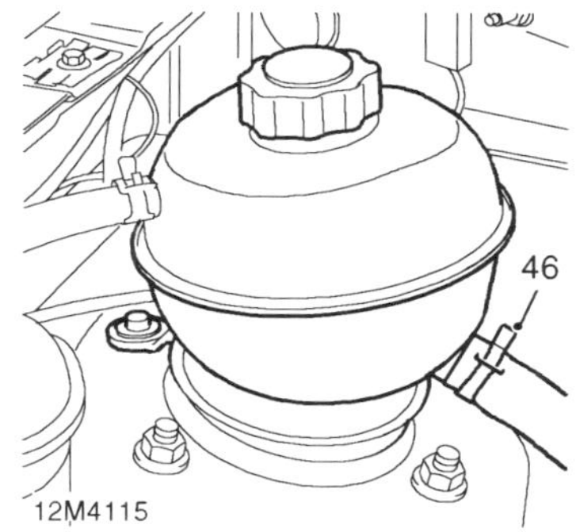

12M4115

46. Release clip and disconnect outlet hose from expansion tank.

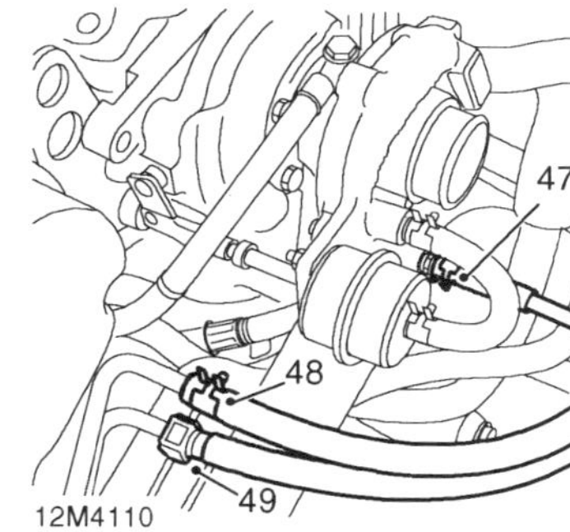

12M4110

47. Release clip and disconnect pressure sensing hose from turbocharger.
48. Release clip and disconnect feed hose from fuel rail.
49. Release return hose from fuel rail.

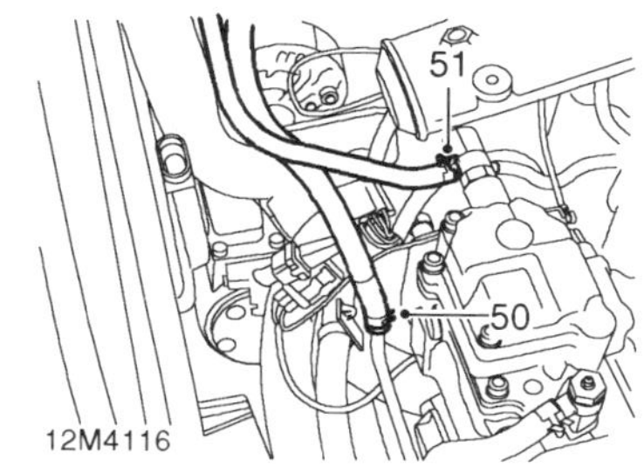

12M4116

50. Release clip and disconnect fuel cooler hose from fuel rail.
51. Release clip and disconnect fuel cooler hose from FIP.

⚠ **CAUTION: Plug the connections.**

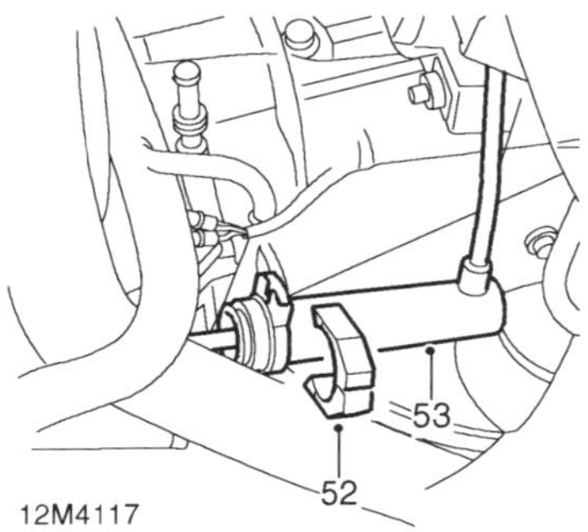

12M4117

52. Remove 'C' clip securing clutch slave cylinder.
53. Remove clutch slave cylinder from bracket and position aside.

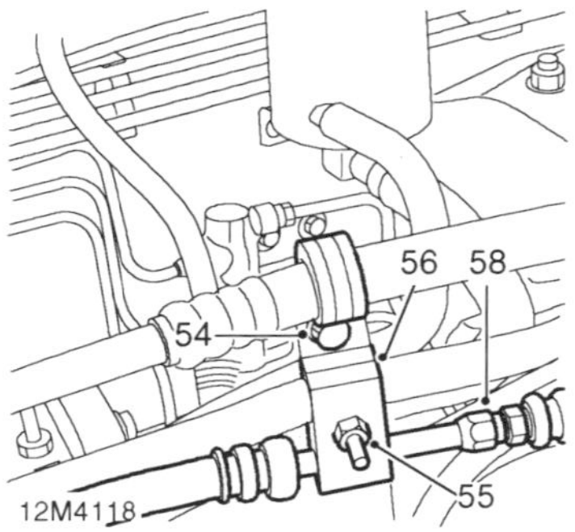

12M4118

Models fitted with air conditioning.

54. Remove screw securing A/C pipe clip to bracket on RH engine mounting.

All models.

55. Remove nut and bolt securing PAS pipe clamp to bracket on RH engine mounting.
56. Remove clamp.
57. Position container to collect PAS fluid spillage.
58. Loosen union and disconnect PAS high pressure pipes at bracket on RH engine mounting.
59. Remove and discard 'O' ring.

⚠ **CAUTION: Plug the connections.**

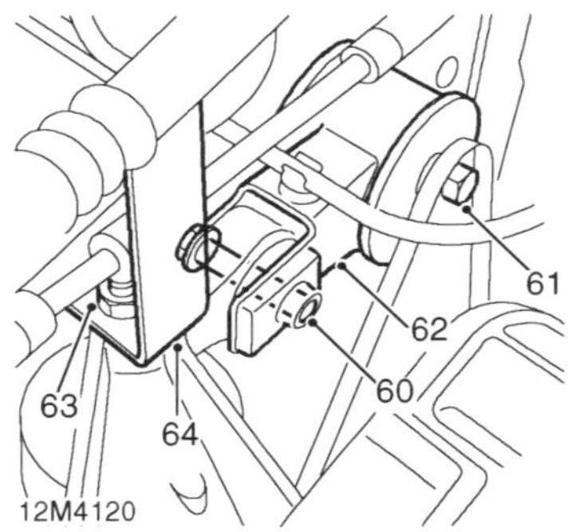

12M4120

60. Remove bolt securing upper tie rod to RH engine mounting bracket.
61. Slacken bolt securing upper tie rod to body.
62. Raise tie rod clear of engine mounting.
63. Remove nut securing bracket to RH engine mounting.
64. Remove PAS hose support bracket.

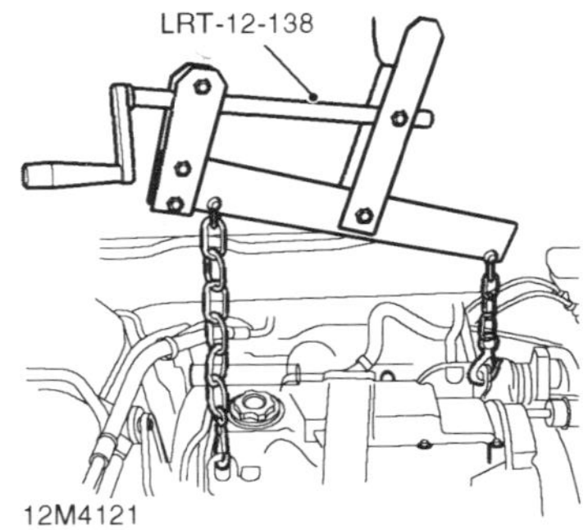

12M4121

65. Fit **LRT-12-138** to suitable lifting chains, and connect to lifting eyes on engine.
66. Take weight of engine on lifting chains.

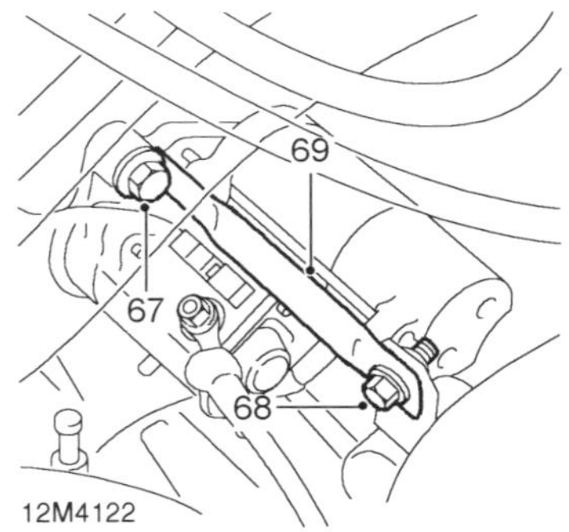

12M4122

67. Remove bolt securing LH engine mounting support strut to starter motor.
68. Remove bolt securing LH engine mounting support strut to mounting.
69. Remove LH engine mounting support strut.

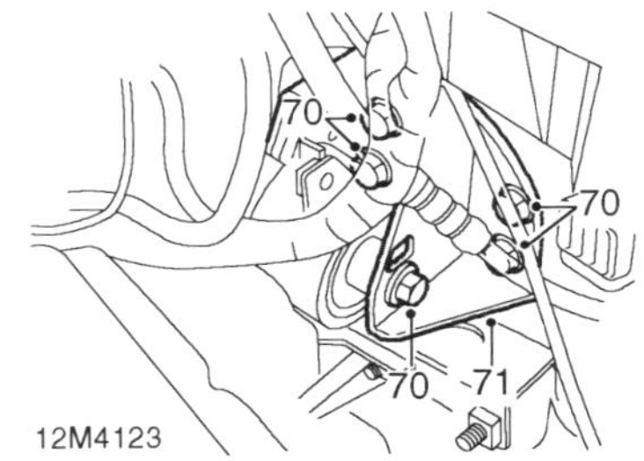

12M4123

70. Remove through bolt from LH engine mounting. remove 4 bolts securing LH engine mounting bracket to body.
71. Remove LH engine mounting bracket.
72. With assistance, lower engine and gearbox from vehicle.

Refit

1. With assistance, raise and position engine and gearbox in vehicle.
2. Fit LH engine mounting to body and tighten bolts to 45 Nm.
3. Align LH engine mounting to bracket on body and fit but do not tighten through bolt at this stage.
4. Fit RH engine mounting bracket to engine and tighten bolts to 120 Nm.
5. Lower engine onto RH engine mounting, fit PAS hose support bracket to stud and tighten nut to 80 Nm.
6. Lower chains to release weight of engine onto mountings and tighten LH mounting through bolt to 80 Nm.
7. Align upper tie rod to RH engine mounting. Fit bolt securing tie rod to mounting and bolt securing tie rod to body. Tighten both bolts to 80 Nm.
8. Fit LH engine mounting support strut.
9. Tighten bolt securing strut to starter motor to 80 Nm.and bolt securing strut to LH engine mounting to 60 Nm.
10. Ensure PAS pipe union is clean.
11. Fit NEW 'O' ring to PAS pipe and tighten union to 22Nm.
12. Connect PAS fluid hose to reservoir and secure with clip.
13. Align PAS fluid pipes to bracket on RH engine mounting, fit clamp and secure with nut and bolt.

Models fitted with air conditioning

14. Align A/C pipe clip to PAS pipe bracket and secure with screw.

All models.

15. Fit clutch slave cylinder to bracket, ensure push rod is engaged with lever and fit clip to secure cylinder to bracket.
16. Connect fuel cooler hose to FIP and secure hose with clip.
17. Connect fuel cooler hose to fuel rail and secure hose with clip.
18. Connect fuel return hose to fuel rail.
19. Connect fuel feed hose to fuel rail and secure hose with clip.
20. Connect outlet hose to expansion tank and secure with clip.
21. Connect hoses to heater matrix and secure with clips.
22. Connect top hose to radiator and secure with clip.
23. Connect vacuum pipe to EGR valve.
24. Connect brake servo hose to pipe at camshaft cover and secure hose with clip.
25. Connect pressure sensing hose to turbo charger and secure hose with clip.
26. Connect multiplug to EGR modulator valve.
27. Connect multiplug to MAP sensor.
28. Connect engine harness multiplug to bracket on LH wing valance.
29. Connect engine harness multiplugs to main harness.
30. Connect engine harness multiplugs to main harness.
31. Connect multiplug to earth lead header.
32. Connect positive leads to fuse box and and tighten screws to 2.75 Nm.
33. Fit cover to fuse box.
34. Connect engine harness multiplug to fuse box.
35. Fit battery carrier. ***See ELECTRICAL, Repairs.***

Models fitted with air conditioning.

36. Fit compressor to water pump housing and tighten bolts to 45 Nm.
37. Connect multiuplug to A/C compressor.

All models

38. Connect hose to intercooler and tighten clip.
39. Align earth lead to gearbox and tighten bolt to 45 Nm.
40. Fit gear selector rod to gearbox and steady rod to IRD adaptor plate.
41. Fit NEW roll pin to selector rod and fit clip to retain roll pin.
42. Fit bolt securing steady rod to IRD adaptor plate and tighten to 25 Nm.
43. Position propeller shaft to IRD drive flange and align reference marks.Tighten nuts and bolts to 40 Nm.
44. Fit exhaust front pipe. ***See MANIFOLD & EXHAUST SYSTEMS, Repairs.***
45. With assistance, use a transmission jack and position rear beam under vehicle.
46. Fit bolts securing beam to body. Tighten 2 front bolts to 190 Nm. and 4 rear bolts to 105 Nm.
47. Connect links to anti roll bar and tighten nuts to 45 Nm.
48. Align engine lower tie bar to bracket on sump and tighten bolt to 80 Nm.
49. Ensure lower arm ball joint tapers are clean and connect swivel hubs to lower arms. Tighten ball joint nuts to 65 Nm.
50. Fit front drive shafts. ***See DRIVE SHAFTS, Repairs.***
51. If required refill engine with oil. ***See MAINTENANCE.***
52. Refill IRD unit with oil. ***See MANUAL GEARBOX, Adjustments.***
53. Refill gear box with oil. ***See MANUAL GEARBOX, Adjustments.***
54. Refill cooling system with coolant. ***See COOLING SYSTEM - 'L' SERIES, Adjustments.***
55. Fill PAS system with PAS fluid. ***See STEERING, Adjustments.***
56. Fit bonnet. ***See BODY, Repairs.***

MOUNTING - ENGINE - LH

Service repair no - 12.45.11

Remove

1. Remove underbelly panel. ***See BODY, Exterior fittings.***
2. Remove air filter assembly. ***See ENGINE MANAGEMENT SYSTEM - EDC, Repairs.***

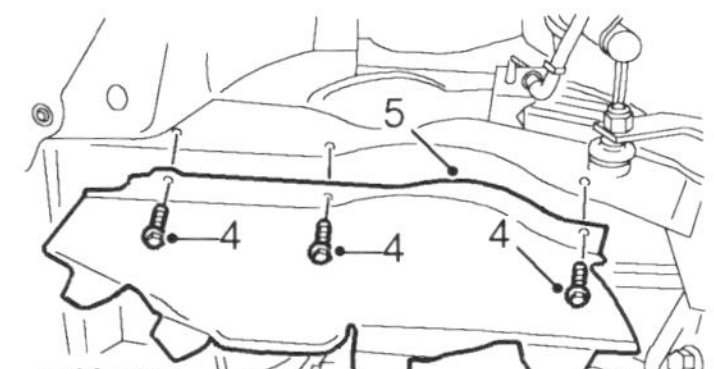

12M3984

3. Remove LH front wheel.
4. Remove 3 bolts securing LH splash shield.
5. Remove LH splash shield.

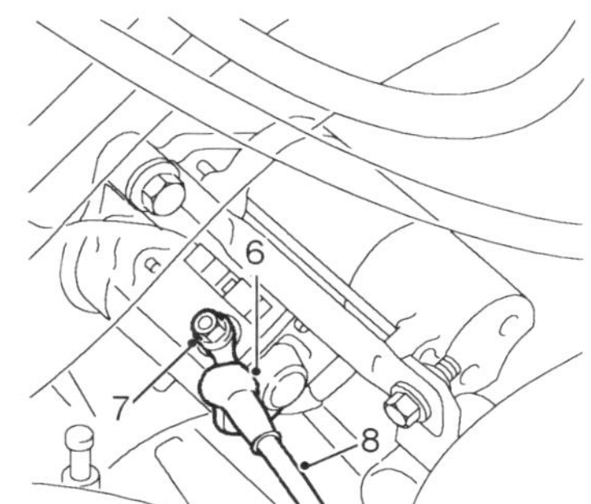

12M4032

6. Release cover from battery lead terminal on starter motor.
7. Remove nut securing battery lead to starter motor terminal.
8. Release battery lead from starter motor terminal.

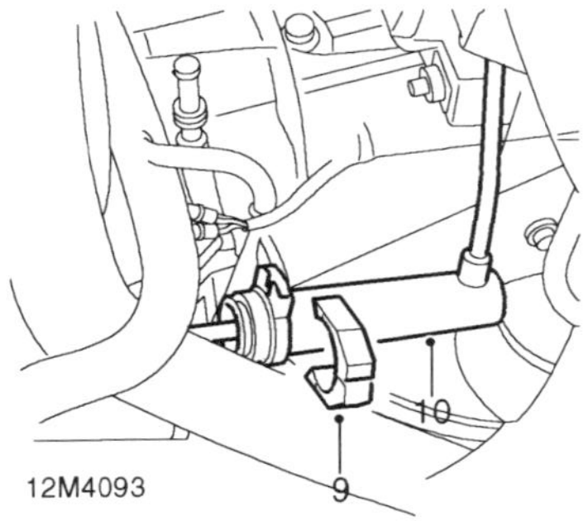

12M4093

9. Remove clip securing clutch slave cylinder to bracket.
10. Move slave cylinder aside.

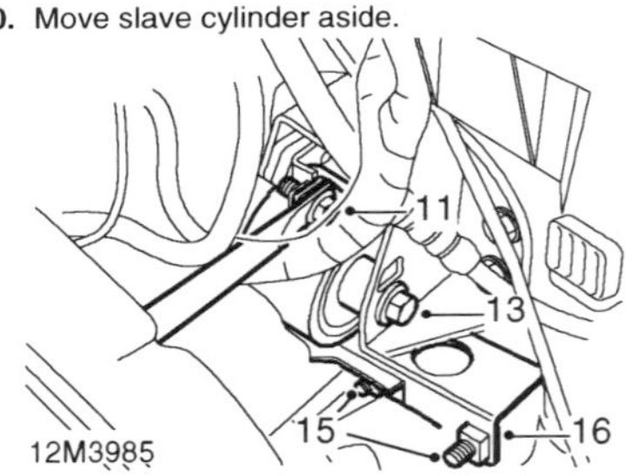

12M3985

11. Remove bolt securing support strut to LH engine mounting.
12. Support engine on a jack.

CAUTION: Fit a suitable block of wood on jack to protect engine.

13. Remove bolt securing LH engine mounting to bracket on body.
14. Lower engine sufficiently only for access to engine mounting bolts.
15. Remove 2 bolts securing engine mounting to gearbox.
16. Remove LH engine mounting.

Refit

1. Fit LH engine mounting to gearbox and tighten bolts to 65 Nm.
2. Raise engine to align LH engine mounting to bracket on body.
3. Fit bolt securing LH engine mounting to bracket on body and tighten to 80 Nm.
4. Remove jack.
5. Fit bolt securing strut to LH engine mounting and tighten to 60 Nm.
6. Fit clutch slave cylinder to bracket, ensure push rod is engaged with lever and fit clip to secure cylinder to bracket.
7. Fit battery lead to starter motor terminal, secure with nut and tighten to 4 Nm.
8. Fit terminal cover.
9. Fit LH splash shield, secure with bolts and tighten to 10 Nm.
10. Fit road wheel(s) and tighten nuts to correct torque. ***See INFORMATION, Torque wrench settings.***
11. Fit air filter assembly. ***See ENGINE MANAGEMENT SYSTEM - EDC, Repairs.***
12. Fit underbelly panel. ***See BODY, Exterior fittings.***

MOUNTING - ENGINE - RH

Service repair no - 12.45.12

Remove

1. Remove engine acoustic cover. ***See ENGINE, Repairs.***
2. Remove underbelly panel. ***See BODY, Exterior fittings.***

Models with air conditioning.

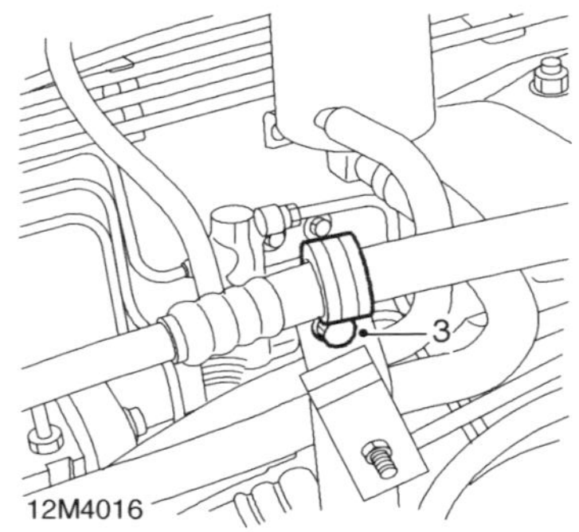

12M4016

3. Remove bolt securing air conditioning hose clip to PAS hose support bracket.

All models.

4. Use a jack to support engine under sump.

CAUTION: Use a block of wood on jack to protect the sump.

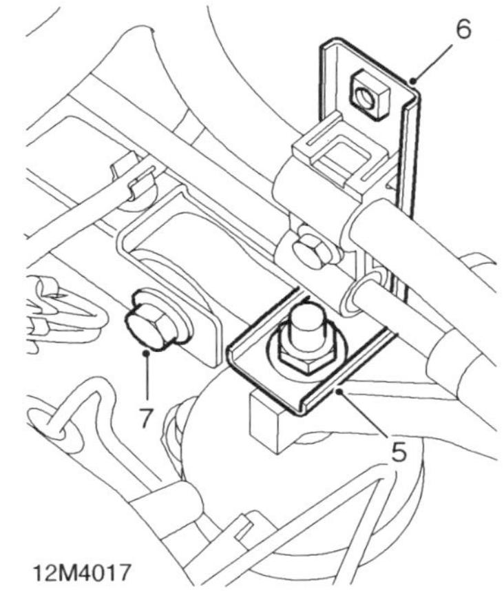

12M4017

5. Remove nut securing PAS hose support bracket to engine mounting stud.
6. Release PAS hose bracket from mounting stud.
7. Remove bolt securing engine upper tie bar to engine mounting bracket.

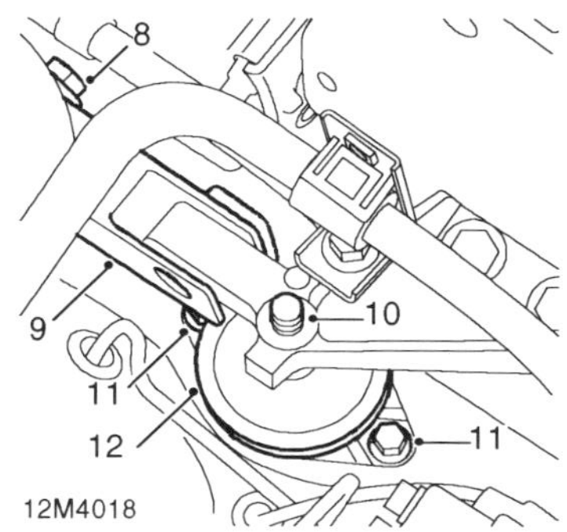

12M4018

8. Slacken bolt securing engine upper tie bar to bracket on body.
9. Raise upper tie bar to clear engine mounting bracket.
10. Raise RH side of engine on jack sufficiently only to clear RH engine mounting stud.
11. Remove 2 bolts securing RH engine mounting to wing valance.
12. Remove RH engine mounting.

Refit

1. Fit RH engine mounting and tighten bolts to 45 Nm.
2. Lower engine onto RH mounting.
3. Fit upper tie bar to engine mounting bracket and tighten both bolts securing tie bar to 80 Nm.
4. Remove jack from under engine.
5. Fit PAS hose bracket to engine mounting stud and tighten nut to 80 Nm.

Models with air conditioning

6. Fit air conditioning hose clip to PAS hose support bracket and secure with bolt.

All models

7. Fit underbelly panel. ***See BODY, Exterior fittings.***
8. Fit acoustic cover. ***See ENGINE, Repairs.***

TIE ROD - UPPER

Service repair no - 12.45.16

Remove

1. Remove engine acoustic cover. ***See ENGINE, Repairs.***

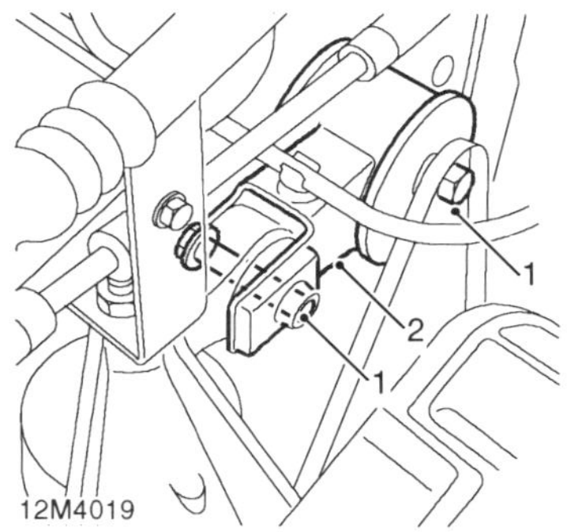

12M4019

2. Remove 2 bolts securing tie rod.
3. Remove tie rod.

Refit

1. Fit tie rod and tighten bolts to 80 Nm.
2. Fit acoustic cover. ***See ENGINE, Repairs.***

TIE ROD - LOWER

Service repair no - 12.45.17

Remove

1. Remove underbelly panel. ***See BODY, Repairs.***

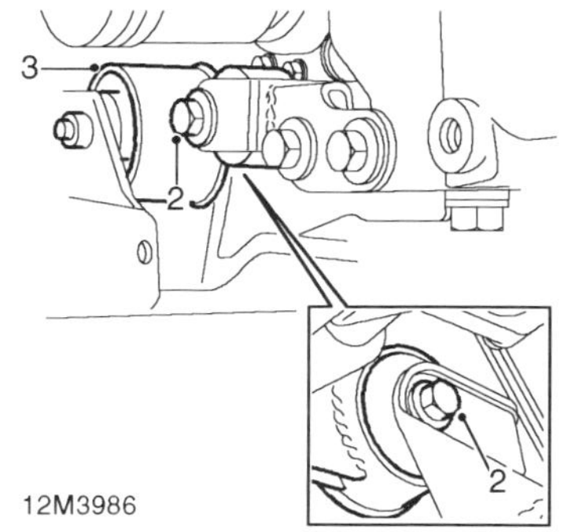

12M3986

2. Remove 2 bolts securing lower tie rod.
3. Remove tie rod.

Refit

1. Fit tie rod and tighten bolts to 80 Nm.
2. Fit underbelly panel. ***See BODY, Repairs.***

FILTER - ENGINE OIL

Service repair no - 12.60.04

Remove

1. Remove underbelly panel. ***See BODY, Exterior fittings.***
2. Clean area around filter head and place a container beneath engine

12M4064

3. Using a strap wrench, unscrew and discard filter.

Refit

1. Clean mating face of filter head.
2. Lubricate sealing ring of NEW filter with clean engine oil.
3. Fit oil filter and tighten by hand until it seats, then tighten a further full turn or to a torque of 17 Nm.
4. Top up engine oil. ***See MAINTENANCE.***
5. Start and run engine and check for leaks.
6. Stop engine, wait a few minutes, then check oil level. Top up if necessary.
7. Fit underbelly panel. ***See BODY, Exterior fittings.***

PUMP - ENGINE OIL

Service repair no - 12.60.26

Remove

1. Remove camshaft timing belt. ***See this section.***

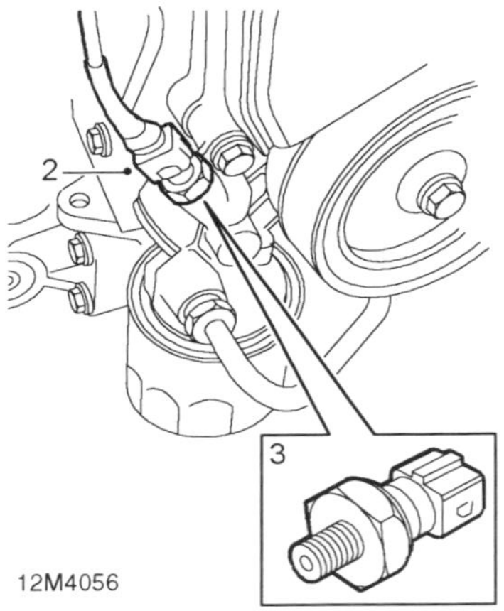

12M4056

2. Disconnect multiplug from oil pressure switch.
3. Remove oil pressure switch.

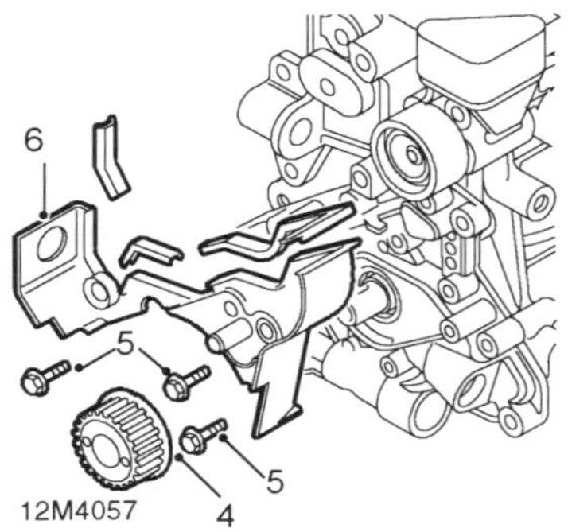

12M4057

4. Remove timing gear from crankshaft.
5. Remove 3 bolts securing camshaft timing belt lower cover backplate.
6. Remove backplate with seal.
7. Remove oil filter.

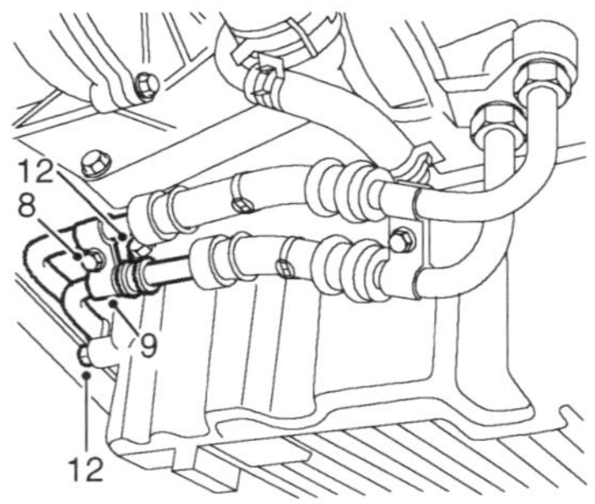

12M4058

8. Remove bolt securing clamp to oil cooler pipes.
9. Remove clamp.
10. Remove 2 bolts securing oil cooler pipe clips to sump.

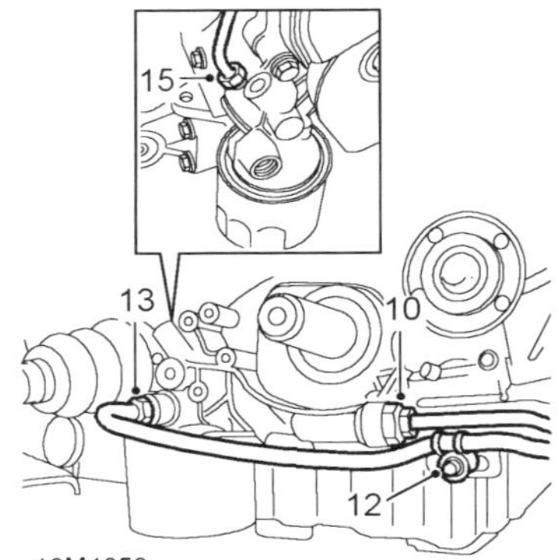

12M4059

11. Remove union nuts and disconnect pipes from oil pump.
12. Remove and discard 'O' ring.
13. Remove union nut and disconnect turbo oil feed pipe from pump.
14. Remove and discard 'O' ring.

CAUTION: Plug the connections.

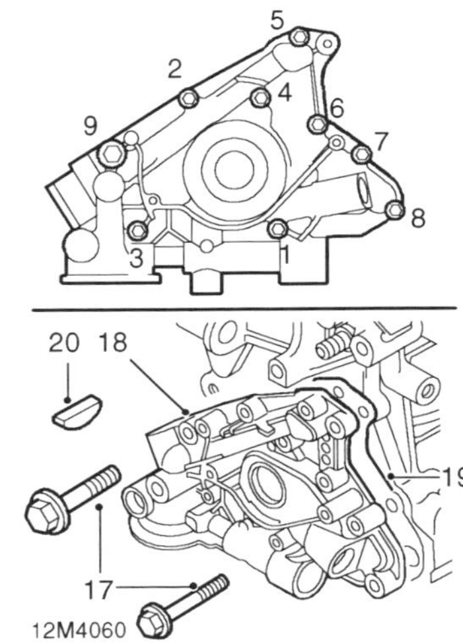

12M4060

15. Using sequence shown, remove 1, M10 and 8, M6 bolts securing oil pump to cylinder block. Note position of longest bolt at position 9.
16. Remove oil pump.
17. Remove and discard gasket.
18. Remove key from crankshaft.

Refit

1. Ensure bolt holes in cylinder block are clean and dry.
2. Remove all traces of gasket from cylinder block.
3. Using suitable solvent, remove all traces of sealant from front main bearing cap.
4. Clean oil seal running surface on crankshaft.
5. Fit Woodruff key to crankshaft.

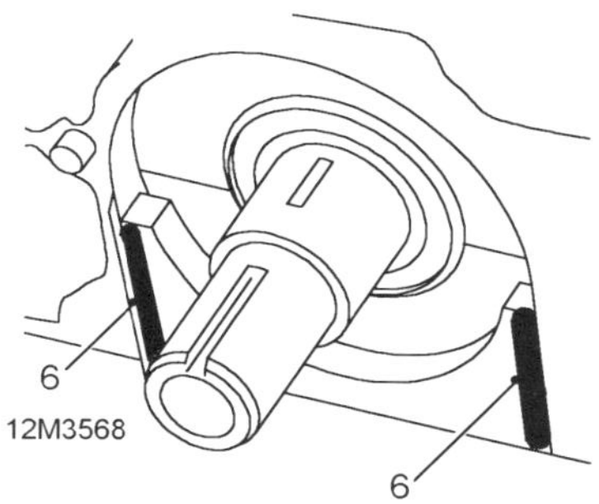

12M3568

6. Using sealant from kit Part No. GUG 705963GM, apply a 1 mm thick bead of sealant to joint line of front main bearing cap and cylinder block.
7. Fit new gasket, dry, to cylinder block.
8. Align key slots in oil pump inner rotor with key.

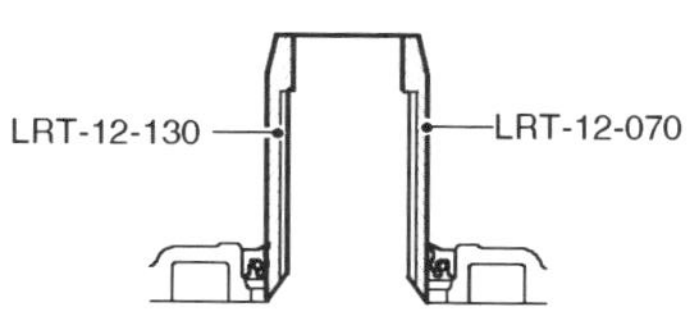

M12 5837

9. Insert oil seal protector **LRT-12-070** and adaptor sleeve **LRT-12-130** into oil pump inner rotor.

NOTE: This will assist in locating oil pump inner rotor on key. Replacement oil pumps are supplied with crankshaft front oil seal fitted. A new oil seal is fitted to existing pumps after pump is fitted. Do not lubricate oil seal or running surface on crankshaft.

10. Fit oil pump over crankshaft ensuring pump rotor is located on key.

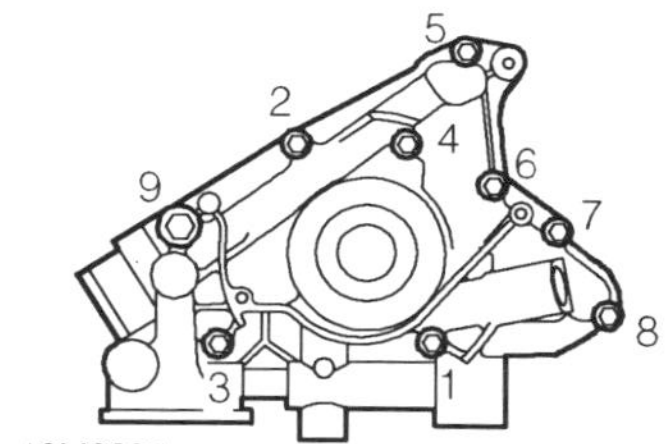

12M2695

11. Fit but do not tighten bolts ensuring that longest bolt is fitted at position 1.
12. Gradually tighten bolts in sequence shown until oil pump is pulled against cylinder block.

CAUTION: Bolt tightening must be done gradually due to tight fit of oil pump rotor on crankshaft. Damage to pump will result if this is not done.

13. Finally, tighten bolts in sequence shown :
    M10 bolt to 45 Nm.
    M6 bolts to 10 Nm.

NOTE: Patchlok bolts may be re-used providing threads are undamaged.

14. *Existing oil pump:* Fit new crankshaft front oil seal. ***See this section.***
15. Ensure sealing strip is fitted to belt lower cover backplate.
16. Fit lower backplate, fit screws and tighten to 8 Nm.
17. Clean oil cooler pipes and turbo feed pipe connections.
18. Fit NEW 'O' rings to turbo feed and oil cooler pipes.

19. Connect turbo oil feed pipe to pump and tighten union nut to 25 Nm.
20. Connect oil cooler pipe to pump and tighten union nut to 25 Nm.
21. Align pipe clips to sump and secure with bolts.
22. Connect oil cooler pipe to pump and tighten union nut to 25 Nm.
23. Fit clamp to oil cooler pipes and secure with bolt.
24. Lubricate oil filter seal with clean engine oil.
25. Fit oil filter and tighten to 17 Nm.
26. Clean oil pressure switch, apply Loctite sealant 242 to thread and tighten switch to 15 Nm.
27. Connect multiplug to oil pressure switch.
28. Clean crankshaft timing gear.
29. Fit timing gear to crankshaft.
30. Fit camshaft timing belt. ***See this section.***
31. Check and top up engine oil.
    See MAINTENANCE.

SUMP - ENGINE

Service repair no - 12.60.44

Remove

1. Disconnect battery earth lead.
2. Raise front of vehicle.

WARNING: Support on safety stands.

3. Remove oil filter. ***See MAINTENANCE.***
4. Drain engine oil. ***See MAINTENANCE.***

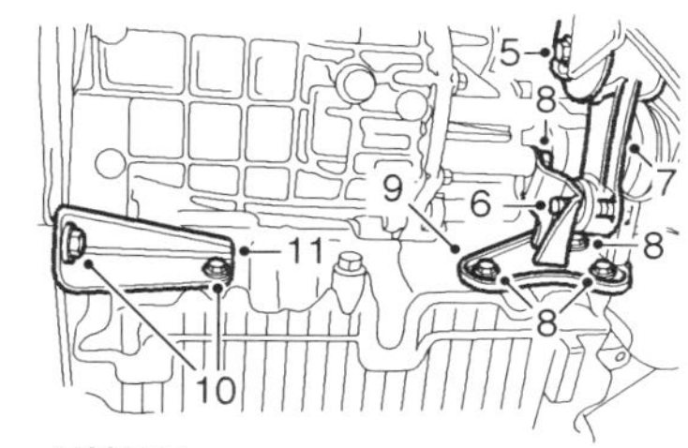

12M4041

5. Loosen bolt, engine lower tie rod to sub frame.
6. Remove bolt securing engine lower tie rod to bracket on sump.
7. Release tie rod from bracket.
8. Remove 4 bolts securing tie rod bracket to IRD unit and engine sump.
9. Remove tie rod bracket.
10. Remove 2 bolts securing support bracket to gearbox and sump.
11. Remove support bracket.
12. Position container to collect spillage from vacuum pump and oil cooler pipe unions.

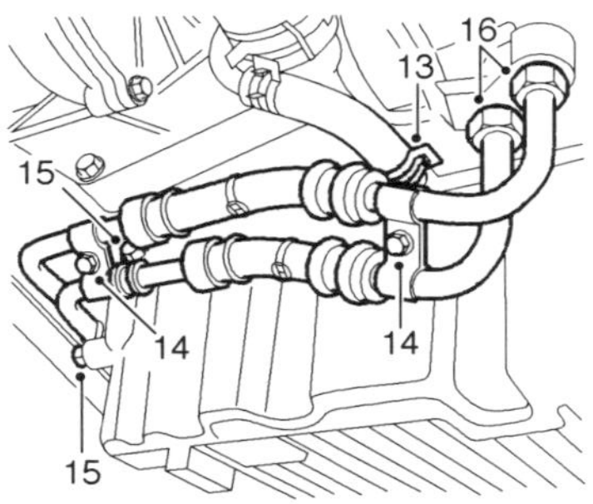

12M4042

13. Release vacuum pump oil return pipe from adaptor on sump.
14. Remove 2 bolts securing oil cooler clamp plates and remove plates.
15. Remove 2 bolts securing oil cooler pipes to sump.
16. Loosen oil cooler pipe unions from oil pump and oil filter.
17. Remove and discard 'O' rings.

CAUTION: Plug the connections.

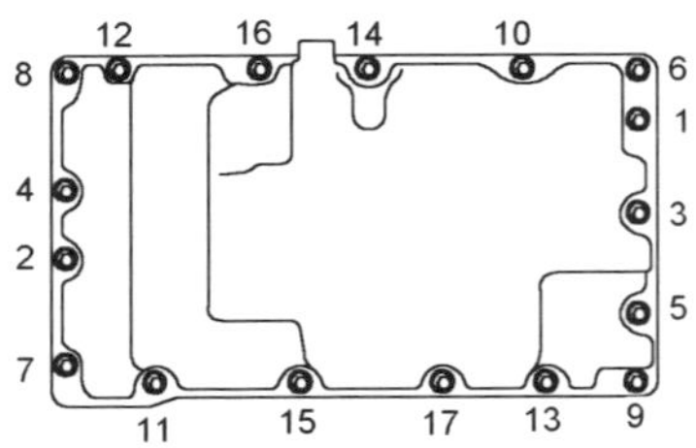

12M1938

18. Using sequence shown, remove 17 bolts securing sump to cylinder block.
19. Remove sump.
20. Remove gasket from sump; discard gasket.

Refit

1. Ensure bolt holes in cylinder block are clean and dry.
2. Clean sump and cylinder block mating faces.
3. Remove all traces of sealant from rear oil seal housing, rear main bearing cap, cylinder block and front main bearing cap using suitable solvent.

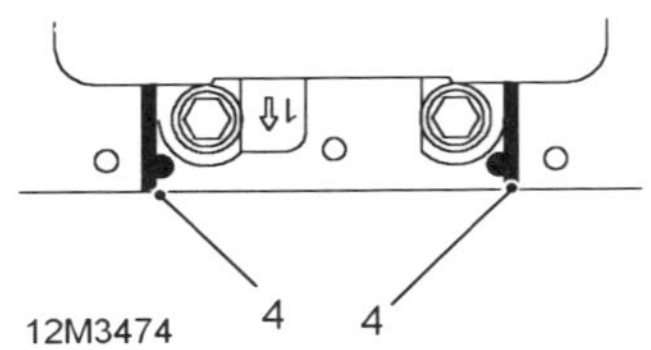

12M3474

4. Using sealant from kit, Part Number GUG 705963GM, fill grooves on each side of front main bearing cap and along joint lines of bearing cap and cylinder block.

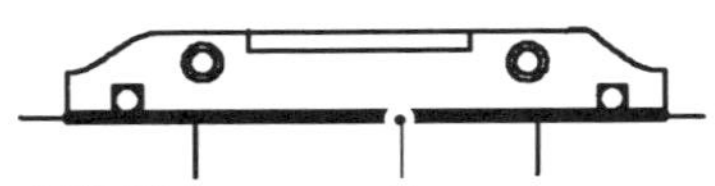

12M3475

5. Apply a 1 mm thick bead of sealant from kit to joint line and around bolt holes of crankshaft rear oil seal housing, rear main bearing cap and cylinder block and sump bolt holes adjacent to rear main bearing cap.

CAUTION: Do not apply sealant until immediately prior to fitting sump. Do not spread sealant bead.

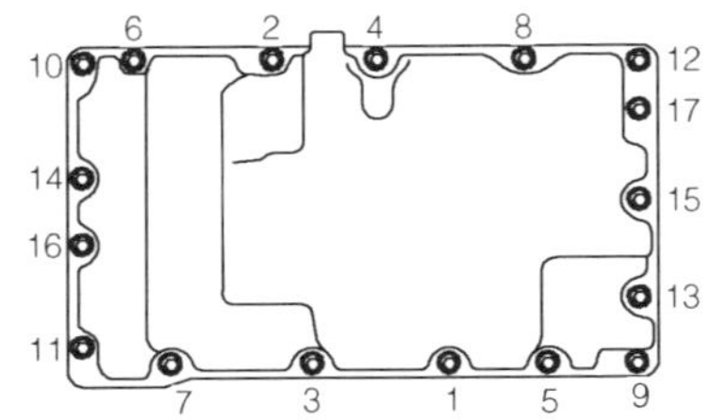

12M1853

6. Fit gasket to sump.
7. Fit sump to cylinder block, fit and finger tighten 17 bolts.
8. Using sequence shown, tighten bolts to 25 Nm.
9. Using same sequence, check that all bolts are torqued to 25 Nm.
10. Clean oil cooler pipe unions.
11. Fit NEW 'O' rings to pipes.
12. Connect pipes and tighten unions to 25 Nm.
13. Fit bolts securing oil cooler pipe clips to sump.
14. Fit oil cooler pipe clamp plates and tighten bolts.
15. Connect vacuum return pipe to sump.
16. Position support bracket, tighten bracket to sump bolt to 45 Nm.and bracket to gearbox bolt to 80 Nm.
17. Fit tie rod bracket.
18. Fit bolts securing bracket to sump and IRD, tighten to 45 Nm.
19. Align lower tie rod to bracket on sump and subframe. Fit bolts and tighten to 80 Nm.
20. Fit oil filter. ***See MAINTENANCE.***
21. Fill with engine oil. ***See MAINTENANCE.***
22. Remove stand(s) and lower vehicle.
23. Connect battery earth lead.

SWITCH - OIL PRESSURE

Service repair no - 12.60.50

Remove

1. Disconnect battery earth lead.
2. Raise front of vehicle, RH side.

WARNING: Support on safety stands.

3. Turn steering wheel to full RH lock.

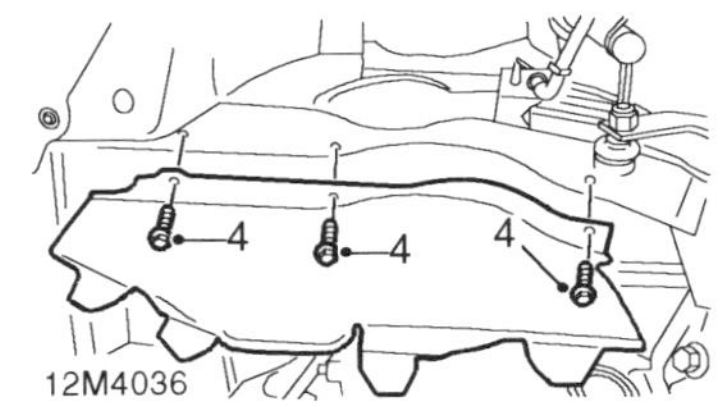

12M4036

4. Remove 3 bolts securing RH splash guard and remove guard.

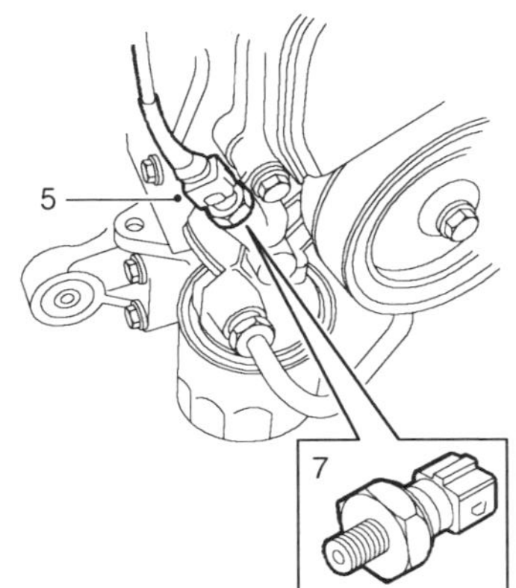

12M4035

5. Disconnect multiplug from oil pressure switch.
6. Position drain tin below switch to catch spillage.
7. Remove oil pressure switch.

Refit

1. Clean oil pressure switch threads.
2. Apply Loctite 577 to threads of switch.
3. Fit oil pressure switch and tighten to 15 Nm.
4. Connect multiplug to oil pressure switch.
5. Position splash guard, fit and tighten bolts to 10 Nm.
6. Position steering wheel straight ahead.
7. Remove stand(s) and lower vehicle.
8. Top-up engine oil. ***See MAINTENANCE.***
9. Connect battery earth lead.

COOLER - ENGINE OIL

Service repair no - 12.60.68

Remove

1. Disconnect battery earth lead.
2. Remove engine acoustic cover. ***See this section.***
3. Drain cooling system. ***See COOLING SYSTEM - 'L' SERIES, Adjustments.***

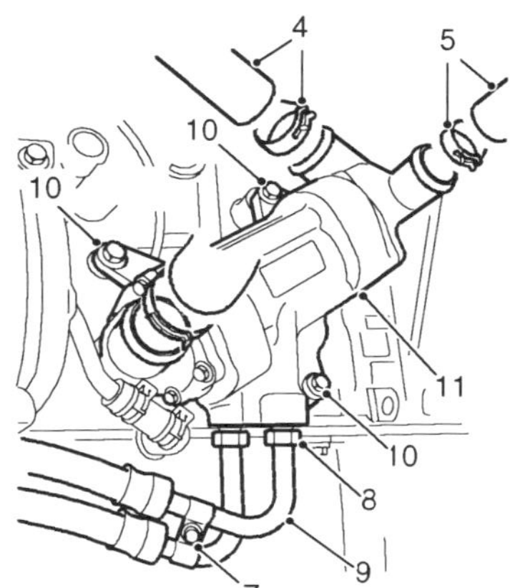

12M4040A

4. Loosen clip and release water pump hose from from oil cooler.
5. Loosen clip and release top hose from oil cooler.
6. Position container to collect fluid loss from oil cooler.
7. Loosen bolt clamping oil cooler pipes together.
8. Using a 22 mm open ended spanner loosen oil pipe unions on cooler.
9. Disconnect oil pipes from cooler, remove and discard 2 'O' rings.

⚠ **CAUTION: Plug the connections.**

10. Remove 3 bolts securing oil cooler to cylinder block.
11. Remove oil cooler.

Refit

1. Position oil cooler.
2. Fit bolts securing oil cooler to cylinder block and tighten:
   M8 bolt to 25 Nm.
   M10 bolts to 45 Nm.
3. Clean oil cooler pipes and unions, fit NEW 'O' rings to pipes.
4. Connect pipes to oil cooler and tighten unions to 25 Nm.
5. Tighten oil pipe clamp bolt.
6. Connect coolant hose to thermostat housing and secure clip.
7. Position top hose and water pump hose to oil cooler and secure clips.
8. Top up engine oil. ***See MAINTENANCE.***
9. Refill cooling system. ***See COOLING SYSTEM - 'L' SERIES, Adjustments.***
10. Fit acoustic cover. ***See this section.***
11. Connect battery earth lead.

BELT - CAMSHAFT DRIVE

Service repair no - 12.65.18

Remove

1. Remove both front drive shafts. ***See DRIVE SHAFTS, Repairs.***

Models fitted with air conditioning

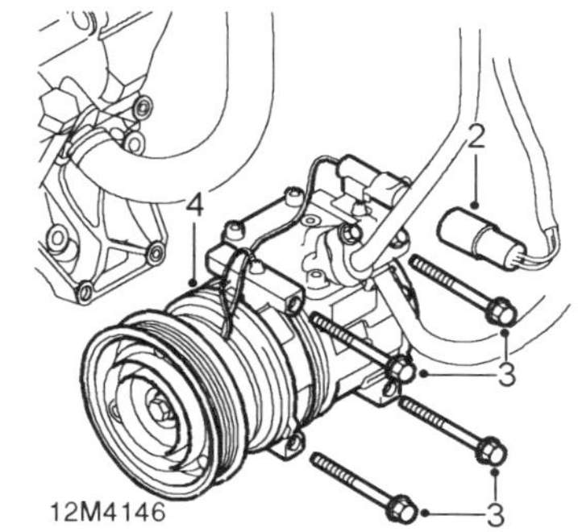

12M4146

2. Disconnect multiplug from compressor.
3. Remove 4 bolts securing compressor to water pump housing.
4. Release compressor from dowels and tie aside.

All models

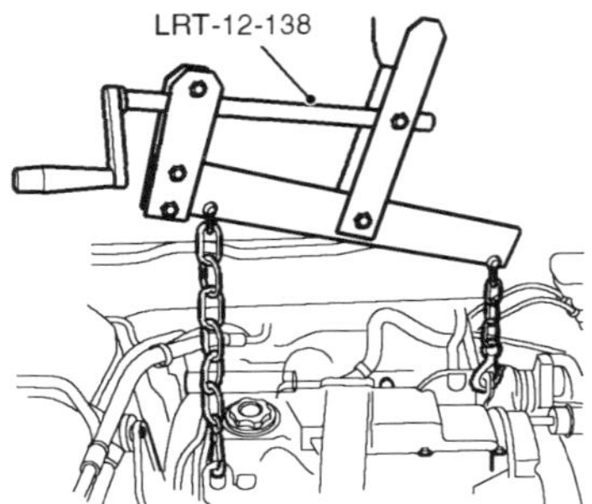

12M4147

5. Fit lifting bracket **LRT-12-138** to lifting chains, and connect to lifting eyes on engine.
6. Take weight of engine and gearbox on lifting chains.

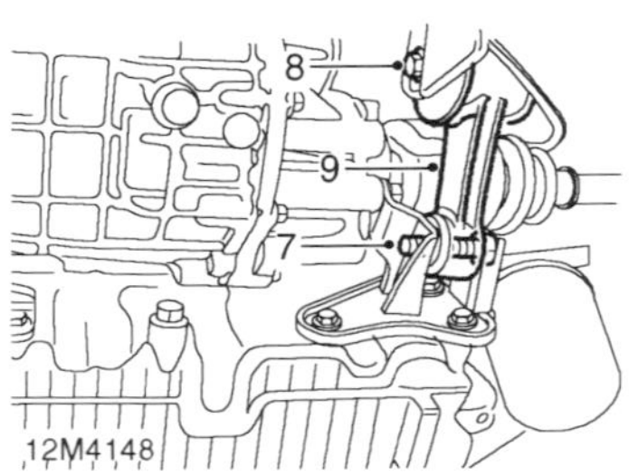

12M4148

7. Remove bolt securing engine lower tie bar to bracket on sump.
8. Loosen bolt securing engine lower tie bar to sub frame.
9. Release tie bar from bracket on sump.
10. Remove LH engine mounting. ***See this section.***

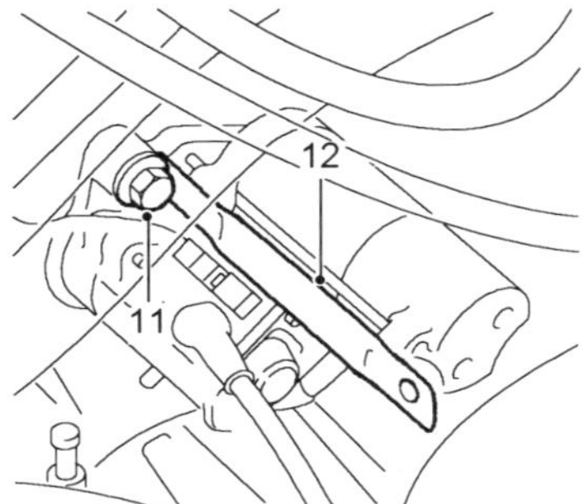

12M4149

11. Remove bolt securing LH mounting strut to starter motor.
12. Remove LH mounting strut.

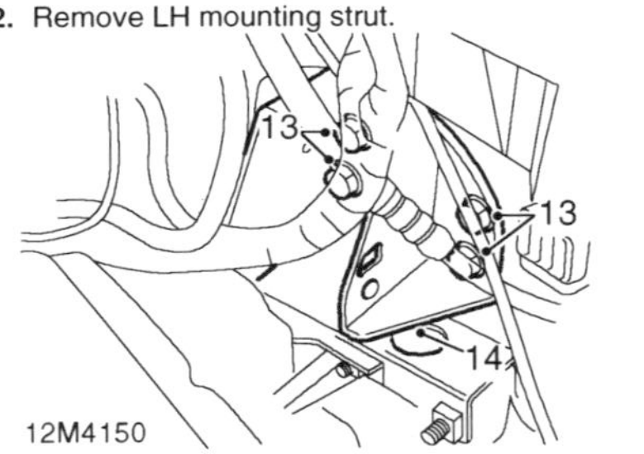

12M4150

13. Remove 4 bolts securing LH engine mounting bracket to body.
14. Remove LH engine mounting bracket.
15. Position engine to LH side of engine bay. If necessary, use a suitable block of wood to hold engine in this position.
16. Remove timing gear lower cover. ***See this section.***

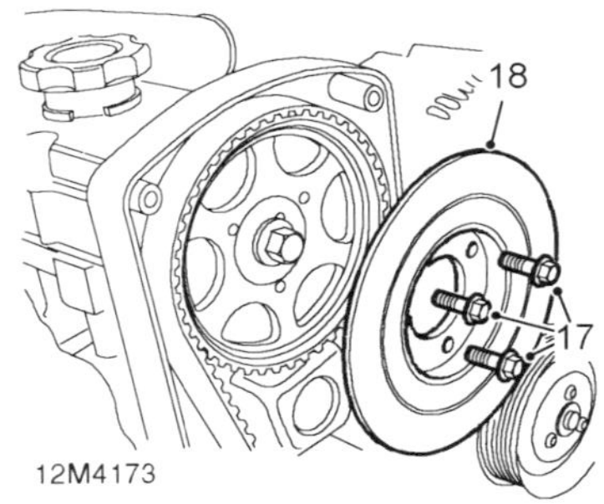

12M4173

17. Remove and discard 3 Torx screws securing damper to camshaft gear.
18. Remove damper from camshaft gear.

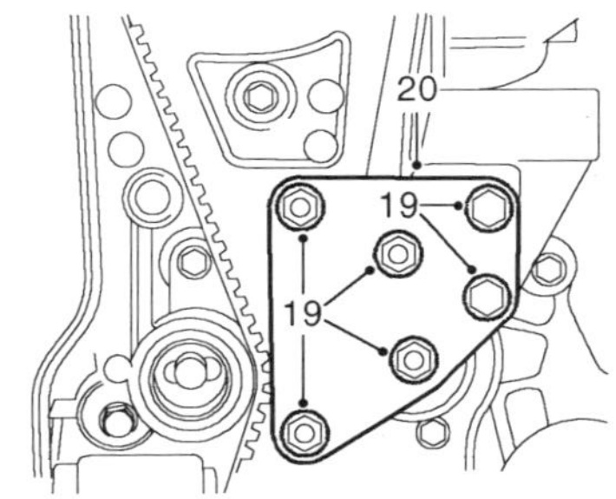

12M4151

19. Remove 4 nuts and 2 bolts from RH engine mounting bracket plate.
20. Remove plate from RH engine mounting bracket.
21. If timing belt is to be refitted, mark direction of rotation.

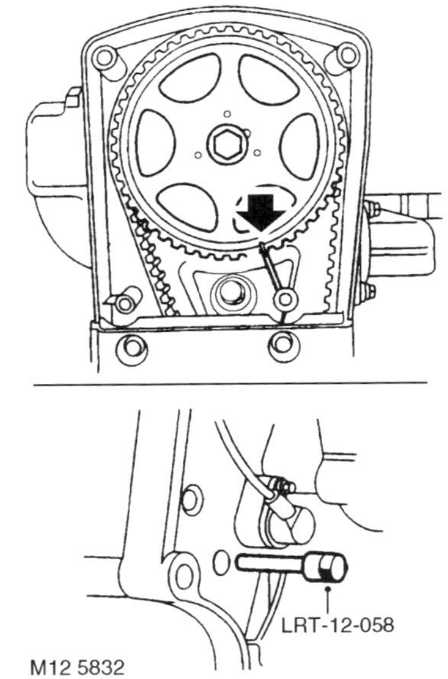

M12 5832

22. Insert timing pin **LRT-12-058** through hole in gearbox mounting plate, hold pin in contact with flywheel and using assistance, rotate crankshaft clockwise until pin can be felt to enter hole in flywheel.

⚠ **CAUTION: Never use the camshaft gear, gear retaining bolt or timing belt to rotate crankshaft.**

23. Check that timing marks on camshaft gear and back cover are aligned.

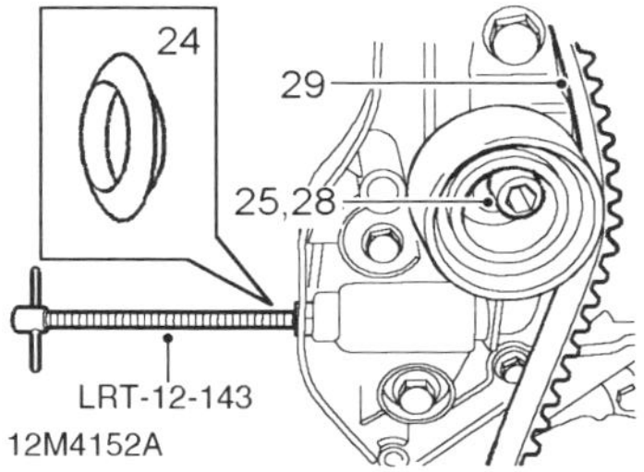

12M4152A

24. Remove timing belt tensioner access plug from belt cover.
25. Loosen Allen bolt securing belt tensioner pulley.
26. Fit **LRT-12-143** to tensioner.
27. Pull back camshaft timing belt tensioner plunger using **LRT-12-143.**
28. Tighten Allen bolt securing belt tensioner pulley.
29. Remove timing belt.

CAUTION: Ease timing belt from gears using fingers only. Metal levers may damage the belt and gears. Do not rotate crankshaft or camshaft with timing belt removed and cylinder head fitted. Timing belts must be stored and handled with care. Store a belt on its edge with a radius greater than 50 mm. Do not use a belt which has been twisted or bent double as this can fracture reinforcing fibres. Do not use an oil or coolant contaminated belt. Cause of contamination must be rectified. Although the belt has a service life of 84,000 miles, (135,000 km) an existing belt should only be refitted if it has completed less than 42,000 miles (65,000 km).

Refit

1. Clean timing belt gears and pulleys.

CAUTION: If the sintered gears have been subjected to prolonged oil contamination, they must be soaked in a solvent bath and thoroughly clean and dry before re-use. The cause of oil contamination must be rectified.

2. Ensure timing marks on camshaft gear and back cover are aligned.
3. Using fingers only, fit timing belt to gears. Ensure the belt run between the crankshaft gear and camshaft gear is kept taut during the fitting procedure.

CAUTION: If the original belt is to be refitted, ensure the direction of rotation is correct.

4. Clean engine mounting bracket plate.
5. Fit engine mounting plate.
6. Fit 4 nuts and 2 bolts, tighten to:
   Nuts 35 Nm
   Bolts 45 Nm

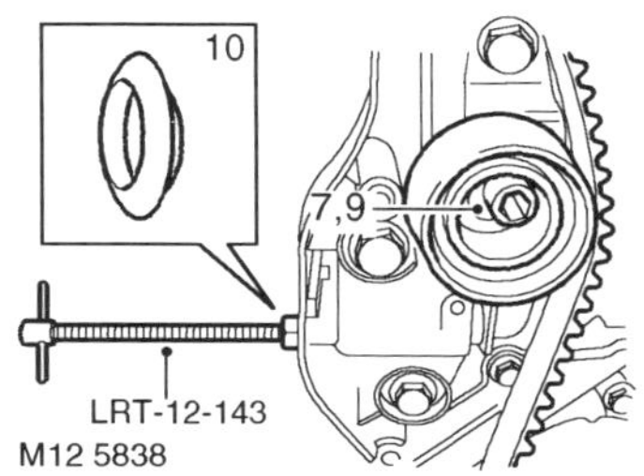

M12 5838

7. Loosen tensioner pulley Allen bolt until tensioner moves easily without tipping.
8. Release timing belt tensioner plunger using tool **LRT-12-143.**
9. Remove tool **LRT-12-143** from camshaft timing belt tensioner and tighten Allen bolt to 55 Nm.

CAUTION: Do not exceed the specified torque figure.

10. Fit belt tensioner access plug to back cover.
11. Remove Allen bolt access plug from timing gear lower cover.
12. Fit camshaft timing gear lower cover. ***See this section.***

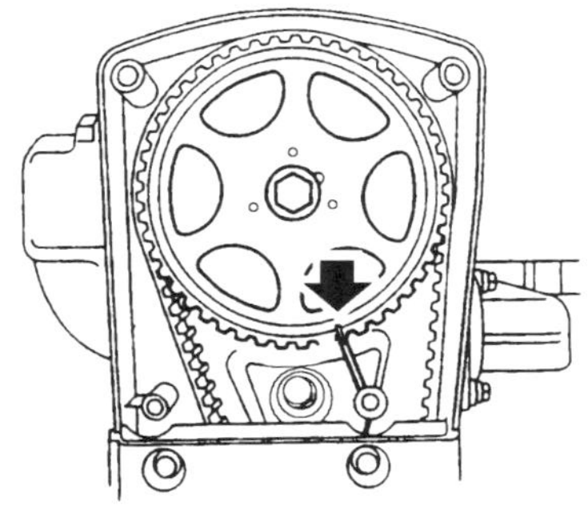

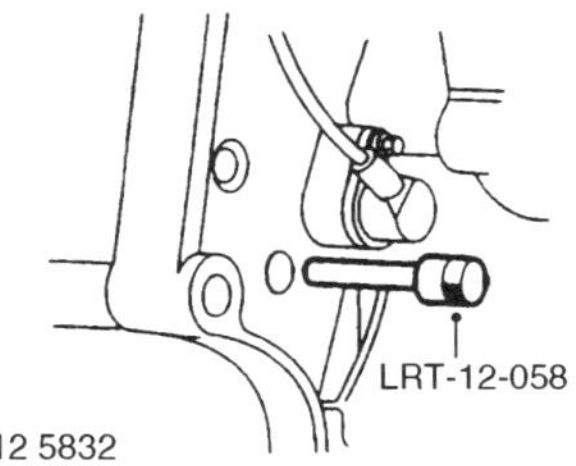

M12 5832

13. Remove timing pin **LRT-12-058** and using a socket and extension bar on crankshaft pulley bolt, rotate crankshaft 2 revolutions clockwise until timing pin **LRT-12-058** can be inserted in hole in flywheel.
14. Check camshaft gear timing mark is aligned with mark on back cover.

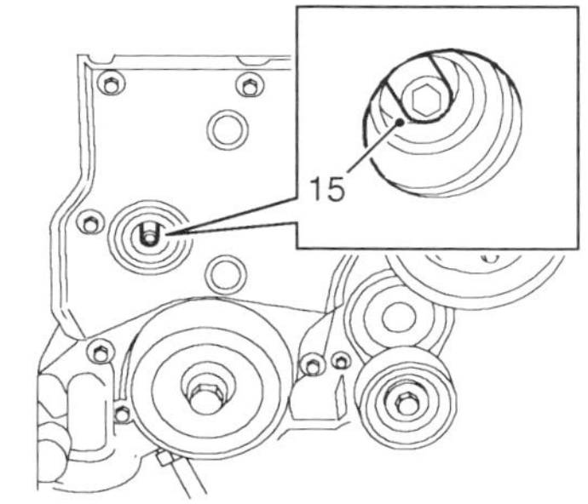

M12 5305

15. Loosen Allen bolt securing tensioner pulley, allow pulley to react then tighten Allen bolt to 55 Nm. Fit Allen bolt access plug.
16. Remove FIP timing belt cover. ***See this section.***

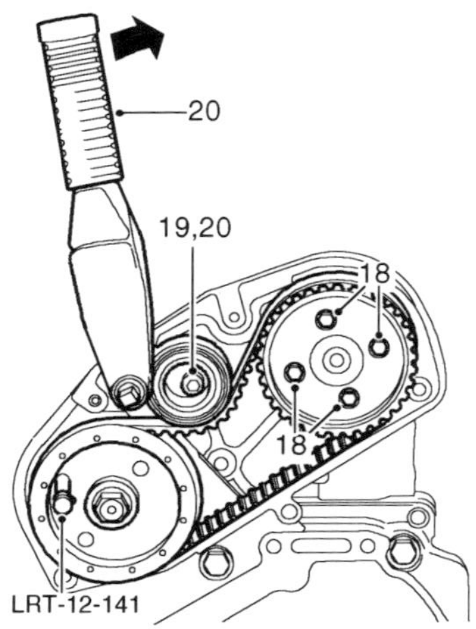

M12 5839

17. Insert locking pin **LRT-12-141** through hole in FIP drive gear and into hole in adapter plate. Locking pin must be a sliding fit. If pin is a tight fit, proceed as follows.
18. Loosen 4 bolts securing FIP timing belt drive gear to hub.
19. Loosen timing belt tensioner pulley Allen bolt.
20. Using a torque wrench fitted to tensioner pulley backplate, apply a **clockwise** (viewed from rear of engine) torque loading of 6 Nm to drive belt. Maintain loading and tighten tensioner pulley Allen bolt to 44 Nm.

CAUTION: Do not exceed the specified torque figure.

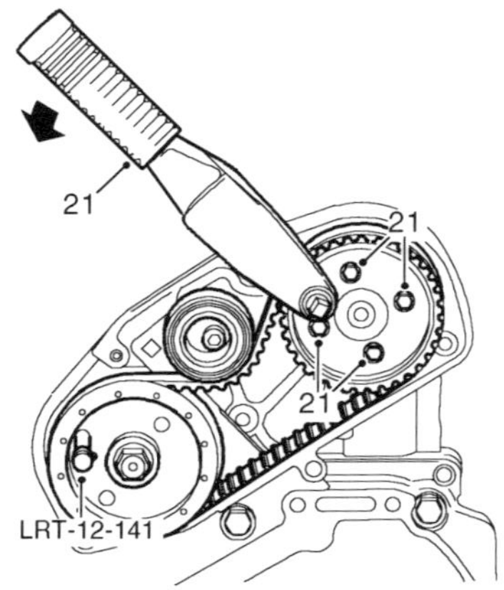

M12 5840

21. Fit torque wrench to square hole in FIP timing belt drive gear as shown and apply an **anti-clockwise** (viewed from rear of engine) torque loading of 25 Nm . Maintain loading and tighten 4 bolts securing gear to 25 Nm.
22. Remove locking pin **LRT-12-141** and timing pin **LRT-12-058.**

ENGINE - 'L' SERIES

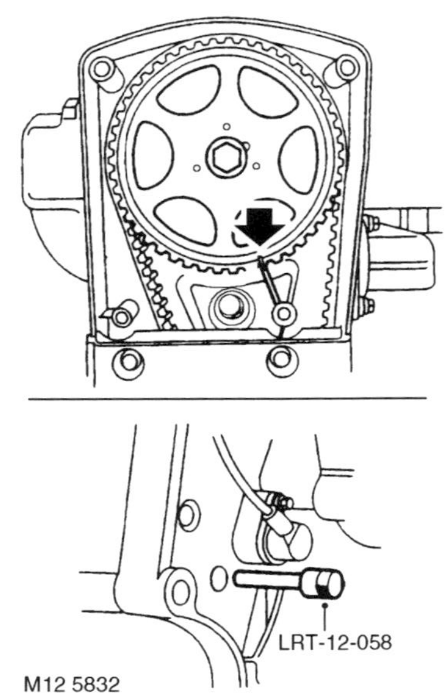

M12 5832

23. Rotate crankshaft 2 revolutions clockwise and fit timing pin **LRT-12-058.**

CAUTION: Ensure pin is fully inserted in hole in flywheel.

24. Check that camshaft gear timing mark is aligned with mark on back cover.

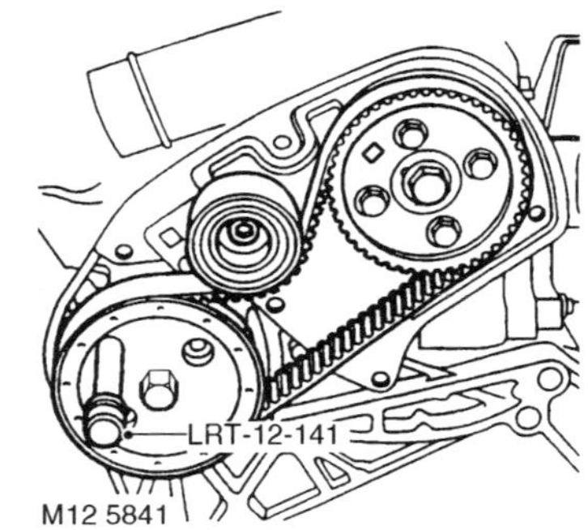

M12 5841

25. Insert locking pin **LRT-12-141** through hole in FIP drive gear and into hole in adapter plate.

CAUTION: To ensure FIP timing is correct, pin must be a sliding fit. If pin is a tight fit, adjustment procedure must be repeated.

26. On completion, remove timing pin **LRT-12-058** and locking pin **LRT-12-141.**
27. Fit FIP timing belt cover. ***See this section.***
28. Clean camshaft gear damper.
29. Fit camshaft gear damper with timing groove in damper aligned with groove in gear.
30. Fit NEW Torx screws and tighten to 10 Nm.
31. Fit timing gear upper cover. ***See this section.***
32. Centralise engine in engine bay.
33. Fit LH engine mounting bracket to body and tighten bolts to 45 Nm.
34. Fit mounting strut to starter motor and tighten bolt to 80 Nm.
35. Fit LH engine mounting. ***See this section.***
36. Align tie bar to bracket on sump.
37. Fit bolts securing tie bar to bracket on sump and subframe and tighten both bolts to 80 Nm.
38. Release lifting chains and remove hooks from lifting eyes on engine.

Models fitted with air conditioning

39. Fit compressor to water pump housing and tighten bolts to 45 Nm.
40. Connect multiplug to compressor.

All models

41. Fit both front drive shafts. ***See DRIVE SHAFTS, Repairs.***

COVER - TIMING GEAR - UPPER

Service repair no - 12.65.41

Remove

1. Remove engine acoustic cover. ***See ENGINE, Repairs.***
2. Remove underbelly panel. ***See BODY, Exterior fittings.***

Models with air conditioning.

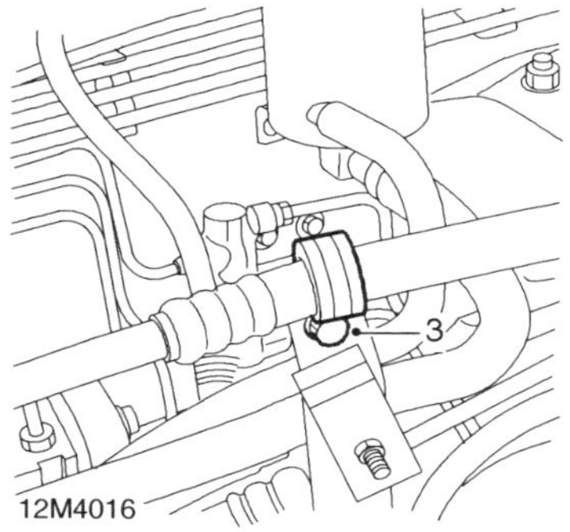

12M4016

3. Remove bolt securing air conditioning hose clip to PAS hose support bracket.

All models

4. Use a jack to support engine under sump.

⚠ **CAUTION: Use a block of wood on jack to protect the sump.**

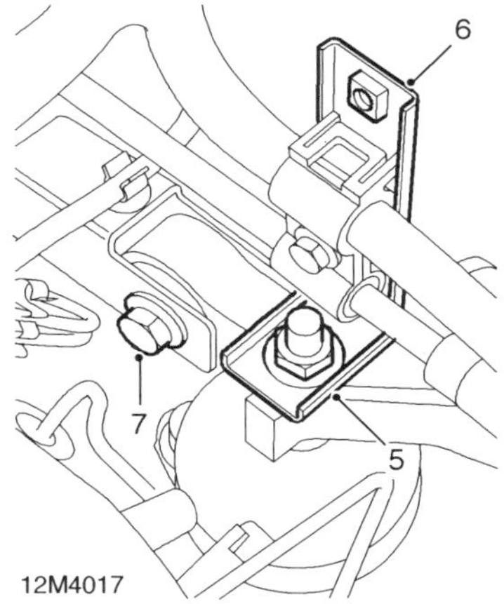

12M4017

5. Remove nut securing PAS hose support bracket to RH engine mounting stud.
6. Release PAS hose bracket from mounting stud.
7. Remove bolt securing engine upper tie bar to RH engine mounting bracket.

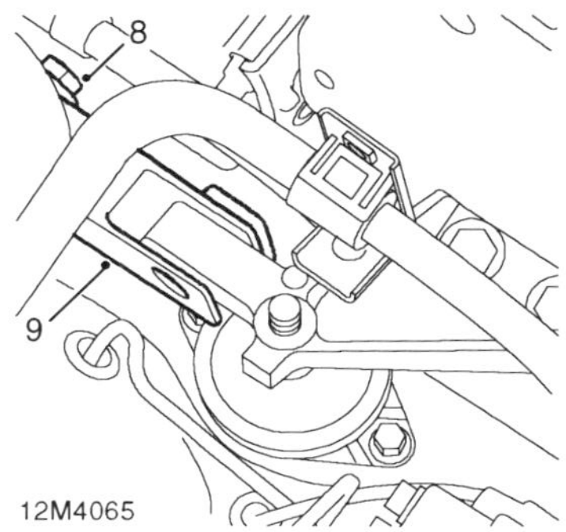

12M4065

8. Slacken bolt securing engine upper tie bar to bracket on body.
9. Raise upper tie bar to clear RH engine mounting bracket.

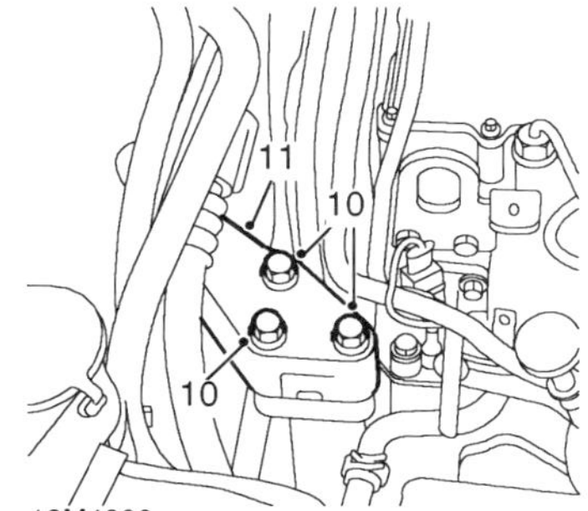

12M4066

10. Remove 3 bolts securing RH engine mounting bracket to engine.
11. Remove RH engine mounting bracket.

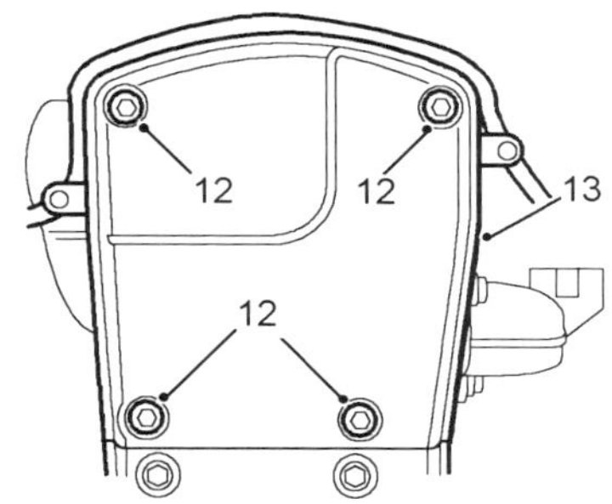

12M4067

12. Remove 4 bolts securing timing gear upper cover.
13. Remove timing gear upper cover.

Refit

1. Fit timing gear upper cover fit bolts and tighten to 5 Nm.
2. Fit engine mounting bracket and tighten bolts securing bracket to engine to 120 Nm.
3. Fit upper tie bar to engine mounting bracket and tighten both bolts securing tie bar to 80 Nm.
4. Remove jack from under engine.
5. Fit PAS hose bracket to engine mounting stud and tighten nut to 80 Nm.

Models with air conditioning

6. Fit air conditioning hose clip to PAS hose support bracket and secure with bolt.

All models

7. Fit underbelly panel. ***See BODY, Exterior fittings.***
8. Fit engine acoustic cover. ***See ENGINE, Repairs.***

COVER - TIMING GEAR - LOWER

Service repair no - 12.65.43

Remove

1. Remove crankshaft pulley. ***See this section.***
2. Remove camshaft timing gear upper cover. ***See this section.***

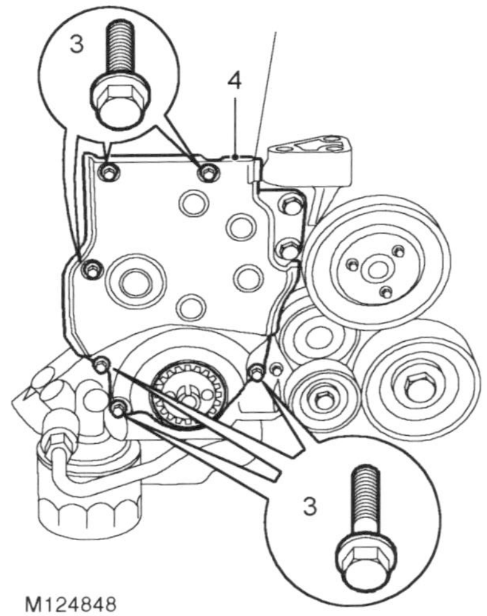

M124848

3. Remove 6 bolts securing lower cover.
4. Remove lower cover.

Refit

1. Fit lower cover to engine and tighten bolts to 5 Nm.
2. Fit timing gear upper cover. ***See this section.***
3. Fit crankshaft pulley. ***See this section.***

FIP TIMING BELT COVER

Service repair no - 12.65.53

Remove

1. Remove engine acoustic cover. ***See this section.***
2. Remove air cleaner. ***See ENGINE MANAGEMENT SYSTEM - EDC, Repairs.***

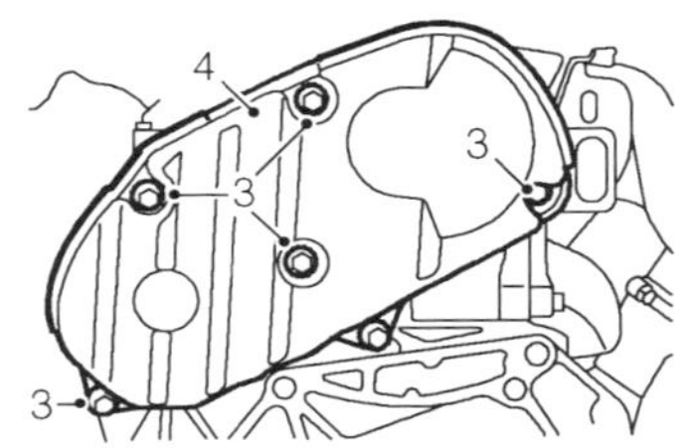

12M1745

3. Remove 6 bolts securing FIP timing belt cover to back plate.
4. Remove timing belt cover.

Refit

1. Fit FIP timing belt cover, fit bolts and tighten to 5 Nm.
2. Fit air cleaner. ***See ENGINE MANAGEMENT SYSTEM - EDC, Repairs.***
3. Fit engine acoustic cover. ***See this section.***

BELT - TIMING - FUEL INJECTION PUMP (FIP)

Service repair no - 12.65.51

Remove

1. Remove FIP timing belt cover. ***See this section.***
2. Remove camshaft timing gear upper cover. ***See this section.***

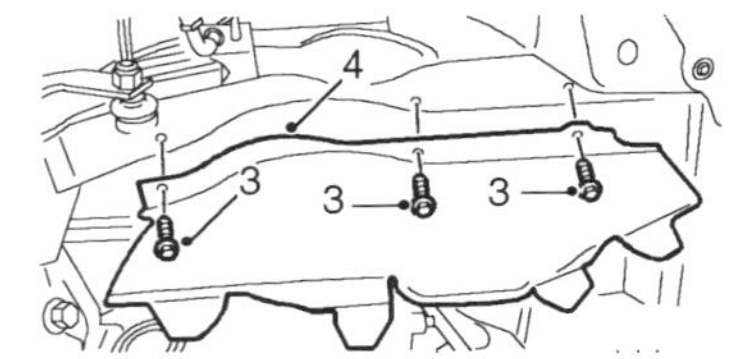

12M4049

3. Remove 3 bolts securing RH splash shield.
4. Remove splash shield.

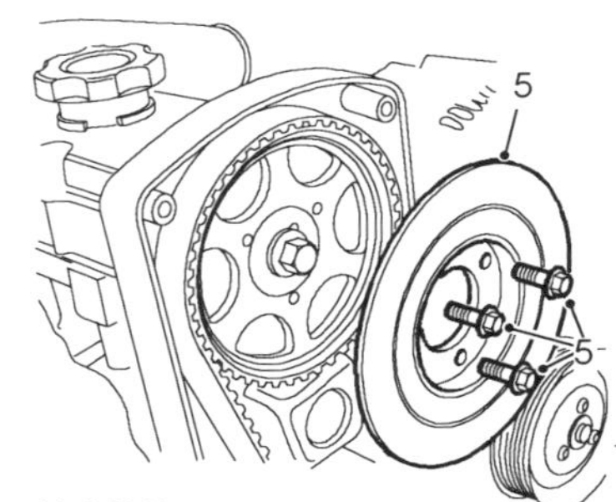

M12 5842

5. Remove and discard 3 Torx screws securing damper to camshaft gear, remove damper.

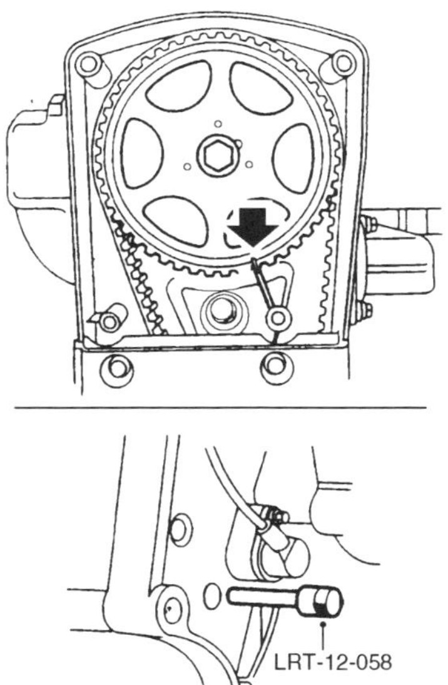

M12 5832

6. Insert timing pin **LRT-12-058** through hole in gearbox mounting plate, hold pin in contact with flywheel and using assistance, rotate crankshaft clockwise until timing pin can be felt to enter hole in flywheel.

CAUTION: Never use the camshaft gear, gear retaining bolt or timing belt to rotate crankshaft.

7. Check that timing marks on camshaft gear and back cover are aligned.

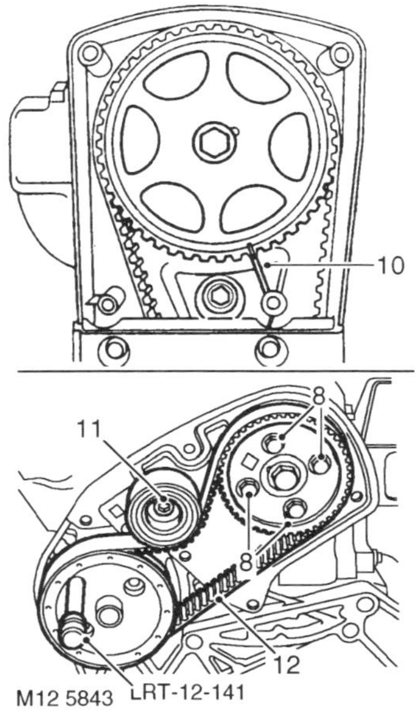

M12 5843

8. Restrain camshaft gear using tool **LRT-12-132** and loosen but do not remove 4 bolts securing FIP timing belt drive gear to hub.
9. Fit locking pin **LRT-12-141** through FIP drive gear and into hole in adapter plate.

CAUTION: Locking pin must be a sliding fit, if pin is tight, rotate pump drive gear slightly using a socket on pump drive gear nut until pin can be inserted correctly.

10. Check that timing marks on camshaft gear and back cover are still aligned.

CAUTION: If drive belt is to be refitted, mark direction of rotation on belt.

11. Loosen Allen bolt securing tensioner pulley, move tensioner away from belt and tighten Allen bolt.

12. Remove FIP timing belt.

CAUTION: Do not rotate camshaft or FIP with timing belt removed.
Ease timing belt from gears using the fingers only, metal levers may damage the belt and gears. Store a belt on its edge with a radius greater than 50 mm. DO NOT use a belt which has been twisted or bent double as this can fracture the reinforcing fibres. Do not use an oil or water contaminated belt. Cause of contamination must be rectified.
Although the belt has a service life of 84,000 miles (135,000 Km), an existing belt should only be refitted if it has completed less than 42,000 miles (65,000 Km).

Refit

1. Clean timing belt gears.

CAUTION: If the sintered gears have been subjected to prolonged oil contamination, they must be soaked in a solvent bath and thoroughly clean and dry before re-use. The cause of oil contamination must be rectified.

2. Leave the 4 bolts securing the FIP belt drive gear to hub just loose enough for the gear to rotate within slots without tipping.
3. Fit timing belt using fingers only rotating the FIP drive gear fully clockwise within the slots and then anti-clockwise until the belt locates in the gear teeth. Fitting the belt in the other possible position will not allow for correct belt adjustment.

CAUTION: If the original belt is to be refitted, ensure direction of rotation is correct.

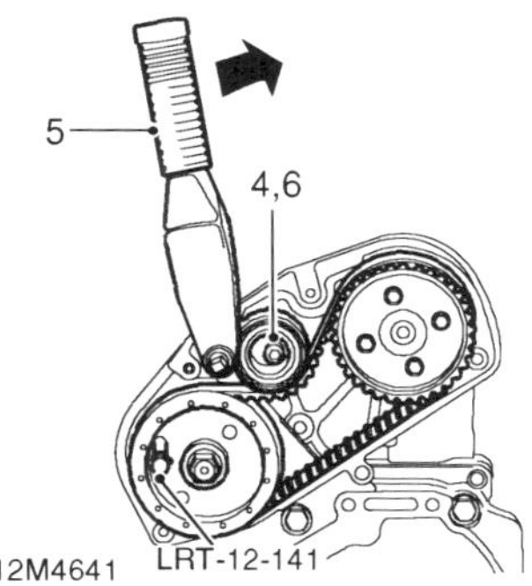

12M4641

4. Loosen tensioner pulley Allen bolt.
5. Using a torque wrench fitted to the tensioner pulley backplate, apply a **clockwise,** as viewed from rear of engine, torque loading of 6 Nm to drive belt.
6. Maintain loading and tighten tensioner pulley Allen bolt to 44 Nm.

CAUTION: Do not exceed the specified torque figure.

7. Remove locking pin **LRT-12-141** and timing pin **LRT-12-058.**

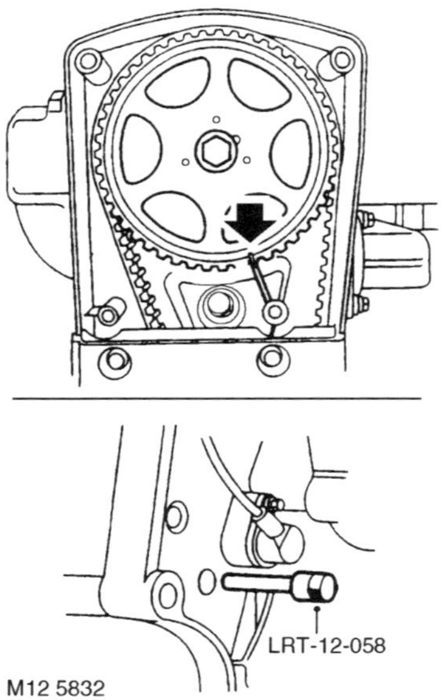

M12 5832

8. Rotate crankshaft clockwise 2 complete revolutions, fit timing pin **LRT-12-058** and check that camshaft gear timing mark is aligned with mark on back cover.

CAUTION: Ensure timing pin is fully inserted into hole in flywheel.

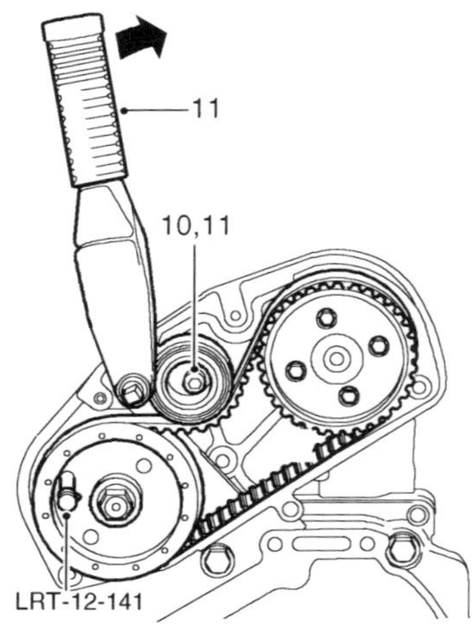

M12 5844

9. Insert locking pin **LRT-12-141** through FIP drive gear and into hole in adapter plate.

NOTE: Locking pin may be a tight fit at this syage.

10. Loosen timing belt tensioner Allen bolt.
11. Using a torque wrench fitted to tensioner pulley backplate, apply a **clockwise,** (as viewed from rear of engine) torque loading of 6 Nm to drive belt. Maintain loading and tighten tensioner Allen bolt to 44 Nm.

CAUTION: Do not exceed the specified torque figure.

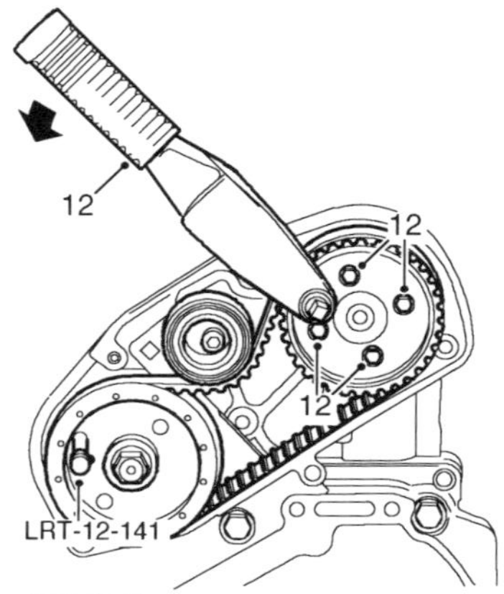

M12 5845

12. Fit torque wrench to square hole in FIP timing belt drive gear as shown and apply an **anti-clockwise** (as viewed from rear of engine) torque loading of 25 Nm. Maintain loading and tighten 4 bolts securing gear to 25 Nm.
13. Remove FIP gear locking pin **LRT-12-141** and timing pin **LRT-12-058.**

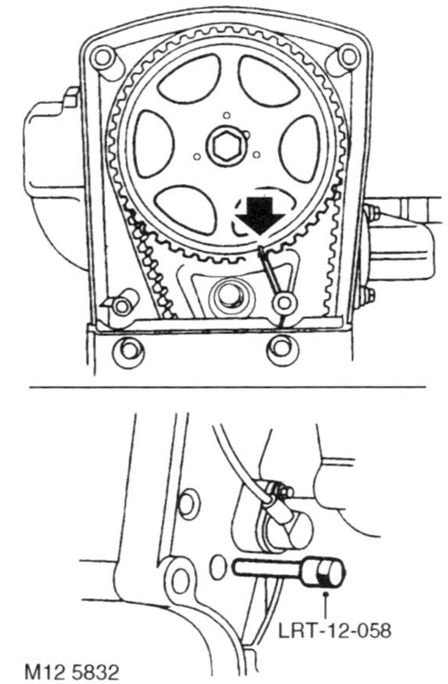

M12 5832

14. Rotate crankshaft clockwise 2 complete revolutions and fit timing pin **LRT-12-058.**

CAUTION: Ensure pin is fully inserted in hole in flywheel.

15. Check that camshaft gear timing mark is aligned with mark on back cover.
16. Insert locking pin **LRT-12-141** through FIP drive gear and into hole in adapter plate.

CAUTION: To ensure FIP timing is correct, locking pin must be a sliding fit. If pin is a tight fit, adjustment procedure must be repeated.

17. On completion, remove timing pin **LRT-12-058** and locking pin **LRT-12-141.**
18. Fit FIP timing belt cover. ***See this section.***
19. Fit damper to camshaft groove and align groove with gear. Secure damper with new Torx screws and tighten to 10 Nm.
20. Fit camshaft timing gear upper cover. ***See this section.***
21. Fit RH splash shield and tighten bolts to 10 Nm.

CONTENTS

TYPES OF EMISSION

Vehicles powered by internal combustion engines produce by-products in the form of emissions which are harmful to the environment. The main by-products are:

- **Carbon Monoxide (CO)** - a colourless, odourless gas which is formed when fuel is burnt in the combustion process and is a result of incomplete combustion.

WARNING: Carbon monoxide is dangerous to inhale and is potentially lethal. Concentrations are particularly high when a vehicle is running at idle speed; it is therefore important to use exhaust extraction equipment when running a vehicle in a workshop or other confined space.

Spark-ignition engines are particularly responsible for carbon monoxide emissions; an air/fuel mixture which is rich in fuel produces an excessive concentration of CO. It is important that vehicles with petrol engines are correctly tuned and maintained to provide the optimum air/fuel mixture and so ensure that carbon monoxide emissions are minimised.

Diesel engines are lean running, so tend to produce less CO emissions than equivalent petrol engines. However, if there is not enough excess air in the combustion chamber, increased emissions of carbon monoxide will result, as well as higher concentrations of soot and hydrocarbons (HC).

- **Hydrocarbons (HC)** - present in exhaust gases and like carbon monoxide, are a result of unburnt fuel during combustion. HC concentrations increase as the air/fuel mixture becomes rich and also increase if a misfire occurs.

- **Carbon Dioxide (CO_2)** - is a by-product of complete combustion and contributes to the "greenhouse effect". Carbon Dioxide is produced even under perfect combustion conditions.

- **Oxides of Nitrogen (NO_x)** - includes Nitric Oxide (NO) and Nitrogen Dioxide (NO_2) and is produced in exhaust gases. Lean mixtures produce more oxides of nitrogen than rich mixtures as the combustion temperature is increased. Oxides of Nitrogen together with Sulphur Dioxide SO_2 contribute to the formation of "acid rain".

EMISSION CONTROL SYSTEMS

In order to minimise emissions of harmful by-products, emission control systems are fitted to Freelander which are designed to keep the emissions within legal limits pertaining at the time of manufacture.

Despite the utilisation of specialised emission control equipment, it is still essential that the engine is correctly maintained and is in good mechanical order so that it operates at its optimal condition. In particular, ignition timing has an effect on the production of HC and NO_2 emissions, with the emissions rising as the ignition timing is advanced.

CAUTION: In many countries it is against the law for a vehicle owner or an unauthorised repair shop to modify or tamper with emission control equipment. In this event the vehicle owner and/or the repairer may be liable for prosecution. Three main types of control system are used to reduce harmful emissions released into the atmosphere from the vehicle. These are:

1. Crankcase emission control - also known as blow-by gas emissions from the engine crankcase.
2. Exhaust emission control - to limit the undesirable by-products of combustion.
3. Fuel vapour evaporative loss control - to restrict the emission of fuel through evaporation from the fuel system.

Crankcase emission control system - 'K' series

The concentration of hydrocarbons in the crankcase of an engine is much greater than that in the vehicle's exhaust system. In order to reduce the emission of these hydrocarbons, crankcase emission-control systems are a standard legal requirement.

The crankcase emission control system is designed to allow the engine crankcase to breathe, but prevent blow-by gas containing HC and CO pollutants from escaping to the atmosphere.

The K-series engine uses a positive crankcase ventilation system to vent the gases from the crankcase to the intake system. Gases from the crankcase are drawn into throttle housing to be burnt in the combustion chambers with the fuel mixture. The system provides effective emission control while the engine is running under all circumstances.

The camshaft cover has two apertures to faciltate engine breathing. The larger orifice is connected upstream of the throttle disc in the throttle housing via a plastic pipe with rubber hose elbows which connect to ports at the camshaft cover and throttle housing. The smaller orifice is connected to a port further downstream in the air intake line via a short rubber hose to the inlet manifold housing. A gauze oil separator is included in the camshaft cover to prevent oil mist being drawn into the engine.

When the engine is running at idle speed, the throttle disc is closed and manifold depression in the inlet manifold side of the disc causes crankcase gases to be drawn through the oil separator and small orifice in the camshaft cover. Clean air enters the crankcase through the large orifice in the camshaft cover, which then mixes with the crankcase gas before it is drawn into the engine via the inlet manifold to be burnt in the combustion chambers with the fuel mixture. This ensures unburnt and partially burnt fuel is returned for combustion and so prevents harmful crankcase gases escaping to the atmosphere.

When the engine is running with the throttle disc wide open, pressure at either side of the disc is equalized and both pipes are subjected to the same manifold depression. In this condition, most of the crankcase gases are drawn through the large orifice in the camshaft cover to be mixed with clean air at the throttle housing before being drawn into the engine for combustion.

In between the fully open and fully closed conditions of the throttle disc, the difference in manifold depression at either side of the throttle housing determines the direction of flow of ventilation through the crankcase.

Crankcase emission control system - 'L'Series

A positive crankcase ventilation system is used to vent crankcase gases to the air induction system. Gases from the crankcase are drawn into the inlet manifold to be burnt in the combustion chambers with the fresh air/fuel mixture. The system provides effective emission control while the engine is running under all circumstances.

Crankcase gases are drawn from the camshaft cover into the turbocharger intake via a depression limiting valve (crankcase pressure limiting valve). The valve closes progressively as engine speed increases, so limiting the maximum depression in the crankcase.

NOTE: Injection timing is extremely important with regards the effects on emissions. The 2.0 L-series engine injection timing is electronically controlled (*Refer to the Engine Management - EDC section of this manual for further information*).

NOTE: The Freelander 2.0 L-series engine incorporates an intercooled turbo-charger. Cooling the intake air increases the density of the oxygen mass per unit volume that is available for combustion, and so improves the engine combustion performance. In addition, the lower combustion temperature helps to inhibit the formation of oxides of Nitrogen (NO_x).

CAUTION: The depression limiting valve taking crankcase fumes to the intake of the turbo-charger must be fitted in the correct orientation.

Exhaust emission control - 'K' Series

The engine management system provides accurately metered quantities of fuel to the combustion chambers to ensure the most efficient air to fuel ratio under all conditions of operation. A further improvement to combustion is made by measuring the oxygen content of the exhaust gases to enable the quantity of fuel injected to be varied, maintaining the optimal ratio necessary for efficient gas conversion by the catalytic converter.

The correct operation of the catalytic converter is dependent upon closed-loop control of the oxygen concentration in the exhaust gas entering the converter. The quantity of oxygen in the exhaust gas is determined by a heated oxygen sensor situated in the exhaust front pipe. The heated oxygen sensor provides the Engine Control Module (ECM) with a signal proportional to the oxygen content. The ECM can then determine whether any adjustment is required to the amount of fuel being injected to achieve the correct exhaust gas content, and implement the required changes.

Catalytic Converter (CAT) 'K' Series

The CAT is mounted between the front pipe and the intermediate pipe assemblies. A flange is welded to each end with three captive bolts in each flange. The CAT is connected to the mating flanges of the front and centre silencer assemblies and secured with three nuts on each flange. A metal gasket seals each flanged joint.

The CAT is fabricated from stainless steel and welded fully at all it's joints. The catalyst element comprises of a ceramic element which is formed into a honeycomb of small squares. The ceramic element is coated with a special surface treatment called 'washcoat'. The washcoat increases the surface area of the catalyst element by approximately 7000 times. A coating is applied to the washcoat which contains the precious metals Platinum, Rhodium and Palladium.

The metallic coating of platinum and palladium oxidize the carbon monoxide and hydrocarbons and convert them into water (H_2O) and carbon dioxide (CO_2). The coating of rhodium removes the oxygen from nitrogen oxide and converts it into nitrogen. The efficient operation of the CAT is highly dependant on the content of oxygen in the exhaust gases which is controlled by the ECM in response to signals from the heated oxygen sensor.

NOTE: Refer to the Engine Management - MEMS section for a desciption of the heated oxygen sensor.

CAUTION: The catalytic converter will be irreparably damaged if leaded fuel is used. Leaks in the exhaust system will also damage the catalyst by drawing oxygen into the exhaust system which causes the catalyst to overheat.
Engine misfires can cause overheating of the catalyst which may lead to overheating and melting the element and partially blocking the exhaust system.
Only use unleaded fuel, the filler neck is designed to accommodate only unleaded fuel pump nozzles.

Exhaust Gas Recirculation (EGR) - 'L' series models

Freelander vehicles fitted with the 2.0 L-series engine utilise an EGR System to reduce NO_x emissions. This is achieved by recirculating exhaust gases back into the combustion process which reduces combustion temperature by delaying the fuel burning rate.

Recirculating too much exhaust gas can result in higher emissions of soot, HC and CO due to insufficient air. Therefore, the precise quantity of recirculated gas is controlled by the Engine Management System - EDC to ensure the optimal operating conditions are maintained.

The exhaust gases pass through an EGR cooler before they are mixed with intake air. The EGR cooler is mounted on the side of the EGR valve which is located on the exhaust manifold. The EGR cooler receives coolant from the cylinder block which then circulates through the cooler to cool the exhaust gases. The cooled gases are drawn from the cooler and mixed in the inlet manifold with the intake air from the intercooler.

NOTE: Refer to the Engine Management System - EDC section for additional descriptions and operations of components and related systems affecting the limitation of emissions (such as the intake air system and fuel injection control).

See ENGINE MANAGEMENT SYSTEM - EDC, Information.

EGR modulator valve

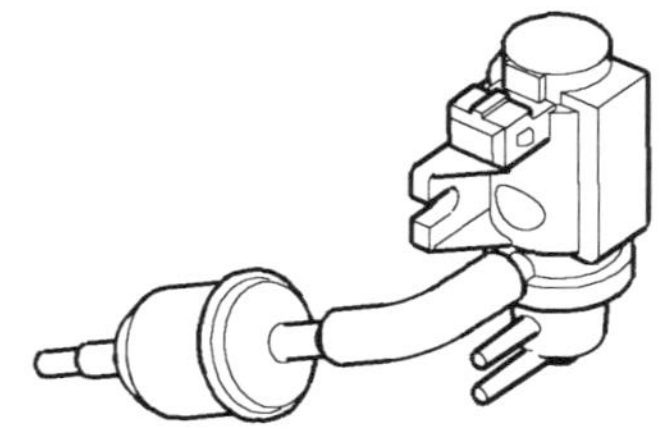

19M2449

The EGR modulator valve is vacuum operated through a solenoid valve, mounted on the bulkhead. When the Engine Control Module (ECM) determines that exhaust gas recirculation should take place, the solenoid valve is modulated and vacuum, supplied by the brake servo vacuum pump, opens the EGR valve. Exhaust gases are then fed through the EGR cooler into the inlet manifold. When EGR is not required the ECM switches the control solenoid to close the EGR valve.

The EGR solenoid valve operates at a frequency of 300 Hz. The signal pressure to the EGR valve from the EGR modulator valve is controlled between the vacuum supplied from the vacuum pump and atmospheric pressure supplied via an air cleaner attached to the EGR modulator valve.

If the EGR modulator valve fails in the stuck open position, a decrease in engine performance, and an increase in visible smoke emissions will be noticed. The effects of a stuck closed modulator valve may not be noticed by the driver.

A MAF sensor is mounted in the air cleaner outlet pipe to sense the volume of air entering the engine. An increase in EGR will cause a corresponding decrease in clean intake air flow, the MAF sensor detects this difference so that the ECM can monitor and control the volume of exhaust gases being recirculated.

Catalytic Converter (CAT) 'L' Series

Hydrocarbon and Carbon Monoxide emissions are reduced through the use of a catalytic converter in the exhaust system where pollutants are burned using the oxygen contained in the exhaust gas.

The CAT is mounted between the downpipe and the intermediate pipe. A flange is welded to each end with three captive bolts in each flange. The CAT is connected to the mating flanges of the downpipe and intermediate pipe and secured with three nuts on each flange. A metal gasket seals each flanged joint.

The CAT is fabricated from stainless steel and welded fully at all it's joints. The catalyst element comprises a ceramic matrix formed into a honeycomb of small squares. The matrix is coated with a special surface treatment called 'washcoat'. The washcoat increases the surface area of the catalyst element by approximately 7000 times. A coating is applied to the washcoat which contains the precious metal Platinum.

The metallic coating of platinum oxidizes the carbon monoxide and hydrocarbons and converts them into water (H_2O) and carbon dioxide (CO_2).

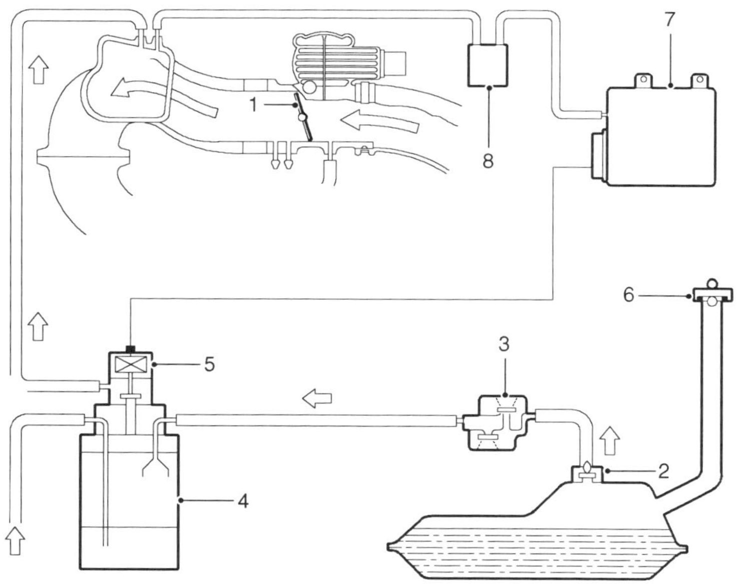

17M0138

Evaporative emission control - 'K' series

1. Throttle disc
2. Fuel cut-off valve
3. Two way valve
4. Evaporative emission canister
5. Evaporative emission canister purge valve
6. Fuel filler cap
7. ECM
8. Fuel trap

The evaporation emission control system is used to reduce the level of hydrocarbons emitted into the atmosphere from the fuel system. The system comprises a carbon canister which stores the hydrocarbons from the fuel tank, pressure valves, vent lines and a purge control solenoid valve.

Fuel vapour generated from within the fuel tank as the fuel heats up is stored in the tank until the pressure exceeds the operating pressure of the two-way valve. When the two way valve opens, the fuel vapour passes along the vent line from the fuel tank (via the fuel tank vapour separator) to the inlet port of the carbon canister.

Fuel vapour is stored in the canister until it is ready to be purged to the inlet manifold under the control of the Engine Control Module (ECM).

As fuel vapour cools, it condenses and is allowed to flow back into the fuel tank from the vent line by way of the two-way valve. A fuel vapour separator is fitted next to the fuel filler neck. This separator allows condensing fuel in the fuel tank to be returned to the tank before it reaches the vent line.

Evaporative emission canister

The evaporative emission canister contains charcoal which absorbs and stores fuel vapour from the fuel tank while the engine is not running. When the canister is not being purged, the fuel vapour remains in the canister and clean air exits the canister via the air inlet port.

When the engine is running, the ECM decides when conditions are correct for vapour to be purged from the canister, and opens the canister purge valve. This connects a manifold vacuum line to the canister and fuel vapour is drawn from the canister's charcoal element to be burned in the engine. Clean air is drawn into the canister through the air inlet port to fill the displaced volume of vapour.

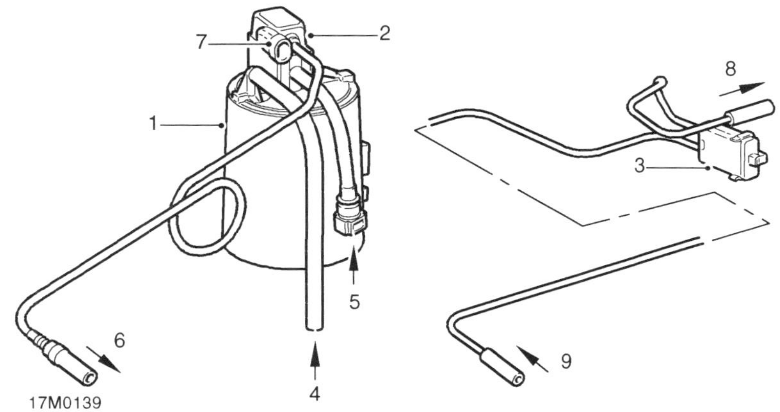

17M0139

1. Carbon canister
2. Purge Control Valve
3. Fuel trap
4. Air inlet port
5. Fuel vapour inlet (from fuel tank)
6. Purge port (from carbon canister to inlet manifold)
7. Harness connector (to ECM)
8. Fuel trap to ECM pipe
9. Inlet manifold to fuel trap pipe

Evaporative emission canister purge valve

The operation of the evaporative emission canister purge valve is controlled by the ECM. The purge valve is located on top of the carbon canister. The valve remains closed below preset coolant and engine speed values to protect engine tune and catalytic converter performance. If the charcoal canister was purged during cold running or at idling speed, the additional enrichment in fuel mixture would delay the catalytic converter light off time and cause erratic idle. When the purge valve is opened, fuel vapour from the charcoal canister is drawn into the throttle housing for combustion.

Fuel Vapour Separator

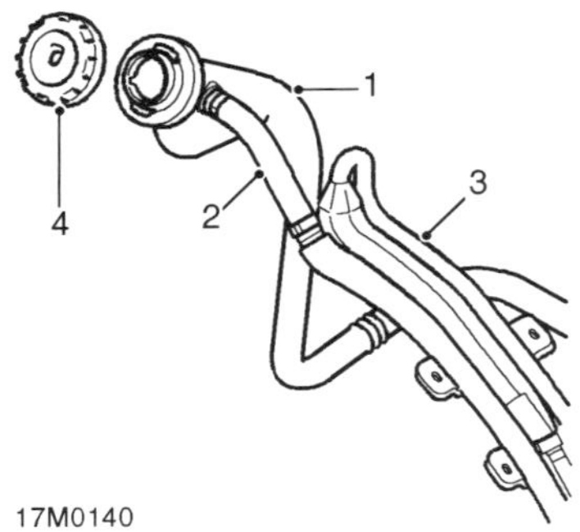

17M0140

1. Fuel filler neck
2. Breather pipe
3. Vapour separator
4. Fuel cap

Fuel vapour evaporating from the fuel tank is routed to the evaporative emission canister through the vapour separator and vent line. Liquid fuel must not be allowed to contaminate the charcoal in the EVAP canister. To prevent this, the vapour separator fitted to the filler neck allows condensed fuel to drain back into the tank.

The fuel vapour separator is located under the rear wheel arch, protected by the wheel arch lining. The connections to the separator unit are quick release devices at the end of flexible hoses which connect the fuel tank to the inlet side of the separator and the outlet of the separator to the evaporation vent line.

Fuel Filler Cap

The fuel tank filler cap incorporates a pressure valve which allows excess pressure to escape (blow-off) at between 10 - 10.8 kPa, (1.50 - 1.57 psi).

Two way Valve

A two way valve is included in the vent line which allows tank pressure to build to 1.80 - 5.03 kPa, (0.26 - 0.73 psi). Above this pressure, vapour is allowed to pass along the vent line to the carbon canister. Vapour is allowed to flow back into the fuel tank as the fuel cools by way of a non return valve within the body of the two way valve.

EVAPORATIVE EMISSION (EVAP) CANISTER - 'K' SERIES

Service repair no - 17.15.13

Remove

1. Disconnect battery earth lead.

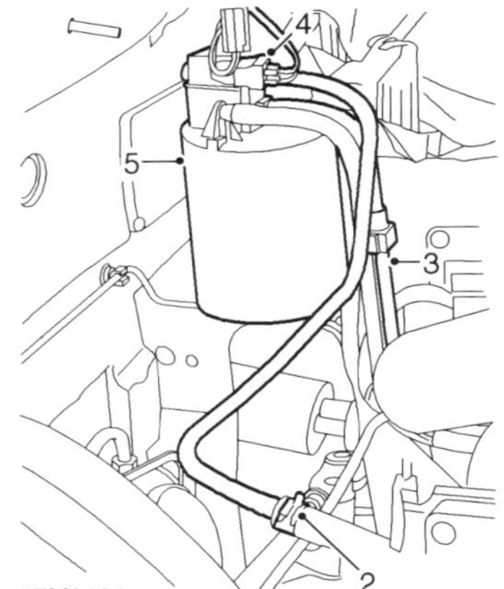

17M0134

2. Release clip and disconnect hose from throttle housing.
3. Disconnect hose from fuel tank vent pipe.
4. Disconnect multiplug from EVAP canister purge valve.
5. Release EVAP canister from mounting bracket.
6. Remove EVAP canister.
   Do not carry out further dismantling if component is removed for access only.

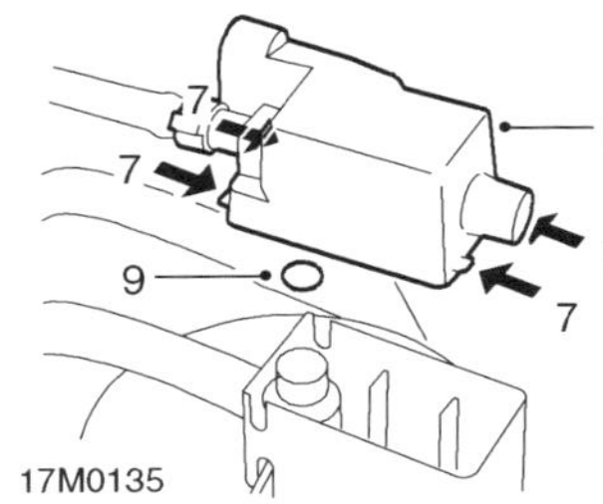

17M0135

7. Release 4 clips securing purge valve to EVAP canister.
8. Remove EVAP canister purge valve.
9. Remove and discard 'O' ring from EVAP canister purge valve.

Refit

1. Clean EVAP canister purge valve and valve seat on EVAP canister.
2. Fit NEW 'O' ring to EVAP canister purge valve.
3. Position purge valve and secure to EVAP canister.
4. Fit EVAP canister to mounting bracket.
5. Connect hose to fuel tank vent pipe.
6. Connect hose to throttle housing and secure with clip.
7. Connect multiplug to EVAP canister purge valve.
8. Connect battery earth lead.

PURGE CONTROL VALVE - EVAPORATIVE EMISSION CANISTER - 'K' SERIES

Service repair no - 17.15.39

Remove

1. Disconnect battery earth lead.

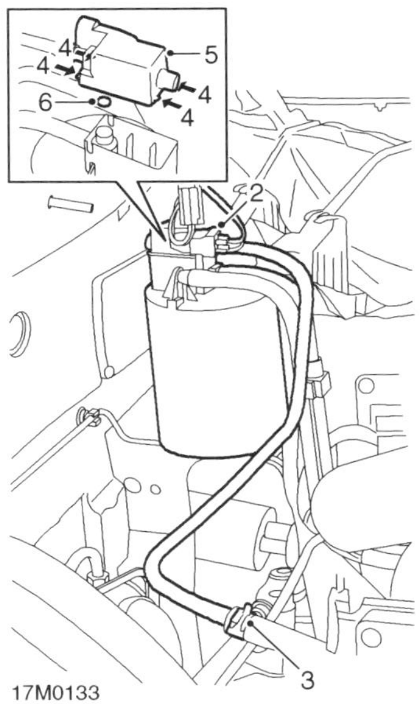

17M0133

2. Disconnect multiplug from EVAP canister purge valve
3. Release clip and disconnect hose from throttle housing.
4. Release 4 clips securing purge valve to EVAP canister.
5. Remove EVAP canister purge valve.
6. Remove and discard 'O' ring from EVAP canister purge valve.

Refit

1. Clean EVAP canister purge valve and valve seat on EVAP canister.
2. Fit NEW 'O' ring to EVAP canister purge valve.
3. Position purge valve and secure to EVAP canister.
4. Connect hose to throttle housing and secure with clip.
5. Connect multiplug to EVAP canister purge valve.
6. Connect battery earth lead.

EXHAUST GAS RECIRCULATION (EGR) VALVE - 'L' SERIES

Service repair no - 17.45.01

Remove

1. Disconnect battery earth lead.
2. Remove engine acoustic cover. *__See ENGINE - 'L' SERIES, Repairs.__*

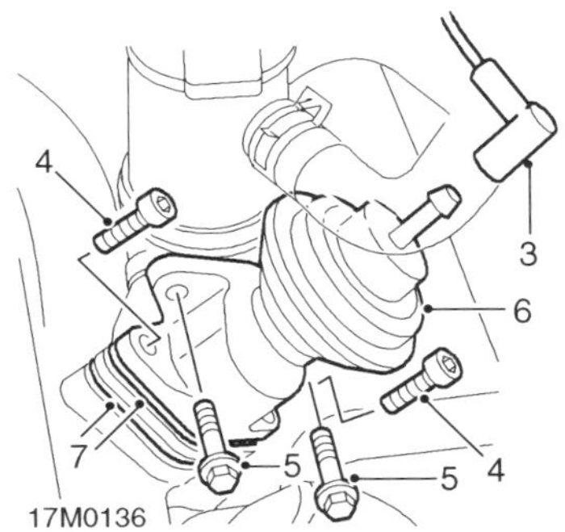

17M0136

3. Disconnect vacuum pipe from EGR valve.
4. Remove 2 Allen screws securing EGR valve to inlet manifold elbow.
5. Remove 2 nuts and bolts securing EGR valve to recirculation pipe.
6. Remove EGR valve.
7. Remove and discard 2 gaskets.

Refit

1. Clean mating faces of EGR valve, inlet manifold elbow and recirculation pipe.
2. Fit NEW gaskets to EGR valve.
3. Align EGR valve to inlet manifold elbow and recirculation pipe.
4. Fit 2 Allen screws securing EGR valve to inlet manifold elbow and tighten to 25 Nm.
5. Fit 2 nuts and bolts to recirculation pipe and tighten to 25 Nm.Connect vacuum pipe from EGR solenoid to EGR valve.
6. Fit engine acoustic cover. *__See ENGINE - 'L' SERIES, Repairs.__*
7. Connect battery earth lead.

SOLENOID VALVE - EGR - 'L' SERIES

Service repair no - 17.45.04

Remove

1. Disconnect battery earth lead.

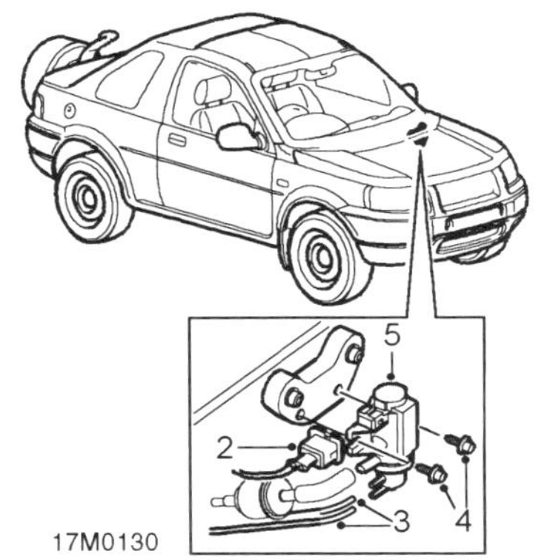

17M0130

2. Disconnect multiplug from EGR solenoid valve.
3. Disconnect 2 vacuum hoses from solenoid valve.
4. Remove 2 screws securing solenoid valve to rubber mounting.
5. Remove EGR solenoid valve.

Refit

1. Position EGR solenoid valve up to rubber mounting, fit and tighten screws.
2. Connect vacuum hoses to EGR solenoid valve.
3. Connect EGR solenoid valve multiplug.
4. Connect battery earth lead.

CATALYTIC CONVERTER

Service repair no - 17.50.01

Remove

1. Raise vehicle on 4 post ramp.

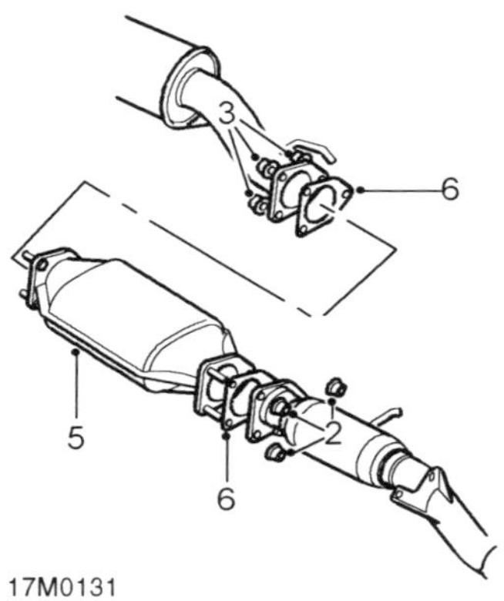

17M0131

2. Remove 3 nuts securing catalytic converter to front pipe.
3. Remove 3 nuts securing catalytic converter to intermediate pipe.
4. Disconnect catalytic converter from intermediate pipe.
5. Remove catalytic converter from front pipe.
6. Remove and discard gaskets.

CAUTION: Catalytic converters are manufactured from ceramic material which is very fragile, avoid heavy impacts on converter casing.

Refit

1. Clean mating faces of catalytic converter, front pipe and intermediate pipe.
2. Fit NEW gasket to each catalytic converter flange.
3. Fit catalytic converter to front pipe and connect to intermediate pipe. Fit nuts and tighten to 34 Nm.
4. Lower vehicle.

CONTENTS

Page

ENGINE MANAGEMENT SYSTEM - MEMS

ENGINE COMPARTMENT COMPONENT LOCATIONS

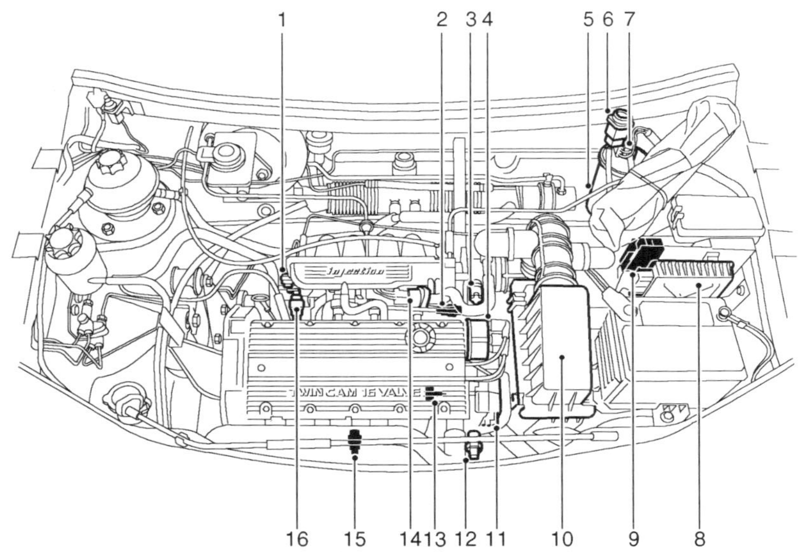

19M2468

1. Fuel pressure accumulator
2. Intake air temperature (IAT) sensor
3. Throttle position (TP) sensor
4. Distributor cap
5. Evaporative (EVAP) emission cannister
6. Inertia fuel shut-off switch
7. Evaporative (EVAP) emission purge valve
8. Engine control module (ECM)
9. Relay module
10. Air cleaner
11. Ignition coil
12. Engine coolant temperature (ECT) sensor
13. Crankshaft position (CKP) sensor
14. Idle air control (IAC) valve
15. Heated oxygen sensor (HO2S)
16. Injectors

PASSENGER COMPARTMENT COMPONENT LOCATIONS

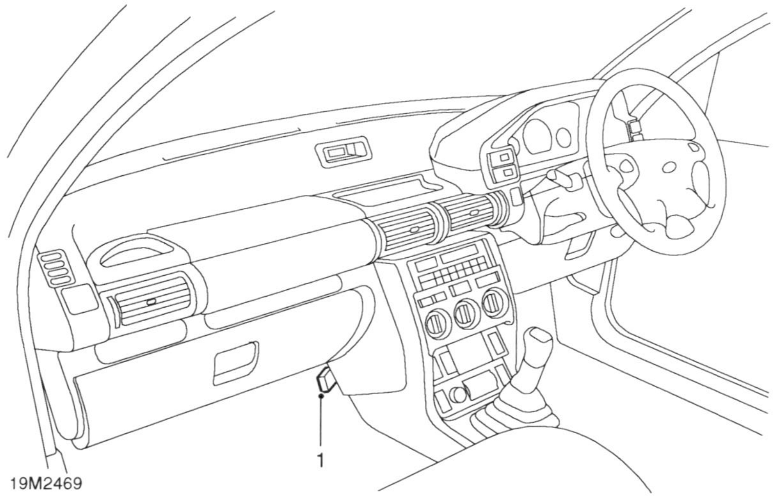

19M2469

1. Diagnostic socket

MODULAR ENGINE MANAGEMENT SYSTEM OPERATION

The Modular Engine Management System (MEMS) is a combined engine management system using a single Engine Control Module to control the multipoint fuel injection, idle speed control and ignition systems.

Electronic Control Module (ECM)

The ECM processes all inputs and outputs related to the operation of the fuel injection and ignition systems. The ECM is located on a mounting plate behind the battery in the engine compartment. The ECM comprises an aluminium cast body with a pressed alloy sealed lid. A socket is positioned on it's side face and receives a multiplug from the engine wiring harness. The socket contains 36 pins, although only the pins corresponding to those in the multiplug are used.

The multiplug is connected to the engine wiring harness to each individual sensor. The multiplug fits into the corresponding socket on the side face of the ECM and is locked in position with a plastic clip. A rubber seal within the body of the multiplug prevents the ingress of moisture. The ECM harness multiplug incorporates plated pins to minimise oxidation and give improved reliability.

The ECM monitors the conditions required for optimum combustion of fuel in the cylinder through sensors located at strategic points around the engine. From these sensor inputs, the engine control module can adjust the fuel quantity and timing of the fuel being delivered to the cylinders.

The main features are as follows:

- A single ECM controls the fuel injection system and the ignition system. The ECM incorporates short circuit protection and can store intermittent faults on certain inputs. TestBook can interrogate the ECM for these stored faults.
- In conjunction with the Throttle Position (TP) sensor, the ECM uses the speed/density method of air flow measurement to calculate fuel delivery. This method measures the crankshaft position/speed, inlet air temperature and inlet manifold pressure and assumes that the engine is a calibrated vacuum pump, with its characteristics stored in the ECM, it can then determine the correct amount of fuel to be injected.
- The ECM contains an integral Manifold Absolute Pressure (MAP) sensor. The MAP sensor reads manifold pressure via a hose connected to the inlet manifold. The manifold pressure is monitored by the ECM, which in turn adjusts the injector pulse width to maintain the correct fuel delivery relative to the air flow ratio. This system removes the need for a fuel pressure regulator and fuel return line on the fuel rail. The device which normally functions as a fuel pressure regulator on other 'K' series applications is now used as an accumulator to damp fuel pump pulses in the fuel rail.
- A separate diagnostic socket, located behind the centre console in the passenger footwell, allows engine diagnostics and tuning to be carried out using TestBook, without disconnecting the ECM harness multiplug.
- The ECM controls the operation of the radiator cooling and air conditioning (if fitted) fans based on signals received from the engine coolant temperature sensor and air conditioning system. If a high engine temperature is detected, the ECM will prevent the air conditioning system from operating.
- If certain system inputs fail, the ECM implements a back-up facility to enable the system to continue functioning, although at a reduced level of performance.

- The ECM also operates the engine immobilisation circuits. When the ignition is switched to position II, a coded signal is sent to the ECM from the Central Control Unit (CCU). If the coded signal does not match the signal programmed into the ECM, the ECM disables the fuel injection function.

NOTE: If an incorrect code is received, but the key is turned very quickly from off to crank, the engine may start for a very short period, then stop. This is quite normal.

- On vehicles fitted with ABS, the ECM provides signal information to the ABS ECU for hill descent control.

The ECM is an adaptive unit which over a period of time learns the load and wear characteristics of the engine it controls. The ECM remembers and updates two main engine requirements when the engine is running at normal operating temperature:

- The position of the idle air control (IAC) valve required to achieve a specified idle speed. This is then used as a reference for IAC valve movement to achieve idle speed under all load conditions.

- The fuelling change or offset required to achieve the correct oxygen sensor signal. This allows the system to provide the correct fuelling without having to apply excessive adjustments to the fuelling which can adversely affect the emissions and driveability.

NOTE: After fitting a different ECM, TestBook will be required to reprogramme the ECM with the code from the CCU and to perform the throttle initialisation procedure.

WARNING: When washing under bonnet, never direct water onto the ECM, as water ingress may occur, resulting in damage to electrical components inside.

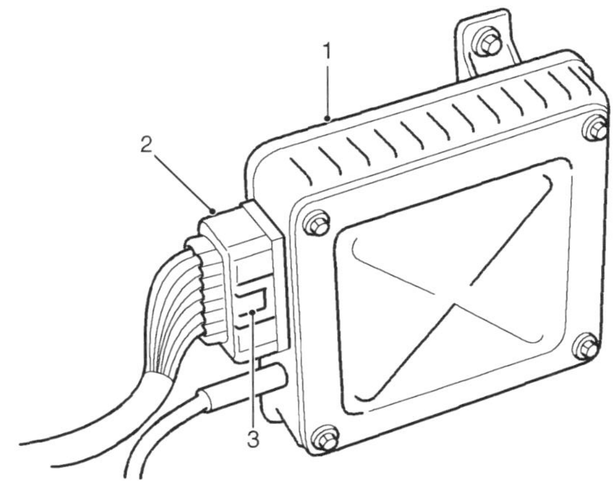

19M2470

1. ECM body
2. Multi plug
3. Locking clip

The ECM inputs and outputs are shown in the following table.

INPUTS		OUTPUTS
Crankshaft position sensor		Ignition coil
Manifold absolute pressure sensor		Injectors
Engine coolant temperature sensor		Idle air control valve
Intake air temperature sensor		Fuel pump relay
Heated oxygen sensor		Diagnostic socket
Throttle position sensor		Heated oxygen sensor relay
Diagnostic input		Main relay
Battery supply (via main relay)		Cooling fan(s) relay(s)
Ignition switch	ECM	A/C clutch relay
Earth supply		(Vehicles with air conditioning only)
A/C request		ABS ECU (Hill Descent Control)
(Vehicles with air conditioning only)		Supply - purge valve and sensors (+5v constant)
Air conditioning fan relay		
Alarm code		
A/C fan request (high pressure)		
Vehicle speed signal from ABS ECU		
(Vehicles with ABS only)		
Vehicle Speed Sensor (VSS)		
(Non ABS vehicles only)		
Request condensor fan (Air conditioning only)		

ECU Harness Pin-out Connections

NOTE: VBATT = Battery Voltage

Pin No.	Function	Voltage	Signal type	State
1	Not Used	-	-	-
2	Stepper drive : Bobbin 2 Phase B	0 - VBATT	Switched	Output
3	Stepper drive : Bobbin 2 Phase A	0 - VBATT	Switched	Output
4	Main Relay Drive	0 - VBATT	Switched	Output
5	Parallel Cooling Fan Relay (Fan 2)	0 - VBATT	Switched	Output
6	Series Cooling Fan Relay (Fan 1)	0 - VBATT	Switched	Output
7	Oxygen Sensor	0 - 1.1V	Analogue	Input
8	Throttle Position Sensor	0 - 5V (Sensor Supply)	Analogue	Input
9	Sensor Supply	5V Nominal	Reference Supply	Output
10	Diagnostic Link K Line	0 - VBATT (ISO9141)	Coded data	Input/ Output
11	Ignition Sense	0 - VBATT	Switched (VBATT = On)	Input
12	Not Used	-	-	-
13	Secutity i/p (From Central Control Unit)	0 - VBATT	Coded Data	Input
14	Not Used	-	-	-
15	A/C Pressure Fan Request i/p	0 - VBATT	Digital (0v = On)	Input
16	Inlet Air Temperature	0 - 5V	Analogue	Input
17	Not Used	-	-	-
18	Oxygen Sensor	0v (nominal)	Analogue	Input

ENGINE MANAGEMENT SYSTEM - MEMS

ECU Harness Pin-out Connections - Continued

NOTE: VBATT = Battery Voltage

Pin No.	Function	Voltage	Signal type	State
19	A/C Clutch Relay	0 - VBATT	Switched (0V = On)	Output
20	Fuel Pump Relay	0 - VBATT	Switched (0v = ON)	Output
21	Purge Valve	0 - VBATT	PWM	Output
22	Stepper Drive : Bobbin 1 Phase A	0 - VBATT	Switched	Output
23	Injectors 2 & 3	0 - VBATT	Switched (0v = ON)	Output
24	Injectors 1 & 4	0 - VBATT	Switched (0v = ON)	Output
25	Ignition Coil Drive	0 - 450v	Switched (0v = coil charge)	Output
26	Hill Descent o/p	0 - VBATT	PWM Data	Output
27	Stepper Drive : Bobbin 1 Phase B	0 - VBATT	Switched	Output
28	Battery Power Supply (via main relay)	VBATT	Power	Input
29	Main ground	0V (nominal)	Power	Ground
30	Sensor Ground	0V Nominal	Reference	Ground
31	Crankshaft Position Sensor +ve	0-100v (peak to peak)	Frequency	Input
32	Crankshaft Position Sensor -ve	0-100v (peak to peak)	Frequency	Input
33	Coolant Temperature Sensor	0 - 5V	Analogue	Input
34	Not Used	-	-	-
35	A/C Request	0 - VBATT	Switched (0v = ON)	Input
36	Oxygen Sensor Heater Relay	0 - VBATT	Switched (0v = ON)	Output

IGNITION SYSTEM

The ECM determines the optimum ignition timing based on the signals it receives from the following sensors:

1. Crankshaft position sensor - Engine speed and crankshaft position
2. Manifold absolute pressure sensor - Engine load
3. Engine coolant temperature sensor - Engine temperature
4. Throttle position sensor - Throttle pedal released
5. Intake Air Temperature sensor - intake air temperature

The engine management system uses no centrifugal or vacuum advance, the timing being controlled by the ECM.

Spark distribution is achieved by means of a rotor arm and distributor mounted at the No.4 cylinder end of the inlet camshaft.

Basic Ignition Timing

Crankshaft Position (CKP) Sensor

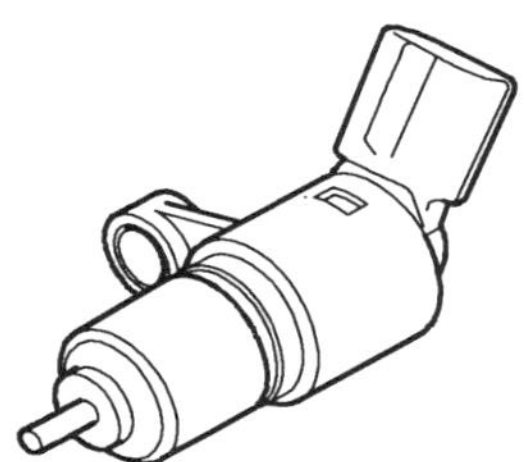

19M2031

The speed and position of the engine is detected by the CKP sensor which is bolted to, and projects through, the engine adapter plate adjacent to the flywheel.

The CKP sensor is an inductive sensor containing a coil and a permanent magnet which provides a magnetic field. The sensor is situated such that an air gap exists between it and the flywheel. Air gap distance is critical for correct operation.

The flywheel incorporates a reluctor ring which consists of 32 poles spaced at 10° intervals, with 4 missing poles at 0°, 50°, 180° and 240°. The missing poles tell the ECM when to operate the injectors. When the flywheel rotates and a pole passes the CKP sensor, it disturbs the magnetic field inducing a voltage pulse in the coil. This pulse is transmitted to the ECM.

By calculating the number of pulses that occur within a given time, the ECM can determine the engine speed. The output from the CKP sensor, when used in conjunction with that from the Manifold Absolute Pressure (MAP) sensor, provides idle stabilisation and reference for injection timing.

If the CKP sensor fails, the engine will stop and cannot be restarted.

Manifold Absolute Pressure (MAP) Sensor

The MAP sensor is located within the ECM and detects manifold pressure via a hose connected to the inlet manifold. A fuel trap is fitted in the hose from the inlet manifold to prevent fuel and oil residues from entering the MAP sensor.

The sensor converts pressure variations into graduated electrical signals which can be read by the ECM. Increases and decreases in the manifold pressure provide the ECM with an accurate representation of the load being placed on the engine, allowing the ECM to adjust the quantity of fuel being injected and the ignition timing to achieve optimum fuelling of the engine.

If the MAP sensor fails, the ECM enters a default mode (called 'Pressure Back-up'), using a substitute value determined from engine speed and throttle position.

Ignition Timing Compensation

Engine Coolant Temperature (ECT) Sensor

The ECT sensor is located in the coolant outlet elbow which is attached at the front of the cylinder head. The sensor is screwed into a threaded port and measures coolant temperature as it leaves the engine via the top hose to the radiator.

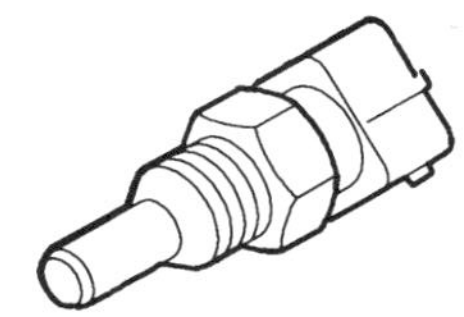

19M0847

The ECT sensor is a 'thermistor' (a temperature dependent resistor) with a Negative Temperature Coefficient, i.e. its resistance reduces as temperature increases. The ECM receives a signal from the ECT sensor which is directly proportional to engine coolant temperature. The ECM uses the information to provide optimum driveability and emissions by advancing or retarding the ignition timing.

If the ECT sensor fails, the ECM enters a default mode using a substitute value of 60.2°C, and activates the cooling fan(s) whilst the engine is running.

Idle Speed Control

With the throttle pedal released and the engine at idle, the ECM uses the fast response of ignition timing to maintain idle stabilisation.

When loads are placed on, or removed from the engine the ECM senses the change in engine speed and in conjunction with adjusting the Idle Air Control (IAC) valve, advances or retards the ignition timing to maintain a specified idle speed. When load is removed from the engine, the IAC returns to its original position and the ignition timing returns to the idle setting.

NOTE: Due to the sensitivity of this system the ignition timing will be constantly changing at idle speed.

Ignition Components

Ignition Coil

The coil for the programmed ignition system is mounted on the cylinder head, adjacent to the distributor cap. The coil is connected to the distributor cap centre connection with a short high tension (ht) lead. The use of a 'dry' ignition coil allows the coil to be mounted on the engine. A two pin plug connects the coil to the engine wiring harness.

The coil has a lower primary winding resistance (0.71 to 0.81 ohms at 20°C) than a coil in a conventional ignition system. This allows the full ht output to be reached faster and so makes the coil operation more consistent throughout the engine speed range. To prevent excessive current draw, and to give a constant energy spark, the ECM constantly varies the ignition coil charge period (dwell period/angle) with engine speed. The faster the engine speed, the larger the dwell period/angle.

If the coil fails, ht output will lost and the engine will stop.

Distributor Cap and Rotor Arm

The distributor cap is located on the left hand end of the cylinder head. A rotor arm is driven directly off the inlet camshaft. The cap is retained on its mounting with two captive bolts.

The cap has five external connections; four for the ht leads to the spark plugs and one to receive the ht lead from the ignition coil. A spring loaded carbon brush is located centrally inside the cap and connects with the rotor arm. The rotor arm is secured by a retaining screw to a 'D' shaped stub shaft, which is press fitted into a vibration absorbing bush in the camshaft. The rotor arm is protected from oil contamination by an anti-flash shield which incorporates an oil drain.

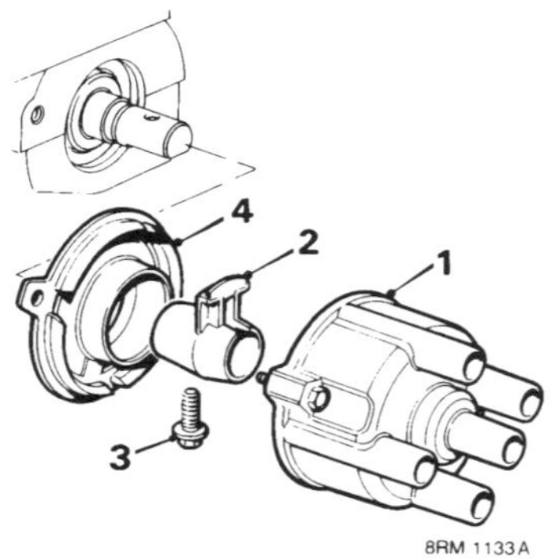

1. Distributor cap
2. Rotor arm
3. Retaining screw
4. Anti-flash shield

Four equally spaced contacts inside the distributor cap provide the electrical path from the coil to the spark plugs. Pulsed current from the coil flows to the rotor arm via the carbon brush and finally to each of the four ht leads in turn as the rotor arm passes each internal contact.

FUEL SYSTEM

Intake Air Temperature (IAT) Sensor

The IAT sensor is located in the side of the inlet tract to the the No. 4 cylinder and can be identified by a green electrical connection.

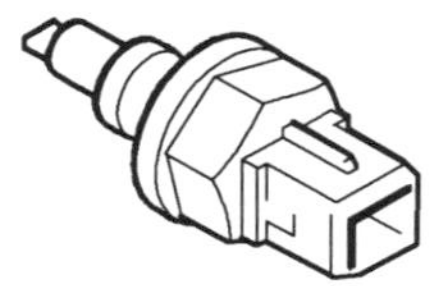

This sensor is of the negative temperature coefficient (NTC) type, designed to reduce its resistance with increasing temperature. The ECM receives a signal proportional to the temperature of the intake air. When used in conjunction with the signal from the MAP sensor, the ECM can calculate the volume of oxygen in the air and adjust the quantity of fuel being injected to achieve optimum fuelling of the engine. The IAT sensor signal is also used to adjust ignition timing.

If the IAT sensor fails, the ECM enters a default mode using a substitute value of 35.5°C.

Injectors

The four fuel injectors are fitted between the pressurised fuel rail and the inlet manifold. Each injector comprises a solenoid operated needle valve and a specially designed nozzle to ensure good fuel atomisation.

The injectors are controlled in grouped mode with 2 & 3 being grouped and 1 & 4 being grouped, with the injectors in each group being operated alternately.

The ECM determines when to operate the injectors based on the signal it receives from the CKP sensor. The ECM provides an earth signal for the period the injectors are required to be open, the injector solenoids are energised and fuel is sprayed into the inlet manifold onto the back of the inlet valves. The ECM carefully meters the amount of fuel injected by adjusting the injector opening period (pulse width). During cranking, when the engine speed is below approximately 400 rev/min, the ECM increases the injector pulse width to aid starting. The amount of increase depends upon engine coolant temperature. To prevent flooding during cranking, the ECM periodically inhibits the operation of the injectors.

Throttle Housing and Inlet Manifold

The plastic throttle housing is located between the plastic inlet manifold and air intake hose and is sealed to the manifold by an 'O' ring. The throttle housing incorporates a throttle disk which is connected to the throttle pedal via the throttle lever and a cable. Mounted on the throttle housing is the throttle position sensor. The throttle housing also provides the attachment point for the throttle cable mounting bracket. The throttle cable is connected to the throttle disk via a semi circular lever. An Idle Air Control (IAC) valve is mounted on the inlet manifold.

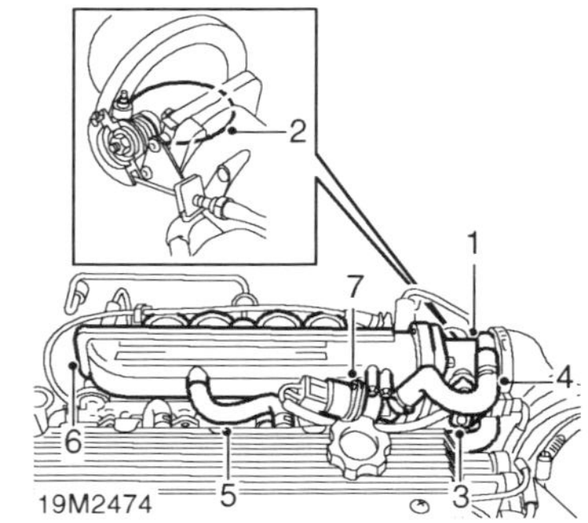

1. Throttle housing
2. Throttle valve
3. TP sensor
4. IAC valve hose
5. Engine ventilation hose
6. Inlet manifold
7. IAC valve

The throttle disk position is set during manufacture and is not adjustable. A throttle position screw is fitted to allow the throttle disk to close at its optimum position.

There are two breather hoses from the camshaft cover; one hose is fitted to the inlet manifold and the other is fitted to the throttle housing. Both pipes are connected to a gauze filter in the camshaft cover to prevent engine oil being drawn into the engine by the substantially greater manifold depression.

The throttle position (TP) sensor is attached to the throttle disk pivot shaft and secured to the throttle housing with two Torx head screws.

The IAC valve is attached to the inlet manifold with four Torx head screws. The valve is connected to the inlet manifold via a port and sealed with an O-ring. A rubber hose connects the valve to the inlet side of the throttle housing.

Throttle Position (TP) Sensor

The TP sensor is located on the throttle housing and secured with two Torx head screws. The sensor is directly attached to the throttle disk spindle and its movement is proportional to throttle movement.

The TP sensor is a rotary potentiometer. The ECM supplies the sensor with a 5 volt supply and an earth path. The sensor returns a signal proportional to throttle disk position. Closed throttle is detected by the TP sensor which prompts the ECM to initiate idle speed control via the IAC valve.

Throttle disk movement causes voltage across the potentiometer to vary. The ECM calculates the rate of change of the voltage signal in positive (acceleration) or negative (deceleration) directions. From this the ECM can determine the required engine speed, rate of acceleration or, rate of deceleration and apply acceleration enrichment, deceleration fuel metering or over-run fuel cut-off.

If the TP sensor fails, the ECM enters a default mode and, using a substitute value, assumes that the throttle disk is fully closed.

NOTE: The position of the throttle disk is preset during manufacture and the throttle position setting screw MUST NOT be adjusted unless directed by TestBook. The TP sensor is not adjustable and the ECM is designed to learn the throttle closed position and adapt to any changes which may occur throughout the life of the engine. If the relationship between the TP sensor and the throttle disc is changed for any reason (renewal of TP sensor etc.), the TestBook throttle initialisation procedure MUST be carried out.

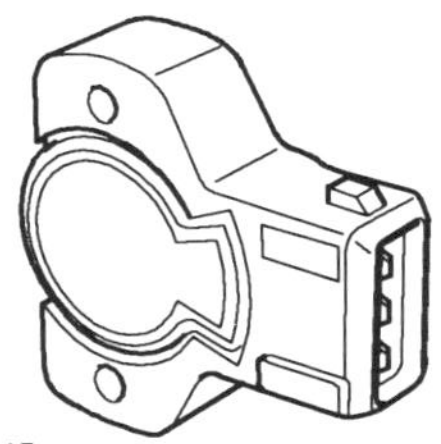

19M2145

Idle Air Control (IAC) Valve

The IAC valve is located on the inlet manifold and is secured with four Torx head screws. The IAC valve comprises a stepper motor and a pintle valve enclosed in a plastic housing. The IAC valve is directly controlled by the ECM.

The IAC valve opens or closes the pintle valve which is situated in an air passage in the throttle housing, allowing air to bypass the throttle disk and flow straight into the inlet manifold. By changing the amount the IAC valve is open, the ECM can control engine idle speed and cold start air flow requirements by adjusting the flow of air through the passage. The position of the IAC valve can be checked using Testbook. When adjusting to the displayed limits, it is important that no electrical or mechanical loads are applied (cooling fan, A/C etc.).

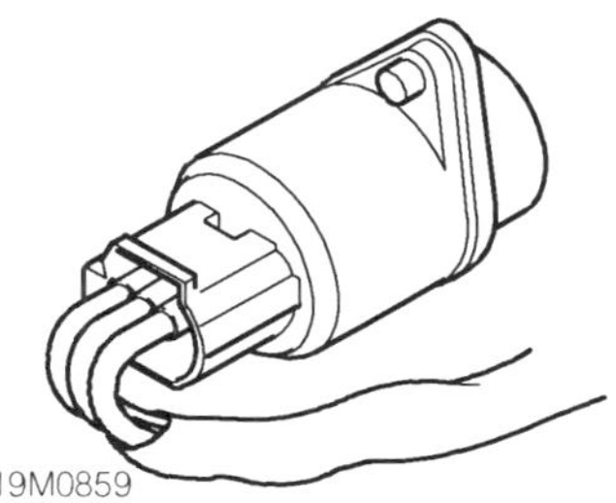

19M0859

During cold starting, the ECM indexes the IAC valve to open a calculated amount to provide a level of fast idle, dependent on engine coolant temperature. As the engine warms, the fast idle is decreased by gradually closing the IAC valve pintle until normal operating temperature is reached.

The position of the IAC valve can be checked using TestBook and should be within the range of 20 to 40 steps when the engine is running at normal operating temperature. If it is identified as being outside this range it can be adjusted to within range using TestBook. This ensures that the IAC valve is at the optimum position within its range for providing further movement to compensate for changes in engine load or temperature in accordance with signals from the ECM.

If the IAC valve fails, the engine may continue to idle depending on the position of the stepper motor prior to failure.

Relay Module

The relay module is located in the engine compartment behind the ECM. The relay module contains the following relays:

- Main relay - energised by the ECM when the ignition is switched on and supplies power to the ECM. The ECM controls the main relay and will maintain the main relay in an energised state for a predetermined period after the ignition is switched off. This allows time for the ECM to 'power down' and prepare itself for the next engine start.
- Fuel pump relay - energised by the ECM for a short period when the ignition is switched on, during cranking and while the engine is running.
- Starter relay - energised by the cranking signal from the ignition switch via the CCU and supplies power to the starter motor solenoid.
- Heated oxygen sensor relay - energised by the ECM and supplies current to the heating element of the heated oxygen sensor.

Fuel Pump

The fuel pump is installed in a unit located inside the top face of the fuel tank. It is accessible by raising the rear passenger seat and removing a sealed cover plate. The electric fuel pump is located inside the fuel tank and is energised by the ECM via the fuel pump relay in the relay module via the inertia fuel shut-off (IFS) switch.

The fuel pump delivers more fuel than the maximum load requirement for the engine, pressure is therefore maintained in the fuel system under all conditions. A fuel pressure regulator is located in the same housing as the fuel pump.

Fuel Pressure Regulator

The fuel pressure regulator is a mechanical device located in the tank unit with the fuel pump.

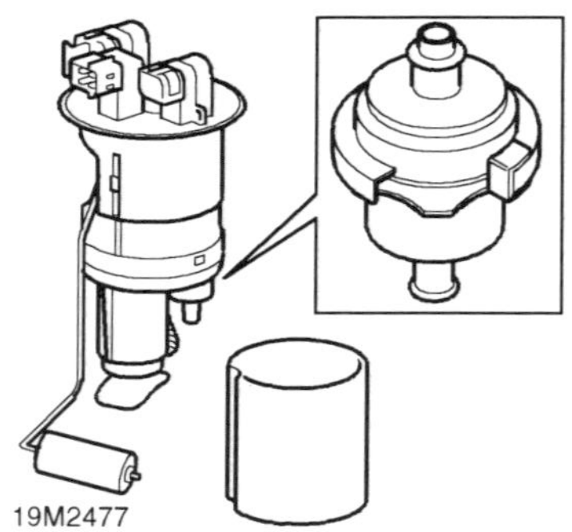

19M2477

The regulator is connected to the fuel delivery pipe from the pump and ensures that constant fuel pressure in the fuel line is maintained. When pressure from the pump exceeds the regulator setting, the pressure overcomes an internal spring in the regulator and fuel is returned to the fuel pump swirl pot.

Fuel Pressure Accumulator

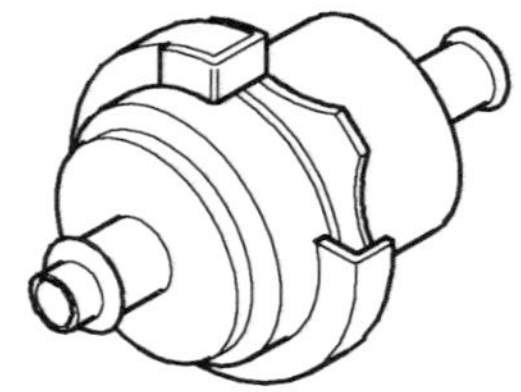

19M0860

The fuel pressure accumulator is located on the end of the fuel rail. The accumulator is connected to the inlet manifold via a hose. The accumulator is the same item normally functioning as the pressure regulator in a feed and return system. In this system, no return line is fitted and the accumulator simply serves to damp out injector pulses and reduce injector noise. The rubber hose connecting the accumulator to the intake manifold must be connected at all times to prevent an intake manifold air leak.

Inertia Fuel Shut-Off (IFS) Switch

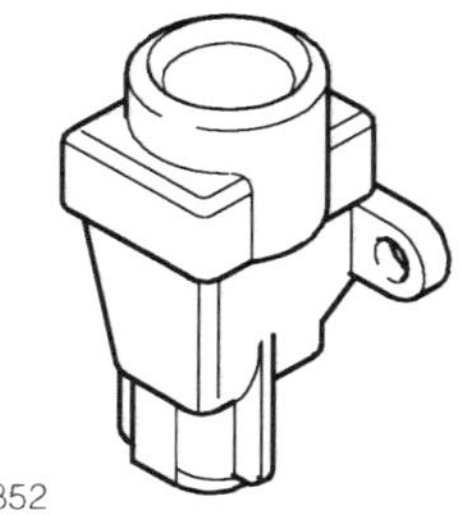

19M0852

The Inertia Fuel Shut-off (IFS) switch is located in the engine compartment on the left hand side of the bulkhead. The switch incorporates a button, covered by a rubber shroud, which is used to reset the switch after operation.

The electrical circuit for the fuel pump incorporates the IFS switch, which in the event of a sudden deceleration, breaks the circuit to the fuel pump stopping fuel delivery to the engine. The switch must be reset by pressing the rubber top before the engine can be restarted.

WARNING: ALWAYS check for fuel leaks and the integrity of fuel system connections before resetting the switch.

Diagnostic Socket

The diagnostic socket is located in a bracket behind the centre console in the passenger footwell. The socket connector is constructed to ISO standard and allows the attachment of TestBook or any other ISO standard scantool. The diagnostic socket allows diagnostic information stored in any of the vehicle's ECU's to be retrieved. It also allows engine tuning and fault diagnosis to be carried out via the ECM.

Heated Oxygen Sensor (HO2S)

The engine management system operates a closed loop emission system to ensure the most efficient level of exhaust gas conversion. The HO2S is fitted in the exhaust manifold and monitors the exhaust gases.

The HO2S supplies a small voltage proportional to exhaust oxygen content to the ECM. As the air/fuel mixture weakens, the exhaust oxygen content increases and the voltage to the ECM decreases. If the mixture becomes richer, the oxygen content decreases and the voltage increases.

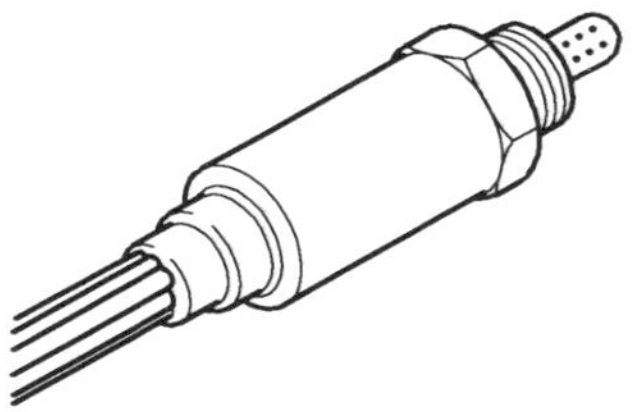

19M0854

From this signal the ECM can determine the air/fuel mixture being delivered to the engine, and can adjust the duration the injectors are open to maintain the ratio necessary for efficient gas conversion by the catalyst.

The HO2S has an integral heating element to ensure an efficient operating temperature is quickly reached from cold. The electrical supply to the heater element is controlled by the ECM via the heated oxygen sensor relay in the relay module.

Acceleration Enrichment

When the throttle pedal is depressed, the ECM receives a rising voltage from the TP sensor and detects a rise in manifold pressure from the MAP sensor. The ECM provides additional fuel by increasing the normal injector pulse width and also provides a small number of extra additional pulses on rapid throttle openings.

If the HO2S fails, the ECM enters a default mode using a substitute value of 100% (open loop).

Over-Run Fuel Cut-Off

The ECM implements over-run fuel cut-off when the engine speed is above 2000 rev/min with engine at normal operating temperature and the TP sensor in the closed position, i.e. the vehicle is 'coasting' with the throttle pedal released.

The ECM indexes the IAC valve open slightly to increase the air flow through the engine to maintain a constant manifold depression to keep emissions low. Fuel is progressively reinstated as the throttle is opened.

Over-Speed Fuel Cut-Off

To prevent damage at high engine speeds the ECM will implement fuel cut-off at engine speeds above 7000 rev/min by inhibiting the earth path for the injectors. As engine speed falls to 6990 rev/min, fuel is progressively reinstated.

Ignition Switch Off

When the ignition is switched off, the ECM will keep the main relay energised for approximately 5 minutes while it drives the IAC valve to its power down position and stores data to permanent memory, ready for the next engine start. During this period, the cooling fan(s) may be operated to reduce engine bay temperature and aid hot starting.

AIR CONDITIONING/COOLING FANS

Air Conditioning (if fitted) / Fan Control

On all models, an electric cooling fan is fitted in a housing at the right hand end of the radiator. Models fitted with air conditioning have an additional condensor fan fitted in the housing on the left hand side of the radiator.

The ECM controls the air conditioning grant output. If an input is received from the air conditioning select button, with the interior blower fan on and the trinary switch set, the ECM will consider engaging the air conditioning clutch. The ECM considers the coolant temperature and the throttle position before the air conditioning grant is operated. When the air conditioning grant is started, the cooling fans operate in slow mode, unless the coolant temperature is above a set value when they operate in fast mode.

The ECM provides two outputs to control the two cooling fans; slow mode and fast mode. The modes of operation vary depending on signals received from the air conditioning thermostat, the ECT sensor and the ECM. In slow mode, both fans operate in series sharing the same electrical feed. In fast mode, both fans operate in parallel, each fan receiving its electrical feed from a separate source.

Cooling Fan (Vehicles without air conditioning)

The ECM controls the operation of the cooling fan. The ECT sensor constantly sends signals to the ECM. When engine coolant reaches 106°C, the ECM switches the cooling fan on, in fast mode, until the engine coolant temperature is reduced to 100°C or less.

When the ignition is turned off, the fan can continue to operate for up to eight minutes if the ECT sensor senses a coolant temperature of 114°C or above. The fan will turn off when the temperature decreases to 112°C or less or when eight minutes has elapsed. If a temperature of 114°C is not sensed within five minutes of ignition off, the fan will not operate.

Cooling Fans (Vehicles with air conditioning)

The ECM controls the operation of the cooling and the condensor fan. The ECT sensor constantly sends signal to the ECM. When engine coolant reaches 112°C, the ECM switches the cooling and condensor fans on, in fast mode, until the engine coolant temperature is reduced to 100°C. The cooling fans will operate at slow speed when A/C is operating unless overriden by a high temperature, fast speed request.

When the ignition is turned off, the fans can continue to operate for up to eight minutes if the ECT sensor senses a coolant temperature of 114°C or above. The fans will turn off when the temperature decreases to 112°C, or less, or when eight minutes has elapsed. If a temperature of 114°C is not sensed within five minutes after ignition off, the fans will not operate.

HILL DESCENT CONTROL (HDC) SIGNAL (Vehicles with ABS Only)

The ECM constantly monitors signal information for throttle position and engine speed and also assesses other engine inputs to produce an engine torque signal. These signals, along with engine and gearbox identifiers, are passed to the ABS ECU to control hill descent.

See BRAKES, Information.

The ECM constantly monitors signal information for throttle position and engine speed and also assesses other engine inputs to produce an engine torque signal. These signals, along with engine and gearbox identifiers, are passed to the ABS ECU to control hill descent.

AIR INTAKE SYSTEM

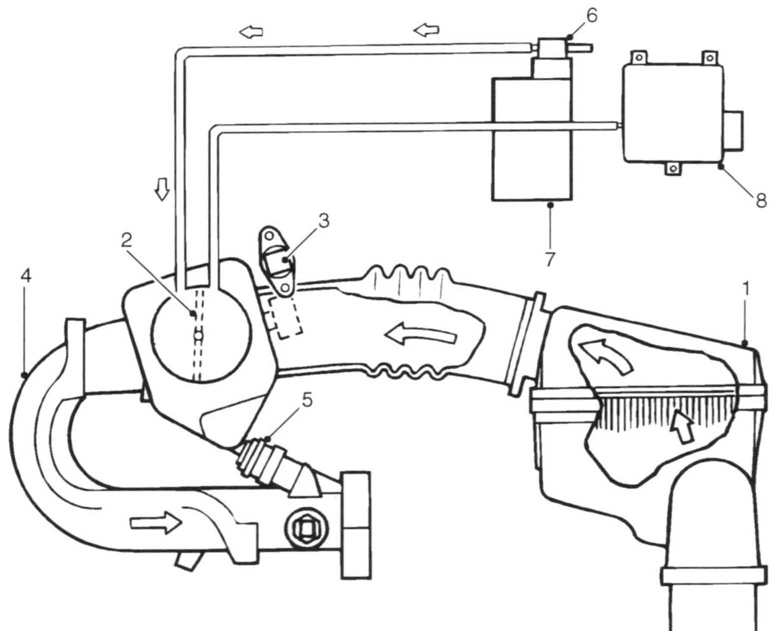

19M0759

1. Air cleaner
2. Throttle disk
3. Idle air control (IAC) valve
4. Inlet manifold
5. Injector
6. Evaporative (EVAP) emission purge valve
7. Evaporative (EVAP) emission cannister
8. Engine Control Module (ECM)

Intake air is drawn into the throttle housing through an air cleaner. Air is passed from the throttle housing via the manifold chamber into the inlet manifold where it is mixed with fuel injected by the injectors before the mixture is drawn into the combustion chamber.

Air Cleaner

The air cleaner housing is located on the left hand side of the engine bay and secured to the battery tray. The air cleaner housing is plastic moulded with a removable lid which is retained with spring clips. Removal of the lid allows access to the corrugated paper filter element.

An air intake pipe is located at the front of the air cleaner housing and draws air from within the engine compartment. A rubber hose is connected to the intake pipe and connects to a resonator box located in the front left hand wheel arch. The resonator box is used to reduce induction noise.

The outlet from the housing is connected to the throttle housing with a flexible rubber hose. The hose incorporates two plastic tubes which provide additional reduction in induction noise.

THROTTLE CABLE - CHECK AND ADJUST

Service repair no - 19.20.05

NOTE: Before adjusting cable, ensure that cable is correctly routed and located. Do not attempt to adjust throttle cable or engine idle speed by means of the throttle stop screw.

Adjust

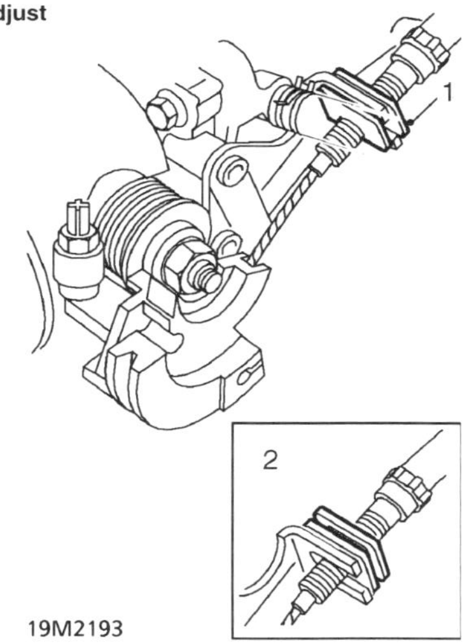

19M2193

1. Release cable adjusting nut from abutment bracket.
2. Position outer cable to abutment bracket so that adjusting nut is in contact with top of abutment bracket.

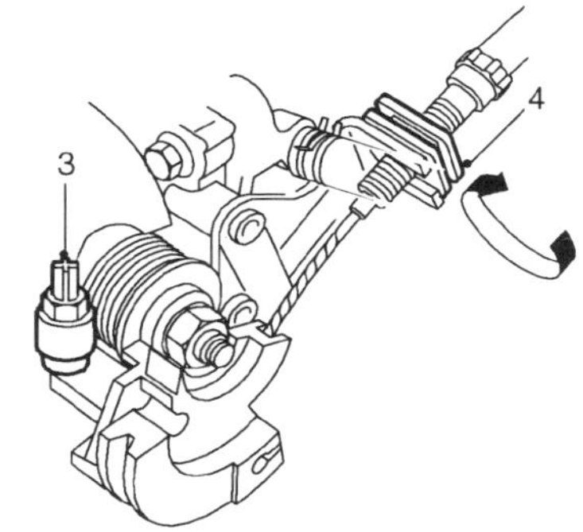

19M0925

3. Hold throttle cam in fully closed position, ensure throttle cam contacts throttle stop screw.
4. Rotate cable adjusting nut until all slack is taken out of inner cable. Ensure throttle does not open.
5. Fit throttle cable adjusting nut in abutment bracket.
6. Operate throttle pedal and ensure that full throttle pedal movement is available.

CAUTION: Ensure that throttle FULLY closes onto the stop and is NOT held open by the cable. If the throttle is held open by the cable, the ECM will not be able to learn and adapt the throttle closed position. This can cause erratic engine idle.

FUEL SYSTEM - DEPRESSURISE

Service repair no - 19.50.02

WARNING: Fuel pressure of up to 3.5 bar will be present in the system of petrol vehicles, even if the engine has not been run for some time. Always depressurise the system before disconnecting any components in the fuel feed line (between the fuel pump and the fuel rail). The spilling of fuel is unavoidable during this operation. Ensure that all necessary precautions are taken to prevent fire and explosion.

1. Position an absorbent cloth around the fuel feed connection at the fuel rail (cloth not shown for clarity).

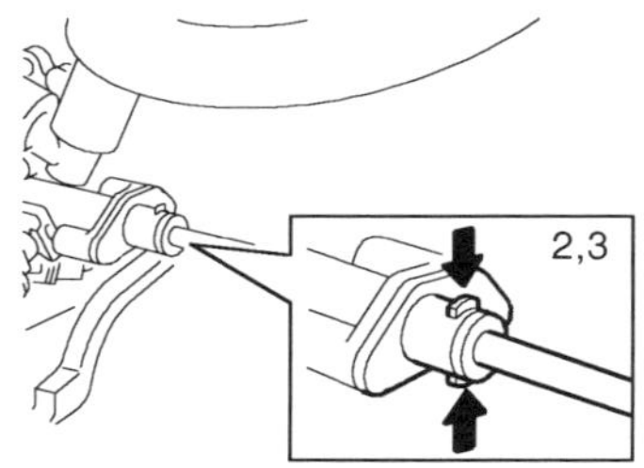

19M2504A

2. Depress tabs on Quick Release connector.
3. Carefully release feed hose from fuel rail.
4. Connect feed hose to fuel rail once pressure has relieved.

AIR - CLEANER

Service repair no - 19.10.01

Remove

1. Remove battery. ***See ELECTRICAL, Repairs.***

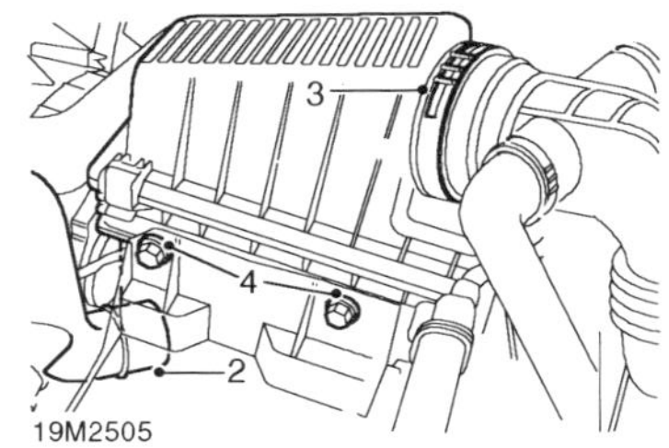

19M2505

2. Release air intake hose from bottom of air cleaner.
3. Release clip and disconnect intake hose from air cleaner.
4. Remove 2 bolts securing air cleaner to battery tray and remove air cleaner.

Refit

1. Position air cleaner to battery tray and secure with bolts.

NOTE: Ensure bottom of air filter is located on peg.

2. Connect intake hose and secure with clip.
3. Connect air intake hose to bottom of air cleaner.
4. Fit battery. ***See ELECTRICAL, Repairs.***

ELEMENT - AIR FILTER

Service repair no - 19.10.10

Remove

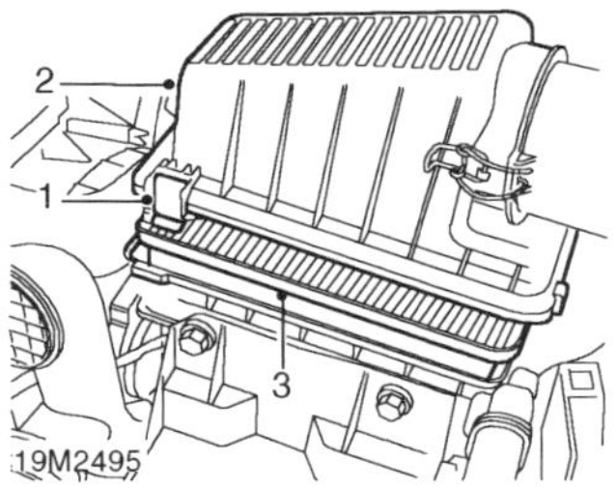

19M2495

1. Release 4 clips retaining air cleaner top cover.
2. Release air filter top cover.
3. Remove and discard air filter element.

Refit

1. Clean inside of air cleaner unit.
2. Fit NEW air filter element.
3. Position air cleaner cover and secure clips.

SWITCH - INERTIA - FUEL CUT-OFF

Service repair no - 19.22.09

Remove

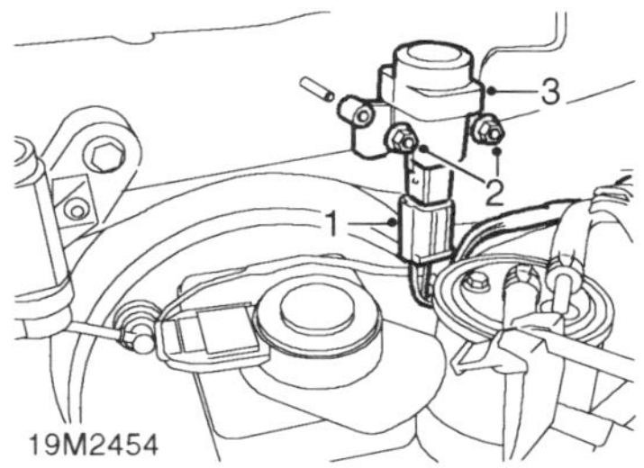

19M2454

1. Disconnect multiplug from fuel cut-off switch.
2. Remove 2 nuts securing switch to bulkhead.
3. Remove switch.

Refit

1. Position switch to bulkhead.
2. Fit 2 nuts securing switch and tighten to 2 Nm.
3. Connect multiplug.
4. Press top of switch to set switch.

ENGINE MANAGEMENT SYSTEM - MEMS

HEATED OXYGEN SENSOR (HO2S)

Service repair no - 19.22.16

Remove

1. Remove exhaust manifold gasket. ***See MANIFOLD & EXHAUST SYSTEMS, Repairs.***

⚠ **CAUTION: Although robust within the vehicle environment, HO2 sensors are easily damaged by dropping, excessive heat and contamination. Care must be exercised when working on the exhaust system not to damage the sensor housing or tip.**

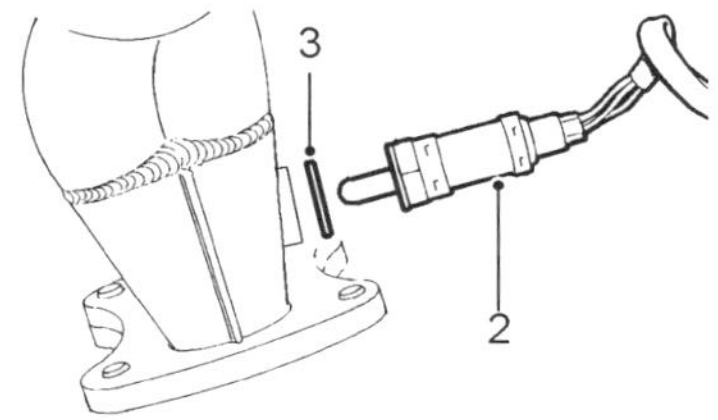

19M2502

2. Remove heated oxygen sensor.
3. Remove and discard sealing washer.

Refit

1. Fit a NEW sealing washer to oxygen sensor.
2. If refitting existing HO2S, coat threads with anti-seize compound.

⚠ **CAUTION: Do not allow anti-seize compound to come into contact with HO2S nose or enter exhaust system.**

3. Fit heated oxygen sensor and tighten to 55 Nm.
4. Fit exhaust manifold gasket. ***See MANIFOLD & EXHAUST SYSTEMS, Repairs.***

HOUSING - THROTTLE

Service repair no - 19.22.45

Remove

1. Disconnect battery earth lead.

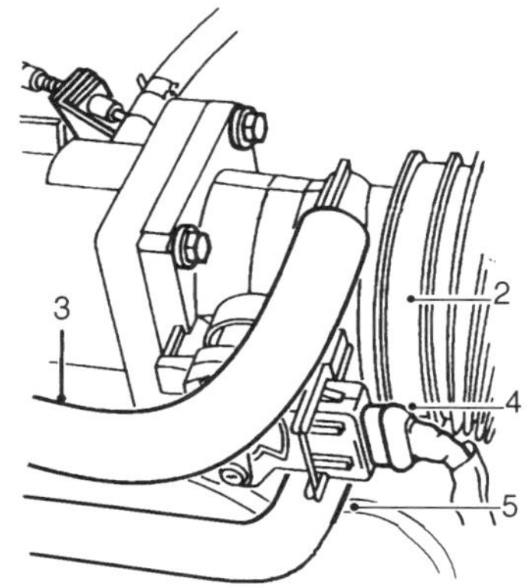

19M2458

2. Release clip and disconnect air intake hose from throttle housing.
3. Disconnect IAC hose from throttle housing.
4. Disconnect multiplug from throttle position sensor.
5. Release clip and disconnect breather hose from throttle housing.

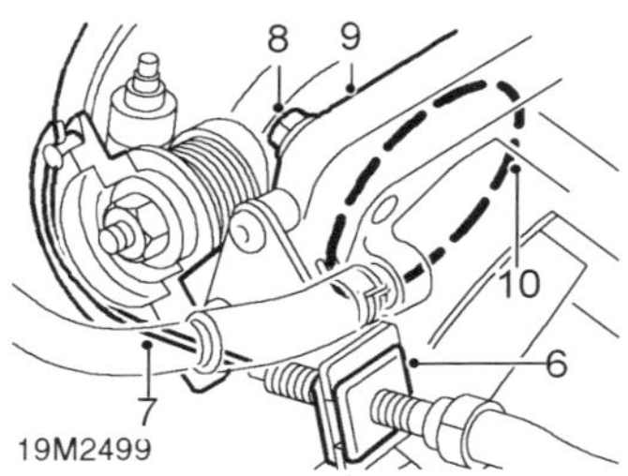

19M2499

6. Release throttle cable adjusting nut from abutment bracket.
7. Disconnect throttle cable from throttle cam.
8. Remove 4 bolts securing throttle housing to inlet manifold.
9. Remove throttle housing.
10. Remove and discard 'O' ring from throttle housing.

Refit

1. Clean mating faces of throttle housing and inlet manifold.
2. Lubricate NEW 'O' ring with silicone grease and fit to throttle housing.
3. Position throttle housing to inlet manifold, fit bolts and tighten to 9 Nm.

⚠ **CAUTION: DO NOT overtighten throttle housing fixings, or distortion of the housing may result.**

4. Connect throttle cable to throttle cam.
5. Locate throttle cable adjusting nut in abutment bracket.
6. Connect breather hose to throttle housing and secure with clip.
7. Connect multiplug to throttle position sensor.
8. Fit IAC hose and align orientation marks.
9. Connect hose to throttle housing.
10. Connect air intake hose to throttle housing and secure with clip.

⚠ **CAUTION: DO NOT overtighten clip, or distortion of the housing may result.**

11. Connect battery earth lead.

THROTTLE CABLE

Service repair no - 19.20.06

Remove

1. Release cable adjusting nut from abutment bracket.
2. Release inner cable from cam.

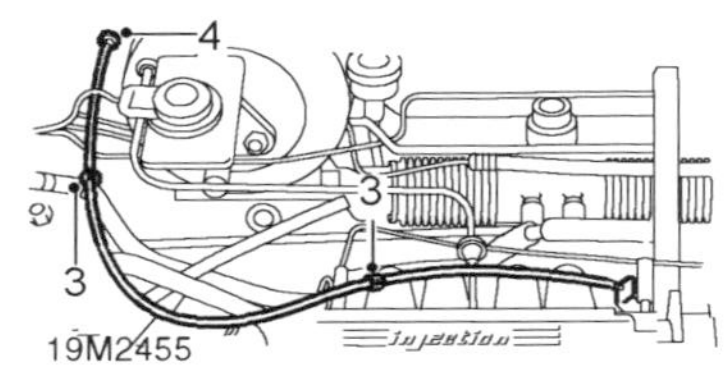

19M2455

3. Release cable from retaining clips.
4. Release cable from bulkhead.

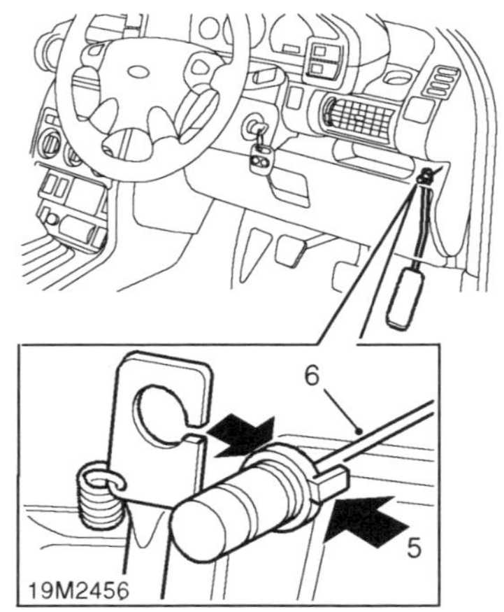

19M2456

5. Depress nylon clips to disconnect throttle cable from pedal.
6. Remove throttle cable.

Refit

1. Feed NEW cable through bulkhead and connect inner cable to pedal.
2. Smear rubber grease on both sides of the rubber seal and secure cable to bulkhead.
3. Refit throttle cable to retaining clips.
4. Connect throttle cable to throttle cam.
5. Adjust throttle cable. ***See Adjustments.***

SPARK PLUGS

Service repair no - 18.20.02

Remove

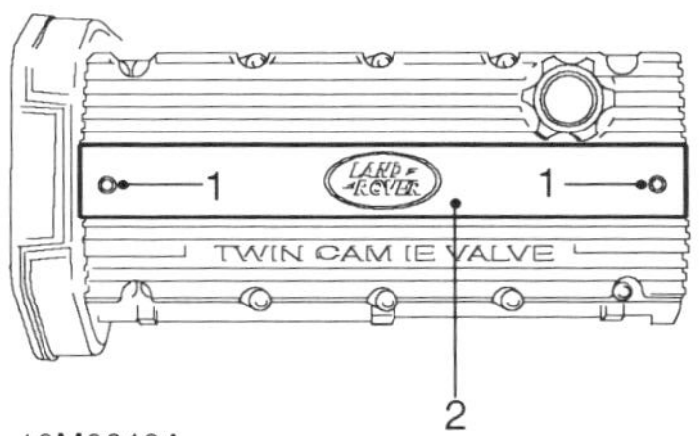

18M0042A

1. Remove 2 screws retaining h.t. lead cover.
2. Remove h.t. lead cover.

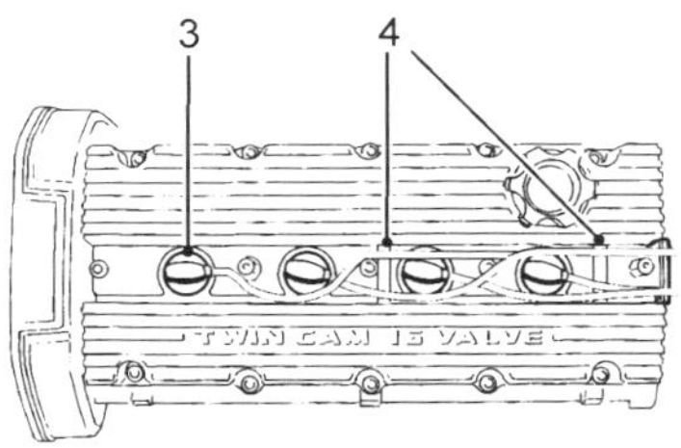

18M0043

3. Disconnect h.t. leads from spark plugs.
4. Release h.t. lead securing rubbers from camshaft cover and place h.t. leads aside.

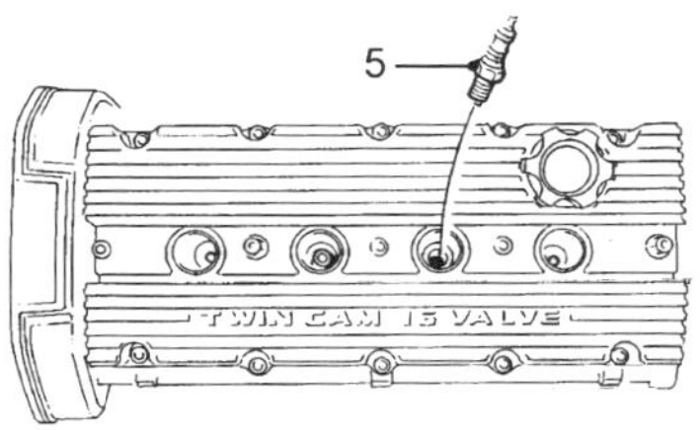

18M0044

5. Using a 16 mm spark plug socket remove 4 spark plugs.

Refit

1. Fit terminals to NEW spark plugs.

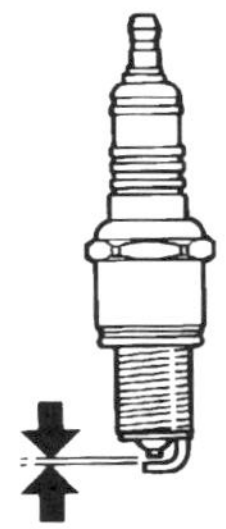

18M0055

2. Set gap of each spark plug to 0.85 mm.
3. Fit spark plugs and tighten to 27 Nm.
4. Connect h.t. leads to spark plugs.
5. Locate h.t. lead securing rubbers in camshaft cover.
6. Fit h.t. lead cover and tighten screws to 10 Nm.

DISTRIBUTOR CAP AND ROTOR ARM

Service repair no - 18.20.23

Remove

1. Remove air cleaner assembly. ***See this section.***

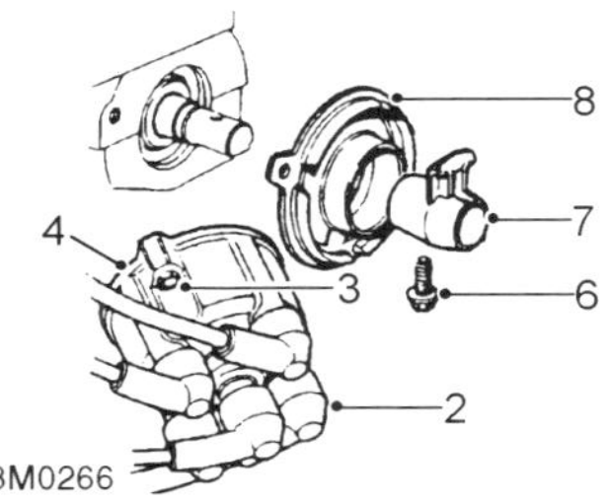

18M0266

2. Noting their fitted positions, disconnect 5 h.t. leads from distributor cap.
3. Loosen 2 screws securing distributor cap to engine.
4. Remove distributor cap.
5. Rotate engine to gain access to rotor arm screw.
6. Remove screw securing rotor arm to camshaft.
7. Remove rotor arm.
8. Remove distributor flash shield.

Refit

1. Clean distributor cap, rotor arm and flash shield.
2. Examine distributor cap and rotor arm for signs of damage or tracking; renew if necessary.
3. Fit flash shield.
4. Clean rotor arm screw thread in camshaft with thread tap.
5. Position rotor arm on camshaft.
6. Fit NEW patchlock screw to secure rotor arm to camshaft and tighten to 8 Nm.
7. Fit distributor cap and align holes in cap and flash shield with those in engine.
8. Fit 2 screws securing distributor cap to engine.
9. Connect h.t. leads to distributor cap.
10. Fit air cleaner assembly. ***See this section.***

COIL - IGNITION

Service repair no - 18.20.44

Remove

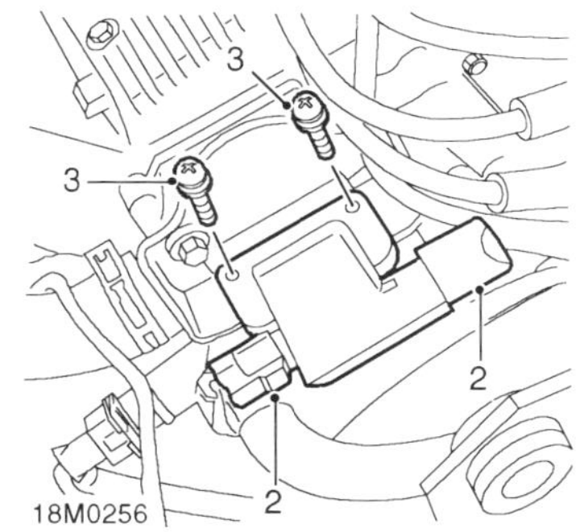

18M0256

1. Disconnect battery earth lead.
2. Disconnect multiplug and h.t. lead from coil.
3. Remove 2 screws and remove coil from mounting bracket.

Refit

1. Position coil to mounting bracket and tighten screws to 9 Nm.
2. Connect multiplug and h.t. lead.
3. Connect battery earth lead.

ENGINE CONTROL MODULE (ECM)

Service repair no - 18.30.01

Remove

1. Disconnect battery earth lead.

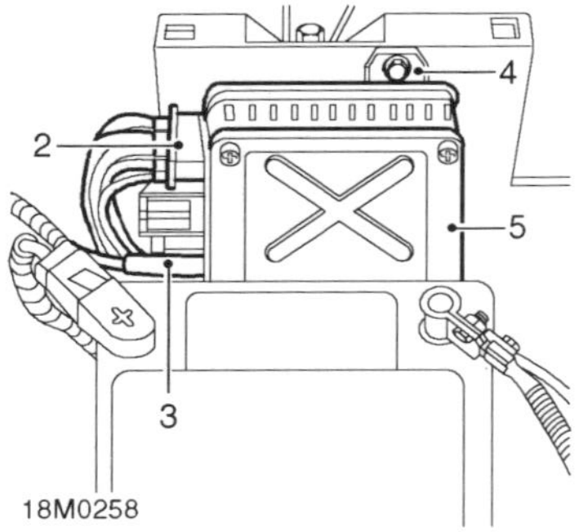

18M0258

2. Disconnect multiplug from ECM.
3. Disconnect vacuum hose from ECM.
4. Remove nut and bolt securing ECM to mounting bracket.
5. Release and remove ECM.

Refit

1. Fit ECM to mounting bracket.
2. Fit nut and bolt securing ECM to mounting bracket and tighten to 9 Nm.
3. Connect vacuum hose to ECM.
4. Connect multiplug to ECM.
5. Connect battery earth lead.

NOTE: If a new ECM has been fitted, the ECM will need to be programmed with the code from the Central Control Unit (CCU) using TestBook, before the engine can be started. In addition, a TestBook 'throttle initialisation' procedure MUST be carried out.

IDLE AIR CONTROL (IAC) VALVE

Service repair no - 18.30.05

Remove

1. Disconnect battery earth lead.

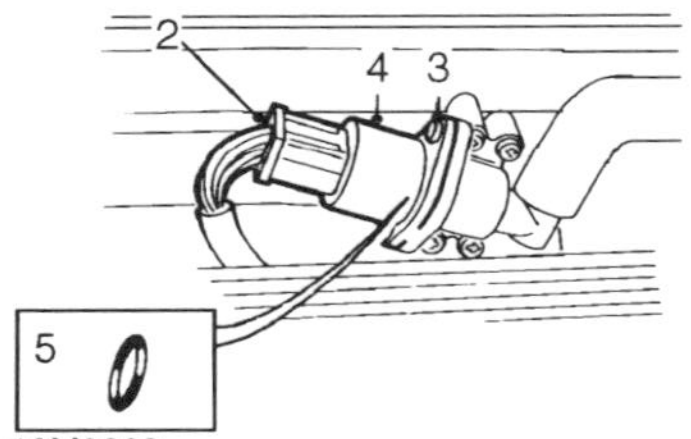

18M0099

2. Disconnect multiplug from IAC valve.
3. Remove 2 Torx screws securing IAC valve to inlet manifold.
4. Remove IAC valve.
5. Remove and discard 'O' ring.

Refit

1. Clean mating faces of IAC valve and inlet manifold.
2. Lubricate NEW 'O' ring with silicone grease and fit to IAC valve.
3. Fit IAC valve to inlet manifold.
4. Fit Torx screws securing IAC valve and tighten to 1.5 Nm.
5. Connect multiplug to IAC valve.
6. Connect battery earth lead.

SENSOR - ENGINE COOLANT TEMPERATURE (ECT)

Service repair no - 18.30.10

Remove

1. Disconnect battery earth lead.

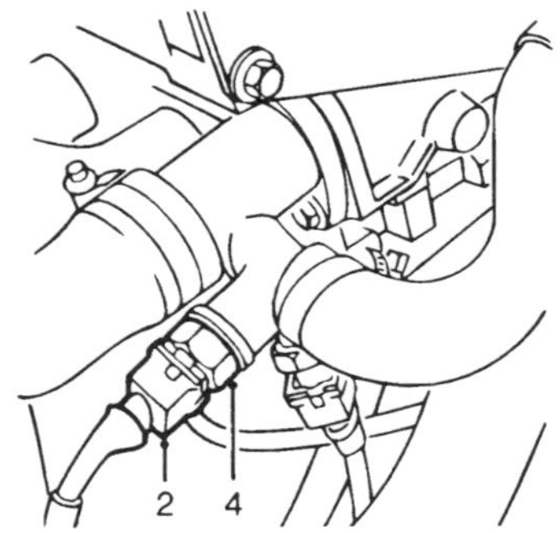

18M0040

2. Disconnect multiplug from ECT sensor.
3. Position drain tin to collect spillage.
4. Remove ECT sensor.

Refit

1. Clean threads of ECT sensor.
2. Apply Loctite 577 to ECT sensor.
3. Fit ECT sensor and tighten to 15 Nm.
4. Connect multiplug to ECT.
5. Connect battery earth lead.
6. Top-up coolant. ***See COOLING SYSTEM - 'K' SERIES, Adjustments.***

SENSOR - CRANKSHAFT POSITION (CKP)

Service repair no - 18.30.12

Remove

1. Disconnect battery earth lead.

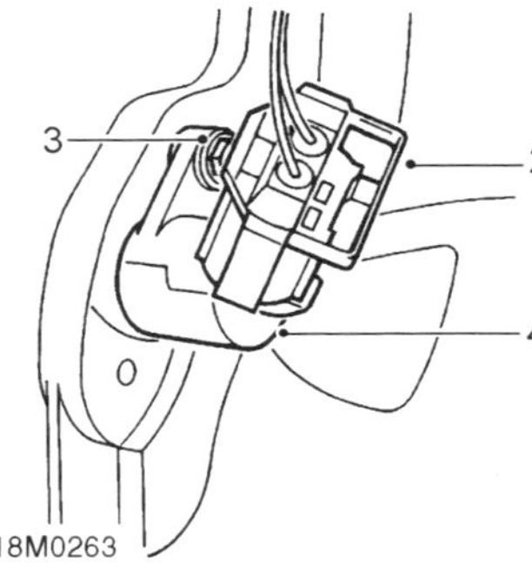

18M0263

2. Disconnect multiplug from CKP sensor.
3. Remove bolt securing CKP sensor to flywheel housing.
4. Remove CKP sensor.

Refit

1. Clean CKP sensor and mating face of flywheel housing.
2. Position CKP sensor, fit bolt and tighten to 6 Nm.
3. Connect multiplug to CKP sensor.
4. Connect battery earth lead.

SENSOR - INTAKE AIR TEMPERATURE (IAT)

Service repair no - 18.30.09

Remove

1. Disconnect battery earth lead.

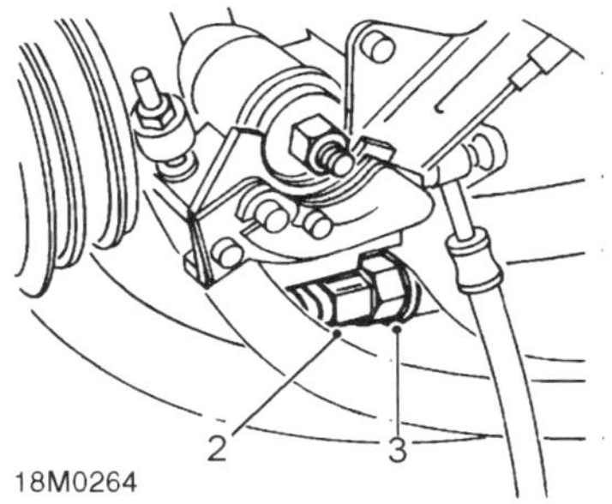

18M0264

2. Disconnect multiplug from IAT sensor.
3. Remove IAT sensor.

Refit

1. Clean threads of IAT sensor
2. Clean mating faces of IAT sensor and intake manifold.
3. Fit sensor to intake manifold and tighten to 7 Nm.
4. Connect multiplug to IAT sensor.
5. Connect battery earth lead.

SENSOR - THROTTLE POSITION (TP)

Service repair no - 18.30.17

Remove

1. Disconnect battery earth lead.

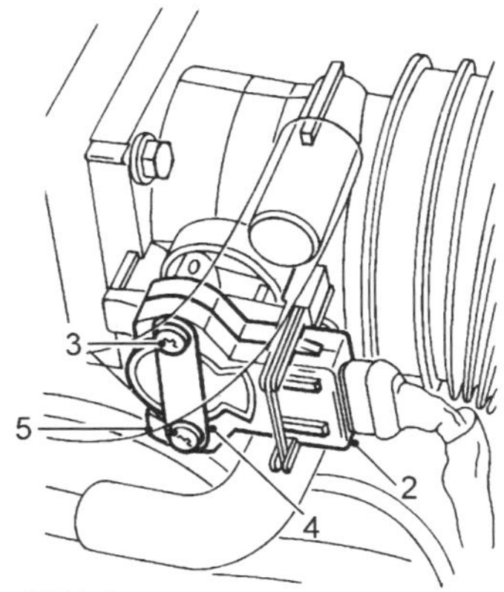

18M0050

2. Disconnect multiplug from TP sensor.
3. Remove and discard 2 Torx screws and wave washers securing TP sensor to inlet manifold.
4. Remove TP sensor specification plate.
5. Pull TP sensor from throttle spindle.

CAUTION: Do not twist or apply leverage to TP sensor.

Refit

1. Clean mating faces of throttle housing and TP sensor.
2. Fit TP sensor to throttle spindle. Ensure that during fitting, the machined flat on the throttle spindle is aligned with the mating portion of the TP sensor.

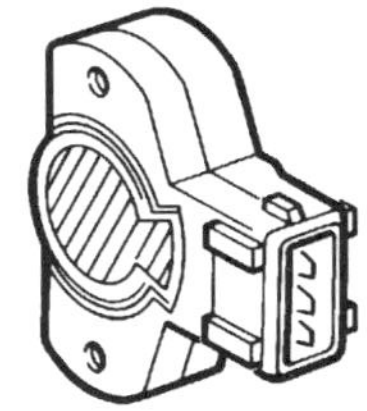

18M0056

CAUTION: The TP sensor can easily be damaged during fitting. When pressing the sensor onto throttle spindle, use fingers only and apply pressure only to the area shown shaded in the illustration.

3. Rotate TP sensor in an anti-clockwise direction to align fixing holes.

CAUTION: Do not rotate TP sensor in a clockwise direction and ensure that it is not rotated beyond its internal stops.

4. Fit TP sensor specification plate.
5. Fit NEW Torx screws and wave washers, tighten Torx screws to 1.5 Nm.

CAUTION: Do not exceed specified torque figure.

6. Connect multiplug to TP sensor.
7. Operate throttle cable cam 2 or 3 times and ensure that full travel to the throttle open and the throttle closed positions is available.
8. Connect battery earth lead.

NOTE: A 'throttle initialisation' procedure MUST be carried out using TestBook whenever the TP sensor is removed or renewed.

FUEL - RAIL

Service repair no - 19.60.04

The procedure for renewing the fuel rail is identical to renewing the injectors. ***See this section.***

INJECTORS - SET

Service repair no - 19.60.12 Injectors - set

Remove

1. Disconnect battery earth lead.
2. Remove air cleaner assembly. ***See this section.***

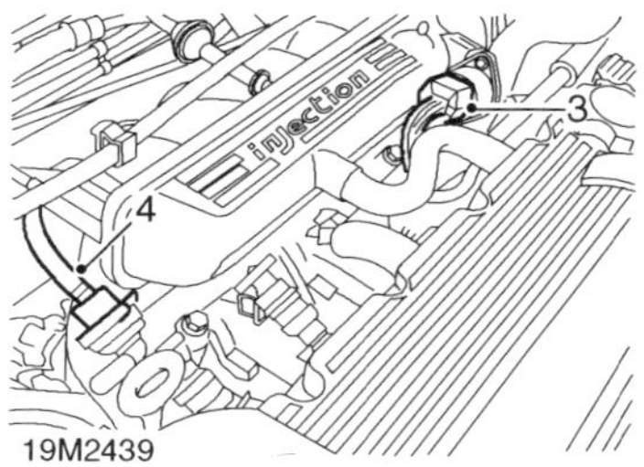

19M2439

3. Disconnect multiplug from IAC valve.
4. Release clip and disconnect vacuum pipe from fuel pressure accumulator.

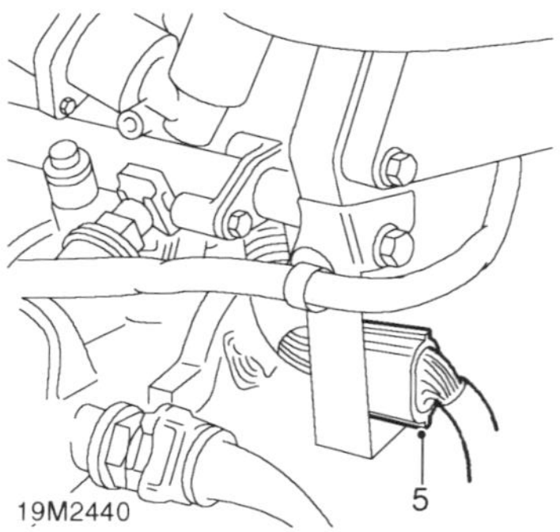

19M2440

5. Release injector harness multiplug from bracket and disconnect multiplug.

WARNING: Fuel pressure of up to 3.5 bar will be present in the system of petrol vehicles, even if the engine has not been run for some time. Always depressurise the system before disconnecting any components in the fuel feed line (between the fuel pump and the fuel rail). The spilling of fuel is unavoidable during this operation. Ensure that all necessary precautions are taken to prevent fire and explosion.

6. Position absorbent cloth beneath fuel rail.

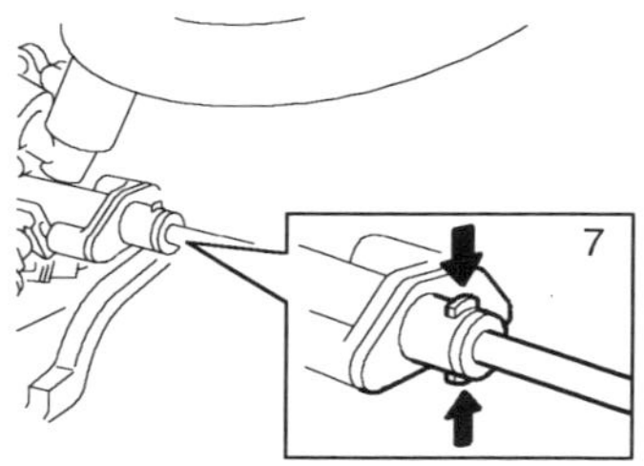

19M2441A

7. Carefully release fuel feed hose from fuel rail.

CAUTION: Plug the connections.

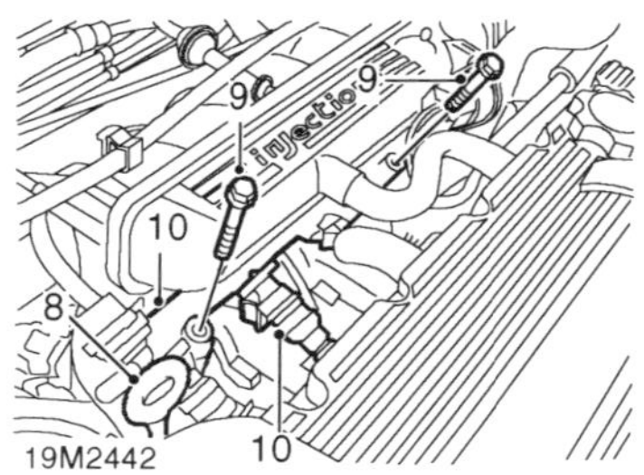

19M2442

8. Remove engine oil dipstick.
9. Remove 2 bolts securing fuel rail to inlet manifold.
10. Release fuel rail and injectors from inlet manifold.
11. Remove the fuel rail complete with injectors and harness.

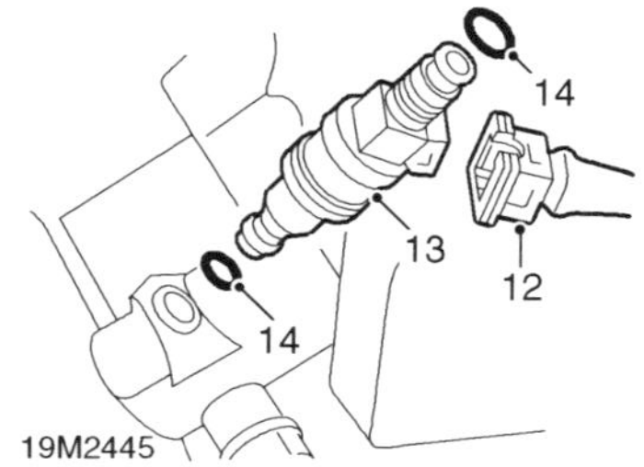

19M2445

12. Disconnect multiplugs from injectors.
13. Release spring clips securing injectors to fuel rail and remove fuel injectors.
14. Remove and discard 2 'O' rings from each injector.
15. Fit protective caps to each end of injectors.

Refit

1. Clean injectors and recesses in fuel rail and inlet manifold.
2. Lubricate NEW 'O' rings with silicone grease and fit to each end of injectors.
3. Fit injectors to fuel rail.
4. Secure injectors to fuel rail with spring clips and connect harness multiplugs.
5. Position fuel rail assembly and push-fit each injector into inlet manifold.
6. Fit bolts securing fuel rail to inlet manifold and tighten to 10 Nm.
7. Connect fuel feed hose to fuel rail.
8. Fit engine oil dipstick.
9. Connect injector harness multiplug to engine harness and secure to bracket.
10. Connect vacuum pipe to fuel pressure accumulator and secure with clip.
11. Connect multiplug to IAC valve.
12. Fit air cleaner assembly. ***See this section.***
13. Connect battery earth lead.

CONTENTS

Page

DESCRIPTION AND OPERATION

REPAIRS

ENGINE COMPARTMENT COMPONENT LOCATIONS

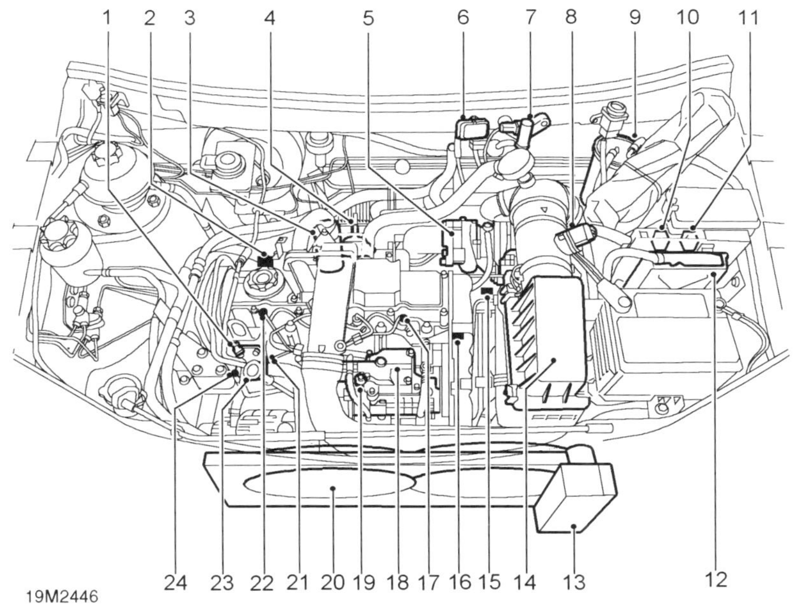

19M2446

1. Engine Coolant Temperature (ECT) sensor
2. Intake Air Temperature (IAT) sensor
3. EGR cooler
4. EGR valve
5. Turbocharger
6. Manifold Absolute Pressure (MAP) sensor
7. EGR modulator valve
8. Mass Air Flow (MAF) sensor
9. Fuel filter
10. Main relay - fuel injection pump
11. Glow plug relay
12. Engine Control Module (ECM)
13. Intercooler
14. Air cleaner
15. Vehicle Speed Sensor (VSS)
16. Crankshaft Position (CKP) sensor
17. Injectors
18. Fuel injection pump
19. Fuel shut off solenoid
20. Cooling fans
21. Glow plugs
22. Needle lift sensor (No. 1 injector)
23. Coolant outlet elbow
24. Coolant temperature gauge sender

PASSENGER COMPARTMENT COMPONENT LOCATIONS

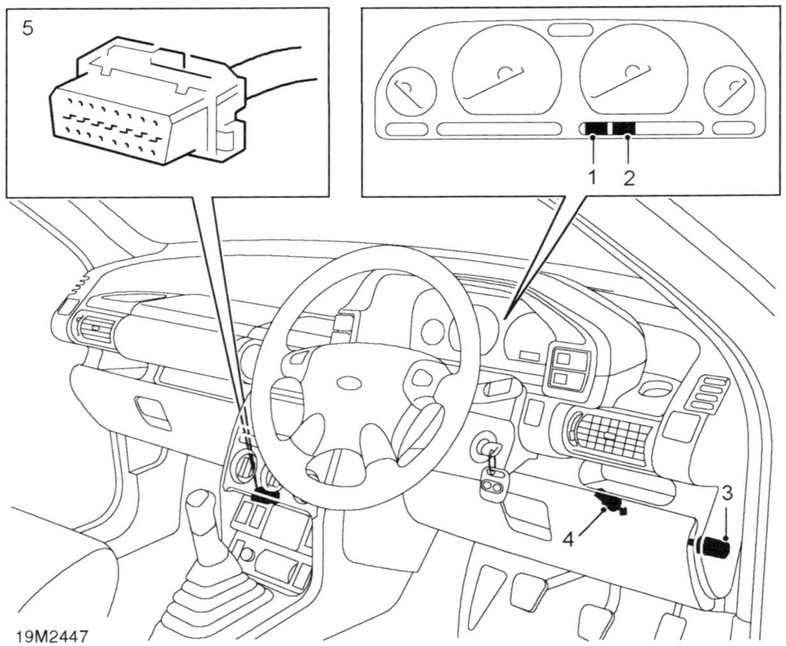

1. Glow plug warning lamp
2. Malfunction indicator lamp (MIL)
3. Throttle Position (TP) sensor
4. Brake pedal switch
5. Diagnostic Socket

ELECTRONIC DIESEL CONTROL OPERATION

Diesel engines operate by compression ignition. The rapid compression of air in the cylinder is heated during the compression cycle. The fuel is injected into the compressed, heated air and spontaneously ignites. Automatically controlled glow plugs are used during cold starting to reduce post start emissions and assist cold starting by raising the temperature of the compressed air to ignition point.

Electronic Control Module (ECM)

The Electronic Control Module (ECM) processes all inputs and outputs related to the operation of the electronic diesel control. The ECM is located on a mounting plate behind the battery in the engine compartment. The ECM comprises an aluminium cast body with a galvanised sealed lid. A socket is positioned on its upper face and receives a multiplug from the engine wiring loom. The socket contains 55 pins although only the pins corresponding to those in the multiplug are used.

The multiplug is connected into the engine compartment wiring loom. All inputs and outputs to and from each sensor is transmitted through the loom and via the multiplug, to the ECM. The multiplug fits into a corresponding socket on the upper face of the ECM and is locked in position with a cam type locking lever. The multiplug pins are plated to minimise oxidation and give improved reliability.

The ECM monitors the conditions required for optimum combustion of fuel in the cylinder through sensors located at strategic points around the engine. From these inputs, the ECM can adjust the quantity and timing of the fuel being delivered to the cylinder.

Main Features

The main features are as follows:
- The ECM incorporates short circuit protection and can store intermittent faults on certain inputs. TestBook can interrogate the ECM for these stored faults.
- The engine management system is a 'Drive by Wire' system, with no mechanical link between the throttle pedal and the fuel injection pump. All throttle movements are monitored by the ECM via a throttle position (TP) sensor which is located on the pedal box. The sensor provides the ECM with a signal proportional to throttle pedal movement. The ECM then adjusts the fuel injection pump to deliver the required amount of fuel.
- In conjunction with the TP sensor, the ECM uses engine speed, calculated from the Crankshaft Position (CKP) sensor, to determine the basic fuelling requirements of the engine. This basic calculation is modified using signals from sensors, strategically positioned around the engine, to ensure that the correct fuel mixture is achieved for optimum performance and emissions.
- If certain system inputs fail, the ECM implements a back-up facility to enable the system to continue functioning, although at a reduced level of performance.
- A separate diagnostic socket, located behind the centre console in the passenger footwell, allows engine tuning or fault diagnosis to be carried out using TestBook.
- The ECM also operates the engine immobilisation circuits. When the ignition is switched to position II, a coded signal is sent to the ECM from the Central Control Unit (CCU). If the coded signal does not match the signal programmed into the ECM, the ECM immobilises the engine starting circuits.
- On vehicles fitted with ABS, the ECM provides signal information to the ABS ECU for hill descent control.

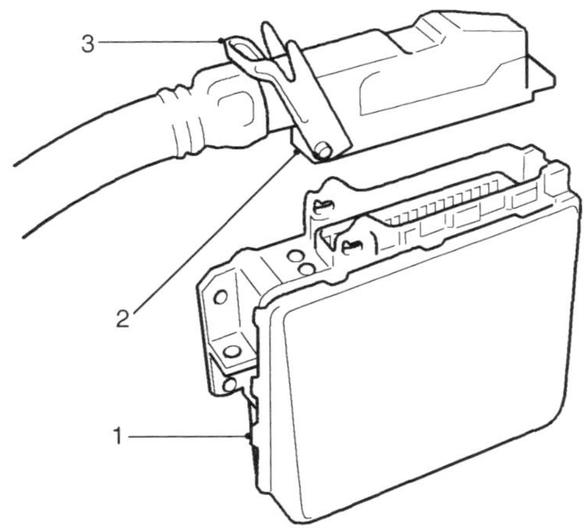

19M2457

1. ECM body
2. Multi plug
3. Locking lever

The ECM inputs and outputs are shown in the following table.

INPUTS		OUTPUTS
Crankshaft Position (CKP) sensor Manifold Absolute Pressure (MAP) Intake Air Temperature (IAT) sensor Engine Coolant Temperature (ECT) sensor Fuel temperature sensor Mass Air Flow (MAF) sensor Injector needle lift sensor Vehicle Speed Sensor (VSS)(Non-ABS) vehicles only) Vehicle Speed Signal from ABS ECU (Vehicles with ABS only) Brake pedal switch Starter signal Diagnostic input A/C request (Vehicles with A/C only) Fuel quantity servo - position Earth supply Alarm code	ECM	Glow plug relay EGR modulator valve Fuel shut off solenoid Glow plug lamp Engine warning lamp Injection timing device Diagnostic socket ABS ECU (if fitted) Fuel quantity servo - control actuator Grant air conditioning (Vehicles with A/C only) Grant cooling fans Grant condenser fan (Vehicles with A/C only)

ECU Harness Pin-out Connections

NOTE: VBATT = Battery Voltage

Pin No.	Function	Voltage	Signal type	State
1	Fuel Quantity Actuator	0 - 12V	PWM	Output
2	Fuel Quantity Actuator	0 - 12V	PWM	Output
3	Fuel Shut-Off Solenoid	0 - 12V	Switched (12V = Fuel on)	Output
4	Malfunction Indicator Lamp	0 - 12V	Switched (0v = On)	Output
5	Injector Needle Lift Sensor	-	Frequency	Input
6	EGR Solenoid	0 - 12V	PWM 5 - 95%	Output
7	Cooling Series Fan	0 - 12V	Switched (0v = On)	Output
8	Glow Plug Control	0 - 12V	Switched (0v = On)	Output
9	Air Grant Clutch relay)	0 - 12V	Switched (0v = On)	Output
10	Injector Timing Solenoid	-	PWM 0 - 95%	Output
11	Glow Plug Lamp	0 - 12V	Switched (0v = On)	Output
12	Injector Needle Lift Sensor Ground	0V	-	Ground
13	Sensor Ground Rail	0V	-	Ground
14	Quantity Servo Potentiometer (Middle tap)	5V	Analogue	Input
15	Main Relay	0 - 12V	Switched (0v = On)	Ground
16	Battery Power Supply	12V	-	Input
17	Battery Power Supply	12V	-	Input
18	Battery Negative	0V	-	Ground
19	Battery Negative	0V	-	Ground

ECU Harness Pin-out Connections - Continued

NOTE: VBATT = Battery Voltage

Pin No.	Function	Voltage	Signal type	State
20	Not Used	-	-	-
21	Fuel Quantity Servo (Reference coil)	5V	-	Supply
22	Not Used	-	-	-
23	Not Used	-	-	-
24	A/C Trinary Switch (Normal)	0 - 12V	Switched (0v = On)	Input
25	Throttle Position Sensor (Idle Switch)	0 - 12V	Switched (0v = On)	Input
26	Brake Pedal Switch	12V	Switched (12V = On)	Input
27	Data Link (L Line)	Serial	-	Input
28	Not Used	-	-	-
29	Road Speed Signal	-	Frequency	Input
30	Not Used	-	-	-
31	Not Used	-	-	-
32	Not Used	-	-	-
33	Throttle Position Sensor	5V	Supply	Output
34	Mass Air Flow Sensor	5V	Supply	-
35	Fuel Temperature Sensor	0 - 5V	Analogue	Input
36	Intake Air Temperature Sensor	0 - 5V	Analogue	Input
37	Throttle Position Sensor - Wiper	0 - 5V	Analogue	Input
38	Mass Airflow Sensor	0 - 5V	Analogue	Input

ECU Harness Pin-out Connections - Continued

NOTE: VBATT = Battery Voltage

Pin No.	Function	Voltage	Signal type	State
39	Fuel Quantity Servo (Measuring Coil)	0 - 5V	Analogue	Supply
40	Hill Descent (MPX Signal)	-	PWM	Output
41	Not Used	-	-	-
42	Data Link (K Line)	-	-	Output
43	Not Used	-	-	-
44	A/C Trinary Switch (High/Low)	0 - 12V	Switched (0v = On)	Input
45	Immobilisation (From Central Control Unit)	-	-	Input
46	Cooling Parallel Fan	0 - 12V	Switched (0v = On)	Output
47	Crankshaft Position Sensor (Signal)	-	Frequency	Input
48	Not Used	-	-	-
49	Not Used	-	-	-
50	Crankshaft Position Sensor (Output Signal)	-	Frequency	Output
51	Mass Absolute Pressure Sensor (Supply)	5V	-	Output
52	Not Used	-	-	-
53	Coolant Temperature Sensor (Signal)	0 - 5V	Analogue	Input
54	Manifold Absolute Pressure Sensor (Signal)	0 - 5V	Analogue	Input
55	Ignition Sense	0 - 12V	Switched (12V = On)	Supply

Fuel Injection Timing

The ECM determines the optimum fuel injection timing for the injection pump based on the signals it receives from the following sensors:

1. Crankshaft Position (CKP) sensor - Engine speed and crankshaft position
2. Needle lift sensor - Start of injection
3. Engine Coolant Temperature (ECT) sensor - Engine temperature
4. Manifold Absolute Pressure (MAP) sensor - Engine load
5. Intake Air Temperature (IAT) sensor

Basic Fuel Injection Timing

Crankshaft Position (CKP) sensor

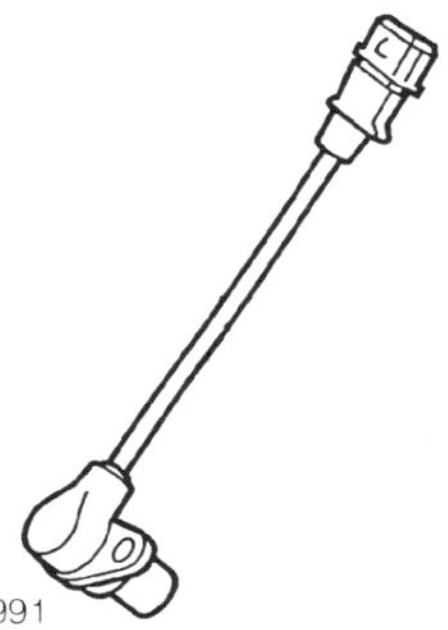

19M0991

The speed and position of the engine is detected by the CKP sensor which is bolted to, and projects through, the gearbox adapter plate adjacent to the flywheel.

The CKP sensor is an inductive sensor containing a coil and a permanent magnet which provides a magnetic field. The sensor is situated such that an air gap exists between it and the flywheel. Air gap distance is critical for correct operation.

The flywheel has four poles positioned equally around the crankshaft circumference at 90 degree intervals. When the flywheel rotates and a pole passes the CKP sensor, it disturbs the magnetic field inducing a voltage pulse in the coil. This pulse is transmitted to the ECM.

Four pulses are transmitted to the ECM for each revolution of the flywheel. By calculating the number of pulses that occur within a given time, the ECM can determine the engine speed. The output from this sensor, when used in conjunction with that from the needle lift sensor, is used for idle stabilisation and reference for injection timing.

If the CKP sensor fails, the malfunction indicator lamp on the instrument panel is illuminated. The ECM enters a default mode and uses signals from the needle lift sensor to enable the ECM to continue functioning but with a reduction in engine performance and a higher than normal idle speed. Starting difficulties may also be experienced.

Needle lift sensor

The needle lift sensor is located in the No. 1 injector body. It operates as the other injectors but has a coil which surrounds the shaft of an extended injection needle. The coil is fed a DC supply from the ECM which produces a magnetic field.

When the needle is moved under the influence of fuel pressure, the magnetic field is disturbed which induces an AC voltage in the coil. The induced voltage is registered in the ECM as a reference point for the start of the injection sequence.

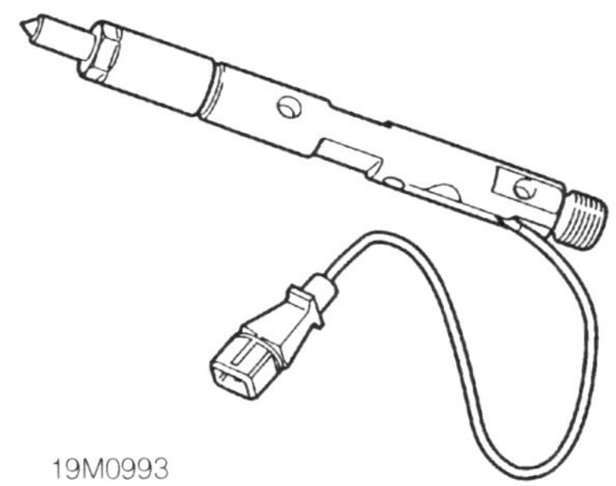

19M0993

The ECM uses the input signals from the needle lift sensor, together with a signal from the CKP sensor, to detect the actual start of injection. The ECM, using inputs from the other sensors, calculates then adjusts the injection timing of the fuel pump to achieve optimum fuelling of the engine.

If the needle lift sensor fails, the malfunction indicator lamp on the instrument panel is illuminated. The ECM, which enters a default mode, continues to function but with a reduction in engine performance and lack of throttle response.

Fuel Injection Timing Compensation

Engine Coolant Temperature (ECT) sensor

19M0985

The ECT sensor is located in the top of the coolant outlet elbow which is attached to the front of the cylinder head. The sensor is screwed into a threaded port and measures the temperature of coolant as it leaves the engine via the top hose to the radiator.

The ECT sensor is a 'thermistor' (a temperature dependent resistor), i.e. the voltage output varies in proportion to temperature. The ECM constantly monitors the signal and uses the information to correct the quantity of fuel injected and the injection timing especially during cold starting. During starting, output from the sensor determines the operating period for the glow plugs.

If the ECT sensor fails, the malfunction indicator lamp on the instrument panel is illuminated. The ECM uses a substitute value of -20°C for the injection timing and uses the fuel temperature to correct the fuel quantity.

Intake Air Temperature (IAT) sensor

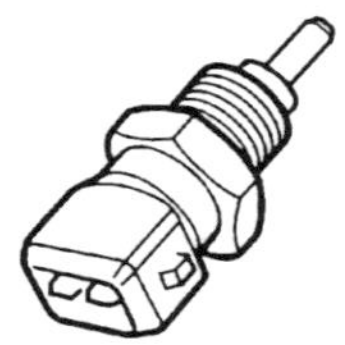

19M0981

The IAT sensor is located in the right hand side of the inlet manifold. This sensor is of the negative temperature coefficient type, designed to reduce its resistance with increasing temperature.

The ECM receives a signal proportional to the temperature of the intake air. When used in conjunction with the signal from the manifold absolute pressure (MAP) sensor and the CKP sensor, the ECM can calculate the volume of oxygen in the air and adjust the quantity of fuel being injected to achieve optimum fuelling of the engine.

Manifold Absolute Pressure (MAP) sensor

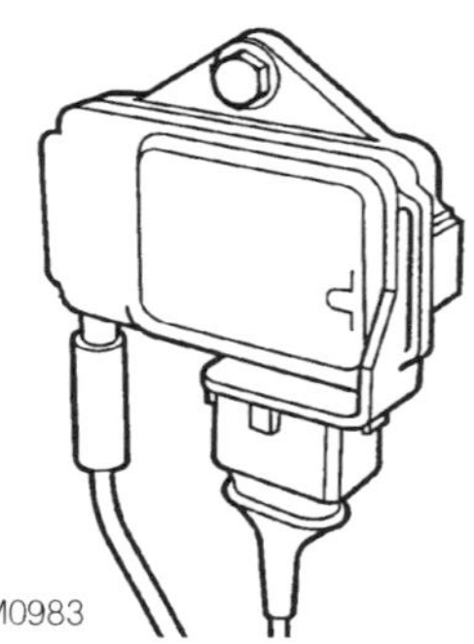

19M0983

The MAP sensor is located on the bulkhead and is connected, via a pressure tube, to the outlet side of the turbocharger.

The MAP sensor is a strain gauge type sensor and monitors the intake air pressure. The sensor is connected electrically to the ECM.

The sensor comprises a plastic body containing a pressure detection chamber. The pressure detection chamber consists of four individual sensors made from glass panels with Silicon diaphragms. The Silicon diaphragms contain resistors which are bonded to the glass panels forming an enclosed vacuum.

When the intake air pressure changes, pressure in the detection chamber causes the diaphragms to deflect. The deflection of the diaphragms alters the length of each resistor, changing their resistance. This change in resistance is converted into an analogue output signal of between 0V and 5V within the pressure sensor. The ECM outputs a reference signal of 5V to the MAP sensor. The ECM compares the output from the MAP sensor to the reference signal and converts the difference into a pressure value.

Manifold absolute pressure, when used in conjunction with the signal from the IAT sensor and the CKP sensor, allows the ECM to accurately calculate the volume of oxygen in the air and adjust the quantity of fuel being injected to achieve optimum fuelling of the engine.

If the MAP sensor fails, the malfunction indicator lamp on the instrument panel is illuminated. The ECM uses a substitute value of 45.5 kPa (6.6 lbf/in^2) which limits the fuel quantity to 21 mg/stroke resulting in a reduction in engine performance.

Vehicle Speed Sensor (VSS)

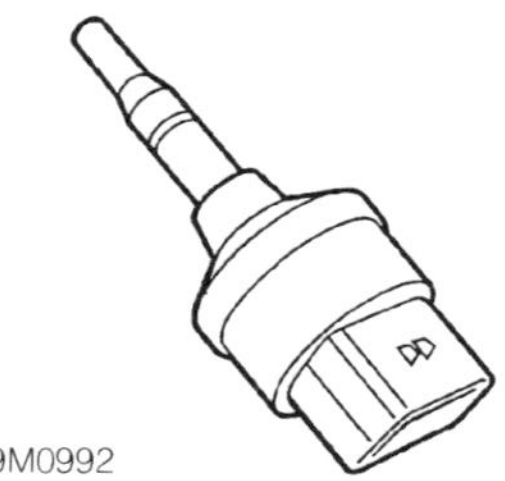

19M0992

The VSS is located on the top face of the gearbox housing at the rear of the engine. The VSS is driven by a shaft from the final drive gear where it is converted into an electrical signal proportional to road speed.

The output from the VSS is used to drive the instrument panel speedometer in addition to providing a signal to the ECM. The ECM uses this signal, along with other inputs, to provide active surge damping, adjust idle stabilisation and the quantity of fuel being delivered to the injectors.

On vehicles fitted with ABS, the speed sensor is not fitted. A dummy sensor is fitted to blank the sensor port. The ECM and the speedometer receive their signals from the ABS ECU, which it calculates from each ABS wheel sensor.

If the VSS fails, the malfunction warning lamp on the instrument panel is illuminated. The ECM uses a substitute value of 1.8 mph (3 km/h), active surge damping is removed and the air conditioning (if fitted) is inoperable.

Throttle Position (TP) sensor

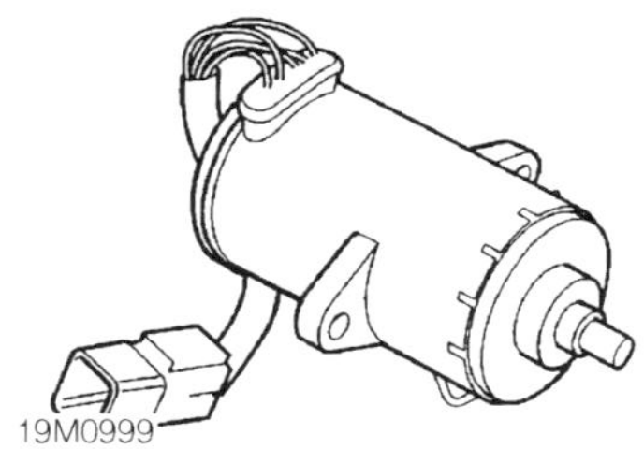

19M0999

The TP sensor is mounted on the pedal box and is connected by a linkage to the throttle pedal. Movements of the throttle pedal are sensed by the TP sensor and a signal sent to the ECM.

The engine management system is a 'Drive by Wire' system. The throttle pedal is not physically connected to the fuel injection pump by a mechanical linkage as in a traditional injection system, but instead the amount of fuel injected is controlled entirely by the ECM.

The TP sensor consists of a thick film potentiometer together with a sender switch. With the throttle pedal at rest the switch is open. The sender switch signal from the potentiometer is used by the ECM to implement idle speed control and over-run fuel shut-off. When the throttle pedal has been moved enough to rotate the potentiometer more than 9 degrees, the switch closes.

When the potentiometer is moved, the sender switch signals a logic input to the ECM. The ECM then checks the voltage signal from the potentiometer. This voltage is compared with a pre-programmed value to check the potentiometer is working correctly.

Throttle pedal movement causes voltage across the potentiometer to vary. The ECM calculates the rate of change of the voltage signal in positive (acceleration) or negative (deceleration) directions. From this, the ECM can determine the required engine speed, rate of acceleration or deceleration and apply acceleration enrichment, deceleration fuel metering, or over-run fuel cut-off.

The ECM calculates the 'maximum allowable fuel quantity' from the input signal according to strategies such as smoke limitation and active surge damping to calculate the final figure. If the signal from the throttle potentiometer is smaller than the maximum allowable quantity, then the requested quantity will be injected. However, if the requested quantity is greater than the maximum allowable quantity, then the maximum allowable quantity will be injected rather than that demanded.

If the TP sensor fails, the malfunction indicator lamp on the instrument panel is illuminated. The ECM limits the engine speed to 1060 rpm and the air conditioning (if fitted) is inoperable.

Brake pedal switch

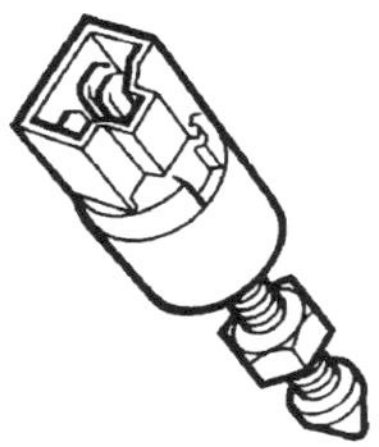

19M0998

The brake pedal switch is mounted on the pedal box. The switch informs the ECM when the vehicle is braking and allows it to implement active surge damping and over-run fuel cut-off.

The ECM has one brake input which is monitored for plausibility with the TP sensor. If the brake pedal switch fails, there will be no effect on the engine management system.

Glow plug relay

The glow plug relay is located behind the battery tray, below the engine compartment fuse box.

When the starter switch is turned to position 'II', the ECM energises the glow plug relay and illuminates the glow plug warning light on the instrument panel. The glow plug relay supplies a current from the battery to the four glow plugs to reduce post start emissions and assist cold starting by raising the temperature of the compressed air to ignition point.

Glow plugs

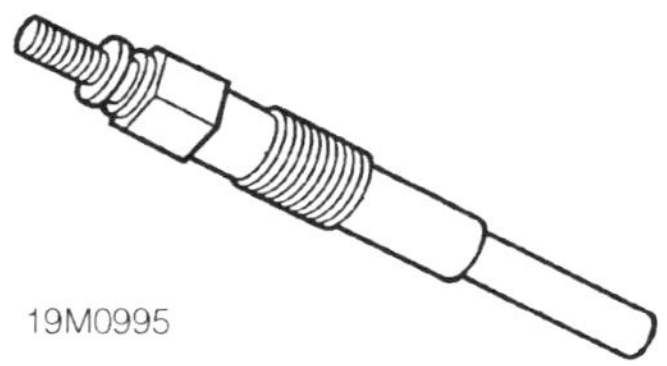

19M0995

The four glow plugs are located in the forward face of the cylinder head below their respective injector. Each glow plug draws a current of 23 to 25 Amps. The current draw has a linear decline to 11 Amps as the glow plug warms.

ENGINE MANAGEMENT SYSTEM - EDC

The operating period of the glow plugs is dependent upon the initial engine temperature determined by the ECM from the ECT sensor. Once the glow plugs have operated for their pre-determined time, the ECM will remove the supply from the glow plug relay and extinguish the glow plug warning light on the instrument panel. Glow plug operation times are as follows (times are approximate):

Temperature	Time
+30°C	2.0 Seconds
+10°C	3.6 Seconds
0°C	4.5 Seconds
-5°C	5.0 Seconds
-7.5°C	5.5 Seconds
-10°C	7.0 Seconds
-12°C	9.0 Seconds
-15°C	11.0 Seconds
-20°C	15.0 Seconds

The ECM can keep the glow plugs on for a short period of time to assist with smooth running and to aid initial driveaway. The time for glow plug operation after the engine is started is dependant on coolant temperature.

With a coolant temperature of 85°C, the ECU will keep the glow plugs on for approximately 2.0 seconds. In very cold conditions, if the ECT sensor reads a coolant temperature of - 25°C, the supply to the glow plugs can remain connected for up to 100 seconds. The supply to the glow plugs is removed if the fuelling to each cylinder exceeds 20 mg/stroke or the engine speed exceeds 1656 rpm.

Mass Air Flow (MAF) sensor

The MAF sensor is located in the air cleaner outlet pipe. The mass air flow is determined from the cooling effect of inlet air flowing over a Hot Film sensor. This signal is fed back to the ECM where it is used to monitor the recirculation of exhaust gases. An increase in the exhaust gas recirculation reduces the amount of intake air being drawn into the system, thereby reducing the cooling effect of the Hot Film resistor.

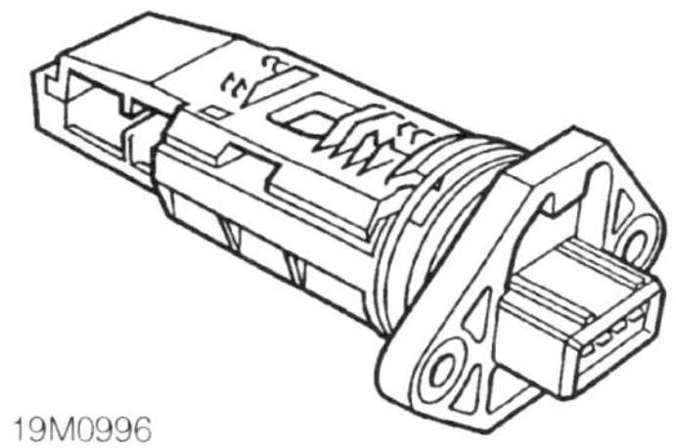

19M0996

Diagnostic Socket

The diagnostic socket is located behind the centre console in the passenger footwell. The diagnostic socket is provided to enable diagnosis via TestBook to be carried out and to allow interrogation of the ECM for triggered fault codes.

Malfunction Indicator Lamp (MIL)

The ECM has a built in self-diagnosis function. If certain faults are detected, the MIL in the instrument panel will illuminate, and the ECM will implement a back-up facility to enable the system to continue functioning, though at a reduced level of performance.

Minor faults will not illuminate the MIL, but will be stored in the ECM's memory and can be retrieved at a later date using TestBook. If a serious fault is detected, the warning light will illuminate and the engine management system will shut down, preventing the vehicle from being started or driven.

The MIL will remain illuminated until the starter switch is turned off. If the fault is still present when the starter switch is turned back on the MIL will illuminate. If the fault is not present when the starter switch is turned on, the MIL will remain extinguished, but a fault code will remain stored in the ECM's memory.

Cooling fans (all models)

On all models, two electric cooling fans are fitted in a housing behind the radiator.

The ECM controls the operation of the cooling fans. The ECT sensor constantly sends signals to the ECM. When engine coolant reaches a temperature of 106°C, the ECM switches the cooling fans on, in slow mode. When the engine coolant reaches a temperature of 112°C, the ECM switches the cooling fans from slow to fast mode. When the engine coolant temperature is reduced to 106°C, the ECM switches the cooling fans to operate in slow mode until the temperature is reduced to below 100°C, when the ECM switches the fans off. When the ignition is turned off, the fans stop.

Cooling fans (Vehicles with air conditioning (A/C) only)

The ECM controls the A/C grant output. If an input is received from the A/C system the ECM will consider engaging the A/C clutch. The ECM considers the coolant temperature and the throttle position before the A/C grant is operated. When the A/C grant is started, the cooling fans turn on in slow mode, unless the coolant temperature is above 112°C when they operate in fast mode.

The ECM provides two outputs to control the two cooling fans; slow mode and fast mode. The modes of operation vary depending on signals received from the A/C thermostat, the ECT sensor and the ECM. In slow mode, both fans operate in series sharing the same electrical feed. In fast mode, both fans operate in parallel, each fan receiving its feed from a separate source. When the ignition is turned off, both fans stop.

If an engine temperature of 117°C is sensed by the ECT sensor, the ECM can override the A/C request to reduce load on the engine. The air conditioning request is reinstated when the coolant temperature reaches a 115°C.

Hill descent control signal (Vehicles with ABS only)

See BRAKES, Information.

The ECM constantly provides signal information of throttle position and engine speed and also assesses other engine inputs to produce an engine torque signal. These signals, together with engine and gearbox identifiers, are passed to the ABS ECU to control hill descent.

FUEL SYSTEM

Fuel is drawn from the tank by the Fuel Injection Pump (FIP) via a filter, located in the engine compartment, which removes particle contamination from the fuel.

The FIP meters a precisely timed, exact quantity of fuel into the injectors in response to throttle variations, injection timing varying with engine speed.

Fuel Injection Pump (FIP)

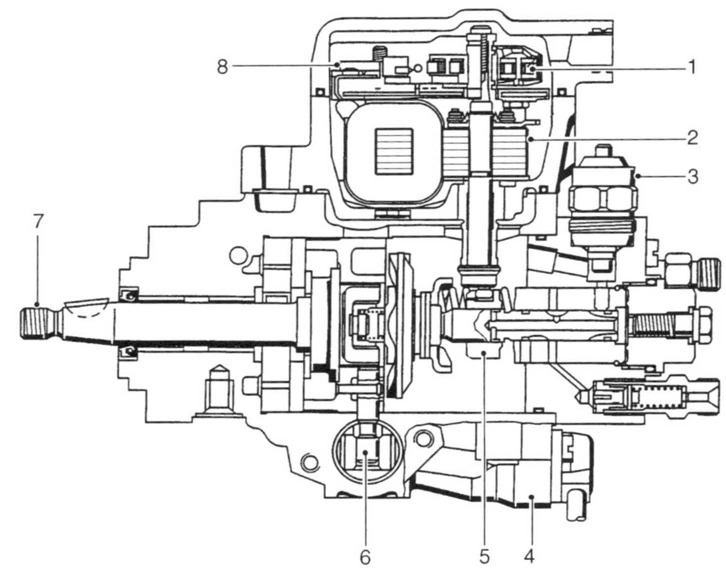

19M2448

1. Fuel quantity servo potentiometer
2. Fuel quantity servo control unit
3. Fuel shut off solenoid
4. Injection timing device solenoid valve
5. Control spool
6. Injection timing device
7. FIP drive shaft
8. Fuel temperature sensor

Any excess fuel delivered to the FIP is not injected, but passed back to the tank via a fuel return line.

Fuel is injected directly into the cylinder head where it ignites. A swirl chamber, machined into the piston crown, promotes efficient mixing of the fuel with the already compressed air. The burning fuel expands rapidly in the combustion chamber, creating extreme turbulence which further mixes the burning fuel with the compressed air, providing complete combustion and reducing emissions.

The FIP is a vane-type pump, which is belt driven from the rear end of the camshaft. Fuel delivery from the pump to the injectors is regulated by the movement of a control spool.

Movement of the control spool increases or decreases the fuel delivery rate to meet engine operating requirements.

The pump houses the following components which either provide feed back to, or are controlled by, the ECM:

Engine Fuel Temperature (EFT) sensor

Fuel temperature is monitored by an EFT sensor located in the FIP. This sensor is of the negative temperature coefficient (NTC) type, designed to reduce its resistance with increasing temperature. The sensor is connected to earth and to a precision resistor inside the ECM. A small current is fed through the resistor.

When the system is operating, the ECM regularly checks the sensor voltage which changes with fuel temperature. This is converted to a digital word that can be read by the microprocessor and converted to a temperature reading. As fuel density varies with temperature, the information received is used to calculate the correct quantity of fuel to inject.

If the fuel temperature sensor fails, the malfunction indicator light on the instrument panel will illuminate. The ECM uses a substitute value of 60°C and slight effects on fuelling may occur.

Quantity servo control unit

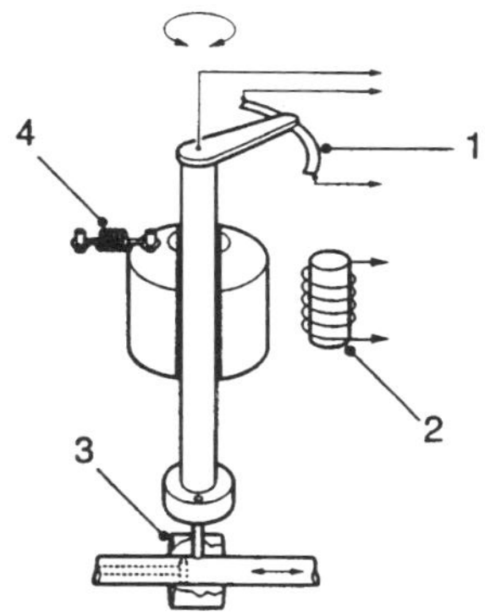

19M 0708

The servo control unit is used to accurately control the amount of fuel delivered to the injectors. The unit consists of a rotary magnet mounted on an eccentric shaft; the shaft engages with the control spool (3) of the pump.

The rotary magnet is fitted with a return spring (4) and moves under the influence of a control coil (2). The magnet rotates through an arc of about 60 degrees moving the control spool from the closed position to the maximum fuel delivery position. The eccentric shaft engages with the control spool at one end, while the opposite end operates a rotary potentiometer (1).

When the control coil is energised the rotary magnet and eccentric shaft move against spring pressure. Rotary movement of the eccentric shaft is converted into linear movement of the control spool. This allows more fuel to be delivered to the injectors.

When the control coil is de-energised the return spring causes the rotary magnet and eccentric shaft to resume their original position. The control spool is moved to the closed position.

ENGINE MANAGEMENT SYSTEM - EDC

Quantity servo potentiometer

Mounted at the top of the servo control unit is a rotary potentiometer. As the eccentric shaft of the servo control unit moves, the wiper of the potentiometer is moved across the resistive part of the potentiometer. The voltage output from the potentiometer is proportional to the position of the control spool. From this input the ECM can calculate the quantity of fuel being delivered by the pump and adjust the amount of fuel being delivered by energising the control coil to move the control spool.

Injection timing device

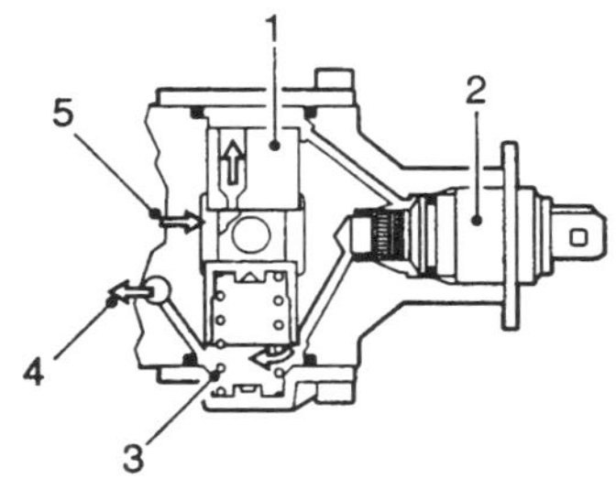

19M 0707

1. Plunger
2. Solenoid
3. Spring
4. Pump feed pressure
5. Pump internal pressure

The injection timing device consists of a spring loaded plunger and a solenoid. The spring loaded plunger acts against a cam plate driven by the FIP shaft. The spring loaded plunger moves under the influence of the pump working pressure.

The injection timing solenoid is responsible for the characteristic 'buzzing' sound when the ignition is turned on. The solenoid operates at 50 Hz and by varying the operating duration, the advance/retard of the fuel injection point can be adjusted.

With the engine stopped and the solenoid de-energised, the plunger (1) is in the fully retarded position. When the engine is started, the fuel pressure (4) passes through the plunger (1) and acts on the plunger face. Simultaneously, the solenoid (2) is energised by the ECM. Depending on the signals received from the sensors, the solenoid (2) is energised for varying lengths of time. This allows the fuel pressure (5) at the plunger face to relieve to the spring side of the plunger, which is at pump inlet pressure (5), retarding the injection timing. As the plunger moves, a cam plate, connected to the plunger via a pin, moves and adjusts the injection timing. The ECM continually modulates the solenoid, advancing or retarding the injection timing to achieve the optimum timing position.

The ECM receives a feedback signal from the needle lift sensor and will attempt to correct the injection timing accordingly by altering the signal to the solenoid (2). If a change does not occur or differs by a substantial amount, the ECM will assume a fault exists and reduce the amount of fuel injected.

Fuel cut-off solenoid

19M0986

The fuel cut-off solenoid is located in the high pressure section of the FIP. When the ignition is switched on the ECM sends a signal to the solenoid. The solenoid energises opening a valve allowing fuel to flow.

When the ignition is switched off, or in the event of a serious engine problem, the ECM will remove the supply to the solenoid, closing the valve and cutting off the fuel supply to the injectors.

EXHAUST GAS RECIRCULATION (EGR)

During certain running conditions the EGR system directs exhaust gases into the intake manifold to be used in the combustion process. The principal effect of this is to reduce combustion temperatures, which in turn reduces Oxides of Nitrogen (NO_x) emissions.

The ECM controls an EGR modulator valve mounted on the bulkhead. This valve, when modulated, opens the exhaust EGR valve and directs exhaust gases into the inlet manifold.

See EMISSION CONTROL, Description and operation.

AIR INTAKE SYSTEM

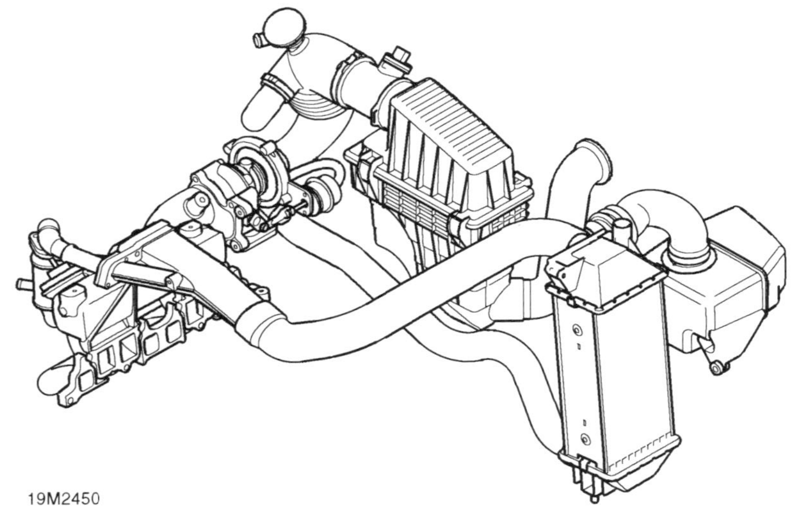

19M2450

The engine is supplied with pre-compressed air by a single stage Garrett GT1549 turbocharger. The turbocharger is mounted on the left hand end of the exhaust manifold at the rear of the engine.

With the engine operating under load, exhaust gases pass into the turbine side of the turbocharger causing the turbine to rotate, driving a compressor mounted on the turbine shaft in the intake side of the turbocharger. Intake air is drawn through the air cleaner to the turbocharger, where it is compressed by the compressor. The compressed air is then fed into the inlet manifold via an intercooler, which reduces the temperature of the compressed air, increasing its density still further.

Turbocharger

The turbocharger unit is located at the left hand end of the exhaust manifold and comprises a die cast housing and a pneumatic actuator.

The housing contains a turbine on a shaft which is driven by exhaust gases. At one end of the turbine shaft is a compressor, mounted on the intake side of the turbocharger. The housing has two main ports. One port receives exhaust gases from the manifold and the other receives clean air from the air filter. Two smaller ports provide an air pressure feed of clean air to the wastegate actuator and the MAP sensor.

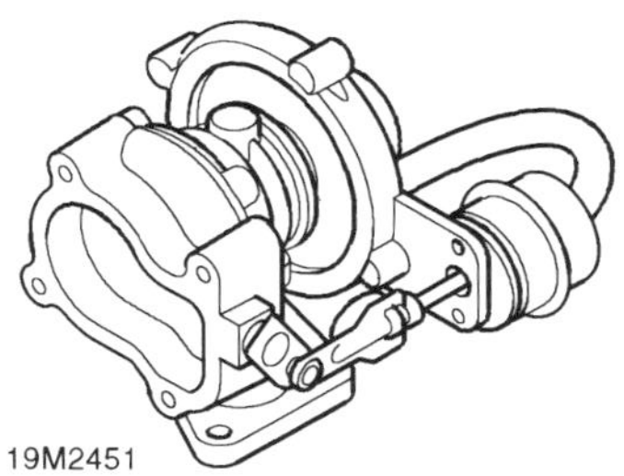

19M2451

The MAP sensor, which is located on the bulkhead, is used to detect intake air pressure changes which enable the ECM to calculate the volume of oxygen in the intake air.

Two oil lines provide lubrication for the turbocharger. A small diameter pipe supplies oil under pressure from the engine oil pump. A larger pipe provides the oil return from the turbocharger to the cylinder block.

Intercooler

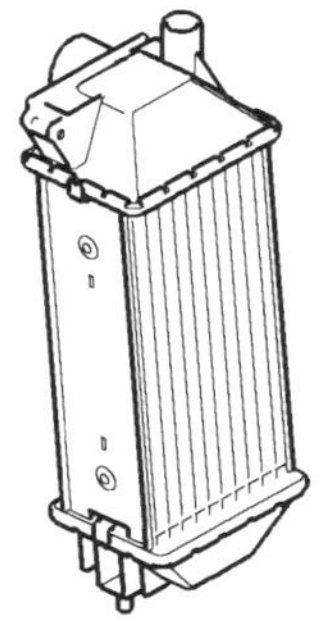

19M2452

The intercooler is positioned at the front of the vehicle to the left of the radiator and is mounted in rubber bushes located on the front body cross member and the bonnet locking platform. The intercooler is an aluminium cross flow construction with plastic mouldings at top and bottom. The plastic mouldings each incorporate a hose connection port.

The intercooler receives a compressed air/exhaust gas mixture from the turbocharger via a hose to the bottom connection port. The top connection port, supplies cooled, compressed air/exhaust gas mixture from the intercooler to the engine inlet manifold via a hose. The intercooler reduces the temperature of the compressed air from the turbocharger which increases the air density.

Boost control

Boost control is achieved by a wastegate actuator operating a mechanical flap, known as a wastegate, situated in the turbocharger. When operated, the wastegate allows exhaust gases to bypass the turbine side of the turbocharger, so decreasing the rotational speed of the turbine thereby reducing the pressure of the intake air.

The wastegate actuator consists of a diaphragm connected to a mechanical linkage which is opposed by an internal spring. Pressure from the compressor side of the turbocharger is applied to the actuator via a sensing pipe. The pressure acting on the actuator diaphragm builds up until it exceeds the opposing force of the internal spring (approx. 17 psi or 1.2 Bar) causing the mechanical linkage to move, thereby opening the wastegate on the turbocharger and so reducing the boost pressure. As boost pressure is reduced the mechanical linkage will move the other way closing the wastegate allowing the pressure to increase again. With the engine under significant load the wastegate actuator will be constantly opening and closing the wastegate.

Air cleaner

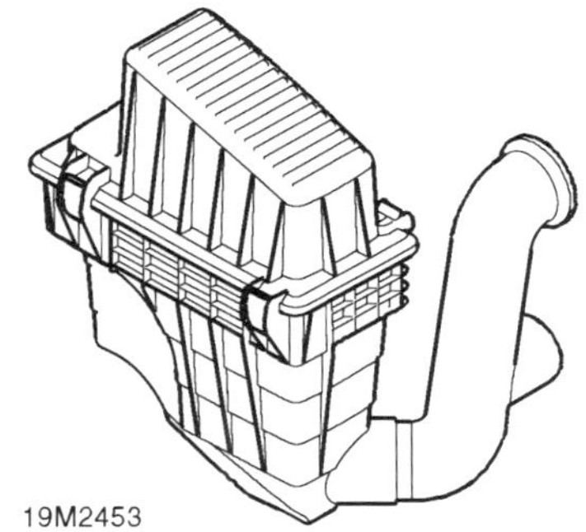

19M2453

The air cleaner housing is located on the left hand side of the engine bay. The air cleaner housing is plastic moulded with a removable lid which is retained with spring clips. Removal of the lid allows access to the corrugated paper filter element.

An air intake pipe is located at the front of the air cleaner housing and draws air from within the engine compartment. A rubber hose is connected to the intake pipe and connects to a resonator box located in the front left hand wheel arch. The resonator box is used to reduce induction noise.

The outlet from the air cleaner housing has a plastic pipe which provides the location for the mass air flow sensor. The outlet pipe is sealed to the housing with an O-ring seal. A gauze filter in the pipe provides additional contamination protection.

A rubber hose connects the outlet pipe to the turbocharger. The rubber hose also connects a breather from the camcover to the air intake system. A plastic tube connected to the rubber hose provides additional reduction of induction noise.

SENSOR - ENGINE COOLANT TEMPERATURE (ECT)

Service repair no - 18.30.10

Remove

1. Disconnect battery earth lead.
2. Remove engine acoustic cover. ***See ENGINE - 'L' SERIES, Repairs.***
3. Position absorbent cloth around ECT sensor to absorb any coolant spillage.

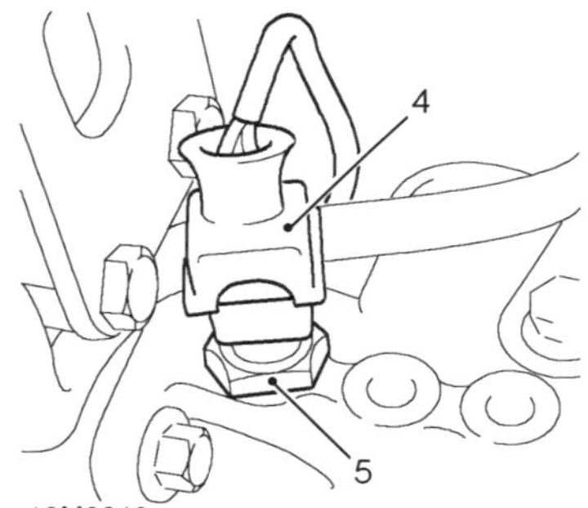

18M0248

4. Disconnect multiplug from ECT.
5. Remove ECT sensor.

Refit

1. Clean threads of ECT sensor and apply Loctite 577.
2. Fit ECT sensor and tighten to 5 Nm.
3. Connect multiplug to ECT sensor.
4. Fit engine acoustic cover. ***See ENGINE - 'L' SERIES, Repairs.***
5. Check and if necessary top up cooling system. ***See INFORMATION, Capacities, fluids and lubricants.***
6. Connect battery earth lead.

SOLENOID - FUEL CUT OFF

Service repair no - 18.30.07

Remove

1. Disconnect battery earth lead.
2. Remove engine acoustic cover. ***See ENGINE - 'L' SERIES, Repairs.***

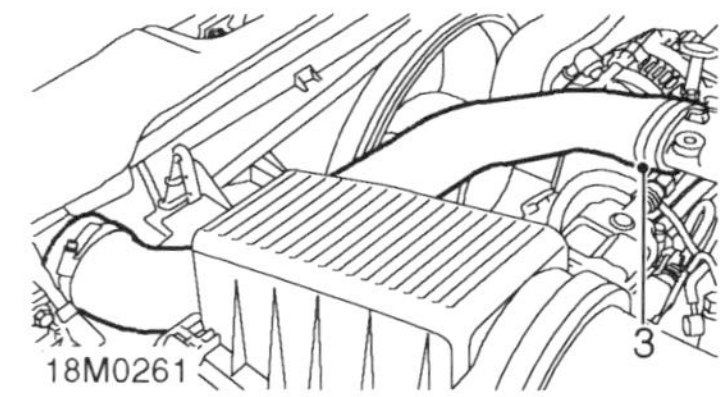

18M0261

3. Release clip and disconnct air hose from plenum chamber.
4. Clean top of FIP around solenoid.
5. Position absorbent cloth around solenoid to absorb any fuel spillage.

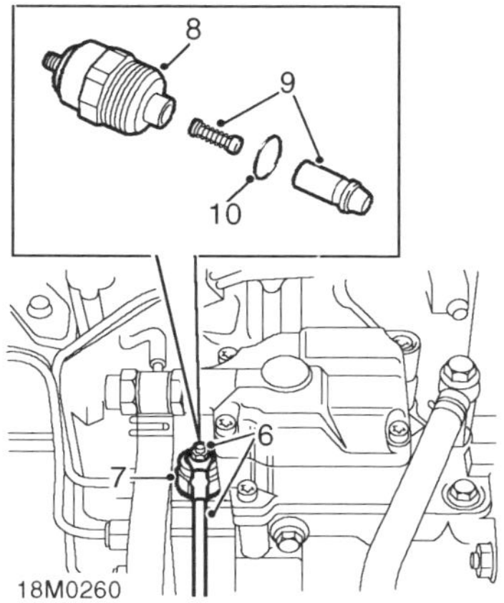

18M0260

6. Remove nut and disconnect lead from solenoid.
7. Using a 24 mm spanner, loosen solenoid from FIP.
8. Unscrew and remove solenoid.
9. Collect solenoid plunger and spring.
10. Remove and discard 'O' ring from solenoid.

Refit

1. Lubricate and fit NEW 'O' ring to solenoid.
2. Clean solenoid plunger.
3. Fit spring and plunger to solenoid.
4. Fit solenoid to FIP and tighten to 20 Nm.
5. Connect lead to solenoid, fit nut and tighten to 2.5 Nm.
6. Connect hose to plenum chamber and secure with clip.
7. Fit acoustic cover. ***See ENGINE - 'L' SERIES, Repairs.***
8. Connect battery earth lead.

SENSOR - CRANKSHAFT POSITION (CKP)

Service repair no - 18.30.12

Remove

1. Remove inlet and exhaust manifold gasket. ***See MANIFOLD & EXHAUST SYSTEMS - 'L' SERIES, Repairs.***

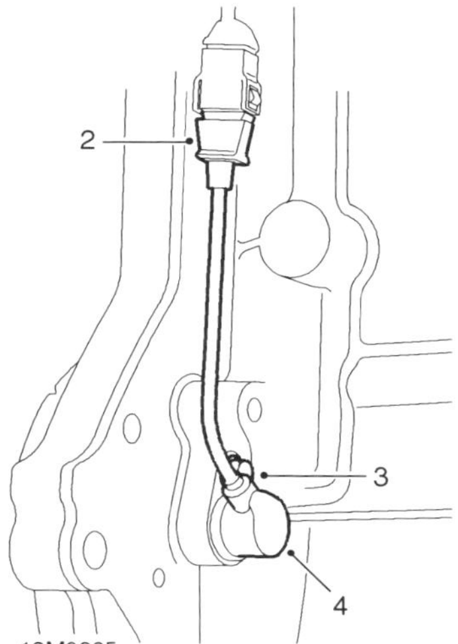

18M0265

2. Disconnect multiplug from CKP sensor.
3. Remove bolt securing CKP sensor to flywheel housing.
4. Remove CKP sensor.

Refit

1. Clean CKP sensor and mating face of flywheel housing.
2. Position CKP sensor, fit bolt and tighten to 6 Nm.
3. Connect multiplug to CKP sensor.
4. Fit inlet and exhaust manifold gasket. ***See MANIFOLD & EXHAUST SYSTEMS - 'L' SERIES, Repairs.***

ELEMENT - AIR FILTER

Service repair no - 19.10.10

Remove

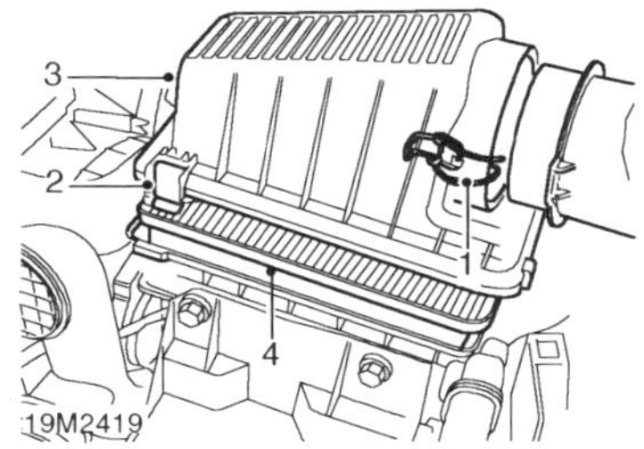

19M2419

1. Release 2 clips securing MAF sensor to air cleaner top cover.
2. Release 4 clips retaining air cleaner cover.
3. Remove air cleaner top cover.
4. Remove and discard air filter element.

Refit

1. Clean inside of air cleaner unit.
2. Fit NEW air filter element.
3. Fit air cleaner top cover and secure clips.
4. Align air cleaner unit with MAF sensor and secure clips.

ENGINE CONTROL MODULE - (ECM)

Service repair no - 18.30.01

Remove

1. Remove battery. ***See ELECTRICAL, Repairs.***

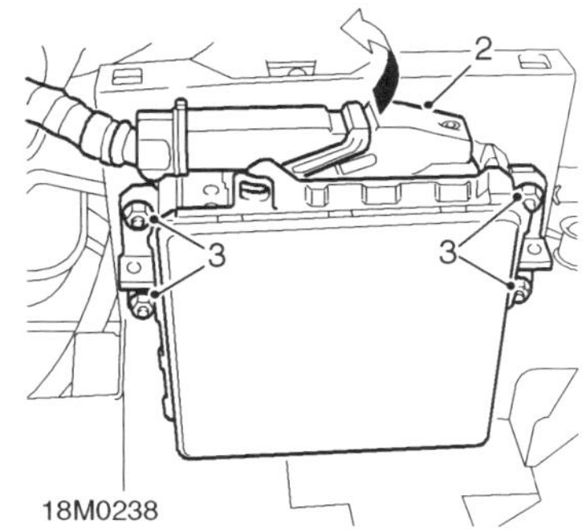

18M0238

2. Using a flat bladed screwdriver release multiplug clamp and release multiplug from ECM.
3. Remove 4 nuts securing ECM to bracket and collect ECM.

Refit

1. Fit ECM to bracket bolts, fit and tighten nuts to 9 Nm.
2. Fit multiplug to ECM and secure with clamp.
3. Fit battery. ***See ELECTRICAL, Repairs.***

SENSOR - INTAKE AIR TEMPERATURE (IAT)

Service repair no - 18.30.09

Remove

1. Disconnect battery earth lead.
2. Remove engine acoustic cover. ***See ENGINE - 'L' SERIES, Repairs.***

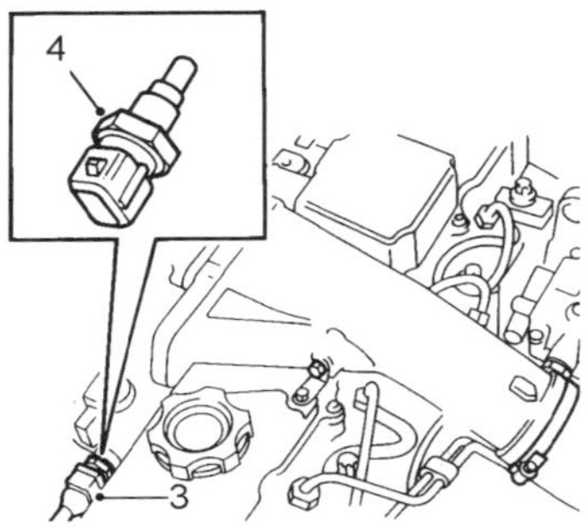

18M0262

3. Disconnect multiplug from IAT sensor.
4. Remove IAT sensor.

Refit

1. Clean threads of IAT sensor.
2. Clean mating faces of IAT sensor and inlet manifold.
3. Apply Loctite 577 to sensor thread
4. Fit IAT sensor and tighten to 12 Nm.
5. Connect multiplug to IAT sensor.
6. Fit engine acoustic cover. ***See ENGINE - 'L' SERIES, Repairs.***
7. Connect battery earth lead.

SENSOR - MANIFOLD ABSOLUTE PRESSURE (MAP)

Service repair no - 18.30.56

Remove

1. Disconnect battery earth lead.

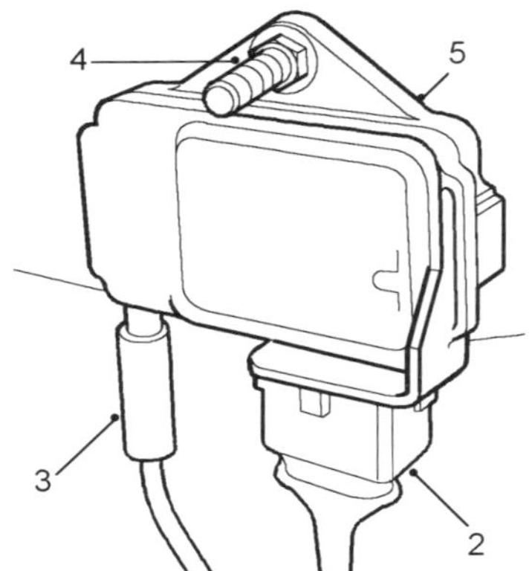

18M0259

2. Disconnect multiplug from MAP sensor.
3. Disconnect boost pressure sensing pipe from MAP sensor.
4. Remove nut securing MAP sensor to bulkhead.
5. Remove MAP sensor.

Refit

1. Position MAP sensor and tighten nut to 5 Nm.
2. Connect boost pressure sensing pipe to MAP sensor.
3. Connect multiplug to MAP sensor.
4. Connect battery earth lead.

RELAY MODULE - ENGINE MANAGEMENT

Service repair no - 18.30.71

Remove

1. Disconnect battery earth lead.

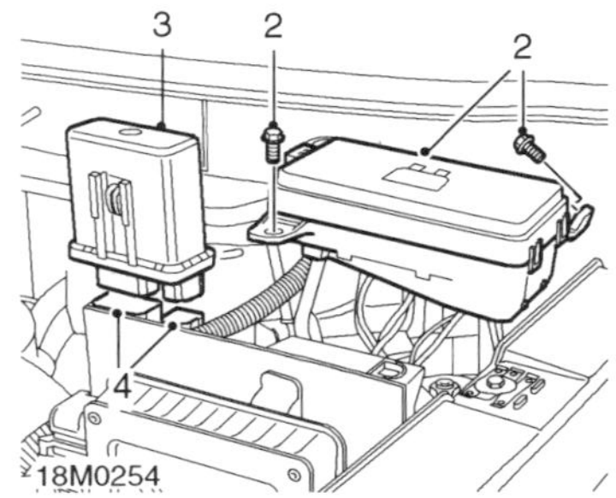

18M0254

2. Remove 2 bolts and position engine compartment fuse box aside.
3. Release relay module from mounting bracket.
4. Disconnect 2 multiplugs from relay module.
5. Remove relay module.

Refit

1. Position relay module and connect multiplugs.
2. Secure relay module to mounting bracket.
3. Position fuse box and tighten bolts to 4 Nm.
4. Connect battery earth lead.

AIR - CLEANER

Service repair no - 19.10.01

Remove

1. Remove battery. ***See ELECTRICAL, Repairs.***

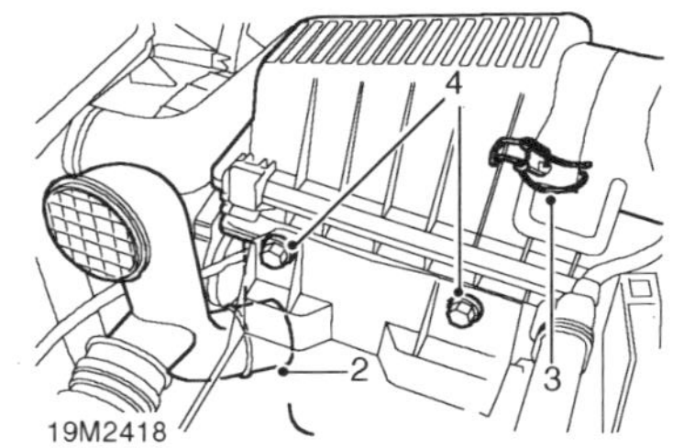

19M2418

2. Release air intake hose from bottom of air cleaner.
3. Release 2 clips and disconnect MAF sensor from air cleaner.
4. Remove 2 bolts securing air cleaner to battery tray and remove air cleaner.

Refit

1. Position air cleaner to battery tray. Fit bolts and tighten to 9 Nm.

> NOTE: Ensure bottom of air filter is located on peg.

2. Connect MAF sensor and secure with clips.
3. Connect air intake hose to bottom of air cleaner.
4. Fit battery. ***See ELECTRICAL, Repairs.***

SENSOR - MASS AIR FLOW (MAF)

Service repair no - 19.22.25

Remove

1. Disconnect battery earth lead.

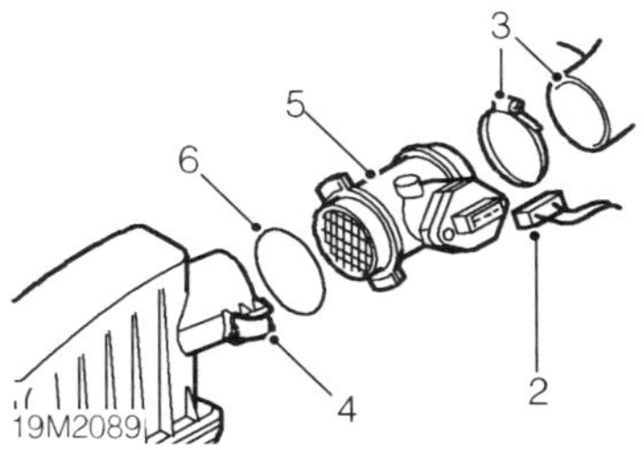

2. Disconnect multiplug from MAF sensor.
3. Release clip securing air intake hose to MAF sensor and disconnect hose.
4. Release 2 clips securing MAF sensor to air filter.
5. Remove MAF sensor.
6. Remove and discard 'O' ring.

Refit

1. Clean 'O' ring recess in air filter.
2. Fit NEW 'O' ring to MAF sensor.
3. Fit MAF sensor to air filter, secure with clips.
4. Fit clip to intake hose.
5. Connect intake hose to MAF sensor and secure clip.
6. Connect multiplug to MAF sensor.
7. Connect battery earth lead.

THROTTLE POTENTIOMETER - RHD

Service repair no - 19.22.49

Remove

1. Remove passenger compartment fuse box. ***See ELECTRICAL, Repairs.***

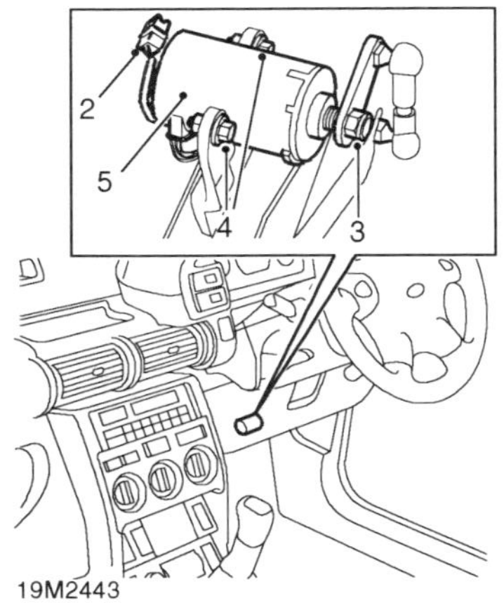

2. Release throttle potentiometer multiplug from bracket and disconnect multiplug from main harness.
3. Remove nut securing lever to potentiometer.
4. Remove 2 nuts and bolts securing potentiometer to throttle pedal bracket.
5. Remove throttle potentiometer.

Refit

1. Fit throttle potentiometer and secure with nuts and bolts.
2. Connect throttle potentiometer multiplug to main harness and secure multiplug to bracket.

Setting

3. Hold throttle pedal up, to ensure throttle is closed. While held in this position, fit lever to potentiometer and secure with nut supplied in kit.
4. Fit passenger compartment fuse box. ***See ELECTRICAL, Repairs.***
5. To ensure the potentiometer is set correctly, the system must be checked using TestBook.

THROTTLE POTENTIOMETER - LHD

Service repair no - 19.22.49

Remove

1. Remove fascia. ***See BODY, Repairs.***

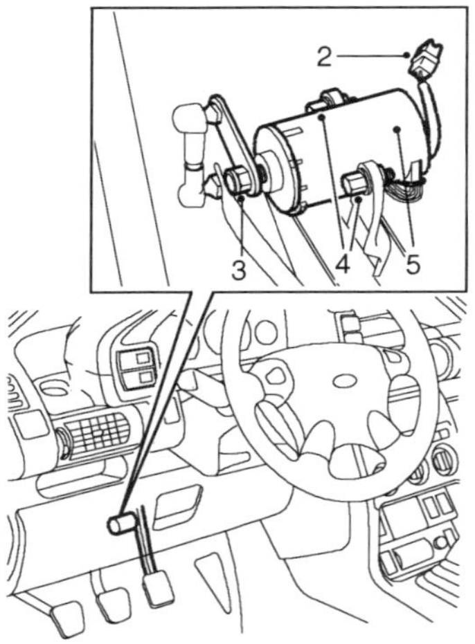

19M2444

2. Release throttle potentiometer multiplug from bracket and disconnect multiplug from main harness.
3. Remove nut securing lever to potentiometer.
4. Remove 2 nuts and bolts securing potentiometer to throttle pedal bracket.
5. Remove throttle potentiometer.

Refit

1. Fit throttle potentiometer and secure with nuts and bolts.
2. Connect throttle potentiometer multiplug to main harness and secure multiplug to bracket.

Setting

3. Hold throttle pedal up to ensure throttle is closed. While held in this position, fit lever to potentiometer and secure with nut supplied in kit.
4. Fit fascia. ***See BODY, Repairs.***
5. To ensure the potentiometer is set correctly, the system must be checked using TestBook. ***See BODY, Doors.***

FILTER - FUEL

Service repair no - 19.25.02

Remove

1. Disconnect battery earth lead.
2. Release straps and remove vehicle jack from retaining bracket.
3. Position absorbent cloth beneath fuel filter.

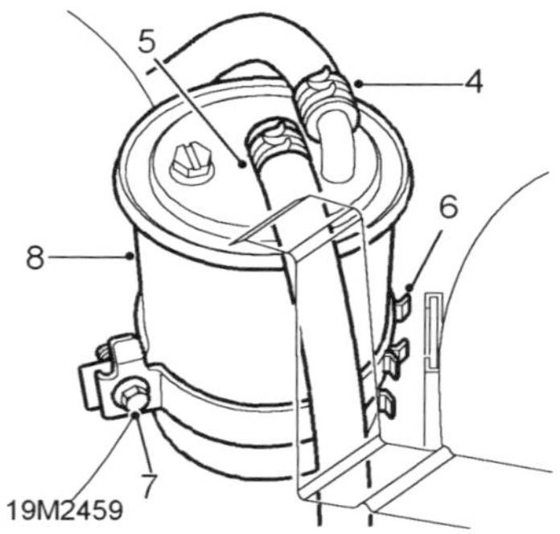

19M2459

4. Release clip and disconnect fuel inlet hose from filter.
5. Release clip and disconnect fuel outlet hose from filter.

CAUTION: Plug the connections.

6. Remove fuel filter bracket from body mounting.
7. Loosen filter bracket clamp bolt.
8. Remove filter from mounting bracket.

Refit

1. Fit NEW filter to mounting bracket.
2. Tighten filter bracket clamp bolt.
3. Fit filter bracket to body mounting.
4. Remove plugs from connections.
5. Connect fuel outlet hose to filter and secure clip.
6. Connect fuel inlet hose to filter and secure clip.
7. Loosen bleed screw.
8. Repeatedly squeeze fuel hand primer until fuel, issuing from bleed screw is free from air bubbles; tighten bleed screw.
9. Connect battery earth lead.
10. Position vehicle jack to mounting bracket and secure retaining straps.

PUMP - FUEL INJECTION (FIP)

Service repair no - 19.30.07

Remove

1. Disconnect battery earth lead.
2. Remove plenum chamber. ***See this section.***
3. Remove FIP timing belt. ***See ENGINE - 'L' SERIES, Repairs.***
4. Drain cooling system. ***See COOLING SYSTEM - 'L' SERIES, Adjustments.***

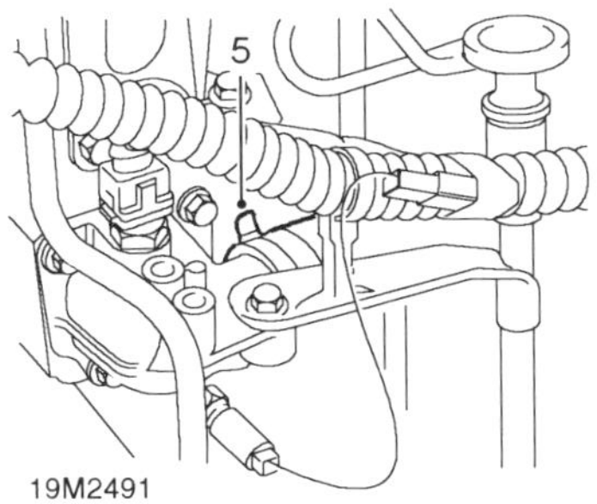

5. Loosen clip and disconnect top hose from cylinder head elbow.

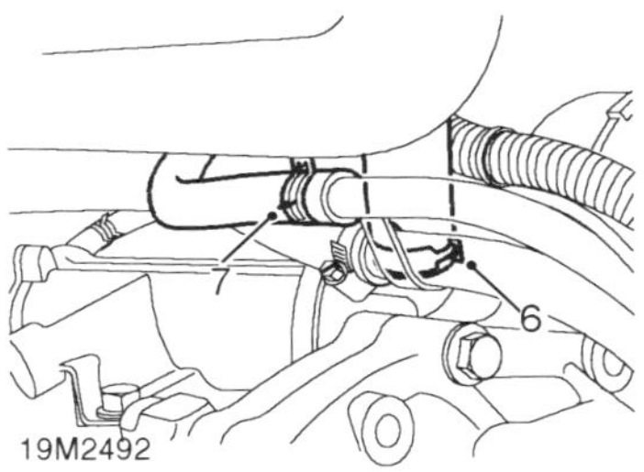

6. Loosen clip and disconnect top hose from engine oil cooler.

7. Loosen clip and disconnect top hose from coolant rail.

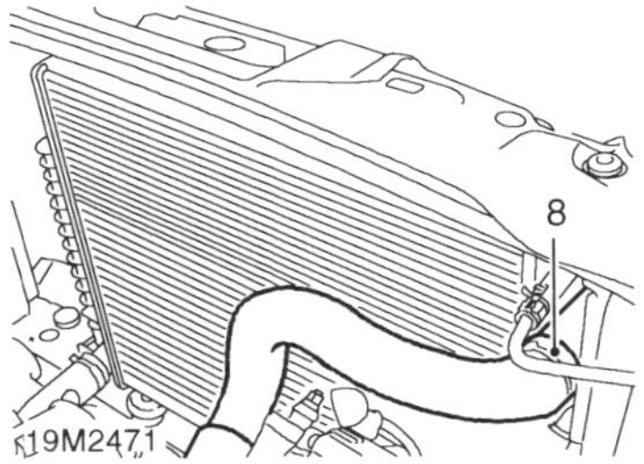

8. Loosen clip and disconnect top hose from radiator.
9. Remove top hose.

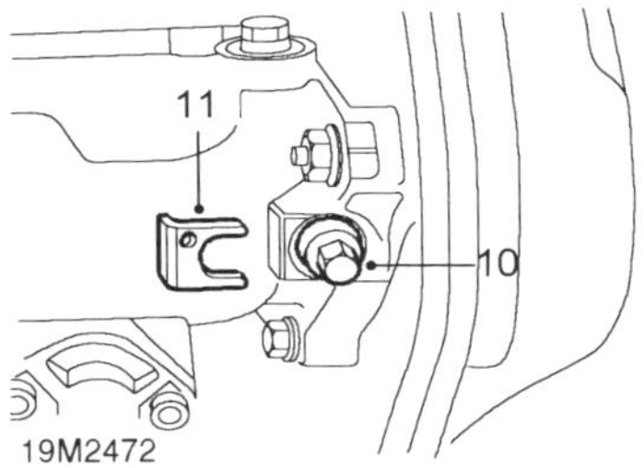

10. Loosen FIP shaft clamp bolt.
11. Remove spacer from clamp bolt.
12. Tighten clamp bolt to 31 Nm.

CAUTION: DO NOT exceed specified torque. Damage to the shaft will render the FIP inoperable.

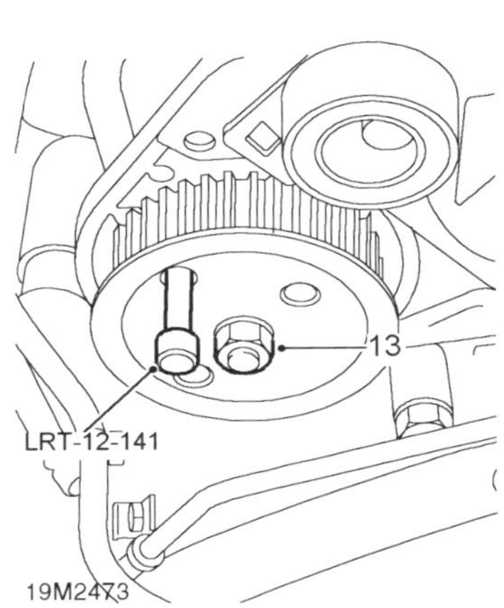

13. Remove FIP drive gear retaining nut.
14. Remove locking pin tool **LRT-12-141** from FIP drive gear.

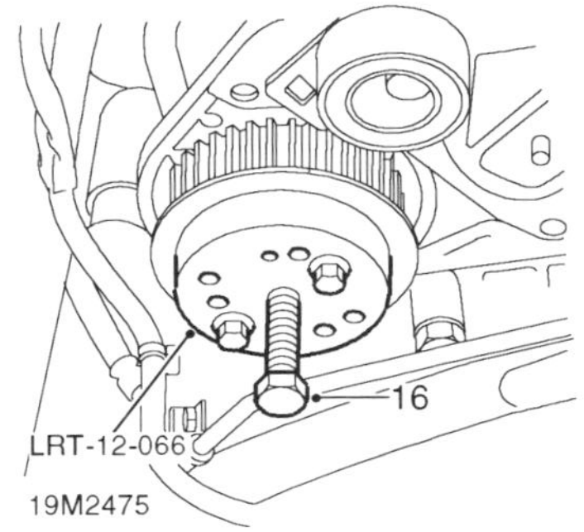

15. Fit tool **LRT-12-066** to FIP drive gear.
16. Rotate tool **LRT-12-066** centre bolt clockwise to release FIP drive gear from taper.
17. Remove tool **LRT-12-066** from drive gear.

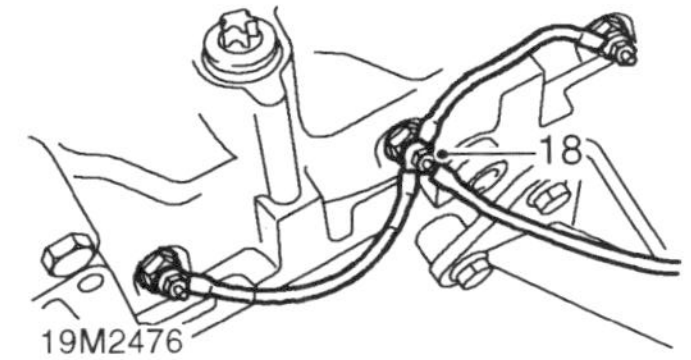

18. Remove nut and disconnect feed lead from No 2 glow plug.

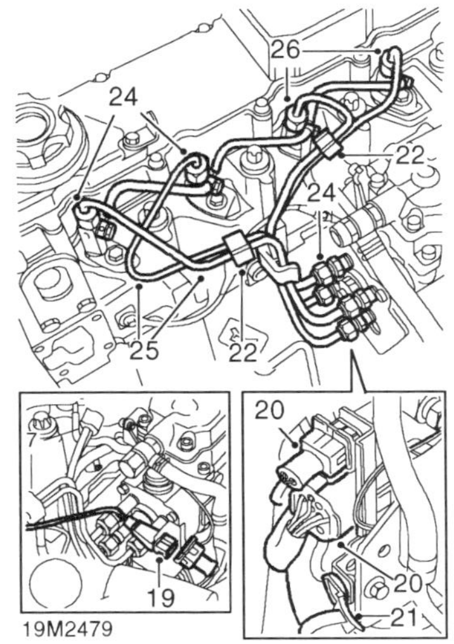

19. Release injector needle lift sensor multiplug from FIP bracket.
20. Disconnect 2 FIP multiplugs.
21. Release engine harness from FIP pump bracket.
22. Remove clamps from the 4 injector pipes.
23. Position absorbent cloth around fuel pipe connections to collect fuel spillage.

24. Loosen No.1 and No.2 injector pipe unions at injector and FIP.

⚠ **CAUTION: To prevent damage to fuel injection pipes or components, use a back up spanner when loosening unions.**

25. Disconnect unions and remove No.1 and No.2 injector pipes.

⚠ **CAUTION: Plug the connections.**

26. Repeat above procedure to remove injector pipes No.3 and No.4
27. Position absorbent cloth to collect fuel spillage.

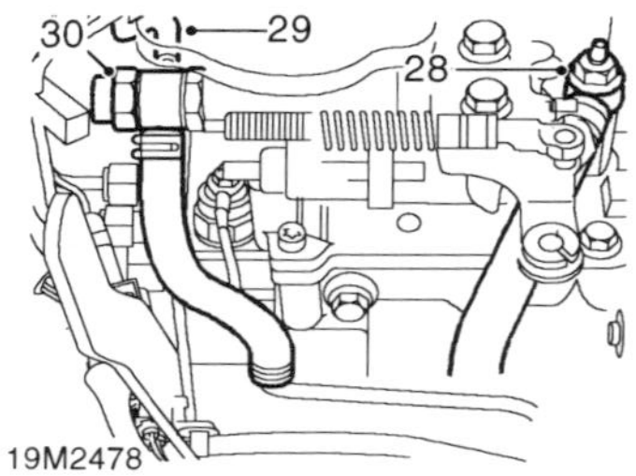

19M2478

28. Remove bolt securing fuel feed pipe banjo to FIP and discard sealing washers.
29. Disconnect fuel return hose to FIP from No 3 injector.
30. Remove cap nut, release fuel return pipe banjo from FIP and discard sealing washers.

⚠ **CAUTION: Plug the connections.**

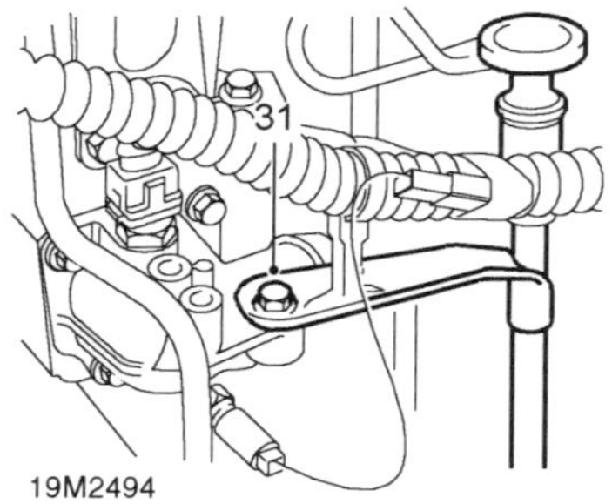

19M2494

31. Remove bolt securing engine dip stick tube to engine.

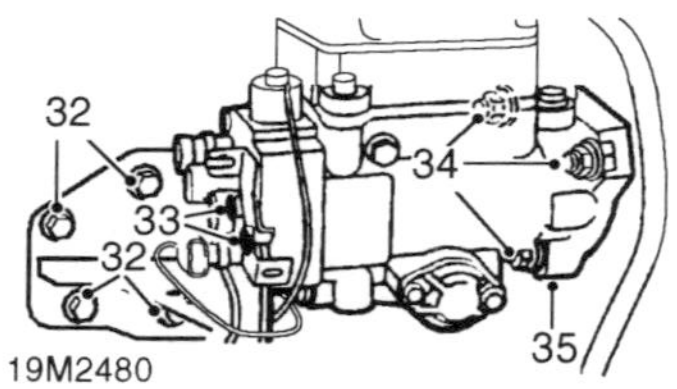

19M2480

32. Remove 4 bolts securing FIP support bracket to engine.
33. Remove 2 nuts and bolts securing bracket to FIP and remove bracket.
34. Remove 3 nuts securing FIP to gearbox mounting plate.
35. Remove FIP.
Do not carry out further dismantling if component is removed for access only.
36. Clean top of FIP around fuel cut-off solenoid.
37. Position absorbent cloth around fuel cut-off solenoid.

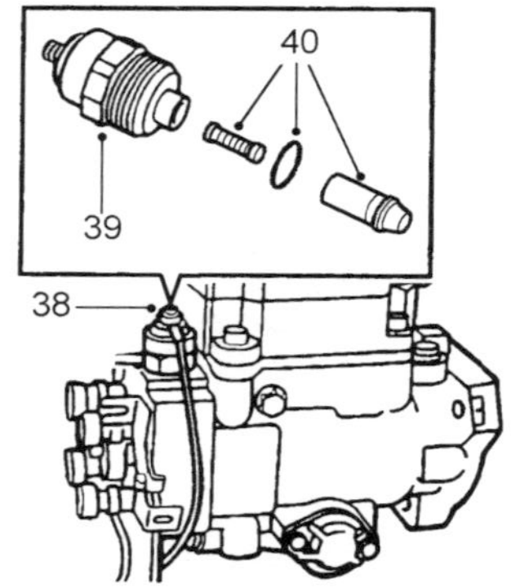

19M2485

38. Remove nut and disconnect lead from fuel cut-off solenoid.
39. Using a 24 mm spanner remove fuel cut-off solenoid from FIP.
40. Collect solenoid plunger, spring and 'O' ring.

⚠ **CAUTION: Plug solenoid aperture in pump.**

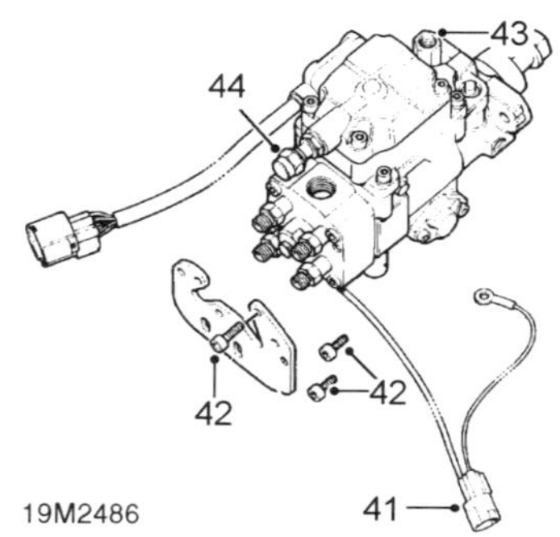

19M2486

41. Release 3 pin multiplug from adaptor bracket.
42. Remove 3 Allen screws securing adaptor bracket to FIP and remove bracket.
43. Remove fuel feed banjo adaptor from FIP and discard sealing washer.
44. Remove fuel return banjo adaptor from FIP and discard sealing washer.

⚠ **CAUTION: Plug the connections.**

45. Fit fuel return banjo adaptor to FIP using NEW sealing washer. Tighten adaptor to 25 Nm.
46. Fit fuel feed banjo adaptor to FIP using NEW sealing washer. Tighten adaptor to 25 Nm.
47. Fit adaptor bracket to FIP and tighten Allen screws to 10 Nm.
48. Connect 3 pin multiplug to adaptor bracket.
49. Lubricate and fit NEW 'O' ring to fuel cut-off solenoid.
50. Clean fuel cut-off solenoid plunger and spring.
51. Fit plunger and spring to solenoid.
52. Fit solenoid to FIP and tighten to 20 Nm.
53. Connect lead to solenoid and secure terminal nut.

Refit

1. Clean mating faces of FIP and gearbox mounting plate.
2. Fit FIP to gearbox mounting plate and tighten nuts to 25 Nm.
3. Fit FIP support bracket.
4. Fit bolts securing bracket to engine but do not tighten at this stage.
5. Fit nuts and bolts securing support bracket to FIP and tighten to 25 Nm.
6. Tighten bolts securing bracket to engine to 25 Nm.
7. Position dip stick tube and tighten bolt to 10 Nm.
8. Connect FIP multiplug to bracket.
9. Clean injector pipes and unions.
10. Fit No.3 and No.4 injector pipes and tighten unions to 20 Nm.

⚠ **CAUTION: To prevent damage to fuel system pipes or components use a back up spanner when tightening unions.**

11. Repeat above procedure to fit No.1 and No.2 injector pipes.
12. Fit clamps to the 4 injector pipes.
13. Connect FIP multiplug to bracket.

14. Using NEW sealing washers fit fuel return pipe banjo to FIP.
15. Fit and tighten cap nut to 28 Nm.
16. Connect fuel return hose to injector No.3.
17. Using NEW sealing washers fit fuel feed pipe banjo to FIP. Tighten bolt to 28 Nm.
18. Connect FIP multiplugs.
19. Connect injector needle lift sensor multiplug to FIP bracket and secure with clip.
20. Connect feed lead to No.2 glow plug and tighten nut to 2.5 Nm.
21. Clean FIP drive gear and shaft.
22. Fit drive gear to FIP.
23. Fit locking pin tool **LRT-12-141** to FIP drive gear and engage into gearbox mounting plate.
24. Fit spring washer and nut to FIP shaft and tighten to 60 Nm.
25. Loosen FIP shaft clamp bolt. Position spacer beneath clamp bolt.
26. Tighten clamp bolt to 10 Nm.
27. Fit FIP timing belt. ***See ENGINE - 'L' SERIES, Repairs.***
28. Fit and position top hose to coolant pipes and secure with clips.
29. Refill cooling system. ***See COOLING SYSTEM - 'L' SERIES, Adjustments.***
30. Fit engine acoustic cover. ***See ENGINE - 'L' SERIES, Repairs.***
31. Connect battery earth lead.

TURBOCHARGER

Service repair no - 19.42.01

Remove

1. Remove exhaust manifold gasket. ***See MANIFOLD & EXHAUST SYSTEMS - 'L' SERIES, Repairs.***

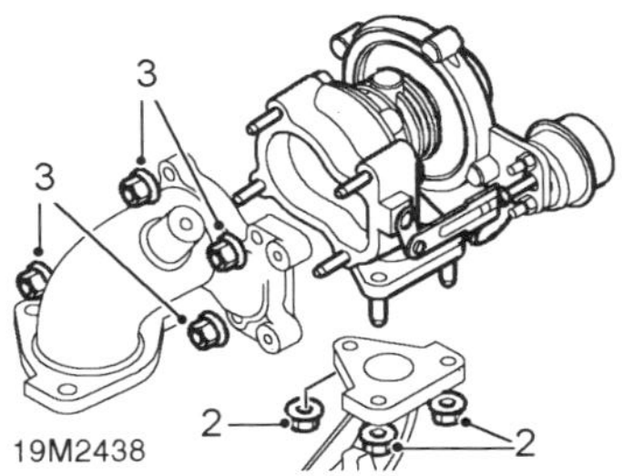

19M2438

2. Remove 3 nuts and remove turbocharger from exhaust manifold.
3. Remove 4 nuts and remove exhaust outlet elbow from turbocharger.

Refit

1. Clean faces of turbocharger and exhaust outlet elbow.
2. Fit exhaust outlet elbow to turbocharger and tighten nuts to 25 Nm.
3. Position turbocharger to exhaust manifold and tighten nuts to 10 Nm. .
4. Fit exhaust manifold gasket. ***See MANIFOLD & EXHAUST SYSTEMS - 'L' SERIES, Repairs.***

CHAMBER - PLENUM

Service repair no - 19.42.02

Remove

1. Remove engine acoustic cover. ***See ENGINE - 'L' SERIES, Repairs.***

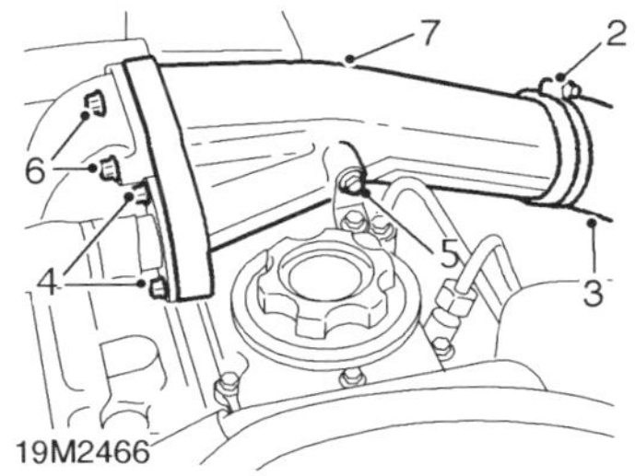

19M2466

2. Loosen clip securing intercooler outlet hose to plenum chamber.
3. Disconnect intercooler outlet hose from plenum chamber.
4. Remove 2 bolts securing EGR pipe to plenum chamber.
5. Remove bolt securing plenum chamber to camshaft cover bracket.
6. Remove 2 bolts securing plenum chamber to inlet manifold.
7. Remove plenum chamber.
8. Remove gasket.

Refit

1. Clean mating faces of inlet manifold and plenum chamber.
2. Use a NEW gasket and fit plenum chamber to inlet manifold. Fit bolts and tighten to 9 Nm.
3. Position EGR pipe to plenum chamber, fit bolts and tighten to 9 Nm.
4. Fit bolt securing plenum chamber to camshaft cover bracket and tighten to 9 Nm.
5. Connect intercooler outlet hose to plenum chamber and tighten clip.
6. Fit engine acoustic cover. ***See ENGINE - 'L' SERIES, Repairs.***

INTERCOOLER

Service repair no - 19.42.15

Remove

1. Remove front grille. ***See BODY, Exterior fittings.***
2. Remove cooling fan assembly. ***See COOLING SYSTEM - 'L' SERIES, Repairs.***

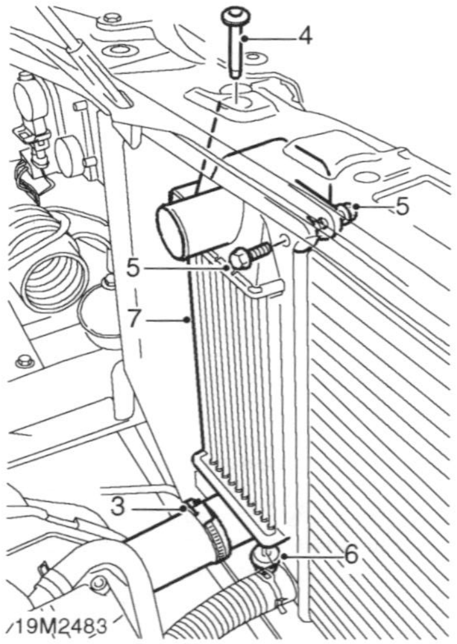

19M2483

3. Release clip securing intercooler bottom hose and disconnect hose.
4. Remove intercooler threaded retainer from top of bonnet platform.
5. Remove nut and bolt from top of intercooler.
6. Lift intercooler to release from lower mounting and radiator.
7. Remove intercooler.

Refit

1. Fit intercooler to radiator and lower mounting locations.
2. Fit nut and bolt to top of intercooler and tighten to 7 Nm .
3. Fit intercooler retainer to top of bonnet platform.
4. Connect bottom hose to intercooler and tighten clip.
5. Fit cooling fan assembly. ***See COOLING SYSTEM - 'L' SERIES, Repairs.***
6. Fit front grille. ***See BODY, Exterior fittings.***

INJECTORS

Service repair no - 19.60.12

Remove

1. Disconnect battery earth lead.
2. Remove plenum chamber. ***See this section.***
3. Position absorbent cloth around fuel injectors to absorb any fuel spillages.

NOTE: No. 1 injector incorporates the needle lift sensor.

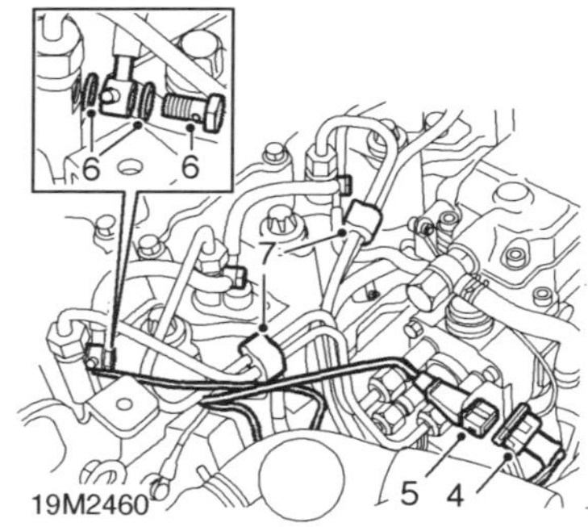

19M2460

4. Disconnect engine harness multiplug from needle lift sensor.
5. Release needle lift sensor harness from bracket on FIP.
6. Remove spill return hose banjo bolts and discard sealing washers.
7. Release clips holding injector pipes together.

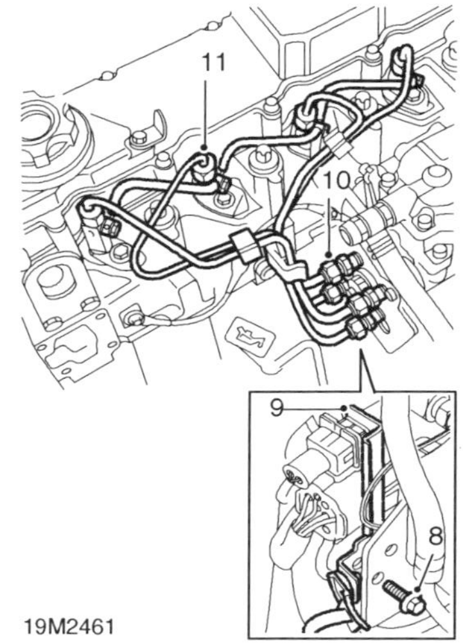

19M2461

CAUTION: To prevent damage to fuel system pipes or components use 2 spanners when loosening or tightening unions.

8. Remove bolt securing multiplug bracket to FIP mounting bracket.
9. Move multiplug bracket clear of injector pipe unions.
10. Loosen injector pipe unions at FIP.
11. Loosen unions and move pipes clear of injectors.

CAUTION: Plug the connections to prevent the ingress of dirt.

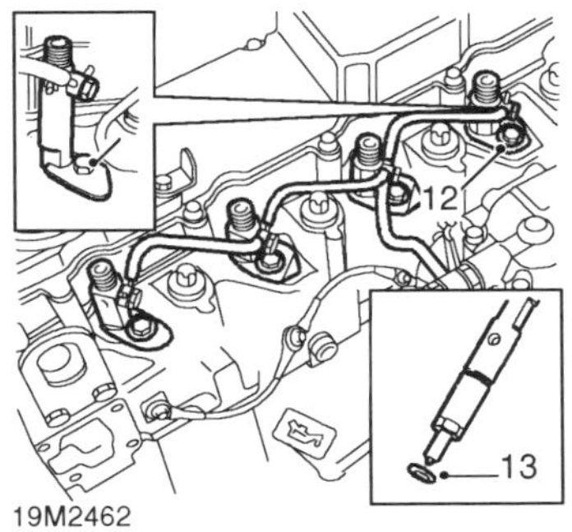

19M2462

12. Remove bolts and collect clamp plates securing injectors to cylinder head.
13. Remove injectors from cylinder head and discard sealing washers.

Refit

1. Thoroughly clean injectors and injector seats in cylinder head.
2. Fit NEW sealing washers to injectors and fit injectors to cylinder head.

CAUTION: Domed surface of sealing washer must face towards injectors.

3. Fit clamp plates to injectors, align injectors and clamp plates to bolt holes in cylinder head.
4. Fit injector clamp plate bolts and tighten to 25 Nm.
5. Using NEW sealing washers, fit spill return hose banjo bolts to injectors and tighten to 9 Nm.
6. Ensure injection pipe unions are clean.
7. Fit injection pipes to injectors and tighten union nuts to 28 Nm.
8. Tighten union nuts at FIP to 28 Nm.

CAUTION: To prevent damage to fuel system pipes or components, use 2 spanners when loosening and tightening unions.

9. Close clips securing injector pipes together.
10. Fit multiplug bracket to FIP bracket and secure with bolt.
11. Connect needle lift sensor multiplug to engine harness and fit to support bracket.
12. Fit plenum chamber. ***See this section.***
13. Connect battery earth lead.

HIGH PRESSURE PIPES - FUEL INJECTION

Service repair no - 19.60.14

Remove

1. Disconnect battery earth lead.
2. Remove plenum chamber. ***See this section.***

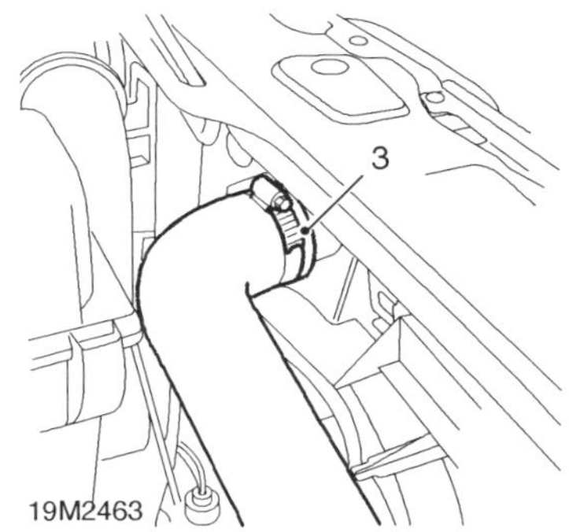

19M2463

3. Loosen clip and remove outlet hose from intercooler.

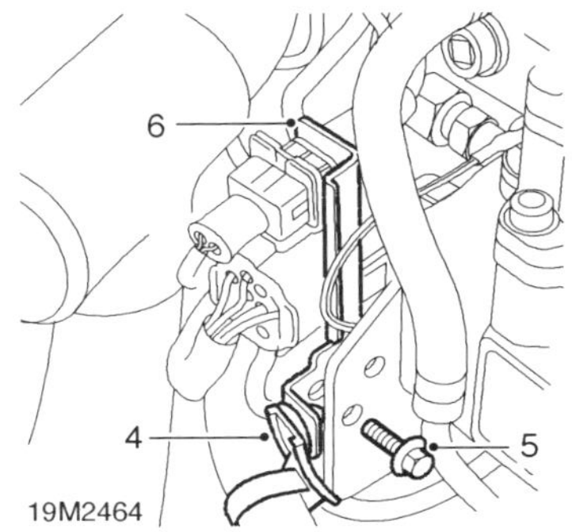

19M2464

4. Release engine harness clip from multiplug bracket on FIP.
5. Remove bolt securing multiplug bracket to FIP support bracket.
6. Pull multiplug bracket clear of FIP.

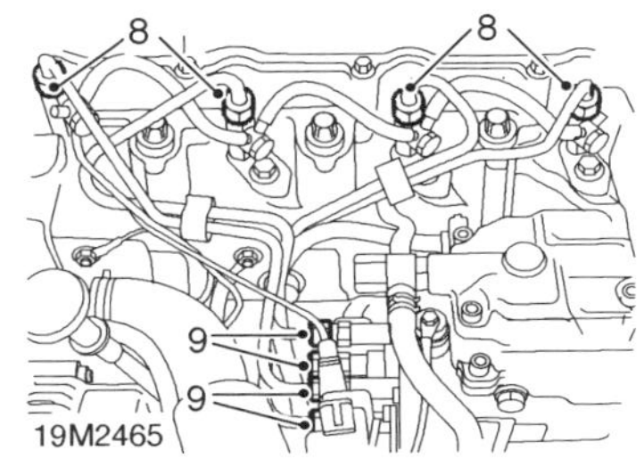

19M2465

7. Position absorbent cloth around fuel injection pipe connections to collect fuel spillage.
8. Loosen injector pipe unions at injectors.
9. Loosen injector pipe unions at FIP.

CAUTION: To prevent damage to fuel injection pipes or components use 2 spanners when loosening unions.

10. Remove injector pipe set.

CAUTION: Plug the connections.

11. Remove clips from injector pipes.

Refit

1. Clean pipes and connections.
2. Position injector pipes to FIP and injectors. Tighten unions to 28 Nm.

CAUTION: To prevent damage to fuel system pipes or components use 2 spanners when tightening unions.

3. Fit clips to injector pipes.
4. Position multiplug bracket and secure with bolt.
5. Fit engine harness clip to multiplug bracket.
6. Fit hose to intercooler and tighten clip.
7. Fit plenum chamber. ***See this section.***
8. Connect battery earth lead.

GLOW PLUGS - SET

Service repair no - 19.60.31

Remove

1. Disconnect battery earth lead.
2. Remove FIP. ***See FUEL DELIVERY SYSTEM, Repairs.***

Models with air conditioning

3. Remove alternator. ***See ELECTRICAL, Repairs.***

All models

4. Drain cooling system. ***See COOLING SYSTEM - 'L' SERIES, Adjustments.***

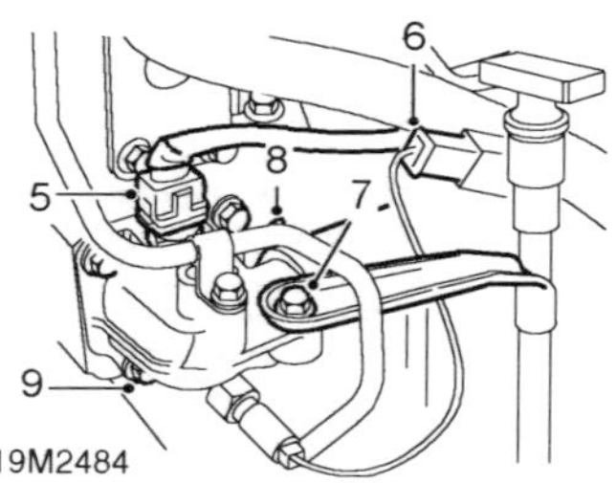

19M2484

5. Disconnect multiplug from coolant temperature sensor.
6. Disconnect temperature gauge sensor.
7. Remove bolt securing dipstick tube bracket to coolant outlet elbow.
8. Release clip and disconnect radiator top hose from coolant outlet elbow.
9. Remove 4 bolts securing coolant outlet elbow to cylinder head.

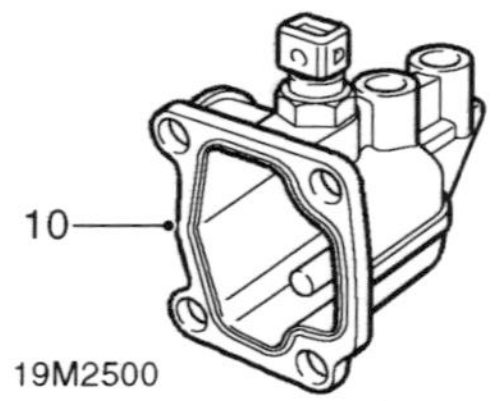

19M2500

10. Remove coolant outlet elbow, remove and discard seal.

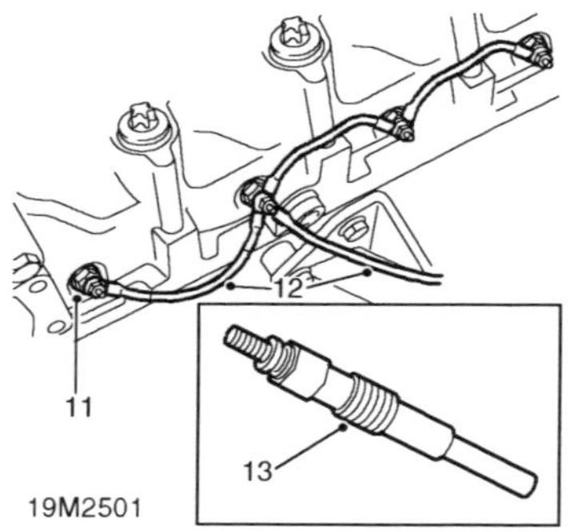

19M2501

11. Remove 4 nuts securing feed leads to glow plugs.
12. Release feed lead from terminal and remove link lead.
13. Remove 4 glow plugs.

Refit

1. Thoroughly clean glow plugs and glow plug seating area in cylinder head.
2. Apply a suitable anti-seize compound to threads of glow plugs.
3. Fit glow plugs and tighten to 20 Nm.
4. Fit link lead and feed leads to glow plugs.

NOTE: Harness feed lead must be connected to glow plug No. 2.

5. Tighten terminal nuts to 2.5 Nm.
6. Clean mating faces of coolant outlet elbow and cylinder head.
7. Fit NEW seal to coolant outlet elbow.
8. Position coolant outlet elbow to cylinder head, fit bolts and tighten to 25 Nm.
9. Connect radiator top hose to coolant outlet elbow and secure clip.
10. Align dipstick tube bracket to coolant outlet elbow and secure with bolt.
11. Connect temperature gauge sensor connector.
12. Connect multiplug to coolant temperature sensor.

Models with air conditioning

13. Fit alternator. ***See ELECTRICAL, Repairs.***

All models

14. Fit FIP. ***See FUEL DELIVERY SYSTEM, Repairs.***
15. Refill cooling system. ***See COOLING SYSTEM - 'L' SERIES, Adjustments.***
16. Connect battery earth lead.

RELAY - GLOW PLUGS

Service repair no - 19.60.34

Remove

1. Disconnect battery earth lead.

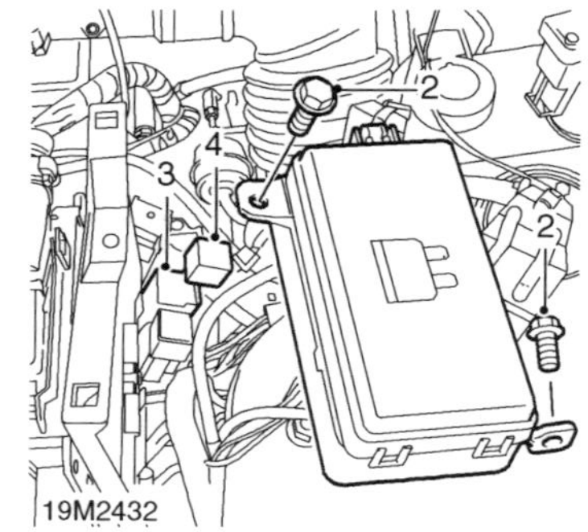

19M2432

2. Remove 2 bolts and position engine compartment fuse box aside.
3. Release relay holder from mounting on battery tray.
4. Remove relay.

Refit

1. Fit relay.
2. Position relay holder to its mounting.
3. Position fuse box and tighten bolts to 4 Nm.
4. Connect battery earth lead.

CONTENTS

Page

FUEL DELIVERY SYSTEM - 'K' SERIES

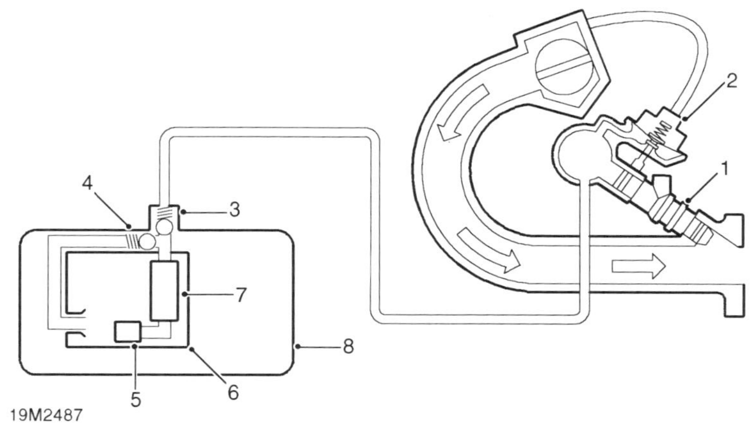

19M2487

1. Injectors
2. Accumulator
3. Non return valve
4. Fuel pressure regulator
5. Fuel filter
6. Swirl pot
7. Fuel pump
8. Fuel tank

FUEL SYSTEM

The fuel delivery system major components comprise a fuel tank, a fuel pump and four injectors.

Fuel Tank

The fuel tank is located on the underside of the vehicle, forward of the rear suspension subframe. The tank is constructed from moulded plastic and is retained by a tubular cradle which is secured to the vehicle floorpan with four bolts. The fuel tank has a capacity of 60 litres (13.2 Gallons).

A reflective metallic covering shields the tank from heat generated from the exhaust system. An aperture in the top surface of the tank allows for the fitment of the fuel pump.

The fuel tank filler is located on the right hand rear wing panel and is protected by a lockable plastic cap. A plastic tube from the filler is connected to the tank by a flexible rubber tube. A vent pipe is connected to the neck of the filler to vent fuel vapour during filling of the tank. A smaller vent pipe is also connected to the tank and vents fuel vapour from the tank to a charcoal cannister located in the engine compartment.

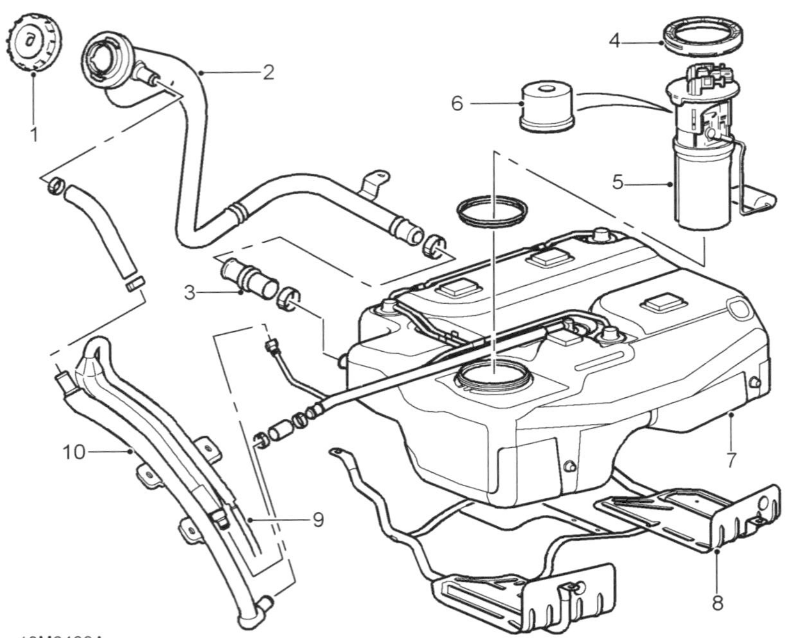

Fuel Tank and Tank Breather

1. Filler cap
2. Filler tube
3. Flexible tube
4. Locking ring
5. Fuel pump and fuel gauge potentiometer
6. Fuel filter
7. Fuel tank
8. Cradle
9. Vent to charcoal canister
10. Vent pipe

Fuel Pump

The fuel pump is electrically operated and is located in the top face of the fuel tank. A notched locking ring retains the fuel pump in the tank and requires a special tool for removal and installation. The fuel pump is housed in a plastic body which incorporates coarse and fine filters. The fuel pump is located in a larger housing which is the swirl pot. The swirl pot maintains a constant fuel level at the pump pick-up.

A pressure regulator which regulates the pressure output of the pump to 3.5 bar is located in the pump housing.

If the pressure exceeds this setting the regulator relieves excess pressure back to the swirl pot. This ensures that the fuel rail and the injectors are supplied with a constant pressure.

An access panel below the rear passenger seats provides access to the fuel pump for maintenance. The top face of the fuel pump has an electrical connector which supplies power and ground to the pump and the rotary potentiometer for the fuel gauge. Two quick fit couplings provide attachment for the fuel feed and the vent pipes.

Fuel Filter

A fine mesh filter is fitted within the fuel pump assembly. This should be renewed at 120,000 mile (200,000 km) intervals.

Injectors

Four injectors held between the fuel rail and the inlet manifold. The injectors are sealed to the fuel rail and the inlet manifold by O-ring seals. Each injector supplies one cylinder with fuel. The injectors receive pressurized fuel from the fuel pump via the fuel rail. The Engine Control Module (ECM) is responsible for the timed injection duration of each injector. The injectors supply a finely atomized spray of the fuel into the cylinder which is mixed with the air prior to ignition.

Accumulator

An accumulator is attached to the right hand end of the fuel rail. The accumulator acts as a damper to damp pulses from the pump and ensure that the fuel pressure in the rail and to the injectors is constant. The accumulator is connected by a pipe to the inlet manifold from which it receives a vacuum to aid the damping process.

FUEL DELIVERY SYSTEM - 'L' SERIES

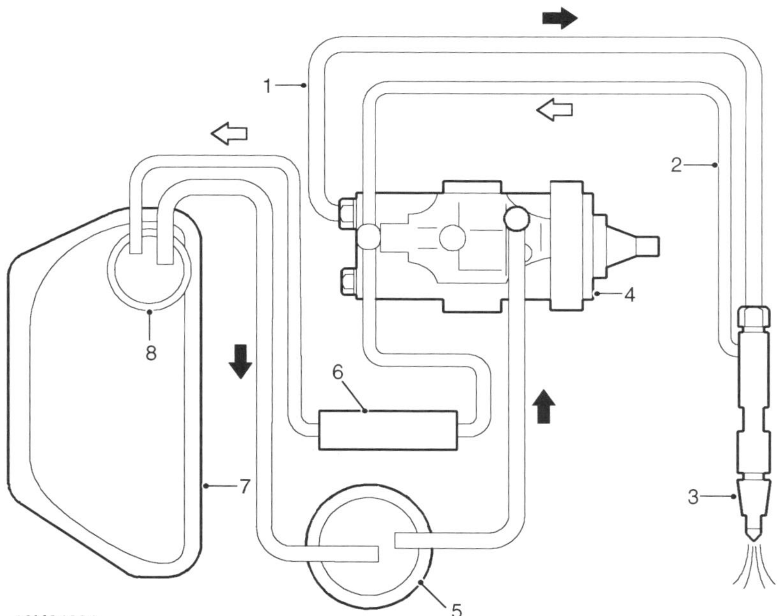

19M2489A

1. Fuel feed line
2. Fuel return line
3. Injectors
4. Fuel injection pump
5. Fuel filter
6. Fuel cooler
7. Fuel tank
8. Fuel pick-up and fuel gauge potentiometer

FUEL SYSTEM

The fuel delivery system major components comprise a fuel tank, a fuel injection pump, a fuel filter and four injectors.

Fuel Tank

The fuel tank is located on the underside of the vehicle, forward of the rear suspension subframe. The tank is constructed from moulded plastic and is retained by a tubular cradle which is bolted to the vehicle floorpan with four bolts. A reflective metallic covering shields the tank from heat generated from the exhaust system. The tank has a capacity of 60 litres (13.2 Gallons).

An aperture in the top surface of the tank allows for the fitment of the fuel pick-up and potentiometer. A notched ring retains the fuel pick-up and potentiometer in the tank and requires a special tool for removal and installation. The fuel pick-up incorporates a swirl pot which maintains a constant fuel level around the pick-up.

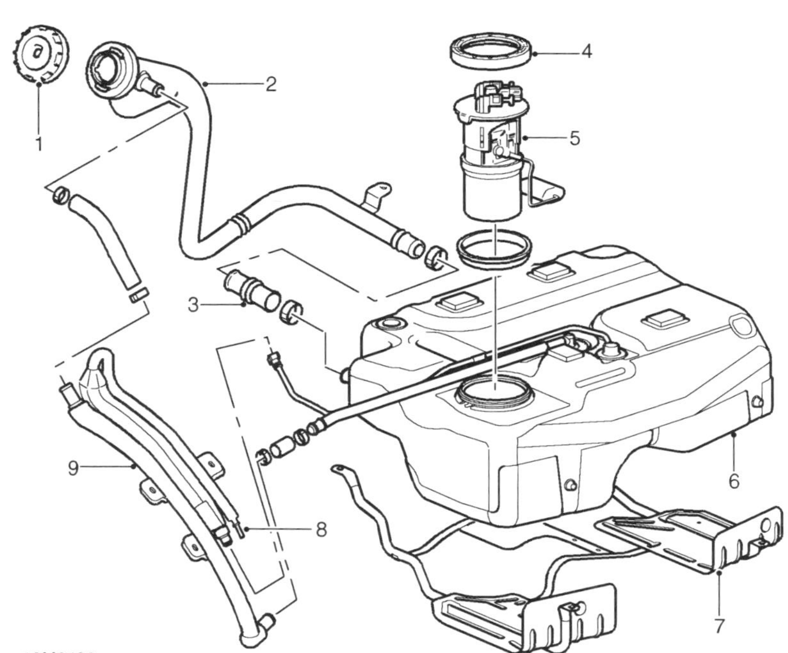

19M2490

Fuel Tank and Tank Breather

1. Filler cap
2. Filler tube
3. Flexible tube
4. Locking ring
5. Fuel pick-up and fuel gauge potentiometer
6. Fuel tank
7. Cradle
8. Atmospheric vent
9. Vent pipe

The swirl pot also mixes warm fuel returned from the injection pump with cool fuel in the tank. An access panel below the rear passenger seats provides access to the fuel tank for maintenance.

The fuel tank filler is located on the right hand rear wing panel and is protected by a lockable plastic cap. A plastic tube from the filler is connected to the tank by a flexible rubber tube.

A vent pipe is connected to the neck of the filler to vent fuel vapour during filling of the tank. A smaller vent pipe is also connected to the tank and vents fuel vapour from the tank to atmosphere.

Fuel Injection Pump

The fuel injection pump is a vane type pump, which is located on the front of the engine and driven by a belt from a pulley on the camshaft. The fuel injection pump draws fuel from the tank through a rubber pipe and the fuel filter. From the fuel filter, the fuel is drawn through a fuel cooler, located behind the bonnet locking platform, to the pump. The fuel injection pump delivers a precisely timed and metered quantity of fuel to each injector. The rubber fuel feed and return pipes connect to metal pipes which are routed around the engine.

Any excess (leak-off) fuel delivered to the pump and injectors is returned to the fuel tank through a rubber return pipe. The returned fuel is delivered to the tank through a port in the fuel pick-up and delivered to the swirl pot.

Fuel Filter

The fuel filter is located in the engine compartment on the left hand side of the bulkhead. Two connections on the top face allow for the fitment of the hoses from the the fuel tank and to the fuel injection pump.

A screw located on the bottom surface allows for drainage of the filter to remove moisture and particle contamination. The feed hose from the filter incorporates a bulb type handpump. The handpump is used, in conjunction with a filter bleed screw on the top face of the filter, to prime the filter and the fuel line after servicing.

Injectors

Three injectors and an injector incorporating a needle lift sensor are fitted to the cylinder head. Each injector supplies fuel to one cylinder and is retained in its port in the cylinder head with a clamp and bolt arrangement.

The injectors receive fuel at pressure from the fuel injection pump. Each injector has a nozzle with five spray orifices. The orifices protrude into the combustion chamber and spray fuel into the chamber, atomizing the fuel and mixing it with the air prior to combustion.

FILTER - FUEL - 'K' SERIES

Service repair no - 19.25.02

Remove

WARNING: The spilling of fuel is unavoidable during this operation. Ensure that all necessary precautions are taken to prevent fire and explosion.

1. Disconnect battery earth lead.
2. Remove fuel gauge sender unit. ***See INSTRUMENTS, Repairs.***

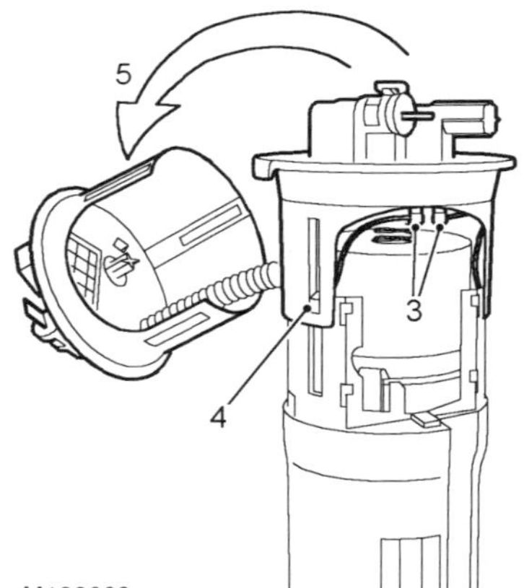

M192662

3. Disconnect 2 Lucar connectors from top of tank unit.
4. Release 3 slots in top of tank unit from lugs in base.
5. Carefully manoeuvre top of tank unit away from base, ensuring that fuel feed hose does not become strained.

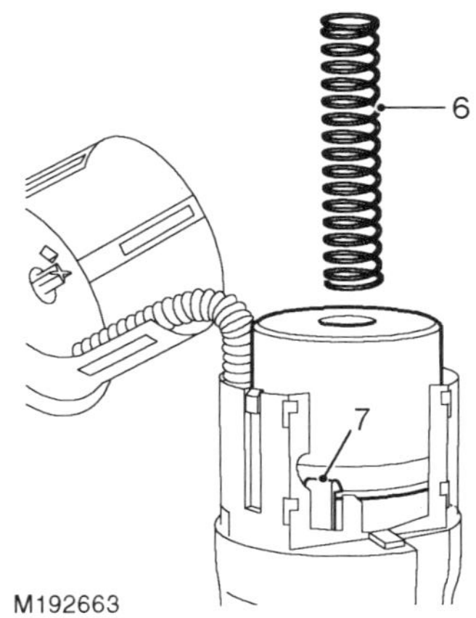

M192663

6. Collect compression spring from fuel filter.
7. Using a long, flat bladed screwdriver, carefully release 3 sprag clips securing fuel filter.

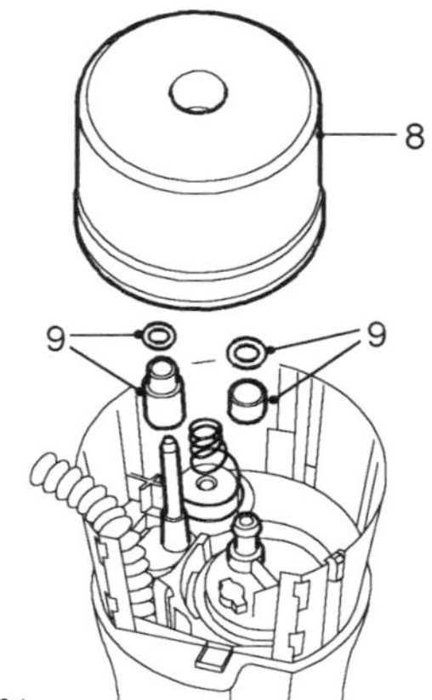

M192664

8. Release fuel filter from inlet and outlet connections. Remove filter.
9. Collect 'O' ring seals and spacers.

NOTE: Early fuel pump assemblies may not have spacers fitted to the inlet and outlet ports for the filter. Spacers supplied in parts kit must be fitted to early type pumps.

Refit

WARNING: During assembly, ensure that all electrical connections are made correctly. Earth tag on fuel pump negative terminal must not become distorted.

1. Position spacers to inlet & outlet ports. Lubricate NEW 'O' ring seals with silicone grease and fit to ports.

NOTE: Early fuel pump assemblies did not have an earthing spring fitted to the fuel pressure regulator. If fitted, ensure spring is correctly located.

2. Carefully fit filter to ports and push fully home, ensuring that sprag clips engage fully.

WARNING: Ensure that the filter earthing tag is correctly located to contact the base of the fuel filter.

3. Position spring to filter recess and engage in top location.
4. Engage pump top to base, ensuring that slots engage correctly with lugs.
5. Fit fuel gauge sender unit. ***See INSTRUMENTS, Repairs.***
6. Connect battery earth lead.

PUMP - FUEL - 'K' SERIES

Service repair no - 19.45.08

WARNING: Fuel pressure of up to 3.5 bar will be present in the system, even if the engine has not been run for some time. Always depressurise the system before disconnecting any components in the fuel feed line (between the fuel pump and the fuel rail). The spilling of fuel is unavoidable during this operation. Ensure that all necessary precautions are taken to prevent fire and explosion. *See ENGINE MANAGEMENT SYSTEM - MEMS, Information.*

NOTE: The fuel pump is an integral part of the fuel pump housing and cannot be renewed separately.

Remove

1. Disconnect battery earth lead.
2. Open tail door and fold rear seat forward.
3. Raise luggage and passenger compartment carpets for access to panel.

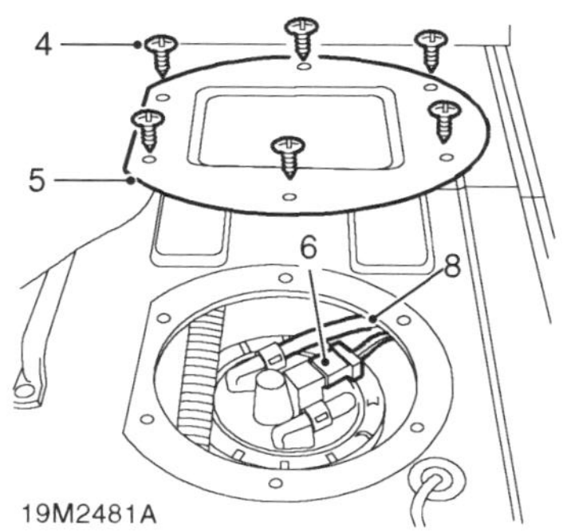

19M2481A

4. Remove 6 screws securing access panel.
5. Remove access panel.
6. Disconnect multiplug from fuel pump and run engine to release fuel line pressure.
7. Disconnect battery earth lead.
8. Disconnect fuel hose from fuel pump.

CAUTION: Plug the connections.

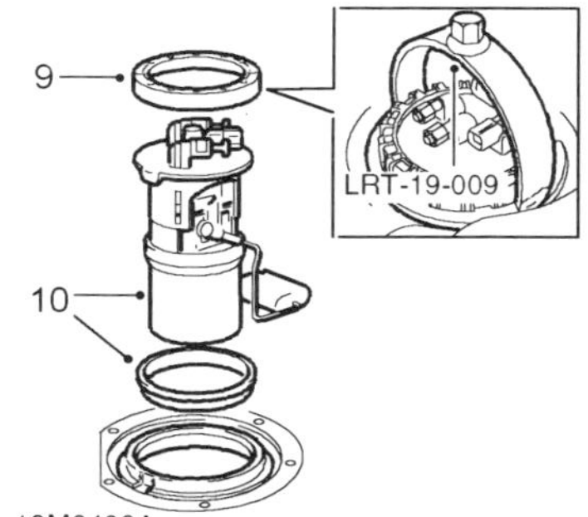

19M2482A

9. Use tool **LRT 19-009** and remove locking ring from pump housing.
10. Remove pump housing and remove sealing ring.

Refit

1. Clean pump housing and mating face on fuel tank.
2. Fit sealing ring to tank aperture.
3. Fit pump housing and secure with locking ring. Tighten to 45 Nm using **LRT 19-009.**
4. Connect multiplug and fuel hose to pump housing.
5. Connect battery earth lead.
6. Run engine and check fuel hose connection for leaks.
7. Fit access panel and secure with screws.
8. Reposition carpets.
9. Raise rear seat.
10. Close rear and tail door.
11. Connect battery earth lead.

FUEL TANK

Service repair no - 19.55.01

Remove

WARNING: Fuel pressure of up to 3.5 bar will be present in the system of petrol vehicles, even if the engine has not been run for some time. Always depressurise the system before disconnecting any components in the fuel feed line (between the fuel pump and the fuel rail). The spilling of fuel is unavoidable during this operation. Ensure that all necessary precautions are taken to prevent fire and explosion. *See ENGINE MANAGEMENT SYSTEM - MEMS, Information.*

CAUTION: Fuel system must be fully drained before fuel tank is removed. *See this section.*

1. Fold rear seat forward and release RH front corner of load space carpet.

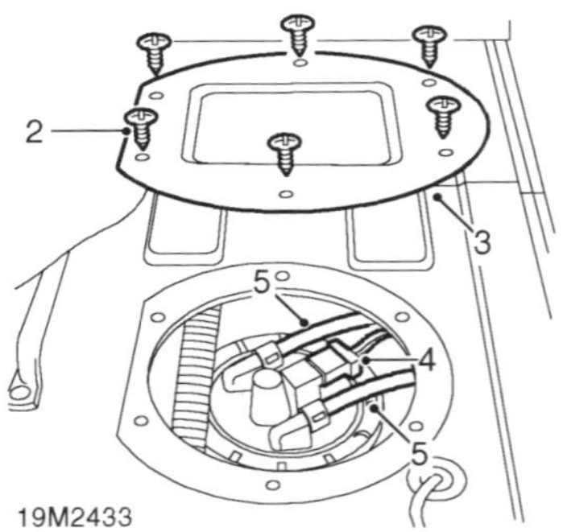

19M2433

2. Remove 6 screws from fuel gauge unit cover.
3. Remove fuel gauge unit cover.
4. Disconnect multiplug from fuel gauge unit.

Diesel models

5. Disconnect fuel feed and return hoses from fuel gauge unit.

Petrol models

6. Disconnect fuel feed hose from fuel gauge unit.

CAUTION: Plug the connections.

All models

7. Remove intermediate exhaust pipe. ***See MANIFOLD & EXHAUST SYSTEMS, Repairs.***
8. Remove propeller shaft. ***See DRIVE SHAFTS, Repairs.***
9. Remove rear road wheels.
10. Remove 4 scrivets from front of RH rear wheel arch liner and release liner from rear wing.
11. Remove clip securing vent hose to filler neck.
12. Disconnect vent hose from filler neck.
13. Disconnect 2 breather hoses from filler neck if petrol model or 1 hose for diesel model.

CAUTION: Plug the connections.

14. Support the weight of the rear sub frame on a transmission jack.
15. Remove 4 bolts securing sub frame to body.
16. Lower sub frame.

CAUTION: Do not allow sub frame to hang on rear brake hoses.

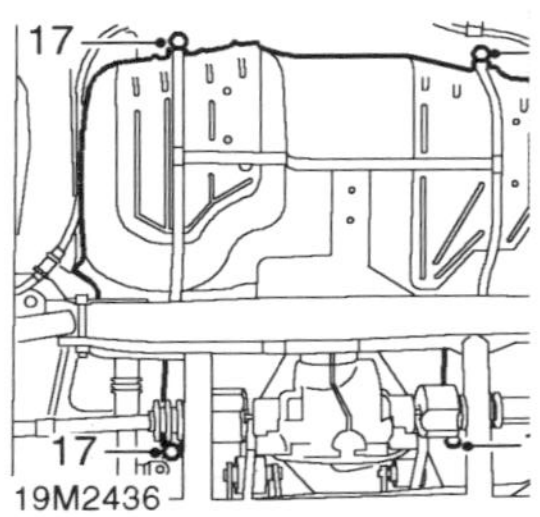

19M2436

17. With assistance, remove 4 bolts securing fuel tank to body.
18. Remove fuel tank.

NOTE: Pull vent and breather hoses through body panel while lowering fuel tank.

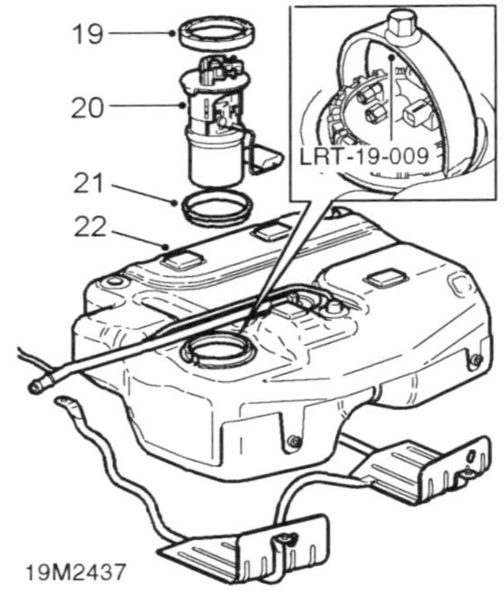

19M2437

19. Use **LRT-19-009** to remove retaining ring from fuel gauge unit.
20. Remove fuel gauge unit.
21. Remove fuel gauge unit seal.
22. Remove fuel tank from cradle.

Refit

1. Fit fuel tank to cradle.
2. Clean mating faces of fuel gauge unit and fuel tank.
3. Fit seal and gauge unit, secure retaining ring with **LRT -19-009** to 45Nm.
4. With assistance, fit fuel tank and tighten bolts to 45 Nm.

NOTE: Pass breather and vent hoses through body while fitting tank.

5. Raise subframe and tighten bolts to 190 Nm.
6. Connect breather hose\s to filler neck.
7. Connect vent hose to filler neck and secure with clip.
8. Position rear wheel arch liner and secure with scrivets.
9. Fit road wheel(s) and tighten nuts to correct torque. ***See INFORMATION, Torque wrench settings.***
10. Fit propeller shaft. ***See DRIVE SHAFTS, Repairs.***
11. Fit intermediate exhaust pipe. ***See MANIFOLD & EXHAUST SYSTEMS, Repairs.***

Diesel models

12. Connect fuel feed and return hose to fuel gauge tank unit.

Petrol models

13. Connect fuel feed hose to tank unit.

All models

14. Connect multiplug to tank unit.
15. Fit fuel gauge unit cover and secure with screws.
16. Reposition carpet and lower the seat.
17. Refill fuel tank.

FUEL TANK DRAINING

Service repair no - 19.55.02

Drain

1. Disconnect both leads from battery, earth lead first.

WARNING: Fuel pressure of up to 3.5 bar will be present in the system of petrol vehicles, even if the engine has not been run for some time. Always depressurise the system before disconnecting any components in the fuel feed line (between the fuel pump and the fuel rail). The spilling of fuel is unavoidable during this operation. Ensure that all necessary precautions are taken to prevent fire and explosion.

2. *Petrol Models:* Depressurise fuel system. ***See ENGINE MANAGEMENT SYSTEM - MEMS, Information.***

WARNING: Petrol/Gasoline vapour is highly flammable and in contained spaces is also explosive and toxic. Always have a fire extinguisher containing FOAM, CO2, GAS OR POWDER close at hand when handling or draining fuel.

3. *Diesel Models:* Remove fuel tank unit assembly. ***See INSTRUMENTS, Repairs.***
4. *Petrol Models:* Remove fuel pump assembly. ***See this section.***
5. Using a fuel recovery appliance, drain the fuel from the tank into a sealed container. Follow the manufacturers instructions for the connection and safe use of the appliance.
6. *Diesel Models:* Fit fuel tank unit assembly. ***See INSTRUMENTS, Repairs.***
7. *Petrol Models:* Fit fuel pump assembly. ***See this section.***
8. Connect battery leads.

FUEL FILLER NECK

Service repair no - 19.55.07

Remove

WARNING: Ensure that fuel handling precautions given in 01 - Introduction, are strictly adhered to when carrying out the following instructions.

WARNING: If the fuel tank is full, the fuel level may be close to the filler neck aperture. If gauge indicates over 50%, drain the fuel tank. *See this section.*

CAUTION: Before disconnecting any part of the system , it is imperative that all dust, dirt and debris is removed from around components to prevent ingress of foreign matter into fuel system.

Remove

1. Disconnect battery earth lead.
2. Remove fuel filler cap.
3. Remove RH rear wheel arch liner. ***See BODY, Repairs.***

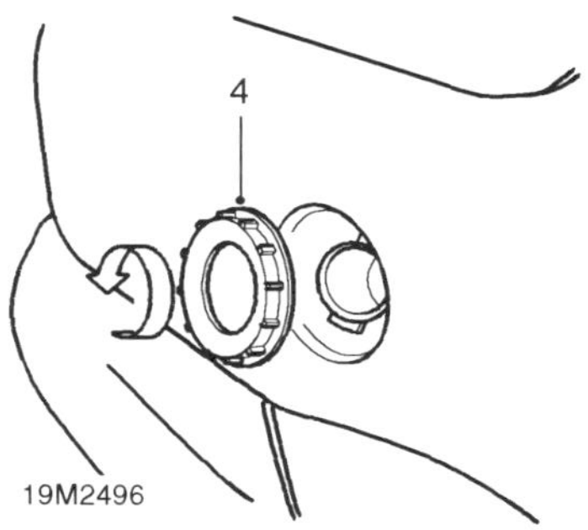

19M2496

4. Remove locking ring securing fuel filler neck to filler cap aperture.

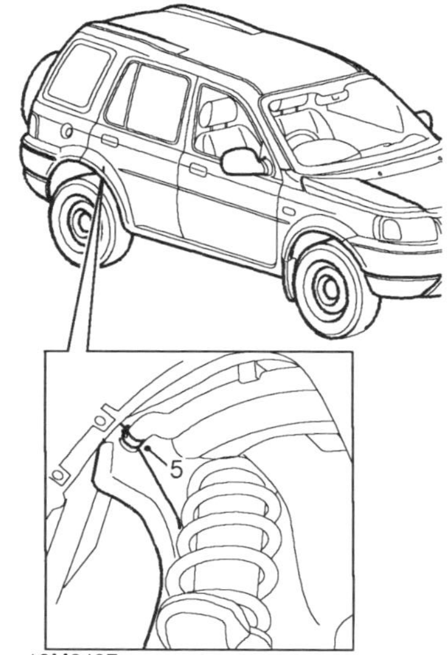

19M2497

5. Release clip from breather hose and disconnect breather hose from filler neck.

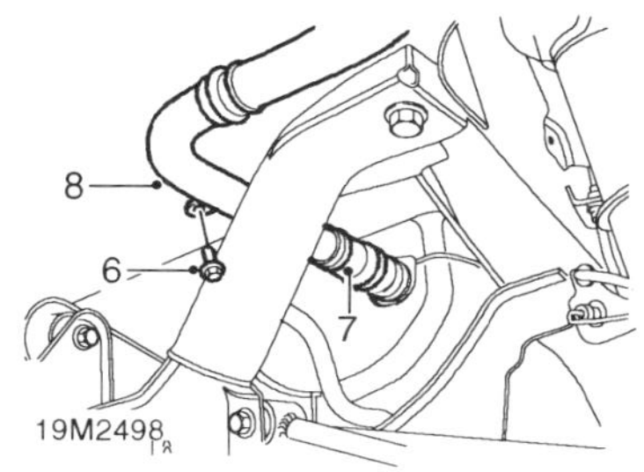

19M2498

6. Remove bolt securing filler neck to body
7. Release clip securing neck assembly to tank.
8. Disconnect filler from tank.
9. Remove filler neck assembly.

Refit

1. Position filler neck, connect to tank, fit and secure clip.
2. Fit tighten bolt securing filler neck to body and tighten to 9 Nm.
3. Connect breather hose to filler neck, fit and secure clip.
4. Position filler neck to fuel cap aperture and fit locking ring.
5. Fit rear wheel arch liner. ***See BODY, Repairs.***
6. Replenish fuel if necessary.
7. Fit filler cap.
8. Connect battery earth lead.

CONTENTS

Page

COOLING SYSTEM COMPONENTS

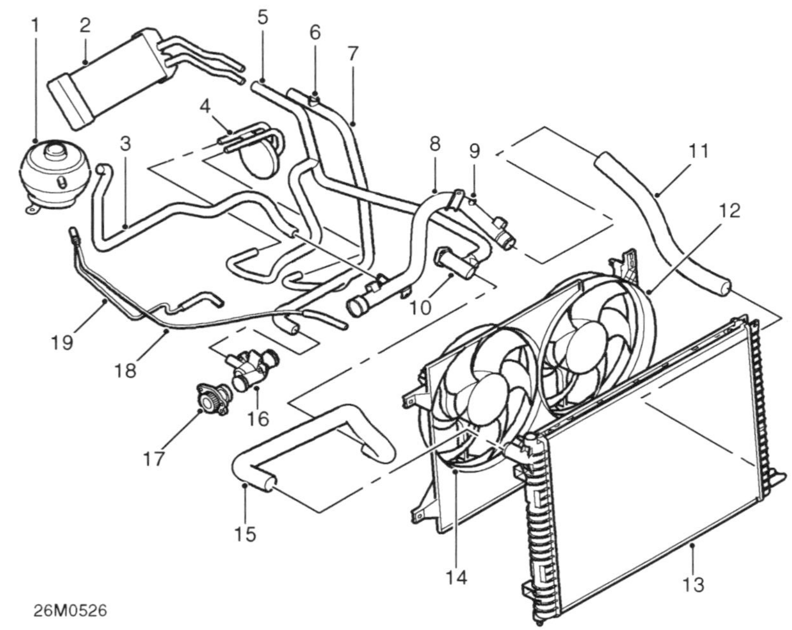

26M0526

1. Expansion tank
2. Heater matrix
3. Hose - Expansion tank to coolant pipe
4. IRD Cooler
5. Hose - Heater inlet
6. Bleed screw
7. Hose - Heater outlet
8. Coolant inlet pipe
9. Bleed screw
10. Coolant outlet pipe
11. Hose - Radiator bottom
12. Air conditioning condenser fan (if fitted)
13. Radiator
14. Cooling fan
15. Hose - Radiator top
16. Thermostat housing
17. Water pump
18. Bleed hose
19. Bleed hose

COOLING SYSTEM OPERATION

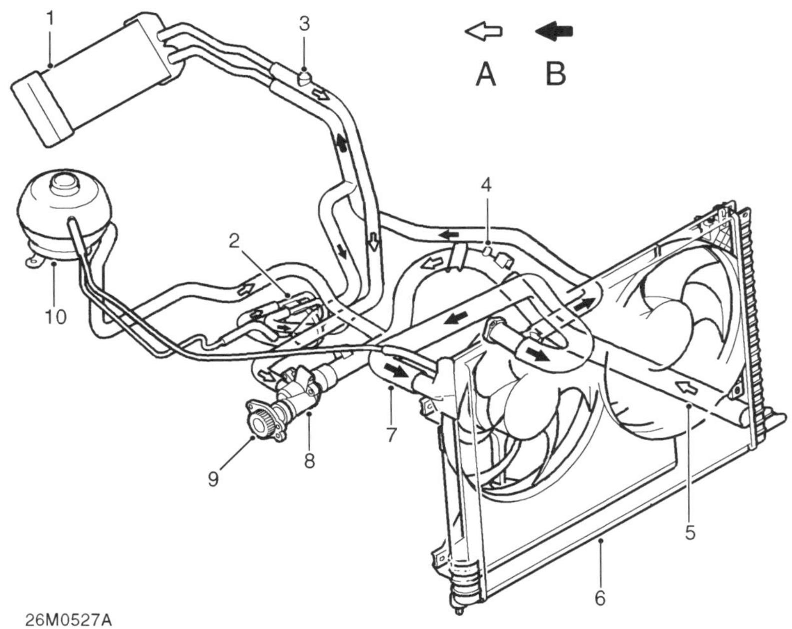

26M0527A

A = COLD
B = HOT

1. Heater matrix
2. IRD Cooler
3. Bleed screw
4. Bleed screw
5. Radiator bottom hose
6. Radiator
7. Radiator top hose
8. Thermostat housing
9. Water pump
10. Expansion tank

The cooling system employed is the by-pass type, allowing coolant to circulate around the engine and the heater circuit while the thermostat is closed.

The thermostat is installed in a housing which is attached to the coolant pump. The thermostat is located in the inlet side of the cooling circuit, which provides a more stable control of the coolant temperature in the engine.

When cold, the thermostat is closed and coolant is prevented from circulating through the radiator. Coolant is able to circulate through the bypass and heater circuits.

As the temperature increases, the thermostat gradually opens, bleeding cool fluid from the radiator bottom hose into the cylinder block and allowing hot coolant to flow to the radiator through the radiator top hose, balancing the flow of hot and cold fluid to maintain the optimum operating temperature. When the thermostat opens fully, the full flow of coolant passes through the radiator.

An expansion tank is fitted to the right hand shock absorber mounting. Any excess coolant, created by heat expansion, is returned to the expansion tank through bleed lines from the top of the radiator and from the cylinder block. The expansion tank has an outlet pipe which is connected into the coolant circuit. The outlet pipe supplies coolant into the system when the engine is cool. This replaces coolant displaced to the expansion tank due to heat expansion.

The coolant is circulated by a rotor type pump. The pump is mounted at the rear of the engine and is driven by a geared pulley from the camshaft timing belt. The pump draws coolant from the radiator bottom hose and circulates it through the engine and heater circuit.

The radiator, positioned at the front of the vehicle, is a copper/brass cross - flow type with moulded plastic end tanks. The radiator is mounted in rubber bushes; the bottom of the radiator is located in the front body cross member, and the top is located in the bonnet locking platform. The top hose from the radiator is connected to the temperature sensor housing and bottom hose is connected, via a pipe, to the thermostat housing.

For additional air flow through the radiator matrix, particularly when the vehicle is stationary, an electric cooling fan is fitted to the rear of the radiator. The temperature of the cooling system is monitored by the Engine Control Module (ECM) via signals from a temperature sensor, which is mounted in a housing attached to the cylinder head. When a temperature of 102°C is reached the ECM switches the cooling fan on via a relay. The fan switches off at 96°C.

Vehicles fitted with air conditioning have 2 fans. These operate either in series or parallel according to engine coolant temperature or air conditioning requirements. The fan operation is controlled by the ECM. The fans operate in series (slow mode) when a temperature of 106°C or higher is sensed. When a temperature of 112°C is sensed, the fans switch from series to parallel operation (fast mode). When the temperature falls to 106°C or below, the fans are switched back to series operation. The fans stop when a temperature of 100°C or lower is sensed.

The cooling system is also used to cool the Intermediate Reduction Drive (IRD). The IRD oil is cooled with fluid from the cylinder block. The fluid passes through a plate which contains waterways and recirculates via the heater circuit.

Bleed screws are installed in the top hose of the heater matrix and the feed pipe to the coolant pump. These are used to bleed air from the cooling system during system filling.

DRAIN AND REFILL

Service repair no - 26.10.01

WARNING: To prevent the risk of scalding ensure engine coolant is COLD before removing expansion tank filler cap.

Drain.

1. Visually check engine and cooling system for signs of coolant leaks.
2. Examine hoses for signs of cracking, distortion and security of connections.
3. Remove underbelly panel. ***See BODY, Exterior fittings.***
4. Remove expansion tank filler cap.
5. Position drain tin to collect coolant.

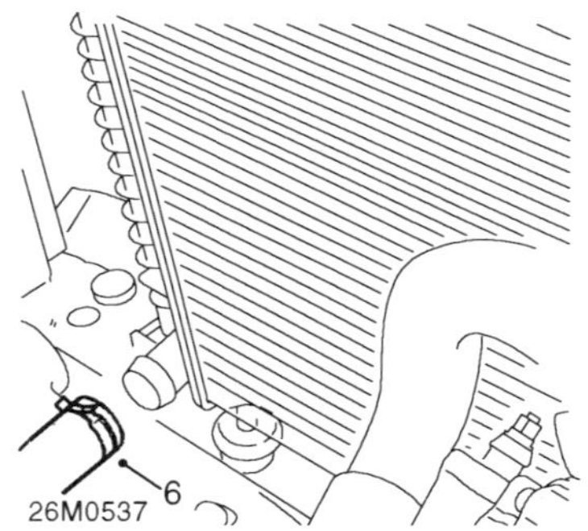

26M0537

6. Release clip and disconnect bottom hose from radiator.
7. Allow cooling system to drain.

Refill

1. Flush system with water under low pressure.

CAUTION: High pressure water could damage the radiator.

2. Connect bottom hose to radiator and fit clip.
3. Prepare coolant to required concentration. ***See INFORMATION, Capacities, fluids and lubricants.***

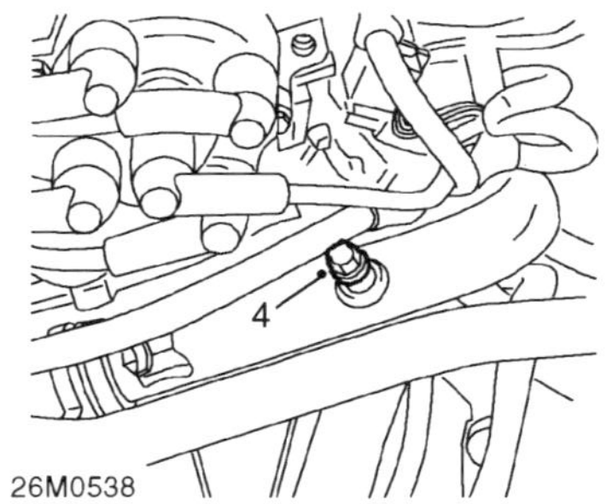

26M0538

4. Remove bleed screw at coolant rail.

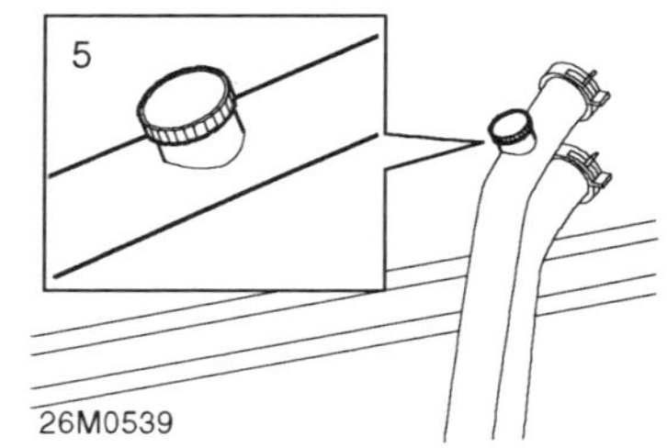

26M0539

5. Slacken bleed screw at heater hose by 2 complete turns.
6. Fill system slowly through coolant expansion tank, until the coolant reaches the 'MAX' mark on expansion tank.
7. Close bleed screws as coolant emerges. Tighten coolant rail bleed screw to 9 Nm. Tighten heater hose bleed screw carefully by hand.

8. Fit expansion tank filler cap.
9. Fit underbelly panel. ***See BODY, Exterior fittings.***
10. Start and run engine until radiator cooling fan operates.

CAUTION: If fitted DO NOT operate air conditioning.

11. Turn heater control to fully hot and ensure that warm air is available at vents.

NOTE: If warm air is not available, an air-lock may be present in heater matrix. If necessary, allow engine to cool, remove expansion tank filler cap and repeat bleed operation at heater hose.

12. Switch off engine and allow to cool.
13. Check for leaks and top-up coolant to 'MAX' mark on expansion tank.
14. Switch off engine and allow to cool.
15. Check for leaks and top-up coolant to 'MAX' mark on expansion tank.

EXPANSION - TANK - COOLANT

Service repair no - 26.15.01

Remove

1. Position container to collect coolant.

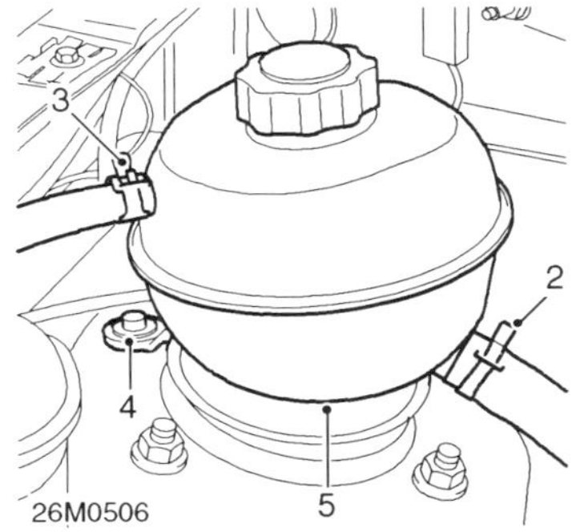

26M0506

2. Release clip and disconnect bottom hose from expansion tank.
3. Release clip and disconnect top hose from expansion tank.
4. Remove scrivet securing expansion tank to inner wing.
5. Remove expansion tank from inner wing location.

Refit

1. Fit expansion tank to inner wing location.
2. Secure expansion tank with scrivet.
3. Connect bottom hose to expansion tank and secure with clip.
4. Connect top hose to expansion tank and secure with clip.
5. Top-up and check level of engine coolant.

MOTOR - COOLING FAN - WITH AIR CONDITIONING

Service repair no - 26.25.22/20

Remove

1. Remove air cleaner. ***See ENGINE MANAGEMENT SYSTEM - MEMS, Repairs.***

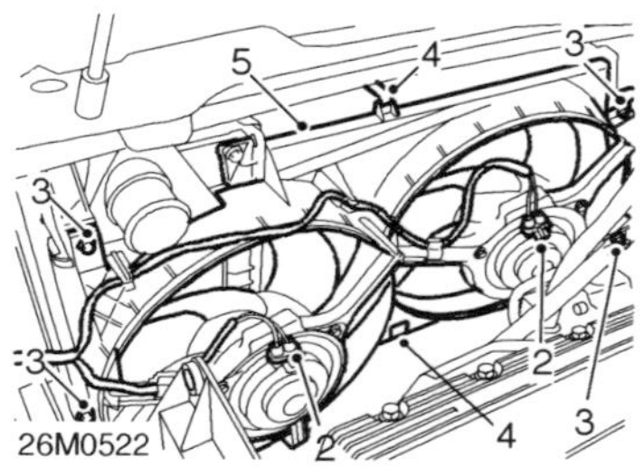

26M0522

2. Disconnect 2 multiplugs from cooling fan motors and release cables from 4 clips.
3. Remove 4 bolts securing fan assembly to radiator.
4. Remove top and bottom clips securing fan assembly to radiator.
5. Remove fan assembly from engine compartment.

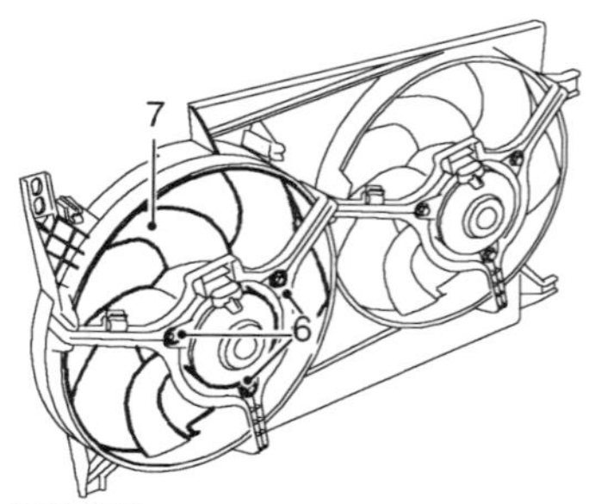

26M0523

6. Remove 3 bolts securing fan motor to fan assembly.
7. Remove fan motor from fan assembly.

Refit

1. Position fan motor to fan assembly, fit and tighten bolts to 6 Nm.
2. Position fan assembly to radiator and secure with clips.
3. Fit and tighten fan assembly bolts to 6 Nm.
4. Connect multiplugs to cooling fan motors and fit cables to clips.
5. Fit air cleaner. ***See ENGINE MANAGEMENT SYSTEM - MEMS, Repairs.***

COOLING SYSTEM - 'K' SERIES

MOTOR - COOLING FAN

Service repair no - 26.25.24

Remove

1. Disconnect battery earth lead.

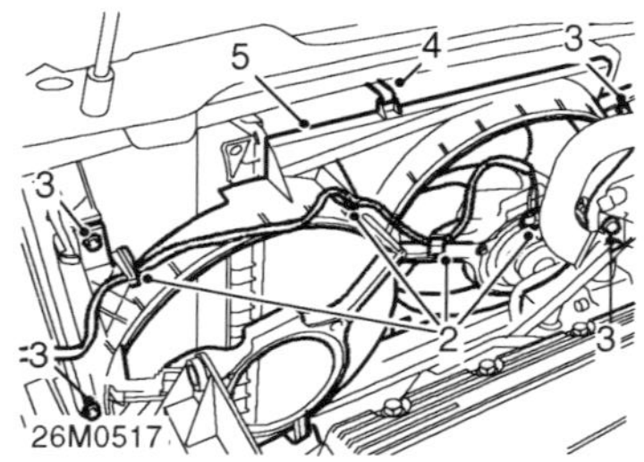

26M0517

2. Disconnect multiplug from cooling fan motor and release cable from 3 clips.
3. Remove 4 bolts securing fan assembly to radiator.
4. Remove top clip securing fan assembly to radiator.
5. Remove fan assembly from engine compartment.

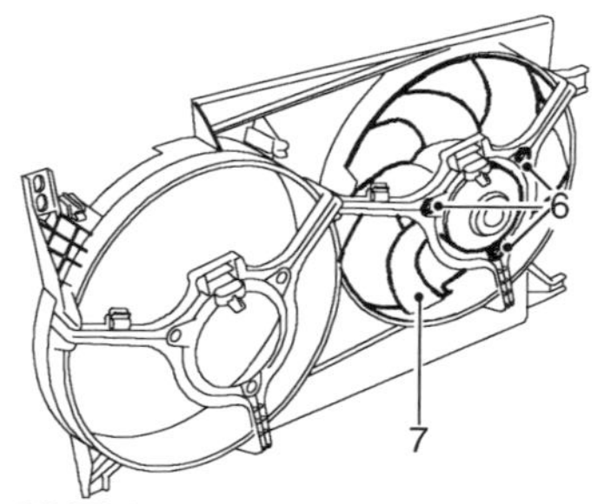

26M0518

6. Remove 3 bolts securing fan motor to fan assembly.
7. Remove fan motor from fan assembly.

Refit

1. Position fan motor to fan assembly, fit and tighten bolts to 6 Nm.
2. Position fan assembly to radiator and secure with clip.
3. Fit and tighten fan assembly bolts to 6 Nm.
4. Connect multiplugs to cooling fan motors and fit cables to clips.
5. Connect battery earth lead.

RADIATOR

Service repair no - 26.40.01

Remove

1. Drain cooling system. ***See Adjustments.***
2. Remove cooling fan. ***See this section.***

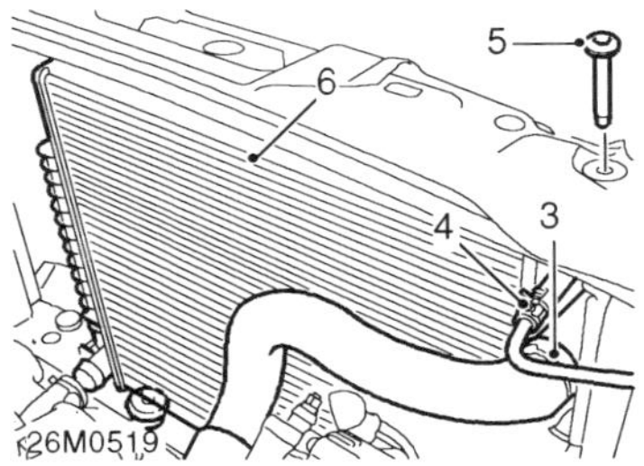

26M0519

3. Release clip and disconnect top hose from radiator.
4. Release clip and disconnect expansion tank hose from radiator.
5. Remove radiator threaded retainers from top of bonnet locking platform.
6. Remove radiator.
7. Remove lower mounting rubbers from radiator.

Refit

1. Fit mounting rubbers to radiator.
2. Position radiator and locate to lower mountings.
3. Fit radiator threaded retainers.
4. Position hoses to radiator and secure clips.
5. Fit cooling fan. ***See this section.***
6. Fill cooling system. ***See Adjustments.***

THERMOSTAT

Service repair no - 26.45.09

Remove

1. Disconnect battery earth lead.
2. Drain cooling system, ***See Adjustments.***

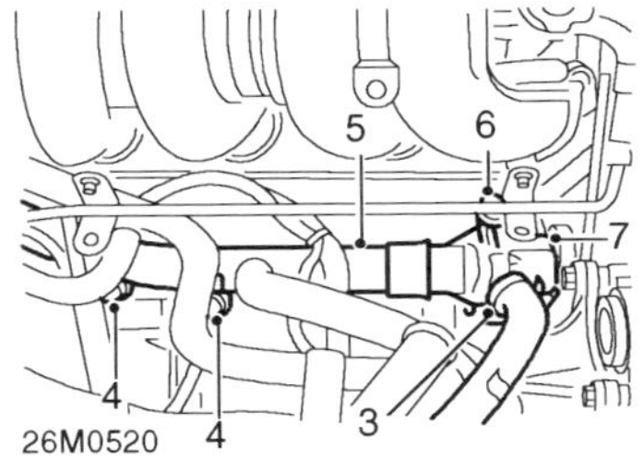

26M0520

3. Loosen clip and disconnect heater hose from thermostat housing.
4. Remove 2 bolts securing coolant rail to cylinder block.
5. Release coolant rail from thermostat housing.
6. Remove bolt securing thermostat housing to cylinder block.
7. Release thermostat housing from coolant pump and remove thermostat housing.

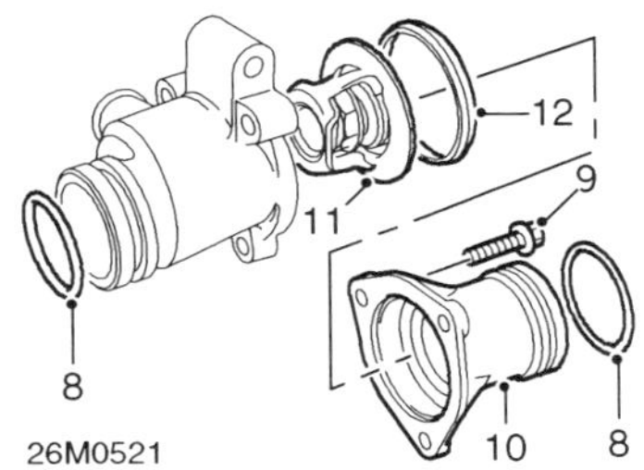

26M0521

8. Remove and discard 2 'O' rings from thermostat housing outlets.
9. Remove 3 bolts securing cover to thermostat housing.
10. Remove thermostat housing cover.
11. Remove thermostat from housing.
12. Remove rubber seal from thermostat.

Refit

1. Examine thermostat rubber seal for signs of deterioration or damage, renew if necessary.
2. Fit rubber seal to thermostat.
3. Clean mating faces of thermostat and cover.

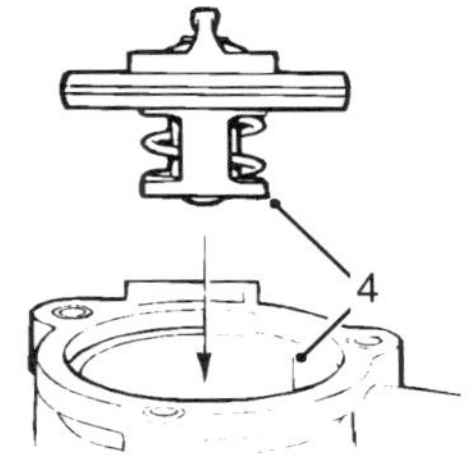

26M0251

4. Align thermostat to shoulder in thermostat housing.
5. Fit thermostat housing cover and tighten bolts to 9 Nm.
6. Clean 'O' ring grooves on thermostat housing outlets.
7. Lubricate NEW 'O' rings with rubber grease and fit to thermostat housing outlets.
8. Position thermostat housing to coolant pump and push into place.
9. Align dipstick tube bracket to thermostat housing.
10. Fit bolt securing thermostat housing to cylinder block and tighten to 9 Nm.
11. Connect coolant rail to thermostat housing.
12. Align coolant rail to cylinder block, fit bolts and tighten to 9 Nm.
13. Connect heater hose to thermostat housing and tighten clip.
14. Refill cooling system. ***See Adjustments.***
15. Connect battery earth lead.

PUMP - COOLANT

Service repair no - 26.50.01

Remove

1. Disconnect battery earth lead.
2. Drain cooling system. ***See COOLING SYSTEM, Adjustments.***
3. Remove camshaft timing belt. ***See ENGINE - 'K' SERIES, Repairs.***
   Do not rotate the engine with timing belt removed from camshaft gears.

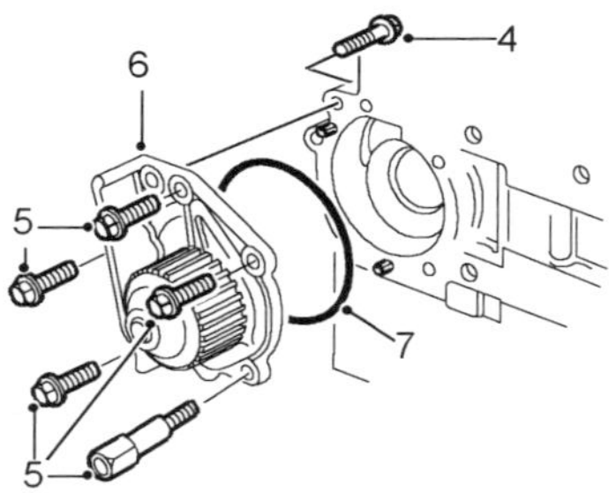

26M0524

4. Remove bolt securing rear cover to coolant pump.
5. Remove 4 bolts and pillar bolt securing coolant pump to cylinder block.
6. Withdraw coolant pump from cylinder block and remove.
7. Remove and discard 'O' ring from coolant pump.

Refit

1. Clean coolant pump and mating face of cylinder block.
2. Clean locating dowel and dowel hole.
3. Lubricate NEW 'O' ring with rubber grease and fit to coolant pump.
4. Fit coolant pump to cylinder block, fit bolts and tighten to 10 Nm.
5. Clean camshaft and coolant pump gears.
6. Inspect camshaft timing belt for signs of uneven wear, splitting or oil contamination. Renew timing belt if necessary.
7. Fit camshaft timing belt. ***See ENGINE - 'K' SERIES, Repairs.***
8. Refill cooling system, ***See Adjustments.***
9. Connect battery earth lead.

CONTENTS

COOLING SYSTEM - 'L' SERIES

This page is intentionally left blank

COOLING SYSTEM COMPONENTS

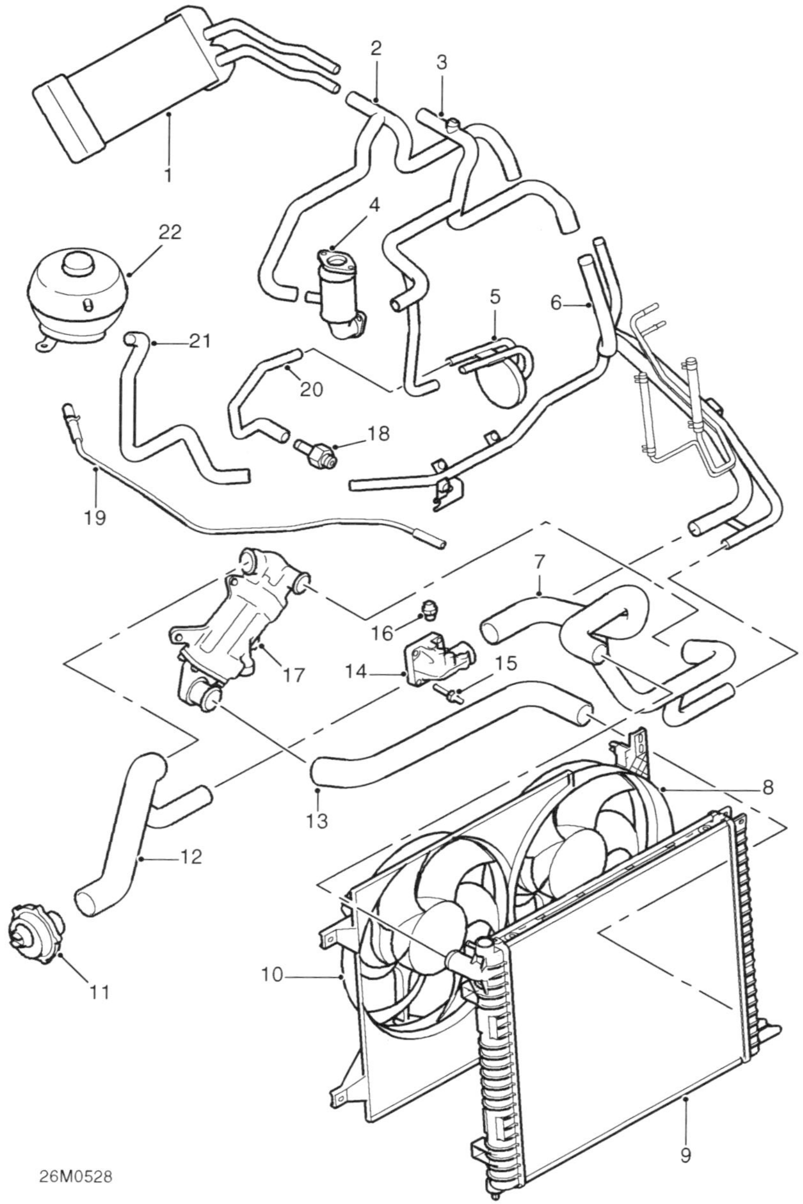

26M0528

1. Heater matrix
2. Hose - Heater inlet
3. Hose - Heater outlet
4. EGR cooler
5. IRD cooler
6. Pipe assembly
7. Engine outlet/radiator top hose
8. Cooling fan
9. Radiator
10. Cooling fan
11. Water pump
12. Hose - Engine inlet
13. Radiator bottom hose
14. Outlet elbow
15. Temperature gauge sensor
16. Temperature sensor
17. Oil cooler (incorporates coolant thermostat)
18. IRD coolant restrictor
19. Bleed hose
20. Hose - IRD inlet
21. Hose - Expansion tank to pipe assembly
22. Expansion tank

COOLING SYSTEM OPERATION

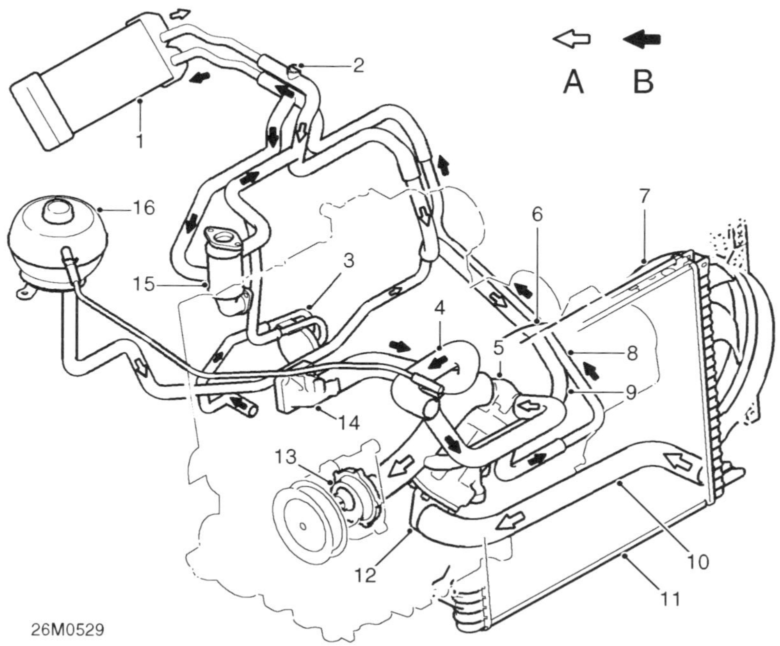

A = COLD
B = HOT

1. Heater matrix
2. Bleed screw
3. IRD cooler
4. Radiator top hose
5. Oil cooler
6. Fan - radiator cooler
7. Fan - radiator cooling/Air Con (if fitted)
8. Heater feed hose/pipe
9. Heater return hose
10. Radiator bottom hose
11. Radiator
12. Thermostat
13. Coolant pump
14. Outlet elbow
15. EGR cooler
16. Expansion tank

The cooling system employed is the by-pass type, allowing coolant to circulate around the engine and the heater circuit while the thermostat is closed.

The thermostat is mounted on the lower end face of the oil cooler. The thermostat is located in the inlet side of the cooling circuit, which provides a more stable control of the coolant temperature in the engine.

When cold, the thermostat is closed and coolant is prevented from circulating through the radiator. Coolant is able to circulate through the bypass and heater circuits.

As temperature reaches 80-84 °C, the thermostat gradually opens, bleeding cool fluid from the radiator bottom hose into the cylinder block and allowing hot coolant to flow through the heater circuit and to the radiator through the radiator top hose, balancing the flow of hot and cold fluid to maintain the optimum operating temperature. When the thermostat opens fully, at 96 °C the full flow of coolant passes through the radiator.

An expansion tank is fitted to the right hand shock absorber mounting. Any excess coolant, created by heat expansion, is returned to the expansion tank through a bleed line from the top of the radiator. The expansion tank has an outlet pipe which is connected into the coolant circuit. The outlet pipe supplies coolant into the system when the engine is cool. This replaces coolant displaced to the expansion tank due to heat expansion.

The coolant is circulated by a rotor type pump. The pump is mounted on the rear face of the PAS pump which is driven by a drive belt. The mounting for the pump is sealed to a port on the cylinder block. The pump draws fluid from the oil cooler and and the heater circuit and circulates it through the the engine via the port on the cylinder block.

The radiator, positioned at the front of the vehicle, is a copper/brass cross - flow type with moulded plastic end tanks. The radiator is mounted in rubber bushes; the bottom of the radiator is located in the front body cross member, and the top is located in the bonnet locking platform. The top hose from the radiator is connected to the coolant outlet elbow on the front of the cylinder head and the bottom hose is connected to the thermostat housing.

For additional air flow through the radiator matrix, particularly when the vehicle is stationary, an electric cooling fan is fitted to the rear of the radiator. The temperature of the cooling system is monitored by the Engine Control Module (ECM) via signals from a twin terminal temperature sensor, which is mounted in the top face of the coolant outlet elbow. When a temperature of 106°C is reached, the ECM switches the cooling fan on via a relay. The fan switches off at 99°C. The coolant outlet elbow also houses a single terminal sensor which provides a coolant temperature output to the instrument panel temperature gauge.

All vehicles have two fans. These operate either in series or parallel according to engine coolant temperature or air conditioning requirements. The fan operation is controlled by the ECM. The fans operate in series (slow mode) when a temperature of 106°C or higher is sensed. When a temperature of 112°C is sensed the fans switch from series to parallel operation (fast mode). When the temperature falls to 106°C or below, the fans are switched back to series operation. The fans stop when a temperature of 100°C or lower is sensed.

The cooling system is also used to cool the engine oil, the Intermediate Reduction Drive (IRD) and the Exhaust Gas Recirculation (EGR) cooler:

An oil cooler is located at the front of the engine cylinder block. A housing at the bottom of the oil cooler contains the system thermostat and also provides the connection for the bottom hose from the radiator. A connection at the top of the oil cooler has two ports; one port supplies coolant from the cooler to the pump and the other port provides the by-pass circuit from the outlet elbow hose. Coolant from the radiator enters the oil cooler body through the thermostat housing and passes through the body of the oil cooler, reducing the engine oil temperature.

The IRD oil cooler is located on the end face of the IRD and comprises a plate, sealed into the end face of the IRD gearbox housing. Coolant from the cylinder block passes through the plate which contains waterways and recirculates via the heater circuit. The coolant supply from the cylinder block flows through a brass connection on the rear of the cylinder block. The connection contains a thermostatically controlled restrictor which controls the flow of coolant to the IRD cooler at certain coolant temperatures. The thermostatic restrictor opens at between 80-84°C and is fully open at 96°C.

The EGR cooler, is located at the rear of the engine and is mounted on the exhaust manifold. The EGR cooler comprises a cylinder, closed at each end with two connection ports. The EGR cooler contains hollow tubes which allow the exhaust gases to pass through the cylinder. The coolant from the heater circuit flows into the lower connection on the cooler, around the hollow tubes cooling the exhaust gases, and flowing out of the upper connection back into the heater circuit.

A bleed screw is installed in the top hose to the heater matrix. This is used to bleed air from the cooling system during system filling.

DRAIN AND REFILL

Service repair no - 26.10.01

WARNING: To prevent the risk of scalding ensure engine coolant is COLD before removing expansion tank filler cap.

Drain.

1. Visually check engine and cooling system for signs of coolant leaks.
2. Examine hoses for signs of cracking, distortion and security of connections.
3. Remove underbelly panel. ***See BODY, Exterior fittings.***
4. Remove expansion tank filler cap.
5. Position drain tin to collect coolant.

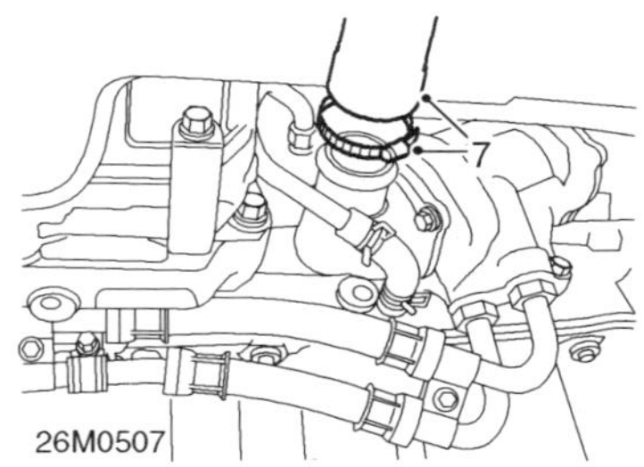

26M0507

6. Release clip and disconnect bottom hose from thermostat housing.
7. Allow cooling system to drain.

Refill

1. Flush system with water under low pressure.

CAUTION: High pressure water could damage the radiator.

2. Connect bottom hose to thermostat housing and fit clip.
3. Prepare coolant to required concentration. ***See INFORMATION, Capacities, fluids and lubricants.***

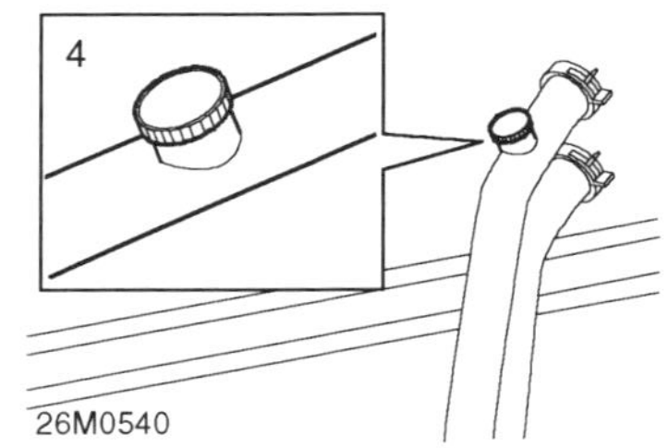

26M0540

4. Slacken bleed screw at heater hose by 2 complete turns.
5. Fill system slowly through coolant expansion tank, until the coolant reaches the 'MAX' mark on expansion tank.
6. Close bleed screw as coolant emerges.
7. Fit expansion tank filler cap.
8. Fit underbelly panel. ***See BODY, Exterior fittings.***
9. Start and run engine until radiator cooling fans operate.

CAUTION: If fitted DO NOT operate air conditioning.

10. Turn heater control to fully hot and ensure that warm air is available at vents.

NOTE: If warm air is not available, an air-lock may be present in heater matrix. If necessary, allow engine to cool, remove expansion tank filler cap and repeat bleed operation at heater hose.

11. Switch off engine and allow to cool.
12. Check for leaks and top-up coolant to 'MAX' mark on expansion tank.

EXPANSION - TANK - COOLANT

Service repair no - 26.15.01

Remove

1. Position container to collect coolant.

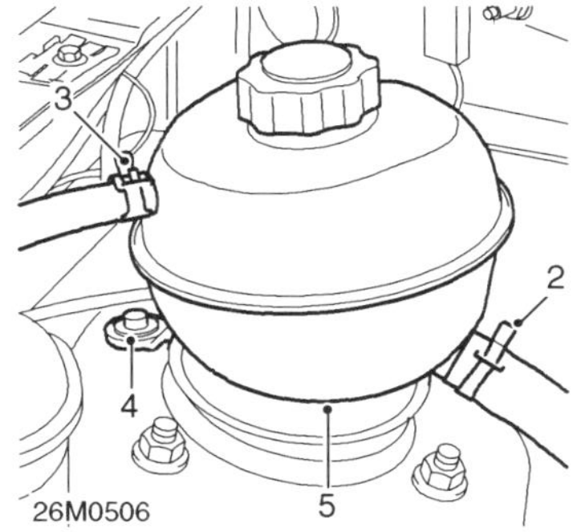

26M0506

2. Release clip and disconnect bottom hose from expansion tank.
3. Release clip and disconnect top hose from expansion tank.
4. Remove scrivet securing expansion tank to inner wing.
5. Remove expansion tank from inner wing location.

Refit

1. Fit expansion tank to inner wing location.
2. Secure expansion tank with scrivet.
3. Connect bottom hose to expansion tank and secure with clip.
4. Connect top hose to expansion tank and secure with clip.
5. Top-up and check level of engine coolant.

MOTOR - COOLING FAN

Service repair no - 26.25.22

Remove

1. Remove engine acoustic cover. ***See ENGINE - 'L' SERIES, Repairs.***

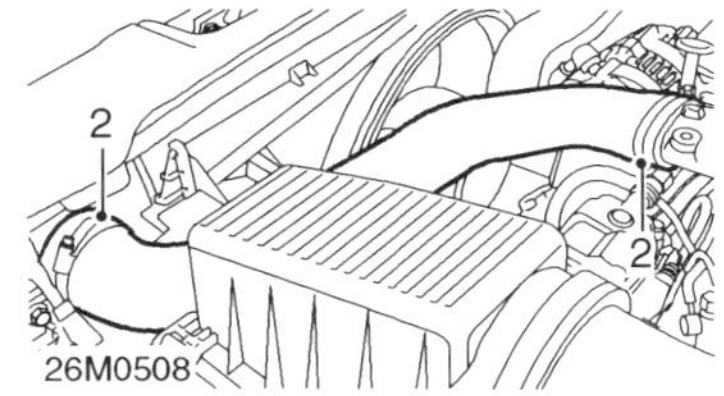

26M0508

2. Release 2 clips securing top intercooler hose and remove hose.
3. Remove battery. ***See ELECTRICAL, Repairs.***

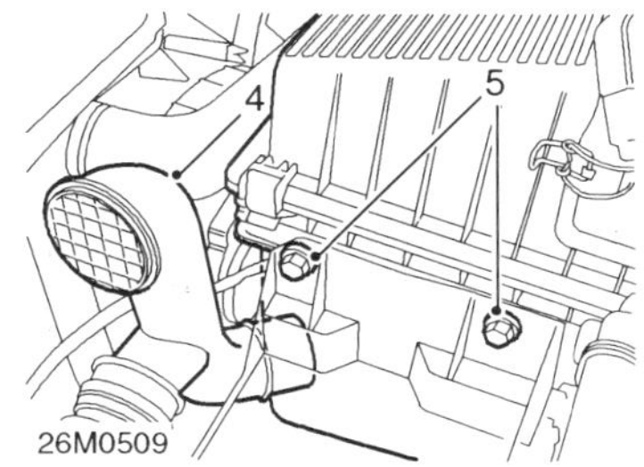

26M0509

4. Disconnect air intake elbow from air cleaner assembly and resonator box, pipe.
5. Remove 2 bolts securing air cleaner assembly to battery carrier, lift assembly off locating peg and position assembly aside.

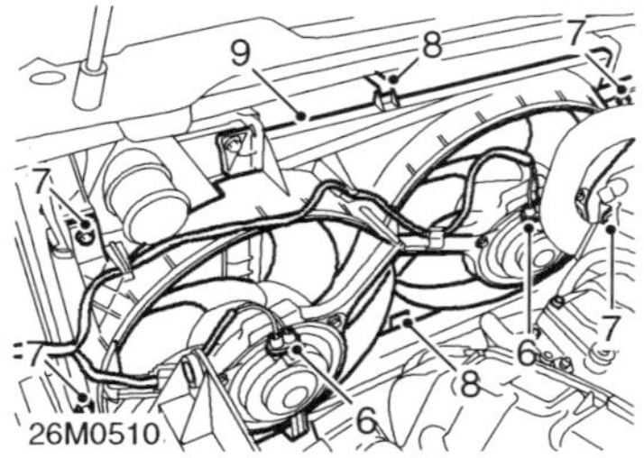

26M0510

6. Disconnect 2 multiplugs from cooling fan motors and release cables from 4 clips.
7. Remove 4 bolts securing fan assembly to radiator.
8. Remove top and bottom clips securing fan assembly to radiator.
9. Remove fan assembly from engine compartment.

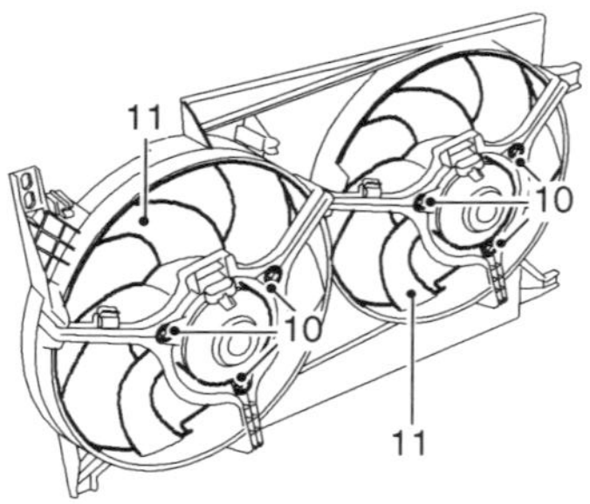

26M0511

10. Remove 3 bolts securing fan motor to fan assembly.
11. Remove fan motor from fan assembly.

Refit

1. Position fan motor to fan assembly, fit and tighten bolts to 6 Nm .
2. Position fan assembly to radiator and secure with clips.
3. Fit and tighten fan assembly bolts to 6 Nm .
4. Connect multiplugs to cooling fan motors and fit cables to clips.
5. Position air cleaner assembly on battery carrier locating peg, fit and tighten bolts.
6. Connect air intake elbow to air cleaner assembly and resonator box, pipe.
7. Fit battery. ***See ELECTRICAL, Repairs.***
8. Fit top intercooler hose and secure clips.
9. Fit engine acoustic cover. ***See ENGINE - 'L' SERIES, Repairs.***

RADIATOR

Service repair no - 26.40.01

Remove

1. Remove intercooler. ***See ENGINE MANAGEMENT SYSTEM - EDC, Repairs.***
2. Drain cooling system. ***See Adjustments.***

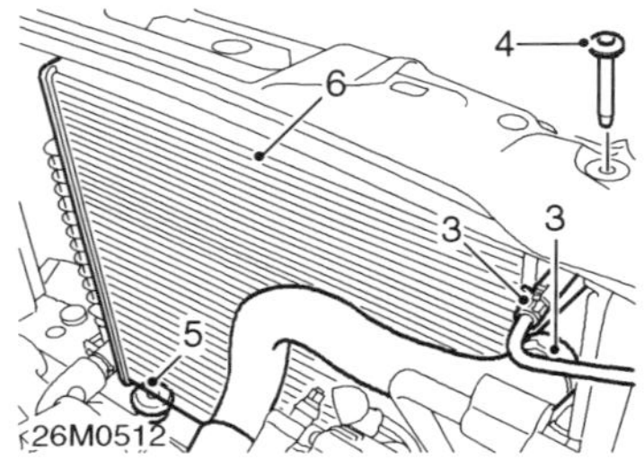

26M0512

3. Release 2 clips from radiator top hoses and disconnect hoses.
4. Remove radiator threaded retainer from top of bonnet platform.
5. Lift radiator to release from lower mounting.
6. Remove radiator.

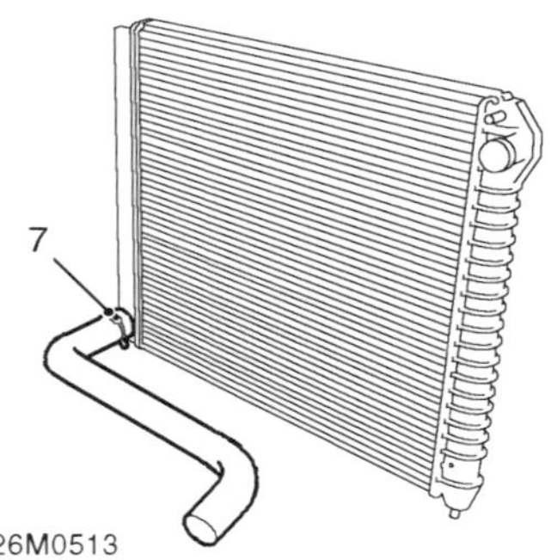

26M0513

7. Release clip from radiator lower hose and disconnect hose.

Refit

1. Connect lower hose to radiator and secure with clip.
2. Fit radiator to lower mounting location.
3. Fit radiator retainer to top of bonnet platform.
4. Connect radiator top hoses and secure with clips.
5. Fill cooling system. ***See Adjustments.***
6. Fit intercooler. ***See ENGINE MANAGEMENT SYSTEM - EDC, Repairs.***

THERMOSTAT

Service repair no - 26.45.09

Remove

1. Drain cooling system. ***See Adjustments.***

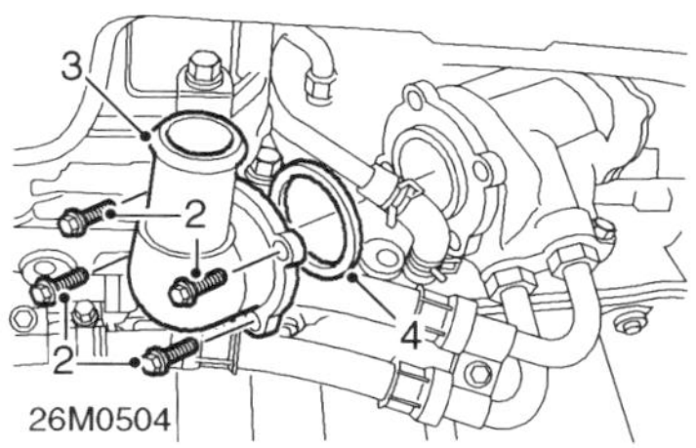

26M0504

2. Remove 4 bolts securing thermostat housing to engine oil cooler housing.
3. Remove thermostat housing.
4. Remove 'O' ring from engine oil cooler housing and discard.

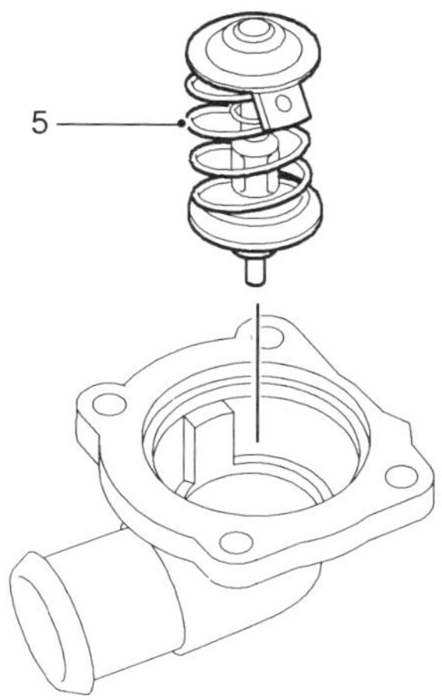

26M0505

5. Remove thermostat from housing.

Refit

1. Clean both thermostat housing and oil cooler housing mating surfaces.
2. Fit NEW 'O' ring to oil cooler housing.
3. Fit thermostat into housing, ensuring thermostat spindle locates housing recess.
4. Position thermostat housing to oil cooler housing, fit bolts and tighten to 9 Nm.
5. Refill cooling system. ***See Adjustments.***

PUMP - COOLANT

Service repair no - 26.50.01

Remove

1. Drain cooling system. ***See Adjustments.***

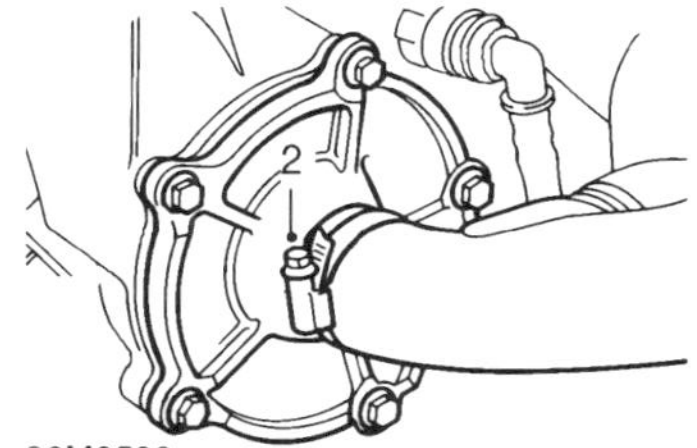

26M0530

2. Release clip and disconnect coolant hose from pump housing.

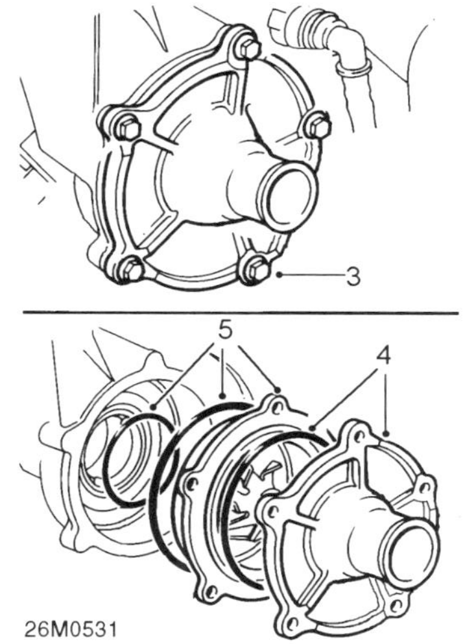

26M0531

3. Remove 5 bolts securing cover to coolant pump.
4. Remove cover and discard 'O' ring.
5. Remove coolant pump from housing and discard 'O' ring.

Refit

1. Clean coolant pump housing and mating faces.
2. Lubricate NEW 'O' rings and fit to coolant pump and coolant pump cover.
3. Fit coolant pump and cover.
4. Fit 5 bolts and tighten to 45 Nm.
5. Connect hose to pump housing and secure clip.
6. Refill cooling system. ***See Adjustments.***

PUMP - COOLANT - WITH AIR CONDITIONING

Service repair no - 26.50.01/20

Remove

1. Drain cooling system. ***See Adjustments.***
2. Remove alternator. ***See ELECTRICAL, Repairs.***

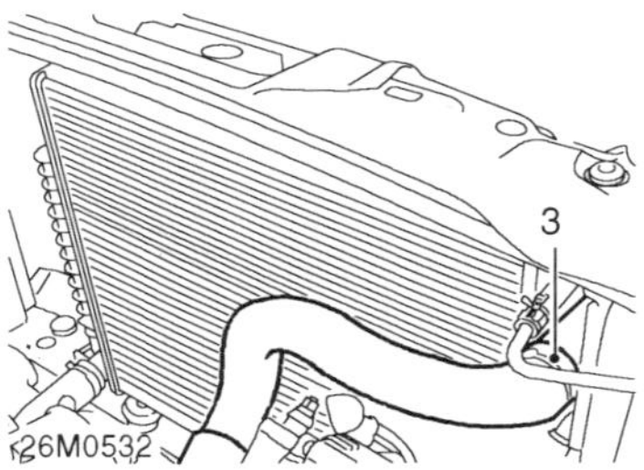

26M0532

3. Loosen clip and release top hose from radiator.

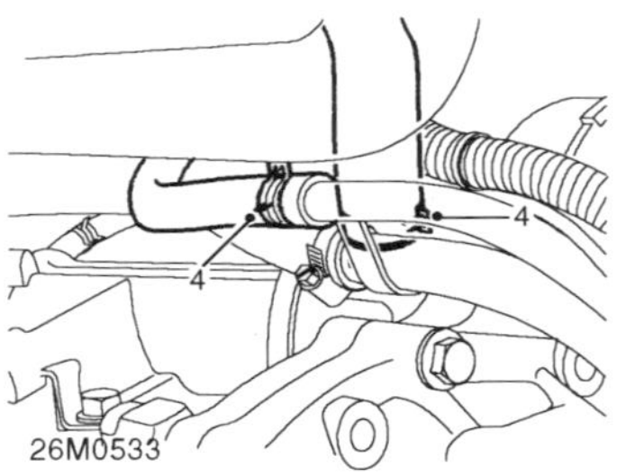

26M0533

4. Loosen clip and release top hose from oil cooler and engine coolant rail.

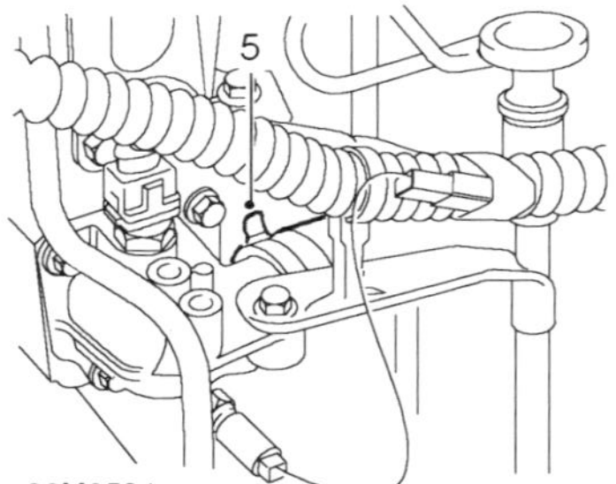

26M0534

5. Loosen clip and remove top hose from engine coolant elbow.

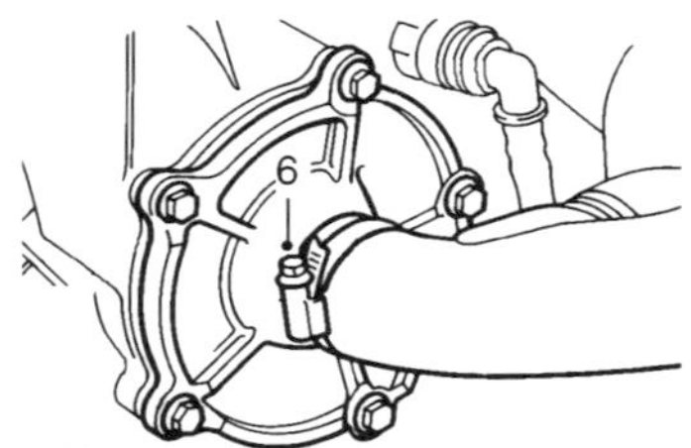

26M0535

6. Loosen clip and release coolant hose from pump housing.

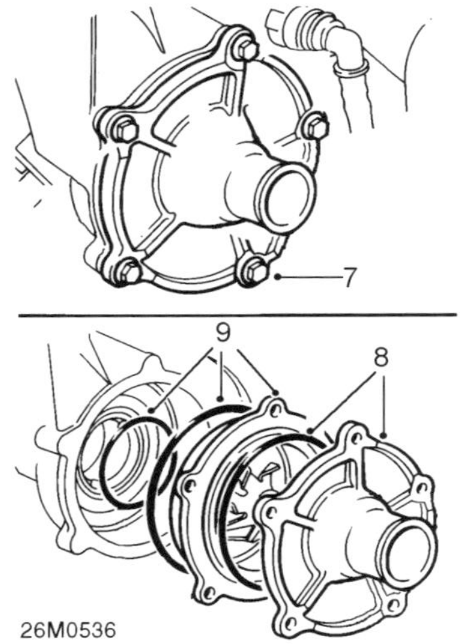

26M0536

7. Remove 5 bolts securing cover to coolant pump.
8. Remove cover and discard 'O' ring.
9. Remove coolant pump from housing and discard 'O' ring.

Refit

1. Clean coolant pump housing and mating faces.
2. Lubricate NEW 'O' rings and fit to coolant pump and coolant pump cover.
3. Fit coolant pump and cover.
4. Fit 5 bolts and tighten to 10 Nm.
5. Connect hose to coolant pump housing and tighten clip.
6. Fit top hose to engine and secure clip.
7. Connect top hose to radiator, coolant rail and oil cooler.Secure hose clips.
8. Fit alternator. ***See ELECTRICAL, Repairs.***
9. Refill cooling system. ***See Adjustments.***

CONTENTS

Page

INLET AND EXHAUST MANIFOLD - 'K' SERIES

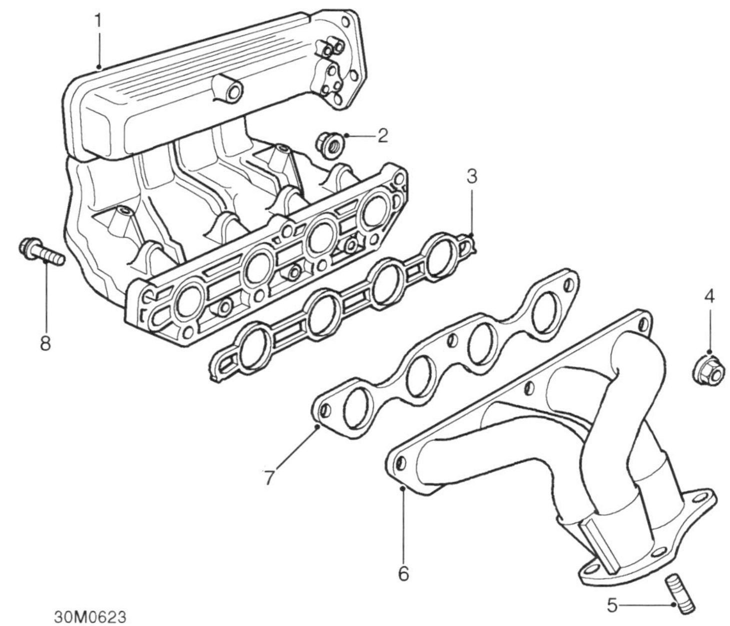

30M0623

1. Inlet manifold
2. Nut 4 off
3. Gasket, inlet manifold
4. Nut 5 off
5. Stud 4 off
6. Exhaust manifold
7. Gasket, exhaust manifold
8. Bolt 4 off

INLET AND EXHAUST MANIFOLD - 'L' SERIES

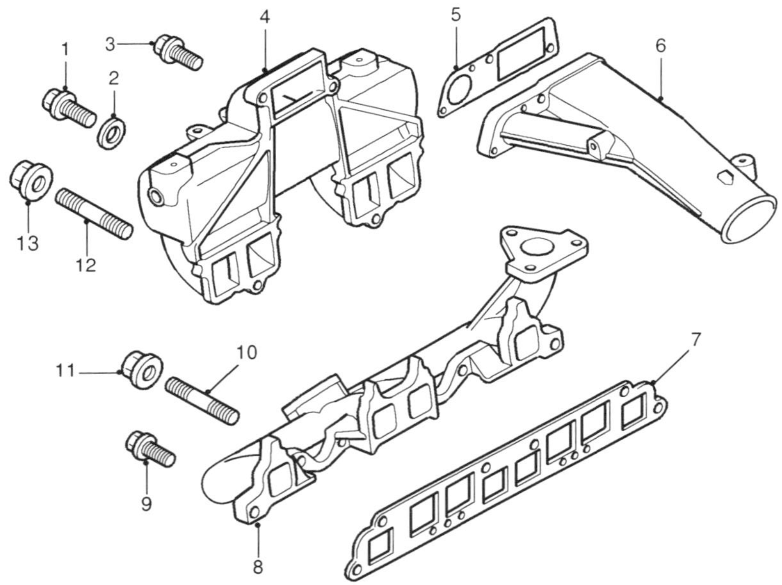

30M0624

1. Bolt 4 off
2. Spacer 4 off
3. Bolt 2 off
4. Inlet manifold
5. Gasket, manifold to plenum chamber
6. Plenum chamber
7. Manifold gasket
8. Exhaust manifold
9. Bolt 2 off
10. Stud 4 off
11. Nut 4 off
12. Stud 2 off
13. Nut 2 off

INLET MANIFOLD

'K' Series Engine

The inlet manifold is a one piece plastic moulding which is attached to the cylinder head on three locating studs and nuts and further retained by four bolts. A rubber moulded gasket, which is located in a corresponding recess in the inlet manifold mounting face, seals the manifold to the cylinder head.

The inlet manifold has vacuum take-off points for the fuel pressure accumulator, the brake servo, the engine control module and the purge valve. A further take-off vents the camshaft cover into the inlet manifold.

Two threaded lugs on the inlet manifold provide for the attachment of the fuel rail. Four ports at the base of each inlet tract house the injectors which are sealed to the manifold with O-ring seals and retained in position by the fuel rail.

The Idle Air Control (IAC) valve is attached to the inlet manifold, adjacent to the throttle housing and is secured with four Torx bolts and sealed to the manifold with an O-ring seal.

The throttle housing is attached to the left hand end of the inlet manifold and is secured with four bolts and sealed with an O-ring seal. The Intake Air Temperature (IAT) sensor is mounted in No.4 inlet tract.

'L' Series Engine

The inlet manifold is a one piece aluminium alloy casting. The inlet manifold is attached to the cylinder head with four bolts and two nuts. A metal laminated gasket seals the inlet manifold to the cylinder head. The same gasket also seals the exhaust manifold to the cylinder head.

An Intake Air Temperature (IAT) sensor is located in the left hand end of the inlet manifold. An air inlet port on the top face of the inlet manifold mates with the plenum chamber. The Exhaust Gas Recirculation (EGR) cooler pipe is attached to the plenum chamber. A paper gasket seals the plenum chamber to the inlet manifold and the EGR cooler pipe to the plenum chamber.

EXHAUST MANIFOLD

'K' Series Engine

The exhaust manifold is a fabricated and welded steel construction. The four branch manifold is located on five studs in the cylinder head and secured with five nuts. A metal corrugated gasket seals the exhaust manifold to the cylinder head. The four separate branches of the manifold merge into one at a siamesed flange. The flange is fitted with four studs which mate with the exhaust system front pipe and sealed with a metal gasket.

A Heated Oxygen Sensor (HO2S) is fitted in the flange and faces the engine block. The HO2S measures the oxygen content of the exhaust gases at the point where the four branches merge.

'L' Series Engine

The exhaust manifold is made from cast iron. The manifold has three separate branches, the centre branch being shared between No's. 2 and 3 cylinders. The manifold is attached to the cylinder head with four nuts and two bolts which also retain the inlet manifold. A laminated metal gasket seals the manifold to the cylinder head. The same gasket also seals the inlet manifold to the cylinder head.

A flanged connection on the left hand end of the exhaust manifold provides for the attachment of the turbocharger. There is no gasket used between the exhaust manifold and the turbocharger. The turbocharger is attached to the flange with three bolts.

A second flange, located centrally at the rear of the exhaust manifold, provides the attachment point for the EGR valve. The EGR valve is attached to the exhaust manifold with two screws. A metal gasket seals the EGR valve to the manifold.

EXHAUST SYSTEM -'K' SERIES

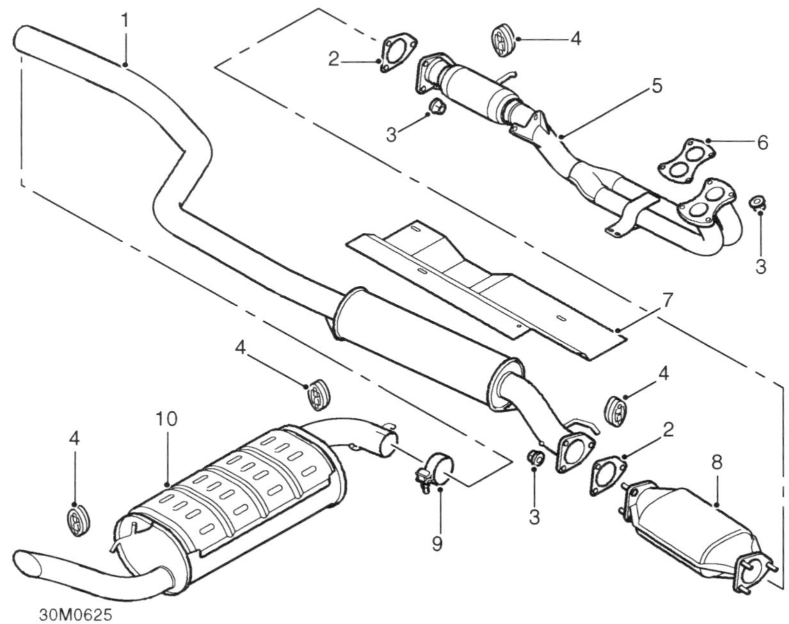

1. Intermediate pipe assembly
2. Gasket - 2 off
3. Nut - 10 off
4. Mounting rubber 4 off
5. Front pipe assembly
6. Gasket
7. Heat shield
8. Catalytic converter
9. Clamp
10. Tailpipe

EXHAUST SYSTEM - 'L' SERIES

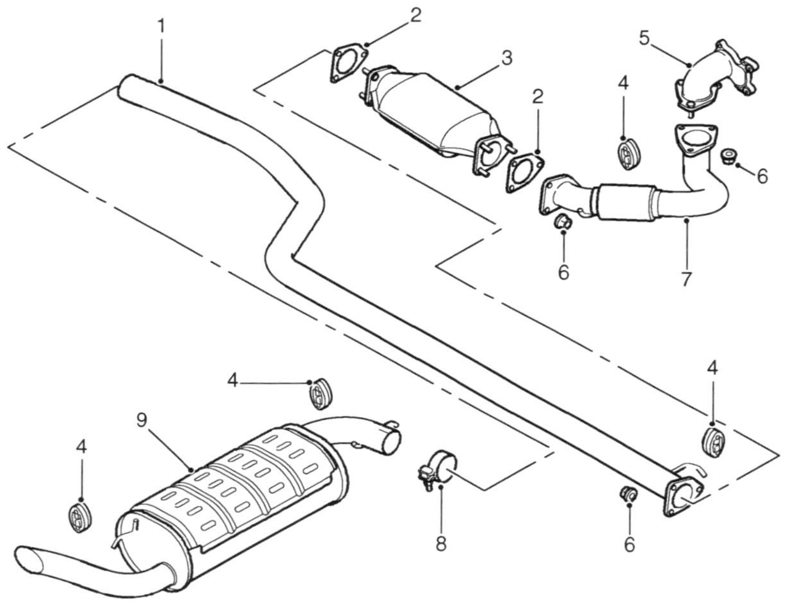

30M0626

1. Intermediate pipe assembly
2. Gasket
3. Catalytic converter
4. Mounting rubber - 4 off
5. Elbow
6. Nut - 6 off
7. Front pipe assembly
8. Clamp
9. Tailpipe assembly

EXHAUST SYSTEM

'K' Series Engine

The exhaust system comprises of a catalytic converter, centre silencer assembly and a tailpipe. The system is constructed of extruded pipe with a 1.5 mm wall thickness.

Front Pipe Assembly

The downpipe assembly is of welded and fabricated tubular construction. The downpipe is connected to the exhaust manifold flange with four nuts and sealed with a metal gasket. Two pipes from its mounting flange merge into one pipe halfway along its length. The pipe then connects into a flexible pipe and terminates in a flanged connection.

The flexible pipe is formed into a concertina shape with woven metal strands around its outer diameter. The flexible pipe allows for ease of exhaust system alignment and also absorbs engine vibration. The woven metal strands increase the longevity of the flexible pipe.

The front pipe is secured with two brackets bolted to the engine sump plate and the intermediate reduction drive and a mounting rubber connected to the body.

Catalytic Converter (CAT)

The CAT is mounted between the front pipe and the centre silencer assembly. A flange is welded to each end of the CAT with three captive bolts in each flange. The CAT connects to mating flanges on the front pipe and centre silencer and is secured with nuts. Metal gaskets seal each flanged joint.

NOTE: Refer to the Emissions section for a description and operation of the catalytic converter.

CAUTION: The catalytic converter will be irreparably damaged if leaded fuel is used. Leaks in the exhaust system will also damage the catalyst by drawing oxygen into the exhaust system which causes the catalyst to overheat. Engine misfires cause overheating of the catalyst which may lead to irreparable damage.

Intermediate Pipe Assembly

A fabricated silencer is mounted at the forward end of the intermediate pipe assembly.A flange at its forward end connects to the catalytic converter flange and is secured with three nuts and sealed with a metal gasket. The rear pipe from the silencer is shaped to go around and over the rear subframe. The flanged end is connected to the vehicle body with a mounting rubber. The silencer is fabricated from 0.6 mm mild steel outer tube with a 0.5 mm stainless steel inner liner. An end plate is secured at each end of the outer tube with seam joints. A perforated baffle tube is welded to each end plate. A stainless steel fibre is packed between the baffle tube and the inner liner to absorb engine noise as exhaust gases pass through the silencer.

Tailpipe Assembly

The tailpipe assembly is of fabricated and welded construction and comprises a large capacity silencer, a connecting pipe and a tail pipe. The curved connecting pipe is welded to the left hand end of the silencer and connects with the rear pipe section of the centre silencer assembly. The tail pipe is welded to the right hand end of the silencer and directs exhaust emissions downwards from the right hand end of the rear bumper.

The connecting pipe is a sliding fit on the centre silencer. A clamp secures the two pipes together. Attachment bars are welded to each end of the tailpipe assembly and provide attachment points for the tailpipe to the body via mounting rubbers.

The tail pipe silencer is fabricated from a 0.6 mm mild steel outer cover with a 0.5 mm stainless steel inner liner and is oval in section. An end plate is secured to each end of the outer cover with seam joints. The inlet and outlet of the silencer are diametrically opposed at each end of the silencer. The inlet and outlet each incorporate a perforated baffle tube welded to each end plate and retained internally by two baffle plates.

Two perforated balance pipes are located between the two baffle plates and exhaust gases from the inlet is forced to flow through the balance pipes before it reaches the outlet. Two open spaces at each end of the silencer act as expansion chambers to further reduce engine exhaust noise.

The upper surface on the outside diameter of the silencer has an additional plate welded, with an air gap between the plate and the silencer body. The air gap is filled with a heat absorbing 'Fibrax' insulating pad which reduces heat from the silencer radiating to the floorpan of the vehicle.

'L' Series Engine

The exhaust system comprises an elbow, downpipe, catalytic converter, centre pipe and a tailpipe. The system is constructed mainly of 60 mm diameter extruded pipe with a 1.5 mm wall thickness.

Elbow

The elbow is made from cast iron and connects the turbocharger to the downpipe of the exhaust system. The elbow is located on four studs on the turbocharger and secured with four nuts. A flanged end with three studs connects with the downpipe and is secured with three nuts. There is a metal gasket between the elbow and the downpipe.

Front Pipe Assembly

The downpipe is of welded and fabricated tubular construction and is connected to the elbow flange with three nuts. The downpipe connects into a flexible pipe and terminates in a flanged connection which mates with the catalytic converter and sealed with a metal gasket.

The flexible pipe is formed into a concertina shape with woven metal strands around its outer diameter. The flexible pipe allows for ease of exhaust system alignment and also absorbs engine vibration. The woven metal strands increase the longevity of the flexible pipe.

The downpipe is secured to the to the gearbox via a metal support bracket with 4 bolts and a mounting rubber connected to the body.

Catalytic Converter (CAT)

The CAT is mounted between the downpipe and the centre pipe. A flange is welded to each end of the CAT with three captive bolts in each flange. The CAT connects to mating flanges on the downpipe and centre pipe and is secured with nuts. Metal gaskets seal each flanged joint.

⚠ NOTE: Refer to the Emissions section for a description and operation of the catalytic converter.

⚠ **CAUTION: Leaks in the exhaust system can damage the catalyst by drawing oxygen into the exhaust system which causes the catalyst to overheat. Engine misfires cause overheating of the catalyst which may lead to irreparable damage.**

Intermediate Pipe Assembly

The centre pipe has a flange at its forward end which connects to the catalytic converter flange, secured with three nuts and sealed with a metal gasket. The rear of the centre pipe shaped to go around and over the rear subframe. The centre pipe is supported at the flanged end to the body via a mounting rubber.

Tailpipe Assembly

The tailpipe assembly is of fabricated and welded construction and comprises a large capacity silencer, a connecting pipe and a tail pipe. The curved connecting pipe is welded to the left hand end of the silencer and connects with the rear pipe section of the centre silencer assembly. The tail pipe is welded to the right hand end of the silencer and directs exhaust emissions downwards from the right hand end of the rear bumper.

The connecting pipe is a sliding fit on the centre pipe. A clamp secures the two pipes together. Attachment bars are welded to each end of the tailpipe assembly and provide attachment points for the tailpipe to the body via mounting rubbers.

The tail pipe silencer is fabricated from a 0.6 mm mild steel outer cover with a 0.5 mm stainless steel inner liner and is oval in section. An end plate is secured to each end of the outer cover with seam joints. The inlet and outlet of the silencer are diametrically opposed at each end of the silencer. The inlet and outlet each incorporate a perforated baffle tube welded to each end plate and retained internally by two baffle plates.

A perforated balance pipe is located between the two baffle plates and exhaust gases from the inlet is forced to flow through the balance pipes before it reaches the outlet. Two open spaces at each end of the silencer act as expansion chambers to further reduce engine exhaust noise.

The upper surface on the outside diameter of the silencer has an additional plate welded, with an air gap between the plate and the silencer body. The air gap is filled with a heat absorbing 'Fibrax' insulating pad which reduces heat from the silencer radiating to the floorpan of the vehicle.

EXHAUST PIPE - FRONT - 'K' SERIES

Service repair no - 30.10.09

Remove

1. Remove underbelly panel. ***See BODY, Exterior fittings.***

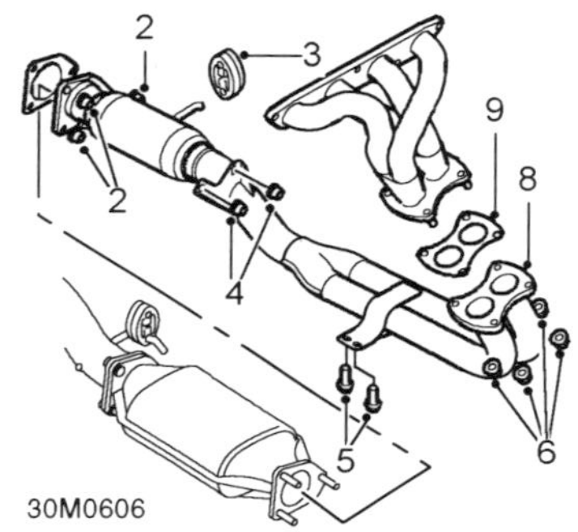

30M0606

2. Remove 3 flange nuts securing front pipe to catalytic converter.
3. Release mounting rubber from pipe bracket.
4. Remove 2 nuts securing front pipe support bracket to IRD unit.
5. Remove 2 bolts securing front pipe to engine sump.
6. Remove 4 flange nuts securing front pipe to manifold.
7. Release front pipe from manifold and remove from catalytic converter.
8. Remove and discard flange gaskets.

Refit

1. Clean pipe flanges.
2. Fit NEW gasket to catalytic converter flange.
3. Fit front pipe to catalytic converter, fit nuts but DO NOT tighten at this stage.
4. Fit new gasket to manifold flange.
5. Raise front pipe and engage flange.
6. Fit manifold to front pipe flange nuts and tighten to 45 Nm.
7. Tighten nuts securing front pipe bracket on IRD unit to 25 Nm.
8. Fit bolts securing front pipe to engine sump and tighten to 25 Nm.
9. Fit flange nuts securing front pipe to catalytic converter and tighten to 60 Nm.
10. Connect rubber mounting to front pipe bracket.
11. Fit underbelly panel. ***See BODY, Exterior fittings.***

EXHAUST PIPE - FRONT - 'L' SERIES

Service repair no - 30.10.09

Remove

1. Remove engine acoustic cover. ***See ENGINE - 'L' SERIES, Repairs.***
2. Remove underbelly panel. ***See BODY, Exterior fittings.***

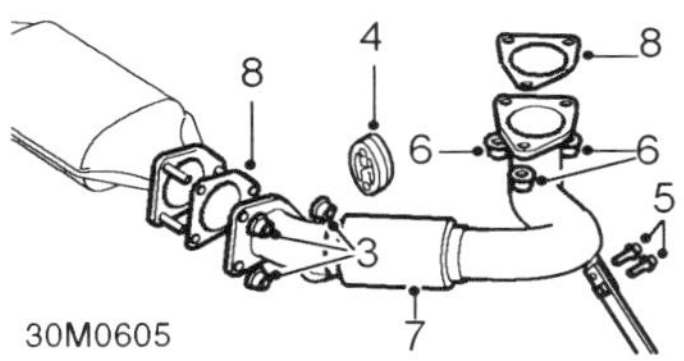

30M0605

3. Remove 3 flange nuts securing front pipe to catalytic converter.
4. Release mounting rubber from pipe bracket.
5. Remove 2 bolts securing front pipe to support bracket on gearbox.
6. Remove 3 flange nuts securing front pipe to manifold.
7. Release front pipe from manifold and remove from catalytic converter.
8. Remove and discard flange gaskets.

Refit

1. Clean pipe flanges.
2. Fit new gasket to catalytic converter flange.
3. Fit front pipe to catalytic converter, fit nuts but DO NOT tighten at this stage.
4. Fit new gasket to manifold flange.
5. Raise front pipe and engage flange.
6. Fit nuts securing front pipe to manifold and tighten to 45 Nm.
7. Fit and tighten bolts securing front pipe to gearbox support bracket to 25 Nm.
8. Fit flange nuts securing front pipe to catalytic converter and tighten to 60 Nm.
9. Connect rubber mounting to front pipe bracket.
10. Fit underbelly panel. ***See BODY, Exterior fittings.***
11. Fit engine acoustic cover. ***See ENGINE - 'L' SERIES, Repairs.***

EXHAUST PIPE - INTERMEDIATE

Service repair no - 30.10.11

Remove

1. Raise vehicle on 4 post ramp.

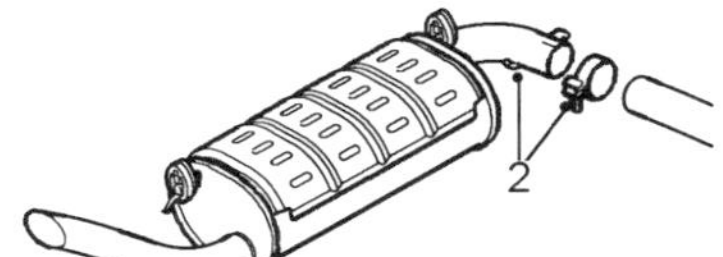

30M0607

2. Loosen tail pipe clamp nut and release tail pipe from intermediate pipe.

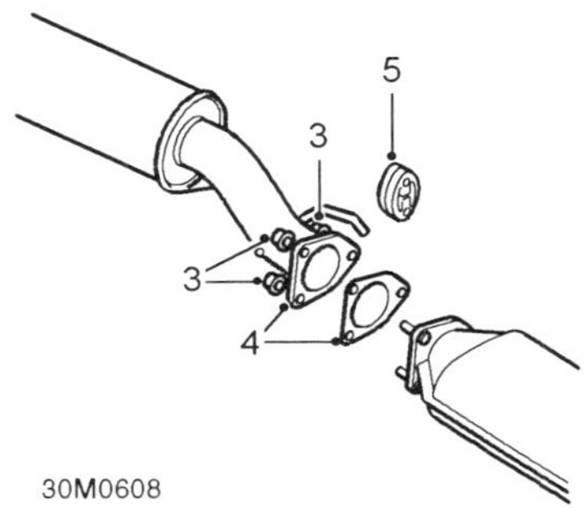

30M0608

3. Remove 3 nuts securing intermediate pipe to catalytic converter.
4. Release intermediate pipe from catalytic converter. Remove and discard gasket.
5. Release rubber mounting from intermediate pipe.
6. With assistance release and remove intermediate pipe.

Refit

1. Clean mating faces of intermediate pipe, catalytic converter and tail pipe.
2. Fit NEW gasket to catalytic converter flange.
3. With assistance fit intermediate pipe to tail pipe and connect to catalytic converter flange.
4. Fit nuts and tighten intermediate pipe flange nuts to 60 Nm.
5. Tighten tail pipe clamp nut to 55 Nm .
6. Connect mounting rubbers.
7. Lower vehicle.

GASKET - INLET AND EXHAUST MANIFOLD - 'L' SERIES

Service repair no - 30.15.15

Remove

1. Disconnect battery earth lead.
2. Remove exhaust front pipe. ***See MANIFOLD & EXHAUST SYSTEMS - 'L' SERIES, Repairs.***
3. Remove air cleaner. ***See ENGINE MANAGEMENT SYSTEM - EDC, Adjustments.***
4. Loosen clip and disconnect breather hose from camshaft cover.

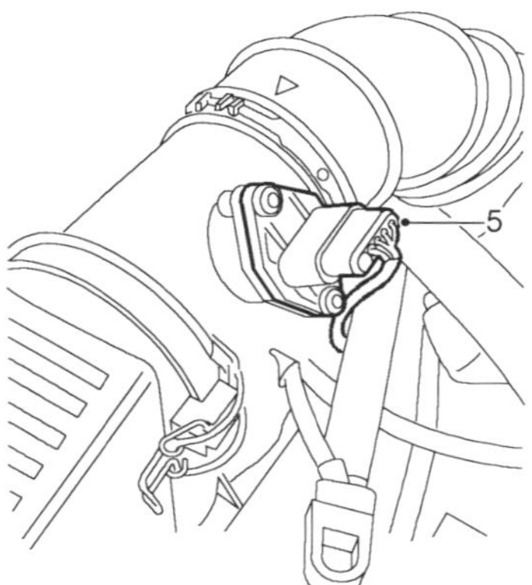

30M0616

5. Disconnect multiplug from MAF sensor.

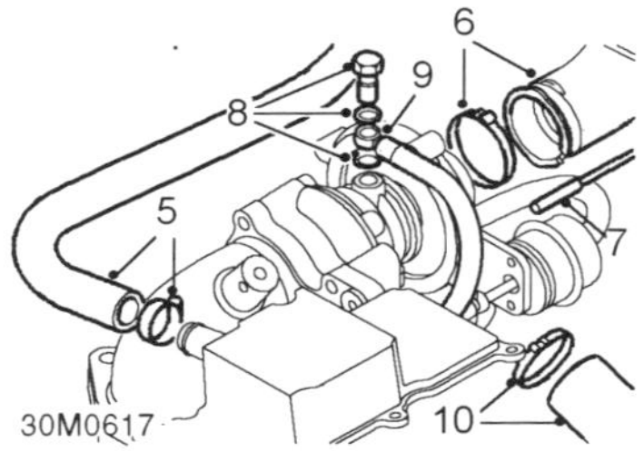

30M0617

6. Release clip and remove air intake hose from turbocharger.
7. Release clip and disconnect boost pressure sensing pipe from turbocharger.
8. Remove banjo bolt securing oil feed pipe to turbocharger, collect 2 sealing washers.
9. Plug oil feed pipe and turbocharger.
10. Loosen clip screw and release air outlet hose from turbocharger.

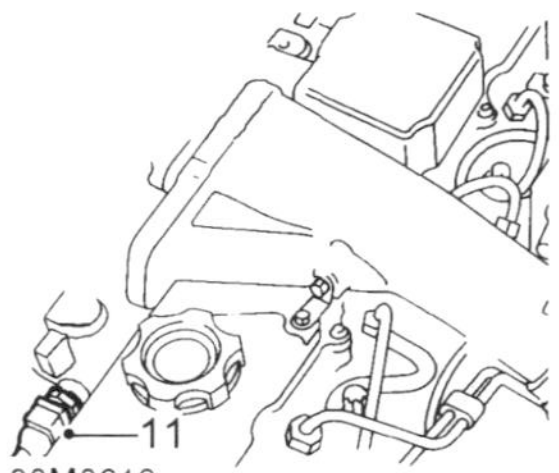

30M0618

11. Disconnect multiplug from IAT sensor.

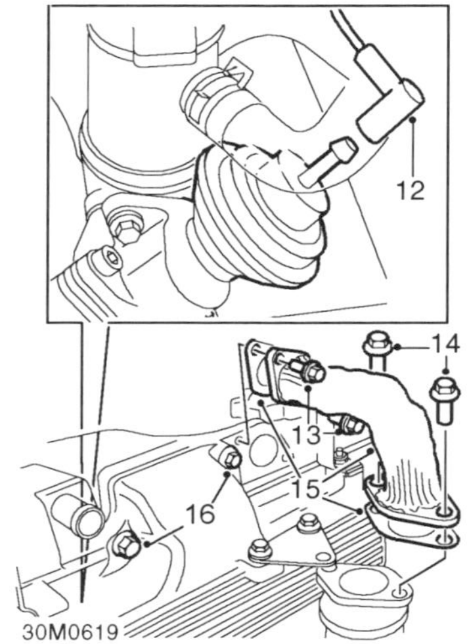

30M0619

12. Disconnect vacuum pipe from EGR valve.
13. Remove 2 bolts securing EGR recirculation pipe to plenum chamber.
14. Remove 2 bolts securing EGR recirculation pipe to EGR valve elbow.
15. Release recirculation pipe and discard gasket.
16. Remove 2 bolts securing inlet manifold to plenum chamber.
17. Remove and discard gasket.

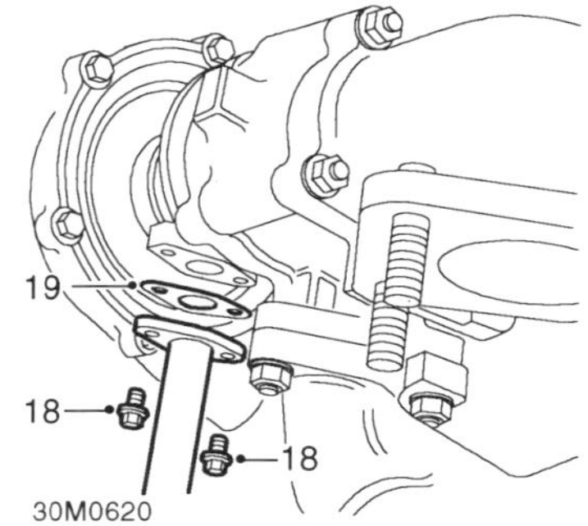

30M0620

18. Remove 2 bolts securing oil drain pipe flange to turbocharger.
19. Remove and discard gasket.

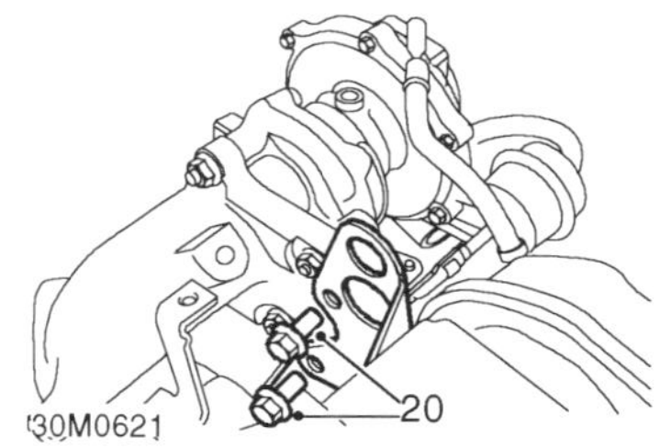

30M0621

20. Remove 2 bolts securing exhaust manifold to engine lifting bracket.

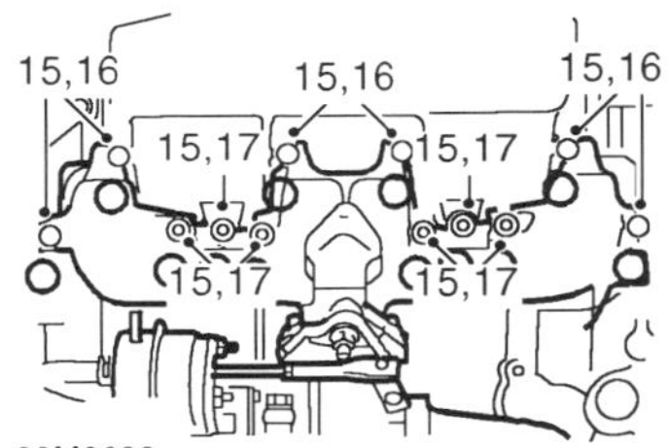

30M0622

21. Remove 6 bolts and 6 nuts securing inlet and exhaust manifold to cylinder head.
22. Release and remove manifolds and turbocharger assembly.
23. Remove and discard manifold gasket.

Refit

1. Clean mating faces of manifolds and cylinder head.
2. Fit NEW manifold gasket.
3. Clean mating faces of EGR recirculation pipe and plenum chamber.
4. Fit NEW gasket to plenum chamber.
5. Manoeuvre manifolds and turbocharger assembly into position and align to cylinder head.
6. Apply Loctite 270 to threads of manifold bolts.
7. Fit nuts, bolts and washers securing manifold to cylinder head. Working in the sequence illustrated tighten manifold nuts to 25 Nm.and manifold bolts to 33 Nm.
8. Fit 2 bolts securing exhaust manifold to mounting bracket.
9. Clean mating faces of oil drain pipe and turbocharger.
10. Fit new gasket to turbocharger oil drain pipe. Align pipe to turbocharger, fit bolts and tighten to 10 Nm.
11. Clean face of EGR recirculation pipe.
12. Fit 2 bolts securing EGR recirculation pipe to plenum chamber and tighten to 9 Nm.
13. Fit 2 bolts securing inlet manifold to plenum chamber and tighten to 9 Nm.
14. Clean face of EGR valve elbow.
15. Fit new gasket to EGR valve elbow.
16. Fit and tighten bolts EGR valve to elbow.
17. Connect vacuum pipe from EGR solenoid to EGR valve.
18. Connect multiplug to intake air temperature IAT sensor.
19. Fit new sealing washers to oil feed banjo bolt, connect oil feed pipe to turbocharger and tighten to 20 Nm.
20. Connect boost pressure sensing pipe to turbocharger and secure clip.
21. Connect air outlet hose to turbocharger and tighten clip screw.
22. Position air intake hose and connect to turbocharger, tighten clip to secure.
23. Connect MAF sensor multiplug.
24. Connect breather hose to camshaft cover and tighten clip.
25. Fit air cleaner. ***See ENGINE MANAGEMENT SYSTEM - EDC, Adjustments.***
26. Fit exhaust front pipe. ***See MANIFOLD & EXHAUST SYSTEMS - 'L' SERIES, Repairs.***
27. Connect battery earth lead.

EXHAUST PIPE - TAIL

Service repair no - 30.10.22

Remove

1. Raise rear of vehicle.

⚠ WARNING: Support on safety stands.

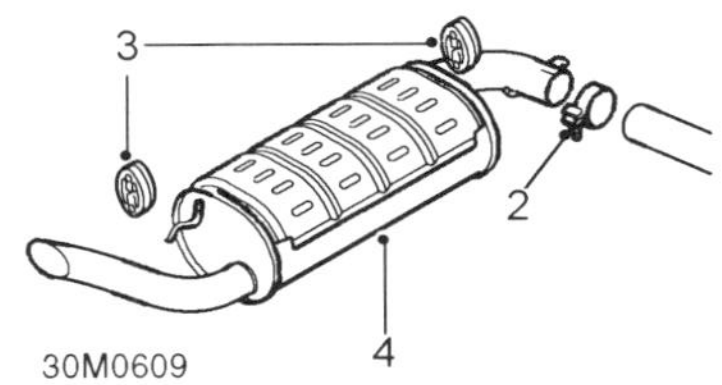

30M0609

2. Loosen tail pipe clamp nut.
3. Release 2 rubber mountings from tail pipe.
4. Remove tail pipe.

Refit

1. Clean intermediate pipe and tail pipe mating faces.
2. Fit tail pipe and connect rubber mountings.
3. Tighten tail pipe clamp nut to 55 Nm.
4. Remove stand(s) and lower vehicle.

GASKET - INLET MANIFOLD - 'K' SERIES

Service repair no - 30.15.08

Remove

1. Disconnect battery earth lead.
2. Drain cooling system. ***See COOLING SYSTEM, Adjustments.***
3. Remove air filter. ***See ENGINE MANAGEMENT SYSTEM - MEMS, Adjustments.***

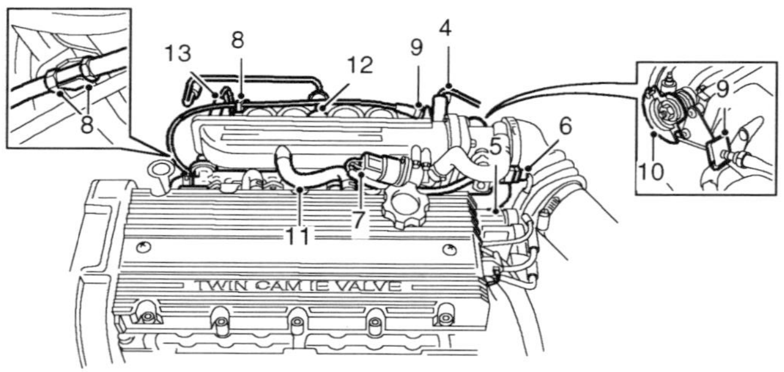

30M0611A

4. Disconnect purge valve hose from inlet manifold.
5. Release clip and disconnect breather hose from throttle body.
6. Disconnect multiplug from TP sensor.
7. Disconnect multiplug from IACV.
8. Release throttle cable from clip on manifold.
9. Release throttle cable adjusting nut from abutment bracket.
10. Release inner cable from throttle cam.
11. Disconnect breather hose from inlet manifold.
12. Depress plastic collar and disconnect brake servo hose from inlet manifold.
13. Disconnect ECM vacuum hose from manifold.

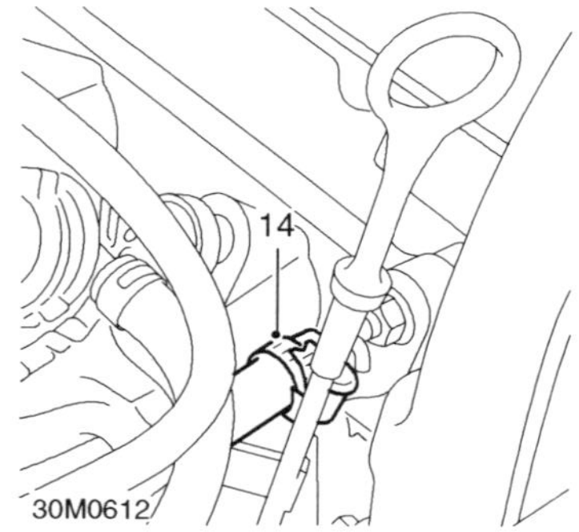

30M0612

14. Release clip and disconnect coolant hose from inlet manifold.

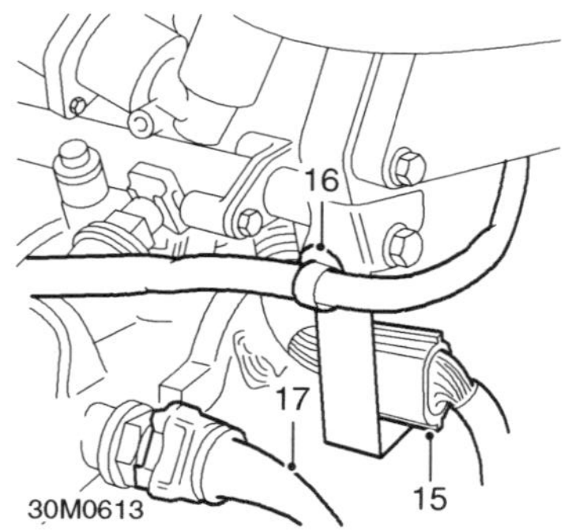

30M0613

15. Release injector harness multiplug from bracket and disconnect multiplug.
16. Release clip securing engine harness to inlet manifold bracket.
17. Disconnect multiplug from Intake Air Temperature (IAT) sensor.
18. Position absorbent cloth beneath fuel rail.

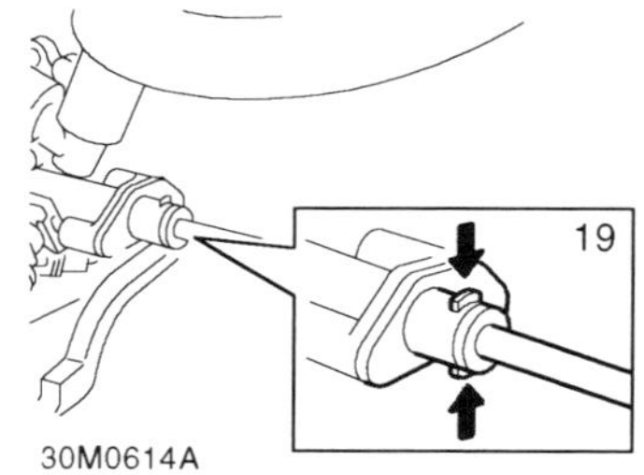

30M0614A

19. Release fuel feed pipe from fuel rail.

CAUTION: Plug the connections.

20. Working from the centre outwards, progressively slacken then remove 3 nuts and 4 bolts securing inlet manifold to cylinder head.
21. Remove inlet manifold, remove and discard gasket.

Refit

1. Ensure mating surfaces are clean and metal inserts are fitted in inlet manifold stud and bolt holes.
2. Fit NEW gasket to inlet manifold.

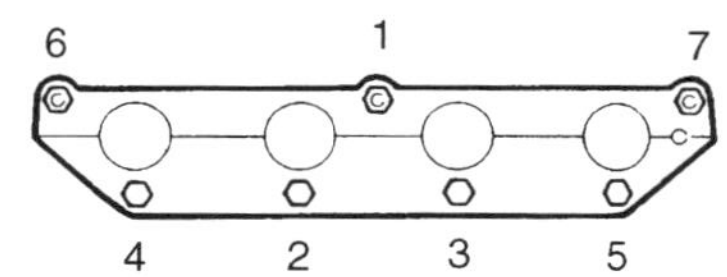

30M0322

3. Fit inlet manifold, fit bolts and nuts and tighten to 17 Nm in the sequence shown.

4. Connect coolant hose to inlet manifold and secure clip.
5. Remove plugs from fuel hose and fuel rail.
6. Position fuel feed pipe to fuel rail.
7. Secure engine harness clip to manifold bracket.
8. Connect IAT sensor multiplug.
9. Connect multiplug to injector harness and secure multiplug to bracket.
10. Connect ECM vacuum pipe and brake servo vacuum hoses to inlet manifold.
11. Connect breather pipe to inlet manifold.
12. Connect throttle cable to throttle cam.
13. Locate throttle cable adjusting nut in abutment bracket.
14. Secure throttle cable in clip on inlet manifold.
15. Connect multiplug to TP sensor.
16. Connect breather hose to throttle body and secure clip.
17. Connect multiplug to IACV.
18. Connect purge hose to inlet manifold and tighten clip.
19. Refit air filter. ***See ENGINE MANAGEMENT SYSTEM - MEMS, Adjustments.***
20. Refill cooling system. ***See COOLING SYSTEM, Adjustments.***
21. Connect battery earth lead.

GASKET - EXHAUST MANIFOLD - 'K' SERIES

Service repair no - 30.15.12

Remove

1. Remove air filter ***See ENGINE MANAGEMENT SYSTEM - MEMS, Repairs.***
2. Remove underbelly panel. ***See BODY, Exterior fittings.***

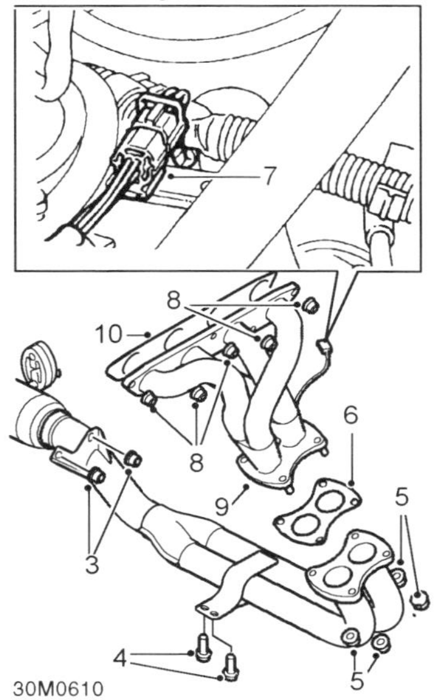

30M0610

3. Remove 2 nuts securing front pipe support bracket to IRD unit.
4. Remove 2 bolts securing front pipe to engine sump.
5. Remove 4 flange nuts securing front pipe to manifold.
6. Release front pipe from manifold and discard gasket.
7. Release oxygen sensor multiplug from coolant rail bracket. Disconnect multiplug.
8. Remove 5 nuts securing exhaust manifold to cylinder head.
9. Remove exhaust manifold.
10. Remove and discard exhaust manifold gasket.

Refit

1. Clean manifold mating faces.
2. Fit NEW gasket to manifold studs.
3. Fit manifold on studs and tighten nuts in the sequence illustrated to 45 Nm.
4. Connect oxygen sensor multiplug and secure to bracket.
5. Clean pipe flanges.
6. Fit NEW gasket to manifold flange.
7. Raise front pipe and engage flange.
8. Fit manifold to front pipe flange nuts and tighten to 45 Nm.
9. Tighten nuts securing front pipe bracket on IRD unit to 25 Nm.
10. Fit bolts securing front pipe to engine sump and tighten to 25 Nm.
11. Fit underbelly panel. ***See BODY, Exterior fittings.***
12. Fit air filter. ***See ENGINE MANAGEMENT SYSTEM - MEMS, Repairs.***

CONTENTS

Page

DESCRIPTION AND OPERATION

REPAIRS

CLUTCH COMPONENTS

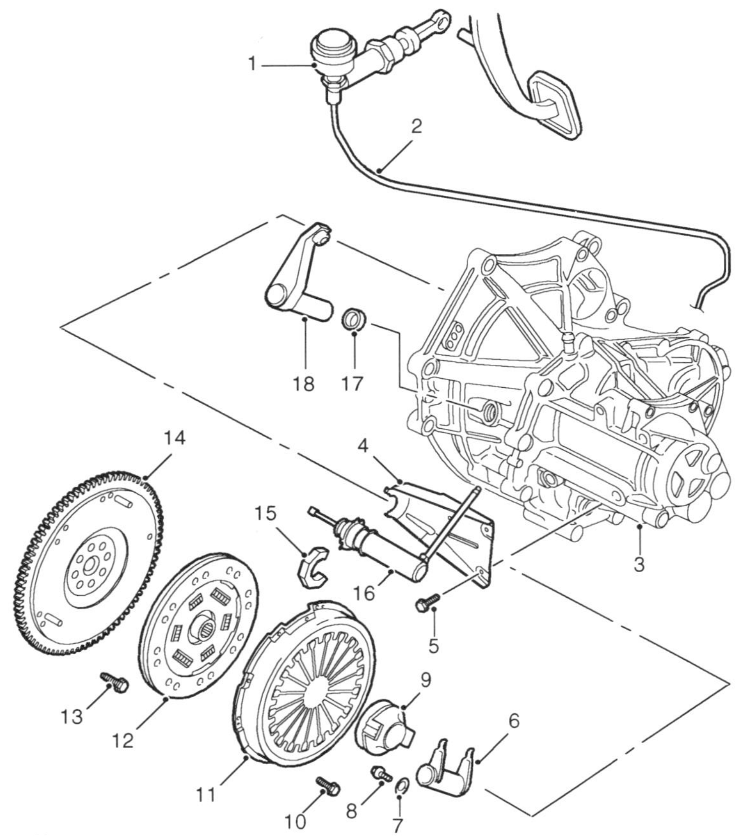

33M0317

1. Clutch master cylinder
2. Tube
3. Gearbox
4. Bracket
5. Bolt 3 off
6. Release fork
7. Spring washer
8. Bolt
9. Release bearing
10. Bolt 6 off
11. Clutch pressure plate
12. Clutch drive plate
13. Bolt 6 off
14. Flywheel
15. Clip
16. Clutch slave cylinder
17. Release shaft oil seal
18. Release lever

CLUTCH SYSTEM DESCRIPTION

The clutch system is a conventional diaphragm type clutch operated by a hydraulic cylinder. The hydraulic system is manufactured from plastic and is sealed for life and can only be replaced in its entirety. The clutch requires no adjustment to compensate for clutch wear.

Hydraulic Clutch

The hydraulic clutch comprises a master cylinder and a slave cylinder connected by a plastic tube. The system comes as a complete assembly, pre filled with hydraulic fluid to ease replacement and minimize repair times. The master and slave cylinders are manufactured from injection moulded thermoplastic which can operate in extremes of temperatures. The hydraulic clutch system is self bleeding.

The master cylinder is mounted in the bulkhead. It locates in a specially designed hole which allows the master cylinder to be installed in the hole at a 45 degree angle from vertical. Once located, the master cylinder is rotated to the vertical position and is automatically secured in this position. The master cylinder has a piston which moves in the cylinder. A rod is attached to the piston and attaches to a spigot on the clutch pedal. A fluid reservoir is mounted on the engine compartment side of the master cylinder and is sealed with a removable rubber cap.

A nylon tube is connected to the master cylinder by a swivel coupling which aids installation and alignment. The other end of the tube is connected to the slave cylinder, also using a swivel coupling. The nylon tube is flexible and allows ease of routing and absorbs engine movements and vibrations.

The slave cylinder comprises a cylinder with a piston and rod. The piston is spring loaded to return to its fully extended position when at rest. A new slave cylinder has the piston locked in the retracted position by a plastic clip. When the clutch is first operated, the hydraulic action of the clutch system breaks the plastic clip and allows the rod to extend. The plastic clip attached to the end of the rod locates in a spherical seat in the release lever. The slave cylinder is located in a bracket which is bolted to the gearbox. A specially shaped slot in the bracket locates the slave cylinder and a plastic clip secures it in position.

Clutch Mechanism

The clutch mechanism comprises a flywheel, drive plate, pressure plate, release lever, release fork and a release bearing. The clutch mechanism is fully enclosed at the end of the engine by a bell housing formed by the gearbox casing.

The spindle of the release lever is located through machined bores in the gearbox casing. The release fork fits on the release lever spindle and is secured to the spindle with a bolt and spring washer. An oil seal is located at the outer face of the gearbox casing and seals against the release lever spindle preventing the ingress of dirt and moisture.

A release bearing is operated by the release fork. The bearing has two lugs which clip onto the forks of the release fork.

The flywheel is bolted to the flange of the engine crankshaft with six bolts. A dowel ensures that the flywheel is correctly located. A ring gear is located on the outside diameter of the flywheel and is seated against a flange. The ring gear is an interference fit on the flywheel and is installed by heating the ring gear and cooling the flywheel. The ring gear is a serviceable item and can be replaced if damaged or worn.

The operating face of the flywheel is machined to provide a smooth surface for the drive plate to engage on. Three dowels are fitted to the outer diameter of the flywheel and provide for the location of the pressure plate. Six threaded holes provide for the attachment of the pressure plate. The flywheel is balanced to ensure that it does not produce vibration when rotating.

The pressure plate comprises a diaphragm, pressure plate and cover. The pressure plate is mounted on and rotates with the flywheel. Three dowels locate the cover and six bolts secure it to the flywheel. The same 228 mm (9.0 in) diameter plate is used on K and L Series engines.

The pressure plate is forged from cast iron and machined to provide a smooth surface for the drive plate to engage on. Three lugs on the outer diameter of the pressure plate connect it via three leaf springs to the cover. The leaf springs have three tempered steel leaves and pull the pressure plate away from the drive plate when the clutch pedal is depressed. The cover is made from pressed steel.

The diaphragm comprises a cast ring with eighteen fingers on its inner diameter. Two circular steel fulcrum rings are attached to the housing and allows the diaphragm to pivot between them. The diaphragm is not physically attached to the pressure plate. When pressure is applied to the diaphragm fingers from the release bearing, the diaphragm pivots between the fulcrum rings and moves away from the pressure plate. The leaf springs attaching the pressure plate to the cover move the plate away from the drive plate.

The drive plate is sandwiched between the flywheel and the pressure plate. The drive plate has a splined hub which engages with the splines on the primary shaft from the gearbox. The splined hub is located in an inner plate which contains four compression pre-damper springs. The inner plate is retained by the springs which can compress in both directions to cushion engine vibration at tickover. The inner plate is located on eight larger compression springs which are located in a central plate. The hub is sandwiched between the central plate and the friction damper. The friction damper comprises friction washers located between the hub and the central plate. The friction washers reduce transmission noises and vibrations.

The drive from the inner plate is transferred to the central plate through the larger compression springs. Two outer plates are located either side of the central plate. The central plate is connected to the outer plate in slots and retained with rivets. The slots allow the central plate to move and compress the springs absorbing shock loads when the clutch is engaged or when the engine is decelerating. One of the outer plates is marked 'flywheel side'. This outer plate must face the flywheel when installed.

One of the outer plates has a spring steel plate riveted to it. The plate provides the attachment surface for the clutch drive plate friction material which is riveted to each side of the plate.

The facing material comprises two discs which are riveted to each side of the spring steel plate. The rivets are secured through recessed holes in the facing material and emerge in clearance holes in the opposite disk.

The drive plates used K and L Series engines are both of the compound centre type. The compound centre drive plate allows angular movement of the hub at low torque levels. The K Series drive plate is 215 mm (8.5 in) diameter and has a facing material manufactured from Raybestos K202. The L Series drive plate is 228 mm (9.0 in) diameter and has a facing material manufactured from APTEC T385.

Pressure plate

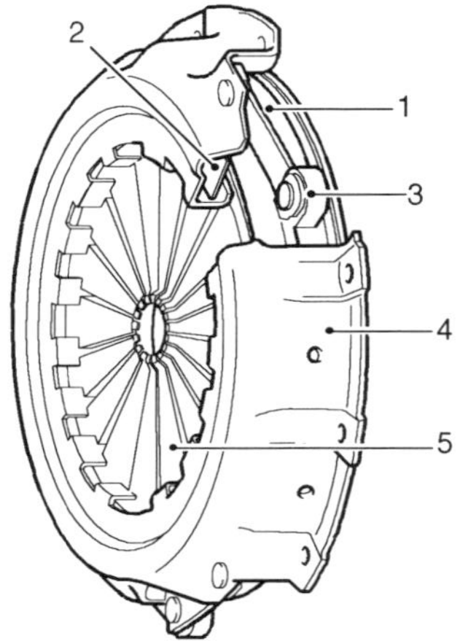

33M0318

1. Leaf springs
2. Fulcrum rings
3. Pressure plate
4. Cover
5. Diaphragm

Drive plate

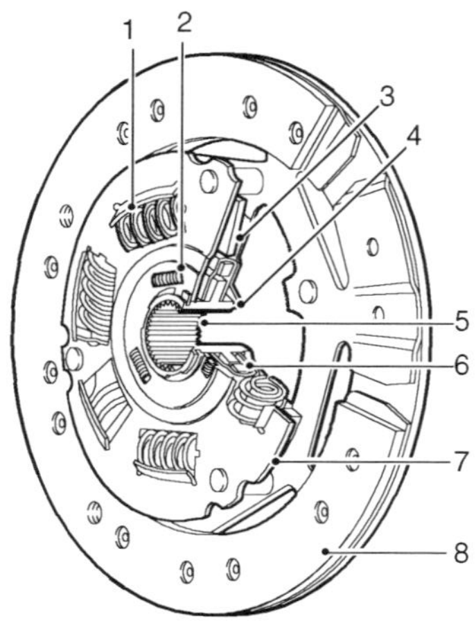

33M0319

1. Damper springs
2. Pre damper springs
3. Inner plate
4. Friction damper
5. Splined hub
6. Central plate
7. Outer plates
8. Friction material

CLUTCH SYSTEM OPERATION

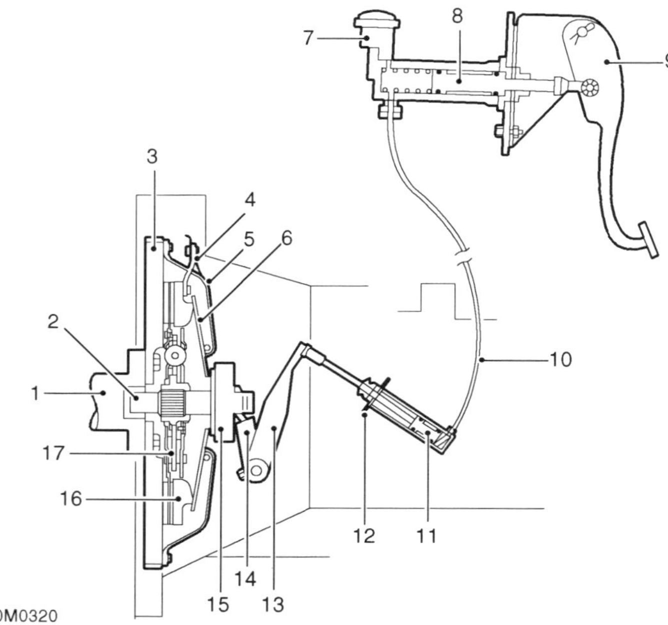

30M0320

1. Engine crankshaft
2. Gearbox primary shaft
3. Flywheel
4. Leaf spring
5. Pressure plate housing
6. Diaphragm
7. Master cylinder
8. Piston
9. Clutch pedal
10. Hydraulic tube
11. Piston
12. Slave cylinder
13. Release lever
14. Release fork
15. Release bearing
16. Pressure plate
17. Drive plate

Hydraulic Operation

When the clutch pedal (9) is depressed, the piston (8) is pushed into the master cylinder (7). The piston pressurizes the fluid in the master cylinder forcing the pressurized fluid along the hydraulic tube (10). The pressure is felt at the piston (11) of the slave cylinder (12) which moves under the hydraulic force applied.

When the clutch pedal (9) is released, force from the compressed fingers of the diaphragm (6), pushes against the release fork (14) through the release bearing. The release fork rotates which in turn rotates the release lever (13).

The release lever pushes the piston (11) back into the slave cylinder (12). This returns hydraulic fluid back up the hydraulic tube (10) and into the master cylinder (7).

Mechanism Operation

When the clutch pedal (9) is depressed, the hydraulic pressure extends the piston (11) rod in the slave cylinder (12). The extension of the piston rod pushes the release lever (13) which transfers its rotary movement to the release fork (14) to which it is connected.

The release fork (14) pivots towards the engine and converts its rotary movement into linear movement of the release bearing (15). The release bearing pushes on the fingers of the diaphragm (6) which pivots about its fulcrum on the pressure plate housing (5). As the diaphragm is deflected, its pressure is removed from the pressure plate (16). The three leaf springs (4) pull the pressure plate away from the drive plate (17).

The removal of force from the pressure plate (16) on the drive plate (17) reduces the friction between the drive plate and the flywheel (3). The drive plate slips against the flywheel and cannot transfer the drive from the flywheel to the gearbox primary shaft (2).

When the clutch pedal is released, hydraulic pressure is removed from the piston (11) in the slave cylinder (12). The removal of the pressure allows the release bearing (15) to be pushed back along the gearbox primary shaft (2) by the fingers of the diaphragm (6). The linear movement of the release bearing is transferred to rotary movement of the release fork (14) and the release lever (13) which pushes the piston (11) into the slave cylinder (12).

The diaphragm (6) pivots on its fulcrum on the pressure plate housing (5). This applies pressure to the pressure plate (16) and overcomes the opposing force applied by the leaf springs (4). The pressure plate moves towards the flywheel (3) and applies force to the drive plate (17).

The force applied to the drive plate (17) by the pressure plate (16) increases the friction between the drive plate and the flywheel (3). As the clutch pedal (9) is released the friction increases and rotary movement of the flywheel is transferred to the drive plate, which in turn rotates the primary shaft (2) of the gearbox.

When the pedal is released fully, the pressure applied to the pressure plate (16) by the diaphragm (6) forces the drive plate (17) onto the flywheel with no slippage.

CLUTCH PLATE AND RELEASE BEARING - 'K' SERIES

Service repair no - 33.10.01

Remove

1. Remove gearbox. ***See MANUAL GEARBOX, Repairs.***

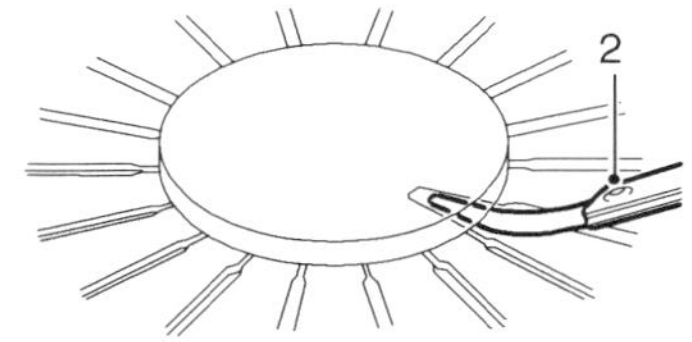

33M0298

2. Place a circular piece of flat plate across diaphragm fingers and insert feeler gauges between plate and fingers; measure finger clearance.
   diaphragm finger clearance - service limit = 1.0 mm
   Renew pressure plate if clearance obtained is outside service limits.

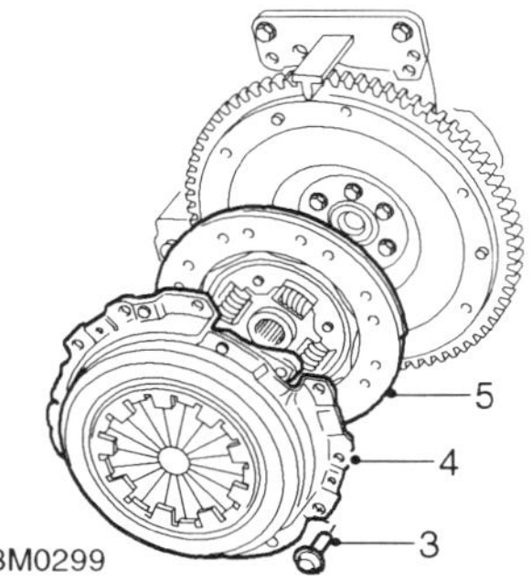

33M0299

3. Progressively loosen then remove 6 bolts securing pressure plate to flywheel.
4. Remove pressure plate.
5. Remove clutch plate.
6. Inspect clutch linings for signs of wear or oil contamination. Check for broken or weak springs and signs of cracking of spring apertures; renew components as necessary.
7. Measure clutch plate thickness, renew plate if less than service limit.
   clutch plate thickness - NEW = 7.40 mm - 6.90 mm
   clutch plate thickness - SERVICE LIMIT = 5.60 mm.
8. Measure rivet depth, renew plate if less than service limit.
   rivet depth - NEW = 1.0 mm
   rivet depth - SERVICE LIMIT = 0.20 mm

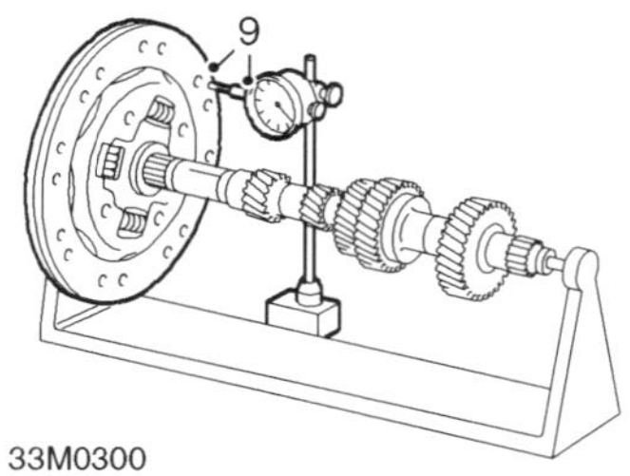

33M0300

9. Measure clutch plate run-out using a dial gauge and a gearbox mainshaft; renew plate if outside service limit.
run-out - NEW = 0.80 mm
run-out - SERVICE LIMIT = 1.0 mm
10. Check clutch plate for signs of wear or damage. Check for signs of overheating on drive straps (deep straw or blue colour); renew pressure plate if necessary.

CAUTION: Renew a pressure plate which has been accidentally dropped.

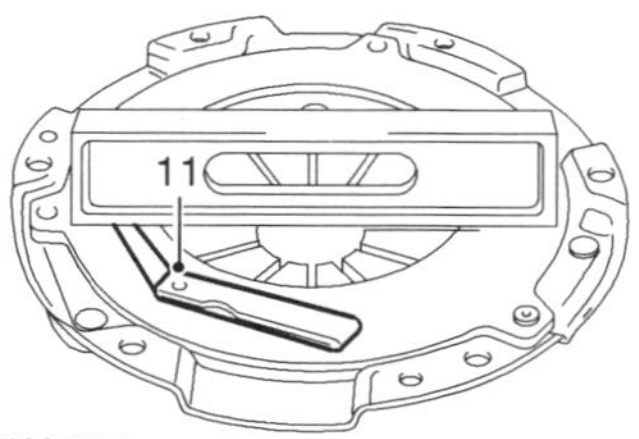

33M0301

11. Using a straight edge and feeler gauges, check surface of pressure plate for warping at 4 seperate points, renew plate if warping exceeds service limit.
pressure plate warping - SERVICE LIMIT = 0.15 mm

Release bearing

12. Remove release bearing.
13. Examine release bearing for signs of wear or damage, renew if necessary.

Refit

Release bearing

1. Clean gearbox input shaft and release bearing mating faces.
2. Fit release bearing.

Clutch assembly

3. Clean all components.
4. Clean flywheel.
5. Ensure locating dowels are fitted in flywheel.
6. Smear clutch plate splines with molybdenum disulphide grease.
7. Position clutch plate to flywheel with 'FLYWHEEL SIDE' marking towards flywheel.
8. Position pressure plate to flywheel ensuring it is located on dowels.

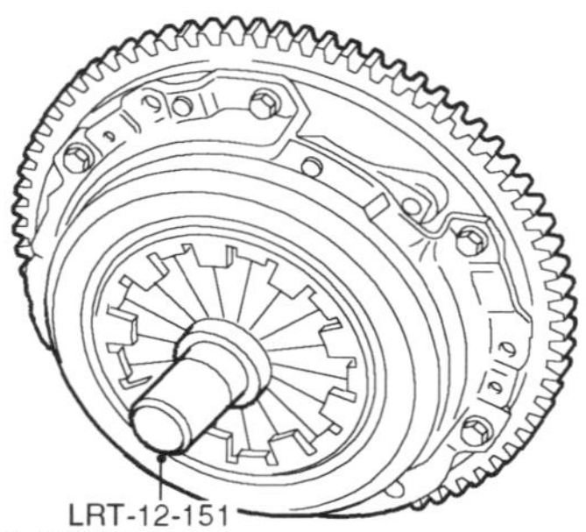

33M0302

9. Fit alignment tool **LRT-12-151.**

10. Fit pressure plate bolts finger tight.
11. Working in diagonal sequence, progressively tighten pressure plate bolts to 25 Nm.

NOTE: During the above procedure, ensure diaphragm fingers do not crimp service tool. When a slight drag is felt between fingers and tool, remove tool.

12. Fit gearbox. ***See MANUAL GEARBOX, Repairs.***

CLUTCH ASSEMBLY AND RELEASE BEARING - 'L' SERIES

Service repair no - 33.10.01

Remove

1. Remove gearbox assembly. ***See MANUAL GEARBOX - 'PG1', Repairs.***

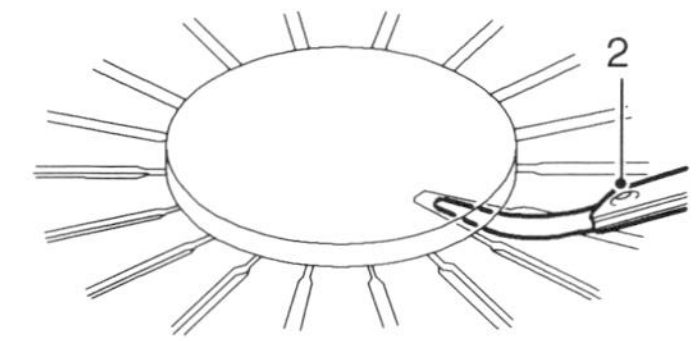

33M0298

2. Place a circular piece of flat plate across diaphragm fingers and insert feeler gauges between plate and fingers.

Diaphragm finger clearance limit = 1.0 mm

3. Measure diaphragm finger height above bolted surface of pressure plate.

Diaphragm finger height:
new clutch plate = 29.1 - 32.0 mm
service limit = 36.5 mm

Renew pressure plate if clearances are outside service limit.
4. Using a socket and extension bar on crankshaft pulley bolt, rotate crankshaft until locking pin **LRT-12-058** can be inserted through hole in gearbox mounting plate and into hole in flywheel.

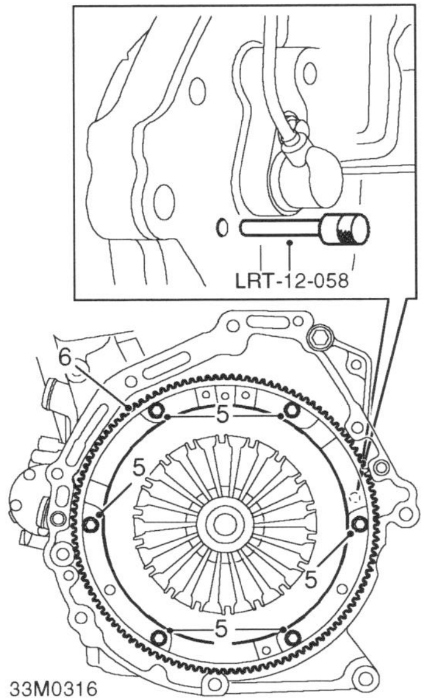

33M0316

5. Progressively loosen and then remove 6 bolts securing pressure plate to flywheel.
6. Remove clutch pressure plate and collect drive plate.
7. Inspect clutch drive plate for signs of wear or oil contamination. Check for broken or loose springs and signs of cracking at spring windows. Renew drive plate if necessary.
8. Measure depth of rivets on drive plate, renew drive plate if less than service limit.

Drive plate rivet depth:
new clutch plate = 1.0 mm minimum
service limit = 0.2 mm

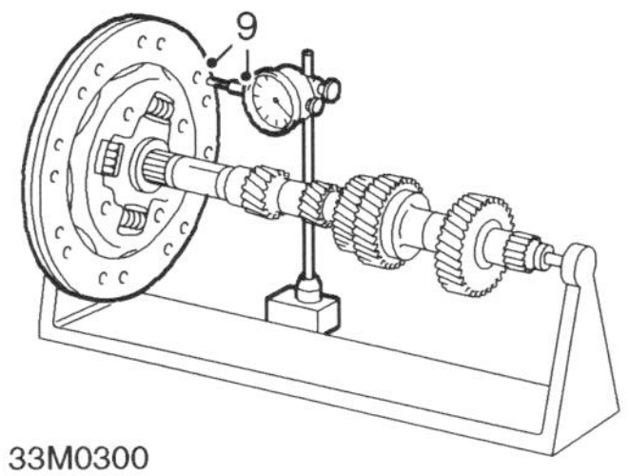

33M0300

9. Measure drive plate run-out by fitting drive plate to a gearbox mainshaft and use a dial gauge as drive plate is rotated. Renew drive plate if outside service limit.

Drive plate run-out:
New clutch plate = 0.8 mm
Service limit = 1.0 mm

10. Check pressure plate for signs of wear or damage. Check for signs of overheating on drive straps (deep yellow to blue colour), renew pressure plate if necessary.

NOTE: Renew a pressure plate which has been accidentally dropped.

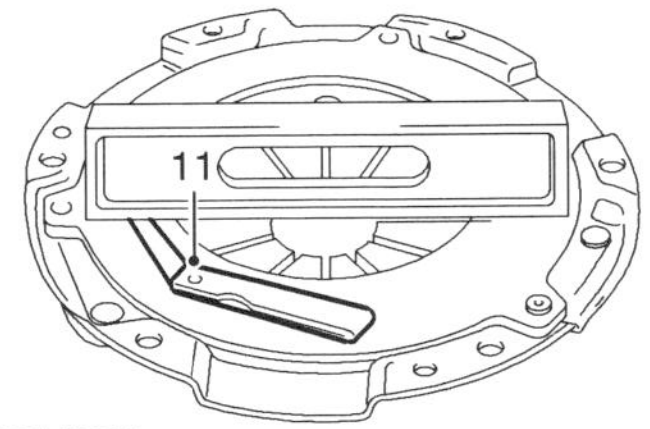

33M0301

11. Using a straight edge and feeler gauges check the surface of the pressure plate for flatness at 4 separate points. Renew pressure plate if warping exceeds service limit.

Pressure plate warping:
service limit = 0.18 mm maximum

Refit

1. Clean pressure plate and flywheel, dowels and dowel holes.
2. Inspect flywheel for signs of scoring or other damage. Renew if worn or damaged.
3. Smear clutch drive plate splines with Molybdenum disulphide grease.

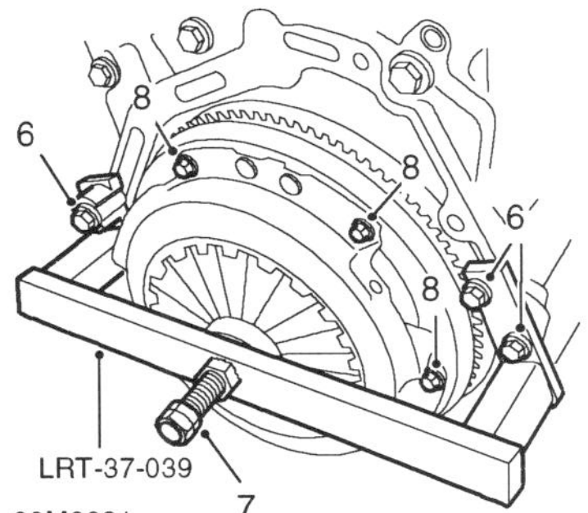

33M0321

4. Position drive plate to flywheel with 'FLYWHEEL SIDE' marking towards flywheel.
5. Fit pressure plate to flywheel and fit but do not tighten bolts.
6. Fit alignment tool **LRT-37-039** to clutch and secure to engine adaptor plate with 3 bolts.
7. Tighten centre screw on alignment tool until clutch is fully depressed.
8. Working in a diagonal sequence, progressively tighten clutch pressure plate bolts to 26 Nm.
9. Remove bolts and tool **LRT-37-039.**
10. Remove locking pin **LRT-12-058.**
11. Clean clutch release fork and release bearing guide sleeve.
12. Smear release fork shaft and release bearing guide with Molybdenum disulphide grease.
13. Operate release lever to ensure that release bearing is correctly located on release fork and slides smoothly on guide sleeve.
14. Fit gearbox assembly. ***See MANUAL GEARBOX - 'PG1', Repairs.***

HYDRAULIC ASSEMBLY - RHD

Service repair no - 33.15.03

Remove

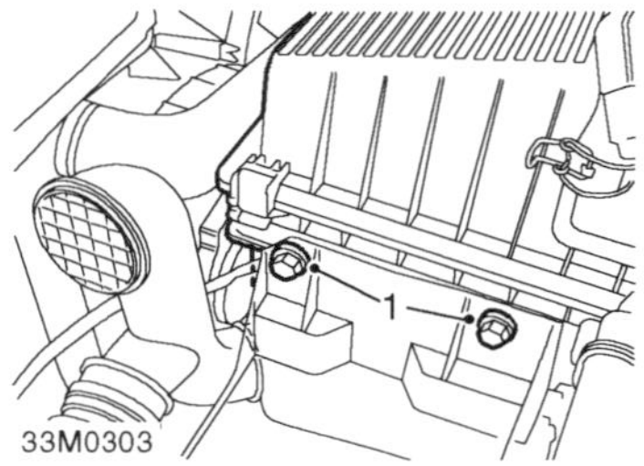

1. Remove 2 bolts securing air filter.

Diesel models.

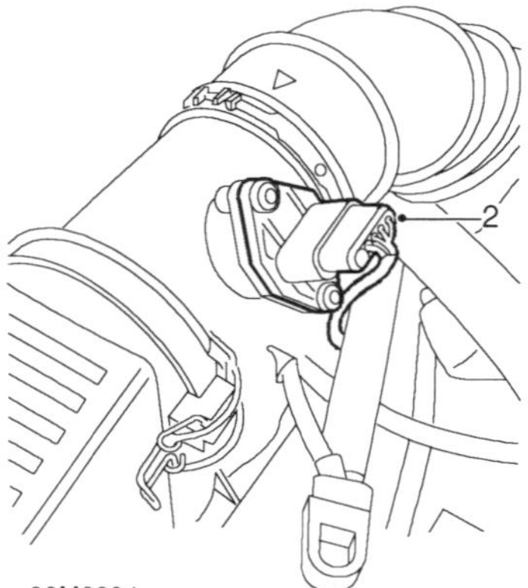

2. Disconnect multiplug from MAF sensor.

All models.

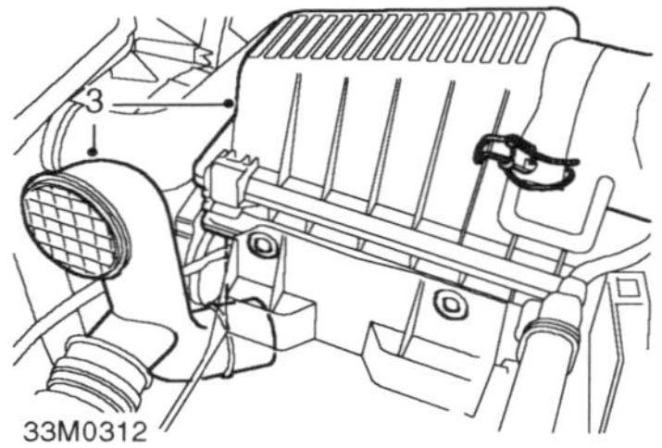

3. Release air filter from battery carrier and intake hose.
4. Position air filter aside.

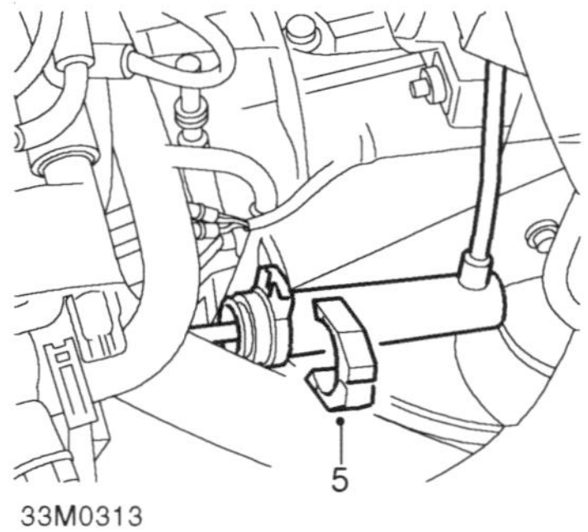

5. Remove 'C' clip from slave cylinder and release cylinder from support bracket.

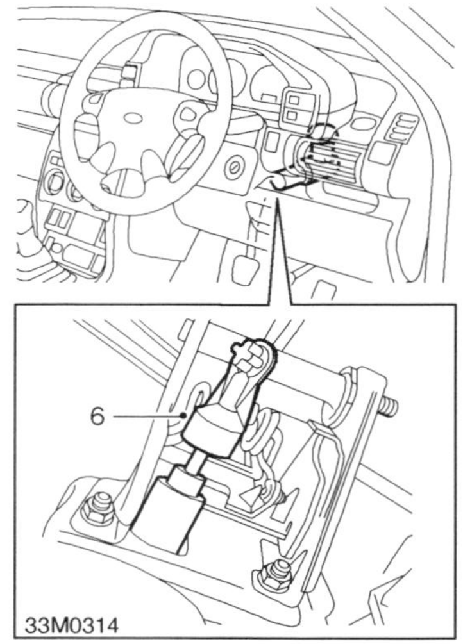

6. Release master cylinder push rod from clutch pedal.
7. Rotate master cylinder clockwise and release from bulkhead.
8. Noting the position of the clutch pipe, release pipe from clips.
9. Manoeuvre the hydraulic assembly from vehicle.

Refit

1. Manoeuvre the hydraulic assembly into position and secure in clips.
2. Position master cylinder, rotate anti-clockwise to secure in position.
3. Connect push rod to clutch pedal.
4. Position slave cylinder in support bracket and secure with 'C' clip.
5. Position air cleaner to battery carrier and air intake hose.

Diesel models

6. Connect multiplug to MAF sensor.

All models

7. Fit and tighten bolts securing air cleaner to 10 Nm.
8. Operate clutch to confirm operation of system.

HYDRAULIC ASSEMBLY - LHD

Service repair no - 33.15.03

Remove

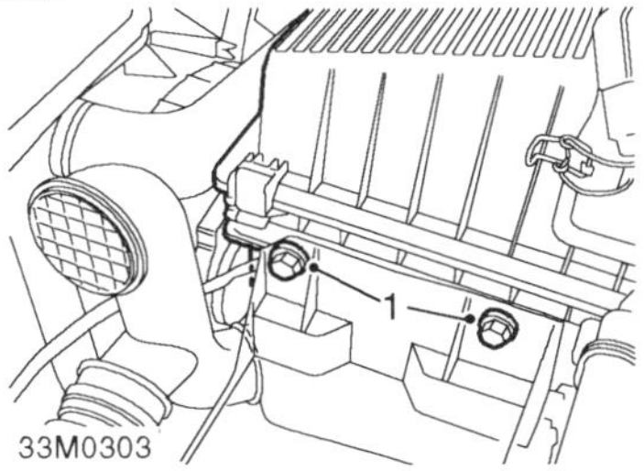

33M0303

1. Remove 2 bolts securing air filter.

Diesel models.

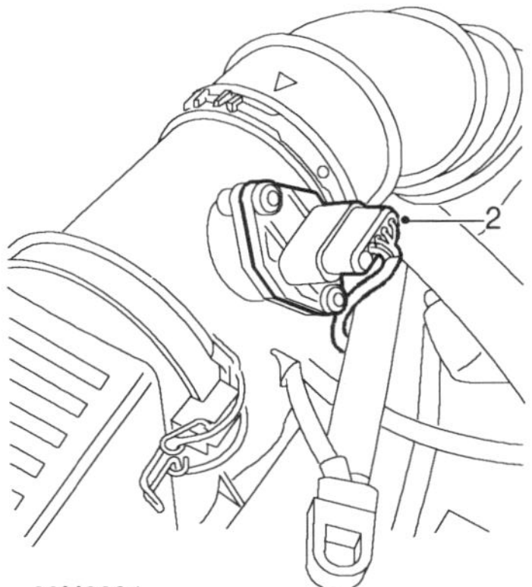

33M0304

2. Disconnect multiplug from MAF sensor.

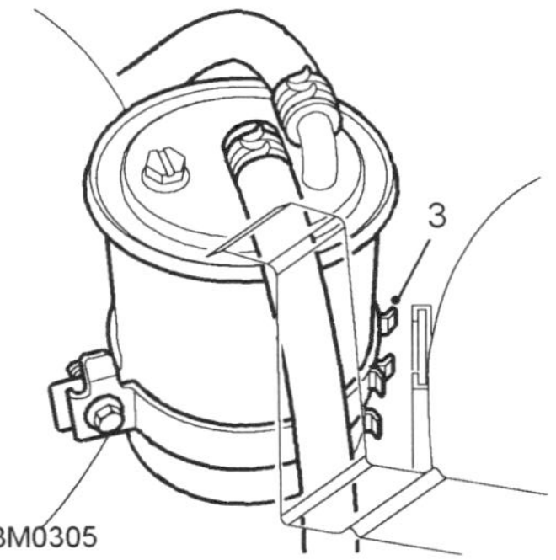

33M0305

3. Release fuel filter and position aside.

Petrol models.

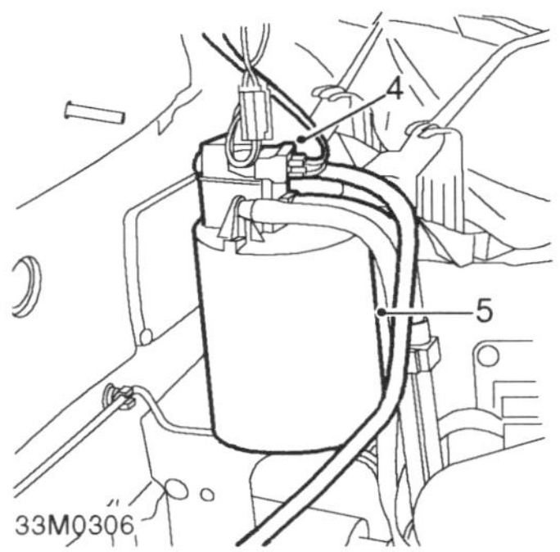

33M0306

4. Disconnect multiplug from charcoal cannister.
5. Release cannister and position aside.

All models.

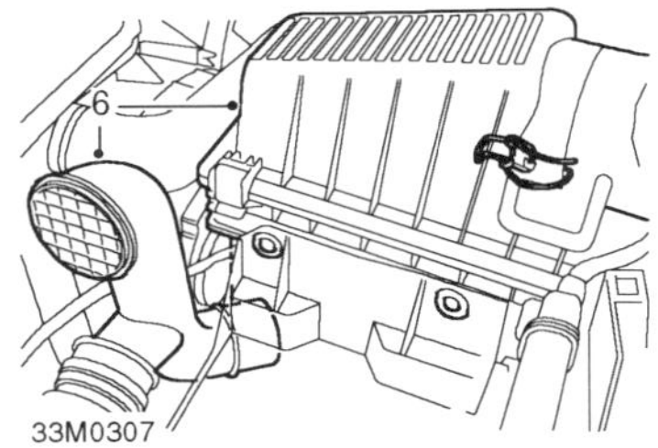

33M0307

6. Release air cleaner from battery carrier and intake hose.
7. Position air cleaner aside.

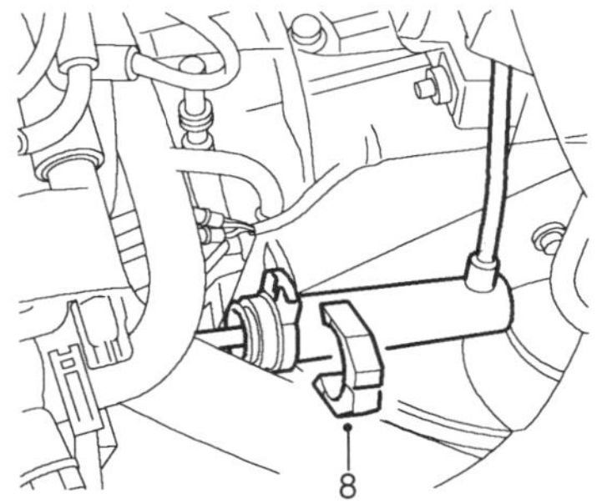

33M0308

8. Remove 'C' clip from slave cylinder and release cylinder from support bracket.

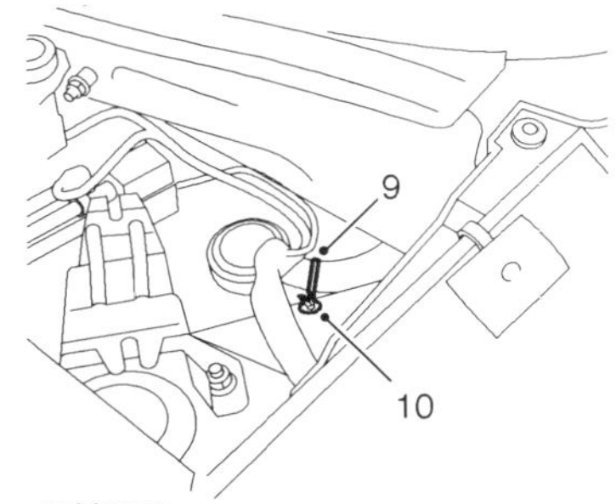

33M0309

9. Carefully cut cable tie, release main harness and position aside.
10. Remove and discard cable tie.

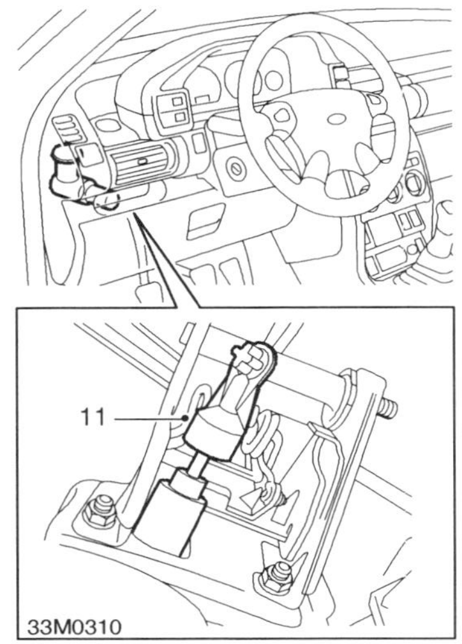

33M0310

11. Release master cylinder push rod from clutch pedal.

12. Rotate master cylinder clockwise and release from bulkhead.

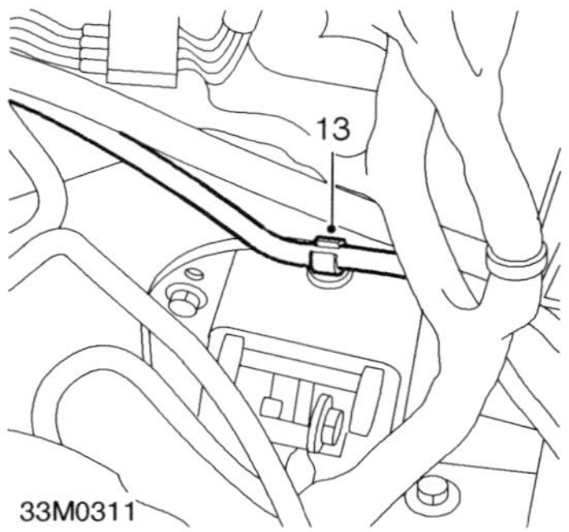

33M0311

13. Noting the position of the clutch pipe, release pipe from clip.
14. Manoeuvre the hydraulic assembly from vehicle.

Refit

1. Manoeuvre the hydraulic assembly into position and secure in clip.
2. Position master cylinder, rotate anti-clockwise to secure in position.
3. Connect push rod to clutch pedal.
4. Using a NEW cable tie, position and secure main harness.
5. Position slave cylinder in support bracket and secure with 'C' clip.
6. Position air cleaner to battery carrier and air intake hose.

Diesel models

7. Connect multiplug to MAF sensor.
8. Position fuel filter.

Petrol models

9. Position charcoal cannister and connect multiplug.

All models

10. Fit and tighten bolts securing air cleaner to 10 Nm.
11. Operate clutch to confirm operation of system.

CONTENTS

Page

REPAIRS

SWITCH - HILL DESCENT

Service repair no - 37.16.80

Remove

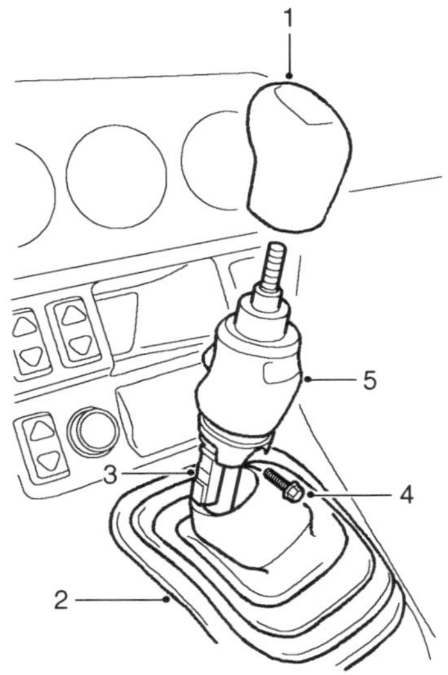

37M1235

1. Remove gear lever knob.
2. Release gear lever gaiter.
3. Disconnect multiplug from hill descent switch.
4. Remove bolt from hill descent switch.
5. Remove hill descent switch assembly.
   Do not carry out further dismantling if component is removed for access only.

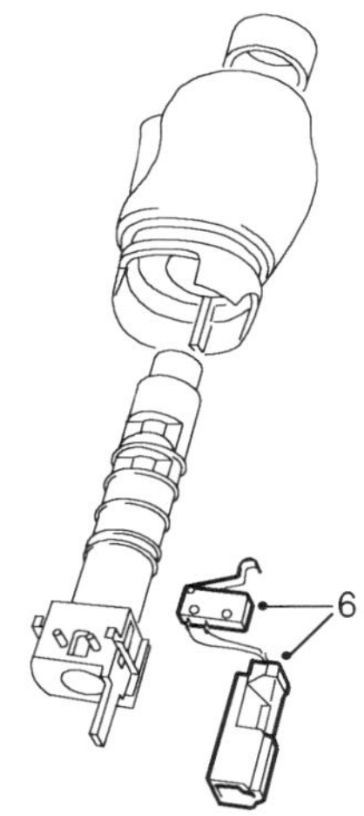

37M1236

6. Release microswitch and multiplug.
7. Remove microswitch.

Refit

1. Position microswitch, secure multiplug and switch retainers.
2. Position hill descent switch to gear lever, fit and tighten bolt.
3. Connect multiplug and secure gear lever gaiter.
4. Screw on gear lever knob fully down to stop on HDC switch, approximately 11 to 12 turns, and ensure that the gear knob is in the 12 o'clock position.

CAUTION: It is important that the gear lever knob is not over-tightened, and the profile of the trigger remains flush with the HDC switch. This will ensure that the trigger is not overloaded unneccessarily.

GEARBOX - 'K' SERIES

Service repair no - 37.20.02/99

Remove

1. Drain lubricating fluid from gearbox. ***See MAINTENANCE.***
2. Drain lubricating fluid from IRD unit. ***See MAINTENANCE.***
3. Remove LH drive shaft. ***See DRIVE SHAFTS, Repairs.***

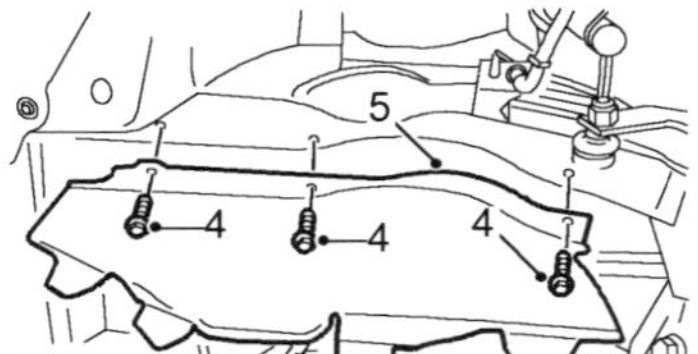

37M1237

4. Remove 3 screws from LH splash shield
5. Remove splash shield.
6. Remove exhaust front pipe. ***See MANIFOLD & EXHAUST SYSTEMS, Repairs.***
7. Remove RH road wheel.

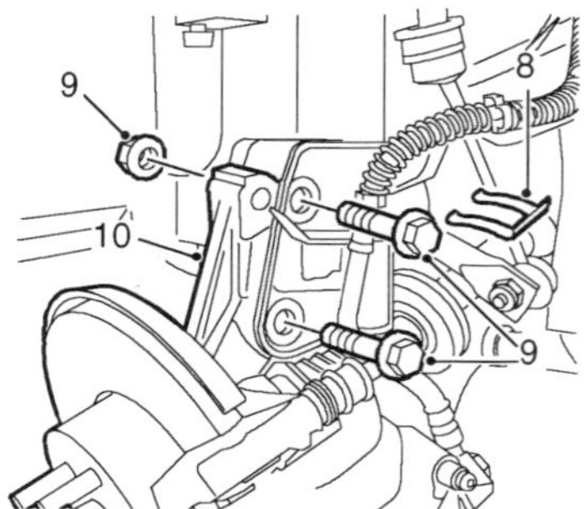

37M1238

8. Remove clip from RH front brake hose and release hose from bracket.
9. Remove 2 nuts and bolts securing hub to damper.
10. Release hub from damper.
11. Remove starter motor. ***See ELECTRICAL, Repairs.***
12. Remove battery carrier. ***See ELECTRICAL, Repairs.***

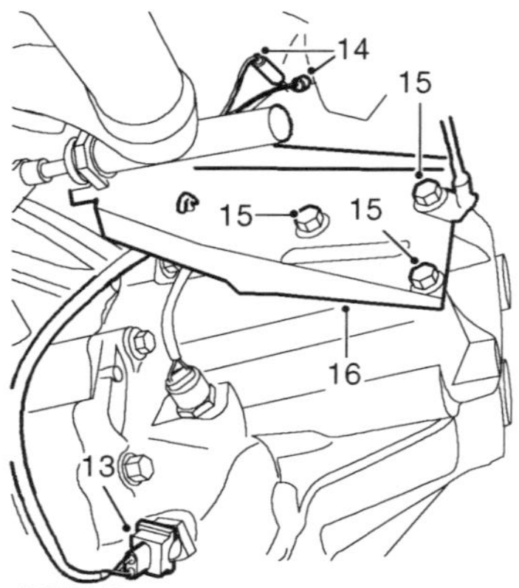

37M1240

13. Disconnect multiplug from 1st gear sensor.
14. Disconnect reverse lamp switch wires.
15. Remove 3 bolts securing clutch slave cylinder bracket.
16. Position bracket and earth lead aside.

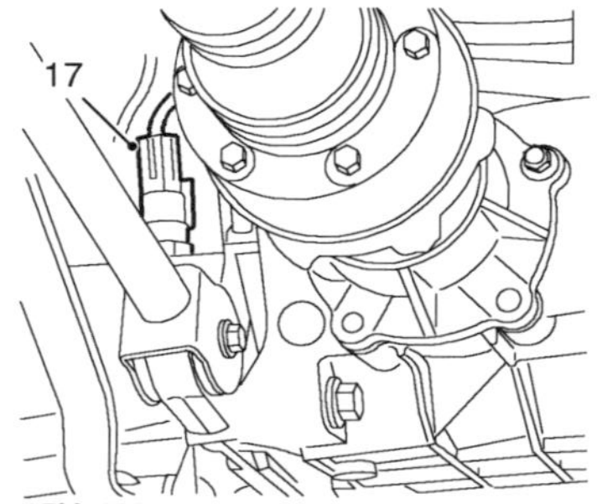

37M1239

17. Disconnect multiplug from VSS.

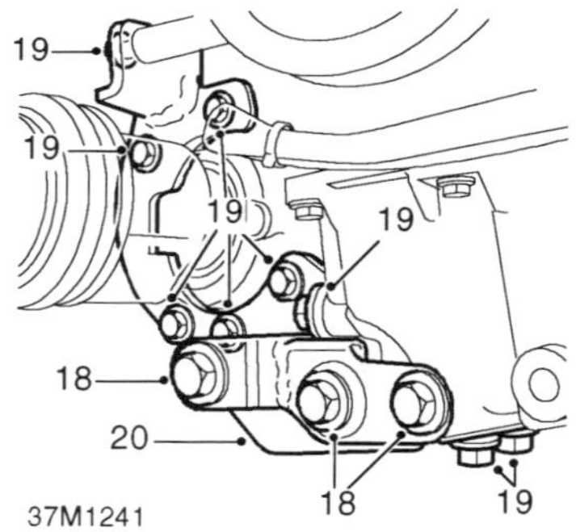

37M1241

18. Remove 3 bolts securing lower tie rod and remove tie rod bracket.
19. Remove 9 bolts securing IRD support bracket.
20. Remove IRD support bracket.

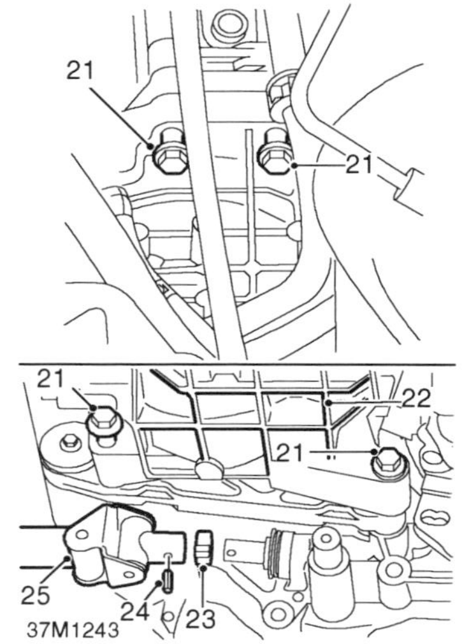

37M1243

21. Remove 4 bolts securing IRD to gearbox.
22. Carefully release IRD unit from gearbox.

CAUTION: Support the IRD unit using a suitable block of wood on top of the sub frame.

23. Remove gear change roll pin retaining clip.
24. Remove and discard roll pin.
25. Release gear change rod from gearbox.

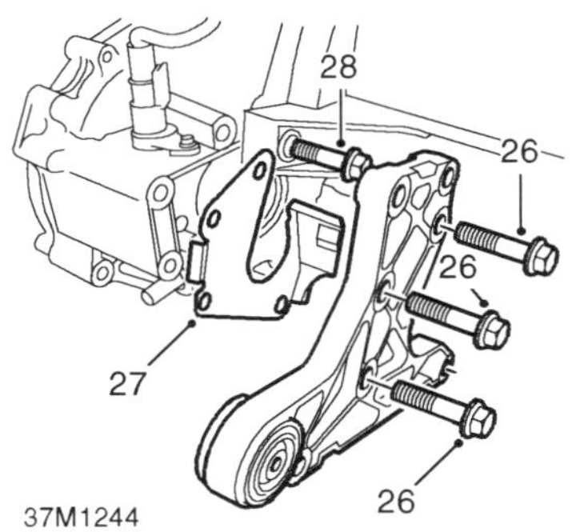

37M1244

26. Remove 3 bolts securing IRD adaptor plate to gearbox.
27. Remove flywheel cover plate.
28. Remove dowel bolt from rear of gearbox.

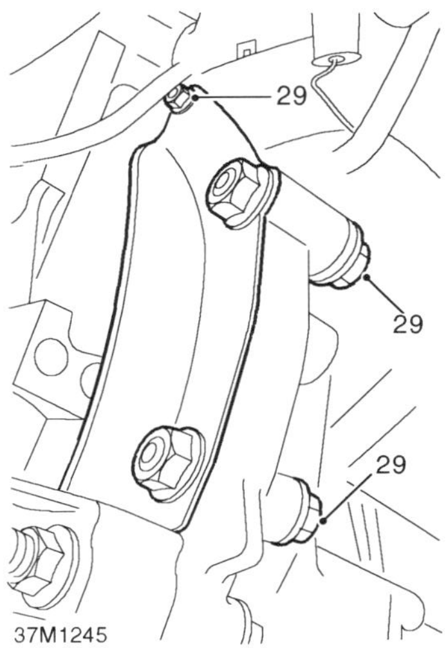

37M1245

29. Remove 3 bolts securing flywheel cover plate and remove cover plate.

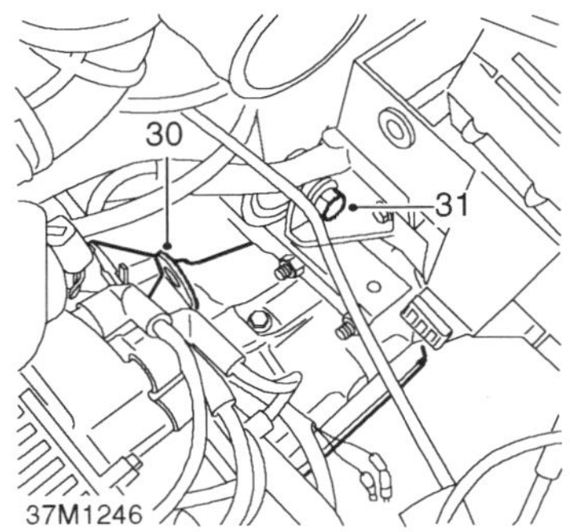

37M1246

30. Fit suitable lifting bracket to gearbox and attach lifting equipment.
31. Remove bolt from gearbox mounting.
32. Lower gearbox.
33. Position jack to support engine.

CAUTION: Use a block of wood between jack and sump.

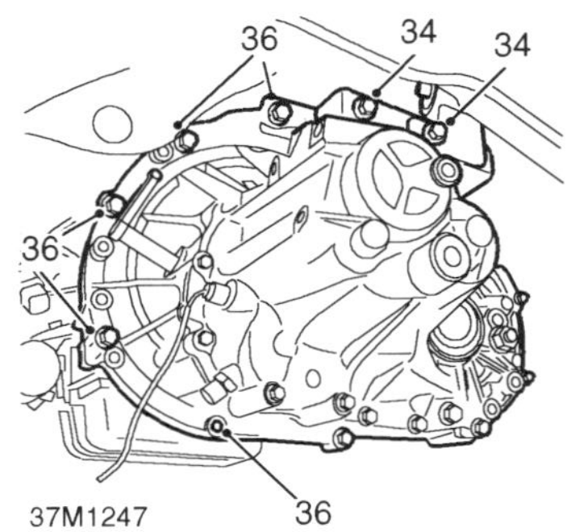

37M1247

34. Remove 2 bolts securing gearbox mounting bracket.
35. Remove gearbox mounting bracket.
36. Remove 5 bolts securing gearbox to engine.

37. With assistance, carefully release gearbox from IRD and clutch.
38. Lower gearbox to the floor and remove lifting equipment.
39. Remove gearbox from beneath vehicle.

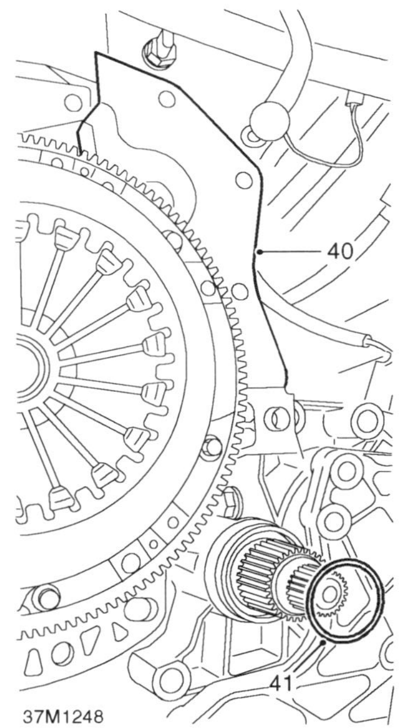

37M1248

40. Collect flywheel rear cover plate.
41. Remove and discard IRD 'O' ring.

Refit

1. Clean mating faces of gearbox and cylinder block.
2. Clean dowels and dowel holes.
3. Clean mating faces of IRD unit and gearbox.
4. Lubricate and fit NEW 'O' ring to IRD unit.
5. Inspect drive shaft seal for damage and renew if necessary.
6. Lightly grease gearbox splines with molybdenum disulphide grease.
7. Locate flywheel rear cover plate.
8. Position gearbox under vehicle and connect lifting equipment.
9. With assistance, raise gearbox and manoeuvre into position.
10. Align gearbox to clutch assembly then locate on dowels.
11. Fit 5 bolts securing gearbox to engine and tighten to 80 Nm.
12. Fit gearbox rear mounting bracket, fit bolts and tighten to 65 Nm.
13. Raise gearbox and locate in rear mounting. Fit through bolt and tighten to 80 Nm.
14. Remove lifting equipment and lifting bracket.
15. Position flywheel front cover. Tighten M10 fixings to 80Nm . Tighten M6 nut to 9 Nm.
16. Fit dowel bolt to rear of gearbox and tighten to 80 Nm.
17. Fit flywheel lower cover plate, align tie rod bracket, fit and tighten bolts to 80 Nm.
18. Position gear change rod, fit NEW roll pin and fit roll pin cover.
19. With assistance, fit IRD unit to gearbox.
20. Fit bolts and tighten to 80 Nm.
21. Fit IRD support bracket and tighten bolts initially only to ensure all mating faces are touching. Tighten in the following sequence:
    5 bolts securing support bracket to IRD 50 Nm
    1 bolt securing IRD support bracket to PAS pump bracket 50 Nm
    3 bolts securing support bracket to sump 90Nm
22. Position tie rod bracket, fit and tighten bolts.
23. Fit clutch slave cylinder bracket and earth lead, fit and tighten bolts to 45 Nm.
24. Connect reverse lamp switch wires.

25. Connect multiplugs to VSS and 1st gear sensor.
26. Fit starter motor. ***See ELECTRICAL, Repairs.***
27. Fit battery carrier. ***See ELECTRICAL, Repairs.***
28. Align hub to damper, fit and tighten both bolts to 205 Nm.
29. Position brake hose in bracket and secure with 'C' clip.
30. Fit exhaust front pipe. ***See MANIFOLD & EXHAUST SYSTEMS, Repairs.***
31. Position LH splash panel, fit and tighten bolts.
32. Fit LH drive shaft. ***See DRIVE SHAFTS, Repairs.***
33. Fit road wheel(s) and tighten nuts to correct torque. ***See INFORMATION, Torque wrench settings.***
34. Remove stand(s) and lower vehicle.
35. Refill IRD unit with lubricating fluid. ***See MAINTENANCE.***
36. Refill gearbox with lubricating fluid. ***See MAINTENANCE.***

GEARBOX - 'L' SERIES

Service repair no - 37.20.02/99

Remove

1. Remove starter motor. ***See ELECTRICAL, Repairs.***
2. Remove battery carrier. ***See ELECTRICAL, Repairs.***
3. Remove exhaust front pipe. ***See MANIFOLD & EXHAUST SYSTEMS - 'L' SERIES, Repairs.***

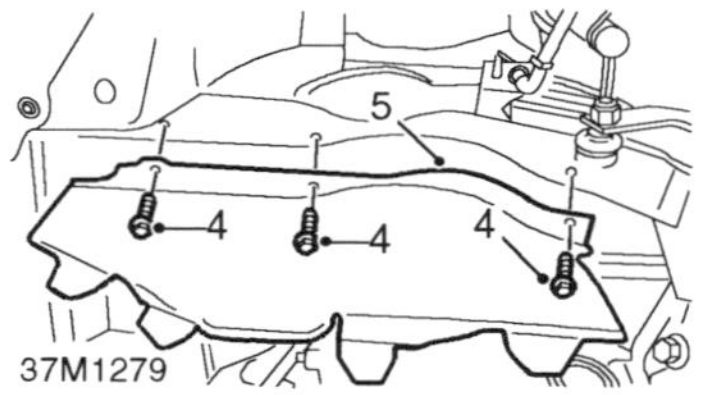

37M1279

4. Remove 3 bolts securing LH splash shield.
5. Remove splash shield.

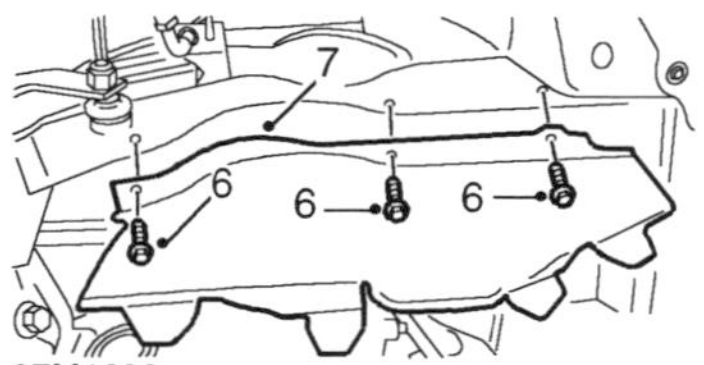

37M1280

6. Remove 3 bolts securing RH splash shield.

7. Remove splash shield.
8. Drain lubricating fluid from gearbox. ***See MAINTENANCE.***
9. Drain lubricating fluid from IRD unit. ***See MAINTENANCE.***
10. Remove LH and RH drive shafts. ***See DRIVE SHAFTS, Repairs.***

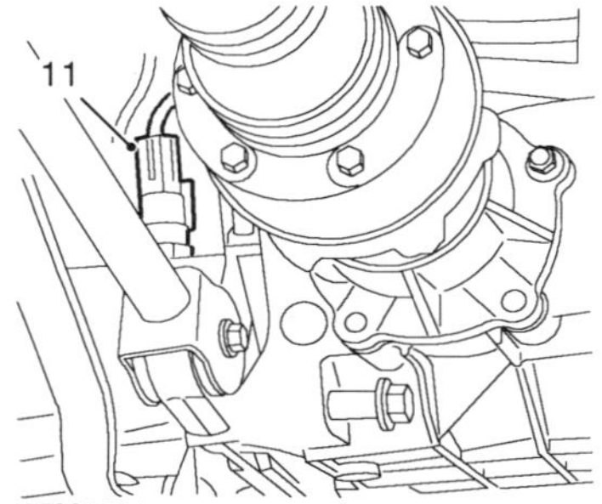

37M1281

11. Disconnect multiplug from VSS.

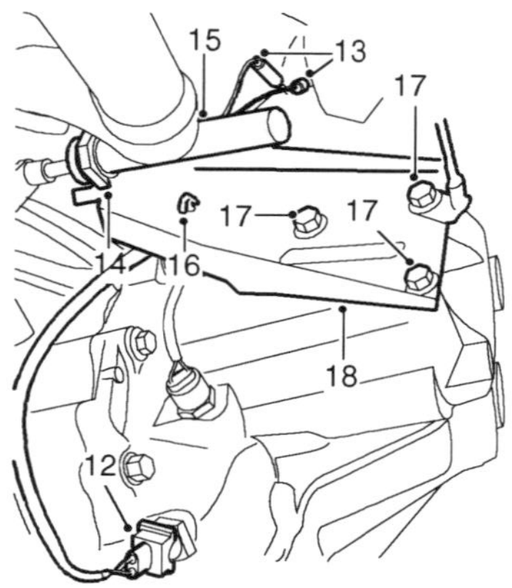

37M1282

12. Disconnect multiplug from 1st gear sensor.

13. Disconnect reverse lamp switch wires.
14. Remove clip securing clutch slave cylinder to bracket.
15. Position slave cylinder aside.
16. Release 1st gear sensor harness clip from clutch slave cylinder bracket.
17. Remove 3 bolts securing clutch slave cylinder bracket.
18. Remove slave cylinder bracket.

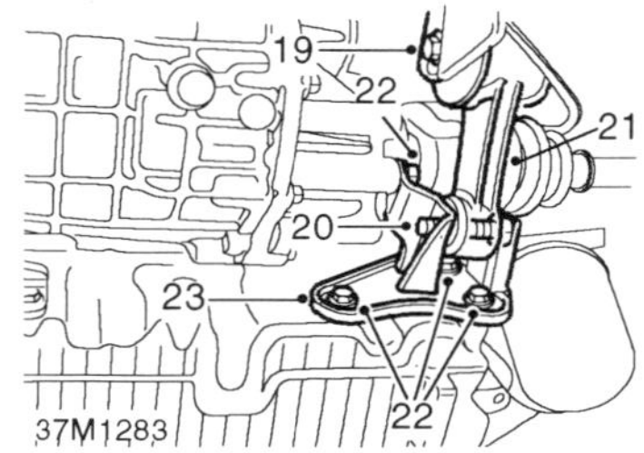

37M1283

19. Remove bolt securing engine lower tie rod to subframe.
20. Remove bolt securing engine lower tie rod to bracket on sump.
21. Remove tie rod from bracket.
22. Remove 4 bolts securing tie rod bracket to sump and IRD.
23. Remove tie rod bracket.

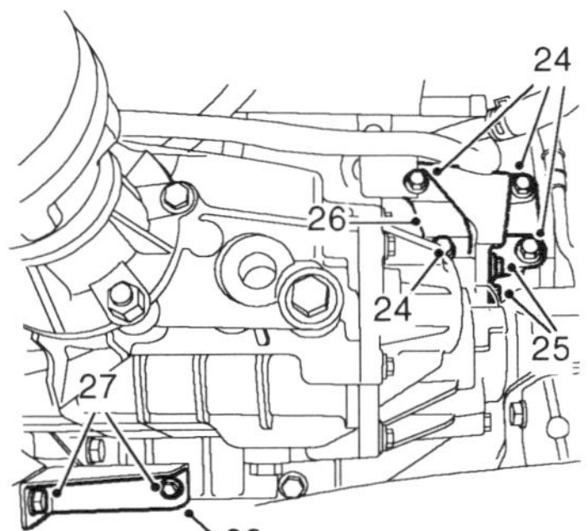

37M1285

24. Remove 4 bolts securing IRD support bracket to cylinder block.
25. Remove 2 bolts securing support bracket to IRD.
26. Remove IRD support bracket.
27. Remove 2 bolts securing bracket to gearbox and sump.
28. Remove support bracket.

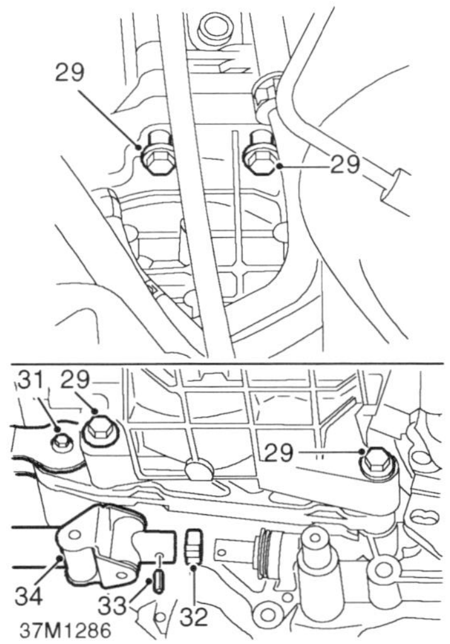

37M1286

29. Remove 4 bolts securing IRD to gearbox.
30. Carefully release IRD unit from gearbox.

⚠ **CAUTION: Support the IRD unit on a suitable block of wood on top of the sub frame and tie IRD in this position.**

31. Remove bolt securing gear change steady rod to IRD adaptor plate.
32. Remove retaining clip from gear selector rod roll pin.
33. Remove and discard roll pin.
34. Release gear selector and steady rods.

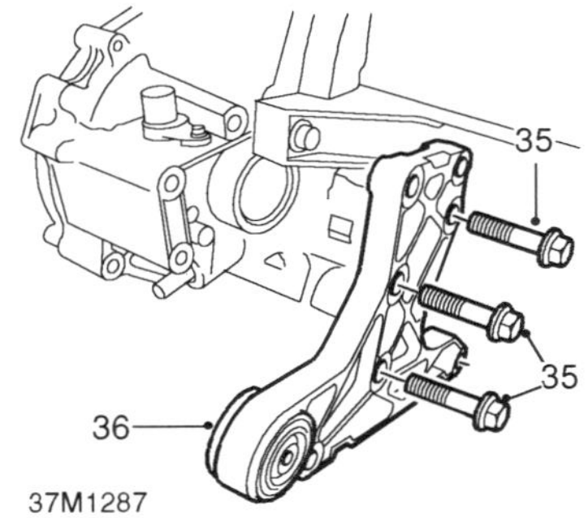

37M1287

35. Remove 3 bolts securing IRD adaptor plate to gearbox.
36. Remove IRD adaptor plate.

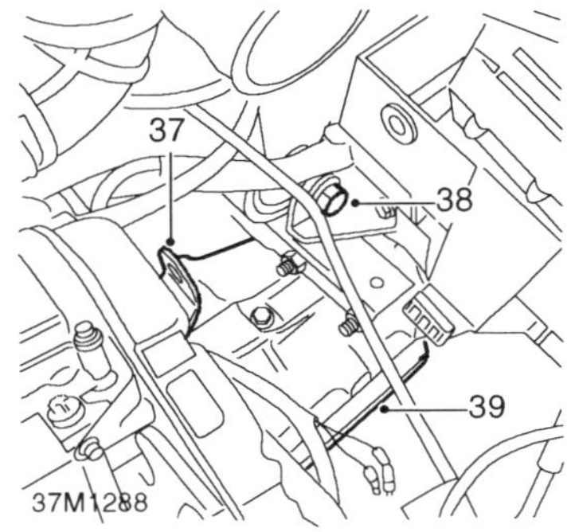

37M1288

37. Fit suitable lifting bracket to gearbox and attach lifting equipment.
38. Remove bolt securing LH mounting to bracket on body.
39. Lower gearbox.

40. Position jack to support engine.

⚠ **CAUTION: Use a block of wood between jack and sump.**

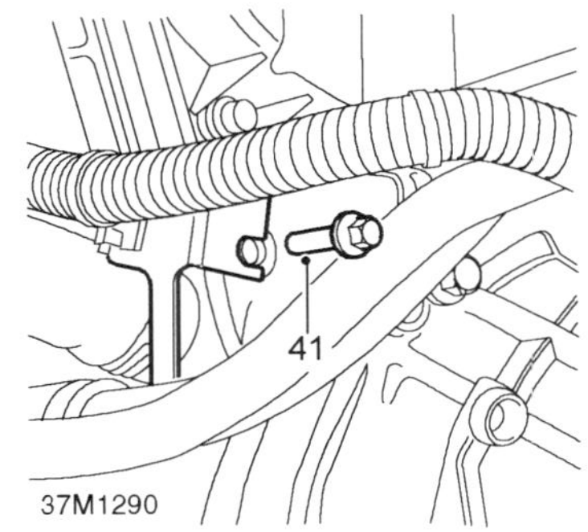

37M1290

41. Remove bolt securing coolant and fuel rails to adaptor plate.

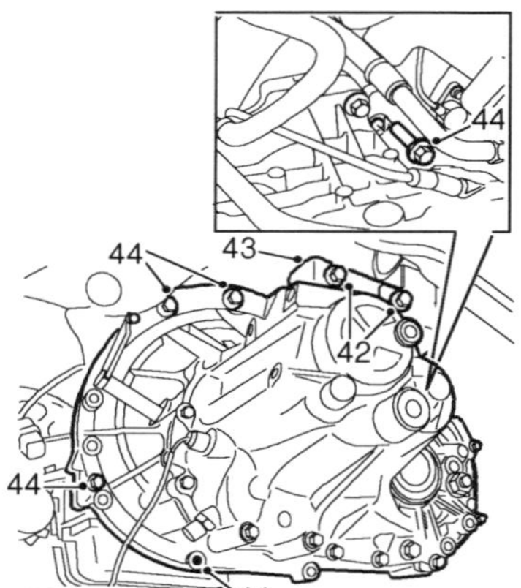

37M1289

42. Remove 2 bolts securing LH mounting bracket to gearbox.
43. Remove gearbox mounting bracket.
44. Remove 6 bolts securing gearbox to gearbox adaptor plate.
45. With assistance, carefully release gearbox from engine.
46. Lower gearbox to the floor and remove lifting equipment.
47. Remove gearbox from under vehicle.

37M1291

48. Remove and discard IRD 'O' ring.

Refit

1. Clean mating faces of gearbox and adaptor plate..
2. Clean mating faces of IRD unit and gearbox.
3. Lubricate and fit NEW 'O' ring to IRD unit.
4. Inspect drive shaft seals for damage and renew if necessary.
5. Lightly grease gearbox splines with molybdenum disulphide grease.
6. Position gearbox under vehicle and connect lifting equipment.
7. With assistance, raise gearbox, manoeuvre into position and locate on dowels.
8. Fit 6 bolts securing gearbox to adaptor plate and tighten to 80 Nm.
9. Align fuel and coolant pipe bracket and secure with bolt.

10. Fit LH engine mounting bracket to gearbox and tighten bolts to 65 Nm.
11. Raise gearbox, align to LH engine mounting bracket on body and tighten bolt to 80 Nm.
12. Remove lifting equipment and lifting bracket.
13. Fit LH drive shaft. ***See DRIVE SHAFTS, Repairs.***

NOTE: The LH drive shaft is fitted to stop rotation of the drive link tube within the gearbox. This will aid engagement of the IRD LH output shaft splines.

14. Fit IRD adaptor plate to gearbox and tighten bolts to 80 Nm.
15. With assistance, fit IRD unit to gearbox.
16. Fit bolts securing IRD to gearbox and tighten sufficiently only to pull mating faces of IRD and gearbox together at this stage.
17. Fit IRD support bracket and tighten bolts sufficiently only to pull mating faces together.

CAUTION: Do not tighten IRD retaining bolts fully until all mating faces of IRD, gearbox and IRD support bracket are touching.

18. Tighten bolts securing IRD to gearbox to 90 Nm.
19. Tighten bolts securing IRD support bracket to 90 Nm.
20. Fit stiffener bracket to gearbox adaptor plate and sump. Tighten gearbox bolt to 80 Nm. Tighten sump bolt to 25 Nm.
21. Fit gear change steady rod to IRD adaptor plate and secure with bolt.
22. Connect gear change selector rod, fit NEW roll pin and fit pin retaining clip.
23. Fit engine lower tie rod bracket to sump and IRD. Tighten bolts to 45 Nm.
24. Fit engine lower tie rod and tighten bolts to 80 Nm.
25. Fit clutch slave cylinder bracket, align earth lead and tighten bolts to 45 Nm.
26. Fit clutch slave cylinder to bracket, ensure push rod is engaged with lever and fit clip to secure cylinder to bracket.
27. Connect multiplug to VSS.
28. Connect reverse lamp switch wires.
29. Connect multiplug to 1st gear sensor.
30. Secure 1st gear sensor harness clip to clutch slave cylinder bracket.
31. Fit RH drive shaft. ***See DRIVE SHAFTS, Repairs.***
32. Fill IRD unit with lubricating fluid. ***See MAINTENANCE.***
33. Fill gearbox with lubricating fluid ***See MAINTENANCE.***
34. Fit LH splash shield and secure with bolts.
35. Fit RH splash shield and secure with bolts.
36. Fit exhaust front pipe. ***See MANIFOLD & EXHAUST SYSTEMS - 'L' SERIES, Repairs.***
37. Fit battery carrier. ***See ELECTRICAL, Repairs.***
38. Fit starter motor. ***See ELECTRICAL, Repairs.***

CONTENTS

Page

INTERMEDIATE REDUCTION DRIVE

Description

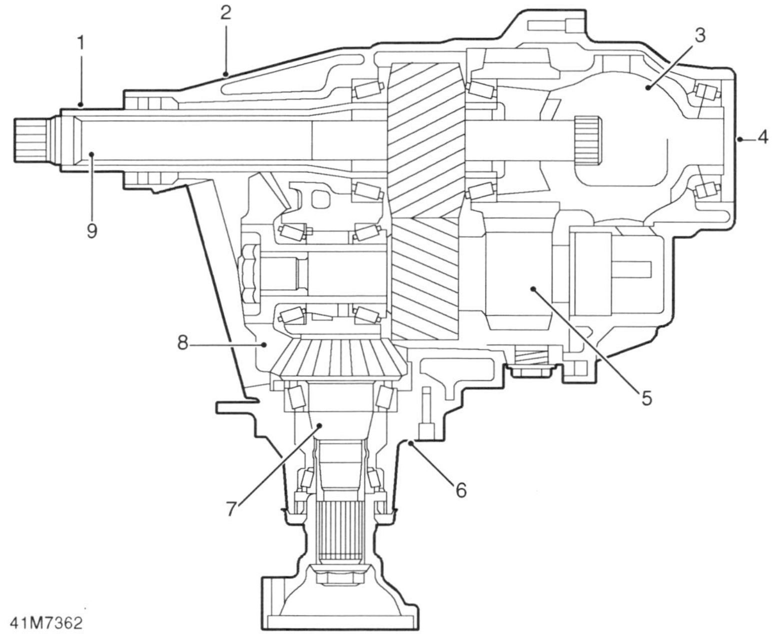

41M7362

The Intermediate Reduction Drive, IRD, is fitted in place of the conventional transfer box, and is attached to the PG1 5 speed manual gearbox. The combination of the two units provides drive to the front and rear wheels. The IRD incorporates a differential unit to control the proportion of drive delivered to each front wheel, and in addition, it operates in conjunction with the viscous coupling to give the vehicle a self-sensing four wheel drive system. The main casing, cover and pinion housing are manufactured from cast aluminium.

The unit comprises of a main casing (2), a RH housing (4), primary shaft (1), an intermediate shaft (9), a differential unit (3), a laygear (5), hypoid gear set (8), a rear output pinion (7) and a pinion housing (6). An oil cooler, connected to the vehicle cooling system, is fitted to prevent overheating of the IRD lubricating fluid. The main casing also incorporates the oil level/drain plugs and a breather outlet. There are a total of seven taper roller bearings and one parallel roller bearing supporting the primary shaft, differential and output shaft assemblies.

Four seals, internal to the IRD, are used to prevent mixing of the IRD and PG1 lubricating fluids.

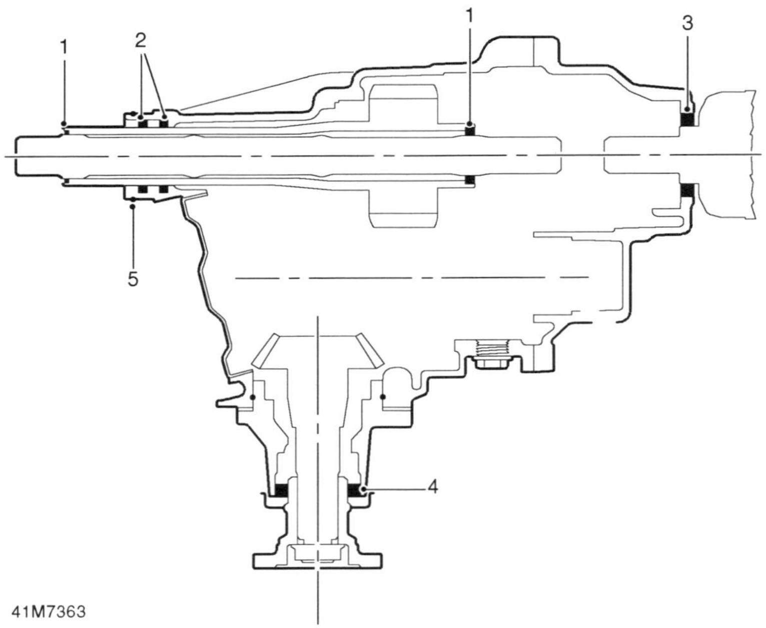

41M7363

Operation

Drive is transmitted from the gearbox to the IRD primary shaft via the splined hub in the gearbox final drive gear carrier. The drive is then transmitted from the primary shaft gear, which is integral with the primary shaft, to the layshaft which in turn drives the differential for the front driveshafts, and via a bevel drive gear and pinion to drive the rear axle. The intermediate shaft passes through the centre of the IRD primary shaft, and is the drive link between the IRD differential, and the left-hand front driveshaft, passing through the centre of the final drive carrier.

Oil Seals

Externally, three oil seals prevent lubricating oil escaping from the PG1 gearbox and the IRD unit. The gearbox gear case houses the oil seal for the left-hand front driveshaft, and the RH housing on the IRD unit houses the oil seal (3) for the right-hand front driveshaft, with the remaining oil seal (4) located in the pinion housing of the IRD.

There are also four internal oil seals in the IRD unit. Two smaller diameter oil seals (1) are fitted internally at each end of the primary shaft. These prevent oil ingress along the intermediate shaft from the IRD unit at the differential end. At the opposite end, the seal prevents oil ingress from the gearbox along the intermediate shaft. Two larger oil seals (2) are fitted in the main casing where the IRD unit enters the gearbox. The inner oil seal prevents oil ingress from the IRD primary shaft entering into the area between the two seals, and the outer oil seal prevents oil ingress from the gearbox entering the same area.

On the underside of the main casing is a 'tell-tale' drilling which is positioned between the inner and outer primary shaft oil seals. Oil leakage from the drilling will indicate either a faulty inner or outer primary shaft oil seal. An 'O' ring seal (5), fitted in a machined groove, seals the IRD main casing to the gearbox clutch housing.

INTERMEDIATE REDUCTION DRIVE (IRD) UNIT

Service repair no - 41.25.01/99

Remove

1. Drain cooling system. ***See COOLING SYSTEM, Adjustments.***
2. Drain lubricating fluid from gearbox. ***See MAINTENANCE.***
3. Drain lubricating fluid from IRD unit. ***See MAINTENANCE.***
4. Remove RH front drive shaft. ***See DRIVE SHAFTS, Repairs.***

'K' Series.

5. Remove exhaust front pipe. ***See MANIFOLD & EXHAUST SYSTEMS, Repairs.***

All models.

6. Mark propeller shaft and IRD drive flange for identification.

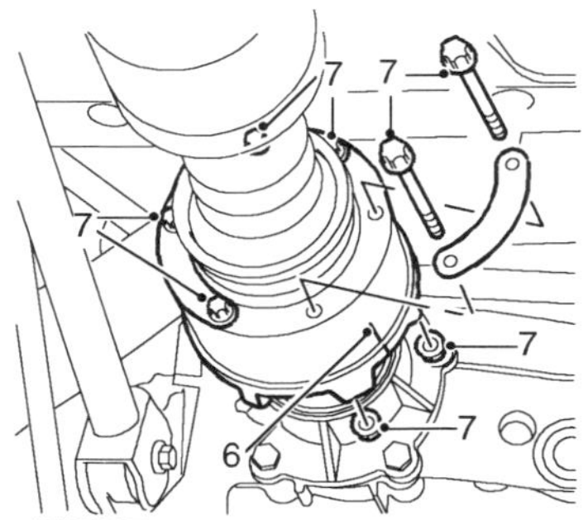

41M7337

7. Remove 6 nuts and bolts securing propeller shaft to IRD drive flange.
8. Release propeller shaft from IRD drive flange.

CAUTION: Care must be taken to support the tripode joint when removed from the IRD unit The joint must not be allowed to fully extend or be dropped as this could damage the joint and reduce its service life.

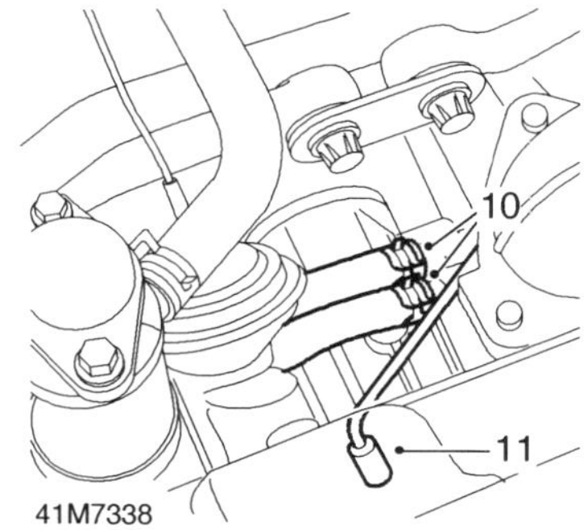

41M7338

9. Release clips securing coolant hoses to IRD unit.
10. Disconnect coolant hoses from IRD unit.
11. Disconnect breather hose from IRD.

'K' series

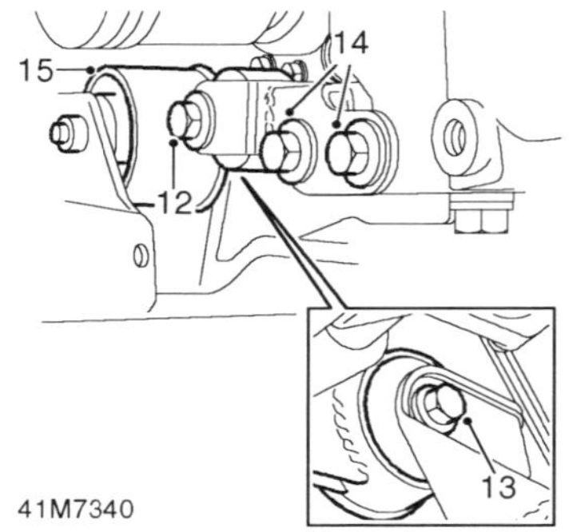

41M7340

12. Loosen bolt securing engine lower tie bar to bracket on sump.
13. Remove bolt securing tie bar to subframe.
14. Remove 2 bolts securing tie bar to sump.
15. Remove tie bar.

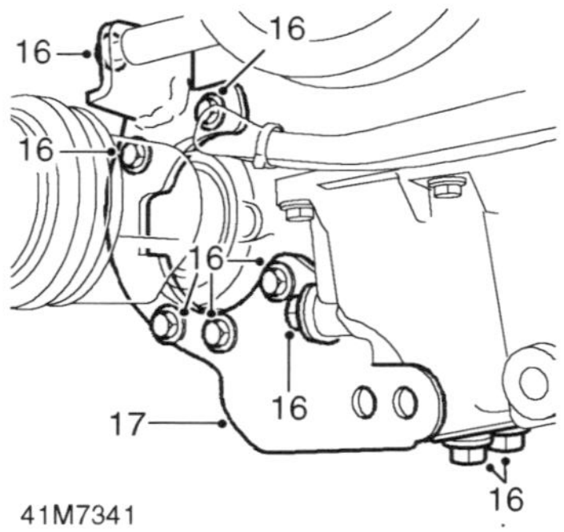

41M7341

16. Remove 9 bolts securing IRD support bracket.
17. Remove IRD support bracket.

L Series

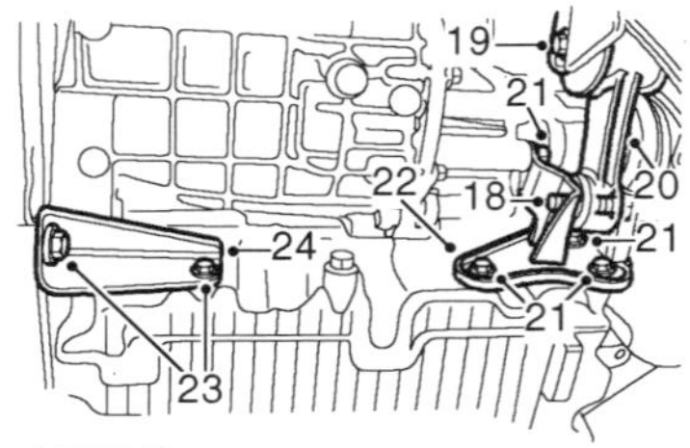

41M7342

18. Remove bolt securing engine lower tie bar to bracket on sump.
19. Remove bolt securing engine tie bar to subframe
20. Remove tie bar.
21. Remove 4 bolts securing tie bar bracket to IRD unit and sump.
22. Remove bracket.
23. Remove 2 bolts securing stiffener bracket to gearbox adaptor plate and sump.
24. Remove bracket.

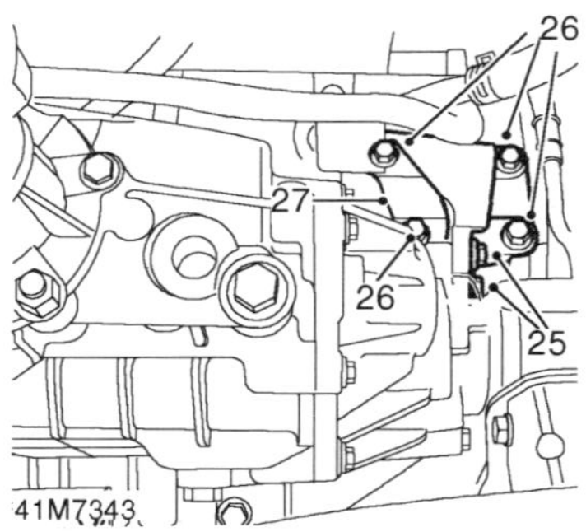

41M7343

25. Remove 2 bolts securing support bracket to IRD unit.
26. Remove 4 bolts securing support bracket to cylinder block.
27. Remove IRD support bracket.

All models

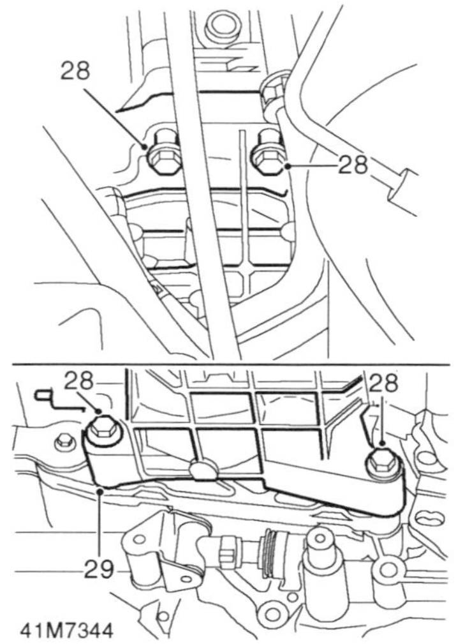

41M7344

28. Remove 4 bolts securing IRD unit.
29. With assistance, release IRD unit from gearbox and remove from vehicle.
30. Remove and discard 'O' ring from IRD unit.

Refit

All models

1. Clean mating face of IRD unit and gearbox.
2. Lubricate NEW 'O' ring with lubricating fluid.
3. Fit 'O' ring to IRD unit.
4. With assistance, fit IRD unit.
5. Fit bolts securing IRD unit to gearbox and tighten sufficiently only to pull mating faces of IRD and gearbox together at this stage.
6. Fit IRD support bracket and tighten bolts sufficiently only to pull mating faces together.

⚠ **CAUTION: Do not tighten IRD retaining bolts fully until all mating faces of IRD, gearbox and IRD support bracket are touching.**

7. Final tighten bolts securing IRD to gearbox to 80 Nm.

'L' series

8. Tighten bolts securing IRD support bracket to 50 Nm.
9. Fit stiffener bracket to gearbox adaptor plate and sump. Tighten gearbox bolt to 80 Nm. Tighten sump bolt to 25 Nm.
10. Fit tie bar bracket and tighten bolts to 45 Nm.
11. Fit lower tie bar and tighten bolts to 80 Nm.

'K' series

12. Fit lower tie bar and bracket assembly.
13. Tighten bolts securing tie bar bracket to sump to 90 Nm.
14. Fit bolt securing tie bar to sub frame and tighten to 80 Nm.
15. Tighten bolt securing tie bar to bracket to 80 Nm.

All models

16. Connect breather hose to IRD.
17. Connect coolant hoses to IRD unit and secure with clips.
18. Clean propeller shaft and drive flange mating faces.
19. Fit propeller shaft to drive flange, align marks and tighten bolts to 40 Nm.

'K' series

20. Fit exhaust front pipe. ***See MANIFOLD & EXHAUST SYSTEMS, Repairs.***

All models

21. Fit RH drive shaft. ***See DRIVE SHAFTS, Repairs.***
22. Fill IRD unit with lubricating fluid. ***See MAINTENANCE.***
23. Fill gearbox with lubricating fluid. ***See MAINTENANCE.***
24. Fill cooling system. ***See COOLING SYSTEM, Adjustments.***

SEAL - DRIVE SHAFT - FRONT LH

Service repair no - 41.29.08

Remove

1. Remove LH drive shaft. ***See DRIVE SHAFTS, Repairs.***
2. Remove and discard drive shaft oil seal.

Refit

1. Thoroughly clean oil seal recess.
2. Lubricate NEW oil seal with gearbox oil.

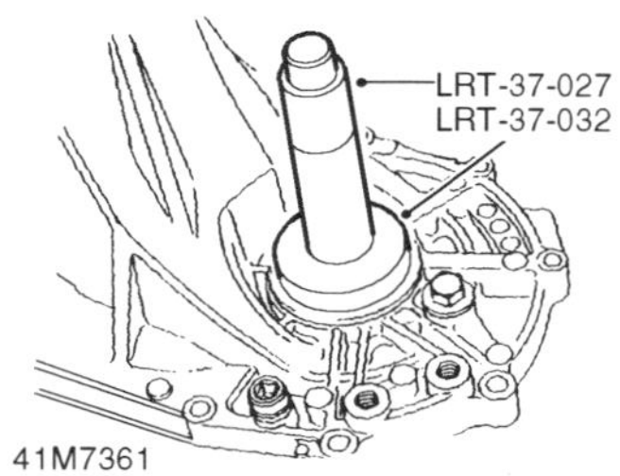

41M7361

3. Locate seal on tool **LRT-37-032** and replacer **LRT-37-027** with sealing lip facing toward housing.
4. Carefully drift oil seal into gearbox housing until it is fully seated in recess.
5. Fit drive shaft. ***See DRIVE SHAFTS, Repairs.***

SEAL - DRIVE SHAFT - RH

Service repair no - 41.29.09

Remove

1. Remove RH drive shaft. ***See DRIVE SHAFTS, Repairs.***
2. Remove and discard drive shaft oil seal.

Refit

1. Thoroughly clean oil seal recess.
2. Lubricate NEW oil seal with gearbox oil. ***See INFORMATION, Capacities, fluids and lubricants.***

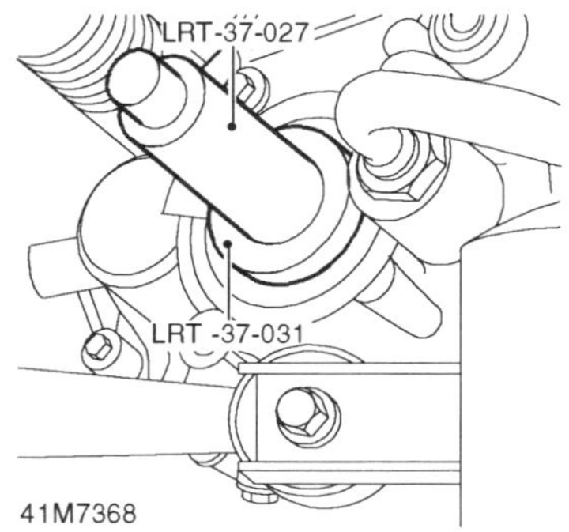

41M7368

3. Locate seal on tool **LRT-37-031** and replacer **LRT-37-027** with sealing lip facing toward housing.
4. Carefully drift oil seal into IRD housing until it is fully seated in recess.
5. Fit drive shaft. ***See DRIVE SHAFTS, Repairs.***

SEAL - PINION GEAR HOUSING

Service repair no - 41.29.11

Remove

1. Raise vehicle on ramp.

Diesel models

2. Remove underbelly panel. ***See BODY, Exterior fittings.***

Petrol models

3. Remove exhaust front pipe. ***See MANIFOLD & EXHAUST SYSTEMS - 'K' SERIES, Repairs.***

All models

4. Drain fluid from IRD. ***See MAINTENANCE.***
5. Raise one wheel on each axle for rotation of propeller shaft to access fixings.

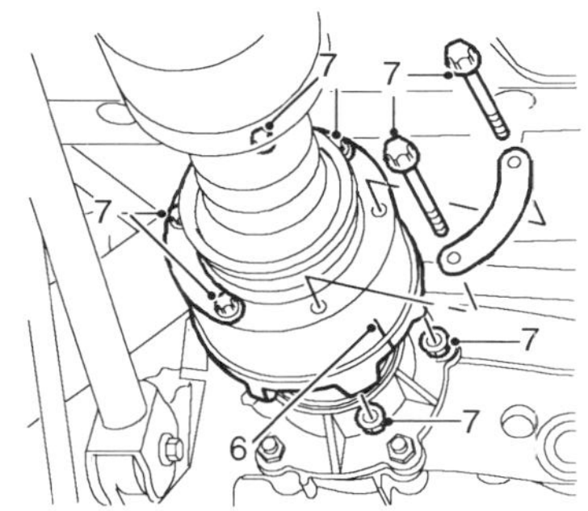

41M7365

6. Reference mark position of propeller and IRD drive flanges.
7. Remove 6 nuts and bolts securing propeller shaft to IRD drive flange.

8. Release propeller shaft from IRD drive flange and tie shaft to one side.

CAUTION: Care must be taken to support the Tripode joint when removed from the IRD unit. The joint must not be allowed to fully extend or be dropped as this could damage the joint and reduce its service life.

Diesel models

9. Remove 5 nuts securing IRD pinion housing to IRD main casing.

Petrol models

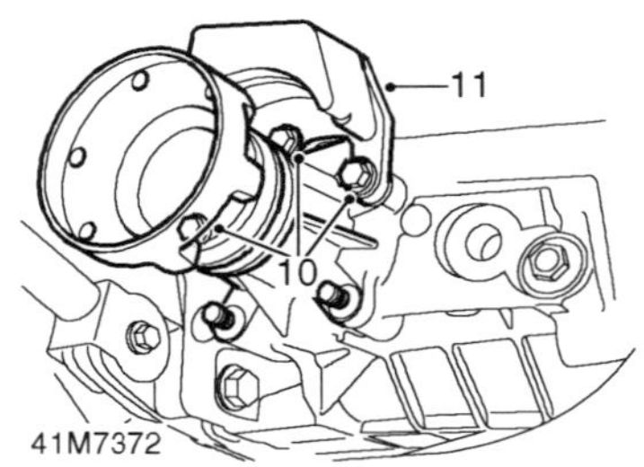

41M7372

10. Remove 3 remaining nuts securing mass damper and IRD pinion housing to IRD main case.
11. Remove mass damper from IRD pinion housing.

All models

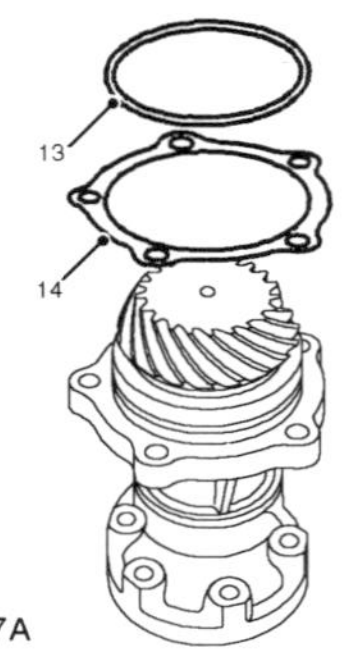

41M7367A

12. Remove pinion housing from IRD.
13. Remove and discard 'O' ring from pinion housing.
14. Remove and retain spacing washer.

Refit

1. Clean pinion housing and mating face on IRD casing.
2. Clean spacing washer.
3. Fit spacing washer to IRD.
4. Lubricate NEW 'O' ring with IRD oil and fit to groove in pinion housing.
5. Fit pinion housing to IRD.

Petrol models

6. Fit mass damper and tighten nuts to 25 Nm.

Diesel models

7. Fit nuts securing pinion housing and tighten to 25 Nm.

All models

8. Ensure mating face of propeller shaft and IRD drive flange are clean.
9. Fit propeller shaft to IRD flange and align marks. Tighten nuts and bolts to 42 Nm.
10. Fill IRD to correct level with fluid ***See MAINTENANCE.***

Petrol models

11. Fit exhaust front pipe. ***See MANIFOLD & EXHAUST SYSTEMS - 'K' SERIES, Repairs.***

Diesel models

12. Fit underbelly panel. ***See BODY, Exterior fittings.***

All models

13. Lower vehicle.

GASKET - END COVER - IRD HOUSING

Service repair no - 41.27.05

Remove

1. Drain lubricating fluid from IRD unit. ***See MAINTENANCE.***
2. Remove RH drive shaft seal. ***See DRIVE SHAFTS, Repairs.***

Petrol Models

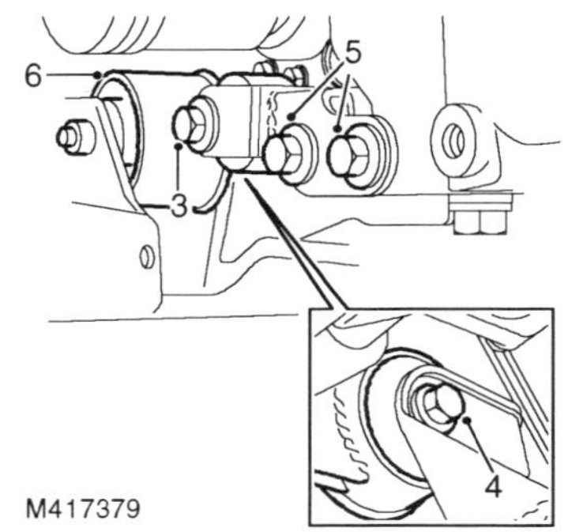

M417379

3. Loosen bolt securing engine lower tie bar to bracket on sump.
4. Remove bolt securing engine lower tie bar bracket to subframe.
5. Remove 2 bolts securing lower tie bar bracket to sump.
6. Remove lower tie bar with bracket.

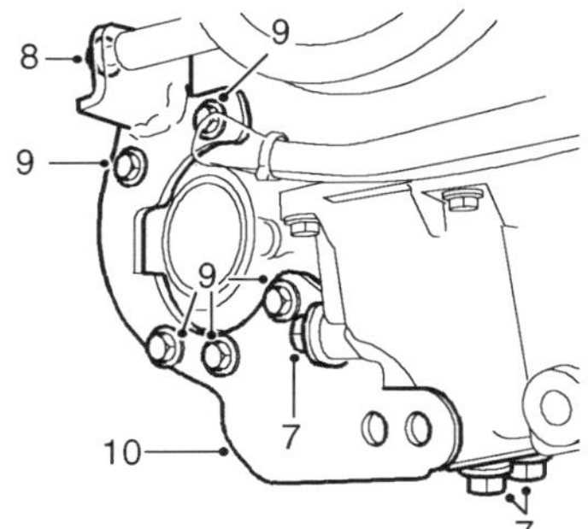

M417380

7. Remove 3 bolts securing IRD support bracket to sump.
8. Remove bolt securing IRD support bracket to PAS pump bracket.
9. Remove 5 bolts securing support bracket to IRD.
10. Remove IRD support bracket.

Diesel Models

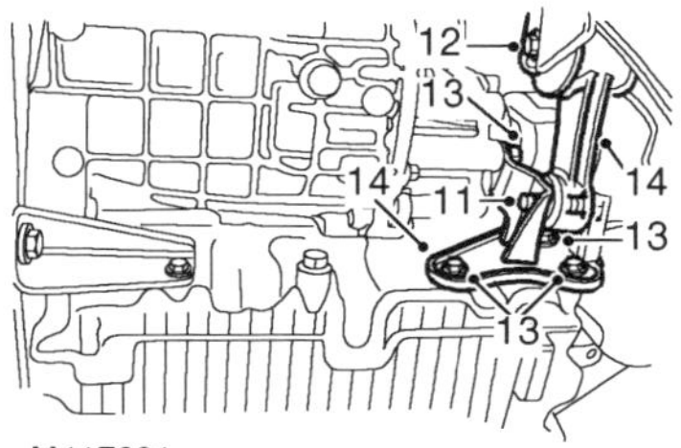

M417381

11. Loosen bolt securing engine lower tie bar to bracket on sump.
12. Remove bolt securing engine lower tie bar to subframe.
13. Remove 6 bolts securing lower tie bar bracket to sump and IRD.
14. Remove lower tie bar with bracket.

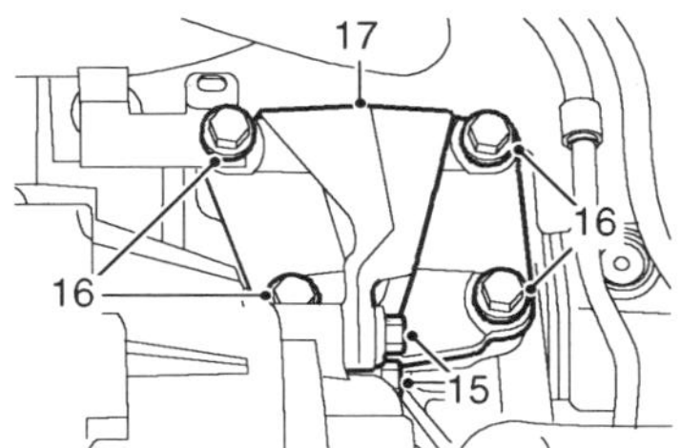

M417382

15. Remove 2 bolts securing support bracket to IRD.
16. Remove 4 bolts securing IRD support bracket to cylinder block.
17. Remove IRD support bracket.

All Models

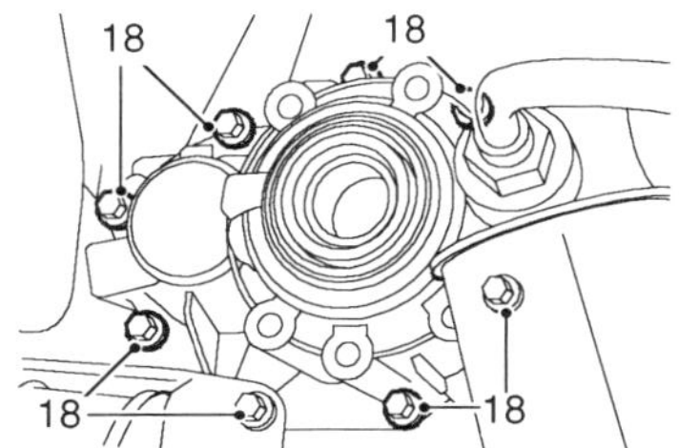

M417383

18. Remove 8 bolts securing end cover to main case of IRD.
19. Remove end cover from IRD main case.

Refit

1. Clean remains of old sealant from mating faces of end cover and IRD main case.

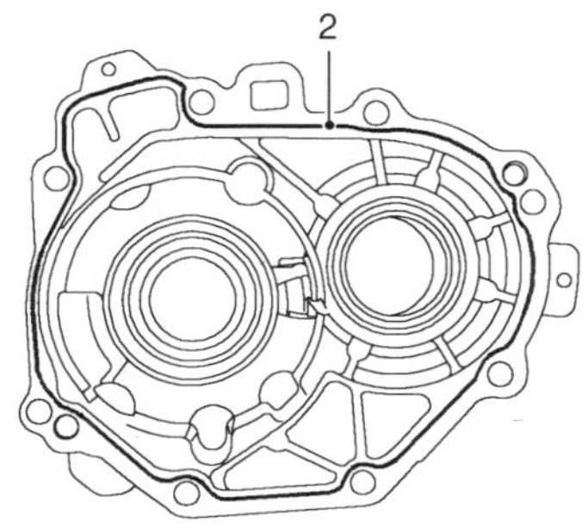

M417384

2. Apply a narrow bead of RTV Silicone sealant to mating face of end cover.
3. Fit end cover to IRD main case and tighten bolts to 30Nm.

Diesel Models

4. Fit IRD support bracket and tighten bolts initially only to ensure all mating faces are touching. Finally tighten bolts to 50 Nm.
5. Fit lower tie bar and bracket and tighten bolts securing bracket to 90 Nm.
6. Fit bolt securing lower tie bar to sub frame and tighten both tie bar bolts to 80 Nm.

Petrol Models

7. Fit IRD support bracket and tighten bolts initially only to ensure all mating faces are touching. Tighten in the following sequence:
   5 bolts securing support bracket to IRD 50 Nm
   1 bolt securing IRD support bracket to PAS pump bracket 50 Nm
   3 bolts securing support bracket to sump 90Nm
8. Fit engine lower tie bar with bracket and tighten bolts securing bracket to sump to 45 Nm.
9. Fit bolt securing engine lower tie bar to sub frame and tighten both tie bar bolts to 80 Nm.

All models

10. Fit RH drive shaft seal. ***See TRANSFER BOX, Repairs.***
11. Fill IRD with fluid. ***See MAINTENANCE.***

SEALS - PRIMARY GEAR SHAFT

Service repair no - 41.29.02

Remove

1. Remove IRD unit. ***See TRANSFER BOX, Repairs.***

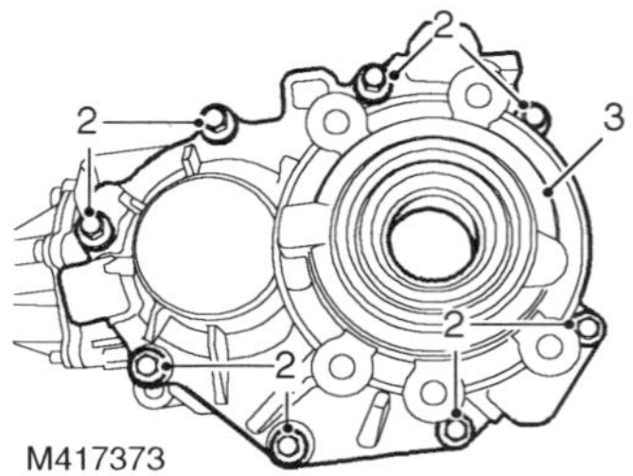

M417373

2. Remove 8 bolts securing end cover to main case.
3. Remove end cover from main case.

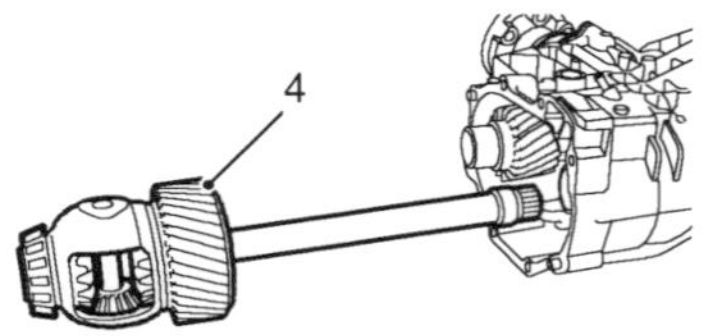

M417374

4. Remove intermediate shaft and differential from primary shaft.

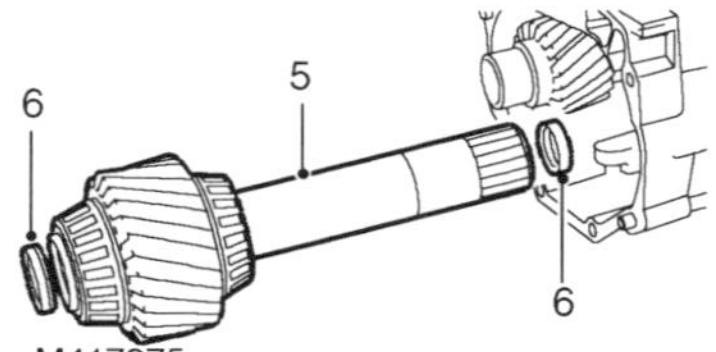

M417375

5. Remove primary shaft from main case.
6. Remove 2 seals from primary shaft.

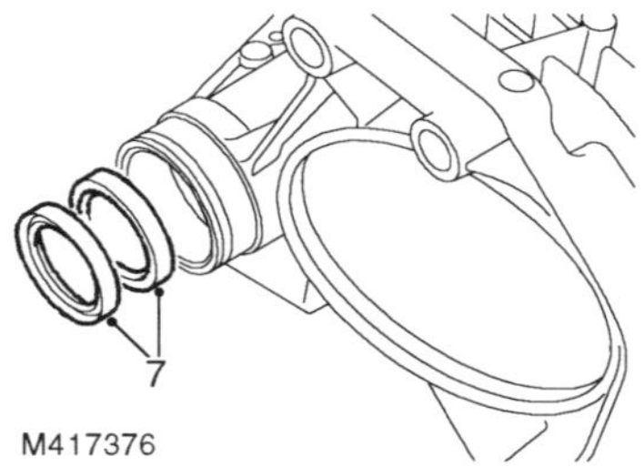

M417376

7. Remove 2 seals from main case.

NOTE: Orientation of seals for reference on refit.

Refit

1. Clean primary gear shaft and intermediate shaft and differential.
2. Clean seal locations.
3. Fit a seal to each end of primary gear shaft with seal lips facing outwards.
4. Fit primary gear shaft to main case.
5. Fit suitable protection over splines on intermediate shaft.
6. Carefully fit intermediate shaft to primary shaft.
7. Ensure end cover and main case mating faces are clean.

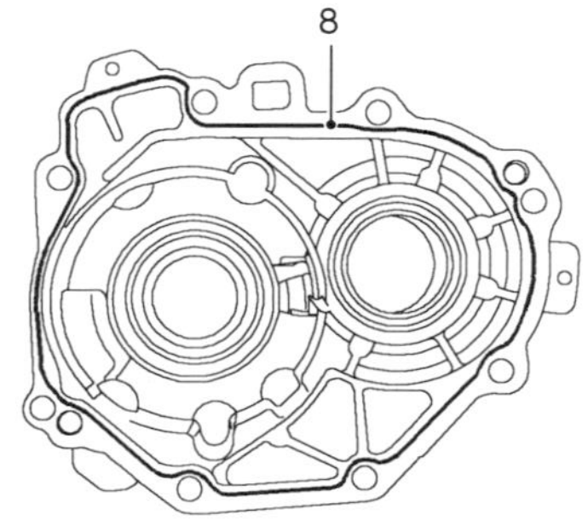

M417377

8. Apply a bead of sealant to sealing face of end cover.
9. Fit end cover and tighten bolts to 30 Nm.

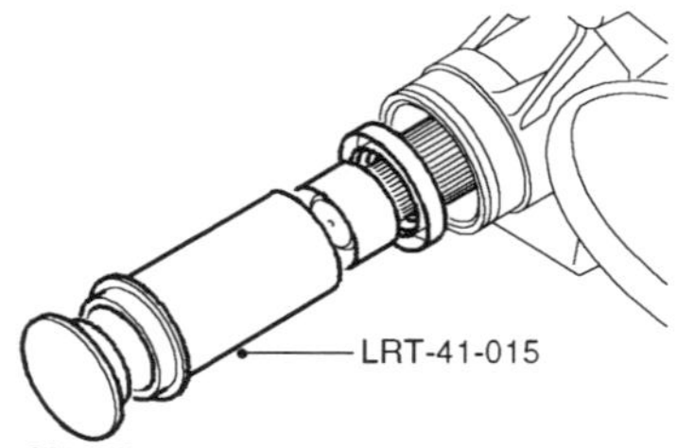

M417514

10. Fit protector of **LRT-41-015** to IRD splines.
11. Using plain end of drift **LRT-41-015** fit inner seal into main case until it contacts the shoulder.

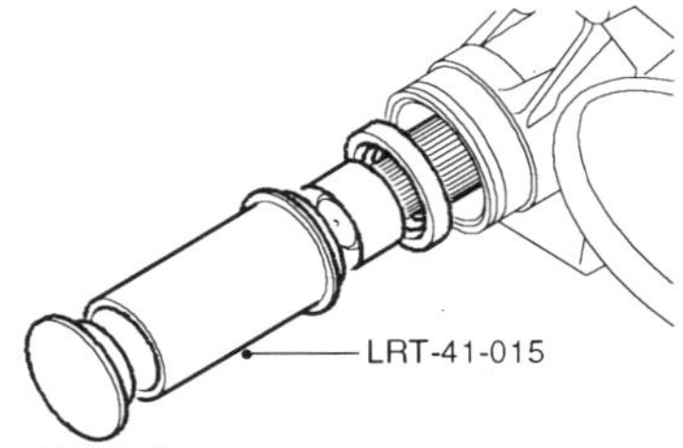

M417378

12. Using flanged end of drift **LRT-41-015** fit outer seal to depth dictated by tool flange.

NOTE: Use end protector of LRT-41-015 to avoid damage to the working surfaces of the tool.

NOTE: The seals are fitted with the main sealing lips facing away from each other.

13. Remove protector.
14. Fit IRD. ***See TRANSFER BOX, Repairs.***

SEAL - PINION GEAR

Service repair no - 41.29.04

1. Remove pinion gear housing. ***See TRANSFER BOX, Repairs.***
2. Attach pinion housing to suitable mounting plate and secure mounting plate in vice.

NOTE: Before dismantling the pinion housing, measure turning torque on existing bearings.

3. Using a torque wrench and a 30 mm socket, rotate pinion shaft 10 complete turns and record reading.

NOTE: Turning torque with NEW bearings is 180 to 200 Ncm. If the recorded figure is below the new bearing figure but above 20 to 30 Ncm, set to figure recorded. If below 20 Ncm, set to 20 to 30 Ncm.

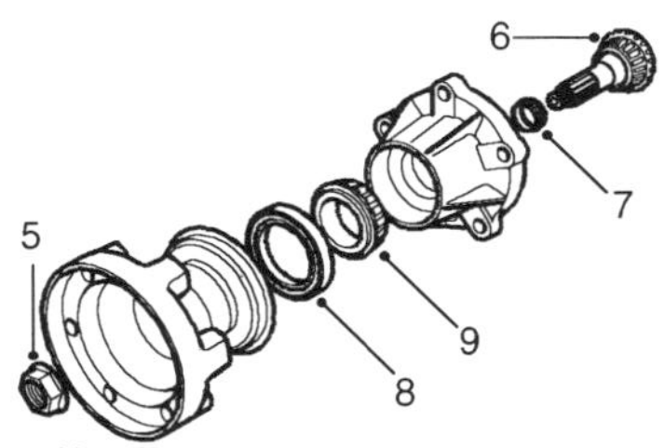

41M7369

4. Mark pinion flange to pinion shaft for assembly purposes.
5. Hold pinion flange using **LRT-51-003,** remove and discard nut.
6. Position pinion housing onto press, fit a suitable adaptor on end of pinion shaft, press pinion shaft from drive flange and housing.
7. Remove and discard collapsible spacer from pinion shaft.
8. Remove and discard pinion oil seal.
9. Remove outer bearing cone from housing.

Refit

1. Clean and dry pinion shaft, drive flange and housing.
2. Lubricate and fit outer bearing to pinion housing.
3. Lubricate new seal with IRD oil, then using a suitable adaptor, press seal into housing.

NOTE: Oil seal should be flush with end of pinion housing.

4. Assemble pinion to housing using a new collapsible spacer.
5. Lightly lubricate drive flange splines with Molybdenum Disulphide grease.
6. Align pinion to drive flange reference marks, and press flange onto pinion shaft until a 2 mm clearance exists at the bearings.
7. Fit pinion assembly to mounting plate and secure in vice.
8. Fit new pinion nut, hold pinion drive flange using **LRT-51-003** and tighten nut to 150 Nm. Remove **LRT-51-003.**
9. Using the torque wrench and 30 mm socket, rotate pinion shaft 10 complete turns and measure turning torque.
   Turning torque limits - used bearings:
   • If recorded figure is higher than 20 Ncm, set to previously recorded figure.
   • otherwise set to 20 to 30 Ncm.
   Turning torque limits - new bearings:
   • 180 to 200 Ncm
10. If turning torque is too low, carefully tighten nut further and recheck reading. If turning torque is too high, the pinion assembly will have to be dismantled, a new collapsible spacer fitted, reassembled using a new nut and the turning torque rechecked.
11. Use a Dial Test Indicator and check drive flange run-out.

NOTE: The drive flange run-out should not exceed 0.05 mm.

12. Remove pinion housing from vice and mounting plate.
13. Fit pinion housing to IRD. ***See TRANSFER BOX, Repairs.***

CONTENTS

DRIVE/PROPELLER SHAFTS

Drive shafts transmit drive from the intermediate reduction drive (IRD) to the front wheels, and from the final drive unit to the rear wheels.

Two propeller shafts and a viscous coupling unit (VCU) transmit drive from theIRD to the final drive unit.

Drivetrain layout

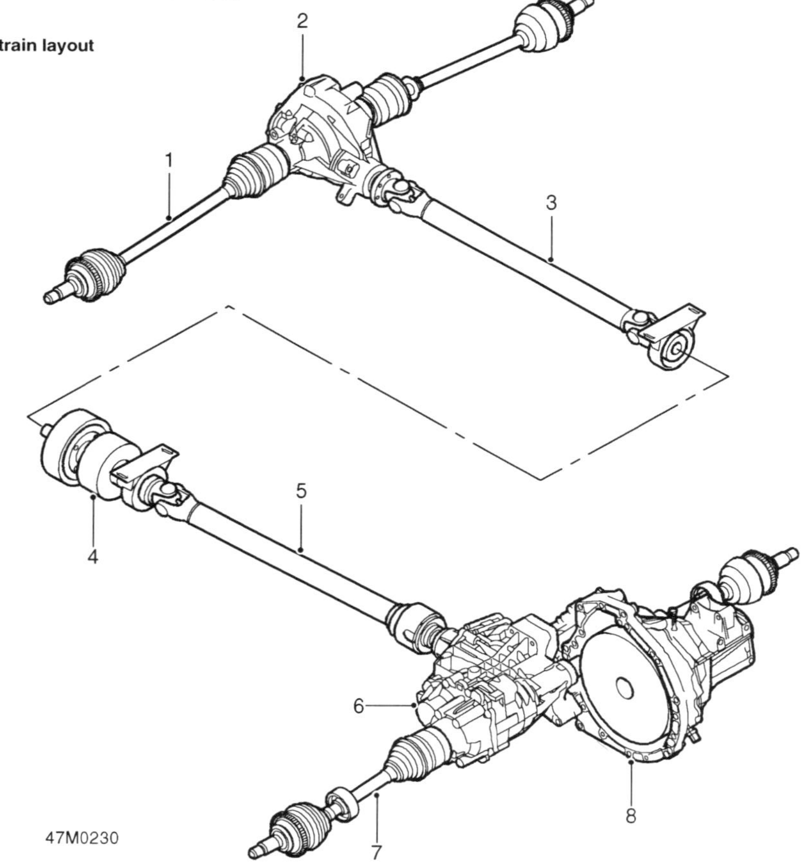

1. Rear drive shaft
2. Final drive unit
3. Rear propeller shaft
4. Viscous coupling unit
5. Front propeller shaft
6. Intermediate reduction drive
7. Front drive shaft
8. Gearbox

DRIVE SHAFTS

All four drive shafts are of similar construction, the main difference being in the lengths of the front and rear drive shafts. The front drive shafts of early vehicles are equipped with dynamic dampers. This feature was deleted soon after first build. Front drive shafts with and without dynamic dampers are interchangeable between early and late vehicles.

Each drive shaft comprises a solid shaft with inner and outer constant velocity joints. The inner joint is of the tripode type with spherical bushing to reduce sliding resistance; the shaft and inner joint are one assembly. The outer joint is of the ball and socket type, with a splined connection between the joint and the shaft. The joints are packed with grease and protected by gaiters.

Front drive shaft components

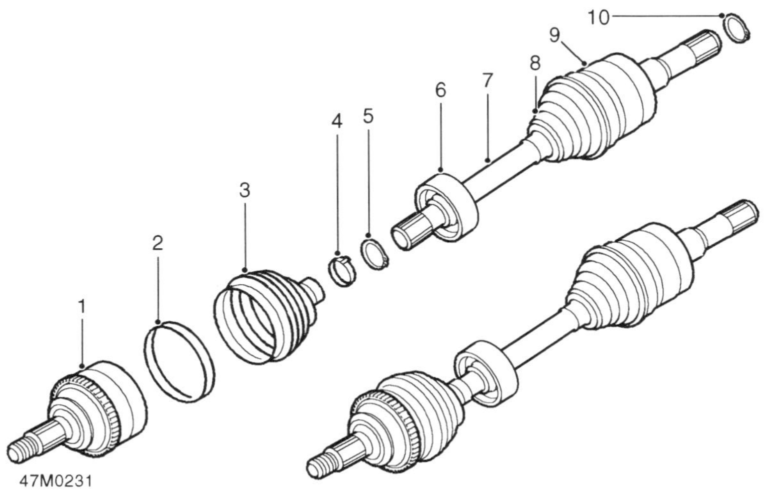

47M0231

1. Outer joint
2. Clamp
3. Gaiter
4. Clamp
5. Circlip
6. Dynamic damper - if fitted
7. Shaft
8. Gaiter
9. Inner joint
10. Circlip

Rear drive shaft components

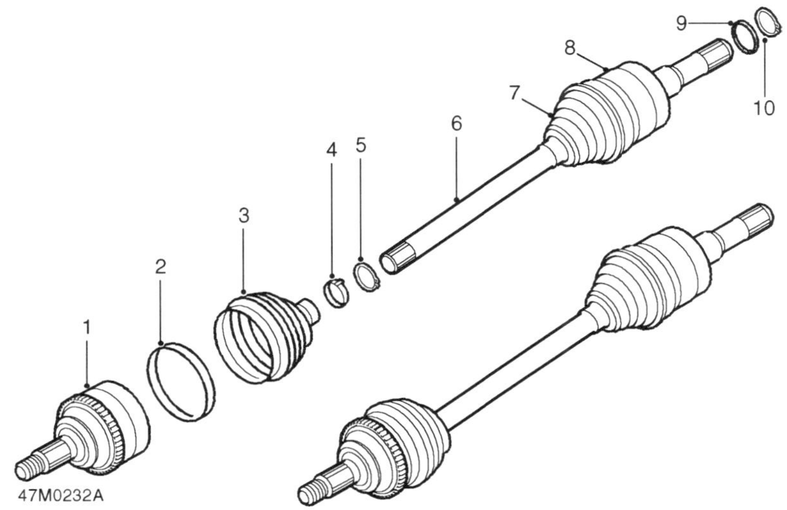

47M0232A

1. Outer joint
2. Clamp
3. Gaiter
4. Clamp
5. Circlip
6. Shaft
7. Gaiter
8. Inner joint
9. Flinger - oil seal
10. Circlip

PROPELLER SHAFTS AND VCU

Front propeller shaft

The front propeller shaft consists of a thin walled tube with a coupling welded to the front end and a conventional universal joint welded to the rear end. The coupling bolts to the output flange of the IRD. The universal joint is splined to the input shaft of the VCU and secured by a bolt.

The coupling reduces vibration and accommodates both angular movement (10 degrees maximum) and axial movement (50 mm maximum) between the propeller shaft and the IRD.

The universal joint incorporates serviceable, sealed needle bearings.

Propeller shaft and VCU components

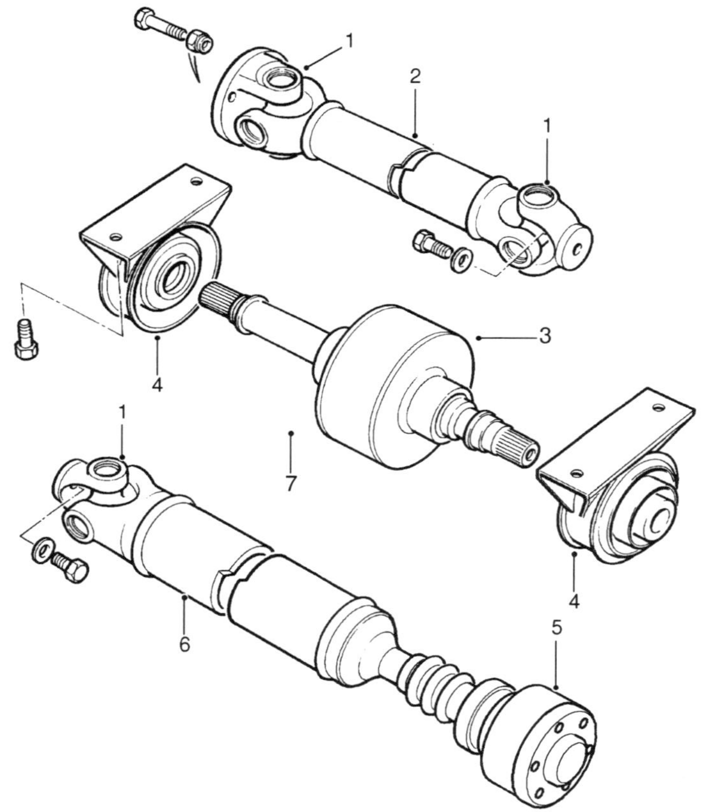

47M0233A

1. Universal joint
2. Rear propeller shaft
3. VCU
4. Propeller shaft bearing
5. Coupling
6. Front propeller shaft
7. Torsional damper

VCU

The VCU automatically controls the transfer of drive to the rear wheels by limiting the speed differential between the front and rear propeller shafts . The unit is supported in two propeller shaft bearings attached to the floor cross member.

The VCU comprises a short cylinder which contains an input shaft supported in a roller bearing race at the front and a ball bearing race at the rear. Within the cylinder, slotted discs are alternately attached to the outer surface of the input shaft and the inner surface of the cylinder. An output shaft is welded onto the rear of the cylinder. A torsional damper is bolted to a flange on the output shaft. The input shaft is attached to the front propeller shaft and the output shaft is attached to the rear propeller shaft.

The cylinder is a sealed unit filled with a silicon jelly. The viscosity of the silicon jelly increases when subjected to shear. When there is a speed differential between the front and rear propeller shafts , adjacent slotted discs in the VCU rotate in relation to each other. The shearing action of the rotating slotted discs increases the viscosity and resistance to rotation of the silicon jelly.

Section through VCU

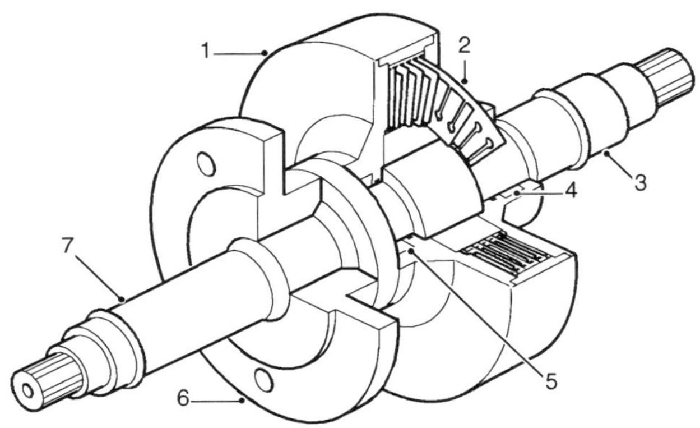

47M0234

1. Cylinder
2. Slotted discs
3. Input shaft
4. Roller bearing
5. Ball bearing
6. Torsional damper flange
7. Output shaft

The rear wheels are 0.8% under driven, so in most conditions the vehicle is effectively front wheel drive, with the rear wheels turning the rear propeller shaft slightly faster than the IRD drives the front propeller shaft. Since the speed differential is low, the increase in viscosity of the silicon jelly is marginal and there is little resistance to relative rotation of the slotted discs.

When there is a significant speed differential between the front and rear propeller shafts , e.g. the front wheels lose traction or traversing rough terrain, the viscosity and resistance to rotation of the silicon jelly increases to a level that slows or stops relative rotation of the slotted discs. With the front and rear propeller shafts locked together, drive is thus transferred from the IRD to the rear wheels.

Torsional damper

The torsional damper reduces vibration from the propeller shafts . The damper consists of a rubber membrane bonded between an outer ring and an inner hub. Three bolts secure the inner hub to the output shaft of the VCU.

Propeller shaft bearings

The two propeller shaft bearings are identical, and each consist of a roller bearing race mounted into a centre bearing housing. The bearing is sealed-for-life and is a press fit on the input/output shaft of the VCU. Bearing covers and flingers prevent the ingress of moisture.

Rear propeller shaft

The rear propeller shaft consists of a thin walled tube with a conventional universal joint welded to each end. The rear universal joint is bolted to the input flange of the final drive unit. The front universal joint is splined to the output shaft of the viscous coupling unit and secured by a bolt: Both universal joints incorporate serviceable, sealed needle bearings.

DRIVE SHAFT - FRONT

Service repair no - 47.10.01

Remove

1. Raise front of vehicle, one side.

WARNING: Support on safety stands.

2. Remove road wheel(s).
3. Remove underbelly panel. ***See BODY, Repairs.***
4. Remove 3 bolts securing splash shield.
5. Remove splash shield.

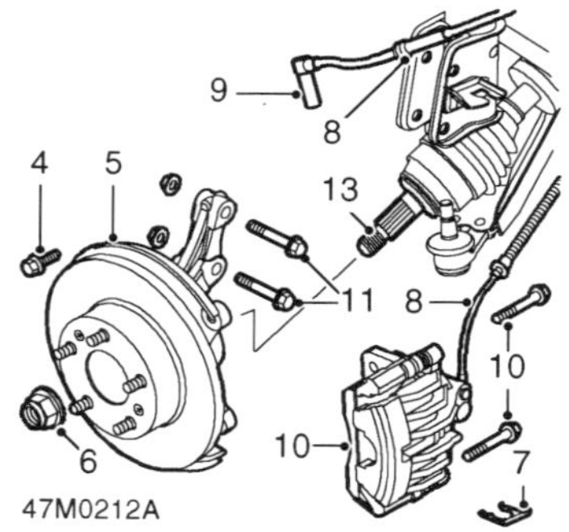

47M0212A

6. Release drive shaft stake nut tag. With an assistant depressing the brake pedal, remove and discard the drive shaft nut.
7. Remove 'C' clip from brake hose.
8. Release brake hose and ABS harness from bracket.
9. Release ABS speed sensor from hub.

CAUTION: Do not allow caliper to hang on brake hose.

10. Remove 2 bolts from brake caliper, release brake caliper from hub and tie aside.
11. Remove 2 bolts securing damper to hub.
12. Release hub from damper.
13. Release drive shaft outer joint from hub.

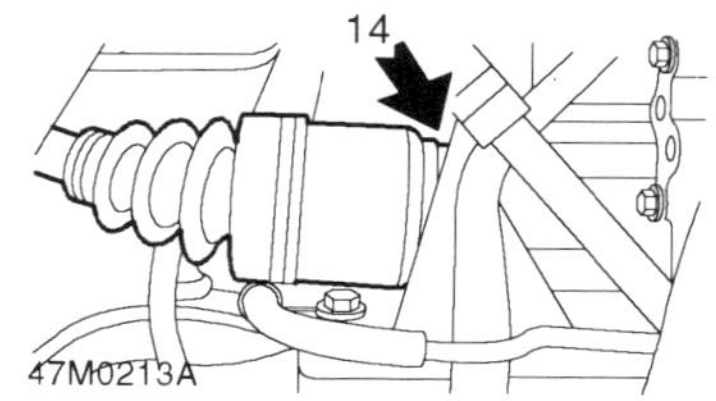

47M0213A

14. Release drive shaft inner joint from gear box.

CAUTION: Care must be taken not to damage oil seal when removing drive shaft from gearbox.

15. Remove drive shaft.

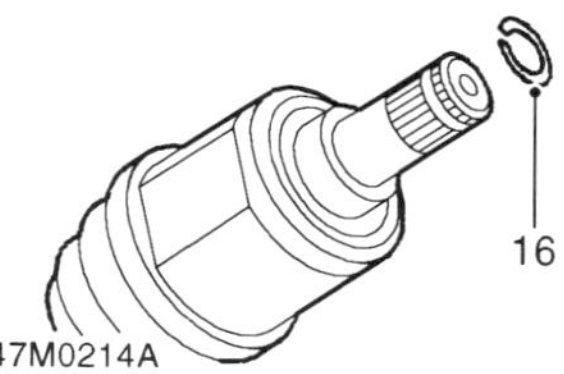

47M0214A

16. Remove and discard circlip from drive shaft.

Refit

1. Inspect gear box seal for signs of wear or damage.
2. Wipe drive shaft ends, gear box oil seal and hub.
3. Lubricate oil seal running surfaces.
4. Fit NEW circlip to drive shaft.

CAUTION: Drive shaft must be fitted with care to prevent damage to gear box oil seal.

5. Fit drive shaft ensuring circlip is fully engaged.
6. Position drive shaft in hub.
7. Fit NEW drive shaft nut but do not tighten at this stage.
8. Align hub to damper and tighten bolts to 205 Nm.
9. Fit brake caliper and tighten bolts to 83 Nm.
10. Fit ABS speed sensor.
11. Position ABS harness and brake hose in bracket and secure hose with 'C' clip.
12. Fit splash shield and secure with bolts.
13. Fit underbelly panel. ***See BODY, Repairs.***
14. Tighten drive shaft nut to 400 Nm.
15. Stake drive shaft nut.
16. Fit road wheel(s) and tighten nuts to correct torque. ***See INFORMATION, Torque wrench settings.***
17. Remove stand(s) and lower vehicle.
18. Check and top up oil level as required. ***See MANUAL GEARBOX, Adjustments.***

DYNAMIC DAMPER - FRONT

NOTE: Dynamic dampers are fitted to the front drive shafts of early vehicles only.

Service repair no - 47.10.33

Remove

1. Remove drive shaft. ***See this section.***
2. Remove drive shaft outer gaiter. ***See this section.***
3. Clean and lubricate shaft to aid removal of dynamic damper.

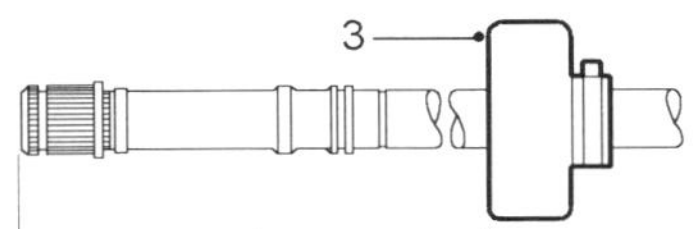

47M0227

4. Mark fitted position of existing damper for reference 'A'
5. Remove dynamic damper.

Refit

1. Lubricate shaft and fit dynamic damper.

CAUTION: Ensure damper is aligned to previously made mark.

2. Fit drive shaft outer gaiter. ***See this section.***
3. Fit drive shaft. ***See this section.***

GAITER - OUTER - FRONT

Service repair no - 47.10.03

Remove

1. Remove drive shaft. ***See this section.***
2. Remove drive shaft outer joint. ***See this section.***

47M0226

3. Slide gaiter from shaft.

Refit

1. Clean drive shaft and gaiter.
2. Fit new gaiter to shaft.
3. Fit drive shaft outer joint. ***See this section.***
4. Fit drive shaft. ***See this section.***

DRIVE SHAFT JOINT - OUTER - FRONT

Service repair no - 47.10.04

Remove

1. Remove drive shaft. ***See this section.***
2. Place drive shaft in vice.
3. Release and discard both gaiter clips.
4. Slide gaiter along shaft to gain access to outer joint.

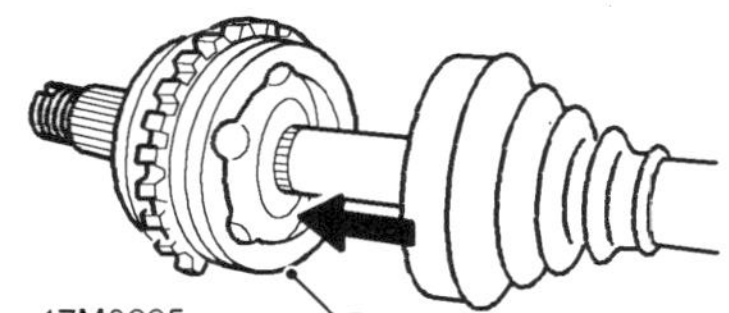

47M0225

5. Using a suitable drift against the inner part of the joint remove the joint.

Refit

1. Clean drive shaft and gaiter.
2. Fit NEW circlip to shaft.
3. Position outer joint to shaft. use a screwdriver to press circlip into its groove and push joint fully onto shaft.
4. Apply grease from sachet to the joint.
5. Position gaiter to joint and use a Band-it thriftool **LRT-99-019** to secure the 2 NEW clips.
6. Fit drive shaft. ***See this section.***

GAITER - INNER - FRONT

Service repair no - 47.10.16

Remove

1. Remove drive shaft. ***See this section.***
2. Remove outer drive shaft joint. ***See this section.***
   Remove dynamic damper if fitted. ***See this section.***

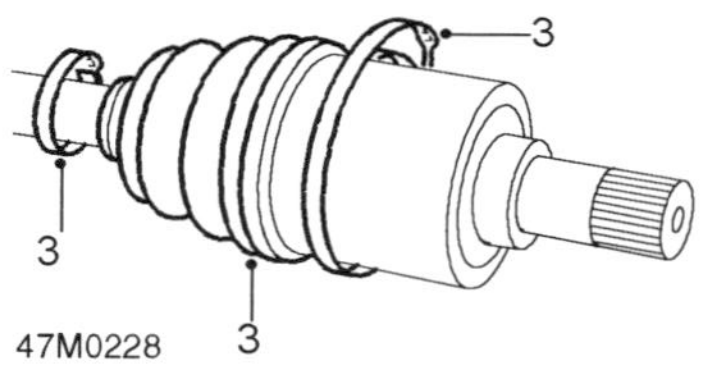

47M0228

3. Release both inner gaiter clips and discard. Remove gaiter from drive shaft.
4. Inspect drive shaft gaiters and dynamic damper for damage and renew if necessary.

Refit

1. Clean drive shaft and joint.
2. Apply grease to joint.
3. Position NEW gaiter to drive shaft and use a Band-it thriftool to secure the new clips.
4. Fit dynamic damper if necessary. ***See this section.***
   Fit outer drive shaft joint. ***See this section.***
5. Fit drive shaft. ***See this section.***

DRIVE SHAFT - REAR

Service repair no - 47.11.01

Remove

1. Raise rear of vehicle.

WARNING: **Support on safety stands.**

2. Remove road wheel(s).

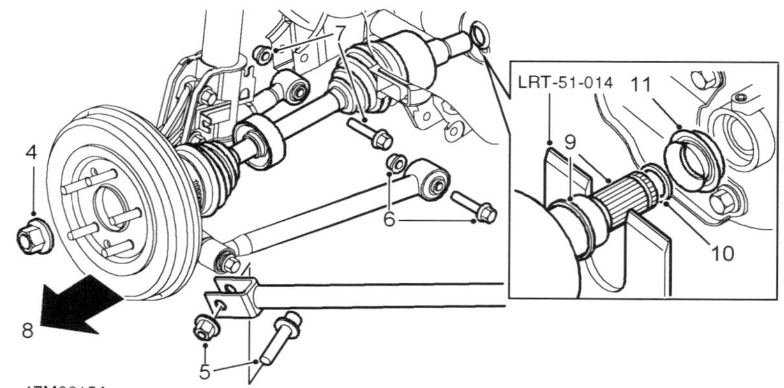

47M0215A

3. Release drive shaft stake nut tag.
4. With an assistant depressing the brake pedal, remove and discard the drive shaft nut.
5. Remove nut and bolt securing trailing link to rear hub.
6. Remove nut and bolt securing fixed transverse link to sub frame.
7. Remove nut and bolt securing adjustable transverse link to sub frame.
8. With assistance pull hub assembly outwards and release drive shaft outer joint from hub assembly.
9. Taking care not to damage 'Flinger', release drive shaft inner joint from differential using **LRT-51-014** and remove drive shaft.
10. Remove and discard drive shaft circlip.
11. Inspect differential oil seal, renew if worn or damaged.

Refit

1. Clean drive shaft ends, differential oil seal and hub.
2. Lubricate oil seal running surfaces.
3. Check condition of oil seal 'Flinger', renew if damaged and fit onto drive shaft.
4. Fit new circlip to drive shaft.

⚠ **CAUTION: When fitting drive shaft into differential, avoid contact between drive shaft spline and oil seal. Seal damage will occur if contact is made.**

5. Fit drive shaft to differential, ensure drive shaft engages in differential.
6. With assistance fit drive shaft to hub.
7. Fit NEW drive shaft nut but do not tighten at this stage.
8. Fit nut and bolt to adjustable transverse link and tighten to 120 Nm.
9. Fit nut and bolt to fixed transverse link and tighten to 120 Nm.
10. Fit nut and bolt to trailing link and tighten to 120 Nm.
11. Tighten drive shaft nut to 400 Nm.
12. Stake drive shaft nut.
13. Fit road wheel(s) and tighten nuts to correct torque. ***See INFORMATION, Torque wrench settings.***
14. Remove stand(s) and lower vehicle.

GAITER - INNER - REAR

Service repair no - 47.11.16

1. Remove drive shaft. ***See this section.***
2. Remove drive shaft outer gaiter. ***See this section.***

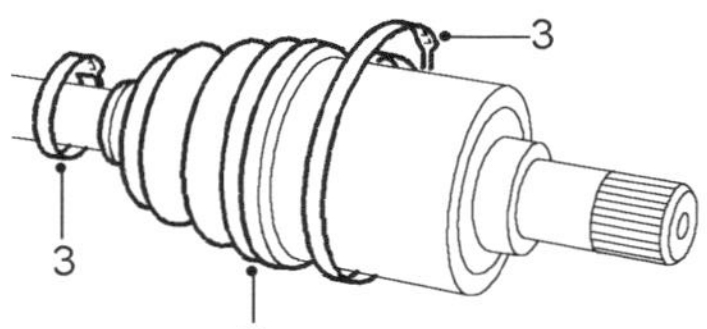

47M0229

3. Release both inner gaiter clips and discard. Remove gaiter from drive shaft.

Refit

1. Clean drive shaft and joint.
2. Apply grease to joint.
3. Position NEW gaiter to drive shaft and use a Band-it thriftool to secure the new clips.
4. Fit drive shaft outer gaiter. ***See this section.***
5. Fit drive shaft. ***See this section.***

GAITER - OUTER - REAR

Service repair no - 47.11.03

1. Remove drive shaft. ***See this section.***
2. Remove drive shaft outer joint. ***See this section.***

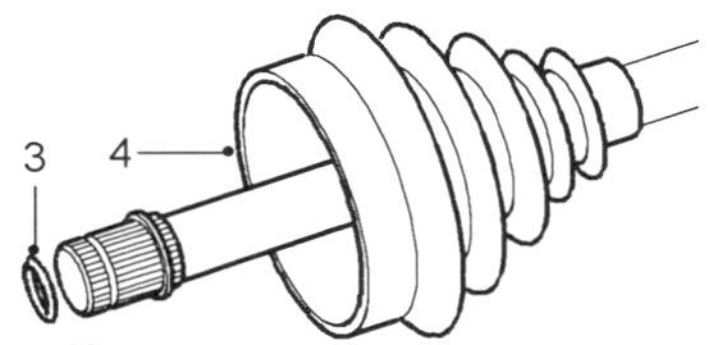

47M0235

3. Remove and discard circlip.
4. Remove outer gaiter.

Refit

1. Clean drive shaft end and outer gaiter, fit gaiter.
2. Fit drive shaft outer joint. ***See this section.***
3. Fit drive shaft. ***See this section.***

JOINT - OUTER - REAR

Service repair no - 47.11.04

Remove

1. Remove drive shaft. ***See this section.***
2. Place drive shaft in vice.
3. Release and discard both gaiter clips.
4. Slide gaiter along shaft to gain access to outer joint.

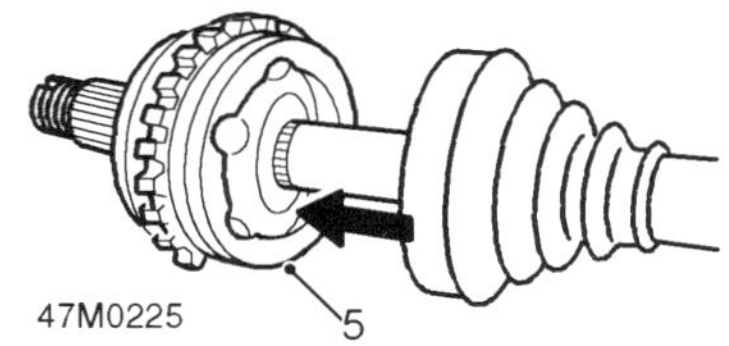

47M0225

5. Using a suitable drift against the inner part of the joint remove the joint.
6. Remove and discard circlip.

Refit

1. Fit NEW circlip to shaft.
2. Position outer joint to shaft. use a screwdriver to press circlip into its groove and push joint fully onto shaft.
3. Apply grease from sachet to the joint.
4. Position gaiter to joint and use a Band-it thriftool **LRT-99-019** to secure the 2 NEW clips.
5. Fit drive shaft. ***See this section.***

PROPELLER SHAFT - ASSEMBLY

Service repair no - 47.15.01

Remove

1. Raise vehicle on a 4 post ramp.

NOTE: Raise one wheel on each axle for rotation of propeller shaft as necessary to access fixings.

CAUTION: When working on the propeller shafts:

- **Always remove the propeller shafts and viscous coupling unit as an assembly. Dismantling individual units on the vehicle may cause damage to components.**
- **Never unbolt the viscous coupling support bearings from the body without first detaching the propeller shafts at the differential and IRD. The weight of the centre section will pull the CV joint apart, causing irreparable damage.**
- **Never allow the CV joint to be manipulated to an acute angle. This will cause the internal roller bearings to break up, leading to excessive backlash and CV joint failure.**

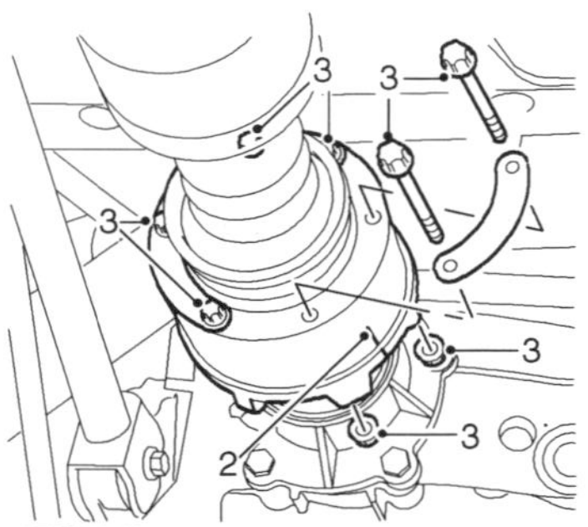

47M0217

2. Reference mark the position of propeller shaft flanges to IRD unit and rear axle flanges to aid reassembly.
3. Remove 6 nuts, bolts and link washers securing CV joint to IRD flange.

CAUTION: DO NOT pull on the propeller shaft when releasing the CV joint from the IRD flange. This will pull the CV joint apart, causing irreparable damage.

4. Release the CV joint from the IRD drive flange by pulling on the main casing of the CV joint. If necessary, position a suitable clamp around the CV joint main body, release the CV joint by levering between the clamp and the IRD flange. Support front of propeller shaft.

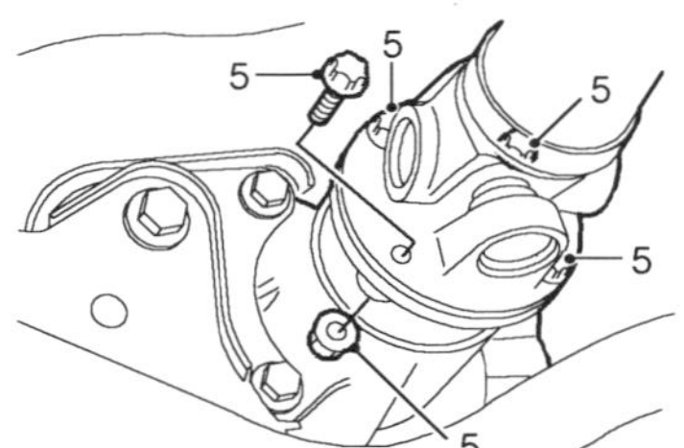

M47 0300

5. Remove 4 nuts and bolts from rear flange, release and support propeller shaft from rear axle flange.

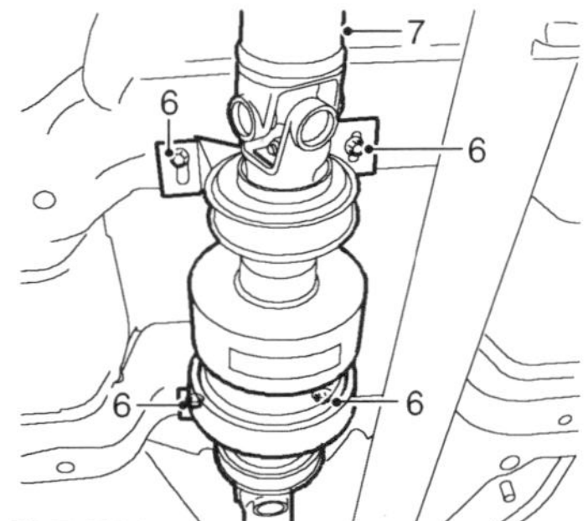

M47 0301

6. Remove 4 bolts from viscous coupling support bearings.
7. With assistance, remove complete propeller shaft assembly.

NOTE: Replace support bearings if worn or damaged.

Refit

1. Clean propeller shaft flanges and mating faces.
2. With assistance, fit propeller shaft in position, support front and rear propeller shafts at each end.
3. Align viscous coupling support bearings, fit bolts but do not tighten at this stage.
4. Position propeller shaft to rear axle and align reference marks.
5. Fit and tighten nuts and bolts securing rear propeller shaft to rear axle to 65 Nm.
6. Position propeller shaft to IRD flange, align flange reference marks.
7. Fit and tighten nuts and bolts to 40 Nm.

CAUTION: It is important that when securing the support bearings to the body that each support bearing is positioned at a right angle to the centre shaft axis before and after tightening the retaining bolts.

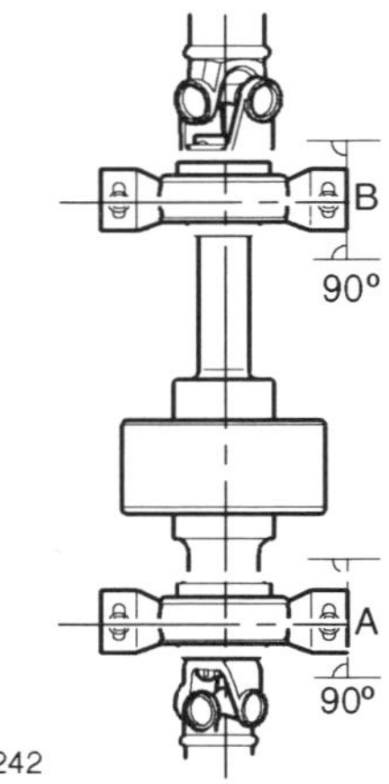

47M0242

8. Correctly position support bearings at 90° to the centre line as shown at points 'A' and 'B', tighten rear then front bolts to 28 Nm.
9. Lower wheels.
10. Lower vehicle.

PROPELLER SHAFT

Service repair no - 47.15.02 - propeller shaft - front
Service repair no - 47.15.03 - propeller shaft - rear

Remove

1. Remove propeller shaft assembly. ***See this section.***

CAUTION: It is important that the propeller shaft assembly is supported on a firm surface before separating the propeller shaft from the viscous coupling.

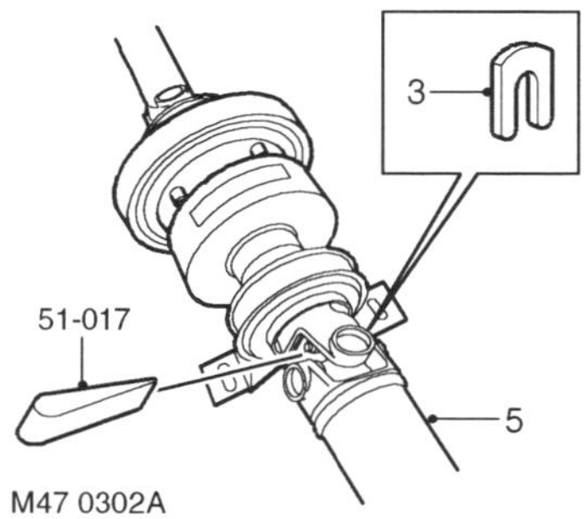

M47 0302A

2. Knock back locktab from bolt securing propeller shaft to viscous coupling.
3. Loosen bolt securing propeller shaft to viscous coupling and slide out 'U' washer.
4. To disengage the spline, insert wedge **51-017** between the bolt head and the universal joint yoke. Screw the bolt in or out to correctly position the wedge between the yoke and the bolt head. Drive the wedge in squarely to separate the components.
5. Adjust bolt engagement as necessary to maintain contact between the wedge and the bolt head.

NOTE: A force is required to remove the splined component due to a helix on the male spline.

CAUTION: Take care that the universal joint seals are not damaged during this operation.

6. Remove bolt and tab washer, pull propeller shaft from viscous coupling, discard tab washer and bolt if damaged.

Refit

1. Clean mating faces and splines on propeller shaft and viscous coupling.
2. Engage splines between propeller shaft and VCU shaft assembly and push home propeller shaft as far as possible.
3. Partially fit bolt and new tab washer, position 'U' spacer between tab washer and spline yoke.
4. Tighten bolt to 65 Nm to fully seat splines and secure with tab washer.
5. Fit propeller shaft assembly. ***See this section.***

PROPELLER SHAFT - FRONT/REAR - OVERHAUL

Service repair no - 47.15.11 - propeller shaft - front
Service repair no - 47.15.12 - propeller shaft - rear

Remove

1. Remove front or rear propeller shaft as applicable. ***See this section.***
2. Thoroughly examine universal joint for signs of damage or wear.
3. Clean universal joint bearing cups and circlips.

CAUTION: To ensure correct assembly and reduce possibility of imbalance, mark position of spider pin relative to spline yoke and tube yoke ears before removing propeller shaft joint.

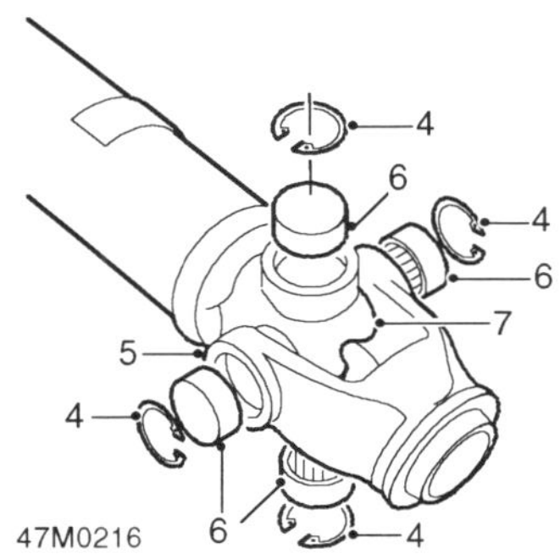

47M0216

4. Remove circlips.
5. Tap yokes to eject bearing cups.
6. Remove bearing cups.
7. Remove spider.
8. Clean yokes and bearing cup locations.

Refit

1. Remove bearing cups from new spider.
2. Check all needle rollers are present and positioned in bearing cups.
3. Ensure bearing cups are one-third full of lubricant. ***See INFORMATION, Capacities, fluids and lubricants.***
4. Enter new spider with seals into ears of flange yoke or spline yoke (dependant on joint being repaired).
5. Partially insert one bearing cup into flange/spline yoke and enter spider trunnion into bearing cup.
6. Insert opposite bearing cup into flange /spline yoke.
7. Press both cups into place.
8. Press each cup into its respective yoke up to lower land of circlip groove. Damage may be caused to cups and seals if cups pass this point.
9. Fit circlips and check no end float exists.
10. Engage spider into tube yokes. Fit bearing cups and circlips as described in instructions 3 to 9.
11. Fit front or rear propeller shaft as applicable. ***See this section.***

VISCOUS COUPLING ASSEMBLY

Service repair no - 47.20.01

Remove

1. Remove front propeller shaft. ***See this section.***

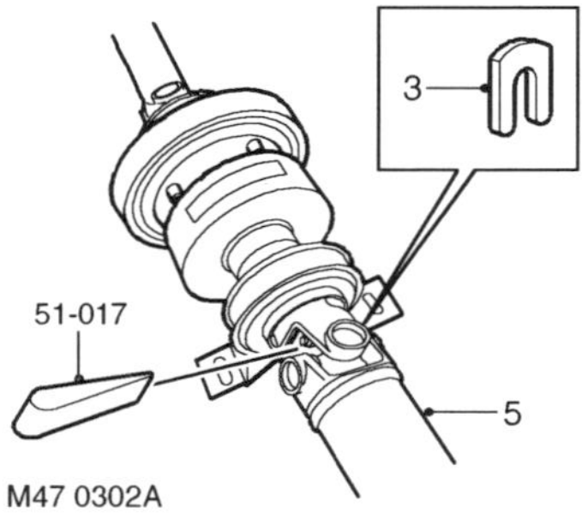

M47 0302A

2. Knock back tab washer from bolt securing rear propeller shaft to viscous coupling.
3. Loosen bolt securing propeller shaft to viscous coupling and slide out 'U' washer.
4. To disengage the spline, insert wedge **51-017** between the bolt head and the universal joint yoke. Screw the bolt in or out to correctly position the wedge between the yoke and the bolt head. Drive the wedge in squarely to separate the components. Adjust the bolt engagement as necessary to maintain contact between the wedge and bolt head.

CAUTION: Take care that the universal joint seals are not damaged during this operation.

NOTE: A force is required to remove the splined component due to a helix on the male spline.

5. Remove bolt and tab washer, pull rear propeller shaft from viscous coupling unit, discard tab washer and bolt if damaged.

CAUTION: It is important that the viscous coupling is fully supported whilst pressing off the support bearing.

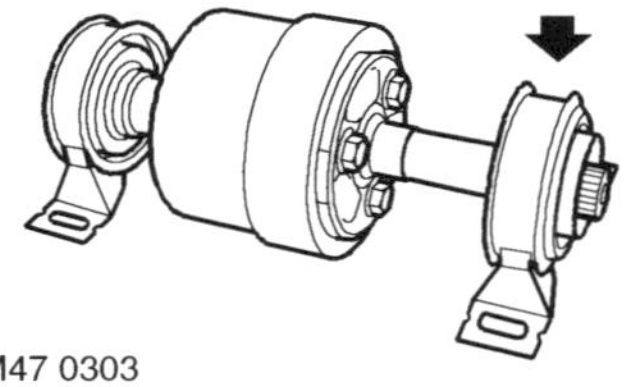

M47 0303

6. Note the orientation of the support bearings on the viscous coupling unit.

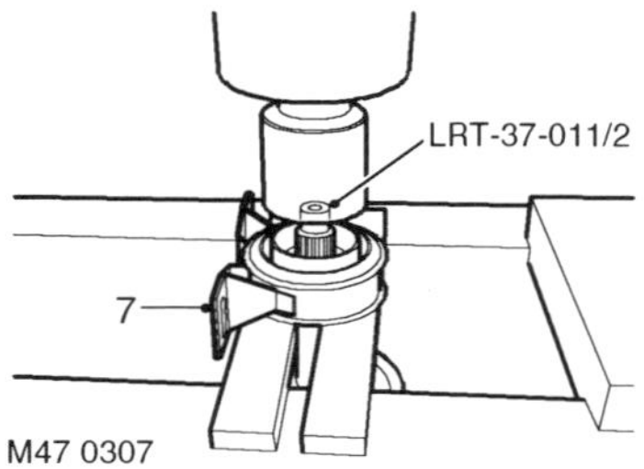

M47 0307

7. With assistance, position viscous coupling unit onto press bed, with suitable press bars located on he support bearing as shown. Take care that the press bars are not positioned on the steel flinger.
8. Position **LRT-37-011/2** thrust button onto viscous coupling unit splines.
9. With assistance, press the splined end of the viscous coupling unit through the bearing.Take care that the viscous coupling unit does not drop when free of support bearing.
10. Repeat the procedure and remove the front support bearing from the viscous coupling unit.
11. Remove 3 bolts securing torsional vibration absorber to the viscous coupling unit.
12. Note orientation of torsional vibration absorber on viscous coupling unit.

Refit

NOTE: Replace support bearings if worn or damaged.

1. Ensure mating face of torsional vibration absorber and viscous coupling are clean and free from burrs.
2. Position torsional vibration absorber to viscous coupling, fit and tighten bolts to 80 Nm.
3. Clean flinger, bearing journal, splines and support bearings.
4. Ensure that the cavities between the bearing and outer shrouds are packed with Texaco Novatex EP2 grease.

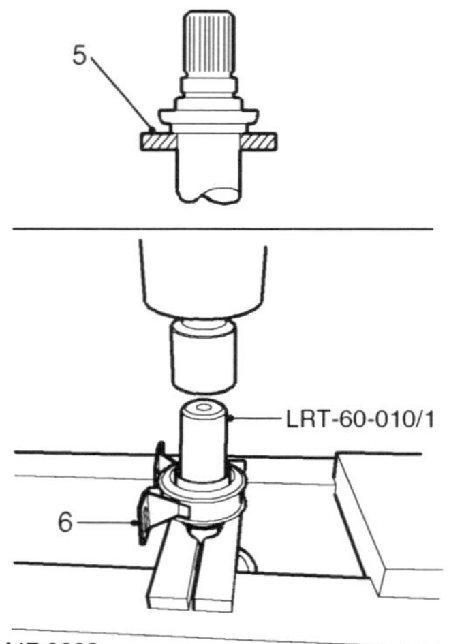

M47 0308

5. With assistance, position viscous coupling unit onto press bed and locate the press bars onto collar as shown.
6. Position front support bearing onto viscous coupling unit.
7. Position **LRT-60-010/1** onto bearing inner race, and with assistance, press support bearing onto viscous coupling unit.
8. Repeat procedure to fit rear support bearing to viscous coupling unit.
9. Spin support bearings and check for true running.
10. Clean mating faces and splines on rear propeller shaft and viscous coupling.
11. Engage splines between propeller shaft and viscous coupling unit shaft and push home propeller shaft as far as possible.
12. Partially fit bolt and new tab washer, position 'U' spacer between tab washer and spline yoke.
13. Tighten bolt to to 65 Nm to fully seat splines and secure with tab washer.
14. Fit front propeller shaft. ***See this section.***

SUPPORT BEARING - VISCOUS COUPLING - FRONT

Service repair no - 47.20.05

Remove

1. Remove front propeller shaft. ***See this section.***

CAUTION: It is important that the viscous coupling is fully supported whilst pressing off the support bearing.

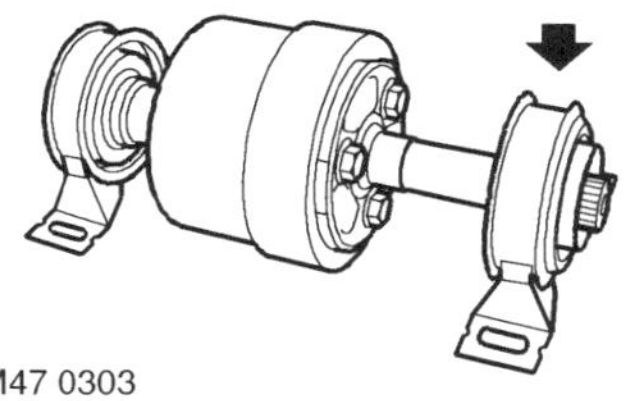

M47 0303

2. Note the fitted position of the support bearing on the viscous coupling.

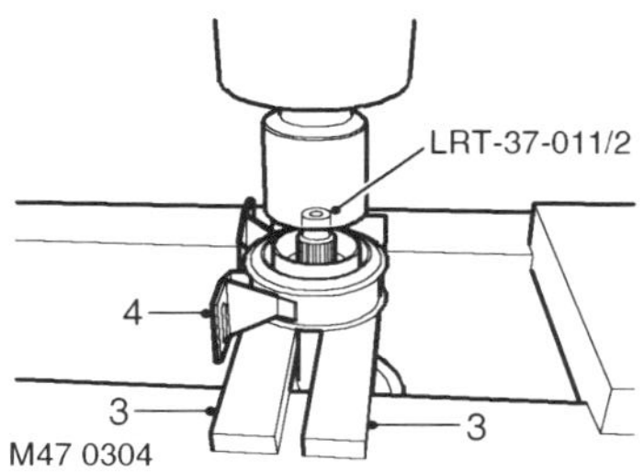

M47 0304

3. Position suitable press bars to support bearing as shown, taking care that the press bars are not positioned on the steel flinger.
4. With assistance, position viscous coupling assembly onto press bed.
5. Position **LRT-37-011/2** thrust button onto viscous coupling splines.
6. With assistance, press the splined end of the viscous coupling unit through the support bearing. Take care that the viscous coupling does not drop when free of the bearing.
7. Remove viscous coupling assembly from press.

NOTE: Replace steel flinger on viscous coupling if damaged during removal of support bearing.

Refit

1. Clean flinger, bearing journal, splines and support bearings
2. Ensure that the cavities between the bearing and outer shrouds are packed with Texaco Novatex EP2 grease.

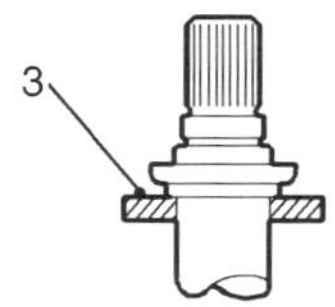

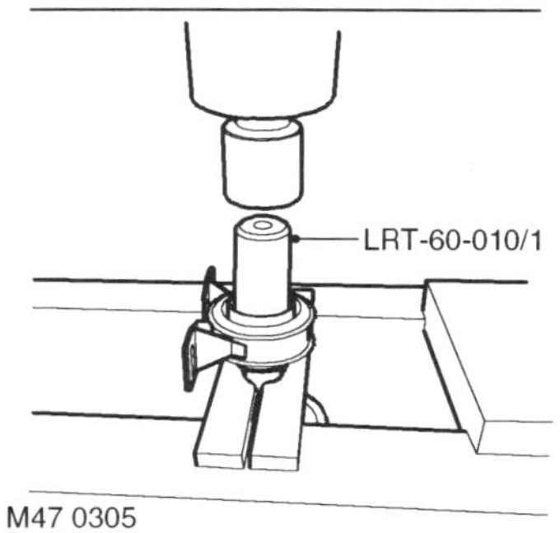

M47 0305

3. With assistance, position viscous coupling assembly onto press bed and locate the press bars onto collar on viscous coupling as shown.
4. Position **LRT-60-010/1** onto bearing inner race, and with assistance, press support bearing onto viscous coupling.
5. Remove viscous coupling assembly from press.
6. Spin support bearing and check for true running.
7. Fit front propeller shaft. ***See this section.***

SUPPORT BEARING - VISCOUS COUPLING - REAR

Service repair no - 47.20.06

Remove

1. Remove rear propeller shaft. ***See this section.***

CAUTION: It is important that the viscous coupling is fully supported whilst pressing off the support bearing.

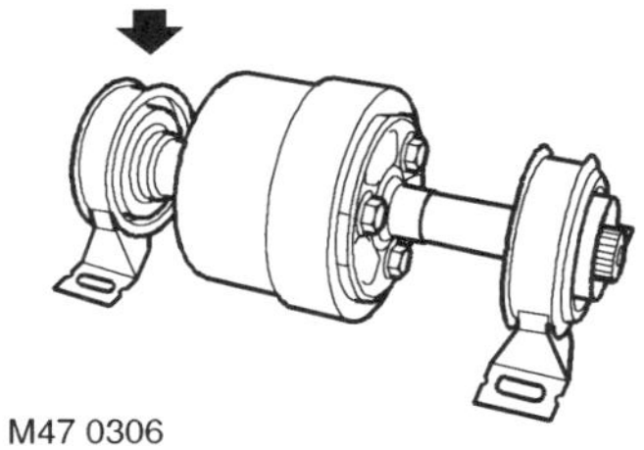

M47 0306

2. Note the fitted position of the support bearing on the viscous coupling.

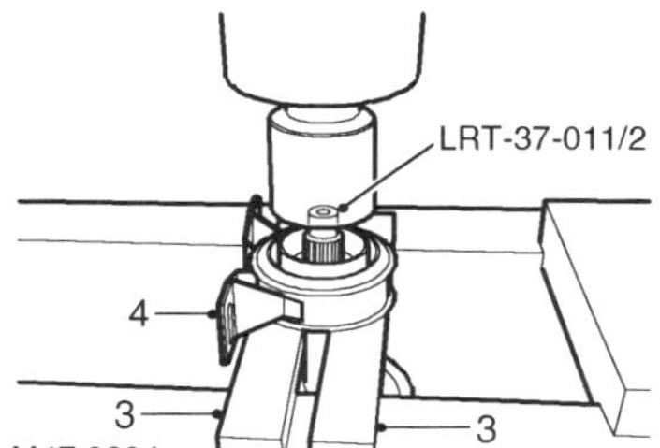

M47 0304

3. Position suitable press bars to support bearing as shown, taking care that the press bars are not positioned on the steel flinger.
4. With assistance, position viscous coupling assembly onto press bed, with suitable press bars located on the support bearings as shown.
5. Position **LRT-37-011/2** thrust button onto viscous coupling splines.
6. With assistance, press the splined end of the viscous coupling unit through the support bearing. Take care that the viscous coupling does not drop when free of the bearing.
7. Remove viscous coupling assembly from press.

NOTE: Replace steel flinger on viscous coupling if damaged during removal of support bearing.

Refit

1. Clean flinger, bearing journal, splines and support bearings
2. Ensure that the cavities between the bearing and outer shrouds are packed with Texaco Novatex EP2 grease.

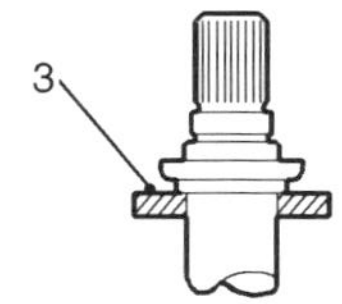

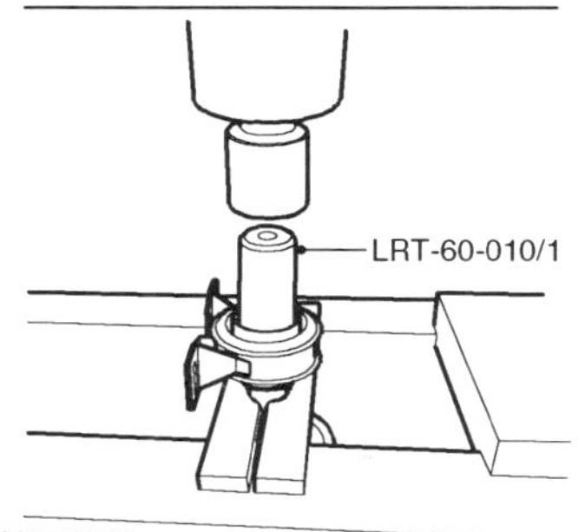

M47 0305

3. With assistance, position viscous coupling assembly onto press bed and locate the press bars onto collar on viscous coupling as shown.
4. Position **LRT-60-010/1** onto bearing inner race, and with assistance, press support bearing onto viscous coupling.
5. Remove viscous coupling assembly from press.
6. Spin support bearing and check for true running .
7. Fit rear propeller shaft. ***See this section.***

CONTENTS

Page

REAR DIFFERENTIAL

Description

The rear differential assembly serves to convert the "angle of drive" through 90° and distribute drive, in the desired proportions, to both rear wheels. The type of rear differential fitted is an integral carrier housing hypoid-gear in which the centre line of the drive pinion is mounted below the centre line of the ring gear. To minimise weight, the differential housing is manufactured in aluminium alloy, and the assembly is secured to the rear subframe by way of three rubber bushed mountings.

The differential housing incorporates the drive pinion gear shaft, which is supported by two opposed taper roller bearings fitted to the pinion and cups assembled into the carrier housing. The pinion bearing pre-load is controlled by a collapsible spacer and the torque of the pinion nut. The pinion position is controlled by a selective shim located between the inner pinion bearing cone and the pinion gear head.

The differential assembly is supported by two opposed taper roller bearings. The bearing cups are secured in the housing by removeable bearing caps. Shims are located between the differential bearing cones and differential case for controlling differential bearing pre-load and ring gear to pinion gear backlash.

The differential casing rear cover is manufactured from pressed steel and is sealed to the casing with RTV silicone sealant. The cover also incorporates the oil filler plug. A breather is located in the top of the differential casing to prevent pressurisation of the casing.

The pinion oil seal, which is fitted in the differential casing, is referred to as a "labyrinth" type seal and is especially designed to prevent contaminant ingress. The oil seal works in conjunction with a pressed steel shield, referred to as a "flinger" which is pressed on to the pinion drive flange. The two drive shafts are also sealed by "labyrinth" type oil seals fitted in the differential housing.

The differential oil level should be maintained to the bottom of the filler plug. No oil changes are specified.

DIFFERENTIAL ASSEMBLY

Service repair no - 51.15.01

Remove

1. Remove both drive shafts. ***See DRIVE SHAFTS, Repairs.***

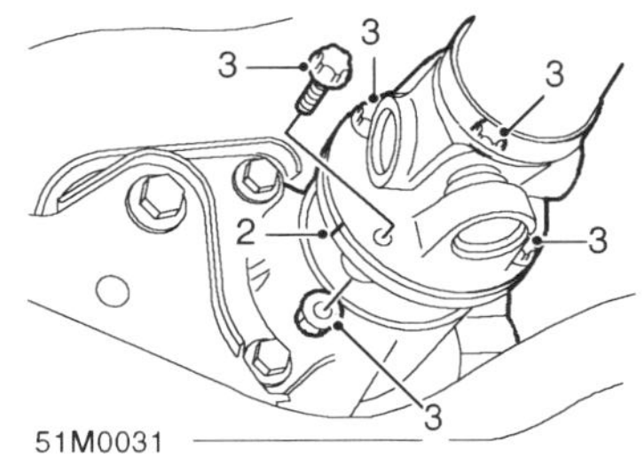

51M0031

2. Reference mark propeller shaft and pinion flanges to aid reassembly.
3. Remove 4 nuts and bolts securing propeller shaft and tie aside.
4. Support the weight of the differential assembly on a jack.

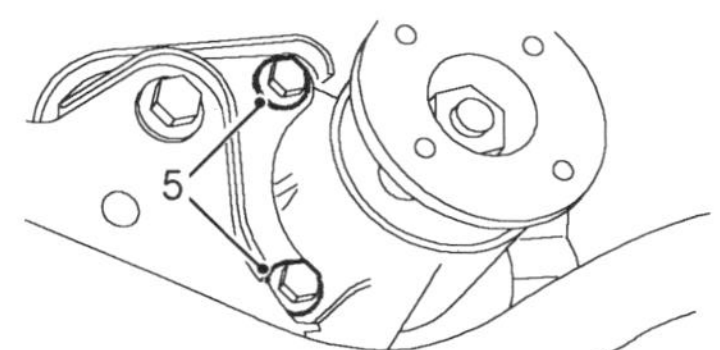

51M0032

5. Remove 2 bolts securing differential to front mounting.

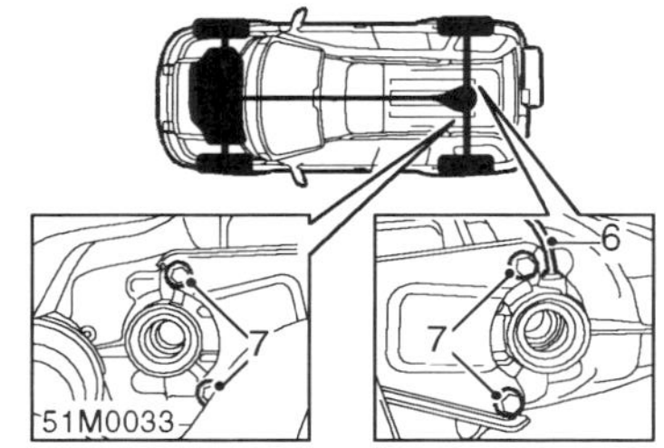

51M0033

6. Depress red locking collar and disconnect breather pipe from differential casing.
7. Remove 4 bolts securing differential to rear mountings.
8. With assistance rotate differential through 90° and remove from sub frame.

Refit

1. With assistance position differential assembly to sub frame and locate in mountings, fit but do not tighten securing bolts at this stage.
2. Position centralising jig **LRT-51-013** to align differential assembly.
3. Tighten forward bolts to 45 Nm.
4. Tighten rearward bolts to 65 Nm.
5. Remove **LRT-51-013.**
6. Connect breather pipe.
7. Align propeller shaft reference marks fit nuts and bolts and tighten to 65 Nm.
8. Fit drive shafts. ***See DRIVE SHAFTS, Repairs.***
9. Check differential oil level. ***See MAINTENANCE.***

PINION SEAL

Service repair no - 51.20.01

Remove

1. Release both rear drive shafts from differential assembly. ***See this section.***

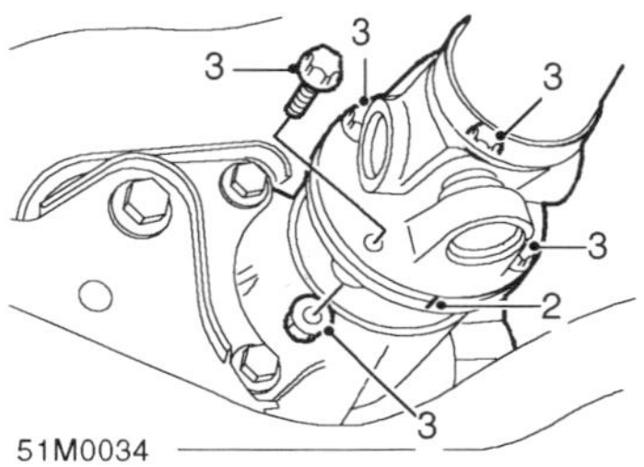

51M0034

2. Reference mark propeller shaft and pinion shaft flanges to aid reassembly.
3. Remove nuts and bolts securing propeller shaft to differential flange.
4. Tie propeller shaft aside.
5. Check and record the torque required to rotate the pinion and differential.

CAUTION: Drive shafts have to be removed to obtain correct torque to turn figure.

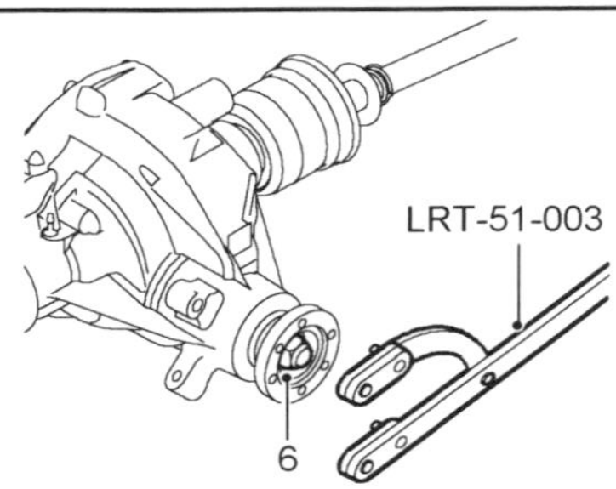

51M0035

6. Using tool **LRT-51-003** to restrain differential flange, remove and discard nut and washer securing flange.

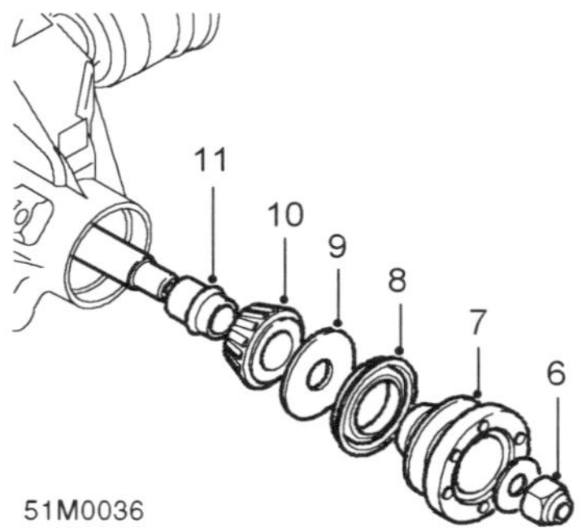

51M0036

7. Remove flange and washer from pinion.
8. Remove oil seal.
9. Remove oil thrower.
10. Remove pinion bearing inner race.
11. Remove and discard collapsible spacer.

Refit

1. Fit NEW collapsible spacer.
2. Fit pinion bearing and oil thrower.
3. Clean flange and seal recess.
4. Lubricate oil seal with clean engine oil.

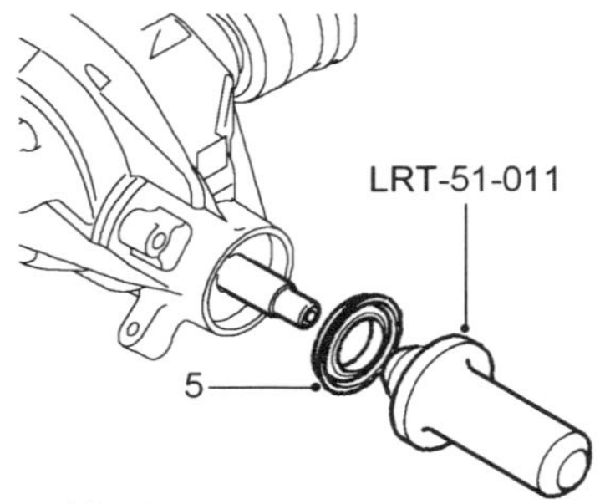

51M0037

5. Fit oil seal using **LRT-51-011.**
6. Fit flange and washer.
7. Restrain flange using **LRT-51-003** and tighten NEW nut to 176 Nm.
8. Check for end float on pinion. If end float exists continue to tighten nut until end float is removed.
9. Check torque to turn pinion figure.

NOTE: Pinion preload is equal to the amount recorded plus 00.56 Nm.

10. Continue to tighten pinion nut until correct preload is obtained.
11. Pinion preload is 1.7-2.8 Nm if higher replace collapsible spacer.

CAUTION: Do not tighten pinion nut to more than 542 Nm, or the collapsible spacer will compress too far.

12. Clean propeller shaft and differential flanges.
13. Position propeller shaft to differential, fit bolts and tighten nuts to 65 Nm.

NOTE: Ensure identification marks are aligned.

14. Fit drive shafts. ***See this section.***
15. Check differential oil level and top up if necessary.

OIL SEAL - DIFFERENTIAL

Service repair no - 51.20.36

Remove

1. Raise rear of vehicle.

WARNING: Support on safety stands.

2. Remove road wheel(s).

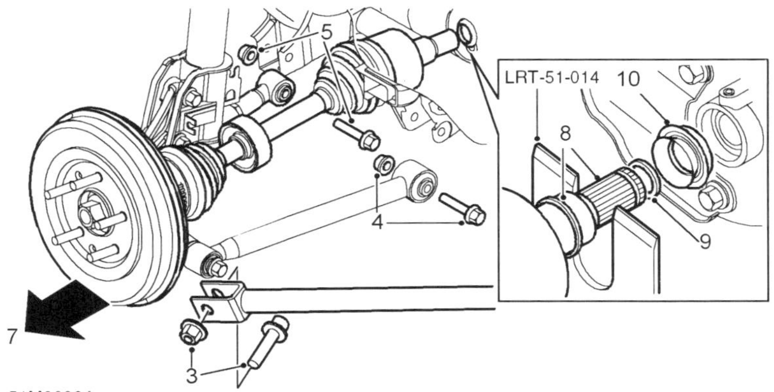

51M0030A

3. Remove nut and bolt securing trailing link to rear hub.
4. Remove nut and bolt securing fixed transverse link to sub frame.
5. Remove nut and bolt securing adjustable transverse link to sub frame.
6. Position drain tin to catch spillage.
7. With assistance pull hub assembly outwards.
8. Taking care not to damage oil seal 'Flinger', release drive shaft inner joint from differential using **LRT-51-014** and position aside.
9. Remove and discard drive shaft circlip.
10. Remove differential oil seal.

Refit

1. Clean oil seal recess.
2. Fit new oil seal using **LRT-51-012.**
3. Clean drive shaft end and differential oil seal.
4. Lubricate oil seal running surfaces.
5. Check condition of oil seal 'Flinger', renew if damaged and fit onto drive shaft.
6. Fit new circlip to drive shaft.
7. With assistance fit drive shaft to differential, push fully home to engage circlip.
8. Fit nut and bolt to adjustable transverse link and tighten to 120 Nm.
9. Fit nut and bolt to fixed transverse link and tighten to 120 Nm.
10. Fit nut and bolt to trailing link and tighten to 120 Nm.
11. Fit road wheel(s) and tighten nuts to correct torque. ***See INFORMATION, Torque wrench settings.***
12. Remove stand(s) and lower vehicle.
13. Check differential oil level. ***See MAINTENANCE.***

CONTENTS

STEERING COMPONENTS - 'K' SERIES

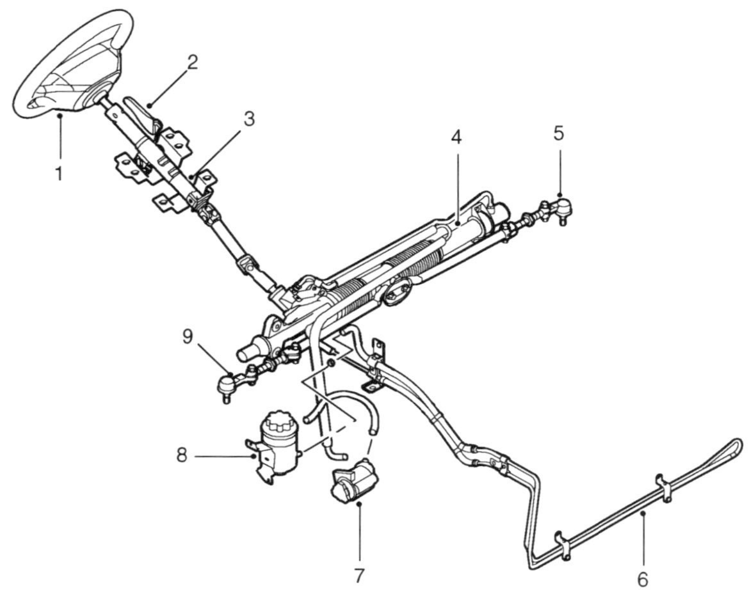

57M0704

RHD shown, LHD similar

1. Steering wheel
2. Column adjuster
3. Telescopic column
4. Steering rack
5. LH Track rod end
6. Fluid cooler
7. PAS Pump
8. Reservoir
9. RH Track rod end

STEERING COMPONENTS - 'L' SERIES

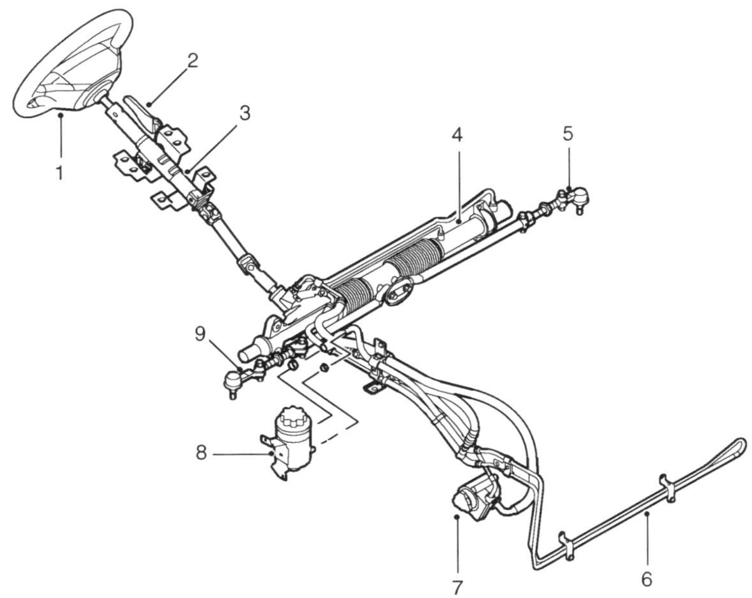

RHD shown, LHD similar

1. Steering wheel
2. Column adjuster
3. Telescopic column
4. Steering rack
5. LH Track rod end
6. Fluid cooler
7. PAS Pump
8. Reservoir
9. RH Track rod end

STEERING DESCRIPTION

The major steering components comprise a shock absorbing telescopic steering column, a power assisted steering rack, a power assisted steering (PAS) pump, a fluid reservoir,a fluid cooler and fluid pipes and hoses.

Steering Column

The steering column design incorporates an energy absorbing mechanism to reduce driver impact loads in the event of a collision. The column is mounted on four captive studs which are located in an extension to the bulkhead. The two lower mountings are fixed and cannot move when loads are applied to them. The upper mounting is designed to dis-engage or deform when a load is applied, allowing the column to collapse in the event of an accident. The steering column is adjustable to allow the steering wheel to be moved vertically up or down to the desired position. The steering column must be replaced as a complete assembly if necessary.

The upper column tube is telescopic and can slide over the lower column tube. The upper column tube provides for the location of the steering lock and ignition switch and also the steering switch gear and a rotary coupler. The rotary coupler provides the electrical connection for the steering wheel mounted airbag and horn switches.

The central shaft comprises of two parts and is located in bearings in the upper and lower column tubes. The upper shaft is located inside the lower shaft. Mating cross holes in each shaft are connected by nylon injection moulded shear pins.

The upper shaft is splined to accept the steering wheel. The lower shaft is connected by a universal joint to the intermediate shaft. A second universal joint on the opposite end of the intermediate shaft is attached to a split adaptor. The adaptor is splined and mates with the splined rotor shaft from the steering rack.

The upper mounting bracket has two open slots with a PTFE coated, metal 'U' clip over each slot. Two soft metal 'curling' plates are riveted to the mounting bracket and cover the slots.

The mounting studs pass through the 'U' clips and the curling plates. The lock nuts that retain the upper mountings to the bulkhead extension are tightened to between 12 and 15 Nm. This torque figure controls the breakout load required to move the upper mounting brackets from the studs in the bulkhead extension and is critical to the crash performance of the column.

Energy absorbtion is achieved by the following mechansim:
When an axial load is applied to the steering column, the mounting bracket deforms or slides out of the 'U' clips and the curling plates deform. The 'U' clips remain captive on the studs When the column mounting moves, the upper column tube slides on the lower column tube and allows approximately 63 mm (2.5 in.) maximum of axial movement. The nylon injection moulded shear pins holding the upper and lower shafts together shear, allowing the central shaft to telescope the same amount as the column tubes.

If, in the event of a collision where the steering rack itself moves, two universal joints in the column allow the intermediate shaft to articulate, minimizing movement of the column towards the driver. If movement continues after articulation of the intermediate shaft, the injection moulded shear pins, retaining the two halves of the central shaft, shear causing the shafts to 'telescope' together reducing further column intrusion.

The steering wheel comprises a cast centre and wire frame onto which the soft polyurethane foam is moulded. A horn switch is located at each side of the wheel. Both switches are connected by wires to the rotary coupler connector.

Protection to the drivers face and upper torso is provided by an SRS airbag located in the centre of the steering wheel under a plastic cover.

The column adjuster is located on the left hand side of the steering column and allows the steering column and wheel to be tilted up or down over a range of approximately 3.5° or 30 mm of vertical movement of the steering wheel. The column adjuster comprises a bolt which passes through each side of the column upper mounting bracket. The column adjustment lever is attached to a two start left hand threaded nut which screws onto the bolt.

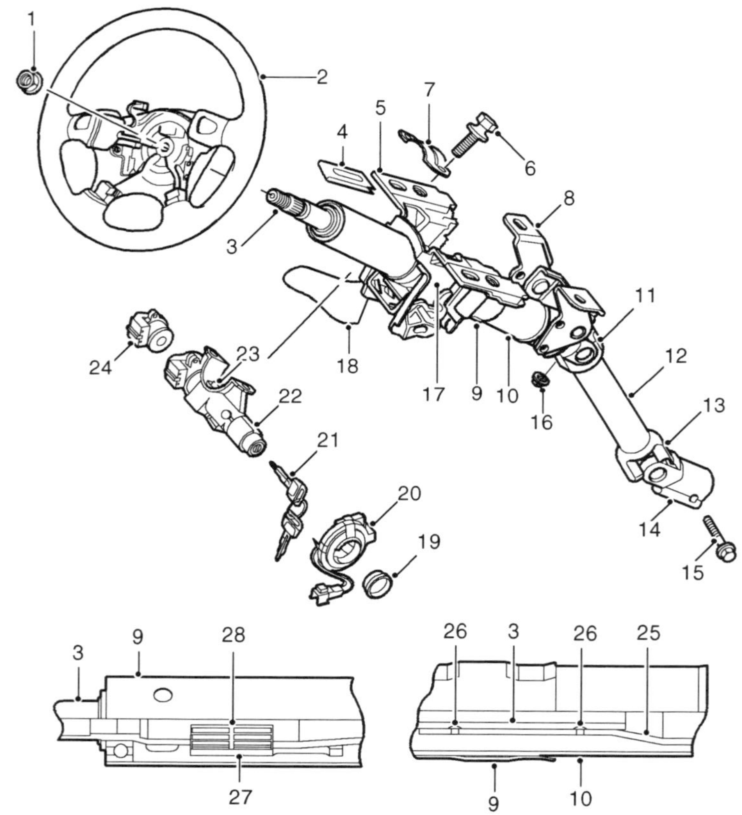

STEERING COLUMN

1. Locknut
2. Steering wheel
3. Upper shaft
4. 'U' Clip - 2 off
5. 'Curling' plate - 2 off
6. Shear bolt - 2 off
7. Clamp plate
8. Lower mounting
9. Upper column tube
10. Lower column tube
11. Universal joint
12. Intermediate shaft
13. Universal joint
14. Adaptor
15. Clamp bolt
16. Locknut, Mounting - 4 off
17. Upper mounting
18. Column adjuster
19. Light ring, ignition switch
20. Passive coil
21. Vehicle key
22. Steering column lock assembly
23. Lock bolt
24. Ignition switch
25. Lower shaft
26. Injection moulded shear pins
27. Lock collar
28. Wave form interference ring

When the lever is lowered the nut is slackened and allows the column to be moved up or down to the desired position. Lifting the lever upwards tightens the nut, clamping the mounting bracket to the column, retaining the steering column in the selected position.

NOTE: The nut tightening torque is 10.5 Nm which gives the correct 'feel' to the lever operation.

The steering lock houses the ignition switch, ignition illumination light ring, key lock barrel and the alarm passive coil

The steering lock is attached to the upper column with a clamp plate and two shear bolts. The bolts are tightened to a torque which shears off the heads of the bolts preventing easy removal of the steering lock.

The steering lock operates by a bolt, which emerges when the ignition key is turned to position 'O' and the ignition key removed. The bolt engages in a lock collar located on the upper shaft in the upper column tube. The lock collar is attached to the upper shaft by a 'wave form' interference ring. The lock collar is allowed to slip on the upper shaft if a torque of 200 Nm or higher is applied. This prevents damage to the steering lock, yet still prevents the vehicle from being driven.

The steering lock is designed to be resistant to slide hammer, shock retraction and scaffold pole attack and cannot be damaged by torque transmitted through the column.

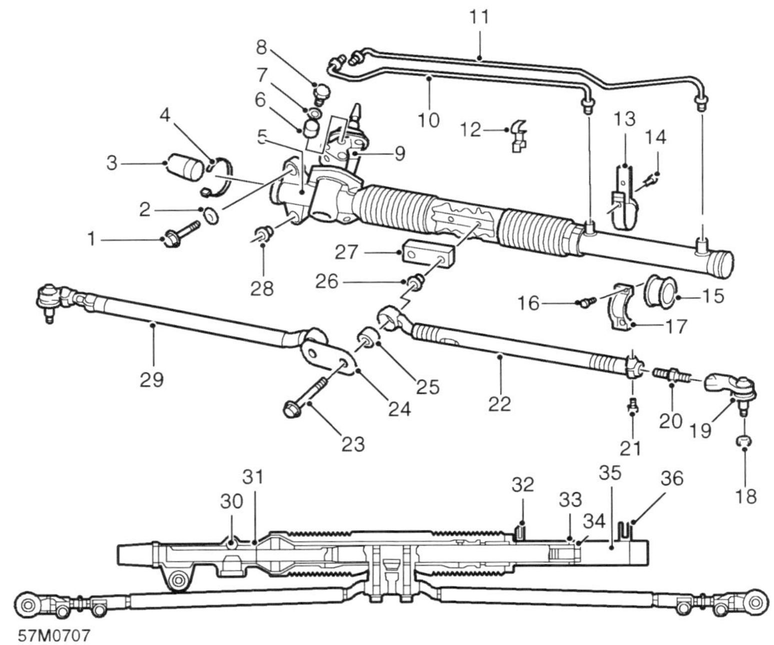

STEERING RACK - RHD SHOWN, LHD SIMILAR

1. Flanged bolt - 2 off
2. Washer - 1 off (lower bolt only)
3. Dust cover
4. Tie
5. Steering rack casting
6. Non return valve
7. Seal
8. Adaptor
9. Valve unit
10. Feed pipe (6 mm dia.)
11. Feed pipe (10 mm dia)
12. Pipe clip - 2 off
13. Pipe support bracket
14. Bolt
15. Rack mounting cushion
16. Bolt - 2 off
17. Rack mounting bracket
18. Nut - 2 off
19. Track rod end - 2 off
20. Turnbuckle - 2 off
21. Bolt - 4 off
22. Track rod LH
23. Track rod bolt - 2 off
24. Support plate
25. Inner track rod bush - 2 off
26. Spacer - 2 off
27. Slider and bush assembly
28. Mounting bush - 2 off
29. Track rod RH
30. Steering pinion
31. Steering rack
32. Cylinder annulus port
33. Piston seal
34. Piston head
35. Cylinder
36. Cylinder full area port

Steering Rack

The steering rack is unique in its design having the track rods mounted at a central location on the rack. The track rods are very long and combined with the optimized steering geometry provide low levels of 'bump steer'.

The steering rack is mounted in the engine compartment on the lower part of the bulkhead. The rack is retained with two bolts through cast lugs near the valve unit and two bolts which secure a clamp over the opposite end of the rack. The lower bolt through the cast lug is fitted with a large washer. The steering rack is handed for left and right hand drive vehicles.

The rack requires 3.16 turns from lock to lock and the rack and pinion has an overall ratio of 19.6:1.

A valve unit is fitted to one end of the steering rack and connects, via a splined rotor shaft, to the adaptor of the steering column. The valve unit has four hydraulic connections; a pressure feed from the PAS pump, a return line and two pressure lines to the annulus and full area of the hydraulic cylinder.

A rotor shaft, which is located through the valve unit, is connected to a pinion gear which drives on a rack which, in turn is connected to the piston rod in the hydraulic cylinder.

At a central position on the rack are two threaded holes which allow for the attachment of the track rods. Rubber bellows cover the movement area of the rack.

Two hydraulic ports at each end of the hydraulic cylinder of the rack are connected by metal pipes to the valve unit. The ports supply hydraulic pressure from the valve unit to the annulus and full area of the cylinder. The cylinder end of the piston rod is fitted with a piston which houses a piston seal.

The track rods are fitted with rubber bushes which are hard enough to give positive feel to the steering but at the same time reduce unwanted feedback through the track rod. Each track rod is fitted with a track rod end. The track rod end is a ball joint which locates on an extended bracket on the suspension strut and secured with a lock nut. A turnbuckle is screwed into the track rod and the track rod end and allows for the adjustment of the steering alignment.

The track rods are located on a bushed slider which locates on the rack. Two spacers are located between the slider and the track rods. Two flanged bolts secure the track rods to the rack.

Valve Unit

The valve unit is an integral part of the steering rack. The principal function of the valve unit is to provide maximum power assistance (ie; when parking) with minimum effort required to turn the steering wheel.

The cast outer casing of the valve unit has four ports which provide the connections for pressure feed from the pump, return to the fluid reservoir and pressure feed from the valve unit to the annulus and full area of the cylinder. A non return valve and seal is fitted in the pressure feed port from the PAS pump.

The valve unit comprises an outer sleeve, rotor, torsion bar and a pinion shaft. The valve unit is coaxial with the pinion shaft which is connected to the steering column via the input shaft. The valve unit components are located in a housing which is screwed to a mating casting on the steering rack main body and secured with screws.

The outer sleeve is located in the main bore of the valve unit. Three annular grooves are machined on its outer diameter. PTFE rings are located between the grooves and seal against the bore of the valve unit. Holes are drilled radially in each annular groove through the wall of the sleeve. The bore of the outer sleeve is machined to accept the input shaft. Six equally spaced slots are machined in the bore of the sleeve. The ends of the slots are closed and do not continue to the ends of the outer sleeve. The radial holes in the outer sleeve are drilled into each slot.

The input shaft is splined at its outer end and has a cross hole for location of the torsion bar. The inner end has splines which are a loose fit in corresponding splines in the pinion shaft. The width of the splines allows the torsion bar to twist several degrees before the splines contact one another. The splined coupling between the input shaft and the pinion shaft ensures that if the power steering fails, the steering can be operated manually without overstressing the torsion bar. The central portion of the input shaft has equally spaced longitudinal slots machined in its circumference. The slots are arranged alternately around the input shaft.

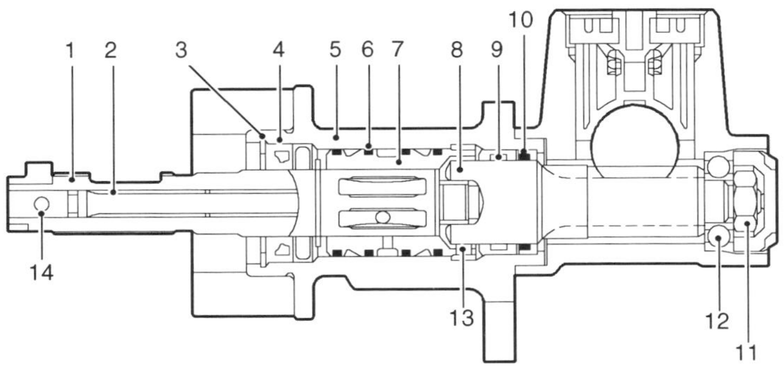

57M0708

VALVE UNIT

1. Input shaft
2. Torsion bar
3. Circlip
4. Oil seal
5. Valve housing
6. PTFE ring - 4 off
7. Outer sleeve
8. Pinion shaft
9. Bearing
10. Oil seal
11. Nut
12. Bearing
13. Pin - Pinion shaft to torsion bar
14. Pin - Rotor to torsion bar

The torsion bar is fitted inside the rotor and is connected to the input shaft and the pinion shaft with pins. The central diameter of the torsion bar is machined to a smaller diameter than at each end. The smaller diameter allows the torsion bar to twist in response to torque applied from the steering wheel in relation to grip of the tyres on the road surface.

The pinion shaft has machined teeth on its central diameter which mate with the teeth on the steering rack. A bore in the upper end is machined with loose splines which mate with similar splines on the rotor. The pinion shaft locates in a cast housing which is part of the steering rack and rotates on ball and roller bearings.

This page is intentionally left blank

Power Assisted Steering (PAS) Pump

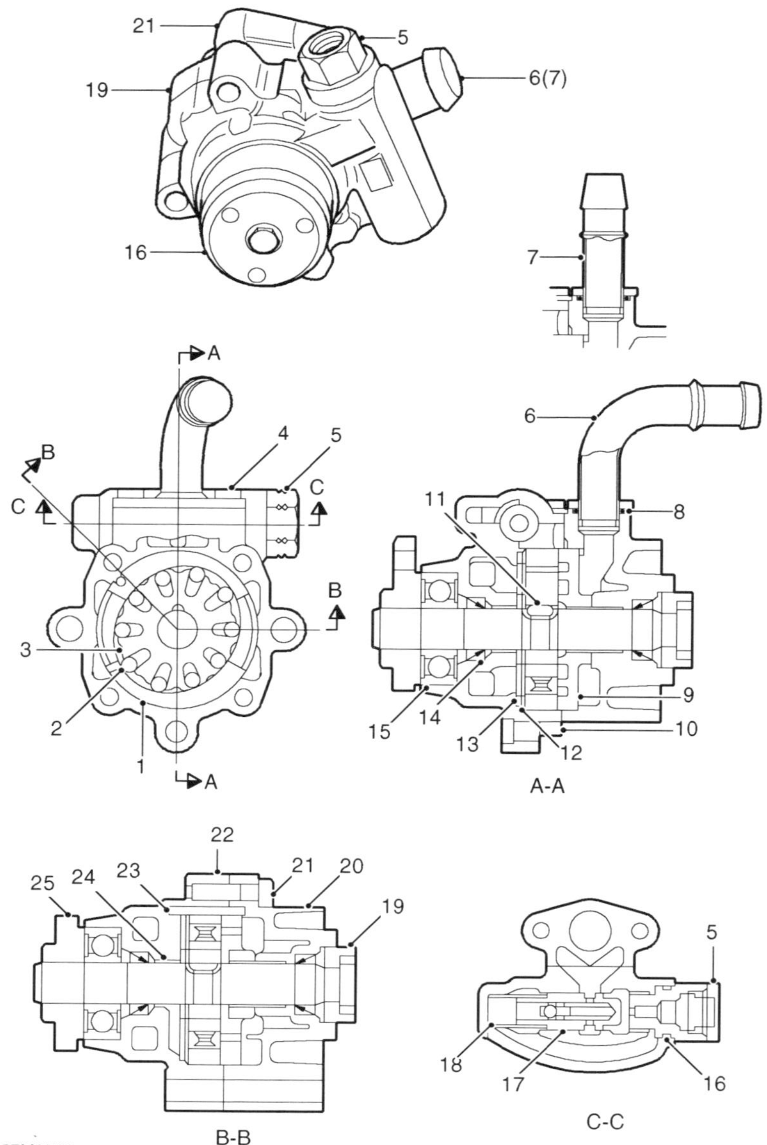

57M0709

1. Cam
2. Roller vane - 10 off
3. Carrier
4. Setscrew - 2 off
5. Discharge adaptor
6. Low pressure feed adaptor (L Series - Non A/C)
7. Low pressure feed adaptor (L Series - A/C and 'K' Series)
8. O-ring
9. End plate
10. Seal
11. Drive pin
12. Port plate
13. Seal plate
14. Oil seal
15. Ball bearing
16. O-ring
17. Valve assembly
18. Control spring
19. Drive coupling (L Series only)
20. Cover
21. Socket capscrew
22. Body
23. Dowel
24. Shaft
25. Pulley hub

PAS Pump

A vane type pump supplies hydraulic pressure to the steering rack valve unit. The pump is driven by a Poly Vee belt from the crankshaft pulley. A self adjusting tensioner is fitted to maintain the correct belt tension.

The pump comprises a body and cover which house the internal components of the pump. A pressure relief valve assembly is installed transversely in the body. The relief valve also operates as a flow control valve. The pressure relief valve limits the maximum pressure to between 89 and 95 bar (1290 and 1377 lbf/in^2). The flow control orifice limits the maximum flow to between 5.0 and 6.0 l/min (1.32 and 1.58 gal/min). The body and cover are retained by four socket capscrews and sealed with a moulded seal plate.

A shaft runs longitudinally through the pump. One end of the shaft has a hub which accepts the drive pulley. On 'L' Series engines, the opposite end has a 'D' shaped drive coupling which mates with the drive for the water pump. On K Series engines, the opposite end is closed by an extended cover. The shaft runs on a ball bearing located in the body. Oil seals at each end of the shaft prevent the leakage of hydraulic fluid.

An oval cam is located in the body. Ten roller vanes are housed in a carrier and rotate within the cam. The carrier is mounted in the centre of the shaft and receives positive drive from the shaft via a drive pin. The carrier is seated against an end plate which is located in the cover. The front of the carrier is covered by a port plate which is located against a seal plate in the body. The port plate controls the fluid flow into and out of the roller vanes during their cycle.

Fluid Reservoir

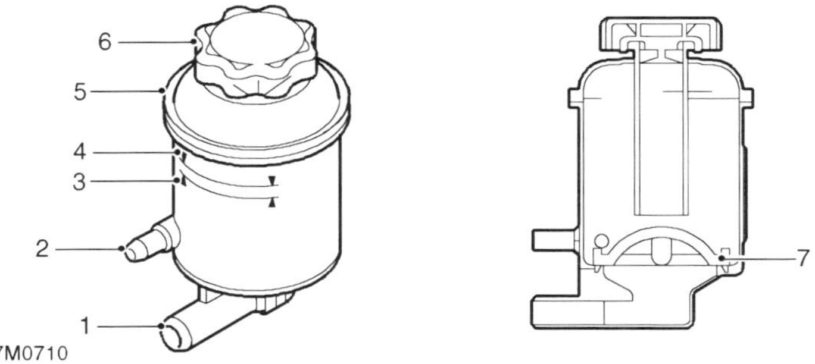

57M0710

1. Supply connection
2. Return connection
3. Lower fluid level mark
4. Upper fluid level mark
5. Reservoir body
6. Cap
7. Filter assembly

The fluid reservoir is mounted in the right hand side of the engine compartment on a bracket which is attached to the inner wing.

The reservoir comprises a body, a cap and a filter assembly. The reservoir has a capacity to the upper level mark of 335 cc (20.4 in^3)

An O-ring seal in the cap prevents leakage. The cap is pushed onto the latch and turned through 90° to lock. A breather hole is incorporated in the cap to allow changes in fluid level during operation.

A filter assembly is fitted into the bottom of the reservoir. The filter is made from fine stainless steel mesh which is moulded into the frame of the filter. The filter removes particulate matter from the fluid before it is drawn into the supply connection and is non-serviceable.

The primary function of the fluid reservoir is to hold a surplus of hydraulic fluid in the system to allow for expansion and contraction of the fluid due to temperature variations. The fluid level ensures that the supply connection is covered with fluid at all operational attitudes. Any air that may be present in the hydraulic system will be exhausted from the fluid at the reservoir.

STEERING OPERATION

PAS Pump Operation

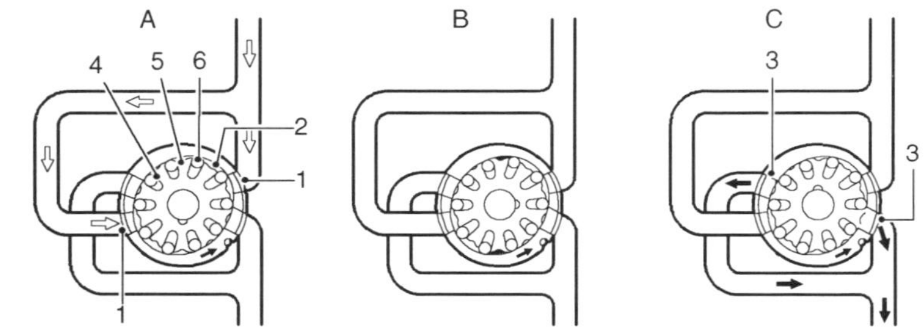

A = Fluid intake
B = Fluid movement
C = Fluid discharge

1. Inlet port
2. Roller vane chamber
3. Discharge port
4. Cam
5. Carrier
6. Roller vanes

As the pump rotates, centrifugal force causes the roller vanes to move outwards in the slots in the carrier and contact the cam. As the carrier rotates, the cam form causes the space between the rollers to increase. The increasing volume between the roller vanes, causes a depression which draws fluid into the space between the rollers.

As the carrier continues to rotate, the inlet port is closed to the roller vanes which have drawn the fluid, trapping the fluid between the rollers. As the carrier rotates further, the cam form causes the space between the roller vanes to decrease, pressurizing the fluid between the rollers.

Further rotation of the carrier, subjects the roller vanes to the discharge port and fluid is displaced under pressure from between the roller vanes into the discharge port. The space between each pair of rollers is subjected to this cycle twice for every revolution of the pump.

Pump Flow Control Valve Operation

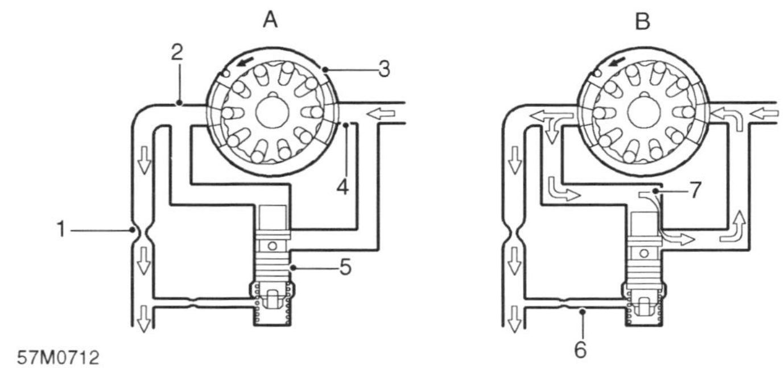

A = Fluid intake
B = Fluid discharge

1. Metering orifice
2. Discharge port
3. Pump
4. Inlet port
5. Flow control valve
6. Relief valve passage
7. Recirculation passage

The pump is a positive displacement type pump and potential output from the pump increases proportionally to engine speed. A flow control valve is fitted to the pump to maintain a constant predetermined flow regardless of engine speed. The flow control valve controls the flow of fluid and increases or decreases the flow discharged from the pump to compensate for engine speed variations.

With the engine at idle the discharge flow from the pump is low and the full flow from the pump is delivered to the valve unit. As engine speed increases, the flow delivered by the pump increases proportionally.

A pressure difference is created between each side of the metering orifice as the engine speed increases, the higher pressure being felt at the pump side of the metering orifice. This higher pressure is also felt at the top of the flow control valve via the recirculation passage. The lower pressure on the discharge side of the metering orifice is felt at the bottom of the flow control valve via the relief valve passage.

When the pressure at the top of the flow control valve exceeds the rating of the flow control valve spring, the valve begins to open against the spring pressure and the lower pressure at the discharge side of the metering orifice. Fluid is allowed to flow through the recirculation passage and recirculate through the pump.

As engine speed increases, the flow control valve is pushed down further, increasing the flow through the recirculation passage.

Pump Pressure Relief Valve Operation

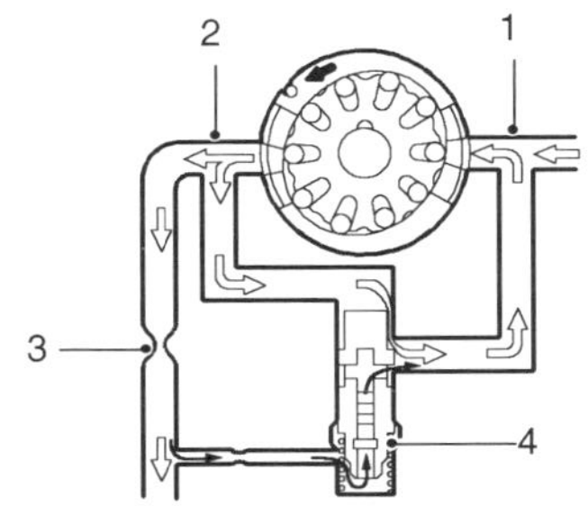

57M0713

A = Fluid intake
B = Fluid discharge

1. Inlet port
2. Discharge port
3. Metering orifice
4. Pressure relief valve

A pressure relief valve is located in the centre of the flow control valve. If the pressure on the discharge side of the metering orifice reaches a predetermined level, a spring loaded ball in the centre of the valve will lift from its seat and allow pressurized fluid to recirculate within the pump.

The pressure relief valve will operate if the discharge from the pump is restricted, steering held at full lock. If the discharge from the pump is completely blocked, all fluid discharged will be recirculated through the pump.

As no fresh oil is drawn into the pump from the reservoir, the fluid temperature inside the pump will increase quickly. Consequentially, periods of operation of full lock should be kept to minimum to avoid overheating the pump and the fluid within it.

Steering Rack Operation

Rotary movement of the steering wheel is transferred via the steering column to the valve unit which is mounted on the steering rack. The rotary movement of the steering is converted into linear movement of the steering rack through the rack and pinion. With the engine running and the PAS pump operating, pressurized fluid is available to the steering rack for power assistance.

Neutral Position

With no movement of the steering wheel being applied, fluid flows from the pump to the valve unit. The slots in the outer sleeve and the rotor are so aligned that the fluid pressure flows across the valve unit. Some pressure is applied to the feed and return ports which in turn is felt at either side of the piston in the hydraulic cylinder. With the forces equal on each side of the cylinder, the steering remains in the neutral position. The majority of the fluid delivered from the pump is returned from the valve unit, and via the fluid cooler, back to the reservoir. With the majority of the fluid being returned to the reservoir, the pressure available at each side of the piston is very low.

Left steering

Anti-clockwise rotation of the steering wheel in turn rotates the rotor and the torsion bar in the same direction. The slots in the rotor move out of their neutral alignment and block the return flow of fluid to the reservoir. Fluid pressure from the pump now flows from the pump into the newly aligned slots in the rotor and outer sleeve. The pressure is directed by the alignment of the slots into the left hand side of the hydraulic cylinder where the pressure increases. The right hand side of the hydraulic cylinder is opened to return and allows fluid displaced from the right hand side of the piston to flow to the reservoir. The pressure difference on the left and right hand sides of the piston in the cylinder gives the power assistance to turn the steering.

Right steering

Clockwise rotation of the steering wheel in turn rotates the rotor and the torsion bar in the same direction. The slots in the rotor move out of their neutral alignment and block the return flow of fluid to the reservoir. Fluid pressure from the pump now flows from the pump into the newly aligned slots in the rotor and outer sleeve. The pressure is directed by the alignment of the slots into the right hand side of the hydraulic cylinder where the pressure increases. The left hand side of the hydraulic cylinder is opened to return and allows fluid displaced from the left hand side of the piston to flow to the reservoir. The pressure difference on the left and right hand sides of the piston in the cylinder gives the power assistance to turn the steering.

Progressive Assistance

Progressive power assistance is dependant on the amount of road wheel resistance opposing the turning of the front wheels. When the steering wheel is turned to the left or right, the rotary movement is transferred through the steering column to the rotor shaft which rotates the same amount as the steering wheel. The rotary movement is also transferred from the rotor to the torsion bar. If the road wheel resistance is high, (when parking), the torsion bar will twist. The twisting of the torsion bar means that the rotary movement of the pinion and the sleeve is slightly less than that of the rotor.

The twisting of the torsion bar moves the slots in the rotor and the torsion bar out of alignment, resulting in the gaps between both sets of slots becoming larger. The greater the resistance of the road wheels to the steering rotary movement, the greater the misalignment of the slots in the rotor and torsion bar. As the misalignment becomes greater, the fluid pressure passing to the applicable side of the hydraulic cylinder increases.

When the road wheel resistance reduces or less effort is applied to the turning of the steering wheel, the reduced torque applied to the rotor allows the torsion bar to unwind. This reduces the misalignment between the slots in the rotor and the torsion bar, reducing the fluid pressure applied to the applicable side of the hydraulic cylinder.

Valve Unit

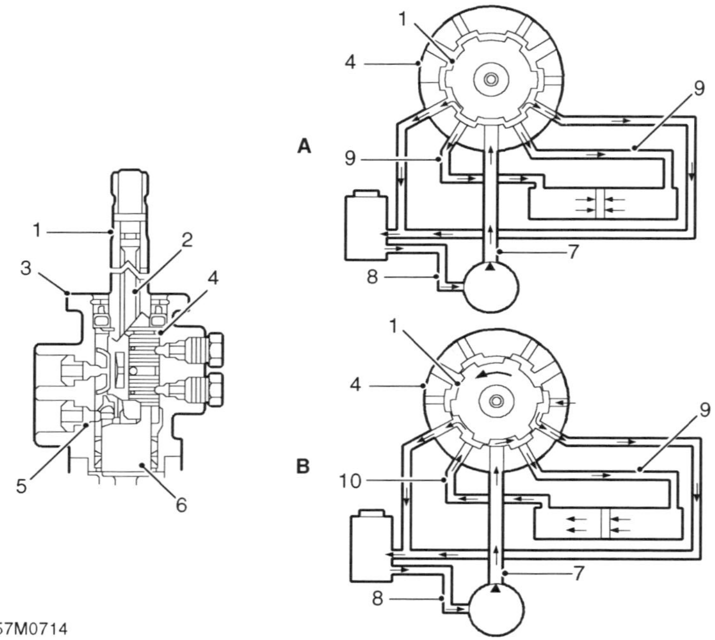

57M0714

A = Neutral Steering
B = Left Steering (Right Steering Similar)

1. Rotor
2. Torsion bar
3. Valve unit
4. Sleeve
5. Pin - Torsion bar to pinion shaft
6. Pinion shaft
7. Pressure from pump
8. Return to pump
9. Pressure flow to hydraulic cylinder
10. Return flow from cylinder

Hydraulic Circuit

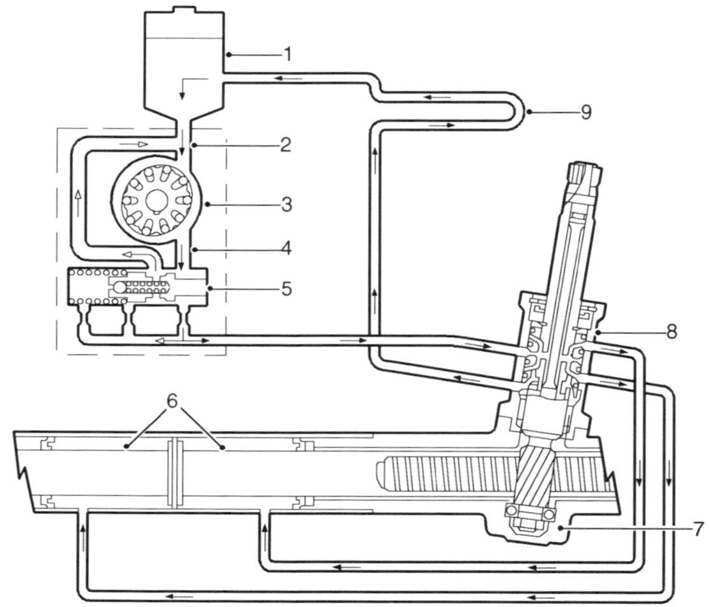

57M0715

1. Reservoir
2. Low pressure suction line
3. PAS Pump
4. Discharge port
5. Flow control/relief valve
6. Hydraulic cylinder pressure area
7. Steering rack and pinion gear
8. Valve unit
9. Fluid cooler

Hydraulic Circuit Operation

When the engine is started, the pump draws fluid from the reservoir down the low pressure suction line. The fluid passes through the pump and emerges as pressurised fluid at the discharge port where it passes through a hose to a valve unit. If no steering effort is applied, the pressure is applied equally to each side of the piston in the hydraulic cylinder. The remainder of the flow is returned from the valve unit to the reservoir via the fluid cooler.

If steering effort is applied in either direction, the fluid pressure is directed to the applicable side of the piston in the hydraulic cylinder, providing power assistance to reduce the steering effort required. The fluid displaced by the movement of the piston in the cylinder is returned through the valve unit to the reservoir via the fluid cooler.

The fluid cooler reduces the fluid temperature which prolongs the life of the hoses and seals in the system.

POWER ASSISTED STEERING (PAS) SYSTEM BLEED

Service repair no - 57.15.02

NOTE: The front road wheels need to be in the straight ahead position when adding fluid to the reservoir.

1. Clean reservoir around filler cap and fluid level indicators.

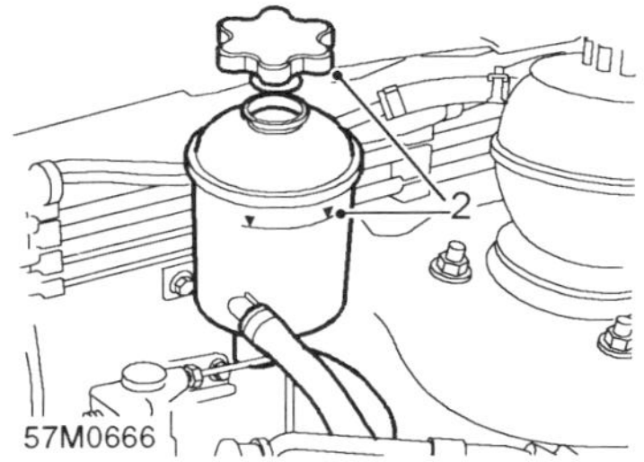

57M0666

2. Remove filler cap from reservoir and fill reservoir to 'UPPER' mark with Dexron II D power steering fluid

Petrol Models

3. Disconnect ignition coil h.t. lead from distributor to prevent engine starting.

Diesel Models

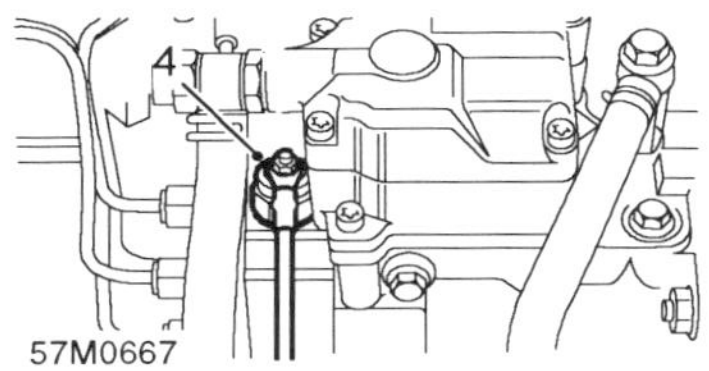

57M0667

4. Remove nut securing lead to fuel cut-off solenoid, disconnect and insulate lead.

All Models

5. Crank engine for 5 seconds to prime steering pump.
6. Top-up steering fluid reservoir.
7. Turn steering to full RH lock and crank engine for 5 seconds.
8. Top-up steering fluid reservoir.
9. Turn steering to full LH lock and crank engine for 5 seconds.
10. Top-up steering fluid reservoir.

Petrol Models

11. Connect ignition coil h.t. lead to distributor.

Diesel Models

12. Remove insulation from fuel cut-off lead, connect lead and tighten nut to 2.5 Nm.

All Models

13. Start and run engine for 2 minutes to circulate fluid through the system.

CAUTION: Do not hold steering at full lock for longer than 10 seconds.

14. Turn steering fully to LH then RH locks.
15. Switch off engine.
16. Check power steering fluid, if aerated, wait until fluid is free from bubbles then top-up reservoir to 'UPPER' level mark.
17. Fit reservoir filler cap.

WHEEL ALIGNMENT - FRONT

Service repair no - 57.65.01

Check

1. Ensure tyre pressures are correct and vehicle is at kerbside weight (unladen).
2. Roll vehicle backwards and forwards to relieve stresses in steering and suspension.
3. Ensure that equipment is properly calibrated.

NOTE: Only use equipment recommended for use by Land Rover.

4. Check front wheel alignment is within tolerance.

NOTE: The following steering geometry settings are given in:
A -Degrees and minutes
B - Decimal parts of a degree
C - Millimetres.
Settings are for a vehicle at unladen weight.

DATA
Front wheel alignment - toe-out - total:
A - 0° 20' ± 0° 15'
B - 0.3° ± 0.25°
C - 5½ J x 15 wheel - 2.211 mm ± 0.710 mm
C - 6J x 16 wheel - 2.360 mm ± 1.811 mm

Adjust

1. Mark position of track rod ends for reference.

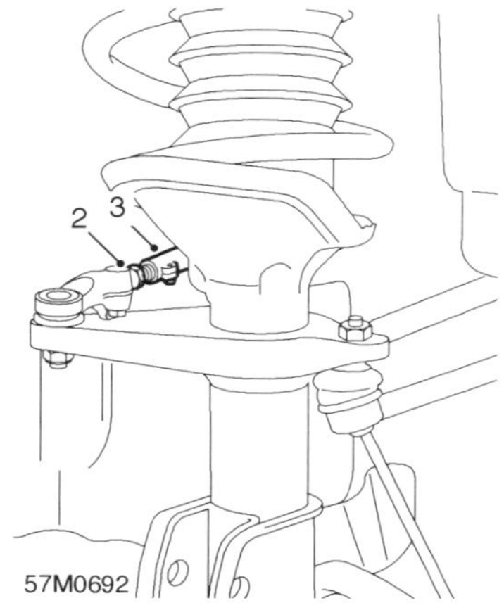

57M0692

2. Loosen track rod and track rod end pinch bolts.
3. Rotate turn buckle to obtain correct alignment. Ensure that ball joint is not rotated.

CAUTION: Both track rods must be rotated an equal amount.

4. Recheck front wheel alignment.
5. Tighten track rod and track rod end pinch bolts to 28 Nm.

WHEEL ALIGNMENT - REAR

Service repair no - 57.65.06

Check

1. Ensure tyre pressures are correct and vehicle is at kerbside weight (unladen).
2. Roll vehicle backwards and forwards to relieve stresses in steering and suspension.
3. Ensure that equipment is properly calibrated.

NOTE: Only use equipment recommended for use by Land Rover.

4. Ensure front wheel alignment is correct. ***See this section.***
5. Check rear wheel alignment is within tolerance.

NOTE: The following steering geometry settings are given in:
A -Degrees and minutes
B - Decimal parts of a degree
C - Millimetres.
Settings are for a vehicle at unladen weight.

DATA
Rear wheel alignment - toe-in - total:
A - 0° 20' ± 0° 15'
B - 0.3° ± 0.25°
C - 5½ J x 15 wheel - 2.211 mm ± 1.710 mm
C - 6J x 16 wheel - 2.360 mm ± 1.811 mm

Adjust

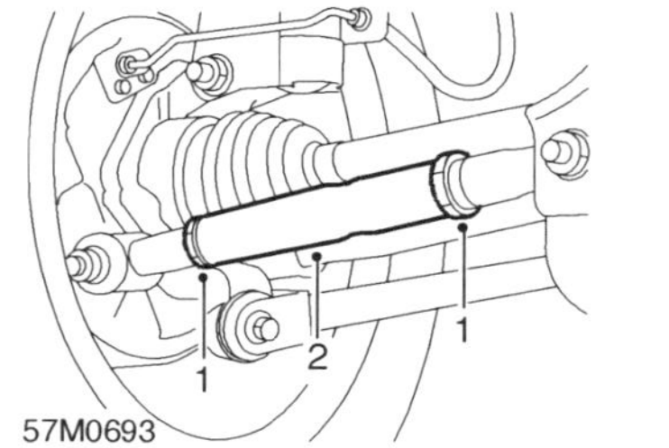

57M0693

1. Hold turnbuckle on adjustable link and loosen both lock nuts.
2. Rotate turnbuckle until toe is correct.
3. Hold turnbuckle and tighten lock nuts to 90 Nm.
4. Roll vehicle backwards and forwards to relieve stresses in suspension.
5. Repeat check and adjust operation on other side of vehicle.

POWER STEERING SYSTEM - PRESSURE TEST

Service repair no - 57.90.10/01

Test Equipment - Assembly

1. Position cloth to collect PAS fluid spillage.

'K' Series

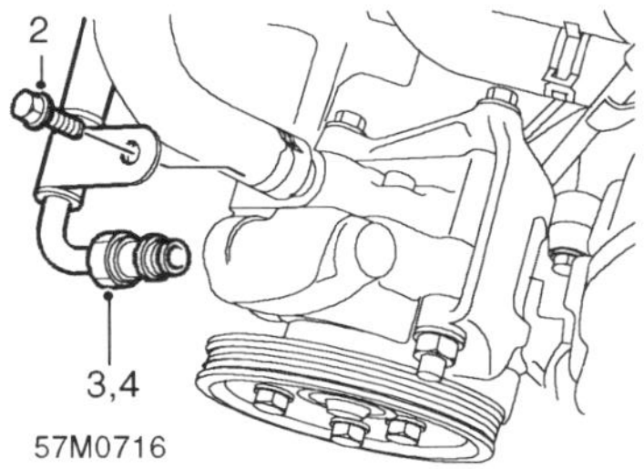

57M0716

2. Remove bolt securing PAS high pressure pipe clip to PAS pump.
3. Loosen union nut securing high pressure pipe to PAS pump.
4. Disconnect high pressure pipe from PAS pump.

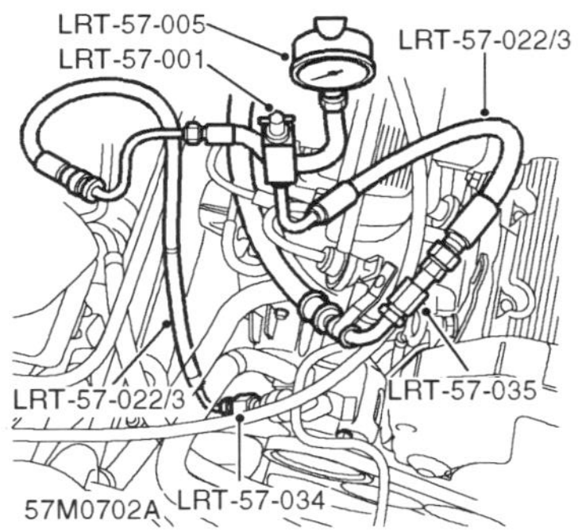

57M0702A

5. Fit adaptor **LRT-57-034** to high pressure port of PAS pump.
6. Fit adaptor **LRT-57-035** to existing high pressure hose.

'L' Series

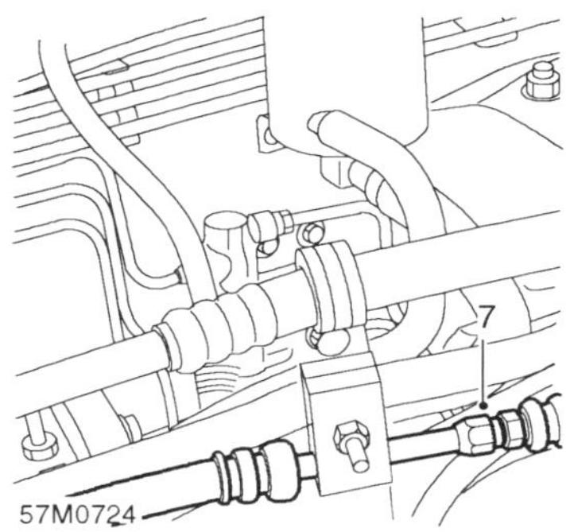

57M0724

7. Loosen union nut and disconnect high pressure pipe at support bracket on RH engine mounting.
8. Fit adaptor **LRT-57-032** to pipe from PAS pump.
9. Fit adaptor **LRT-57-033** to existing high pressure hose.

All Models

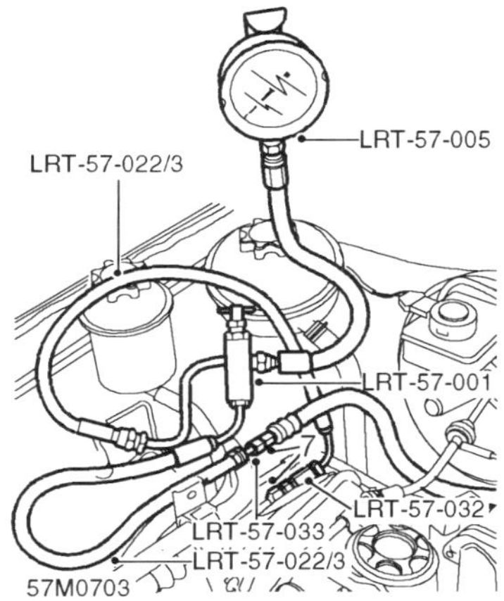

57M0703

10. Fit hose **LRT-57-022/3** to each adaptor.
11. Fit pressure gauge **LRT-57-005** to test valve **LRT-57-00.1**
12. Connect hoses **LRT-57022/3** to **LRT-57-001** and tighten all unions.

Test Procedure

13. Ensure steering system is free from leaks and maintain maximum fluid level during test.
14. With the test valve open, start the engine.
15. With the engine at idle, slowly turn the steering wheel and hold on lock.
16. Repeat pressure check in opposite lock.
17. The test pressure should be between 27 and 55 bar, dependant on road surface.
18. With the engine at idle, release the steering wheel. Pressure should read below 7 bar.
19. Pressures outside the above tolerance indicates a fault.
20. To determine if fault is in steering pump or steering rack, close the test valve for a maximum of five seconds.

CAUTION: Pump damage will occur if test valve is closed for longer periods.

21. If the gauge does not register between 85 and 97 bar (maximum pump pressure), the pump is faulty.
22. If maximum pump pressure is correct, suspect the steering rack.
23. On completion, stop the engine and remove test equipment.

'K' Series

24. Fit NEW 'O' ring to high pressure pipe, connect pipe to PAS pump and tighten union nut to 25 Nm.
25. Fit bolt securing high pressure pipe clip to pump.

'L' Series

26. Fit NEW 'O' ring, connect high pressure pipes and tighten union nut to 25 Nm.

All Models

27. Check PAS fluid level. ***See this section.***

RACK - POWER ASSISTED STEERING (PAS)

Service repair no - 57.10.01

Remove

1. Raise front of vehicle.

WARNING: Support on safety stands.

2. Remove road wheel(s).

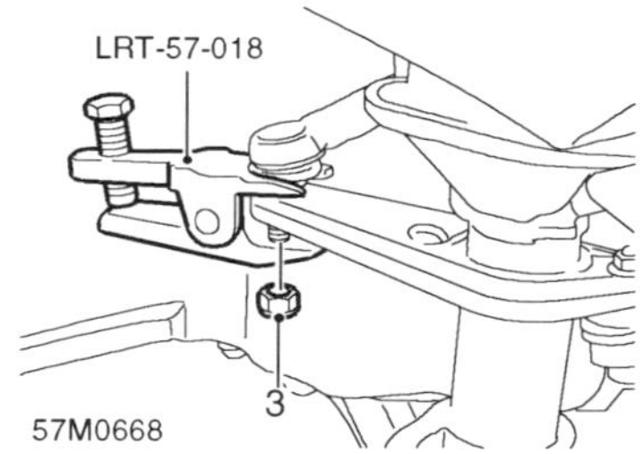

57M0668

3. Remove and discard nuts securing track rod ball joints to steering arms.
4. Use **LRT-57-018** to disconnect track rod ball joints.

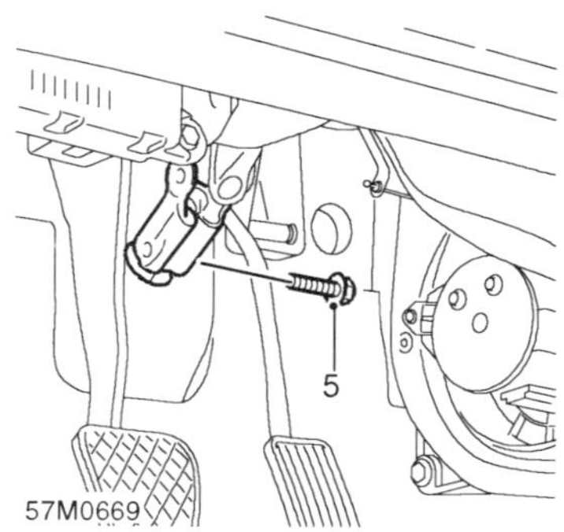

57M0669

5. Remove pinch bolt, securing steering column to PAS rack pinion.

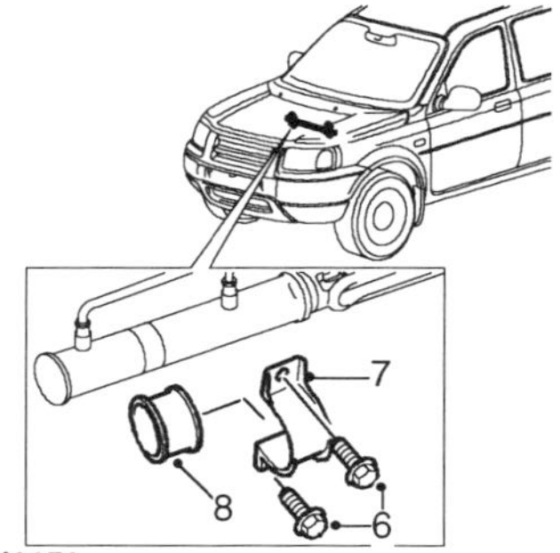

57M0670

6. Remove 2 bolts and washer securing PAS rack clamp to bulkhead.
7. Remove PAS rack clamp.
8. Remove rubber mount.

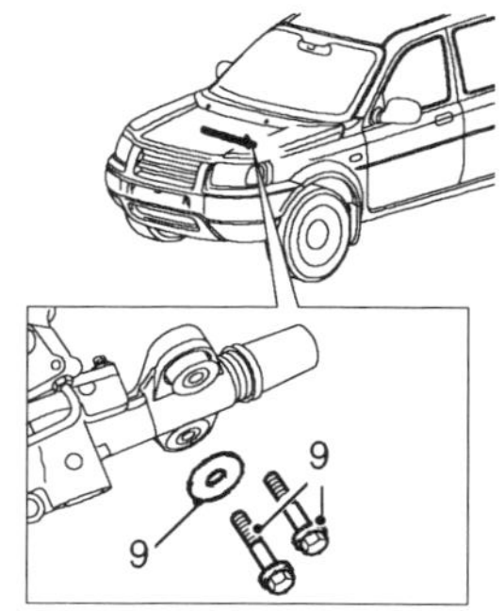

57M0671

9. Remove 2 bolts securing PAS rack mounting to bulkhead.
10. Release PAS rack pinion from steering column.

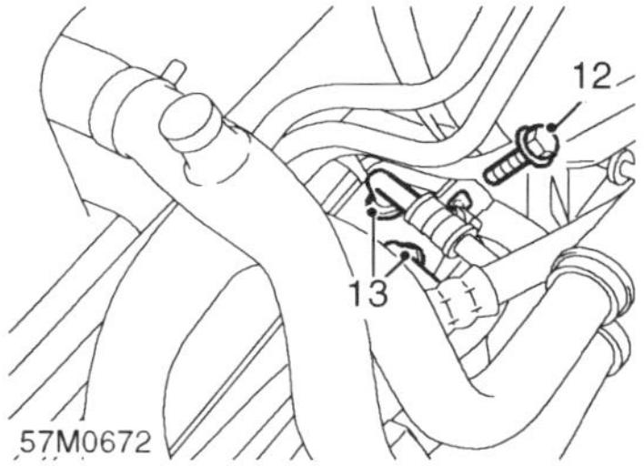

57M0672

11. Position container to collect PAS fluid spillage.
12. Remove bolt, securing pipe bracket to PAS rack.
13. Release pipe unions and disconnect fluid pipes from PAS rack.

⚠ **CAUTION: Plug the connections.**

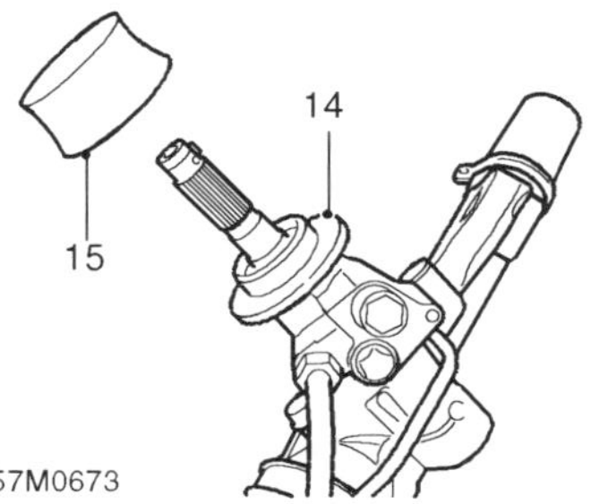

57M0673

14. With assistance, remove PAS rack from passenger side of vehicle.
15. Remove dust seal from pinion housing.

Refit

1. Fit PAS rack to vehicle from passenger side.
2. Fit dust seal to pinion housing.
3. Ensure pipe unions are clean.
4. Fit fluid pipes to PAS rack but do not tighten unions at this stage.
5. Align fluid pipe bracket to PAS rack, fit bolt but do not tighten at this stage.
6. With assistance, fit PAS rack pinion to steering column ensuring that column coupling is aligned with gear input shaft flag.
7. Fit 2 bolts, and washer on lower bolt, securing steering rack mounting to bulkhead but do not tighten at this stage.

△ NOTE: Ensure large washer is fitted to lower bolt.

8. Fit rubber mount and clamp to PAS rack.
9. Fit bolts securing clamp to bulkhead but do not tighten at this stage.
10. Tighten PAS rack mounting bolts to 45 Nm.
11. Tighten PAS clamp bolts to 45 Nm.
12. Tighten PAS rack fluid feed pipe union nut to 18 Nm.
13. Tighten PAS rack fluid return pipe union nut to 22 Nm.
14. Tighten fluid pipe bracket bolt to 8 Nm.
15. Fit pinch bolt to steering column and tighten to 32 Nm.
16. Fit ball joints to steering arms using new nuts, and tighten nuts to 55 Nm.
17. Fit road wheel(s) and tighten nuts to correct torque. ***See INFORMATION, Torque wrench settings.***
18. Remove stand(s) and lower vehicle.
19. Bleed power assisted steering system. ***See Adjustments.***
20. Check and adjust front wheel alignment. ***See Adjustments.***

GAITER - STEERING RACK

Service repair no - 57.10.29

Remove

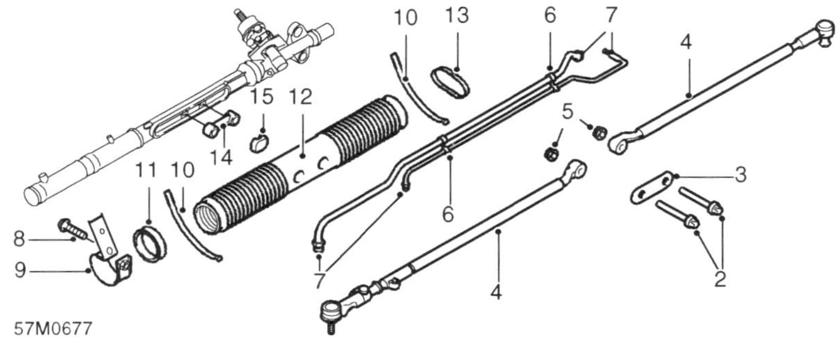

57M0677

1. Remove PAS rack assembly. ***See this section.***
2. Hold PAS rack securely and remove 2 Torx bolts securing track rods. Discard bolts.
3. Remove support plate.
4. Remove track rods.
5. Remove spacers.
6. Remove clips from PAS rack ram feed pipes.
7. Loosen 4 pipe unions and remove both ram feed pipes.

⚠ **CAUTION: Plug the connections.**

8. Remove clamp bolt from fluid pipe support bracket.
9. Remove support bracket.
10. Remove 2 gaiter securing clips.
11. Remove gaiter sealing ring.
12. Remove gaiter.
13. Remove gaiter sealing band.
14. Remove slider and clip assembly.
15. Remove clip from slider.

Refit

1. Clean remains of lubricant from PAS rack slider and clip.
2. Cut 2 hacksaw slots along thread of one of the discarded Torx bolts and use this to remove remains of patch lock from the 2 threaded holes in rack.
3. Fit the clip to slider.
4. Fit the slider and clip assembly to rack.
5. Apply grease supplied in gaiter kit to exposed rack shaft, slider and clip.
6. Fit gaiter sealing band.
7. Fit gaiter.
8. Fit gaiter sealing ring.
9. Align gaiter to slider and having ensured slider is correctly located, use track rod securing bolts to hold gaiter in position without tightening bolts so to activate Loctite.
10. Ensure gaiter is not twisted, and fit gaiter securing clips.
11. Fit fluid pipe support bracket and secure with bolt.
12. Ensure pipe unions and rack ports are clean.
13. Fit both ram feed pipes and tighten small diameter pipe union nuts to 18 Nm. and large diameter pipe union nuts to 24 Nm.
14. Fit clips to pipes.
15. Remove track rod securing bolts used to align gaiter, fit spacers, track rods and support plate to PAS rack.
16. Hold track rods parallel with PAS rack and tighten NEW Torx bolts to 100 Nm.
17. Fit PAS rack. ***See this section.***

BELT - DRIVE - PAS PUMP - 'K' SERIES

Service repair no - 57.20.02

Remove

1. Turn steering to full RH lock.

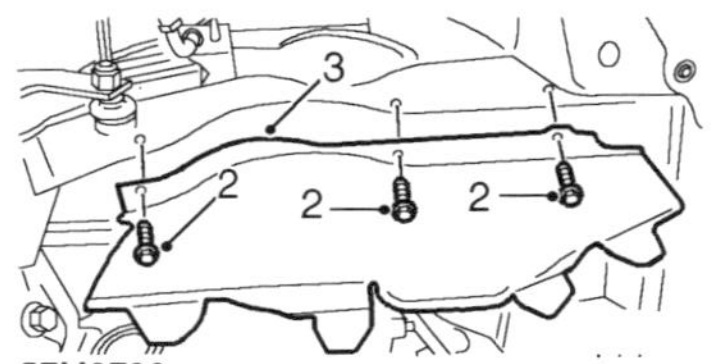

57M0726

2. Remove 3 bolts securing RH splash shield.
3. Remove RH splash shield.

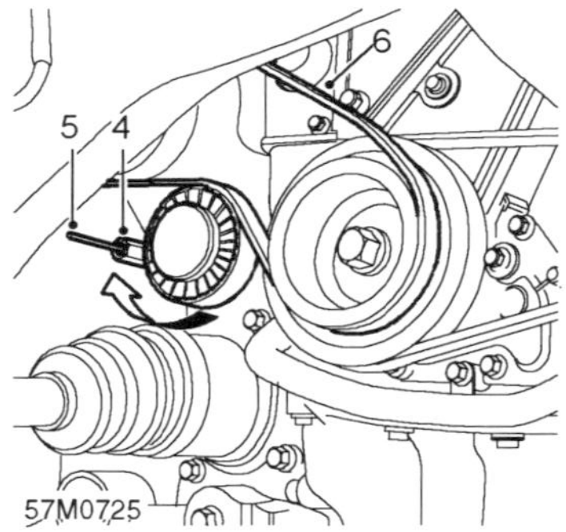

57M0725

4. Fit a 13mm spanner to hexagon on belt tensioner and rotate clockwise to release tension on drive belt.
5. Hold tensioner in this position using a suitable pin not exceeding 3mm diameter.

NOTE: Fit pin through centre of hexagon into tensioner backplate.

6. Remove and discard drive belt.

Refit

1. Ensure PAS pump belt pulleys are clean and damage free.
2. Fit NEW drive belt.

NOTE: Check belt is correctly located in pulley grooves.

3. Use a 13mm spanner and release tension from retaining pin.
4. Remove retaining pin and lower tensioner pulley onto PAS belt.
5. Fit RH splash shield and secure with bolts.

PUMP - POWER ASSISTED STEERING - L SERIES

Service repair no - 57.20.14 Models without air conditioning
Service repair no - 57.20.14/20 Models with air conditioning

Remove

1. Remove underbelly panel. ***See BODY, Exterior fittings.***
2. Remove engine acoustic cover. ***See ENGINE - 'L' SERIES, Repairs.***
3. Use a jack to support the engine under sump.

CAUTION: Place block of wood on jack to protect sump.

Models without air conditioning

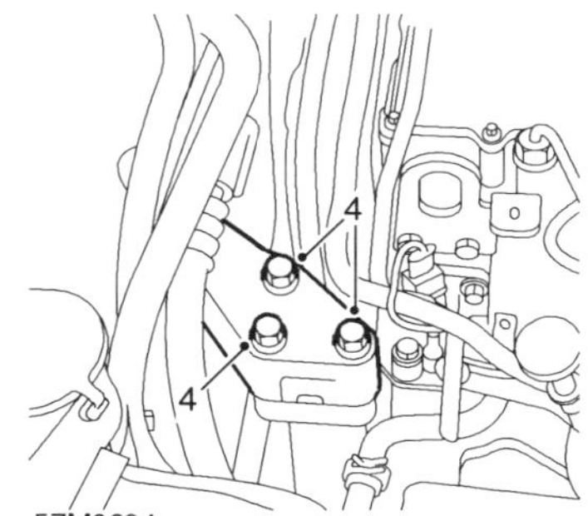

57M0694

4. Remove 3 bolts securing RH engine mounting bracket to engine.
5. Lower engine sufficient to allow access to PAS pump.

Models with air conditioning

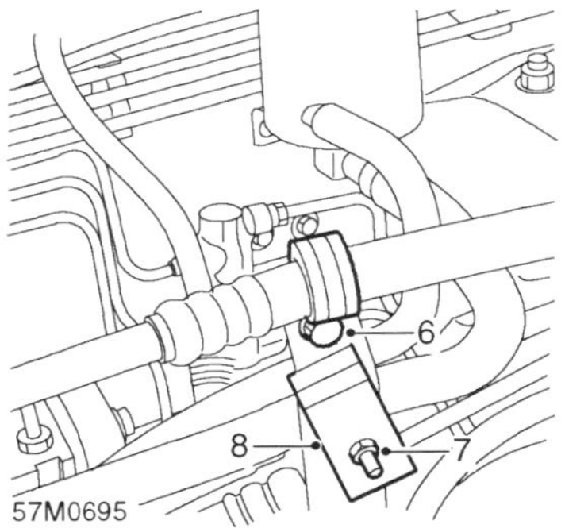

57M0695

6. Remove bolt securing air conditioning hose clip to PAS hose support bracket.
7. Remove nut and bolt securing PAS fluid hose clamp to support bracket.
8. Remove clamps from hose.

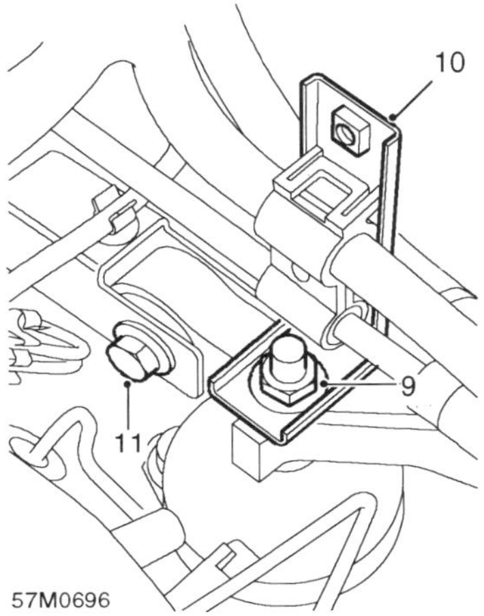

57M0696

9. Remove nut securing PAS hose support bracket to engine mounting stud.
10. Remove PAS hose support bracket.
11. Remove bolt securing engine upper tie bar to engine mounting bracket.

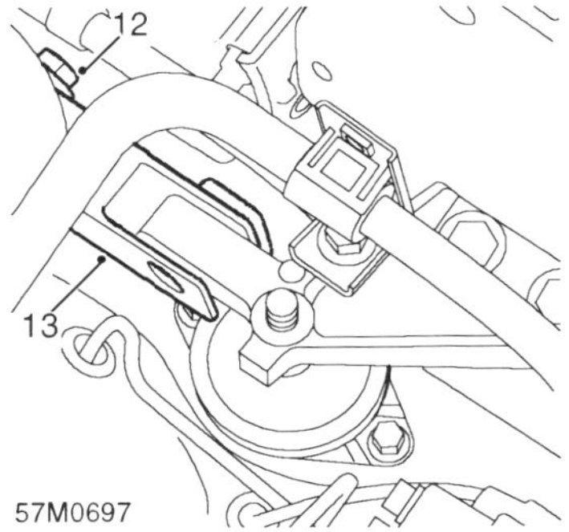

57M0697

12. Loosen bolt securing engine upper tie bar to bracket on body.
13. Raise upper tie bar to clear engine mounting bracket.

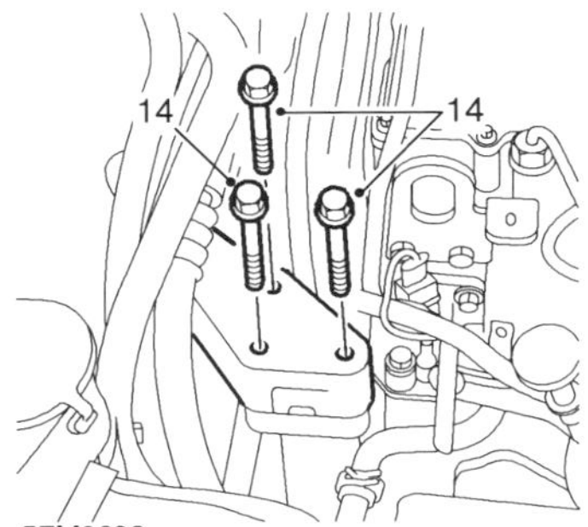

57M0698

14. Remove 3 bolts securing engine mounting bracket to engine.
15. Remove engine mounting bracket.
16. Raise engine sufficient to allow access to PAS pump.

All Models

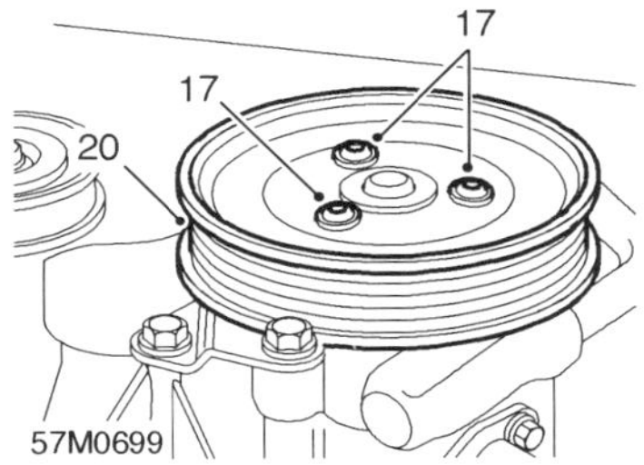

57M0699

17. Loosen 3 Torx screws securing PAS pump pulley.
18. Remove auxiliary drive belt. ***See ELECTRICAL, Repairs.***
19. Remove 3 Torx screws securing PAS pump pulley.
20. Remove PAS pump pulley.
21. Position container to collect fluid loss from PAS system.

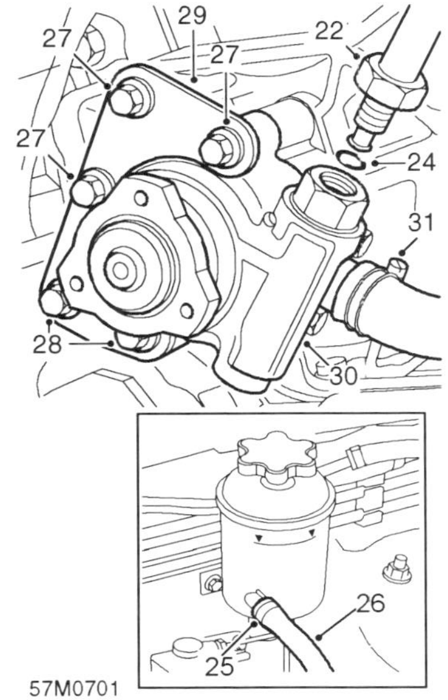

57M0701

22. Loosen union securing high pressure fluid pipe to PAS pump.

CAUTION: To prevent damage to components, use two spanners when loosening or tightening unions.

23. Disconnect high pressure pipe from pump.
24. Remove and discard 'O' ring.
25. Remove clip securing fluid feed hose to PAS fluid reservoir.
26. Disconnect feed hose from reservoir.

CAUTION: Plug the connections.

27. Remove 3 short bolts securing support bracket to PAS pump and coolant pump.
28. Remove 2 long bolts securing support bracket to PAS pump and coolant pump.
29. Remove support bracket.

30. Remove PAS pump.
31. Remove clip securing fluid feed hose to PAS pump.
32. Remove feed hose from PAS pump.

Refit

1. Fit fluid feed hose to PAS pump and secure hose with clip.
2. Clean mating face of PAS pump and coolant pump housing.
3. Align drive coupling and fit PAS pump to coolant pump.
4. Fit support bracket and tighten bolts securing pump and bracket to 25 Nm.
5. Lubricate and fit NEW 'O' ring to high pressure pipe.
6. Connect high pressure pipe to PAS pump, but do not tighten at this stage.
7. Connect fluid feed hose to reservoir and secure with clip.
8. Tighten high pressure pipe to PAS pump union to 25 Nm.
9. Ensure pulley and mating face is clean.
10. Fit PAS pump pulley and tighten screws.
11. Fit auxiliary drive belt. ***See ELECTRICAL, Repairs.***
12. Tighten PAS pump pulley screws to 9 Nm.

Models without air conditioning

13. Raise engine on jack to align to mounting bracket.
14. Fit bolts securing engine to mounting bracket and tighten to 120 Nm.

Models with air conditioning

15. Lower engine on jack to fit engine mounting.
16. Fit engine mounting bracket and tighten bolts securing bracket to engine to 80 Nm.
17. Fit upper tie bar to engine mounting bracket and tighten both bolts securing tie bar to 120 Nm.
18. Fit PAS hose bracket to engine mounting stud and tighten nut to 80 Nm.
19. Fit clamps to PAS hoses and fit nut and bolt securing hose clamp to bracket.
20. Fit air conditioning hose clip to PAS hose support bracket and secure with bolt.

All Models

21. Connect PAS fluid feed hose to reservoir and secure with clip.
22. Fit underbelly panel. ***See BODY, Exterior fittings.***
23. Fit engine acoustic cover. ***See ENGINE - 'L' SERIES, Repairs.***
24. Bleed PAS system. ***See Adjustments.***

COOLER - PAS FLUID

Service repair no - 57.15.11

Remove

1. Remove front bumper. ***See BODY, Repairs.***
2. Position container beneath PAS rack.

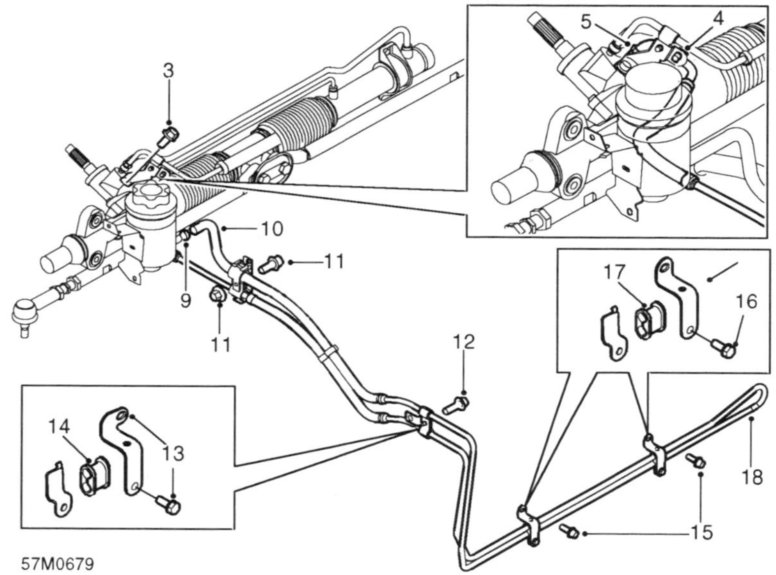

57M0679

3. Remove bolt securing PAS fluid pipe bracket to PAS rack pinion housing.
4. Release clip from PAS fluid return pipe.
5. Remove union nut and disconnect fluid return pipe from PAS rack.
6. Remove and discard 'O' ring.

CAUTION: Plug the connections.

7. Release return pipe from clips on support bracket.
8. Position container to collect fluid spillage from PAS fluid reservoir hose connection.
9. Remove clip securing return hose to PAS fluid reservoir.
10. Disconnect fluid hose from reservoir

CAUTION: Plug the connections.

11. Remove nut and bolt securing PAS fluid pipes to bracket on RH engine mounting.
12. Remove bolt securing PAS fluid pipe to bracket at RH side of front panel.
13. Remove bolt and clamp.
14. Remove rubber sleeve.
15. Remove 2 bolts securing PAS fluid cooler to brackets on front cross member.
16. Remove 2 bolts and clamps from fluid cooler.
17. Remove rubber sleeve's from cooler.
18. Remove PAS fluid cooler.

Refit

1. Fit PAS fluid cooler.
2. Fit rubber sleeves to cooler.
3. Fit clamps and secure with bolts to brackets on front cross member. Tighten bolts to 10 Nm.
4. Fit rubber sleeve to pipes.
5. Fit clamp and secure pipe to front panel with bolt. Tighten bolt to 10 Nm.
6. Fit clamp and tighten nut and bolt securing PAS fluid pipe to bracket on RH engine mounting to 10 Nm.
7. Connect PAS fluid hose to reservoir and secure with clip.
8. Ensure PAS fluid pipe union is clean.
9. Lubricate NEW 'O' ring with PAS fluid and fit seal to PAS fluid pipe.
10. Fit fluid pipe to PAS rack and tighten union nut to 22 Nm.
11. Fit clip to fluid pipe and fit bolt to secure bracket to PAS rack pinion housing. Tighten bolt to 8 Nm.
12. Fit PAS fluid pipe to remaining clips on PAS rack.
13. Fit front bumper. ***See BODY, Repairs.***
14. Bleed PAS system. ***See Adjustments.***

NACELLE - STEERING COLUMN

Service repair no - 57.40.29

Remove

1. Remove key from starter switch.

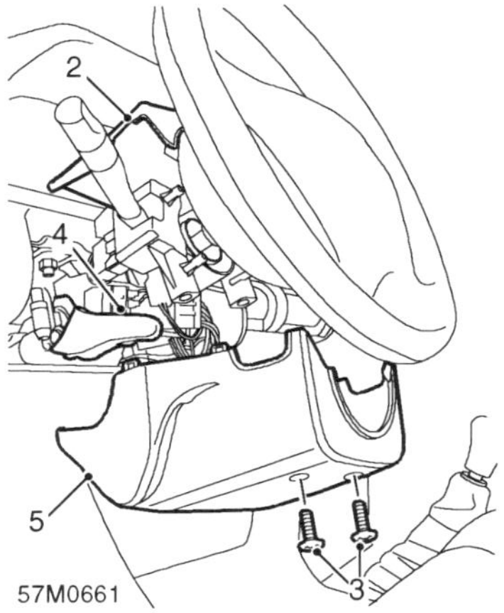

57M0661

2. Carefully remove upper half of nacelle. Take care when releasing clips from lower half of nacelle.
3. Remove 2 screws securing lower half of nacelle to steering column.
4. Lower steering column tilt lever.
5. Carefully pull lower half of nacelle from retaining clip on column lock.

Refit

1. Ensure that steering column tilt lever is lowered.
2. Position lower half of nacelle and engage with clip on column lock.
3. Raise column tilt lever.
4. Fit and tighten 2 screws securing lower half of nacelle to steering column.
5. Fit upper half of nacelle and ensure that clips engage with lower half.

LOCK - STEERING COLUMN

Service repair no - 57.40.31

Remove

1. Remove steering column. ***See this section.***
2. Position steering column assembly in a vice.

NOTE: If steering column is to be re-used, take care not to deform or damage column in vice.

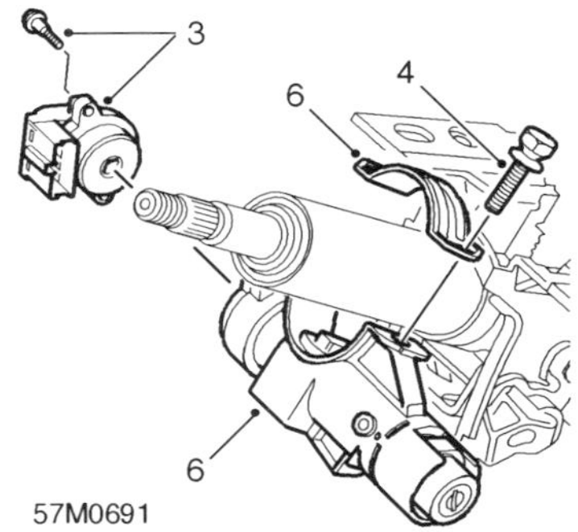

57M0691

3. Remove 2 screws and remove ignition switch.
4. Mark shear bolts with a centre punch.
5. Drill out shear bolt heads.
6. Remove lock saddle from column and remove lock from column.

Refit

1. Position lock to column, fit saddle and shear bolts, finger tighten at this stage.
2. Insert starter key, check operation of steering lock and key turns freely.
3. Tighten shear bolts fully and shear heads off.
4. Position ignition switch to column, fit and tighten screws.
5. Remove column from vice.
6. Fit steering column. ***See this section.***

STEERING COLUMN ASSEMBLY

Service repair no - 57.41.01

WARNING: *See GENERAL INFORMATION, SRS Precautions.*

Remove

1. Make the SRS system safe. ***See GENERAL INFORMATION, SRS Precautions.***
2. Remove rotary coupler. ***See BODY, Repairs.***

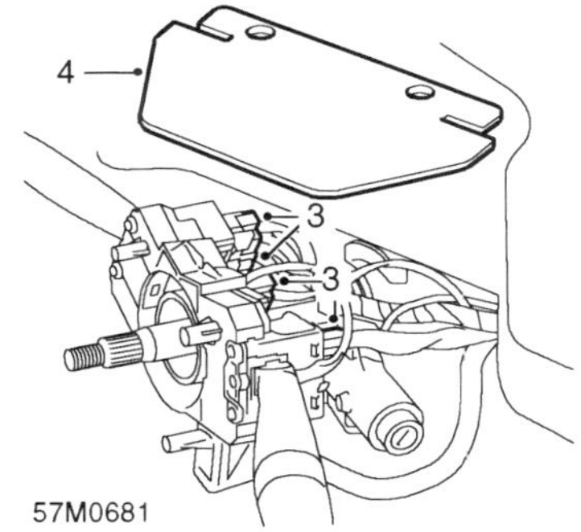

57M0681

3. Disconnect 4 multiplugs from indicator /wiper switch.
4. Move aside rubber column cover fitted to instrument pack lower cover.

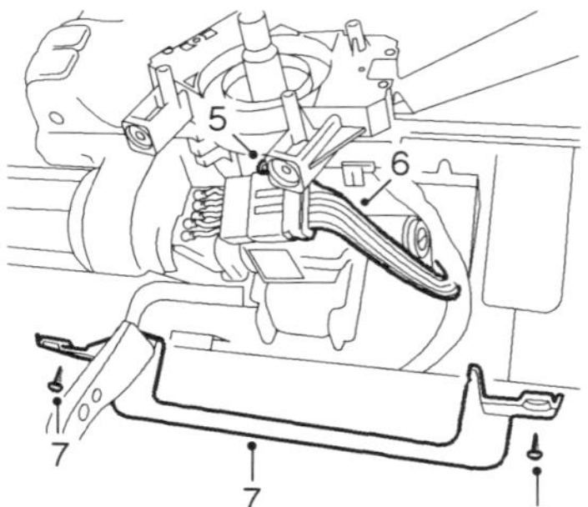

57M0682

5. Loosen screw securing switch assembly to steering column and remove switch assembly.
6. Disconnect multiplug from ignition switch.
7. Remove 2 screws from steering column aperture trim and remove trim.

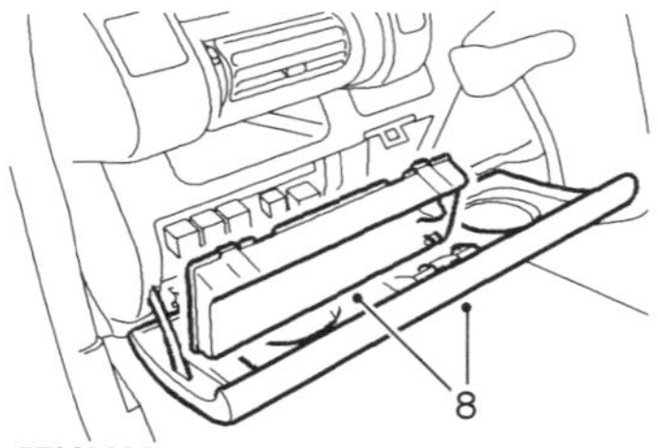

57M0683

8. Lower glove box lid and remove fuse box cover.

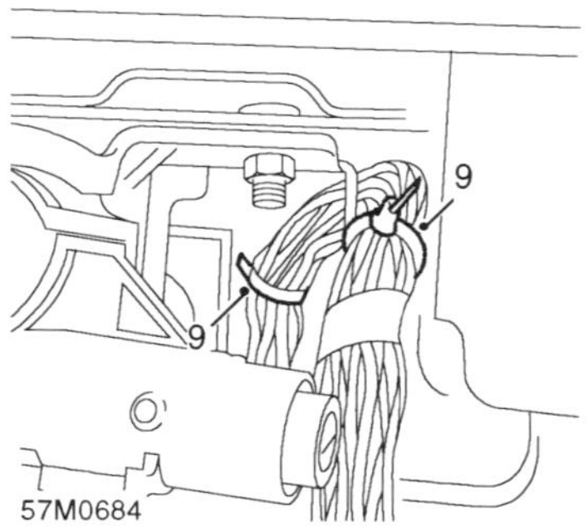

57M0684

9. Carefully cut 2 harness clips and release harness from column.

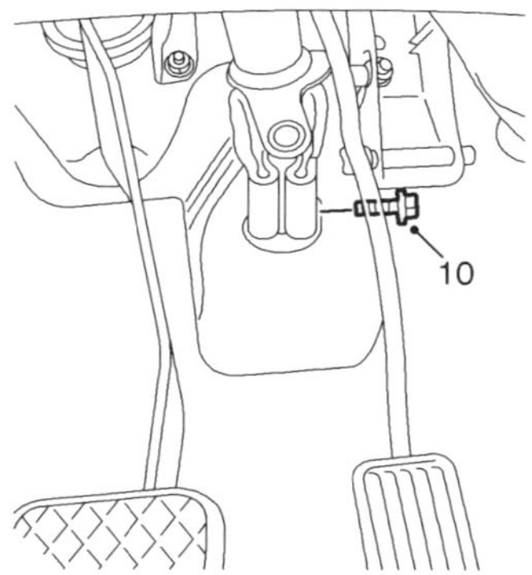

57M0685

10. Remove steering column to steering rack clamp bolt, and release column.

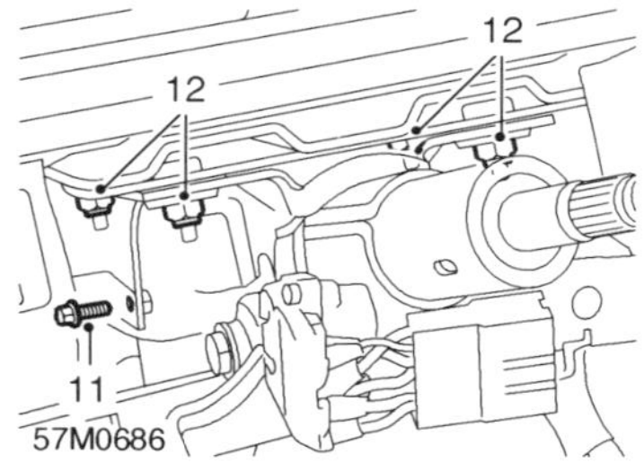

57M0686

11. Remove bolt securing side of steering column to fuse box support bracket.
12. Remove 4 nuts securing column to fascia.
13. Remove column from vehicle.

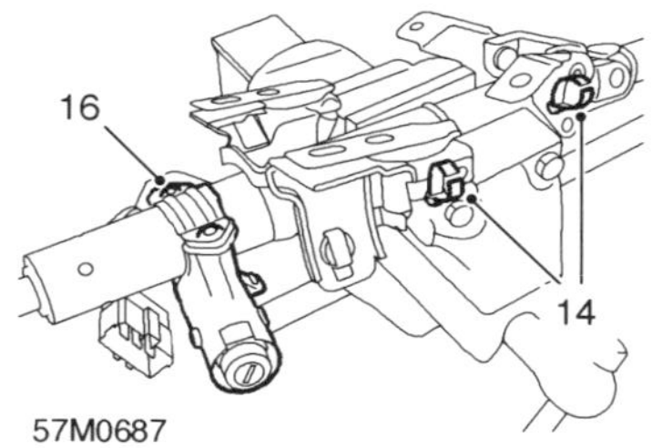

57M0687

14. Remove 2 cable ties from column.
15. Position steering column in vice.

CAUTION: If steering column is to be re-used, take care not to deform or damage column in vice.

16. Centre punch shear bolts securing lock to column.
17. Using a 5mm drill, drill out 2 shear bolts securing column to lock.

CAUTION: Take care not to damage steering lock body if the lock is to be refitted.

18. Remove steering column lock.

Refit

1. Locate steering column lock in position on steering column, fit but do not tighten shear bolts at this stage.
2. Insert key, confirm correct operation of steering lock and that key turns freely.
3. Tighten shear bolts until heads shear off.
4. Remove steering column assembly from vice.
5. Fit NEW cable ties to harness.
6. Position column to vehicle, locate column on steering rack aligning column coupling with rack input shaft flag.
7. Fit nuts and and tighten to 14 Nm.
8. Fit side support bolt and tighten to 10 Nm.
9. Fit clamp bolt and tighten to 32 Nm.
10. Position harness and secure with clips to column.
11. Fit fuse box cover and close glove box lid.
12. Position rubber column cover over steering column.
13. Fit aperture trim and secure with screws.
14. Position indicator/wiper switch assembly, tighten screw and connect multiplugs.
15. Fit rotary coupler. ***See BODY, Repairs.***

TRACK ROD

Service repair no - 57.55.09

Remove

1. Raise front of vehicle.

WARNING: Support on safety stands.

2. Remove road wheel(s).
3. If necessary, position steering to gain access to track rod to PAS rack fixing bolt.

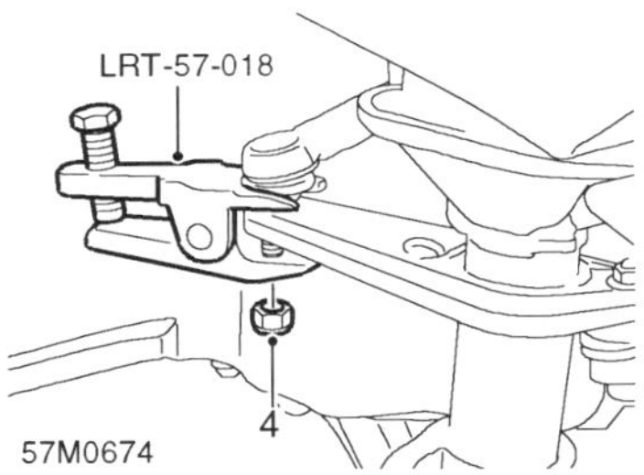

57M0674

4. Remove and discard nut securing track rod end ball joint to steering arm.
5. Use **LRT-57-018** to disconnect track rod end ball joint from steering arm.

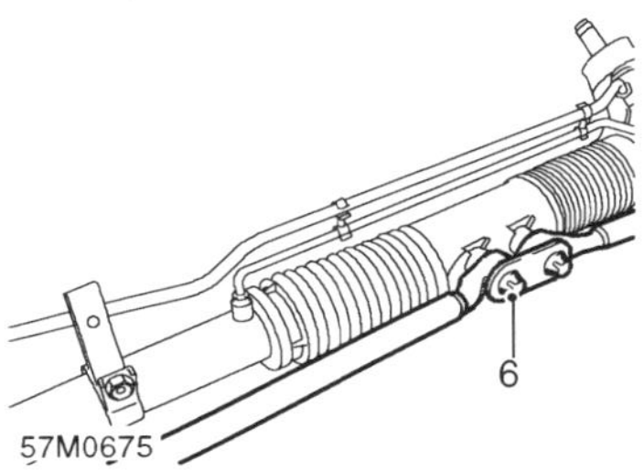

57M0675

6. Remove Torx bolt securing track rod to PAS rack, discard Torx bolt.
7. Remove spacer.
Do not carry out further dismantling if component is removed for access only.

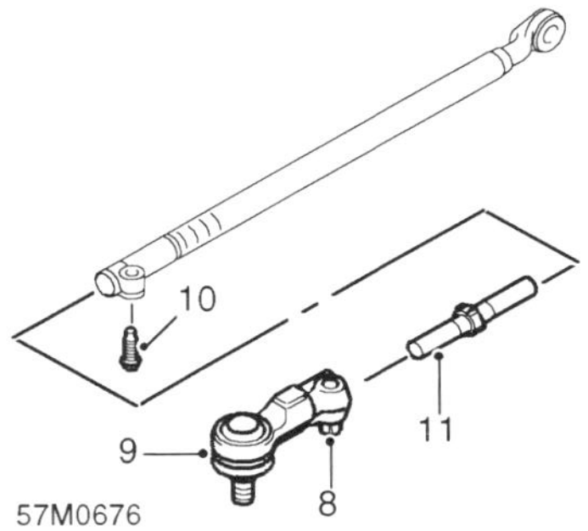

57M0676

8. Hold track rod securely and loosen pinch bolt in track rod end.
9. Remove track rod end and note number of turns for refit.
10. Remove pinch bolt from track rod.
11. Remove turnbuckle and note number of turns for refit.

NOTE: Turnbuckle has a LH thread into the track rod.

Refit

1. Fit turnbuckle to track rod to number of turns as noted in remove.
2. Fit pinch bolt to track rod but do not tighten at this stage.
3. Fit track rod end to turnbuckle to number of turns as in remove.
4. Do not tighten pinch bolt in track rod end at this stage.
5. Cut 2 hacksaw slots along thread of discarded Torx bolt and use this to remove remains of patch lock from threaded hole in rack.
6. Fit spacer to PAS rack.
7. Fit track rod to PAS rack.
8. Hold track rod parallel to PAS rack and tighten NEW Torx bolt to 100 Nm.
9. Fit track rod end ball joint to steering arm using new nut, and tighten nut to 55 Nm.
10. Fit road wheel(s) and tighten nuts to correct torque. ***See INFORMATION, Torque wrench settings.***
11. Remove stand(s) and lower vehicle.
12. Check and adjust front wheel alignment. ***See Adjustments.***

WARNING: Ensure all track rod pinch bolts are tightened to 28 Nm on completion of front wheel alignment check.

STEERING WHEEL

Service repair no - 57.60.01

Remove

1. Remove steering wheel air bag. ***See RESTRAINT SYSTEMS, Repairs.***

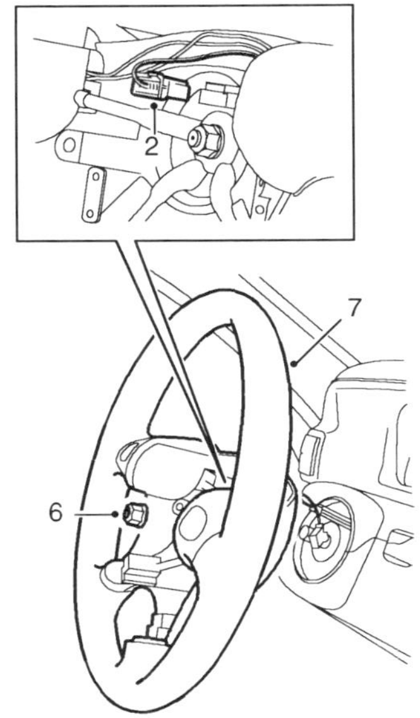

2. Disconnect multiplug from rotary coupler.
3. Centralise steering wheel with road wheels in straight ahead position.
4. Restrain steering wheel and loosen self-locking nut securing steering wheel to column.
5. Pull steering wheel from column splines.
6. Remove and discard self-locking nut.
7. Remove steering wheel.

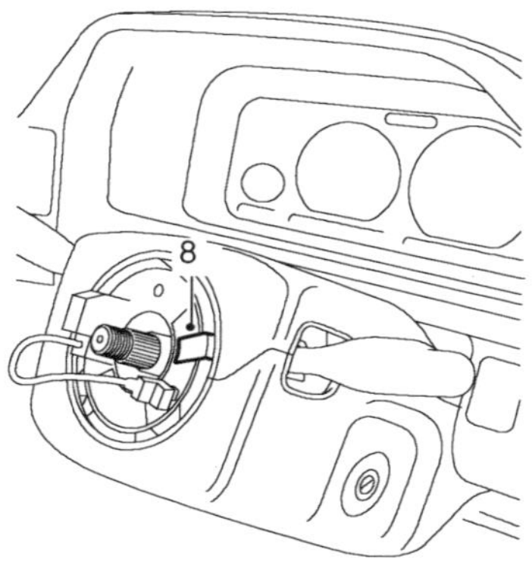

57M0690

8. Attach tape across edge of rotary coupler to retain correct setting.

Refit

1. Remove retaining tape from rotary coupler.
2. Ensure road wheels are in straight ahead position and indicator cancelling cam is aligned horizontally.
3. Fit steering wheel to column and ensure spokes are horizontal.

NOTE: On factory fitted columns, there is a reference mark on column shaft and steering wheel for steering wheel alignment.

4. Fit NEW self-locking nut, tighten to 18 Nm.
5. Connect multiplug to rotary coupler.
6. Fit driver's airbag. ***See RESTRAINT SYSTEMS, Repairs.***

PUMP - POWER ASSISTED STEERING - K SERIES

Service repair no - 57.20.14

Remove

1. Raise front of vehicle.

WARNING: Support on safety stands.

2. Loosen pulley bolts to finger tight and remove power steering pump drive belt.
3. Position drain tin.

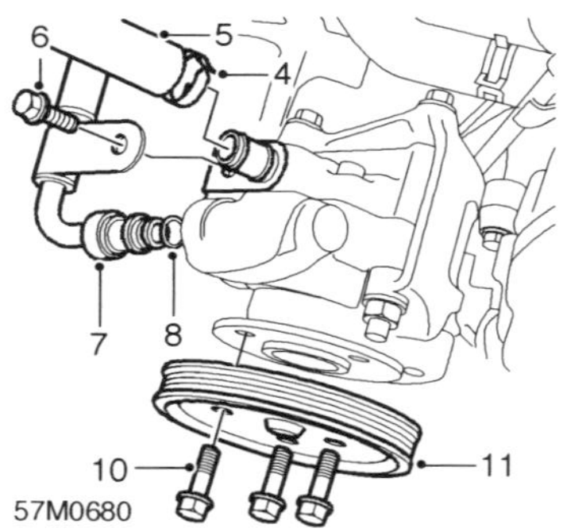

57M0680

4. Release clip securing fluid inlet hose to power steering pump.
5. Disconnect fluid inlet hose from power steering pump.
6. Remove bolt securing fluid outlet hose clamp to bracket.
7. Loosen union and disconnect fluid outlet hose from power steering pump.

CAUTION: To prevent damage to components, use two spanners when loosening or tightening unions.

8. Remove and discard 'O' ring seal from fluid outlet hose.
9. Plug hose and power steering pump connections to prevent excess fluid loss and the ingress of dirt and moisture into the system.
10. Remove 3 bolts securing pulley to power steering pump.
11. Remove power steering pump pulley.

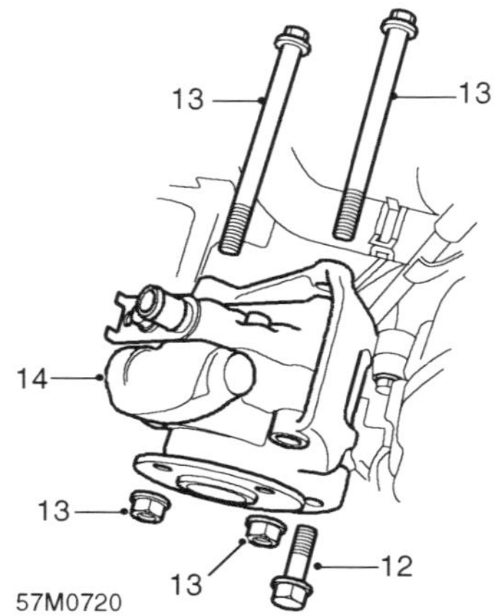

57M0720

12. Remove bolt securing power steering pump to mounting bracket.
13. Remove 2 through bolts and nuts securing power steering pump to mounting bracket.
14. Remove power steering pump.

CAUTION: Plug the connections.

Refit

1. Remove plugs from hose connections on new power steering pump and fit to old pump.
2. Position power steering pump and align to mounting bracket.
3. Fit nuts and bolts securing power steering pump to mounting bracket and tighten to 25 Nm.
4. Fit pulley to power steering pump and tighten bolts finger tight.
5. Remove plug from fluid outlet hose.
6. Lubricate and fit NEW 'O' ring to fluid outlet hose.
7. Loosely connect fluid outlet hose to power steering pump.
8. Align fluid outlet hose clamp to bracket and secure with bolt.

CAUTION: To prevent damage to components, use two spanners when loosening or tightening unions.

9. Tighten fluid outlet hose to 25 Nm.
10. Remove plug from fluid inlet hose and connect to power steering pump.
11. Fit clip securing fluid inlet hose to power steering pump.
12. Remove drain tin.
13. Fit power steering pump drive belt.
14. Tighten pulley bolts to 9 Nm.
15. Bleed power steering system, see **Adjustments.**

CONTENTS

FRONT SUSPENSION COMPONENT LOCATIONS

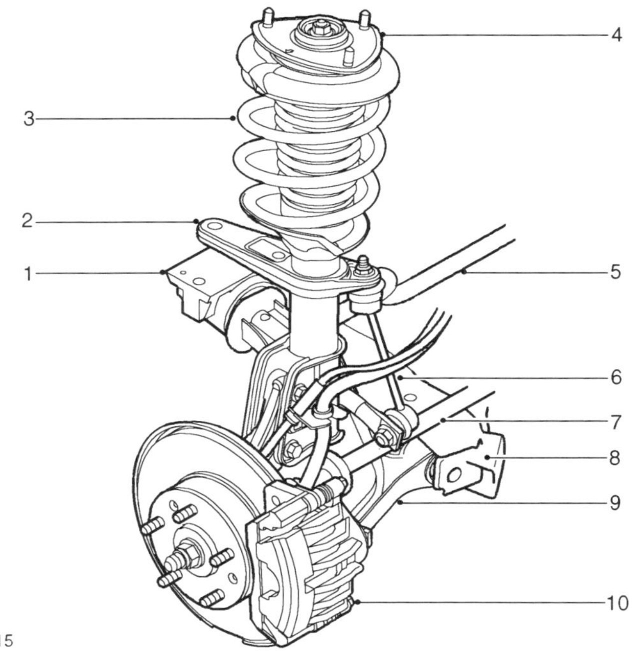

60M0515

RH Front suspension shown - LH is mirror image

1. Bush and housing assembly
2. Damper
3. Road spring
4. Top mount
5. Anti-roll bar
6. Anti-roll bar link
7. Drive shaft
8. Front subframe
9. Lower arm
10. Brake caliper and hub assembly

FRONT SUSPENSION COMPONENT DETAIL

1. Damper
2. Road spring
3. Rebound washer
4. Top mount
5. Bearing
6. Spring seat
7. Bump washer
8. Spring aid
9. Dust cover
10. Bump cup
11. Anti-roll bar
12. Anti-roll bar link
13. Subframe
14. Bush
15. Lower arm
16. Bush
17. Snubber washer
18. Rear bush housing

RH Front suspension shown - LH is mirror image

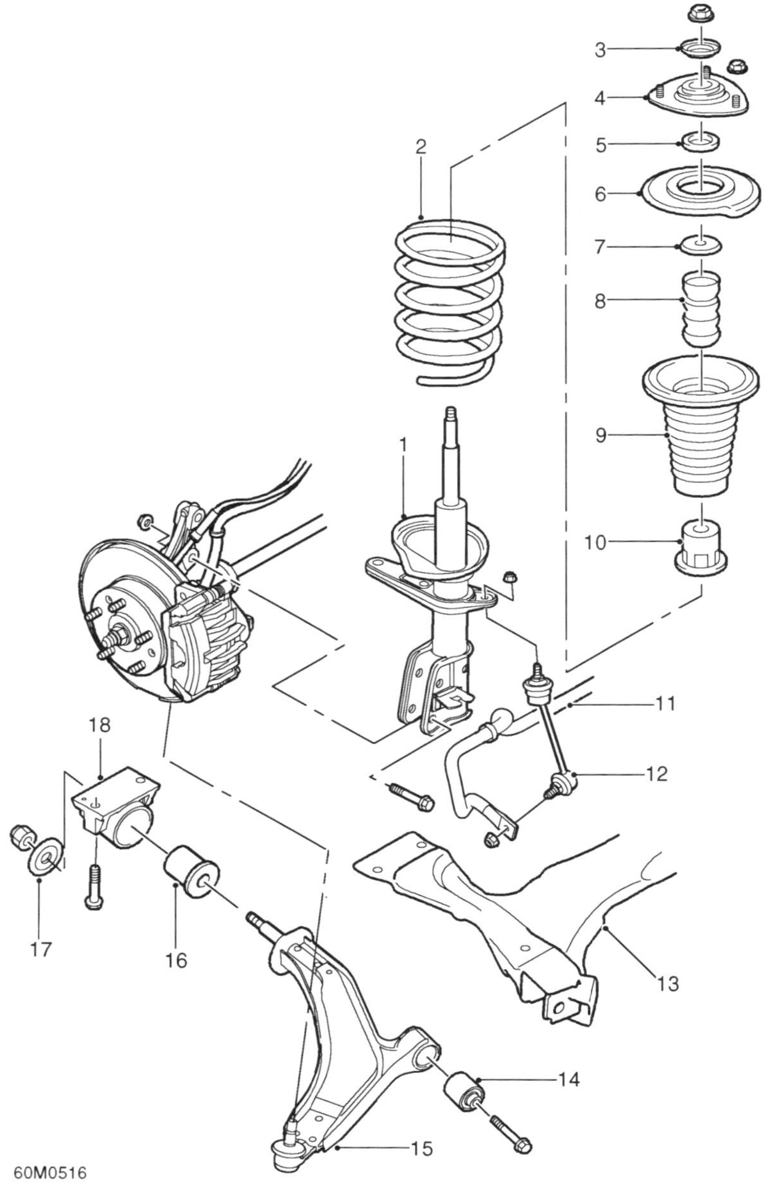

60M0516

FRONT SUSPENSION DESCRIPTION

The front suspension comprises two MacPherson strut dampers with coil springs, two lower suspension arms and an anti-roll bar. A front subframe is bolted to the body and provides mounting points for the lower suspension arms. Each damper has a steering arm,which provides for the attachment of the track rods from the power steering rack.

The suspension is designed to allow longitudinal movement of the wheel, which allows the wheel to move rearwards and upwards in response to surface undulations. The longitudinal movement allows the springs and dampers time to react to surface changes which improves ride quality.

MacPherson Struts

The left and right hand dampers are handed but otherwise similar in construction. The front dampers are similar to the rear dampers but have slightly different damping characteristics. The damping characteristics of the front dampers also differs between petrol and diesel variants. The spring rates also differ between the front and rear suspension, petrol and diesel variants and also between vehicles with and without air conditioning.

The damper has a forged steering arm which provides for the attachment of the track rod via a ball joint and the anti-roll bar link. The damper body is fabricated from thick walled tubing and has welded brackets for attachment of the swivel hub. A smaller welded bracket provides for the attachment of the brake hose to the caliper and the ABS sensor cable (if fitted).

Each damper is fitted with a coil spring. The coil spring locates in a fabricated seat and is retained in a partially compressed condition on the damper by a spring seat, top mount and nut. The top mount is fitted with three studs which locate in mating holes in the inner wing turret. The top mount is fitted with a bearing which allows the damper rod to pivot when the steering is turned.

On vehicles fitted with air conditioning, the front springs are approximately 5 mm longer. This maintains the correct ride height with respect to the additional weight of the air conditioning equipment.

A spring aid and a bump cup are fitted to the damper to prevent shock loads when the damper is fully compressed. A dust cover prevents the ingress of dirt and water to maintain the integrity of the chromium plated damper rod.

The damper functions by restricting the flow of a hydraulic fluid through internal galleries within the damper. A chromium plated damper rod moves axially within the damper. As the rod moves, its movement is limited by the flow of fluid through the galleries thus providing damping of undulations in the terrain. The damper rod is sealed at its exit point from the damper body to maintain fluid within the unit and to prevent the ingress of dirt and moisture. The seal also acts as a wiper to keep the rod outer diameter clean.

Anti Roll Bar

The anti-roll bar is mounted to the upper face of the front subframe in two places. Rubber bushes fitted to the anti-roll bar are held in position by two clamps retained with bolts. The outer ends of the anti-roll bar are each connected to a link, which in turn is attached to the damper.

The links have a ball joint at each end. The other end is attached to the anti-roll bar and secured with a nut. The link transmits suspension movements directly to the anti-roll bar. The design of the links reduces the steer effects commonly found in this type of suspension.

Lower Suspension Arms

The lower suspension arms are fabricated from steel and each arm is handed. The arms are attached at two pivot points. The forward end of the arm contains a bush and is attached to lugs on the front subframe with a bolt. A spigot on the rear mounting of the arm engages with a bush and housing assembly and is retained with a snubber washer and a nut. A ball joint is located on the outer part of the arm and is connected to the swivel hub and secured with a nut.

The two pivot bushes have a significant role in vehicle handling. The bushes control the longitudinal movement of the wheel due to braking, acceleration or surface undulations.

Front bush

The front bush is located at a specified angle to the axis of rotation of the lower suspension arm. The front bush is deflected radially and axially as the wheel moves rearwards. The angle of the bush ensures that the wheel moves directly rearward reducing the effects of longitudinal steer to a minimum.

Rear Bush

The rear bush is mounted on the axis of rotation of the lower suspension arm. In the radial direction the bush is relatively soft in its construction. In the axial direction, the bush is very soft for the first 2 mm of movement. Snubbing areas to the front and rear of the bush provides a progressive increase in the hardness of the bush as the deflection of the wheel increases. The rear bush controls the amount that the wheel can move forward or rearward.

ANTI-ROLL BAR

Service repair no - 60.10.01

Remove

1. Raise front of vehicle.

WARNING: Support on safety stands.

2. Remove road wheel(s).
3. Remove underbelly panel. ***See BODY, Repairs.***

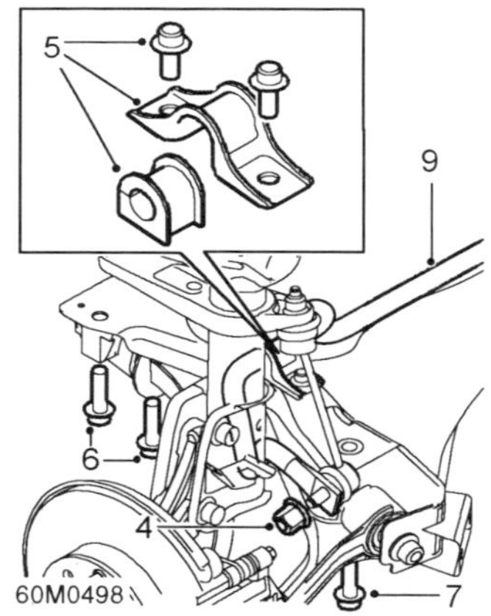

4. Remove nuts securing each end of anti-roll bar to links.
5. Remove 4 bolts securing anti-roll bar saddles, collect saddles and rubber bushes.
6. Remove 4 bolts securing both lower arm rear bush housings.
7. Remove and discard 2 bolts securing front subframe to body.
8. Lower front subframe to release anti-roll bar.
9. Remove anti-roll bar.

Refit

1. Position anti-roll bar.
2. With assistance raise front subframe.
3. Fit new bolts securing front subframe to body and tighten to 190 Nm.
4. Fit bolts securing lower arm rear bush housings and tighten to 105 Nm.
5. Position anti roll bar rubbers, bushes and saddles.
6. Fit saddle bolts and tighten to 23 Nm .
7. Fit nuts to anti-roll bar links and tighten to 55 Nm.
8. Fit underbelly panel. ***See BODY, Repairs.***
9. Fit road wheel(s) and tighten nuts to correct torque. ***See INFORMATION, Torque wrench settings.***
10. Remove stand(s) and lower vehicle.

BEARING - HUB - FRONT

Service repair no - 60.25.14

Remove

1. Raise front of vehicle.

WARNING: Support on safety stands.

2. Remove road wheel(s).

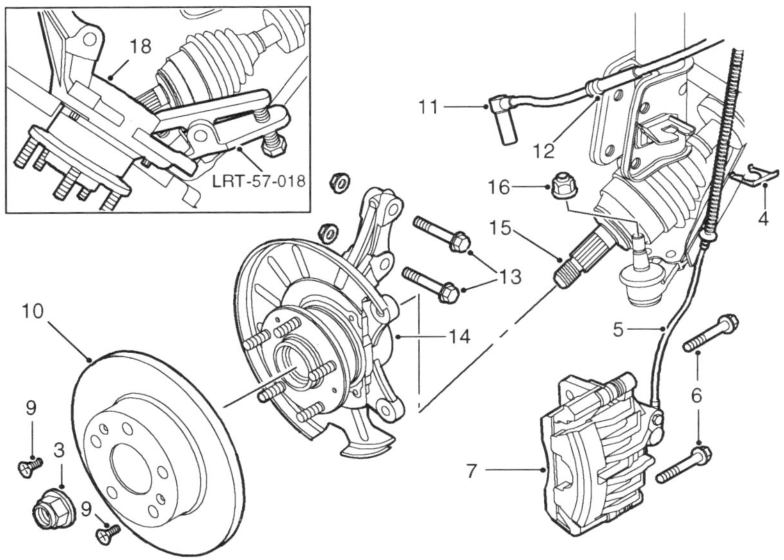

60M0489

3. Remove drive shaft nut.
4. Remove clip securing brake hose to bracket.
5. Remove brake hose from bracket.
6. Remove 2 bolts securing caliper.
7. Remove caliper from hub and tie aside.

CAUTION: Do not allow caliper to hang on brake hose.

8. Mark brake disc to hub relationship.
9. Remove 2 screws from disc.
10. Remove disc.
11. Remove ABS sensor from hub.
12. Remove ABS sensor lead from bracket.
13. Remove 2 nuts and bolts securing swivel hub to suspension damper.
14. Release hub from damper.
15. Remove drive shaft from hub.
16. Restrain hub from rotating and remove nut from lower swivel.
17. Break taper joint using tool **LRT-57-018.**
18. Remove swivel hub.
Do not carry out further dismantling if component is removed for access only.

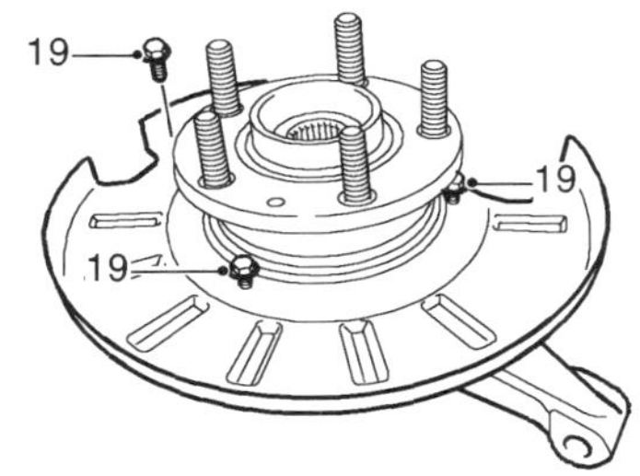

60M0490

19. Remove 3 screws securing brake disc shield.

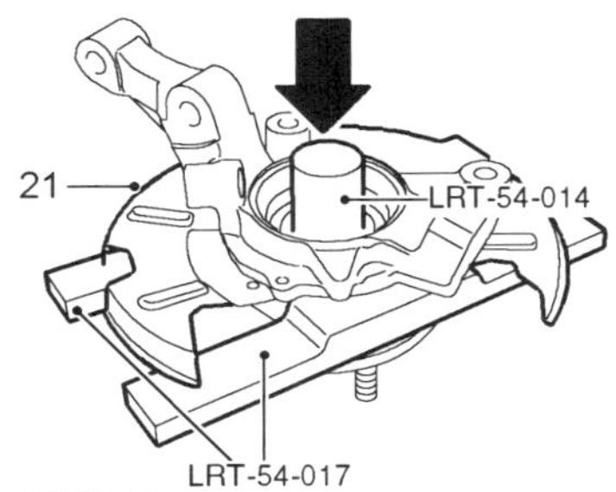

60M0491

20. Position swivel hub assembly to press, support on tools **LRT-54-017** and press out drive flange using tool **LRT-54-014.**
21. Remove brake disc shield.

NOTE: Outer bearing inner track will remain on drive flange.

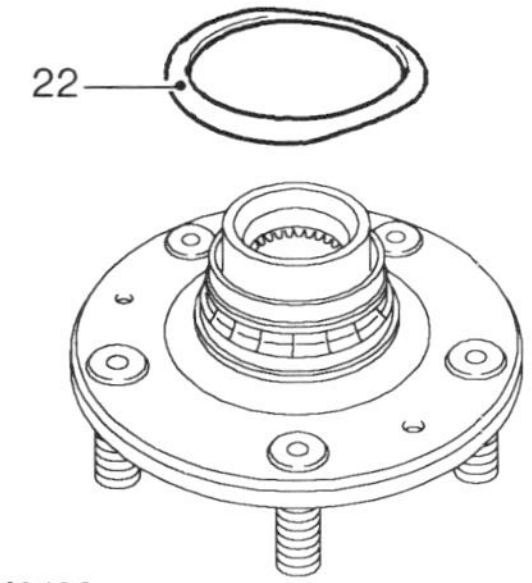

60M0492

22. Remove bearing sealing plate from inner track.
23. Position drive flange in a vice.

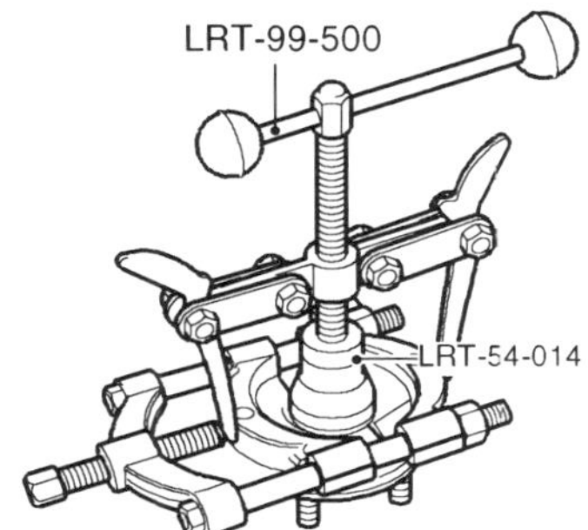

60M0493

24. Clamp both halves of bearing separator around bearing inner track ensuring that inner lip fits in groove on the inner track.
25. Using tool **LRT-99-500** and thrust pad **LRT-54-014** withdraw inner track from drive flange.

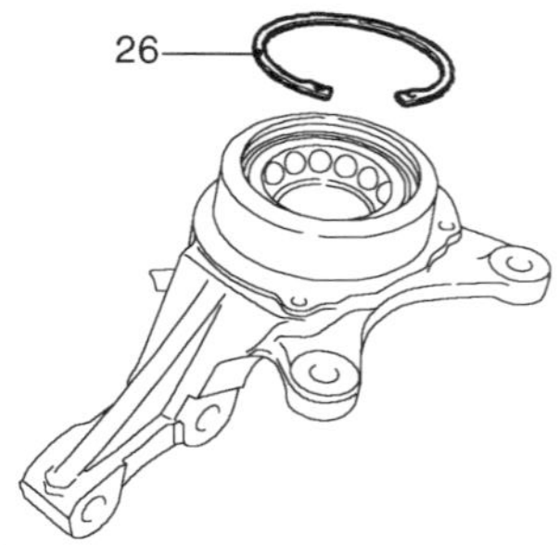

60M0494

26. Remove circlip retaining bearing.

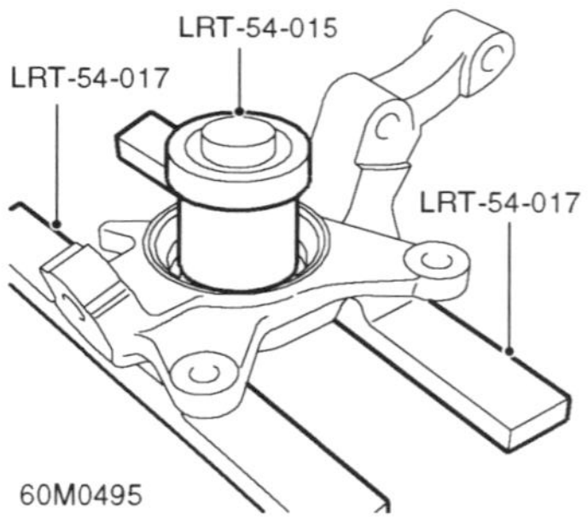

60M0495

27. Position hub to press and press out bearing using tools **LRT-54-017** and **LRT-54-015.** discard bearing.

⚠ **CAUTION: Never re-use existing bearing.**

28. Clean swivel hub assembly and drive flange.

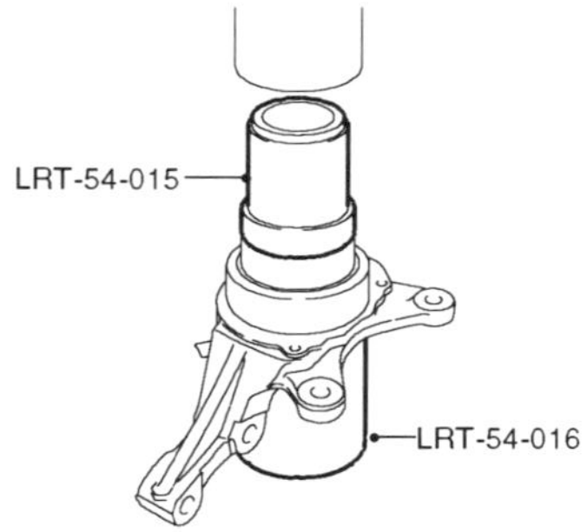

60M0496

29. Support hub on tool **LRT-54-016** and press in new bearing using tool **LRT-54-015.**
30. Fit circlip.
31. Fit disc shield, fit bolts and tighten to 8.5 Nm.

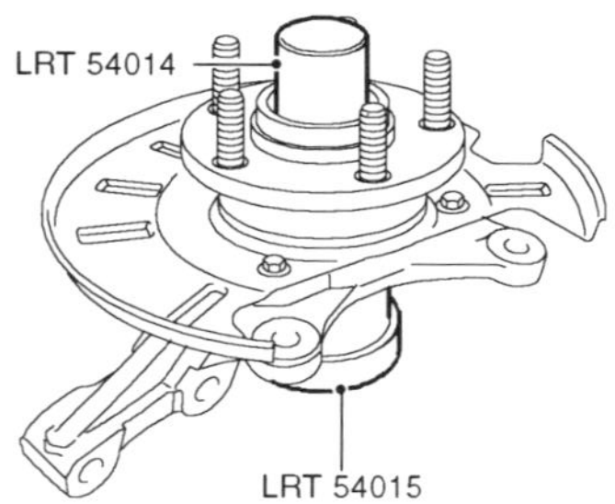

60M0497

32. Support hub on tool **LRT-54-015** and press flange into bearing using tool **LRT-54-014.**

Refit

1. Fit hub assembly to lower ball joint, fit nut and tighten to 65 Nm.
2. Fit drive shaft to hub.
3. Fit hub to suspension damper and tighten nuts and bolts to 205 Nm.
4. Clean disc and drive flange mating faces.
5. Fit disc to drive flange, align reference marks, fit screws and tighten to 5 Nm.
6. Fit caliper, fit bolts and tighten to 83 Nm.
7. Align brake hose to bracket and fit clip.
8. Clean ABS sensor, apply anti-seize grease and fit sensor to hub.
9. Fit sensor lead to bracket.
10. Fit NEW drive shaft nut and tighten to 400 Nm. Stake nut to shaft.
11. Fit road wheel(s) and tighten nuts to correct torque. ***See INFORMATION, Torque wrench settings.***
12. Remove stand(s) and lower vehicle.

DAMPER - FRONT

Service repair no - 60.30.02 Damper - front
Service repair no - 60.20.01 Spring - front

Remove

1. Raise front of vehicle, one side.

WARNING: Support on safety stands.

2. Remove road wheel(s).

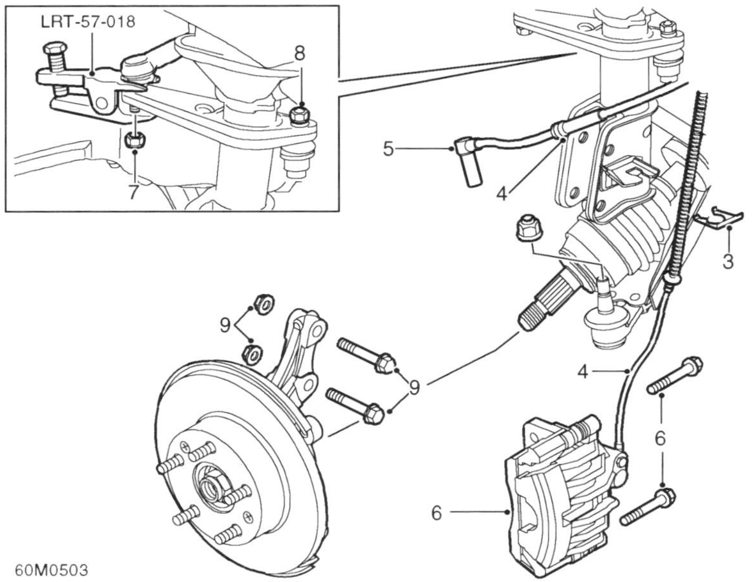

60M0503

3. Remove 'C' clip from brake hose.
4. Release brake hose and ABS harness from bracket.
5. Release ABS sensor from hub assembly.
6. Remove 2 bolts securing brake caliper to hub, release caliper and tie aside.
7. Remove nut from track rod end ball joint and use **LRT-57-018** to break ball joint taper.
8. Remove upper nut from anti-roll bar link, release link and position aside.

CAUTION: Use a spanner and an Allen key to prevent ball joint rotating when undoing link.

9. Remove 2 bolts securing damper to swivel hub, release damper from hub.

10. *LH Damper only* : Remove jacking kit from mounting.

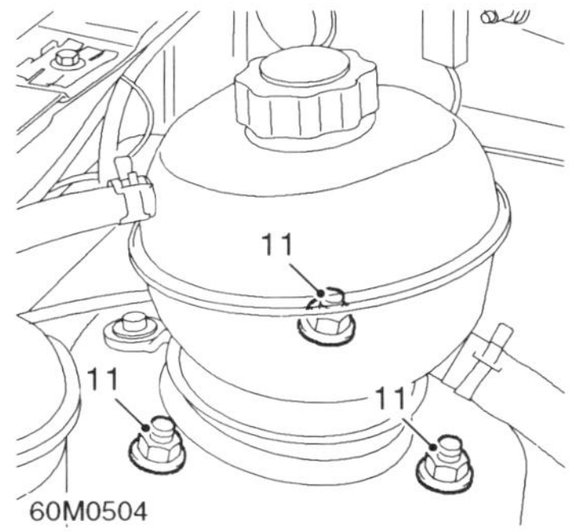

60M0504

11. Remove 3 nuts securing damper top mounting to body.
12. *LH Damper* : Collect jacking kit mounting.
13. Remove damper and spring assembly.

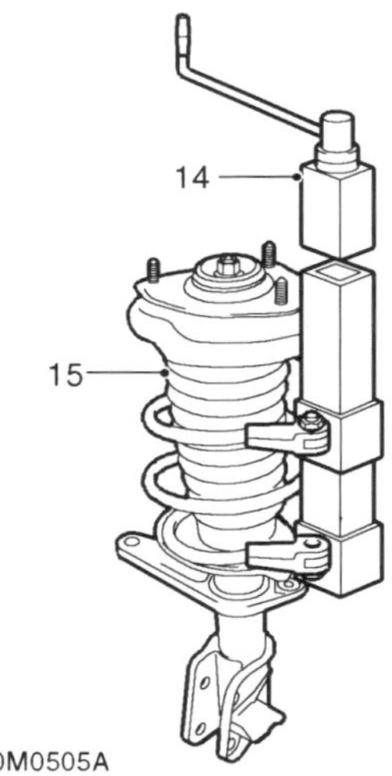

60M0505A

14. Position a suitable spring compressor tool in vice.
15. Position damper and spring assembly to spring compressor and locate in arms.

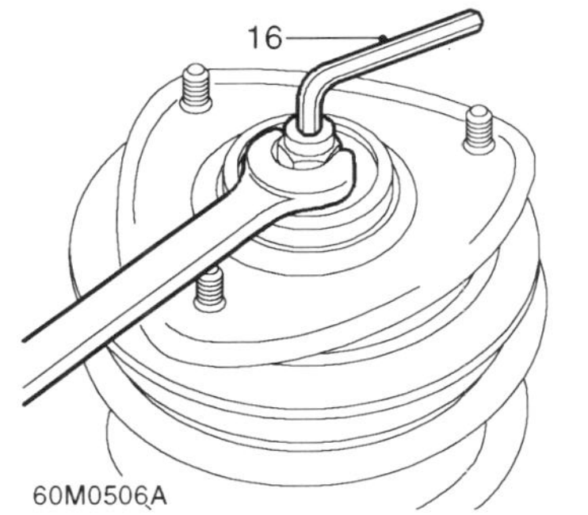

60M0506A

16. Compress spring by 2 to 3 cm until loose, hold damper shaft with Allen key, remove and discard mounting plate nut.

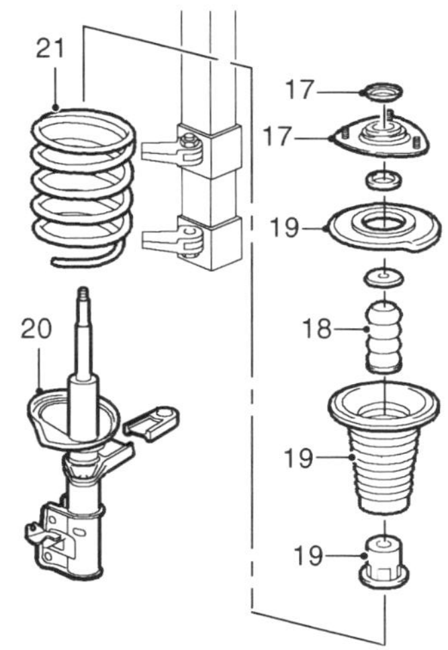

60M0510A

17. Remove rebound washer and top mounting plate.
18. Remove bump washer and spring aid.
19. Remove spring seat, dust cover and bump cup.
20. Remove damper from spring.
21. Release and remove spring from spring compressor.

Refit

1. Inspect damper, mounting plate rubber and dust cover for deterioration and damage.
2. Clean mating faces of spring, damper and mounting plate.
3. Clean damper shaft and bump stop plate.
4. Position spring in spring compressor, locate spring in arms and compress spring by 2 to 3 cm.
5. Fit damper to spring, ensure spring is located in cut recess in damper plate.
6. Fit spring seat dust cover and bump cup.
7. Fit spring aid and bump washer.
8. Fit mounting plate and rebound washer.
9. Using a NEW nut, hold damper shaft with an Allen key and tighten nut to 57 Nm.
10. Release spring and remove assembly from spring compressor.
11. Clean mating face of top mounting plate.
12. *LH Damper* : position jacking kit bracket.
13. Position damper assembly, align top mounting to body and tighten nuts to 45 Nm.
14. *LH Damper* : Fit jacking kit to bracket and secure with straps.
15. Fit bolts securing damper to swivel hub and tighten to 205 Nm.
16. Connect anti-roll bar link and tighten nut to 45 Nm.

CAUTION: Use a spanner and an Allen key to prevent ball joint rotating when tightening link.

17. Position track rod end and tighten nut to 55 Nm.
18. Locate brake hose and ABS harness in bracket.
19. Secure brake hose with 'C' clip.
20. Fit road wheel(s) and tighten nuts to correct torque. ***See INFORMATION, Torque wrench settings.***
21. Remove stand(s) and lower vehicle.

LOWER ARM - FRONT

Service repair no - 60.35.02

Remove

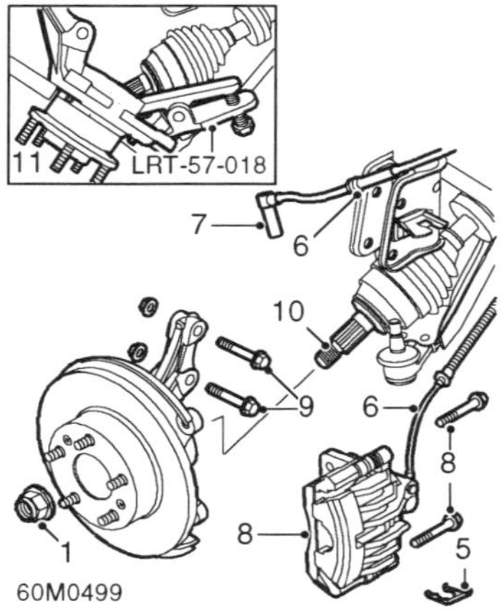

60M0499

1. Remove and discard front hub nut.
2. Raise front of vehicle, one side.

WARNING: Support on safety stands.

3. Remove road wheel(s).
4. Remove underbelly panel. ***See BODY, Repairs.***
5. Remove 'C' clip from brake hose.
6. Release brake hose and ABS harness from bracket.
7. Release ABS speed sensor from hub.

CAUTION: Do not allow brake caliper to hang on brake hose.

8. Remove 2 bolts from brake caliper, release brake caliper from hub and tie aside.
9. Remove 2 bolts securing hub to damper and release damper.
10. Release drive shaft from hub and tie aside.
11. Remove nut from lower arm ball joint and, using **LRT-57-018,** release tapered joint.
12. Remove hub assembly.
13. Remove 2 bolts from lower arm rear mounting.
14. Remove bolt from lower arm front bush housing.
15. Remove lower arm assembly.

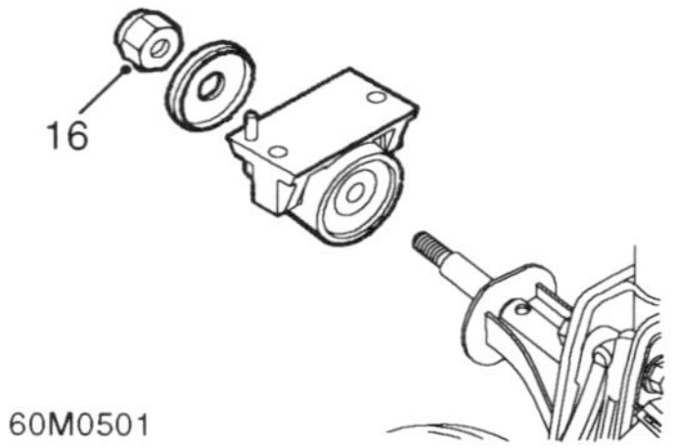

60M0501

CAUTION: Note orientation of snubber washer.

16. Remove nut from rear mounting, remove snubber washer and remove rear bush housing.

Refit

CAUTION: Ensure correct orientation of snubber washer. Ensure that 'OUT' is visible on snubber washer when fitted.

1. Fit rear bush housing and snubber washer to lower arm but do not tighten nut at this stage.
2. Position lower arm, secure but do not tighten bolts at this stage.
3. Fit hub assembly to lower arm ball joint and tighten nut to 65 Nm.
4. Clean drive shaft mating faces and position drive shaft in hub.
5. Fit but do not tighten NEW hub nut at this stage.
6. Align hub to damper and tighten bolts to 205 Nm.
7. Fit brake caliper and tighten bolts to 83 Nm.
8. Clean ABS sensor, apply anti-seize grease and fit ABS speed sensor to hub.
9. Position ABS harness and brake hose in bracket and secure hose with 'C' clip.

CAUTION: Nuts and bolts must be tightened with the weight of the vehicle on the suspension.

10. Fit road wheel(s) and tighten nuts to correct torque. ***See INFORMATION, Torque wrench settings.***
11. Remove stand(s) and lower vehicle.
12. Tighten lower arm front bush bolt to 190 Nm.
13. Tighten 2 bolts for lower arm rear bush housing to 105 Nm.
14. Tighten rear mounting nut to 140 Nm.
15. Fit underbelly panel. ***See BODY, Repairs.***
16. Tighten front hub nut to 400 Nm.
17. Stake front hub nut.

CONTENTS

Page

REAR SUSPENSION COMPONENT LOCATIONS

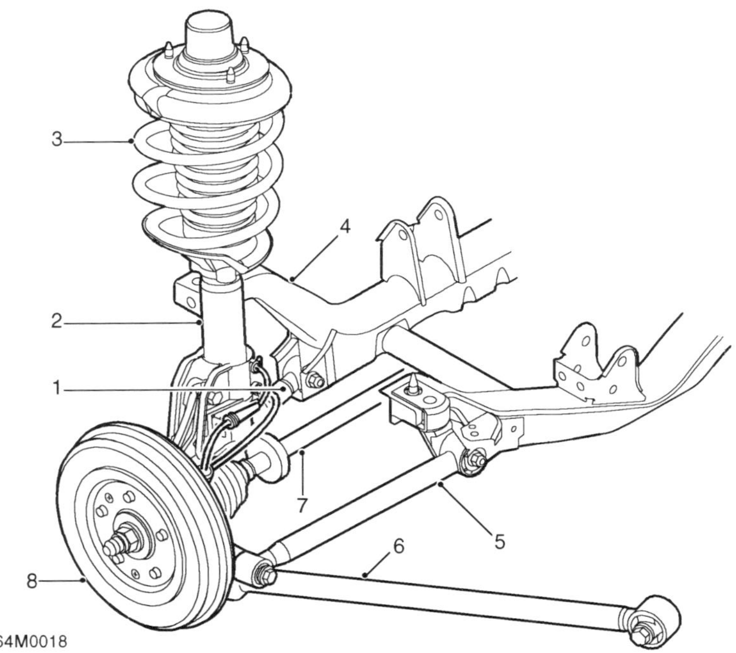

64M0018

RH Rear suspension shown - LH is mirror image

1. Adjustable transverse link
2. Damper
3. Road spring
4. Rear subframe
5. Fixed transverse link
6. Trailing link
7. Drive shaft
8. Brake and hub assembly

REAR SUSPENSION COMPONENT DETAIL

1. Damper
2. Road spring
3. Spring aid
4. Dust cover
5. Bump cup
6. Cover
7. Rebound washer
8. Seal
9. Top mount
10. Spring seat
11. Bump plate
12. Rear subframe
13. Fixed transverse link
14. Trailing link
15. Bush
16. Adjustable transverse link

RH Rear suspension shown - LH is mirror image

REAR SUSPENSION

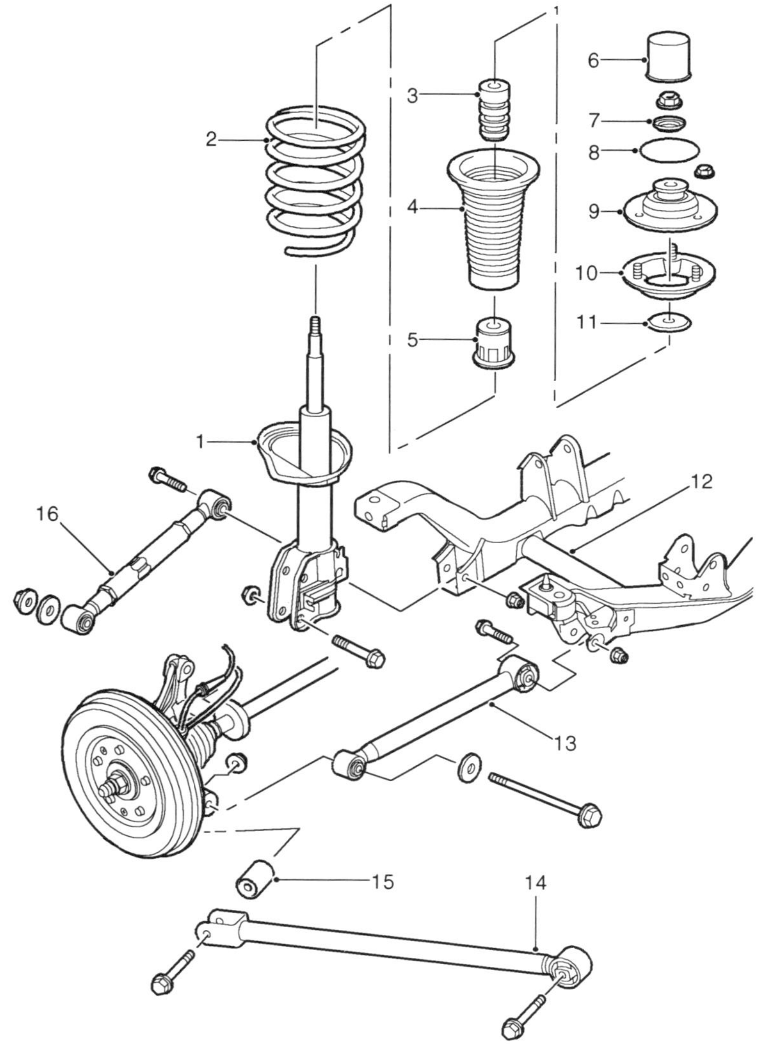

64M0019

REAR SUSPENSION DESCRIPTION

The rear suspension comprises two MacPherson strut dampers with coil springs and two sets of three links (known as "trapezoidal links"). A rear subframe is bolted to the body and provides the mounting points for the fixed and adjustable links. The third link is known as the trailing link and is attached from the hub carrier to the body.

The suspension is designed to allow longitudinal movement of the wheel, which allows the wheel to move rearwards and upwards in response to surface undulations. The longitudinal movement allows the springs and dampers time to react to surface changes and improves ride quality.

MacPherson Struts

The left and right hand dampers are handed but otherwise similar in construction. The rear dampers are similar to the front dampers but have slightly different damping characteristics.

The damper body is fabricated from thick walled tubing and has welded brackets for attachment of the hub carrier. Two smaller welded brackets provide for the attachment of the brake hose to the brake pipe and the ABS sensor cable (if fitted).

Each damper is fitted with a coil spring. The coil spring locates in a fabricated seat and is retained in a compressed condition on the damper by a top mount and nut. The top mount is fitted with three studs which locate in mating holes in the inner wing turret and retained with three self locking nuts. A bump plate is fitted which accommodates a spring aid. The bump plate is sealed against the inner wing turret to prevent the ingress of moisture into the interior load space.

The spring rates differ between the front and rear suspension.

A spring aid and a bump cup are fitted to the damper to prevent shock loads when the damper is fully compressed. A dust cover prevents the ingress of dirt and water to maintain the integrity of the chromium plated damper rod.

The damper functions by restricting the flow of a hydraulic fluid through internal galleries within the damper. A chromium plated damper rod moves laterally within the damper. As the rod moves, its movement is limited by the flow of fluid through the galleries thus providing damping of undulations in the terrain. The damper rod is sealed at its exit point from the damper body to maintain fluid within the unit and to prevent the ingress of dirt and moisture. The seal also acts as a wiper to keep the rod outer diameter clean.

Trapezoidal Links

Three links make up the trapezoidal linkage. The fixed transverse link is fabricated and is not adjustable. The adjustable transverse link comprises a tube, threaded at each end. A threaded fitting is screwed into each end of the tube and locked with lock nuts to a prescribed distance between centres. Each fitting has a pressed bush installed. The trailing link is fabricated and is not adjustable.

The fixed transverse link is bushed at each end and is located in the forward mounting of the rear subframe and the forward attachment on the hub. The adjustable transverse link is also bushed at each end and is located in the rearward mounting of the rear subframe and the rearward attachment on the hub. The fixed transverse link and the adjustable transverse link are attached to the rear subframe with individual bolts and nuts and are attached to the hub with a single bolt and nut with a washer at each end.

The trailing link is bushed at one end. The bushed end is located in a separate bracket which is bolted to the body. The link is secured with a bolt which screws through the bracket into a captive nut in the body rail. The opposite end is forked and locates over a bushed lug on the hub and secured with a bolt and nut.

The fixed transverse links, the adjustable transverse links and the trailing link have a significant role in the vehicle handling. The bushes in each link control the longitudinal movement of the wheel due to braking, acceleration or surface undulations.

The adjustable transverse link allows for the toe-in of the wheel to be adjusted if necessary. The fixed transverse link is slightly shorter than the adjustable link which promotes a small amount of toe-in during cornering. This also minimizes the effects of bump steer. The bush attaching the fixed transverse link to the rear subframe has a very soft initial movement rate which becomes progressively harder as the rate of deflection increases. The three remaining bushes in the fixed transverse and the adjustable transvserse links are of hard construction which give precise handling and minimizes transient steer effects. The soft bush allows for small amounts of toe-in during cornering.

BUSH - TRAILING LINK - REAR

Service repair no - 64.15.11

Remove

1. Raise rear of vehicle.

WARNING: Support on safety stands.

2. Remove road wheel(s).

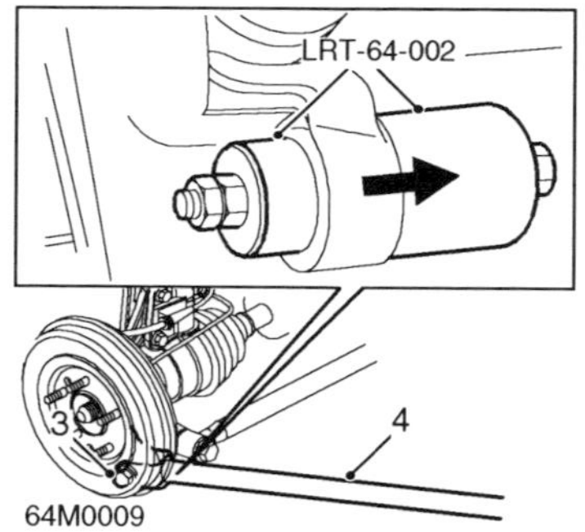

64M0009

3. Remove nut and bolt securing trailing link to hub.
4. Remove link from hub and tie aside.
5. Using **LRT-64-002** remove trailing link bush from hub.

Refit

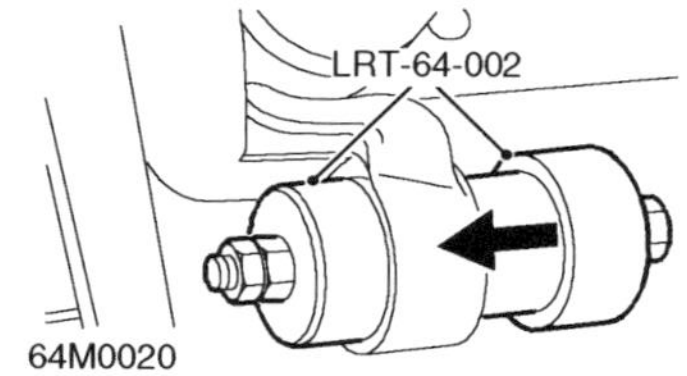

64M0020

1. Ensure bush bore in hub is clean.
2. Using **LRT-64-002** fit new bush into hub.
3. Fit trailing link to hub, fit nut and bolt but do not tighten at this stage.

CAUTION: Nuts and bolts must be tightened with weight of vehicle on suspension.

4. Support weight of vehicle with jack under rear hub.
5. Tighten trailing link to hub nut and bolt to 120 Nm.
6. Fit road wheel(s) and tighten nuts to correct torque. ***See INFORMATION, Torque wrench settings.***
7. Remove stand(s) and lower vehicle.
8. Check and if necessary adjust rear wheel alignment. ***See STEERING, Adjustments.***

BEARING - HUB - REAR

Service repair no - 64.15.14

Remove

1. Raise front of vehicle.

WARNING: Support on safety stands.

2. Remove road wheel(s).

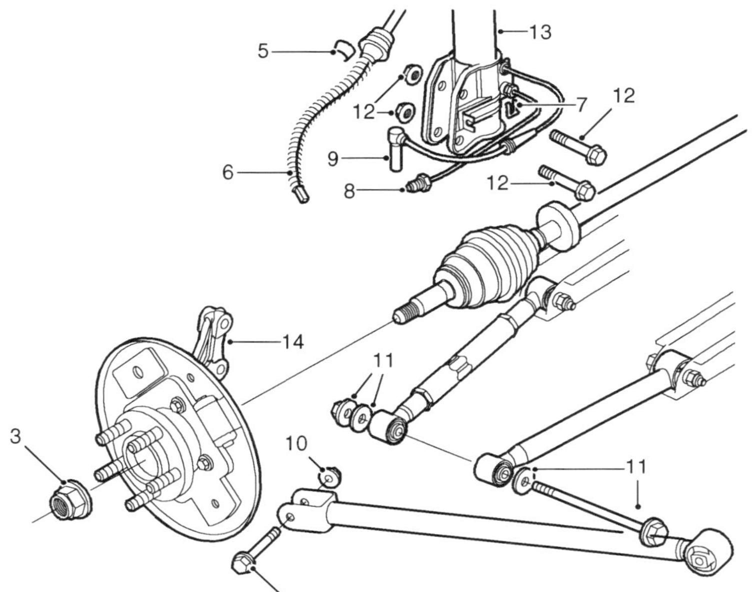

64M0001

3. Remove and discard drive shaft nut.
4. Remove brake shoes as an assembly. ***See BRAKES, Repairs.***
5. Release handbrake cable retainer from backplate.
6. Remove cable from backplate.
7. Remove clip securing brake pipe to bracket.
8. Remove brake pipe union from wheel cylinder.

CAUTION: Plug the connections.

9. Remove ABS sensor from hub.
10. Remove nut and bolt securing trailing link to hub.
11. Remove nut, bolt and washers securing transverse links to hub.
12. Remove 2 nuts and bolts securing hub to damper.
13. Release damper from hub.
14. Remove hub from drive shaft.
Do not carry out further dismantling if component is removed for access only.

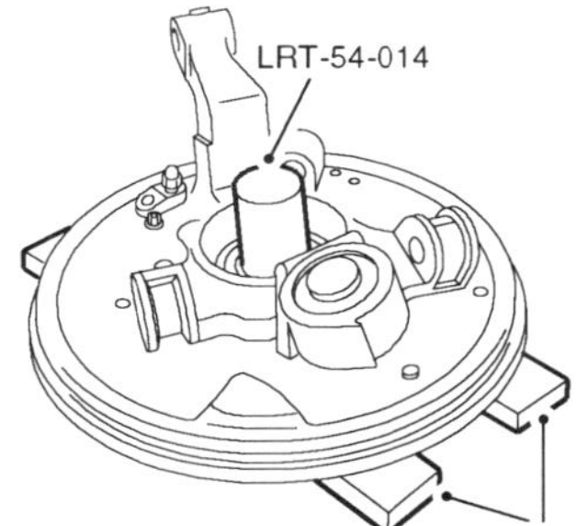

64M0002

15. Position swivel hub assembly to press, support on tools **LRT-54-017** and press out drive flange using tool **LRT-54-014.**

NOTE: Outer bearing inner track will remain on drive flange.

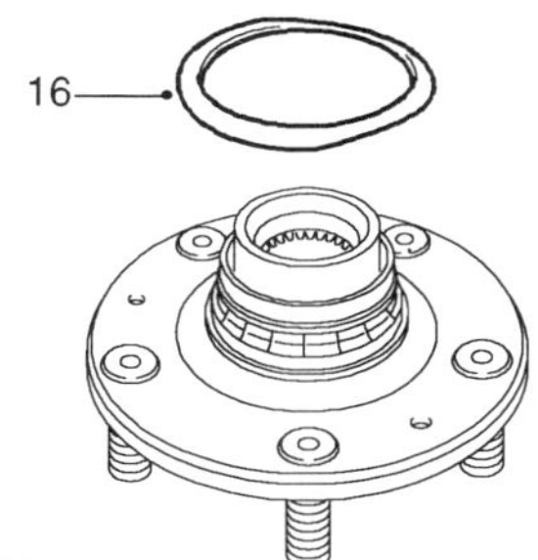

64M0013

16. Remove bearing sealing plate from inner track
17. Position drive flange in a vice.

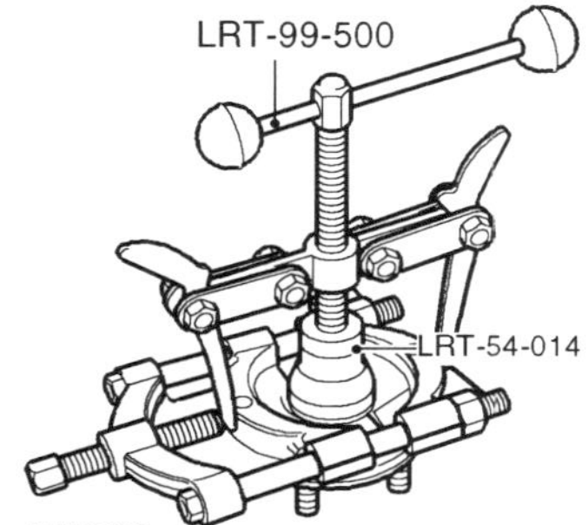

64M0003

18. Clamp both halves of a suitable bearing separator around bearing inner track ensuring that inner lip fits in groove on inner track.
19. Using tool **LRT-99-500** and thrust pad **LRT-54-014** withdraw inner track from drive flange.

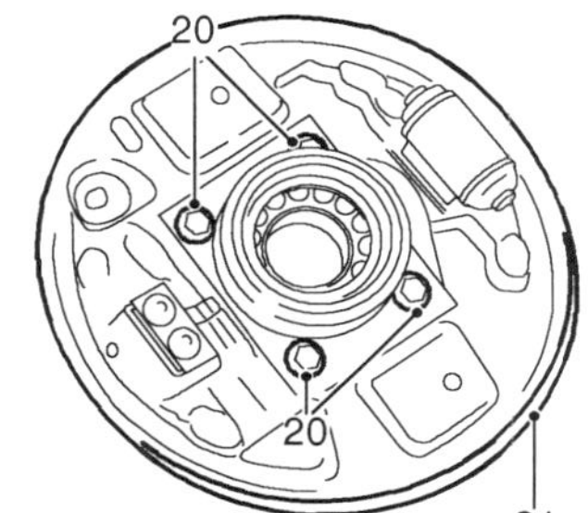

64M0004

20. Fit hub to vice and remove 4 bolts securing backplate to hub.
21. Remove backplate.

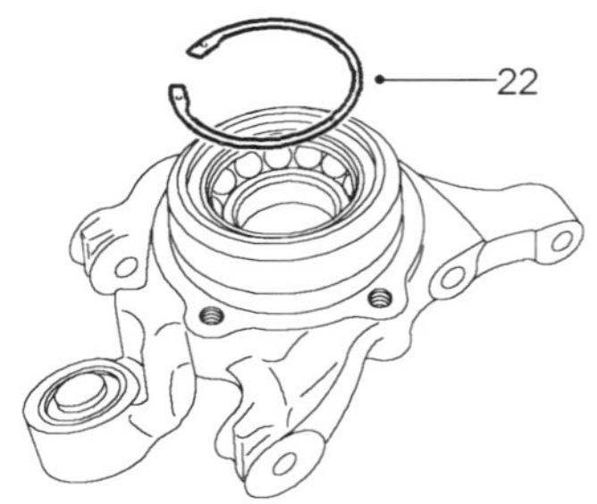

64M0005

22. Remove circlip from bearing.

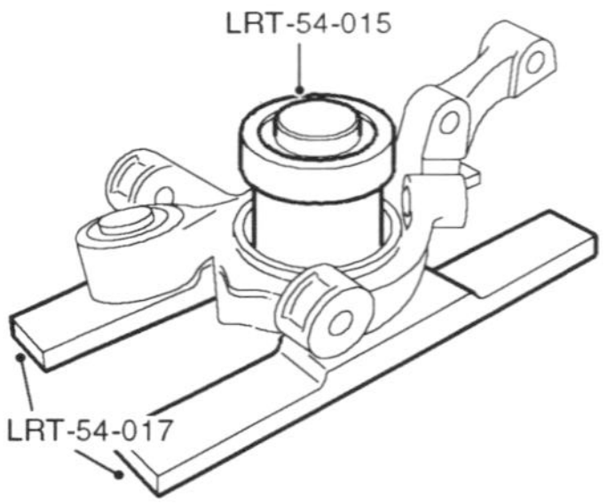

64M0006

23. Position hub to press and press out bearing using tool **LRT-54-015** and **LRT-54-017** discard bearing.

CAUTION: Never re-use existing bearing.

24. Clean hub assembly and drive flange.

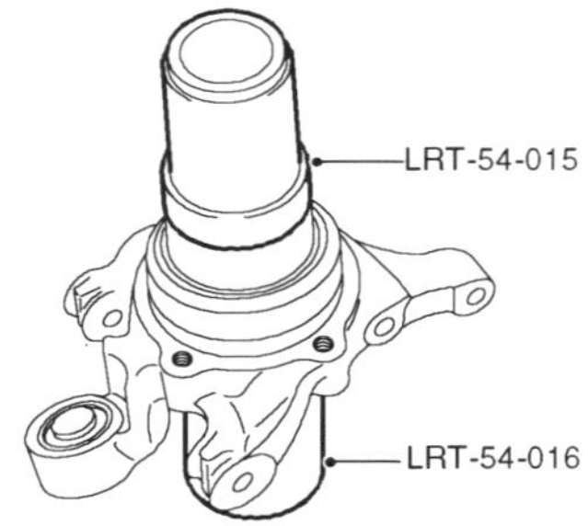

64M0007

25. Support hub on tool **LRT-54-016** and press in new bearing using tool **LRT-54-015.**
26. Fit circlip.
27. Fit hub to vice, fit back plate and tighten bolts to 45 Nm.

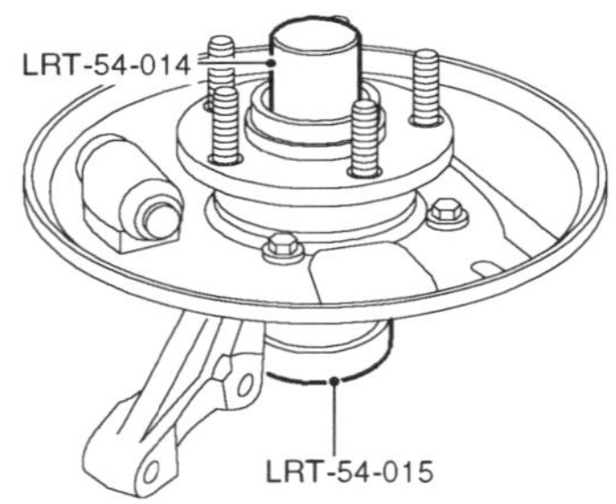

64M0008

28. Support hub on tool **LRT-54-015** and press flange into bearing using tool **LRT-54-014.**

Refit

1. Fit hub to drive shaft.
2. Fit hub to damper and tighten nuts and bolts to 205 Nm.

NOTE: Ensure that washers are fitted to both ends of bolt.

3. Fit nut, bolt and washers securing transverse links to hub and tighten nut to 120 Nm.
4. Fit trailing link to hub, tighten nut and bolt to 120 Nm.
5. Clean ABS sensor, smear sensor with an anti-seize grease and fit sensor to hub.
6. Fit brake pipe to wheel cylinder and tighten nut to 14 Nm.
7. Fit clip securing brake pipe to bracket.
8. Fit handbrake cable to back plate.
9. Fit brake shoe assembly. ***See BRAKES, Repairs.***
10. Fit NEW drive shaft nut and tighten to 400 Nm. Stake nut to shaft.
11. Fit road wheel(s) and tighten nuts to correct torque. ***See INFORMATION, Torque wrench settings.***
12. Remove stand(s) and lower vehicle.

DAMPER - REAR

Service repair no - 64.30.02
Service repair no - 64.20.01 Spring - rear

Remove

1. Raise rear of vehicle, one side.

WARNING: Support on safety stands.

2. Remove road wheel(s).
3. Fit clamp to brake hose.

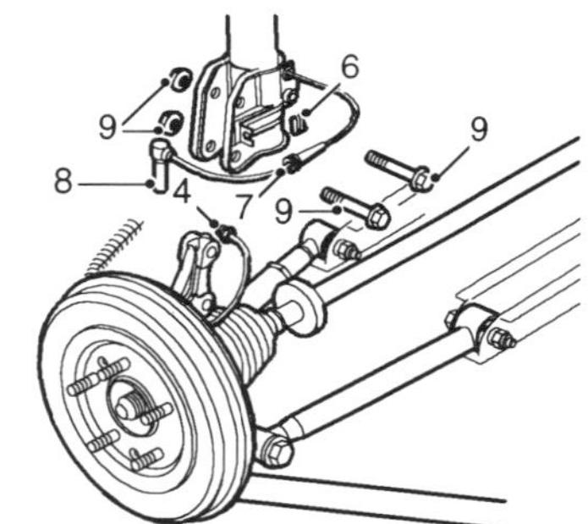

64M0014

4. Disconnect brake pipe from brake hose.
5. Position cloth to collect spillage.

CAUTION: Plug the connections.

6. Remove 'C' clip from brake hose.
7. Release ABS harness from brackets.
8. Release ABS sensor from hub assembly.
9. Remove 2 bolts securing damper to hub carrier. Release damper from hub carrier.

CAUTION: Support the hub assembly.

10. Remove rear quarter lower trim casing. ***See BODY, Interior trim components.***

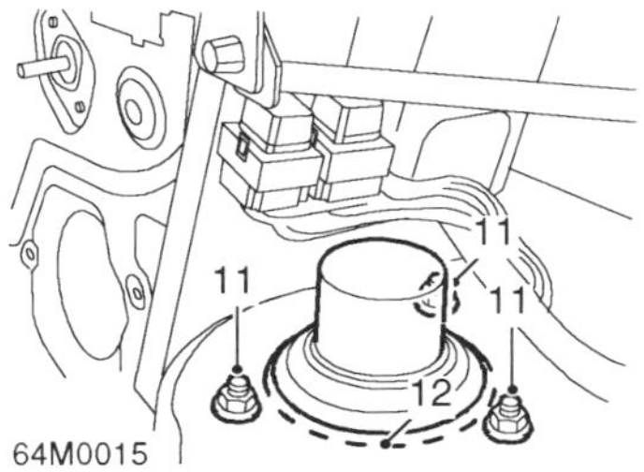

64M0015

11. Remove 3 nuts from damper top mounting and remove spring and damper assembly.
12. Remove rubber seal from top mounting.

CAUTION: Note alignment of top mounting, spring and damper dust cover.

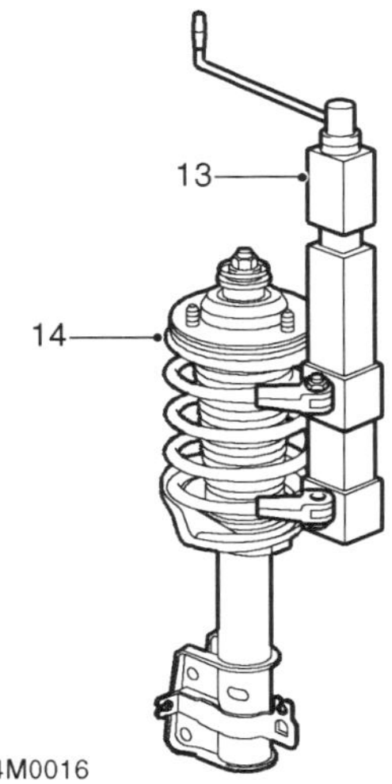

64M0016

13. Position a suitable spring compressor tool in vice.
14. Position damper and spring assembly to spring compressor and locate in arms.
15. Add a reference mark between the top mount and the spring.

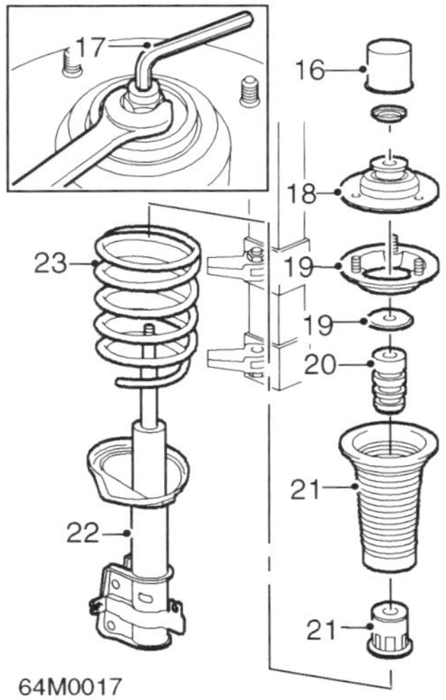

64M0017

16. Remove cover from top mounting.
17. Compress spring by 2 to 3 cm until loose, hold damper shaft with Allen key, remove and discard mounting plate nut.
18. Remove top mounting plate.
19. Remove rebound washer and mounting plate.
20. Remove spring aid and bump plate.
21. Remove spring seat, dust cover and bump stop cup.
22. Remove damper from spring.
23. Release and remove spring from spring compressor.

Refit

1. Inspect damper, mounting plate rubber and dust cover for deterioration and damage.
2. Clean mating faces of spring, damper and mounting plate.
3. Clean damper shaft and bump stop plate.
4. Position spring in spring compressor, locate spring in arms and compress spring by 2 to 3 cm.
5. Fit damper to spring, ensure spring is located in recess in damper plate.
6. Fit dust cover and bump stop cup.
7. Fit spring aid and bump plate.
8. Fit mounting plate and rebound washer.

CAUTION: Align tag on dust cover to damper.

9. Using a NEW nut, hold damper shaft with an Allen key and tighten nut to 57 Nm.
10. Fit top mounting cover.
11. Release spring and remove assembly from spring compressor.
12. Clean mating face of top mounting plate.
13. Fit rubber seal to top mounting.
14. Position damper assembly and align top mounting to body and tighten nuts to 45 Nm.
15. Fit rear quarter lower trim casing. ***See BODY, Interior trim components.***
16. Fit bolts securing damper to hub carrier and tighten to 205 Nm.
17. Clean ABS sensor, smear sensor with anti-seize grease and fit sensor to hub carrier.
18. Locate brake hose and ABS harness in bracket.
19. Secure brake hose with 'C' clip.
20. Connect brake pipe to brake hose.
21. Remove clamp from brake hose.
22. Bleed brakes. ***See BRAKES, Adjustments.***
23. Fit road wheel(s) and tighten nuts to correct torque. ***See INFORMATION, Torque wrench settings.***
24. Remove stand(s) and lower vehicle.

TRANSVERSE LINK - ADJUSTABLE - REAR

Service repair no - 64.35.70

Remove

1. Raise rear of vehicle.

WARNING: Support on safety stands.

2. Remove road wheel(s).

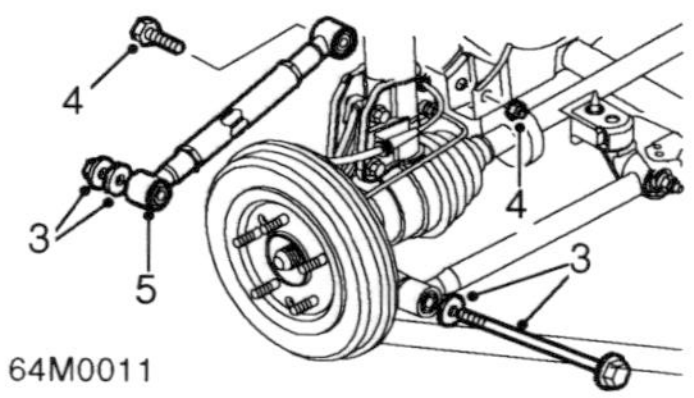

64M0011

3. Remove nut and bolt securing link to hub.
4. Remove nut, bolt and washers securing link to subframe.
5. Remove link.

Refit

1. Fit link.

NOTE: Ensure that washers are fitted to both ends of bolt.

2. Fit nuts, bolts and washers securing link to hub and subframe but do not tighten.

CAUTION: Nuts and bolts must be tightened with weight of vehicle on suspension.

3. Support weight of vehicle with jack under rear hub.
4. Tighten nuts and bolts to 120 Nm.
5. Fit road wheel(s) and tighten nuts to correct torque. ***See INFORMATION, Torque wrench settings.***
6. Remove stand(s) and lower vehicle.
7. Check and if necessary adjust rear wheel alignment. ***See STEERING, Adjustments.***

CONTENTS

Page

BRAKES

Vehicle braking is provided by disc brakes on the front wheels and drum brakes on the rear wheels. The foot brakes are operated by a diagonally split, dual circuit hydraulic system with vacuum servo power assistance. A cable operated handbrake operates on the two rear brakes.

The hydraulic system has two variants, a non anti-lock braking system and an ABS variant. The ABS variant features 4-wheel electronic traction control and hill descent functions as well as anti-lock braking.

FRONT BRAKES

The front brakes each comprise a hub mounted, single piston caliper assembly and a solid disc. The inboard side of the disc is protected by a mudshield.

When hydraulic pressure is supplied to the caliper, the piston extends and forces the inner pad against the disc. The caliper body reacts and slides on the guide pins to bring the outer pad into contact with the disc.

REAR BRAKES

The rear brakes each comprise a hub mounted backplate and drum containing leading and trailing brake shoes. An adjuster rod is incorporated to automatically adjust the brake shoes to compensate for wear of the brake linings. Adjustment occurs during operation of the foot brake.

When hydraulic pressure is supplied to the wheel cylinder, the cylinder extends and forces the brake shoes against the drum.

Brake system layout - non ABS (RH drive shown, LH drive similar)

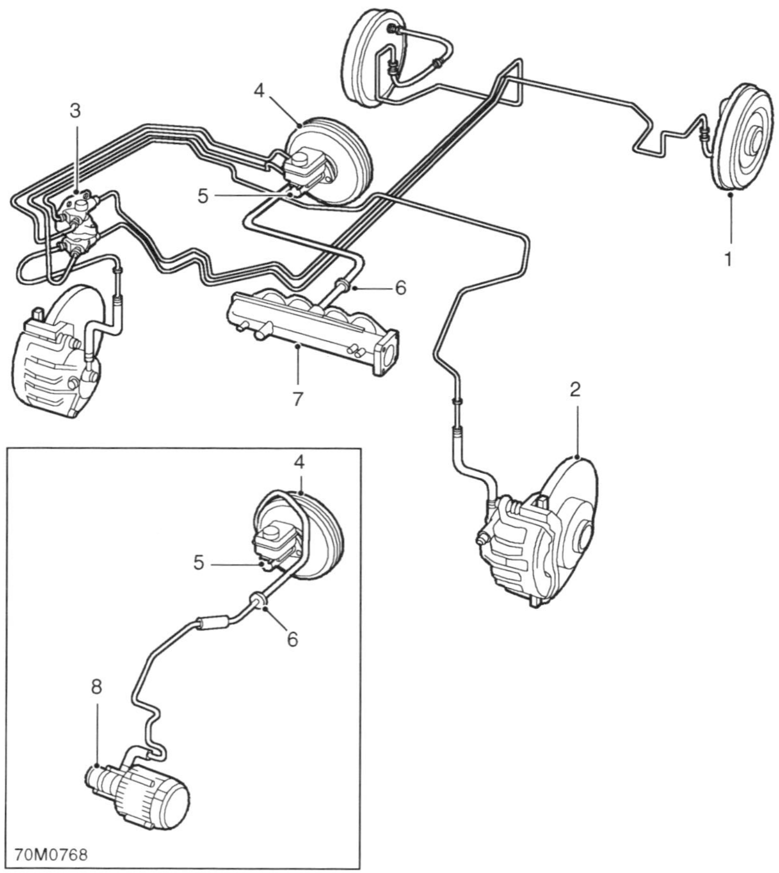

1. Rear brake
2. Front brake
3. Pressure conscious reducing valve
4. Brake servo assembly
5. Master cylinder assembly
6. Vacuum check valve
7. Engine inlet manifold (petrol models)
8. Vacuum pump (diesel models)

Brake system layout - ABS (RH drive shown, LH drive similar)

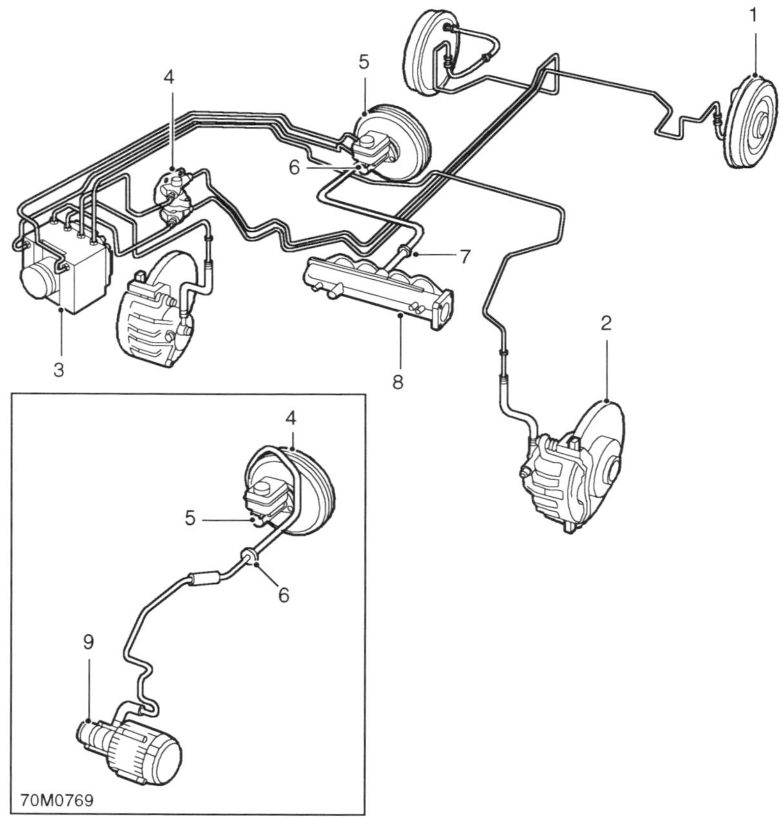

1. Rear brake
2. Front brake
3. ABS modulator
4. Pressure conscious reducing valve
5. Brake servo assembly
6. Master cylinder assembly
7. Vacuum check valve
8. Engine inlet manifold (petrol models)
9. Vacuum pump (diesel models)

Front brake components

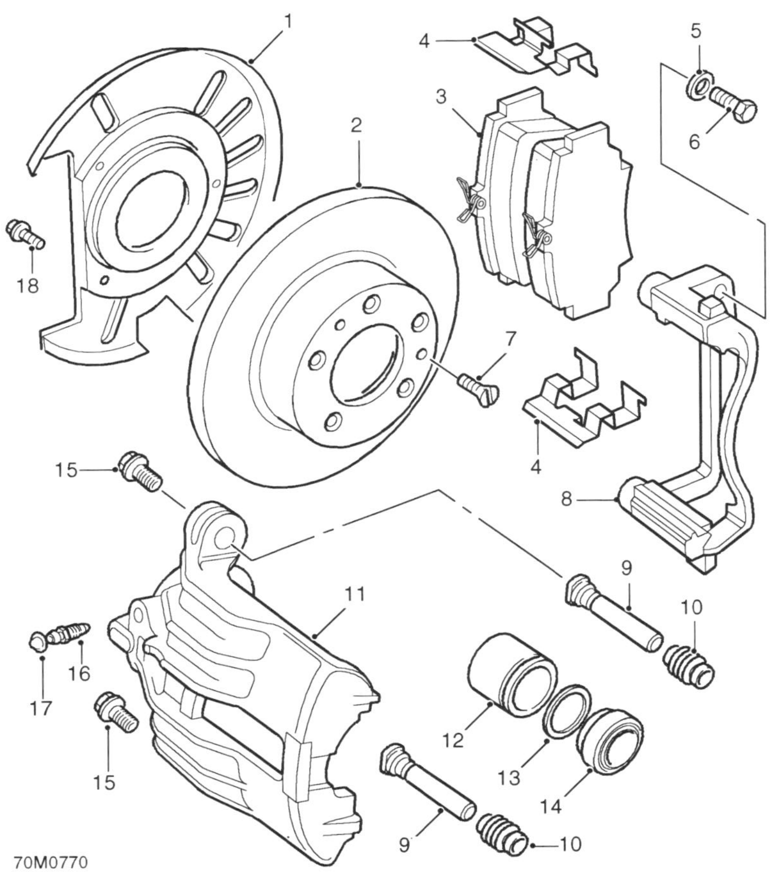

70M0770

1. Mudshield
2. Brake disc
3. Brake pads
4. Pad retainer
5. Washer
6. Caliper fixing bolt
7. Brake disc fixing screw
8. Caliper carrier
9. Guide pin
10. Guide pin dust cover
11. Caliper body
12. Piston
13. Piston seal
14. Piston dust cover
15. Guide pin bolt
16. Bleed screw
17. Bleed screw cap
18. Mudshield fixing bolt

Rear brake components

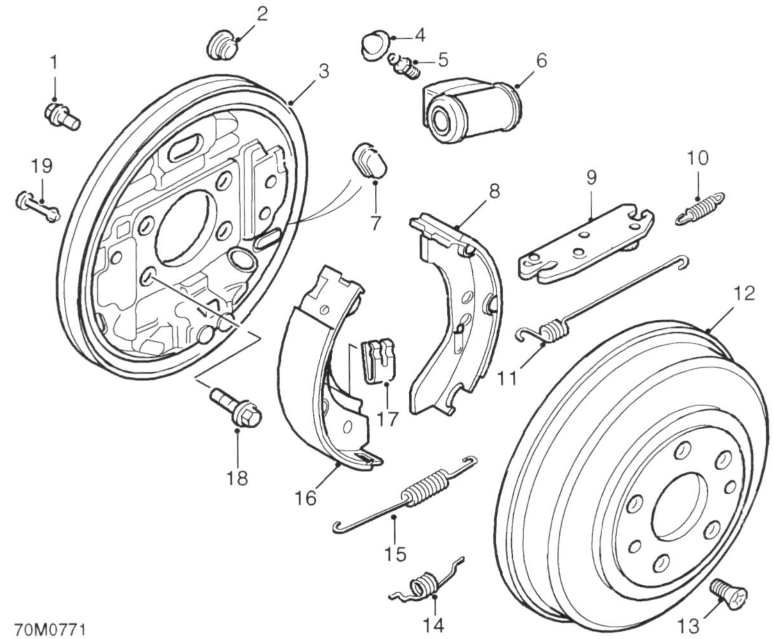

70M0771

1. Wheel cylinder fixing bolt
2. Blanking plug
3. Backplate
4. Bleed screw cap
5. Bleed screw
6. Wheel cylinder
7. Blanking plug
8. Leading brake shoe
9. Adjuster rod
10. Adjuster spring
11. Upper shoe return spring
12. Brake drum
13. Drum fixing screw
14. Bias spring
15. Lower shoe return spring
16. Trailing brake shoe
17. Shoe retaining pin spring clip
18. Backplate fixing bolt
19. Shoe retaining pin

HYDRAULIC SYSTEM

The hydraulic system operates the brakes in response to brake pedal movement and, on ABS variants, operation of the ABS modulator.

For normal brake operation, brake pedal movement is assisted by the brake servo assembly and transmitted to the master cylinder assembly. The master cylinder assembly converts brake pedal movement to hydraulic pressure. Primary and secondary brake pipe circuits supply the hydraulic pressure to the brakes: the primary circuit supplies the front left and rear right brakes; the secondary circuit supplies the front right and rear left brakes. A Pressure Conscious Reducing Valve (PCRV) regulates the pressure to the rear brakes to give front/rear differential braking.

A red, brake warning lamp in the instrument pack illuminates if the fluid level in the hydraulic system falls to an unsafe level.

Vacuum for the brake servo assembly is obtained from the engine inlet manifold (petrol models) or a vacuum pump (diesel models) through a vacuum line and non return valve.

Hydraulic system schematic - non ABS

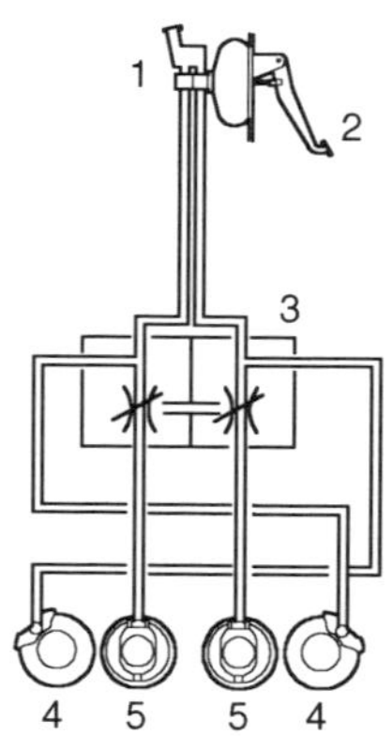

70M0772

1. Servo/Master cylinder assembly
2. Brake pedal
3. Pressure conscious reducing valve
4. Front brake
5. Rear brake

To reduce operating noise on vehicles with ABS, sleeving is installed on some of the brake pipes in the engine compartment and the pipes are located in sprung pipe clips.

Hydraulic system schematic - ABS

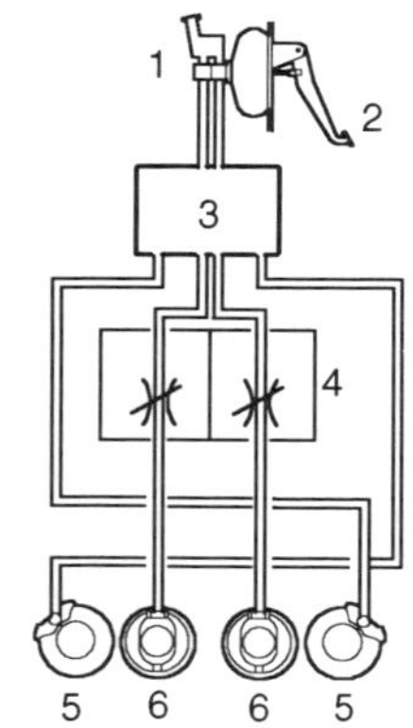

70M0773

1. Servo/Master cylinder assembly
2. Brake pedal
3. ABS modulator
4. Pressure conscious reducing valve
5. Front brake
6. Rear brake

Brake servo assembly

The brake servo assembly provides power assistance to reduce the pedal load when braking.

The assembly is attached to the front of the pedal box and comprises a circular housing containing a diaphragm, push rods, valve and filter. A push rod at the rear of the housing is connected to the brake pedal. The vacuum line is connected to a port in the front face of the housing.

With the brake pedal released and the engine running, vacuum pressure is present on both sides of the diaphragm. When the brake pedal is pressed, the rear push rod moves forward and opens the valve to allow atmospheric pressure through the filter into the pedal side of the diaphragm. The pressure differential acting on the diaphragm increases the pressure being applied by the brake pedal, which is transmitted to the master cylinder via the forward push rod.

If the servo fails, the hydraulic system will still function but will require greater pedal effort due to the lack of vacuum assistance.

Sectioned view of brake servo assembly

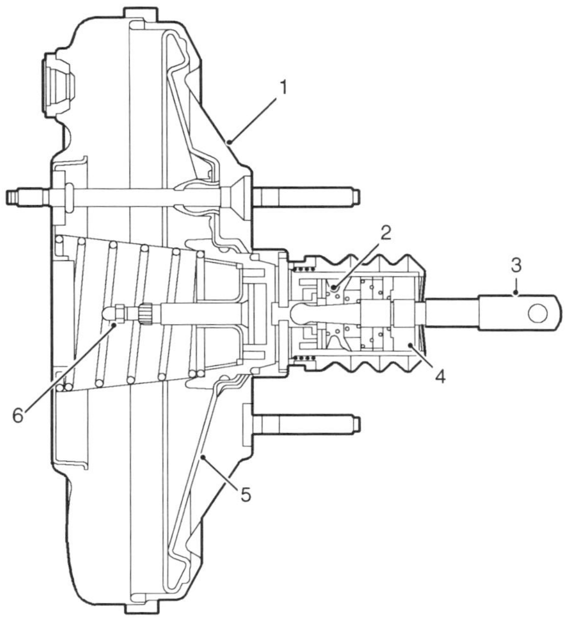

70M0777

1. Housing
2. Control valve
3. Rear push rod
4. Filter
5. Diaphragm
6. Forward push rod

Vacuum pump (diesel models only)

As the diesel engine air inlet system does not produce sufficient depression to operate the brake servo assembly, an engine driven vacuum pump is installed. The vacuum pump is integrated with the engine alternator and driven by the accessory drive belt. The pump is a rotary vane type, lubricated and cooled by engine oil supplied through a pipe connected to the centre front of the engine block and returned through a pipe connected to the centre front of the oil sump. Air extracted from the brake servo assembly is vented into the oil sump with returning lubricating oil.

NOTE: Normally, only a small volume of air is drawn from the brake servo assembly. However, a leak in the brake servo assembly or vacuum pipe may cause excessive crankcase pressure.

Vacuum pump installation

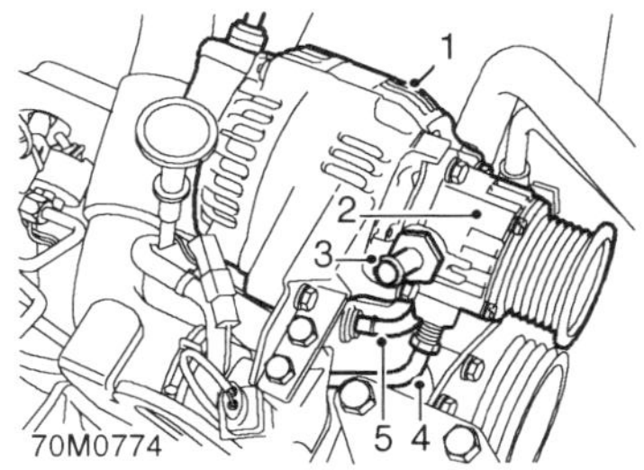

1. Alternator
2. Vacuum pump
3. Brake servo assembly vacuum connection
4. Oil feed pipe
5. Oil drain pipe

Master cylinder assembly

The master cylinder assembly produces hydraulic pressure to operate the brakes when the brake pedal is pressed. The assembly is attached to the front of the brake servo assembly, and comprises a cylinder containing two pistons in tandem. The rear piston produces pressure for the primary circuit and the front piston produces pressure for the secondary circuit.

Installed on top of the cylinder is a brake fluid reservoir. The reservoir is internally divided to provide an independent supply of fluid to each brake circuit, and so prevent a single fluid leak from disabling both primary and secondary brake circuits.

Should a failure occur in one circuit, the remaining circuit will still operate effectively, although brake pedal travel and vehicle braking distances will increase. If the fluid level in the reservoir is too low, the brake fluid level switch in the reservoir filler cap connects an earth to the instrument pack and illuminates the brake warning lamp.

Non ABS master cylinder

When the brake pedal is pressed, the front push rod in the brake servo assembly pushes the primary piston along the cylinder bore. This produces pressure in the primary pressure chamber which, in conjunction with the primary spring, overcomes the secondary spring and, simultaneously, moves the secondary piston along the cylinder bore. The initial movement of the pistons takes the recuperating seals past the cut-off holes in the cylinder wall. Further movement of the pistons then pressurizes the fluid in the primary and secondary pressure chambers, and thus the brake circuits. The fluid in the chambers behind the pistons is unaffected by movement of the pistons and can flow unrestricted through the feed holes between the chambers and the reservoir.

When the brake pedal is released, the primary and secondary springs push the pistons back down the bore of the cylinder. This creates a depression in the pressure chambers, which causes the recuperation seals to momentarily collapse and allows fluid from the chambers behind the pistons to flow into the pressure chambers. Fluid from the reservoir flows through the feed holes to compensate for the loss of fluid from the chambers behind the pistons. The final return movement of the pistons exposes the cut-off holes and allows excess fluid in the pressure chambers to flow into the reservoir.

ABS master cylinder

When the brake pedal is pressed, the front push rod in the brake servo assembly pushes the primary piston along the cylinder bore. This produces pressure in the primary pressure chamber which, in conjunction with the primary spring, overcomes the secondary spring and simultaneously moves the secondary piston along the cylinder bore. The initial movement of the pistons, away from the piston stops, closes the primary and secondary centre valves. Further movement of the pistons then pressurizes the fluid in the primary and secondary pressure chambers, and thus the brake circuits. The fluid in the chambers, behind the pistons, is unaffected by movement of the pistons and can flow unrestricted through the feed holes between the chambers and the reservoir.

When the brake pedal is released, the primary and secondary springs push the pistons back down the bore of the cylinder. As the pistons contact the piston stops, the primary and secondary centre valves open, which allows fluid to circulate unrestricted between the two hydraulic circuits and the reservoir, through the centre valves, the chambers behind the pistons and the feed holes.

Sectioned view of master cylinder assembly - non ABS

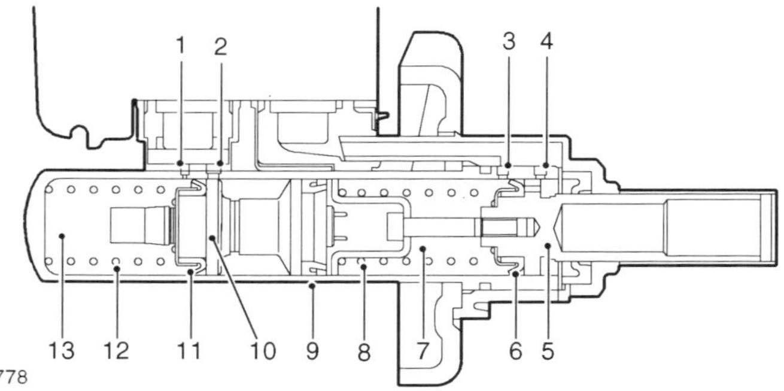

1. Secondary cut-off hole
2. Secondary feed hole
3. Primary cut-off hole
4. Primary feed hole
5. Primary piston
6. Recuperating seal
7. Pressure chamber
8. Primary spring
9. Cylinder
10. Secondary piston
11. Recuperating seal
12. Secondary spring
13. Pressure chamber

Sectioned view of master cylinder assembly - ABS

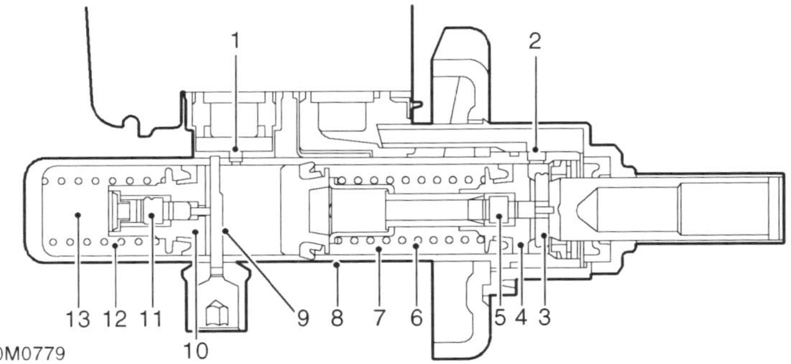

70M0779

1. Secodary feed hole
2. Primary feed hole
3. Valve pin
4. Primary piston
5. Centre valve
6. Primary spring
7. Pressure chamber
8. Cylinder
9. Valve pin
10. Secondary piston
11. Centre valve
12. Secondary spring
13. Pressure chamber

PCRV

The PCRV is a twin valve unit that reduces the hydraulic pressure supplied to the rear brakes to maintain vehicle stability under braking. A mounting bracket attaches the PCRV to the RH inner wing.

The PCRV comprises two cast housings, one connected to the primary brake circuit and one connected to the secondary brake circuit. The two housings are bolted together and connected by an internal passageway. The passageway in each housing contains a piston sleeve, poppet valve and associated seals and springs. One housing incorporates a vent from the internal passageway, which is sealed by a rubber vent plug.

On ABS variants, only the rear brake pipes are connected to the PCRV. On non ABS variants, both the front and the rear brake pipes are connected to the PCRV, but the flow to the front brake pipes is unregulated.

When the brakes are applied, pressurized brake fluid from the inlet ports passes through the piston sleeves and the open poppet valves to the rear brake outlet ports. On non ABS variants, pressurized brake fluid also passes directly from the inlet ports to the front brake outlet ports. Hydraulic pressure, on the outer ends of the piston sleeves, moves the piston sleeves against spring pressure towards the centre of the PCRV. When the piston sleeves contact the poppet valves, the rear brake outlet ports are isolated from the inlet ports.

As the pressure from the master cylinder increases, the poppet valves remain closed until, at approximately 25 bar (367.5 $lbf.in^2$), hydraulic pressure overcomes poppet valve spring pressure to allow a restricted flow through to the rear brake outlet ports. The restriction causes a pressure drop across the poppet valves, to give a front : rear brake pressure differential of 10 : 3.

Sectioned view of PCRV - non ABS

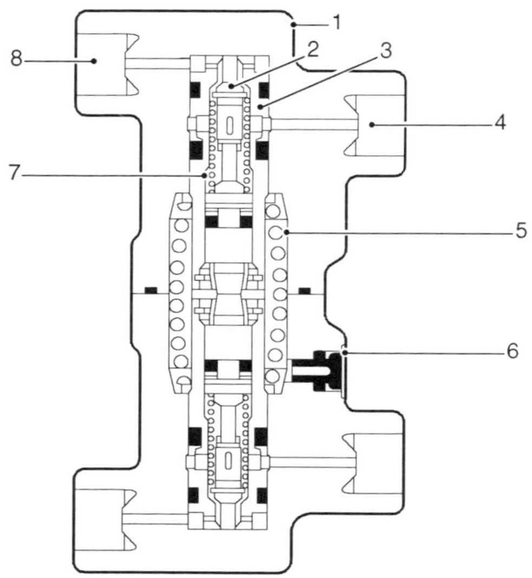

70M0780

1. Housing
2. Poppet valve
3. Piston sleeve
4. Rear brake outlet port
5. Spring
6. Vent plug
7. Spring
8. Inlet port

On non ABS variants, in order to balance the hydraulic pressure to the rear brake outlets, the two piston sleeves act in opposition to each other at either end of a common spring. Any difference in pressure at the two inlet ports causes the position of the piston sleeves to be biased towards the lower pressure circuit. This causes an increase in the pressure drop across the poppet valve of the circuit with the higher pressure. The subsequent pressure at the outlet port is then approximately the same as the pressure at the outlet port of the low pressure circuit.

When the brakes are released, the piston sleeves are moved outwards by spring pressure. This opens the poppet valves, releasing hydraulic pressure from the rear brakes and allowing brake fluid to flow back towards the master cylinder.

In the event of failure of an internal seal, fluid will enter the centre chamber of the PCRV and, when the brake pedal is applied, will cause the vent plug to rupture and allow brake fluid to escape.

Sectioned view of PCRV - ABS

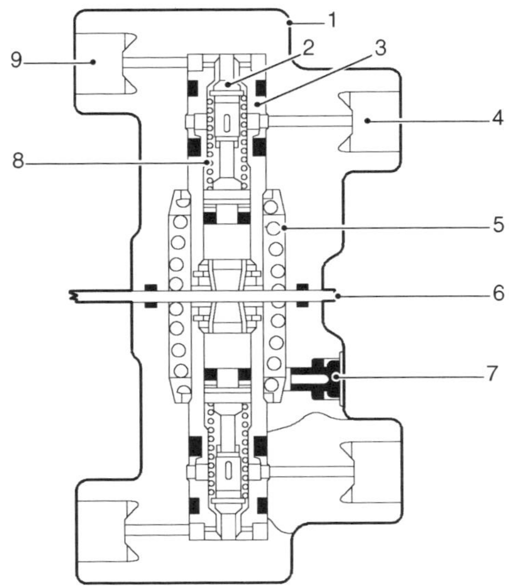

70M0781

1. Housing
2. Poppet valve
3. Piston sleeve
4. Rear brake outlet port
5. Spring
6. Mounting bracket
7. Vent plug
8. Spring
9. Inlet port

ABS

The ABS is a full time, four channel system that gives individual speed control of all four wheels to provide the vehicle with anti-lock braking (ABS), Electronic Traction Control (ETC) and Hill Descent Control (HDC) functions. In addition to the components of the non ABS brake system, vehicles with ABS have an ABS modulator, four ABS sensors and an ABS Electronic Control Unit (ECU).

ABS modulator

The ABS modulator controls the supply of hydraulic pressure to the brakes in response to inputs from the ABS ECU. The modulator is attached by three mounting bushes to a bracket on the RH inner wing, and connected to the primary and secondary hydraulic circuits downstream of the master cylinder assembly. Three electrical connectors link the ABS modulator to the vehicle wiring.

Internal passages in the ABS modulator, separated into primary and secondary circuits, connect to the various components that control the supply of hydraulic pressure to the brakes. Shuttle valves and check valves control the flow through the internal circuits. Shuttle valve switches, connected in series to the ABS ECU, provide a brakes on/off signal. A damper chamber and restrictor are included in each circuit to refine system operation. Inlet and outlet solenoid valves control the flow to the individual brakes. An expansion chamber is connected to each circuit to absorb pressure. A return pump is connected to both circuits to provide a pressure source.

The ABS modulator has three operating modes:

- Normal braking mode: When the brake pedal is pressed, pressurized fluid from the master cylinder assembly moves the shuttle valves to open lines A' and close the shuttle valve switches. Pressurized fluid then flows through the open inlet solenoid valves to operate the brakes. The shuttle valve switches supply a brakes on signal to the ABS ECU.
- ABS braking mode: When in the normal braking mode, if the ABS ECU detects that a wheel is about to lock, it energizes the inlet and outlet solenoid valves of the related brake and starts the return pump. The inlet solenoid valve closes to isolate the brake from pressurized fluid; the outlet solenoid valve opens to release pressure from the brake into the expansion chamber and the return pump circuit. The brake releases and the wheel begins to accelerate. The ABS ECU then operates the inlet and outlet valves to control the supply of hydraulic pressure to the brake and apply the maximum braking effort (for the available traction) without locking the wheel.
- Active braking mode: When ETC or HDC are enabled, and the ABS ECU determines that active braking is required, it starts the return pump. Hydraulic fluid, drawn from the reservoirs through the master cylinder, shuttle valves and lines B', is pressurized by the return pump and supplied to lines A'. The ABS ECU then operates the inlet and outlet solenoid valves to control the supply of hydraulic pressure to the individual brakes and slow the wheel(s).

ABS sensors

The ABS sensors supply the ABS ECU with a speed signal from each wheel. An inductive sensor is installed in a bush in each wheel hub, sensing off a 60 tooth exciter ring. A fly-lead connects each sensor to the vehicle wiring. The exciter rings are fitted to the outer diameter of the constant velocity joint on each drive shaft and shielded by the hub centre boss.

ABS modulator schematic

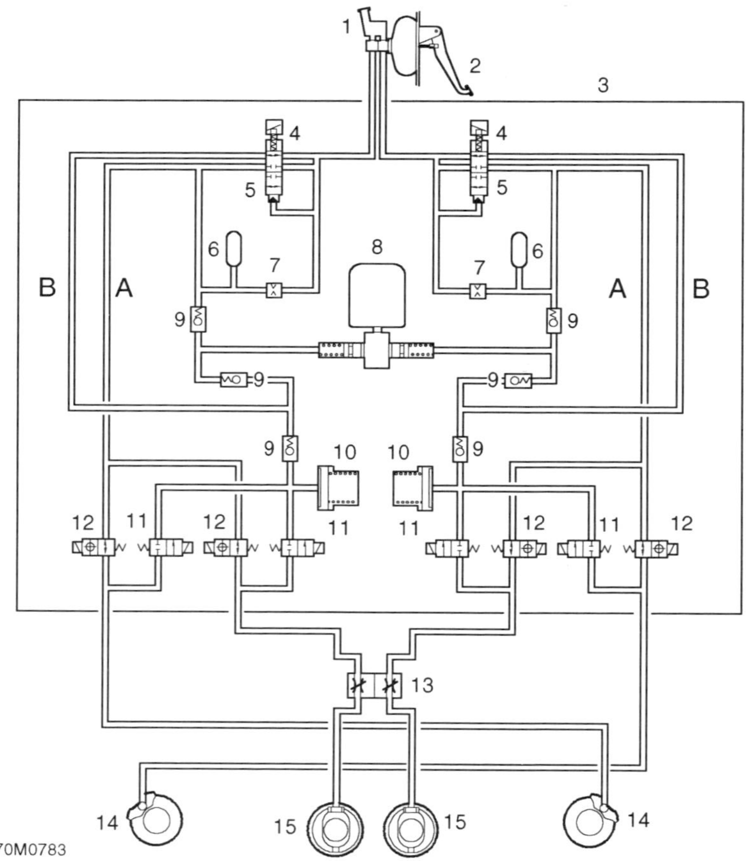

70M0783

1. Master cylinder assembly
2. Brake pedal
3. ABS modulator
4. Shuttle valve switch
5. Shuttle valve
6. Damper chamber
7. Restrictor
8. Return pump
9. Check valve
10. Expansion chamber
11. Outlet solenoid valve
12. Inlet solenoid valve
13. Pressure conscious reducing valve
14. Front brake
15. Rear brake

ABS ECU

The ABS ECU controls the operation of the ABS modulator to provide the ABS, ETC and HDC functions. It also operates warning lamps in the instrument pack to provide the driver with status information on each function. The ABS ECU is attached to a bracket below the RH front seat, beneath a protective cover. Incorporated into the ABS ECU are integrated circuits and software for system control and diagnostics. Three electrical connectors interface the unit with the vehicle wiring.

The warning lamps consist of:
- An amber ABS graphic.
- An amber TC graphic.
- Two inclined vehicle graphics for HDC, one amber (fault), which includes an exclamation mark, and one green (information).

The warning lamp bulbs are serviceable items that can be renewed from the rear of the instrument pack.

When the ignition is switched on, the ABS ECU performs a bulb check of the warning lamps as part of the power up procedure. The ABS warning lamp is extinguished briefly, after 1.3 to 2 seconds, then remains illuminated until vehicle speed exceeds 4.4 mph (7 kph). The ETC and HDC warning lamps are extinguished after 4 to 5 seconds. If a fault warning lamp remains illuminated after the lamp check, a fault has been detected and repair action is required.

The ABS ECU continually calculates vehicle speed using the inputs from all four ABS sensors. Vehicle speed is used as a reference against which individual wheel speeds are monitored for unacceptable acceleration or deceleration. Vehicle speed is also output to the instrument pack for the speedometer.

ABS operation

The purpose of ABS is to prevent vehicle wheels locking during brake application, thus maintaining vehicle steerability and stability. This allows the vehicle to be steered while the brakes are applied, even under emergency conditions, and to avoid obstacles where there is sufficient space to redirect the vehicle.

WARNING: ABS is an aid to retaining steering control and stability while braking. ABS cannot defy the natural laws of physics acting on the vehicle. ABS will not prevent accidents resulting from excessive cornering speeds, following another vehicle too closely or aquaplaning, i.e. where a layer of water prevents adequate contact between tyre and road surface. The additional control provided by ABS must never be exploited in a dangerous or reckless manner which could jeopardise the safety of driver or other road users. The fitting of ABS does not imply that the vehicle will always stop in a shorter stopping distance.

NOTE: During normal braking the feel of the brake pedal on vehicles equipped with ABS will be the same as that on non ABS vehicles. During anti-lock braking operation the driver will experience feedback in the form of a pulsating brake pedal and solenoid/pump motor noise from the ABS modulator.

The anti-lock braking function is automatically enabled whenever the ABS modulator is in the normal braking mode.

While the anti-lock braking function is enabled, if the ABS ECU detects a wheel decelerating faster than the average, indicating it is about to lock, it operates the ABS modulator in the ABS braking mode for the affected wheel.

ABS ECU

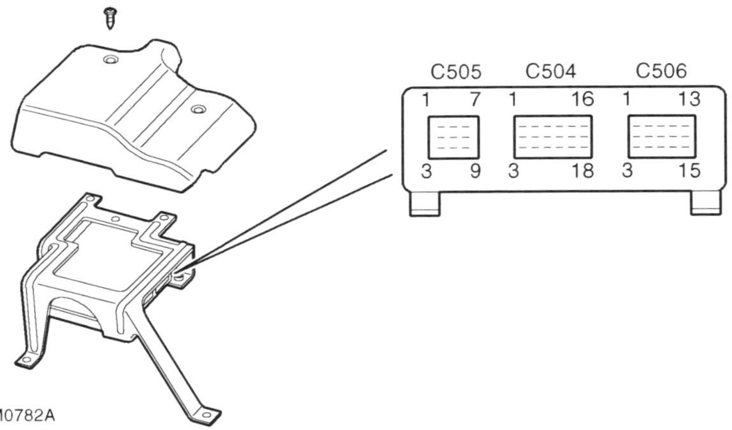

70M0782A

ABS ECU connector pin-out details

Connector C504

1. Battery power
2. Ignition power
3. Road speed
4. Not used
5. ISO 9141 K line
6. Not used
7. Reverse gear selected
8. Return pump monitor
9. Not used
10. ECM input
11. First gear selected
12. Earth
13. ETC warning lamp
14. HDC selected
15. Not used
16. HDC fault warning lamp
17. HDC information warning lamp
18. ABS warning lamp

Connector C505

1. Front LH ABS sensor
2. Front LH ABS sensor
3. Rear RH ABS sensor
4. Front RH ABS sensor
5. Front RH ABS sensor
6. Rear RH ABS sensor
7. Rear LH ABS sensor
8. Rear LH ABS sensor
9. Not used

Continued.....

Connector C506

1. Front LH outlet valve
2. Front LH inlet valve
3. Reference earth
4. Front RH outlet valve
5. Front RH inlet valve
6. Shuttle valve switches
7. Rear LH outlet valve
8. Rear LH inlet valve
9. Not used
10. Rear RH outlet valve
11. Rear RH inlet valve
12. Brake lamps relay coil
13. Not used
14. Not used
15. Return pump relay coil

NOTE: ECM input (C504/10) contains data on throttle position, engine torque, engine speed and engine type.

ABS control schematic

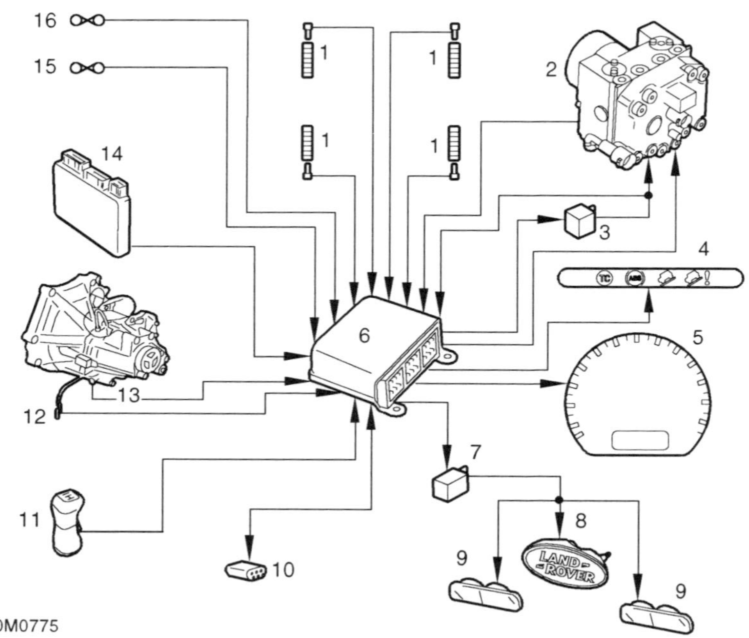

70M0775

1. ABS sensor
2. ABS modulator
3. Return pump relay
4. Warning lamps
5. Speedometer
6. ABS ECU
7. Brake lamp relay
8. Centre high mounted stop lamp
9. Bumper brake lamp
10. Diagnostic socket
11. HDC switch
12. Reverse gear switch
13. First gear switch
14. Engine control module
15. Battery power supply
16. Ignition power supply

ETC operation

ETC uses brake intervention to prevent wheel spin. The ETC function operates on all four wheels and is automatically enabled at speeds up to 31.3. mph (50 kph) provided the brakes are off.

While the ETC function is enabled, if the ABS ECU detects a wheel accelerating faster than the average, indicating loss of traction, it operates the ABS modulator in the active braking mode for the affected wheel. The ABS ECU also illuminates the ETC warning lamp, for a minimum of 2 seconds or for the duration that ETC is active. If the brake pedal is pressed while ETC is active, the ABS ECU reverts to ABS mode.

HDC operation

HDC uses brake intervention to provide a controlled descent ability in off road conditions when engine braking is insufficient to maintain a comfortable speed. The HDC function operates with the vehicle travelling forwards or backwards and is selected on/off by a switch on the gear lever. When selected, HDC is enabled at speeds of 3.6 mph (5.7 kph) and above provided the vehicle is in first or reverse gear with the clutch engaged. In off road conditions this allows the driver to leave HDC selected and to control the vehicle's descent speed, down to the system's minimum target speed, using only the accelerator pedal.

When HDC is selected, the HDC information warning lamp illuminates permanently if HDC is enabled or flashes if HDC is not enabled (i.e. the vehicle is not in first or reverse gear, or the clutch is disengaged). When HDC is enabled, the ABS ECU calculates a target speed from the throttle position element of the engine ECU input, and compares this with actual speed. If the actual speed is higher than the target speed, the ABS ECU operates the ABS modulator in the active braking mode to achieve and then maintain the target speed. While the braking force is being applied, the ABS ECU also energizes the ABS brake lamp relay to put the brake lamps on. Active braking is discontinued while vehicle speed is below the target speed or if the foot brakes are applied. Applying the foot brakes during active braking may result in a pulse through the brake pedal, which is normal.

Minimum target speeds with the throttle closed are 6 mph (9.6 kph) in first gear and 4 mph (6.5 kph) in reverse gear. The first gear target speed is decreased to 4.4 mph (7 kph) if rough terrain or sharp bends (detected from ABS sensor inputs) are encountered while already travelling at the minimum target speed. Minimum target speeds are increased at cold idle to prevent conflict between the brakes and the engine caused by HDC trying to impose a lower vehicle speed than is normal for the increased engine speeds at cold idle. Minimum target speeds at cold idle are 7.5 mph (12 kph) in first gear and 4.4 mph (7 kph) in reverse gear.

During active braking, the brakes are operated in axle pairs on one or both axles. The braking effort is distributed between the front and rear axles as necessary to maintain vehicle stability. Distribution of the braking effort is dependant on direction of travel and braking effort being applied. To prevent wheel lock, anti-lock braking is also enabled during active braking.

The ABS ECU incorporates a fade out strategy that, if a fault occurs or HDC is deselected during active braking, provides a safe transition from active braking to brakes off. The fade out strategy increases the target speed at a low constant acceleration rate, independent of actual throttle position. If active braking is in operation, this causes the braking effort to be gradually reduced and then discontinued. The HDC information warning lamp flashes while fade out is in progress.

If the clutch is disengaged during active braking, the HDC information warning lamp flashes after a delay of 3 seconds. After 60 seconds, if the clutch is still disengaged, the HDC fault warning lamp flashes and active braking operation fades out.

To prevent the brakes overheating, the ABS ECU monitors the amount of active braking employed and, from this, calculates brake temperature. If the ABS ECU determines brake temperature has exceeded a preset limit, it extinguishes the HDC information warning lamp and flashes the HDC fault warning lamp to indicate that HDC should be deselected. If active braking continues and the ABS ECU determines that brake temperature has increased a further 50 °C, it fades out active braking and disables HDC. After fade out, the HDC fault warning lamp continues to flash, while HDC is selected, until the ABS ECU calculates brake temperature to be at an acceptable level. This calculation continues even if the ignition is turned off, so turning the ignition off and back on will not reduce the disabled time. When the ABS ECU calculates the brake temperature to be acceptable, it extinguishes the HDC fault warning lamp and illuminates the HDC information warning lamp to indicate HDC is available again. The disabled time is dependant on vehicle speed; typical times at constant vehicle speeds are as follows:

Typical brake overheat disabled times

Vehicle speed, mph (kph)	Time, minutes
1.3 (2)	40
12.5 (20)	33
15.6 (25)	17
25 (40)	9
31.3 (50)	6

Diagnostics

While the ignition is on, the diagnostics function of the ABS ECU monitors the system for faults. In addition, the return pump is tested by pulsing it briefly immediately after the engine starts provided vehicle speed exceeded 4.4 mph (7 kph) during the previous ignition cycle. If a fault is detected at any time, the ABS ECU stores a related fault code in memory and illuminates the appropriate warning lamps in the instrument pack. If a fault exists in a warning lamp circuit, the lamp will not illuminate during the lamp check at ignition on, but, provided there are no other faults, the related function will otherwise be fully operational.

Checks performed by diagnostics

Item	Check
ABS ECU	Internal failure
Shuttle valve switches	Plausibility of input
ECM input	Sticking throttle, signal failures and data corruption
First and reverse gear inputs	Plausibility of inputs
Reference earth	Connection to earth (by comparison with ABS ECU earth)
ABS sensors	Resistance (to check status and air gap)
Inlet valves	Open/Short circuit
Outlet valves	Open/Short circuit
Return pump	Correct pump operation
Return pump relay	Open/Short circuit
Brake lamps relay	Open/Short circuit
Supply voltages	Range (10 to 16 V)

After detecting a fault, the ABS ECU selects an appropriate default strategy which, where possible, retains some operational capability. A shuttle valve switch fault, sticking throttle and implausible gear input are classified as permanent faults. If a permanent fault is detected, the related warning lamp illumination and default strategies are automatically employed in subsequent ignition cycles, even if the fault is intermittent, until the fault has been rectified and cleared from memory. If a non permanent fault is detected, the related warning lamp illumination and default strategies will only be employed in subsequent ignition cycles if the fault is still present.

After rectification of an ABS sensor fault, the ABS and ETC functions are disabled, and their warning lamps remain illuminated, until vehicle speed exceeds 9.4 mph (15 kph) (to allow additional checks to be performed).

Fault retrieval and diagnosis of the ABS ECU are done using Testbook.

Fault lamp indications and default strategies

Fault	Status of Warning Lamps				Default Strategy
	ABS	ETC	HDC Fault	HDC Information	
ABS ECU internal failure	On	On	On	Off	ABS: Disabled. ETC: Disabled. HDC: Disabled.
Shuttle valve switch	On	On	On	Off	ABS: Deceleration threshold increased, return pump activated if sum of output valve actuation on one axle exceeds 120 milliseconds. ETC: Disabled. HDC: Disabled.
ECM input failure	Off	On	On	Off *	ABS: Enabled. ETC: Disabled. HDC: Immediately disabled if not in active braking mode, faded out then disabled if in active braking mode.
Sticking throttle	Off	Off	On	Off *	ABS: Enabled. ETC: Enabled. HDC: Immediately disabled if not in active braking mode, faded out then disabled if in active braking mode.
Implausible gear position input	Off	Off	On	Off *	ABS: Enabled. ETC: Enabled. HDC: Immediately disabled if not in active braking mode, faded out then disabled if in active braking mode.
No reference earth	On	On	On	Off	ABS: Disabled. ETC: Disabled. HDC: Disabled.
Failure of ABS sensor	On	On	On	Off †	ABS: Enabled. ETC: Enabled. HDC: Immediately disabled if not in active braking mode; if in active braking mode, remains enabled until braking inactive for 10 seconds, then disabled.

Fault lamp indications and default strategies - continued

Fault	Status of Warning Lamps				Default Strategy
	ABS	ETC	HDC Fault	HDC Information	
Failure of two ABS sensors	On	On	On	Off *	ABS: Enabled on unaffected hydraulic circuit (if applicable), disabled on affected hydraulic circuit(s). ETC: Disabled. HDC: Immediately disabled if not in active braking mode, faded out then disabled if in active braking mode.
Failure of more than two ABS sensors	On	On	On	Off	ABS: Disabled. ETC: Disabled. HDC: Disabled.
Failure of input valve	On	On	On	Off *	ABS: Enabled on unaffected hydraulic circuit, disabled on affected hydraulic circuit. ETC: Disabled. HDC: Immediately disabled if not in active braking mode, faded out then disabled if in active braking mode.
Failure of more than one input valve	On	On	On	Off *	ABS: Enabled on unaffected hydraulic circuit (if applicable), disabled on affected hydraulic circuit(s). ETC: Disabled. HDC: Immediately disabled if not in active braking mode, faded out then disabled if in active braking mode.
Failure of output valve	On	On	On	Off *	ABS: Enabled on unaffected hydraulic circuit, disabled on affected hydraulic circuit. ETC: If front valve, enabled on rear wheels, disabled on front wheels; if rear valve, disabled. HDC: Immediately disabled if not in active braking mode, faded out then disabled if in active braking mode.
Failure of more than one output valve	On	On	On	Off *	ABS: Enabled on unaffected hydraulic circuit (if applicable), disabled on affected hydraulic circuit(s). ETC: Disabled. HDC: Immediately disabled if not in active braking mode, faded out then disabled if in active braking mode.

Fault lamp indications and default strategies - continued

Fault	Status of Warning Lamps				Default Strategy
	ABS	**ETC**	**HDC Fault**	**HDC Information**	
Battery short in more than two input or output valve circuits	On	On	On	Off	ABS: Disabled. ETC: Disabled. HDC: Disabled.
Return pump or relay fault	On	On	On	Off	ABS: Disabled. ETC: Disabled. HDC: Disabled.
Brake lamp relay fault	Off	Off	On	Off	ABS: Enabled. ETC: Enabled. HDC: Enabled.
Supply voltage out of limits	On	On	On	Off *	ABS: Disabled. ETC: Disabled. HDC: Immediately disabled if not in active braking mode, faded out then disabled if in active braking mode.

*= Flashes if HDC faded out; †= Flashes if HDC in active braking mode

Electrical data

Component	Resistance, Ohms
ABS brake lamp relay coil	73 to 89
ABS pump relay coil	44.4 to 54.4
ABS sensor	950 to 1100
Shuttle valve switches, both open (brakes off)	2977 to 3067
Shuttle valve switches, both closed (brakes on)	1007 to 1037
Shuttle valve switches, one open, one closed	1992 to 2052
Inlet solenoid valve	5.9 to 7.3
Outlet solenoid valve	3.0 to 3.6

Component	Signal
First gear switch	Earth when first gear selected Open circuit when first gear not selected
HDC switch	Battery voltage when HDC selected Open circuit when HDC not selected
Reverse gear switch	Battery voltage when reverse gear selected Open circuit when reverse gear not selected

HANDBRAKE

The handbrake operates on both rear brakes via two handbrake cables, a cable equaliser and an intermediate rod on the handbrake lever.

As the handbrake lever is applied, movement is transmitted by the intermediate rod and the cable equaliser to the two handbrake cables. Each handbrake cable pulls on a lever on the trailing brake shoe. The lever pivots against the brake's adjuster rod, which forces the brake shoes apart and brings the brake linings into contact with the drum.

The cables are adjusted by the handbrake adjust nut that locates the cable equaliser on the intermediate rod.

A warning switch, on the base of the handbrake lever, operates the brake warning lamp in the instrument pack. When the handbrake is applied and the ignition is on, the warning switch connects an earth to the instrument pack and illuminates the brake warning lamp. In some markets, the central control unit performs a bulb check of the brake warning lamp each time the ignition is switched on.

Handbrake components

70M0776

1. Cable/Console bracket
2. Rear brake
3. Rear brake cable
4. Cable equaliser
5. Warning switch
6. Handbrake lever
7. Gaiter

BRAKE BLEED

Service repair no - 70.25.02

The following procedure covers bleeding the complete system but where only the primary or secondary circuit have been disturbed in isolation, it should only be necessary to bleed that system. Partial bleeding of the hydraulic system is only permissable if a brake pipe or hose has been disconnected with only minor loss of fluid.

CAUTION:
Never reuse fluid that has been bled from the brake system.
- **Do not allow fluid level in master cylinder to fall below 'MIN' mark during bleeding.**
- **Do not fill reservoir above 'MAX' level.**

Adjust

1. Raise front and rear of vehicle.

WARNING: Support on safety stands.

2. Check all pipe and hose connections are tight and there are no signs of leakage.
3. Top-up fluid level in brake reservoir to 'MAX' mark. ***See INFORMATION, Capacities, fluids and lubricants.***

CAUTION: Use only new brake fluid of the recommended grade. Bleed sequence: LH front to RH front, LH rear to RH rear.

4. Attach bleed tube to either front brake caliper bleed screw, submerge free end in a clear container containing brake fluid.
5. Apply pressure to brake pedal several times, then apply steady pressure.
6. Loosen bleed screw to release brake fluid and air. Allow pedal to return unassisted.
7. Depress brake pedal steadily through its full stroke and allow to return unassisted. Repeat procedure until a flow of clean air-free fluid is purged into container. Then, whilst holding pedal at end of downward stroke, tighten bleed screw to 10 Nm on calipers and 7 Nm on wheel cylinders.

CAUTION: Maintain brake fluid level above 'MIN' mark during this procedure.

8. Top-up brake fluid level.

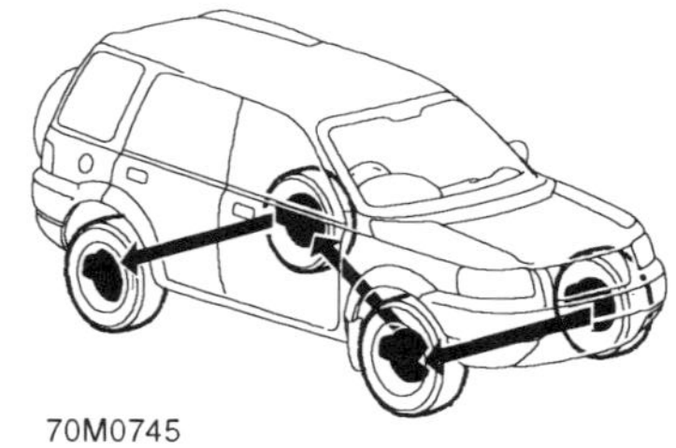

70M0745

9. Repeat procedure at each wheel in the sequence given above.

CAUTION: Braking efficiency may be seriously impaired if wrong bleed sequence is used.

10. Remove bleed tube. Apply brakes and check for leakage.
11. Remove stand(s) and lower vehicle.
12. Road test vehicle. Check brake pedal for short firm travel when brakes are applied.

CABLE - HANDBRAKE

Service repair no - 70.35.10

Check

1. Remove rear console. ***See BODY, Interior trim components.***
2. Apply handbrake lever one notch at a time and count number of notches required to apply the brakes firmly, equivalent to a pull of 20 kgf applied at mid point of handbrake lever grip. Handbrake lever travel = 4 to 7 notches.
3. Adjust handbrake cable tension if travel is outside limits.

CAUTION: Travel must not be less than 4 notches

Adjust

NOTE: If carrying out handbrake adjustment after brake drum installation, start engine and depress brake pedal several times to set self-adjusting mechanism before adjusting handbrake cable.

1. Raise rear of vehicle.

WARNING: Support on safety stands.

2. Check handbrake cable connections for free movement in handbrake equalizer.
3. Apply handbrake one notch.

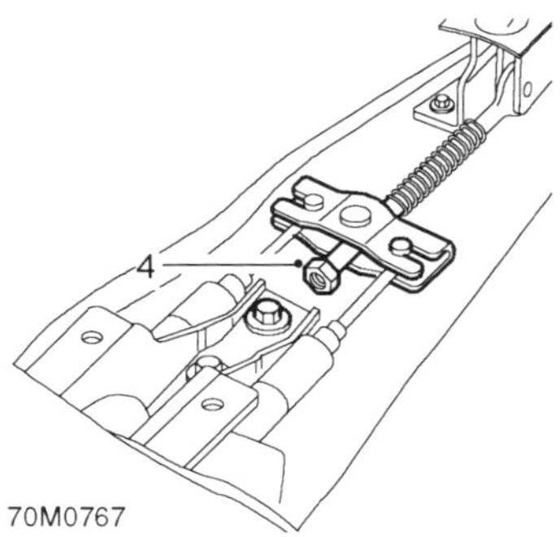

70M0767

4. Tighten equalizer adjusting nut until rear wheels drag slightly when turned.
5. Release handbrake lever and check that rear wheels do not drag when turned. Adjust if necessary.
6. Apply handbrake one notch at a time and count the number of notches until both rear wheels lock. This should be a minimum of 4 and a maximum of 7 clicks. Adjust if necessary.
7. Release handbrake lever.
8. Fit rear console. ***See BODY, Interior trim components.***

SWITCH - BRAKE LIGHT

Service repair no - 70.35.41

Adjust

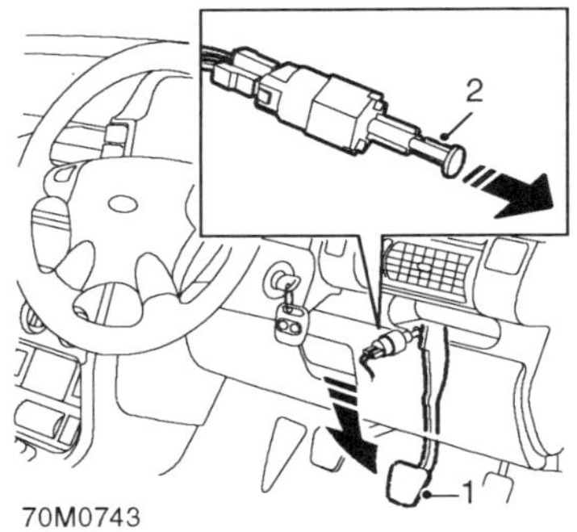

70M0743

1. Depress and hold brake pedal.
2. Reset switch by pulling plunger.
3. Release brake pedal slowly to set switch adjustment.

BRAKE DRUM - REAR

Service repair no - 70.12.03

Remove

1. Raise rear of vehicle.

WARNING: Support on safety stands.

2. Remove road wheel(s).
3. Release handbrake.

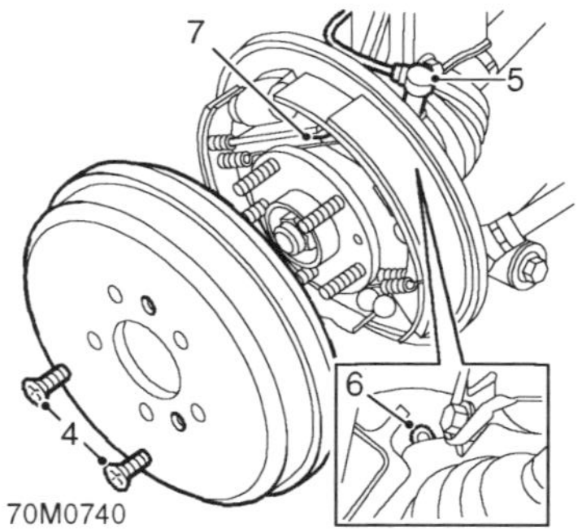

70M0740

4. Remove 2 screws securing brake drum and remove drum.

NOTE: If brake drum cannot be removed, release brake shoe adjustment as follows:

5. If fitted, release ABS sensor from rear hub.
6. Remove rubber grommet from rear of backplate.
7. Using a flat bladed screwdriver, disengage brake shoe adjuster cam to increase shoe to drum clearance.
8. Remove brake drum.
9. Clean backplate and brake drum with brake cleaning fluid.

WARNING: Do not use an air line to blow dust from brake assembly.

WARNING: Do not use petroleum based fluid as damage will occur to rubber components.

10. Renew brake drum if scored, grooved or cracked.

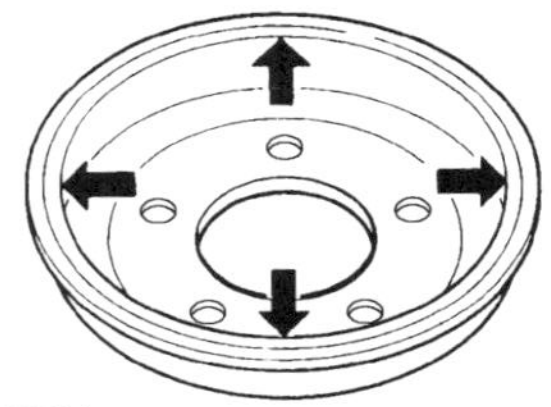

70M0741

11. Measure inside diameter of drum at 2 points.
    Drum internal diameter:
    New = 254 mm
    Service limit = 255.49 mm
    Drum ovality limit = 0.012 mm
    Renew drum if outside limits.
12. Examine wheel cylinder dust seals for signs of brake fluid leakage, a certain amount of dampness is usual. However, if free fluid is apparent, lift dust seal and check for excessive leakage.
    Renew wheel cylinder and brake linings if linings are contaminated.
13. Check wheel cylinder pistons for freedom of movement.

Refit

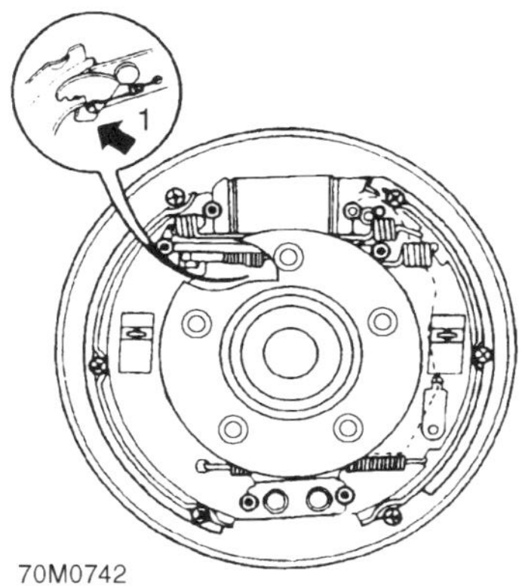

70M0742

1. Check adjuster cam and if necessary set to minimum adjustment position as follows: Lever leading shoe away from wheel cylinder; Move adjuster cam back fully; Ease shoe back into position.

WARNING: Ensure grease does not come into contact with brake shoe linings or wheel cylinder covers.

2. Apply Molycote 111 grease to brake shoe and spring contact points.

NOTE: Clean inside of NEW brake drum with brake cleaning fluid.

CAUTION: Ensure that brake shoes are correctly engaged with wheel cylinder pistons before fitting brake drum.

3. Fit brake drum, tighten screws to 7 Nm.
4. If necessary, fit grommet and ABS sensor.
5. Fit road wheel(s) and tighten nuts to correct torque. ***See INFORMATION, Torque wrench settings.***
6. Remove stand(s) and lower vehicle.
7. Check handbrake operation, adjust if necessary. ***See Adjustments.***

BRAKE DISC - FRONT

Service repair no - 70.12.10

Remove

CAUTION: Brake discs must be renewed in pairs, unless one disc requires changing before 1000 miles (1500 km) from new.

1. Raise front of vehicle.

WARNING: Support on safety stands.

2. Remove road wheel(s).

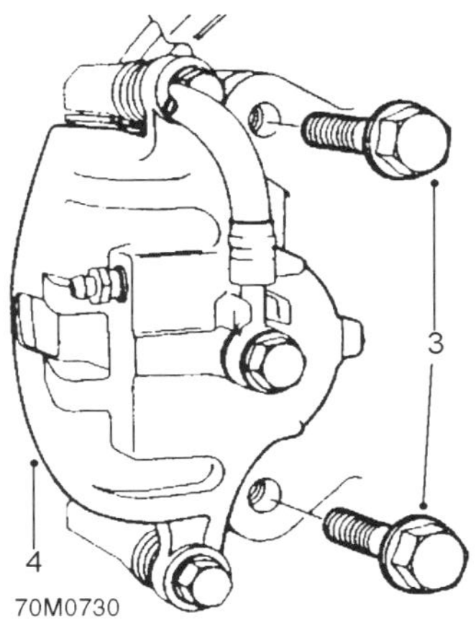

70M0730

3. Remove 2 bolts securing brake caliper to swivel hub.
4. Release caliper and tie aside clear of brake disc.

CAUTION: Do not allow caliper to hang on brake hose.

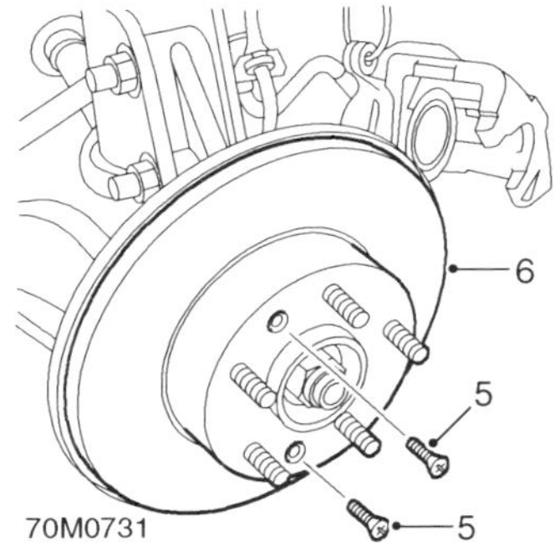

70M0731

5. Remove 2 screws securing disc to drive flange.
6. Remove brake disc from drive flange.

Refit

1. Clean mating faces of drive flange and new disc.
2. Fit brake disc to drive flange, fit and tighten screws to 5 Nm.
3. Clean mating faces of caliper and hub.
4. Fit caliper, and tighten bolts to 83 Nm.
5. Fit road wheel(s) and tighten nuts to correct torque. ***See INFORMATION, Torque wrench settings.***
6. Remove stand(s) and lower vehicle.

MASTER CYLINDER

Service repair no - 70.30.08

Remove

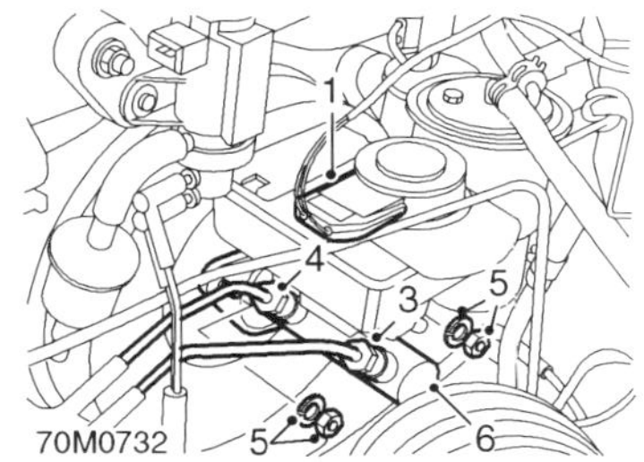

70M0732

1. Disconnect fluid level switch multiplug.
2. Position cloth under master cylinder to absorb spilled fluid.

CAUTION: Do not allow brake fluid to contact paint finished surfaces as paint may be damaged. If spilled, remove fluid and clean area with clean warm water.

3. Disconnect secondary system pipe union from master cylinder.
4. Disconnect primary system pipe union from master cylinder.

CAUTION: Plug the connections.

5. Remove 2 nuts and washers securing master cylinder.
6. Remove master cylinder.

Refit

1. Clean master cylinder and servo mating surfaces.
2. Align servo push rod and fit master cylinder to servo.
3. Fit nuts and washers, tighten to 14 Nm.
4. Connect primary and secondary brake pipes, tighten unions to 14 Nm.
5. Connect fluid level switch multiplug.
6. Bleed brake system. ***See Adjustments.***
7. Remove stand(s) and lower vehicle.

CABLE - HANDBRAKE

Service repair no - 70.35.25

Remove

1. Raise rear of vehicle.

WARNING: Support on safety stands.

2. Remove road wheel(s).
3. Remove rear console. ***See BODY, Interior trim components.***

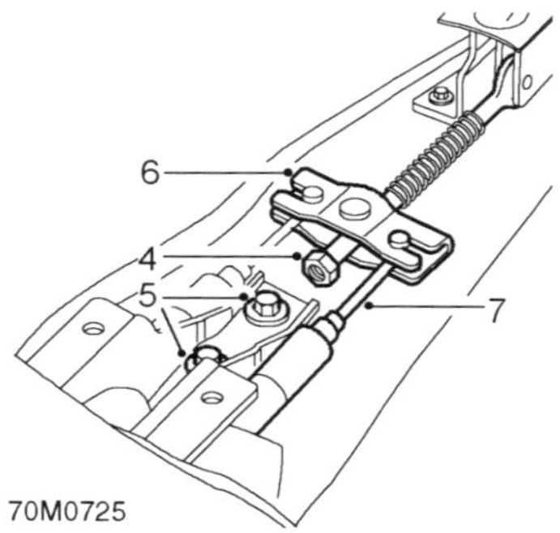

70M0725

4. Remove cable adjusting nut.
5. Remove 2 bolts securing cable retaining plate to body and remove plate.
6. Release equalizer from adjusting rod.
7. Release cable from equalizer plate.

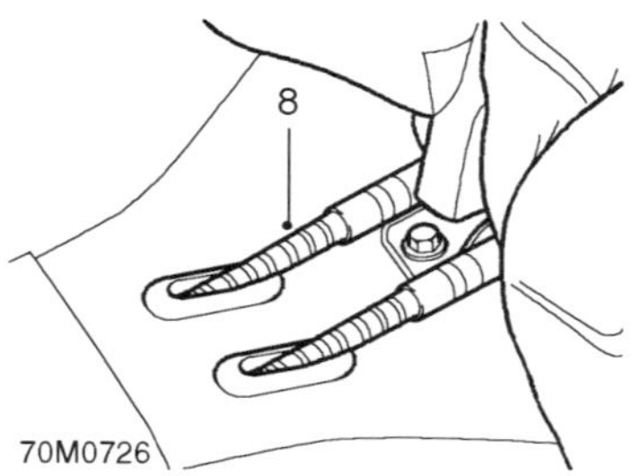

70M0726

8. Reach under carpet and release grommet from body.

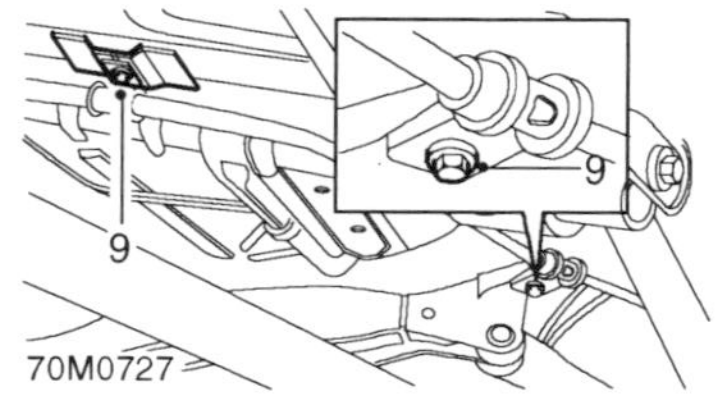

70M0727

9. Remove 2 bolts securing handbrake cable clips to body and rear subframe.

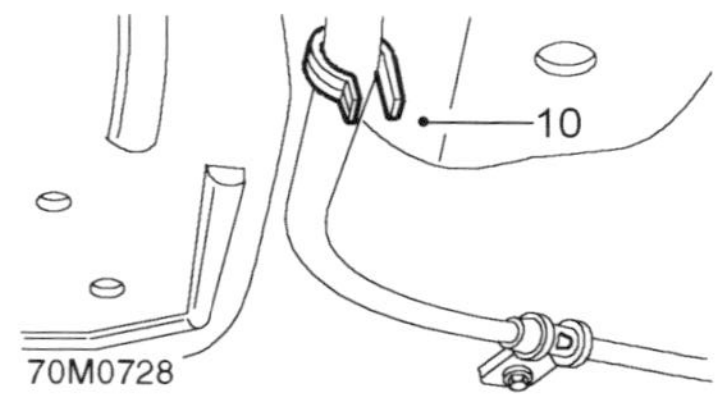

70M0728

10. Release handbrake cable from body clip.
11. Remove rear brake shoes. ***See this section.***

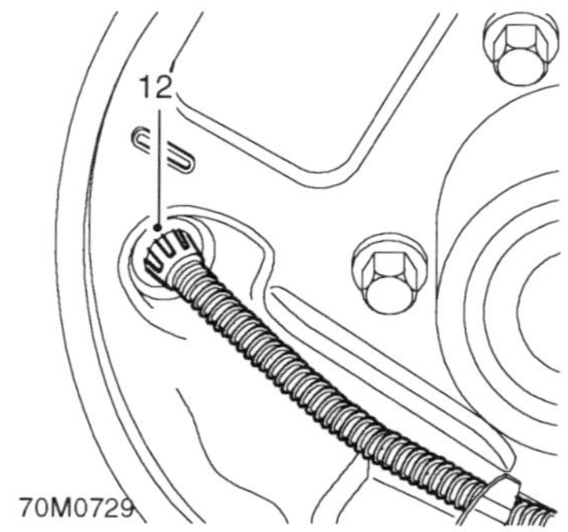

70M0729

12. Release cable retainer from backplate and withdraw cable from backplate.
13. Remove handbrake cable from vehicle.

Refit

1. Manoeuvre handbrake cable into position, fit grommet and connect cable to equalizer plate.
2. Connect cable to backplate.
3. Fit brake shoes. ***See this section.***
4. Position cable clips and tighten bolts to 22 Nm.
5. Secure cable to body clip.
6. Connect handbrake cable to equalizer.
7. Ensure spring is in place and fit equalizer to adjusting rod.
8. Fit cable adjusting nut.
9. Fit cable retaining plate and tighten bolts to 22 Nm.
10. Adjust handbrake cable. ***See Adjustments.***
11. Fit rear console ***See BODY, Interior trim components.***
12. Fit road wheel(s) and tighten nuts to correct torque. ***See INFORMATION, Torque wrench settings.***
13. Remove stand(s) and lower vehicle.

SWITCH - BRAKE LIGHT

Service repair no - 70.35.42

Remove

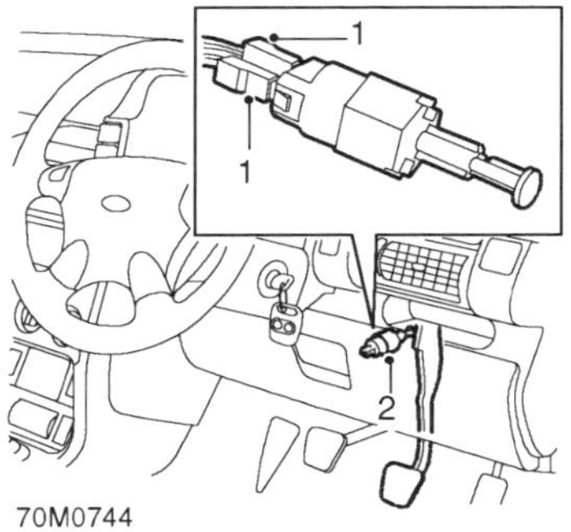

70M0744

1. Release 2 Lucar connectors from switch.
2. Release bayonet fixing and remove switch.

Refit

1. Fit switch to pedal box.
2. Connect Lucar connectors.
3. Adjust switch ***See Adjustments.***

BRAKE PADS - FRONT SET

Service repair no - 70.40.02

Remove

1. Raise front of vehicle.

WARNING: Support on safety stands.

2. Remove road wheel(s).

WARNING: Brake pads must be renewed in axle sets only. Braking efficiency may otherwise be impaired.

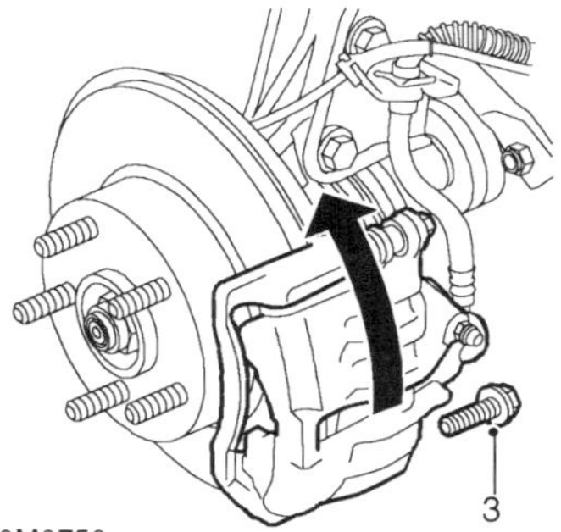

70M0753

3. Remove lower guide pin bolt from caliper and pivot caliper housing upwards.

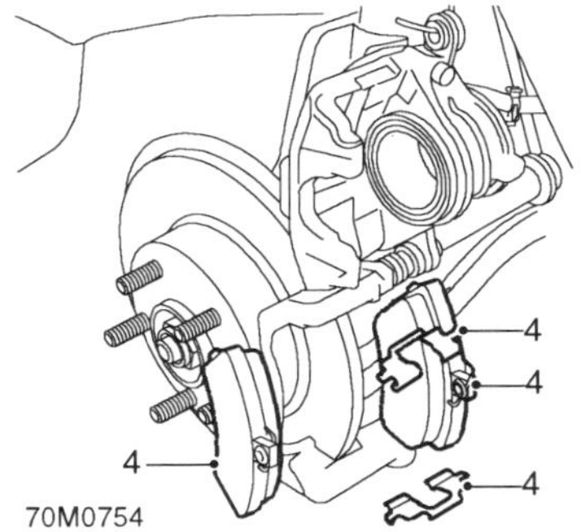

70M0754

4. Remove 2 brake pads and retainers from caliper bracket.

Refit

1. Rotate disc by hand and scrape all scale and rust from around edge of disc.
2. Scrape rust from pad locating surfaces on caliper.
3. Clean dust from calipers using brake cleaning fluid or industrial alcohol.

WARNING: Do not use an air line to blow dust from brake assembly. Do not use petroleum based fluid as damage will occur to rubber components.

4. Position bleed bottle, connect bleed hose to bleed screw and loosen screw.
5. Press piston back into housing.
6. Tighten bleed screw to 10 Nm.
7. Remove bleed bottle.

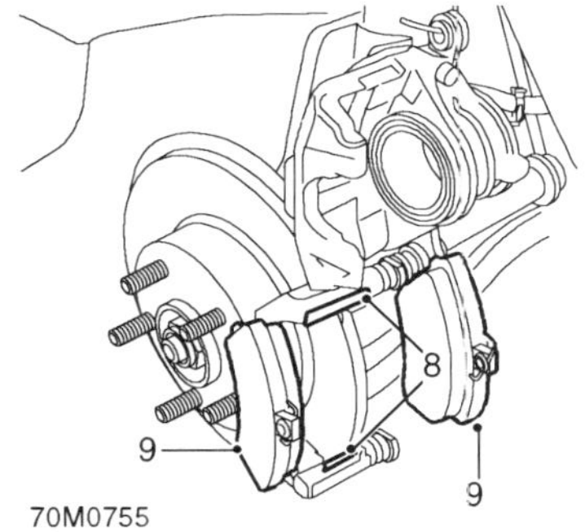

70M0755

8. Fit pad retainers to caliper bracket.
9. Fit pads to caliper bracket.

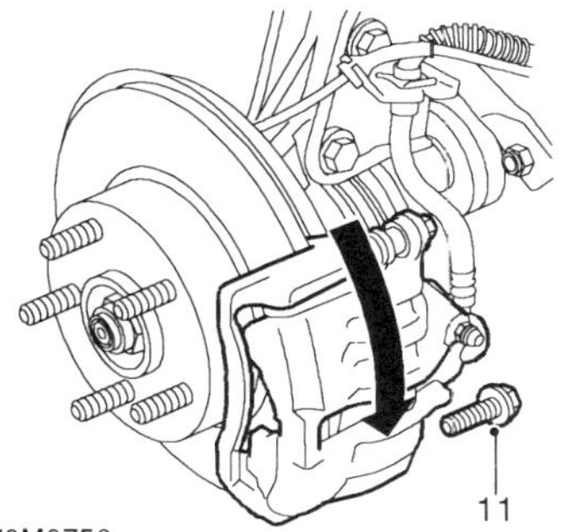

70M0756

10. Lower caliper housing over pads.
11. Ensure flats on guide pins locate with lugs on caliper housing. Fit bolt and tighten to 27 Nm.
12. Repeat procedure for other side.
13. Fit road wheel(s) and tighten nuts to correct torque. ***See INFORMATION, Torque wrench settings.***
14. Remove stand(s) and lower vehicle.
15. Depress brake several times to set pad disc clearance.
16. Check and top-up brake fluid. ***See INFORMATION, Capacities, fluids and lubricants.***

BRAKE SHOES - REAR SET

Service repair no - 70.40.09

Remove

1. Raise rear of vehicle.

WARNING: Support on safety stands.

2. Remove road wheel(s).
3. Release handbrake.
4. Remove rear brake drum. ***See this section.***

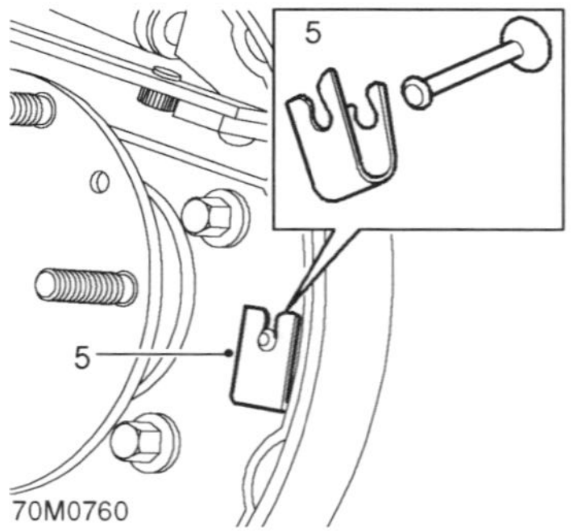

70M0760

5. Depress brake shoe clips and turn to release, remove 2 clips and 2 retaining pins.
6. Ease one shoe out of retaining groove in abutment followed by other shoe.

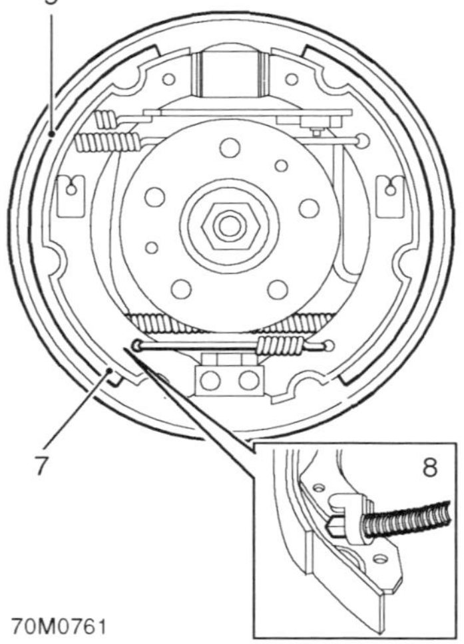

70M0761

7. Detach shoe abutment return spring from leading shoe end and remove spring.

NOTE: The forward shoe is the LEADING shoe, the TRAILING shoe has the handbrake lever attached to it.

8. Release hand brake cable from lever on brake shoe.
9. Manoeuvre shoe assembly around wheel cylinder and remove shoe assembly.

CAUTION: Ensure edges of brake shoes do not damage wheel cylinder dust covers.

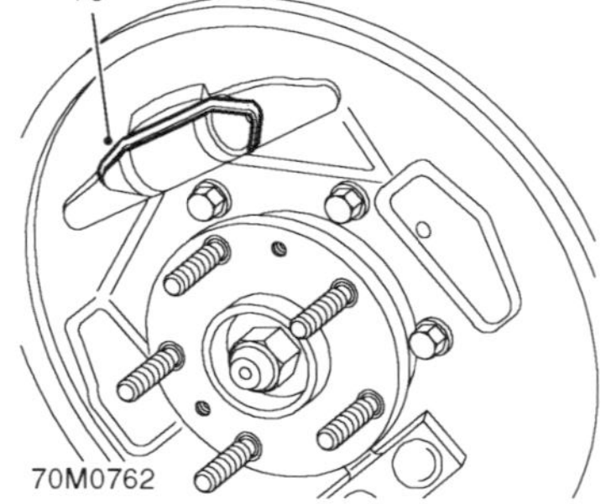

70M0762

10. Fit an elastic band around wheel cylinder to retain pistons.
Do not carry out further dismantling if component is removed for access only.

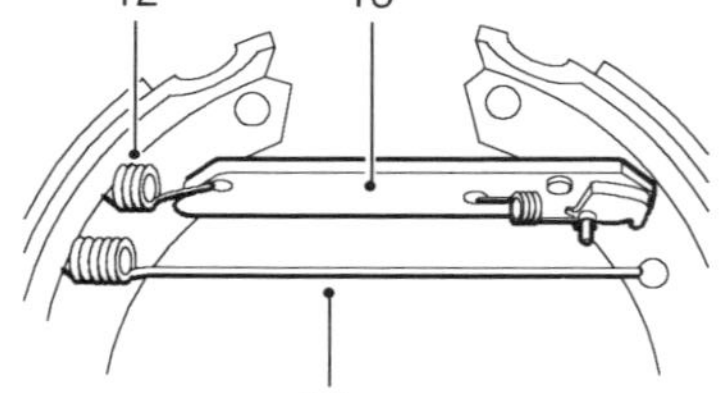

70M0763

11. Detach upper return spring from leading shoe and remove spring.
12. Detach short spring from adjuster strut and remove from trailing shoe.
13. Remove adjuster strut from leading shoe by pulling on shoe and fully extending cam so that shoe pivots out of engagement.
14. Remove strut from trailing shoe.

Inspect

1. Clean backplate and drum with brake cleaning fluid.

WARNING: Do not use an air line to blow dust from brake assembly.

WARNING: Do not use petroleum based fluid as damage will occur to rubber components.

2. Use a wire brush to remove any corrosion taking care not to damage wheel cylinder covers.
3. Inspect all parts for wear or damage.
4. Examine adjuster strut to ensure it is in working order with no signs of wear or damage. The quadrant lever, when pulled away from the knurled wheel against spring pressure, should move smoothly and freely within its slot in the strut.
5. Ensure teeth on quadrant and knurled wheel are undamaged and wheel is firmly attached to strut.
6. Examine wheel cylinder dust seals for signs of brake fluid leakage, a certain amount of dampness is usual. However, if excessive fluid is apparent, lift dust seal and check for leakage.
Renew wheel cylinder and brake linings if lining are contaminated.
7. Check wheel cylinder pistons for freedom of movement.
8. Check condition of springs, renew if necessary.

Refit

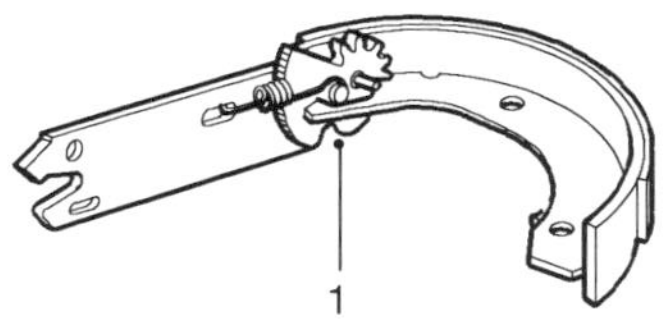

70M0765

1. Fully extend cam on strut and rotate leading shoe into strut slot.
2. Engage trailing shoe to adjuster strut fit adjuster spring to trailing shoe and secure spring to adjuster strut.
3. Fit upper return spring to trailing shoe and connect to leading shoe.
4. Smear shoe contact points with Molykote 111 grease.

WARNING: Ensure grease does not contact brake shoe linings or wheel cylinder dust covers.

5. Manoeuvre shoe assembly into position between hub and wheel cylinder and connect hand brake cable to brake shoe lever.
6. Fit lower return spring to trailing shoe and connect spring to leading shoe.
7. Remove elastic band from wheel cylinder.
8. Engage leading shoe in wheel cylinder followed by trailing shoe and align.

NOTE: During this operation the adjuster may become extended, it must be reset prior to fitting brake drum.

9. Fit trailing shoe into abutment bracket followed by leading shoe.

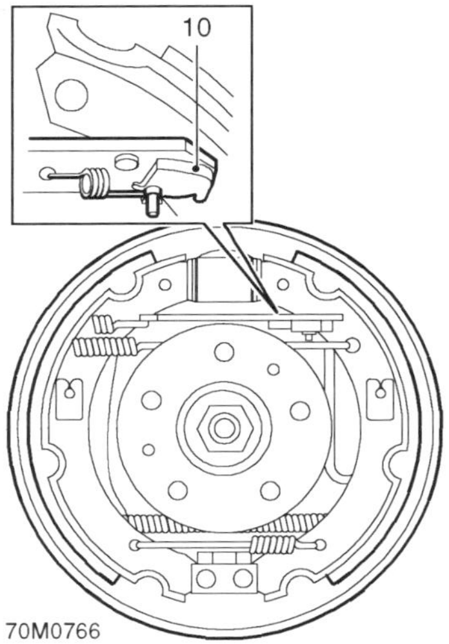

70M0766

10. Check adjuster cam and if necessary set to minimum adjustment position as follows: lever leading shoe away from wheel cylinder. Move adjuster cam back fully and ease shoe back into position.
11. Fit shoe steady pins through backplate, fit clips and turn to lock.
12. Clean brake drum, scrape ridge from edge of drum.
13. Fit brake drum. ***See this section.***
14. Fit road wheel(s) and tighten nuts to correct torque. ***See INFORMATION, Torque wrench settings.***
15. Remove stand(s) and lower vehicle.
16. Apply brake pedal several times to set self adjust mechanism.
17. Check and top up master cylinder.
18. Check handbrake operation, adjust if necessary. ***See Adjustments.***

SERVO - LHD

Service repair no - 70.50.01

Remove

1. Remove brake master cylinder. ***See this section.***
2. Remove air cleaner. ***See ENGINE MANAGEMENT SYSTEM - EDC, Repairs.***

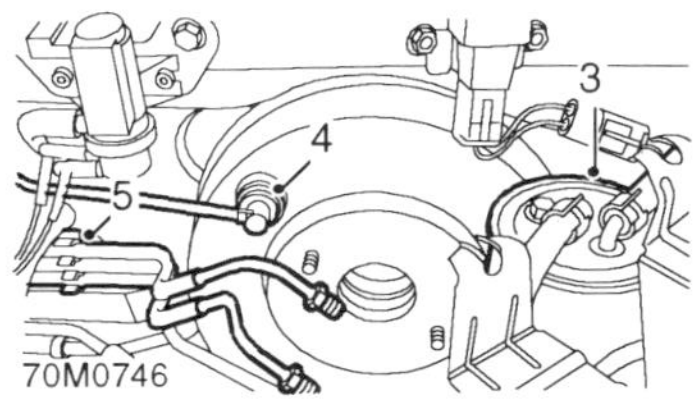

70M0746

3. Release fuel filter from bracket on LH front suspension turret.
4. Release and disconnect vacuum hose from servo.
5. Release brake pipes from clips on bulkhead.

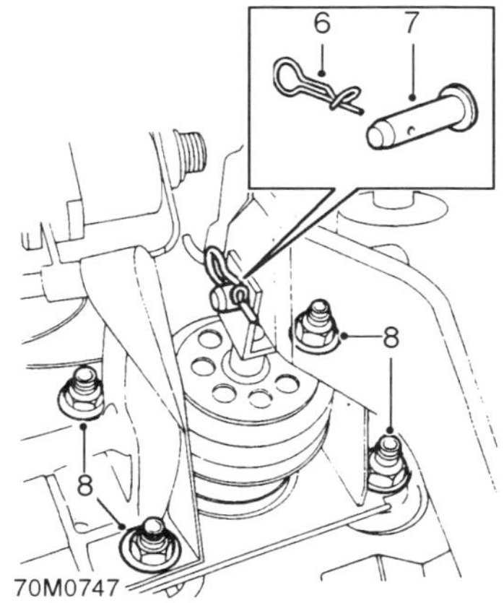

70M0747

6. Remove and discard spring clip from clevis pin.
7. Remove clevis pin securing brake pedal to servo push rod.
8. Remove 4 flange nuts securing servo to bulkhead.
9. Remove servo.
10. Remove and discard gasket.

Refit

1. Fit NEW gasket to servo.
2. Fit servo to bulkhead with vacuum connection uppermost, tighten nuts to 22 Nm.
3. Align push rod to brake pedal, fit clevis pin and secure with NEW spring clip.
4. Position fuel filter to retaining bracket.
5. Connect brake vacuum hose to servo.
6. Fit brake master cylinder. ***See this section.***
7. Secure brake pipes to retaining clips.
8. Fit air cleaner. ***See ENGINE MANAGEMENT SYSTEM - EDC, Repairs.***

SERVO - RHD

Service repair no - 70.50.01

Remove

1. Remove brake master cylinder. ***See this section.***

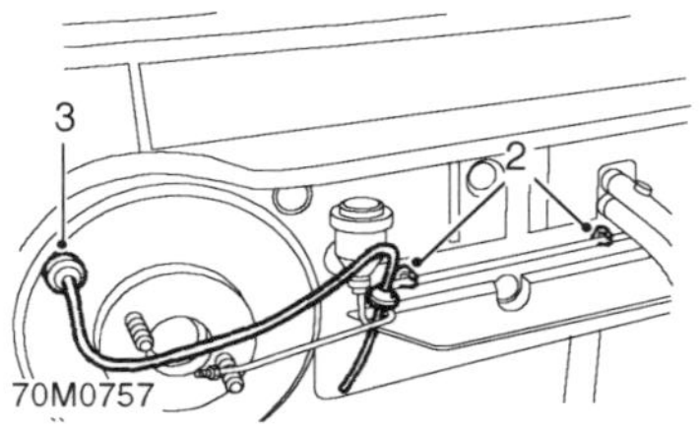

70M0757

2. Release brake pipes from clips on bulkhead.
3. Release and disconnect vacuum hose from servo.

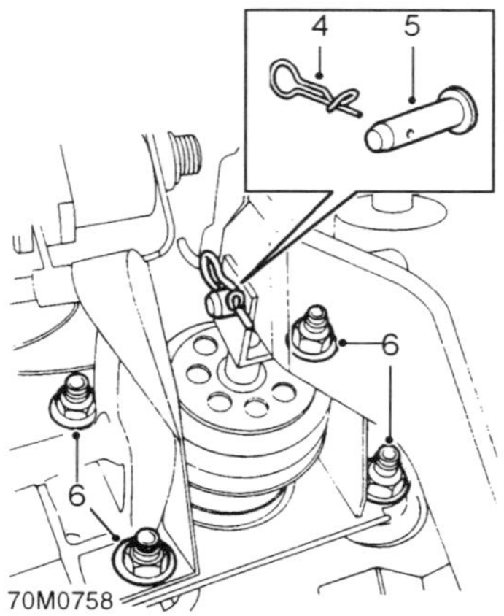

70M0758

4. Remove and discard spring clip from clevis pin.
5. Remove clevis pin securing brake pedal to servo push rod.
6. Remove 4 flange nuts securing servo to bulkhead.
7. Remove servo.
8. Remove and discard gasket.

Refit

1. Fit NEW gasket to servo.
2. Fit servo to bulkhead with vacuum connection uppermost, tighten nuts to 22 Nm..
3. Align push rod to brake pedal, fit clevis pin and secure with NEW spring clip.
4. Connect brake vacuum hose to servo.
5. Fit brake master cylinder. ***See this section.***
6. Secure brake pipes to retaining clips.

PUMP - VACUUM - BRAKE SERVO - 'L' SERIES

Service repair no - 70.50.19

Remove

1. Remove alternator. ***See ELECTRICAL, Repairs.***

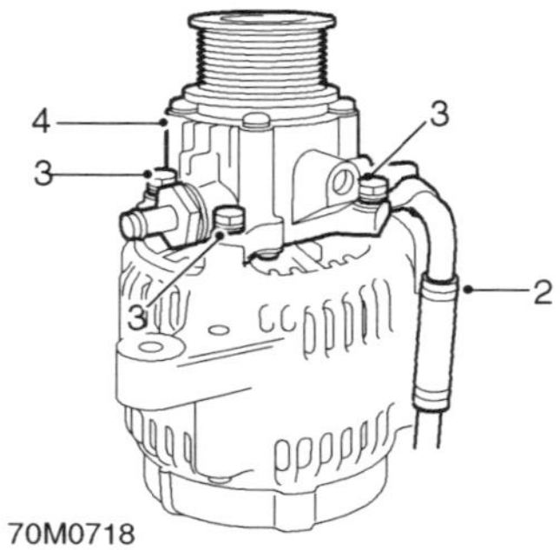

70M0718

2. Release clip and disconnect oil return hose from oil return pipe.
3. Remove 4 bolts securing vacuum pump to alternator.
4. Remove vacuum pump.

CAUTION: Plug the connections.

Refit

1. Clean mating face of alternator and vacuum pump.
2. Fit vacuum pump to alternator, fit bolts and tighten to 8 Nm.
3. Remove plugs from vacuum pump, drain hose connections.
4. Clean drain hose connections.
5. Connect oil return hose to oil return pipe and secure with clip.
6. Fit alternator. ***See ELECTRICAL, Repairs.***

HOUSING - CALIPER - FRONT

Service repair no - 70.55.24

Remove

1. Raise front of vehicle, one side.

WARNING: Support on safety stands.

2. Remove road wheel(s).

CAUTION: A brake hose clamp must be used.

3. Clamp brake hose to prevent fluid loss.
4. Remove brake hose banjo bolt.
5. Discard 2 sealing washers.

CAUTION: Plug the connections.

6. Remove 2 guide pin bolts.
7. Remove caliper housing from carrier.

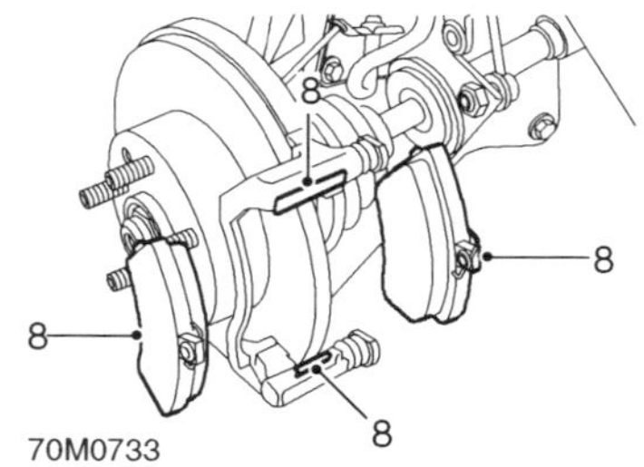

70M0733

8. Remove 2 brake pads and retainers from caliper bracket.

Refit

1. Rotate disc by hand and scrape all scale and rust from around edge of disc. Scrape clean location surfaces on caliper bracket.

WARNING: **Do not use an air line to blow dust from brake assembly. Do not use petroleum based fluid as damage will occur to rubber components.**

2. Clean dust from brake parts using brake cleaning fluid.
3. Fit pad retainers to caliper bracket.
4. Fit brake pads to caliper housing.
5. Position caliper housing to carrier, align flats **'A'** on guide pins with caliper housing.
6. Fit and tighten guide pin bolts to 27 Nm.
7. Clean banjo bolt and fit NEW sealing washers.
8. Position hose to caliper and tighten banjo bolt to 28 Nm.
9. Remove clamp from brake hose.
10. Bleed brakes.***See Adjustments.***
11. Fit road wheel(s) and tighten nuts to correct torque. ***See INFORMATION, Torque wrench settings.***
12. Remove stand(s) and lower vehicle.

WHEEL CYLINDER - REAR

Service repair no - 70.60.19

Remove

1. Remove rear brake shoes. ***See this section.***

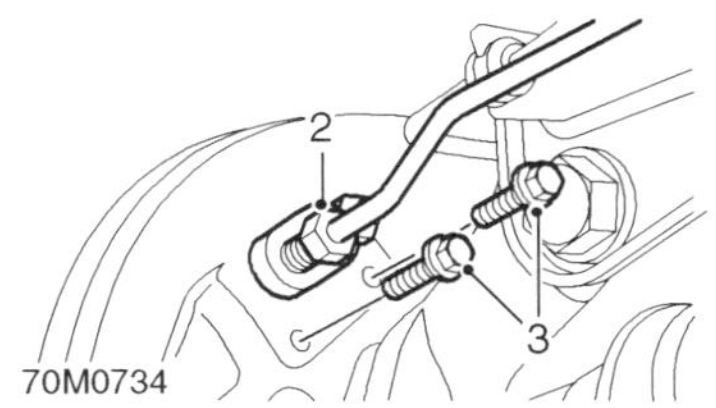

70M0734

2. Disconnect pipe union from wheel cylinder.

CAUTION: Plug the connections.

3. Loosen 2 bolts and remove wheel cylinder.
4. Remove and discard sealing ring.

WARNING: **Clean backplate and drum with brake cleaning fluid. Do not use an air line to blow dust from brake assembly. Do not use petroleum based fluid as damage will occur to rubber components.**

5. Use a wire brush to remove any corrosion.

Refit

1. Fit NEW sealing ring to wheel cylinder.
2. Fit wheel cylinder to backplate, tighten screws to 8 Nm.
3. Connect brake pipe to wheel cylinder and tighten union to 14 Nm.
4. Fit brake shoes. ***See this section.***
5. Bleed brakes. ***See Adjustments.***
6. Remove stand(s) and lower vehicle.

ELECTRONIC CONTROL UNIT (ECU) - ABS

Service repair no - 70.65.01

Remove

1. Slide RH front seat fully rearwards.

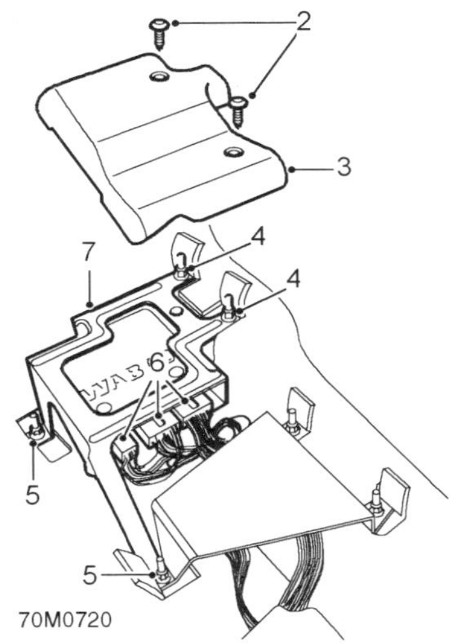

70M0720

2. Remove 2 Torx screws from ECU cover.
3. Remove ECU cover.
4. Remove 2 nuts from front of support bracket.
5. Slide RH front seat fully forward and remove 2 nuts from rear of support bracket.
6. Disconnect 3 multiplugs from ECU.
7. Remove support bracket and ECU.

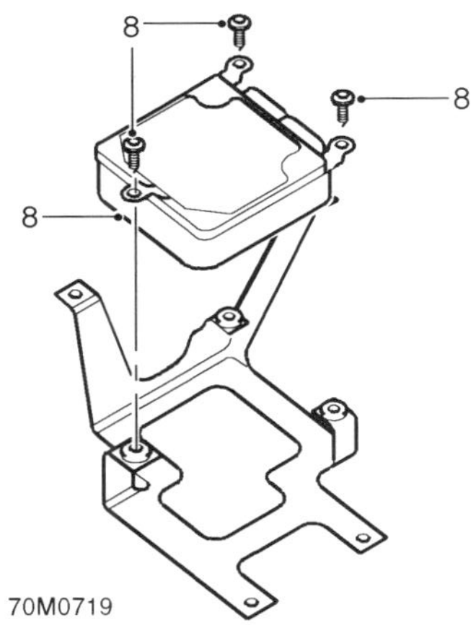

70M0719

8. Remove 3 Torx screws from ECU and remove ECU from support bracket.

Refit

1. Position ECU to support bracket and tighten Torx screws.
2. Position ECU support bracket to floor and tighten rear nuts.
3. Connect multiplugs to ECU.
4. Slide seat fully rearward and tighten front nuts.
5. Position ECU cover and tighten Torx screws.
6. Reset seat position.

SENSOR AND HARNESS - ABS - FRONT

Service repair no - 70.65.30

Remove

1. *LH sensor only:* Remove battery carrier. ***See ELECTRICAL, Repairs.***
2. Remove wheel arch liner. ***See BODY, Exterior fittings.***

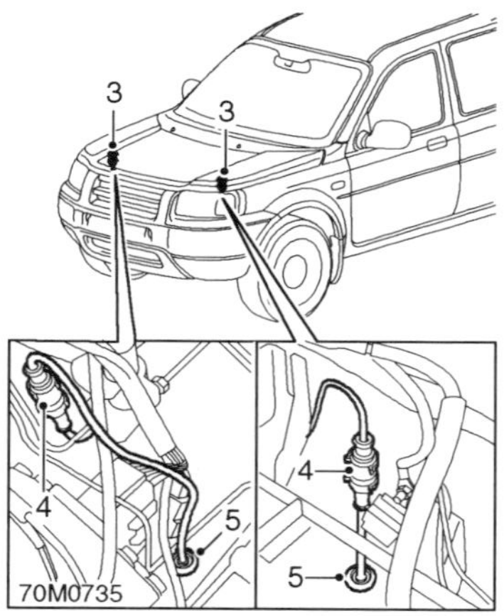

3. Locate sensor harness multiplug on RH or LH under wing valance.
4. Release multiplug from clip and disconnect multiplug.
5. Release grommet from wing valance and pull harness through.

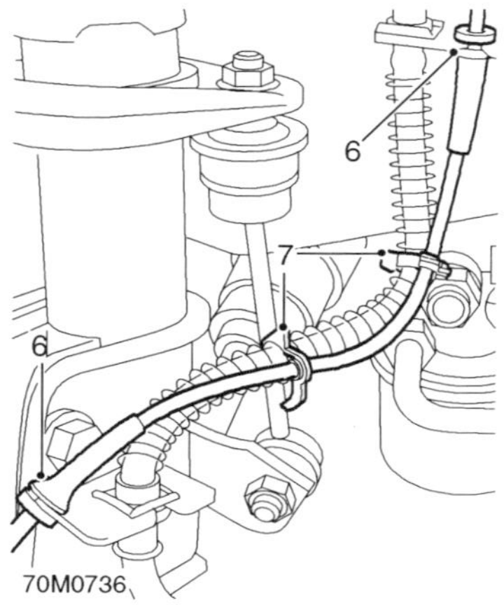

6. Release 2 sensor harness grommets from wing valance and suspension bracket.
7. Release harness from brake hose clips.

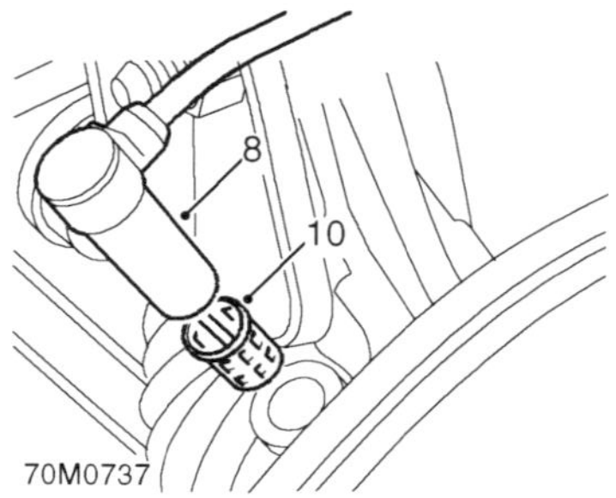

8. Release sensor from front hub.
9. Remove sensor and harness.
10. Remove bush from front hub.

Refit

1. Clean mating surfaces of sensor and hub.
2. Fit NEW bush to hub.
3. Apply anti-seize grease to sensor.
4. Fit sensor to hub. Ensure sensor is fully seated in hub.
5. Secure harness grommets to brackets.
6. Pass sensor harness through wing valance and secure grommet.
7. Ensuring 'O' ring is in place, connect sensor harness multiplug to body harness and secure multiplug in clip.
8. Fit wheel arch liner. ***See BODY, Exterior fittings.***
9. Fit battery carrier. ***See ELECTRICAL, Repairs.***
10. To ensure correct operation, the system MUST be tested using TestBook.

SENSOR AND HARNESS - ABS - REAR

Service repair no - 70.65.31

Remove

1. Raise rear of vehicle, one side.

WARNING: Support on safety stands.

2. Remove road wheel(s).

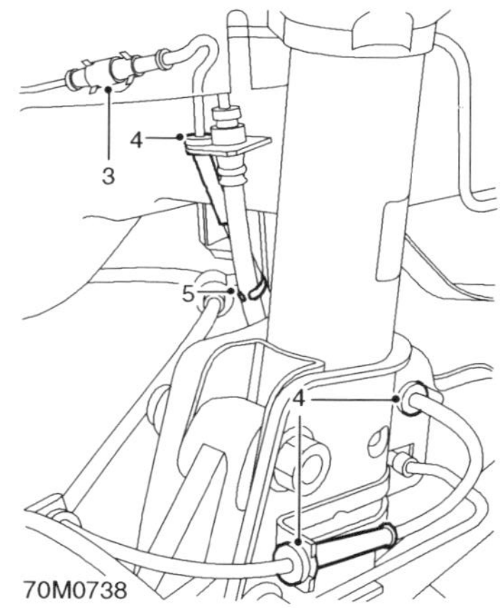

3. Release sensor multiplug from body clip and disconnect multiplug.
4. Release 3 sensor harness grommets from rear suspension and body brackets.
5. Release sensor harness from clip on rear brake hose.

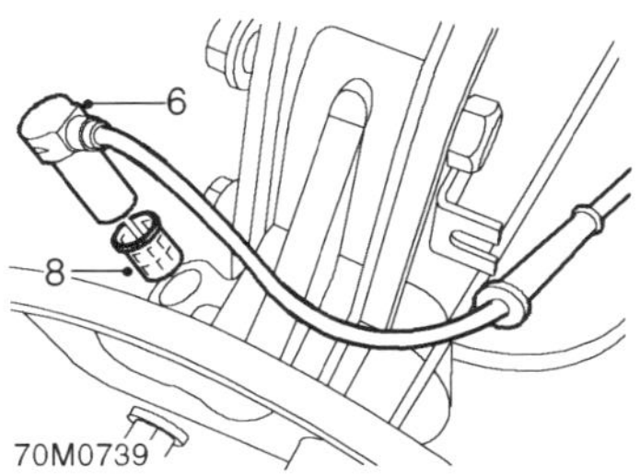

70M0739

6. Release sensor from rear hub.
7. Remove sensor and harness.
8. Remove bush from rear hub.

Refit

1. Clean sensor and hub mating face.
2. Fit NEW bush to hub.
3. Apply anti-seize grease to sensor.
4. Fit sensor to hub. Ensure sensor is fully seated in hub.
5. Secure harness grommets to brackets.
6. Ensure 'O' ring is in place and connect sensor multiplug to body harness.
7. Secure multiplug to clip.
8. Secure harness to clip on brake hose.
9. Fit road wheel(s) and tighten nuts to correct torque. ***See INFORMATION, Torque wrench settings.***
10. Remove stand(s) and lower vehicle.
11. To ensure correct operation, the system MUST be tested using TestBook.

MODULATOR - ABS

Service repair no - 70.65.49

Remove

1. Remove RH headlamp. ***See ELECTRICAL, Repairs.***
2. Position cloth under modulator to absorb fluid spillage.

WARNING: Do not allow brake fluid to contact paint finished surfaces as paint may be damaged. If spilled, remove fluid and clean area with clean warm water.

NOTE: Note position of brake pipe to ensure correct fitment.

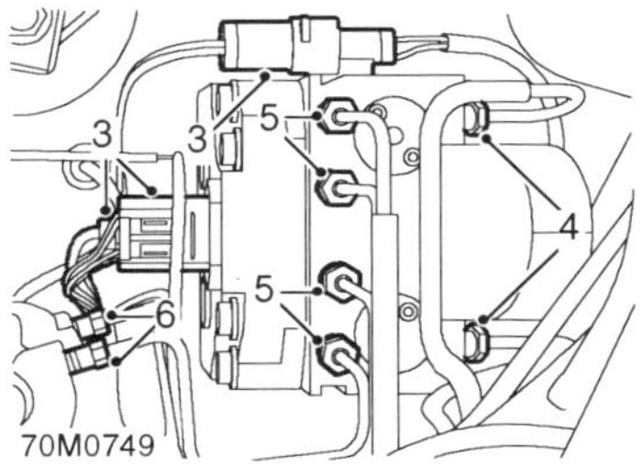

70M0749

3. Disconnect 3 multiplugs from ABS modulator
4. Disconnect 2 inlet brake pipe unions from front of modulator.
5. Disconnect 4 outlet brake pipe unions from top of modulator.
6. Disconnect 2 modulator outlet pipe unions to pressure conscious reducing valve (PCRV) and remove pipes.

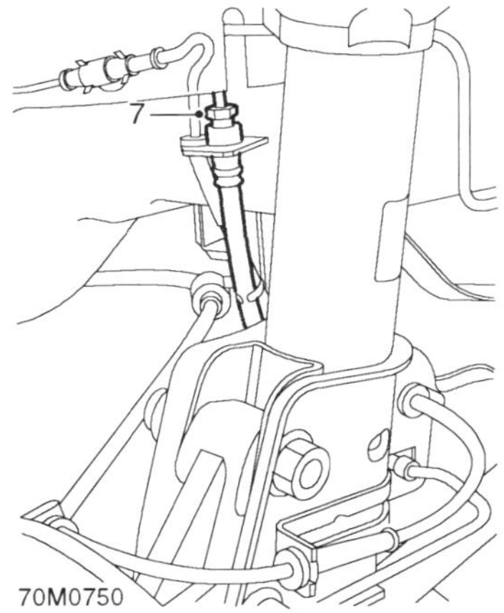

70M0750

7. Disconnect RH front brake pipe union at hose connection.

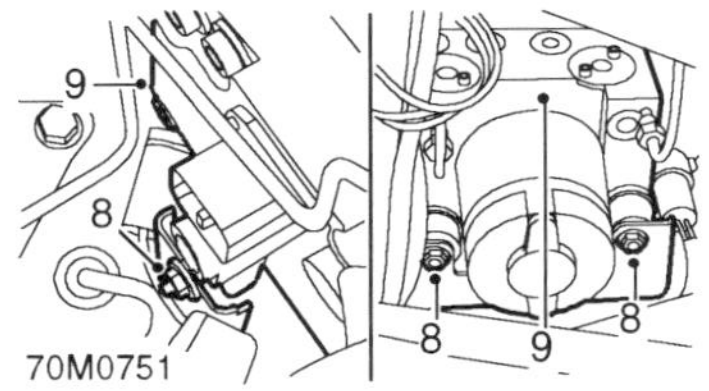

70M0751

8. Loosen 3 nuts securing modulator assembly to mounting bracket.
9. Release and remove modulator from mounting bracket.

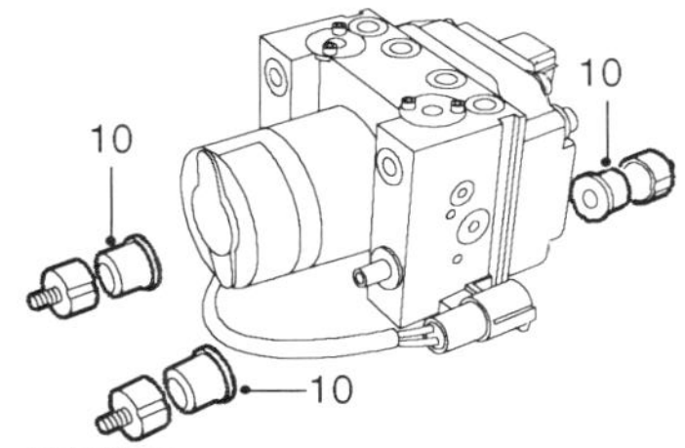

70M0752

Do not carry out further dismantling if component is removed for access only.

10. Remove 3 mounting rubbers from modulator.
11. Fit mounting rubbers to replacement modulator.

Refit

1. Fit modulator assembly to mounting bracket and tighten nuts to 9 Nm.
2. Clean brake pipe unions.
3. Position brake pipes to PCRV and tighten unions to 14 Nm.
4. Connect brake pipe unions to modulator, ensuring pipes are connected to their correct ports.
5. Tighten unions to 14 Nm.
6. Connect pipe union to RH hose connector and tighten to 14 Nm.
7. Connect multiplugs to modulator.
8. Fit RH headlamp. ***See ELECTRICAL, Repairs.***
9. Bleed brakes. ***See Adjustments.***
10. To ensure correct operation, the system MUST be tested using TestBook.
11. Remove stand(s) and lower vehicle.

CONTENTS

Page

SEAT BELTS & SUPPLEMENTARY RESTRAINT SYSTEM

Seat belts are provided as the primary restraint for all occupants. The supplementary restraint system provides additional protection for front seat occupants.

SEAT BELTS

An inertia reel, three point seat belt is installed at each seat position. The inertia reels are of the Emergency Locking Retractor (ELR) type which incorporate a liftshaft locking system with webbing sensor and car sensor activating mechanisms. The webbing sensor activates the locking system if the webbing is subjected to a sharp pull. The car sensor activates the locking system if the vehicle is subjected to sudden deceleration or a severe tilt angle.

Front seat belts

The inertia reel of each front seat belt is attached to the related B/C post, behind the finishers. The webbing runs from the inertia reel, through a height adjuster, to an anchor point either at the base of the B/C post (five door models), or on a bar attached to the inner sill (three door models).

The buckle assembly for each belt, consisting of a buckle attached to a flexible stalk and an integrated pretensioner, is secured to the inboard side of the related front seat frame.

Front seat belt components

Three door models *Five door models*

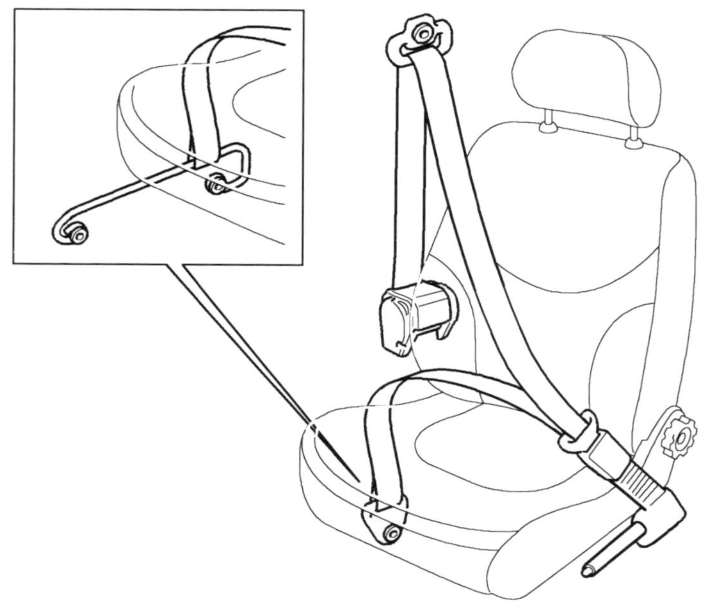

76M2697

Rear seat belts

Three door models

The inertia reel of each rear seat belt is attached to a bracket on top of the related rear suspension turret, behind the loadspace rear quarter trim. The webbing runs from the inertia reel, through a loop on the D post, to an anchor point in the rear wheel arch.

The buckle for each belt is directly attached to the inboard side of the related rear seat frame.

Rear seat belt components - three door models

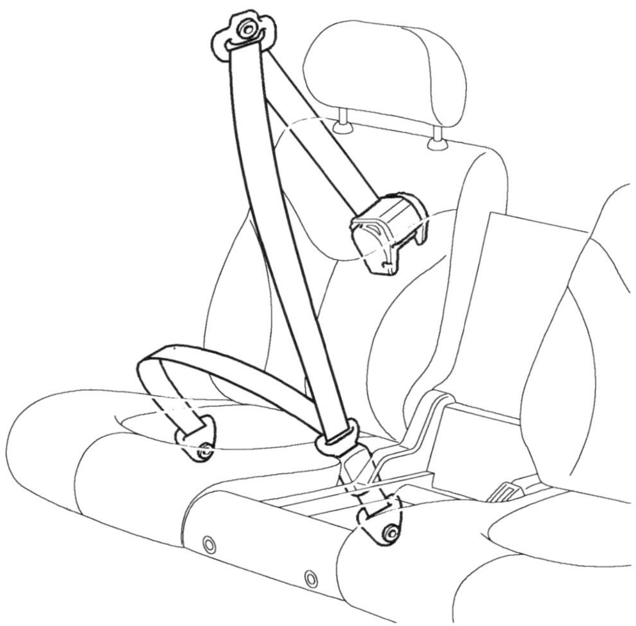

76M2698

Five door models

The inertia reel of each outboard rear seat belt is attached to the related D post, behind the D/E post finisher. The webbing runs from the inertia reel, through a loop on the D post, to an anchor point in the rear wheel arch.

The inertia reel for the centre rear seat belt is installed in a recess in the back of the rear seat. The webbing runs from the inertia reel, over the top of the seat, to an anchor point in the lower frame of the right rear seat.

The buckle assembly for each belt, consisting of a buckle attached to a length of webbing, is fixed to the lower frames of the rear seats. The buckle assembly for the right seat belt shares an anchor point with the webbing of the centre seat belt.

Rear seat belt components - five door models

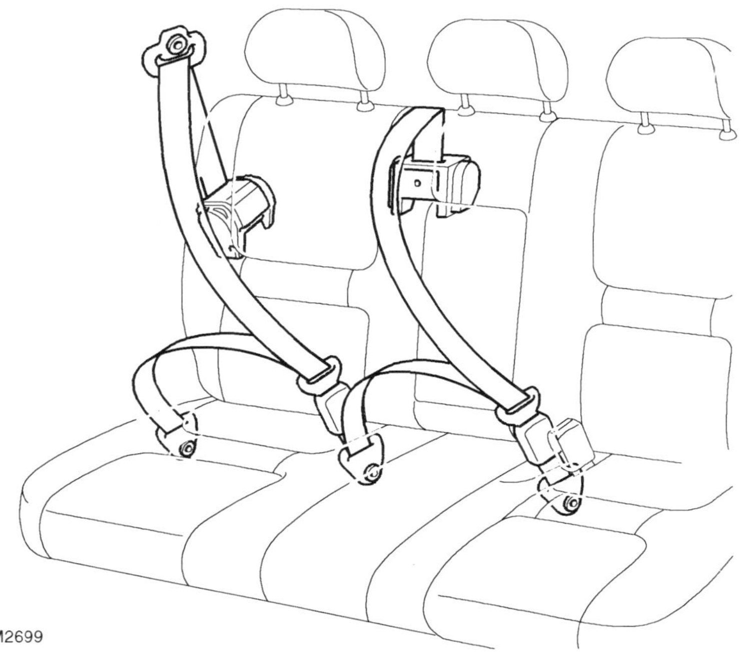

76M2699

SUPPLEMENTARY RESTRAINT SYSTEM (SRS)

Precautions

Making the system safe

Before working on, or in the area of, the SRS, make the system safe as follows:
1. Remove the key from ignition switch.
2. Disconnect both battery leads, earth lead first.
3. Wait 10 minutes to allow the SRS back-up power to fully discharge.

General

Carefully inspect SRS parts before installation. Do not install a part that shows signs of being dropped or improperly handled, such as dents, cracks or deformation.

The airbag ECU is a shock sensitive device and must be handled with extreme care. Because the crash sensor is incorporated inside the airbag ECU, it is imperative that the bolts securing the airbag ECU and its bracket are tightened to their correct torque.

Do not install used SRS parts from another vehicle. When repairing a SRS, use only new parts.

Always use new fixings when replacing SRS parts.

Do not use a multimeter or other general test equipment to check SRS parts or connectors.

After completing work, check that the electrical connectors are installed correctly.

Handling and storage

WARNING: If the airbag is improperly stored face down, accidental deployment could propel the unit with enough force to cause serious injury.

CAUTION: Improper handling or storage can internally damage the airbag module, making it inoperative. If you suspect the airbag module has been damaged, install a new unit and refer to the Workshop Manual for Deployment/Disposal Procedures.

Do not allow anything to rest on an airbag module.

When carrying an airbag module, hold it by the cover, with the cover uppermost and the base away from your body. Do not wrap your arms around the module.

Do not try to disassemble an airbag module or seat belt pretensioner. They have no serviceable parts and, once deployed, cannot be repaired or reused.

Do not expose an airbag module or seat belt pretensioner to heat exceeding 85°C (185°F) or allow it to be contaminated with oil, grease, detergent or water.

For temporary storage of an airbag module or seat belt pretensioner during service, place in a designated storage area or, if no designated storage area is available, in the loadspace of the vehicle; always lock the vehicle and inform the workshop supervisor.

Airbag modules and seat belt pretensioners are classed as explosive articles. For overnight and longer term storage, they must be stored in an approved, secure steel cabinet which has been registered by the local authority.

SRS wiring

Never attempt to modify, splice or repair SRS wiring.

Never install electronic equipment such as a mobile telephone, two way radio or in car entertainment system in such a way that it interferes electrically with the SRS wiring.

Always ensure SRS wiring is routed correctly. Be careful to avoid trapping or pinching the SRS wiring. Ensure the are no possible chafing points.

Always use specified earth fixings tightened to the correct torque. Poor earthing can cause intermittent problems that are difficult to diagnose.

Ensure all SRS wiring connectors are mated correctly and securely fastened. Do not leave the connectors hanging loose.

Warning labels

Warning labels are displayed on SRS parts and prominent places on the vehicle to indicate:
- The need for caution when working in close proximity to SRS parts.
- That, if a passenger airbag module is installed, rearward facing child seats are prohibited on front passenger seats.
- The publication where suitable reference and advice can be found (usually the Workshop Manual or Owner's Handbook).

System description

The supplementary restraint system (SRS) provides additional protection for front seat occupants during a frontal collision above a preset severity.

Impact zone for SRS activation (approximate)

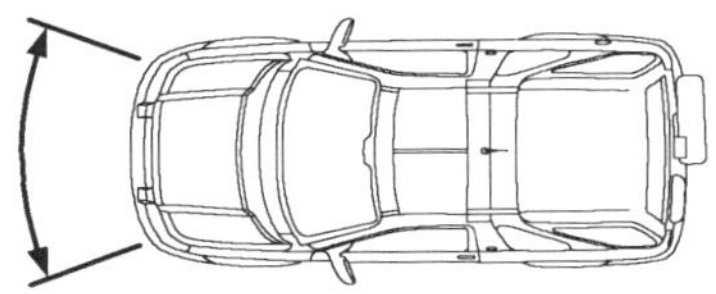

76M2701

SRS component location

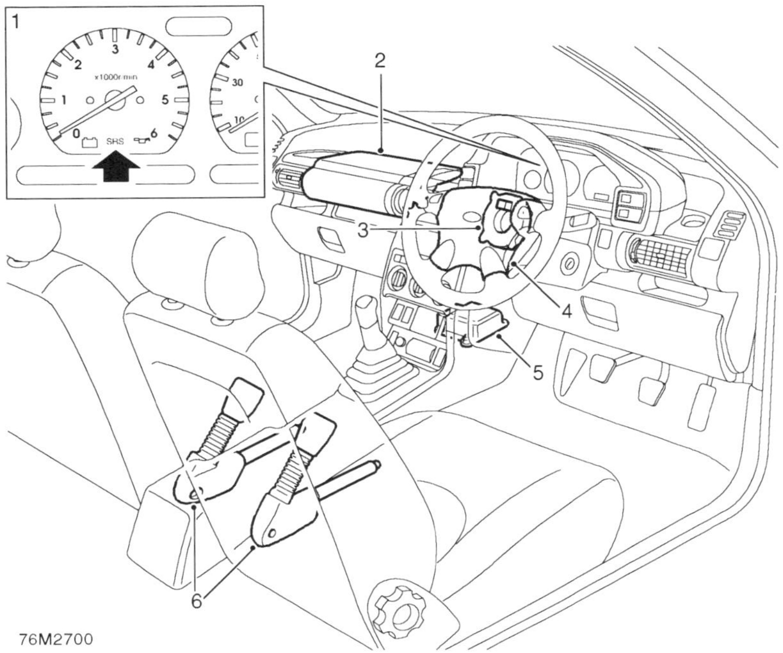

76M2700

1. SRS warning lamp
2. Passenger's airbag module (optional)
3. Rotary coupler
4. Driver's airbag module
5. Airbag ECU
6. Seat belt pretensioners

The SRS is an electronically controlled, single point sensing system. The system comprises an airbag Electronic Control Unit (ECU), a driver's airbag module, a passenger's airbag module (optional), two seat belt pretensioners and a warning lamp. Interconnecting wiring for the system is contained in yellow sleeving and integrated into the vehicle harnesses. A rotary coupler connects the vehicle harness to the driver' airbag module. On vehicles with a passenger's airbag module, a link lead connects the module to the vehicle harness. An ISO 9141 K line (bi-directional) serial communication link connects the airbag ECU to the vehicle's diagnostic socket.

The system is operational only while the ignition is on. With the ignition on, any frontal collision is detected by the airbag ECU. If the impact is above the preset severity, the ECU sends out simultaneous fire signals to the airbag modules and the seat belt pretensioners. The airbag modules then deploy protective airbags in front of the driver and front seat passenger, and the seat belt pretensioners retract to tighten the front seat belts. Collision detection to full deployment of the airbags and pretensioners takes approximately 45 milliseconds.

WARNING: All the SRS parts, including the wiring harness, link lead (where fitted) and rotary coupler, must be renewed after the airbags and pretensioners have deployed.

SRS schematic

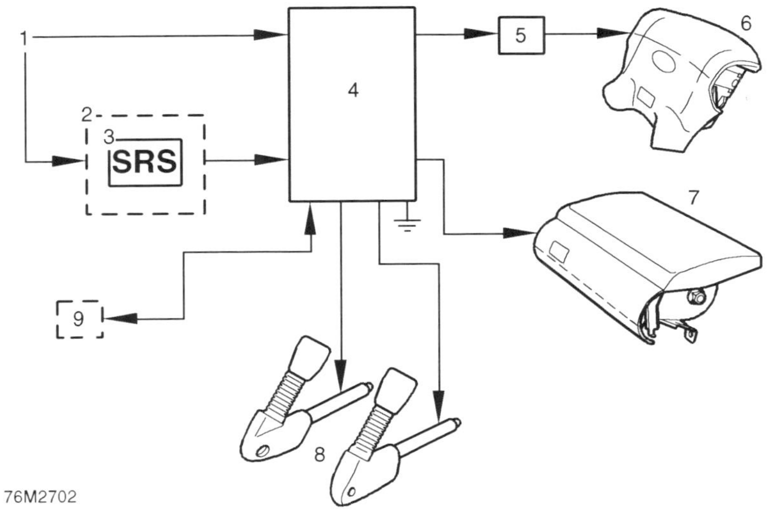

76M2702

1. Ignition power supply
2. Instrument pack
3. Warning lamp
4. Airbag ECU
5. Rotary coupler
6. Driver's airbag module
7. Passenger's airbag module
8. Seat belt pretensioners
9. Diagnostic socket

Airbag ECU

The airbag ECU controls the operation of the system and also contains the collision detection sensors. The airbag ECU is attached to a bracket on the transmission tunnel, directly below the heater. A vehicle earth output connects to one of the fixings. A 30 pin connector provides the airbag ECU connection with the vehicle harness.

Incorporated into the airbag ECU is a mechanical safing sensor, an electronic single point sensor and integrated circuits for control and diagnostics. The mechanical safing sensor is a normally open switch that closes at the preset deceleration limit. The single point sensor is an accelerometer that produces an output proportional to the vehicle's deceleration .

Airbag ECU

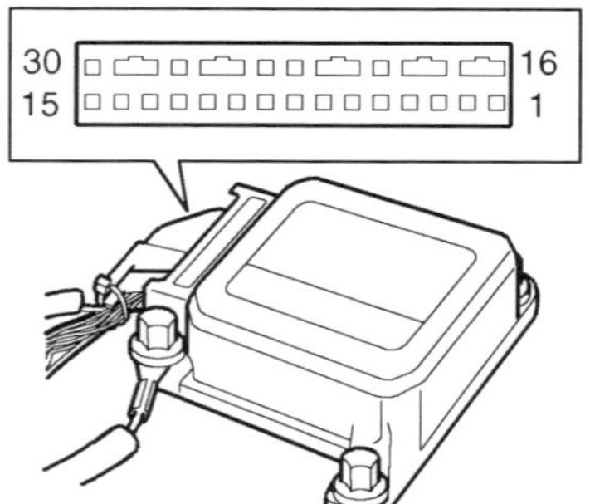

76M2703

Airbag ECU pin connections

Pin	Description
1.	RH pretensioner (+ve)
2.	RH pretensioner (-ve)
3.	LH pretensioner (+ve)
4.	LH pretensioner (-ve)
5.	Vehicle supply
6.	Vehicle earth
7.	SRS warning lamp
8.	Not used

Pin	Description
9.	ISO 9141 K line
10.	Driver airbag module (+ve)
11.	Driver's airbag module (-ve)
12.	Not used
13.	Passenger's airbag (+ve) - where fitted
14.	Passenger's airbag (-ve) - where fitted
15.	to **30.** Not used

Power back-up

The airbag ECU incorporates capacitors to ensure the system will function if the external power supply is disconnected during a collision:

- A hardware capacitor provides power for 200 milliseconds to enable system operation and collision recording.
- Individual capacitors for each fire signal output provide power for 150 milliseconds.

The capacitors are kept charged while the ignition is on by a dc-dc voltage converter incorporated into the airbag ECU. It can take up to 10 minutes from the ignition being switched off for the energy stored in the capacitors to fully dissipate and make the system inert.

Operation

When the ignition is switched on, the airbag ECU performs a bulb check of the SRS warning lamp as part of the power up procedure. The lamp should be extinguished after approximately 5 seconds, indicating that the system is fully operational. If the lamp remains illuminated, a fault has been detected and repair action is required.

While the ignition is on, data from the single point sensor is continuously monitored by the airbag ECU. If the data from the single point sensor indicates vehicle deceleration is at or above the preset limit, and the mechanical safing sensor is closed, the ECU interprets this as a collision that requires deployment of the airbags and retraction of the seat belt pretensioners. It then activates transistors to send fire signals to the airbag modules and the seat belt pretensioners. Simultaneously, the airbag ECU records in memory the following information:

- The error code of the last permanent fault (if any) detected before the collision.
- Internal program information about the collision as seen by the airbag ECU.
- The diagnostic status of the airbag and seat belt pretensioner circuits before deployment.
- The voltage of each power backup capacitor before deployment.
- Information on the airbag ECU internal program status.

If external power is lost during the collision, recording of the last three above items only occurs if there is sufficient power in the backup capacitors after outputting the fire signals.

When deployment and collision event recording has been completed, the airbag ECU enters crash locked mode and illuminates the SRS warning lamp. In crash locked mode the airbag ECU is permanently disabled and must be replaced during subsequent repair action. Crash locked mode cannot be cleared using Testbook.

Diagnostics

While the ignition is on the diagnostic function of the airbag ECU monitors the SRS for faults. If a fault is detected, the airbag ECU stores a related fault code in memory and switches the earth output to illuminate the SRS warning lamp. With a supply voltage range fault, the warning lamp is illuminated only for the duration of the fault. With all other faults, including intermittent faults, the warning lamp is illuminated for the remainder of the drive cycle. At the next ignition on, if the fault is still present the warning lamp remains illuminated after the lamp check; if the fault does not recur, the warning lamp extinguishes but the fault code remains stored in memory. An intermittent fault will be cleared from memory if 40 drive cycles are completed without its recurrence.

After detecting a fault, the system may retain some operational capability:

- If a fault is detected in an airbag or pretensioner circuit, only that circuit is disabled; the other airbag and pretensioner circuits remain operational and their related components will still be deployed in a collision.
- If an internal or power supply fault is detected, the complete system will be disabled.
- If a fault exists in the SRS warning lamp circuit, the lamp will not illuminate during the lamp check at ignition on, but, provided there are no other faults, the system will otherwise be fully operational.

Fault code retrieval and fault diagnosis of the SRS can only be done using Testbook. Additional SRS information that can be read using Testbook is the:

- Airbag ECU bar code.
- Evolution number of the hardware, software and diagnostic protocol.
- Status of the crash locked mode.
- Vehicle identification number (VIN) data.

Diagnostic checks performed by the airbag ECU include:

- Monitoring of the airbag and pretensioner circuits for open/short circuits.
- Internal errors.
- Supply voltage (limits are 8.6 to 19.0 V at power up, 6.0 to 19.0 V during drive cycle).

Airbag modules

During a frontal collision each airbag module deploys a gas filled bag to form a protective cushion between the front seat occupant and the steering wheel or fascia/windshield. The driver's airbag module is attached to the centre of the steering wheel. Where fitted, the passenger's airbag module is installed in the fascia, above the glovebox.

Each airbag module has a gas generator attached to a folded airbag installed in a housing. The driver's airbag has an inflated volume of 45 litres; the passenger's airbag has an inflated volume of 120 litres. The gas generator of the driver's airbag module is filled with a nitrocellulose based material; the gas generator of the passenger's airbag module is filled with a sodium azide based material.
The outlet of the gas generators incorporates a filter screen to prevent solid combustion by-products entering the airbag during deployment. An igniter (squib) in each generator provides an ignition source when triggered by a fire signal from the airbag ECU. A 2 pin connector provides the interface between the igniter and the vehicle wiring.

On the driver's airbag module, the housing is closed by a cover that forms the steering wheel centre pad; split lines are formed in the inner surface of the cover to direct the airbag through the required exit point during deployment. On the passenger's airbag module, the housing is closed by a trim panel profiled to match the fascia; a tethered deployment door forms an integral part of the trim panel.

Both airbag modules operate in the same way. On receipt of a fire signal from the airbag ECU, the igniter ignites the material in the gas generator. The burning material rapidly produces a large amount of nitrogen gas which passes through the filter screen into the airbag, forcing the airbag to unfold. On the driver airbag module, the unfolding airbag ruptures the cover along the split lines; on the passenger airbag module, the unfolding airbag breaks the deployment door fixings to the module housing and trim panel, and the deployment door lifts off the fascia (but remains tethered to the module housing). Once free of the housing the airbag inflates to its full extent. Vents in the airbag prevent excess pressure bursting the bag and, as soon as the material in the gas generator is exhausted, allows the airbag to instantly deflate.

Driver's airbag module components

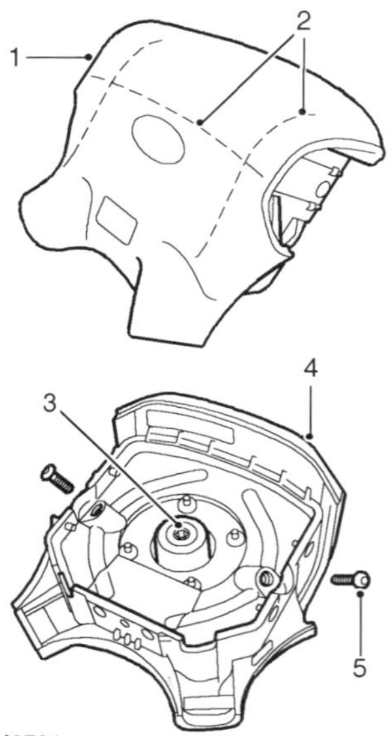

76M2704

1. Cover
2. Split lines
3. Electrical connector
4. Housing
5. Fixing

Passenger's airbag module components

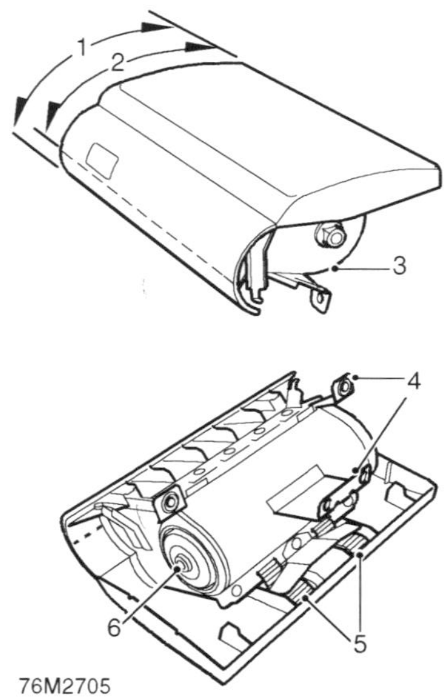

76M2705

1. Trim panel
2. Deployment door section
3. Housing
4. Fixing bracket
5. Tethers
6. Electrical connector

Seat belt pretensioners

During a frontal collision the seat belt pretensioners tighten the front seat belts to ensure the occupants are securely held in their seats. A pretensioner is integrated into the buckle assembly of each front seat belt.

The two pretensioners are handed, but otherwise identical. Each pretensioner has a tube containing propellant and a piston. The piston is attached to a steel cable, the opposite end of which is attached to the seat belt buckle. An igniter (squib) in the base of tube provides an ignition source when triggered by a fire signal from the airbag ECU. A fly lead with a 2 pin connector links the igniter to the vehicle wiring.

On receipt of a fire signal from the airbag ECU, the igniter ignites the propellant. The burning propellant rapidly produces nitrogen gas that drives the piston along the tube, pulling on the cable and drawing the buckle towards the buckle assembly fixing point on the seat.

SRS warning lamp

The SRS warning lamp provides system status information for the driver. The lamp consists of a bulb behind a red SRS graphic at the base of the tachometer in the instrument pack. The bulb is a serviceable item that can be renewed from the rear of the instrument pack.

Seat belt pretensioner components

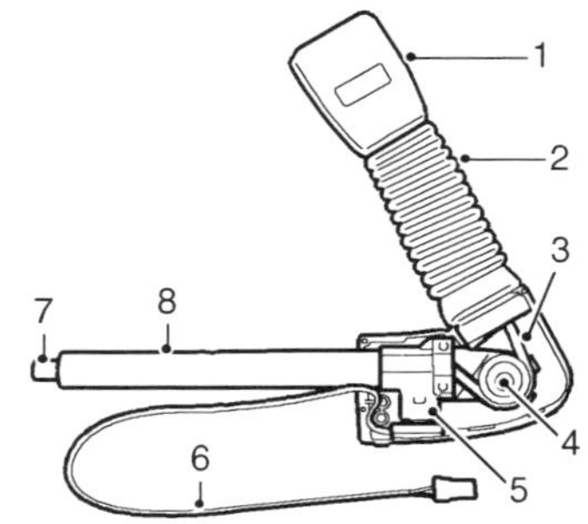

76M2706

1. Seat belt buckle
2. Gaiter
3. Steel cable
4. Fixing
5. Igniter
6. Fly lead
7. Vent
8. Tube

Rotary coupler

The rotary coupler is installed on the steering column to provide the interface between the fixed wiring harness and the moveable driver airbag module and horn buttons on the steering wheel.

A rotating link harness is encapsulated into a plastic cassette comprising outer and inner housings with integral connectors. Screws attach the outer housing to the steering column switch assembly and the inner housing is keyed to the steering wheel by its connector. The inner housing can turn a maximum of six revolutions in relation to the outer housing. For maintenance purposes the outer housing incorporates a position indicator wheel; a white tab is visible on the wheel when the rotary coupler is centralised. To prevent breaking the rotating link harness, both the steering and the rotary coupler must be centralised when removing and installing the steering wheel.

Rotary coupler components

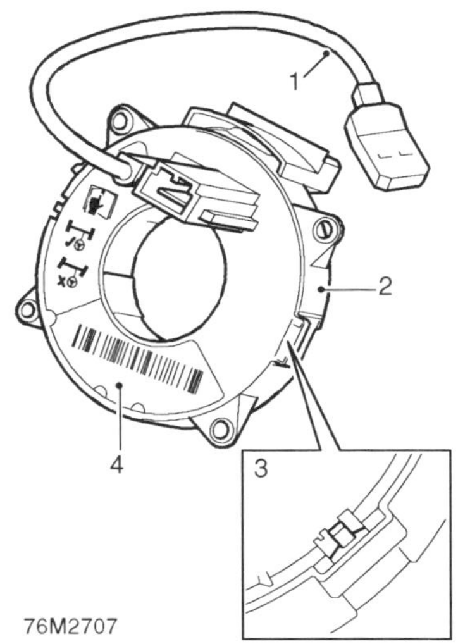

76M2707

1. Fly lead (to airbag module)
2. Outer housing
3. Position indicator wheel
4. Inner housing

SEAT BELT - FRONT - 3 DOOR

Service repair no - 76.73.13

Remove

1. Remove seat base finisher. ***See BODY, Seats and seat belts.***
2. Remove body side rear trim casing. ***See BODY, Interior trim components.***

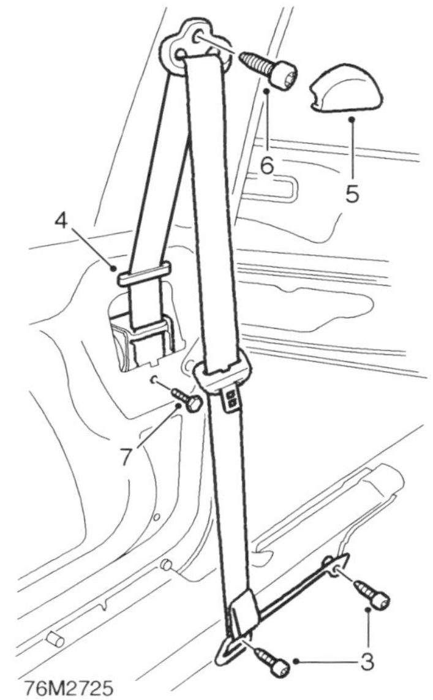

76M2725

3. Remove 2 Torx bolts securing seat belt lower mounting and remove mounting from seat belt.
4. Release seat belt retaining strap.
5. Remove cover from upper mounting.
6. Remove Torx bolt from upper mounting.
7. Remove bolt from seat belt reel and remove reel.

Refit

1. Position reel and tighten bolt to 31 Nm.
2. Extend belt, position top mounting and tighten Torx bolt to 31 Nm.
3. Fit top mounting cover.
4. Secure belt retaining strap.
5. Fit lower mounting to seat belt, position mounting, fit and tighten Torx bolts to 40 Nm.
6. Fit trim casing. ***See BODY, Interior trim components.***
7. Fit seat base finisher. ***See BODY, Seats and seat belts.***

SEAT BELT - FRONT - 5 DOOR

Service repair no - 76.73.13

Remove

1. Remove seat base finisher. ***See BODY, Seats and seat belts.***
2. Remove 'B/C' post upper finisher. ***See BODY, Interior trim components.***

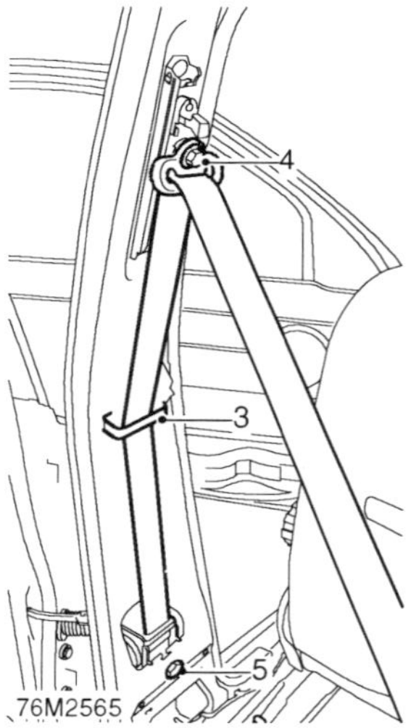

3. Release seat belt retaining strap.
4. Remove nut from seat belt upper mounting.
5. Remove bolt from seat belt reel and remove reel.

Refit

1. Position reel and tighten bolt to 31 Nm.
2. Extend belt, position top mounting and tighten nut to 31 Nm.
3. Secure belt retaining strap.
4. Fit 'B/C' post upper finisher. ***See BODY, Interior trim components.***
5. Fit seat base finisher. ***See BODY, Seats and seat belts.***

SEAT BELT - CENTRE - REAR - 5 DOOR

Service repair no - 76.73.20

Remove

1. Remove RH rear seat. ***See BODY, Seats and seat belts.***

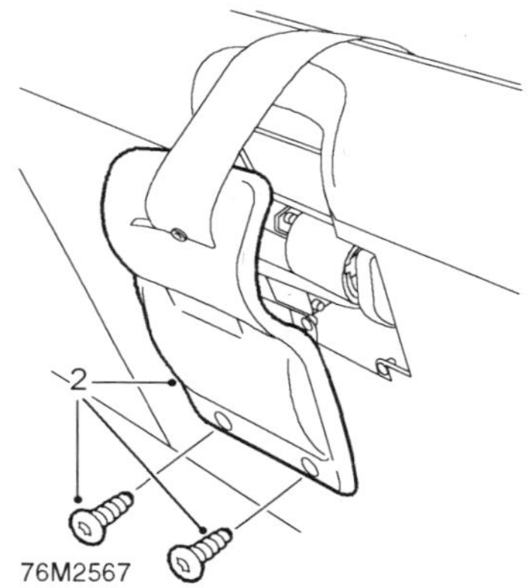

2. Remove 2 screws and remove seat belt reel cover.

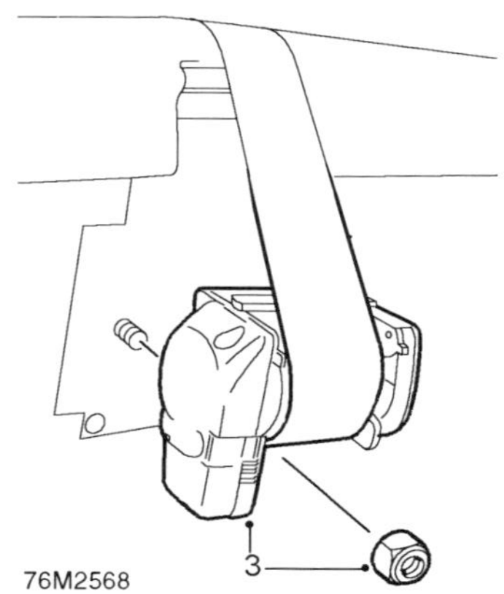

3. Remove nut and release seat belt reel.

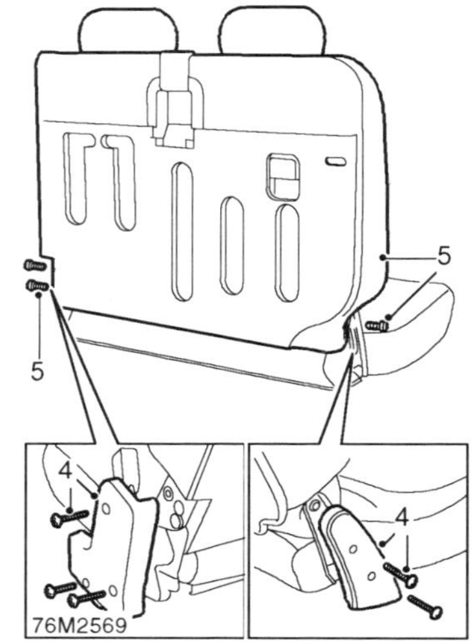

4. Remove 5 screws and remove both end covers from seat hinges.
5. Remove 3 Torx bolts and remove squab from cushion.

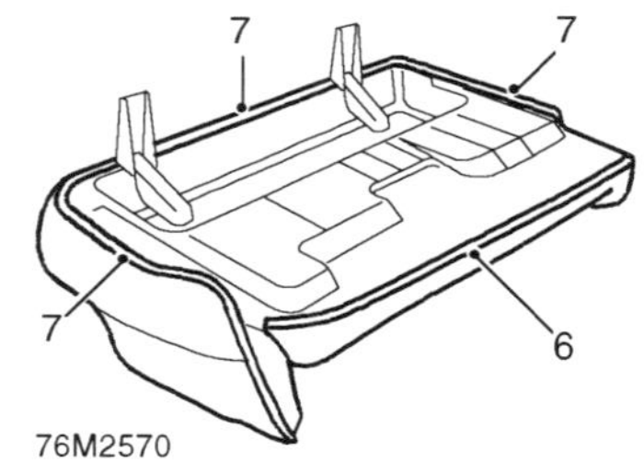

6. Release rear of cushion cover from seat frame.
7. Release sides and front of cushion cover from seat frame.

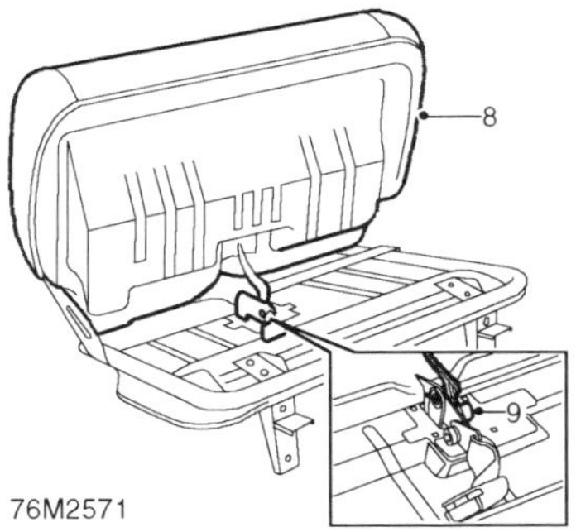

76M2571

8. Release cover and pad from seat frame.
9. Remove Torx bolt from centre seat belt anchor/right seat belt buckle.
10. Remove seat belt and right seat belt buckle.

Refit

1. Position centre seat belt anchor and right seat belt buckle to seat and tighten Torx bolt to 32 Nm.
2. Fit cover and pad to seat frame.
3. Fit front and sides of cushion cover to seat frame.
4. Fit rear of cushion cover to seat frame.
5. Fit cushion to squab and tighten Torx bolts.
6. Fit end covers and tighten screws.
7. Position seat belt reel and tighten nut to 32 Nm.
8. Fit seat belt reel cover and tighten screws.
9. Fit rear seat. ***See BODY, Seats and seat belts.***

SEAT BELT - SIDE - REAR - 5 DOOR

Service repair no - 76.73.23

Remove

1. Remove rear quarter upper trim casing. ***See BODY, Interior trim components.***

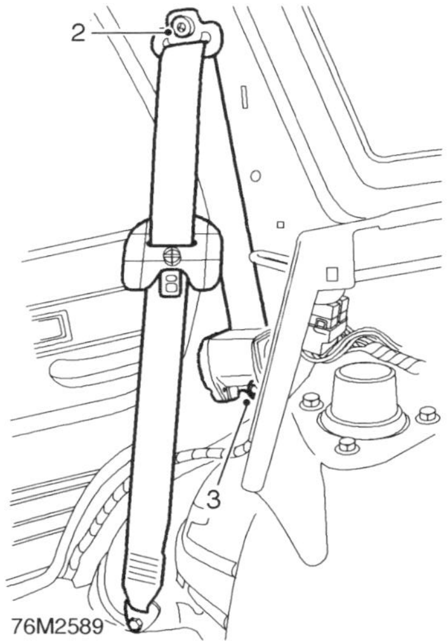

76M2589

2. Remove Torx bolt from seat belt upper mounting.
3. Remove Torx bolt from seat belt reel and remove reel.

Refit

1. Position reel and tighten Torx bolt to 50 Nm.
2. Extend belt, position top mounting and tighten Torx bolt to 32 Nm.
3. Fit rear quarter upper trim casing. ***See BODY, Interior trim components.***

ADJUSTABLE MOUNTING - SEAT BELT - 'B/C' POST

Service repair no - 76.73.26

Remove

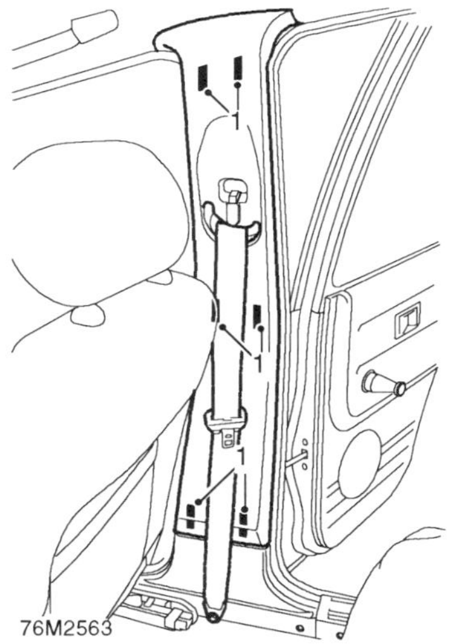

76M2563

1. Release 'B/C' post upper finisher from 6 clips and position aside.

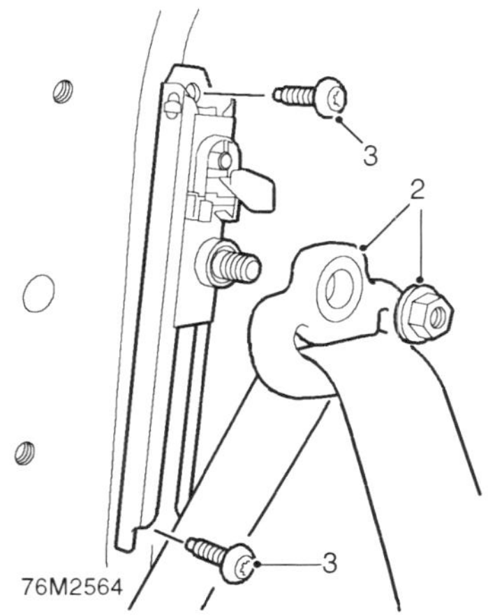

76M2564

2. Remove nut from seat belt upper mounting and remove belt bracket.
3. Remove 2 Torx screws from mounting and remove mounting.

Refit

1. Position mounting and tighten Torx screws to 26 Nm.
2. Fit upper belt bracket and tighten nut to 31 Nm.
3. Position 'B/C' post upper finisher and secure with clips.

SEAT BELT BUCKLE - REAR - 3 DOOR

Service repair no - 76.73.32

Remove

1. Remove rear seat. ***See BODY, Seats and seat belts.***

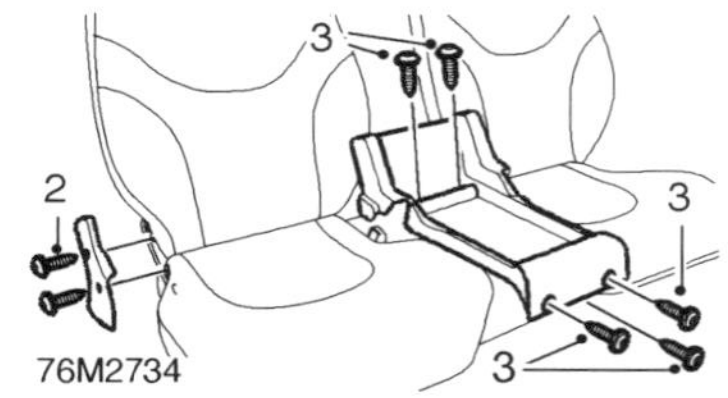

76M2734

2. Remove 2 screws from hinge cover and remove cover from seat hinge.
3. Remove 4 screws and remove rear seat centre console.

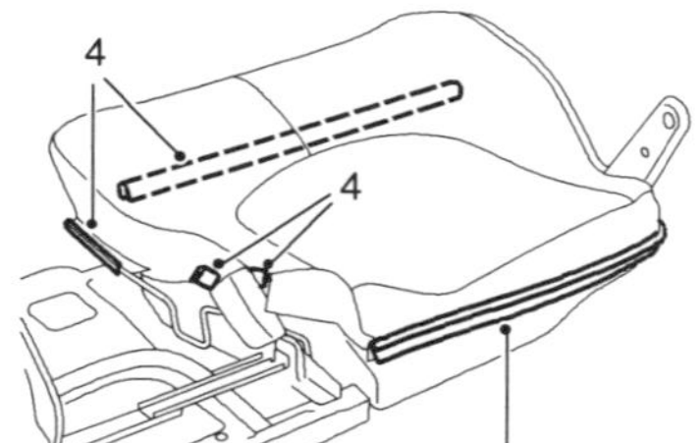

76M2735

4. Release rear seat cushion cover retainers and position cushion aside.

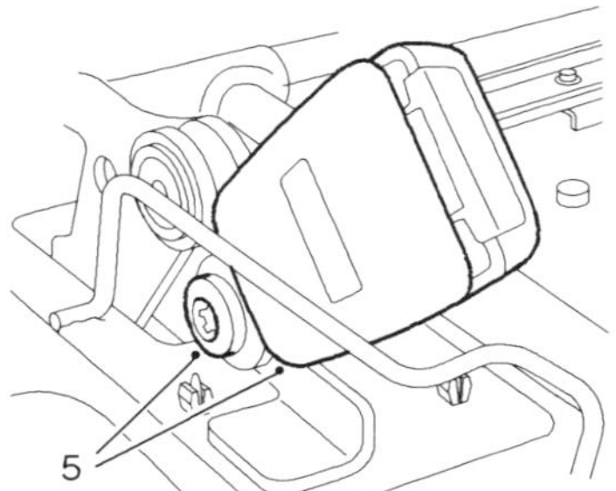

76M2736

5. Remove Torx bolt and remove seat belt buckle.

Refit

1. Fit buckle to seat frame and tighten Torx bolt to 32 Nm.
2. Position seat cushion and secure cover retainers.
3. Fit centre console and tighten screws.
4. Fit hinge cover and tighten screws.
5. Fit rear seat. ***See BODY, Seats and seat belts.***

SEAT BELT BUCKLE - REAR - 5 DOOR

Service repair no - 76.73.32

Remove

1. Position rear seat forward.

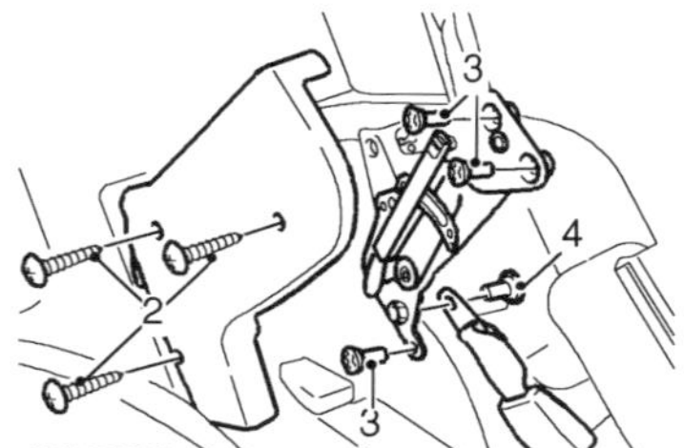

76M2566

2. Remove 3 screws from end cover and remove covers from seat hinges.
3. Remove 4 Torx bolts from seat lock down catch and remove catch assembly.
4. Remove Torx bolt from seat belt buckle and remove buckle.

Refit

1. Fit buckle to catch assembly and tighten Torx bolt to 32 Nm.
2. Fit catch assembly to seat, fit Torx bolts but do not tighten at this stage.
3. Fold seat down and check that seat unfolds on lockdown bar correctly. Adjust catch assembly if required.
4. Tighten Torx bolts to 32 Nm.
5. Re-check seat fold.
6. Fit end cover and tighten screws.
7. Reposition seat.

PRETENSIONER - SEAT BELT - FRONT

Service repair no - 76.73.75

Remove

WARNING: *See GENERAL INFORMATION, SRS Precautions.*

1. Make the SRS system safe. ***See GENERAL INFORMATION, SRS Precautions.***
2. Remove rear console. ***See BODY, Interior trim components.***

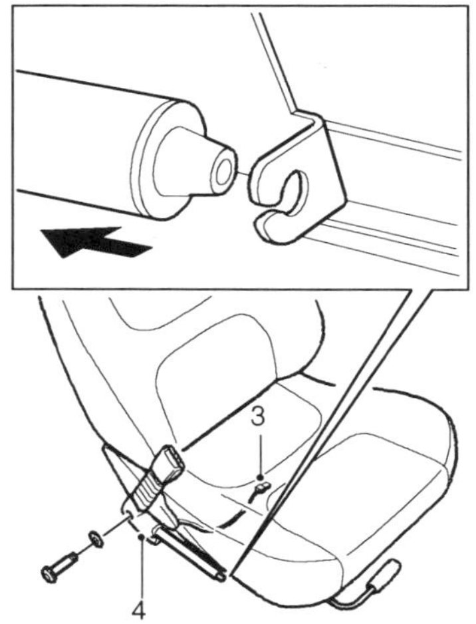

76M2573

3. Disconnect and secure pretensioner multiplug.
4. Remove Torx bolt from pretensioner, release pretensioner from seat location and remove pretensioner assembly.

WARNING: Store the pretensioner in accordance with the storage procedures. *See GENERAL INFORMATION, SRS Precautions.*

Refit

NOTE: If the pretensioner is to be replaced, the bar code of the new pretensioner must be recorded.

1. Position pretensioner in seat location and tighten Torx bolt to 32 Nm.
2. Connect and secure pretensioner multiplug.
3. Fit rear console. ***See BODY, Interior trim components.***
4. Connect battery leads, earth lead last.
5. Carry out system check by turning the ignition on and checking that the SRS warning lamp illuminates, then extinguishes after approximately 5 seconds.

SEAT BELT BUCKLE - CENTRE - REAR - 5 DOOR

Service repair no - 76.73.98

Remove

1. Remove RH rear seat. ***See BODY, Seats and seat belts.***

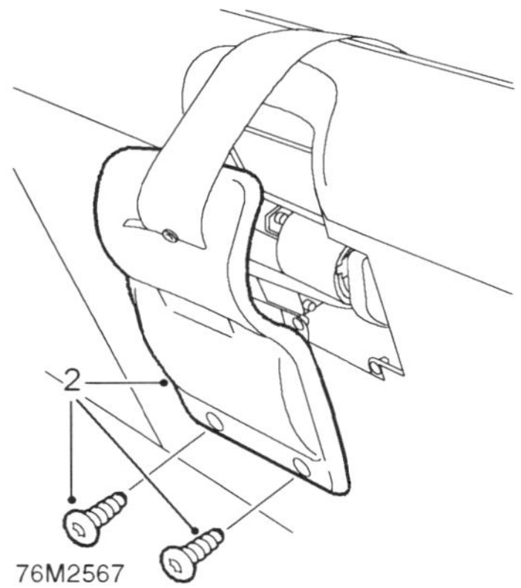

76M2567

2. Remove 2 screws and remove seat belt reel cover.

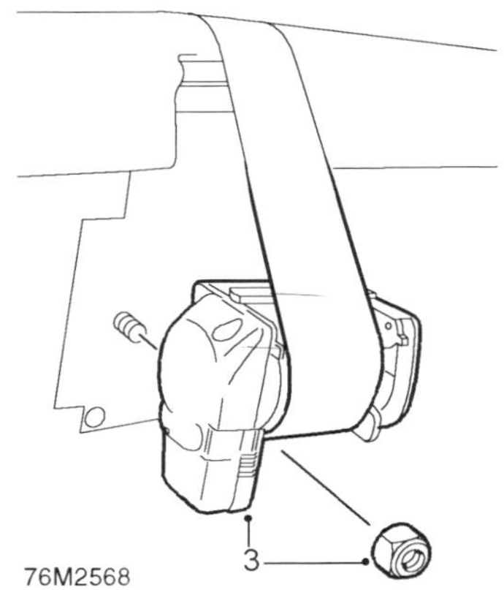

76M2568

3. Remove nut and release seat belt reel.

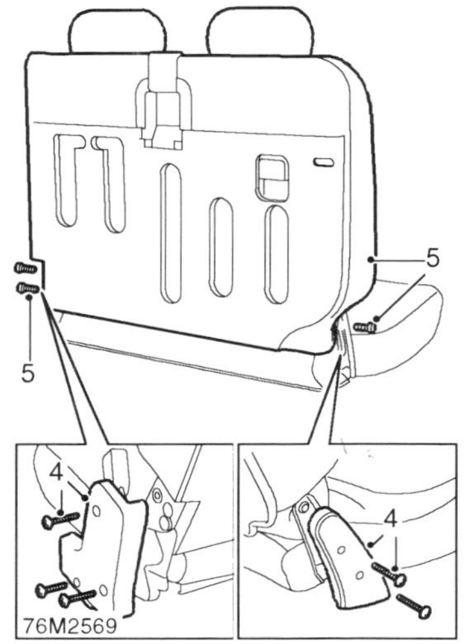

76M2569

4. Remove 5 screws and remove both end covers from seat hinges.
5. Remove 3 Torx bolts and remove squab from cushion.

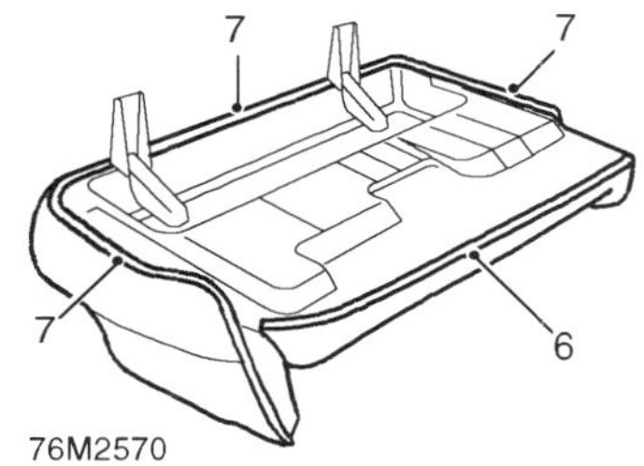

76M2570

6. Release rear of cushion cover from frame.
7. Release sides and front of cushion cover from frame.

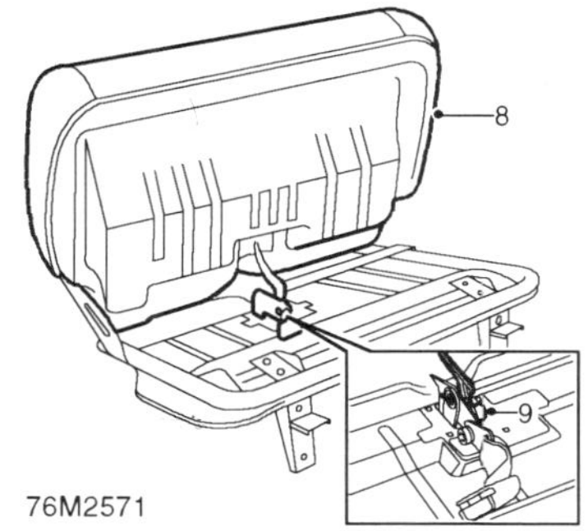

76M2571

8. Release cover and pad from frame.
9. Remove Torx bolt from seat belt buckle and remove buckle.

Refit

1. Position seat belt buckle and tighten Torx bolt to 32 Nm.
2. Fit cover and pad to frame.
3. Fit front and sides of cushion cover to frame.
4. Fit rear of cushion cover to frame.
5. Fit cushion to squab and tighten Torx bolts to 32 Nm.
6. Fit end covers and tighten screws.
7. Position seat belt reel and tighten nut to 32 Nm.
8. Fit seat belt reel cover and tighten screws.
9. Fit rear seat. ***See BODY, Seats and seat belts.***

AIRBAG - STEERING WHEEL

Service repair no - 76.74.01

Remove

WARNING: *See GENERAL INFORMATION, SRS Precautions.*

1. Make the SRS system safe. ***See GENERAL INFORMATION, SRS Precautions.***

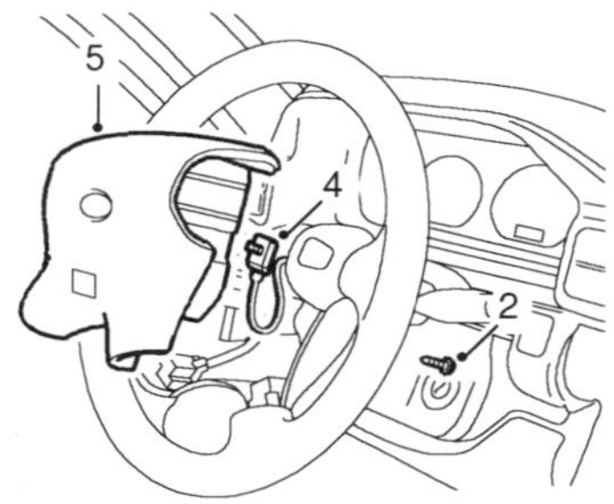

76M2594

2. Remove 2 Torx bolts securing the airbag module to steering wheel.
3. Release airbag module from steering wheel.

CAUTION: Do not allow the airbag module to hang by the harness.

4. Disconnect harness connector from the airbag module.
5. Remove airbag module.

WARNING: Store the airbag module in accordance with the storage procedures. *See GENERAL INFORMATION, SRS Precautions.*

Refit

NOTE: If the airbag module is to be replaced, the bar code of the new module must be recorded.

1. Position airbag module and make connection with harness upwards as shown in illustration.
2. Fit airbag to steering wheel and hand start the 2 Torx screws. Tighten screws to 9 Nm.
3. Connect battery leads, earth lead last.

AIRBAG - PASSENGER

Service repair no - 76.74.02

Remove

WARNING: *See GENERAL INFORMATION, SRS Precautions.*

1. Make the SRS system safe. ***See GENERAL INFORMATION, SRS Precautions.***

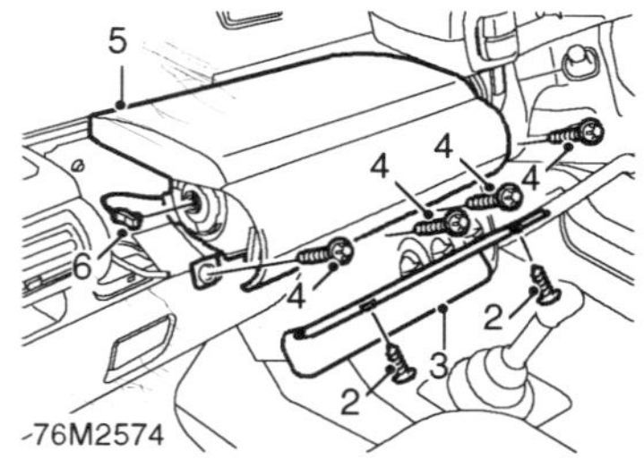

76M2574

2. Remove 2 screws securing airbag lower finisher.
3. Remove finisher.
4. Remove 4 Torx screws securing airbag to fascia.
5. Release airbag from fascia.

CAUTION: Do not allow the airbag module to hang by the harness.

6. Disconnect multiplug holder and multiplug from airbag.
7. Remove airbag.

WARNING: Store the airbag module in accordance with the storage procedures. *See GENERAL INFORMATION, SRS Precautions.*

Refit

NOTE: If the airbag module is to be replaced, the bar code of the new module must be recorded.

1. Position airbag to fascia, connect multiplug and multiplug holder.
2. Align airbag to fascia and tighten torx screws to 9 Nm.
3. Position airbag lower finisher and tighten screws.
4. Connect battery leads, earth lead last.

ROTARY COUPLER

Service repair no - 76.74.20

Remove

WARNING: *See GENERAL INFORMATION, SRS Precautions.*

1. Make the SRS system safe. ***See GENERAL INFORMATION, SRS Precautions.***

CAUTION: Ensure front road wheels are in the straight ahead position.

2. Remove steering wheel. ***See STEERING, Repairs.***

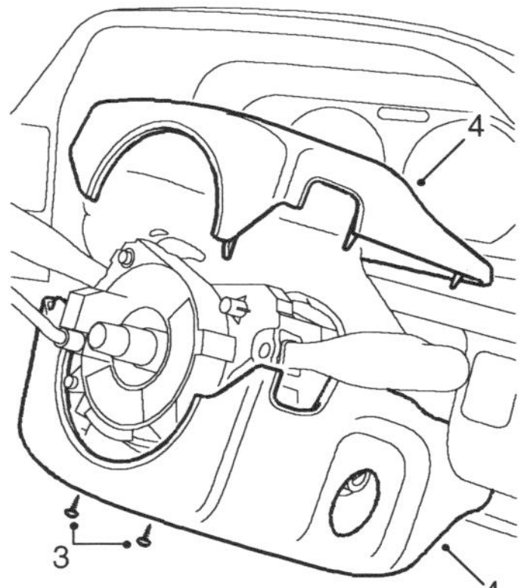

76M2595

3. Remove 2 screws securing lower half of steering column nacelle.
4. Remove lower and upper halves of nacelle.

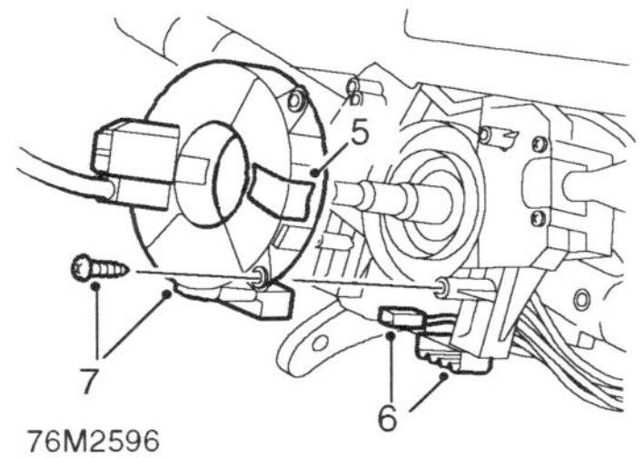

76M2596

5. If the rotary coupler is being re-used place adhesive tape around moulding to prevent rotation.
6. Disconnect 2 multiplugs from rotary coupler.
7. Remove 4 screws and remove rotary coupler.

CAUTION: Do not dismantle the rotary coupler, it has no serviceable parts and must be replaced as a complete assembly.

Refit

CAUTION: Ensure front road wheels are in the straight ahead position.

1. Ensure the rotary coupler is installed in its centred position, as indicated by the white segment on the indicator wheel.
2. Fit rotary coupler and secure with screws.
3. Connect multiplugs to rotary coupler.
4. Fit upper and lower halves of nacelle to steering column and tighten screws.
5. If fitting existing rotary coupler, remove retaining tape from rotary coupler. If fitting new rotary coupler, remove blue locking tab from rotary coupler.
6. Fit steering wheel. ***See STEERING, Repairs.***

DIAGNOSTIC CONTROL UNIT (DCU)

Service repair no - 76.74.68
Service repair no - 76.74.68/20

Remove

WARNING: *See GENERAL INFORMATION. SRS Precautions.*

1. Make the SRS system safe. ***See GENERAL INFORMATION, SRS Precautions.***
2. Remove heater assembly. ***See HEATING & VENTILATION, Repairs.***

Models with air conditioning fitted

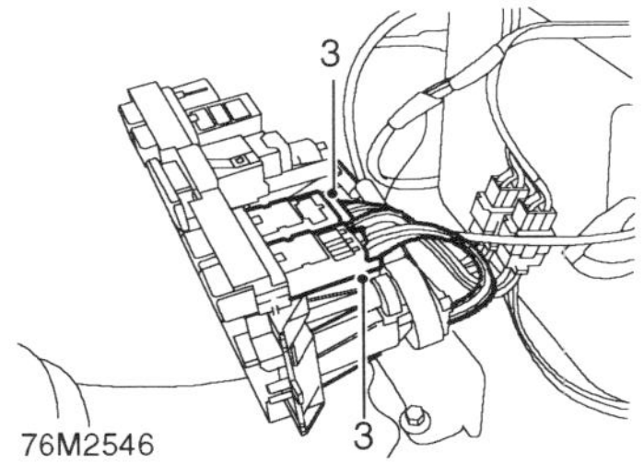

76M2546

3. Disconnect 2 multiplugs from air conditioning switches.

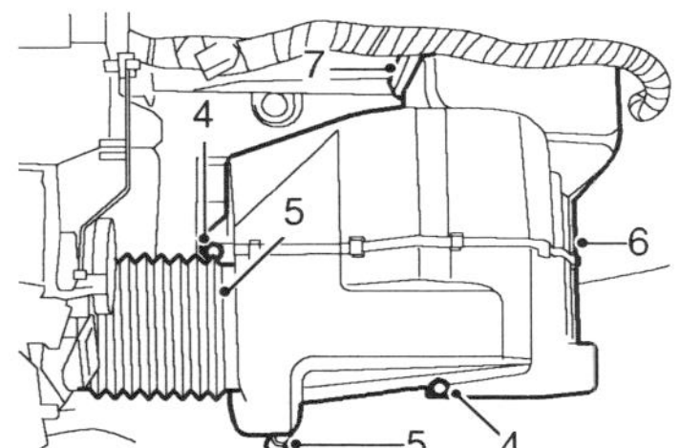

76M2547

4. Remove 2 nuts securing evaporator.
5. Release evaporator from drain hose and air intake.
6. Remove evaporator.
7. Collect air duct and pipe seal.

All models

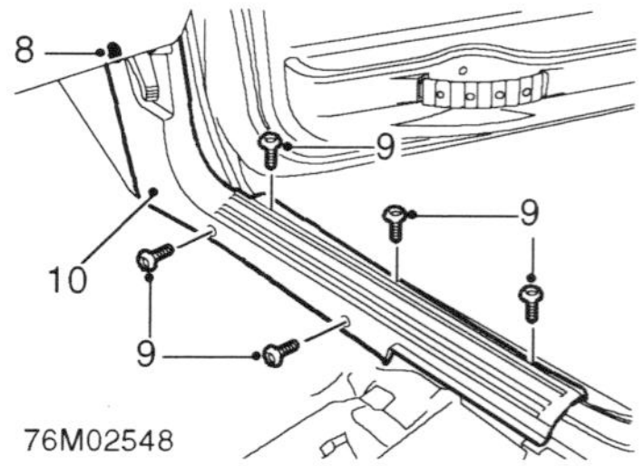

76M02548

8. Remove scrivet from front of passenger side carpet retainer.
9. Remove 5 Torx screws from carpet retainer.
10. Remove carpet retainer.

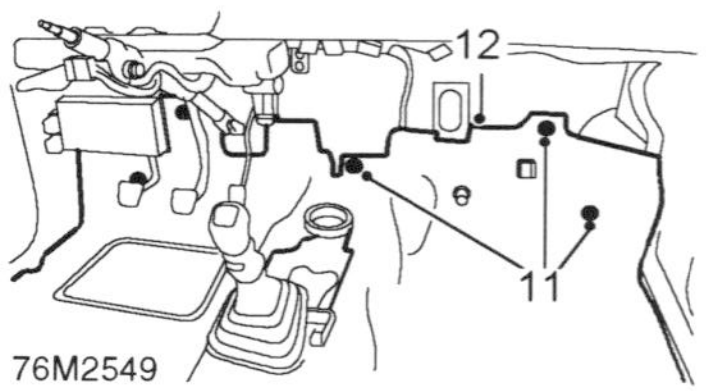

76M2549

11. Remove 3 retainers securing carpet to bulkhead.
12. Pull carpet back for access to DCU.

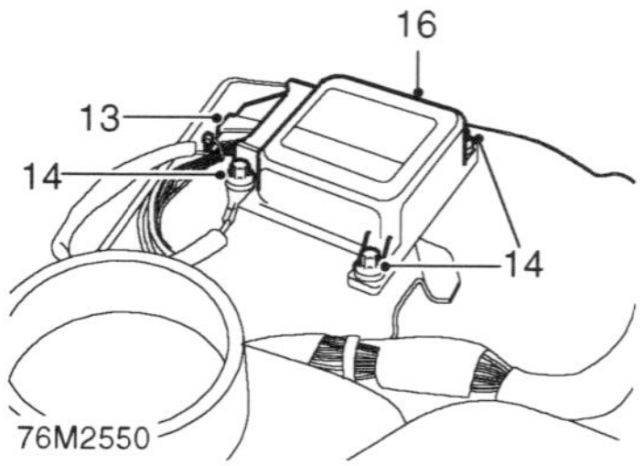

76M2550

13. Disconnect multiplug from DCU.
14. Remove 3 bolts securing DCU.
15. Release earth lead.
16. Remove DCU.

Refit

1. Fit DCU.
2. Fit earth lead and tighten bolts to 9 Nm.

WARNING: The vehicle crash sensor is incorporated inside the DCU, it is imperative that bolts securing the DCU are tightened to their correct torque.

3. Connect multiplug to DCU.
4. Fit carpet and secure to bulkhead.
5. Fit carpet retainer, fit and tighten Torx screws.
6. Fit scrivet to front of carpet retainer.

Models with air conditioning fitted

7. Fit air duct and pipe seal.
8. Fit evaporator assembly to drain hose and air intake.
9. Fit evaporator to studs and secure with nuts.
10. Connect multiplugs to air conditioning switches.
11. Fit NEW receiver drier. ***See AIR CONDITIONING, Repairs.***

All models

12. Fit heater assembly. ***See HEATING & VENTILATION, Repairs.***
13. Connect battery leads, earth lead last.

CONTENTS

CONTENTS

CONTENTS

FRONT WINDOW REGULATOR

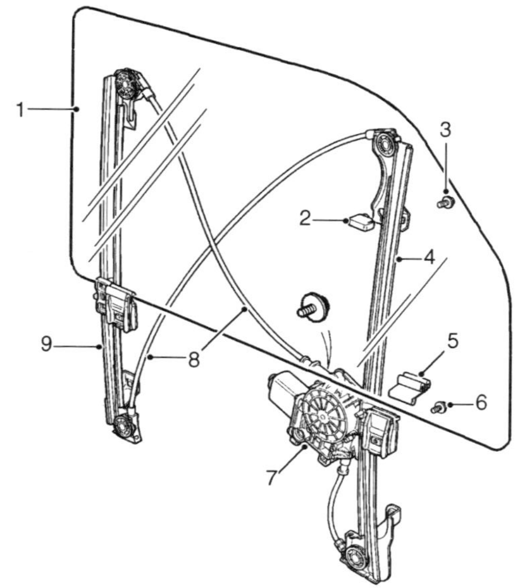

76M2783

LH REGULATOR SHOWN - RH SIMILAR

1. Front window glass
2. Glass stop damper
3. Mounting screw 4 off
4. Forward runner
5. Friction pad
6. Glass clamp screw
7. Motor assembly
8. Cables
9. Rear runner

The front windows are electrically operated and are controlled from two rocker type switches located in the centre of the fascia. The windows can only be operated with the ignition in position II.

The front window regulator and motor are supplied as an assembly and are handed. The assembly comprises a front and rear runner, a continuous cable and a motor.

The runners are secured in the door frame with four screws. The door glass is located in two carriers which are located in tracks in the runners. The glass is retained in friction pads in each carrier and secured with clamp screws.

Each carrier is attached to the cable which in turn is attached to a drum which is driven by the motor. When the motor is operated the drum pulls the cable in the required direction to raise or lower the glass.

REAR WINDOW REGULATOR

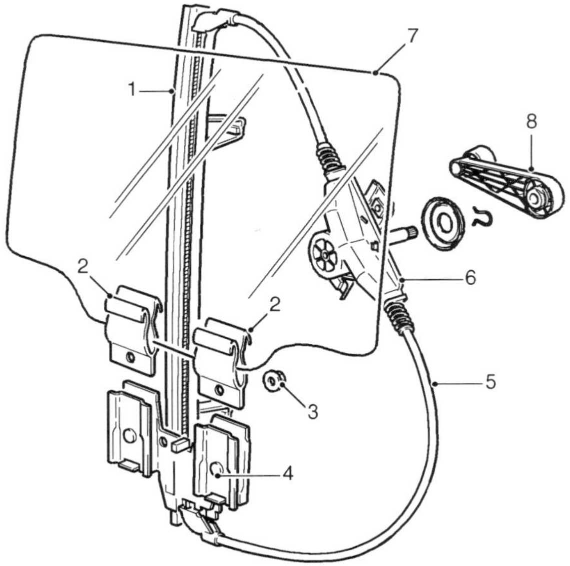

76M2784

RH REGULATOR SHOWN - LH SIMILAR

1. Runner
2. Friction pad
3. Mounting nut 2 off
4. Mounting screw 2 off
5. Cable
6. Regulator
7. Rear window glass
8. Regulator handle

Each rear window is manually operated using the regulator handle located on rear door.

The rear window regulators are supplied as an assembly and are handed. The assembly comprises a runner, regulator mechanism, cable and regulator handle.

The runner is secured in the door frame with four bolts, two bolts securing the runner and two bolts securing the regulator. The door glass is located in two carriers which are connected to a track in the runner. The glass is retained in friction pads in each carrier and secured with clamp screws and nuts.

The carrier is attached to the cable which, in turn, is attached to a drum driven by the manual regulator. When the regulator handle is rotated in the required direction, the drum pulls the cable to raise or lower the glass.

TAIL DOOR WINDOW REGULATOR

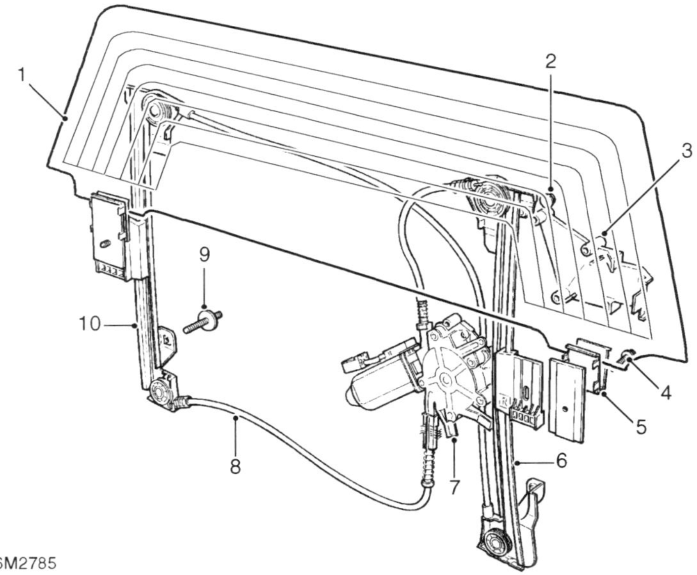

76M2785

1. Tail door glass
2. Nut 3 off
3. Base plate
4. Clamp screw 2 off
5. Friction pad 2 off
6. Runner RH
7. Motor
8. Cable
9. Mounting screw 4 off
10. Runner LH

The tail door window is electrically operated and is controlled principally by the central control unit. The window can be operated from a rocker switch on the fascia, reverse gear selected with front windscreen wipers operating, remote handset request, key operation in tail door key barrel and, on 3 door models, removal of the roof.

The tail door window regulator comprises left and right hand runners, a continuous cable and a motor. The runners are secured in the tail door frame with four screws. The glass is located in two carriers which are located in tracks in the runners. The glass is retained in friction pads in each carrier and secured with clamp screws.

Each carrier is attached to the cable which, in turn, is attached to a drum driven by a motor. When the motor is operated, the drum pulls the cable in the required direction to raise or lower the glass.

FRONT DOOR CENTRAL LOCKING COMPONENTS

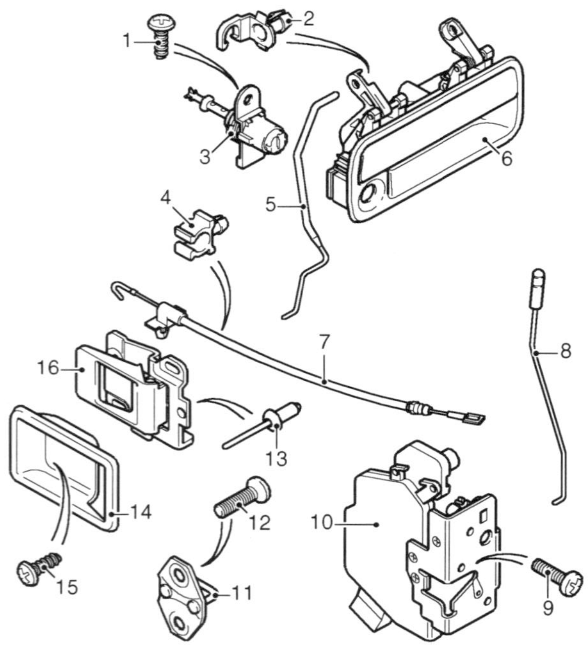

76M2786

DRIVER'S DOOR MECHANISM SHOWN - PASSENGER DOOR MECHANISM SIMILAR

1. Screw
2. Linkage clip
3. Lock assembly (driver's door only)
4. Release cable clip
5. Link - Latch to outer door handle
6. Outer door handle
7. Release cable
8. Link - Sill button
9. Screw 3 off
10. Latch assembly
11. Striker
12. Screw 2 off
13. Rivet 2 off
14. Screw
15. Handle finisher
16. Release handle

REAR DOOR CENTRAL LOCKING COMPONENTS

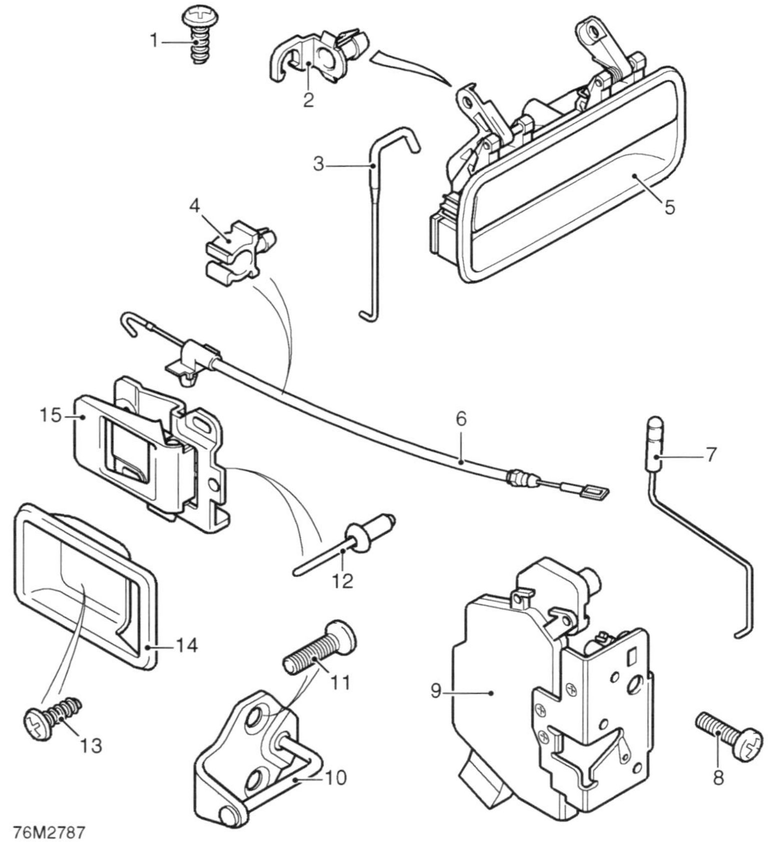

76M2787

1. Screw 2 off
2. Linkage clip
3. Link - Handle to latch
4. Cable clip 2 off
5. Outer door handle
6. Release cable
7. Link - Sill button
8. Screw 3 off
9. Latch assembly
10. Striker
11. Screw 2 off
12. Rivet 2 off
13. Screw
14. Handle finisher
15. Release handle

TAIL DOOR LOCKING COMPONENTS

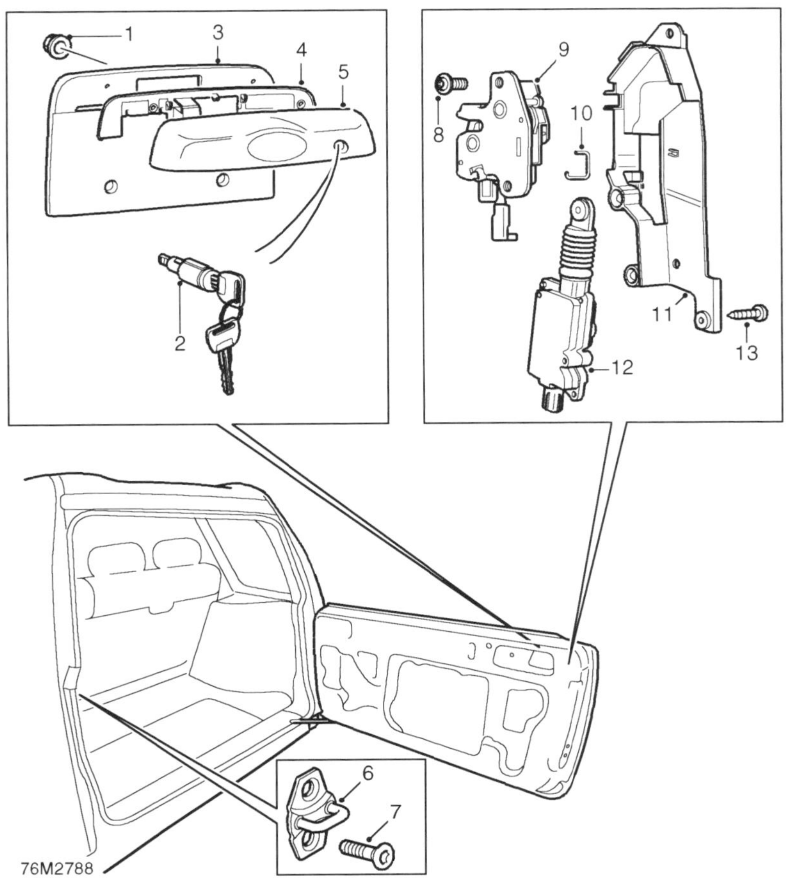

1. Flanged nut 3 off
2. Key barrel
3. Number plate plinth (Selected markets only)
4. Handle gasket
5. Tail door handle
6. Striker
7. Screw 2 off
8. Screw 2 off
9. Latch assembly
10. Link - Latch to actuator
11. Shield
12. Latch actuator
13. Self tapping screw 2 off

CENTRAL DOOR LOCKING OPERATION

Driver and Passenger Door(s)

The central door locking can be operated from either the Central Door Locking (CDL) switch on the fascia, the remote handset or the vehicle key in the driver's door lock.

All aspects of the central door locking system are controlled by the Central Control Unit (CCU). The driver and the passenger doors can be CDL locked or superlocked.

Locking or unlocking the driver's door using the vehicle key, mechanically operates the driver's door latch. The mechanical operation simultaneously operates a switch within the latch mechanism which completes an earth path to the CCU. The CCU uses the earth path as a signal to electrically operate the remaining door lock motor(s) and lock or unlock the passenger door(s). Each latch assembly contains separate motors for CDL locking and superlocking.

Locking and unlocking using the CDL switch or the remote handset is controlled electrically by the CCU.

Each outer door handle is connected to its respective latch assembly via a linkage. Each interior release handle is connected to the latch assembly via a cable. A door sill button is connected to each latch assembly and gives a visual indication to the locked or unlocked condition of each door. The button also allows each door to be individually locked from inside the vehicle.

On 5 door models, both rear doors have a child door lock facility. A small lever near the latch, when selected, prevents the doors from being opened from the interior of the vehicle. The doors can only be opened using the outside door handles.

Each door latch assembly also contains a switch which informs the CCU if a door is open. A warning lamp on the instrument panel warns if an open door condition is sensed by the CCU. The switch also operates in conjunction with the vehicle alarm system if a door is opened when the alarm is armed.

Tail Door

The tail door has no locking facility. When the vehicle is locked, the CCU ignores operation of the tail door handle. The door cannot be opened until the CCU authorises electrical operation of the tail door actuator which mechanically operates the tail door latch.

The tail door handle contains a switch, which is operated when the handle is pulled. The switch completes an earth path to the CCU. The CCU uses the earth path as a signal to electrically operate the latch actuator to open the tail door latch.

The tail door latch assembly also contains a switch which informs the CCU if the tail door is open. A warning lamp on the instrument panel warns if an open door condition is sensed by the CCU. The switch also operates in conjunction with the vehicle alarm system if the tail door is opened when the alarm is armed.

DOOR STRIKER - CHECK AND ADJUST

Service repair no - 76.28.05

Check

1. A closed door should be flush with adjacent panels and edges have equal gap.

Adjust

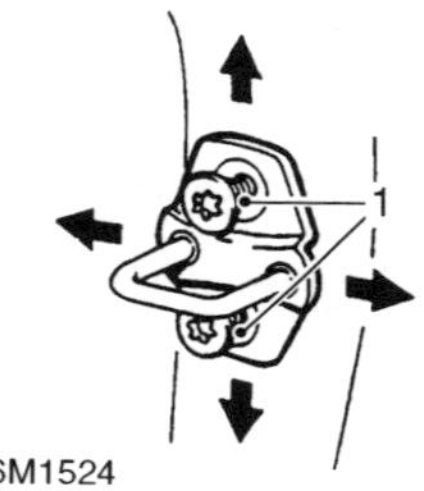

76M1524

1. Loosen 2 Torx screws securing striker.
2. Adjust striker to obtain required door to panel fit and open and close operation.
3. Tighten Torx screws to 10 Nm.

DOOR - ALIGN ON HINGES

Service repair no - 76.28.07 - FRONT
Service repair no - 76.28.08 - REAR

Check

1. Check door for flush fit to adjacent panels and edges for equal gap.

Adjust

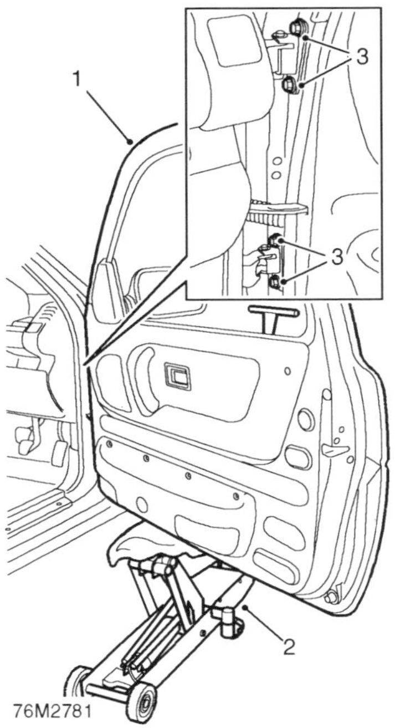

Front door illustrated

1. Open front door.
2. Place wooden block on jack and position jack to support door under lower edge.
3. Loosen 4 bolts securing hinges to door.
4. Loosen 2 Torx screws securing door striker.
5. Use jack to assist with door alignment.
6. Tighten hinge bolts.
7. Remove jack and close door to check for correct alignment.
8. When alignment satisfactory:
   Tighten hinge bolts to 30 Nm.
   Adjust door striker. ***See this section.***

DOOR ASSEMBLY - FRONT

Service repair no - 76.28.01/99

Remove

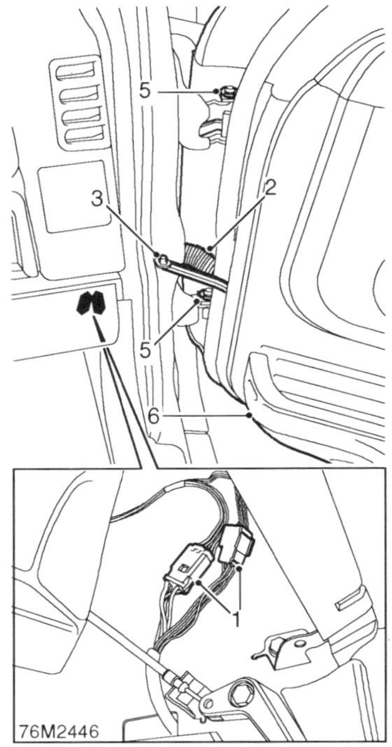

1. Release and disconnect 2 multiplugs from lower 'A' post.
2. Release harness sheath from 'A' post and pull door harness through 'A' post.
3. Remove roll pin from door check strap, and release check strap from 'A' post.
4. Discard roll pin.
5. Remove 2 'C' clips from door hinges.
6. With assistance raise and remove door.

Refit

1. With assistance position door to hinges.
2. Fit 'C' clips to hinge pins.
3. Position check strap to 'A' post and secure with NEW roll pin.
4. Feed door harness through 'A' post and secure harness sheath.
5. Connect and secure multiplugs at base of 'A' post.
6. Check door alignment. ***See Adjustments.***

DOOR ASSEMBLY - REAR

Service repair no - 76.28.02/99

Remove

1. Release 'B/C' post upper finisher and position aside. ***See Interior trim components.***

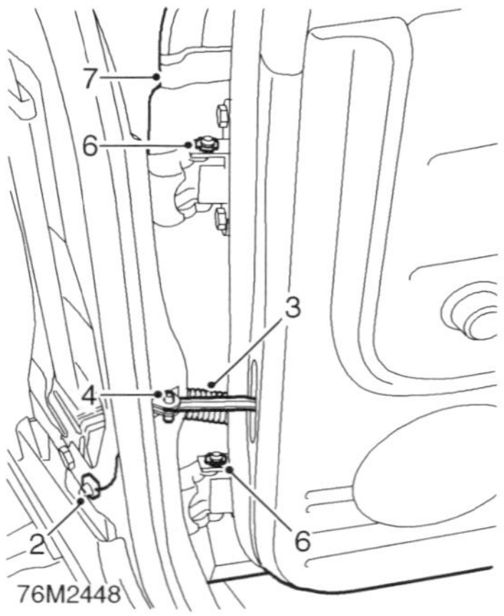

76M2448

2. Release and disconnect multiplug from lower 'B/C' post.
3. Release harness sheath from 'B/C' post and pull door harness through 'B/C' post.
4. Remove roll pin from door check strap, and release check strap from 'B/C' post.
5. Discard roll pin.
6. Remove 2 'C' clips from door hinges.
7. With assistance raise and remove door.

Refit

1. With assistance position door to hinges.
2. Fit 'C' clips to hinge pins.
3. Position check strap to 'B/C' post and secure with NEW roll pin.
4. Feed door harness through 'B/C' post and secure harness sheath.
5. Connect and secure multiplug at base of 'B/C' post.
6. Fit 'B/C' post upper finisher. ***See Interior trim components.***
7. Check door alignment. ***See Adjustments.***

DOOR ASSEMBLY - TAIL

Service repair no - 76.28.29/99

Remove

1. Remove spare wheel from tail door.
2. Remove RH rear quarter lower trim casing. ***See Interior trim components.***

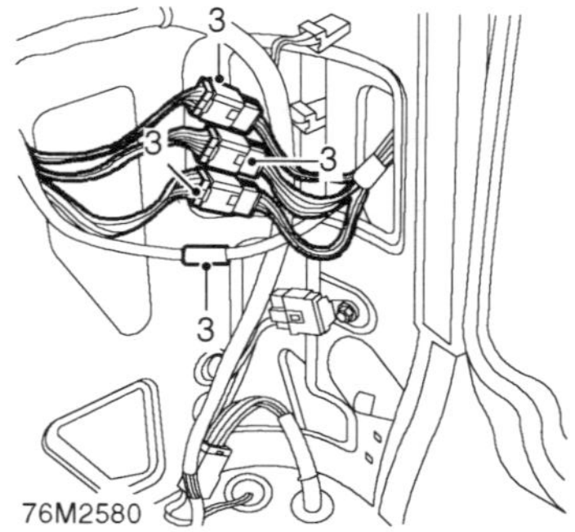

76M2580

3. Release and disconnect 3 multiplugs and rear washer tube from lower 'E' post.

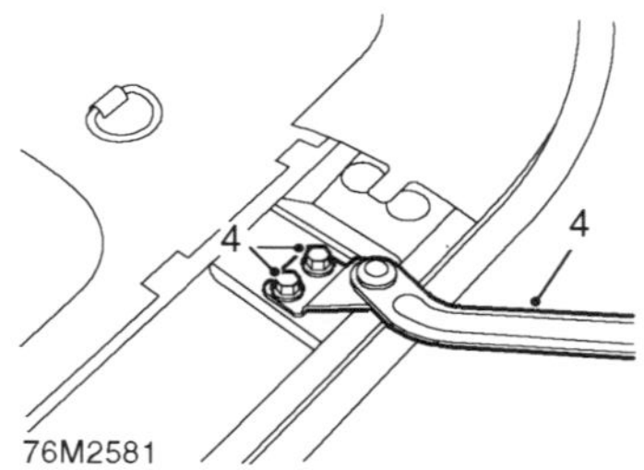

76M2581

4. Remove 2 screws from tail door check strap, release strap and position aside.

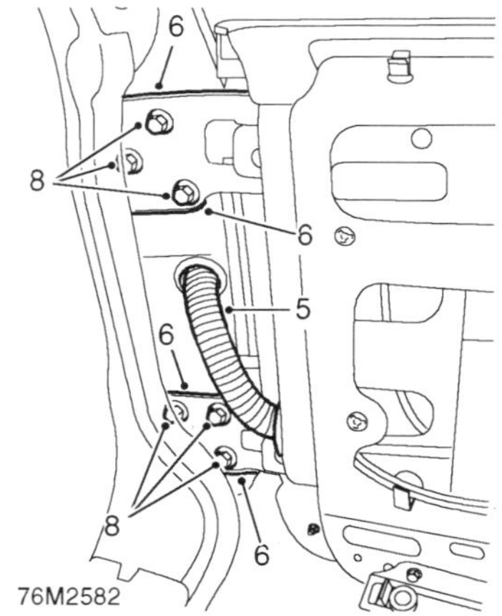

76M2582

5. Release door harness sheath from 'E' post and pull harness through 'E' post.
6. Mark the outline of hinges to body.
7. Support the weight of the tail door.
8. Remove 6 bolts securing tail door to body.
9. With assistance remove door.

Refit

1. With assistance position door, fit but do not tighten securing bolts.
2. Position check strap, fit and tighten bolts.
3. Align hinges and tighten bolts to 30 Nm.
4. Feed door harness through 'E' post and secure harness sheath.
5. Connect and secure multiplugs and rear washer tube at 'E' post.
6. Fit rear quarter lower casing. ***See Interior trim components.***
7. Fit spare wheel to tail door.

GLASS - FRONT DOOR

Service repair no - 76.31.01

Remove

1. Remove front door water shedder. ***See this section.***

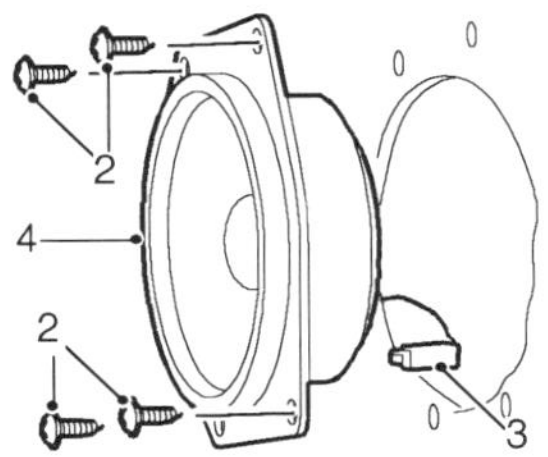

76M2777

2. Remove 4 screws securing door speaker.
3. Disconnect multiplug from door speaker.
4. Remove door speaker.

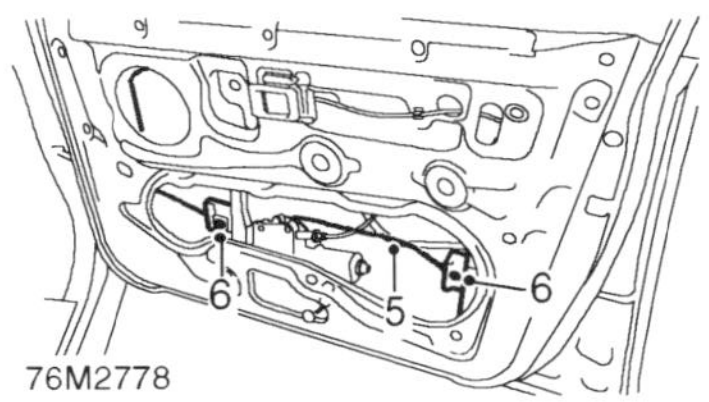

76M2778

5. Lower glass to access clamp bolts.
6. Loosen 2 bolts securing glass to clamps.

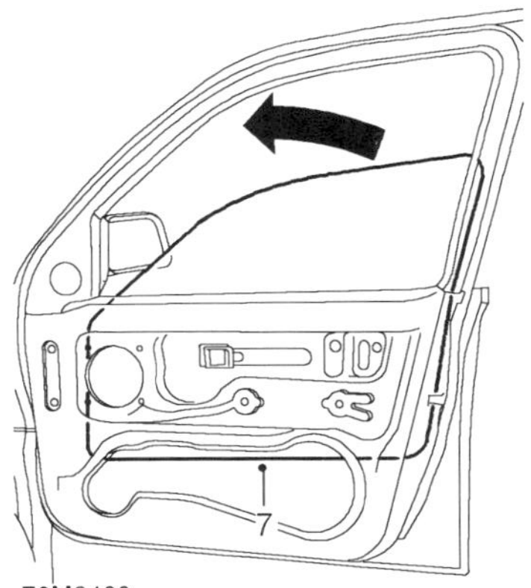

76M2460

7. Release glass from clamps, raise and rotate glass to remove from door frame.

Refit

1. Locate glass in door frame and rotate into position to engage seal and clamps.
2. Tighten bolts securing glass to 8 Nm.
3. Raise/lower glass to check operation.
4. Position door speaker, connect multiplug, fit and tighten screws.
5. Fit water shedder. ***See this section.***

GLASS - REAR DOOR

Service repair no - 76.31.02

Remove

1. Remove rear door water shedder. ***See this section.***

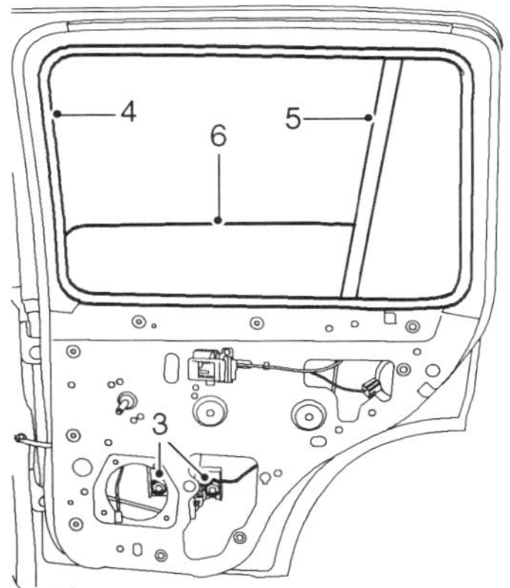

76M2422

2. Lower glass to access nuts on clamps.
3. Loosen 2 nuts securing clamps to glass.
4. Remove seal from door.
5. Release glass from quarter light seal.
6. Raise glass and remove from door.

Refit

1. Fit glass to door and locate in quarter light seal.
2. Fit seal to door.
3. Position glass in clamps and tighten nuts to 8 Nm.
4. Raise/lower glass to check seal fit.
5. Fit water shedder. ***See this section.***

SEAL - GLASS CHANNEL - FRONT

Service repair no - 76.31.13

Remove

1. Remove exterior mirror. ***See Repairs.***
2. Lower door glass.
3. Remove inner seal.

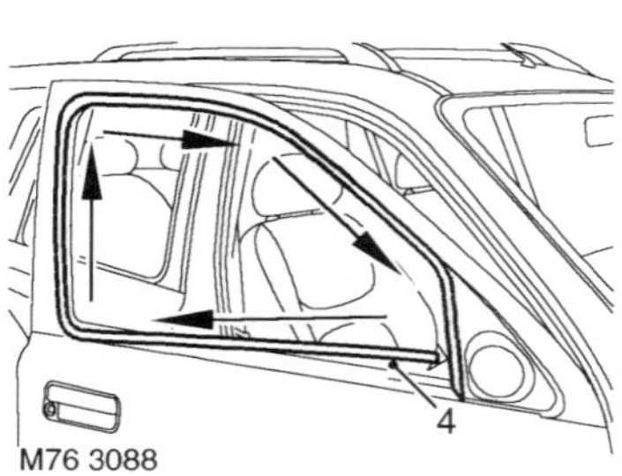

4. Carefully release seal from door flange, starting from the cheater panel, working along the waist rail and around the door flange.

CAUTION: Excess force will damage the seal.

Refit

CAUTION: This seal assembly uses an internal metal former. Take care not to bend the seal during fitment, or the former will become kinked.

1. Lubricate corners of seal with soapy water.

2. Starting at the rearmost top corner of the glass aperture, seat the seal onto the flange, ensuring that the radius of the seal matches the door profile.
3. Secure seal to flange across cantrail and down 'A' post.
4. Secure seal in corner at base of 'A' post.
5. Carefully pull 'B' post length of seal away from flange until bottom corner is just clear of flange, seal will then locate over flange. Ensure seal has not become twisted. Starting from the top, push the seal onto the flange

NOTE: The bottom radius should match the door profile.

6. Secure the seal to the bottom flange by rotating the seal onto the flange and pushing evenly on its length along the waist rail.
7. Fit inner seal
8. Raise/lower glass to check operation. Adjust the seal as necessary.
9. Fit exterior mirror. ***See Repairs.***

SEAL - GLASS CHANNEL - REAR DOOR

Service repair no - 76.31.14

Remove

1. Remove rear door glass. ***See this section.***

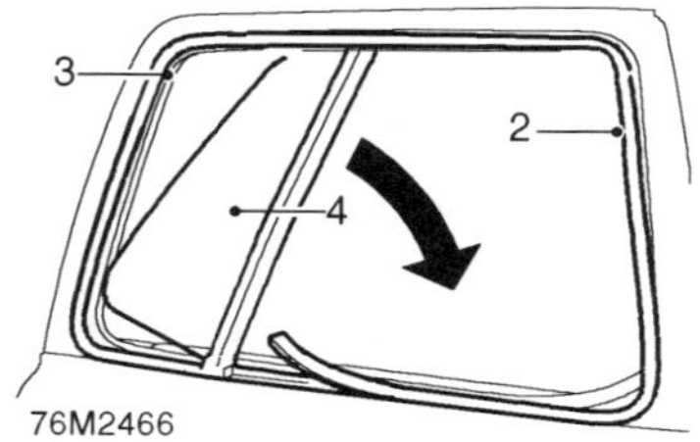

2. Release seal from flange. Remove lower section first, then the front vertical section, followed by the top section.

CAUTION: If seal is to be re-used, do not use excessive force or seal will be damaged.

3. Release top corner of quarter light from frame. Rotate quarter light and seal, release rest of seal from flange and remove quarter light and seal from door.
4. Remove quarter light from seal.

Refit

1. Fit quarter light to seal.
2. Lubricate seal around quarter light with soft soap.
3. Position quarter light and seal to flange at bottom rear corner of window aperture and rotate into top rear corner. Using dividing bar, pull quarter light rearwards to locate seal around quarter light on flange.
4. Starting at top of divider bar, push seal onto top flange and locate in top front corner. Ensure radius of seal matches door profile.
5. Ease seal away from front flange and locate seal in bottom front corner. Ensure radius of seal at bottom front corner matches profile of door and that seal is still correctly located in top front corner, then push seal onto front flange.
6. Push seal onto bottom flange.
7. Fit rear door glass. ***See this section.***

SCREEN - REAR

Service repair no - 76.31.20

Remove

1. Remove tail door water shedder. ***See this section.***

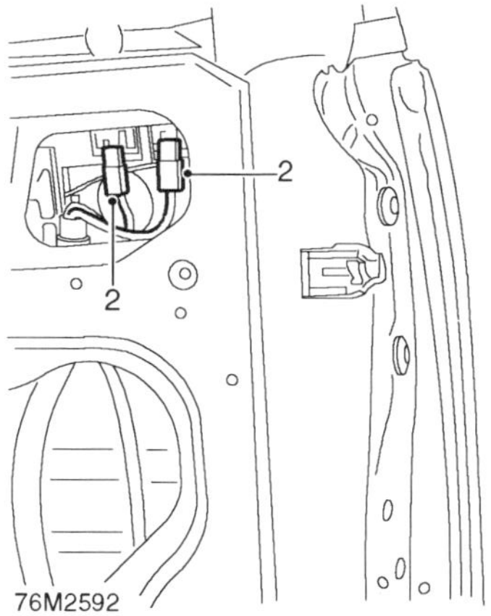

76M2592

2. Disconnect 2 Lucars from heater element.

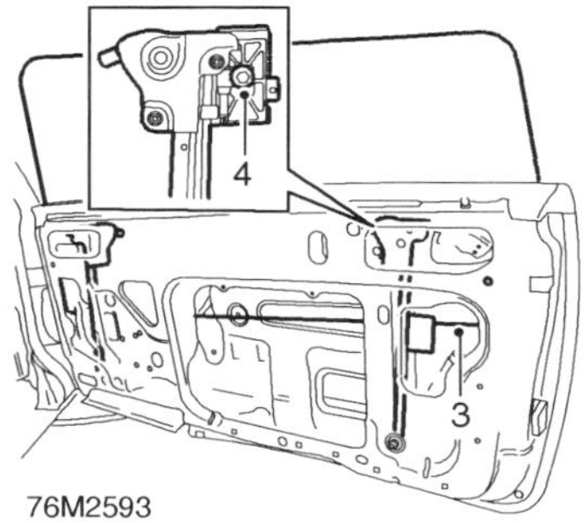

76M2593

3. Lower screen to access clamp bolts.

CAUTION: Remove screen carefully to avoid damaging element connections.

4. Loosen both clamp bolts, release and remove rear screen.

CAUTION: Do not fully remove clamp screws.

Refit

CAUTION: Fit screen carefully to avoid damaging heater element connections.

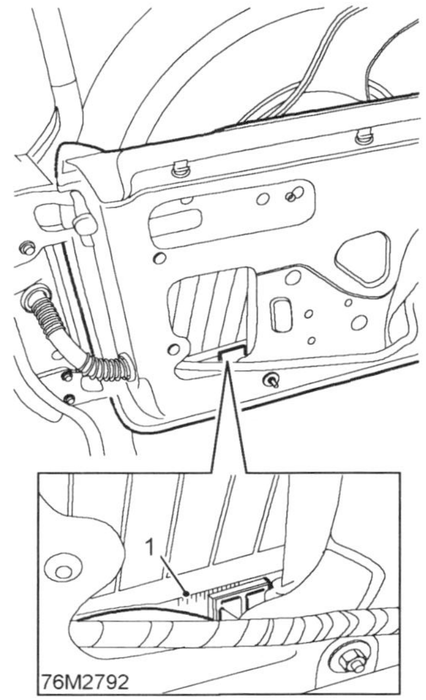

76M2792

1. Position screen to door and align in clamps using timing marks on screen.
2. Ensure glass is fully pushed down in clamp closest to door hinge, then tighten clamp bolt. Position screen horizontally by lifting clamp closest to door latch so that screen heater element is aligned with waist seal.

CAUTION: Ensure that glass remains seated in base of clamp.

3. Tighten clamp bolts to 8 Nm.
4. Raise screen and connect Lucars to screen heater element.
5. Ensure a 5mm equal gap exists between screen and both 'E' post finishers. If required, adjust screen again using timing marks.
6. Loosen lower adjuster lock nuts.
7. Loosen pre-load screws so screen clears seal.
8. Adjust pre-load screws until screen is just in contact with seal.
9. Adjust pre-load screws until screen applies a 1mm pre-load on seal.
10. Ensure there is full screen to seal contact.
11. Lower glass and tighten lock nuts to 14 Nm.

CAUTION: Always tighten lock nuts with the screen lowered.

12. Recheck pre-load.
13. Raise and lower screen to confirm correct alignment.
14. Fit water shedder. ***See this section.***

QUARTER LIGHT - REAR DOOR

Service repair no - 76.31.31

The procedure for renewing the quarter light is identical to renewing the rear door glass channel seal. ***See this section.***

REGULATOR - REAR DOOR GLASS

Service repair no - 76.31.46

Remove

1. Remove water shedder from rear door. ***See this section.***
2. Lower glass to access clamp nuts.

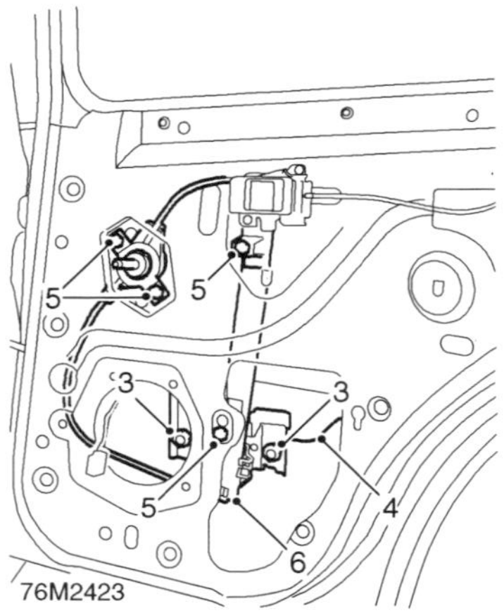

76M2423

3. Loosen 2 nuts securing glass to clamps.
4. Release glass from clamps, raise glass and secure in position with a suitable wedge.
5. Remove 4 bolts securing regulator to door.
6. Manoeuvre regulator into bottom of door and remove through aperture.

Refit

1. Position regulator in door and align to bolt holes, fit and tighten bolts.
2. Remove wedge and lower glass.
3. Locate glass to clamps and tighten clamp nuts to 8 Nm .
4. Raise and lower glass to ensure correct operation.
5. Fit water shedder. ***See this section.***

REGULATOR - REAR SCREEN

Service repair no - 76.31.65

Remove

1. Remove rear screen. ***See this section.***

76M2576

2. Disconnect multiplug from regulator motor.

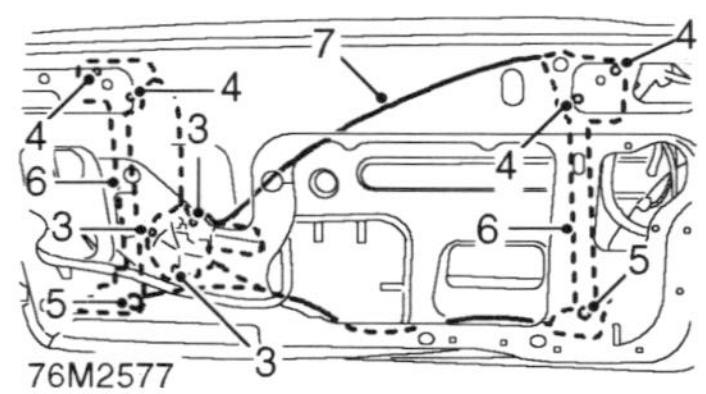

76M2577

3. Slacken 3 nuts securing regulator motor and rotate motor to release from door.
4. Slacken 4 nuts securing top of cable guides and release guides from door.
5. Remove 2 nuts securing pre-load adjusters and rotate adjusters fully clockwise to improve access.
6. Release regulator from door and detach electrical harness from LH glass clamp.
7. Remove regulator from door.

Refit

1. Position regulator to door and unclip motor transit package from rail.
2. Connect multiplug to regulator motor.
3. Connect harness clip and align regulator to door.
4. Fit nuts to pre-load adjusters, but do not tighten at this stage.
5. Position tops of cable guides to door, leaving fixings finger tight.
6. Tighten regulator motor fixings.
7. Fit rear screen and secure centrally within clamps, but do not adjust fully at this stage. ***See this section.***
8. Fully lower glass and tighten top cable guide fixings to 8 Nm.

NOTE: Ensure that glass is raised and lowered at least twice before making final adjustments. Failure to do so could prevent smooth operation of the glass mechanism.

9. Complete the glass fitting and adjustment procedure. ***See this section.***

WAIST SEAL - TAIL DOOR

Service repair no - 76.31.67

Remove

1. Lower rear screen.

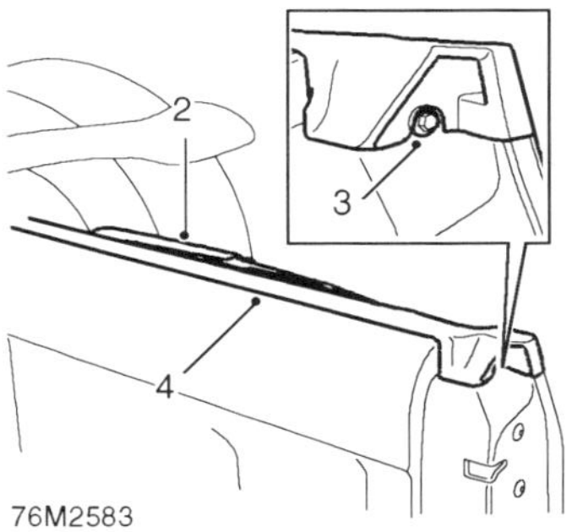

76M2583

2. Raise wiper blade away from seal.
3. Remove 2 screws from ends of seal.
4. Release seal from door flanges.
5. Remove waist seal.

Refit

1. Position seal to door flanges.
2. Fit and tighten screws.
3. Lower wiper blade onto seal.
4. Raise rear screen.

CASING - FRONT DOOR - 3 DOOR

Service repair no - 76.34.01

Remove

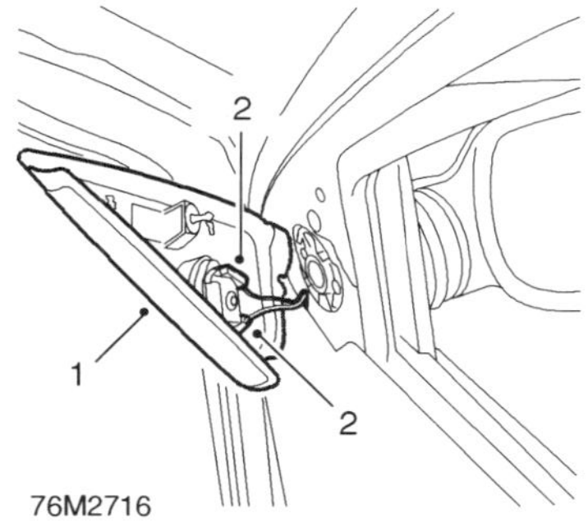

76M2716

1. Release cheater panel.
2. Disconnect Lucars and remove cheater panel.

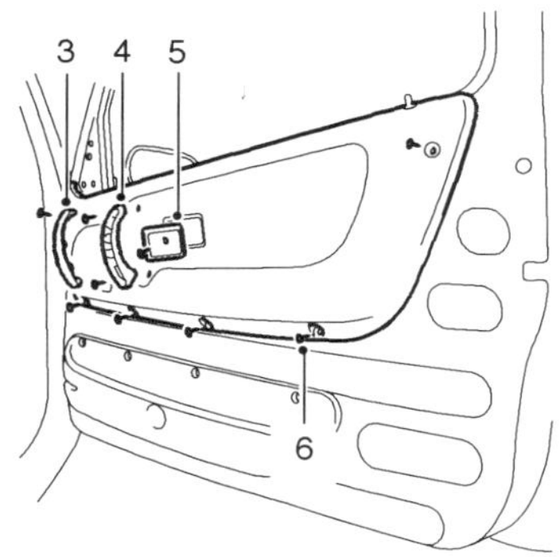

76M2717

3. Remove door pull centre trim.
4. Remove 2 screws securing door pull and remove door pull.
5. Remove screw securing door handle escutcheon and remove escutcheon.
6. Remove 6 Torx screws securing door casing, release casing from 3 studs and sill button, remove casing.

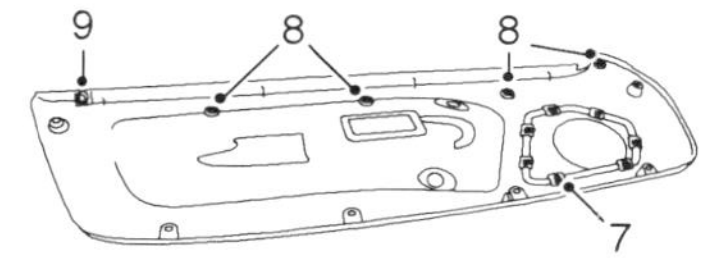

76M2718

7. Release 7 clips securing speaker grill and remove grill.
8. Remove 4 casing studs.
9. Remove sill button support.

Refit

1. Position speaker grill and secure clips.
2. Fit sill button support.
3. Ensure casing studs are in position.
4. Position casing to door, locate sill button and secure in studs.
5. Fit and tighten Torx screws.
6. Position door escutcheon, fit and tighten screw.
7. Position door pull, fit and tighten screws.
8. Fit door pull centre trim.
9. Connect Lucars to cheater panel and locate panel in position.

CASING - FRONT DOOR - 5 DOOR

Service repair no - 76.34.01

Remove

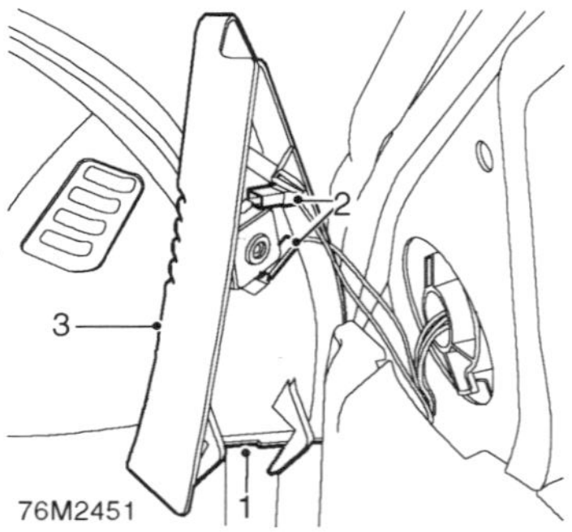

76M2451

1. Release cheater panel from door.
2. Disconnect Lucars from tweeter speaker.
3. Remove cheater panel.

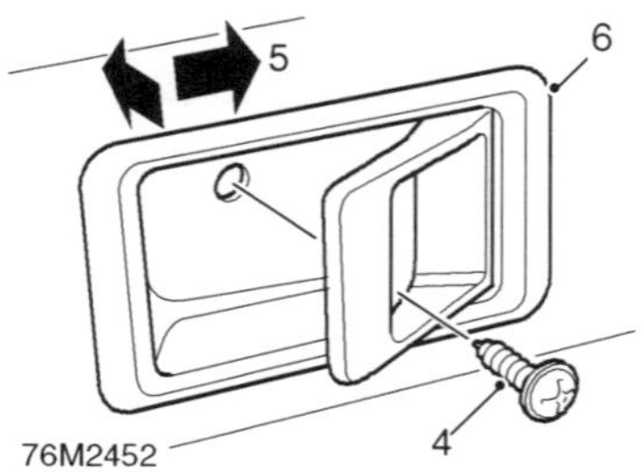

76M2452

4. Remove screw securing door release escutcheon.
5. Push escutcheon in and to the rear of door to release securing catch.
6. Remove escutcheon.

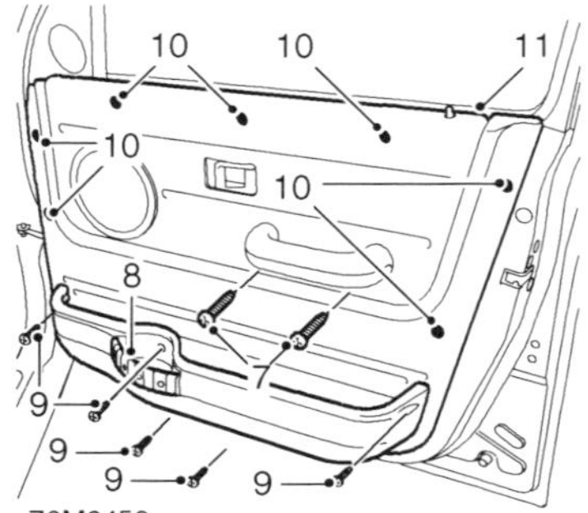

76M2453

7. Remove 2 screws from door pull.
8. Remove cup retainer.
9. Remove 5 screws securing door pocket.
10. Release 7 trim studs.
11. Remove casing.

Do not carry out further dismantling if component is removed for access only.

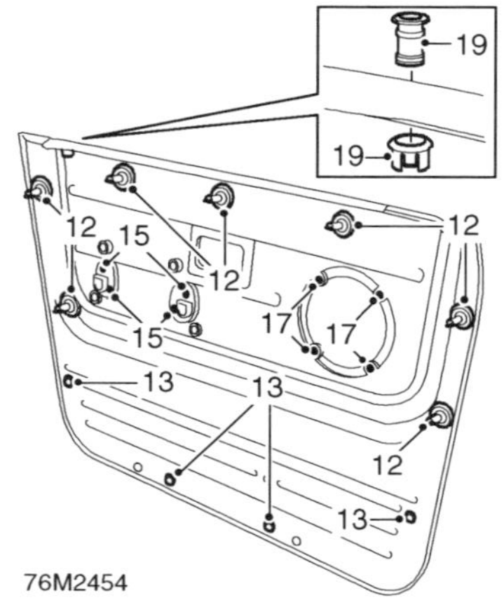

76M2454

12. Remove 7 trim studs from casing.
13. Remove 4 Torx screws securing door pocket.
14. Remove door pocket.
15. Remove 4 Torx screws from door pull.
16. Remove door pull.
17. Remove 4 Torx screws from door speaker grille.
18. Remove speaker grille.
19. Release retainer and remove sill button guide.
20. Fit sill button guide to replacement casing and secure with retainer.
21. Fit speaker grille to replacement casing and secure with Torx screws.
22. Fit door pull to replacement casing and secure with Torx screws.
23. Fit door pocket to replacement casing and secure with Torx screws.
24. Fit trim studs to replacement casing.

Refit

1. Position casing to door and engage trim studs.
2. Fit screws securing door pocket.
3. Fit cup holder.
4. Fit door pull.
5. Position door release escutcheon and secure with screw.
6. Connect Lucars to tweeter speaker.
7. Fit cheater panel.

CASING - REAR DOOR

Service repair no - 76.34.04

Remove

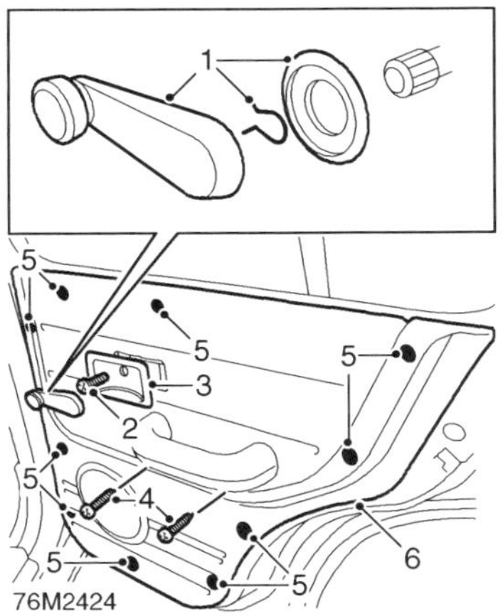

76M2424

1. Remove clip from window winder handle, remove handle and escutcheon.
2. Remove screw securing door release escutcheon.
3. Push escutcheon in and to the rear of door to release from securing catch, remove escutcheon.
4. Remove 2 screws from door pull.
5. Release 10 trim studs.
6. Remove casing.

Do not carry out further dismantling if component is removed for access only.

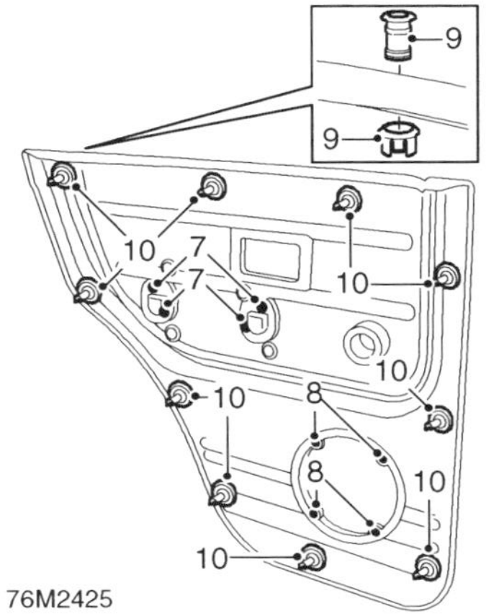

76M2425

7. Remove 4 Torx screws from door pull, and remove door pull.
8. Remove 4 Torx screws from speaker grille and remove grille.
9. Release retainer and remove sill button guide.
10. Remove 10 trim studs.
11. Fit trim studs to replacement trim casing.
12. Fit sill button guide to replacement casing and secure with retainer.
13. Fit speaker grille to replacement casing and secure with Torx screws.
14. Fit door pull to replacement casing and secure with Torx screws.

Refit

1. Position casing to door and engage trim studs.
2. Fit door pull screws.
3. Position door release escutcheon and secure with screw.
4. Fit window winder escutcheon and window winder and secure with clip.

CASING - TAIL DOOR

Service repair no - 76.34.10

Remove

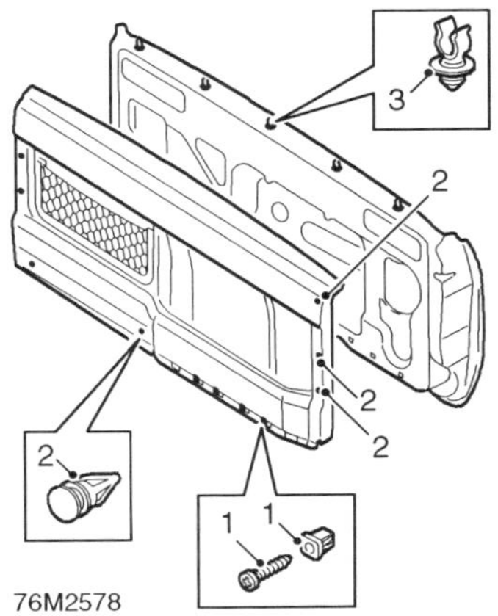

76M2578

1. Remove 4 screws securing bottom of casing.
2. Release 7 clips securing sides and bottom of casing.
3. Release 5 clips securing top of casing.

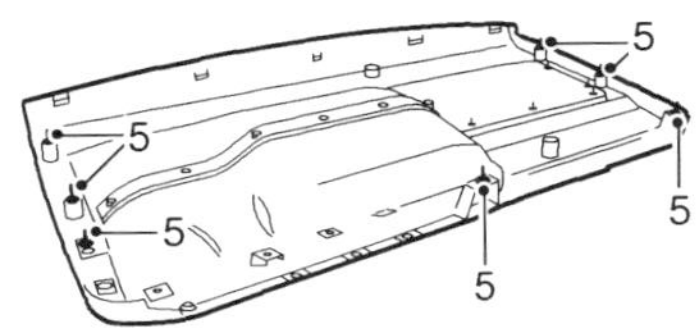

76M2579

4. Remove casing.
5. Remove 7 trim studs.

Refit

1. Ensure trim studs are in position.
2. Position casing and secure in top clips.
3. Secure clips on side and bottom of casing.
4. Fit screws to bottom of casing.

WATER SHEDDER - LOWER - 3 DOOR

Service repair no - 76.34.18

NOTE: Always replace a damaged water shedder.

Remove

1. Remove front door pocket. ***See this section.***

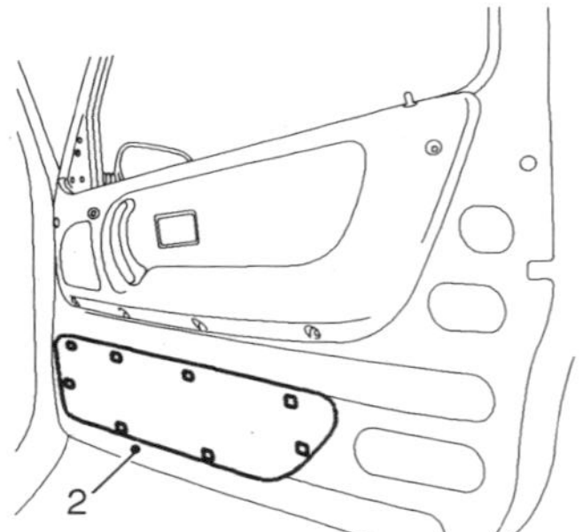

76M2720

2. Release and discard water shedder.

Refit

1. Clean door contact area with white spirit.
2. Position NEW water shedder to door and seal in position, by applying hand pressure to centre bottom of shedder first then move out from this point in both directions applying an even pressure to the seal, smooth out any creases.

CAUTION: It is crucial that no creases are present along the base of the water shedder.

NOTE: To obtain an effective seal when fitting a new water shedder, ensure that the water shedder and door contact surface are at room temperature: 18 C to 30 C.

3. Fit front door pocket. ***See this section.***

POCKET - FRONT DOOR - 3 DOOR

Service repair no - 76.34.19

Remove

1. Remove 8 Torx screws securing pocket to door and remove pocket.

Refit

1. Position pocket, fit and tighten Torx screws.

WATER SHEDDER - UPPER - 3 DOOR

Service repair no - 76.34.24

NOTE: Always replace a damaged water shedder.

Remove

1. Remove front door casing. ***See this section.***

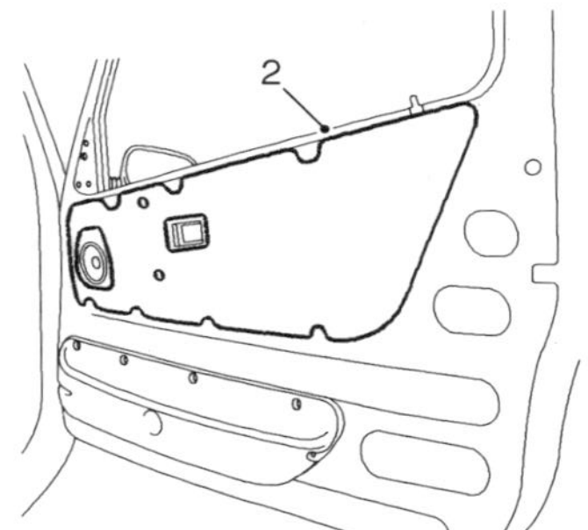

76M2719

2. Release and discard water shedder.

Refit

1. Clean door contact area with white spirit.
2. Position NEW water shedder to door and seal in position, by applying hand pressure to centre bottom of shedder first then move out from this point in both directions applying an even pressure to the seal, smooth out any creases.

CAUTION: It is crucial that no creases are present along the base of the water shedder.

NOTE: To obtain an effective seal when fitting a new water shedder, ensure that the water shedder and door contact surface are at room temperature: 18 C to 30 C.

3. Fit front door casing. ***See this section.***

WATER SHEDDER - TAIL DOOR

Service repair no - 76.34.25

NOTE: Always replace a damaged water shedder.

Remove

1. Remove tail door casing. ***See this section.***

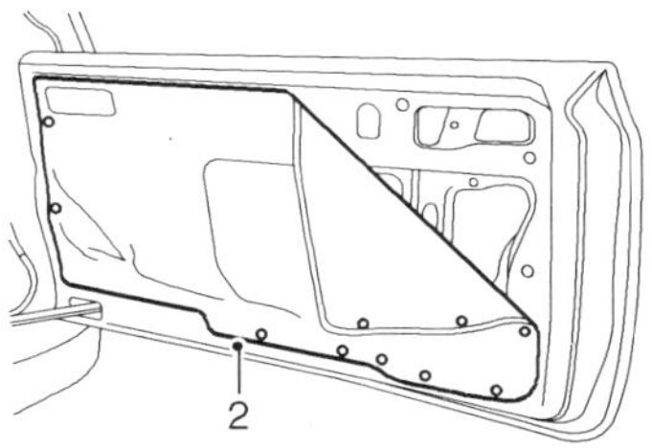

76M2551

2. Release and discard water shedder.

Refit

1. Clean door contact area with white spirit.
2. Position NEW water shedder to door and seal in position, by applying hand pressure to centre bottom of shedder first then move out from this point in both directions applying an even pressure to the seal, smooth out any creases.

CAUTION: It is crucial that no creases are present along the base of the water shedder.

NOTE: To obtain an effective seal when fitting a new water shedder, ensure that the water shedder and door contact surface are at room temperature: 18 C to 30 C.

3. Fit tail door casing. ***See this section.***

WATER SHEDDER - FRONT DOOR - 5 DOOR

Service repair no - 76.34.26

NOTE: Always replace a damaged water shedder.

Remove

1. Remove front door speaker. ***See ELECTRICAL, Repairs.***

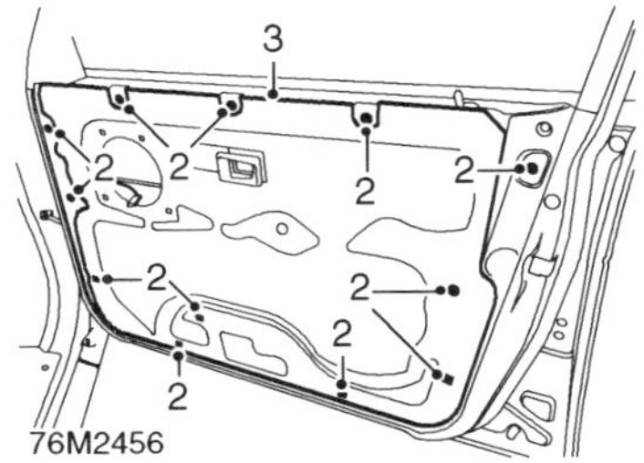

76M2456

2. Noting their fitted position, remove door casing retainers.
3. Release and discard water shedder.

Refit

1. Clean door contact area with white spirit.
2. Position NEW water shedder to door and seal in position, by applying hand pressure to centre bottom of shedder first then move out from this point in both directions applying an even pressure to the seal, smooth out any creases.

CAUTION: It is crucial that no creases are present along the base of the water shedder.

NOTE: To obtain an effective seal when fitting a new water shedder, ensure that the water shedder and door contact surface are at room temperature: 18 C to 30 C.

3. Fit door casing retainers.
4. Fit front door speaker. ***See ELECTRICAL, Repairs.***

WATER SHEDDER - REAR DOOR

Service repair no - 76.34.28

NOTE: Always replace a damaged water shedder.

Remove

1. Remove rear door speaker. ***See ELECTRICAL, Repairs.***

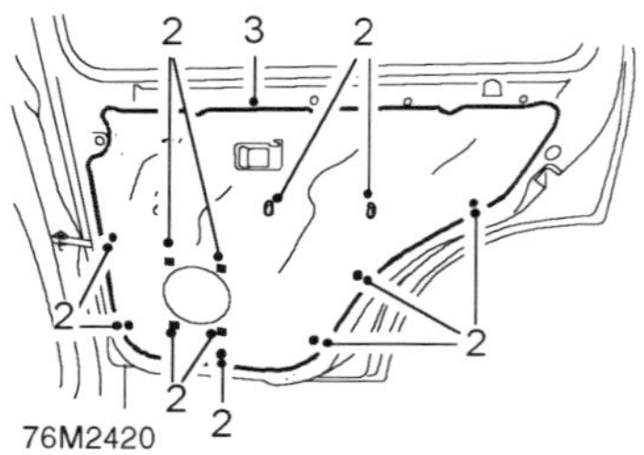

76M2420

2. Noting their fitted position, remove 10 trim stud retainers and 2 door pull securing screw retainers.
3. Release and discard water shedder.

Refit

1. Clean door contact area with white spirit.
2. Position NEW water shedder to door and seal in position, by applying hand pressure to centre bottom of shedder first then move out from this point in both directions applying and even pressure to the seal, smooth out any creases.

CAUTION: It is crucial that no creases are present along the base of the water shedder.

NOTE: To obtain an effective seal when fitting a new water shedder, ensure that the water shedder and door contact surface are at room temperature: between 18 C to 30 C.

3. Fit 10 trim stud retainers and 2 door pull securing screw retainers.
4. Fit rear door speaker. ***See ELECTRICAL, Repairs.***

LATCH - FRONT DOOR - 3 DOOR

Service repair no - 76.37.12

Remove

1. Remove upper water shedder. ***See this section.***

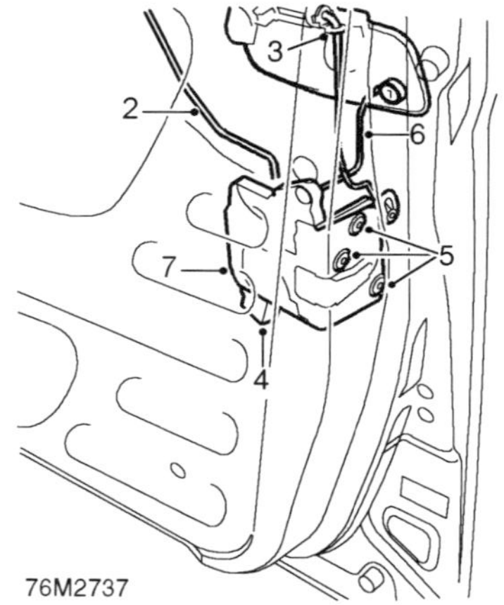

76M2737

2. Remove sill button lock rod from latch.
3. Release control rod from exterior handle.
4. Disconnect multiplug from latch.
5. Remove 3 Torx screws from latch
6. On driver's door, release door lock barrel paddle from latch.
7. Remove latch from aperture.

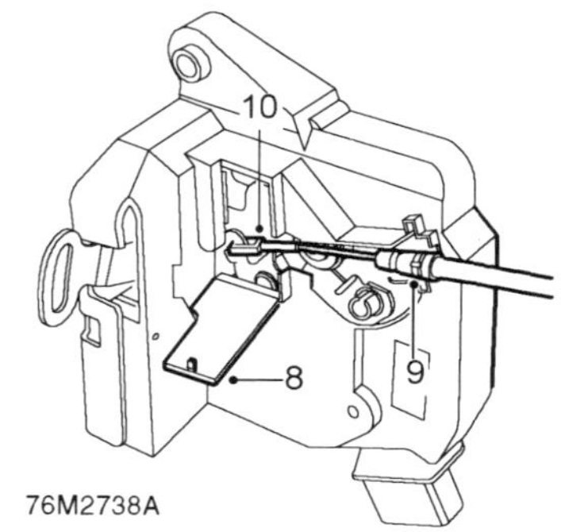

76M2738A

8. Open latch security flap.
9. Release interior release cable clamp from latch.
10. Disengage interior release cable from latch.

Refit

1. Secure interior release cable to latch and close latch security flap.
2. Fit interior release cable clamp to latch.
3. Position latch to door. On driver's door, align lock barrel paddle to latch.
4. Fit and tighten Torx screws securing latch.
5. Connect multiplug to latch.
6. Connect exterior handle control rod to latch.
7. Fit sill button lock rod to latch.
8. Check operation of latch.
9. Fit front door water shedder. ***See this section.***

LATCH - FRONT DOOR - 5 DOOR

Service repair no - 76.37.12

Remove

1. Remove water shedder from front door. ***See this section.***

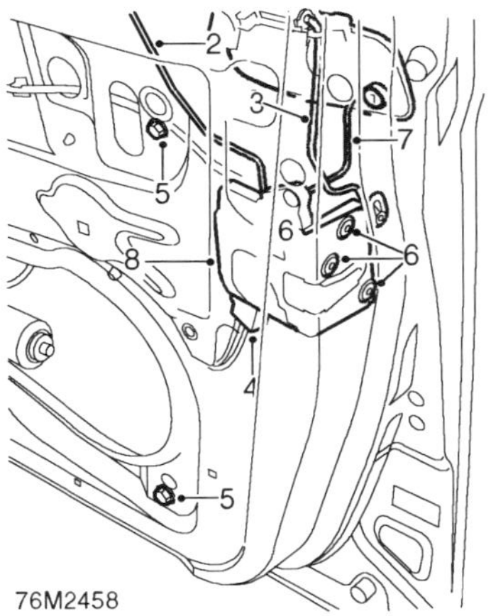

76M2458

2. Remove sill button lock rod from latch.
3. Release control rod from exterior handle.
4. Disconnect multiplug from latch.
5. Remove 2 screws securing RH glass cable guide and position guide aside.
6. Remove 3 Torx screws from latch
7. On driver's door, release door lock barrel paddle from latch.
8. Remove latch from aperture.

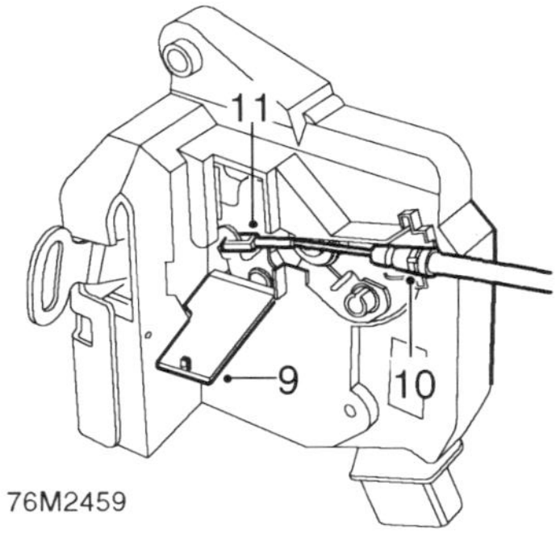

76M2459

9. Open latch security flap.
10. Release interior release cable clamp from latch.
11. Disengage interior release cable from latch.

Refit

1. Secure interior release cable to latch and close latch security flap.
2. Fit interior release cable clamp to latch.
3. Position latch to door. On driver's door, align lock barrel paddle to latch.
4. Fit and tighten Torx screws securing latch.
5. Position RH glass cable guide and tighten screws.
6. Connect multiplug to door latch.
7. Connect exterior handle control rod to latch.
8. Fit sill button lock rod to latch.
9. Check operation of door latch.
10. Fit front door water shedder. ***See this section.***

LATCH - REAR DOOR

Service repair no - 76.37.13

Remove

1. Remove rear door water shedder ***See this section.***

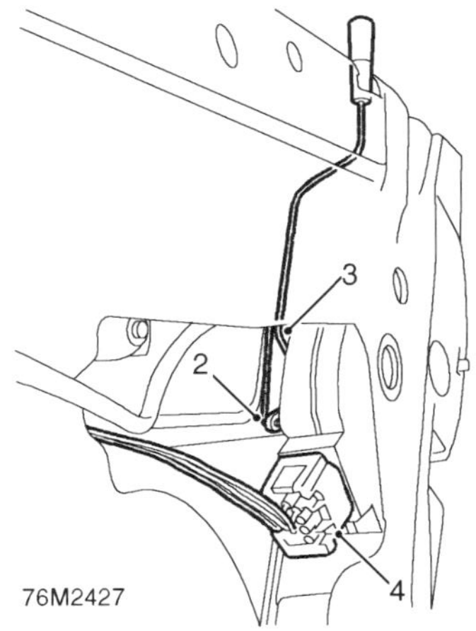

76M2427

2. Release exterior handle control rod from latch.
3. Release sill button lock rod and remove lock rod.
4. Disconnect multiplug from latch.

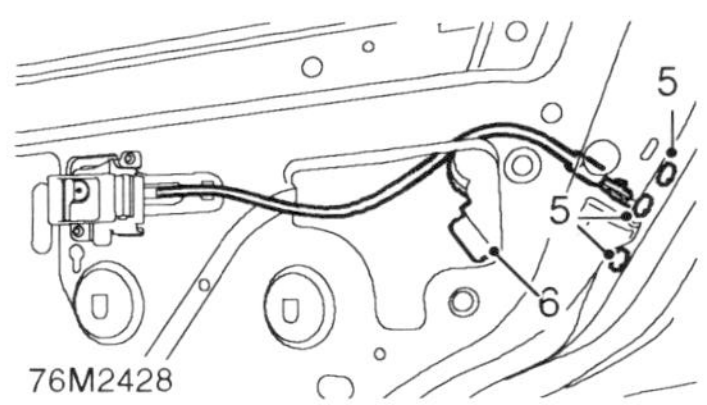

76M2428

5. Remove 3 Torx screws securing latch.
6. Remove latch through aperture.

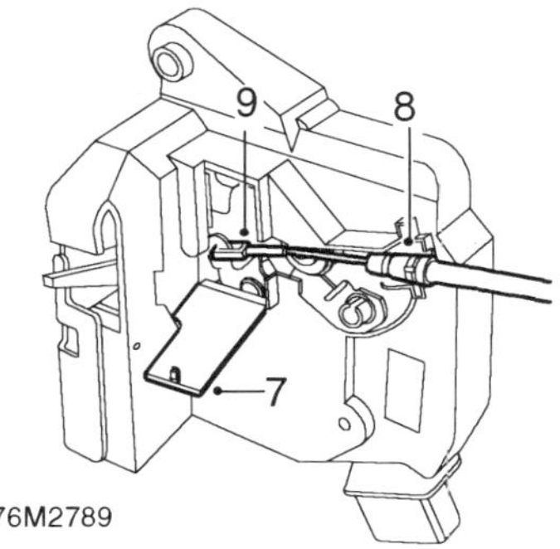

76M2789

7. Open latch security flap.
8. Release interior release cable clamp from latch.
9. Disengage interior release cable from latch.

Refit

1. Secure interior release cable to latch and close latch security flap.
2. Position latch to door, fit and tighten torx screws.
3. Connect multiplug to latch.
4. Connect exterior handle control rod to latch.
5. Fit and secure sill button lock rod.
6. Check operation of latch.
7. Fit water shedder. ***See this section.***

LATCH - TAIL DOOR

Service repair no - 76.37.16

Remove

1. Remove tail door water shedder. ***See this section.***

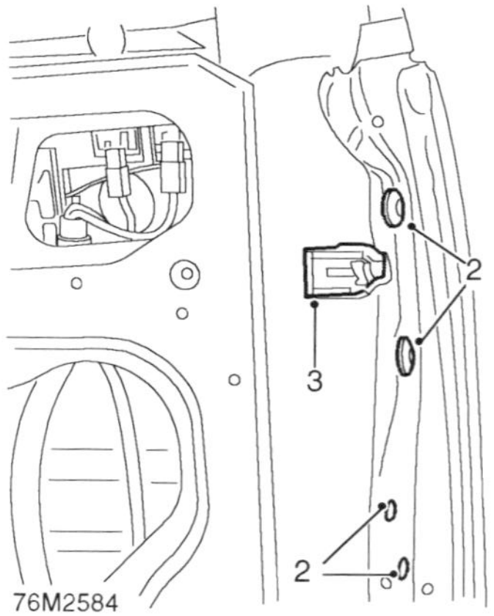

76M2584

2. Remove 4 screws securing door latch.
3. Release door latch to access harness clips and multiplugs.

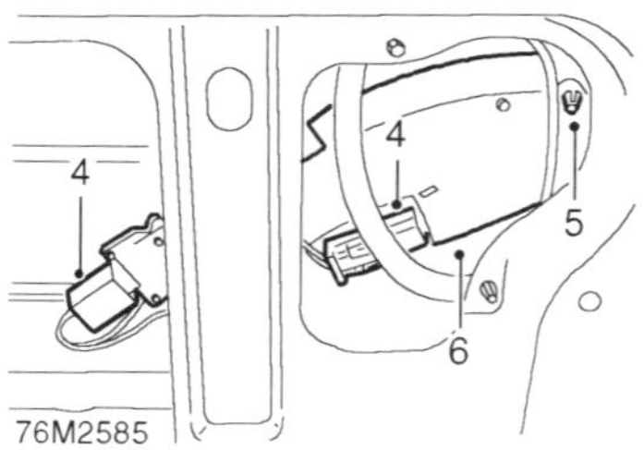

76M2585

4. Disconnect 2 multiplugs from door latch.
5. Release door harness clip from latch.
6. Remove door latch.

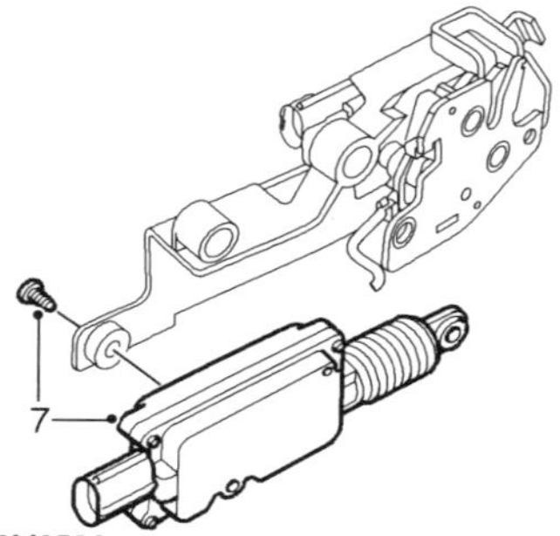

76M2586

7. Remove screw from solenoid motor and remove motor from latch.

Refit

1. Position solenoid motor to latch, fit and tighten screw.
2. Position door latch, connect multiplugs and harness clips.
3. Locate door latch in position, fit and tighten screws.
4. Fit water shedder. ***See this section.***

DOOR RELEASE - INTERIOR - FRONT DOOR - 3 DOOR

Service repair no - 76.37.31

Remove

1. Remove upper water shedder. ***See this section.***

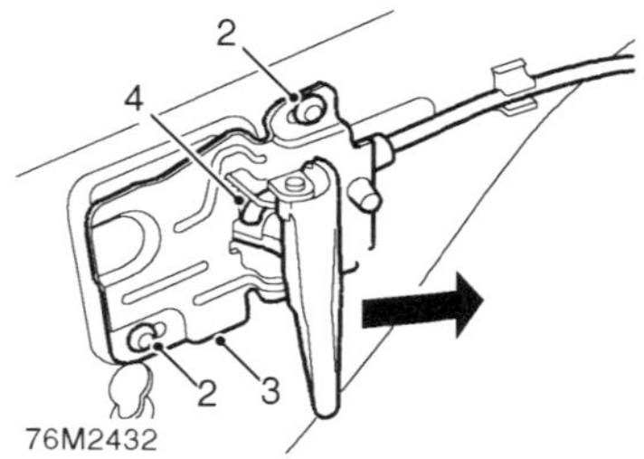

76M2432

2. Drill out 2 rivets from door release.
3. Remove door release.
4. Release cable from door release.

Refit

1. Connect cable to door release.
2. Position door release and secure with rivets.
3. Fit water shedder. ***See this section.***

DOOR RELEASE - INTERIOR - FRONT DOOR - 5 DOOR

Service repair no - 76.37.31

Remove

1. Remove front door water shedder. ***See this section.***

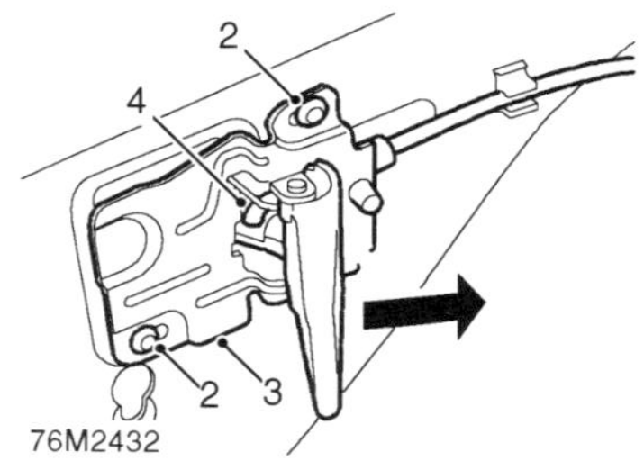

76M2432

2. Drill out 2 rivets from door release.
3. Remove door release.
4. Release cable from door release.

Refit

1. Connect cable to door release.
2. Position door release and secure with rivets.
3. Fit water shedder. ***See this section.***

DOOR RELEASE - INTERIOR - REAR DOOR

Service repair no - 76.37.32

Remove

1. Remove rear door water shedder. ***See this section.***

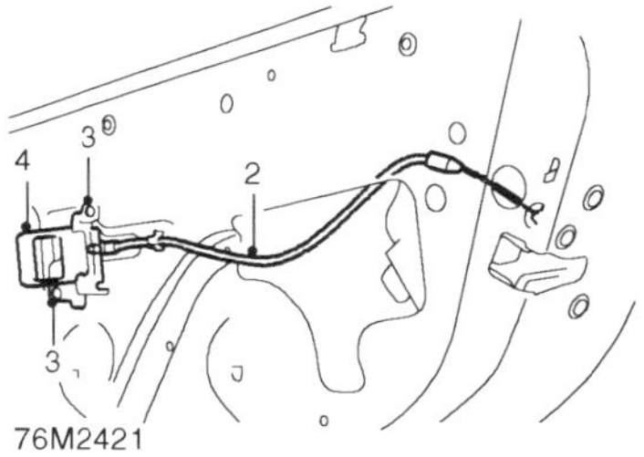

76M2421

2. Release cable from door release.
3. Drill out 2 rivets from door release.
4. Remove door release.

Refit

1. Connect cable to door release.
2. Position door release and secure with rivets.
3. Fit water shedder. ***See this section.***

CABLE - INTERIOR DOOR RELEASE - FRONT DOOR

Service repair no - 76.37.60

Remove

1. Remove front door latch. ***See this section.***

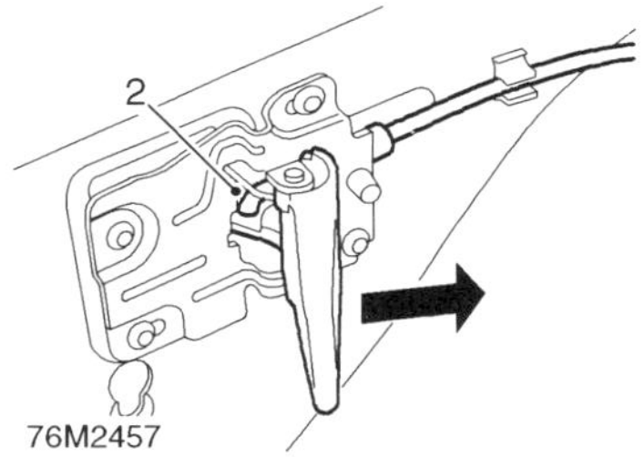

76M2457

2. Release cable from interior door release and remove cable.

Refit

1. Connect cable to interior door release.
2. Fit door latch. ***See this section.***

CABLE - INTERIOR DOOR RELEASE - REAR DOOR

Service repair no - 76.37.61

Remove

1. Remove rear door latch. ***See this section.***

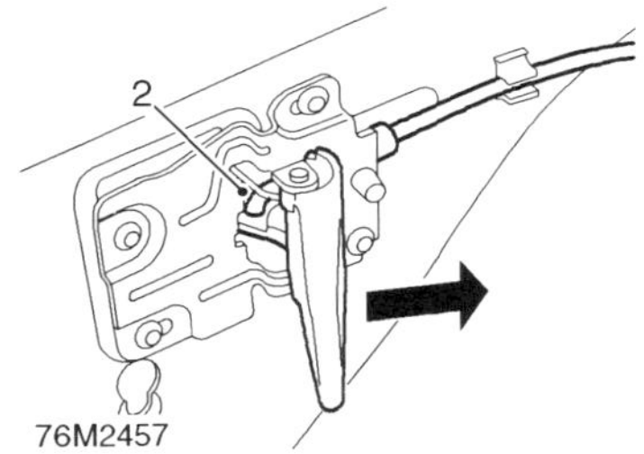

76M2457

2. Release cable from door release and remove cable.

Refit

1. Connect and secure cable to door release.
2. Fit door latch. ***See this section.***

FINISHER - UPPER - TAIL DOOR GLASS

Service repair no - 76.43.74

Remove

1. Remove tail door glass side finishers. ***See this section.***

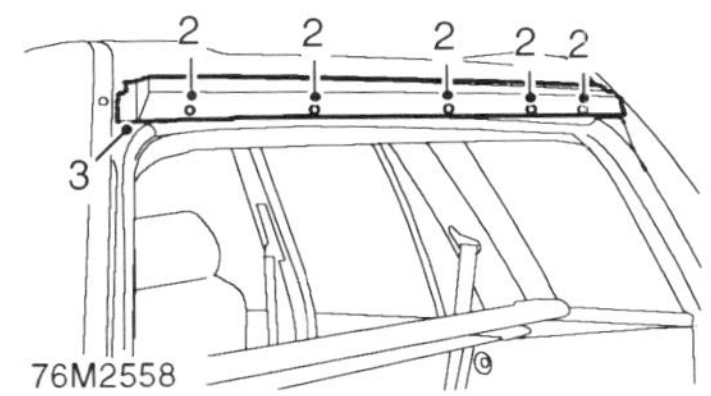

76M2558

2. Release 5 clips securing finisher to bracket.
3. Remove tail door glass upper finisher.
4. Remove and discard clips from finisher and/or bracket.

Refit

1. Fit NEW clips to finisher.
2. Fit finisher and secure clips to bracket.
3. Fit tail door glass side finishers. ***See this section.***

FINISHER - SIDE - TAIL DOOR GLASS

Service repair no - 76.43.81

Remove

1. Open tail door.

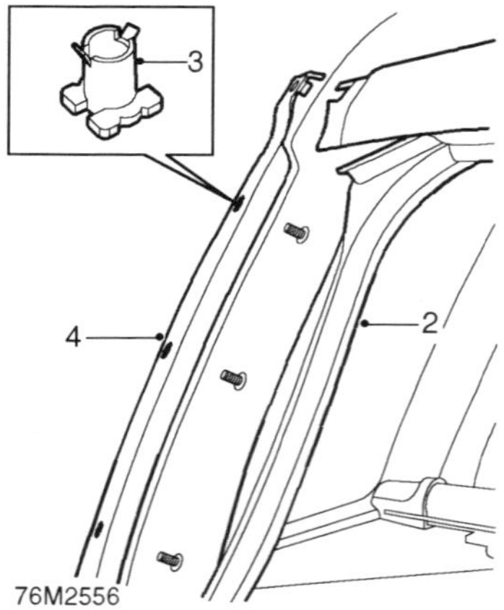

76M2556

2. Release tail door glass seal from aperture for access to side finisher fixings.
3. Using a suitable trim stud removal tool, release 3 side finisher fixings from studs on body.
4. Remove side finisher from upper fixing.
5. Remove and discard fixings from finisher.

Refit

1. Fit NEW fixings to finisher.
2. Fit door glass seal to flange.
3. Fit finisher and secure fixings.

HANDLE - EXTERIOR - REAR DOOR

Service repair no - 76.58.02

Remove

1. Remove rear door water shedder. ***See this section.***

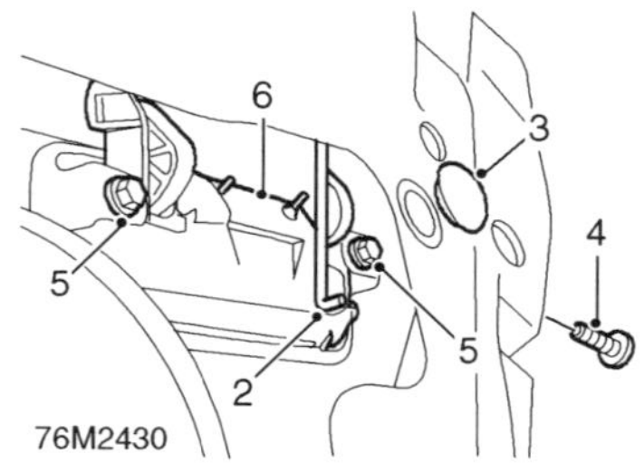

76M2430

2. Release door latch control rod.
3. Remove grommet to access screw.
4. Remove 3 Torx screws securing door latch release and lower latch to access screw.
5. Remove 2 screws securing door handle.
6. Remove door handle.

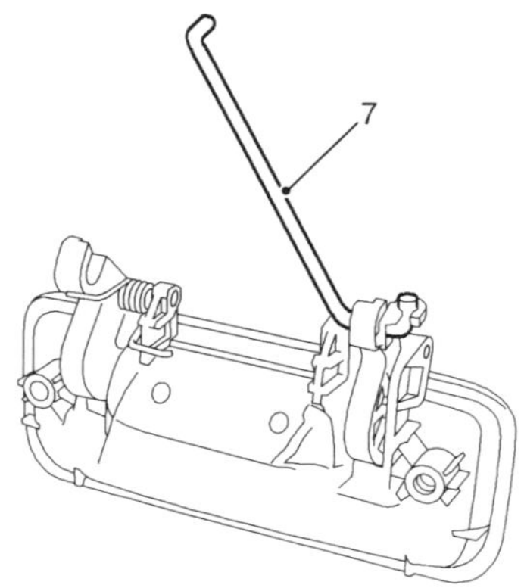

76M2431

7. Remove door latch control rod.

Refit

1. Fit door latch control rod to handle.
2. Position handle to door and tighten securing screws.
3. Position door latch, fit and tighten Torx screws.
4. Fit grommet.
5. Connect door latch control rod.
6. Fit water shedder. ***See this section.***

HANDLE - EXTERIOR - TAIL DOOR

Service repair no - 76.58.05

Remove

1. Remove tail door water shedder. ***See this section.***
2. Raise glass by clicking latch.

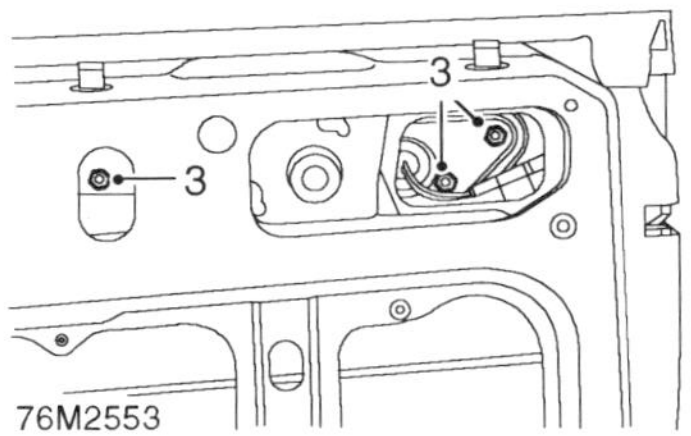

76M2553

3. Remove 3 nuts securing handle to tail door.
4. Release handle from tail door.

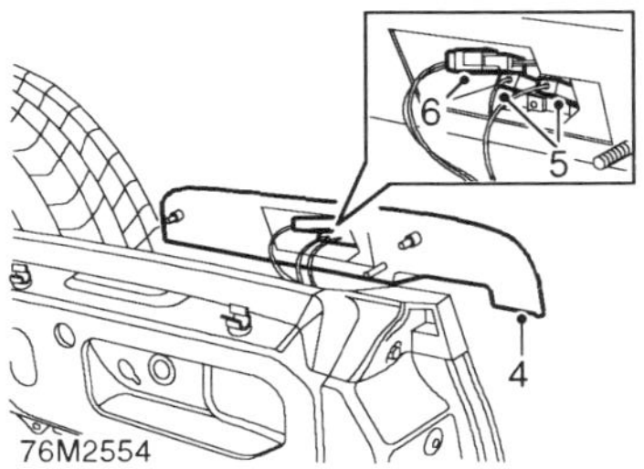

76M2554

5. Disconnect 2 Lucars from number plate lamp.
6. Disconnect multiplug from locking mechanism and remove handle.

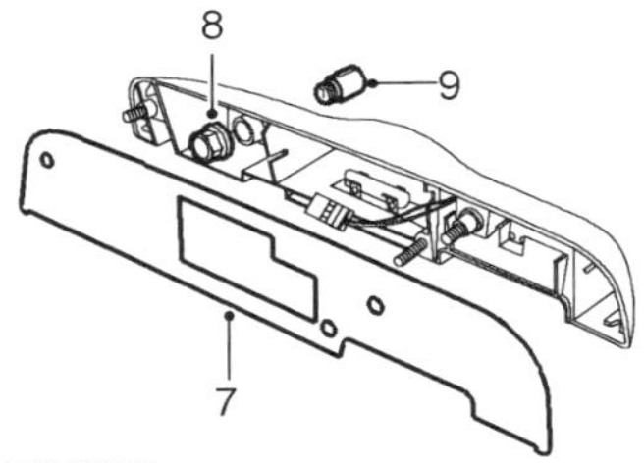

76M2555

7. Collect gasket.
   Do not carry out further dismantling if component is removed for access only.
8. Remove nut from lock barrel.
9. Remove lock barrel from handle.
10. Fit lock barrel to replacement handle. Fit and tighten nut.

Refit

1. Position gasket on handle.
2. Connect multiplug to handle locking mechanism.
3. Connect Lucars to number plate lamp.
4. Position housing on door, fit and tighten nuts to 5 Nm.
5. Fit water shedder. ***See this section.***
6. Reset latch to lower glass.
7. Close door.

HANDLE - EXTERIOR - FRONT DOOR

Service repair no - 76.58.07

Remove

3 door models

1. Remove upper water shedder. ***See this section.***

5 door models

2. Remove front door water shedder. ***See this section.***

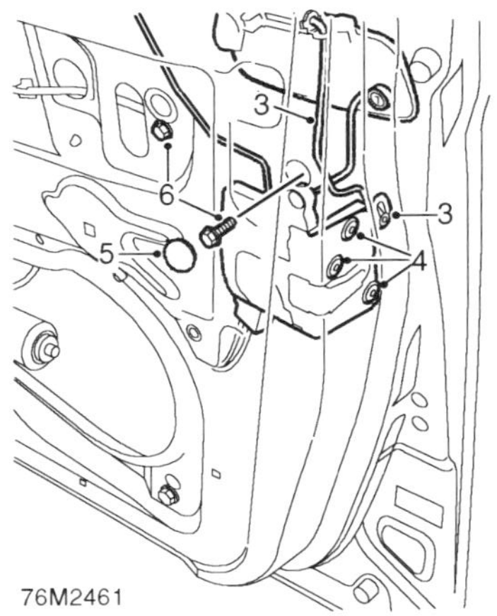

76M2461

All models

3. Release clip securing latch control rod to door latch, and release rod.

5 door models

4. Remove Torx screws securing door latch, lower latch and release door lock paddle.

All models

5. Remove grommet to access screw.
6. Remove 2 screws securing door handle.

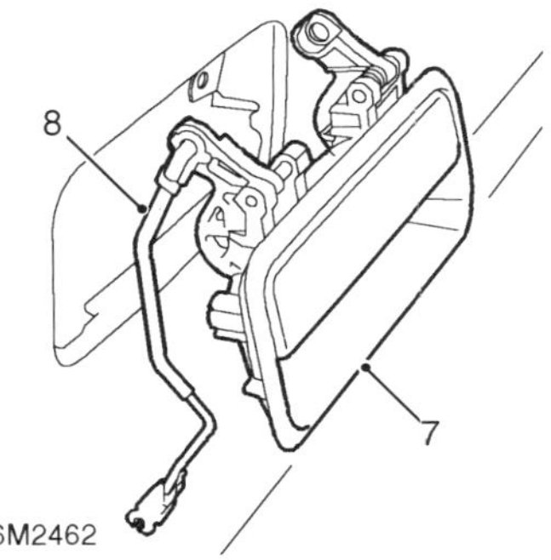

76M2462

7. Remove door handle.
8. Remove latch control rod from handle.

Refit

1. Fit door latch control rod to handle.
2. Position handle to door, fit and tighten screws.
3. Fit grommet.

5 door models

4. Position latch, locate door lock paddle, fit and tighten Torx screws.

All models

5. Connect control rod to door latch.
6. Fit water shedder. ***See this section.***

DOOR PULL - FRONT

Service repair no - 76.58.25

Remove

1. Remove front door casing. ***See this section.***

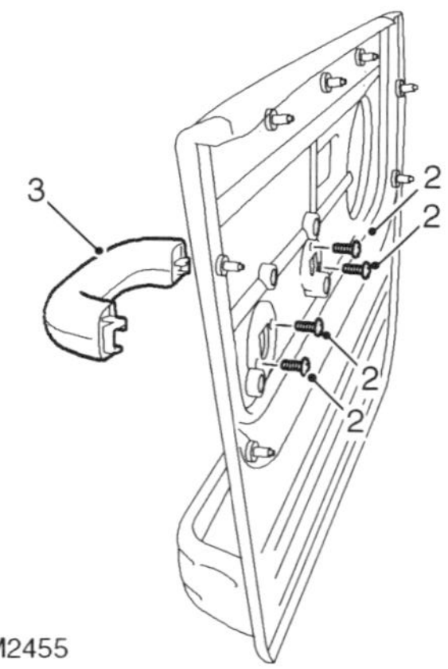

76M2455

2. Remove 4 Torx screws securing door pull to door casing.
3. Remove door pull.

Refit

1. Position door pull to door casing, fit and tighten Torx screws.
2. Fit front door casing. ***See this section.***

WING - FRONT

Service repair no - 76.10.24

Remove

1. Remove front mud flap. ***See this section.***
2. Remove lower sill finisher. ***See this section.***

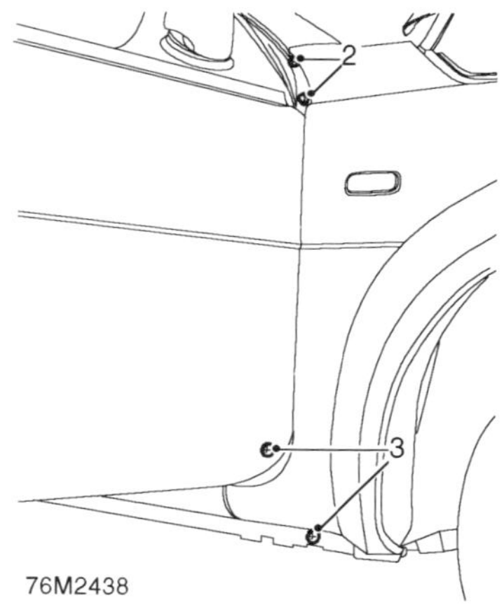

76M2438

3. Remove 3 Torx screws and 1 bolt securing rear of front wing.

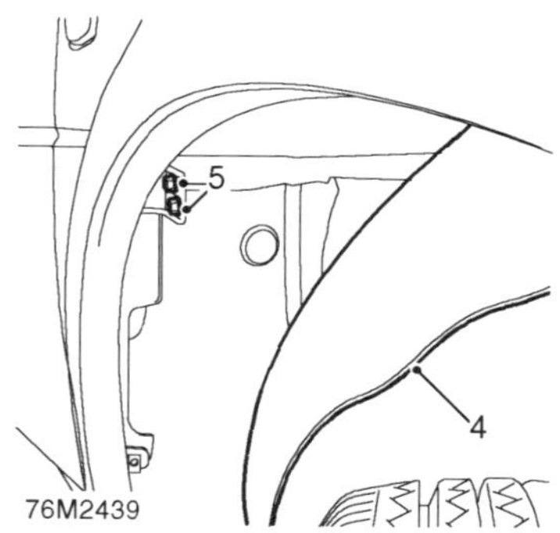

76M2439

4. Release wheel arch liner from rear of front wing.
5. Remove 2 bolts securing wing bracket to 'A' post.

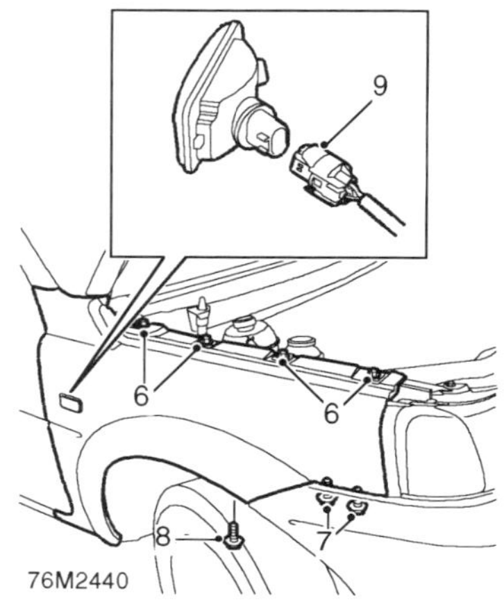

76M2440

6. Remove 4 bolts securing top of wing.
7. Remove 2 bolts securing front of wing.
8. Remove screw securing wheelarch liner to under side of wing.
9. Release wing from body, disconnect multiplug from repeater lamp.
10. Remove front wing from body.

Refit

1. Position front wing to body.
2. Connect repeater lamp multiplug.
3. Align front wing to body.
4. Fit, but do not tighten, the following:
   Torx screws and bolt securing rear of wing to 'A' post
   Bolts securing wing bracket to 'A' post.
   Bolts securing top of wing.
   Bolts securing front of wing.

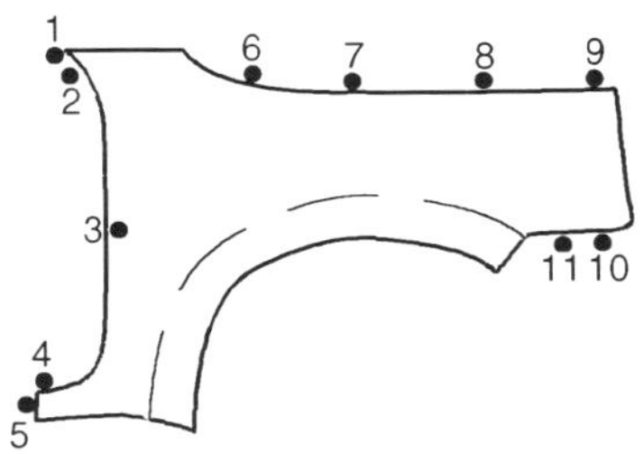

76M2791

5. Align wing and tighten bolts and Torx screws, in sequence shown above, to 5 Nm.
6. Align wheel arch liner to rear of wing.
7. Fit screw securing wheelarch liner to under side of wing.
8. Fit lower sill finisher. ***See this section.***
9. Fit front mud flap. ***See this section.***

WHEEL ARCH LINER - FRONT

Service repair no - 76.10.48

Remove

1. Raise front of vehicle, one side.

WARNING: Support on safety stands.

2. Remove road wheel(s).
3. Remove front mud flap. ***See this section.***

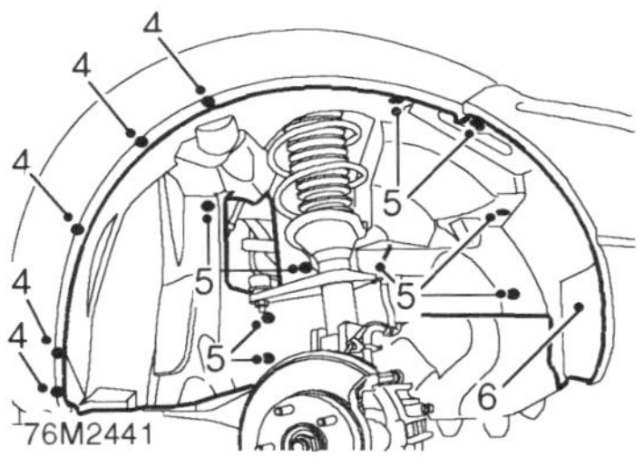

76M2441

4. Remove 5 screws securing wheel arch to front wing.
5. Remove 8 scrivets securing wheel arch to inner wing.
6. Remove wheel arch liner from inner wing.

Refit

1. Position wheel arch liner to inner wing, locate behind wheel arch cladding.
2. Fit scrivets securing wheel arch liner to inner wing.
3. Fit screws securing wheel arch liner to front wing.
4. Fit mud flap. ***See this section.***
5. Fit road wheel(s) and tighten nuts to correct torque. ***See INFORMATION, Torque wrench settings.***
6. Remove stand(s) and lower vehicle.

PANEL - UNDERBELLY

Service repair no - 76.10.50

Remove

1. Raise front of vehicle.

WARNING: Support on safety stands.

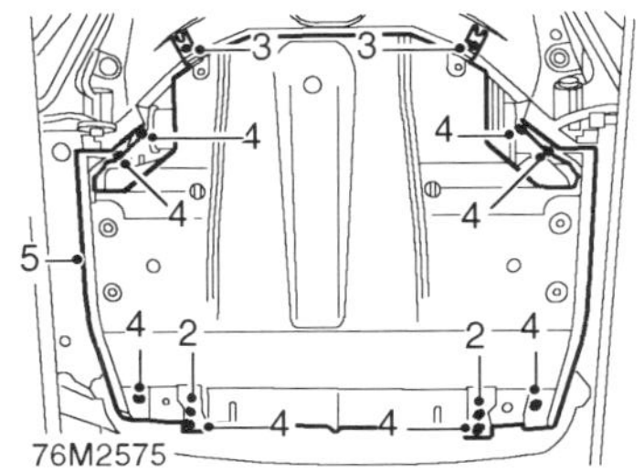

76M2575

2. Remove 2 screws securing bumper valance to underbelly panel brackets.
3. Remove 2 bolts securing rear of underbelly panel.
4. Remove 8 bolts securing underbelly panel frame.
5. Remove underbelly panel.

Refit

1. Position underbelly panel to vehicle.
2. Fit bolts securing frame and tighten to 45 Nm.
3. Fit bolts securing rear of panel and tighten to 8 Nm.
4. Fit screws securing bumper valance to brackets.
5. Remove stand(s) and lower vehicle.

MIRROR - EXTERIOR - ELECTRIC

Service repair no - 76.10.57

Remove

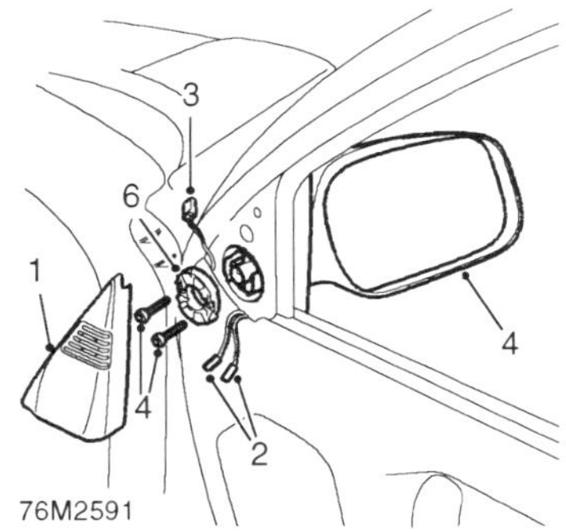

76M2591

1. Remove cheater panel.
2. Disconnect 2 Lucars from tweeter and place cheater panel aside.
3. Disconnect multiplug from mirror.
4. Hold mirror and remove 2 Torx screws.
5. Remove mirror.
6. Collect clamping plate.

Refit

1. Position mirror, locate clamping plate, fit and tighten Torx screws to 6 Nm.
2. Connect multiplug to mirror.
3. Connect Lucars to tweeter in cheater panel.
4. Fit cheater panel.

MUD FLAP - FRONT

Service repair no - 76.10.83

Remove

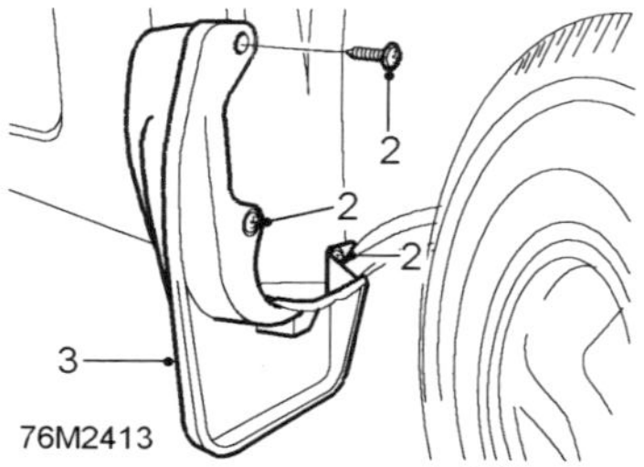

76M2413

1. Turn steering wheel to full lock.
2. Remove 3 screws securing mud flap.
3. Remove mud flap.

Refit

1. Position mud flap to body and secure with screws.
2. Straighten steering.

MUD FLAP - REAR

Service repair no - 76.10.85

Remove

1. Raise rear of vehicle.

WARNING: Support on safety stands.

2. Remove road wheel(s).

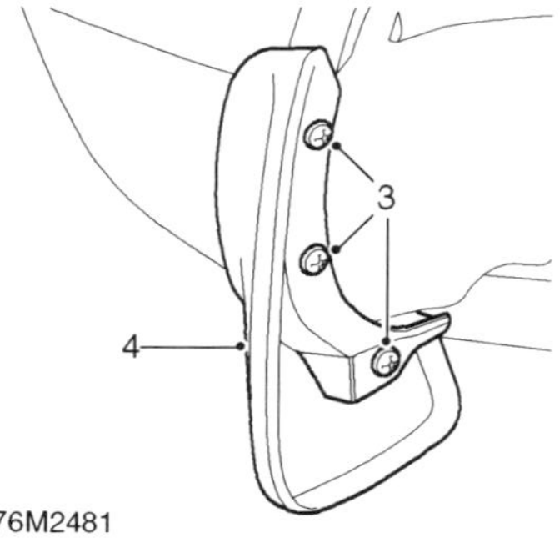

76M2481

3. Remove 3 screws securing mud flap.
4. Remove mud flap.

Refit

1. Position mud flap to body and secure with screws.

MOUNTING BRACKET - SPARE WHEEL

Service repair no - 76.11.18

Remove

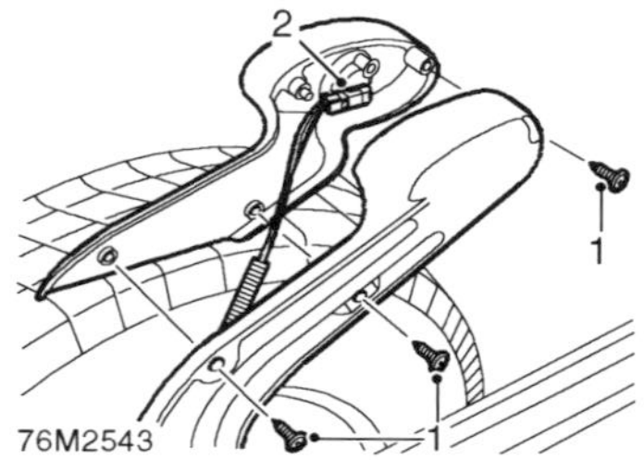

76M2543

1. Lower tail door glass and remove 3 screws securing high mounted stop lamp.
2. Disconnect multiplug and remove lamp.

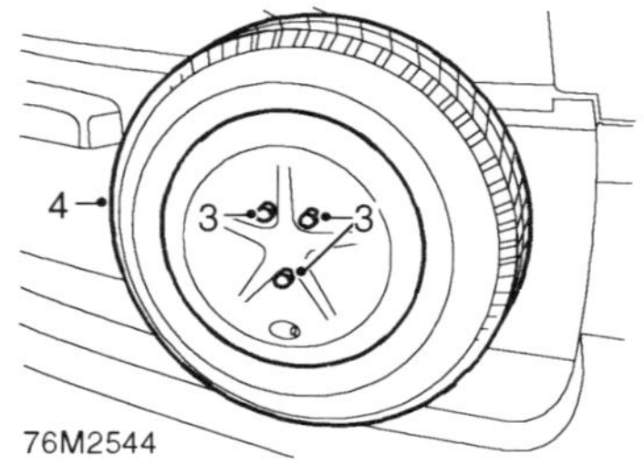

76M2544

3. Remove 3 nuts securing spare wheel to mounting bracket.
4. Remove spare wheel from mounting bracket.

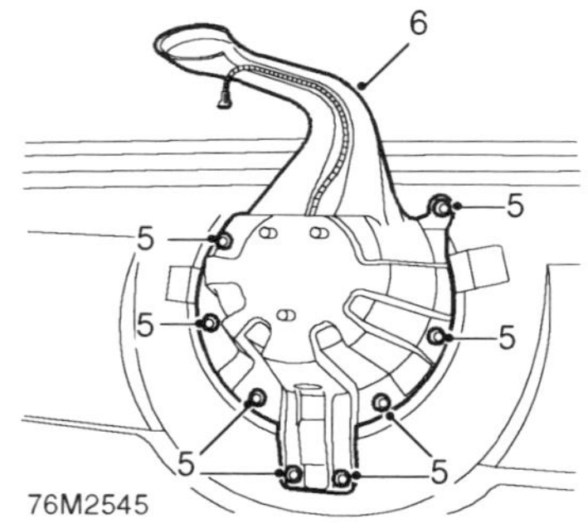

76M2545

5. Remove 6 bolts and 2 nuts securing spare wheel mounting bracket to tail door.
6. Remove mounting bracket.

Refit

1. Position spare wheel mounting bracket to tail door and tighten bolts to 13 Nm.
2. Tighten mounting bracket nuts to 25 Nm.
3. Position stop lamp and connect multiplug.
4. Fit and tighten screws securing stop lamp.
5. Fit spare wheel and tighten nuts to 45 Nm.
6. Raise tail door glass.

SIDE RAIL - ROOF RACK - 5 DOOR

Service repair no - 76.11.30

Remove

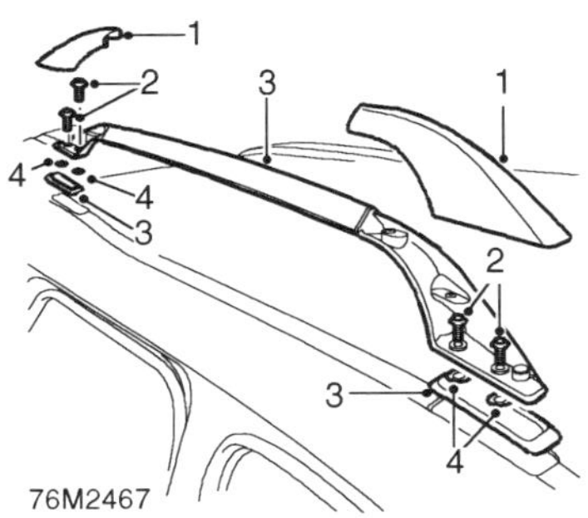

1. Remove finishers from feet of side rail.
2. Unscrew 4 Torx bolts securing side rail to roof panel.
3. Remove side rail and 2 gaskets.
   Do not carry out further dismantling if component is removed for access only.
4. Remove seal from each Torx bolt.
5. Remove Torx bolts from side rail.
6. Fit Torx bolts and seals to replacement side rail.

Refit

1. Fit gaskets to side rail.
2. Position side rail and tighten Torx bolts to 22 Nm.
3. Fit finishers to feet of side rail.

BONNET

Service repair no - 76.16.01/99

Remove

1. Support bonnet in open position.
2. Fit protection covers to wings and mark hinge outline on bonnet if bonnet is to be refitted.

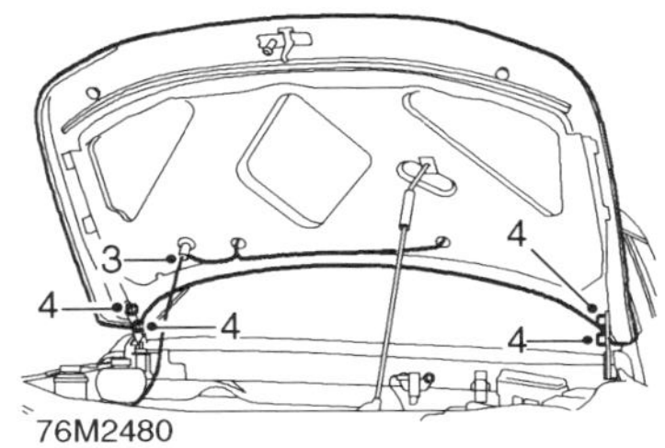

3. Disconnect windscreen washer tube at elbow joint.
4. With assistance, remove bolts securing bonnet and remove bonnet.

Refit

1. With assistance, position bonnet and align hinges to marks on bonnet.
2. Lightly tighten bolts.
3. Connect windscreen washer tube.
4. Close bonnet to safety catch position, check that bonnet is aligned to both front wings and that gaps are equal.
5. Finally tighten hinge bolts to 9 Nm.

CABLE - BONNET RELEASE

Service repair no - 76.16.29

Remove

1. Remove front grille. ***See this section.***

Models with air conditioning:

2. Remove condenser. ***See AIR CONDITIONING, Repairs.***

All models:

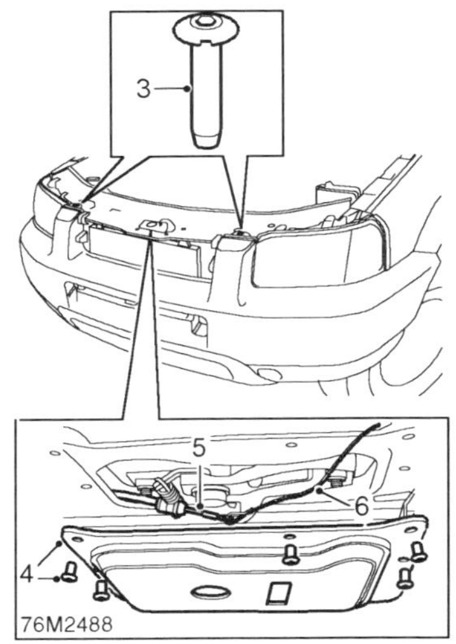

3. Remove radiator threaded retainers from bonnet locking platform.
4. Drill out 5 rivets and remove bonnet bonnet latch shield.
5. Disconnect bonnet release cable from lock.
6. Tie a draw string to end of bonnet release cable and pull cable from bonnet locking platform.
7. Untie draw string.
8. Remove 3 cable ties securing bonnet release cable to main harness.

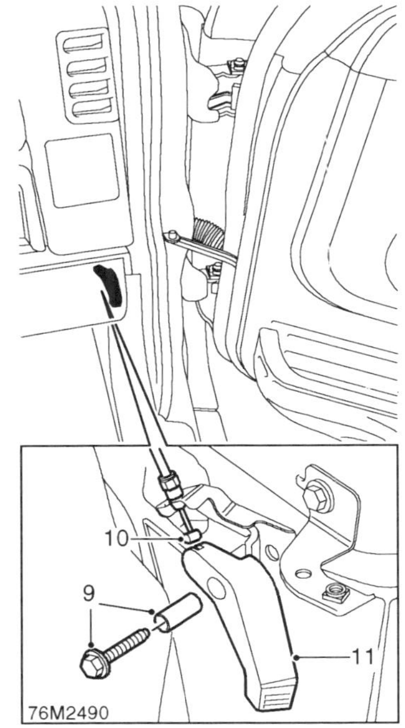

9. Remove bolt securing bonnet release lever to 'A' post lower panel.
10. Remove bonnet release cable from lever.
11. Remove release lever.

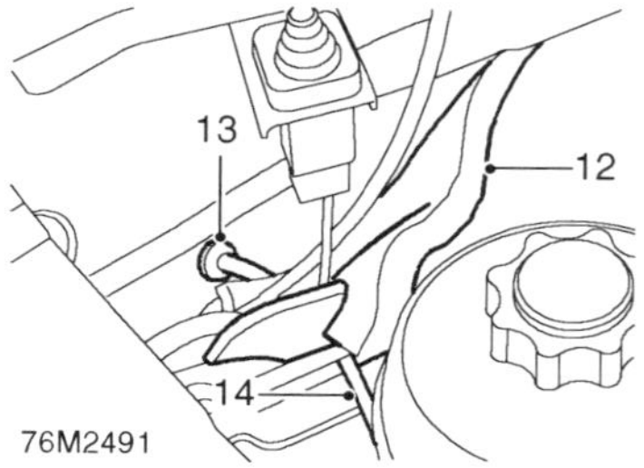

76M2491

12. Pull sound insulation away from bulkhead for access to bonnet release cable grommet.
13. Remove grommet from bulkhead.
14. Remove bonnet release cable.

Refit

1. Fit bonnet release cable through bulkhead.
2. Position bonnet release lever.
3. Connect bonnet release cable to lever.
4. Fit release lever to 'A' post and tighten bolt to 9 Nm.
5. Fit bonnet release cable grommet to bulkhead.
6. Fit cable ties and secure bonnet release to main harness.
7. Fit sound insulation material to bulkhead.
8. Tie draw string to end of bonnet release cable.
9. Pull on draw string to feed bonnet release cable through bonnet locking platform.
10. Untie draw string and connect bonnet release cable to bonnet lock lever.
11. Fit bonnet latch shield and secure with 5 rivets.
12. Fit and tighten radiator threaded retainers in bonnet locking platform.

Models with air conditioning:

13. Fit condenser. ***See AIR CONDITIONING, Repairs.***

All models:

14. Fit front grille. ***See this section.***
15. Close bonnet and check for correct locking operation.

BUMPER VALANCE - FRONT

Service repair no - 76.22.72

Remove

1. Remove front grille. ***See this section.***

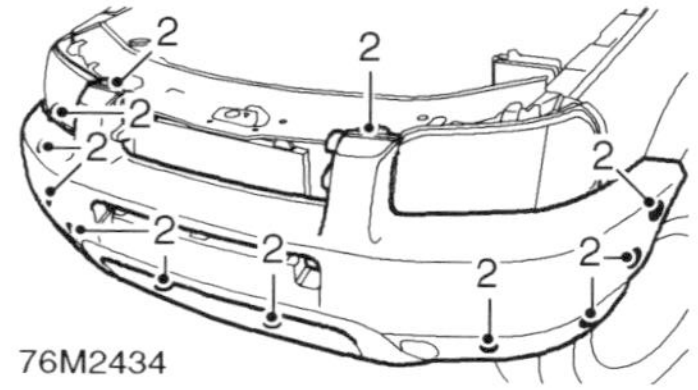

76M2434

2. Remove 12 screws securing bumper valance to body.

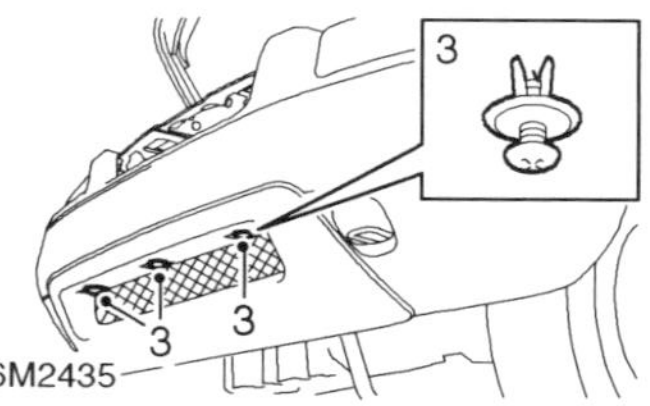

76M2435

3. Remove 3 scrivets from bumper valance.

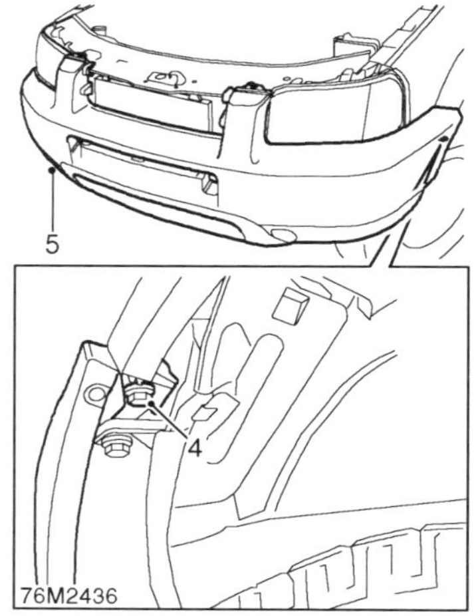

76M2436

4. Remove wheelarch liner access panel and loosen bolts under front of each wing.
5. With assistance, remove bumper valance. ***Do not carry out further dismantling if component is removed for access only.***
6. Remove number plate.

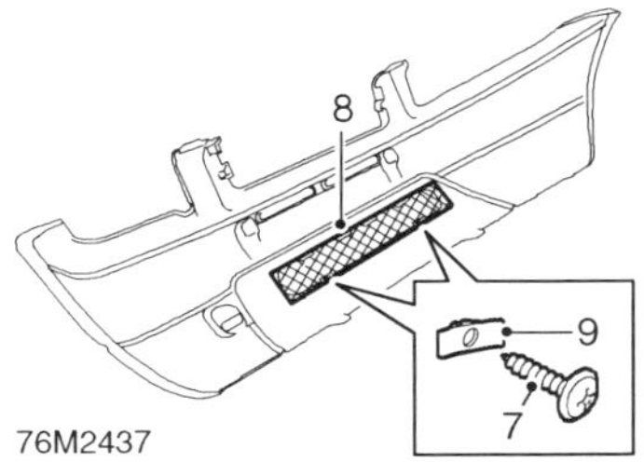

76M2437

7. Remove 2 screws from bumper grille.
8. Remove bumper grille.
9. Remove 2 spire nuts.
10. Fit spire nuts to replacement bumper valance.
11. Position bumper grille on replacement bumper valance and secure with screws.
12. Fit number plate on replacement bumper valance.

Refit

1. With assistance position bumper valance to body.
2. Tighten bolts under each front wing to 5 Nm.
3. Fit wheelarch liner access panel.
4. Fit scrivets.
5. Fit screws securing bumper valance to body.
6. Fit front grille. ***See this section.***

BUMPER VALANCE - REAR

Service repair no - 76.22.74

Remove

1. Remove rear mud flaps. ***See this section.***
2. Remove both tail lamps. ***See ELECTRICAL, Repairs.***
3. Remove rear wheel arch extensions. ***See this section.***

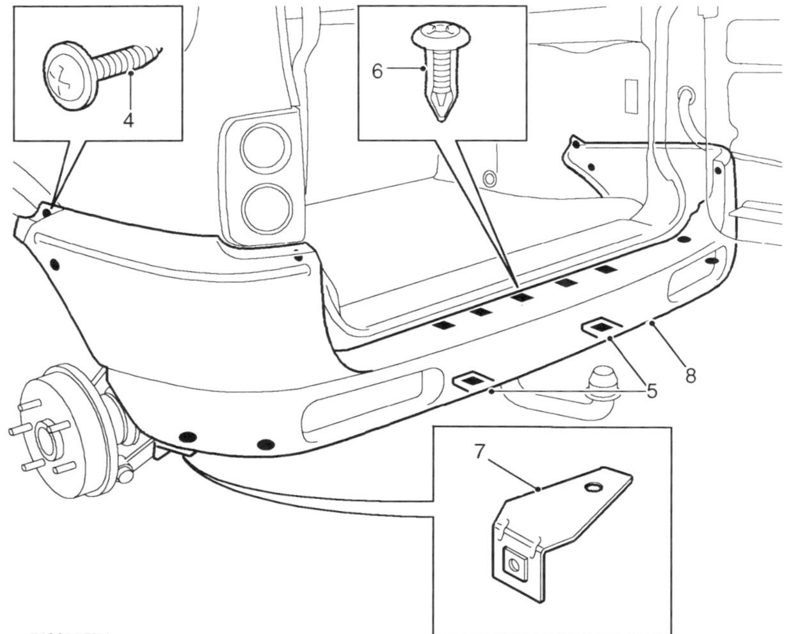

76M2557A

4. Remove 10 screws securing bumper valance.
5. Remove 2 nuts and bolts securing bumper valance to armature.
6. Remove 5 scrivets securing bumper valance.
7. Remove 2 mud flap brackets.
8. With assistance, remove bumper valance.

Refit

1. With assistance, fit bumper valance. Secure bumper valance with scrivets, screws and nuts and bolts.
2. Fit mud flap brackets and secure with screws.
3. Fit rear wheel arch extensions. ***See this section.***
4. Fit both tail lamps. ***See ELECTRICAL, Repairs.***
5. Fit mud flaps. ***See this section.***

FINISHER - SILL - LOWER

Service repair no - 76.43.28

Remove

1. Raise front of vehicle.

WARNING: Support on safety stands.

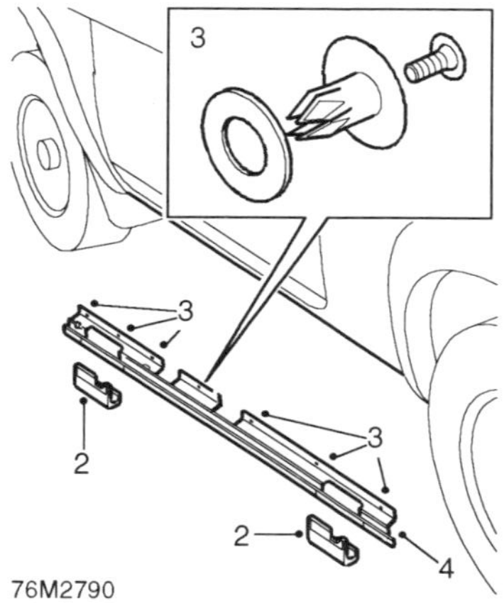

76M2790

2. Remove both jacking point covers.
3. Remove 7 scrivits securing finisher.
4. Release and remove finisher from sill.

Refit

1. Clean mating faces of finisher.
2. Position finisher to sill, locate over jacking points and secure with scrivits.
3. Fit jacking point covers.
4. Remove stand(s) and lower vehicle.

FINISHER - ROOF PANEL

Service repair no - 76.43.68

Remove

1. Remove tail door glass side finisher. ***See Doors.***

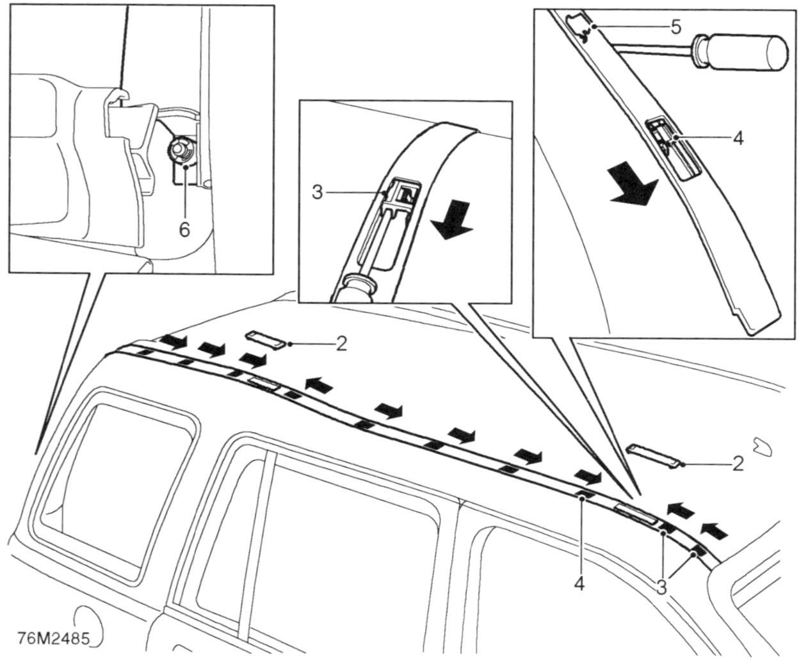

76M2485

2. Remove roof finisher caps or, if roof rack fitted, remove side rail. ***See this section.***
3. Using a suitable hooked tool in the front foot hole of the roof finisher, slide the finisher's 2 forward clips rearward from the roof channel.
4. Slide the clip rear of the foot hole forward from the roof channel.
5. Slide the remaining 7 clips from the roof channel.
6. Remove nut securing rear end of roof finisher.
7. Remove finisher.

Refit

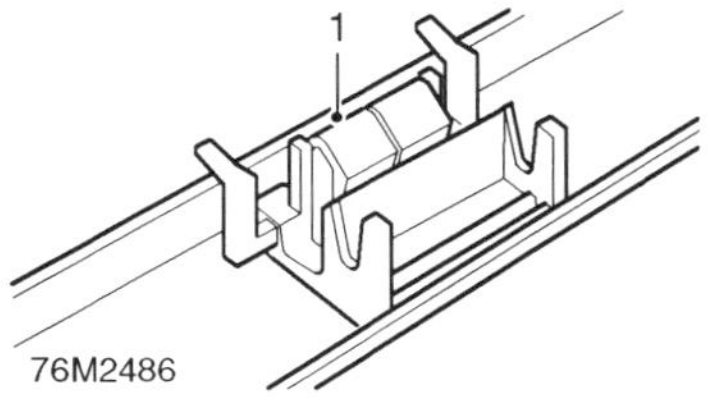

76M2486

1. Fit clips to finisher.
2. Fit finisher to roof channel with forward two clips.
3. Slide finisher to align with screen. Feed forward clip below screen seal.
4. Fit remaining clips to roof channel.
5. Fit nut to secure rear end of finisher.
6. Ensure full length of finisher is correctly seated in roof channel.
7. Fit roof finisher caps or roof rack side rail. ***See this section.***
8. Fit tail door glass side finisher. ***See Doors.***

WHEEL ARCH EXTENSION - REAR

Service repair no - 76.43.94

Remove

1. Raise rear of vehicle.
2. Remove road wheel(s).

5 door models

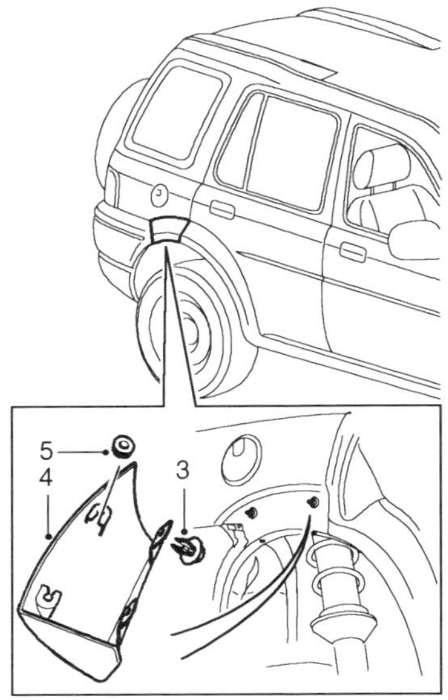

76M2779

3. Remove 2 scrivets securing extension to edge of wheel arch.
4. Remove wheel arch extension from 2 fixing studs.
5. Remove fasteners from arch extension.

3 door models

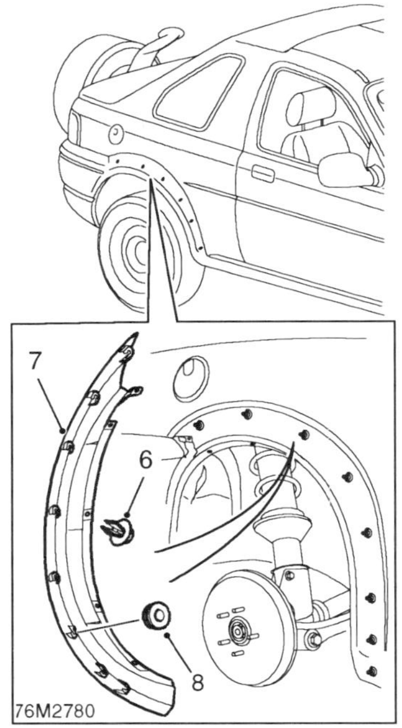

76M2780

6. Remove 6 scrivets securing extension to edge of wheel arch and sill panel.
7. Remove wheel arch extension from 8 fixing studs.
8. Remove fasteners from arch extension

Refit

1. Fit fasteners to arch extension.
2. Fit wheel arch extension to studs.
3. Fit scrivets securing extension to wheel arch.
4. Fit road wheel(s) and tighten nuts to correct torque. ***See INFORMATION, Torque wrench settings.***
5. Remove stand(s) and lower vehicle.

GRILLE - FRONT

Service repair no - 76.55.03

Remove

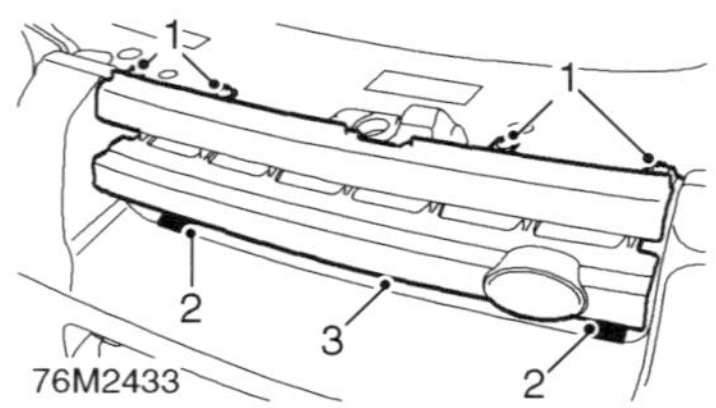

1. Remove 4 screws from grille.
2. Release 2 catches securing bottom of grille.
3. Remove grille.

Refit

1. Position grille to body, locate with securing catches.
2. Fit and tighten screws.

VENT - REAR QUARTER

Service repair no - 76.81.24

Remove

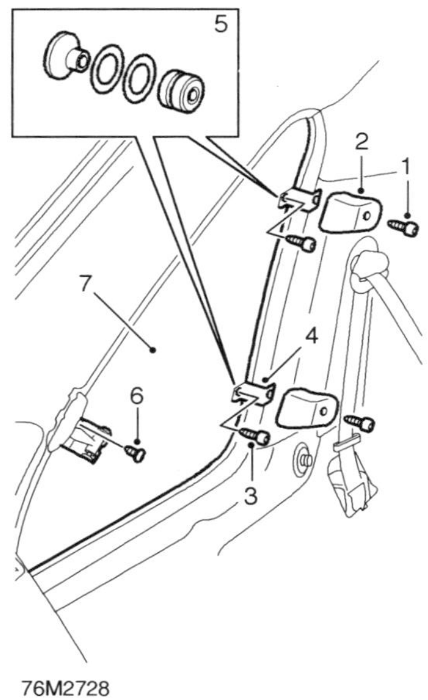

1. Remove 2 Torx screws securing vent hinge covers.
2. Remove covers from hinges.
3. Remove 2 screws securing hinges to vent.
4. Remove hinges from vent.
5. Remove nuts from vent and discard sealing washers.
6. With assistance remove screw securing vent catch to body.
7. Remove vent.

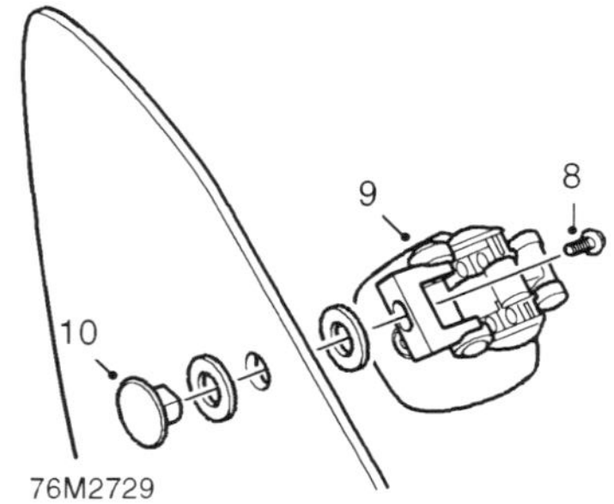

8. Remove screw securing catch to vent.
9. Remove catch from vent.
10. Remove nut from vent and discard sealing washers.

Refit

1. Fit nut and NEW sealing washer to vent.
2. Fit catch and tighten screw.
3. With assistance fit vent and tighten catch screw.
4. Using NEW sealing washers fit nuts and hinges to vent. Fit and tighten hinge screws to vent.
5. Fit hinge covers and tighten Torx screws.

SUN VISOR

Service repair no - 76.10.47

Remove

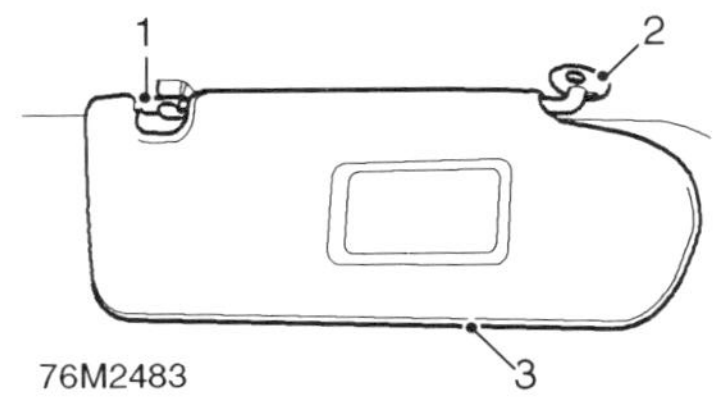

76M2483

1. Release sun visor from retaining clip.
2. Remove 2 screws securing sun visor.
3. Remove sun visor.

Refit

1. Fit sun visor and secure with screws.
2. Secure sun visor in clip.

FINISHER - 'A' POST

Service repair no - 76.13.07

Remove

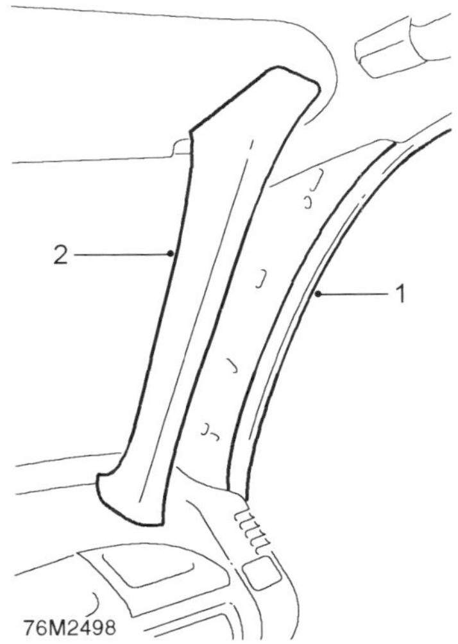

76M2498

1. Release seal from door aperture.
2. Release 4 clips and remove 'A' post finisher.
3. Remove clips from finisher.

Refit

1. Fit clips to 'A' post finisher.
2. Fit finisher to 'A' post and secure with clips.
3. Fit seal to door aperture.

CASING - REAR QUARTER LOWER - 3 DOOR

Service repair no - 76.13.12

Remove

1. Release rear seat squab and fold seat forward.

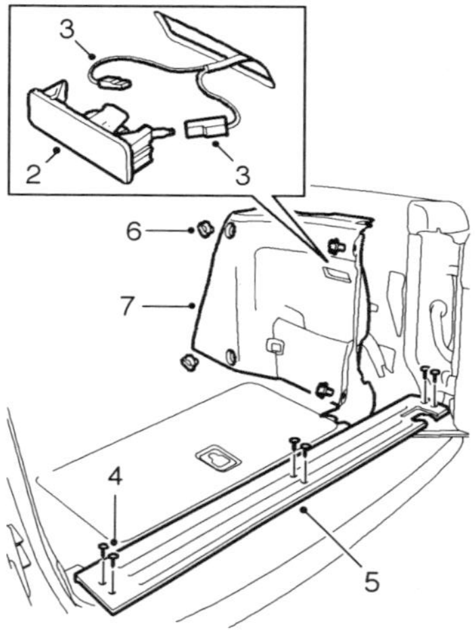

76M2711

2. Release load space lamp from trim casing.
3. Disconnect 2 Lucars and remove load space lamp.
4. Remove 6 Torx screws securing luggage compartment carpet retainer.
5. Remove carpet retainer.
6. Release 4 turn buckles securing trim casing.
7. Release and remove trim casing from luggage compartment.

Refit

1. Position casing in luggage compartment.
2. Fit turn buckles
3. Fit luggage compartment carpet retainer and fit Torx screws.
4. Position load space lamp to casing, connect Lucars and secure lamp in casing.
5. Reposition rear seat.

CASING - REAR QUARTER LOWER - 5 DOOR

Service repair no - 76.13.12

Remove

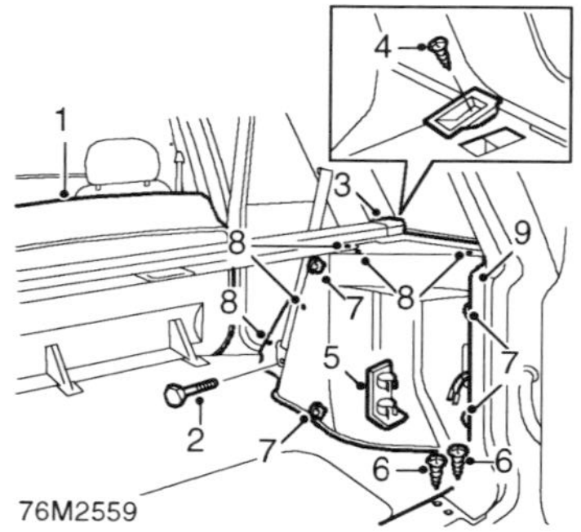

76M2559

1. Release back of rear seat and fold forward.
2. Remove bolt securing rear seat belt lower mounting and position seat belt aside.
3. Release load space cover from retainers and remove cover.
4. Remove screw securing load space cover retainer and remove retainer.
5. Release load space lamp from trim casing. Disconnect 2 Lucars and remove load space lamp.
6. Remove 2 screws securing casing to load space carpet retainer.
7. Release 4 turn buckles securing trim casing.
8. Release trim casing from 5 retaining clips.
9. Remove trim casing from load space.

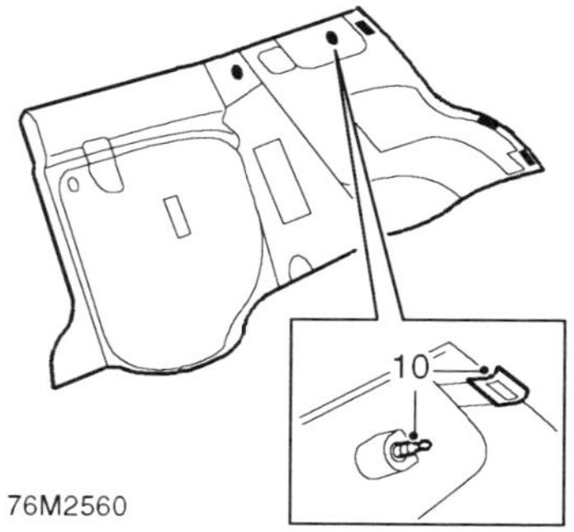

76M2560

10. Remove 5 retaining clips from casing.

Refit

1. Fit retaining clips to casing.
2. Position casing in load space, locate and secure retaining clips.
3. Fit turn buckles
4. Fit screws securing casing to carpet retainer.
5. Position load space lamp to casing, connect Lucars and secure lamp in casing.
6. Position load space cover retainer and secure with screw.
7. Fit load space cover and secure in retainers.
8. Position rear seat belt and tighten bolt to 40 Nm
9. Lower seats and secure back of seat in position.

CASING - REAR QUARTER UPPER - 3 DOOR

Service repair no - 76.13.13

Remove

1. Remove rear quarter lower casing. ***See this section.***
2. Remove body rear side casing. ***See this section.***

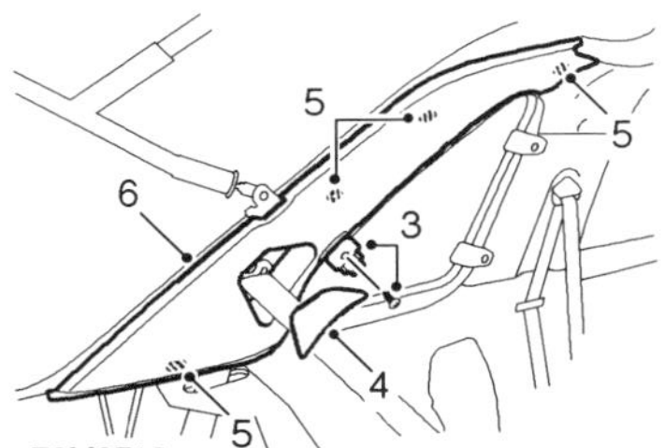

76M2712

3. Remove screw and release rear vent catch.
4. Remove seat belt access cover from upper casing.
5. Release 4 clips securing upper casing.
6. Remove upper casing.

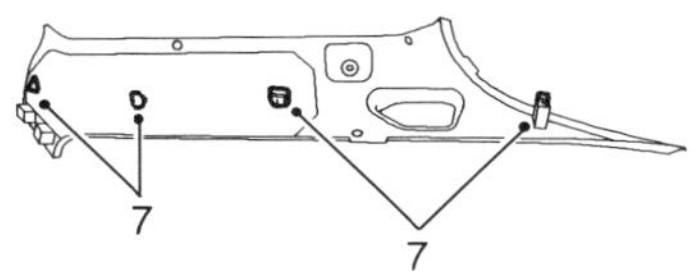

76M2713

7. Remove 4 retaining clips from casing

Refit

1. Fit retaining clips to casing.
2. Position casing, align seat belt and secure casing retaining clips.
3. Fit seat belt access cover.
4. Position rear vent sealing rubber to upper casing.
5. Position rear vent catch and tighten screw.
6. Fit side casing. ***See this section.***
7. Fit lower casing. ***See this section.***

CASING - REAR QUARTER UPPER - 5 DOOR

Service repair no - 76.13.13

Remove

1. Remove rear quarter lower casing. ***See this section.***

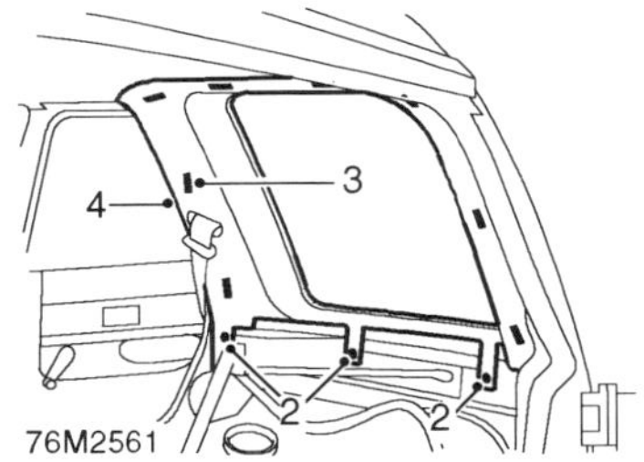

76M2561

2. Remove 3 screws securing upper casing to body.
3. Release casing from 8 retaining clips.
4. Remove upper casing from load space.

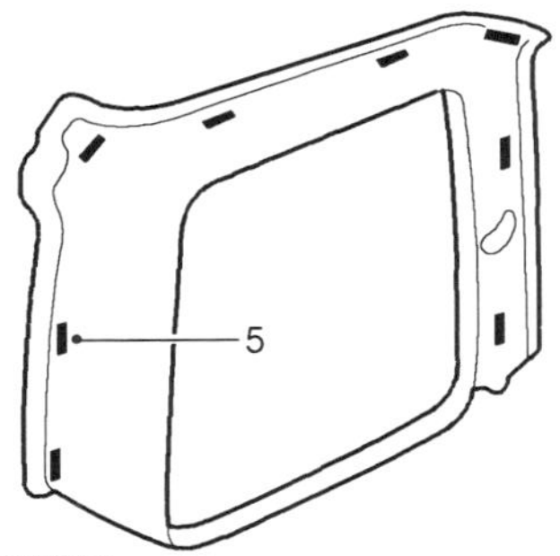

76M2562

5. Remove 8 retaining clips from casing

Refit

1. Fit retaining clips to casing.
2. Position casing to body and secure retaining clips.
3. Fit screws securing bottom of casing.
4. Fit rear quarter lower casing. ***See this section.***

FINISHER - 'B/C' POST UPPER - 5 DOOR

Service repair no - 76.13.28

Remove

1. Remove seat base finisher. ***See this section.***

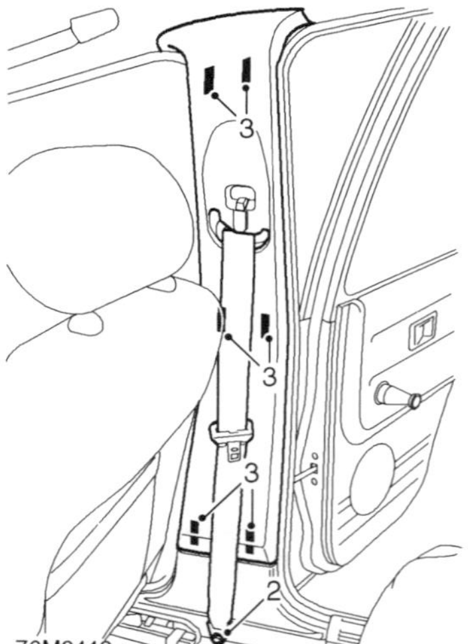

76M2442

2. Remove Torx bolt retaining seat belt lower mounting and position seat belt aside.
3. Release finisher from 6 retaining clips and remove finisher.

Do not carry out further dismantling if component is removed for access only.

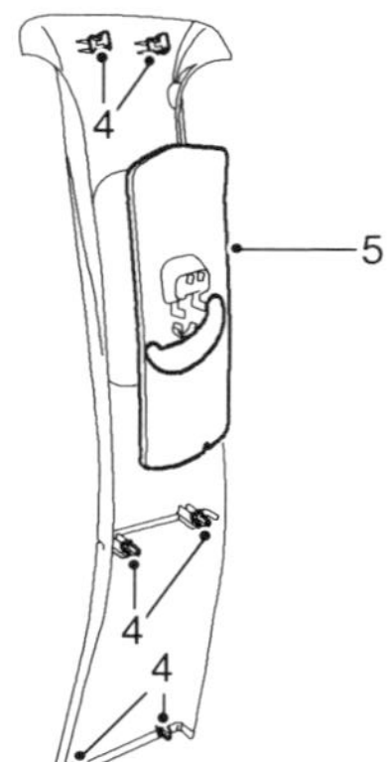

76M2443

4. Remove 6 clips from finisher.
5. Remove seat belt slide.
6. Fit seat belt slide to replacement finisher.
7. Fit clips to replacement finisher.

Refit

1. Position finisher and engage retaining clips.
2. Position seat belt lower mounting. Fit and tighten Torx bolt to 40 Nm.
3. Fit seat base finisher. ***See this section.***

FINISHER -'B/C' POST LOWER - 5 DOOR

Service repair no - 76.13.29

Remove

1. Remove cushion side finisher. ***See Seats and seat belts.***

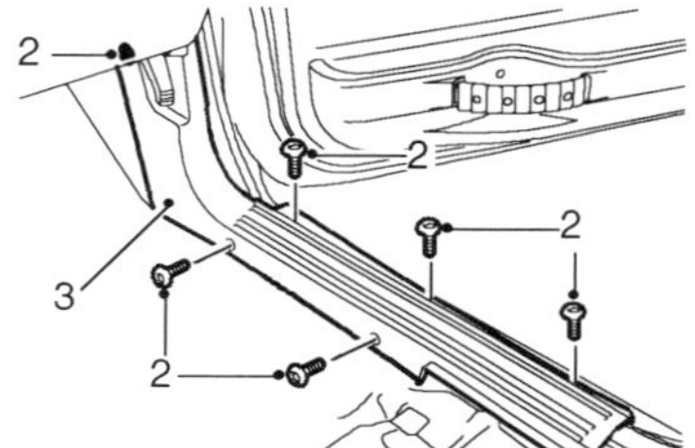

78M0251

2. Remove scrivet and 5 Torx screws from carpet retainer.
3. Remove front carpet retainer.
4. Release B/C' post upper finisher and position aside.

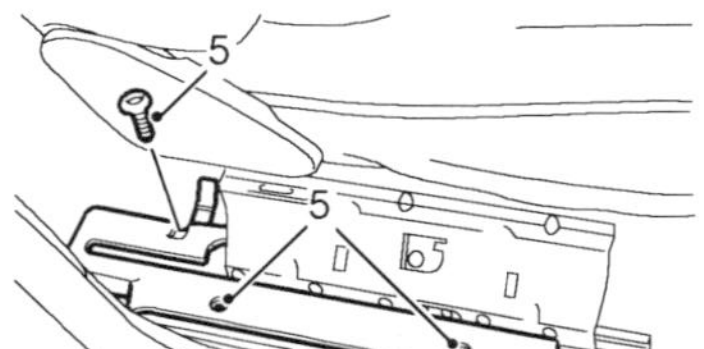

76M2444

5. Remove 3 Torx screws from top of seat base finisher.

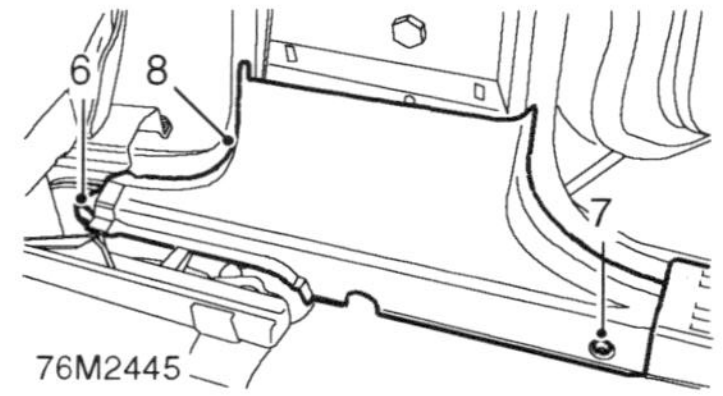

76M2445

6. Remove scrivet from front of B/C' post lower finisher.
7. Remove Torx screw from rear of B/C' post lower finisher.
8. Release and remove B/C' post lower finisher from seat base finisher.

Refit

1. Locate B/C' post lower finisher under seat base finisher and rear carpet retainer.
2. Fit Torx screw to rear of B/C' post lower finisher.
3. Fit scrivet to B/C' post lower finisher.
4. Fit Torx screws to seat base finisher.
5. Align and secure B/C' post upper finisher.
6. Fit cushion side finisher. ***See Seats and seat belts.***
7. Fit front carpet retainer and secure with Torx screws and scrivet.

CASING - BODY SIDE - REAR

Service repair no - 76.13.57

Remove

1. Remove rear seat. ***See Seats and seat belts.***

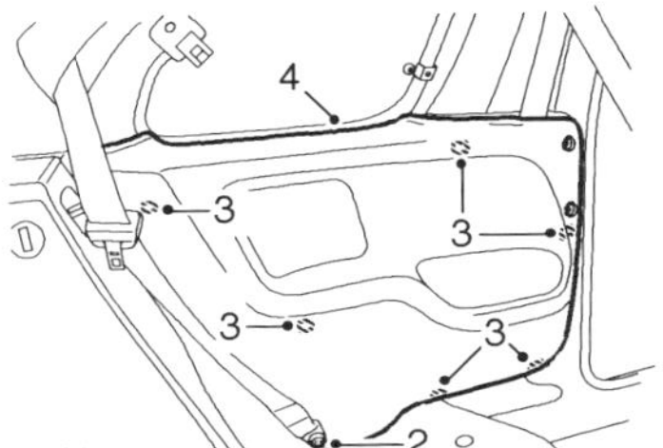

76M2714

2. Remove Torx bolt securing rear seat belt lower to body and position seat belt aside.
3. Release 6 trim clips and remove trim casing.
4. Remove 6 trim fasteners from body panel.
Do not carry out further dismantling if component is removed for access only.

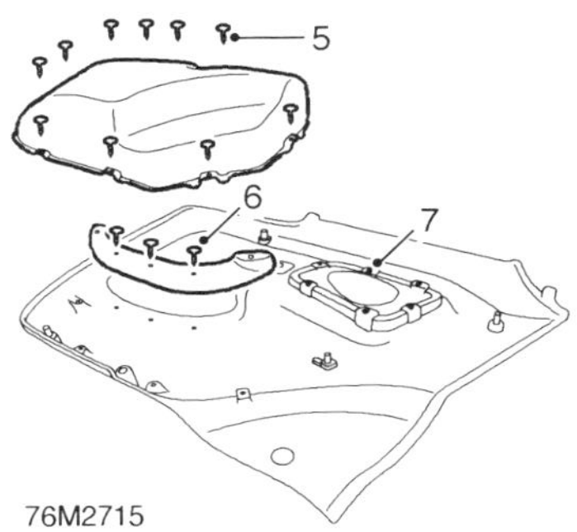

76M2715

5. Noting the position of the 3 long screws, remove 10 Torx screws and remove pocket from trim casing.
6. Remove 3 screws and remove pocket finisher.
7. Release 6 tags and remove speaker grille.
8. Position speaker grille on replacement casing and secure tags.
9. Position pocket finisher and tighten screws.
10. Position pocket and tighten Torx screws

Refit

1. Fit trim fasteners to trim casing.
2. Position trim casing and secure clips.
3. Position seat belt and tighten Torx bolt to 50 Nm.
4. Fit rear seat. ***See Seats and seat belts.***

CONSOLE - FRONT

Service repair no - 76.25.01

Remove

1. Remove rear console. ***See this section.***
2. Remove radio. ***See ELECTRICAL, Repairs.***

76M2469

3. Remove 3 heater control knobs.
4. Remove 2 screws from heater control panel.
5. Remove heater control panel.

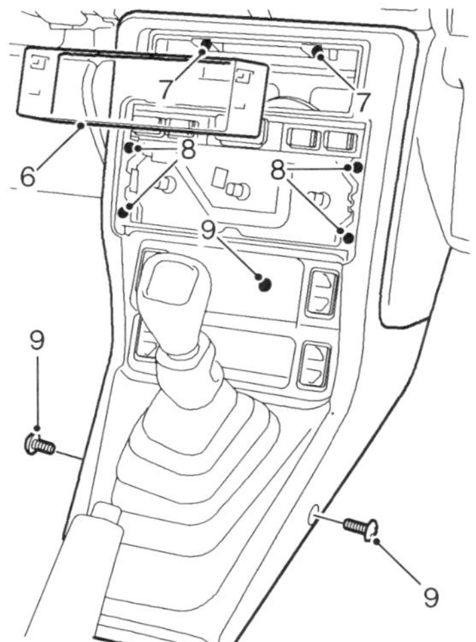

76M2470

6. Release tags and remove radio cage.
7. Remove 2 screws from top of console.
8. Remove 4 screws securing switch pack to console.
9. Remove 3 screws from centre and sides of console.

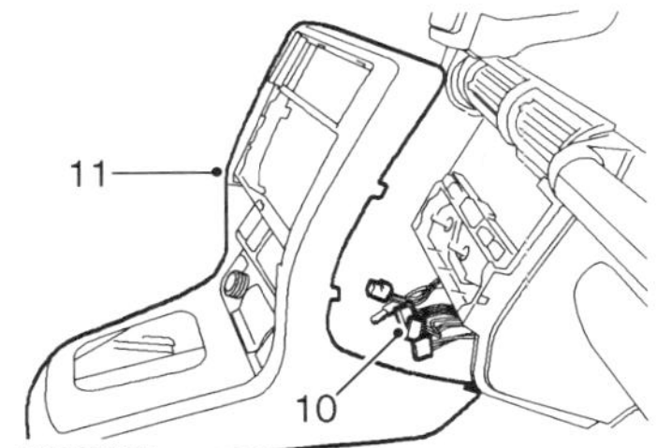

76M2471

10. Release 5 multiplugs and bulb holder from switch pack.
11. Remove console.

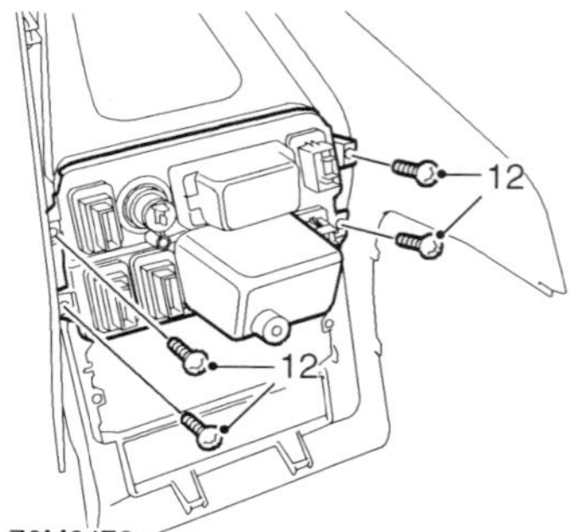

76M2472

12. Remove 4 screws from switch pack assembly and remove assembly.

Refit

1. Position switch pack assembly, fit and tighten screws.
2. Position console to fascia.
3. Connect multiplugs and bulb holder to switch pack.
4. Fit and tighten screws securing centre and sides of console.
5. Fit and tighten screws securing switch pack to console.
6. Fit and tighten screws to top of console.
7. Position radio cage to console and secure with retaining tags.
8. Position heater control panel, fit and tighten screws.
9. Fit heater control knobs.
10. Fit radio. ***See ELECTRICAL, Repairs.***
11. Fit rear console. ***See this section.***

CONSOLE - REAR

Service repair no - 76.25.04

Remove

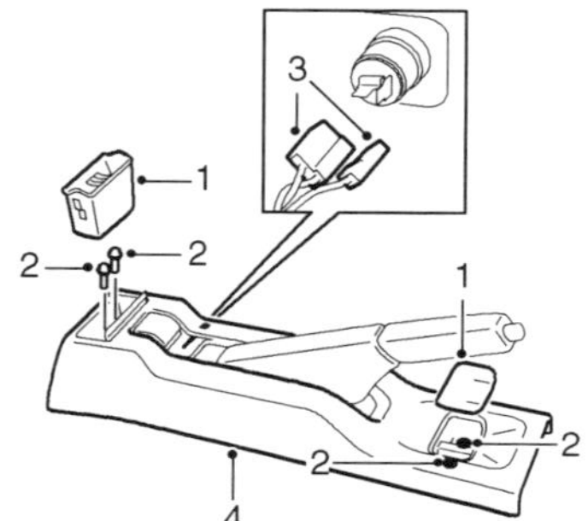

76M2473

1. Remove ashtray and screw cover.
2. Remove 4 screws from console.
3. Raise console and disconnect Lucar and multiplug from cigar lighter.
4. Remove rear console.

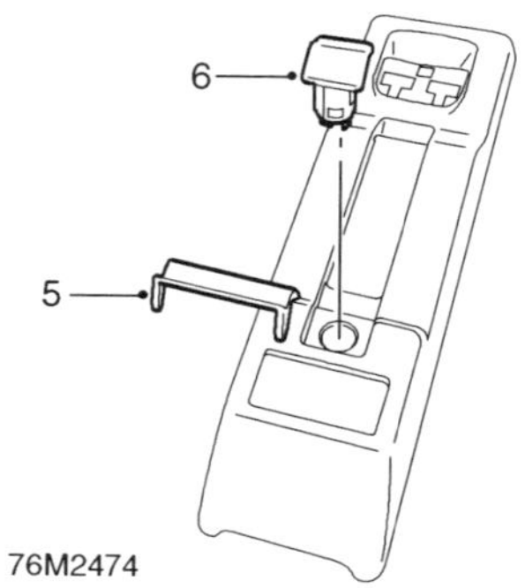

76M2474

5. Remove ashtray lid.
6. Remove cigar lighter.

Refit

1. Fit cigar lighter.
2. Fit ashtray lid.
3. Position rear console and connect Lucar and multiplug to cigar lighter.
4. Fit and tighten screws.
5. Fit ashtray and screw cover.

FASCIA

Service repair no - 76.46.23

Remove

1. Remove front console. ***See this section.***
2. Remove rotary coupler. ***See RESTRAINT SYSTEMS, Repairs.***

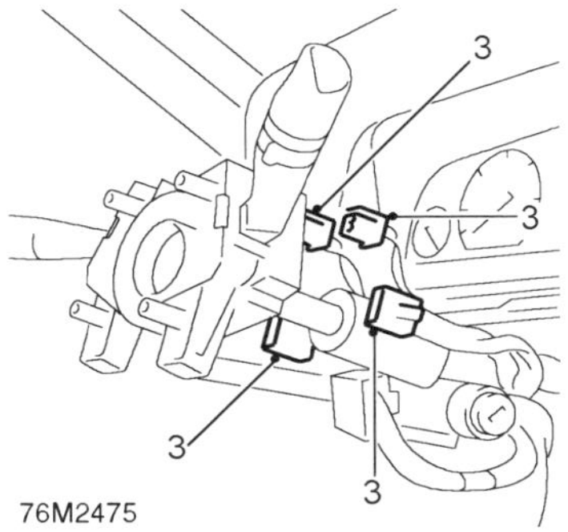

76M2475

3. Disconnect 4 multiplugs from wiper/ indicator switch.

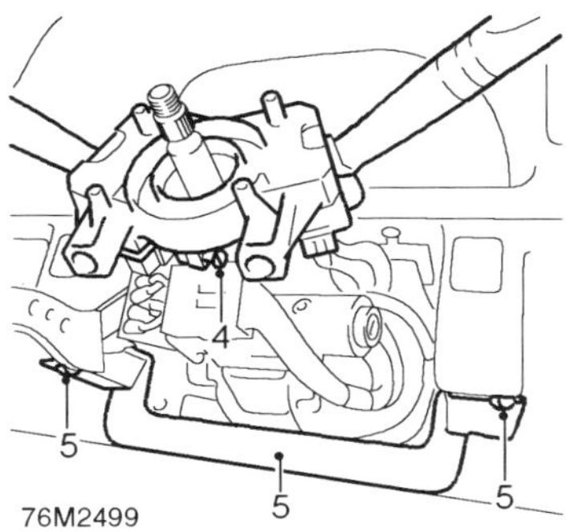

76M2499

4. Loosen clamping screw and remove wiper/ indicator switch.
5. Remove 2 screws from steering column lower finisher and remove finisher.

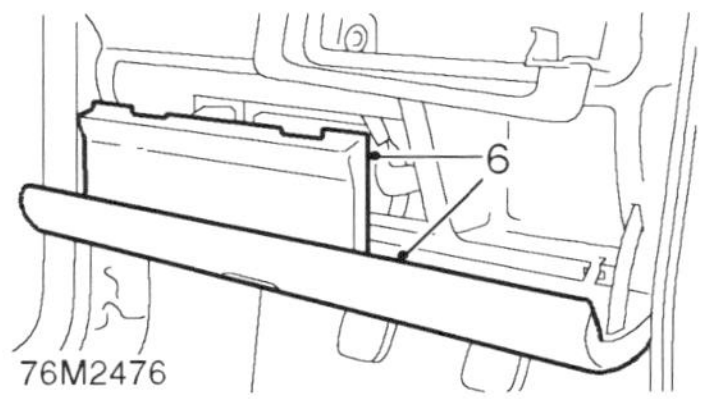

76M2476

6. Open driver's glove box lid and remove fuse box cover.

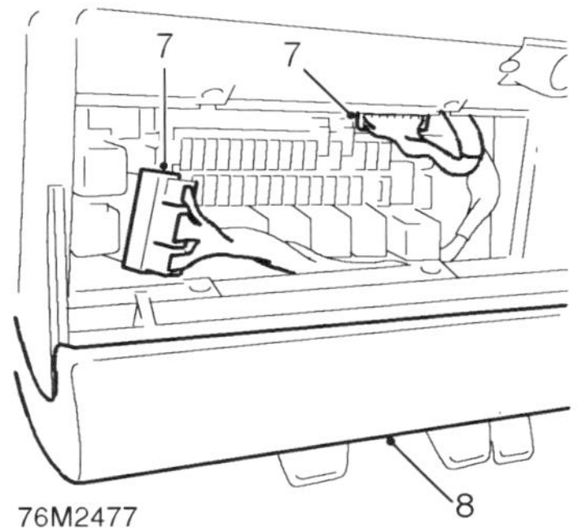

76M2477

7. Disconnect 2 multiplugs from fuse box.
8. Close glove box lid.
9. Remove clock. ***See ELECTRICAL, Repairs.***
10. Remove both 'A' post finishers ***See this section.***
11. ***Models without passenger airbag:*** Remove fascia stowage box. ***See this section.***

Models with passenger airbag:
Remove passenger airbag. ***See RESTRAINT SYSTEMS, Repairs.***

All models:

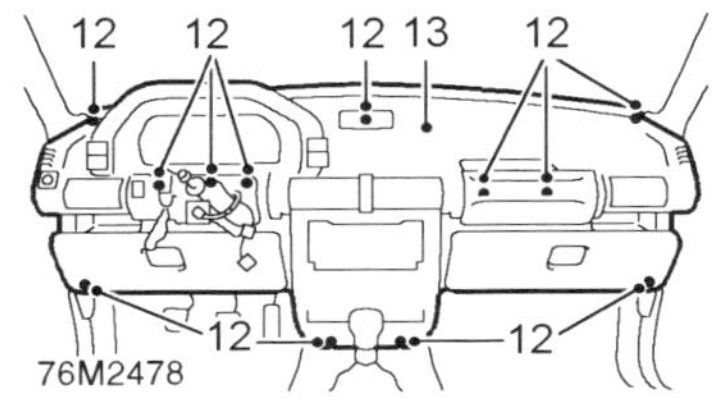

76M2478

12. Remove 12 bolts securing fascia.
13. With assistance remove fascia.
Do not carry out further dismantling if component is removed for access only.

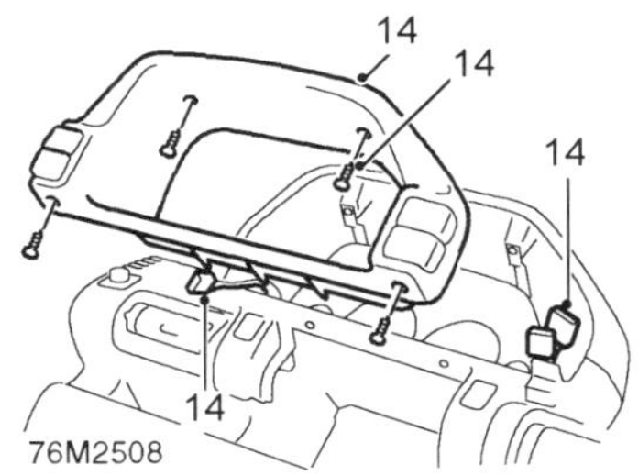

76M2508

14. Remove 4 screws, disconnect 3 multiplugs from switches, and remove instrument bezel finisher.

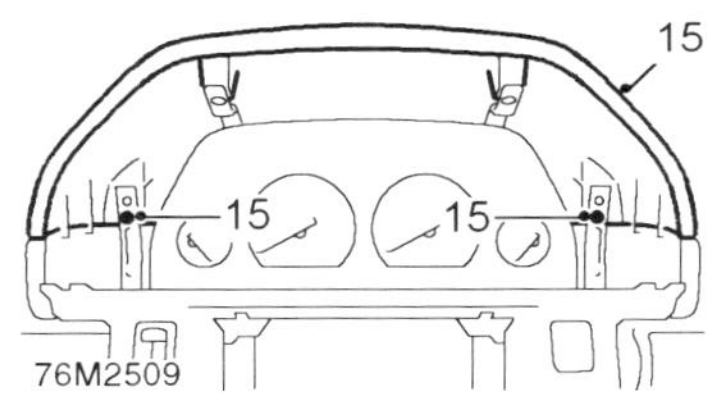

76M2509

15. Remove 2 screws from instrument upper cover and remove cover.

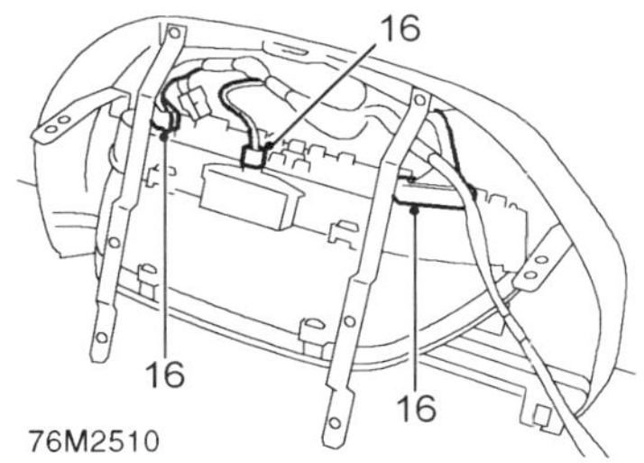

76M2510

16. Disconnect 3 multiplugs from instrument pack.

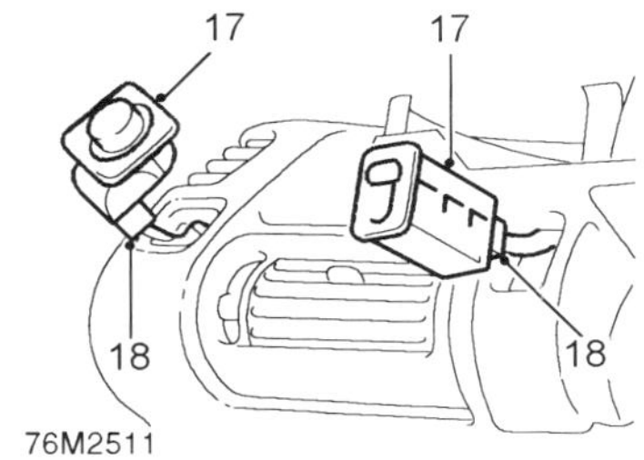

76M2511

17. Release mirror and headlamp leveling switches.
18. Disconnect multiplugs from mirror switch and headlamp leveling switch.

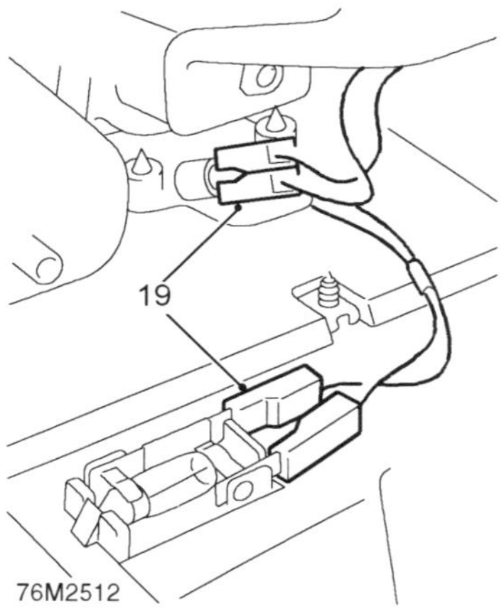

76M2512

19. Disconnect 4 Lucars from glove box lamp and switch.

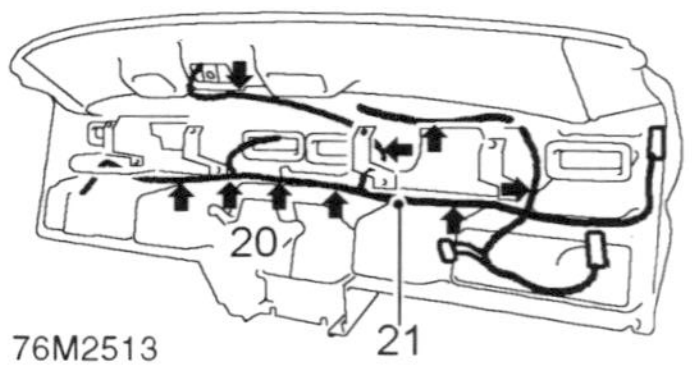

76M2513

20. Release 9 harness clips.
21. Feed harness through fascia and remove harness.

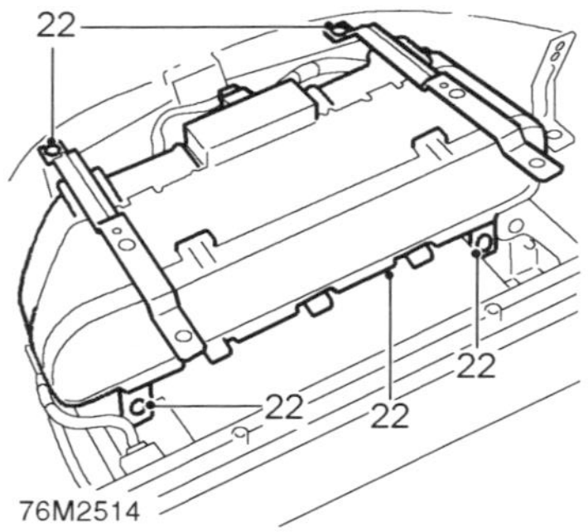

76M2514

22. Remove 4 screws from instrument pack and remove instrument pack.

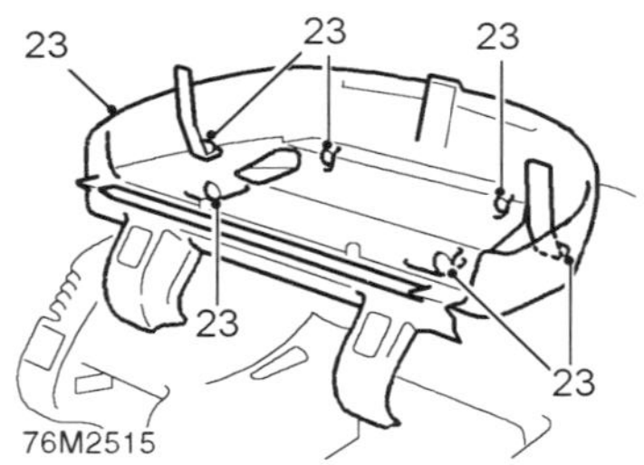

76M2515

23. Remove 6 screws from instrument pack lower cover and remove cover.

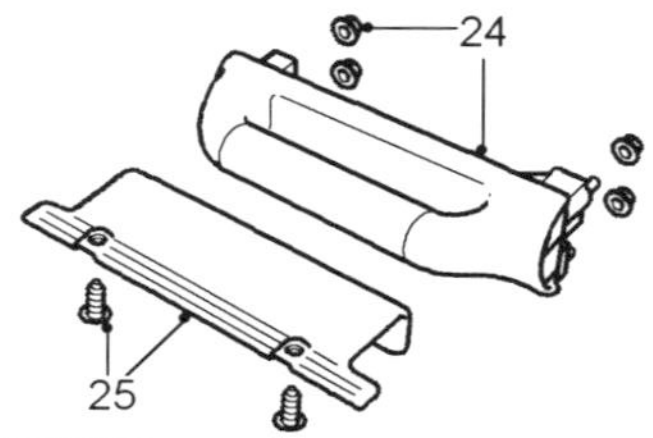

76M2516

Models without passenger airbag:

24. Remove 4 nuts from grab handle and remove handle.

Models with passenger airbag:

25. Remove 2 screws from airbag lower finisher and remove finisher.

All models:

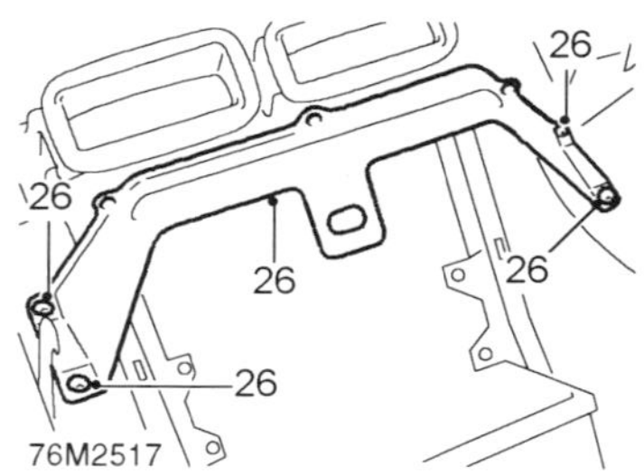

76M2517

26. Remove 4 screws from centre bracket and remove bracket.

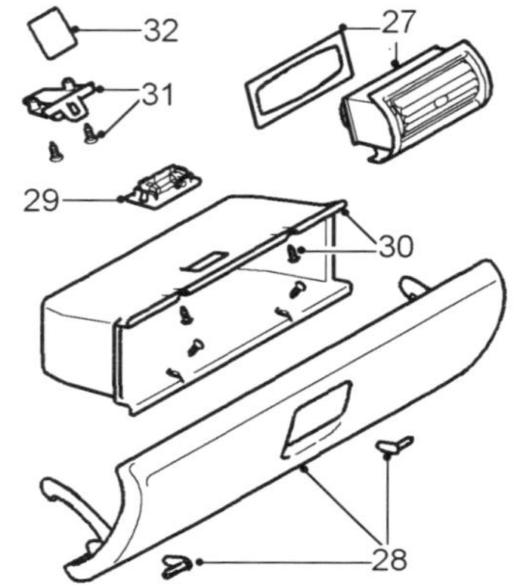

76M2518

27. Remove 4 face level vents and collect seals.
28. Remove glove box hinge pins and remove glove box lids.
29. Remove glove box lamp and mat.
30. Remove 4 screws from glove box and remove glove box.
31. Remove 2 screws from each glove box lock and remove locks.
32. Remove switch blank.
33. Noting their fitted positions, remove 11 spire nuts and 3 harness clips.
34. Remove fascia and coin tray mats.

35. Fit fascia and coin tray mats to replacement fascia. Ensure mats are fully located in position.
36. Fit spire nuts and harness clips.
37. Fit switch blank.
38. Fit glove box locks and secure with screws.
39. Fit glove box and secure with screws.
40. Fit glove box lamp and mat.
41. Fit glove box lids and secure hinge pins.
42. Position seals to face level vents and fit vents.
43. Fit centre bracket and secure with screws.

Models without passenger airbag:

44. Fit grab handle and secure with nuts.

Models with passenger airbag:

45. Fit airbag lower finisher and secure with screws.

All models:

46. Fit instrument pack lower cover and secure with screws.
47. Fit instrument pack and secure with screws.
48. Position harness and secure harness in clips.
49. Fit mirror and headlamp leveling switches.
50. Feed harness through fascia and connect multiplugs to instrument pack, mirror switch and headlamp leveling switch.
51. Connect Lucars to glove box lamp and switch.
52. Fit instrument upper cover and secure with screws.
53. Position instrument bezel finisher, connect multiplugs and secure finisher with screws.

Refit

1. With assistance position fascia.
2. Fit and tighten screws.

Models without passenger airbag:

3. Fit fascia stowage box. ***See this section.***

Models with passenger airbag:

4. Fit passenger airbag. ***See RESTRAINT SYSTEMS, Repairs.***

All models:

5. Fit 'A' post finishers. ***See this section.***
6. Fit clock. ***See ELECTRICAL, Repairs.***
7. Open driver's glove box lid and connect multiplugs to fuse box.
8. Fit fuse box cover and close glove box lid.
9. Fit steering column lower finisher and secure with screws.
10. Fit wiper/indicator switch and tighten clamping screw.
11. Connect multiplugs to wiper/indicator switch.
12. Fit rotary coupler. ***See RESTRAINT SYSTEMS, Repairs.***
13. Fit front console ***See this section.***

STOWAGE BOX - FASCIA

Service repair no - 76.46.45

Remove

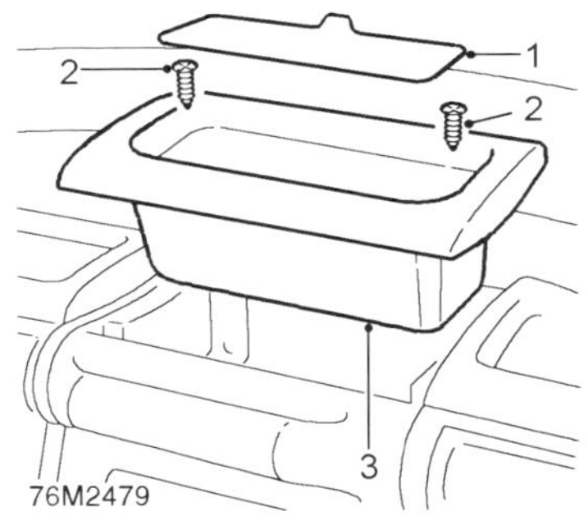

1. Remove mat from stowage box to access screws.
2. Remove 2 screws.
3. Remove stowage box form fascia.

Refit

1. Position stowage box and secure with screws.
2. Fit mat to stowage box.

CARPET - LOADSPACE

Service repair no - 76.49.04

Remove

1. Remove both rear quarter lower trim casings. ***See this section.***

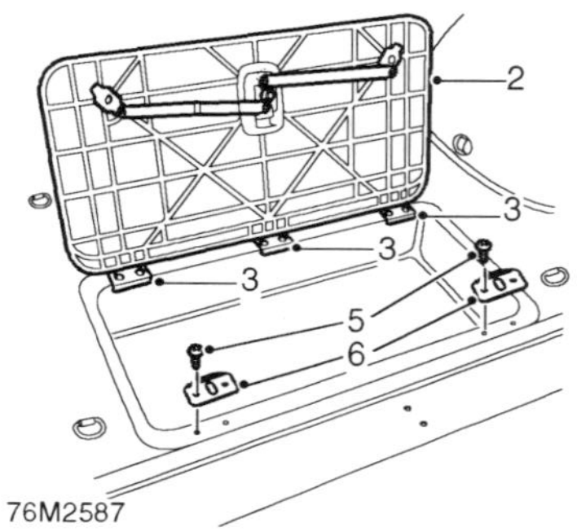

76M2587

2. Open lid on security box.
3. Remove 6 screws securing lid.
4. Remove lid.
5. Remove 4 screws securing lid latch strikers.
6. Remove both strikers.

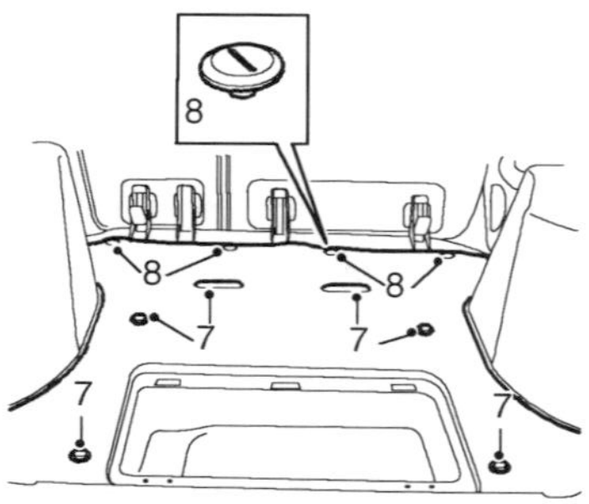

76M2588

7. Release carpet from rear seat strikers and lashing eyes.
8. Remove 4 buckles from rear carpet.
9. Remove carpet.

Refit

1. Position carpet in loadspace.
2. Fit buckles to rear carpet.
3. Fit lid latch strikers and secure with screws.
4. Fit lid and secure with screws.
5. Close lid.
6. Fit rear quarter lower trim casings. ***See this section.***

BODY

GLOVE BOX

Service repair no - 76.52.03

Remove

1. Open glove box lid.
2. Remove glove box mat.

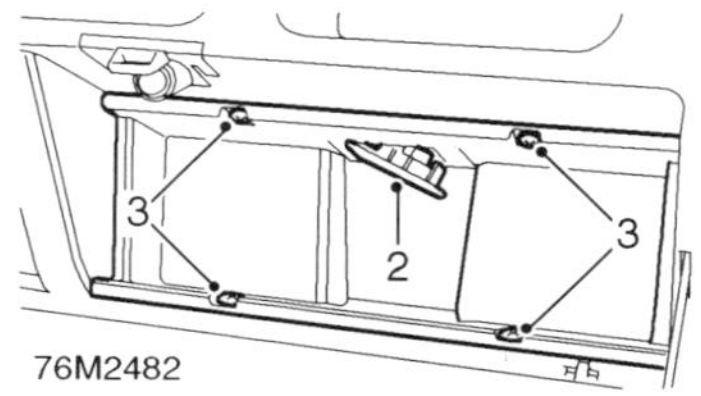

76M2482

3. Release illumination lamp from glove box.
4. Remove 4 screws and remove glove box.

Refit

1. Position glove box and tighten screws.
2. Position and secure illumination lamp.
3. Fit glove box mat.
4. Close glove box lid.

HEADLINING - 5 DOOR

Service repair no - 76.64.01
Service repair no - 76.64.15

Remove

1. Remove both A' post trims. ***See this section.***
2. Remove both rear quarter upper trim casings. ***See this section.***
3. Remove both sun visors. ***See this section.***

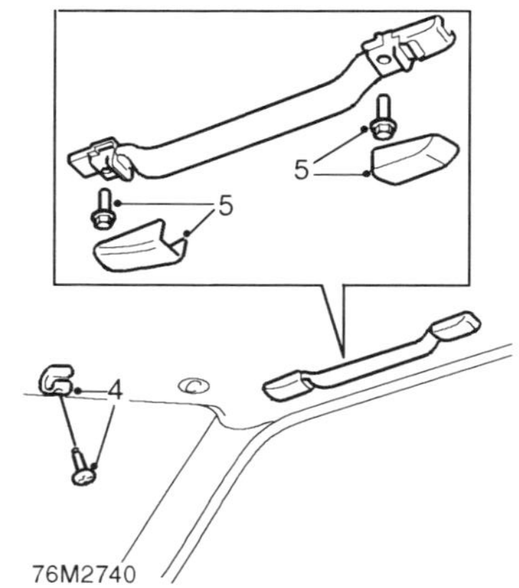

76M2740

4. Remove screw from each sun visor clip and collect clips.
5. Remove screw covers and screws from grab handles and remove grab handles.
6. Remove grab handle blanking plugs.

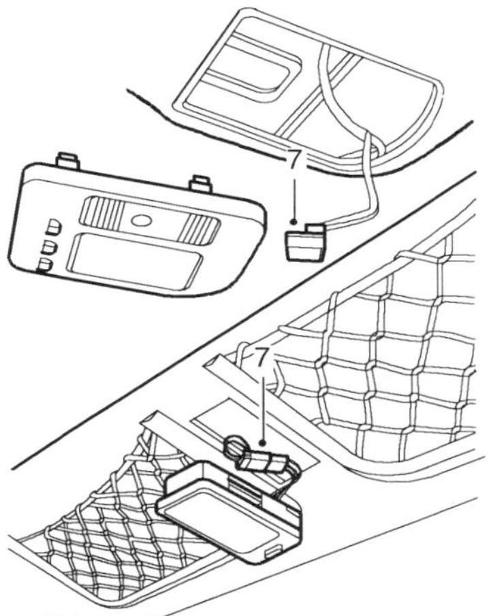

76M2741

7. Release roof lamps, disconnect multiplugs and remove roof lamps.

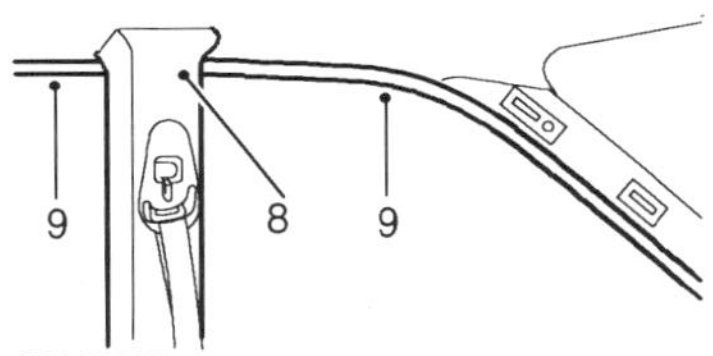

76M2742

8. Release both B/C' post upper finishers and position aside.
9. Release headlining from front and rear door aperture seals.

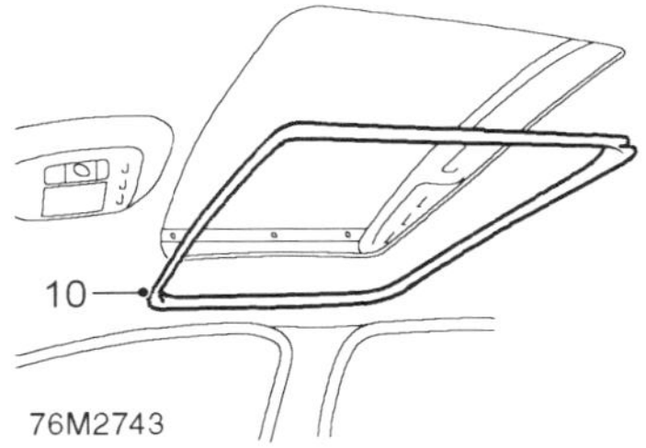

76M2743

Models with sun roof:

10. Release and remove sun roof surround finisher from sunroof aperture.

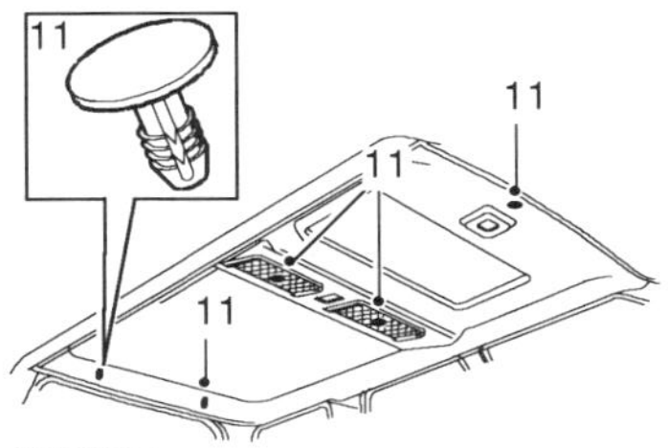

76M2744

All models:

11. Remove 5 retaining studs from headlining.
12. With assistance remove headlining through tail door.

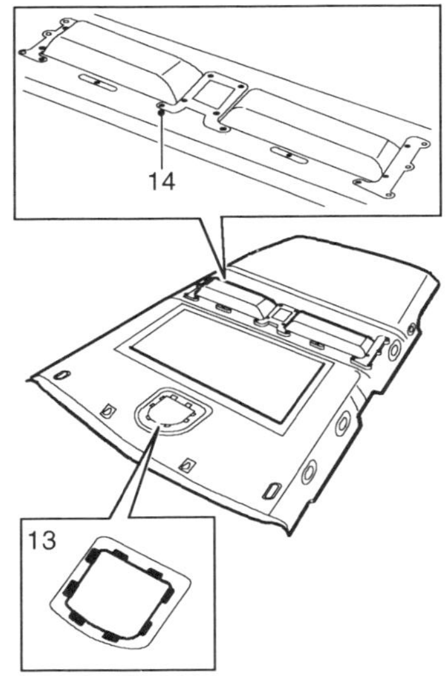

76M2745

Do not carry out further dismantling if component is removed for access only.

13. Release 8 tags securing front roof lamp support and remove support.
14. Remove 14 nuts from stowage pockets, collect backing plates and remove stowage pockets.
15. Position stowage pockets and backing plates on replacement headlining and secure with nuts.
16. Position roof lamp support on replacement headlining and secure retaining tags.

Refit

1. With assistance, position headlining and secure with retaining studs.

Models with sun roof:

2. Position sunroof surround finisher and secure in position.

All models:

3. Locate headlining to front and rear door aperture seals.
4. Fit and secure 'B/C' post upper finishers.
5. Connect multiplugs and fit roof lamps.
6. Fit grab handle blanking plugs.
7. Fit grab handles, tighten screws and fit screw covers.
8. Fit sun visor clips and tighten screws.
9. Fit both sun visors. ***See this section.***
10. Fit both 'A' post trims. ***See this section.***
11. Fit rear quarter upper trim casings. ***See this section.***

HEADLINING - 3 DOOR

Service repair no - 76.64.15

Remove

1. Fold front seat squabs forward.
2. Remove both sun visors. ***See this section.***
3. Remove both 'A' post trims. ***See this section.***

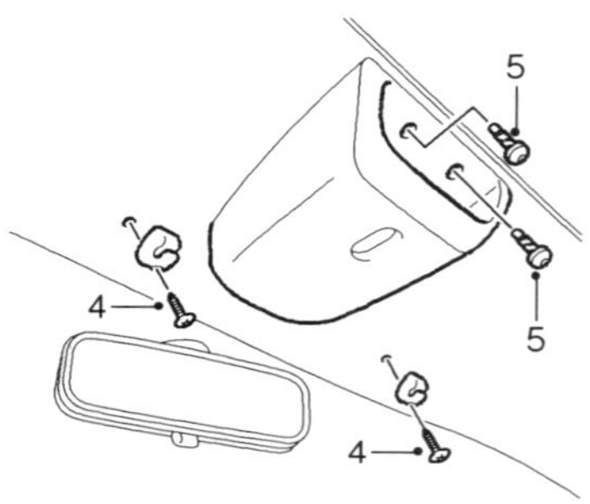

76M2721

4. Remove 2 screws from both sun visor clips and collect clips.
5. Remove 2 screws securing headlining to front end of roof panel.

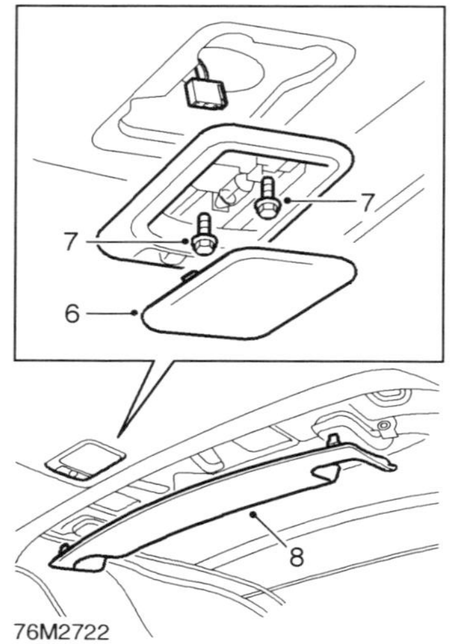

76M2722

6. Remove roof lamp lens.
7. Remove 2 screws, release roof lamp and disconnect multiplug.
8. Release headlining rear finisher from roof panel and remove finisher.

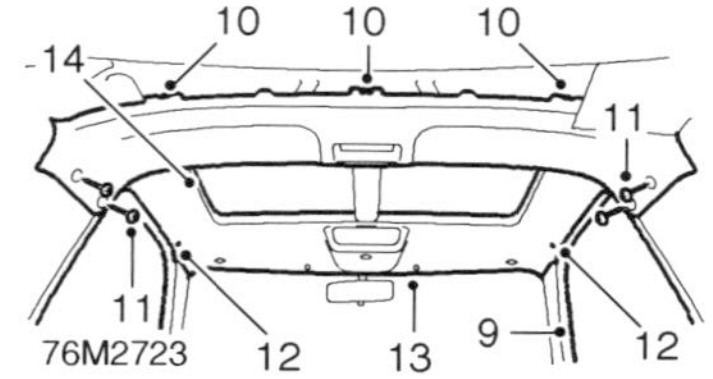

76M2723

9. Release door aperture seals to release headlining.
10. Release 3 studs securing rear edge of headlining to roof panel.
11. Remove 4 screws securing headlining to 'B' posts.
12. Release 2 studs at LH and RH side of headlining.
13. Lower front edge of headlining.
14. Release sun roof seal and remove headlining.

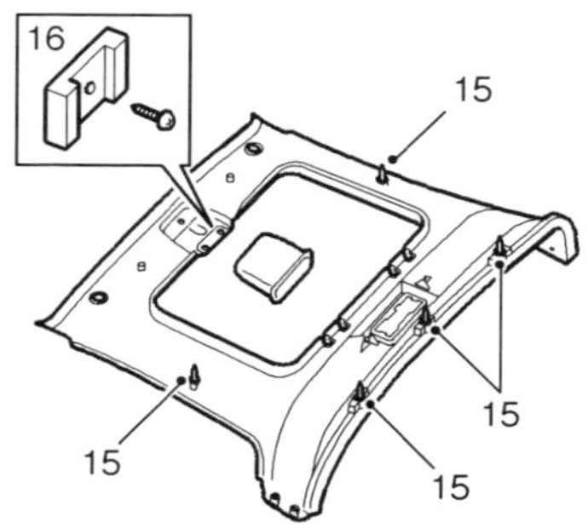

76M2724

15. Remove studs from headlining.
16. Remove 3 screws and remove pocket from headlining.

Refit

1. Fit pocket to headlining and secure with screws.
2. Fit studs to headlining.
3. Position headlining and secure studs to roof panel.
4. Fit and tighten screws to 'B' posts and roof panel.
5. Secure headlining behind rear vent rubbers.
6. Fit headlining rear finisher.
7. Refit door aperture seals.
8. Position sun roof seal to headlining.
9. Position roof lamp and connect multiplug.
10. Tighten roof lamp screws and fit lens.
11. Position sun visor clips and tighten screws.
12. Fit sun visors. ***See this section.***
13. Fit both 'A' post finishers. ***See this section.***
14. Reposition front seat squabs.

SEAT - FRONT

Service repair no - 78.10.44/99

WARNING: *See GENERAL INFORMATION, SRS Precautions.*

Remove

1. Make the SRS system safe. ***See GENERAL INFORMATION, SRS Precautions.***
2. Remove seat base finisher. ***See this section.***

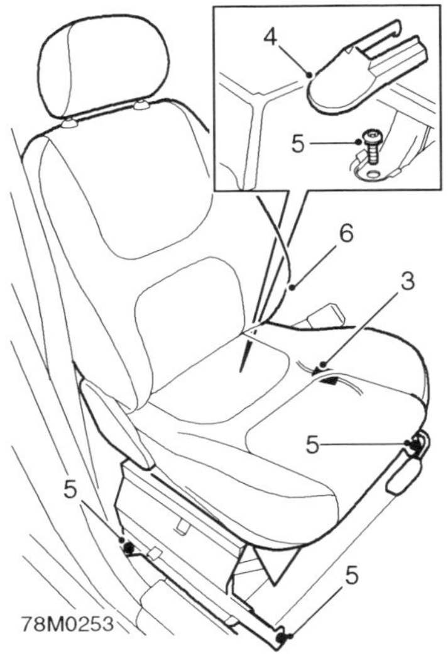

3. Release pretensioner multiplug from seat frame. Disconnect pretensioner multiplug.
4. Remove cover from rear securing bolt.
5. Remove 4 Torx screws securing seat.
6. Remove seat.

Refit

1. Position seat and secure with screws. Tighten screws to 45 Nm.
2. Fit cover to rear bolt.
3. Connect pretensioner multiplug. Secure pretensioner multiplug to seat frame.
4. Fit seat base finisher. ***See this section.***

SEAT - RH REAR - 5 DOOR

Service repair no - 78.10.49/99

Remove

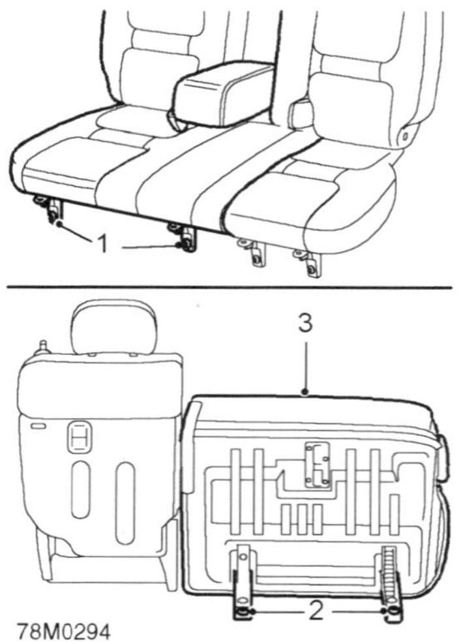

78M0294

1. Release carpet from heel board and remove 2 Torx bolts from seat hinges.
2. Fold seat forward and remove 2 Torx bolts from seat hinges.
3. Remove seat.

Refit

1. Position seat in vehicle and align hinges.
2. Fit Torx bolts to seat hinges. Tighten Torx bolts to 25 Nm.
3. Lower seat.
4. Fit Torx bolts to heel board. Tighten Torx bolts to 25 Nm.
5. Reposition carpet.

CUSHION AND SQUAB - REAR SEAT - 3 DOOR

Service repair no - 78.10.57/99

Remove

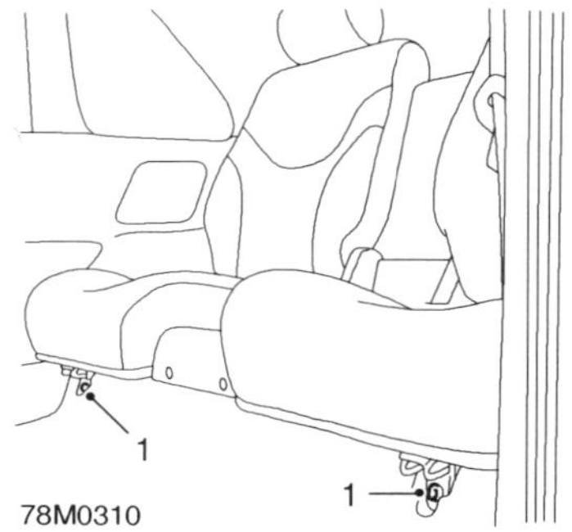

78M0310

1. Remove 2 Torx bolts securing seat to heel board.

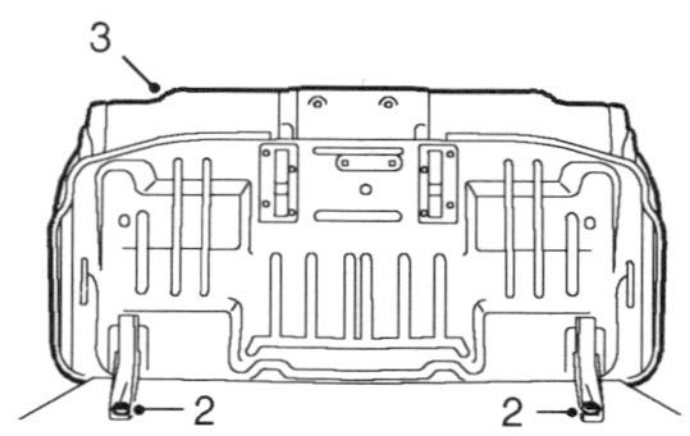

78M0311

2. Fold seat forward and remove 2 Torx bolts from seat hinges.
3. With assistance, remove seat.

Refit

1. With assistance, position seat in vehicle and align hinges.
2. Fit Torx bolts and lower seat. Tighten Torx bolts to 25 Nm.
3. Fit Torx bolts to heel board. Tighten Torx bolts to 25 Nm.

CUSHION COVER - FRONT SEAT

Service repair no - 78.30.01

Remove

1. Remove front seat. ***See this section.***

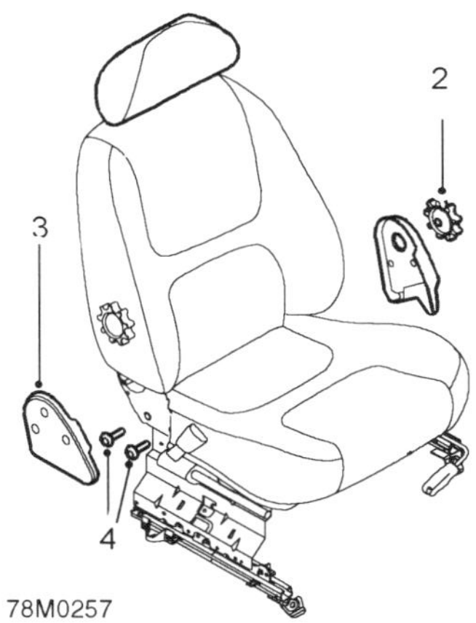

78M0257

2. Remove recline control knob.
3. Release retaining studs from side covers and remove covers.
4. Remove 4 Torx bolts from squab frame and remove squab frame from cushion frame.

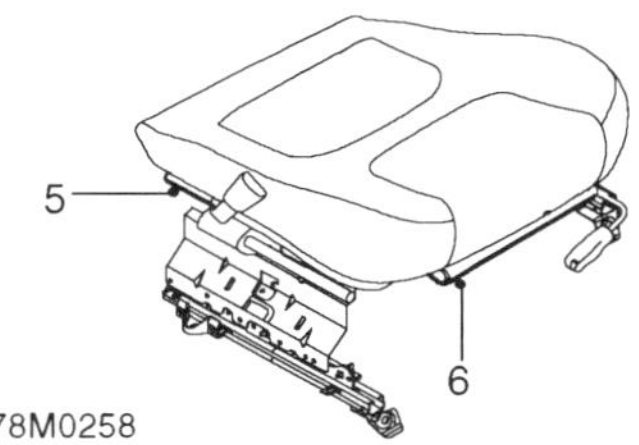

78M0258

5. Release sides of cushion cover from frame.
6. Release front of cushion cover from frame.

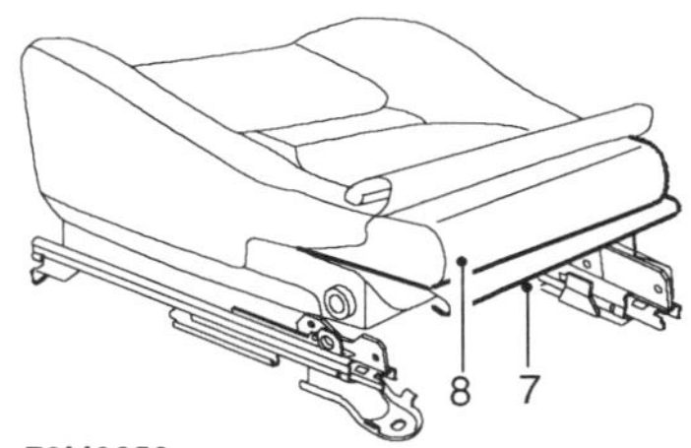

78M0259

7. Release rear of cushion cover from frame.
8. Release rear of cushion pad from frame.
9. Remove cushion cover and pad.

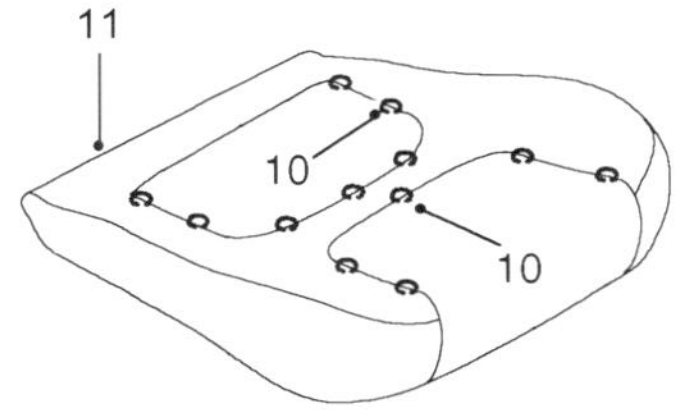

78M0260

10. Remove and discard 12 hog rings holding cushion cover to cushion pad.
11. Remove cushion cover.

Refit

1. Position cushion cover to pad.
2. Pull cover into position and secure with NEW hog rings.
3. Position cushion cover and pad and secure to frame.
4. Fit squab frame to cushion frame and tighten Torx bolts to 45 Nm .
5. Fit side covers and secure retaining studs.
6. Fit recline control knob.
7. Fit front seat. ***See this section.***

CUSHION COVER - RH REAR SEAT - 5 DOOR

Service repair no - 78.40.04

Remove

1. Remove RH rear seat. ***See this section.***

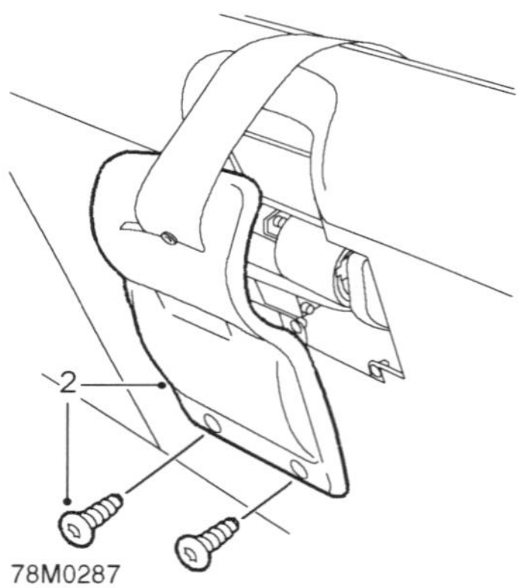

78M0287

2. Remove 2 screws and remove seat belt reel cover.

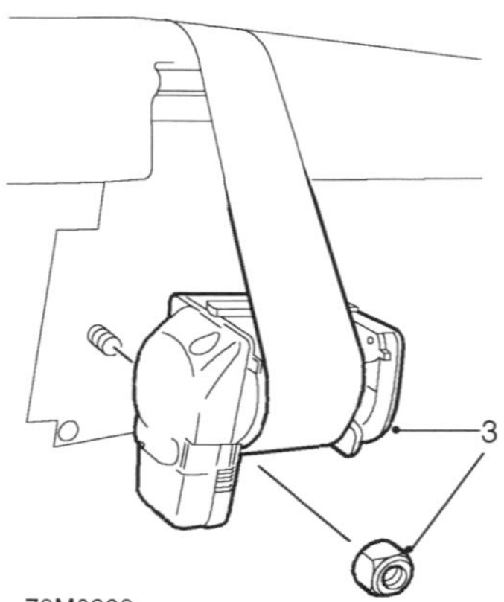

78M0268

3. Remove nut and release seat belt belt reel.

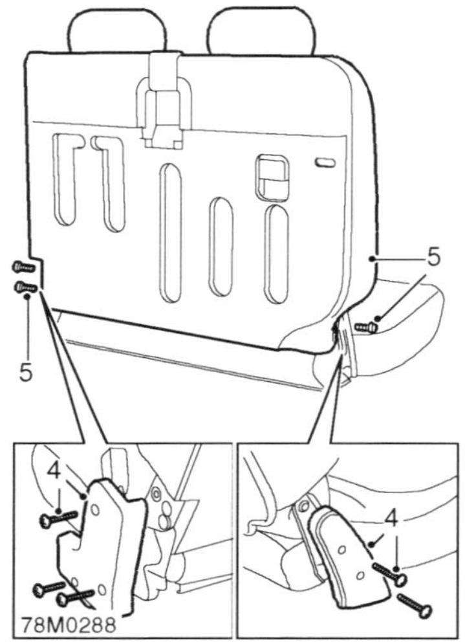

78M0288

4. Remove 5 screws and remove both end covers.
5. Remove 3 Torx bolts and remove squab from cushion.

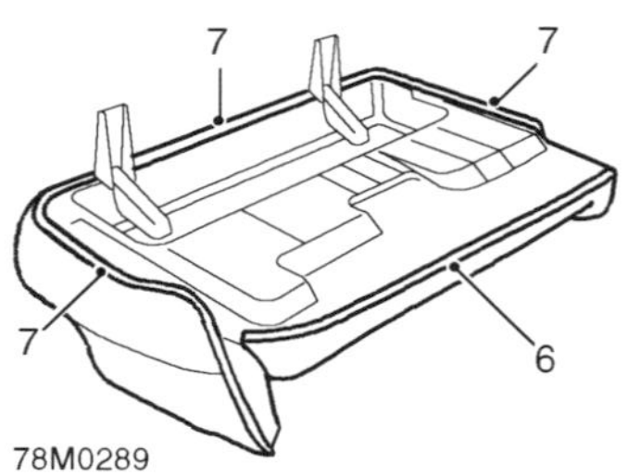

78M0289

6. Release rear of cushion cover from frame.
7. Release sides and front of cushion cover from frame.
8. Release cover and pad from frame.

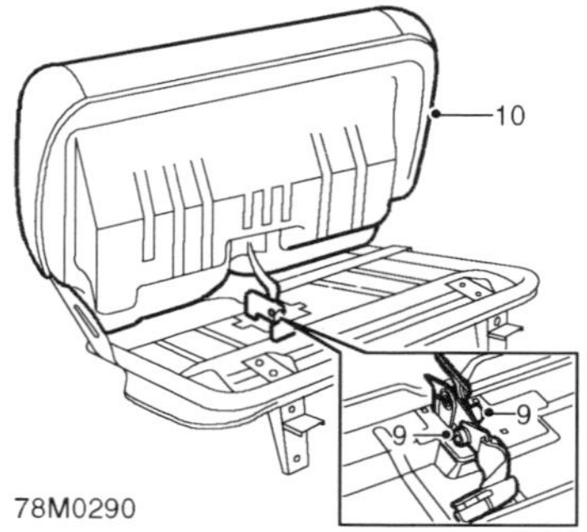

78M0290

9. Remove 2 Torx bolts from seat belt/seat belt buckle. Remove seat belt/seat belt buckle from frame.
10. Remove cover and pad from frame.

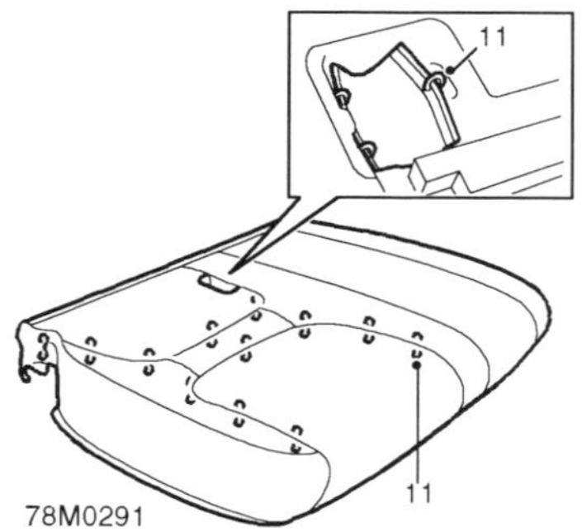

78M0291

11. Remove and discard 17 hog rings and remove cover from pad.

Refit

1. Position cover to pad and secure with NEW hog rings.
2. Position seat belt/seat belt buckle on frame and tighten Torx bolts to 32 Nm.
3. Fit cover and pad to frame.
4. Fit front and sides of cushion cover to frame.
5. Fit rear of cushion cover to frame.
6. Fit cushion to squab and tighten Torx bolts.
7. Fit end covers and tighten screws.
8. Position seat belt reel in seat squab and tighten nut to 32 Nm.
9. Fit seat belt reel cover and tighten screws.
10. Fit rear seat. ***See this section.***

CUSHION COVER - REAR SEAT - 3 DOOR

Service repair no - 78.40.05

Remove

1. Remove rear seat assembly. ***See this section.***

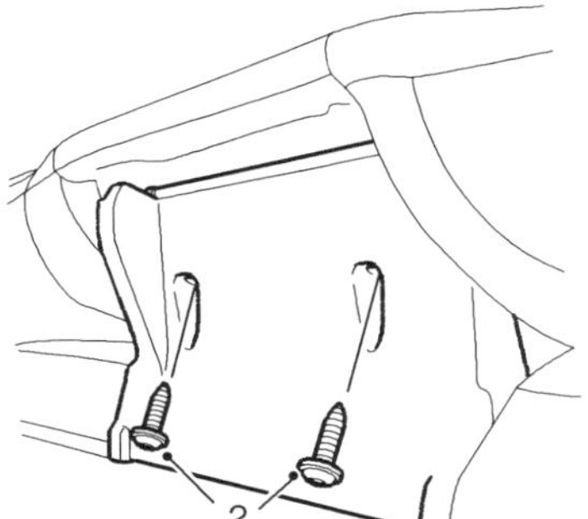

78M0300

2. Remove 2 screws securing console cover and remove cover.

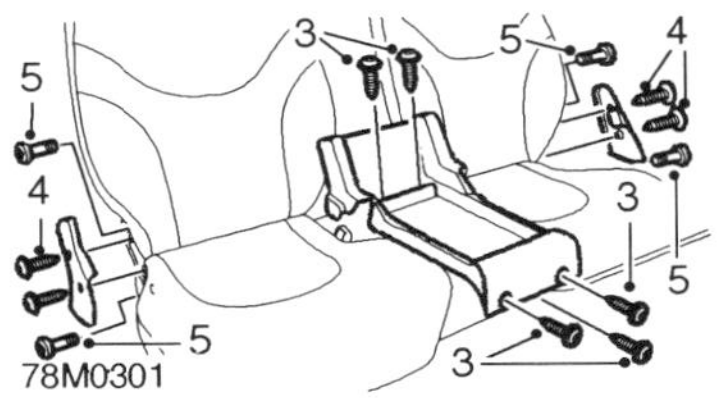

78M0301

3. Remove 4 screws securing rear seat console and remove console.
4. Remove 4 screws securing end covers and remove covers.
5. Remove 4 Torx bolts and remove squab assembly from cushion assembly.

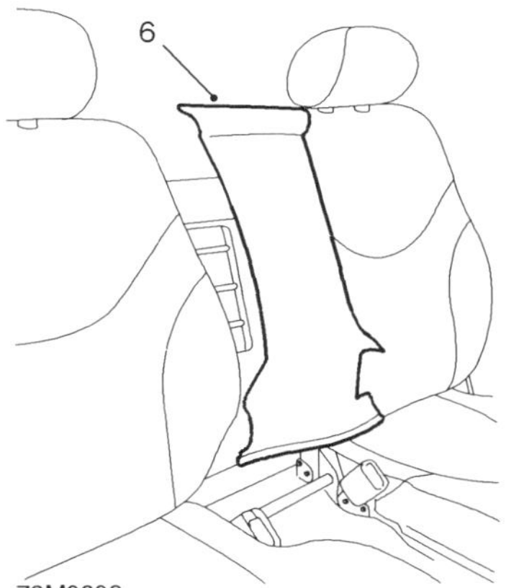

78M0302

6. Release back board assembly from squab frame and remove back board.

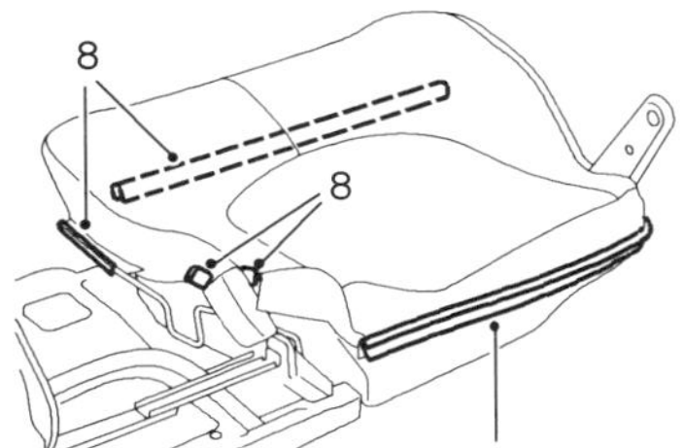

78M0303

7. Release rear of cushion cover from frame.
8. Release sides and front of cushion cover from frame.

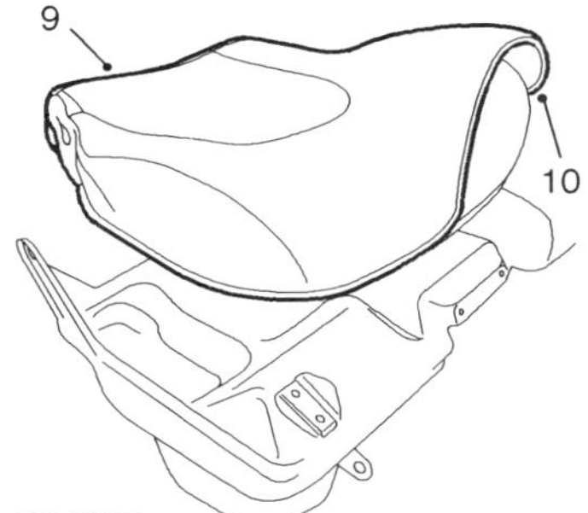

78M0304

9. Remove cover and pad from frame.
10. Release cushion cover from pad.

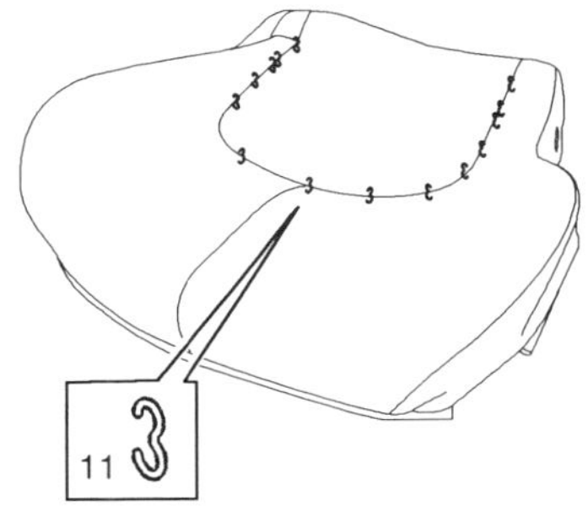

78M0305

11. Remove and discard 13 hog rings and remove cover from pad.

Refit

1. Position cover to pad and secure with NEW hog rings.
2. Fit cover to pad.
3. Position cover and pad and secure to frame.
4. Fit cushion to squab and tighten Torx bolts to 28 Nm.
5. Position back board and secure to frame.
6. Fit end covers and tighten screws.
7. Position rear seat console, fit and tighten screws.
8. Position console cover, fit and tighten screws.
9. Fit rear seat. ***See this section.***

CUSHION COVER - LH REAR SEAT - 5 DOOR

Service repair no - 78.40.05

Remove

1. Remove LH rear seat. ***See this section.***

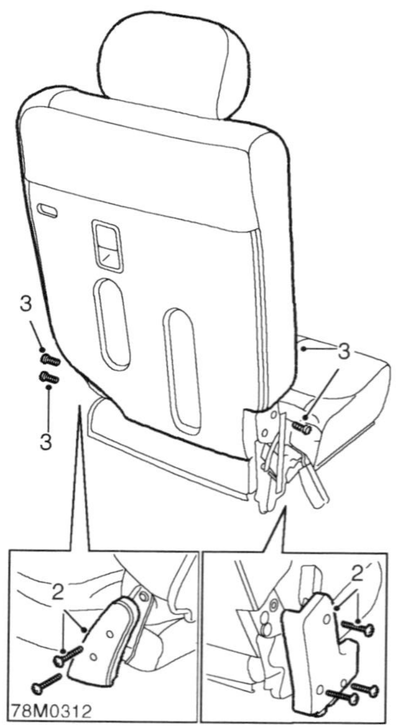

78M0312

2. Remove 5 screws and remove both end covers.
3. Remove 3 Torx bolts and remove squab from cushion.

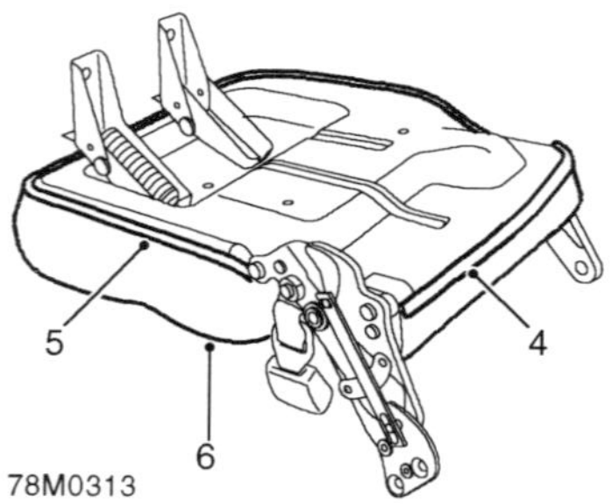

78M0313

4. Release rear of cushion cover from frame.
5. Release sides and front of cushion cover from frame.
6. Remove cover and pad from frame.

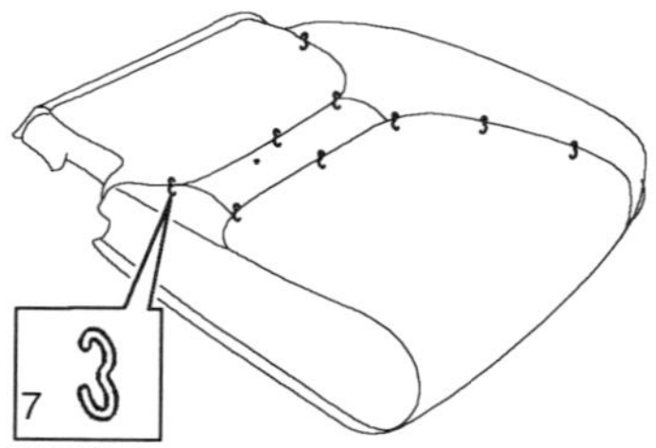

78M0314

7. Remove and discard 16 hog rings and remove cover from pad.

Refit

1. Position cover to pad and secure with NEW hog rings.
2. Fit cover and pad to frame.
3. Fit front and sides of cushion cover to frame.
4. Fit rear of cushion cover to frame.
5. Fit cushion to squab and tighten Torx bolts to 28 Nm.
6. Fit end covers and tighten screws.
7. Fit rear seat. ***See this section.***

FINISHER - SEAT BASE - FRONT SEAT

Service repair no - 78.55.01

Remove

1. Remove front seat cushion side finisher. ***See this section.***

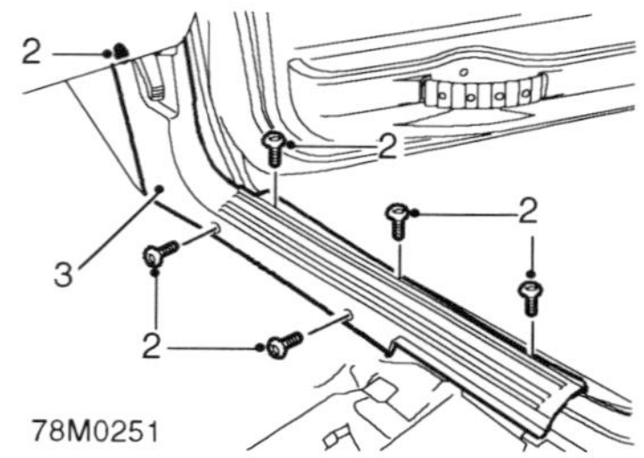

78M0251

2. Remove scrivet and 5 Torx screws from carpet retainer.
3. Remove front carpet retainer.

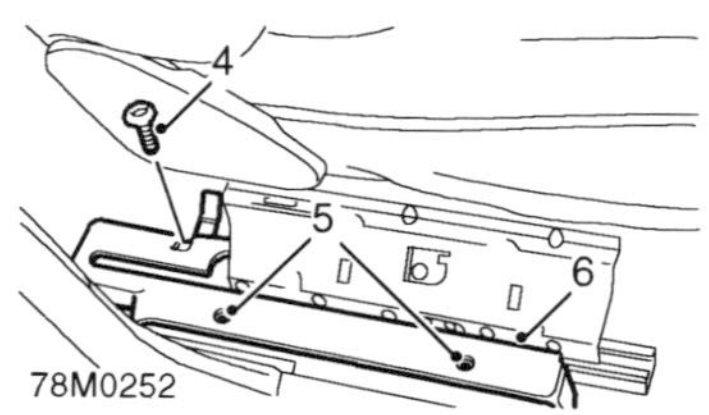

78M0252

4. Release cover to access Torx screw under front seat, remove Torx screw.
5. Remove 2 Torx screws securing finisher to seat runner.
6. Remove finisher.

Refit

1. Position finisher to seat runner.
2. Fit and tighten Torx screws.
3. Fit and tighten Torx screw under front seat and close cover.
4. Fit front carpet retainer and secure with scrivet and Torx screws.
5. Fit front seat cushion side finisher. ***See this section.***

FINISHER - CUSHION SIDE - FRONT SEAT

Service repair no - 78.55.06

Remove

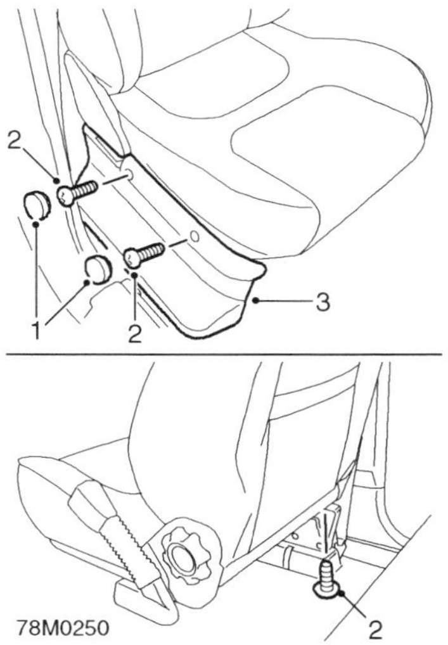

78M0250

1. Remove 2 covers to access screws.
2. Remove 3 screws securing finisher.
3. Release catches at front and side of seat and remove finisher.

Refit

1. Position finisher to seat, locate catches, fit and tighten securing screws.
2. Fit screw covers.

LUMBAR SUPPORT - FRONT SEAT

Service repair no - 78.60.07

Remove

1. Remove front seat. ***See this section.***

78M0254

2. Release and remove head restraint.
3. Remove recline control knob.
4. Release retaining studs from side covers and remove covers.
5. Remove 4 Torx bolts from squab frame and remove squab frame from cushion frame.
6. Remove lumbar control knob.

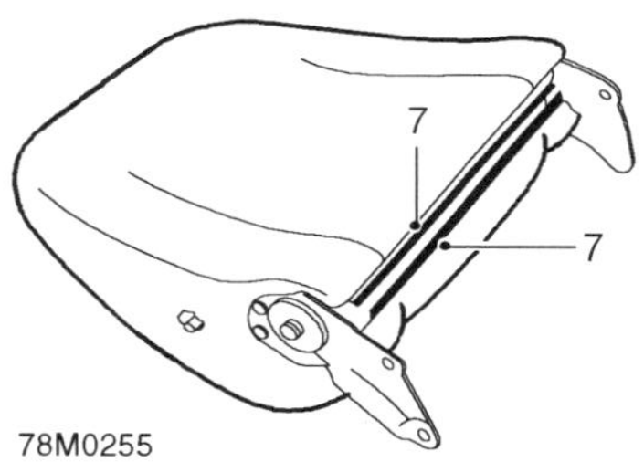

78M0255

7. Release squab cover at base of seat frame.

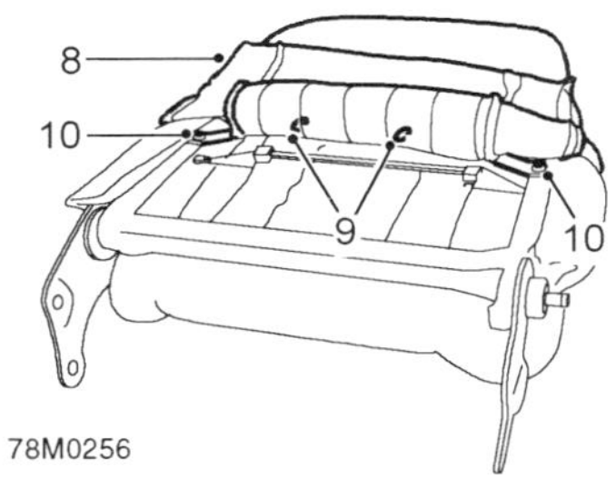

78M0256

8. Release squab cover from squab frame and squab pad.
9. Remove and discard 2 hog rings from rear of cover.
10. Drill out 2 pop rivet from squab frame.

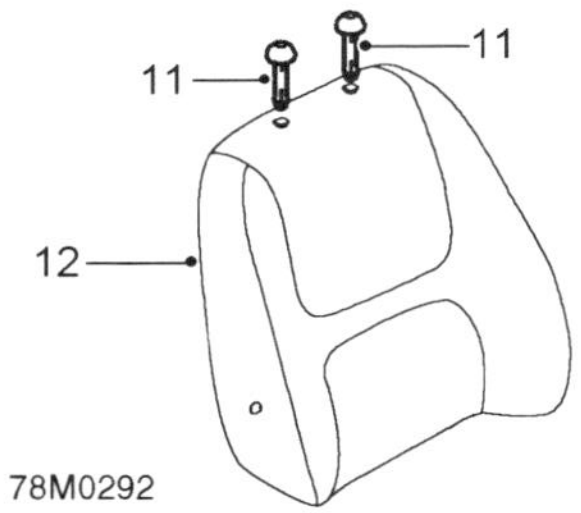

78M0292

11. Remove head restraint guide tubes.
12. Remove squab cover and pad.

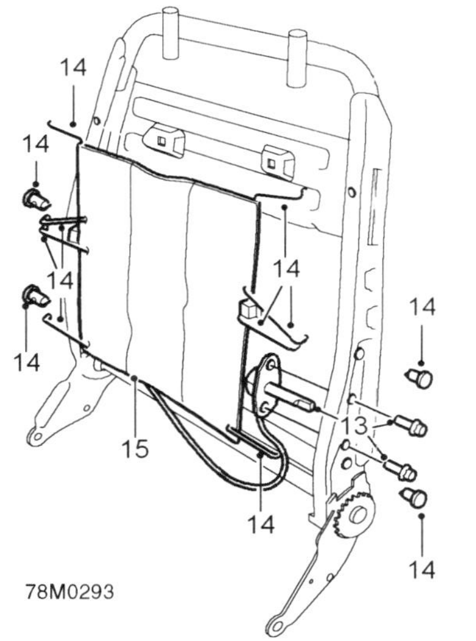

78M0293

13. Remove 2 bolts from cable control and release cable control.
14. Release 8 lumbar support retainers from squab frame and collect 4 hook retainers
15. Remove lumbar support mechanism.

Refit

1. Position lumbar support to squab frame, locate hook retainers.
2. Fit lumbar support retainers to squab frame.
3. Position cable control and tighten bolts.
4. Fit squab cover and pad to frame.
5. Fit head restraint guide tubes.
6. Fit new hog rings to rear of cover.
7. Position straps and secure with pop rivets.
8. Fit squab cover to squab pad and frame.
9. Secure squab cover at base of frame.
10. Fit lumbar support control knob.
11. Fit squab frame to cushion frame and tighten Torx bolts to 45 Nm.
12. Fit side covers and secure retaining studs.
13. Fit head restraint.
14. Fit recline control knob.
15. Fit front seat. ***See this section.***

LATCH ASSEMBLY - REAR SQUAB - RH

Service repair no - 78.80.05

Remove

1. Remove rear seat squab cover. ***See this section.***

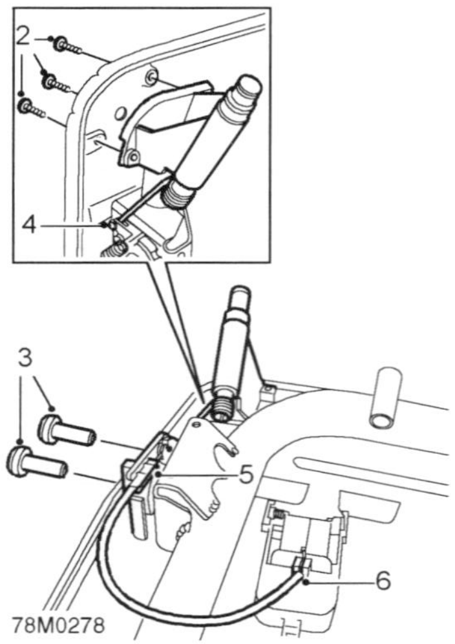

78M0278

2. Remove 3 screws from lock button.
3. Remove 2 Torx screws from squab lock.
4. Release lock button from lock.
5. Release cable from abutment and remove from lock.
6. Release cable from lever abutment and remove from lever.

Refit

1. Position cable to lever and locate in abutment.
2. Fit cable to lock and locate in abutment.
3. Fit lock button to lock.
4. Fit Torx screws to squab lock and tighten to 20 Nm. .
5. Fit screws to lock button.
6. Fit squab cover. ***See this section.***

LATCH ASSEMBLY - REAR SQUAB - LH

Service repair no - 78.80.16

Remove

1. Remove rear seat squab cover. ***See this section.***

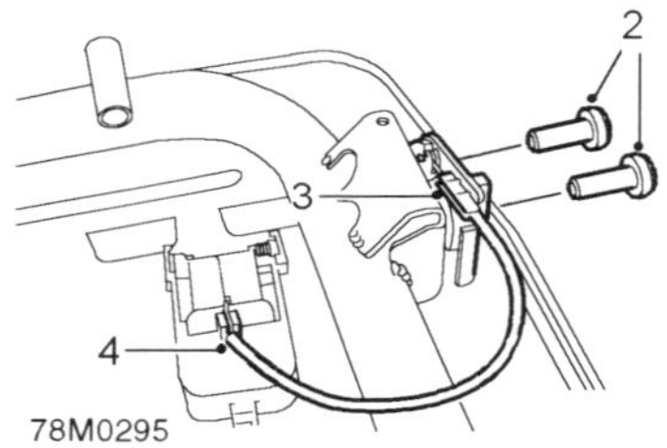

78M0295

2. Remove 2 Torx screws from squab lock.
3. Release cable from abutment and remove from lock.
4. Release cable from lever abutment and remove from lever.

Refit

1. Position cable to lever and locate in abutment.
2. Fit cable to lock and locate in abutment.
3. Fit and tighten Torx screws to lock.
4. Fit squab cover. ***See this section.***

SQUAB COVER - FRONT SEAT

Service repair no - 78.90.08

Remove

1. Remove front seat. ***See this section.***

78M0254

2. Release and remove head restraint.
3. Remove recline control knob.
4. Release retaining studs from side covers and remove covers.
5. Remove 4 Torx bolts from squab frame and remove squab frame from cushion frame.
6. Remove lumbar control knob.

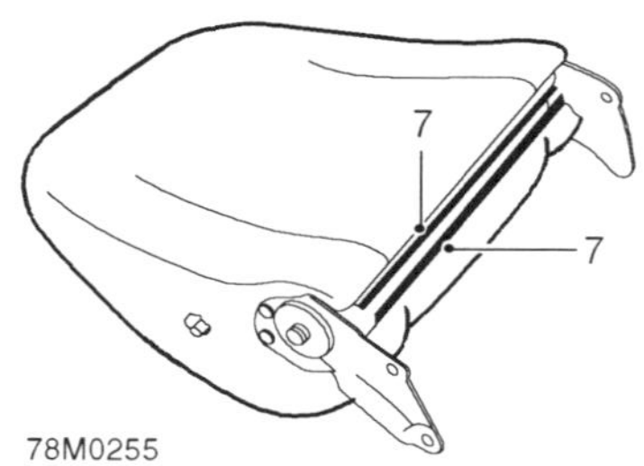

78M0255

7. Release squab cover at base of seat frame.

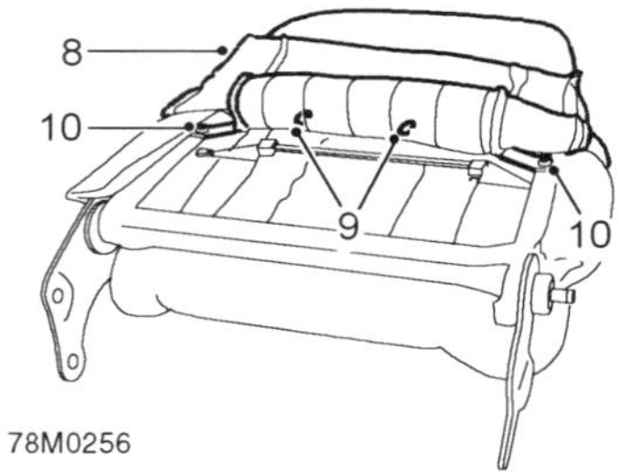

78M0256

8. Release squab cover from squab frame and squab pad.
9. Remove and discard 2 hog rings from rear of cover.
10. Drill out 2 pop rivet from squab frame.

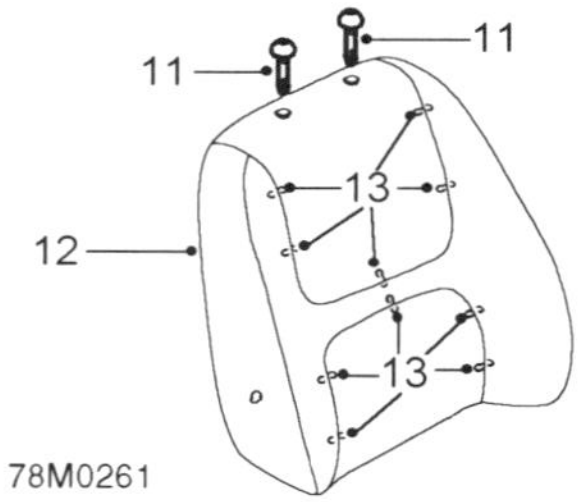

78M0261

11. Remove head restraint guide tubes.
12. Remove squab cover and pad from frame.
13. Remove and discard 10 hog rings holding cover to squab pad.
14. Remove squab cover.

Refit

1. Position squab cover to pad.
2. Pull cover into position and secure with NEW hog rings.
3. Fit squab cover and pad to frame.
4. Fit head restraint guide tubes.
5. Fit NEW hog rings to rear of cover.
6. Position straps and secure with pop rivets.
7. Fit squab cover to squab pad and squab frame.
8. Secure squab cover at base of squab frame.
9. Fit lumbar support control knob.
10. Fit squab frame to cushion frame and tighten Torx bolts to 45 Nm.
11. Fit side covers and secure retaining studs.
12. Fit recline control knob.
13. Fit head restraint.
14. Fit front seat. ***See this section.***

SQUAB COVER - REAR SEAT - 3 DOOR

Service repair no - 78.90.12

Remove

1. Remove rear seat assembly. ***See this section.***

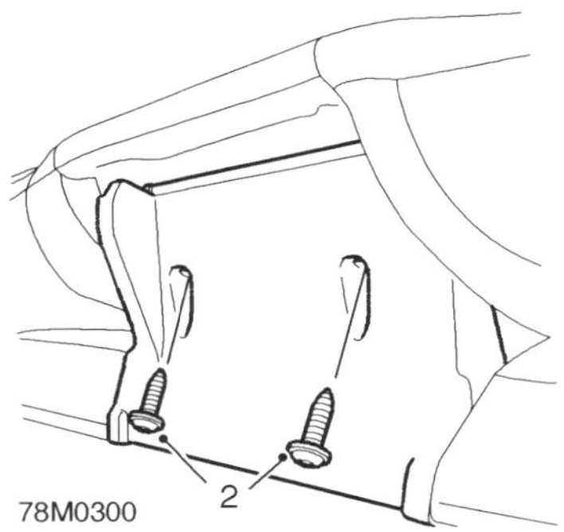

78M0300

2. Remove 2 screws securing console cover and remove cover.

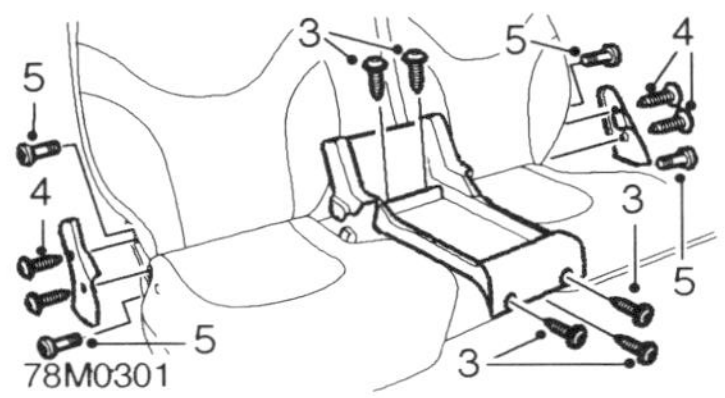

78M0301

3. Remove 4 screws securing rear seat console and remove console.
4. Remove 4 screws securing end covers and remove covers.
5. Remove 4 Torx bolts and remove squab assembly from cushion assembly.

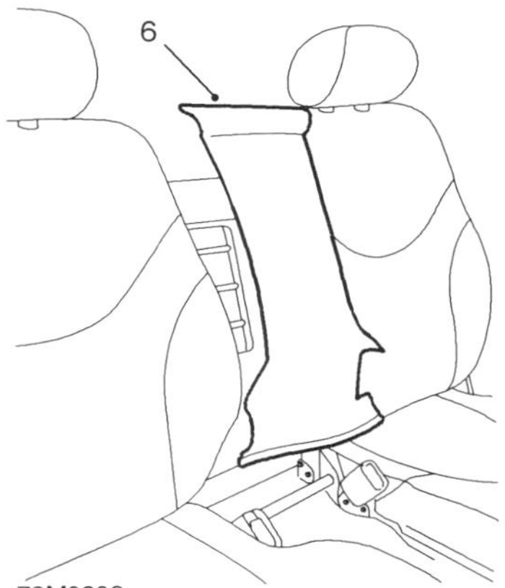

78M0302

6. Release back board assembly from squab frame and remove back board.

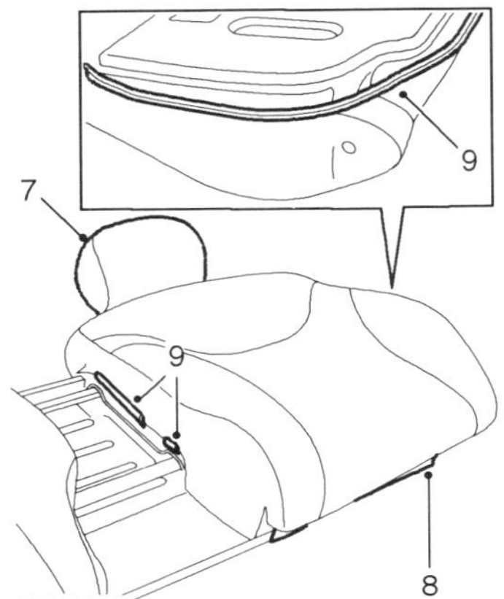

78M0306

7. Remove head restraint.
8. Release bottom of squab cover from frame.
9. Release sides of squab cover from frame.

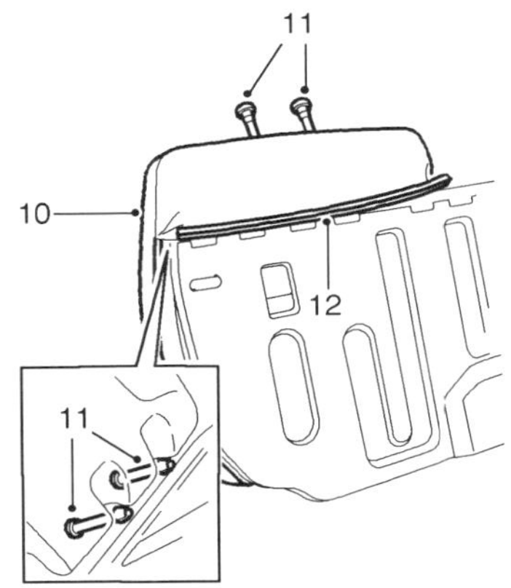

78M0307

10. Raise cover and pad to access head restraint guide tubes.
11. Remove guide tubes.
12. Release cover from top of frame.

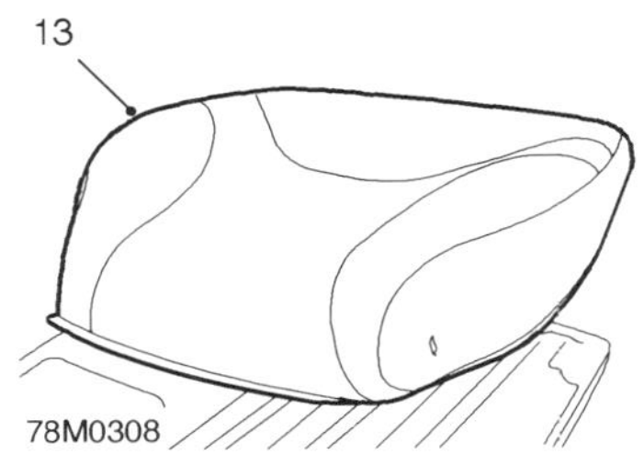

78M0308

13. Remove cover and pad.

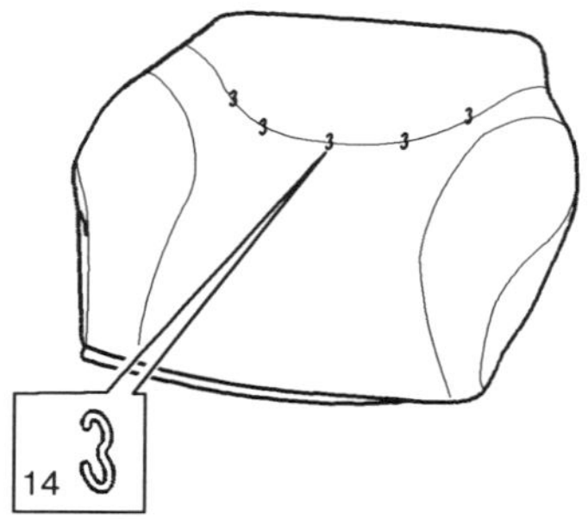

78M0309

14. Release cover from pad, remove and discard 5 Hog rings.
15. Remove cover from pad.

Refit

1. Locate cover to pad and secure with NEW hog rings.
2. Fit cover to pad.
3. Secure cover to top of frame.
4. Fit guide tubes.
5. Secure sides and bottom of cover to frame.
6. Fit head restraint
7. Fit cushion to squab and tighten Torx bolts to 28 Nm.
8. Position back board and secure to frame.
9. Fit end covers and tighten screws.
10. Position rear seat console, fit and tighten screws.
11. Position console cover, fit and tighten screws.
12. Fit rear seat. ***See this section.***

SQUAB COVER - LH REAR SEAT - 5 DOOR

Service repair no - 78.90.12

Remove

1. Fold LH rear seat forward.

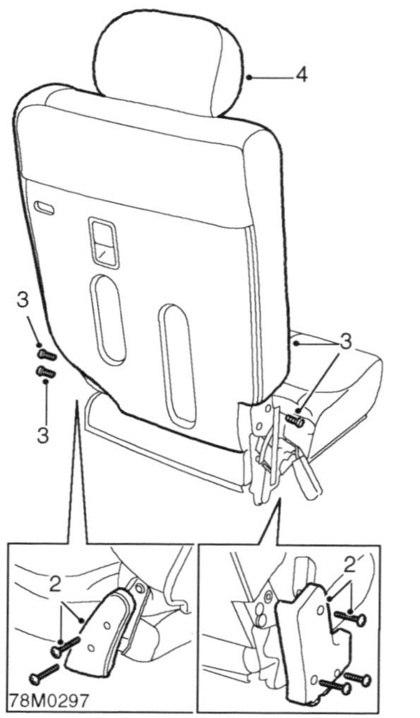

2. Remove 5 screws from end covers and remove covers.
3. Remove 3 bolts from seat squab and remove squab from cushion.
4. Remove head restraint.

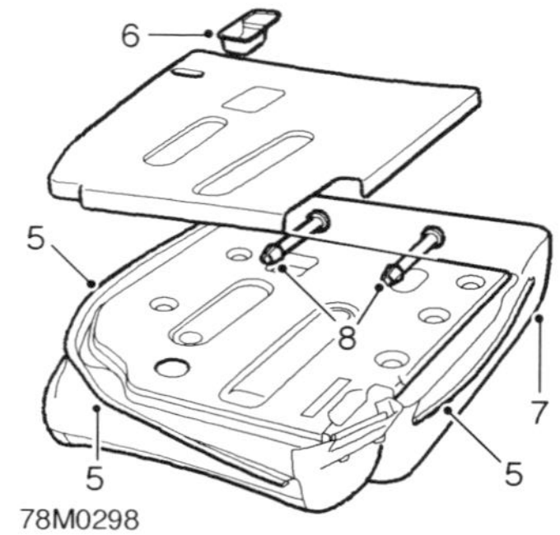

78M0298

5. Release squab from sides and bottom of frame.
6. Release latch escutcheon and remove seat frame back cloth.
7. Release cover from rear of frame.
8. Release and remove 2 head restraint guide tubes.
9. Remove cover and pad from frame.

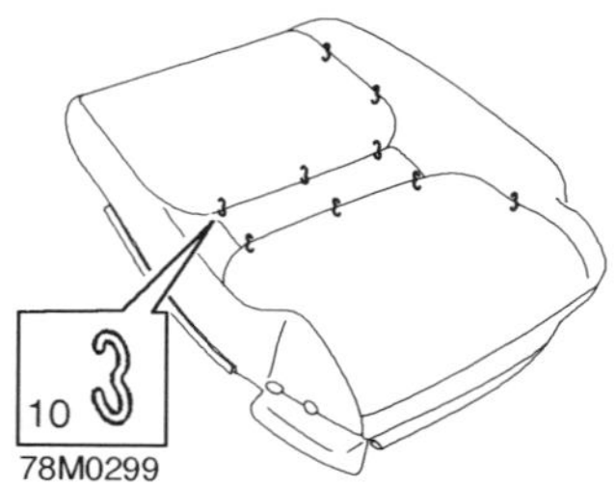

78M0299

10. Remove 9 hog rings and remove cover from pad.

Refit

1. Position latch escutcheon to back cloth and fit to frame. Ensure that latch escutcheon is secured correctly into latch housing.
2. Position squab cover to pad and secure hog rings.
3. Fit cover and pad to squab frame.
4. Fit head restraint guide tubes.
5. Fit cover to sides and bottom of frame.
6. Fit cover to rear of frame .
7. Fit head restraint.
8. Fit squab to cushion and tighten bolts.
9. Fit side covers and tighten screws.
10. Secure rear seat in locked position.

SQUAB COVER - RH REAR SEAT - 5 DOOR

Service repair no - 78.90.13

Remove

1. Fold RH rear seat forward.

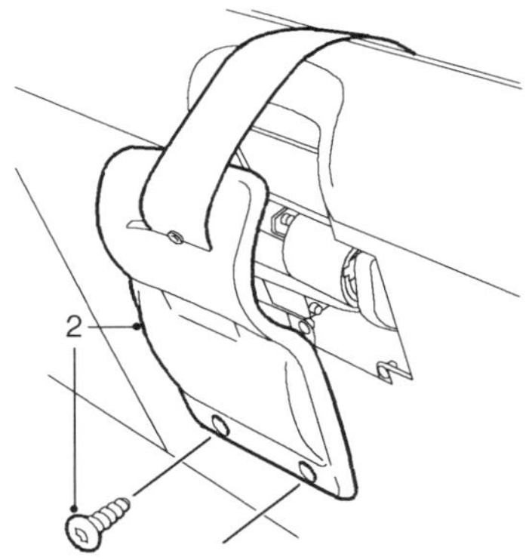

78M0267

2. Remove 2 screws from seat belt reel cover and remove cover.

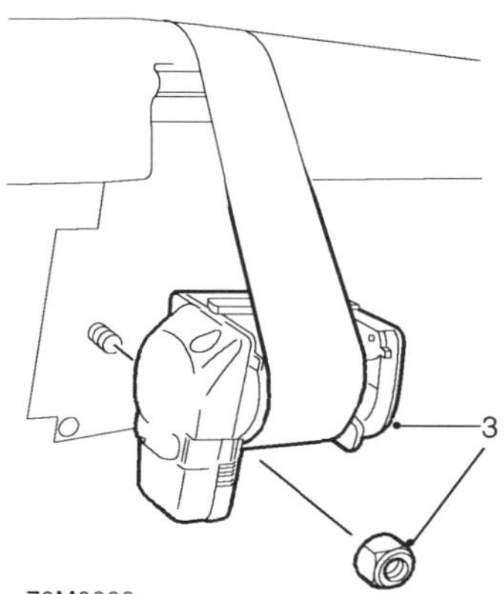

78M0268

3. Remove nut from seat belt reel, release reel and position aside.

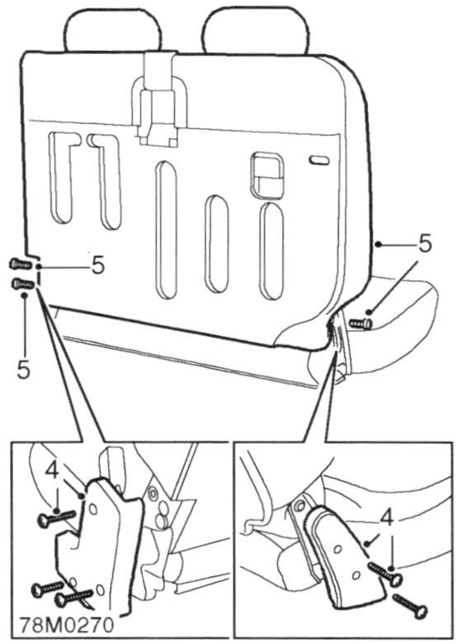

78M0270

4. Remove 5 screws from end covers and remove covers.
5. Remove 3 bolts from seat squab and remove squab from cushion.

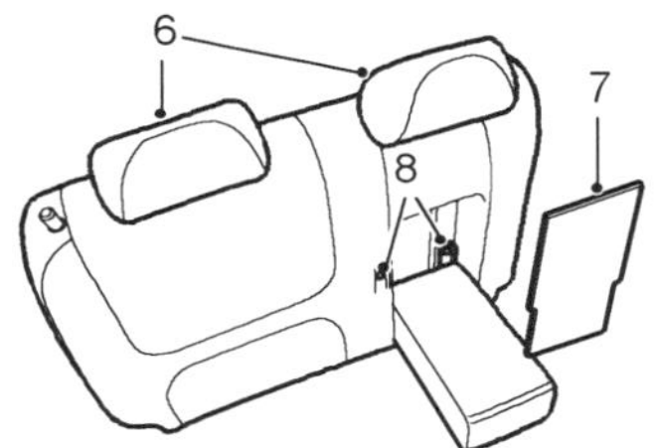

78M0269

6. Remove both head restraints.
7. Remove arm rest aperture trim.
8. Remove 2 screws from arm rest and remove arm rest.

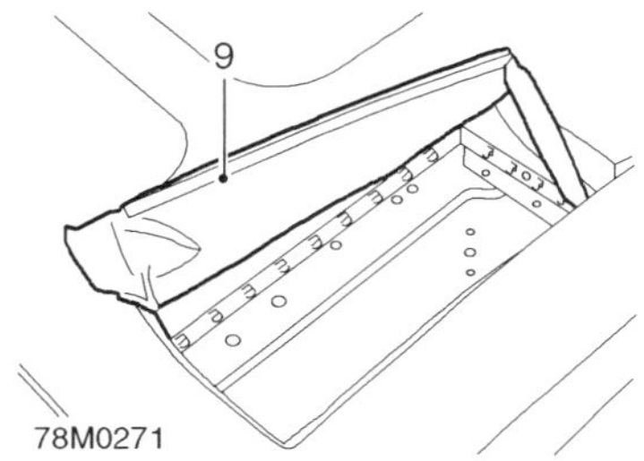

78M0271

9. Release squab from arm rest aperture.

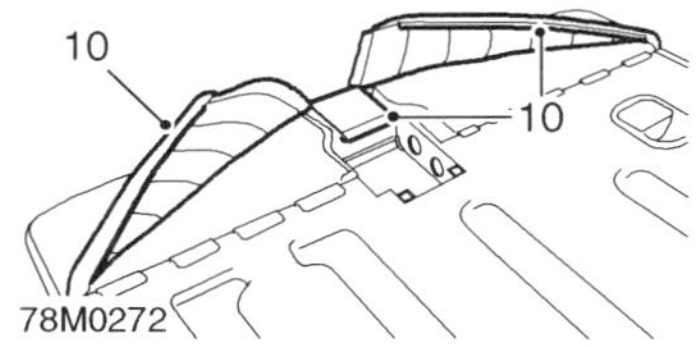

78M0272

10. Release squab from seat belt aperture and from rear of frame.

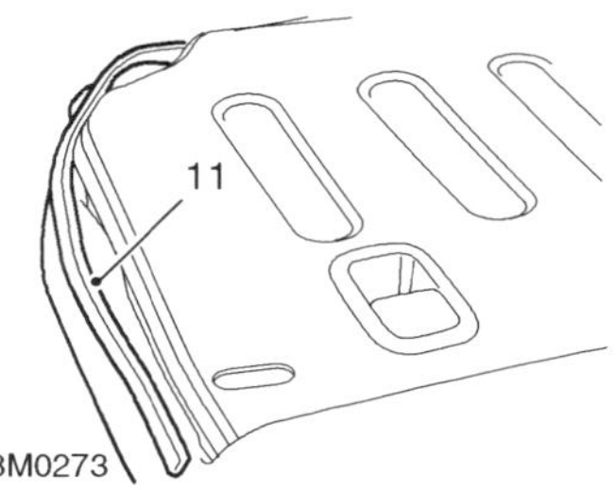

78M0273

11. Release squab from sides and bottom of frame. Release latch escutcheon and remove back cloth.

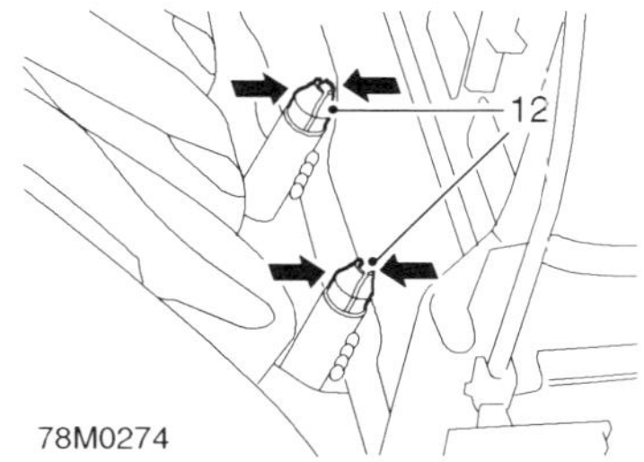

78M0274

12. Release and remove 4 head restraint guide tubes.

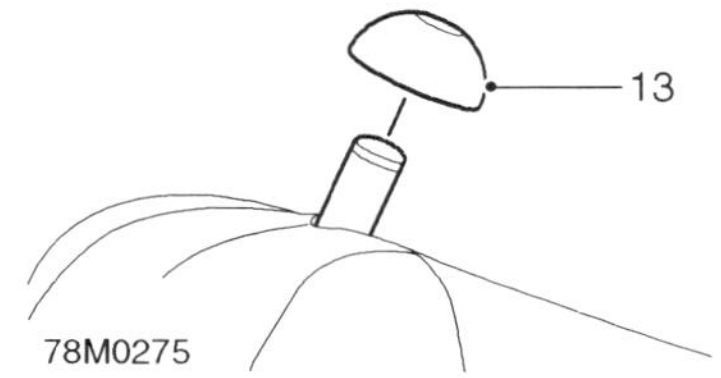

78M0275

13. Release squab lock warning button escutcheon.

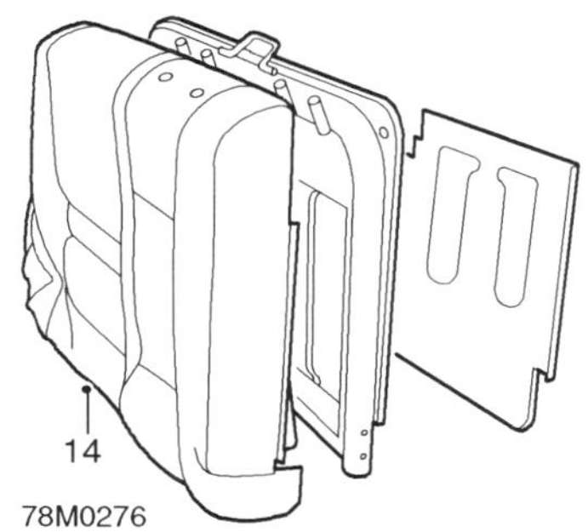

78M0276

14. Remove cover and pad from frame.

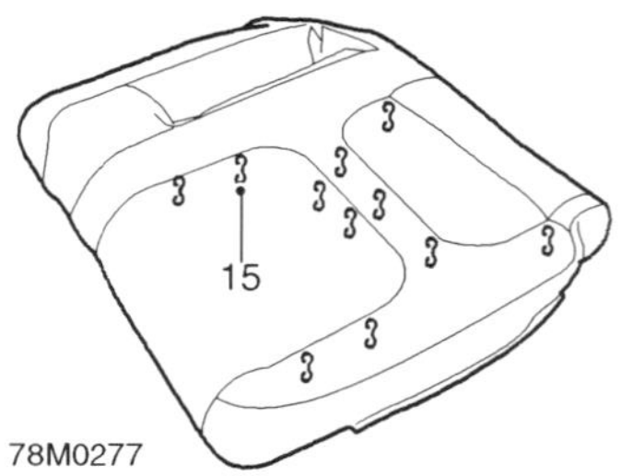

78M0277

15. Remove 12 hog rings and remove cover from pad.

Refit

1. Position squab cover to pad and secure hog rings.
2. Fit cover and pad to squab frame.
3. Fit head restraint guide tubes and seat lock warning button escutcheon.
4. Fit cover to sides and bottom of frame.
5. Fit cover to rear of frame and seat belt aperture.
6. Fit back cloth and secure latch escutchion.
7. Fit cover to arm rest aperture.
8. Fit arm rest and tighten screws.
9. Fit arm rest aperture trim.
10. Fit head restraints.
11. Fit squab to cushion and tighten bolts.
12. Fit side covers and tighten screws.
13. Position seat belt reel and tighten nut to 32 Nm.
14. Fit seat belt reel cover and tighten screws.
15. Secure rear seat in locked position.

WINDSCREEN

Service repair no - 76.81.01

NOTE: The following equipment is required:
Cutting wire and handles
Windscreen repair kit
Sealer applicator gun
Suction cups

WARNING: Wear protective gloves when handling glass, solvents and primers.

WARNING: Wear suitable eye protection when removing and refitting glass.

Remove

1. Remove air intake panel and wipers. ***See HEATING & VENTILATION, Repairs.***
2. Remove sun visors and sun visor retaining clips.
3. Remove 'A' post trims. ***See Interior trim components.***
4. Remove retaining stud from front of headlining.
5. Remove interior mirror. ***See Interior trim components.***
6. Fit protection to bonnet and areas around screen.
7. Cover heater ducts with masking tape.
8. Cover interior of vehicle with protective sheet.
9. Make knife cut in sealant at bottom of 'A' post.

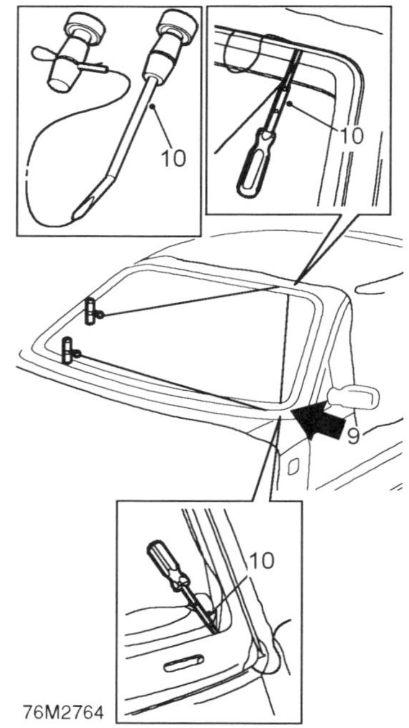

76M2764

10. Insert cutting wire through previously made knife cut and fit handles as shown, with approximately 200 mm of wire between handles.
11. Using suitable cutting wire, with assistance if required, carefully cut sealer. Ensure that glass is retained as last sealant is cut.

NOTE: If multi-strand cutting wire is used, a sawing action can be used to cut through heavy sealant deposits around corners.

CAUTION: Use of a sawing action may overheat and break single strand wire.

12. Attach suction cups and use assistance to remove glass from body.

CAUTION: Lay glass on felt covered supports. Do not stand on edge. Any chipping of glass edge may develop into cracks.

13. Collect screen support blocks.

Refit

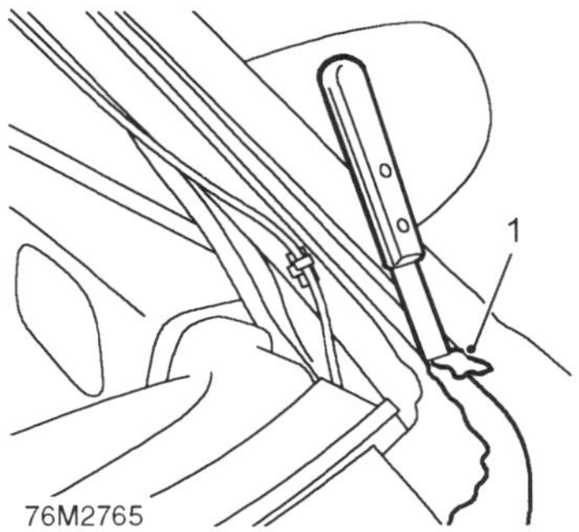

76M2765

1. Carefully remove excess sealer from body leaving a smooth surface.
2. Use a vacuum cleaner to clear away any waste.
3. Original glass: Carefully cut back old sealer to obtain a smooth surface without damaging obscuration band on glass.
4. Fit spacer blocks to body.
5. With assistance, locate screen to body.
6. Apply masking tape reference marks to aid fitment.
7. With assistance, remove screen and place aside.
8. Clean frame and edge of screen with solvent.

CAUTION: Do not touch cleaned or primed surfaces with fingers.

9. Apply etch primer to any bare metal on frame.
10. Apply bonding agent to screen and allow to cure.
11. Apply primer over etch primer on frame.
12. Apply activator over old sealer on frame.
13. Allow activator to cure.
14. Fit pre-cut nozzle to sealer cartridge, remove lid and shake out crystals, and install in applicator gun.

NOTE: Nozzle will need modification to achieve required bead section.

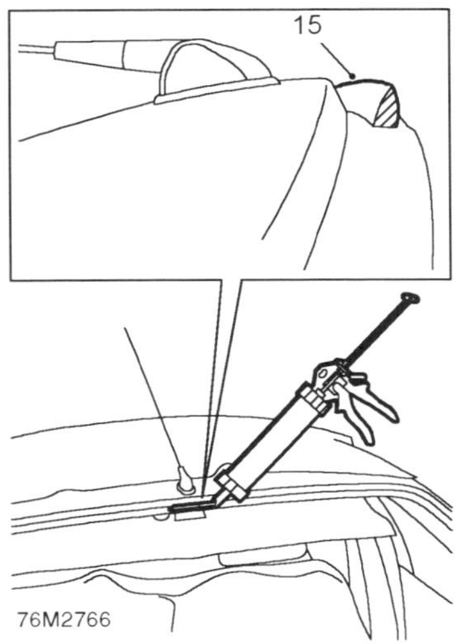

76M2766

15. Apply a continuous bead of sealer around edge of frame as shown.
16. Check for breaks and air bubbles in sealer.

17. With assistance, lift screen into place and align to screen supports and tape. Raise screen up to roof on ratchet support blocks. Lightly press glass to fully seat sealer.
18. Remove protective covers and tape.
19. Test sealer for leaks, apply additional sealer if necessary. If water is used, allow sealer to dry before testing. Spray water around glass and check for leaks. Mark any area that leaks. Dry glass and sealer then apply additional sealer.
20. Fit 'A' post trims. ***See Repairs.***
21. Fit headlining retaining stud.
22. Fit sun visor retaining clips and sun visors.
23. Fit interior mirror. ***See Repairs.***
24. Fit air intake panel and wipers. ***See HEATING & VENTILATION, Repairs.***

CAUTION: A curing time of 6 hours is desirable, during this time leave a window open and do not slam the doors. If the car must be used, drive slowly.

GLASS - BODY SIDE - REAR

Service repair no - 76.81.18

NOTE: The following equipment is required:

- Cutting wire and handles.
- Windscreen repair kit.
- Sealer applicator gun.
- Suction cups.

WARNING: Wear protective gloves when handling glass, solvents and primers.

WARNING: Wear suitable eye protection when removing and refitting glass.

Remove

1. Remove rear quarter upper casing. ***See Interior trim components.***
2. Cover interior of vehicle with protective sheet.

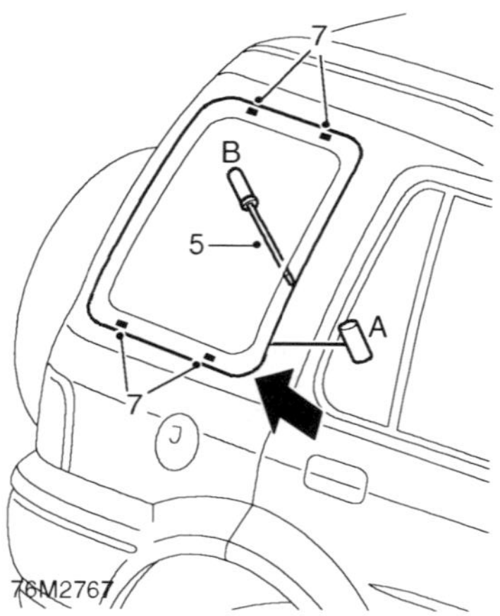

3. Make knife cut in sealant at bottom of 'D' post.
4. Insert cutting wire through previously made knife cut and fit handles as shown, with approximately 200 mm of wire between handles.
5. With assistance, wedge tube of handle A between glass and body, ahead of cutting position, and carefully cut sealer using a continuous pull on handle B from the outside. Ensure that glass is retained as last sealant is cut.

NOTE: If multi-strand cutting wire is used, a sawing action can be used to cut through heavy sealant deposits around corners.

CAUTION: Use of a sawing action may overheat and break single strand wire.

6. Attach suction cup and remove glass body.

CAUTION: Lay glass on felt covered supports. Do not stand on edge. Any chipping of glass edge may develop into cracks.

7. Collect 4 spacer blocks.

Refit

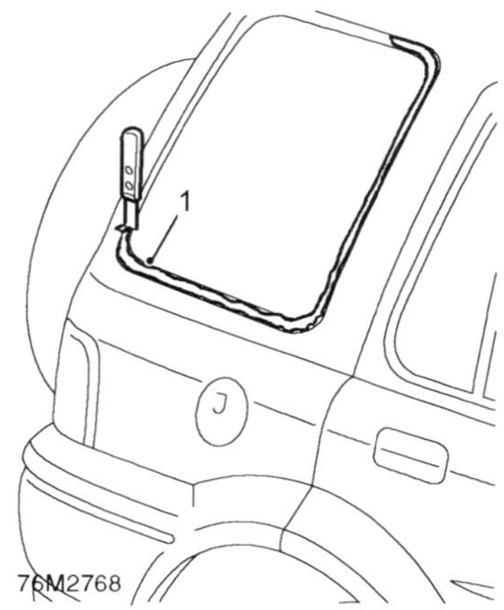

1. Carefully remove excess sealer from body leaving a smooth surface.
2. Use a vacuum cleaner to clear away any waste.
3. Original glass: Carefully cut back old sealer to obtain a smooth surface without damaging obscuration band on glass.
4. Fit rubber spacer blocks to body.
5. With assistance, locate screen to body.
6. Apply masking tape reference marks to aid fitment.
7. Remove screen and place aside.
8. Clean frame and edge of screen with solvent.

CAUTION: Do not touch cleaned or primed surfaces with fingers.

9. Apply etch primer to any bare metal on frame.
10. Apply bonding agent to screen and allow to cure.
11. Apply primer over etch primer on frame.
12. Apply activator over old sealer on frame.
13. Allow activator to cure.
14. Fit pre-cut nozzle to sealer cartridge, remove lid and shake out crystals. Install cartridge in applicator gun.

NOTE: Nozzle will need modification to achieve required bead section.

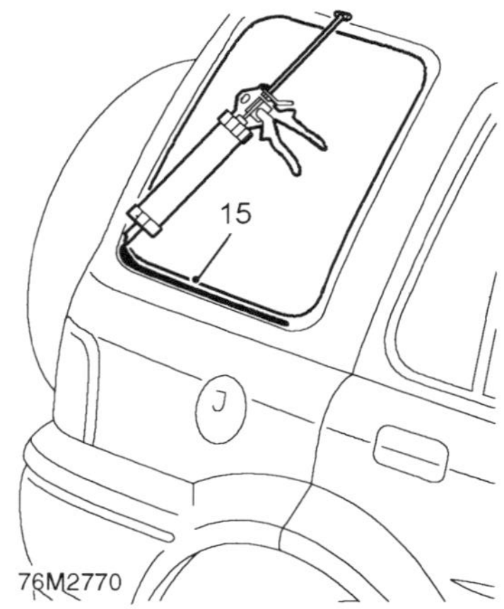

15. Apply a continuous bead of sealer around edge of frame as shown. Make bead slightly thicker at each corner.
16. Check for breaks and air bubbles in sealer.
17. Position glass to body and align to reference tape.
18. Lightly press glass to fully seat sealer.
19. Secure glass with tape until sealer has cured.
20. Remove protective covers and tape.
21. Test sealer for leaks, apply additional sealer if necessary. If water is used, allow sealer to dry before testing. Spray water around glass and check for leaks. Mark leakage points and apply additional sealer as necessary when area is completely dry.
22. Fit rear quarter upper casing. ***See Interior trim components.***

This page is intentionally left blank

HOOD OUTER COVER

Service repair no - 76.61.11

Remove

CAUTION: Always position trim components on a soft covered, clean work surface.

NOTE: Where necessary, transfer witness marks from the old cover to aid assembly. New outer covers are supplied complete with the header rail.

NOTE: The following operation involves the bonding of fabric backed vinyl. If adhesive is to be applied to the fabric backing, Dunlop 758 adhesive or equivalant should be used. For direct application on vinyl surfaces, use Dunlop S1588 adhesive or equivalant. A thin coating of adhesive should be applied to both surfaces and then allowed to cure, until touch dry, for between 5 and 10 mins before bond is made.

1. Remove hood assembly. **See Owner's Handbook.**

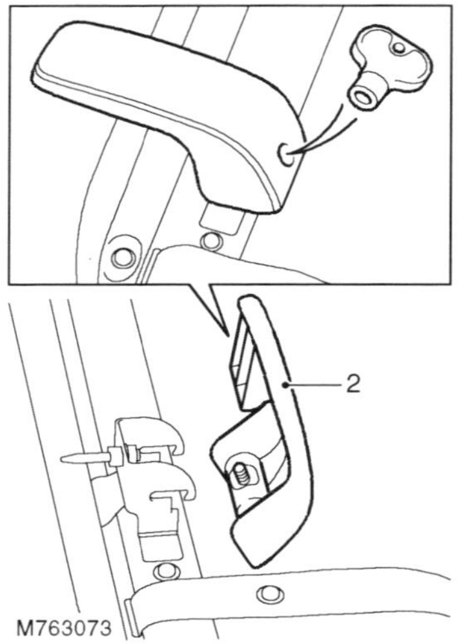

M763073

2. Loosen catch screws with special key, release catches from hood and remove both catches.

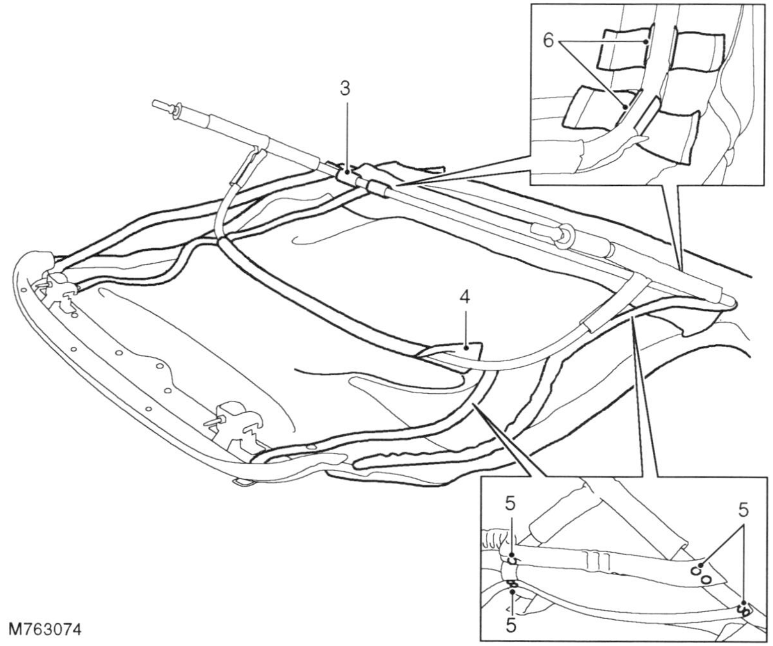

M763074

3. Release fabric flaps from rear of frame.
4. Release fabric flap from front of frame.
5. Remove 14 screws securing tension straps
6. Release frame from outer cover retainers.
7. Remove frame from outer cover.

Refit

1. Clean excess adhesive from frame using a suitable solvent.
2. Position frame to hood outer cover and locate in retainers.
3. Position tension straps and secure with screws.
4. Apply adhesive to fabric flap and secure to front of frame.
5. Apply adhesive to fabric flaps and secure to rear of frame.

CAUTION: Ensure adhesive does not contact frame.

NOTE: The fabric flaps should be free to move on the frame.

6. Fit hood catches and secure with special key.
7. Fit soft back assembly. **See Owner's Handbook.**

GLASS - BODY SIDE - HARD BACK

Service repair no - 76.61.29

CAUTION: Always position trim components on a soft covered, clean work surface.

WARNING: Wear protective gloves when handling glass, solvents and primers.

WARNING: Wear suitable eye protection when removing and refitting glass.

NOTE: The following equipment is required:
- Cutting wire and handles
- Sharp knife
- Windscreen repair kit
- Sealer applicator gun
- Suction cups

Remove

1. Remove hard-back. **See Owner's Handbook.**

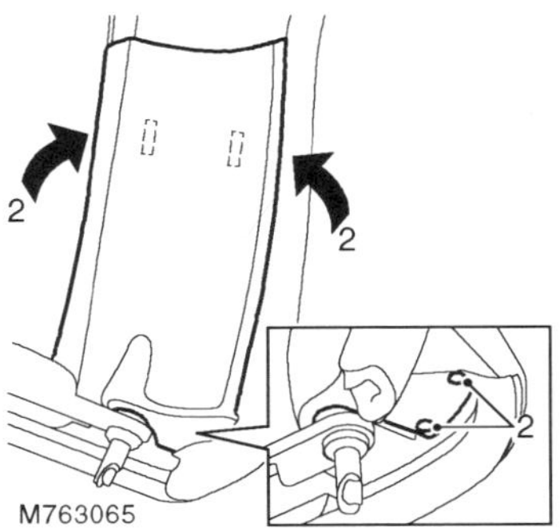

M763065

2. Remove 2 screws securing 'E' post finisher, release finisher from clips and remove finisher.

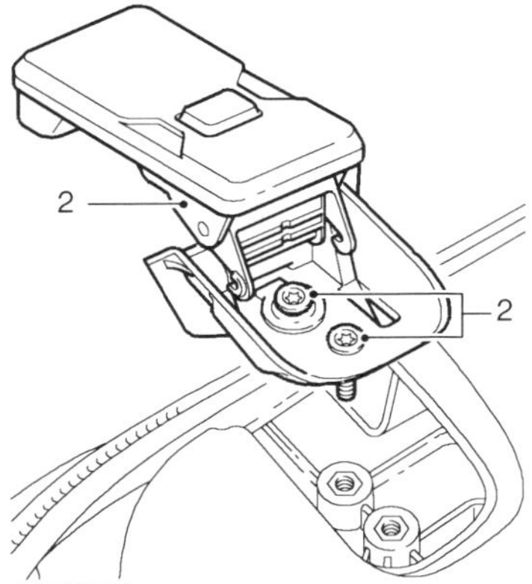

M763063

3. Remove 4 Torx screws securing hard-back catches, slide catches from position and remove catches.

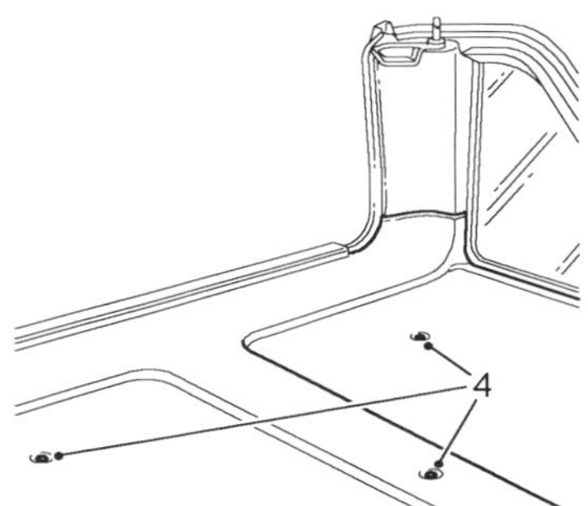

M763077

4. Remove 3 Torx screws securing headlining release headlining from hard-back seal and remove headlining.
5. Cover interior of hard-back with protective sheet.
6. Apply masking tape to protect paintwork.

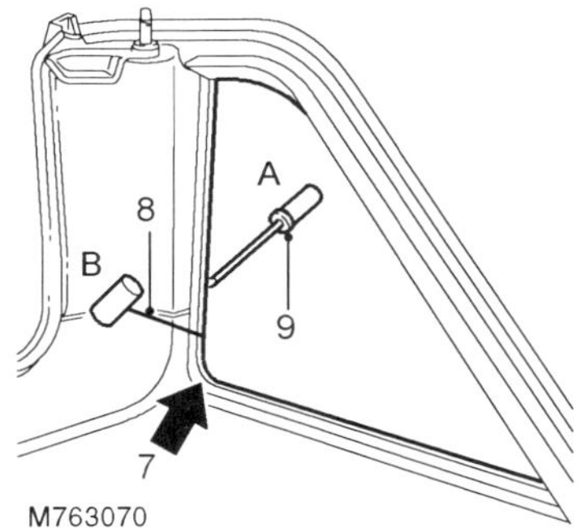

M763070

7. Make knife cut in sealant at bottom of 'E' post.
8. Insert cutting wire through previously made knife cut and fit handles as shown, with approximately 200 mm of wire between handles.
9. With assistance, wedge tube of handle **A** between glass and body, ahead of cutting position, and carefully cut sealer using a continuous pull on handle **B** from the outside. Ensure that glass is retained as last sealant is cut.

NOTE: If multi-strand cutting wire is used, a sawing action can be used to cut through heavy sealant deposits around corners.

CAUTION: Use of a sawing action may overheat and break single strand wire.

10. Attach suction cup and remove glass body.

CAUTION: Lay glass on felt covered supports. Do not stand on edge. Any chipping of glass edge may develop into cracks.

Refit

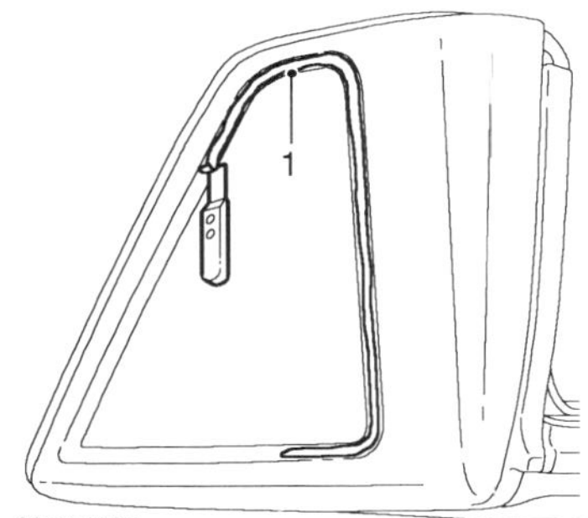

M763071

1. Carefully remove excess sealer from body leaving a smooth surface.
2. Use a vacuum cleaner to clear away any waste.
3. Original glass: Carefully cut back old sealant to obtain a smooth surface without damaging obscuration band on glass.
4. With assistance, locate glass to body.
5. Apply masking tape reference marks to aid fitment.
6. Remove glass and place aside.
7. Clean frame and edge of glass with solvent.

CAUTION: Do not touch cleaned or primed surfaces with fingers.

8. Repair any damaged paintwork as necessary.
9. Apply bonding agent to glass and allow to cure.
10. Apply activator over old sealer on frame.
11. Allow activator to cure.
12. Apply primer to frame.
13. Fit pre-cut nozzle to sealer cartridge, remove lid and shake out crystals, and install in applicator gun.

NOTE: Nozzle will need modification to achieve required bead section.

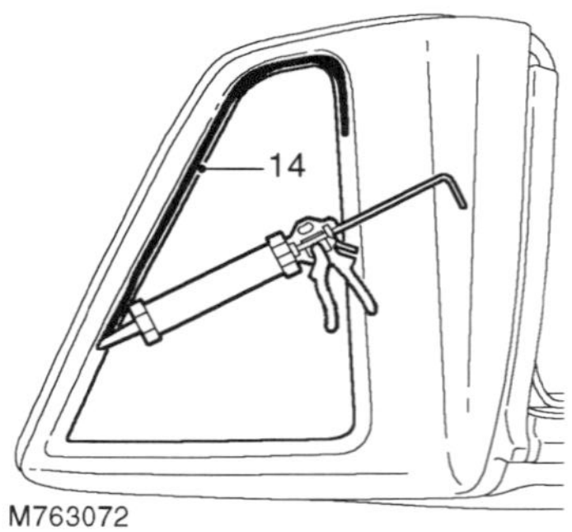

M763072

14. Apply a continuous bead of sealer around edge of frame as shown. Make bead slightly thicker at each corner.
15. Check for breaks and air bubbles in sealer.
16. Position glass to body and align to reference tape.
17. Lightly press glass to fully seat sealer.
18. Secure glass with tape until sealer has cured.
19. Remove protective covers and tape.
20. Test seal for leaks, apply additional sealer if necessary. If water is used, allow sealer to dry before testing. Spray water around glass and check for leaks. Dry affected area and apply additional sealer if necessary.
21. Position headlining and locate hardback seal.
22. Secure headlining with Torx screws.
23. Position catches, fit Torx screws and tighten to 10 Nm.
24. Fit 'E post finishers, engage in clips and secure with screws.
25. Fit Hard-back. **See Owner's Handbook.**

SEAL - HARD BACK - PRIMARY

Service repair no - 76.61.34

CAUTION: Always position trim components on a soft covered, clean work surface.

Remove

1. Remove hard back. **See Owner's Handbook.**

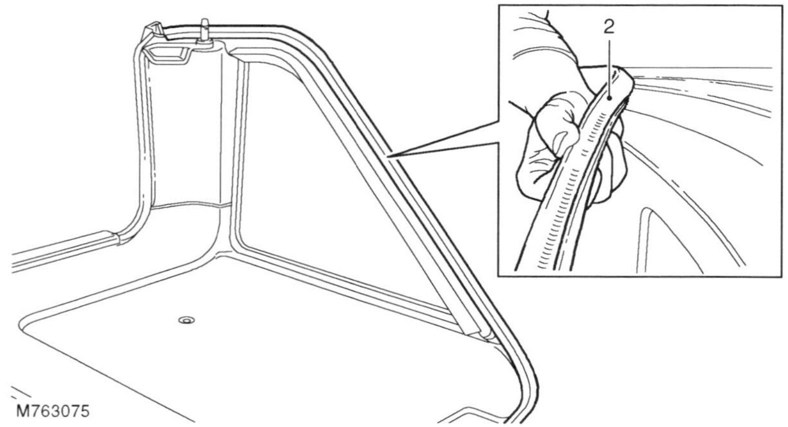

M763075

2. Release seal from flange around hard back frame and remove seal.

Refit

1. Clean seal flange.
2. Position seal and secure to flange.
3. Secure ends of seal to hard-back frame using Butyl Rubber adhesive if necessary.
4. Fit hard back. **See Owner's Handbook.**

CATCH AND RETAINER - HARD-BACK - FRONT

Service repair no - 76.61.94

Remove

1. Remove hard-back. **See Owner's Handbook.**

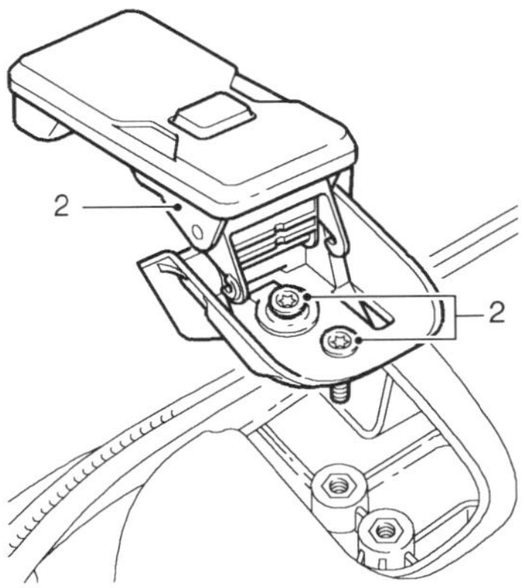

M763063

2. Remove 2 Torx screws securing catch, slide catch from position and remove catch.

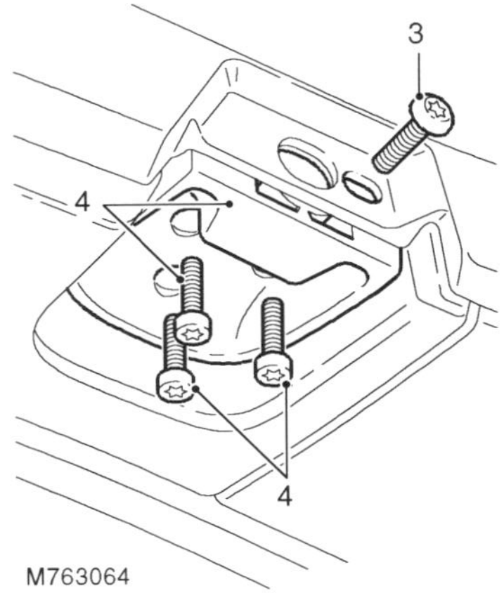

M763064

3. Remove Torx screw securing roof finisher to hard-back retainer.
4. Remove 3 Torx screws securing hard-back retainer and remove retainer.

Refit

1. Position hard-back retainer, fit Torx screws and tighten to 10Nm.
2. Fit Torx screw securing roof finisher.
3. Position catch, fit Torx screws and tighten to 10 Nm.

CAUTION: Ensure formed washer is correctly located in catch recess.

4. Fit hard-back. **See Owner's Handbook.**

CATCH AND RETAINER - HARD-BACK - REAR

Service repair no - 76.61.95

Remove

1. Remove hard-back or soft-back. **See Owner's Handbook.**

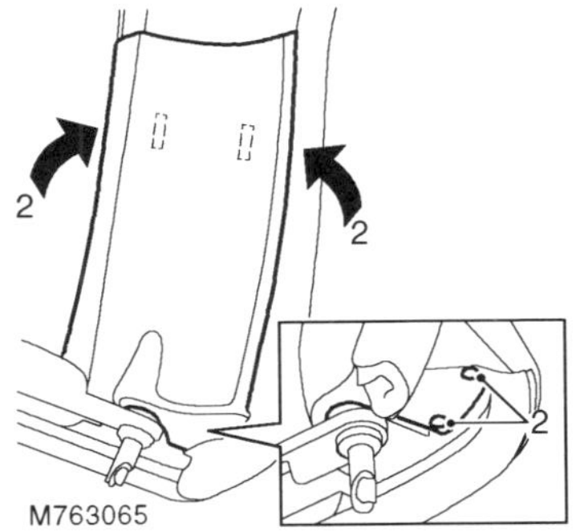

M763065

2. Remove 2 screws securing 'E' post finisher, release finisher from 2 clips and remove finisher.

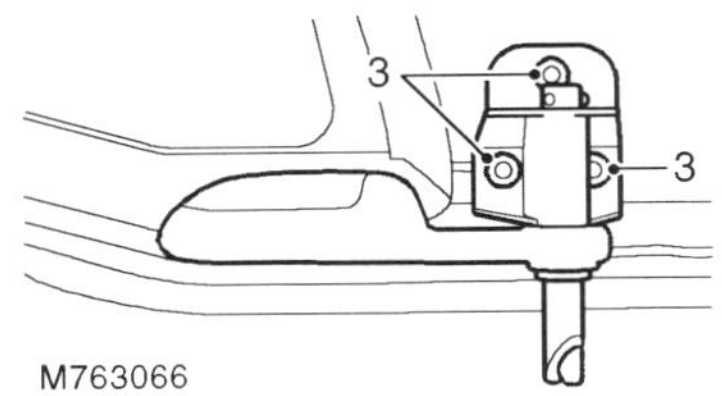

M763066

3. Remove 3 Torx screws securing catch and remove catch.
4. Remove lower rear quarter trim casing. ***See Interior trim components.***

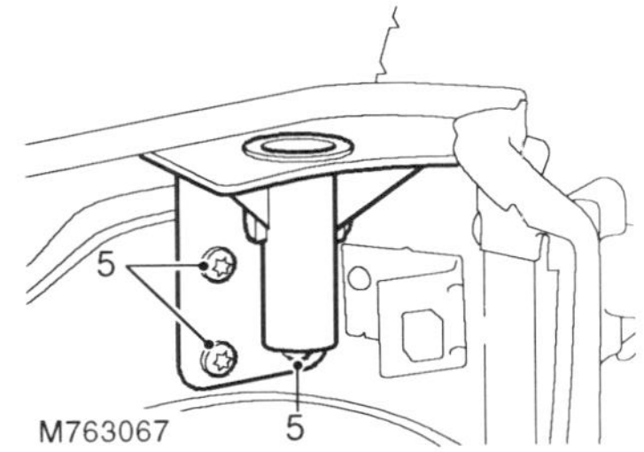

M763067

5. Remove 3 Torx screws securing hard-back retainer and remove retainer.

Refit

1. Position catch, fit Torx screws and tighten to 10Nm.
2. Position 'E' post finisher, engage in clips and secure with screws.
3. Position hard-back retainer, fit Torx screws and tighten to 10 Nm.
4. Fit lower rear quarter trim casing. ***See Interior trim components.***
5. Fit hard-back. **See Owner's Handbook.**

SUN ROOF ASSEMBLY - 3 DOOR

Service repair no - 76.83.01

Remove

WARNING: Wear protective gloves when handling solvents and primers.

WARNING: Wear suitable eye protection when cutting out sun roof.

1. Remove headlining. ***See Interior trim components.***

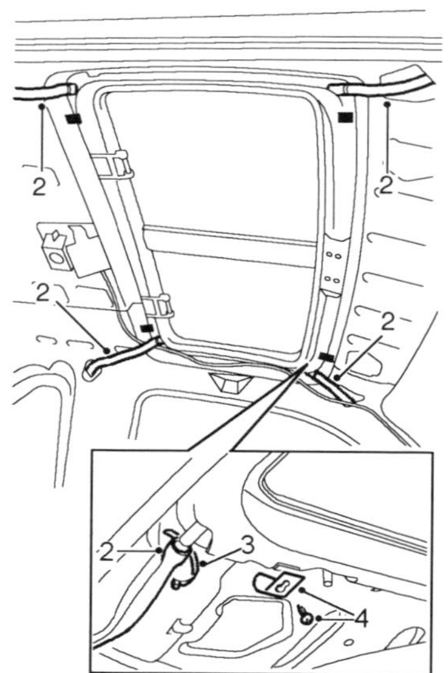

76M2772

2. Disconnect drain tubes from sun roof.
3. Remove and discard cable ties.
4. Loosen 4 Torx screws securing clamping plates and remove plates.

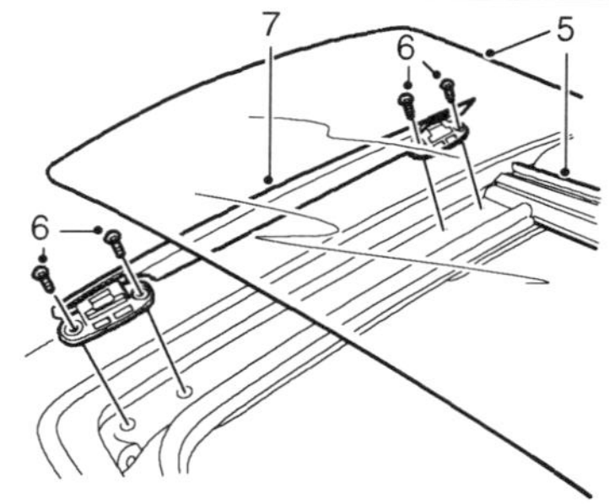

76M2773

5. Remove glass panels and 'T' bar.
6. Remove 8 screws securing wind deflectors.
7. Remove wind deflectors.

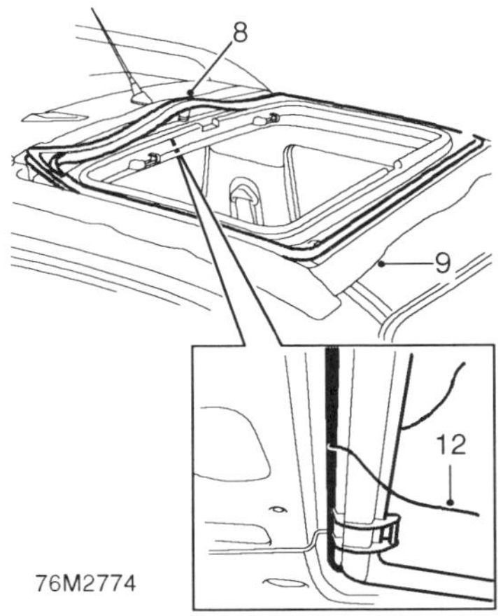

76M2774

8. Remove sun roof tray seal. ***See this section.***
9. Mask up roof and sun roof aperture.
10. Cover interior trim with protective sheet.
11. Make a cut through the sealer at the back of the sun roof, a 90° bend in the cutting tool will help.

CAUTION: Take care not to damage paint or roof aperture flange when cutting out sunroof.

12. Using suitable cutting wire, cut through PU sealer securing sunroof to roof.

NOTE: Multi-strand cutting wire is advised, as a sawing action may be required on the corners. Single strand wire may overheat and break during sawing action.

13. Remove section of sunroof.

Refit

1. Clean surrounding area with solvent.
2. Use a vacuum cleaner to clear away dust and debris.
3. Cut sealer on roof flange down to a smooth even finish.
4. Etch prime and paint any damaged areas.
5. Apply primer over etch primer on flange.
6. Apply activator over old sealer on flange.
7. Allow activator to cure.
8. Fit pre-cut nozzle to sealer cartridge, remove lid and shake out crystals, install in applicator gun.

NOTE: Modify nozzle as required.

9. Apply a continuous bead of sealer around roof flange as shown. Make bead slightly thicker at the corners.

NOTE: Sealer bead should be 8 mm by 8 mm.

10. Check for breaks and air bubbles in the sealer.
11. With assistance position sunroof and align to roof aperture.
12. Fit sun roof tray seal. ***See this section.***
13. Position sunroof clamping plates, fit and tighten screws.
14. Connect drain tubes and secure with NEW cable ties.
15. Remove body and trim protection.
16. Position wind deflectors, fit and tighten screws.
17. Fit 'T' bar and glass panels.
18. Fit headlining. ***See Interior trim components.***

WIND DEFLECTOR - GLASS SUN ROOF - 3 DOOR

Service repair no - 76.83.28

Remove

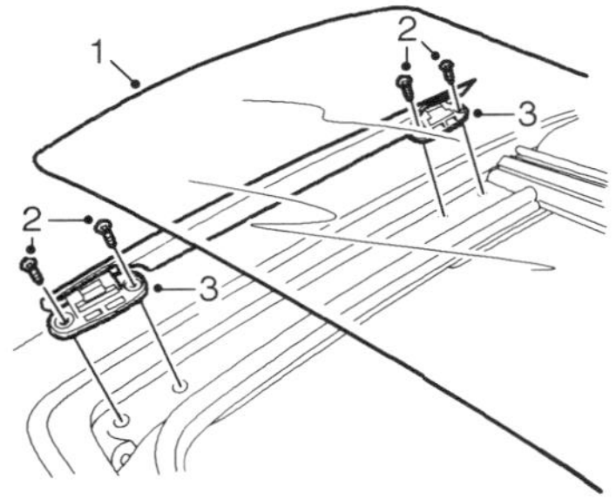

76M2739

1. Release and remove sun roof glass panel.
2. Remove 4 screws securing hinges, and remove wind deflector.
3. Collect hinges.

NOTE: Hinges are handed.

Refit

1. Locate hinges to wind deflector, position wind deflector, fit and tighten screws.
2. Position glass panel and secure catch.

SEAL - SUN ROOF TRAY

Service repair no - 76.83.61

Remove

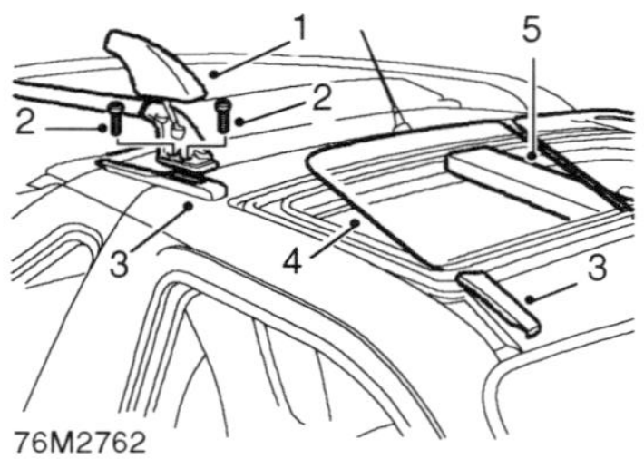

76M2762

1. Remove side rail front end covers.
2. Unscrew 4 Torx bolts securing front of side rails and side rails.
3. Remove front and rear roof finishers.
4. Remove roof glass.
5. Remove 'T' bar.

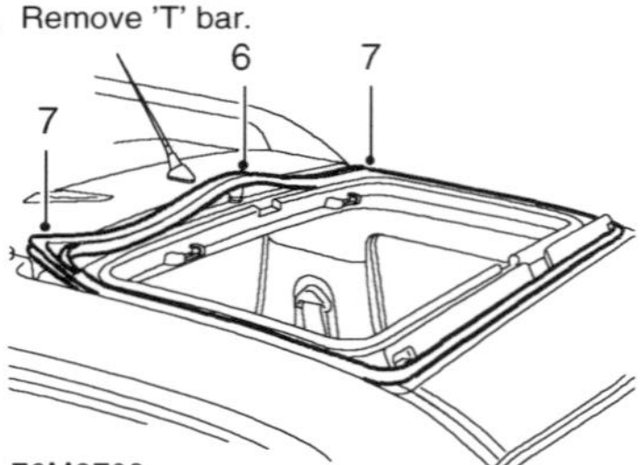

76M2763

6. Release seal from inner part of tray.
7. Release seal from corners of tray and ease from between roof and tray.
8. Remove tray seal.

Refit

1. Position seal to roof.

CAUTION: Do not use sharp tools to locate seal

2. Locate seal to corners of tray and fit between roof and tray.
3. Fit seal to inner part of tray.
4. Fit 'T' bar.
5. Fit roof glass.
6. Fit roof finishers.
7. Ensure gaskets are in position on side rails. Tighten Torx bolts to 22 Nm. to secure side rails.
8. Fit side rail end covers.

SUN ROOF ASSEMBLY - 5 DOOR

Service repair no - 76.84.01

Remove

1. Remove headlining. ***See Interior trim components.***

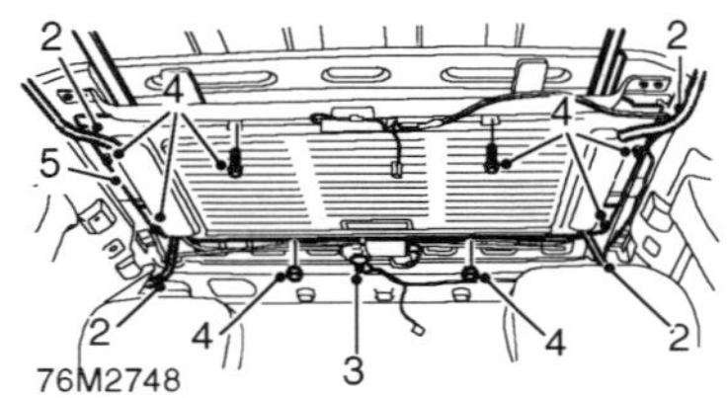

76M2748

2. Disconnect drain tubes from sun roof.
3. Disconnect multiplug from sun roof motor.
4. With assistance, remove 6 nuts and 2 bolts securing sun roof.
5. Remove sun roof assembly.

Refit

1. Ensure plastic washers and tray seal are in position.
2. With assistance position sun roof assembly, fit and tighten nuts and bolts.
3. Connect multiplug to sun roof.
4. Connect drain tubes to sun roof and secure with cable ties.
5. Fit headlining. ***See Interior trim components.***

PANEL GLASS - SUN ROOF - 5 DOOR

Service repair no - 76.84.03

Remove

1. Open sun roof blind.

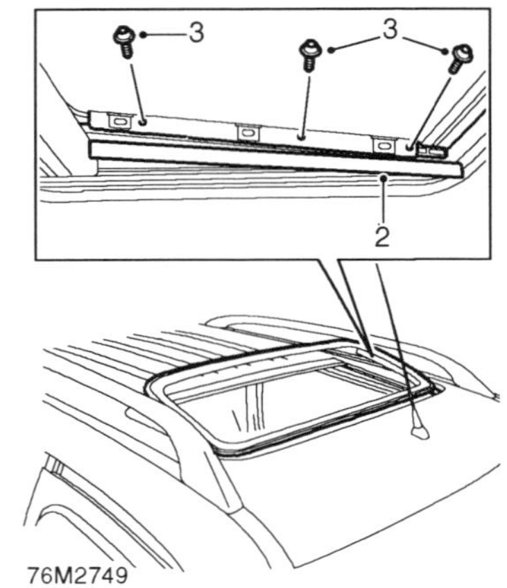

76M2749

2. Remove covers from glass securing screws.
3. Remove 6 screws securing glass.
4. Remove glass.

Refit

1. Position glass, fit screws but do not tighten at this stage.
2. Align glass to roof and tighten screws.

NOTE: The sunroof should be aligned evenly within the aperture. Set the glass height flush with the roof panel at each side.
Set the glass height flush to 1mm low at the front.
Set the glass height flush to 1mm high at the rear.

3. Fit screw covers.
4. Operate sun roof and recheck alignment. Adjust if necessary.
5. Close sun roof blind.

SEAL - PANEL GLASS - SUN ROOF - 5 DOOR

Service repair no - 76.84.05

Remove

1. Remove glass panel. ***See this section.***

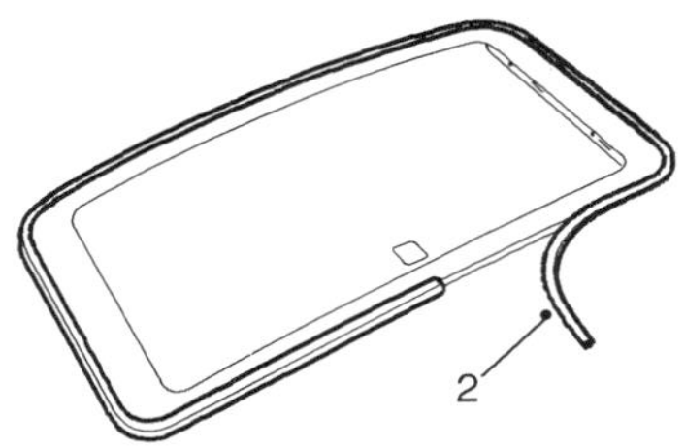

76M2752

2. Release ends of seal from glass and remove seal .

Refit

1. Clean adhesive from glass.
2. Position seal; apply adhesive to ends of seal and secure to glass panel.
3. Fit glass panel. ***See this section.***

MOTOR - SUN ROOF

Service repair no - 76.84.07

Remove

1. Remove front roof lamp. ***See ELECTRICAL, Repairs.***
2. Remove headlining to sun roof finisher. ***See Repairs.***
3. Carefully lower front of headlining to access motor.

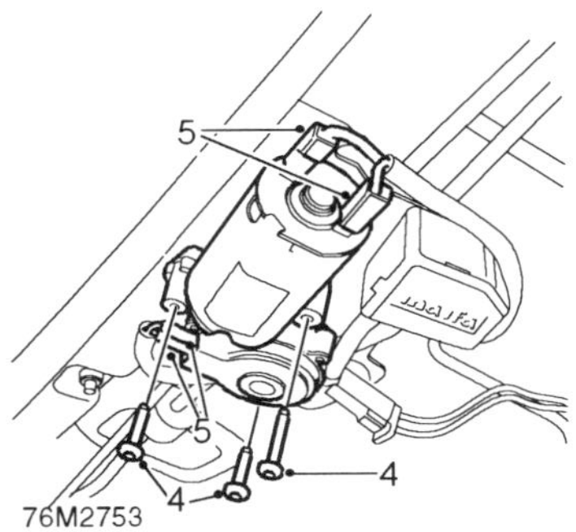

76M2753

4. Remove 3 Torx screws securing motor.
5. Release motor from gearbox, lower through headlining, disconnect 4 Lucars and remove motor.

Refit

1. Position motor, connect Lucars and fit motor to gearbox.
2. Position sun roof in tilt mode, power motor forward to the first stop (motor and lifting assemblies are then timed together).
3. Fit and tighten Torx screws.
4. Carefully reposition headlining.
5. Fit sun roof finisher. ***See Repairs.***
6. Fit roof lamp. ***See ELECTRICAL, Repairs.***

DRIVE CABLES & SLIDE ASSEMBLIES

Service repair no - 76.84.09

Remove

1. Remove sun roof motor. ***See this section.***
2. Remove glass panel. ***See this section.***
3. Open sun roof.
4. Release and remove wind deflector.
5. Position sun roof in tilt mode.

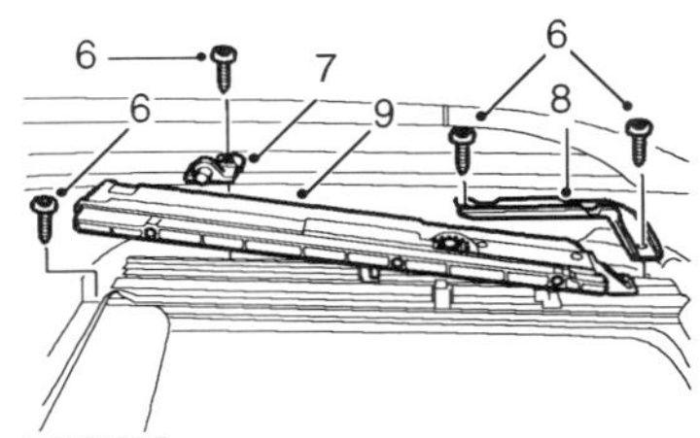

76M2757

6. Remove 4 Torx screws securing lifting assembly to roof.
7. Collect rear cam guide.
8. Slide assembly forward, remove cable guide clamp.
9. Remove lifting assembly and cable.

Refit

1. Ensure cable tubes are in position, lightly grease the end of cable tube.
2. Engage cable in tube and fit lifting assembly to roof.
3. Fit cable guide clamp, place lifting assembly in tilt mode.
4. Fit rear cam guide.
5. Fit and tighten Torx screws.
6. Fit sun roof motor. ***See this section.***
7. Open sun roof.
8. Position wind deflector and secure to sun roof.
9. Fit glass panel. ***See this section.***

DRAIN TUBE - SUN ROOF - FRONT - 5 DOOR

Service repair no - 76.84.20

Remove

1. Remove headlining. ***See Interior trim components.***

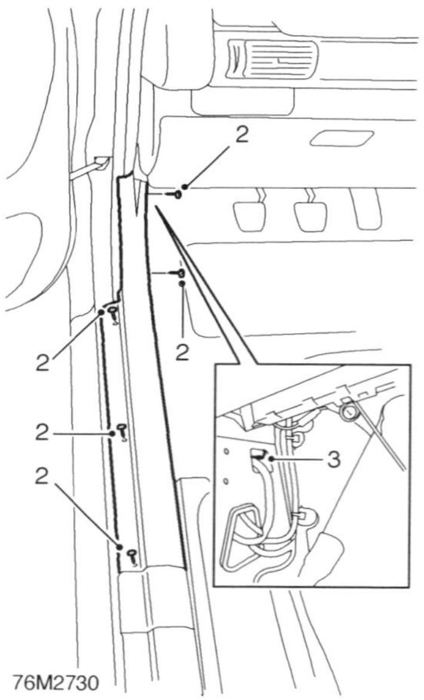

76M2730

2. Remove 5 Torx screws securing carpet retainer and remove retainer.
3. Release drain tube from wheel arch grommet.

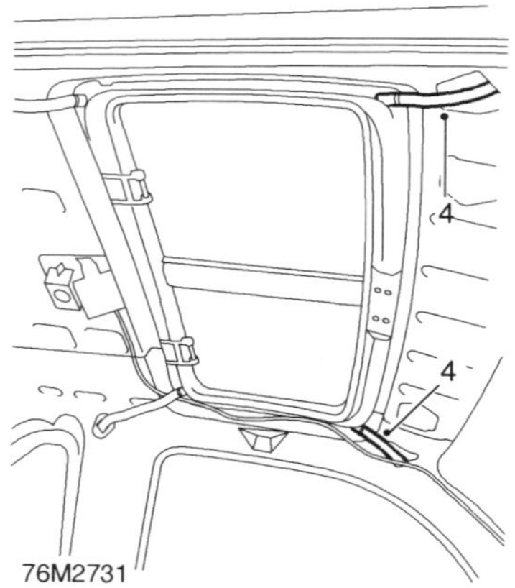

76M2731

4. Disconnect drain tube from sun roof, discard cable tie.
5. Attach draw string and remove drain tube.

Refit

1. Attach draw string to NEW drain tube and pull into position.
2. Connect drain tube to sun roof and secure with NEW cable tie.
3. Connect drain tube to wheel arch grommet.
4. Secure wheel arch grommet.
5. Position carpet retainer, fit and tighten Torx screws.
6. Fit headlining. ***See Interior trim components.***

DRAIN TUBE - SUN ROOF - REAR - 5 DOOR

Service repair no - 76.84.21

Remove

1. Remove headlining. ***See Interior trim components.***

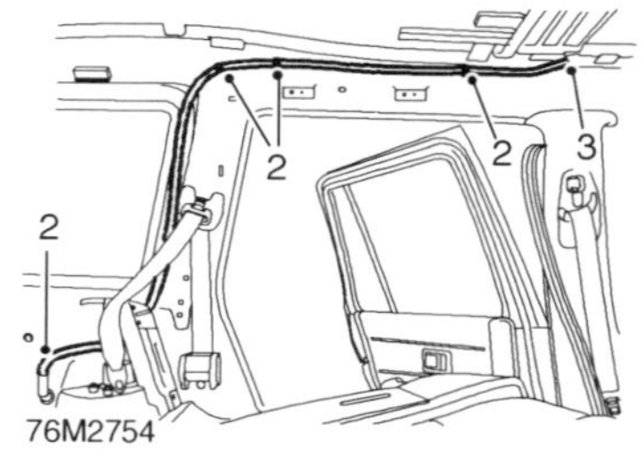

76M2754

2. Release drain tube from wheel arch grommet and 3 securing clips.
3. Disconnect drain tube from sun roof and discard cable tie.
4. Remove drain tube.

Refit

1. Position NEW drain tube.
2. Connect drain tube to sun roof and secure with NEW cable tie.
3. Connect drain tube to wheel arch grommet and secure in clips.
4. Secure wheel arch grommet.
5. Fit headlining. ***See Interior trim components.***

FINISHER - SUN ROOF FLANGE TO HEADLINING

Service repair no - 76.84.25

Remove

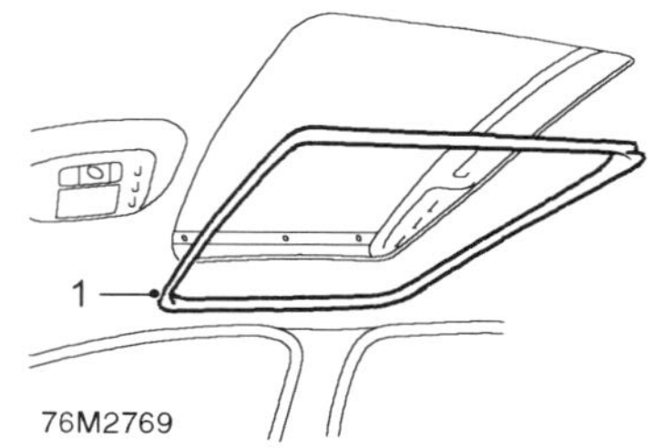

76M2769

1. Release sun roof surround finisher from sunroof aperture and remove finisher.

Refit

1. Position sunroof surround finisher and secure in position ensure locating lug is in position at the front of finisher.

WIND DEFLECTOR - SUN ROOF - 5 DOOR

Service repair no - 76.84.28

Remove

1. Open sun roof.

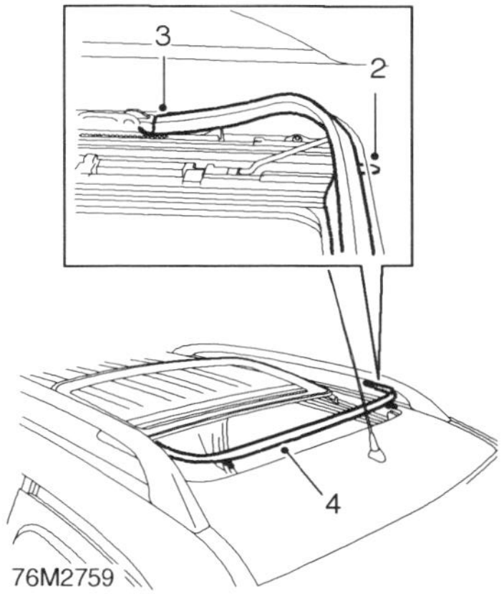

76M2759

2. Carefully release wind deflector retaining pegs from roof.
3. Release wind deflector from lifting assemblies.
4. Remove wind deflector.

Refit

1. Position wind deflector to lifting assemblies and secure in position.
2. Carefully locate retaining pegs under roof.
3. Close sun roof.

BLIND - SUN ROOF - 5 DOOR

Service repair no - 76.84.30

Remove

1. Remove headlining. ***See Interior trim components.***

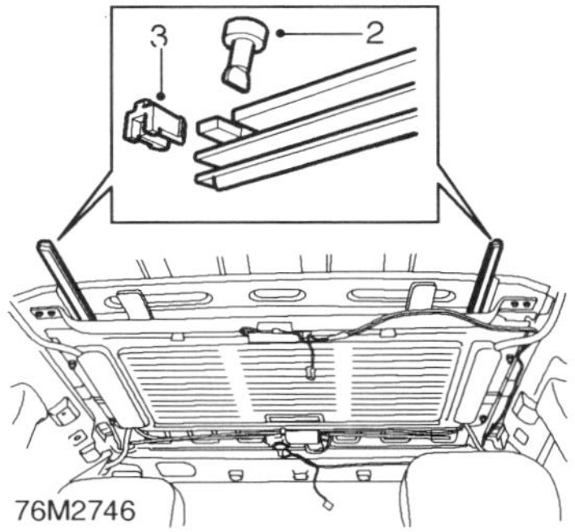

76M2746

2. Remove 2 blind stops.
3. Remove 2 rubber buffers.
4. Slide blind to the rear of sun roof and remove from guides.

Refit

1. Lubricate guides with isoflex grease.
2. Fit blind to guides and slide into position.
3. Fit blind stops and rubber buffers.
4. Fit headlining. ***See Interior trim components.***

SWITCH - SUN ROOF

Service repair no - 76.84.40

Remove

1. Remove front console. ***See Interior trim components.***
2. Remove switch from console.

Refit

1. Fit switch to console.
2. Fit front console. ***See Interior trim components.***

SEAL - SUN ROOF TRAY - 5 DOOR

Service repair no - 76.84.61

Remove

1. Remove sun roof assembly. ***See this section.***

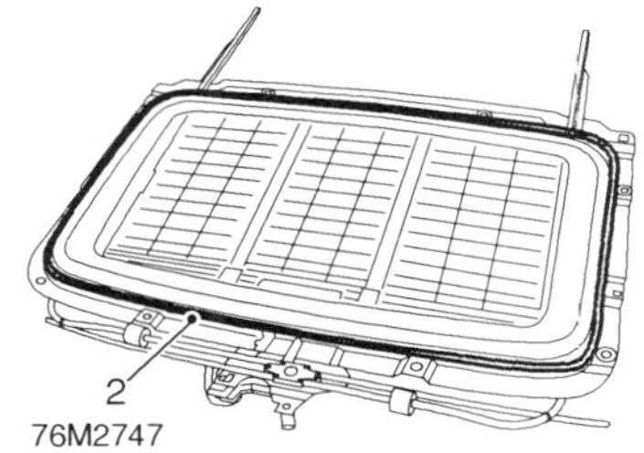

76M2747

2. Remove seal from tray.

Refit

1. Clean old adhesive from tray.
2. Remove backing from NEW seal and fit seal to tray.
3. Fit sun roof assembly. ***See this section.***

CONTENTS

Page

HEATING AND VENTILATION

The heating and ventilation system controls the temperature and distribution of air supplied to the vehicle interior. Air is drawn into a heater assembly through a connector hose and an air inlet duct or, on vehicles with air conditioning, the cooling unit. **See Air Conditioning, Description and Operation**.

In the heater assembly, the air can be heated and supplied as required to fascia and floor level outlets. An electrical variable speed blower, and/or ram effect when the vehicle is in forward motion, forces the air

through the system. Temperature, distribution and blower controls are installed on a panel on the centre console.

Heating and ventilation system component layout (RH drive shown, LH drive similar)

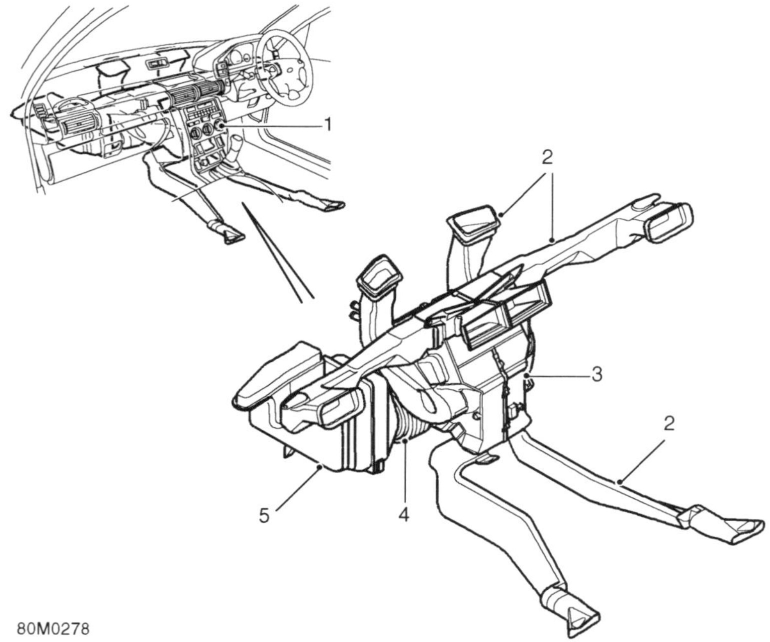

1. Control panel
2. Distribution ducts
3. Heater assembly
4. Connector hose
5. Air inlet duct

AIR INLET DUCT

The air inlet duct connects the passenger's side of the plenum to the heater assembly, to provide the fresh air inlet. The upper end of the duct locates in a slot in the body and the lower end of the duct is connected to the heater assembly via a corrugated connector hose. A pollen filter is installed in the air inlet duct and retained by two scrivets.

Air inlet duct components (RH drive shown, LH drive similar)

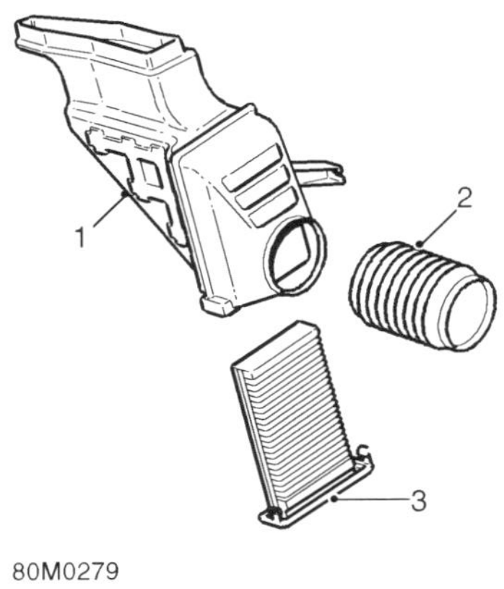

1. Air inlet duct
2. Connector hose
3. Pollen filter

HEATER ASSEMBLY

The heater assembly heats and distributes air as directed by selections made on the control panel. The assembly is installed on the vehicle centre-line, between the fascia and the engine bulkhead.

The heater assembly consists of a two-piece plastic casing containing a blower, resistor pack, heater matrix and control flaps. Integral passages guide the air through the casing from the inlet to the distribution outlets. A wiring harness connects the blower and resistor pack to the blower switch on the control panel.

Heater assembly components (RH drive shown, LH drive similar)

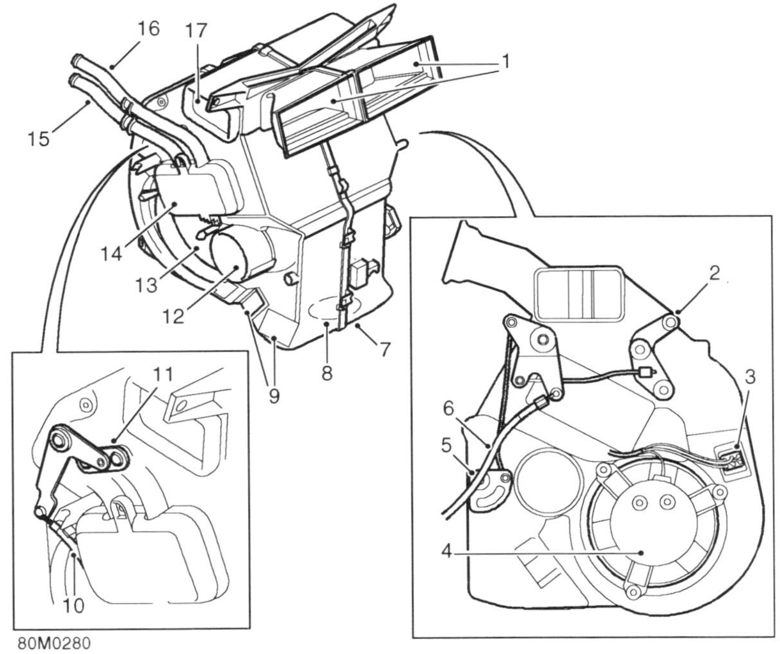

1. Centre face level air outlets
2. Fresh air flap lever
3. Resistor pack
4. Blower
5. Main flap lever
6. Distribution control cable
7. Casing
8. Rear footwells air outlet
9. Front footwell air outlets
10. Blend flap control cable
11. Blend flap lever
12. Windscreen and side window air outlet
13. Air inlet
14. Heater matrix cover
15. Engine coolant feed
16. Engine coolant return
17. Outer face level air outlet

Blower

The blower controls the volume of air being supplied to the distribution outlets. The blower is installed in the driver's side of the casing and consists of an open hub, centrifugal fan powered by an electric motor. The open end of the fan surrounds the air inlet, which is on the passenger's side of the casing. The blower switch and the resistor pack control the operation of the blower, which can be selected to run at one of four speeds.

Resistor pack

The resistor pack supplies reduced voltages to the blower motor for blower speeds 1, 2 and 3. For blower speed 4, the resistor pack is bypassed and

battery voltage drives the motor at full speed. The pack is installed in the RH side of the casing, in the air outlet from the blower fan, so that any heat generated is dissipated by the air flow.

Interior view of heater assembly (RH drive shown, LH drive similar)

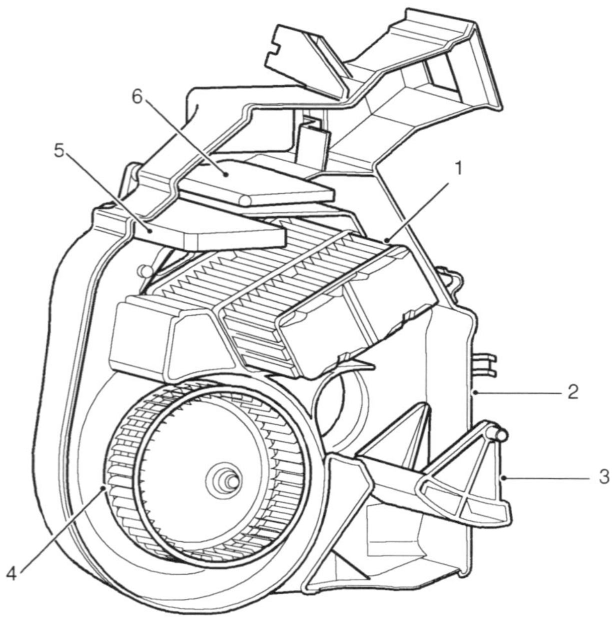

80M0281

1. Heater matrix
2. Casing
3. Distribution main flap
4. Blower fan
5. Blend flap
6. Distribution fresh air flap

Heater matrix

The heater matrix provides the heat source to warm the air being supplied to the distribution outlets. It is installed in the LH side of the casing behind a protective cover. The matrix is a copper and brass, two pass, fin and tube heat exchanger. Engine coolant is supplied to the matrix through two brass tubes that extend through the bulkhead into the engine compartment. When the engine is running, coolant is constantly circulated through the heater matrix by the engine coolant pump.

Control flaps

Three control flaps are installed in the heater assembly to control the temperature and distribution of air. A blend flap controls the temperature and two distribution flaps control the distribution.

Blend flap

The blend flap regulates the flow of air through the heater matrix to control the temperature of the air leaving the heater assembly. It consists of a hinged flap between the cold air bypass and the heater matrix. The flap hinge is connected to a lever mechanism on the LH side of the casing. A control cable is installed between the lever mechanism and the temperature knob on the control panel to operate the flap. Turning the temperature knob turns the flap and varies the proportions of air going through the cold air bypass and the heater. The proportions vary, between full bypass no heat and no bypass full heat, to correspond with the selection on the temperature knob. When the flow is split between the cold air bypass and the heater matrix, the two flows are mixed downstream of the heater matrix to produce an even air temperature at the individual outlets.

Temperature control

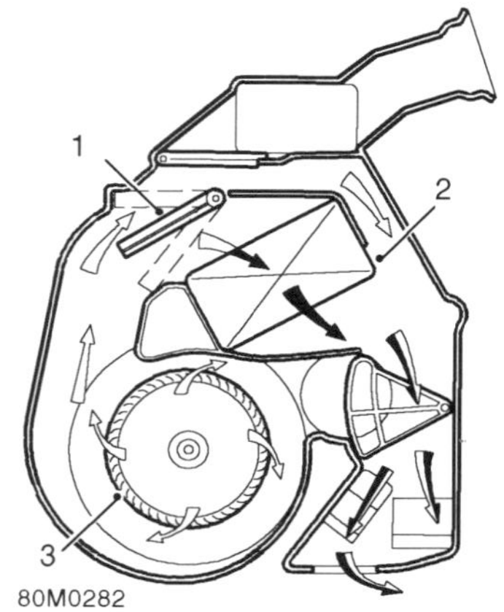

80M0282

1. Blend flap
2. Heater matrix
3. Blower

Distribution flaps

A main flap and a fresh air flap control the flow of air to the distribution outlets in the casing. The main flap is a rotating segment that controls the flow to the windscreen/side window and footwell outlets. The fresh air flap is a hinged door that controls the flow to the face level outlets. The hinge of each flap is connected to a common lever mechanism on the RH side of the casing. A control cable is installed between the mechanism and the distribution knob on the control panel to operate the flaps together. Turning the distribution knob turns the flaps to direct air through the corresponding outlets in the casing.

Distribution control

Face level

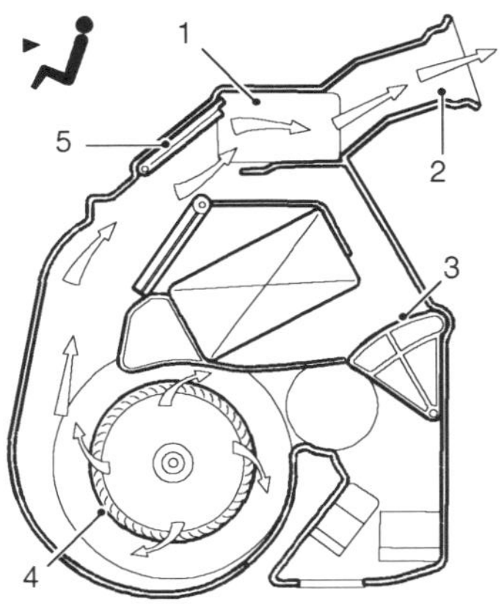

80M0283

Face level and footwells

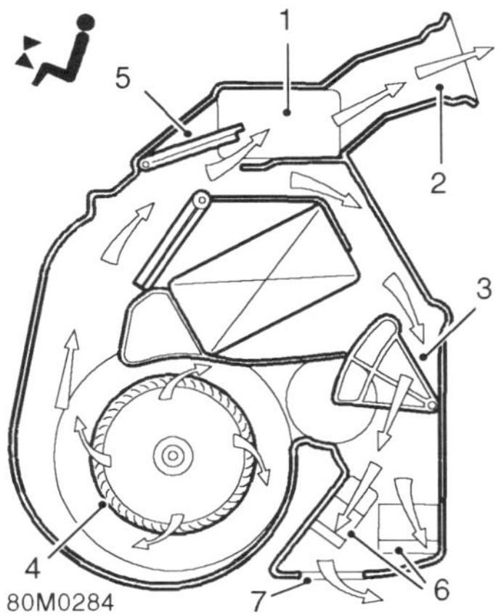

80M0284

Footwells

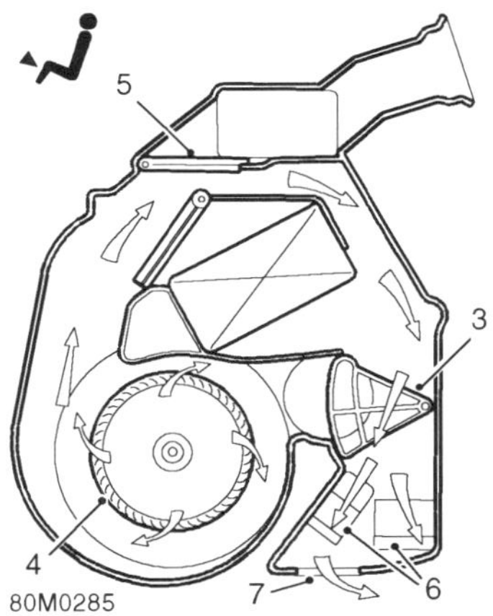

80M0285

Windscreen/Side windows demist

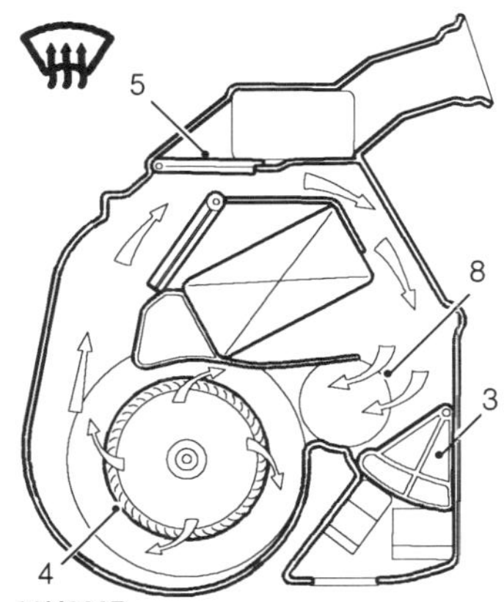

80M0287

Footwells and windscreen/side windows demist

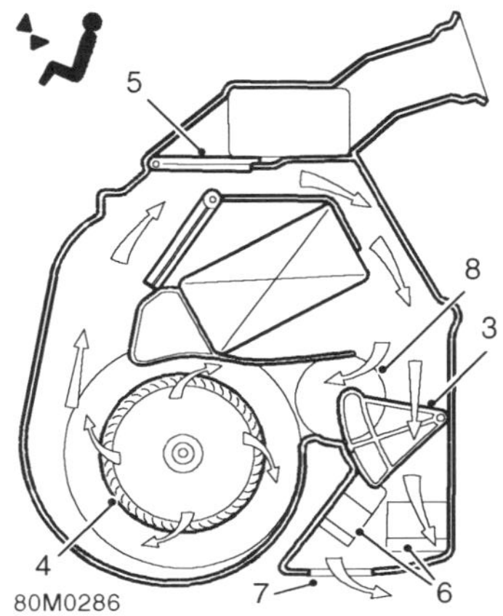

80M0286

Key to distribution control figures

1. Outer face level air outlet
2. Centre face level air outlet
3. Distribution main flap
4. Blower
5. Distribution fresh air flap
6. Front footwell air outlets
7. Rear footwells air outlet
8. Windscreen and side window air outlet

DISTRIBUTION

Air from the heater assembly is distributed around the vehicle interior through fascia and floor level outlets. Fascia outlets consist of fixed vents for the windscreen and side windows, and adjustable vent assemblies for face level air. Floor level outlets consist of fixed vents for the front and rear footwells.

The front footwell vents are integrated into the heater assembly. Two central vent assemblies for face level air are connected directly onto the related outlets of the heater assembly. Air for the rear footwell, outer face level vent assemblies and windscreen/side windows is distributed through ducts.

Fascia outlets

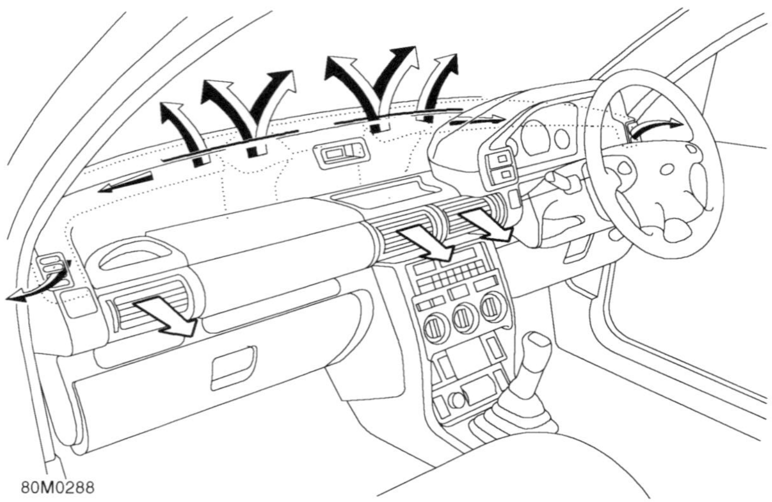

80M0288

Ducts

The rear footwell ducts extend along each side of the transmission tunnel and vent into the rear footwells from below the front seats. The outer face level ducts attach to the underside of the fascia and connect to the vent assembly at each end of the fascia. The windscreen/side window ducts connect to a duct integrated into the top of the fascia.

Vent assemblies

The vent assemblies allow occupants to control the flow and direction of face level air. Each vent assembly incorporates a thumbwheel to regulate flow and moveable vanes to control direction.

CONTROLS

Rotary knobs are installed on the centre console to control air distribution, blower speed and air temperature. The air distribution and temperature knobs operate cables connected to the control flaps in the heater assembly. The blower speed knob operates a rotary switch in the blower's electrical circuit.

Heating and ventilation controls

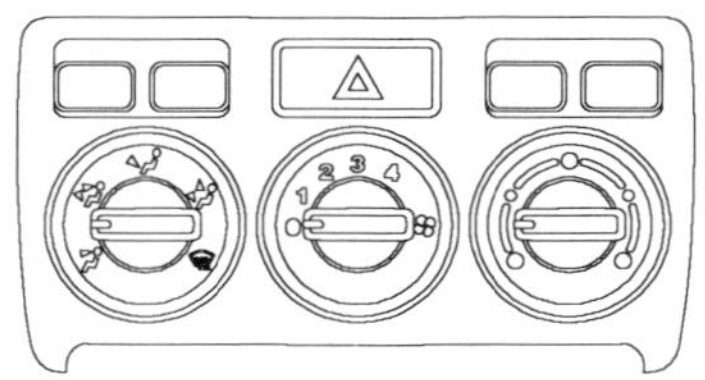

80M0289

OPERATION

Air flow through the heater assembly is directed to the outlets selected by the distribution control knob. The temperature of the air from all except the face level vents depends on the setting of the temperature control knob. Hot air is available from the face level vents only when the temperature control knob is at the maximum heat setting. As the temperature control knob is turned towards cold, the temperature of the air from the face level vents rapidly decreases to ambient (non A/C vehicles) or evaporator outlet temperature (A/C vehicles). The forward speed of the vehicle and the setting of the blower control knob determines the volume of air flowing through system.

SERVO - AIR RECIRCULATION

Service repair no - 80.10.18

Remove

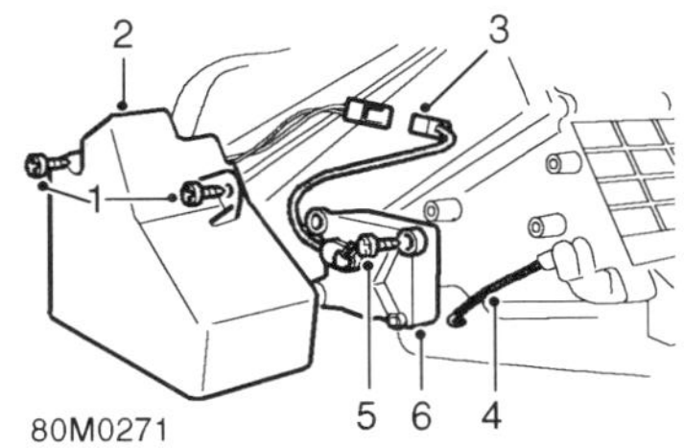

80M0271

1. Remove 2 screws from servo cover.
2. Remove servo cover.
3. Release and disconnect servo multiplug.
4. Release operating rod.
5. Remove 3 screws from servo.
6. Remove servo.

Refit

1. Position servo, fit and tighten securing screws.
2. Connect operating rod.
3. Connect multiplug to servo.
4. Fit servo cover and secure with screws.

SWITCH - RECIRCULATION CONTROL

Service repair no - 80.10.21

Remove

1. Remove radio. ***See ELECTRICAL, Repairs.***

80M0260

2. Remove heater control knobs.
3. Remove 2 screws and remove heater control face plate.

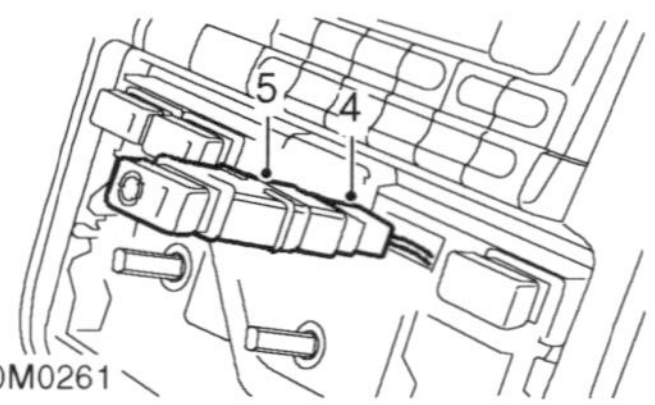

80M0261

4. Disconnect multiplug from switch.
5. Remove switch from heater control mounting.

Refit

1. Fit switch and connect multiplug.
2. Fit heater control face plate and tighten screws.
3. Fit heater control knobs.
4. Fit radio. ***See ELECTRICAL, Repairs.***

SWITCH - HEATER FAN

Service repair no - 80.10.22

Remove

1. Remove front console. ***See BODY, Interior trim components.***

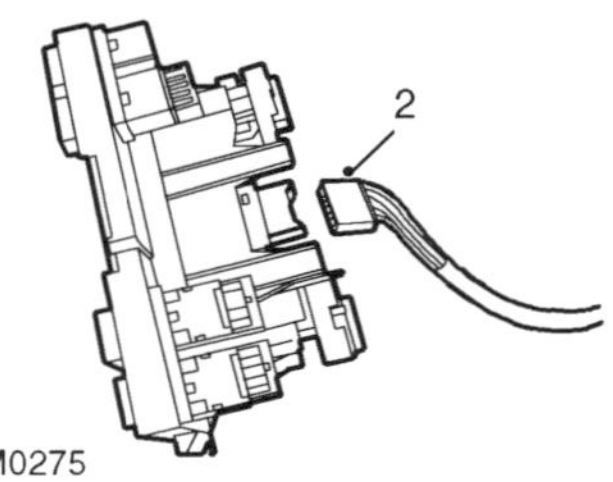

80M0275

2. Disconnect multiplug from switch.

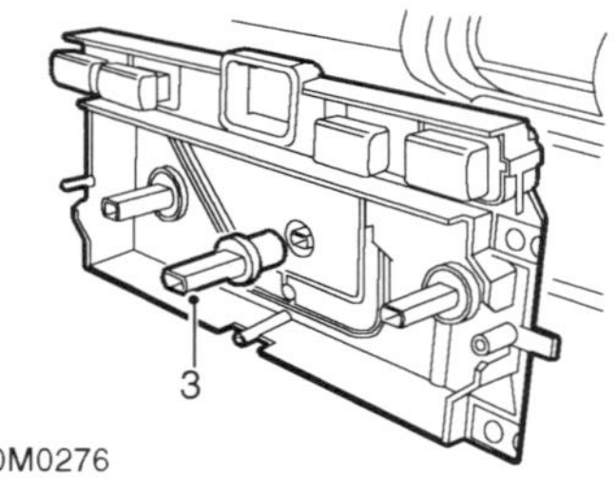

80M0276

3. Remove drive shaft from switch.

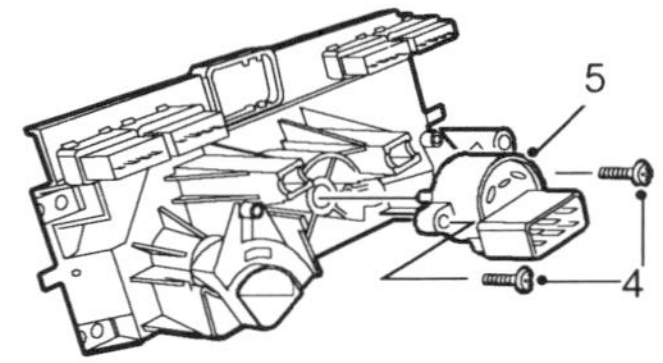

80M0277

4. Remove 2 screws securing switch.
5. Remove switch.

Refit

1. Fit switch and secure with screws.
2. Fit drive shaft.
3. Connect multiplug to switch.
4. Fit front console. ***See BODY, Interior trim components.***

VENTILATOR - FACE LEVEL

Service repair no - 80.15.05

Remove

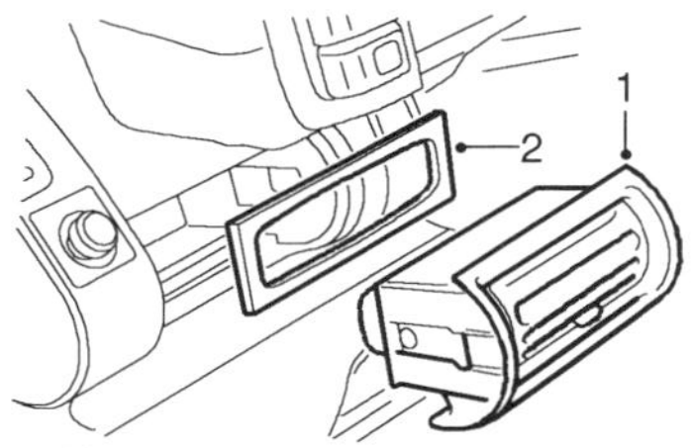

80M0274A

1. Protect fascia and carefully lever vent from fascia.
2. Discard seal.

Refit

1. Fit NEW seal to vent.
2. Fit vent to fascia.

PLENUM - AIR INTAKE MOULDING

Service repair no - 80.15.62

Remove

1. Remove wiper arms. ***See WIPERS & WASHERS, Repairs.***

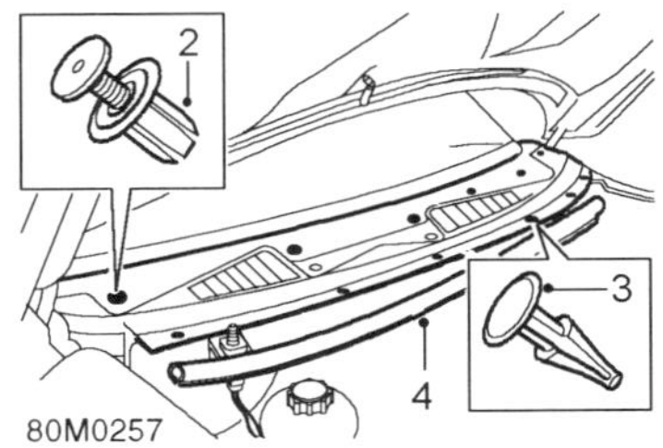

80M0257

2. Remove 6 studs securing rear edge of air intake moulding.
3. Releases 6 studs securing front edge of moulding and bonnet sealing rubber to engine bulkhead. Remove air intake moulding and bonnet sealing rubber.
   Do not carry out further dismantling if component is removed for access only.
4. Remove bonnet sealing rubber from air intake moulding.
5. Position bonnet sealing rubber on replacement air intake moulding and secure with studs.

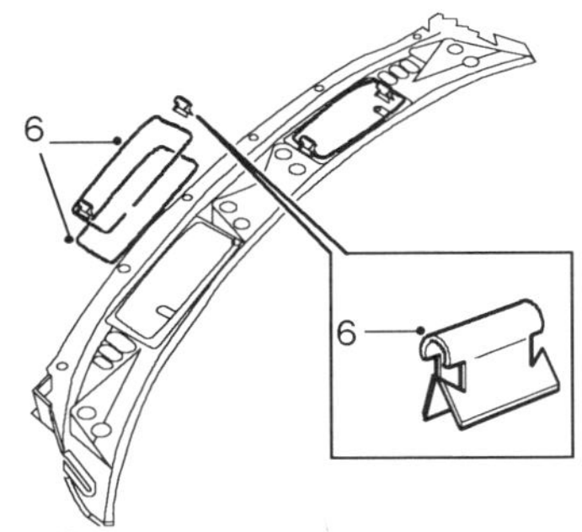

80M0258

6. Remove 4 clips securing air intake filter retainers. Remove retainers and filters.
7. Fit filters and retainer to replacement air intake moulding. Fit clips to retainers.

Refit

1. Position air intake moulding and secure with studs. Fit front studs first.
2. Fit wiper arms. ***See WIPERS & WASHERS, Repairs.***

HEATER

Service repair no - 80.20.01

Remove

1. Drain cooling system. ***See COOLING SYSTEM, Adjustments.***

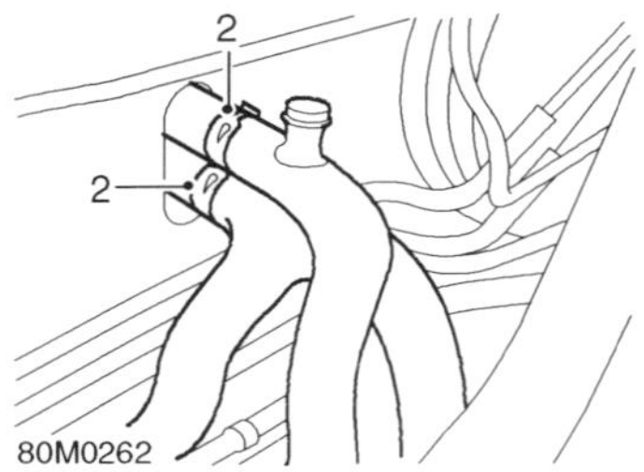

80M0262

2. Release hose clips and release heater hoses from heater pipes.
3. Remove fascia assembly. ***See BODY, Interior trim components.***

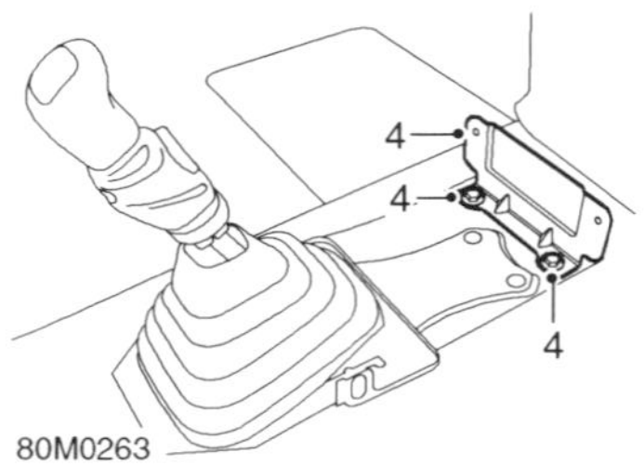

80M0263

4. Remove 2 bolts from console support bracket and remove bracket.

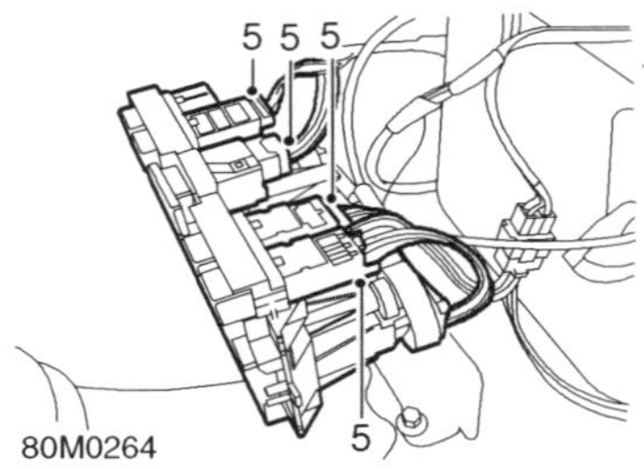

80M0264

5. Disconnect 4 multiplugs from heater control switch pack.

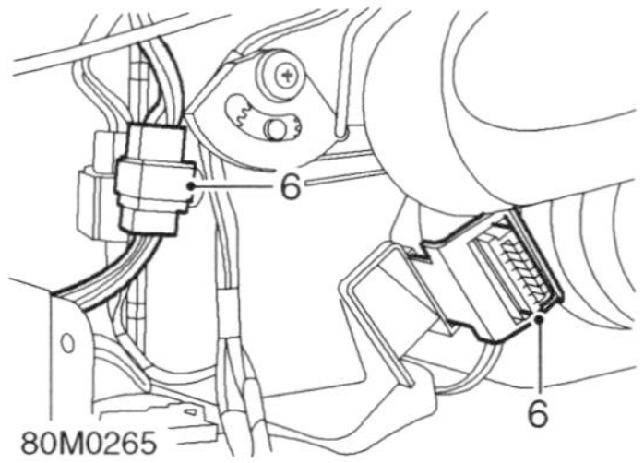

80M0265

6. Disconnect multiplug from heater and release diagnostic socket.

Models with A/C

7. Disconnect multiplug from evaporator.

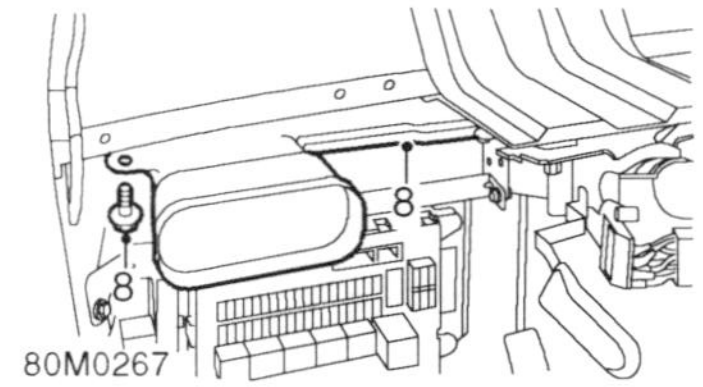

80M0267

All models

8. Remove bolt from duct of LH outer face level vent and remove duct.

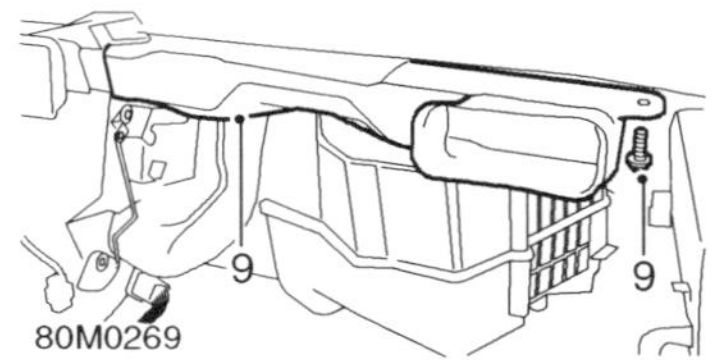

80M0269

9. Remove bolt from duct of RH outer face level vent and remove duct.

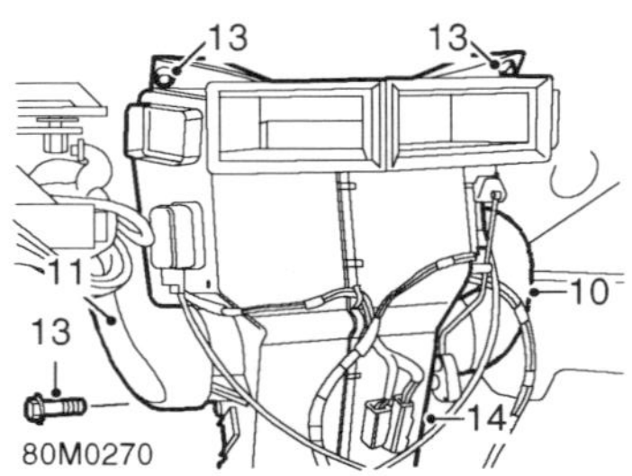

80M0270

10. Remove duct of RH demister vent.
11. Remove duct of LH demister vent.
12. Remove air inlet connector hose.
13. Remove 2 nuts and 1 bolt from heater.
14. Remove heater.

Do not carry out further dismantling if component is removed for access only.

15. Release air blend cable from lever and abutment.
16. Release air distribution cable from lever and abutment.
17. Remove heater control.
18. Position heater control to replacement heater.
19. Connect air distribution cable to lever and abutment.
20. Connect air blend cable to lever and abutment.

Refit

1. Position heater. Fit and tighten nuts and bolt.
2. Fit air inlet connector hose.
3. Fit duct of RH demister vent.
4. Fit duct of RH outer face level vent. Fit and tighten bolt.
5. Fit duct of LH demister vent.
6. Fit duct of LH outer face level vent. Fit and tighten bolt.

Models with A/C

7. Connect multiplug to evaporator.

All models

8. Connect multiplug to heater and secure diagnostic socket.
9. Connect multiplugs to heater control switch pack.
10. Fit console support bracket. Fit and tighten bolts.
11. Fit fascia assembly. ***See BODY, Interior trim components.***
12. Connect hoses to heater pipes and secure clips.
13. Refill cooling system. ***See COOLING SYSTEM, Adjustments.***

MOTOR AND FAN ASSEMBLY

Service repair no - 80.20.12

Remove

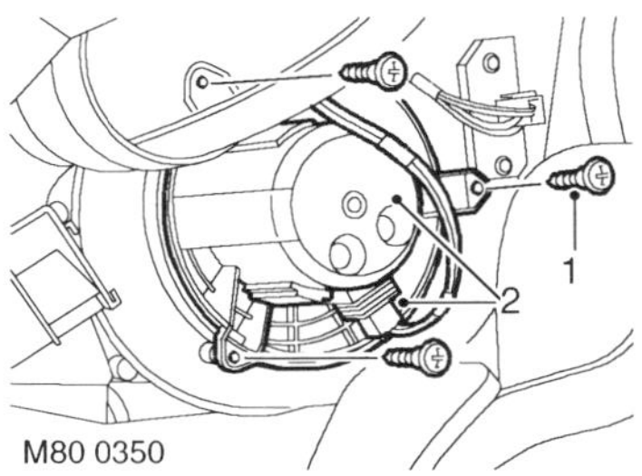

1. Remove 3 screws securing fan motor assembly to heater casing.
2. Release fan assembly from heater and disconnect mutiplug.
3. Remove fan assembly

Refit

1. Position fan assembly to heater and connect multiplug.
2. Align fan assembly to heater casing and secure with screws.

RESISTOR - FAN MOTOR

Service repair no - 80.20.17

Remove

1. *LHD Models Only:* Remove air inlet connector hose.

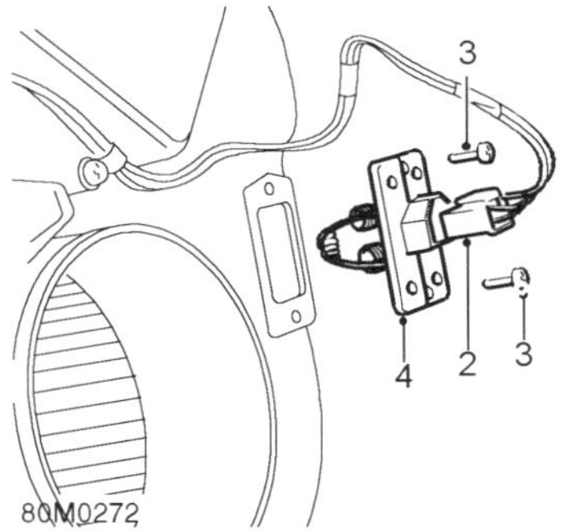

2. Disconnect multiplug from resistor.
3. Remove 2 screws from resistor.
4. Remove resistor from heater.

Refit

1. Fit resistor to heater.
2. Fit and tighten screws.
3. Connect multiplug to resistor.
4. *LHD Models Only:* Fit air inlet connector hose.

MATRIX - HEATER

Service repair no - 80.20.29

Remove

1. Remove heater assembly. ***See this section.***

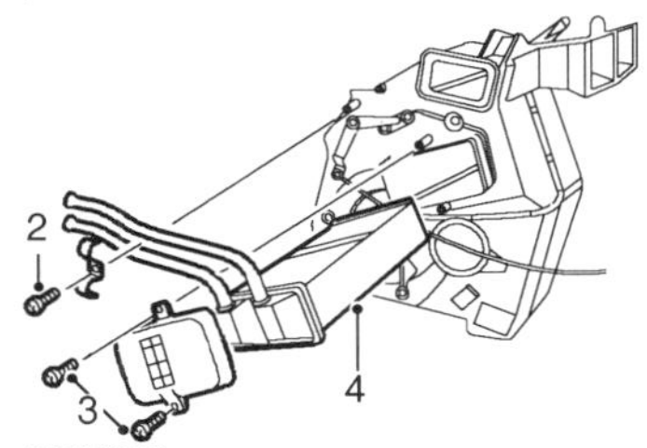

2. Remove screw from pipe clamp and remove pipe clamp.
3. Remove 2 screws from matrix cover and remove cover.
4. Remove heater matrix.

Refit

1. Fit heater matrix to heater body.
2. Fit matrix cover and secure with screws.
3. Fit pipe clamp and secure with screw.
4. Fit heater assembly. ***See this section.***

CONTENTS

Page

AIR CONDITIONING

Where fitted, the air conditioning system supplies cooled and dehumidified, fresh or recirculated air to the interior of the vehicle. Air is cooled by drawing it through the matrix of an evaporator. The air is then ducted into the heater assembly, from where it is distributed to the vehicle interior through the heating and ventilation system air ducts.

Schematic of air conditioning system

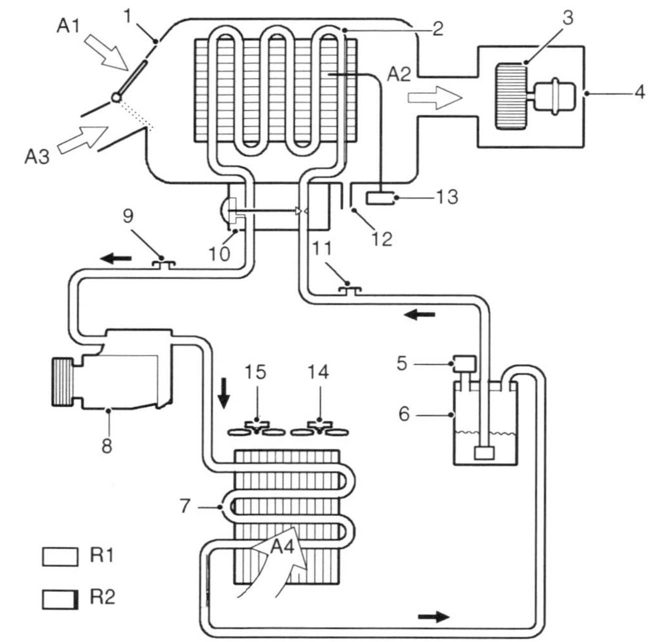

82M0474

1. Cooling unit
2. Evaporator
3. Blower
4. Heater assembly
5. Trinary pressure switch
6. Receiver drier
7. Condenser
8. Compressor
9. Low pressure servicing connection
10. Thermostatic expansion valve
11. High pressure servicing connection
12. Water condensate drain
13. Thermostat
14. Condenser fan
15. Cooling fan

A1. Recirculated air flow
A2. Cooled air flow to heater assembly
A3. Fresh air flow
A4. Ambient air flow through condenser

R1. Refrigerant vapour
R2. Refrigerant liquid

In the heater assembly, the temperature of the air distributed to the vehicle interior can be adjusted by passing a proportion, or all, of the cooled air through the heater matrix. The volume of air being distributed is controlled by the variable speed blower in the heater assembly. For details of temperature control and distribution. **See Heating & Ventilation, Description and Operation**.

The air conditioning system comprises a refrigerant system, a cooling unit and a control system.

REFRIGERANT SYSTEM

The refrigerant system transfers heat from the vehicle interior to the outside atmosphere. The system comprises a compressor, condenser, receiver drier, thermostatic expansion valve and evaporator, joined together by refrigerant lines. The system is a sealed, closed loop, filled with a 725 ± 25 g charge weight of R134a refrigerant as the heat transfer medium. ND oil 8 is added to the refrigerant to lubricate the internal components of the compressor (new compressors come pre filled with ND8 oil 8).

To accomplish the transfer of heat, the refrigerant is circulated around the system, where it passes through two pressure/temperature regimes. In each of the pressure/temperature regimes, the refrigerant changes state, during which process maximum heat absorbtion or release occurs. The low pressure/temperature regime is from the thermostatic expansion valve, through the evaporator to the compressor; the refrigerant decreases in pressure and temperature at the thermostatic expansion valve, then changes state from liquid to vapour in the evaporator, to absorb heat. The high pressure/temperature regime is from the compressor, through the condenser and receiver drier to the thermostatic expansion valve; the refrigerant increases in pressure and temperature as it passes through the compressor, then releases heat and changes state from vapour to liquid in the condenser.

Compressor

The compressor circulates the refrigerant around the system by compressing low pressure, low temperature vapour from the evaporator and discharging the resultant high pressure, high temperature vapour to the condenser.

The compressor is attached to a mounting bracket at the bottom right front of the engine. The drive pulley and refrigerant line connections differ between petrol and diesel engined models, but otherwise the compressor is the same on both engine variants. The compressor is a ten cylinder swash plate unit with a fixed displacement of 177.7 cc/rev. The auxiliary drive belt drives the compressor via a pulley and an electrically actuated magnetic clutch.

Operation of the clutch is controlled by the engine control module (ECM). To protect the refrigerant system from unacceptably high pressure, a pressure relief valve is installed in the outlet side of the compressor. The pressure relief valve is set to operate at 3430 kPa (497.5 lbf.in^2) and vents excess pressure into the engine compartment.

Refrigerant system component layout (LH drive shown, RH drive similar)

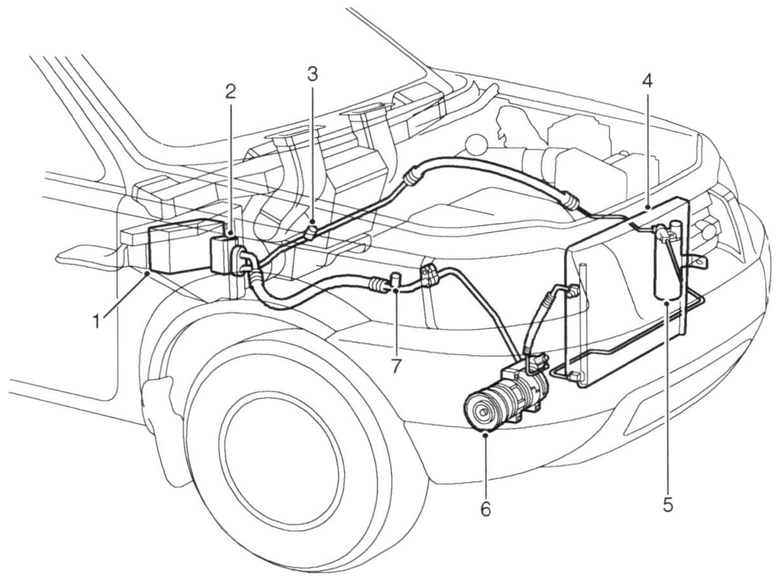

1. Evaporator
2. Thermostatic expansion valve
3. High pressure servicing connection
4. Condenser
5. Receiver drier
6. Compressor
7. Low pressure servicing connection

Compressor components

Petrol models

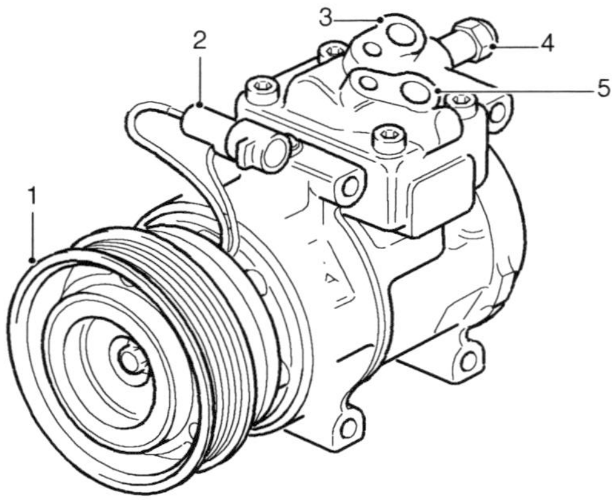

82M0477

Diesel models

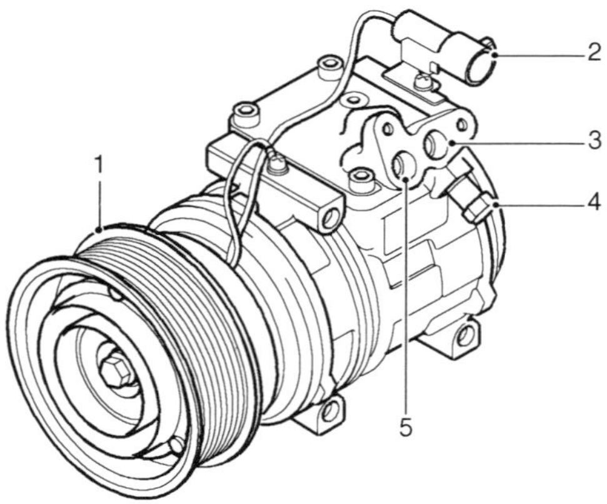

82M0478

1. Pulley
2. Clutch connector
3. Outlet connection
4. Pressure relief valve
5. Inlet connection

Condenser

The condenser transfers heat from the refrigerant to the surrounding air.

The condenser is installed immediately in front of the radiator assembly. Rubber mounting bushes are used to mount the condenser to brackets on the front crossmember and the bonnet locking platform. The condenser is a four pass heat exchanger, of fin and tube brazed aluminium construction, with inlet and outlet connections in the RH end tank.

Ambient air, passing through the condenser matrix due to ram effect and/or the cooling and condenser fans, absorbs heat from the refrigerant, which changes state from a vapour to a liquid.

Condenser components

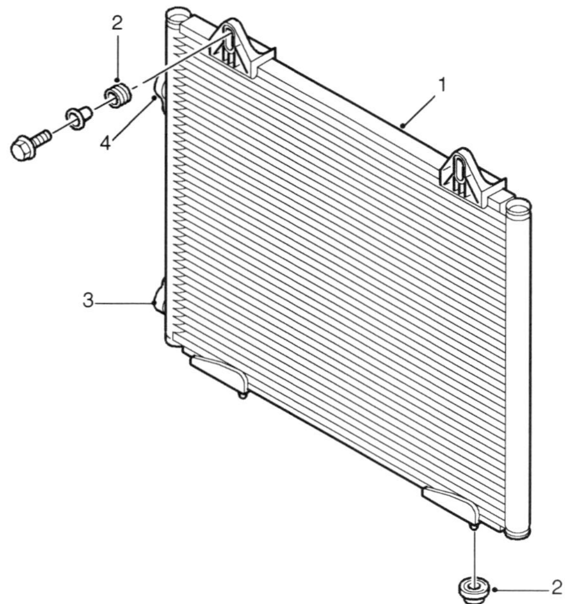

82M0479

1. Condenser matrix
2. Rubber mounting
3. Outlet connection
4. Inlet connection

Cooling and condenser fans

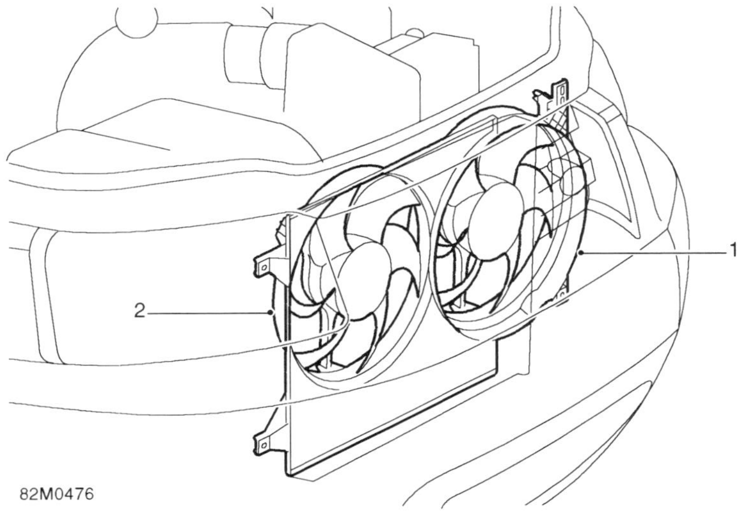

82M0476

1. Condenser fan
2. Cooling fan

Receiver drier

The receiver drier removes moisture and solid impurities from the refrigerant and also acts as a refrigerant reservoir.

Two screws secure the receiver drier to the LH front sidemember in the engine compartment. The receiver drier housing is manufactured in aluminium and contains zeolite desicant to absorb moisture. A mesh screen in the housing removes solid impurities. Inlet, outlet and trinary pressure switch connections are located in the top of the housing.

Liquid refrigerant enters the receiver drier, passes through the desicant and mesh screen, and through a tube to the outlet connection.

Receiver drier components and section

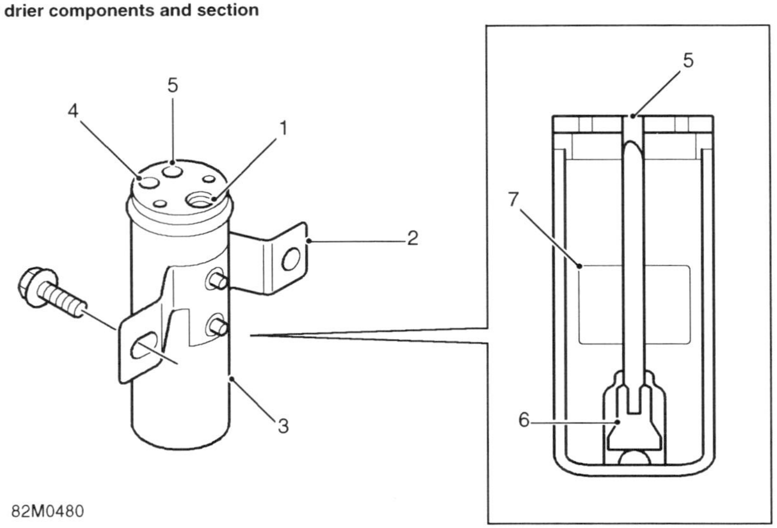

82M0480

1. Trinary pressure switch connection
2. Mounting bracket
3. Housing
4. Inlet connection
5. Outlet connection
6. Screen
7. Desicant

Thermostatic expansion valve (TXV)

The thermostatic expansion valve meters the flow of refrigerant into the evaporator to match the refrigerant flow with the heat load of the air passing through the evaporator matrix.

The thermostatic expansion valve is attached to the evaporator, in the cooling unit behind the passenger's side of the fascia. The valve is the parallel charge type, consisting of an aluminium housing containing inlet and outlet passages. A ball and spring metering valve is installed in the inlet passage and a temperature sensor is installed in the outlet passage. The temperature sensor consists of a push rod connected to a diaphragm. The bottom end of the push rod acts on the ball of the metering valve. Pressure on top of the diaphragm is controlled by evaporator outlet temperature conducted through the push rod. The bottom of the diaphragm senses evaporator outlet pressure via internal passages.

Liquid refrigerant flows through the metering valve into the evaporator. The restriction across the metering valve reduces the pressure and temperature of the refrigerant. The restriction also changes the solid stream of refrigerant into a fine spray, to improve the evaporation process. As the refrigerant passes through the evaporator, it absorbs heat from the air flowing through the evaporator matrix. The increase in temperature causes the refrigerant to vapourize and increase in pressure.

The temperature and pressure of the refrigerant leaving the evaporator are sensed by the temperature sensor, which regulates the metering valve opening to control the volume of refrigerant flowing through the evaporator. The warmer the air flowing through the evaporator matrix, the more heat available to evaporate refrigerant and thus the greater the volume of refrigerant allowed through the metering valve.

Evaporator

The evaporator absorbs heat from the exterior or recirculated air being supplied to the heater assembly.

The fin and plate, brazed aluminium evaporator is installed in the cooling unit behind the passenger's side of the fascia. Inlet and outlet connections on the evaporator are attached to the thermostatic expansion valve.

Low pressure, low temperature refrigerant changes from liquid to vapour in the evaporator, absorbing large quantities of heat as it changes state.

Refrigerant lines

To maintain similar flow velocities around the system, the diameter of the refrigerant lines varies to suit the two pressure/temperature regimes. The larger diameters are installed in the low pressure/temperature regime and the smaller diameters are installed in the high pressure/temperature regime. Low and high pressure charging connections are incorporated into the refrigerant lines for system servicing.

Thermostatic expansion valve components and section

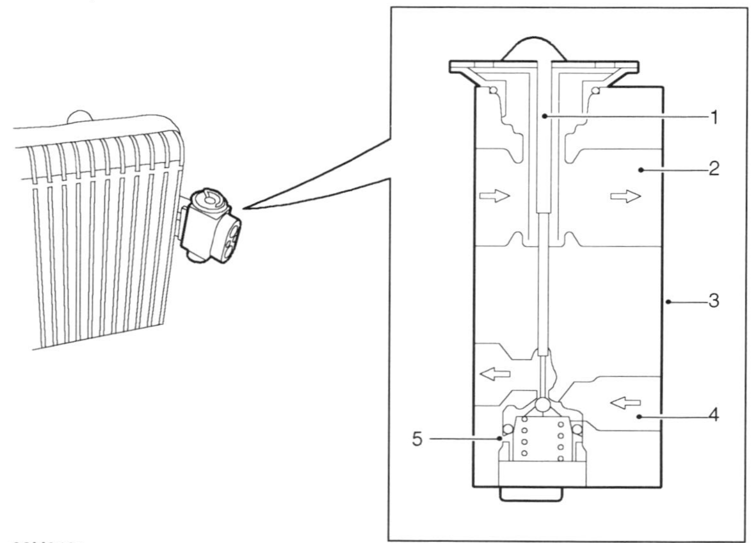

82M0481

1. Temperature sensor
2. Outlet passage
3. Housing
4. Inlet passage
5. Metering valve

COOLING UNIT

The cooling unit directs the flow of air, from the plenum or the vehicle interior, through the evaporator to the heater assembly.

The cooling unit is installed in place of the air inlet duct of non air conditioned vehicles, and contains the evaporator, thermostatic expansion valve and thermostat. It also incorporates the water condensate drain and the fresh and recirculated air inlets. A control flap, operated by a recirculated air motor, opens and closes the fresh and recirculated air inlets. On the downstream side of the evaporator, the casings are lined with polstyrene insulation.

Cooling unit components (LH drive shown, RH drive similar)

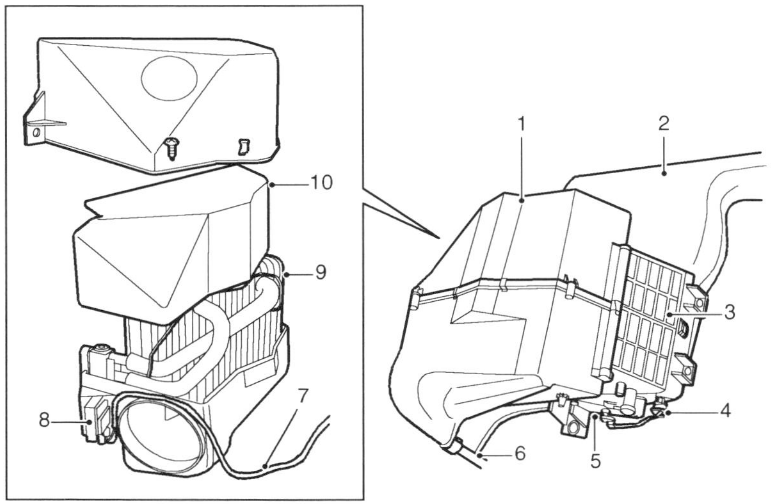

82M0482

1. Evaporator casing
2. Air intake
3. Recirculated air inlet
4. Control flap lever
5. Recirculated air motor
6. Water condensate drain hose
7. Wiring harness
8. Thermostat
9. Evaporator
10. Insulation

CONTROL SYSTEM

In conjunction with the Engine Control Module (ECM), the air conditioning control system operates the condenser fan, cooling fan and compressor clutch to control the operation of the refrigerant system. The control system also operates the recirculated air motor. The control system comprises of two control switches, a trinary pressure switch, a thermostat and a relay module.

Control system components (RH drive shown, LH drive similar)

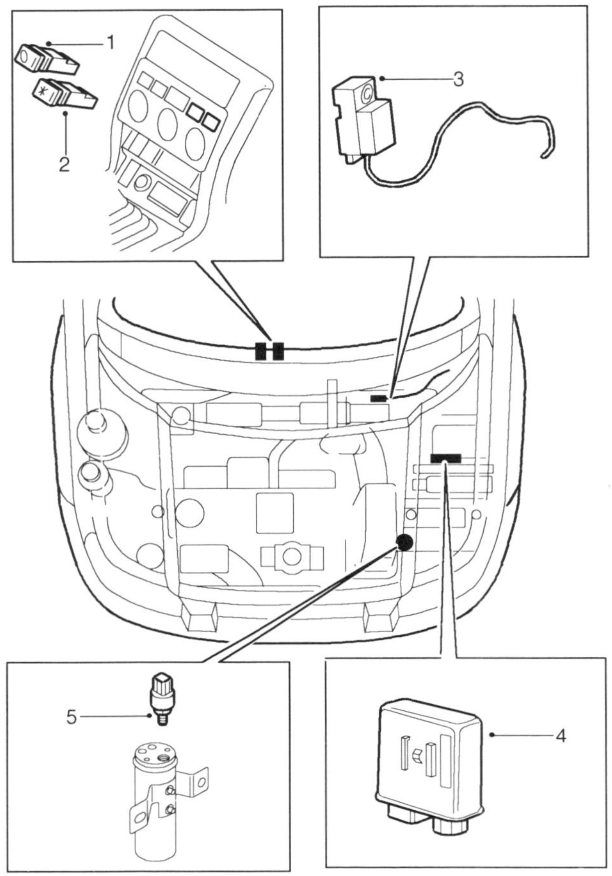

82M0483

1. Fresh/Recirculated air switch
2. Air conditioning switch
3. Thermostat
4. Relay module
5. Trinary pressure switch

Control switches

The control switches consist of two latching push switches installed in the centre console, an air conditioning switch and a fresh/recirculated air switch. Each switch contains an amber indicator lamp which illuminates when air conditioning or recirculated air is selected, as applicable.

Trinary pressure switch

The trinary pressure switch senses refrigerant pressure to protect the compressor, control the refrigerant condensing pressure and limit the maximum refrigerant pressure. Three separate switches, low, normal and high, are contained in the trinary pressure switch, which is installed in the top of the receiver drier.

Since the compressor is lubricated by oil suspended in the refrigerant, the low pressure switch prevents operation of the compressor unless there is a minimum refrigerant pressure, and thus refrigerant charge, in the system. The switch is normally closed, and opens if refrigerant pressure decreases to less than the minimum.

The normal pressure switch provides fan speed request signals for the ECM. Below a given pressure the switch is open, producing a slow speed request signal. When refrigerant pressure increases to a value that indicates additional condensing is required, the switch closes to produce a fast speed request signal.

The high pressure switch is normally closed and opens if refrigerant pressure exceeds the maximum limit.

The three switches operate at the following pressures:

Switch	Opening Pressure, kPa ($lbf.in^2$)	Closing Pressure, kPa ($lbf.in^2$)
Low	100 (14.5) pressure decreasing	140 (20.3) pressure increasing
Normal	1650 (239) pressure decreasing	2150 (319) pressure increasing
High	2850 (413) pressure increasing	2250 (326) pressure decreasing

Thermostat

The thermostat prevents ice formation on the evaporator. The thermostat is installed in the cooling unit, and consists of a pressure operated switch connected to a capillary tube filled with a temperature sensitive fluid. The end of the capillary tube is located between the fins of the evaporator core. If the temperature at the evaporator falls low enough for ice to form on the fins, the fluid in the capillary tube contracts sufficient to open the contacts of the switch. The switch is calibrated to open at -1°C and close at +1°C.

Relay module

The relay module switches power to the compressor clutch, cooling fan and condenser fan under the control of the ECM. The relay module is installed in the engine compartment, on the rear of the battery tray, and consists of four relays in a plastic housing. Two electrical connectors in the housing connect the relay module to the vehicle wiring. The compressor clutch is energized to engage and de-energized to disengage. The motors of the two fans are switched together, in series (6 volts nominal) for slow speed and in parallel (12 volts nominal) for fast speed.

OPERATION

Air conditioning operates only while the engine is running and the blower in the heater assembly is on (any speed). Fresh or recirculated air can be selected with or without the air conditioning being on, provided the ignition is on.

Air conditioning

When the air conditioning switch is selected on, the indicator lamp in the switch illuminates and an air conditioning request signal is input to the ECM. The air conditioning request signal consists of an earth through the blower switch, air conditioning switch, thermostat and trinary pressure switch (low and high switches in series). The ECM is also in receipt of a fan speed request input from the trinary pressure switch (normal switch). The fan speed request signal consists of an open circuit (slow speed) or earth (fast speed).

On receipt of the air conditioning request signal, the ECM switches air conditioning on by signalling the relay module to engage the compressor clutch and run the cooling and condenser fans at the appropriate speed. The engine drives the compressor to circulate the refrigerant. The blower draws fresh or recirculated air through the evaporator. As the air flows through the evaporator, moisture condenses out from the relatively warm air onto the cold evaporator. The dehumidified air is then fed into the heater assembly, from where it is distributed to the vehicle interior.

When the air conditioning switch is selected off, or if the blower is selected off, the indicator lamp in the air conditioning switch extinguishes and the air conditioning request signal is removed from the ECM. The ECM then switches air conditioning off by signalling the relay module to disengage the compressor clutch and stop the cooling and condenser fans.

Refrigerant pressure control

Under most conditions, refrigerant pressure is kept within limits by the ECM switching the fans between slow and fast speeds in response to the fan speed request signal from the trinary pressure switch. However, if refrigerant pressure goes outside the upper or lower limit, the trinary pressure switch removes the air conditioning request signal from the ECM. The ECM then switches air conditioning off (the indicator lamp in the air conditioning switch remains on). When the pressure returns within limits, the ECM automatically switches air conditioning on again.

Evaporator anti-icing

If the temperature of the air leaving the evaporator decreases to -1°C, the thermostat removes the air conditioning request signal from the ECM. The ECM then switches air conditioning off (the indicator lamp in the air conditioning switch remains on). When the temperature of the air leaving the evaporator increases to +1°C, the thermostat reinstates the air conditioning request signal, and the ECM switches air conditioning on again.

Engine overheat protection

If engine coolant temperature reaches 117.5°C (diesel models) or 118°C (petrol models), the ECM switches the air conditioning off to reduce the load on the engine (the indicator lamp in the air conditioning switch remains on). When engine coolant decreases to 115°C (diesel models) or 114°C (petrol models), the ECM switches air conditioning on again.

Fresh/Recirculated air selection

When recirculated air is selected, the amber indicator lamp in the switch illuminates and the recirculated air motor turns the control flap to open the recirculated air inlet and close the fresh air inlet. When fresh air is selected, the amber indicator lamp extinguishes and the recirculated air motor turns the control flap to open the fresh air inlet and close the recirculated air inlet.

Control schematic

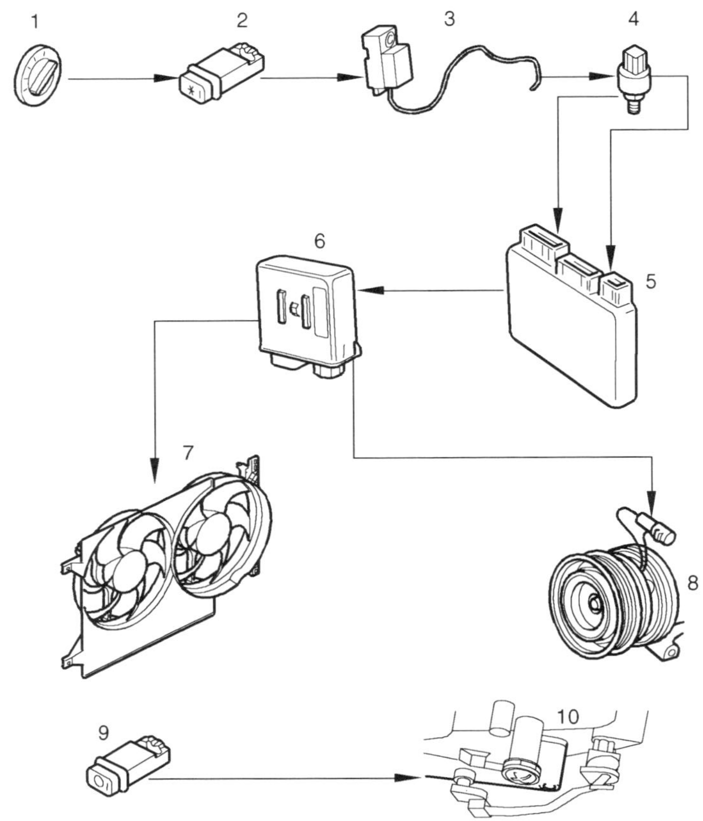

82M0484

1. Blower switch
2. Air conditioning switch
3. Thermostat
4. Trinary pressure switch
5. ECM
6. Relay module
7. Cooling and condenser fans
8. Compressor clutch
9. Fresh/Recirculated air switch
10. Recirculated air motor

RECOVERY AND RECYCLING

NOTE: An air conditioning portable Refrigerant Recovery, Recycling and Recharging Station for use with R134a refrigerant incorporates all the features necessary to recover refrigerant R134a from the A/C system, to filter and remove moisture, to evacuate and recharge with reclaimed refrigerant. The unit can also be used for performance testing and air conditioning system analysis.

1. Connect a refrigerant station to high and low pressure servicing connections.
2. Operate the refrigerant recovery system in accordance with the manufacturer's instructions.

WARNING: Refrigerant must always be recycled before re-use, to ensure that the purity of the refrigerant is high enough for safe use in the air conditioning system.

Recycling should always be carried out with equipment which is design certified by Underwriter Laboratory Inc. for compliance with SAE - J1991. Other equipment may not recycle refrigerant to the required level of purity.

A R134a Refrigerant Recovery Recycling Recharging Station must not be used with any other type of refrigerant.

Refrigerant R134a from domestic and commercial sources must not be used in motor vehicle air conditioning systems.

EVACUATION AND RECHARGING

WARNING: Servicing must be carried out by personnel familiar with both the vehicle system and the charging and testing equipment. All operations must be carried out in a well ventilated area away from open flame and heat source.

1. Add calculated refrigerant oil to the compressor as necessary.
2. Renew receiver/dryer. ***See Repairs.***
3. Connect a Refrigerant Station to the high and low pressure servicing connections.

CAUTION: Whenever the refrigerant system is opened, the receiver/dryer must be renewed immediately before evacuating and recharging the system.

4. Operate the refrigerant evacuation system according to the manufacturers instructions.

NOTE: If the vacuum reading is below 700 mm/Hg after 15 minutes, suspect a leak in the system. Partially recharge the system and check for leaks using an electronic leak tester.

CAUTION: The system must be evacuated immediately before recharging commences. Delay between evacuation and recharging is not permitted.

5. Operate the refrigerant recharging system according to the manufacturers instructions. Amount of refrigerant required to charge system is 725 ± 25 g.
6. If the full charge has not been accepted by the system, start the engine and run it at 1500 rev/min for a minimum of 2 minutes.
7. Switch on the air conditioning system, open the car windows, set the temperature control to cold and switch the blower to maximum speed.
8. Consult the Refrigerant Station Manual for the correct procedure to complete the charge.
9. Carry out the air conditioning system performance test.
10. Switch off air conditioning and wait for pressures to equalize, before disconnecting charging hoses from vehicle.

PERFORMANCE GUIDE-LINES

Carry out this test with bonnet, doors or windows open; air conditioning switched on, temperature control set to cold, face vent mode and blower at maximum speed. Set the air supply control to supply fresh air.

1. Close low pressure valve on Refrigerant Station.
2. Close high pressure valve on Refrigerant Station.
3. Connect Refrigerant Station to the high and low pressure servicing connections.
4. With a thermometer measure the air intake temperature, close to the outside air inlet at the plenum.
5. With a thermometer measure the air outlet temperature, at the centre vent outlet.
6. Run the engine at idle speed for 10 minutes or until normal operating temperature is reached.
7. Read both pressure gauges and thermometers. Check readings against the guide-lines shown in the table below.

	Ambient Temperature °C			
	20 - 24	**25 - 29**	**30 - 34**	**35 - 40**
Intake Temperature, °C	35 - 37	33 - 40	44 - 46	46 - 45
Outlet Temperature, °C	11 - 13	13 - 15	16 - 21	18 - 20
Low Pressure, kPa	250 - 268	266 - 276	288 - 316	306 - 325
High Pressure, kPa	1875 - 1832	1814 - 1789	1841 - 1897	1851 - 1983

The temperatures and pressures may be slightly increased for high humidity conditions. The refrigerant pressure will dictate whether the fans operate in series or parallel, which will itself cause the temperatures and pressures to fluctuate. Fans could operate as follows:

- Condenser and cooling fan both running at half speed (series).
- Condenser and cooling fan both running at full speed (parallel).
- Fans switching from series to parallel.

COMPRESSOR - 'K' SERIES

Service repair no - 82.10.20

Remove

1. Disconnect battery earth lead.
2. Recover refrigerant from A/C system. ***See Adjustments.***
3. Remove alternator. ***See ELECTRICAL, Repairs.***

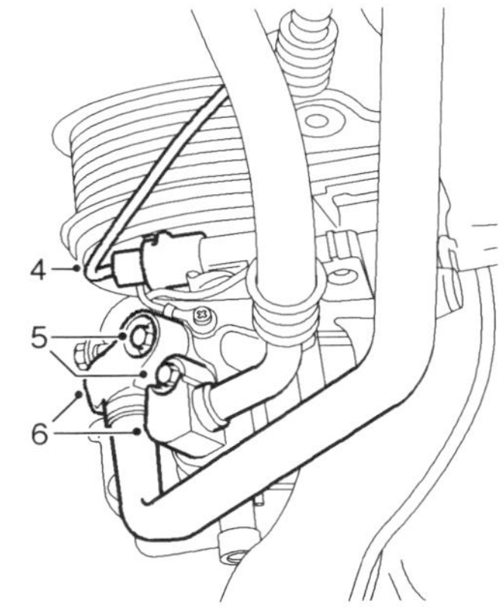

82M0471

4. Disconnect multiplug from A/C compressor.
5. Remove 2 bolts securing A/C pipe unions to compressor.
6. Release A/C pipe unions from compressor.
7. Remove and discard 2 'O' rings from compressor.

CAUTION: Immediately cap all air conditioning pipes to prevent ingress of dirt and moisture into the system.

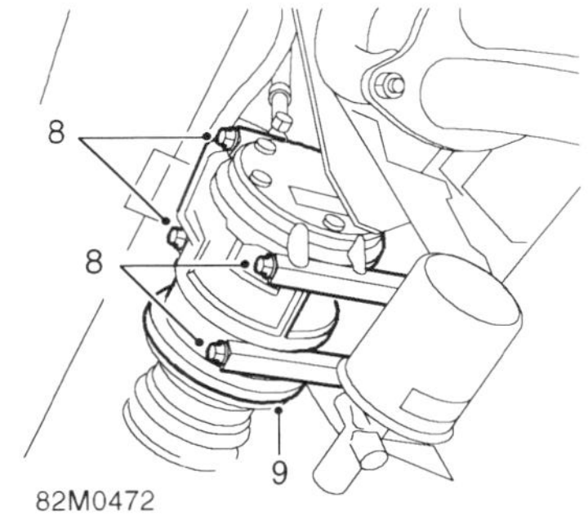

82M0472

8. Remove 4 through bolts securing compressor to engine.
9. Manoeuvre compressor from mounting bracket, remove compressor from beneath vehicle.

Fitting a new compressor

A new compressor is sealed and pressurised with Nitrogen gas, slowly release the sealing cap, gas pressure should be heard to release as the seal is broken.

NOTE: A new compressor should always have it's sealing cap in place and must not be removed until immediately prior to fitting.

A new compressor is supplied with an oil fill quantity (Xcm^3) of 150 ± 20 cm^3. A calculated quantity of oil must be drained from a new compressor before fitting.

To calculate the quantity to be drained:

1. Remove the drain plug from the old compressor.
2. Invert compressor and gravity drain the oil into a calibrated measuring cylinder. Rotating the compressor clutch plate will assist complete draining.
3. Note the quantity of oil drained (Ycm^3)

4. Calculate the quantity of oil to be drained from the NEW compressor using the following formula:

   $Xcm^3 - (Ycm^3 + 20cm^3) = Qcm^3$

5. Remove drain plug from new compressor and drain Qcm^3 of oil. Fit and tighten compressor drain plug.

Fitting an existing compressor

When refitting an existing compressor a quantity of refrigerant oil equivalent to the amount obtained when the system was discharged must be added to the compressor.

Use only an approved refrigerant lubricating oil:

Nippon Denso ND-8
Unipart ND-8

CAUTION: Do not use any other type of refrigerant oil.

Refrigerant oil easily absorbs water and must not be stored for long periods. Do not pour unused oil back into the container.

Refit

1. Fit compressor and manoeuvre onto mounting bracket.
2. Fit through bolts securing compressor to mounting bracket and tighten to 45 Nm.
3. Clean compressor and pipe connections.
4. Remove caps from compressor and pipe connections.
5. Lubricate NEW 'O' rings with refrigerant oil and fit to compressor.
6. Position A/C pipe unions to compressor, fit securing bolts and tighten to 7 - 10 Nm.
7. Connect multiplug to compressor.
8. Fit alternator. ***See ELECTRICAL, Repairs.***
9. Fit NEW receiver/drier. ***See this section.***
10. Connect battery earth lead.
11. Recharge A/C system. ***See Adjustments.***

COMPRESSOR - 'L' SERIES

Service repair no - 82.10.20

Remove

1. Disconnect battery earth lead.
2. Recover refrigerant from A/C system. ***See Adjustments.***
3. Remove auxiliary drive belt ***See ELECTRICAL, Repairs.***

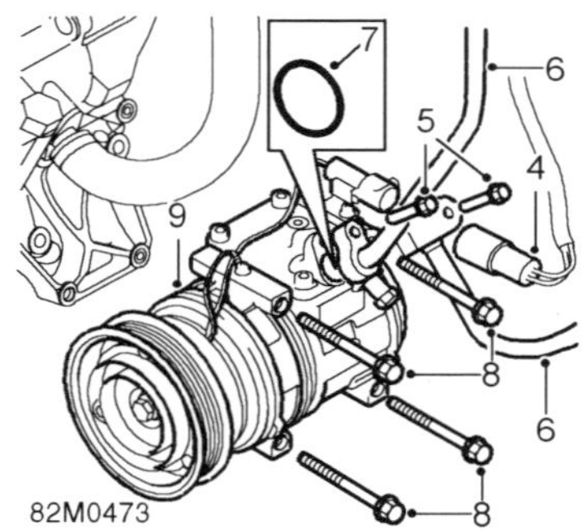

82M0473

4. Disconnect multiplug from A/C compressor.
5. Remove 2 bolts securing A/C pipe unions to compressor.
6. Release A/C pipe unions from compressor.
7. Remove and discard 2 'O' rings from compressor.

CAUTION: Immediately cap all air conditioning pipes to prevent ingress of dirt and moisture into the system.

8. Remove 4 through bolts securing compressor to engine.
9. Manoeuvre compressor from mounting bracket, remove compressor from beneath vehicle.

Fitting a new compressor

A new compressor is sealed and pressurised with Nitrogen gas, slowly release the sealing cap, gas pressure should be heard to release as the seal is broken.

NOTE: A new compressor should always have it's sealing cap in place and must not be removed until immediately prior to fitting.

A new compressor is supplied with an oil fill quantity (Xcm^3) of 150 ± 20 cm^3. A calculated quantity of oil must be drained from a new compressor before fitting.

To calculate the quantity to be drained:

1. Remove the drain plug from the old compressor.
2. Invert compressor and gravity drain the oil into a calibrated measuring cylinder. Rotating the compressor clutch plate will assist complete draining.
3. Note the quantity of oil drained (Ycm^3)
4. Calculate the quantity of oil to be drained from the NEW compressor using the following formula:

   $Xcm^3 - (Ycm^3 + 20cm^3) = Qcm^3$

5. Remove drain plug from new compressor and drain Qcm^3 of oil. Fit and tighten compressor drain plug.

Fitting an existing compressor

When refitting an existing compressor a quantity of refrigerant oil equivalent to the amount obtained when the system was discharged must be added to the compressor.

Use only an approved refrigerant lubricating oil:

Nippon Denso ND-8
Unipart ND-8

CAUTION: Do not use any other type of refrigerant oil.

Refrigerant oil easily absorbs water and must not be stored for long periods. Do not pour unused oil back into the container.

Refit

1. Clean compressor and mating faces.
2. Fit compressor and manoeuvre onto mounting bracket.
3. Fit through bolts securing compressor to mounting bracket and tighten to 45 Nm.
4. Clean compressor and pipe connections.
5. Remove caps from compressor and pipe connections.
6. Lubricate NEW 'O' rings with refrigerant oil and fit to compressor.
7. Position A/C pipe unions to compressor, fit securing bolts and tighten to 7 - 10 Nm.
8. Connect multiplug to compressor.
9. Fit auxiliary drive belt. ***See ELECTRICAL, Repairs.***
10. Replace receiver/drier. ***See this section.***
11. Connect battery earth lead.
12. Recharge A/C system. ***See Adjustments.***

CONDENSER

Service repair no - 82.15.07

Remove

1. Disconnect battery earth lead.
2. Recover refrigerant from A/C system. ***See Adjustments.***
3. Remove front bumper. ***See BODY, Exterior fittings.***

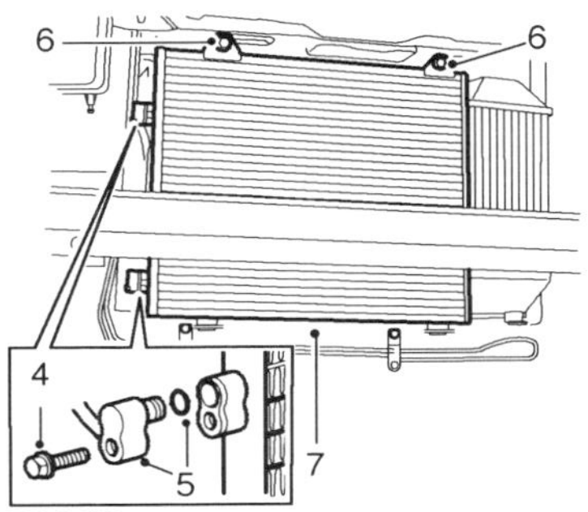

82M0470

4. Remove 2 bolts securing A/C pipes to condenser.
5. Release pipes from condenser, remove and discard 'O' rings.

CAUTION: Immediately cap all air conditioning pipes to prevent ingress of dirt and moisture into the system.

6. Remove 2 bolts securing condenser to upper mounting brackets.
7. Remove condenser.

Refit

1. Clean condenser and pipe connections.
2. Position condenser and tighten bolts to 9 Nm.
3. Lubricate NEW 'O' rings with refrigerant oil and fit to condenser pipes.
4. Position A/C pipes to condenser, fit bolts and tighten to 7 - 10 Nm.
5. Fit NEW receiver drier. ***See this section.***
6. Fit front bumper. ***See BODY, Exterior fittings.***
7. Recharge A/C system. ***See Adjustments.***
8. Connect battery earth lead.

RECEIVER DRIER

Service repair no - 82.17.02/03

Remove

1. Disconnect battery earth lead.
2. Recover refrigerant from A/C system. ***See Adjustments.***

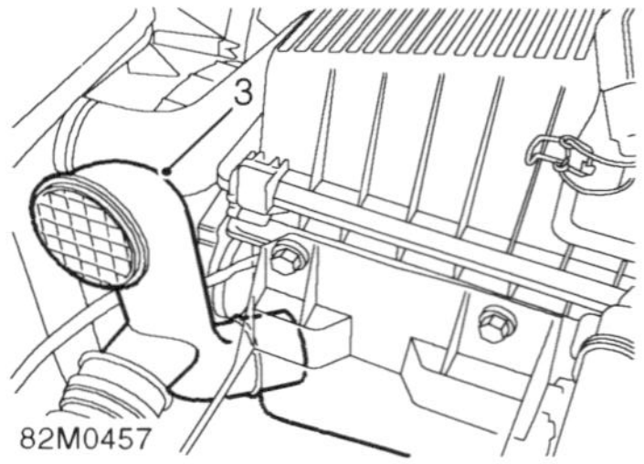

3. Disconnect air intake elbow from air cleaner assembly and resonator box, pipe.

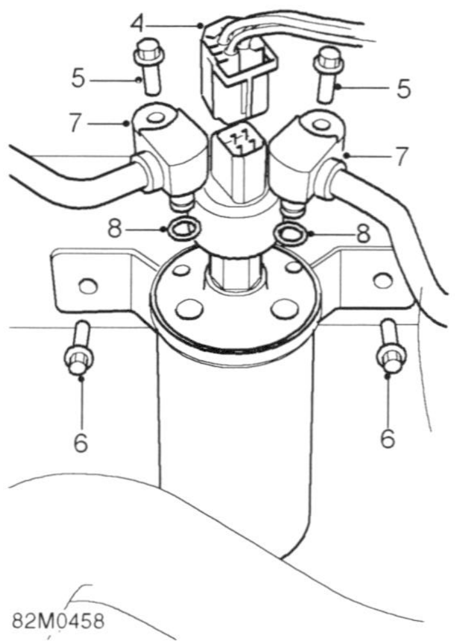

4. Release multiplug from trinary switch.
5. Remove 2 bolts from pipe unions.
6. Remove 2 bolts from receiver drier bracket.
7. Release pipe unions and discard receiver drier.
8. Remove 1 'O' ring from each pipe union, discard 'O' rings.

⚠ **CAUTION: Immediately cap all air conditioning pipes to prevent ingress of dirt and moisture into the system.**

Refit

1. Lubricate NEW 'O' rings with refrigerant oil and fit to pipe unions.
2. Position NEW receiver drier to vehicle, fit and tighten bracket bolts.
3. Fit pipe unions to receiver drier, fit and tighten bolts to 7 - 10 Nm.
4. Fit multiplug to trinary switch.
5. Fit air intake elbow.
6. Recharge A/C system. ***See Adjustments.***
7. Connect battery earth lead.

SWITCH - CONTROL

Service repair no - 82.20.07

Remove

1. Remove radio. ***See ELECTRICAL, Repairs.***

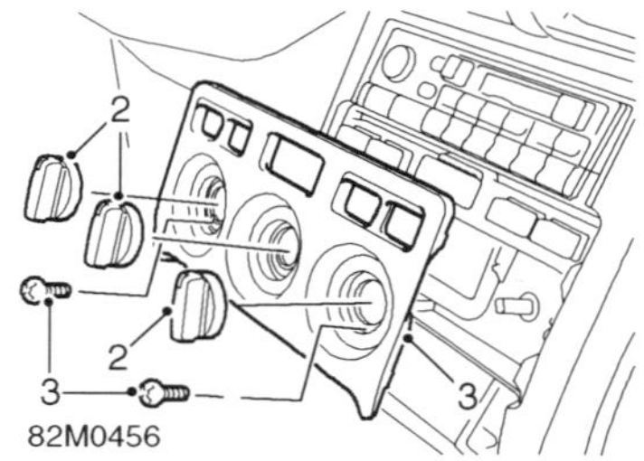

2. Remove heater control knobs.
3. Remove 2 screws and remove heater control face plate.

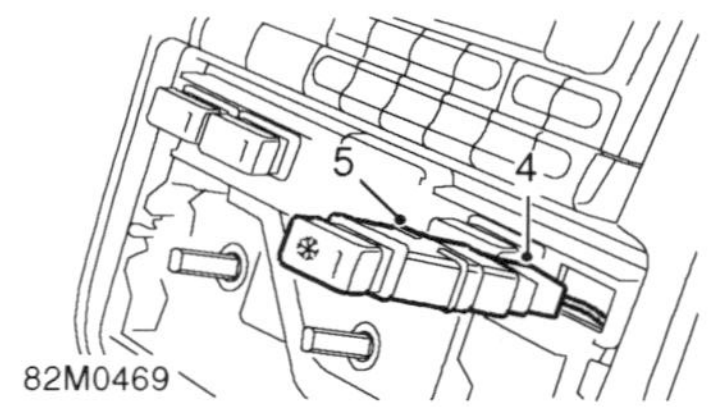

4. Disconnect multiplug from air conditioning control switch.
5. Remove switch from heater control mounting.

Refit

1. Fit switch and connect multiplug.
2. Fit heater control face plate and tighten screws.
3. Fit heater control knobs.
4. Fit radio. ***See ELECTRICAL, Repairs.***

THERMOSTATIC EXPANSION VALVE (TXV)

Service repair no - 82.25.01

Remove

1. Remove receiver drier. ***See this section.***

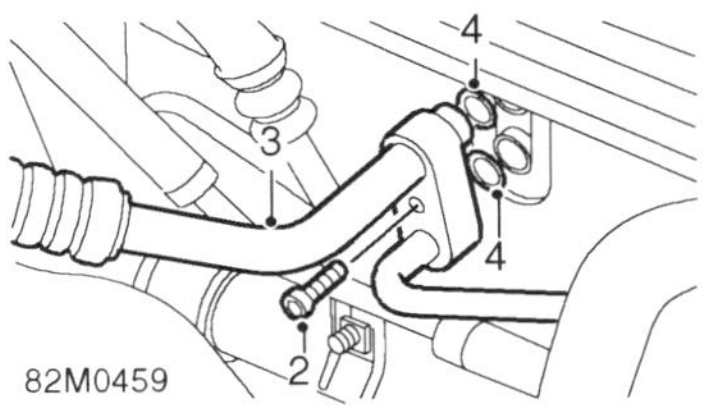

82M0459

2. Remove bolt securing pipe to evaporator.
3. Release pipe from evaporator.
4. Remove and discard 2 'O' rings.

⚠ **CAUTION: Immediately cap all air conditioning pipes to prevent ingress of dirt and moisture into the system.**

5. Remove fascia. ***See BODY, Interior trim components.***

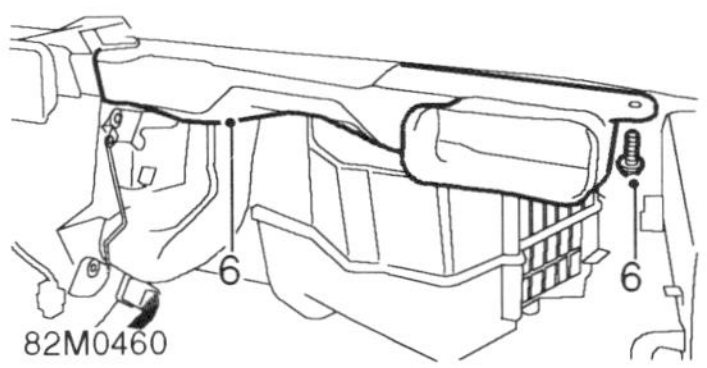

82M0460

6. Remove bolt from face level ducting, and remove ducting.

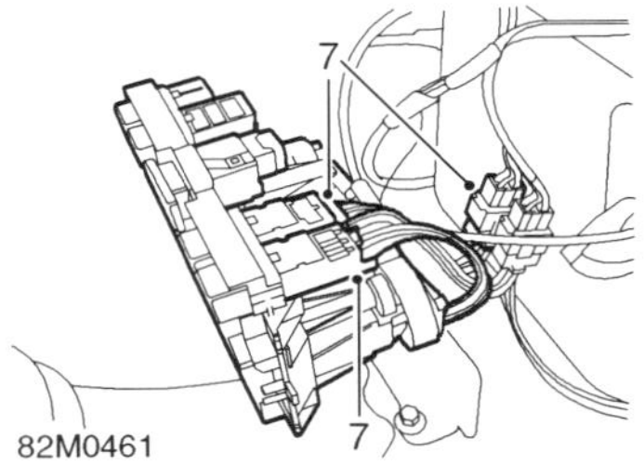

82M0461

7. Disconnect 3 multiplugs from air conditioning switches and heater harness.

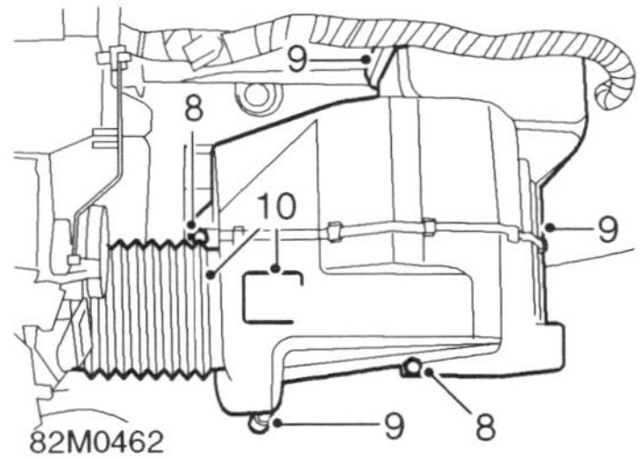

82M0462

8. Remove 2 nuts securing evaporator to body.
9. Release evaporator from drain hose and air intake, remove evaporator assembly.
10. Collect air duct and pipe seal.

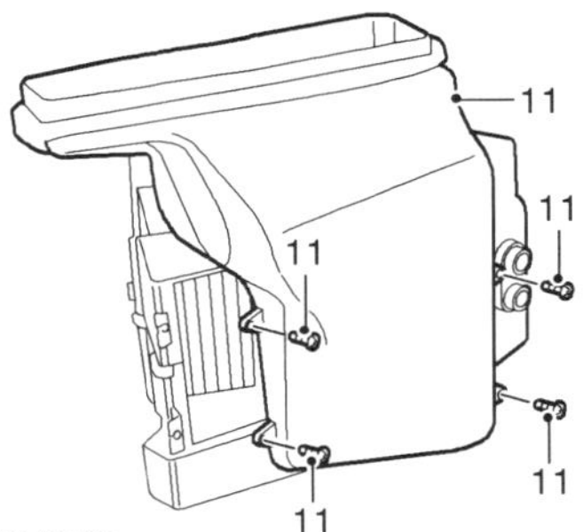

82M0464

11. Remove 4 screws from air ducting and remove ducting.

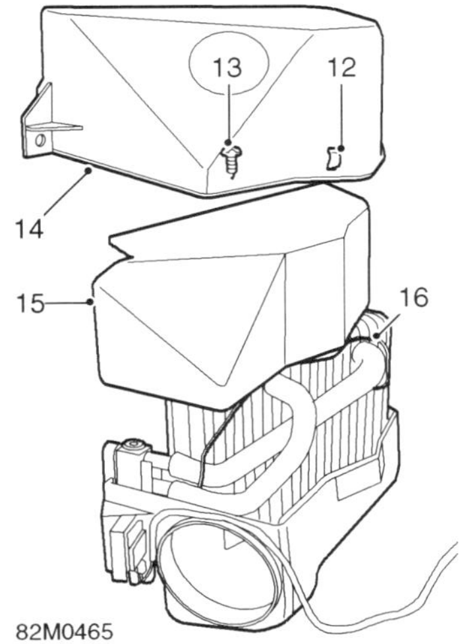

82M0465

12. Remove 5 clips from evaporator casing.
13. Remove 3 screws from evaporator casing.
14. Remove top half of evaporator casing.
15. Remove insulation from evaporator matrix.
16. Release thermostat pipe and ease to one side.

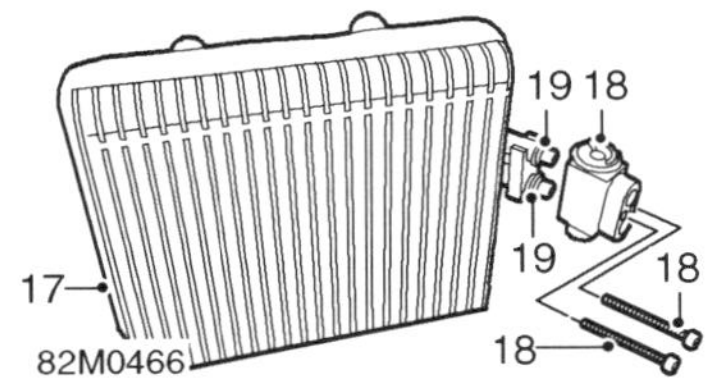

82M0466

17. Remove evaporator matrix.
18. Remove 2 Allen screws from TXV and and remove valve.
19. Remove and discard 2 'O' rings.

Refit

1. Clean evaporator pipes.
2. Lubricate NEW 'O' rings with refrigerant oil and fit to TXV.
3. Fit TXV to evaporator matrix.
4. Fit and tighten Allen screws.
5. Position evaporator matrix in casing.
6. Locate thermostat pipe in matrix.
7. Fit insulation to evaporator matrix.
8. Fit top half of evaporator casing.
9. Fit screws to casing.
10. Fit clips to casing.
11. Fit air ducting.
12. Fit and tighten ducting screws.
13. Position air duct and pipe seal.
14. Locate evaporator assembly to drain hose and air intake, position evaporator to body.
15. Fit and tighten securing nuts.
16. Connect multiplugs to heater harness and air conditioning switches.
17. Fit face level vent ducting, fit and tighten bolt.
18. Fit fascia. ***See BODY, Interior trim components.***
19. Remove plugs from evaporator pipe.
20. Clean evaporator pipe.
21. Lubricate NEW 'O' rings with refrigerant oil.
22. Fit 'O' rings to evaporator pipe.
23. Position evaporator pipe to evaporator, fit and tighten bolt.
24. Fit receiver drier. ***See this section.***

EVAPORATOR

Service repair no - 82.25.20

The procedure for renewing the evaporator is identical to renewing the thermostatic expansion valve (TXV). ***See this section.***

THERMOSTAT - EVAPORATOR

Service repair no - 82.25.50

Remove

1. Remove receiver drier. ***See this section.***

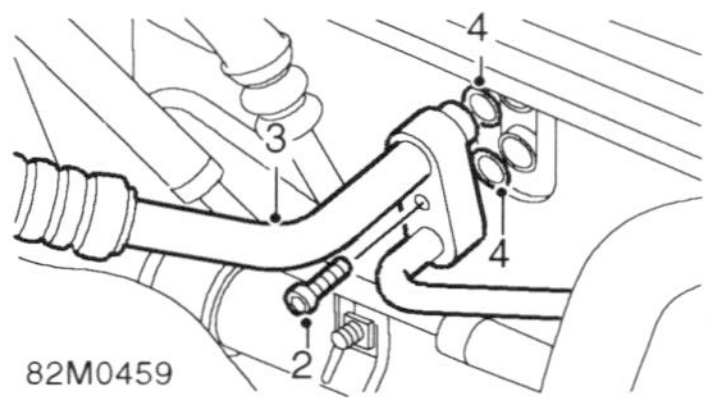

82M0459

2. Remove bolt securing pipe to evaporator.
3. Release pipe from evaporator.
4. Remove and discard 2 'O' rings.

⚠ **CAUTION: Immediately cap all air conditioning pipes to prevent ingress of dirt and moisture into the system.**

5. Remove fascia. ***See BODY, Interior trim components.***

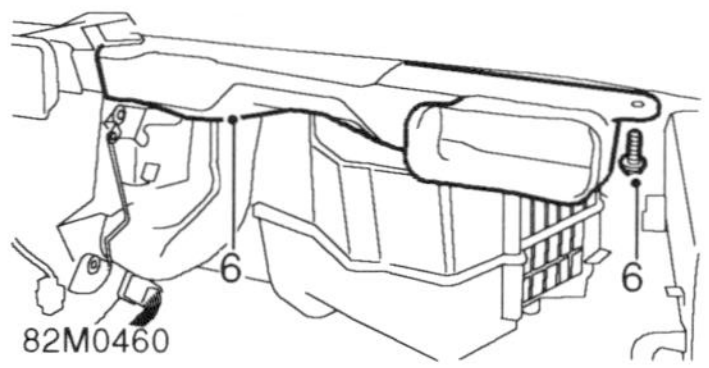

82M0460

6. Remove bolt from face level ducting, and remove ducting.

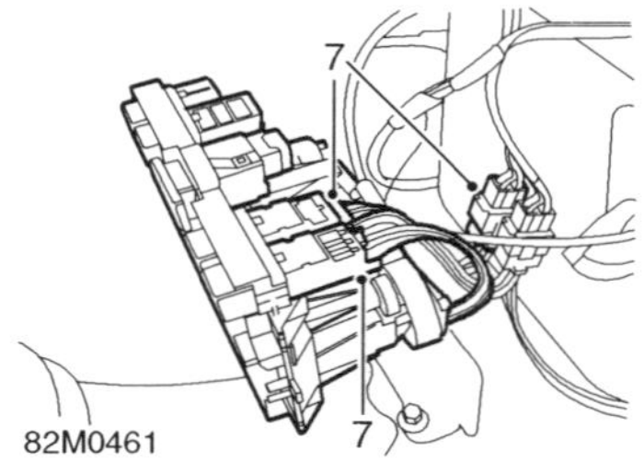

82M0461

7. Disconnect 3 multiplugs from air conditioning switches and heater harness.

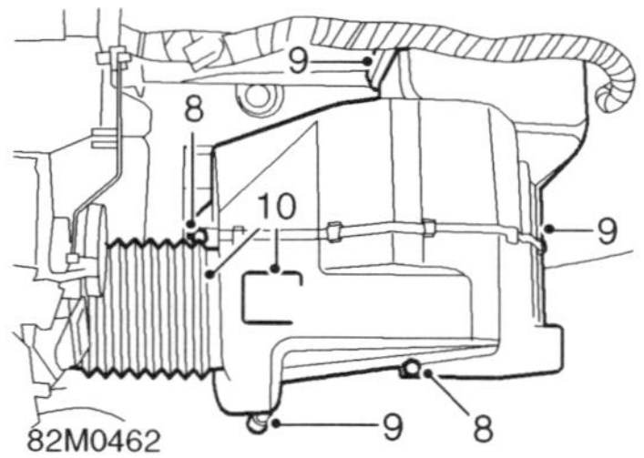

82M0462

8. Remove 2 nuts securing evaporator to body.
9. Release evaporator from drain hose and air intake, remove evaporator assembly.
10. Collect air duct and pipe seal.

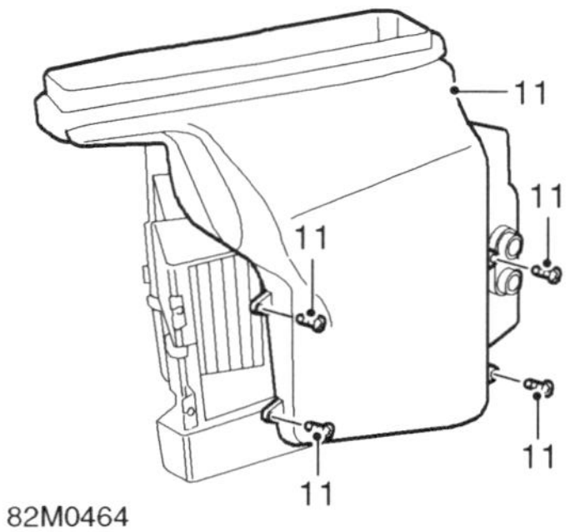

82M0464

11. Remove 4 screws from air ducting and remove ducting.

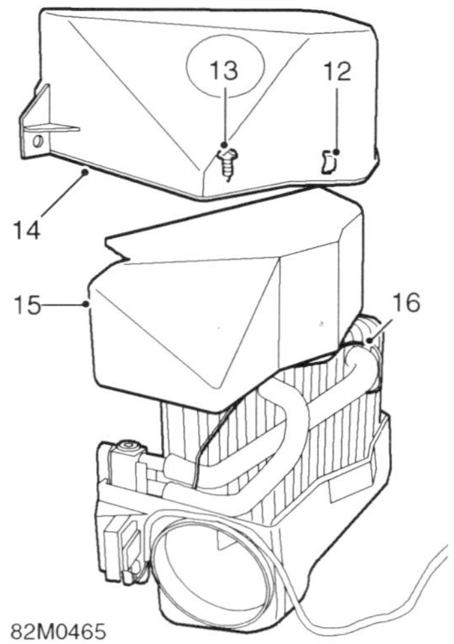

82M0465

12. Remove 5 clips from evaporator casing.
13. Remove 3 screws from evaporator casing.
14. Remove top half of evaporator casing.
15. Remove insulation from evaporator matrix.
16. Release thermostat pipe and ease to one side.

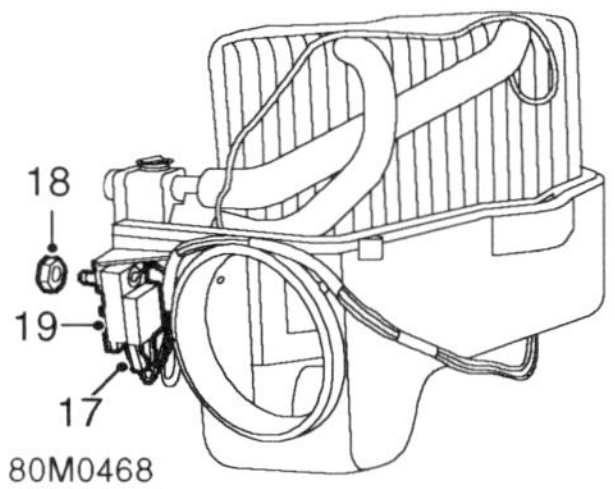

80M0468

17. Disconnect Lucars from thermostat.
18. Remove nut from thermostat.
19. Remove thermostat complete with sensor pipe.

Refit

1. Locate thermostat pipe and secure to evaporator matrix.
2. Position thermostat and tighten nut.
3. Connect Lucars to thermostat.
4. Fit insulation to evaporator matrix.
5. Fit top half of evaporator casing.
6. Fit screws to casing.
7. Fit clips to casing.
8. Fit air ducting.
9. Fit and tighten ducting screws.
10. Position air duct and pipe seal.
11. Locate evaporator assembly to drain hose and air intake, position evaporator to body.
12. Fit and tighten securing nuts.
13. Connect multiplugs to heater harness and air conditioning switches.
14. Fit face level vent ducting, fit and tighten bolt.
15. Fit fascia. ***See BODY, Interior trim components.***
16. Remove plugs from evaporator pipe.
17. Clean evaporator pipe.
18. Lubricate NEW 'O' rings with refrigerant oil.
19. Fit 'O' rings to evaporator pipe.
20. Position evaporator pipe to evaporator, fit and tighten bolt.
21. Fit receiver drier. ***See this section.***

CONTENTS

Page

WIPERS & WASHERS

WINDSCREEN WIPER COMPONENTS

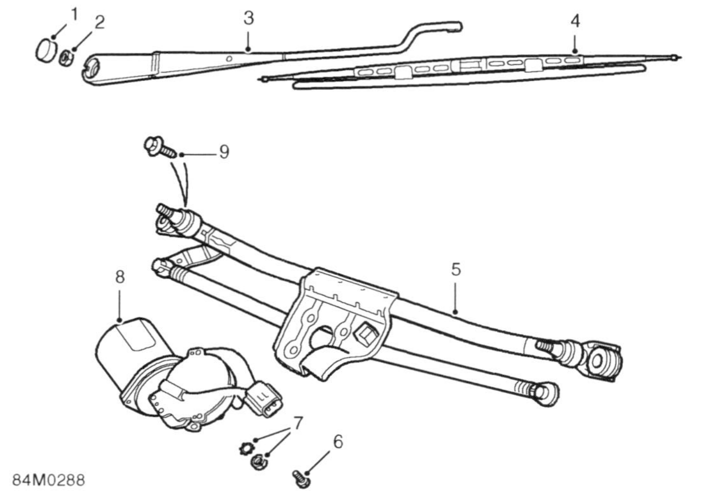

RHD shown, LHD mirror image

1. Cap 2 off
2. Nut 2 off
3. Wiper arm 2 off
4. Wiper blade 2 off
5. Wiper link assembly
6. Motor mounting bolt 3 off
7. Nut and washer, spindle to link
8. Wiper motor
9. Mounting bolt 3 off

REAR SCREEN WIPER COMPONENTS

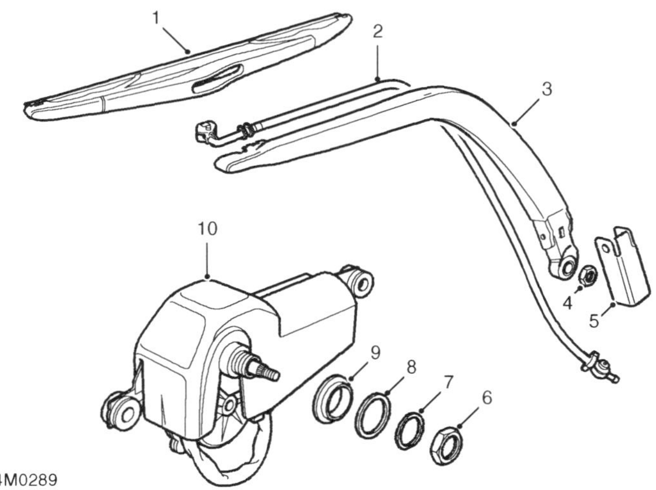

84M0289

1. Wiper blade
2. Washer jet and hose
3. Wiper arm
4. Nut
5. Cover
6. Nut
7. Washer
8. Rubber washer
9. Rubber spacer
10. Wiper motor

WASHER COMPONENTS

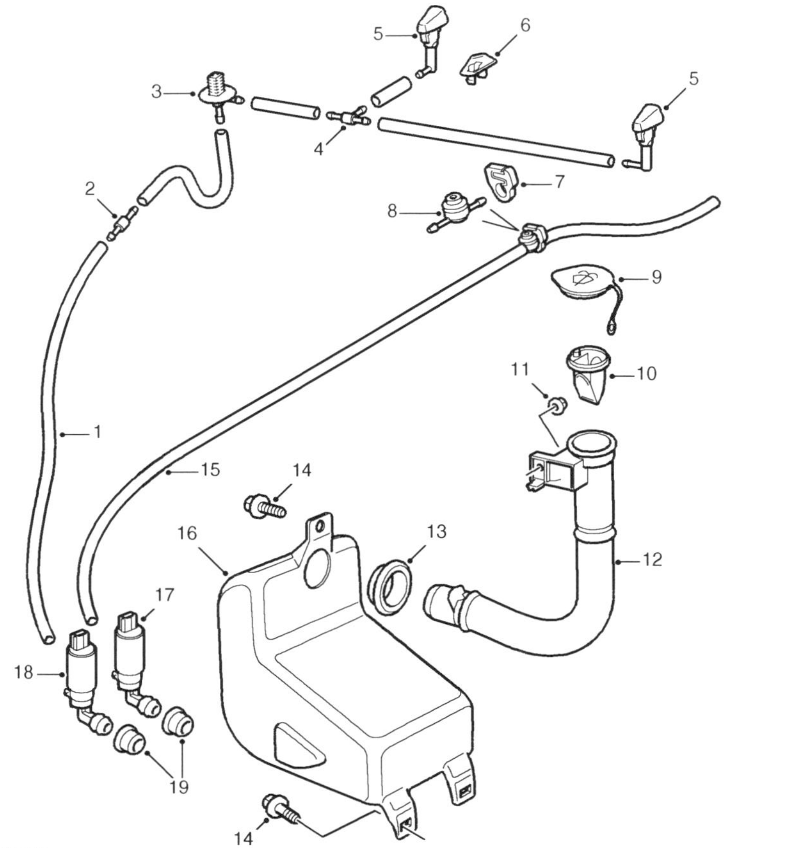

84M0290

1. Hose - Windscreen
2. Non return valve
3. Connector elbow
4. Connector T' piece
5. Washer jet 2 off
6. Washer jet holder 2 off
7. 4 mm hose clip
8. Non return valve
9. Filler cap
10. Filler filter
11. Mounting nut
12. Filler neck tube
13. Filler neck seal
14. Mounting bolt 3 off
15. Hose - Rear screen
16. Washer reservoir
17. Rear screen washer pump
18. Windscreen washer pump
19. Grommet 2 off

WINDSCREEN WIPERS DESCRIPTION

The windscreen wiper functions are controlled from the wash/wipe stalk located on the right hand side of the steering column. The wash/wipe stalk is a multi-function switch which controls the windscreen wiper, intermittent and washer operation. The Central Control Unit (CCU) is responsible for the operation of the intermittent wipe facility and the park facility when the wipers are turned off.

Two front windscreen wipers are operated by a single electric motor. The motor and a link assembly are located below the plenum grill at the base of the windscreen.

The link assembly is handed for left and right hand drive vehicles. All other wiper components remain common to both versions. The component descriptions and operation are the same for both left and right hand drive.

The parallel coupled link assembly comprises a curved galvanized tube which has a cast wheel box pushed into each end of the tube and crimped for retention. A galvanized link arm is attached to a lever at the base of each wheel box.

Each link is attached by a spherical bearing which is permanently attached to the lever and the link. The opposite end of each link also has a spherical bearing, which are both attached to a spigot which in turn is attached to a lever. The lever has a splined bore and mates with a splined shaft from the motor. A spring washer and nut secure the lever to the shaft.

Each wheel box comprises a cast housing, through which a splined shaft is located on bearings. The outer end of each shaft has splines which provide positive location for the wiper arms. The link assembly is a sealed unit and is not serviceable. The motor is attached to the link assembly with three bolts. The motor can operate at two speeds for fast and slow wiper operation. The motor is a DC motor with permanent magnets. The central shaft of the motor is fitted with a worm drive which in turn rotates a gear connected to the splined drive shaft.

The two speed operation is achieved by three brushes in the motor. One brush is the common earth. The slow speed is initiated by a brush positioned 180° to the common brush. The fast speed is initiated by a brush positioned at approximately 45° to the common brush. The fast speed operates by the brushes transferring direct current to a smaller portion of the armature coils, which causes the armature to rotate faster, but with a lower torque than the slow speed.

A wiper arm is located on the splined shaft of each wheel box and secured with a nut. The wiper arm attachment to the splined shaft has a pivot to which the remainder of the arm is attached. The two parts of the arm are connected by a spring which controls the pressure of the blade on the screen to a predetermined amount.

Each wiper blade is attached to its wiper arm with a clip that allows the blade to pivot. Each wiper blade comprises a number of levers and yokes to which the rubber wiper is fitted. The levers and yokes ensure that the pressure applied by the arm spring is distributed evenly along the full length of the blade. The rubber wiper is held in the yokes by a pair of stainless steel strips, which also distribute the spring pressure evenly. The driver's side wiper blade is fitted with an airfoil, which presses the wiper blade onto the windscreen at high speed. This prevents the wiper blade from lifting off the screen and maintains the wiping performance.

REAR SCREEN WIPER DESCRIPTION

The rear screen wiper functions are controlled from a push button switch located to the right of the instrument pack or by the selection of reverse gear when the front wipers are operating. The Central Control Unit (CCU) is responsible for monitoring and controlling the operations of the rear screen wiper motor.

The rear screen wiper has three modes of operation; programmed mode, intermittent and slow.

- Programmed mode operates when the rear screen wiper is selected by operation of the wash/wipe switch. The rear screen washer and the wiper operate when the switch is depressed. When the switch is released, the washers stop and the wiper continues for five cycles before stopping.
- Intermittent operates when the rear screen wiper is selected using the latching push button switch. The wiper operates for three complete cycles, then the CCU operates the wiper intermittently every five seconds until the wiper is selected off.
- Slow mode operates when reverse gear is selected and the front wipers are on. The rear wiper operates until reverse gear is disengaged or the front wipers are switched off.

The rear screen wiper is operated by a single electric motor which indirectly drives, via an eccentric drive mechanism, a splined shaft to which the wiper arm is attached.

The motor is a single speed dc motor with permanent magnets. The motor shaft is fitted with a worm drive which rotates a gear wheel. The gear wheel has an offset spigot to which an eccentric cam is fitted which can rotate through 180° in each direction. A coil spring is located around the cam and operates as a simple friction clutch to enable the cam to be rotated when the motor is driven in reverse. A connecting link is attached to the cam and drives two gears located in a link. The connecting link converts the rotary motion of the gear wheel into linear movement of the link. The linear movement is converted back into rotary movement of the splined shaft which moves the wiper arm in an arc in two directions across the rear screen.

The wiper motor has the ability to park the wiper arm off the rear screen when the wiper is selected off. When the motor is operating to wipe the rear screen, the motor shaft is rotating in a clockwise direction. When the rear screen wiper is selected off, the CCU allows the wiper arm to reach the vertical position on the screen. A micro switch actuated by a slip ring on the underside of the gear wheel, signals that the wiper arm has reached this position. The CCU then reverses the polarity of the supply to the motor which causes the motor shaft to rotate in an anti-clockwise direction.

When the motor changes direction, the eccentric cam is rotated through 180° which effectively lengthens the linear movement of the connecting link. This causes the wiper arm to sweep across the screen to its park position. The longer linear movement of the connecting link, causes the wiper arm to rotate further than during normal wiping, parking the wiper arm and blade off screen. A second slip ring on the underside of the gear wheel, signals the CCU that the wiper arm has reached its off screen position and the CCU removes the supply to the rear screen wiper motor.

The wiper arm is located on the splined shaft from the motor and secured with a nut. The wiper arm attachment to the splined shaft has a pivot to which the remainder of the arm is attached. The two parts of the arm are connected by a spring which controls the pressure of the blade on the screen to a predetermined amount.

The wiper blade is pushed onto the wiper arm which has a clip-on feature that allows the blade to pivot. The wiper blade comprises a lever, two yokes and a plastic strip. The rubber wiper is fitted to the plastic strip and held in the yokes. The lever, yokes and plastic strip ensure that pressure applied by the arm spring is distributed evenly along the length of the blade.

Rear Wiper Operation

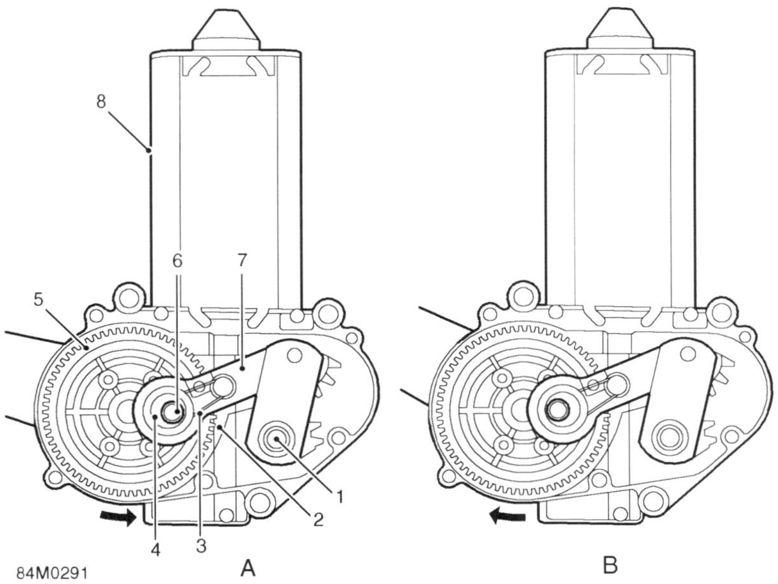

A = Motor operating (Forward operation - Wiper at bottom of screen)
B = Park position (Reverse operation - Off-screen parked)

1. Splined shaft
2. Motor worm drive
3. Coil spring
4. Cam
5. Gear wheel
6. Spigot
7. Link
8. Motor

WINDSCREEN WASHERS DESCRIPTION

The windscreen washers are operated from the wash/wipe stalk located on the right hand side of the steering column. Operation of the windscreen washers will also operate the windscreen wipers.

If the wash/wipe stalk is pulled quickly and released, the washers will operate and the wipers will operate at slow speed for one cycle. If the stalk is pulled and held, the washers will operate and the wipers will operate at slow speed for as long as the switch is operated. When the stalk is released, the washers will stop but the wipers will continue for several cycles before stopping.

Two washer jets are located on the top surface of the bonnet. Each jet contains two adjustable jets which can be moved to obtain the correct coverage of the windscreen. The two jets are connected in series to a flexible pipe which is routed in the electrical harness to a washer reservoir. The reservoir is located inside the right hand wheel arch behind the wheel arch liner. A non-return valve is located in the feed pipe to the windscreen washer jets to prevent washer fluid siphoning back to the reservoir.

The reservoir is moulded from plastic and has a capacity of approximately 4.0 litres (7 pints). The reservoir has two ports which allow for the attachment of two washer pumps. The flexible pipe from the windscreen washer jets is connected to the forward of the two electric washer pumps. The reservoir has a filler tube which protrudes into the engine compartment. The tube is sealed by a removable cap. A filter is located in the neck of the filler tube and prevents the ingress of particulate matter when replenishing the reservoir. The filter can be removed for cleaning.

REAR SCREEN WASHER DESCRIPTION

The rear washer is operated from a non-latching push switch located on the fascia to the right of the instrument pack. Operation of the rear washer switch operates the washer and the rear wiper for as long as the switch is depressed. When the switch is released the rear wiper operates for five cycles before stopping.

The rear washer uses the same reservoir as the windscreen washers. A second electric washer pump is fitted to the reservoir and supplies washer fluid, via a pipe located in the wiring harness, to a single washer jet which is fitted in the rear wiper arm. The jet has four jets which direct washer fluid to each side of the wiper blade. A non-return valve is located in the feed pipe to the rear screen washer jet to prevent washer fluid siphoning back to the reservoir.

RESERVOIR - WINDSCREEN WASHER

Service repair no - 84.10.01

Remove

1. Remove front bumper. ***See BODY, Exterior fittings.***
2. Position container to collect any fluid loss.

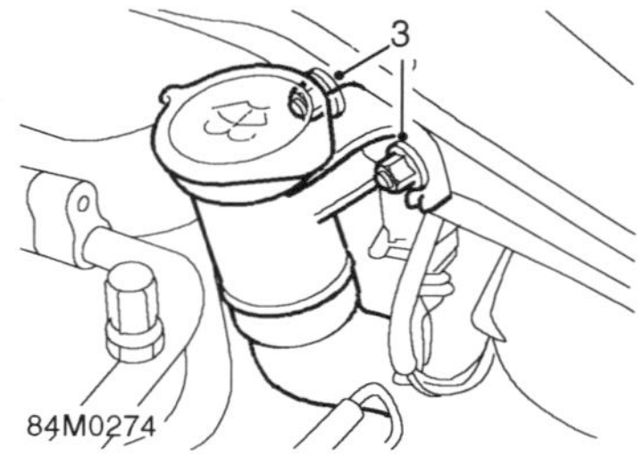

3. Remove 2 nuts securing reservoir filler neck and remove filler neck.

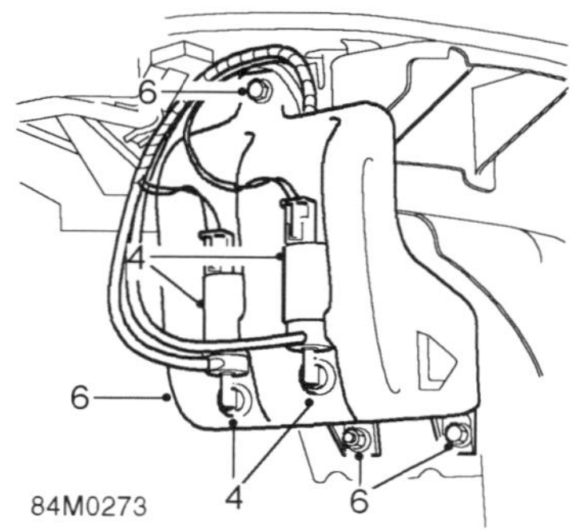

4. Release both washer pumps from reservoir.
5. Remove and discard pump sealing grommets.
6. Remove 3 bolts securing washer reservoir and remove.

Refit

1. Position reservoir and secure with bolts.
2. Fit NEW pump sealing grommets to reservoir.
3. Fit pumps to reservoir.
4. Position filler neck and secure with nuts.
5. Fit front bumper. ***See BODY, Exterior fittings.***

WASHER JET - WINDSCREEN

Service repair no - 84.10.08

Remove

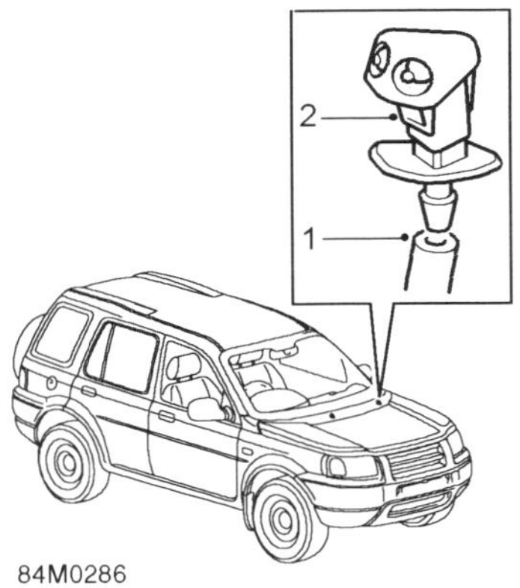

84M0286

1. Disconnect tube from washer jet.
2. Depress plastic lugs and remove washer jet from bonnet.

Refit

1. Fit washer jet to bonnet and connect tube.
2. Adjust jet so the inside spray is to centre of the screen, and the outer spray is to the top of the screen.

PUMP - WINDSCREEN WASHER

Service repair no - 84.10.21

Remove

1. Remove front bumper. ***See BODY, Exterior fittings.***
2. Position container to catch windscreen washer fluid.

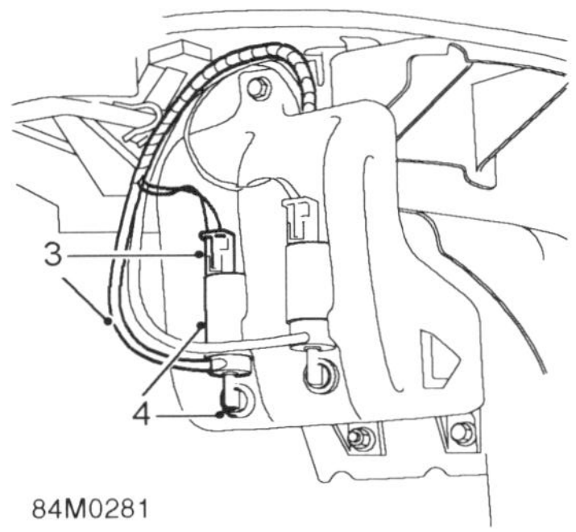

84M0281

3. Disconnect multiplug and hose from windscreen washer pump.
4. Release pump from reservoir.
5. Remove and discard pump sealing grommet.

Refit

1. Fit NEW pump sealing grommet to reservoir.
2. Fit pump to reservoir.
3. Connect hose and multiplug to pump.
4. Refit front bumper. ***See BODY, Exterior fittings.***

WIPER ARM - WINDSCREEN

Service repair no - 84.15.02

Remove

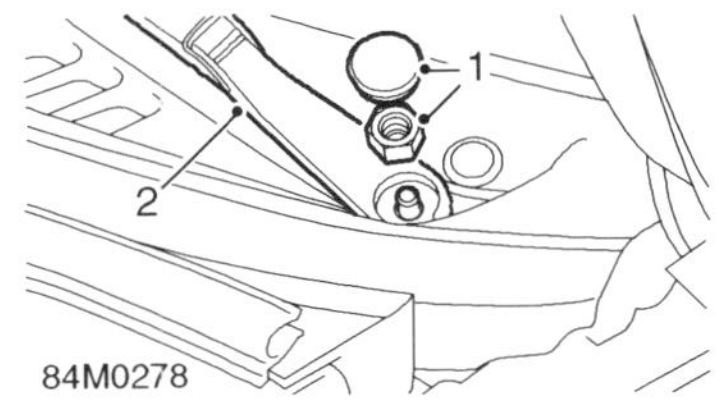

84M0278

1. Remove nut cover on wiper arm and remove nut.
2. Remove wiper arm from spindle.
   Do not carry out further dismantling if component is removed for access only.
3. Remove wiper blade. ***See this section.***
4. Fit wiper blade to replacement wiper arm. ***See this section.***

Refit

1. Fit wiper arm to spindle, with tip of wiper blade aligned to screen marks.
2. Fit nut and tighten to 18 Nm. Fit nut cover.

WIPER BLADE - WINDSCREEN

Service repair no - 84.15.06

Remove

1. Lift wiper arm from screen.

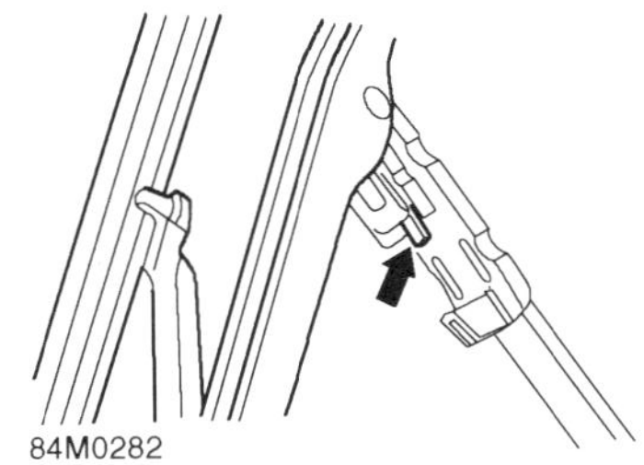

84M0282

2. Press retaining lever.
3. Slide blade down arm and withdraw.

Refit

1. Position new blade to wiper arm.
2. Push blade into engagement with arm, and check blade is retained.
3. Lower wiper arm onto screen.

MOTOR AND LINKAGE - WINDSCREEN WIPER

Service repair no - 84.15.11

Remove

1. Remove air intake moulding. ***See AIR CONDITIONING, Repairs.***

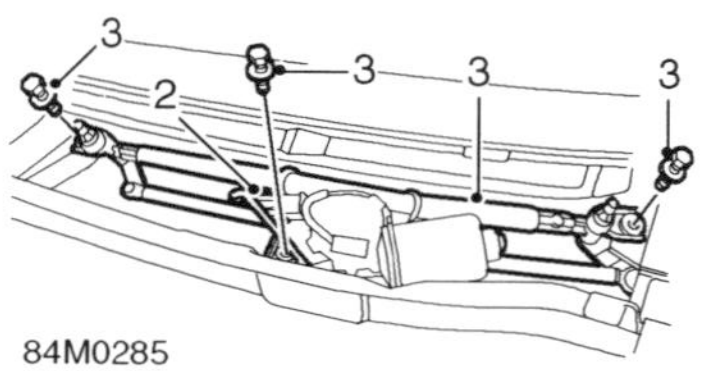

84M0285

2. Disconnect harness multiplug from wiper motor.
3. Remove 3 bolts securing wiper motor and linkage. Remove motor and linkage.

Refit

1. Fit motor and linkage assembly, fit and tighten bolts to 5 Nm.
2. Connect harness multiplug to wiper motor.
3. Fit air intake moulding. ***See AIR CONDITIONING, Repairs.***

SWITCH - WINDSCREEN WASHER AND WIPER

Service repair no - 84.15.34

Remove

1. Remove rotary coupler. ***See RESTRAINT SYSTEMS, Repairs.***

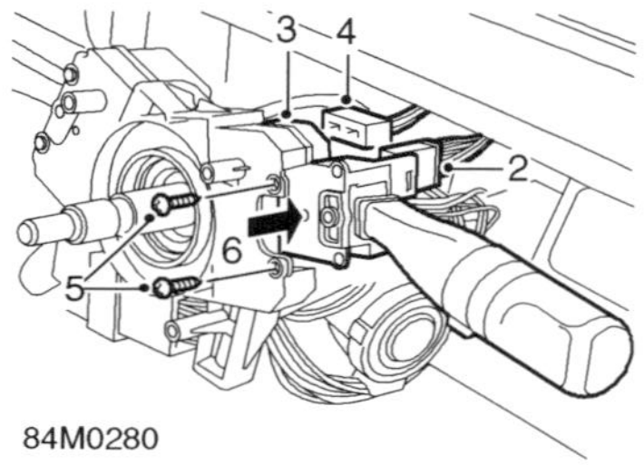

84M0280

2. Disconnect multiplug from washer and wiper switch.
3. Using a small flat blade release the multiplug connector from the switch base on steering column.
4. Disconnect multiplug from the connector.
5. Remove 2 screws from wiper switch.
6. Depress retaining tag and remove switch.

Refit

1. Fit washer and wiper switch assembly and secure with screws.
2. Connect multiplugs to switch.
3. Fit rotary coupler. ***See RESTRAINT SYSTEMS, Repairs.***

PUMP - REAR SCREEN WASHER

Service repair no - 84.30.21

Remove

1. Remove front bumper. ***See BODY, Exterior fittings.***
2. Position container to catch windscreen washer fluid.

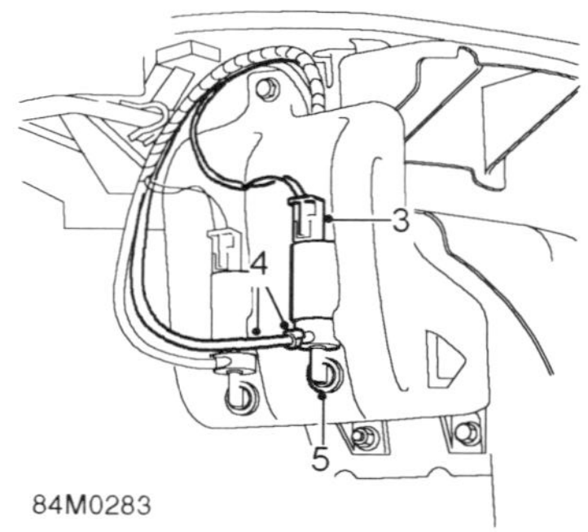

84M0283

3. Disconnect multiplug from washer pump.
4. Release hose from pump.
5. Remove pump from reservoir and discard pump sealing grommet.

Refit

1. Fit NEW pump sealing grommet to reservoir.
2. Fit pump to reservoir.
3. Connect hose and multiplug to pump.
4. Refit front bumper. ***See BODY, Exterior fittings.***

WIPER ARM - REAR SCREEN

Service repair no - 84.35.01

Remove

1. Remove wiper blade. ***See this section.***
2. Remove spare wheel mounting bracket. ***See BODY, Exterior fittings.***

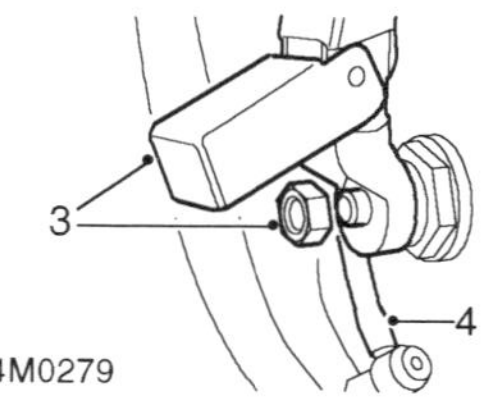

84M0279

3. Raise nut cover on wiper arm and remove nut.
4. Release washer jet tube and remove wiper arm.
Do not carry out further dismantling if component is removed for access only.
5. Release washer jet and tube from wiper arm.
6. Position and secure washer tube and jet to wiper arm.

Refit

1. Position wiper arm and connect washer tube.
2. Set wiper arm with tip contacting joint line between waist seal and rear door. Fit and tighten wiper arm nut to 13 Nm.
3. Fit wiper blade. ***See this section.***
4. Fit spare wheel mounting bracket. ***See BODY, Exterior fittings.***

WIPER BLADE - REAR SCREEN

Service repair no - 84.35.02

Remove

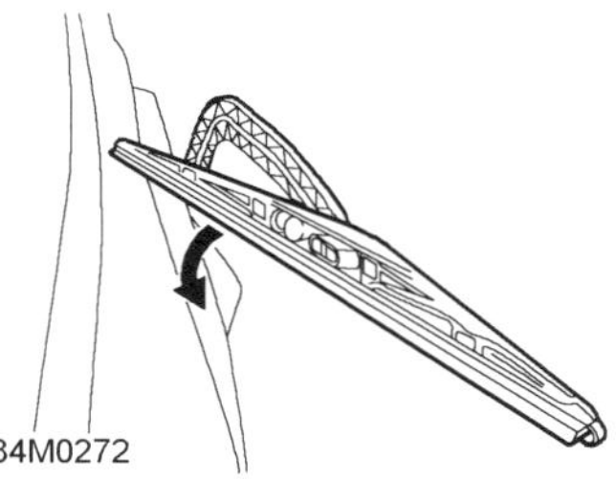

84M0272

1. Release wiper arm from tail door glass.
2. Remove wiper blade from arm.

Refit

1. Position NEW blade to wiper arm.
2. Push blade into engagement with arm and check blade is retained.

MOTOR - REAR SCREEN WIPER

Service repair no - 84.35.12

Remove

1. Remove rear wiper arm. ***See this section.***
2. Remove tail door water shedder. ***See BODY, Doors.***

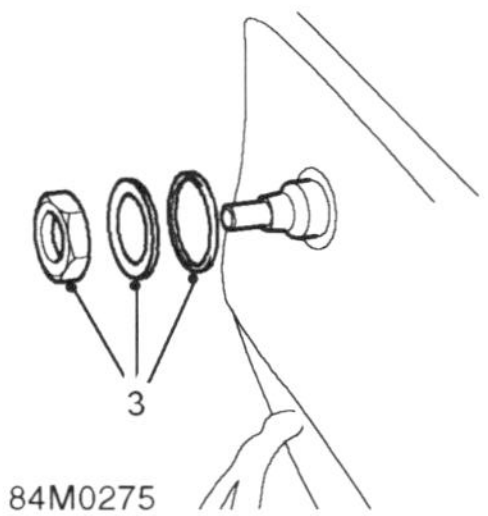

84M0275

3. Remove spindle nut, flat washer and discard rubber seal.

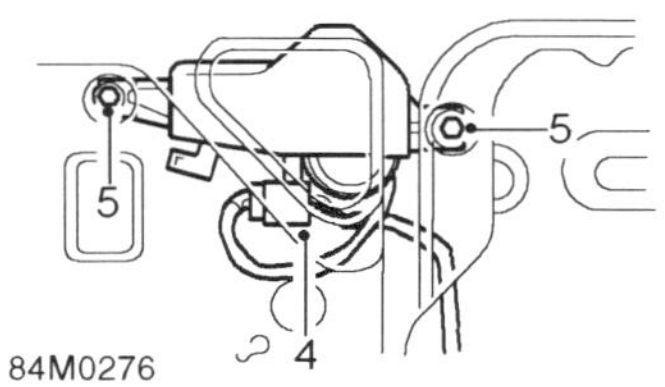

84M0276

4. Disconnect tailgate harness from wiper motor.
5. Remove 2 bolts and remove wiper motor.

Do not carry out further dismantling if component is removed for access only.

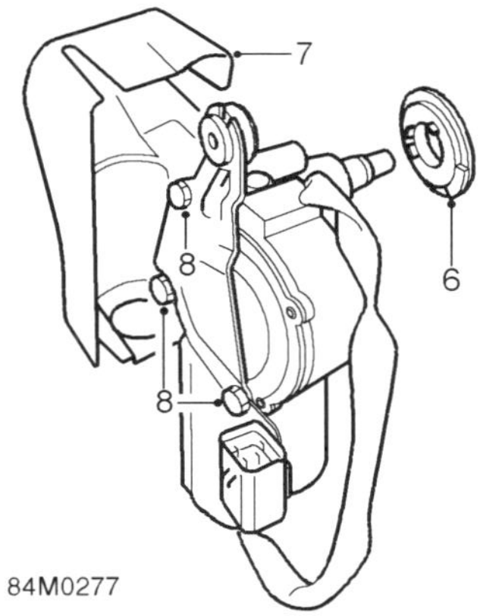

84M0277

6. Remove and discard spindle sealing washer.
7. Remove motor water shield.
8. Remove 3 bolts securing mounting plate to wiper motor.
9. Release multiplug and remove mounting plate.
10. Position mounting plate, tighten bolts and secure multiplug.
11. Fit motor water shield and NEW sealing washer to spindle.

Refit

1. Fit wiper motor and tighten bolts to 5 Nm.
2. Connect multiplug to wiper motor.
3. Fit NEW rubber seal to wiper motor spindle.
4. Fit flat washer and tighten spindle nut to 5 Nm.
5. Fit water shedder. ***See BODY, Doors.***
6. Fit wiper arm. ***See this section.***

SWITCH - REAR SCREEN WASHER AND WIPER

Service repair no - 84.35.34

Remove

1. Remove instrument panel cowl. ***See INSTRUMENTS, Repairs.***

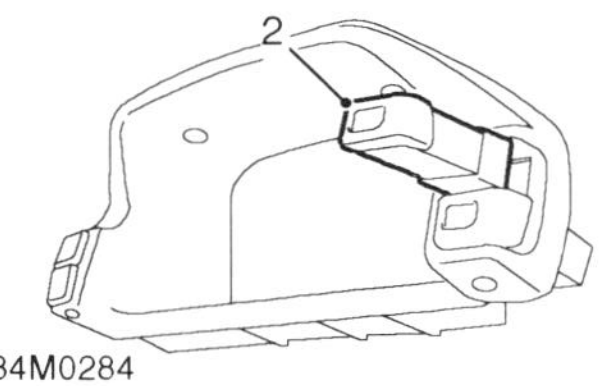

84M0284

2. Remove rear wiper switch from instrument panel cowl.

Refit

1. Fit switch to instrument panel cowl.
2. Fit instrument panel cowl. ***See INSTRUMENTS, Repairs.***

RELAY - REAR SCREEN WIPER MOTOR

Service repair no - 84.35.38

Remove

1. Remove RH rear quarter, lower casing. ***See BODY, Interior trim components.***

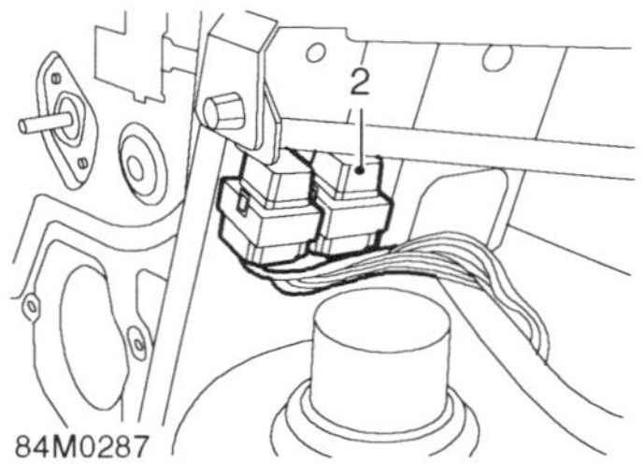

84M0287

2. Remove rear wiper motor relay.

Refit

1. Fit relay.
2. Fit lower casing. ***See BODY, Interior trim components.***

CONTENTS

CONTENTS

CENTRAL CONTROL UNIT (CCU)

The CCU is located on the back of the passenger compartment fusebox below the fascia. The CCU is responsible for controlling the following functions:

- Transit mode
- Anti theft alarm system
- Windscreen wipers
- Courtesy lamp delay
- Door open warning light
- Rear fog guard lights
- Lights on alarm
- Catalyst overheat
- Seat belt warning
- Handbrake warning
- Overspeed warning
- Rear screen wiper
- Tail door window
- Heated rear window

NOTE: Some of the above features controlled by the CCU are are market selectable and may not be operative or available in specific markets.

TestBook can be used to configure the CCU to enable/disable market selectable features, tailor anti theft alarm features to customer requirements and can also interrogate the CCU for stored fault codes and alarm triggers. TestBook is connected to the CCU via a diagnostic socket which is located in the passenger footwell.

The CCU is attached to the passenger compartment fusebox by five multiplugs. All inputs and outputs, to and from the CCU are transmitted through the fusebox.

The following sections describe the functions controlled by the CCU. For more detailed descriptions and operation, refer to the relevant section in the Electrical Reference Library (ERL).

TRANSIT MODE

The transit mode feature is to minimise battery usage when the vehicle is being stored to sale. When the CCU is programmed in transit mode, the following functions are disabled:

- RF receiver
- Tail door actuator
- Tail door window
- Central Door Locking (CDL)
- Interior lamps.

If the ignition is switched to position II, the CCU buzzer will sound an alarm to warn that the vehicle is in transit mode. The dealer can remove the transit mode feature and programme the CCU to the applicable market specification at the Pre Delivery Inspection (PDI) using TestBook.

ANTI THEFT ALARM SYSTEM

The anti theft alarm system controls the central locking and alarm functions for the vehicle. The vehicle locking and alarm system comprises the following components:

- Remote handset (RF transmitter)
- RF receiver
- Passive coil
- Volumetric sensor
- Door lock actuators
- Drivers door key barrel
- Central door locking (CDL) switch
- Door switches
- Tail door switch
- Bonnet switch
- Horn or BBUS
- Alarm LED
- Starter relay
- Inertia switch
- Engine immobilisation

Central Locking

The vehicle can be locked and unlocked by three methods; CDL switch, vehicle key or remote handset.

CDL Switch

The CDL switch is located in the centre console. The CDL switch allows the occupants to CDL lock the vehicle from inside without arming the alarm. The CDL switch is inoperative if the inertia switch is tripped. The CDL locked state can be removed by operation of the CDL switch, remote handset or key unlock in the drivers door key barrel. If the inertia switch is tripped while the doors are CDL locked and the ignition is on, all doors will automatically unlock.

Key locking

The vehicle can be CDL locked using the vehicle key in the driver's door key barrel. Turning the top of the key to the rear of the vehicle will CDL lock all doors. Turning the key a second time, within one second of the first turn, will superlock all doors.

Key Unlocking

On vehicles with alarm selected:

With the vehicle CDL or superlocked, turning the top of the key once to the front of the vehicle will mechanically unlock the driver's door only. The vehicle will enter the Emergency Key Access (EKA) state. Refer to Emergency Key Access (EKA) in this section.

On vehicles with alarm not selected (market option):

With the vehicle CDL locked, turning the top of the key once to the front of the vehicle will unlock all the doors.

If the vehicle is superlocked, turning the top of the key once to the front of the vehicle will only unlock the driver's door for Single Point Entry (SPE). The remaining door(s) will unlock to the CDL state. If the key is turned a second time, the remaining door(s) will unlock.

NOTE: If the vehicle is superlocked and SPE has not been selected in the CCU, turning the top of the key once to the front of the vehicle will unlock all the doors.

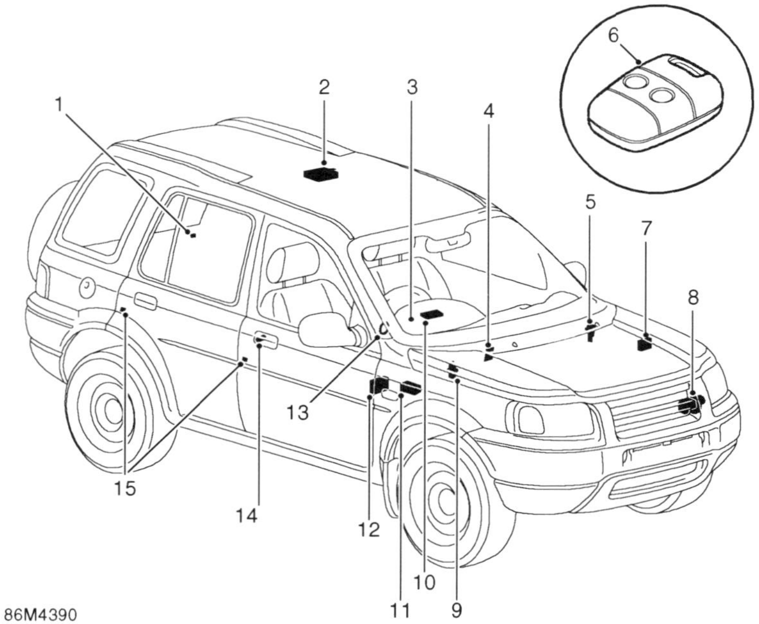

86M4390

1. Tail door switch
2. Volumetric sensor
3. Alarm LED
4. CDL switch
5. Inertia switch
6. Remote handset
7. Starter relay
8. Horn
9. Bonnet switch
10. RF receiver
11. Battery backed-up sounder (BBUS)
12. Central Control Unit (CCU)
13. Transponder
14. Key barrel
15. Door switches

Remote Locking

On vehicles with alarm selected:

The vehicle can be superlocked by pressing the lock button on the remote handset once.

On vehicles with alarm not selected (market option):

The vehicle can be CDL locked by pressing the lock button on the remote handset once.

Remote Unlocking

With the vehicle CDL locked, pressing the unlock button on the remote handset once will unlock all doors.

If the vehicle is superlocked, pressing the unlock button once on the remote handset will only unlock the drivers door for SPE. The remaining door(s) will unlock to the CDL state. If the button is pressed a second time, the remaining door(s) will unlock.

NOTE: If the vehicle is superlocked and SPE has not been selected in the CCU, pressing the unlock button once on the remote handset will unlock all the doors.

Central Locking Notes:

- Locking or unlocking using the vehicle key or remote handset is prevented if the CCU senses that the ignition is on.
- Superlocking is prevented if the CCU senses that one or more doors are open. The CCU will attempt to CDL lock all doors.

Inertia Switch

The inertia switch is located on the bulkhead in the engine compartment. With the ignition on and the alarm disarmed, if the inertia switch is tripped all the doors will unlock irrespective of their state at the time. Further locking is prevented unless:

- the ignition is switched off and the driver's door is opened and closed
- the driver's door is opened and closed and the inertia switch is manually reset by depressing the button on the top of the switch.

Tail Door

The CCU also controls the tail door release. The tail door can only be opened if the vehicle is unlocked, the alarm is not armed and the vehicle is travelling at not more than 3 mph (5 km/h).

Slam Locking

The driver's door is designed to prevent slam locking. The remaining door(s) can be slam locked.

Latch Motor Protection

To protect the door lock latches from damage, the CCU will only allow eight changes of state of the locks in any sixteen second period or less. If eight changes of state occurs within the sixteen second period, the CCU will prevent further operation of the latch motors for a further sixteen second period.

The CCU will always prevent further operation only when the latch motors are in an unlocked condition. If SPE is operational, the CCU will override the SPE function and all doors will unlock if eight operations is exceeded in the sixteen second period.

The CCU central locking inputs and outputs are shown in the following table:

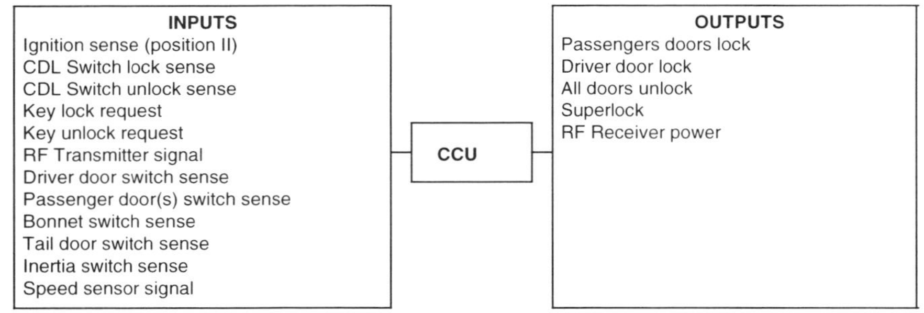

Alarm/Immobilisation System

The alarm system can be armed and disarmed using the vehicle key or the remote handset. An Emergency Key Access (EKA) facility is also available to disarm the alarm and mobilise the engine in the event of the remote handset becoming inoperative or unavailable. The alarm system monitors the driver's door, passenger door(s), tail door, bonnet and roof (3 door models only) using perimetric sensing. It also monitors movement within the passenger compartment using volumetric sensing.

The alarm system also controls the mobilisation and immobilisation of the engine starter operation and engine management system. The vehicle can be immobilised and mobilised using the remote handset or the vehicle key. Passive immobilisation will occur if the vehicle is left unattended for a predetermined period with the alarm not armed.

In certain countries, the alarm system is programmed not to arm under any circumstances.

NOTE: Hazard warning light confirmation of alarm arm or disarm is market programmable and therefore may not be operative on certain variants.

Perimetric Sensing

Perimetric sensing is invoked by the CCU to monitor entry to the vehicle after the alarm has been set. The panel open switches on the driver's door, passenger door(s), tail door, bonnet and roof (3 door only) are all monitored by the CCU.

If a panel is opened after the alarm has been set, the alarm will be triggered. The horn or BBUS will sound and the hazard warning lights will operate. On 3 door models, if the roof is off when the alarm is armed, further operation of the roof off switch will not trigger the alarm.

Volumetric Sensing

The volumetric sensor is located in a central position on the roof panel, behind the headlining. The volumetric sensor monitors movement inside the vehicle to detect any possible intrusion. The vehicle can be armed with the volumetric sensor disabled to avoid accidental triggering of the alarm if a pet is in the vehicle for instance. The volumetric sensor is also inoperative if the CCU senses that a panel has been left open, with the exception of the bonnet.

A fifteen second delay is initiated after arming of the alarm before signals from the volumetric sensor are interpreted as an intrusion. This precaution is included in the CCU software to avoid accidental or nuisance triggering of the alarm.

If the alarm has been triggered, the CCU will ignore further volumetric sensor signals for the duration of the alarm sounding. The CCU will delay volumetric sensing for a further 15 seconds after the alarm has stopped sounding, unless ten triggers have been sensed by the volumetric sensor since the alarm was last armed.

The volumetric gain setting is controlled by the VIN stored in the CCU. The VIN informs the CCU of the vehicle body and roof type to avoid under or over sensitivity.

If battery supply voltage falls to below 9 Volts, the CCU will ignore inputs from the volumetric sensor.

Alarm - Key Operation

Arming and disarming using the vehicle key in the driver's door key barrel will be ignored if the CCU senses that the ignition is on. In certain markets the alarm system is programmed not to arm under any circumstances, in these cases key operation will only operate the door locking facility as described in Key Locking/Unlocking.

NOTE: Using the vehicle key in the driver's door key barrel will not enable the volumetric sensing.

Key Arm

The vehicle alarm can be fully armed by turning the top of the key to the rear of the vehicle once with all panels closed. The Vehicle will be CDL locked, the hazard warning lights will flash three times. The alarm LED will fast flash for ten seconds and then change to slow flash. Perimetric sensing, engine immobilisation and starter relay disable will be activated.

The vehicle alarm can also be fully armed by turning the top of the key to the rear of the vehicle a second time, within one second of the first turn, with all the panels closed. The vehicle will be superlocked, the hazard warning lights will flash three times. The alarm LED will fast flash for ten seconds and then change to slow flash. Perimetric sensing, engine immobilisation and starter relay disable will be activated.

Key Disarm

The driver's door only will be mechanically unlocked.

The alarm LED will continue to slow flash, perimetric and volumetric sensing will be disabled, but engine immobilisation and starter relay disable will remain activated.

To deactivate the engine immobilisation and starter relay disable, the EKA code must be correctly entered (Refer to EKA description in this section).

Alarm - Remote Handset Operation

In certain markets, the alarm system is programmed not to arm under any circumstances. In these cases the remote handset will only operate the door locking facility as described in remote handset lock/unlock.

Remote Handset Arm

The vehicle alarm can be fully armed by pressing the lock button on the remote handset once with all panels closed. The Vehicle will be superlocked, the hazard warning lights will flash three times. The alarm LED will fast flash for ten seconds and then change to slow flash. Perimetric and volumetric sensing, engine immobilisation and starter relay disable will be activated.

Remote Handset Disarm

The vehicle can be fully disarmed by pressing the unlock button once on the remote handset. The hazard warning lights will flash once and the alarm LED will go off. The perimetric and volumetric sensing will be disabled and engine immobilisation and starter relay disable will be deactivated.

Partial Arming

If one or more of the panels is left open, the CCU will attempt to partially arm as much of the vehicle as possible. If a failure of a panel open switch or wiring occurs, the CCU will partially arm the alarm in the same manner as if a panel is left open.

When the alarm is armed with one or more panels open, the CCU will sound a miss-lock warning from the horn or BBUS to tell the driver that a panel is open.

The miss-lock warning sound is market selectable and therefore may not be operative in specific markets. When the CCU enters a partially armed state, there is no hazard warning flasher operation, the alarm LED will be extinguished for 10 seconds and will then slow flash.

The CCU will partially alarm the vehicle according the priority of the panel left open. The panel priority is driver's door, passenger door(s), tail door and bonnet with the driver's door being the highest priority and the bonnet being the lowest.

Drivers Door

If the driver's door is open and a lock request is made, the CCU will CDL lock the closed doors, suspend superlocking and volumetric sensing and monitor the panel left open.

Vehicle state changes:

- If the driver's door is open and a lower priority panel closes, the CCU will give a miss-lock sound and remain in the driver's door partial arm condition.
- If the driver's door closes, the CCU will sound a miss-lock warning and remain in the driver's door partial arm condition. If the driver's door is opened, the alarm will be triggered.
- If the driver's door closes and one or more lower priority panels are open and a lock request is made, the CCU will CDL lock the closed door(s) and enter the partial arm state of the panel open with the next highest priority.
- If the driver's door closes and all other panels are closed and a lock request is made, the CCU will lock the doors and arm the alarm.

Passenger Door(s)

If one or more of the passenger doors are open and the driver's door closes and a lock request is made, the CCU will CDL lock the closed door(s), suspend superlocking and volumetric sensing and monitor the panel(s) left open. *Vehicle state changes:*

- If one or more passenger door(s) are open and a lower priority panel closes, the CCU will sound a miss-lock warning and remain in the passenger door partial arm condition.
- If the passenger door(s) close(s) and one or more lower priority panels remain open, the CCU will sound a miss-lock warning and enter the partial arm condition of the panel with the next highest priority.
- If the passenger door(s) closes and all other panels are closed, the CCU will arm the alarm door sense switches for the closed door(s).

NOTE: The passenger door(s) can be slam locked.

Tail Door

If the tail door is open and all higher priority panels are closed and a lock request is made, the CCU will allow superlocking of the passenger and driver's doors, suspend volumetric sensing and monitor the panel(s) left open.

Vehicle state changes:

- If the tail door is open and the bonnet closes, the CCU will sound a miss-lock warning and remain in the tail door partial arm condition.
- If the tail door closes and the bonnet remains open, the CCU will suspend operation of the tail door open actuator until the next unlock request is made and enter the bonnet partial arm condition.
- If the tail door closes and the bonnet and all other panels are closed, the CCU will lock the doors and arm the alarm.

Bonnet

If the bonnet is open and all higher priority panels are closed and a lock request is made, the CCU will allow superlocking of the passenger and driver's doors and volumetric sensing and monitor the panel left open.

Vehicle state changes:

- If the bonnet closes and all other panels are closed, the CCU will enter the locked and armed condition.

Miss-lock Warning

When the CCU enters a partial armed condition or the alarm is armed with the tail door window down, the CCU will sound a miss-lock warning. The miss-lock warning is market selectable. The miss-lock warning is sounded from either the vehicle horn for a period of 0.02 seconds or from the BBUS for a period of 0.1 seconds.

Alarm Activated

The audible and visual warning activated by the CCU when an alarm trigger is received by the CCU, is market selectable. The audible warnings can be a constant tone from the horn for a period of 30 seconds or an intermittent tone from the horn for 30 seconds, with the horn sounding for 0.5 seconds and off for 0.5 seconds. The visual warning is flashing of the hazard warning lights for 30 seconds.

When a BBUS is fitted, all alarm and miss-lock warnings will be sounded via the BBUS.

Alarm Reset

When the alarm has been activated, it can be silenced with the ignition off by either disarming or repeat arming using the vehicle key or the remote handset.

Battery Backed-Up Sounder (BBUS)

The BBUS is market selectable and, when fitted, is located in the driver's side wing above the wheel arch liner, near the side repeater flasher. The BBUS provides all security alarm and miss-lock warning sounds. In the event of tampering with the BBUS, power loss will sound the alarm and the BBUS can only be silenced by reconnection to the power supply and a disarm and arm request made with the vehicle key or remote handset.

If the BBUS is disconnected with the alarm activated, the BBUS will sound. The BBUS can be removed with the alarm deactivated without sounding. The battery life of the BBUS is approximately three years, after which, replacement is recommended.

Emergency Key Access (EKA)

The EKA feature permits an armed vehicle to be fully disarmed using the key. This feature is useful if the remote handset is not available or is inoperative.

When the vehicle has been locked using the key or the remote handset, unlocking and disarming of the alarm system is normally achieved by means of the remote handset. If the remote handset is not available or inoperative, access to the vehicle can be obtained by unlocking the driver's door with the vehicle key which initiates the EKA status.

When the vehicle enters the EKA state, the following occurs:

- The driver's door unlocks (other doors remain in their locked condition)
- The alarm LED continues to slow flash
- Perimetric protection is suspended on all panels, except the bonnet
- Engine immobilisation and crank disable remain activated
- Volumetric protection is deactivated.

EKA requires the entry of a four number code in the CCU. The code is randomly generated and is not connected with the VIN. Each number in the code can be between 1 and 15. The EKA code is entered by turning the key in the driver's door lock to the lock and unlock positions in accordance with the code.

If the EKA code, for example is 3, 6, 2 and 11, the following procedure would be required to fully unlock and disarm the vehicle:

NOTE: When entering the code, unlocking and locking will operate as normal on the first turn of the key. The procedure starts with the vehicle in the locked condition and the first turn to the unlock position initiates the EKA state.

- Turn the key once to the unlock position and wait for a minimum of six minutes before proceeding to enter the EKA code
- Turn the key to the unlock position three times
- Turn the key to the lock position six times
- Turn the key to the unlock position two times
- Turn the key to the lock position eleven times
- Finally, turn the key to the unlock position once.

If the code is entered correctly, the CCU will unlock all doors, fully disarm the alarm and mobilise the ignition and starter relay circuits. If the code is entered incorrectly, the vehicle will remain in the EKA state. Three incorrect attempts at code entry will result in the CCU initialising a thirty minute time out period. The CCU will fail to respond to any further code entry attempt during this period.

If a code is entered incorrectly, the system can be reset by opening and closing the driver's door or turning the ignition on and off. An aborted attempt will not count on the CCU's tally of incorrect attempts.

Remote Handset (RF Transmitter)

Two remote handsets are supplied with each vehicle. Two buttons on the handset control the locking and unlocking and alarm arm and disarm functions remotely. The remote handset transmits a coded signal which is recognized by the RF receiver. If the handset battery is removed or changed, or the vehicle battery is disconnected, the synchronization of the handset and the RF receiver will be lost.

Remote Handset Re-synchronization

Re-synchronization can be achieved by inserting the vehicle key in the ignition switch. Turning on the ignition causes the CCU to transmit a signal from the passive coil which surrounds the ignition switch. This in turn causes the handset to transmit a re-synchronization code and will synchronize the handset with the CCU automatically.
Re-synchronization can also be achieved using the handset by operating either handset button five times in quick succession with the ignition off.

Remote Handset Battery Low Warning

If the remote handset battery voltage becomes low, when the handset transmits a signal to the CCU, it also transmits a low battery signal when the driver's door is opened. The CCU buzzer sounds a 10 second warning and the alarm LED flashes for 10 seconds to signify to the driver that the handset battery requires replacement. When the battery is replaced, the remote handset will require re-synchronization with the CCU.

Mobilisation/Immobilisation

Engine immobilisation

The engine immobilisation feature disables the starter relay operation and also prevents the CCU sending a coded signal to the Engine Control Module to enable the engine management system. If the engine is immobilised with the alarm disarmed and the ignition off, the alarm LED will slow flash. If the engine is immobilised with the ignition on, the alarm LED will be permanently illuminated.

Passive Immobilisation

Passive immobilisation occurs, following a delay of 5 seconds, if the ignition is turned off and the driver's door is opened. Turning off the ignition and the CCU not sensing the ignition for 5 minutes will also invoke the passive immobilisation.

Passive Re-Mobilisation

Passive re-mobilisation occurs when the CCU receives an unlock request from the remote handset.

Passive re-mobilisation will also occur by turning on the ignition with the remote handset within 70 mm of the passive coil surrounding the ignition switch attached to the key ring. When the ignition is turned on, with the vehicle disarmed and immobilised, the CCU transmits a 'ringing waveform' signal through the passive coil. The passive coil in turn, excites the remote handset to transmit a re-mobilisation signal. If the CCU does not receive a valid code within 60 seconds of the ignition being turned on, the handset will stop transmitting the signal until the ignition is turned off and on again.

If two handsets are on the same key ring, passive re-mobilisation will not occur because both handsets will transmit together and corrupt each handset signal.

MEMS Coded Signal

The CCU sends a coded signal to the engine control module, activating the MEMS electronic engine management systems when ignition on is sensed. The MEMS coded signal is as follows:

- If vehicle is mobilised, the CCU will initiate MEMS coded signal transmission from ignition on until passive immobilisation occurs.

Passive Immobilisation Repeat

If the re-mobilisation of the engine occurs by whatever means and the CCU does not sense ignition on in 5 minutes, the passive immobilisation will be activated and the engine and ignition will be immobilised.

The CCU alarm inputs and outputs are shown in the following table:

INPUTS		OUTPUTS
Ignition sense (position II)	CCU	Passive coil (out)
Key lock request		Starter relay enable
Key unlock request		MEMS coded signal
RF signal		Alarm LED
Driver door sense		BBUS
Passenger door sense		BBUS ST
Bonnet sense		Hazard flasher relay
Tail door sense		Horn relay
Volumetric signal		Volumetric power
Roof off sense		Volumetric link
		RF power

The CCU immobilisation inputs and outputs are shown in the following table:

INPUTS		OUTPUTS
Ignition sense (position II)	CCU	Passive coil (out)
RF signal		Starter relay enable
Driver door sense		MEMS coded signal
Key unlock request		Alarm LED
Oil pressure sense		RF power

WINDSCREEN WIPERS

The CCU is programmed to control the windscreen wipers intermittent wipe and programmed wash/wipe facilities. The windscreen wipers are operated from the right hand stalk switch on the steering column.

Intermittent Wipe

A five position rotary potentiometer, inboard of the wiper control switch, operates the intermittent wipe delay function. The five positions operate the wipers intermittently at time delays of approximately 3, 5, 8, 12 and 17 seconds. The CCU monitors the resistance through the intermittent switch and adjusts the delay to suit the position selected.

The following table details the wiper switch position and corresponding switch resistance and time delay:

Switch Position	Switch Resistance	Delay (seconds)
1	less than 500 Ohms	3 ±1
2	1500 ± 500 Ohms	5 ±1
3	3000 ± 500 Ohms	8 ±2
4	4500 ± 500 Ohms	12 ±2
5	more than 5400 Ohms	17 ±3
Default	Open circuit	8 ±2

The CCU windscreen wiper inputs and outputs are shown in the following table:

INPUTS		OUTPUTS
Ignition sense (position II) Front wiper intermittent request Front wiper intermittent speed Front wash sense Front wiper park power	CCU	Front wiper slow

Programmed Wash/Wipe

The programmed wash/wipe is operated by pushing the right hand stalk on the steering column downwards. The length of time that the wash/wipe function operates is determined by the time that the switch is operated.

When the switch is operated, the washers operate immediately. The CCU suspends wiper operation for approximately 0.6 seconds before energising the wiper relay coil, allowing the wipers to operate.

When the switch is released the washers immediately stop. The CCU continues to energise the wiper relay coil for a further 2 seconds after the switch is released, which allows the wipers to wipe the screen after the washers have stopped.

COURTESY LAMP DELAY

The CCU controls the operation of the interior courtesy lamp. Opening any of the doors will illuminate the courtesy lamp. The lamp will be extinguished in the following ways:

- The lamp will extinguish 15 seconds after all the doors have been closed.
- The lamp will extinguish if all doors are closed and ignition is selected on within the 15 second delay period.
- The lamp will extinguish if a lock request is made within the 15 second delay period.
- The lamp will extinguish after a period of 10 minutes if a door is left open, or a door switch fault occurs.

If the vehicle is locked, an unlock request using the vehicle key or the remote handset will illuminate the courtesy lamp for 15 seconds unless one of the above conditions is met.

The courtesy lamp can also be switch on using a manual switch on the lamp unit.

The CCU courtesy lamp inputs and outputs are shown in the following table:

INPUTS		OUTPUTS
Ignition sense (position II) Driver door sense Passenger door(s) sense Tail door sense Key lock request Key unlock request Remote handset unlock request Remote handset lock request	CCU	Courtesy lamp

DOOR OPEN WARNING LIGHT

The CCU monitors all vehicle panels and will illuminate a warning light on the instrument panel if the driver's door, passenger door(s), tail door or bonnet is open and the ignition is on.

The CCU door open warning light inputs and outputs are shown in the following table:

INPUTS		OUTPUTS
Ignition sense (position II) Driver door sense Passenger door(s) sense Tail door sense Bonnet sense	CCU	Door open warning light

REAR FOG GUARD LIGHTS

The CCU controls the operation of the rear fog guard lights via a rear fog guard light relay. The rear fog guard lights will be enabled when the CCU senses:

- a rear fog guard light request signal from the switch
- the ignition on
- the headlights and/or front fog lights on (if fitted).

If the rear fog guard lights switch is pushed or one of the above CCU senses is removed, the rear fog guard lights will go off. When the rear fog guard lights have been extinguished, ignition switched off for example, the rear fog guard lights will remain off until requested. This feature prevents unwanted rear fog guard light operation.

The CCU rear fog guard light inputs and outputs are shown in the following table:

INPUTS		OUTPUTS
Ignition sense (position II) Headlamp sense Front fog light sense (if fitted) Rear fog guard light request	CCU	Rear fog guard light relay Rear fog guard warning lamp

LIGHTS ON ALARM

If the side lights or headlights are on, ignition off and the driver's door is opened, the CCU will sound a continuous warning buzzer to warn the driver that the side lights or headlights are turned on. The CCU senses signals from the headlight switch, ignition off and driver's door open.

The CCU lights on alarm inputs and outputs are shown in the following table:

INPUTS		OUTPUTS
Ignition sense off Lighting switch side lights or headlights sense Driver's door sense	CCU	Internal sounder

CATALYST OVERHEAT WARNING (MARKET SELECTABLE)

A warning light to warn the driver of catalyst overheat is located in the instrument panel. The warning light is only fitted on certain variants. After the ignition is switched on, the catalyst warning lamp will illuminate for a period of approximately 5 seconds to show that the warning lamp is operative. After 5 seconds, the warning lamp will go off and should only illuminate if the CCU senses catalyst overheat and ignition 1 on signals.

The CCU catalyst overheat warning light inputs and outputs are shown in the following table:

INPUTS		OUTPUTS
Ignition sense (position II) Catalyst overheat sense	CCU	Catalyst overheat warning lamp

HANDBRAKE WARNING

A warning light to warn the driver that the handbrake is on is located in the instrument panel.

On certain variants, when the ignition is switched on, the handbrake warning lamp will illuminate for a period of approximately 5 seconds to show that the warning lamp is operative. After 5 seconds, the lamp will go off if the handbrake is released. The warning lamp will illuminate at all times when the ignition is on and the handbrake is applied.

On other variants, the warning lamp will only illuminate when the ignition is on and the handbrake is applied.

The CCU handbrake warning light inputs and outputs are shown in the following table:

INPUTS		OUTPUTS
Ignition sense (position II)	CCU	Handbrake warning lamp

OVERSPEED WARNING (MARKET SELECTABLE)

On certain variants, an audible overspeed warning is sounded by the CCU if the vehicle speed exceeds 75 mph (120 km/h).

The audible warning is in the form of a 2 kHz chime from the CCU. The chime comes on at 72.8 mph (116.58 km/h) and goes off when vehicle speed falls below 70.98 mph (113.57 km/h).

The CCU overspeed warning inputs and outputs are shown in the following table:

INPUTS		OUTPUTS
Ignition sense (position II) Speed signal	CCU	Internal sounder

REAR SCREEN WIPER

The rear screen wiper is controlled from a latching push button switch located on the right hand side of the instrument pack. A second non-latching switch, also on the right hand side of the instrument pack, operates the rear screen wash/wipe facility.

The CCU controls all functions of the rear screen wiper. The wiper will not operate if; the tail door window is lowered or not calibrated or, on 3 door models, if the roof is removed. The wiper motor drives a geared wheel which has three tracks on one face. The tracks communicate with three contacts and provide signal information to the CCU.

When the wiper is operating, one of the tracks signals the CCU of this condition. When the wiper reaches its 'out wipe' position, the second of the tracks completes a circuit which signals the CCU of this position. When the wiper reaches its off-screen position, the third track signals the CCU, which removes the power supply from the reverse relay.

The off-screen park is operated by the CCU reversing the motor rotational direction. This, in turn, activates a cam within the motor linkage, lengthening the stroke of the wiper and parking the wiper off-screen.

The CCU operates the wiper motor via a forward and a reverse relay. The forward relay is energised when the wiper is operating in programmed, intermittent and slow mode. The reverse relay is energised to reverse the rotational direction of the motor to activate the off-screen park function.

The CCU operates the rear screen wiper in four different modes; off-screen parked, intermittent, programmed and slow.

Off-Screen Parked

When the rear screen wiper is not selected, no power is supplied to the wiper relays and the wiper is parked off-screen.

Intermittent

With the ignition on, the rear window wiper switch selected on, the tail door window closed and, on 3 door models, the roof is on, the wiper operates intermittently with a fixed delay of five seconds between wipes.

Programmed

If the ignition is on, the tail door window is closed, on 3 door models the roof is on and the rear screen wash/wipe is selected, the CCU operates the wiper in programmed mode, washing and wiping the rear screen until the wash/wipe switch is released.When the switch is released, the washer stops and the CCU continues to energise the forward relay for a further six seconds before parking off-screen.

Slow

If the ignition is on, the tail door window is closed, the front screen wipers are on, on 3 door models the roof is on and reverse gear is engaged, the CCU operates the wiper in slow mode, wiping the rear screen until reverse gear is disengaged or the front wipers are turned off.

Intermittent, Programmed, Slow operation to Off-Screen Parked

The off-screen park function operates as follows: The CCU energizes the forward relay until the rear screen wiper out wipe sense is detected. The forward relay is then de-energised and the reverse relay is energised. The reverse relay operates the motor in the opposite direction, which lengthens the stroke of the wiper arm. When the wiper arm reaches the off-screen position, the CCU senses a signal from the applicable contact in the wiper motor and de-energizes the reverse relay.

Rear Screen Wiper Motor Fuse Blow

If the rear screen wiper fuse blows, for whatever reason, when the rear wiper is operating, a requested timer of approximately 3.2 seconds is initiated by the CCU. If an off-screen park signal is not sensed within the timed period, the CCU removes power from the rear wiper relays. Tail door window functions will be inhibited with the exceptions that the tail door can be opened and closed, removal of the roof will cause the tail door window to lower and window calibration will be allowed.

When the fault has been corrected, selection of a rear screen wiper function is required to recalibrate the rear wiper and the rear screen operation.

The CCU rear screen wiper inputs and outputs are shown in the following table:

INPUTS		OUTPUTS
Ignition sense (position II)	CCU	Rear wiper forward relay
Rear wiper request		Rear wiper reverse relay
Rear wiper wash sense		
Reverse gear sense		
Rear wiper park sense		
Rear wiper out wipe sense		
Tail door window position		
Roof off sense (3 door only)		
Front wiper park power		
Front wiper intermittent request		

TAIL DOOR WINDOW

The tail door window can be lowered using the console switch or the remote handset. On 3 door models, removal of the roof will automatically lower the window. The window can be raised using the console switch or the vehicle key in the tail door key barrel. When the tail door is opened, the tail door window lowers to a 'clear of seal position' and when the door is closed the window automatically raises to its fully up position.

Power-Up and Calibration

If the vehicle battery has been disconnected, reconnection will require the tail door window to be recalibrated as follows (provided that the alarm is disarmed):

1. Battery voltage applied and sensed by the CCU.
2. The CCU energizes the tail door window down relay until the window stalls.
3. The CCU de-energizes the tail door window.
4. With the roof on or roof lowered, switch ignition on and operate tail door window, using console switch, to the fully closed stall position or using the vehicle key in the tail door key barrel until the tail door window is fully closed.

If the vehicle is changed from transit mode to a valid market, the tail door window will be driven fully down and will require the above calibration procedure.

If the tail door window does not complete the calibration procedure successfully, the CCU will sound a warning for approximately 0.8 seconds and the window will lower fully.

Tail door window calibration can fail for the following reasons:

- Window stops before minimum travel is achieved
- Window does not achieve a stall
- Window request removed before stall is achieved
- Tail door opened while driving window up.

Tail Door Open

If the vehicle is unlocked and unarmed and travelling at less than 3 mph (5 km/h), opening the tail door will signal the CCU to initially lower the tail door window to the 'clear of seal' position and stop. After a delay of approximately 0.5 seconds, the CCU operates the door actuator to allow the door to be opened. If the rear screen wiper is operating it will off-screen park.

Tail Door Close

When the tail door is closed, the tail door window will still be at the 'clear of seal' position. The CCU will power the window to the fully up position after delay of approximately 0.5 seconds after the door closed signal is sensed by the CCU.

Tail Door Window Lower

NOTE: The rear screen wiper must be parked off-screen before the CCU will allow the tail door window to lower. If the heated rear window (HRW) is operating, the CCU will turn off the HRW when the window is lowered.

Remote Handset Lower

When requesting unlock using the remote handset, if the unlock button remains pressed for a minimum of 1 second with the ignition off and the tail door closed, the CCU will energise the tail door window down relay and lower the window fully.

Console Switch Lower - Inch Down

With the ignition on, pressing the console switch in the down position will signal the CCU to lower the tail door window for as long as the switch is held. The window will stop at the chosen position when the switch is released. When the window is almost fully open, the CCU will continue to lower the window irrespective of whether the switch is pressed or not.

Console Switch Lower - One Shot

With the ignition on, pressing the console switch in the down position for a period of approximately 0.2 seconds or less, will signal the CCU to lower the tail door window fully. This feature is market programmable.

Roof Removal - 3 Door Models Only

If the alarm is not armed, removal of the roof will trip the roof off switch. This signals the CCU which automatically lowers the tail door window even if the tail door is open. If the roof is removed and the alarm is armed, operation of the roof off switch will trigger the alarm and the CCU will not lower the tail door window.

Tail Door Window Raise

NOTE: If the rear screen wiper was selected on when the tail door window was lowered, when the window is raised fully, the CCU will resume operation of the wiper providing the switch is still selected on.

Tail Door Key Barrel Raise

With the tail door closed and, on 3 door models the roof is on, inserting the key in the tail door key barrel and holding in the turned condition will signal the CCU to raise the tail door window. If the key is released before the window has reached the fully up position, the signal will be removed from the CCU and the window will fully lower.

Console Switch Raise

With the ignition on and, on 3 door models the roof is on, and the tail door closed, pressing the console switch in the up position will signal the CCU to raise the tail door window. The switch must be pressed until the window is fully raised (stalled position). If the switch is released and the window has not reached its stalled position, the raise signal is removed from the CCU and the window will be fully lowered.

Motor Timeout

To protect the tail door window lift motor from damage, the motor outputs have a fail-safe inhibit relative to the window height. This prevents the motor from being overdriven. If the fail-safe limit is reached, the CCU will energise the tail window down relay to lower the window and the CCU sets the window to an uncalibrated setting. The calibration procedure will need to be performed to recalibrate the tail door window.

Tail Door Window Open Warning.

If the tail door window is calibrated and open and, on 3 door models the roof is on, and a lock request is made from the remote handset or the vehicle key in the driver's door key barrel, the CCU will sound an audible miss-lock warning to advise that the window is open. The window can be closed using the console switch or the tail door key barrel.

The CCU tail door window inputs and outputs are shown in the following table:

INPUTS		OUTPUTS
Ignition sense (position II)	CCU	Tail window up relay
Battery 1 (unfused)		Tail window down relay
Tail window up request		Tail door actuator
Tail window key up request		Internal sounder
Rear wiper park request		
Rear wiper top window sense		
Roof off sense		
Tail door sense		
Tail window position signal		
Tail window software flags		
Tail door open request		
Remote handset (RF transmitter) lock/unlock signals		
Vehicle locked (software sensed)		

NOTE: The tail window flags are derived from the CCU tracking the window movement using the tail window position signal.

HEATED REAR WINDOW (HRW)

The HRW is controlled from a non-latching push button switch located on the centre of the fascia.

The CCU controls all functions of the HRW. When the HRW switch is pressed and released a signal is sent to the CCU.

With the ignition on and oil pressure sense present, tail window not lower than the 'clear of seal' position and, on 3 door models the roof is on, the CCU will grant the HRW on. The CCU will energise the HRW relay for approximately 8 minutes after which the CCU will de-energise the HRW relay. A warning lamp on the HRW switch shows when the HRW is operating.

If the switch is pressed before the timed 8 minute period, the CCU will switch off the HRW. Removal of any of the input signals to the CCU will also stop HRW operation. The HRW switch will require re-selection to operate again.

The CCU HRW inputs and outputs are shown in the following table:

INPUTS		OUTPUTS
Ignition sense (position II) Tail window software flags Tail door open request Roof off sense Oil pressure sense HRW request (on/off)	CCU	HRW relay

NOTE: The tail window flags are derived from the CCU tracking the window movement using the tail window position signal.

DRIVE BELT - ALTERNATOR - K SERIES - WITHOUT AIR CONDITIONING

Service repair no - 86.10.05

Check

1. Disconnect battery earth lead.
2. Check condition of drive belt, renew a drive belt that shows signs of wear or splitting.

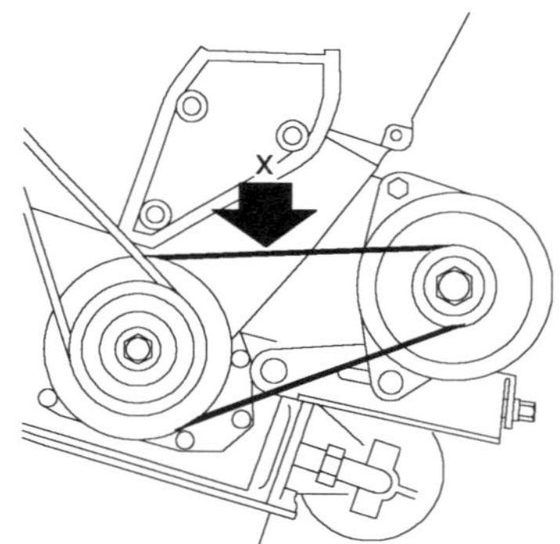

86M4421

3. Apply a force of 10 kg to drive belt at position X and measure deflection between crankshaft pulley and alternator pulley. Deflection must be 6 - 8 mm.

Adjust

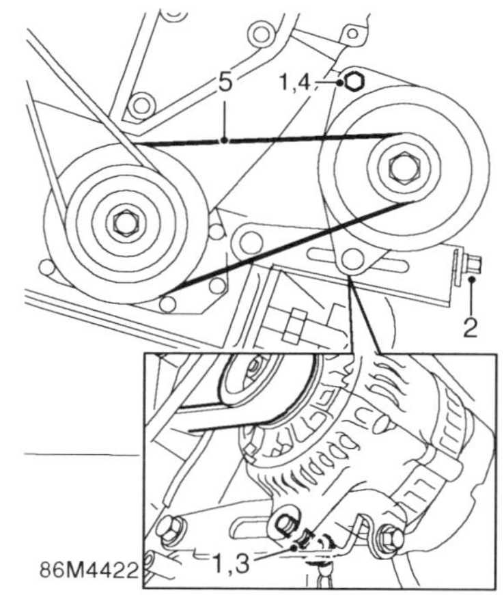

86M4422

1. Loosen 2 alternator mounting bolts.

CAUTION: Ensure that bolts are loosened sufficiently for alternator to move freely.

2. Adjust drive belt tension by turning tensioner bolt.

CAUTION: Do not apply excessive torque to adjusting bolt or damage to bolt will result. If bolt appears to be seized or is difficult to turn, apply suitable anti-seize lubricant to bolt.

3. Tighten mounting bolt securing alternator to adjusting link to 25 Nm.
4. Tighten upper mounting nut and bolt to 45 Nm.
5. Recheck drive belt tension.
6. Connect battery earth lead.

DRIVE BELT - ALTERNATOR - K SERIES - WITH AIR CONDITIONING

Service repair no - 86.10.05/20

Check

1. Disconnect battery earth lead.
2. Remove underbelly panel. ***See BODY, Exterior fittings.***
3. Check condition of drive belt, renew a drive belt that shows signs of wear or splitting.

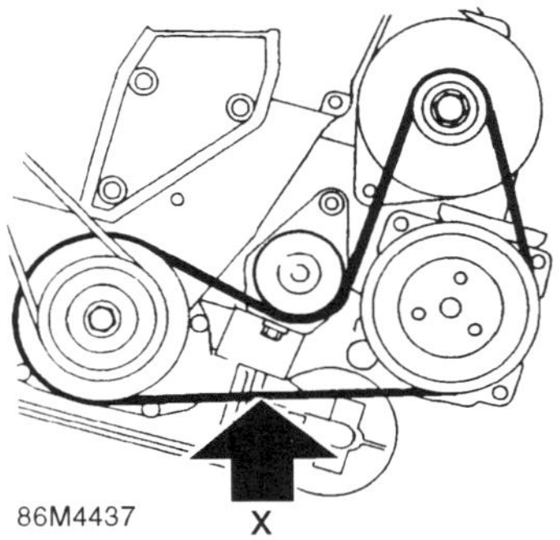

86M4437

4. Apply a force of 10 kg to the drive belt at position X and measure the deflection between the crankshaft pulley and air conditioning compressor pulley. Deflection must be 9 - 10 mm.

Adjust

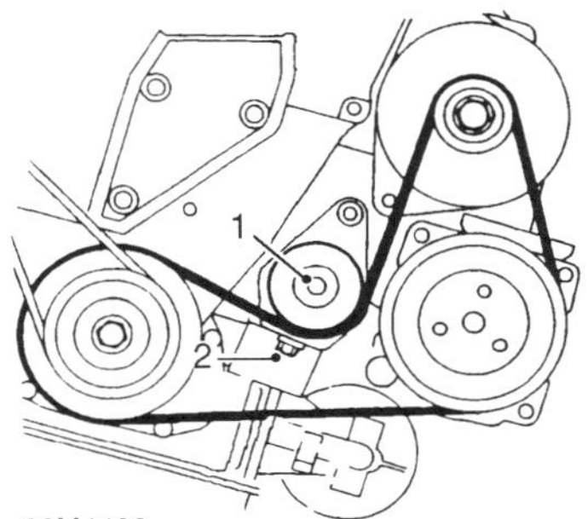

86M4438

1. Loosen tensioner pulley retaining nut.
2. Increase drive belt tension by turning the tensioner adjusting bolt clockwise.
3. Tighten tensioner pulley retaining nut to 25 Nm.
4. Recheck drive belt tension.
5. Fit underbelly panel. ***See BODY, Exterior fittings.***
6. Connect battery earth lead.

HEADLAMPS ADJUSTMENT

Service repair no - 86.40.17

Inspect

1. Align suitable beam setting equipment to headlamp.
2. Switch on headlamps.
   Headlamp setting 1.2% below horizontal and parallel.

Adjust

1. Adjust headlamp using a 6 mm Allen key.

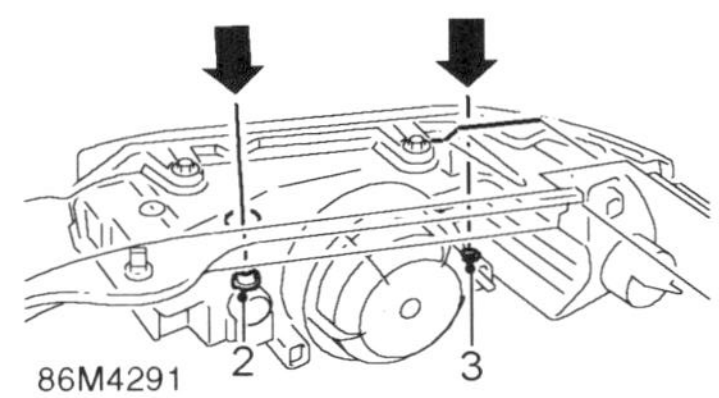

86M4291

2. Turn Allen screw for vertical alignment.
3. Turn Allen screw for horizontal alignment.
4. Align beam setting equipment to 2nd headlamp.
5. Adjust 2nd headlamp as detailed in steps 1 to 3 above.
6. Switch off headlamps.
7. Remove beam setting equipment.

ALTERNATOR - 'L' SERIES

Service repair no - 86.10.02

Remove

1. Disconnect battery earth lead.
2. Remove auxiliary drive belt. ***See this section.***

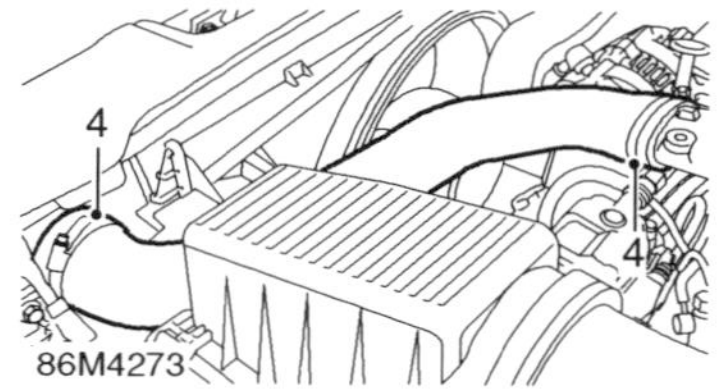

86M4273

3. Release 2 clips securing intercooler top hose, and remove hose.

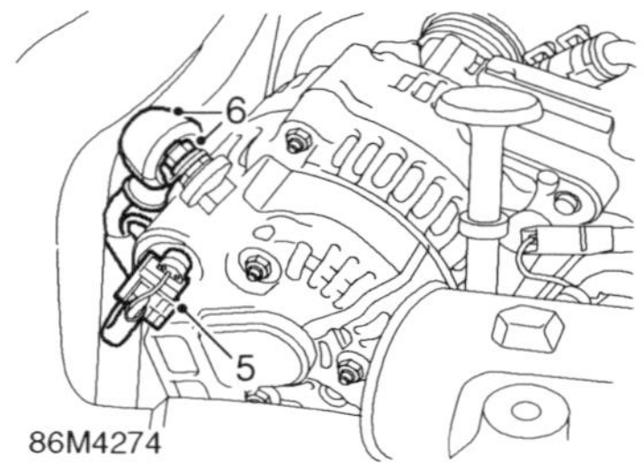

86M4274

4. Disconnect multiplug from alternator.
5. Release cover, remove nut and disconnect battery cable from alternator.

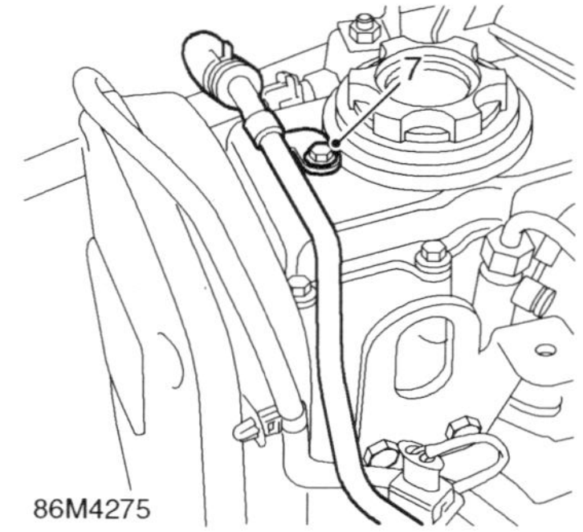

86M4275

Models with Air Conditioning fitted:

6. Remove bolt securing brake servo vacuum pipe to camshaft cover.

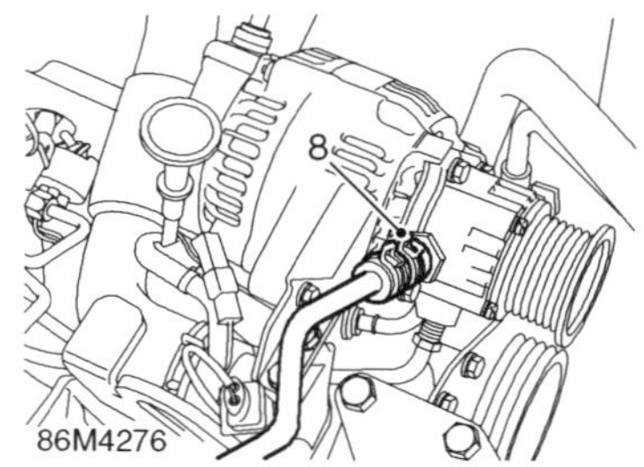

86M4276

All Models:

7. Release clip and disconnect vacuum hose from vacuum pump.
8. Position drain tin to collect oil spillage.

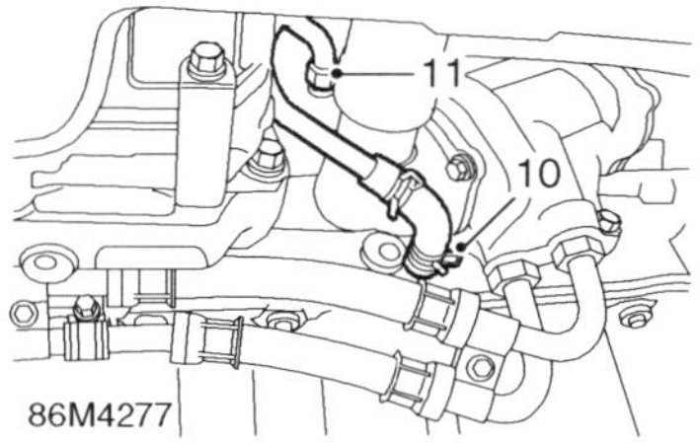

86M4277

9. Disconnect vacuum pump, oil return pipe from sump.
10. Disconnect vacuum pump, oil feed pipe union from cylinder block.

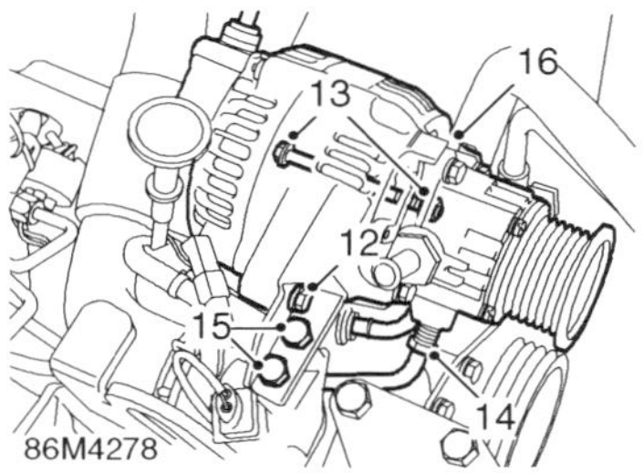

86M4278

11. Remove bolt securing alternator to top mounting bracket.
12. With assistance, remove nut and bolt securing alternator to lower mounting bracket.
13. Disconnect oil feed pipe from vacuum pump.
14. Remove 2 bolts securing alternator top mounting bracket, and remove bracket.
15. Remove alternator from vehicle.

CAUTION: Plug the connections.

Do not carry out further dismantling if component is removed for access only.

16. Remove 4 bolts securing vacuum pump to alternator.
17. Remove vacuum pump.
18. Clean mating face of vacuum pump and replacement alternator.
19. Fit vacuum pump to replacement alternator. Fit bolts and tighten to 8 Nm.

Refit

1. Remove plugs from connections.
2. Clean all pipe connections.
3. Position alternator to lower mounting bracket.
4. Fit top mounting bracket and tighten bolts to 25 Nm.
5. Connect oil feed pipe to cylinder block and tighten union.
6. With assistance fit lower mounting nut and bolt and tighten to 45 Nm.
7. Fit upper mounting bolt and tighten to 25 Nm.
8. Tighten oil feed pipe union to vacuum pump.
9. Connect vacuum hose to vacuum pump and secure hose with clip.

Models with Air Conditioning fitted:

10. Align vacuum pipe bracket to camshaft cover and tighten bolt.

All Models:

11. Connect oil return pipe to sump.
12. Connect battery cable to alternator stud. Tighten nut to 4 Nm. and position cover.
13. Connect multiplug to alternator.
14. Fit intercooler top hose and tighten clips.
15. Fit auxiliary drive belt. ***See this section.***
16. Connect battery earth lead.

ALTERNATOR - 'K' SERIES WITHOUT AIR CONDITIONING

Service repair no - 86.10.02

Remove

1. Disconnect battery earth lead.

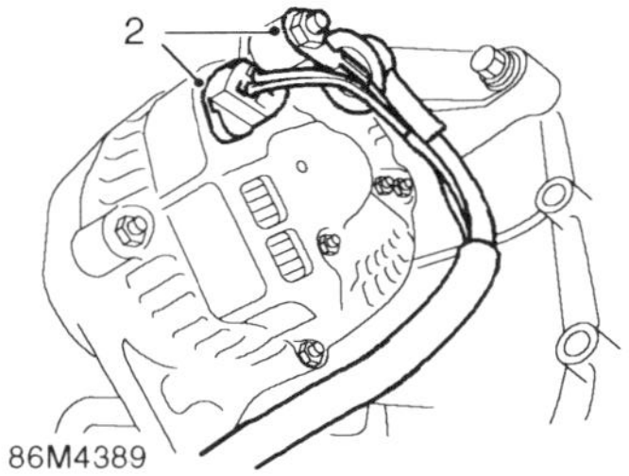

86M4389

2. Disconnect multiplug from alternator. Remove nut and disconnect battery cable from alternator.
3. Remove alternator drive belt. ***See this section.***

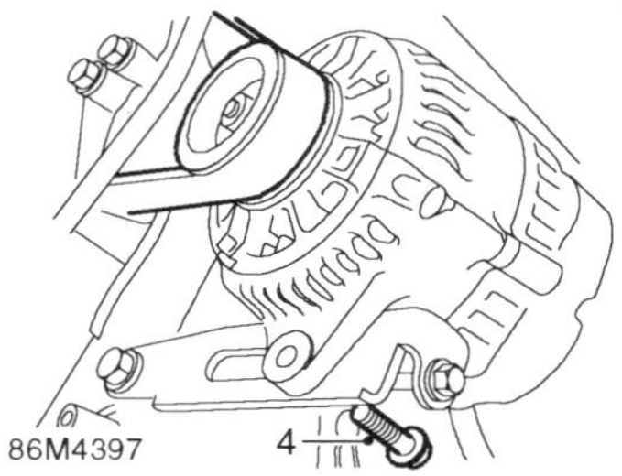

86M4397

4. Remove bolt securing alternator to adjusting link.

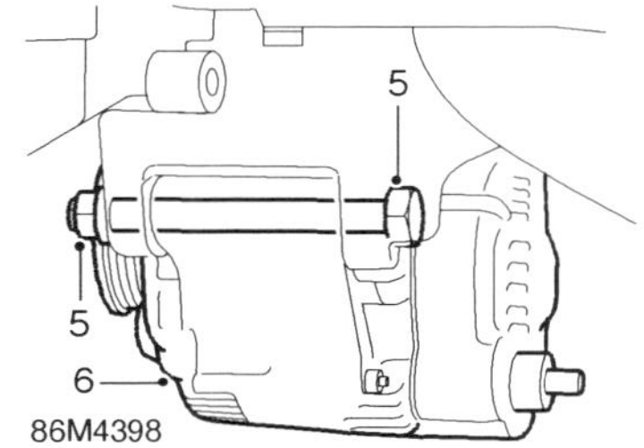

86M4398

5. Remove nut and bolt from alternator top mounting.
6. Gently tap alternator on rear of upper lug to free slip bush, release alternator from mounting and remove alternator from vehicle.

Refit

1. Position alternator to engine.
2. Fit nut and bolt securing alternator to top mounting and tighten sufficiently to clamp slip bush onto alternator.
3. Fit bolt securing alternator to adjusting link, but do not tighten at this stage.
4. Fit alternator drive belt. ***See this section.***
5. Connect battery cable to alternator and secure with nut. Tighten nut to 4 Nm.
6. Connect multiplug to alternator.
7. Connect battery earth lead.

ALTERNATOR -'K' SERIES WITH AIR CONDITIONING

Service repair no - 86.10.02/20

Remove

1. Disconnect battery earth lead.
2. Remove alternator drive belt. ***See this section.***
3. Remove cooling fan motor. ***See COOLING SYSTEM - 'K' SERIES, Repairs.***

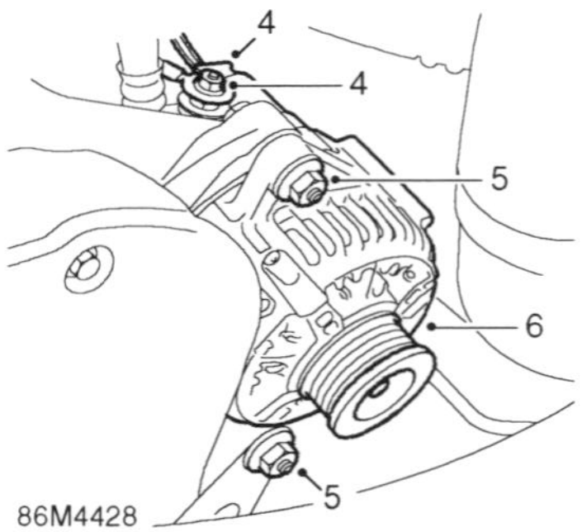

86M4428

4. Disconnect multiplug from alternator. Remove nut and disconnect lead from alternator
5. Remove upper and lower mounting bolts from alternator.
6. Gently tap alternator on rear of lower lug to free slip bush, release alternator from mounting and remove from vehicle.

Refit

1. Position alternator to mounting.
2. Fit mounting bolts and tighten to 45 Nm.
3. Connect battery lead to alternator and tighten nut to 4 Nm.
4. Connect multiplug to alternator.
5. Fit cooling fan motor. ***See COOLING SYSTEM - 'K' SERIES, Repairs.***
6. Fit alternator drive belt. ***See this section.***
7. Connect battery earth lead.

DRIVE BELT - AUXILIARY - 'L' SERIES

Service repair no - 86.10.03

Remove

1. Disconnect battery earth lead.
2. Remove engine acoustic cover. ***See ENGINE - 'L' SERIES, Repairs.***
3. Remove underbelly panel. ***See BODY, Exterior fittings.***

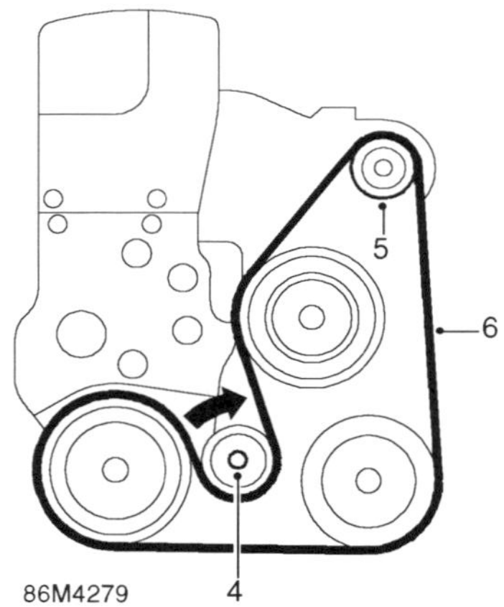

86M4279

4. Using a 15 mm ring spanner on pulley bolt of drive belt tensioner, rotate pulley clockwise and hold.
5. With assistance, release drive belt from alternator pulley.
6. Remove drive belt from remaining pulleys and remove from vehicle.

Refit

1. Clean drive belt pulley grooves and ensure grooves are not damaged.
2. Fit drive belt around pulleys, except alternator pulley, ensure belt is correctly aligned in pulley grooves.
3. Hold tensioner pulley fully clockwise, with assistance fit drive belt around alternator pulley.
4. Fit underbelly panel. ***See BODY, Exterior fittings.***
5. Fit engine acoustic cover. ***See ENGINE - 'L' SERIES, Repairs.***
6. Connect battery earth lead.

DRIVE BELT - ALTERNATOR - 'K' SERIES WITHOUT AIR CONDITIONING

Service repair no - 86.10.03

Remove

1. Disconnect battery earth lead.
2. Remove PAS pump drive belt. ***See STEERING, Repairs.***

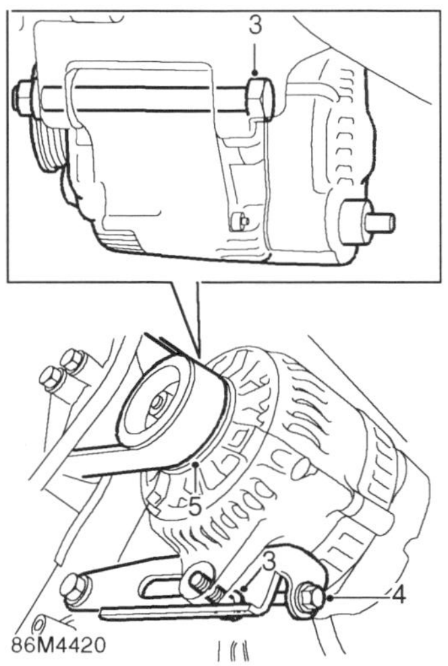

3. Loosen 2 alternator mounting bolts.

CAUTION: Ensure that bolts are loosened sufficiently for alternator to move freely.

4. Release drive belt tension by turning tensioner bolt anti-clockwise.

CAUTION: Do not apply excessive torque to adjusting bolt or damage to bolt will result. If bolt appears to be seized or is difficult to turn, apply suitable anti-seize lubricant to bolt.

5. Release drive belt from alternator pulley.
6. Remove drive belt.

Refit

1. Clean drive belt pulley grooves and ensure grooves are not damaged.
2. Fit drive belt to crankshaft pulley and connect to alternator pulley. Ensure grooves on pulleys and drive belt are correctly located.
3. Adjust drive belt tension. ***See Adjustments.***
4. Fit and adjust PAS pump drive belt. ***See STEERING, Repairs.***
5. Connect battery earth lead.

DRIVE BELT - ALTERNATOR - 'K' SERIES WITH AIR CONDITIONING

Service repair no - 86.10.03/20

Remove

1. Disconnect battery earth lead.
2. Remove underbelly panel. ***See BODY, Exterior fittings.***
3. Remove PAS drive belt. ***See STEERING, Repairs.***

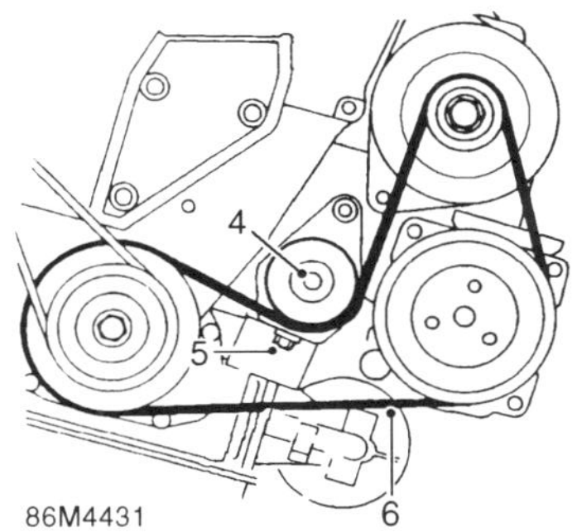

4. Loosen tensioner pulley retaining nut.
5. Loosen drive belt tension by turning tensioner adjusting bolt anti-clockwise.
6. Remove drive belt from remaining pulleys and remove from vehicle.

Refit

1. Clean drive belt pulley grooves and ensure grooves are not damaged.
2. Fit drive belt around pulleys, ensure belt is correctly aligned in pulley grooves.
3. Tension auxiliary drive belt. ***See Adjustments.***
4. Fit PAS drive belt. ***See STEERING, Repairs.***
5. Fit underbelly panel. ***See BODY, Exterior fittings.***
6. Connect battery earth lead.

BATTERY

Service repair no - 86.15.01

Remove

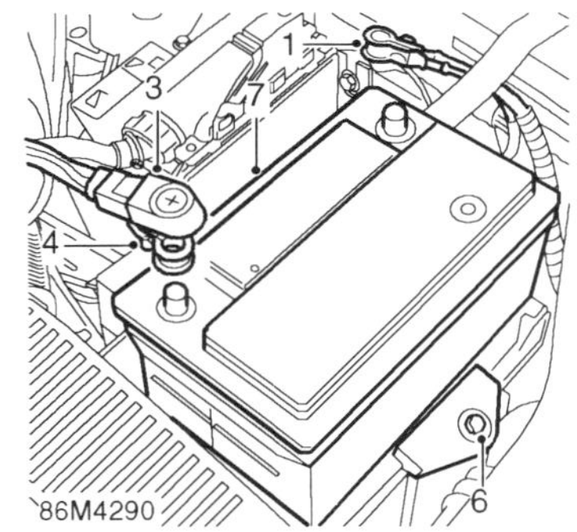

1. Loosen connector nut on negative lead.
2. Remove negative lead from battery terminal.
3. Release cover from positive terminal.
4. Loosen connector nut on positive lead.
5. Remove positive lead from battery terminal.
6. Remove bolt securing battery clamp and collect clamp.
7. Remove battery from vehicle.

Refit

1. Fit battery to vehicle.
2. Fit battery clamp and tighten bolt.
3. Fit positive lead to positive terminal and tighten connector nut.
4. Fit cover to positive terminal.
5. Fit negative lead to negative terminal, and tighten connector nut.

BATTERY CARRIER

Service repair no - 86.15.11

Remove

1. Remove battery. ***See this section.***

2. Remove 2 bolts and move engine compartment fuse box aside.
3. Release 3 relay holders and relay module from battery carrier.

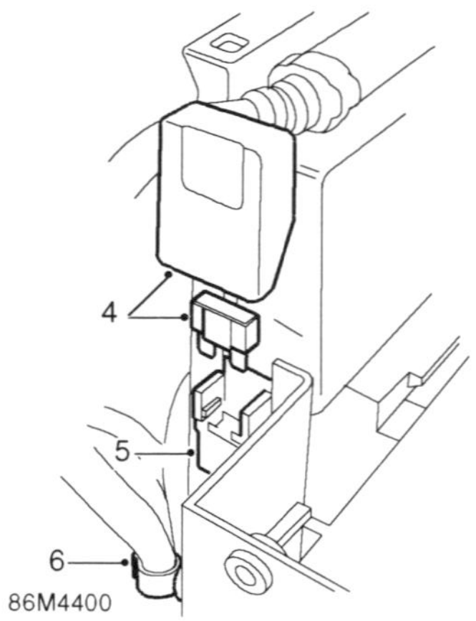

4. Remove cover and 70 ampere fuse from battery carrier.
5. Release fuse holder from battery carrier
6. Release clip securing engine harness to battery carrier.

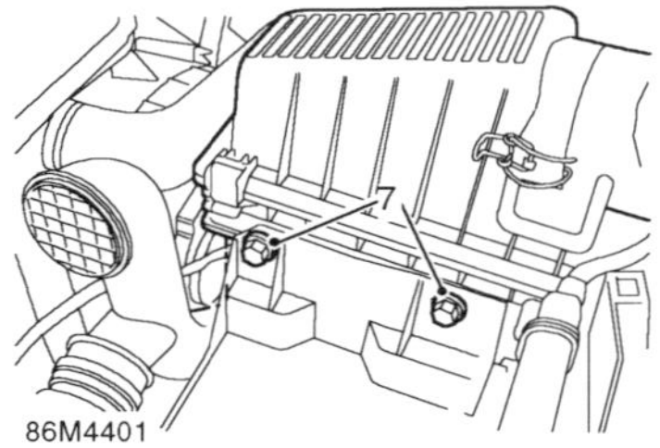

7. Remove 2 bolts and release air cleaner.

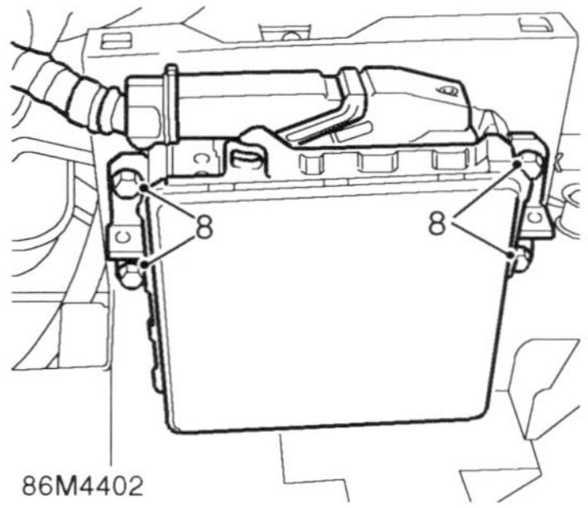

8. Remove 4 bolts and move ECM aside.

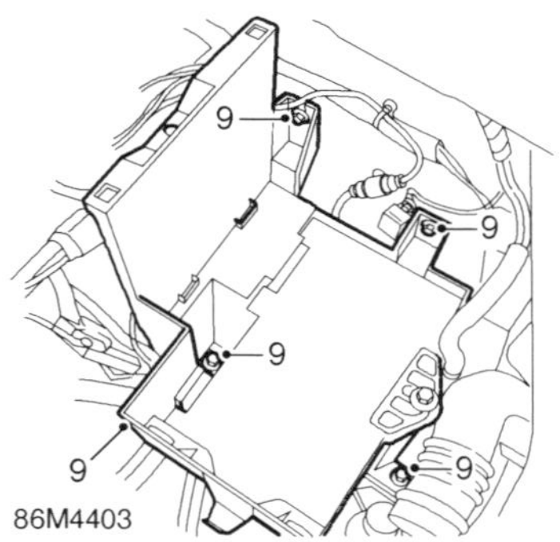

9. Remove 4 bolts and remove battery carrier.

Refit

1. Position battery carrier and tighten bolts to 10 Nm.
2. Position ECM and tighten bolts to 9 Nm.
3. Position air cleaner and tighten bolts.
4. Secure engine harness clip to battery carrier.
5. Position relays and relay module to carrier.
6. Fit fuse holder into battery carrier.
7. Fit fuse and fuse cover.
8. Position engine compartment fuse box and tighten bolts to 4 Nm.
9. Fit battery. ***See this section.***

MOTOR AND CONTROL UNIT - FRONT DOOR GLASS - 3 DOOR

Service repair no - 86.25.01

Remove

1. Remove front door upper water shedder. ***See BODY, Doors.***
2. Remove front door lower water shedder. ***See BODY, Doors.***

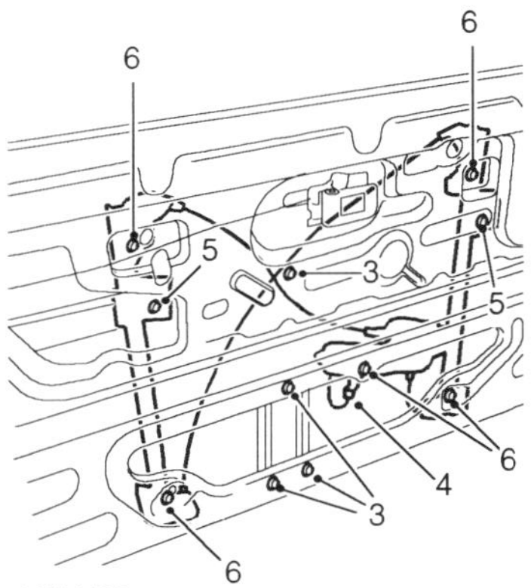

86M4436

3. Remove 4 Torx screws securing door stiffener, release bowden cable from clip and remove door stiffener.
4. Disconnect multiplug from door glass motor.
5. Loosen 2 screws clamping control unit to glass and release glass from clamps.
6. Remove 5 screws securing control unit to door.
7. Manoeuvre motor and control unit out from door aperture.

Refit

CAUTION: It is very important when fitting the control unit that the cable with the anti-rattle sleeve is next to the trim casing and the motor cable is next to the glass.

1. Position motor and control unit in door aperture and locate to glass.
2. Fit and tighten screws securing control unit to door.
3. Tighten clamps securing control unit to glass, to 9 Nm .
4. Connect multiplug to door glass motor.
5. Position door stiffener, fit and tighten Torx screws to 9 Nm.
6. Secure cable in door stiffener clip.
7. Fit front door lower water shedder. ***See BODY, Doors.***
8. Fit front door upper water shedder. ***See BODY, Doors.***

MOTOR AND CONTROL UNIT - FRONT DOOR GLASS - 5 DOOR

Service repair no - 86.25.01

Remove

1. Remove front door water shedder. ***See BODY, Doors.***

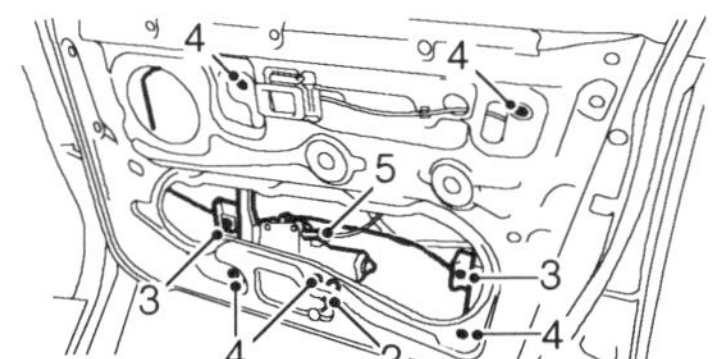

86M4260

2. Disconnect multiplug from door glass motor.
3. Loosen 2 screws clamping control unit to glass.
4. Remove 5 screws securing control unit to door.
5. Release bowden cable from door clip and manoeuvre motor and control unit out from door aperture.

Refit

CAUTION: It is very important when fitting the control unit that the cable with the anti-rattle sleeve is next to the trim casing and the motor cable next to the glass.

1. Position motor and control unit in door aperture and locate to glass.
2. Fit and tighten screws securing control unit to door.
3. Secure bowden cable in door clip.
4. Tighten clamps securing control unit to glass, to 9 Nm .
5. Connect multiplug to door glass motor.
6. Fit front door water shedder. ***See BODY, Doors.***

SWITCH - CONSOLE

Service repair no - 86.25.19

Remove

1. Remove front console. ***See BODY, Interior trim components.***

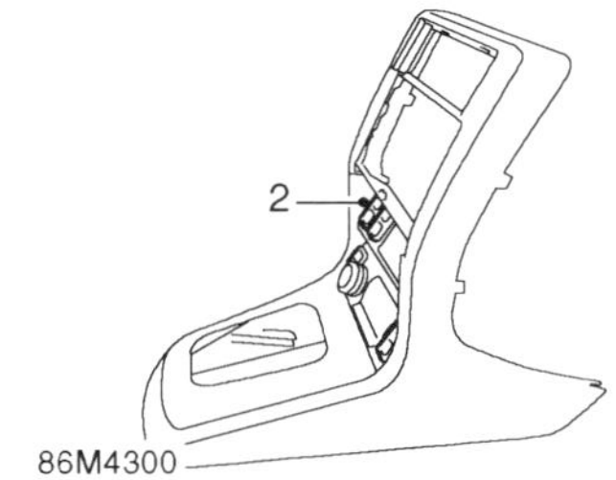

86M4300

2. Remove switch from console.

Refit

1. Fit switch to console.
2. Fit front console. ***See BODY, Interior trim components.***

RELAY - CONTROL - TAIL DOOR GLASS

Service repair no - 86.25.45

Remove

1. Remove RH rear quarter lower casing. ***See BODY, Interior trim components.***

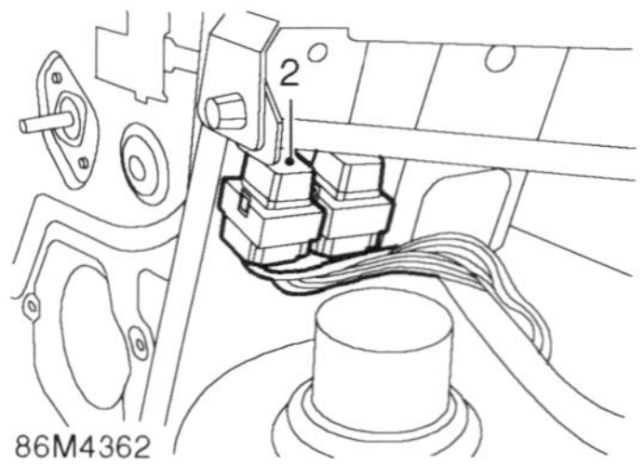

86M4362

2. Remove tail door glass control relay.

Refit

1. Fit relay.
2. Fit RH rear quarter lower casing. ***See BODY, Interior trim components.***

MICRO-SWITCH - HARD-BACK

Service repair no - 86.25.46

Remove

1. Remove hard-back or soft-back. **See Owner's Handbook.**
2. Remove RH upper trim casing. ***See BODY, Interior trim components.***

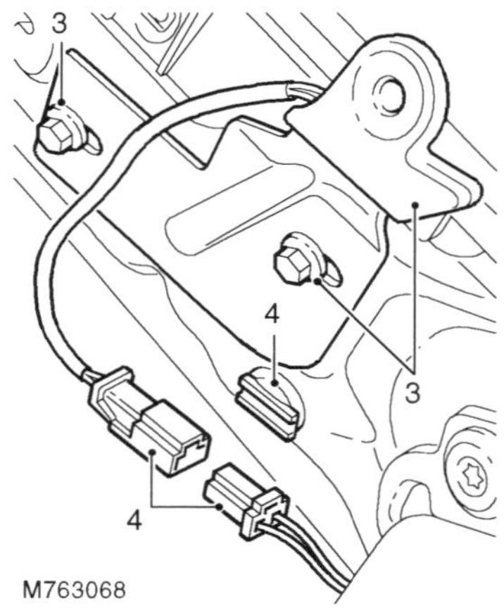

M763068

3. Remove 2 bolts securing soft-back support bracket and remove bracket.
4. Disconnect micro-switch multiplug and release from retainer.

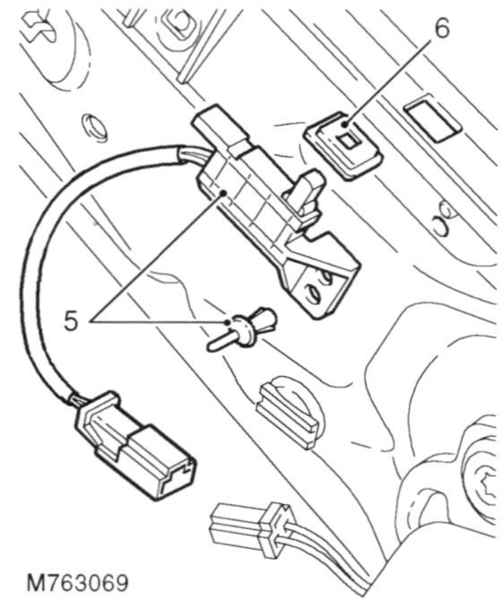

M763069

5. Remove peg securing-micro switch, and remove micro-switch.
6. Collect micro-switch seal.

Refit

1. Locate micro-switch seal, position micro-switch and secure with peg.
2. Connect multiplug and secure to retainer
3. Position soft-back support bracket, fit bolts and tighten to 25 Nm.
4. Fit upper trim casing. ***See BODY, Interior trim components.***
5. Fit hard-back. **See Owner's Handbook.**

MOTOR - TAIL DOOR

Service repair no - 86.26.02

Remove

1. Remove tail door water shedder. ***See BODY, Doors.***

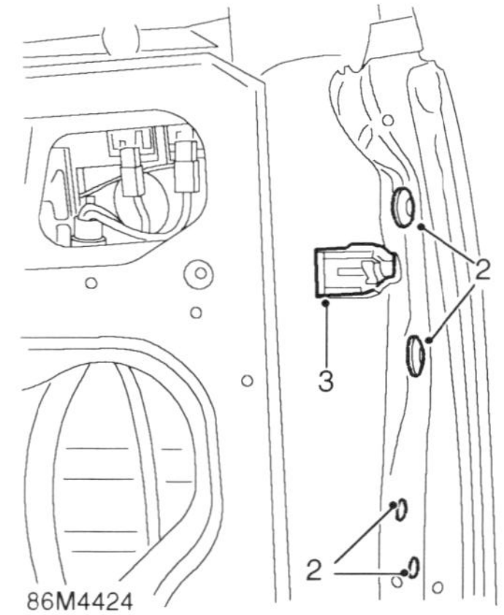

86M4424

2. Remove 4 screws securing door latch.
3. Release door latch to access harness clips and multiplugs.

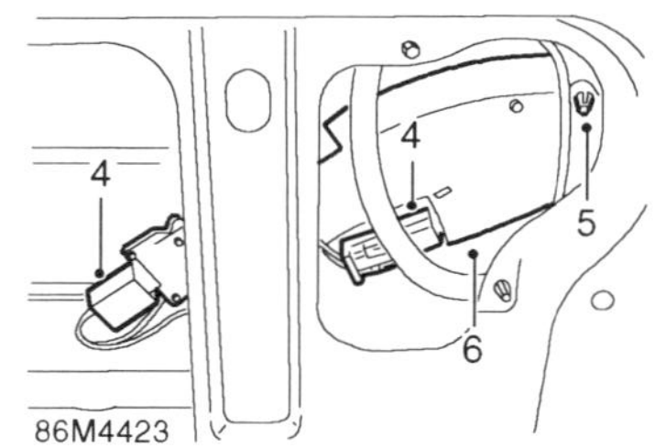

86M4423

4. Disconnect 2 multiplugs from door latch.
5. Release door harness clip from latch.
6. Remove door latch.

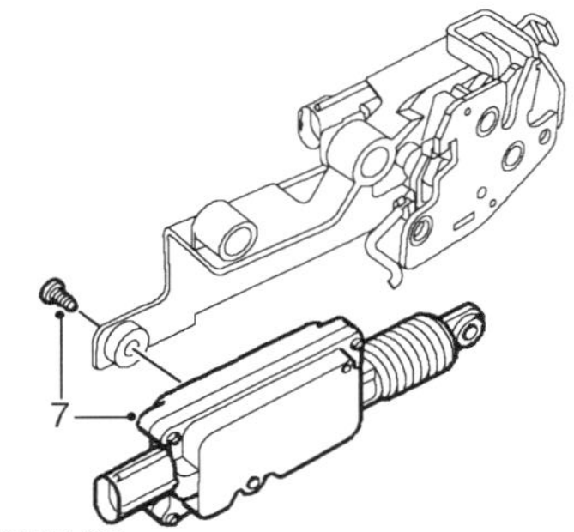

86M4425

7. Remove screw from motor and remove motor from latch.

Refit

1. Position motor to latch, fit and tighten screw.
2. Position door latch, connect multiplugs and harness clips.
3. Locate in position, fit and tighten screws.
4. Fit water shedder. ***See BODY, Doors.***

SWITCH - HORN PUSH

Service repair no - 86.30.01

Remove

1. Remove air bag from steering wheel. ***See RESTRAINT SYSTEMS, Repairs.***

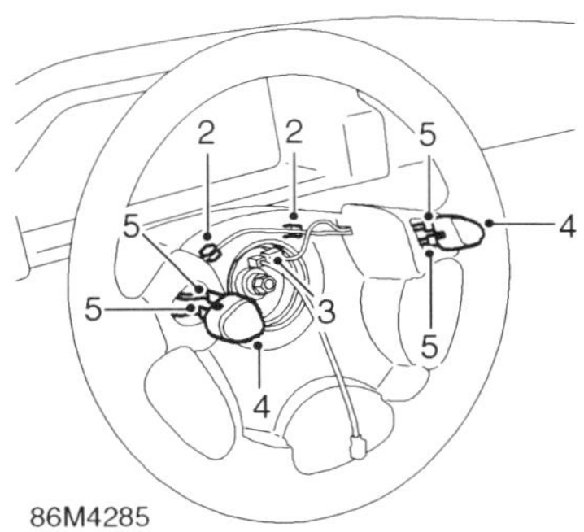

86M4285

2. Release horn switch leads from retainers on steering wheel base.
3. Disconnect multiplug from rotary coupler.
4. Using a broad round edged tool, carefully prise horn switch from steering wheel while feeding harness through foam channel.

CAUTION: The tool must be inserted to a depth of 15mm. midway along lower edge of switch.

5. Note fitted position of harness connection and disconnect 2 Lucars from switch.

Refit

1. Position NEW switch and connect Lucars.
2. Carefully fit switch to steering wheel while gently pulling on harness.
3. Connect multiplug to rotary coupler and secure leads to base of steering wheel.
4. Fit air bag to steering wheel. ***See RESTRAINT SYSTEMS, Repairs.***

HORN

Service repair no - 86.30.10

Remove

1. Remove battery. ***See this section.***

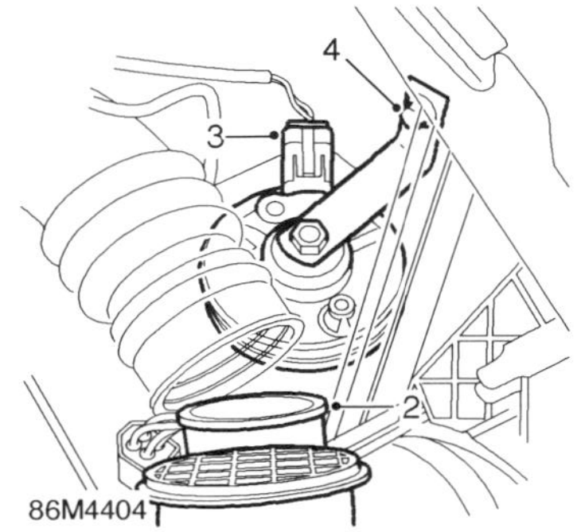

86M4404

2. Release air intake hose from intake elbow.
3. Disconnect multiplug from horn.
4. Remove bolt securing horn mounting bracket and remove horn.

Refit

1. Position horn and tighten bolt.
2. Connect multiplug to horn.
3. Connect air intake hose to elbow.
4. Fit battery. ***See this section.***

HEADLAMP ASSEMBLY

Service repair no - 86.40.49

Remove

1. Remove front bumper valance. ***See BODY, Exterior fittings.***

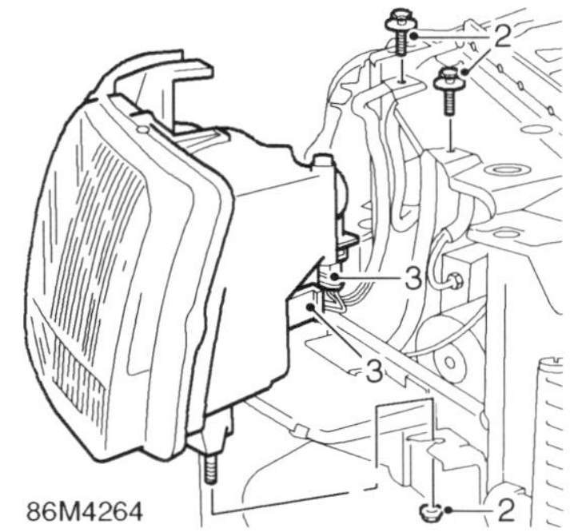

86M4264

2. Remove 2 bolts and 1 nut securing head lamp.
3. Disconnect 2 multiplugs and remove headlamp.

Refit

1. Position headlamp and connect multiplugs.
2. Fit and tighten bolts and nut.
3. Fit front bumper valance. ***See BODY, Exterior fittings.***
4. Check headlamps adjustment. ***See Adjustments.***

LAMP - SIDE REPEATER

Service repair no - 86.40.53

Remove

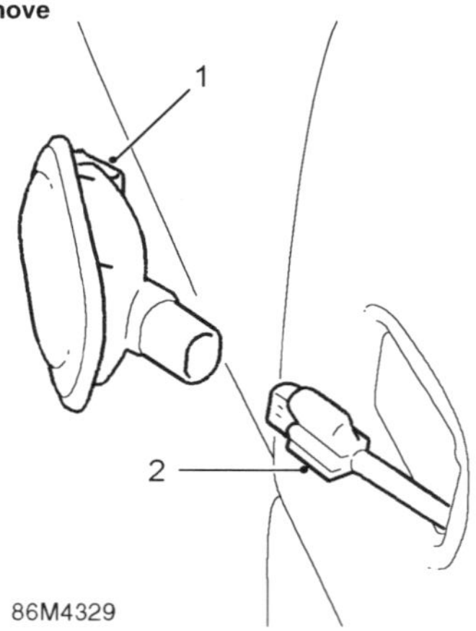

86M4329

1. Push lamp towards rear of vehicle to release spring clip, and release lamp from wing.
2. Disconnect multiplug.

Refit

1. Connect multiplug to lamp and secure lamp to wing.

LAMP - TAIL

Service repair no - 86.40.70

Remove

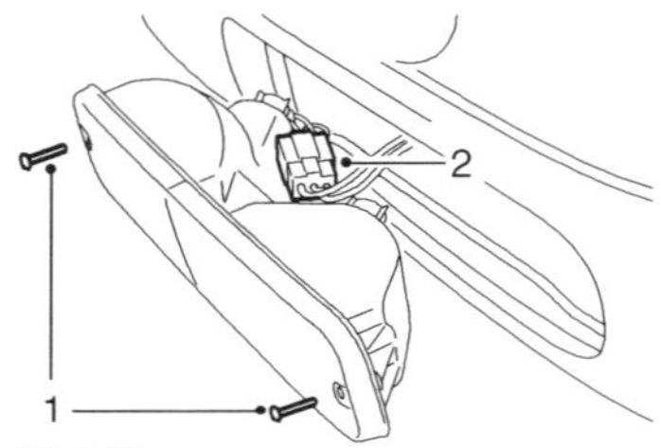

86M4265

1. Remove 2 screws securing tail lamp to rear bumper.
2. Release lamp, disconnect multiplug and remove lamp.

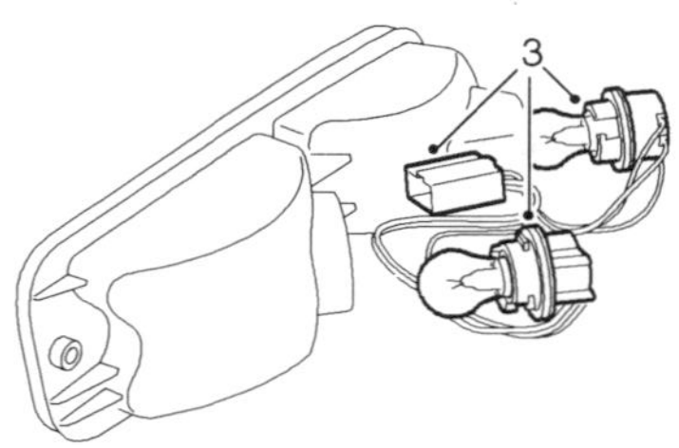

86M4266

Do not carry out further dismantling if component is removed for access only.

3. Remove multiplug and bulb holders from tail lamp.
4. Fit multiplug and bulb holders to replacement tail lamp.

Refit

1. Position tail lamp and connect multiplug. Fit and tighten screws.

LAMP - NUMBER PLATE

Service repair no - 86.40.86

Remove

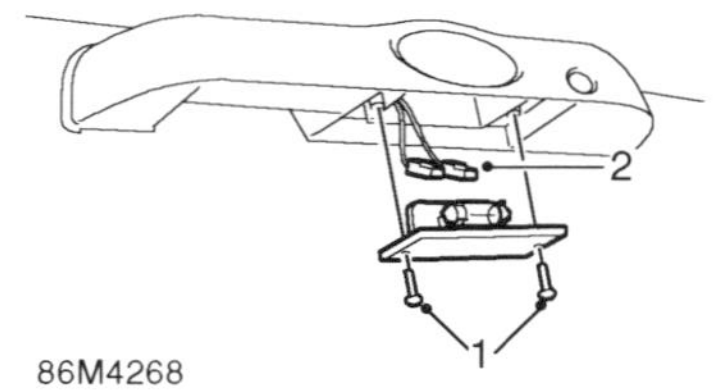

86M4268

1. Remove 2 screws securing lamp to tail door handle.
2. Disconnect Lucars and remove lamp.

Refit

1. Position lamp and connect Lucars. Fit and tighten screws.

LAMP - REAR FOG GUARD

Service repair no - 86.41.15

Remove

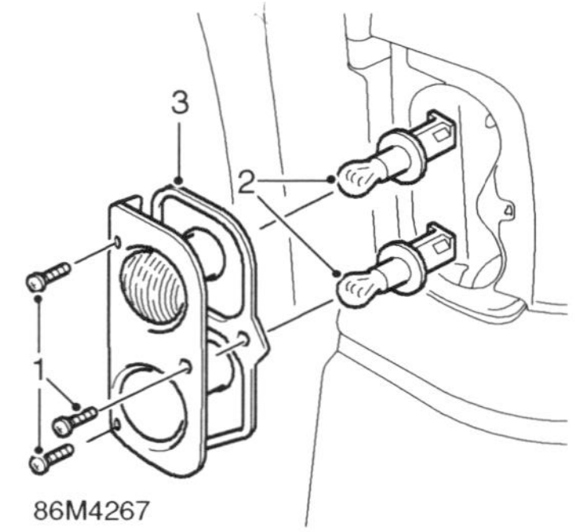

86M4267

1. Remove 3 screws securing lamp to body.
2. Release lamp, disconnect 2 bulb holders and remove lamp.
3. Remove lamp sealing rubber.

Refit

1. Fit sealing rubber and bulb holders to lamp.
2. Position lamp, fit and tighten screws.

STOP LAMP - CENTRE - HIGH MOUNTED

Service repair no - 86.41.32

Remove

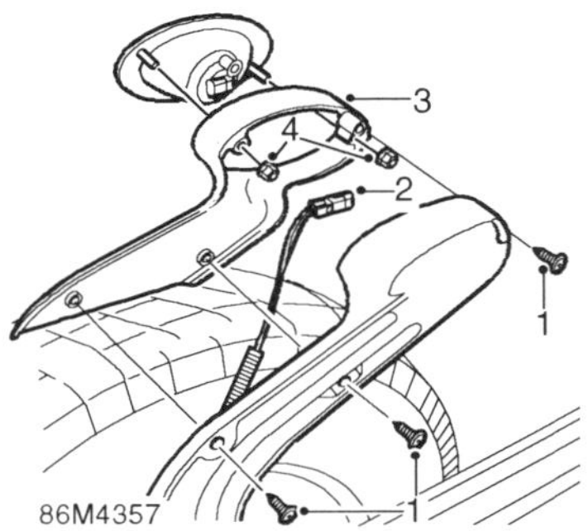

86M4357

1. Remove 3 screws securing high mounted stop lamp bracket to spare wheel carrier.
2. Release lamp bracket and disconnect multiplug.
3. Remove lamp and bracket.
4. Remove 2 nuts and remove lamp from bracket.

Refit

1. Position lamp to bracket and tighten nuts.
2. Position lamp bracket and connect multiplug to lamp.
3. Position lamp bracket to spare wheel carrier and tighten screws.

LAMP - GLOVE BOX COMPARTMENT

Service repair no - 86.45.08

Remove

1. Open glove box lid.

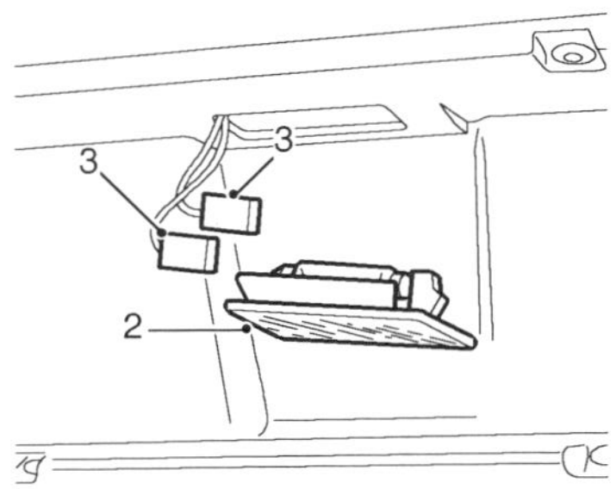

86M4269

2. Release lamp from glove box.
3. Disconnect Lucars and remove lamp.

Refit

1. Position lamp and connect Lucars.
2. Secure lamp and close glove box lid.

LAMP - LOAD SPACE

Service repair no - 86.45.16

Remove

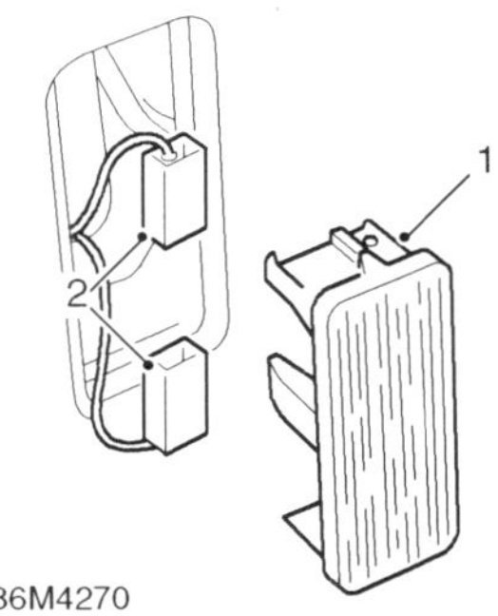

86M4270

1. Release lamp from trim casing.
2. Disconnect Lucars and remove lamp.

Refit

1. Position lamp and connect Lucars.
2. Secure lamp to trim casing.

RADIO

Service repair no - 86.50.03

Remove

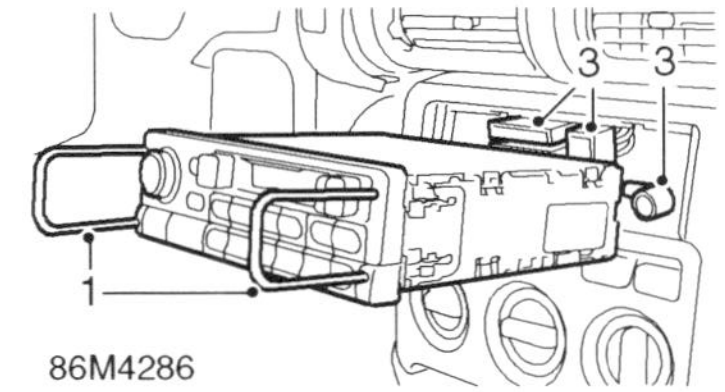

86M4286

1. Fit radio removal tools **SMD 4091** to retaining clips.
2. Pull on tool to release radio from fascia.
3. Disconnect multiplugs and aerial lead.
4. Remove radio.

Refit

1. Position radio to aperture, connect multiplugs and aerial lead.
2. Slide radio into fascia until retaining clips engage.
3. Enter security code and check radio for correct operation.

SPEAKER - REAR - 3 DOOR

Service repair no - 86.50.12

Remove

1. Remove body side rear trim casing. ***See BODY, Interior trim components.***

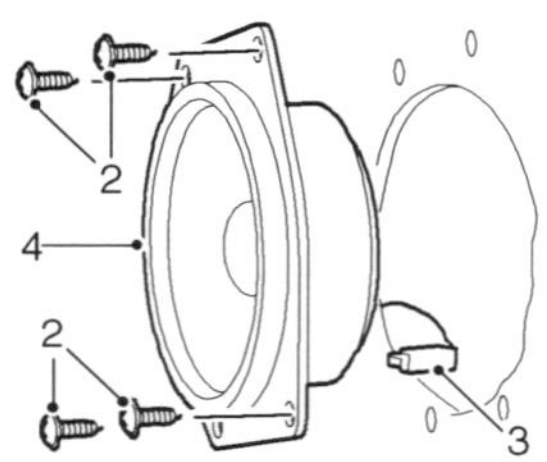

86M4257

2. Remove 4 screws securing speaker to door.
3. Disconnect multiplug from speaker.
4. Remove speaker from door.

Refit

1. Position speaker to door, and connect multiplug.
2. Fit and tighten securing screws.
3. Fit trim casing. ***See BODY, Interior trim components.***

SPEAKER - REAR - 5 DOOR

Service repair no - 86.50.12

Remove

1. Remove rear door trim casing. ***See BODY, Doors.***

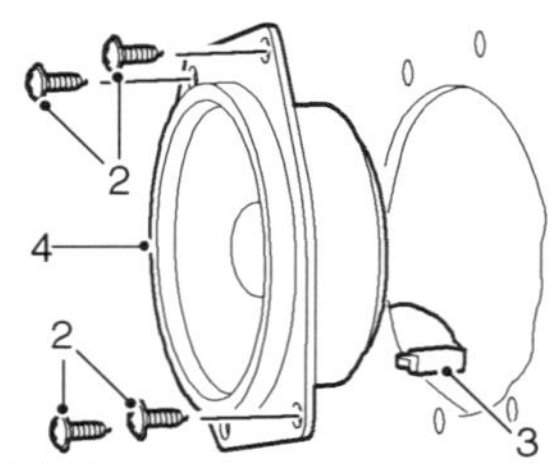

86M4257

2. Remove 4 screws securing speaker to door.
3. Disconnect multiplug from speaker.
4. Remove speaker from door.

Refit

1. Position speaker to door, and connect multiplug.
2. Fit and tighten securing screws.
3. Fit trim casing. ***See BODY, Doors.***

SPEAKER - FRONT - 3 DOOR

Service repair no - 86.50.15

Remove

1. Remove front door trim casing. ***See BODY, Doors.***

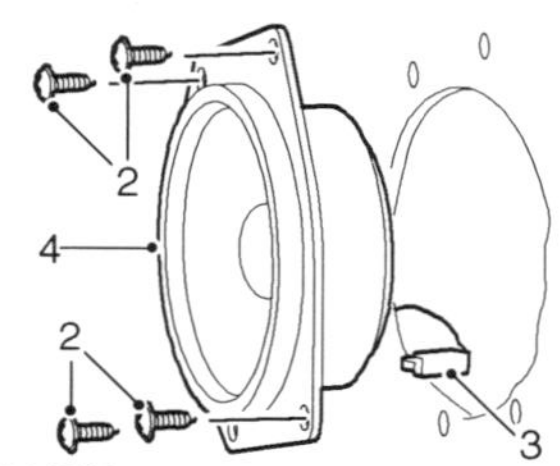

86M4257

2. Remove 4 screws securing speaker to door.
3. Disconnect multiplug from speaker.
4. Remove speaker from door.

Refit

1. Position speaker to door, and connect multiplug.
2. Fit and tighten securing screws.
3. Fit front door trim casing. ***See BODY, Doors.***

SPEAKER - FRONT - 5 DOOR

Service repair no - 86.50.15

Remove

1. Remove front door trim casing. ***See BODY, Doors.***

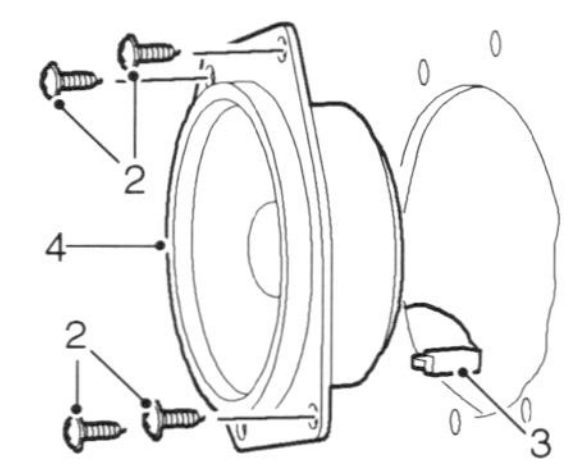

86M4257

2. Remove 4 screws securing speaker to door.
3. Disconnect multiplug from speaker.
4. Remove speaker from door.

Refit

1. Position front speaker to door, and connect multiplug.
2. Fit and tighten securing screws.
3. Fit trim casing. ***See BODY, Doors.***

AERIAL - 3 DOOR

Service repair no - 86.50.18

Remove

1. Remove headlining. ***See BODY, Interior trim components.***

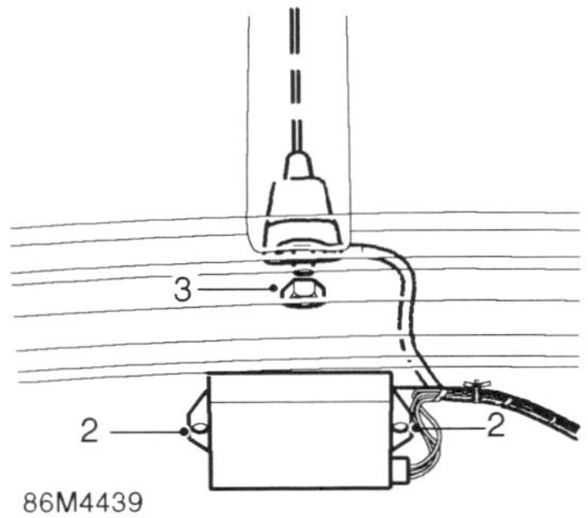

86M4439

2. Remove 2 screws and release volumetric sensor mounting bracket.
3. Remove nut securing coaxial cable to aerial base.

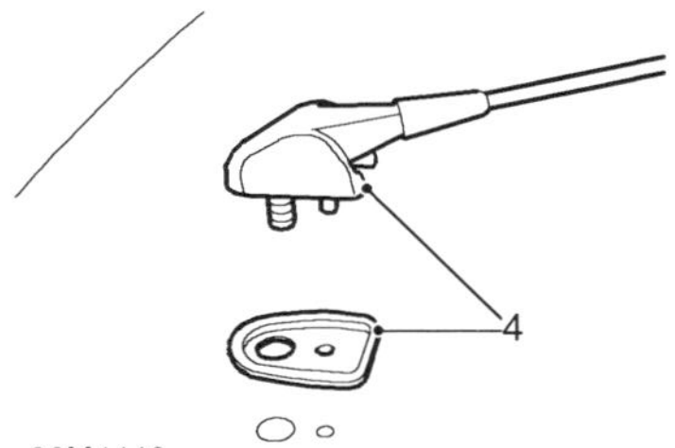

86M4440

4. Remove aerial base from roof panel and remove rubber seal.

Refit

1. Fit rubber seal and position aerial base to roof panel.
2. Connect coaxial cable and tighten nut.
3. Position volumetric sensor bracket and tighten screws.
4. Fit headlining. ***See BODY, Interior trim components.***

AERIAL - 5 DOOR

Service repair no - 86.50.18

Remove

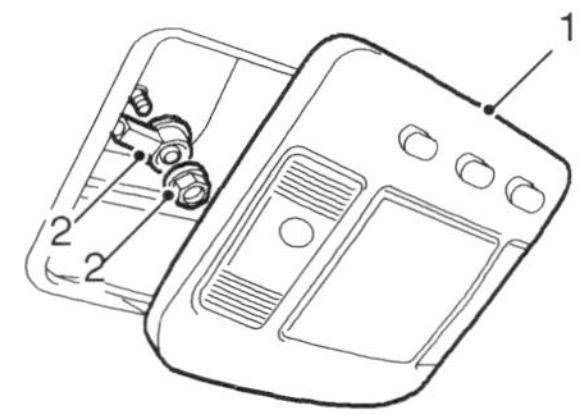

86M4271

1. Release roof lamp from headlining.
2. Remove nut securing coaxial cable to aerial base.

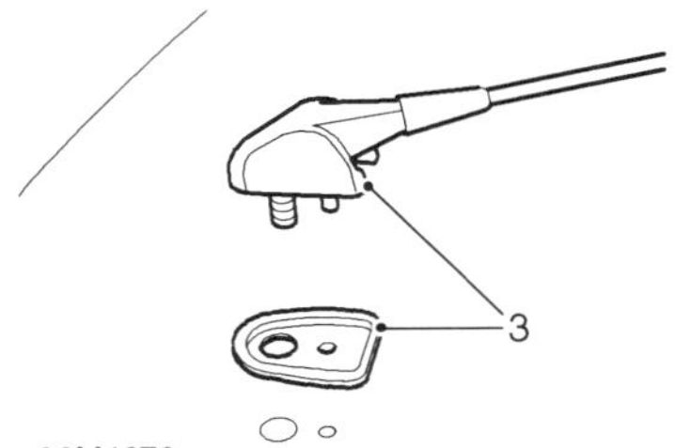

86M4272

3. Remove aerial base from roof panel and remove rubber seal.

Refit

1. Fit rubber seal and position aerial base to roof panel.
2. Connect coaxial cable and tighten nut.
3. Position and secure roof lamp.

COAXIAL LEAD - AERIAL - 3 DOOR

Service repair no - 86.50.24

Remove

1. Remove aerial. ***See this section.***

NOTE: Original coaxial lead cannot be removed as it is part of the body harness.

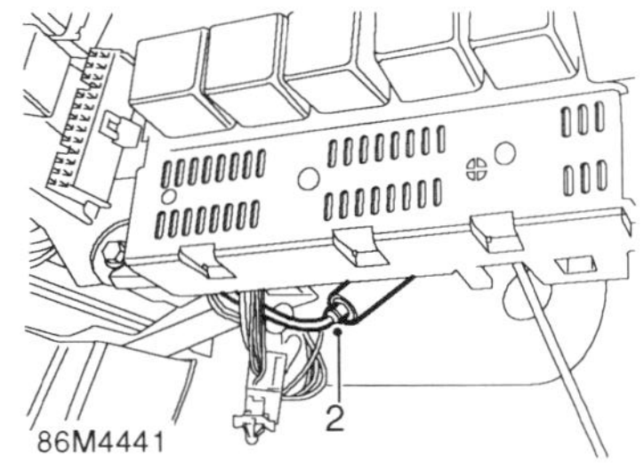

86M4441

2. Disconnect coaxial lead from link lead behind fuse box.

Refit

1. Position NEW coaxial lead to roof panel.
2. Align coaxial lead behind fascia and connect to link lead.
3. Secure coaxial lead to harness with cable ties.
4. Fit aerial. ***See this section.***

COAXIAL LEAD - AERIAL - 5 DOOR

Service repair no - 86.50.24

Remove

1. Remove aerial. ***See this section.***
2. Remove 'A' post finisher. ***See BODY, Interior trim components.***
3. Remove sun visor. ***See BODY, Interior trim components.***

NOTE: Original coaxial lead cannot be removed as it is part of the body harness.

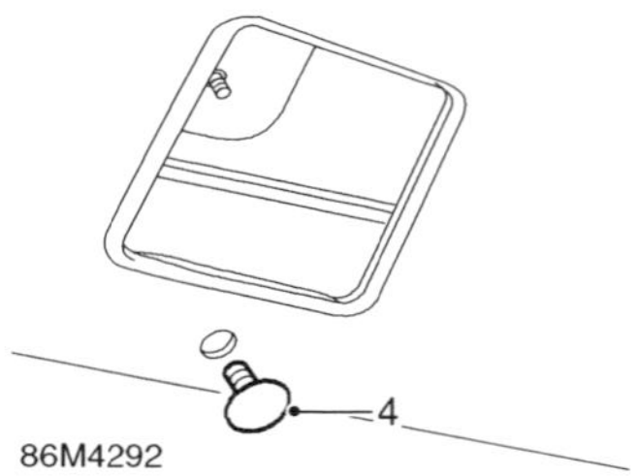

86M4292

4. Remove stud securing front edge of head lining.

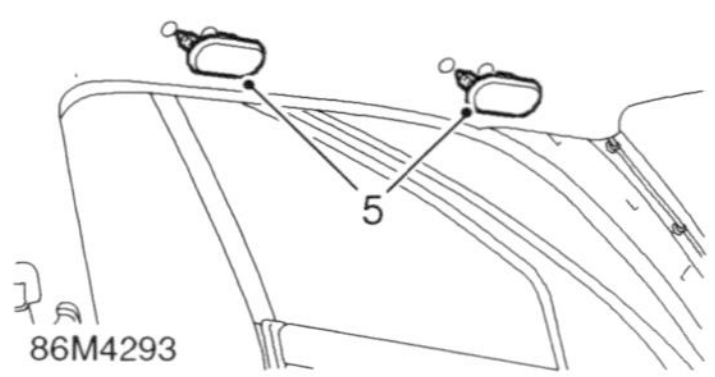

86M4293

5. Remove 2 grab handle blanks from head lining.

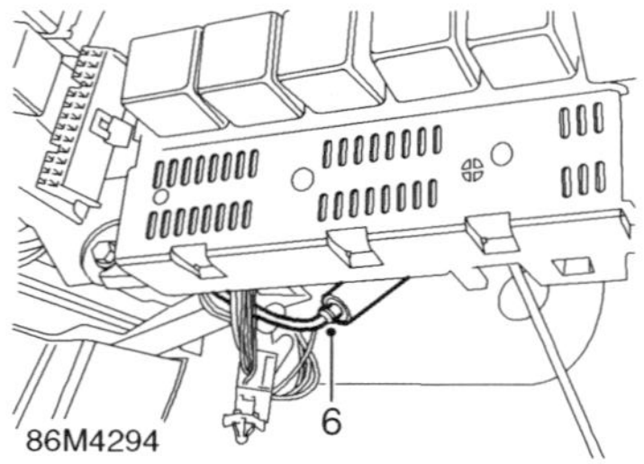

86M4294

6. Disconnect coaxial lead from link lead behind fuse box.

Refit

1. Position NEW coaxial lead to roof panel.
2. Align coaxial lead behind fascia and connect to link lead.
3. Secure coaxial lead to harness with cable ties.
4. Fit stud and grab handle blanks to head lining.
5. Fit 'A' post finisher. ***See BODY, Interior trim components.***
6. Fit sun visor. ***See BODY, Interior trim components.***
7. Fit aerial. ***See this section.***

SPEAKER - TWEETER - FRONT

Service repair no - 86.50.34

Remove

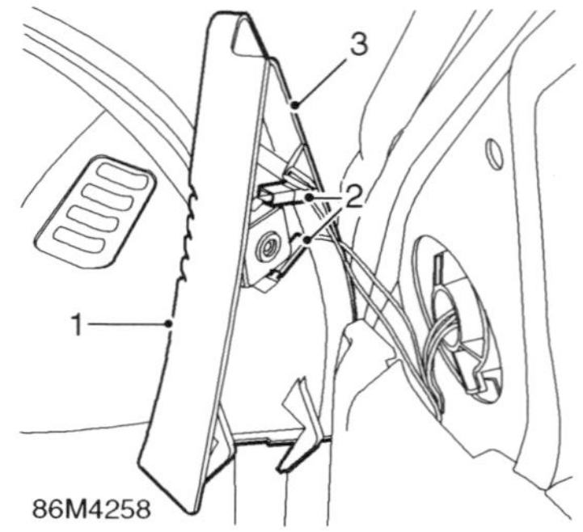

86M4258

1. Release cheater panel from door.
2. Disconnect Lucars from tweeter speaker.
3. Remove cheater panel.

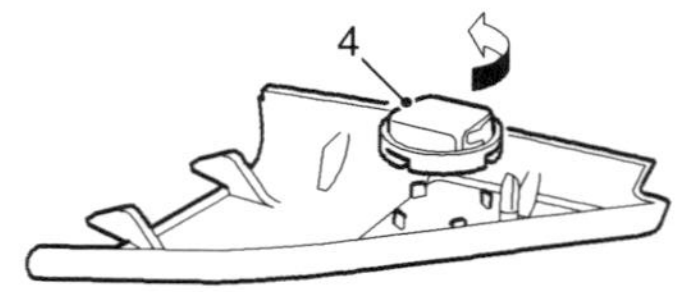

86M4259

4. Remove tweeter speaker.

Refit

1. Fit tweeter speaker to cheater panel, and connect Lucars.
2. Fit cheater panel to door.

COAXIAL LINK LEAD

Service repair no - 86.50.65

Remove

1. Remove radio. ***See this section.***

NOTE: Original coaxial link lead cannot be removed as it is part of the main harness.

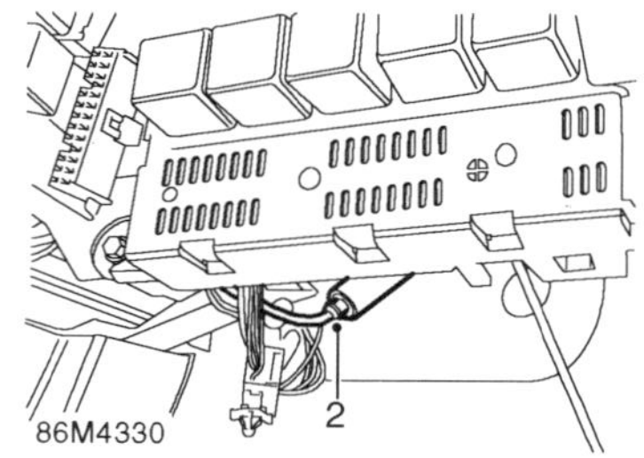

86M4330

2. Disconnect coaxial link lead from aerial lead.

Refit

1. Fit replacement extension lead and route to radio position.

WARNING: Ensure link lead does not foul control pedals or steering column.

2. Secure lead as necessary with cable ties.
3. Connect link lead to aerial lead.
4. Fit radio. ***See this section.***

RELAY - MAIN

Service repair no - 86.55.08

Remove

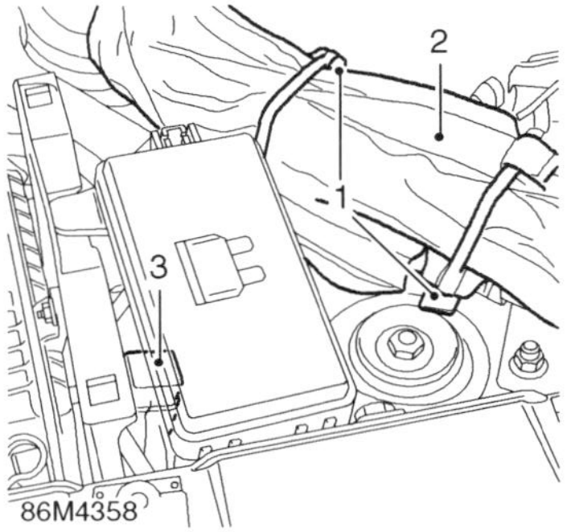

1. Remove 2 straps securing vehicle jack.
2. Remove jack.
3. Remove relay from holder on battery tray.

Refit

1. Fit relay.
2. Position vehicle jack to its mounting.
3. Fit securing straps.

RELAY MODULE

Service repair no - 86.55.72

Remove

1. Disconnect battery earth lead.

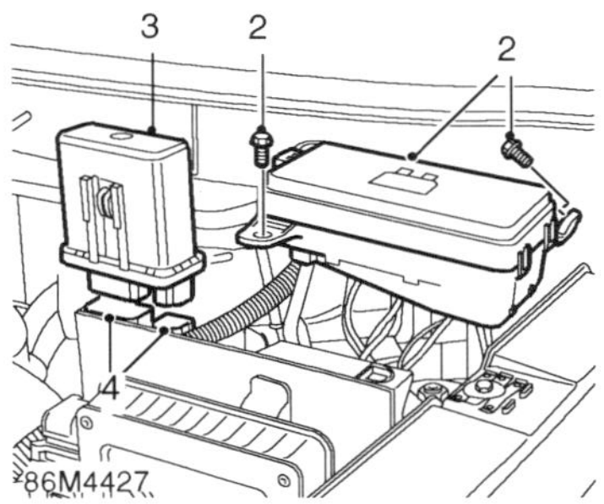

2. Remove 2 bolts and position engine compartment fuse box aside.
3. Release relay module from mounting bracket.
4. Disconnect 2 multiplugs from relay module.
5. Remove relay module.

Refit

1. Position relay module and connect multiplugs.
2. Secure relay module to mounting bracket.
3. Position fuse box and tighten bolts.
4. Connect battery earth lead.

CENTRAL CONTROL UNIT - (CCU)

Service repair no - 86.55.75

Remove

1. Disconnect battery earth lead.

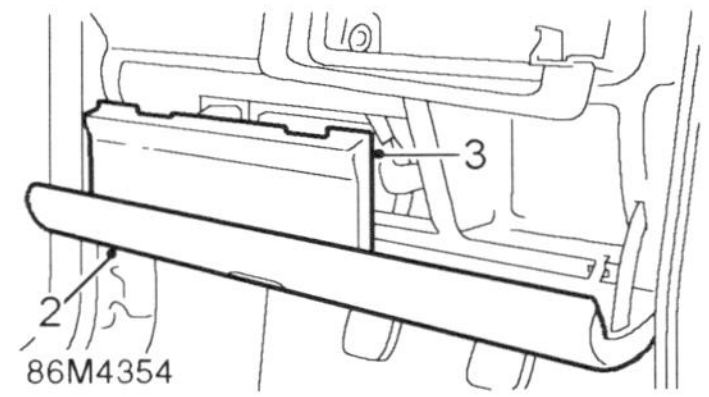

2. Open driver's side glove box
3. Remove fuse box cover.

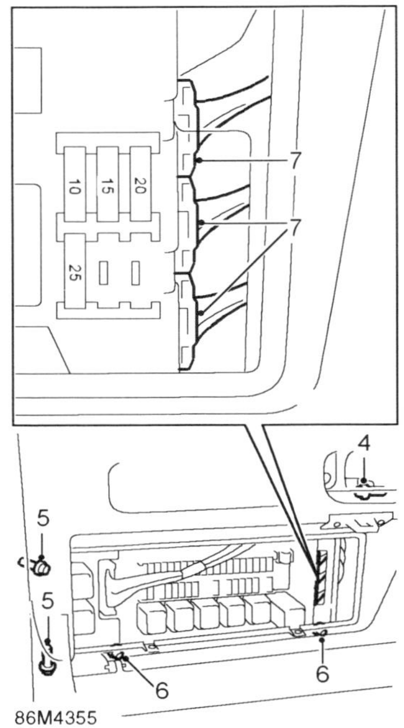

4. Remove bolt securing fuse box mounting plate to steering column bracket.
5. Remove 2 bolts securing mounting plate to body.
6. Remove 2 bolts securing fuse box to mounting plate.
7. Disconnect 3 multiplugs from CCU in rear fuse box.

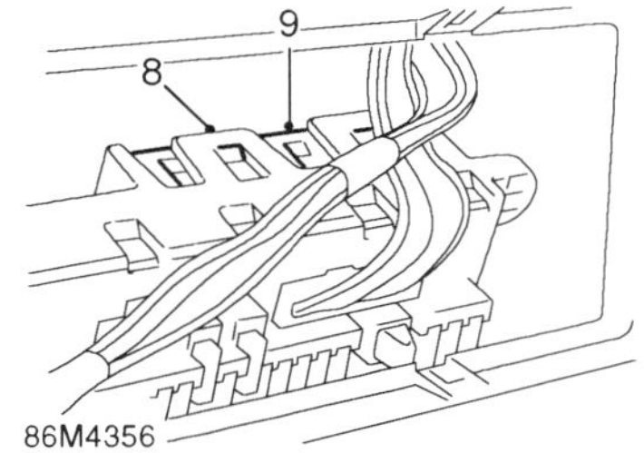

8. Manoeuvre fuse box to gain access to CCU and release retaining clips.
9. Remove CCU.

Refit

1. Position CCU and secure in clips.
2. Align fuse box into position with mounting plate.
3. Connect multiplugs to CCU.
4. Fit bolts securing fuse box to mounting bracket and tighten to 8 Nm.
5. Position mounting plate and tighten bolts to 8 Nm.
6. Fit fuse box cover.
7. Close glove box.
8. Connect battery earth lead.

STARTER MOTOR - 'K' SERIES

Service repair no - 86.60.01

Remove

1. Disconnect battery earth lead.
2. Remove air cleaner. ***See ENGINE MANAGEMENT SYSTEM - MEMS, Repairs.***

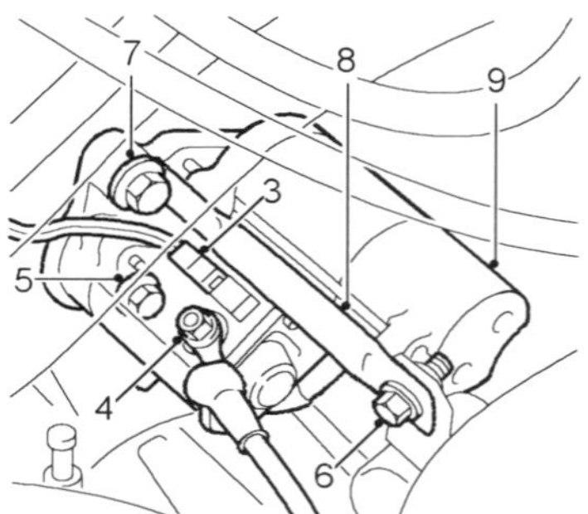

86M4350

3. Disconnect Lucar from starter solenoid.
4. Remove nut and disconnect battery lead from starter solenoid.
5. Remove lower bolt securing starter motor.
6. Remove bolt securing engine steady bar to gearbox mounting.
7. Remove upper bolt securing starter motor.
8. Remove engine steady bar.
9. Remove starter motor.

Refit

1. Clean mating faces of starter motor and gearbox.
2. Fit starter motor and fit lower bolt but do not tighten at this stage.
3. Fit engine steady bar and fit bolt to gearbox mounting.
4. Fit starter motor upper bolt.
5. Tighten both upper and lower starter motor bolts to 85 Nm.
6. Connect battery cable to starter solenoid, fit nut and tighten to 4 Nm.
7. Connect Lucar to solenoid.
8. Fit air cleaner. ***See ENGINE MANAGEMENT SYSTEM - MEMS, Repairs.***
9. Connect battery earth lead.

STARTER MOTOR - 'L' SERIES

Service repair no - 86.60.01

Remove

1. Disconnect battery earth lead.
2. Remove air cleaner. ***See ENGINE MANAGEMENT SYSTEM - EDC, Repairs.***

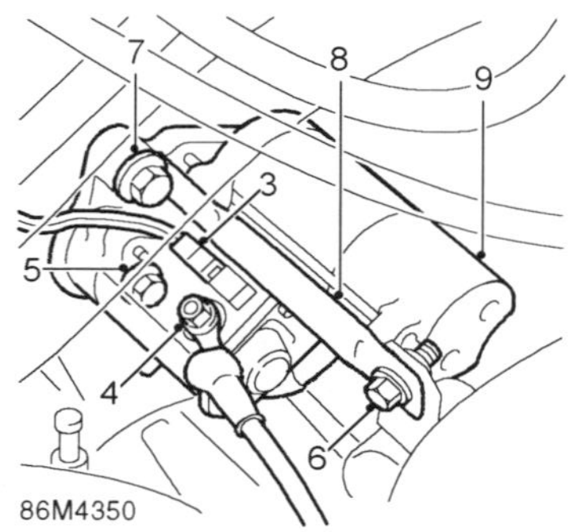

86M4350

3. Disconnect Lucar from starter solenoid.
4. Remove nut and disconnect battery lead from starter solenoid.
5. Remove lower bolt securing starter motor.
6. Remove bolt securing engine steady bar to gearbox mounting.
7. Remove upper bolt securing starter motor.
8. Remove engine steady bar.
9. Remove starter motor.

Refit

1. Clean mating faces of starter motor and gearbox.
2. Fit starter motor and fit lower bolt but do not tighten at this stage.
3. Fit engine steady bar and fit bolt to gearbox mounting.
4. Fit starter motor upper bolt.
5. Tighten both upper and lower starter motor bolts to 85 Nm.
6. Connect battery cable to starter solenoid, fit nut and tighten to 4 Nm.
7. Connect Lucar to solenoid.
8. Fit air cleaner. ***See ENGINE MANAGEMENT SYSTEM - EDC, Repairs.***
9. Connect battery earth lead.

RELAY - STARTER

Service repair no - 86.60.10

Remove

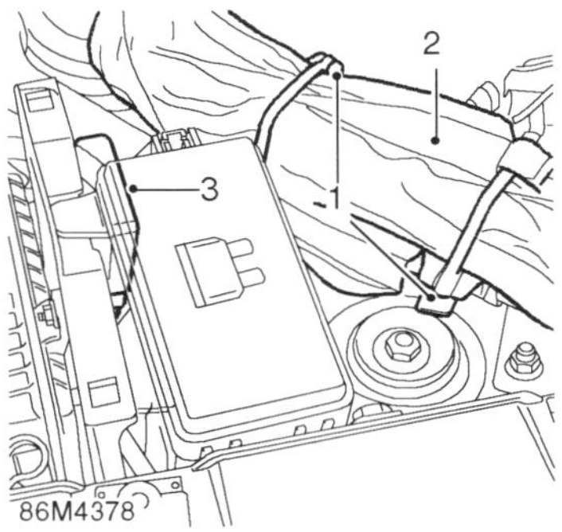

86M4378

1. Remove 2 straps securing vehicle jack.
2. Remove jack.
3. Remove relay from holder on battery tray.

Refit

1. Fit relay.
2. Position vehicle jack to its mounting.
3. Fit securing straps.

SWITCH - STARTER

Service repair no - 86.65.02

WARNING: *See GENERAL INFORMATION, SRS Precautions.*

Remove

1. Make the SRS system safe. ***See GENERAL INFORMATION, SRS Precautions.***
2. Remove steering column nacelle. ***See STEERING, Repairs.***

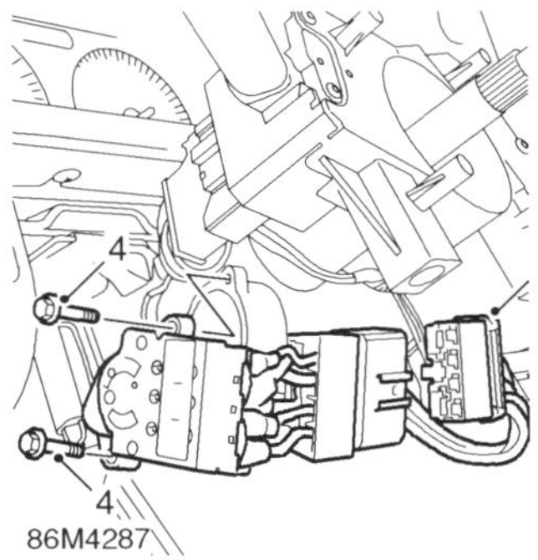

86M4287

3. Disconnect multiplug from starter switch.
4. Remove 2 screws securing starter switch to lock and remove switch.

Refit

1. Fit starter switch and tighten retaining screws.
2. Connect multiplug to starter switch.
3. Fit steering column nacelle. ***See STEERING, Repairs.***
4. Connect battery, earth lead last.

SWITCH - HEADLAMP LEVELLING

Service repair no - 86.65.16

Remove

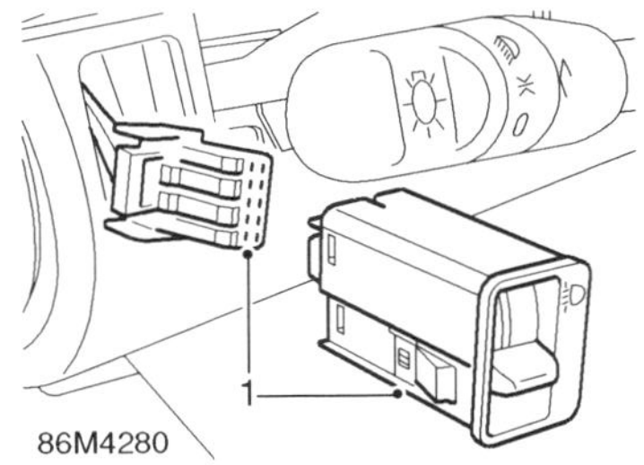

86M4280

1. Release headlamp levelling switch from fascia and disconnect multiplug.

Refit

1. Position switch, connect multiplug and secure switch to fascia.

SWITCH - GLOVE BOX LAMP

Service repair no - 86.65.24

Remove

1. Remove glove box. ***See BODY, Interior trim components.***

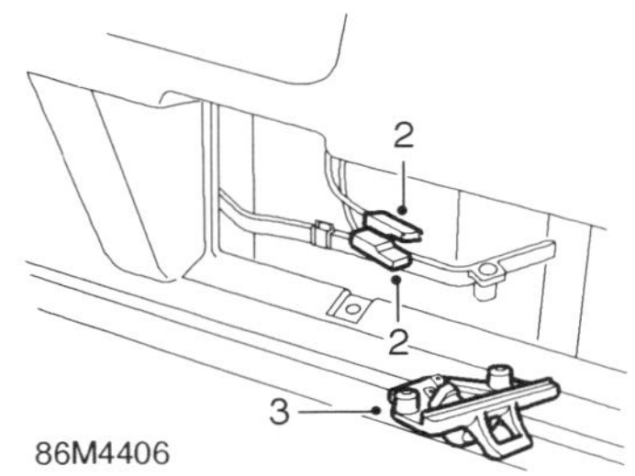

86M4406

2. Disconnect 2 Lucars from glove box lamp switch.
3. Remove switch from glove box latch.

Refit

1. Fit switch and connect Lucars.
2. Fit glove box. ***See BODY, Interior trim components.***

SWITCH - HEATED REAR SCREEN

Service repair no - 86.65.36

Remove

1. Remove radio. ***See this section.***

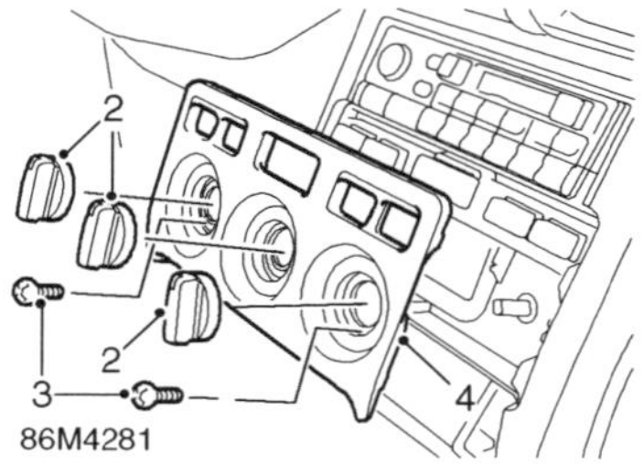

2. Remove heater control knobs.
3. Remove 2 screws from heater control face plate.
4. Remove heater control face plate.

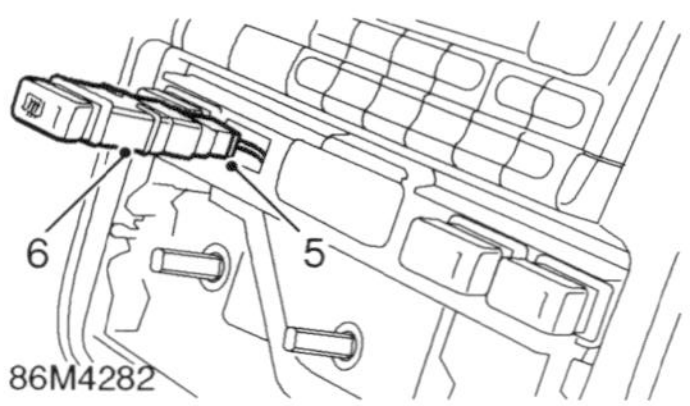

5. Disconnect multiplug from heated rear screen switch.
6. Remove switch.

Refit

1. Fit switch and connect multiplug.
2. Fit heater control, face plate and tighten screws.
3. Fit heater control knobs.
4. Fit radio. ***See this section.***

SWITCH - HANDBRAKE WARNING

Service repair no - 86.65.45

Remove

1. Remove rear console. ***See BODY, Interior trim components.***

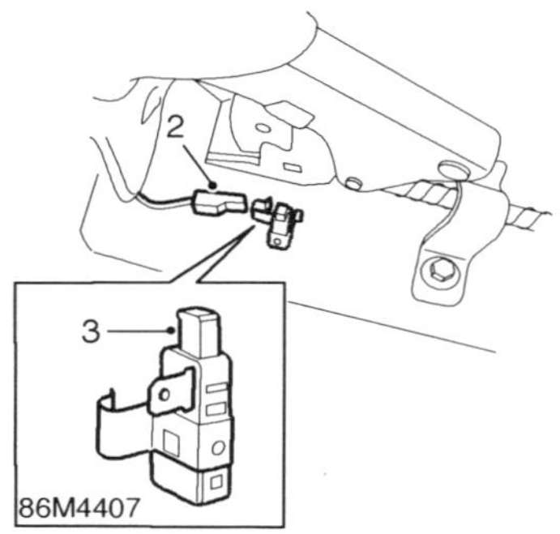

2. Disconnect Lucar from handbrake warning switch.
3. Release switch from handbrake.

Refit

1. Fit switch to handbrake and connect Lucar.
2. Fit rear console. ***See BODY, Interior trim components.***

SWITCH - HAZARD WARNING LIGHTS

Service repair no - 86.65.50

Remove

1. Remove radio. ***See this section.***

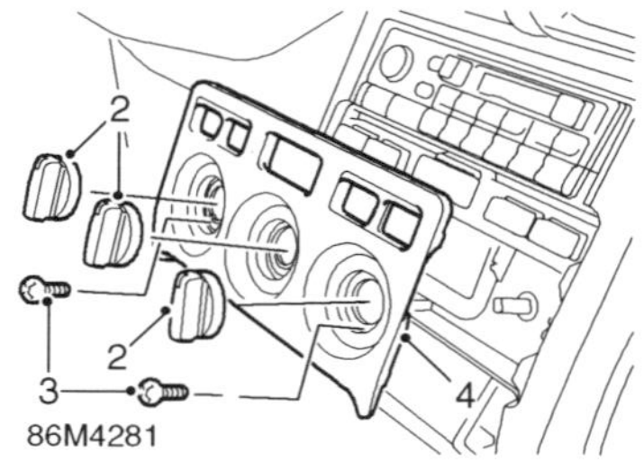

2. Remove heater control knobs.
3. Remove 2 screws from heater control face plate.
4. Remove face plate.

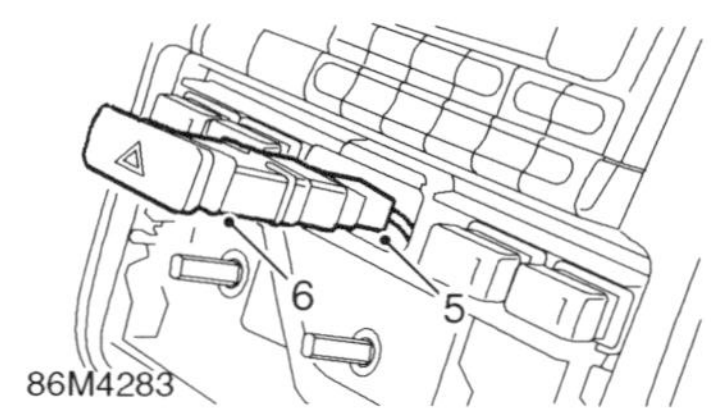

5. Disconnect multiplug from hazard warning light, switch.
6. Remove switch.

Refit

1. Fit switch and connect multiplug.
2. Fit heater control, face plate and tighten screws.
3. Fit heater control knobs.
4. Fit radio. ***See this section.***

SWITCH - INDICATOR AND LIGHTS

Service repair no - 86.65.55

Remove

1. Remove steering column nacelle. ***See STEERING, Repairs.***

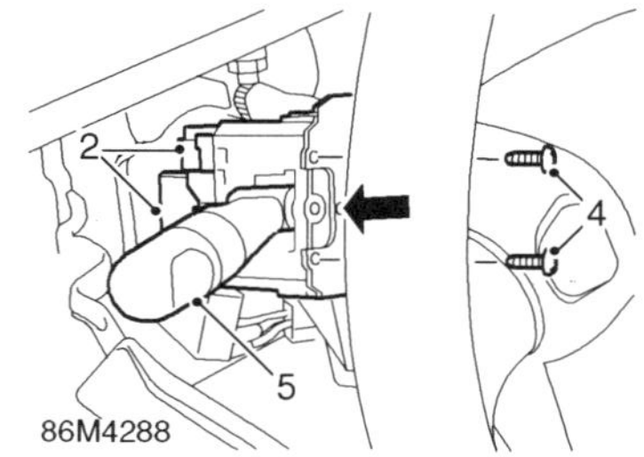

2. Disconnect 2 multiplugs from indicator and light switch.
3. Rotate steering wheel to access switch securing screws.
4. Remove 2 screws securing switch.
5. Depress retaining tag and remove switch

Refit

1. Fit switch and secure with screws.
2. Connect multiplugs to switch.
3. Fit steering column nacelle. ***See STEERING, Repairs.***

CIGAR LIGHTER - FRONT

Service repair no - 86.65.60

Remove

1. Remove front console. ***See BODY, Interior trim components.***

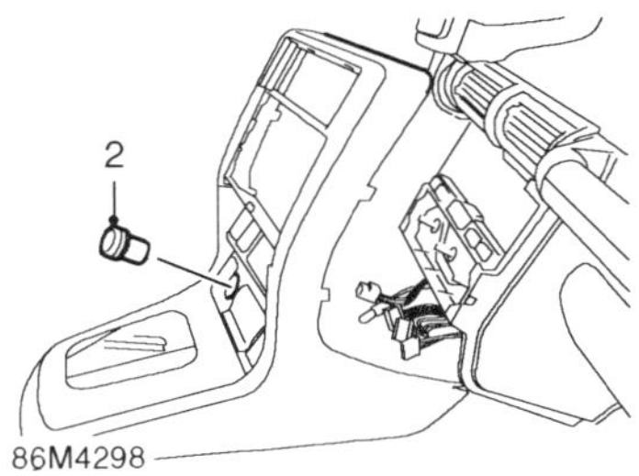

2. Remove cigar lighter element.

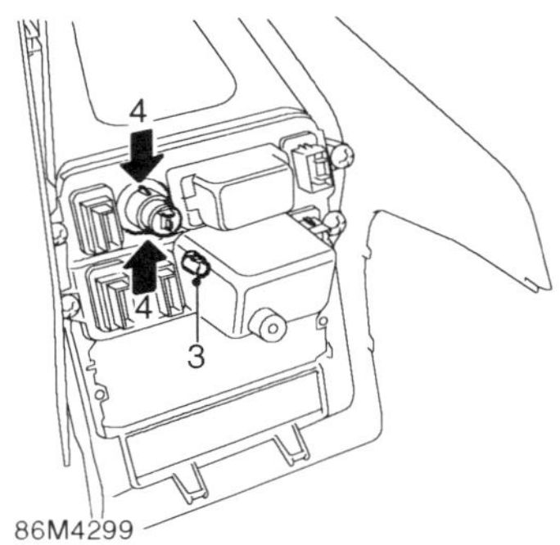

3. Remove bulb holder from lighter.
4. Release clips and remove lighter from console.

Refit

1. Fit lighter to console.
2. Fit bulb holder to lighter.
3. Fit lighter element.
4. Fit front console. ***See BODY, Interior trim components.***

SWITCH - REAR FOG LAMP

Service repair no - 86.65.65

Remove

1. Remove instrument panel cowl. ***See INSTRUMENTS, Repairs.***

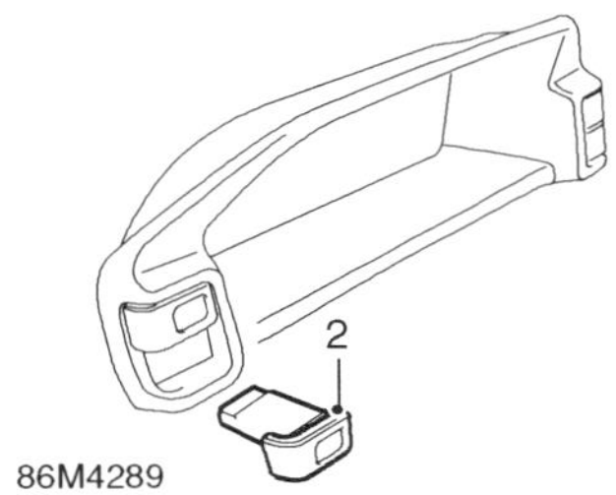

2. Remove rear fog lamp switch from instrument panel cowl.

Refit

1. Fit switch to instrument panel cowl.
2. Fit instrument panel cowl. ***See INSTRUMENTS, Repairs.***

SWITCH - EXTERIOR MIRROR

Service repair no - 86.65.75

Remove

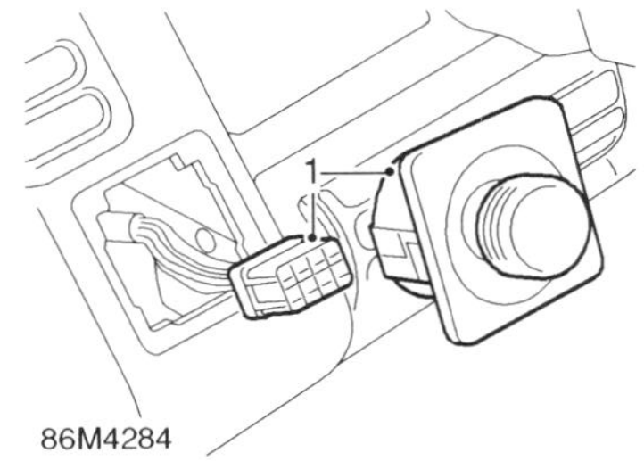

1. Release mirror switch from fascia and disconnect multiplug.

Refit

1. Position switch, connect multiplug and secure switch to fascia.

HARNESS - MAIN - 5 DOOR

Service repair no - 86.70.07

WARNING: *See GENERAL INFORMATION, SRS Precautions.*

Remove

1. Make the SRS system safe. ***See GENERAL INFORMATION, SRS Precautions.***
2. Remove complete carpet. ***See BODY, Interior trim components.***
3. Remove windscreen washer reservoir. ***See WIPERS & WASHERS, Repairs.***
4. Pull reservoir harness and washer tubes into engine bay.

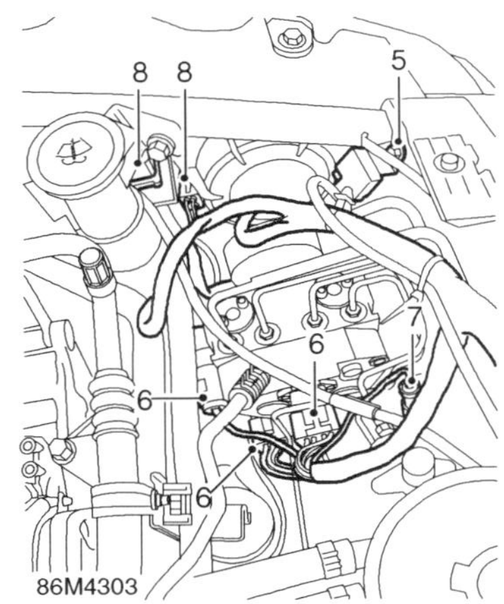

5. Remove nut and release earth header from RH inner wing.

Models with ABS:

6. Disconnect 3 multiplugs from ABS modulator.
7. Disconnect multiplug from front RH ABS speed sensor and release harness from clips.

All models:

8. Disconnect 2 multiplugs from RH headlamp and headlamp levelling motor.

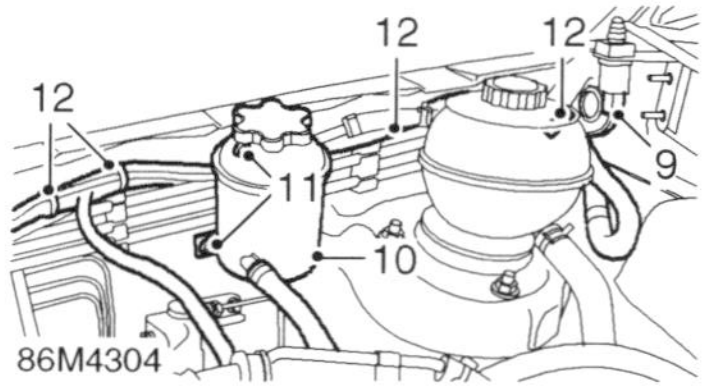

9. Disconnect multiplug from bonnet switch.
10. Release PAS reservoir and position aside.
11. Remove 2 bolts from reservoir support bracket and remove bracket.
12. Release 4 harness retaining clips.
13. Release front screen washer tube from harness and position aside.
14. With assistance feed harness through bulkhead into vehicle interior.
15. Remove battery carrier. ***See this section.***

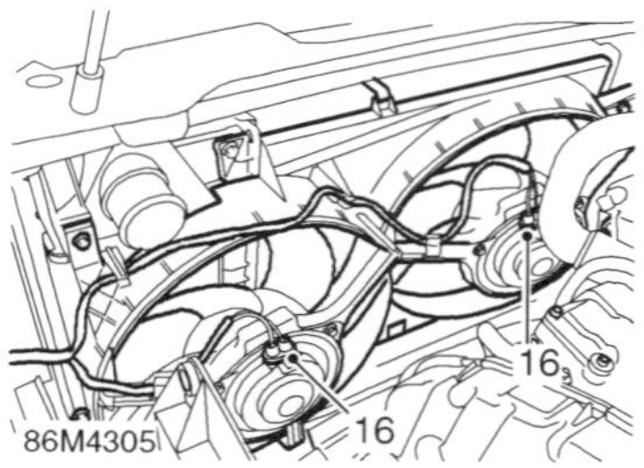

16. Disconnect 2 multiplugs from cooling fans and release harness from clips.

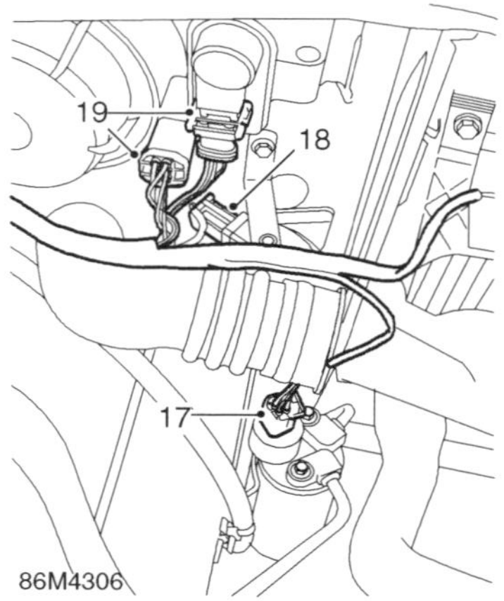

17. Disconnect multiplug from receiver/ drier.
18. Disconnect multiplug from horn.
19. Disconnect 2 multiplugs from LH headlamp and headlamp levelling motor.

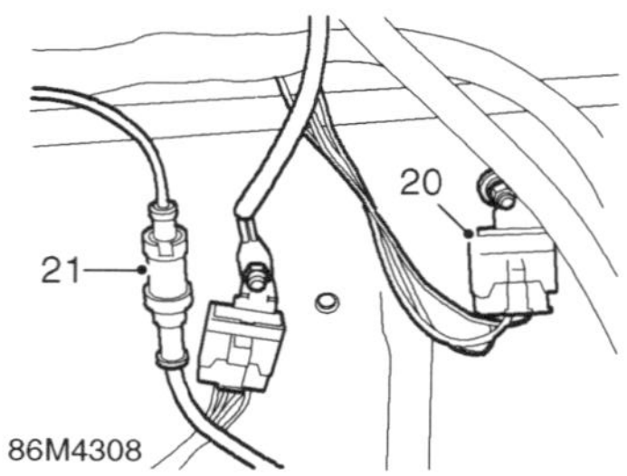

20. Remove nut securing LH earth header and release header.

Models with ABS:

21. Disconnect multiplug from front LH ABS speed sensor and release harness from clips.

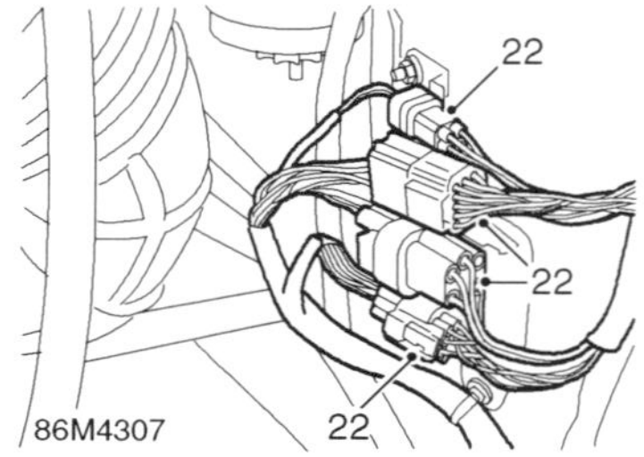

All models:

22. Disconnect 4 multiplugs from engine harness.

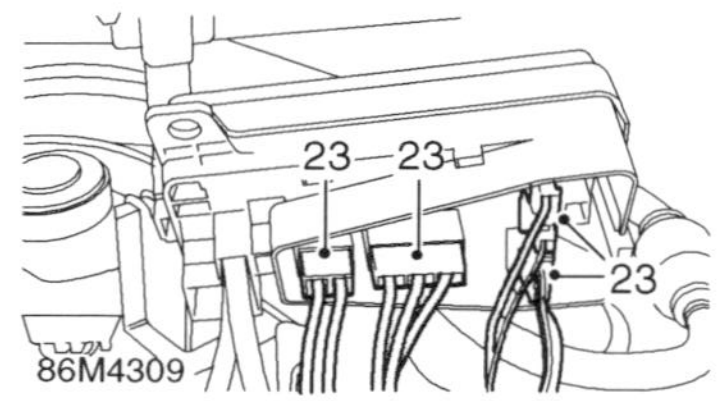

23. Disconnect 4 multiplugs from fuse box.

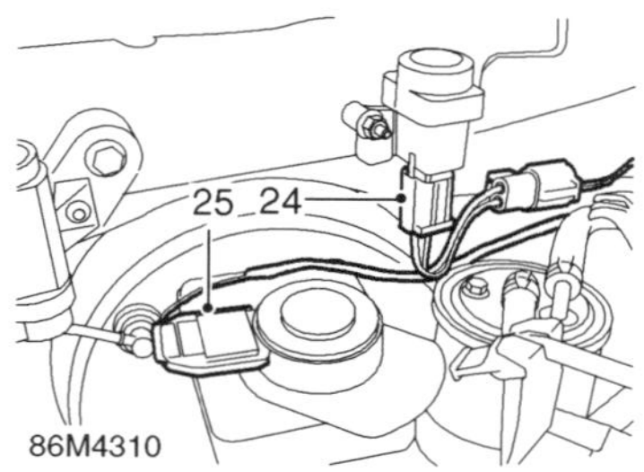

24. Disconnect multiplug from inertia fuel shut-off switch.
25. Disconnect multiplug from brake fluid level switch.

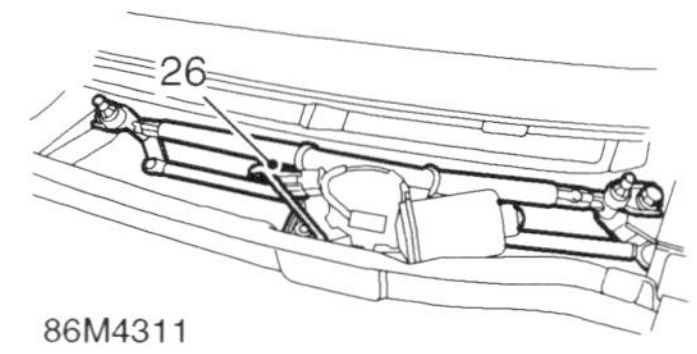

26. Disconnect multiplug from wiper motor and pull into engine bay.

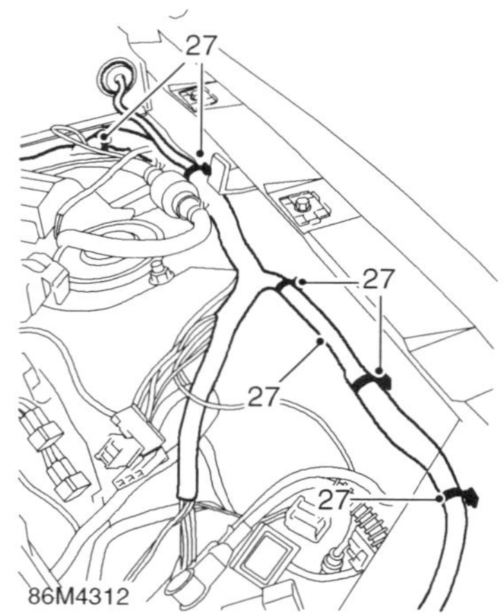

27. Release 5 harness clips from LH inner wing.
28. With assistance pull main harness into vehicle interior.
29. Remove 6 screws from front mudflaps and remove mudflaps.
30. Release rear edge of front wing liner.
31. Release side repeater lamps, disconnect multiplugs and remove lamps.

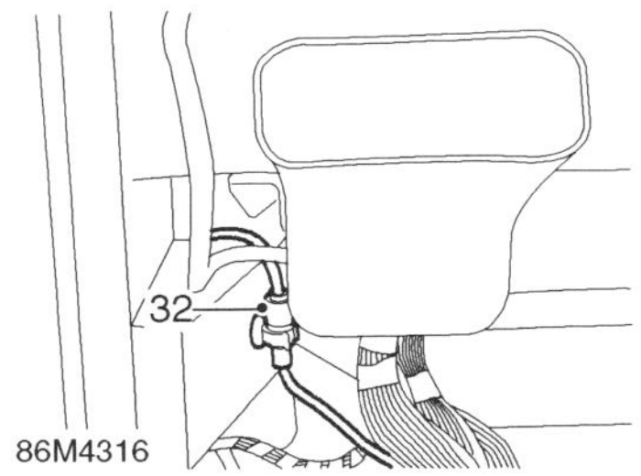

32. Release and disconnect multiplugs from 'A' post.

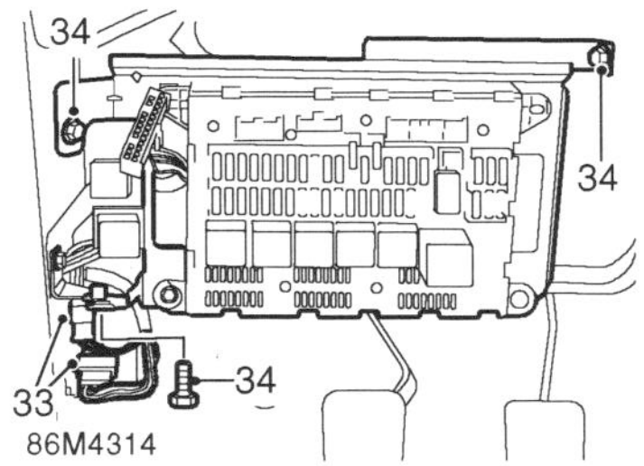

33. Release and disconnect multiplugs from brake light and ABS modulator relays.
34. Remove 3 bolts from passenger compartment fuse box.

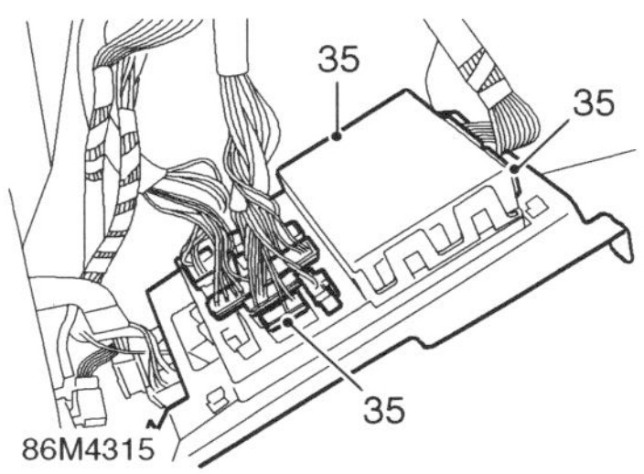

35. Release fuse box and disconnect 11 multiplugs, remove fuse box.

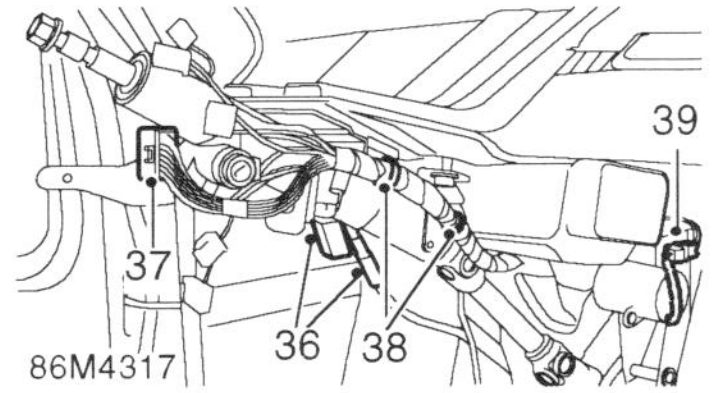

36. Release and disconnect roof harness multiplug and aerial socket.
37. Disconnect multiplug from steering column switch.
38. Release 2 harness clips from steering column.
39. Disconnect multiplug from throttle position sensor.

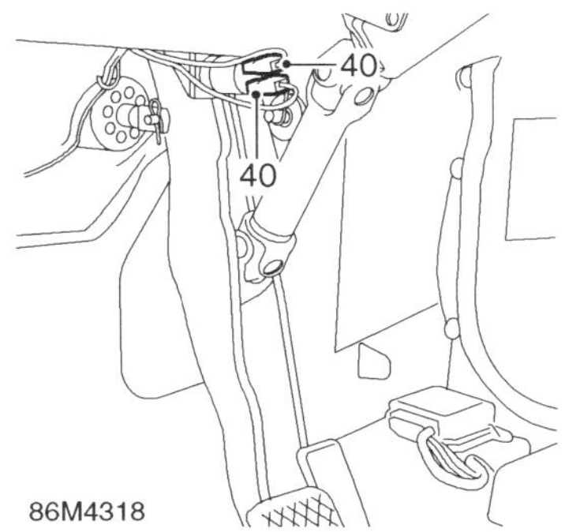

40. Disconnect 2 Lucars from brake light switch.

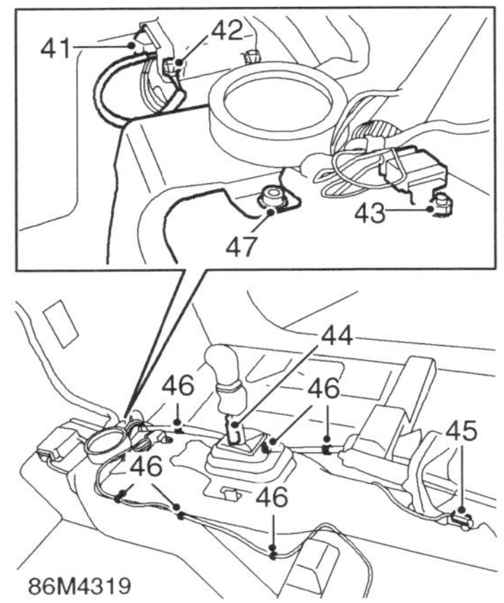

41. Release and disconnect multiplug from airbag ECU.
42. Remove airbag ECU securing bolt and release earth lead.
43. Remove nut from earth header and release header from floor tunnel.

Models with ABS:

44. Disconnect multiplug from gear lever hill descent switch.

All models:

45. Disconnect Lucar from handbrake switch.
46. Release 6 clips from SRS harness.
47. Remove nut from rear heater ducting and remove ducting.

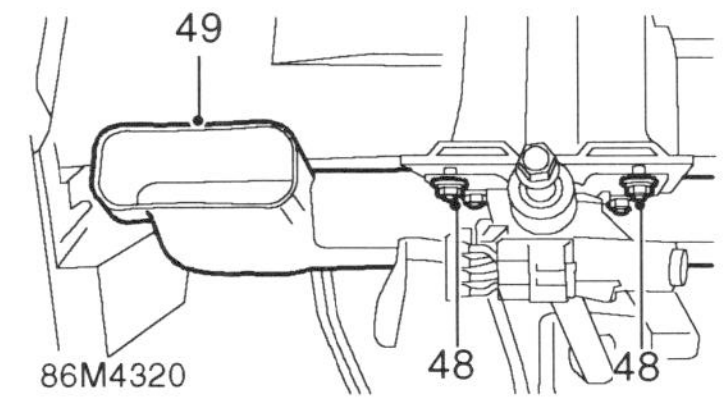

48. Remove 4 nuts from steering column and lower column.
49. Remove face level vent ducting to access main harness clips.
50. Release all harness clips from fascia and sills.

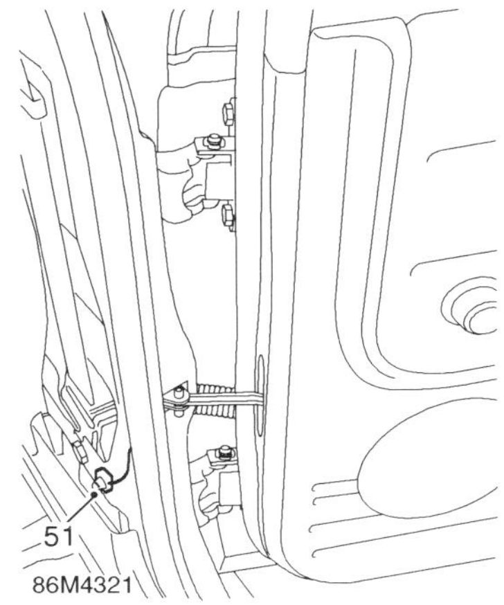

51. Release and disconnect multiplugs from base of 'B/C' posts.
52. Remove luggage compartment carpet. ***See BODY, Interior trim components.***

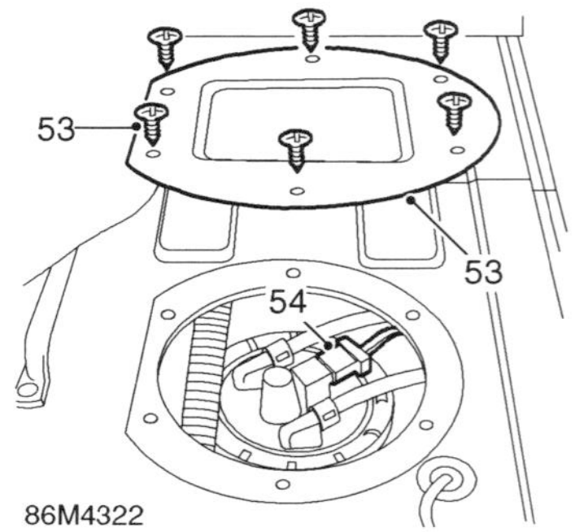

86M4322

53. Remove 6 screws from access cover and remove cover.
54. Disconnect multiplug from tank unit.

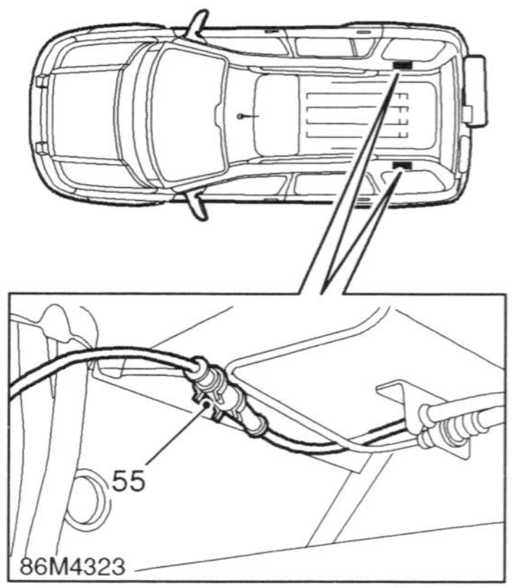

86M4323

Models with ABS:

55. Release both rear ABS speed sensor harnesses and disconnect multiplugs.
56. Pull harness into vehicle interior.

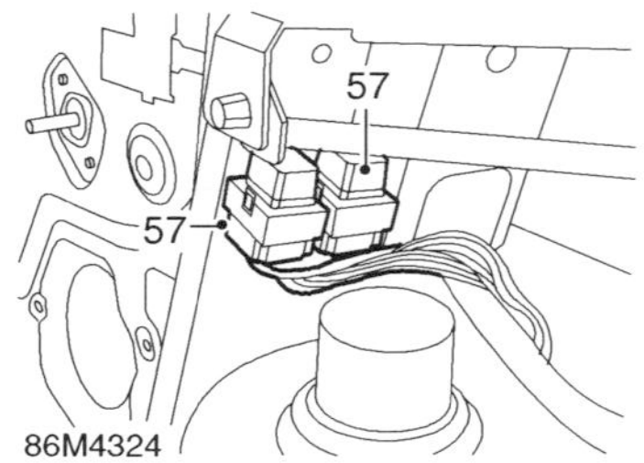

86M4324

All models:

57. Release and disconnect rear window lift and wash/wipe relays.

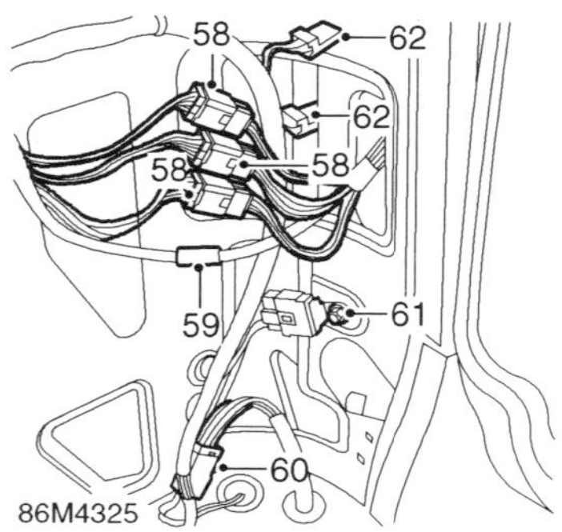

86M4325

58. Disconnect 3 multiplugs from tail door harness.
59. Disconnect rear screen washer tube.
60. Disconnect multiplug from towing electrics.
61. Remove nut from RH rear earth header and release header.
62. Disconnect multiplugs from reverse and hazard lamps.
63. Remove nut from LH rear earth header and release header.

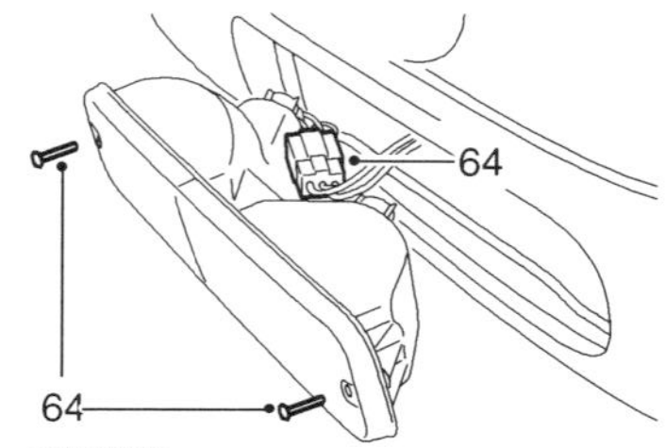

86M4326

64. Remove 4 screws from rear lamps, release lamps and disconnect multiplugs.
65. Release harness clips and pull harness into luggage compartment.
66. Release main harness retaining clips and pull harness into vehicle interior.
67. Remove main harness from vehicle.

Refit

1. Lay main harness in vehicle.
2. Locate rear section and secure in retaining clips.
3. Feed harness to rear lamps, secure in clips and grommets.
4. Connect multiplugs to rear lamps, fit rear lamps and secure with screws.
5. Fit LH rear earth header and secure nut.
6. Connect multiplugs to reverse and hazard lamps.
7. Fit RH rear earth header and secure nut.
8. Connect multiplug to towing electrics.
9. Connect rear screen washer tube.
10. Connect tail door multiplugs.
11. Connect and secure rear window lift and wash/wipe relays.

Models with ABS:

12. Connect both rear ABS speed sensor multiplugs and secure harness in grommets and clips.

All models:

13. Connect multiplug to tank unit and secure grommet.
14. Fit tank access cover and tighten screws.
15. Fit luggage compartment carpet. ***See BODY, Interior trim components.***
16. Connect and secure multiplugs at base of 'B/C' post.
17. Position harness to sills and fascia and secure harness clips.
18. Fit face level vent ducting.
19. Raise steering column, fit and tighten nuts to 14 Nm.
20. Fit rear heater ducting and tighten nut.
21. Secure SRS section of harness in clips.
22. Connect Lucar to handbrake switch.

Models with ABS:

23. Connect multiplug to gear lever hill descent switch.

All models:

24. Connect floor tunnel earth header and tighten nut.
25. Connect earth lead to airbag ECU securing bolt. Fit bolt and tighten to 9 Nm.
26. Connect and secure multiplug to airbag ECU.
27. Connect multiplug to throttle position sensor.
28. Connect Lucars to brake lamp switch.
29. Secure harness clips to steering column.
30. Connect multiplug to steering column switch.
31. Connect roof harness multiplug and aerial socket and secure in position.
32. Connect and secure multiplugs to brake light and ABS modulator relays.
33. Connect fuse box multiplugs, position fuse box fit and tighten screws.
34. Connect and secure multiplugs at both 'A' posts.
35. Connect multiplugs to side repeater lamps, locate and secure lamps.

36. Secure harness grommets.
37. Locate rear of wing liners.
38. Position mudflaps and tighten screws.
39. With assistance pull harness into LH inner wing and secure in clips.
40. Secure bulkhead grommets.
41. Connect wiper motor multiplug and secure harness.
42. Connect multiplug to brake fluid level switch.
43. Connect multiplug to inertia fuel shut-off switch.
44. Connect multiplugs to fuse box.

Models with ABS:

45. Connect front LH ABS speed sensor multiplug and secure harness.

All models:

46. Connect multiplugs to engine harness.
47. Locate LH earth header and tighten nut.
48. Connect multiplugs to LH headlamp and headlamp levelling motor.
49. Connect multiplug to horn.
50. Connect multiplug to receiver/drier.
51. Connect multiplugs to cooling fans and secure harness.
52. Fit battery carrier. ***See this section.***
53. With assistance pull harness into RH inner wing.
54. Secure front screen washer tube to harness.
55. Secure harness in retaining clips.
56. Fit PAS reservoir support bracket and tighten bolts.
57. Fit PAS reservoir.
58. Connect multiplug to bonnet switch.
59. Connect multiplugs to RH headlamp and headlamp levelling motor.

Models with ABS:

60. Connect multiplug to front RH ABS speed sensor and secure harness.
61. Connect multiplugs to ABS modulator.

All models:

62. Fit RH earth header and tighten nut.
63. Feed harness and washer tube to washer reservoir.
64. Fit washer reservoir. ***See WIPERS & WASHERS, Repairs.***
65. Fit complete carpet. ***See BODY, Repairs.***

HARNESS - FASCIA

Service repair no - 86.70.10

Remove

1. Remove fascia. ***See BODY, Interior trim components.***

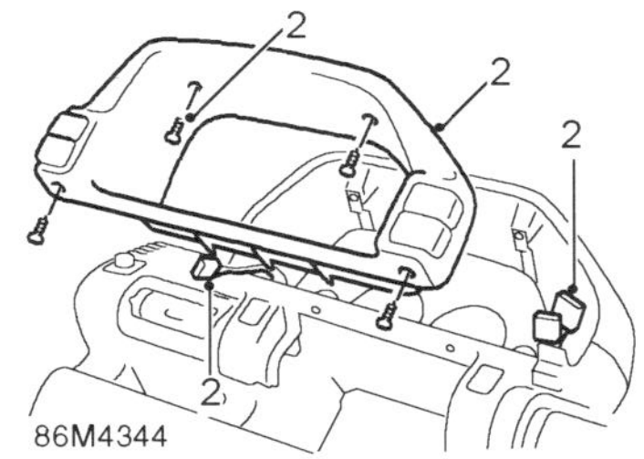

86M4344

2. Remove 4 screws, disconnect 3 multiplugs from switches, and remove instrument bezel finisher.

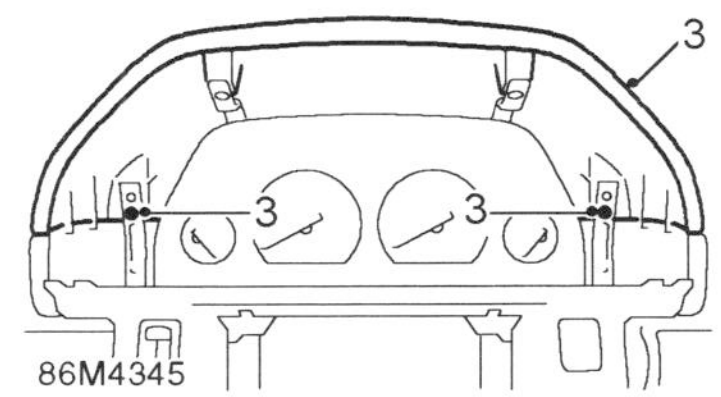

86M4345

3. Remove 2 screws from instrument upper cover and remove cover.

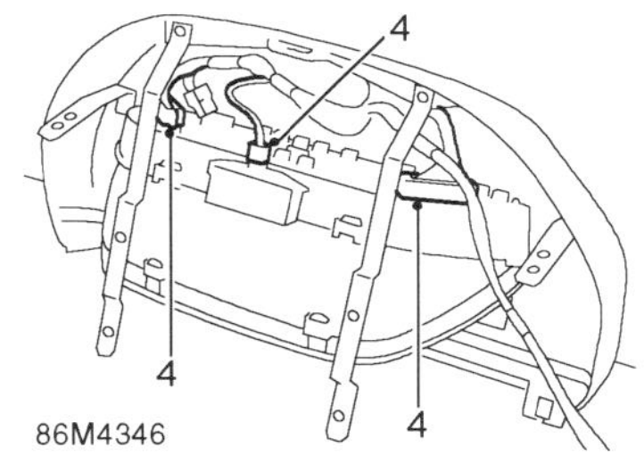

86M4346

4. Disconnect 3 multiplugs from instrument pack.

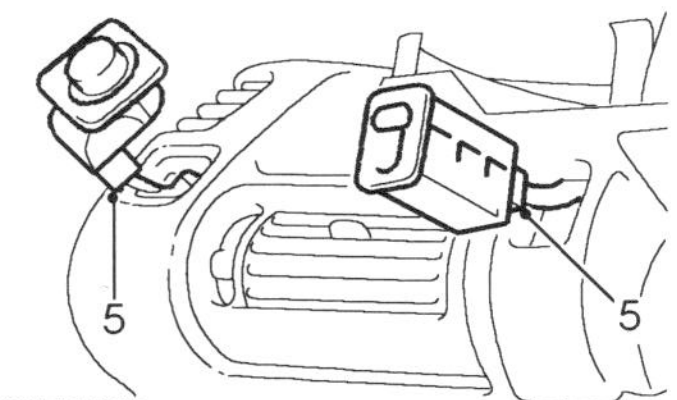

86M4347

5. Disconnect multiplugs from mirror switch and headlamp leveling switch.

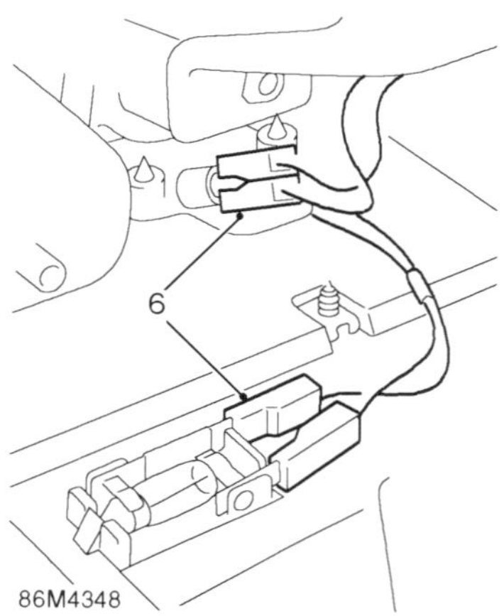

6. Disconnect 4 Lucars from glove box light and switch.

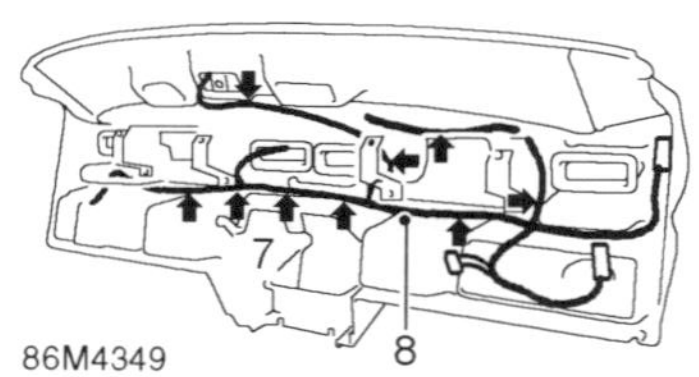

7. Release harness from 9 clips.
8. Feed harness through fascia and remove harness.

Refit

1. Position harness and secure harness in clips.
2. Feed harness through fascia and connect multiplugs to instrument pack, mirror switch and headlamp levelling switch.
3. Position upper cover and tighten screws.
4. Connect Lucars to glove box light and switch.
5. Position instrument bezel finisher, connect multiplugs and secure retaining screws.
6. Fit fascia. ***See BODY, Interior trim components.***

HARNESS - ENGINE - 'K' SERIES

Service repair no - 86.70.17

Remove

1. Remove air cleaner. ***See ENGINE MANAGEMENT SYSTEM - MEMS, Repairs.***
2. Remove battery carrier. ***See this section.***
3. Remove underbelly panel. ***See BODY, Exterior fittings.***

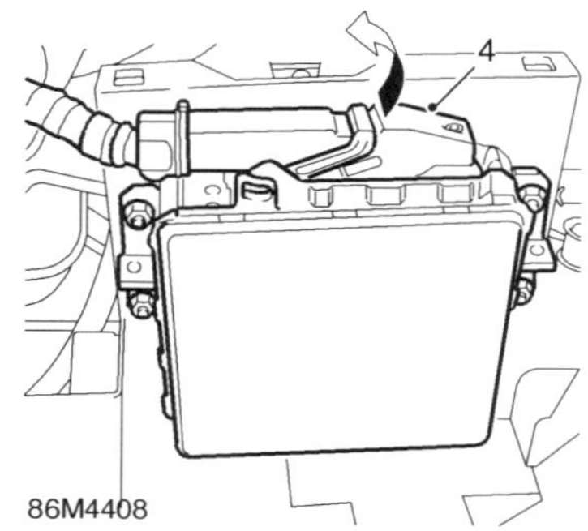

4. Disconnect multiplug from ECM.

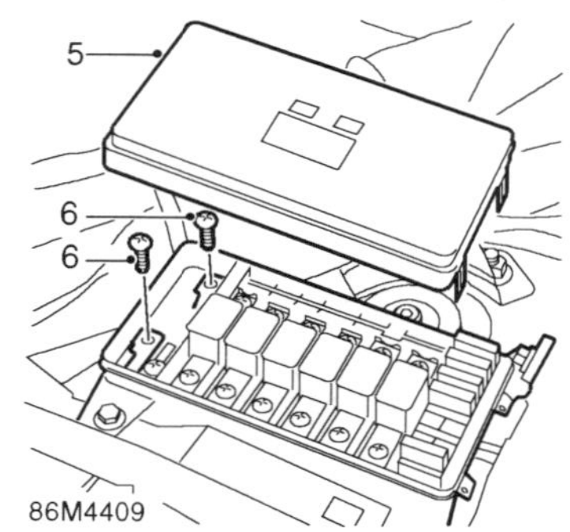

5. Remove engine fuse box cover.
6. Remove 2 screws and release harness leads from fuse box.

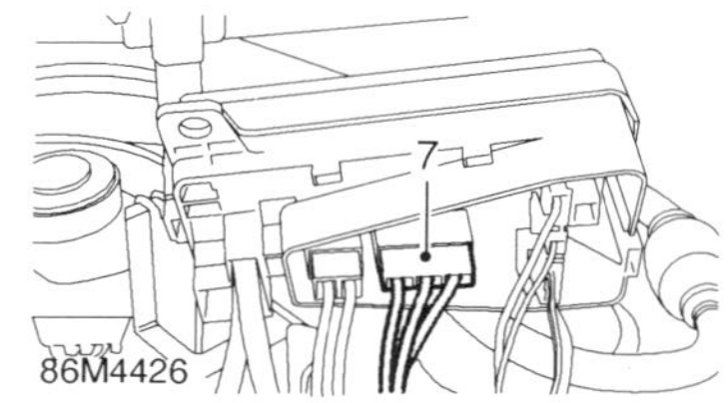

7. Disconnect harness multiplug from fuse box.

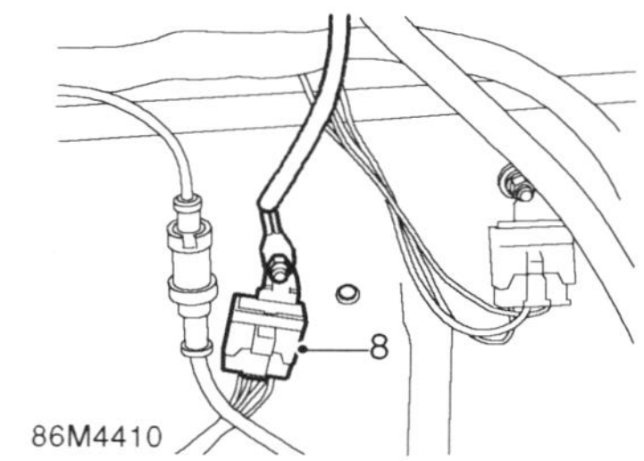

8. Disconnect earth lead multiplug.

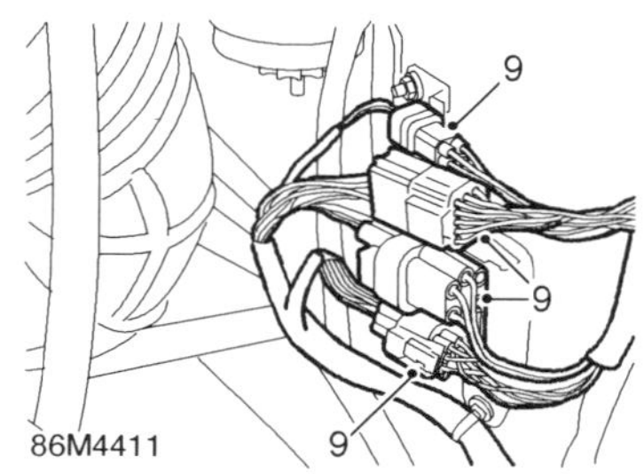

9. Disconnect 3 engine harness multiplugs from main harness.

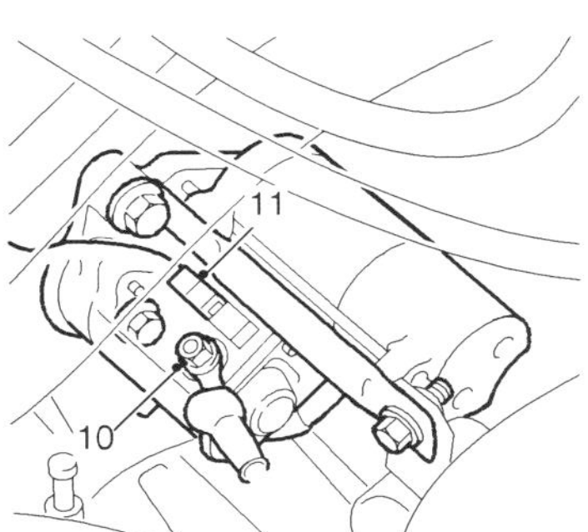

86M4412

10. Loosen nut and disconnect lead from starter solenoid.
11. Release Lucar from starter solenoid.

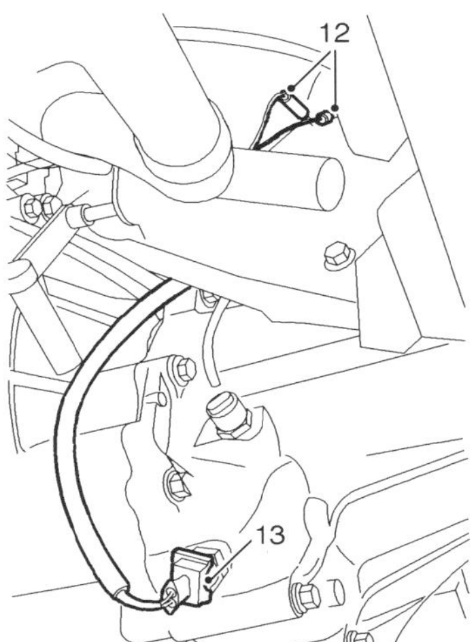

86M4413

12. Disconnect reverse lamp switch leads.
13. Disconnect multiplug from 1st gear switch on gearbox.

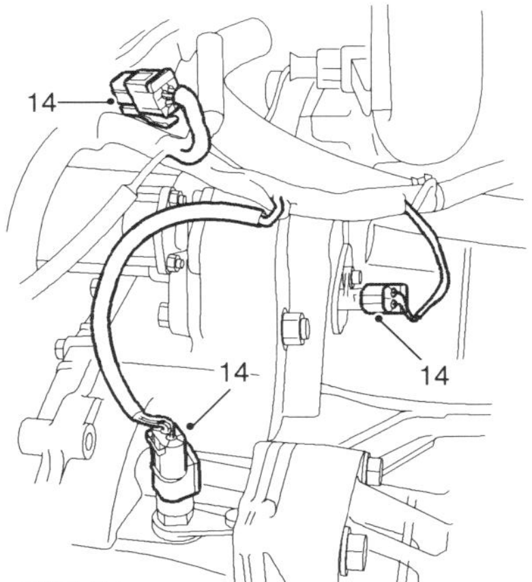

86M4414

14. Disconnect multiplugs from gearbox speed sensor, crankshaft sensor and oxygen sensor.

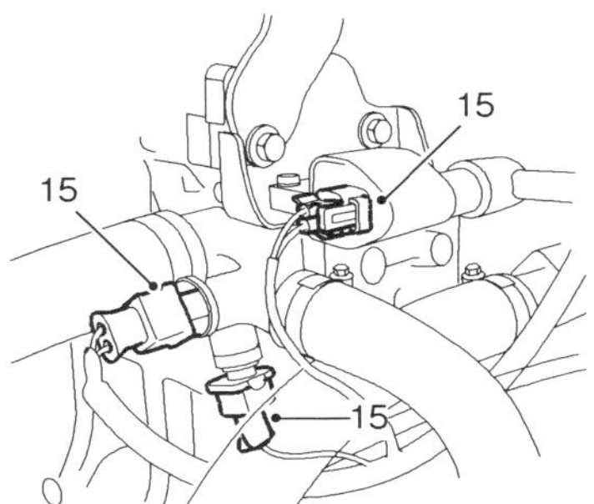

86M4415

15. Disconnect multiplugs from coolant sensors and ignition coil.

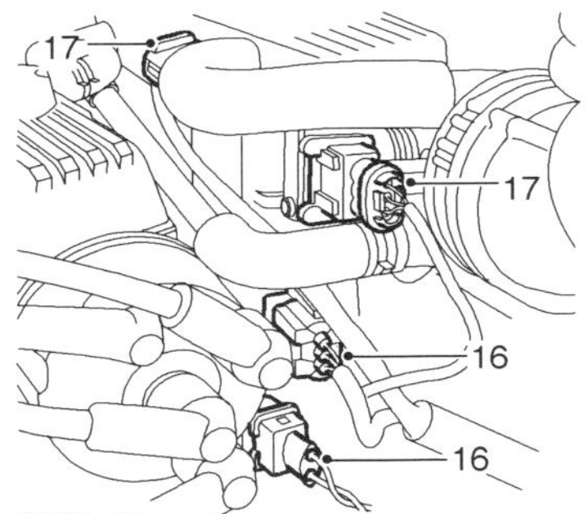

86M4416

16. Disconnect multiplugs from IAT sensor and injector harness.
17. Disconnect multiplugs from IAC and TP sensors.

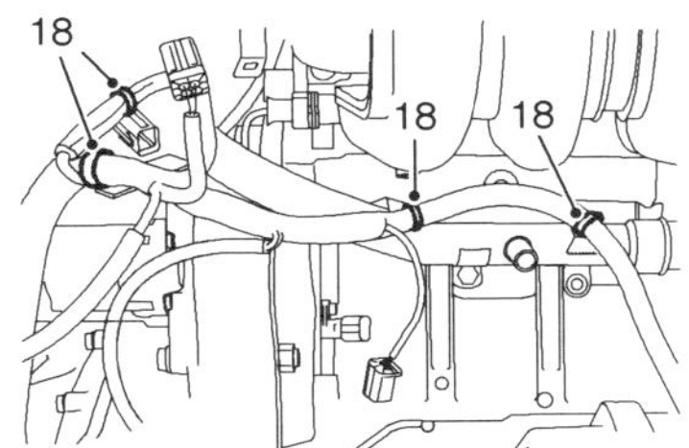

86M4417

18. Release 4 harness clips from engine coolant rail.

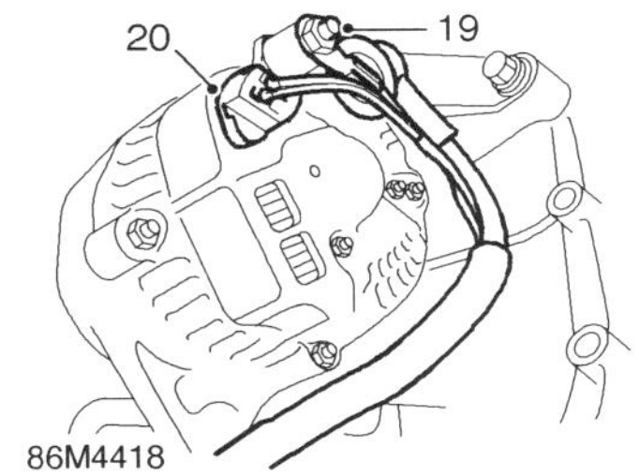

86M4418

19. Remove nut and release lead from alternator.
20. Disconnect multiplug from alternator.

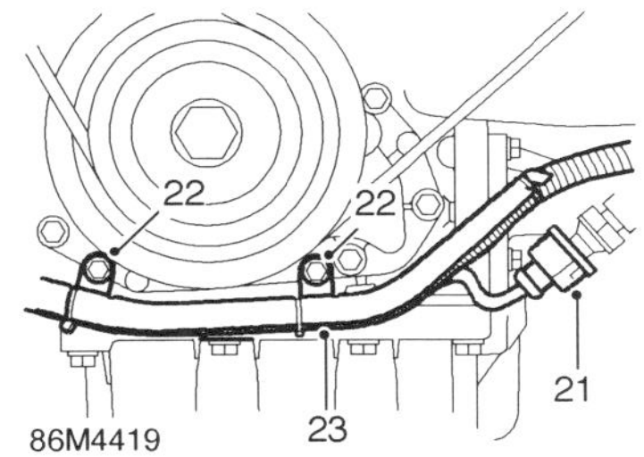

86M4419

21. Disconnect multiplug from oil pressure sensor.
22. Remove 2 bolts securing engine harness shield to oil pump.
23. Remove engine harness.

Refit

1. Position harness to engine.
2. Tighten bolts securing harness shield to oil pump.
3. Connect multiplug to oil pressure sensor.
4. Connect multiplug to alternator.
5. Connect lead to alternator and tighten nut.
6. Connect harness clips to engine coolant rail.
7. Connect multiplugs to TP and IAC sensors.
8. Connect multiplugs to IAT sensor and injector harness.
9. Connect multiplugs to coolant sensors and ignition coil.
10. Connect multiplugs to gearbox speed sensor, crankshaft sensor and oxygen sensor.
11. Connect multiplug to 1st gear switch.
12. Connect reverse lamp leads.
13. Connect Lucar to starter solenoid.
14. Connect lead to starter solenoid and tighten nut.
15. Connect multiplugs to main harness.
16. Connect earth lead multiplug.
17. Connect harness multiplug to fuse box.
18. Position harness leads to fuse box and tighten screws.
19. Fit fuse box cover.
20. Connect multiplug to ECM.
21. Fit battery carrier. ***See this section.***
22. Fit air cleaner. ***See ENGINE MANAGEMENT SYSTEM - EDC, Repairs.***
23. Fit underbelly panel. ***See BODY, Exterior fittings.***

HARNESS - ENGINE - L SERIES

Service repair no - 86.70.17

Remove

1. Remove alternator. ***See this section.***
2. Remove air cleaner. ***See ENGINE MANAGEMENT SYSTEM - EDC, Repairs.***
3. Remove battery carrier. ***See this section.***

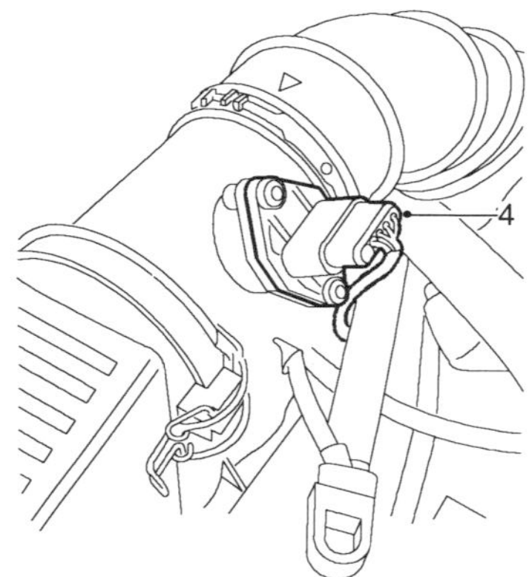

86M4363

4. Disconnect multiplug from MAF sensor.

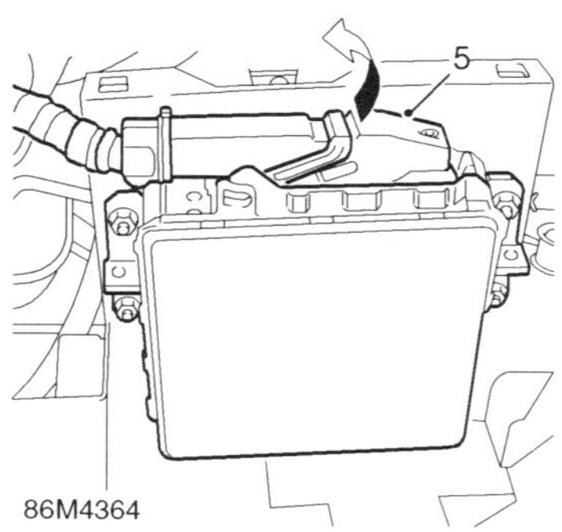

86M4364

5. Disconnect multiplug from ECM.

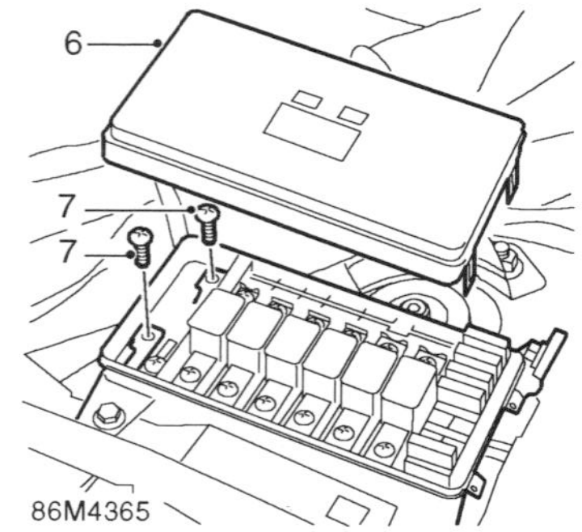

86M4365

6. Remove engine fuse box cover.
7. Remove 2 screws and release harness leads from fuse box.

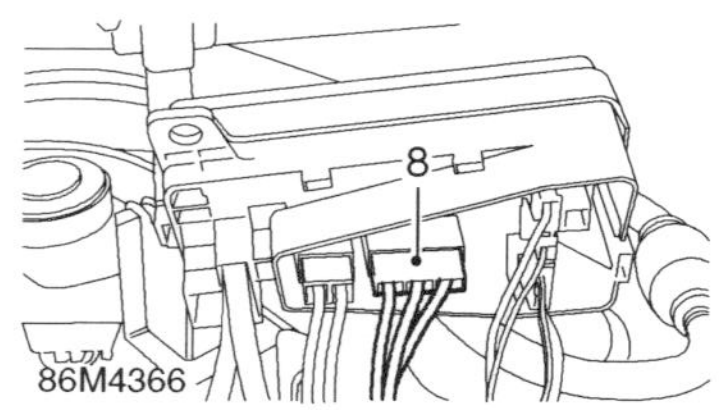

86M4366

8. Disconnect harness multiplug from fuse box.

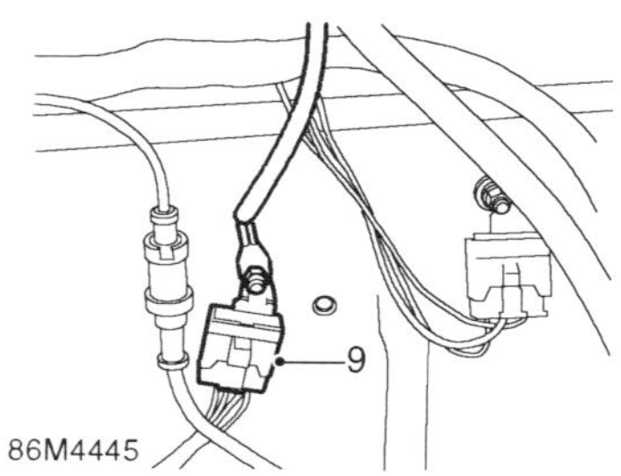

86M4445

9. Disconnect earth lead multiplug.

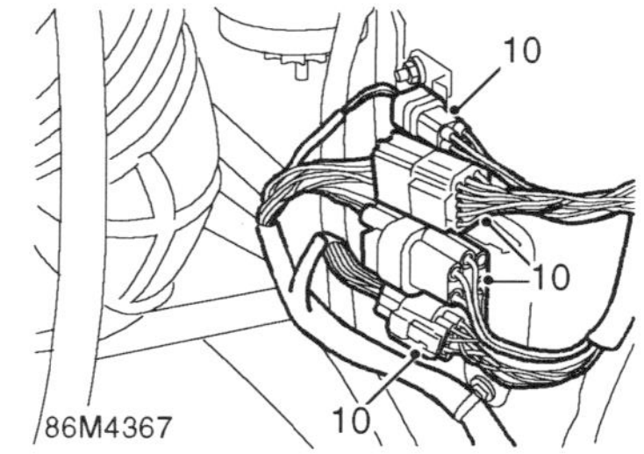

86M4367

10. Disconnect 4 engine harness multiplugs from main harness.

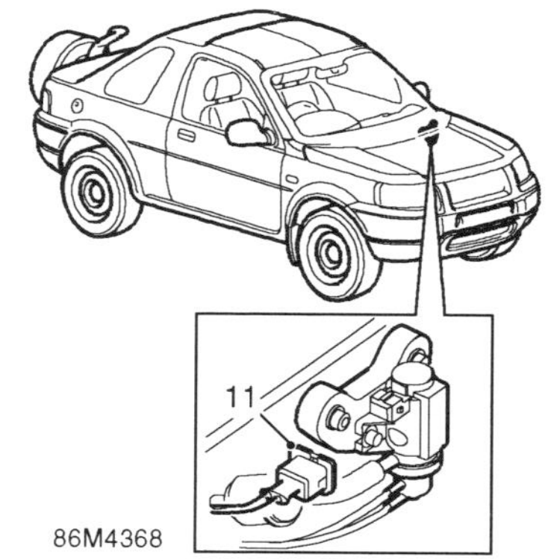

86M4368

11. Disconnect multiplug from EGR solenoid valve.

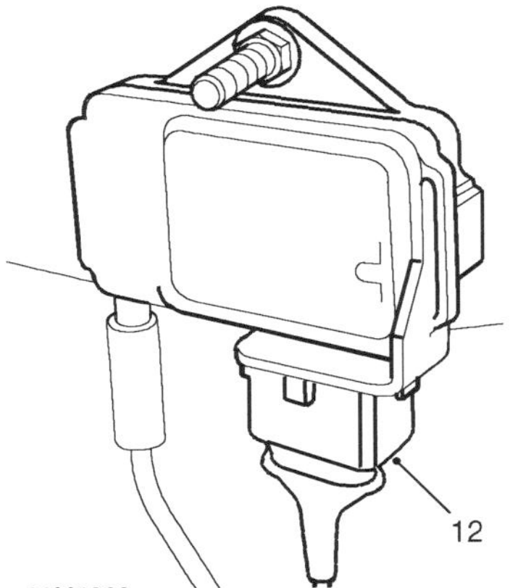

86M4369

12. Disconnect multiplug from MAP sensor.

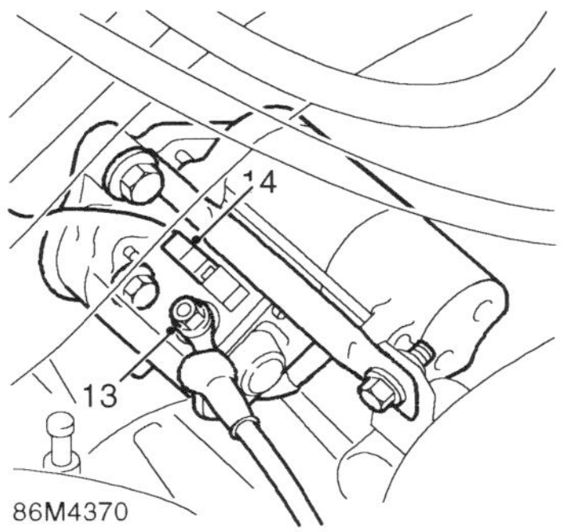

86M4370

13. Loosen nut and disconnect lead from starter solenoid.
14. Release Lucar from starter solenoid.

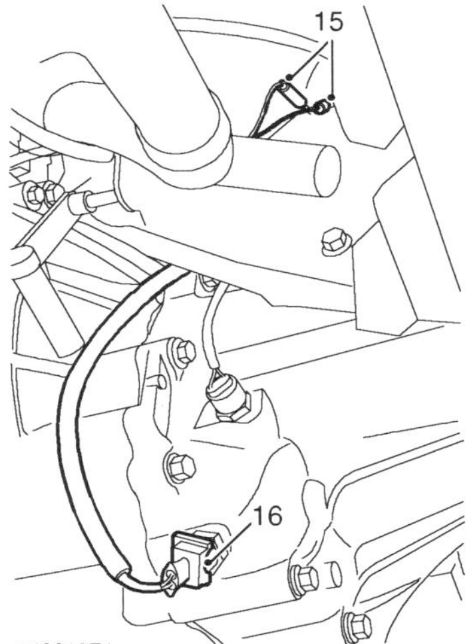

86M4371

15. Disconnect reverse lamp switch leads.
16. Disconnect multiplug from 1st gear switch on gearbox.

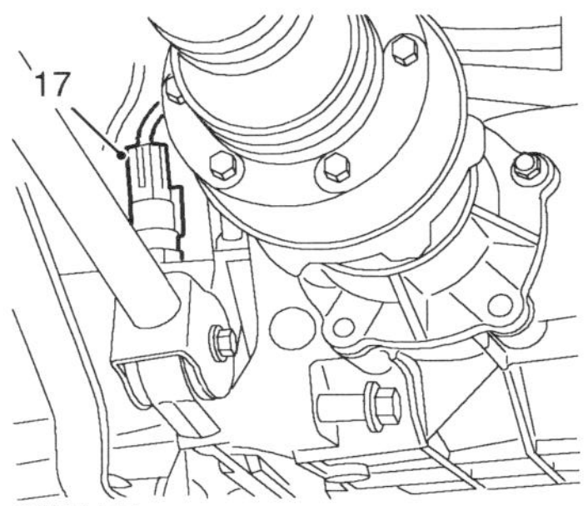

86M4444

17. Disconnect multiplug from gearbox speed sensor.

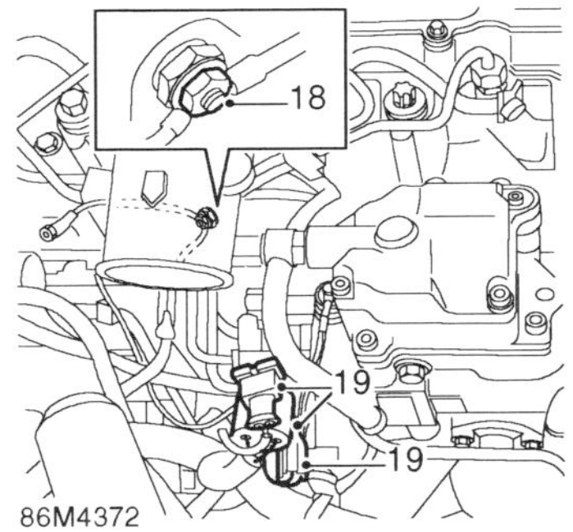

86M4372

18. Loosen nut and disconnect lead from No.2 glow plug.
19. Disconnect 3 multiplug from FIP leads.

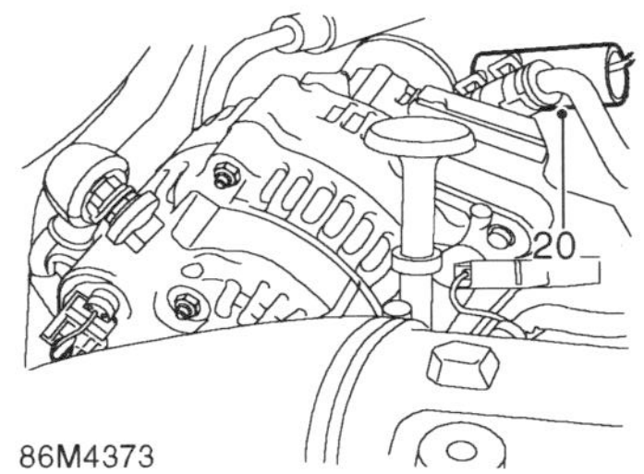

86M4373

20. Disconnect multiplug from air conditioning compressor.

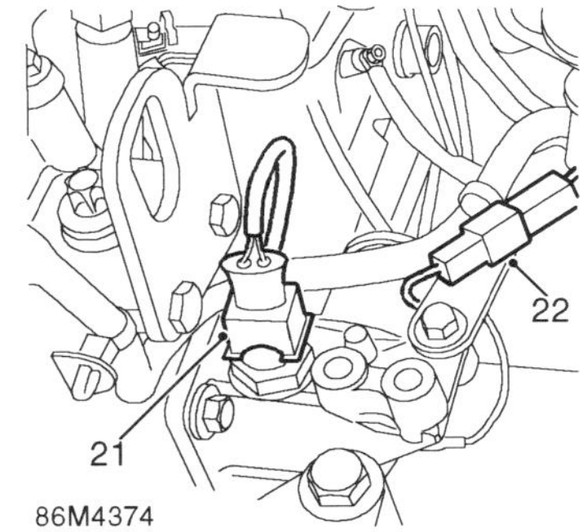

86M4374

21. Disconnect multiplug from engine temperature sensor.
22. Disconnect Lucar from engine temperature transmitter.

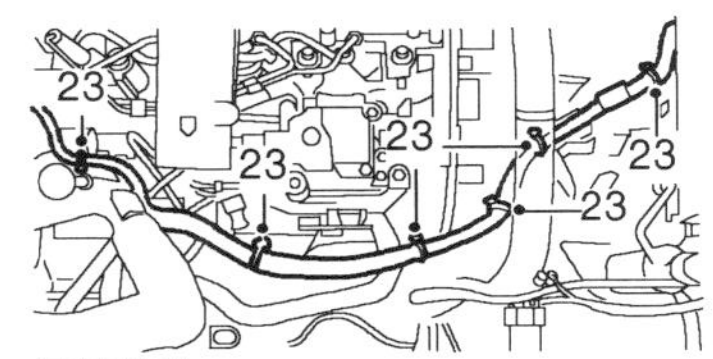

86M4375

23. Remove 6 cable ties securing harness to engine.

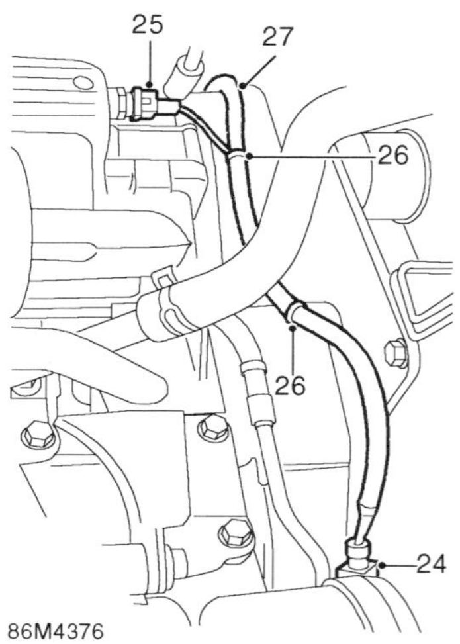

86M4376

24. Disconnect multiplug from oil pressure sensor.
25. Disconnect multiplug from intake air temperature sensor.
26. Release 2 clips securing harness to camshaft belt cover.
27. Remove engine harness.

Refit

1. Position harness to engine.
2. Connect multiplugs to oil pressure and intake air temperature sensors.
3. Connect Lucar to engine temperature transmitter.
4. Connect multiplugs to engine temperature sensor and air conditioning compressor.
5. Connect multiplugs to FIP.
6. Connect lead to glow plug and tighten nut.
7. Connect gearbox speed sensor multiplug.
8. Connect multiplug to 1st gear switch.
9. Connect reverse lamp leads.
10. Connect Lucar and lead to starter solenoid. Tighten starter lead nut.
11. Connect multiplugs to EGR valve and MAP sensor.
12. Connect multiplugs to main harness.
13. Connect earth lead multiplug.
14. Connect harness multiplug to fuse box.
15. Position harness leads to fuse box and tighten screws. Fit fuse box cover.
16. Connect MAF sensor and ECM multiplugs.
17. Fit battery carrier. ***See this section.***
18. Fit air cleaner. ***See ENGINE MANAGEMENT SYSTEM - EDC, Repairs.***
19. Fit alternator. ***See this section.***

HARNESS - TAIL DOOR

Service repair no - 86.70.19

Remove

1. Remove RH rear lower trim casing. ***See BODY, Interior trim components.***
2. Remove tail door water shedder. ***See BODY, Doors.***

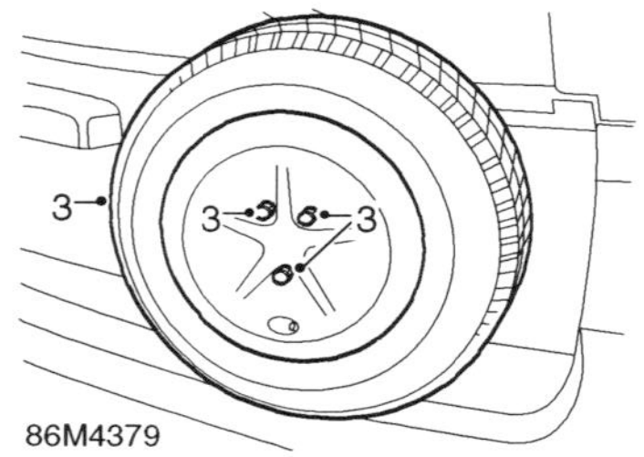

86M4379

3. Remove 3 nuts and remove spare wheel.

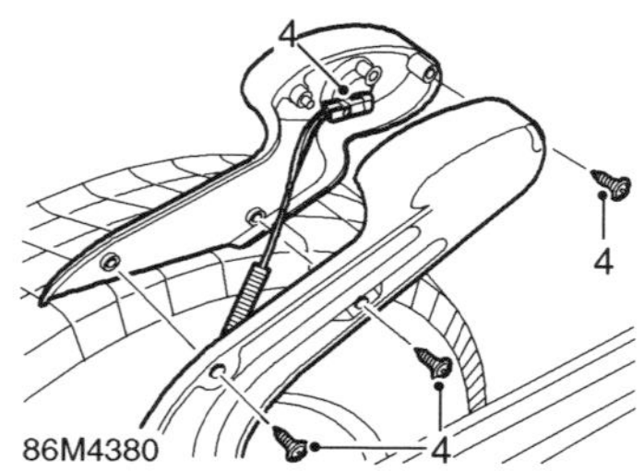

86M4380

4. Remove 3 screws securing CHMSL, disconnect multiplug and remove CHMSL.
5. Release 2 harness clips.

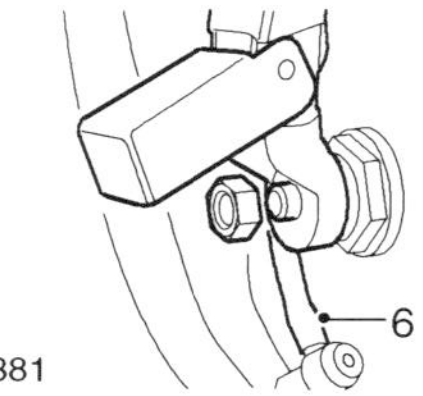

86M4381

6. Disconnect rear washer tube from behind spare wheel carrier.

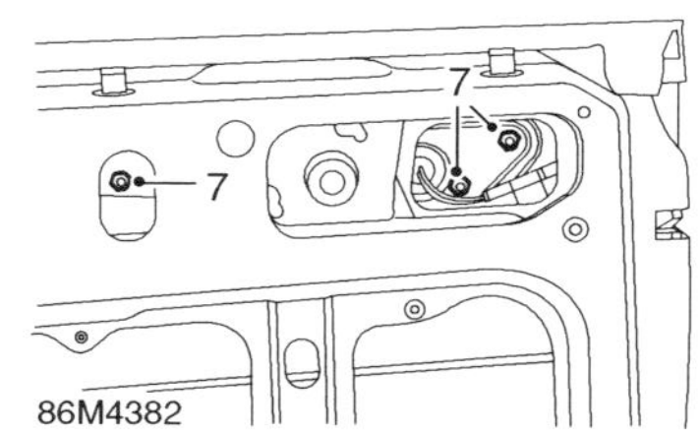

86M4382

7. Remove 3 nuts from number plate lamp housing, release housing.

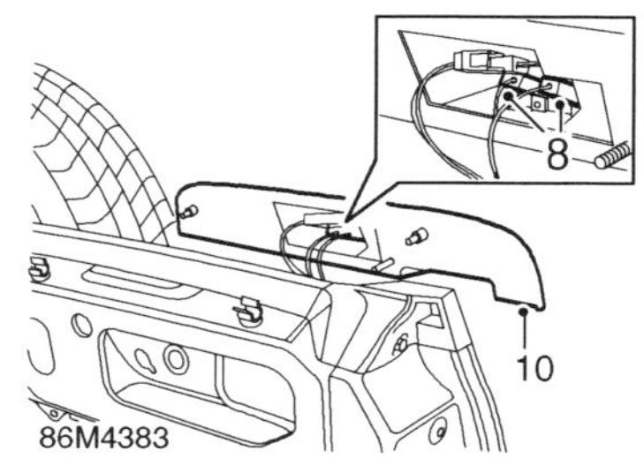

86M4383

8. Disconnect 2 Lucars and multiplug from housing.
9. Collect 2 spacers and housing seal.
10. Remove housing.

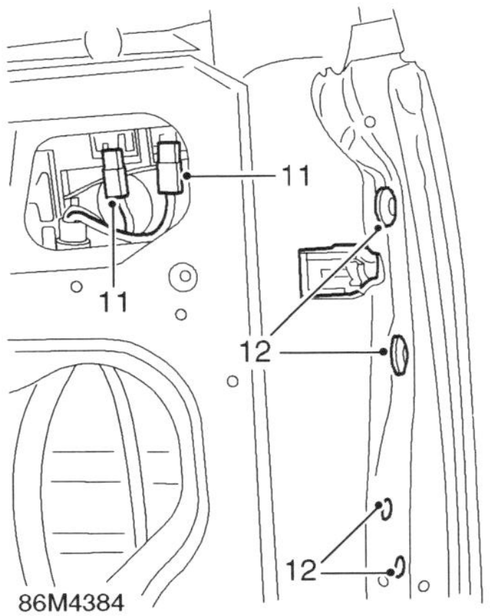

86M4384

11. Disconnect 2 Lucars from rear screen element.
12. Remove 4 screws from door latch, release door latch to access multiplugs and harness clips.

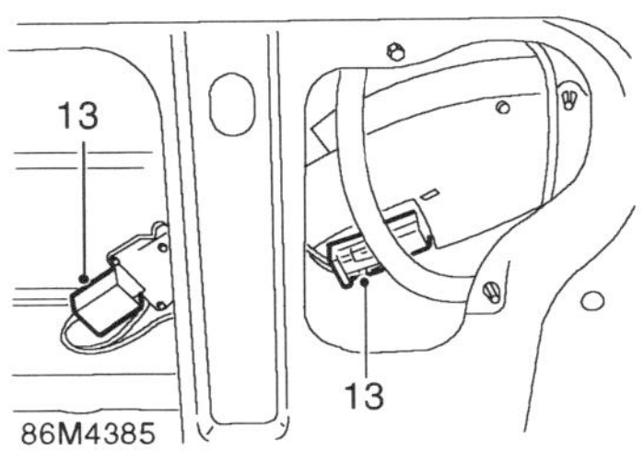

86M4385

13. Disconnect 2 multiplugs from door lock.

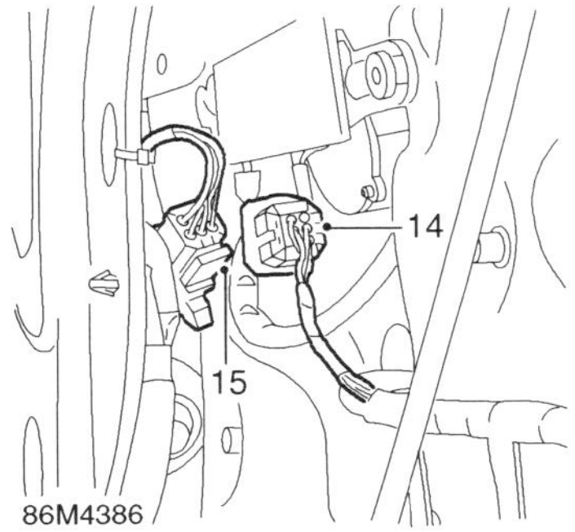

86M4386

14. Disconnect multiplug from rear wiper motor.
15. Disconnect multiplug from rear window motor.

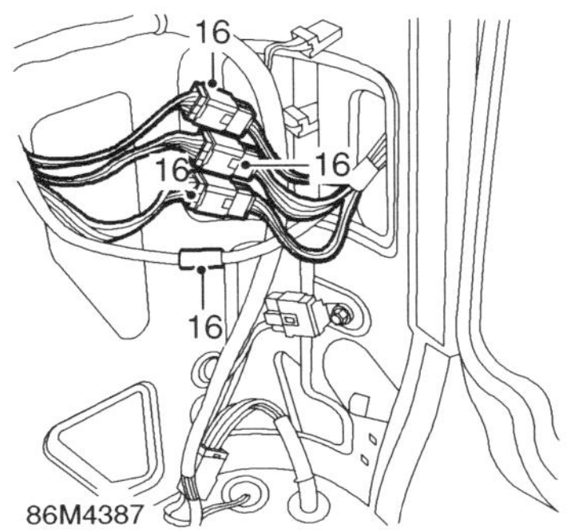

86M4387

16. Release and disconnect 3 multiplugs and washer tube from main harness at 'E' post.

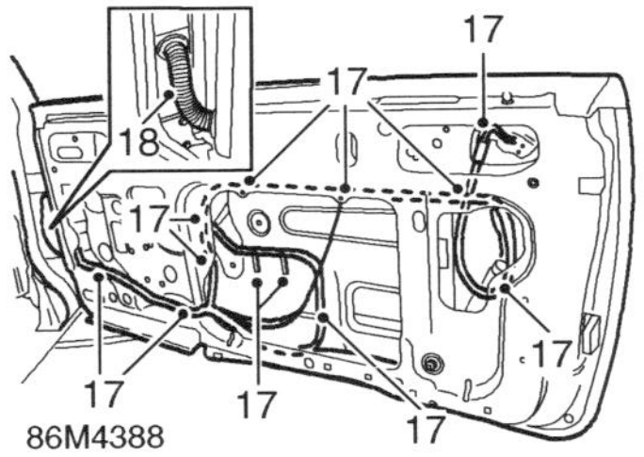

86M4388

17. Release tail door harness from 13 retaining clips.
18. Release harness sheath from tail door and 'E' post.
19. Remove harness from vehicle.

Refit

1. Position harness to vehicle and secure in retaining clips.
2. Secure harness sheath to tail door and 'E' post.
3. Connect multiplugs and washer tube to main harness, secure multiplugs to body.
4. Connect multiplugs to window motor, wiper motor and door lock.
5. Position door latch, fit and tighten screws.
6. Connect Lucars to heated rear screen.
7. Position number plate lamp housing, locate seal and fit spacers.
8. Connect multiplug and Lucars to housing.
9. Fit housing and tighten nuts.
10. Connect washer tube behind spare wheel carrier.
11. Secure harness clips to spare wheel carrier, connect multiplug to CHMSL, fit CHMSL and secure with screws.
12. Fit spare wheel, fit and tighten nuts.
13. Fit water shedder. ***See BODY, Doors.***
14. Fit lower trim casing. ***See BODY, Interior trim components.***

HARNESS - INTERIOR LIGHTS

Service repair no - 86.70.44

Remove

1. Remove fascia assembly. ***See BODY, Interior trim components.***
2. Remove headlining. ***See BODY, Interior trim components.***

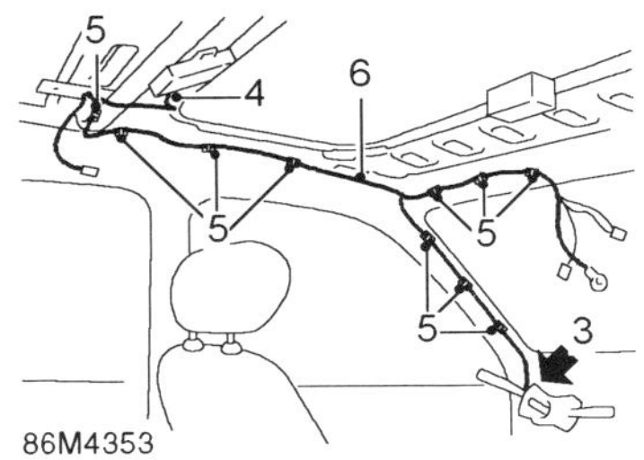

86M4353

3. Disconnect aerial connection and interior light harness from main harness.
4. Disconnect multiplug from volumetric sensor.
5. Release 10 harness clips.
6. Remove harness.

Refit

1. Position harness and secure harness clips.
2. Connect multiplug to volumetric sensor.
3. Connect multiplug and aerial connection to main harness.
4. Fit headlining. ***See BODY, Interior trim components.***
5. Fit fascia assembly. ***See BODY, Interior trim components.***

HARNESS - FRONT DOOR

Service repair no - 86.70.65

Remove

1. Disconnect battery earth lead.
2. Remove front door water shedder. ***See BODY, Doors.***

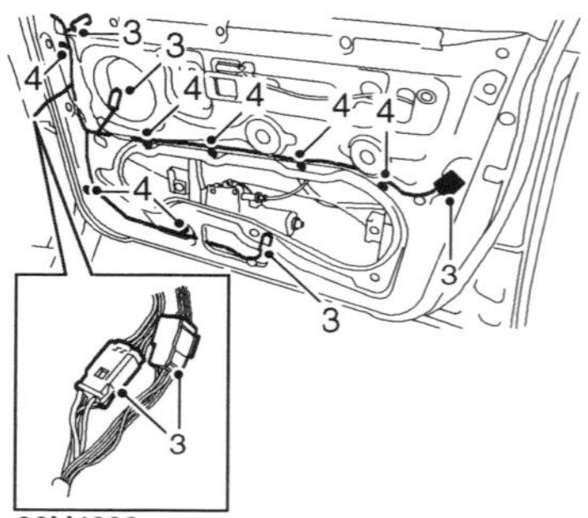

86M4262

3. Release multiplugs from door speaker, door lock, door mirror and window motor.
4. Release 7 clips securing door harness to door.
5. Release 2 multiplugs from location at base of 'A' post and disconnect multiplugs.
6. Release sheath from front edge of door, and pull harness from door.
7. Release sheath from 'A' post, and pull harness from 'A' post.
8. Remove door harness.

Refit

1. Position harness to 'A' post and feed harness partly into 'A' post.
2. Feed sheath onto harness and locate sheath to 'A' post.
3. Feed harness through front edge of door and secure sheath to door.
4. Connect and secure multiplugs at base of 'A' post.
5. Position harness in door and secure with clips.
6. Connect multiplugs to door mirror, door speaker, door lock and window motor.
7. Fit water shedder. ***See BODY, Doors.***
8. Connect battery earth lead.

HARNESS - REAR DOOR

Service repair no - 86.70.66

Remove

1. Disconnect battery earth lead.
2. Remove rear door water shedder. ***See BODY, Doors.***

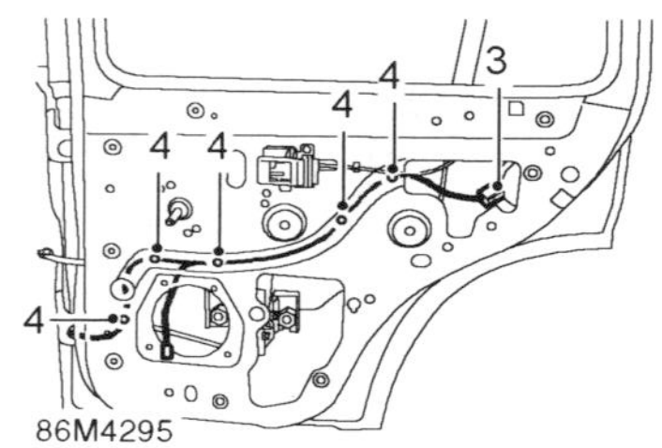

86M4295

3. Release multiplug from door latch.
4. Release 5 clips securing door harness to door.

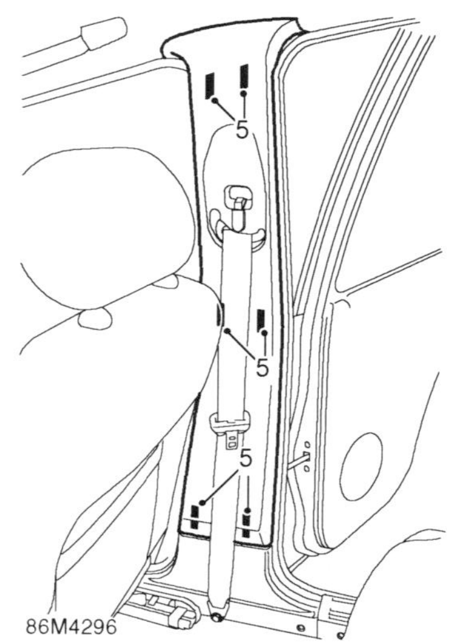

86M4296

5. Release 6 clips securing B/C' upper finisher, position finisher aside.

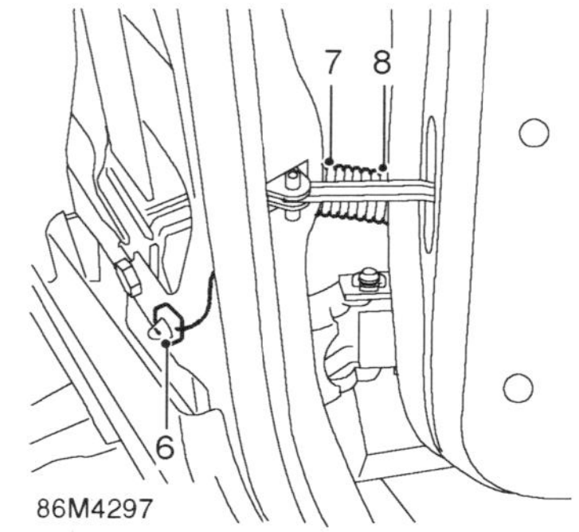

86M4297

6. Release multiplug from location at base of B/C' post and disconnect multiplug.
7. Release sheath from B/C' post, and pull harness from B/C' post.
8. Release sheath from front edge of door and pull harness into door.
9. Remove door harness.

Refit

1. Position harness in door and secure retaining clips.
2. Connect multiplug to door latch.
3. Feed harness through front edge of door and secure sheath to door.
4. Feed harness into B/C' post, and secure sheath to B/C' post.
5. Connect and secure multiplug at base of B/C' post.
6. Position B/C' post upper finisher and secure with retaining clips.
7. Fit water shedder. ***See BODY, Doors.***
8. Connect battery earth lead.

SENSOR - VOLUMETRIC - ALARM SYSTEM - 5 DOOR

Service repair no - 86.77.29

Remove

1. Remove LH rear quarter upper trim casing. ***See BODY, Interior trim components.***
2. Remove LH 'A' post finisher. ***See BODY, Interior trim components.***

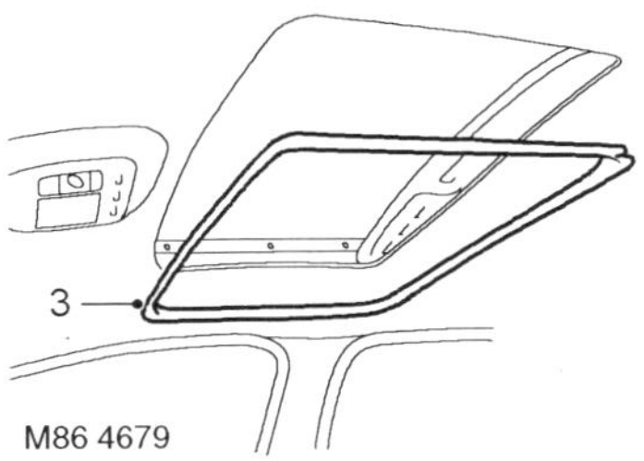

M86 4679

3. Release and remove sunroof finisher.
4. Remove LH front and rear grab handles. ***See BODY, Interior trim components.***

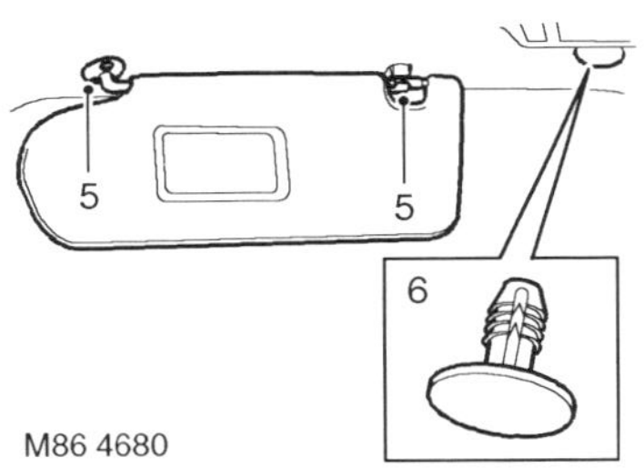

M86 4680

5. Remove 3 screws and remove LH sun visor.
6. Remove trim stud from centre of headlining.

M86 4681

7. Release LH 'B' post upper finisher.
8. Carefully lower headlining to gain access to volumetric sensor.

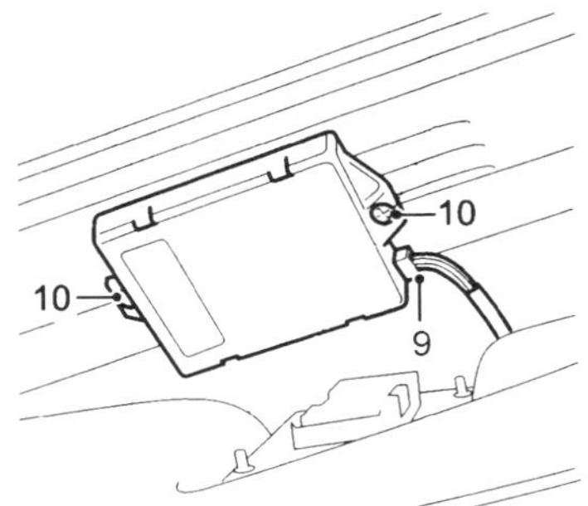

M86 4682

9. Disconnect multiplug from volumetric sensor.
10. Remove 2 screws and remove sensor.

Refit

1. Position sensor to roof bracket and tighten screws.
2. Connect multiplug.
3. Position and secure 'B' post finisher.
4. Position sun visor and tighten screws.
5. Fit front and rear grab handles. ***See BODY, Interior trim components.***
6. Fit 'A' post finisher. ***See BODY, Interior trim components.***
7. Position and secure sunroof finisher.
8. Fit LH rear quarter upper trim casing. ***See BODY, Interior trim components.***
9. Secure front and rear door seals.

SENSOR - VOLUMETRIC - ALARM SYSTEM - 3 DOOR

Service repair no - 86.77.29

Remove

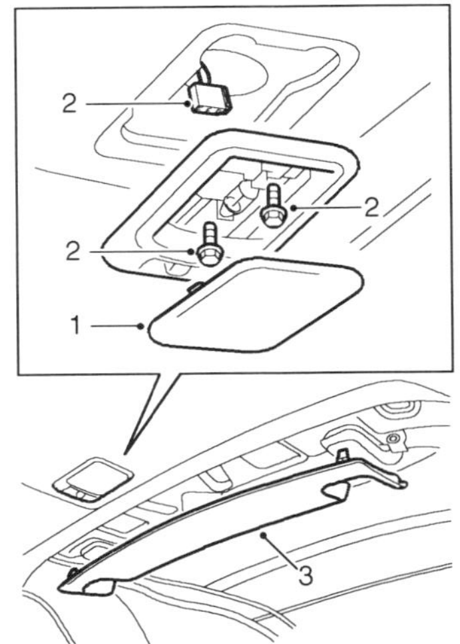

M86 4683

1. Remove lens from roof lamp.
2. Remove 2 screws securing roof lamp, disconnect multiplug and remove lamp assembly.
3. Release headlining rear finisher from roof panel and remove finisher.

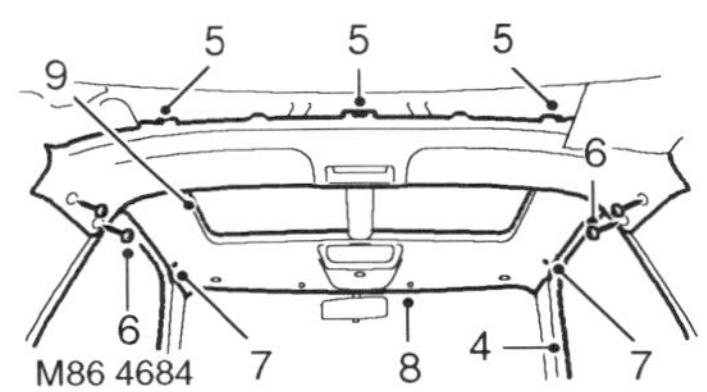

M86 4684

4. Release door aperture seals to clear headlining.
5. Release 3 studs securing rear edge of headlining to roof panel.
6. Remove 4 screws securing headlining to 'B' posts.
7. Release 2 studs at LH and RH side of headlining.
8. Lower front edge of headlining.
9. Release sun roof seal.

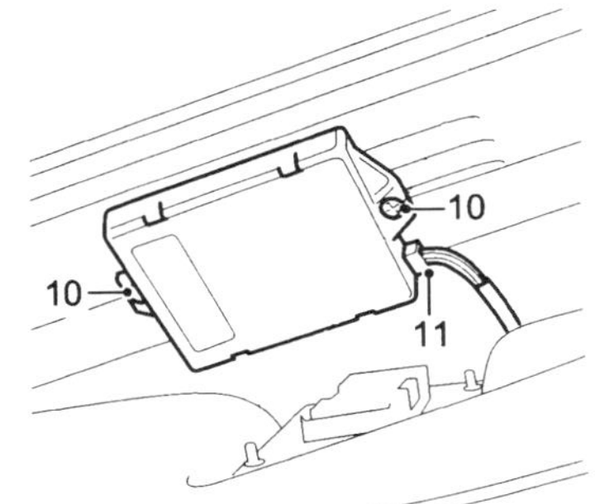

M86 4685

10. Remove screws from volumetric sensor.
11. Disconnect multiplug and remove sensor.

Refit

1. Position sensor and connect multiplug.
2. Fit and tighten sensor screws.
3. Fit and tighten screws securing headlining to 'B' posts.
4. Secure headlining behind rear vent rubbers.
5. Fit headlining rear finisher.
6. Refit door aperture seals.
7. Position sun roof seal to headlining.
8. Position roof lamp and connect multiplug.
9. Tighten roof lamp screws and fit lens.

RECEIVER - ALARM SYSTEM

Service repair no - 86.77.31

Remove

1. Remove instrument bezel finisher. ***See INSTRUMENTS, Repairs.***

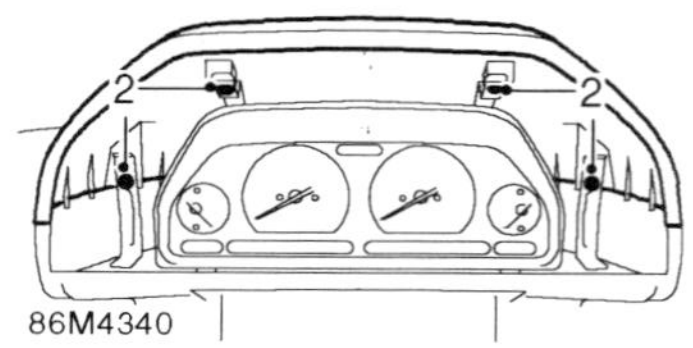

86M4340

2. Remove 4 screws and remove instrument panel upper cover.

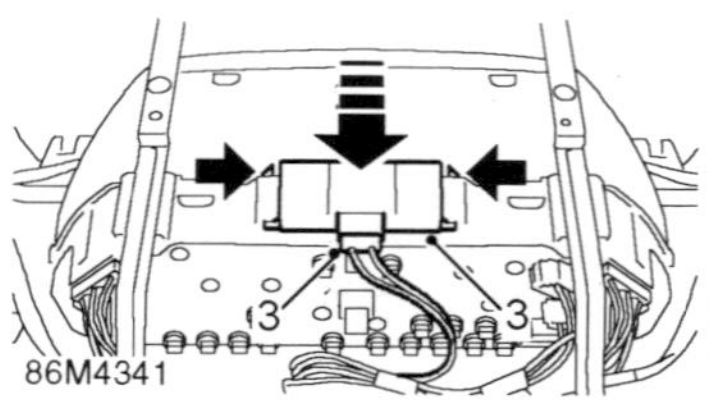

86M4341

3. Disconnect multiplug and remove alarm receiver from instrument pack.

Refit

1. Fit alarm receiver and connect multiplug.
2. Fit instrument panel upper cover and secure with screws.
3. Fit instrument bezel finisher. ***See INSTRUMENTS, Repairs.***

PASSIVE COIL

Service repair no - 86.77.35

Remove

1. Remove steering column nacelle ***See STEERING, Repairs.***

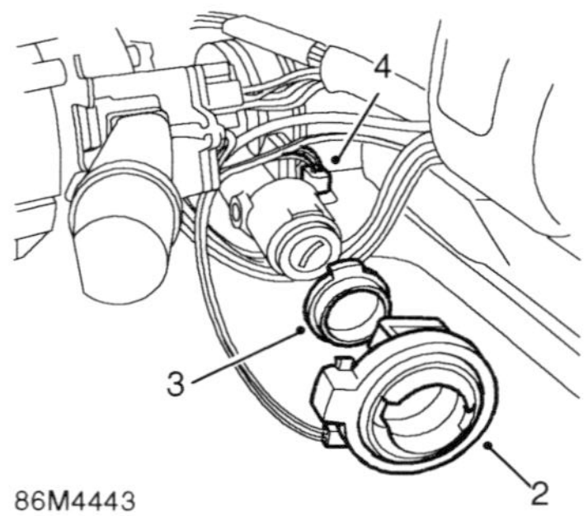

86M4443

2. Release passive coil from column lock
3. Collect illumination ring.
4. Release and disconnect multiplug and remove passive coil.

Refit

1. Fit illumination ring.
2. Position passive coil, connect and secure multiplug.
3. Fit steering column nacelle. ***See STEERING, Repairs.***

CONTENTS

INSTRUMENTS

INSTRUMENT PACK

Indications of vehicle and system status are relayed to the driver by the instruments and warning lamps contained in the fascia mounted instrument pack.

The instrument pack comprises a case, a cowl and a meter lens which are secured together by integral clips. A print panel (printed circuit) is located on the rear of the case. Three electrical connectors from the vehicle wiring locate in recesses in the case and mate with the print panel. Bulb sockets for warning and illumination lamps are installed through the print panel and located in the case. Colour filters that incorporate appropriately coloured graphics are installed over the warning lamp bulbs. The instruments are installed in the case and secured by screws that also pass through the print panel. The screws and the bulb sockets provide the electrical connections between the print panel and their related components. A reset knob is installed through the cowl and meter lens and connected to the speedometer.

Instrument pack components

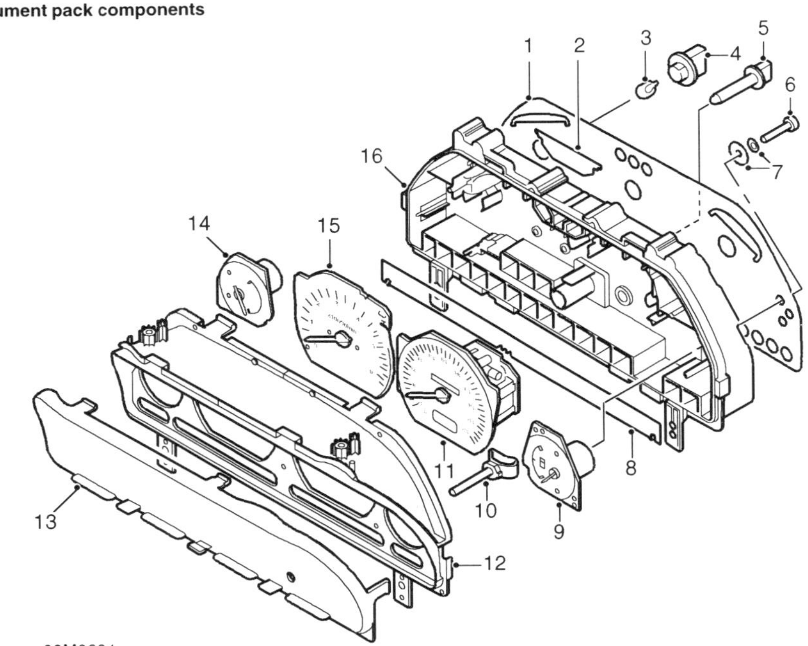

88M0201

1. Print panel
2. Warning lamp filter
3. Bulb
4. Bulb socket
5. Alarm LED and socket
6. Screw
7. Washers
8. Warning lamp filter
9. Fuel gauge
10. Trip distance reset knob
11. Speedometer
12. Cowl
13. Meter lens
14. Engine coolant temperature gauge
15. Tachometer
16. Case

Each warning lamp incorporates a serviceable bulb. The colour of the warning lamp graphic denotes the category of the information the lamp is conveying:

- Red for warning.
- Amber for caution.
- Green and blue for information.

All of the warning lamps are concealed until illuminated.

Additional serviceable bulbs are installed to illuminate the odometer and provide background illumination. The alarm warning indicator consists of a serviceable, red LED and socket assembly.

The instruments receive electrical signals from sender units and transpose them into analogue gauge readouts. The fuel gauge pointer remains fixed at the latest fuel level reading when the ignition is switched off; the pointer's of the other gauges return to the zero/rest position.

Engine coolant temperature gauge

The engine coolant temperature gauge is controlled by a voltage signal from the temperature gauge sensor. The electrical resistance across the temperature gauge sensor is proportional to temperature, so the voltage of the control signal and the resultant deflection of the gauge pointer are directly related to coolant temperature.

Model Type	Sensor Resistance, Ohms	Nominal Gauge Reading
Diesel	135.9	Wide sector at cold
	22.9 to 71.0	5 degrees below horizontal (engine normal operating temperature)
	18.1	Between red and white sectors at hot
Petrol	142.0	Wide sector at cold
	32.1 to 49.0	10 degrees below horizontal (engine normal operating temperature)
	16.9	Red sector at hot

Speedometer

The speedometer and integrated odometer are controlled by a road speed signal that is input from either the gearbox mounted speed sensor (non ABS models) or the ABS ECU (ABS models). The signal consists of 4 pulses per revolution of the speed sensor, or equivalent on ABS models. The speedometer is calibrated to 5000 pulses/min at 60 mph (3107.6 pulses/min at 60 km/h). The odometer is a Liquid Crystal Display (LCD) that shows total and trip distances: Pushing the reset knob for less than 1 second switches between the six digit total distance display and the four digit trip distance display. When the trip distance display is showing, pressing and holding the reset knob for more than 1 second will zero the trip distance reading. The odometer is calibrated at 5160 pulses to 1 mile (3206.8 pulses to 1 kilometre).

Tachometer

The tachometer uses an engine speed signal from the ignition coil (petrol models) or engine control module (diesel models). The signal consists of 2 pulses per engine revolution.

Fuel contents gauge

The fuel contents gauge is controlled by a voltage signal from the float operated sender unit in the fuel tank. Movement of the sender unit float arm varies the electrical resistance across the sender unit, so the voltage of the control signal and the resultant deflection of the gauge pointer are directly related to the level of fuel in the tank.

Sender Unit Resistance, Ohms	Nominal Gauge Reading
105	Red sector at empty
32.5	Horizontal (half full)
5	White sector at full

Rear view of instrument pack

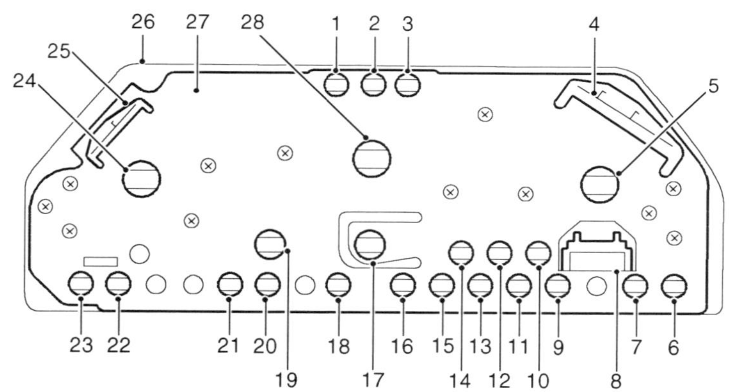

88M0202

1. Right direction indicator warning lamp
2. Main beam warning lamp
3. Left direction indicator warning lamp
4. Electrical socket
5. Background illumination lamp
6. Door open warning lamp
7. Hazard warning lamp
8. Electrical socket
9. Traction control warning lamp
10. Ignition/no charge warning lamp
11. Anti-lock braking warning lamp
12. SRS warning lamp
13. Hill descent control information warning lamp
14. Engine oil pressure warning lamp
15. Hill descent control fault warning lamp
16. Brake fault/handbrake on warning lamp
17. Alarm warning indicator
18. Glow plug warning lamp (diesel models only)
19. Odometer illumination lamp
20. MIL warning lamp (diesel models only)
21. Seat belt warning lamp (if fitted)
22. Trailer direction indicator/ hazard warning lamp
23. Rear fog guard warning lamp
24. Background illumination lamp
25. Electrical socket
26. Case
27. Print panel
28. Background illumination lamp

CLOCK

Service repair no - 88.15.07

Remove

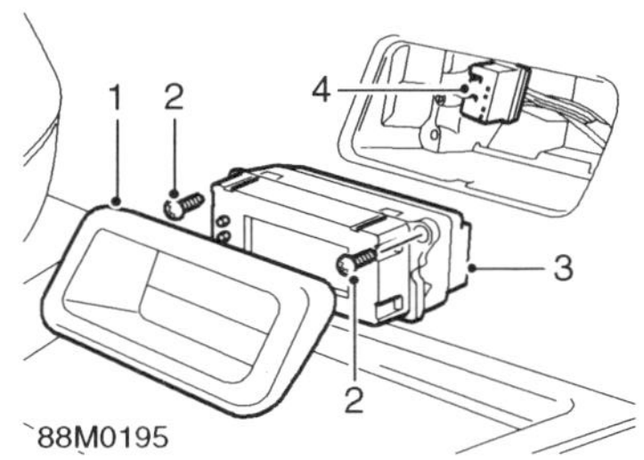

88M0195

1. Remove clock finisher from fascia.
2. Remove 2 screws securing clock to fascia.
3. Release clock to gain access to multiplug.
4. Disconnect multiplug and remove clock.

Refit

1. Position clock to fascia and connect multiplug.
2. Fit and tighten screws securing clock to fascia.
3. Fit finisher to fascia.

PANEL - INSTRUMENT

Service repair no - 88.20.01

WARNING: *See GENERAL INFORMATION, SRS Precautions.*

Remove

1. Make the SRS system safe. ***See GENERAL INFORMATION, SRS Precautions.***
2. Remove instrument bezel finisher. ***See this section.***

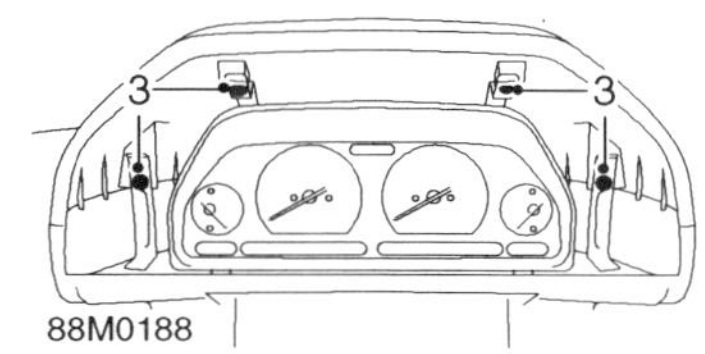

88M0188

3. Remove 4 screws and remove instrument panel upper cover.

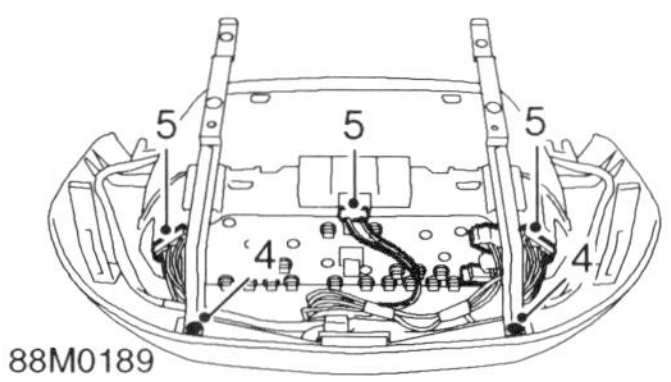

88M0189

4. Remove 4 screws securing instrument panel.
5. Disconnect 4 multiplugs and remove instrument panel.

Refit

1. Position instrument panel, fit and tighten screws.
2. Connect multiplugs to instrument panel.
3. Fit instrument panel upper cover and tighten screws.
4. Fit instrument bezel finisher. ***See this section.***
5. Connect battery, earth lead last.

FINISHER - INSTRUMENT BEZEL

Service repair no - 88.20.02

Remove

88M0196

1. Remove 4 screws and release finisher.
2. Disconnect multiplugs from switches and remove finisher.
   Do not carry out further dismantling if component is removed for access only.

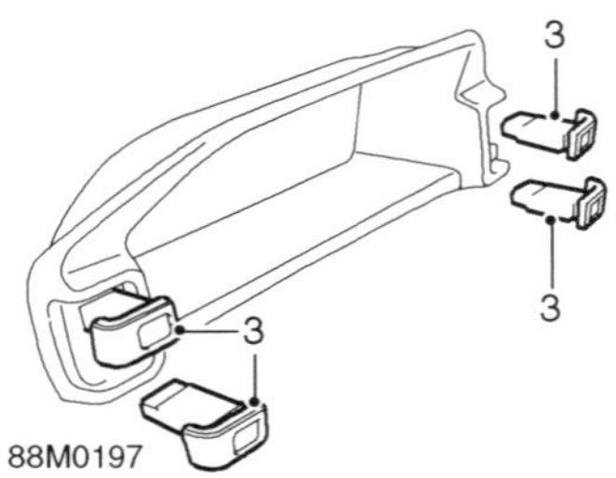

88M0197

3. Remove switches/switch blanks from finisher.
4. Fit switches/switch blanks to replacement finisher.

Refit

1. Position finisher and connect multiplugs to switches.
2. Fit and tighten screws.

PRINTED CIRCUIT - INSTRUMENT PANEL

Service repair no - 88.20.19

Remove

1. Remove instrument panel. ***See this section.***

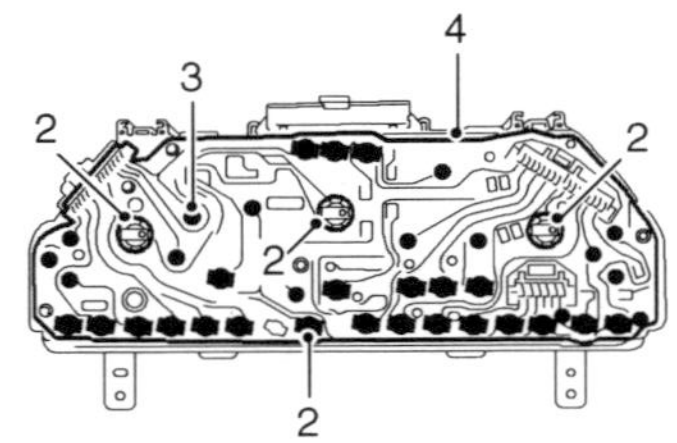

88M0190

2. Remove 26 illumination and warning lamp bulb holders.
3. Remove 13 screws securing printed circuit.
4. Release and remove printed circuit.

Refit

1. Fit and secure printed circuit to instrument pack, fit and tighten screws
2. Fit bulb holders to instrument panel.
3. Fit instrument panel. ***See this section.***

GAUGE - COOLANT TEMPERATURE

Service repair no - 88.25.14

Remove

1. Remove instrument panel. ***See this section.***

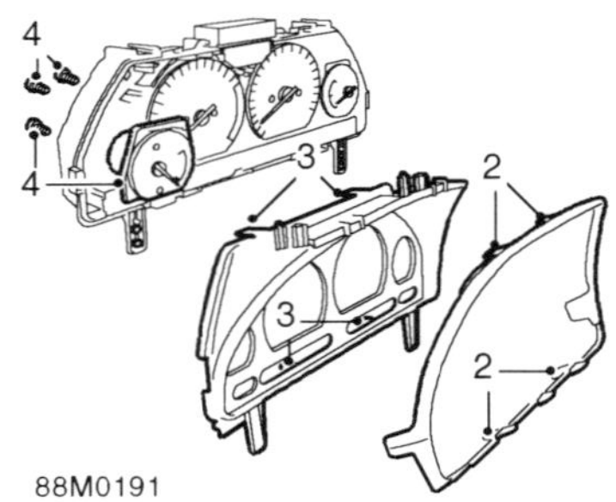

88M0191

2. Release 6 clips securing meter lens to cowl and remove meter lens.
3. Release 4 clips securing cowl to case and remove cowl.
4. Remove 3 screws and remove coolant temperature gauge.

Refit

1. Fit coolant temperature gauge and secure with screws.
2. Fit cowl to case.
3. Fit meter lens to cowl.
4. Fit instrument panel. ***See this section.***

TRANSMITTER - COOLANT TEMPERATURE GAUGE - 'L' SERIES

Service repair no - 88.25.20

Remove

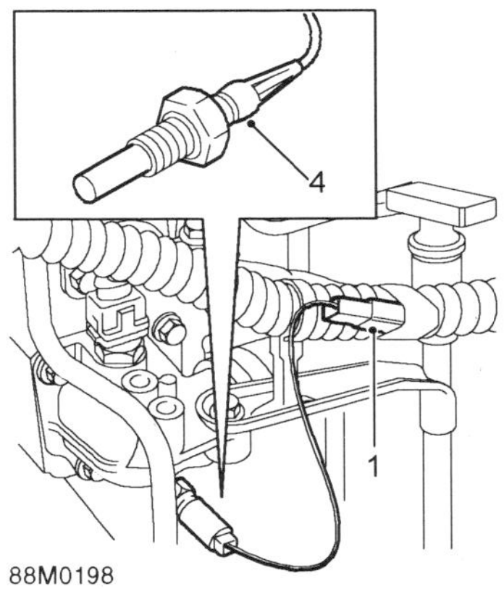

88M0198

1. Disconnect coolant temperature gauge transmitter lead from engine harness.

Models with air conditioning

2. Remove alternator. ***See ELECTRICAL, Repairs.***

All models

3. Position drain tin to collect spillage.
4. Remove coolant temperature gauge transmitter.

Refit

1. Clean threads of coolant temperature gauge transmitter.
2. Apply Loctite 577 to threads of coolant temperature gauge transmitter.
3. Fit coolant temperature gauge transmitter and tighten to 10 Nm.
4. Connect lead to engine harness
5. Top-up coolant. ***See INFORMATION, Capacities, fluids and lubricants.***

Models with air conditioning

6. Fit alternator. ***See ELECTRICAL, Repairs.***

GAUGE - FUEL

Service repair no - 88.25.26

Remove

1. Remove instrument panel. ***See this section.***

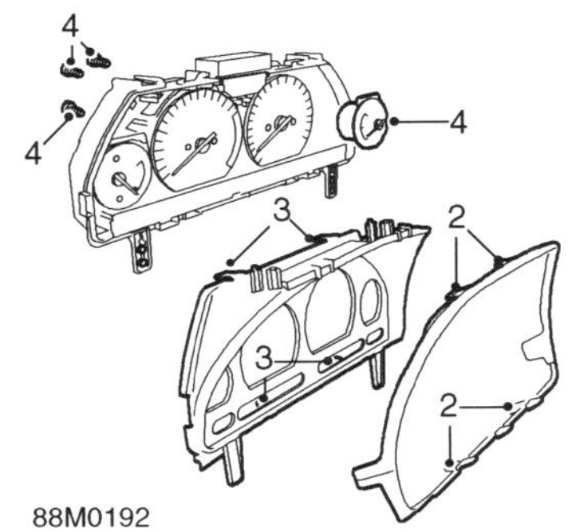

88M0192

2. Release 6 clips securing meter lens to cowl and remove meter lens.
3. Release 4 clips securing cowl to case and remove cowl.
4. Remove 3 screws and remove fuel gauge.

Refit

1. Fit fuel gauge and secure with screws.
2. Fit cowl to case.
3. Fit meter lens to cowl.
4. Fit instrument panel. ***See this section.***

TANK UNIT ASSEMBLY - DIESEL

Service repair no - 88.25.32

Remove

1. Disconnect battery earth lead.

WARNING: The spilling of fuel is unavoidable during this operation. Ensure that all necessary precautions are taken to prevent fire and explosion.

2. Open RH rear and tail doors.
3. Release and roll RH rear seat forward.
4. Raise luggage and passenger compartment carpets for access to panel.

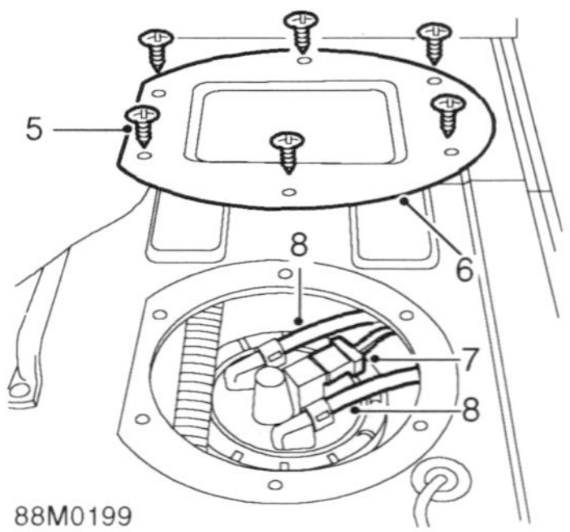

88M0199

5. Remove 6 screws securing access panel.
6. Remove access panel.
7. Disconnect multiplug from tank unit.
8. Disconnect fuel hoses from tank unit.

CAUTION: Plug the connections.

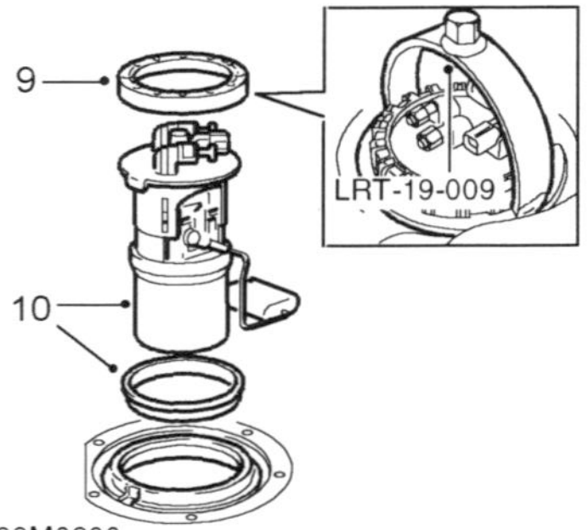

88M0200

9. Use tool **LRT 19-009** and remove locking ring from tank unit.
10. Remove tank unit and sealing ring.

Refit

1. Clean mating faces of tank unit and fuel tank.
2. Fit seal to tank unit.
3. Fit tank unit and secure with locking ring.
4. Connect multiplug to tank unit.
5. Connect fuel hoses to tank unit.
6. Fit access panel and secure with screws.
7. Reposition carpets.
8. Raise rear seat.
9. Close rear and tail doors.
10. Connect battery earth lead.

SENDER - FUEL GAUGE

Service repair no - 88.25.32

Remove

1. Disconnect battery earth lead.

WARNING: The spilling of fuel is unavoidable during this operation. Ensure that all necessary precautions are taken to prevent fire and explosion.

2. *Petrol Models:* Remove fuel pump assembly. ***See FUEL DELIVERY SYSTEM, Repairs.*** *Diesel Models:* Remove tank unit assembly. ***See this section.***

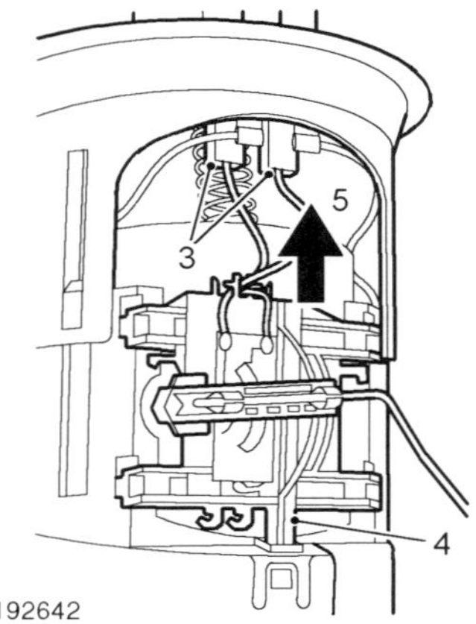

M192642

3. Disconnect 2 Lucar terminals from top of tank unit assembly.
4. Using a flat bladed screwdriver, carefully release sprag clip securing sender to tank unit.
5. Remove sender unit.

Refit

1. Position sender to location slots and engage sprag clip.

CAUTION: Ensure that each of the 4 location lugs on the sender are engaged with corresponding slots in the tank unit.

2. Connect Lucar terminals to top of tank unit assembly.
3. *Petrol Models:* Fit fuel pump assembly. ***See FUEL DELIVERY SYSTEM, Repairs.*** *Diesel Models:* Fit tank unit assembly. ***See this section.***
4. Connect battery earth lead.

SPEEDOMETER

Service repair no - 88.30.01

Remove

1. Remove instrument panel. ***See this section.***

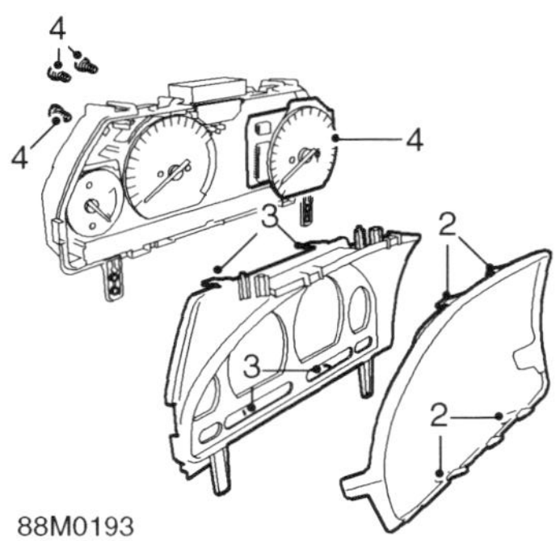

88M0193

2. Release 6 clips securing meter lens to cowl and remove meter lens.
3. Release 4 clips securing cowl to case and remove cowl.
4. Remove 3 screws and remove speedometer.

Refit

1. Fit speedometer and secure with screws.
2. Fit cowl to case.
3. Fit meter lens to cowl.
4. Fit instrument panel. ***See this section.***

TACHOMETER

Service repair no - 88.30.21

Remove

1. Remove instrument panel. ***See this section.***

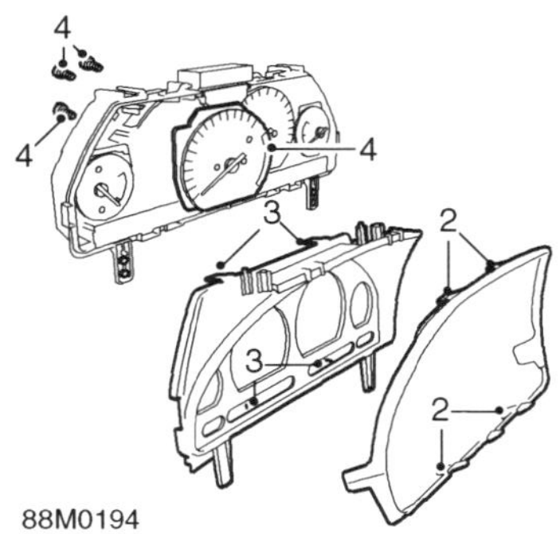

88M0194

2. Release 6 clips securing meter lens to cowl and remove meter lens.
3. Release 4 clips securing cowl to case and remove cowl.
4. Remove 3 screws and remove tachometer.

Refit

1. Fit tachometer and secure with screws.
2. Fit cowl to case.
3. Fit meter lens to cowl.
4. Fit instrument panel. ***See this section.***

'L' SERIES DIESEL ENGINE

OVERHAUL MANUAL

This engine is fitted to the following model:

Land Rover Freelander

'L' SERIES DIESEL ENGINE OVERHAUL MANUAL

CONTENTS

Page

INTRODUCTION

How to use this manual

To assist in the use of this manual the section title is given at the top and the relevant sub-section is given at the bottom of each page.

This manual contains procedures for overhaul of the 'L' Series Diesel engine on the bench with the gearbox and clutch removed. For all other information regarding General Information, Adjustments, removal of oil seals, engine units and ancillary equipment, consult the Repair Manual for the model concerned.

This manual is divided into 3 sections, Description and Operation, Overhaul and Data, Torque & Tools. To assist filing of revised information each sub-section is numbered from page 1.

The individual overhaul items are to be followed in the sequence in which they appear. Items numbered in the illustrations are referred to in the text.

Overhaul operations include reference to Service Tool numbers and the associated illustration depicts the tool. Where usage is not obvious the tool is shown in use. Operations also include reference to wear limits, relevant data, torque figures, and specialist information and useful assembly details.

WARNINGS, CAUTIONS and Notes have the following meanings:

WARNING: Procedures which must be followed precisely to avoid the possibility of injury.

CAUTION: Calls attention to procedures which must be followed to avoid damage to components.

NOTE: Gives helpful information.

References

With the engine and gearbox assembly removed, the crankshaft pulley end of the engine is referred to as the front.

Operations covered in this manual do not include reference to testing the vehicle after repair. It is essential that work is inspected and tested after completion and if necessary a road test of the vehicle is carried out particularly where safety related items are concerned.

Dimensions

The dimensions quoted are to design engineering specification with Service limits where applicable.

REPAIRS AND REPLACEMENTS

When replacement parts are required it is essential that only Land Rover recommended parts are used.

Attention is particularly drawn to the following points concerning repairs and the fitting of replacement parts and accessories.

Safety features and corrosion prevention treatments embodied in the vehicle may be impaired if other than Land Rover recommended parts are fitted. In certain territories, legislation prohibits the fitting of parts not to the manufacturer's specification.

Torque wrench setting figures given in this Manual must be used. Locking devices, where specified, must be fitted. If the efficiency of a locking device is impaired during removal it must be renewed.

The terms of the vehicle Warranty may be invalidated by the fitting of other than Land Rover recommended parts. All Land Rover recommended parts have the full backing of the vehicle Warranty.

Land Rover dealers are obliged to supply only Land Rover recommended parts.

SPECIFICATION

Land Rover are constantly seeking to improve the specification, design and production of their vehicles and alterations take place accordingly. While every effort has been made to ensure the accuracy of this Manual, it should not be regarded as an infallible guide to current specifications of any particular component or vehicle.

This Manual does not constitute an offer for sale of any particular component or vehicle. Land Rover dealers are not agents of Land Rover and have no authority to bind the manufacturer by any expressed or implied undertaking or representation.

CONTENTS

CONTENTS

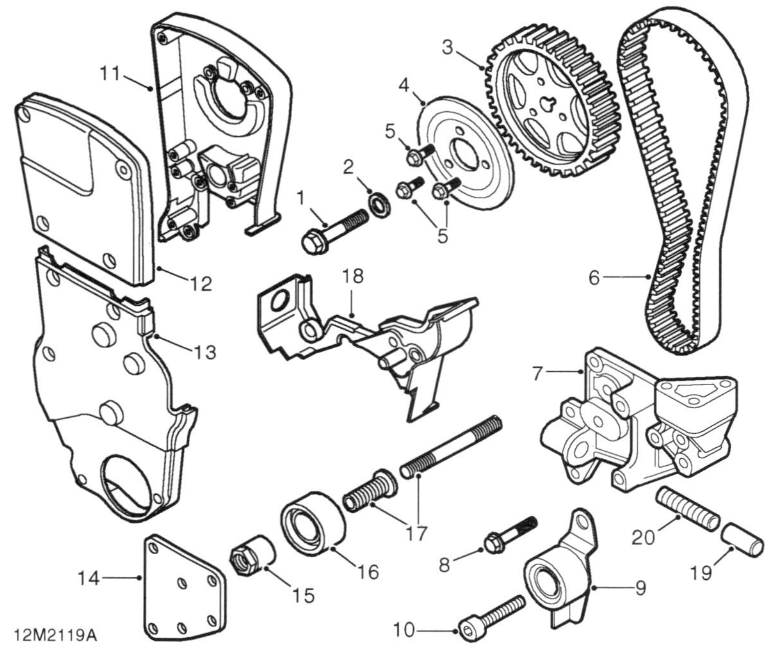

12M2119A

CAMSHAFT TIMING BELT COMPONENTS

1. Bolt - timing belt gear
2. Washer
3. Timing belt gear
4. Timing belt gear - damper
5. Torx screws - damper to timing gear
6. Camshaft timing belt
7. Tensioner housing
8. Bolt - tensioner pulley
9. Tensioner pulley
10. Allen screw - tensioner pulley
11. Timing belt upper rear cover
12. Timing belt upper front cover
13. Timing belt lower front cover
14. Engine front mounting cover plate
15. Nut - idler pulley
16. Idler pulley
17. Stud and adaptor - idler pulley
18. Timing belt lower rear cover
19. Tensioner plunger
20. Tensioner spring

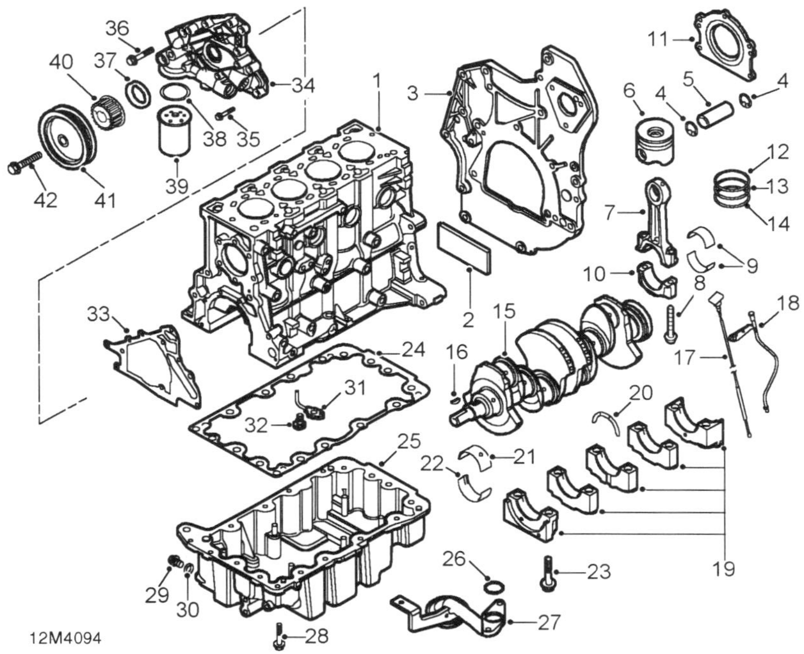

12M4094

CYLINDER BLOCK COMPONENTS

1. Cylinder block
2. Foam pad
3. Gearbox adaptor plate
4. Circlip - gudgeon pin
5. Gudgeon pin
6. Piston
7. Connecting rod
8. Bolt - connecting rod
9. Big-end bearing shells
10. Big-end bearing cap
11. Crankshaft rear oil seal and housing
12. Top compression ring
13. 2nd compression ring
14. Oil control ring
15. Crank shaft
16. Woodruff key
17. Dipstick
18. Dipstick tube
19. Main bearing cap
20. Thrust washer
21. Upper main bearing shell - grooved
22. Lower main bearing shell - plain
23. Bolt - main bearing cap
24. Gasket - sump
25. Sump
26. 'O' ring
27. Oil strainer and pick-up pipe
28. Bolt - sump
29. Drain plug
30. Sealing washer
31. Oil squirt jet
32. Banjo bolt
33. Gasket - oil pump
34. Oil pump
35. Bolt - M6
36. Bolt - M10
37. Crankshaft front oil seal
38. Sealing ring
39. Oil filter element
40. Timing gear
41. Crankshaft pulley
42. Bolt - crankshaft pulley

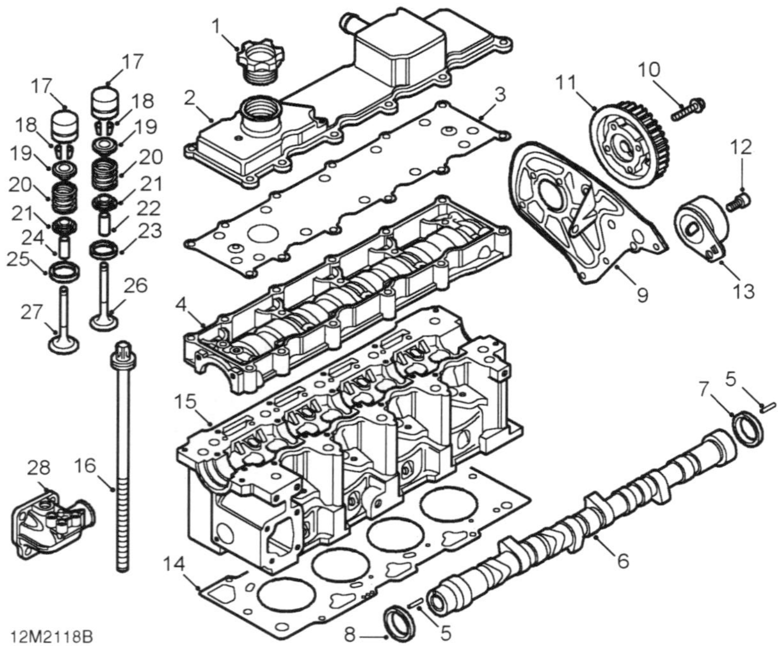

12M2118B

CYLINDER HEAD COMPONENTS

1. Oil filler cap
2. Camshaft cover
3. Gasket - camshaft cover
4. Camshaft carrier
5. Drive pin
6. Camshaft
7. Camshaft rear oil seal
8. Camshaft front oil seal
9. Fuel injection pump drive belt rear cover
10. Bolt - fuel injection pump drive gear
11. Fuel injection pump drive gear
12. Allen screw
13. Fuel injection pump drive belt tensioner
14. Gasket - cylinder head
15. Cylinder head
16. Bolt - cylinder head
17. Tappet
18. Collets
19. Spring cap
20. Valve spring
21. Spring seat and valve stem oil seal
22. Valve guide - exhaust
23. Valve seat insert - exhaust
24. Valve guide - inlet
25. Valve seat insert - inlet
26. Exhaust valve
27. Inlet valve
28. Coolant outlet elbow

DESCRIPTION

The ' L' Series 2.0 litre engine is a 4 cylinder, in-line, direct injection diesel engine having 2 valves per cylinder operated by a single overhead camshaft.
A cast iron cylinder block incorporates direct bored cylinders, each pair of cylinders being strategically positioned to reduce engine length and give good structural rigidity.
An alloy camshaft carrier is bolted directly to the alloy cylinder head, the camshaft bearing journals are line bored between the two components. The camshaft operates the valves via hydraulic tappets, the camshaft gear, which incorporates a tortional damper, is driven by an internally toothed drive belt by a gear on the front of the crankshaft. Belt tension is achieved by means of a semi-automatic tensioner and an idler pulley is also fitted. A gear on the rear end of the camshaft drives the fuel injection pump belt.
A single spring is fitted to each valve, the valve stem oil seals are moulded onto a metal base which also forms the valve spring seat on the cylinder head. The valve stems run in guides pressed into the cylinder head.

The aluminium alloy, graphite coated pistons are fitted with two compression and an oil control ring, the top ring is located in a steel insert which helps to provide a minimal reaction to compression forces. The piston crowns are domed in the centre, the combustion chamber being formed in a bowl around the dome. Fully floating gudgeon pins retain the pistons to the connecting rods, the pins are offset towards the thrust side of the pistons which are retained in the pistons by circlips. Oil squirt jets, located in the cylinder block provide additional piston cooling and gudgeon pin lubrication. Plain big-end bearing shells without location tags are fitted, with the connecting rod bearing caps retained by flange headed bolts to the connecting rods. The big-end has a 'Fracture Split' type joint between the connecting rod and the bearing cap. There are no identification marks, however, to prevent incorrect fitment of the the bearing cap to connecting rod, the bolts are off-set by 1mm.

The crankshaft runs in 5 main bearings, grooved shells are fitted in the cylinder block with plain bearing shells in each main bearing cap. Positive location of each main bearing cap is by means of hollow dowels. Crankshaft end-float is controlled by single size thrust washers,located each side of the centre - Number 3 main bearing in the cylinder block. The crankshaft front oil seal is located in the oil pump body whilst the rear oil seal is integral with a housing bolted to the rear of the cylinder block. Additional oil sealing is provided by RTV sealant injected into grooves and along the joint lines of the front main - Number 1 bearing cap and the crankshaft rear oil seal.

A rotor type oil pump is driven from the front of the crankshaft, the pump is sealed to the cylinder block with a gasket.

The cast alloy sump is bolted to the cylinder block and rear main bearing cap and is sealed to the block with a rubber gasket which incorporates location lugs for the block and sump. Compression limiters in the bolt holes prevent distortion of the gasket.

>

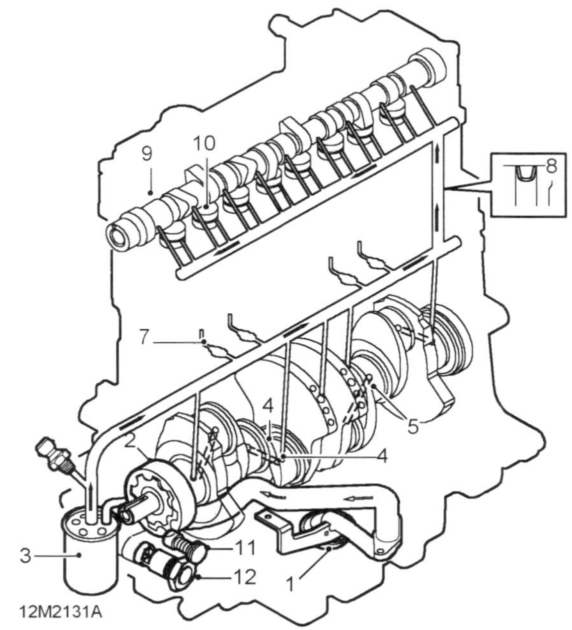

12M2131A

Lubrication

Oil is drawn through a gauze strainer (1) and through a passage in the cylinder block to the oil pump (2). Pressurised oil flows via the full flow filter (3) to the main oil gallery in the cylinder block.
Drillings from the main oil gallery direct oil to the crankshaft main bearings (4) and cross drillings in the crankshaft direct oil to the big-end bearings (5).
Additional drillings in the cylinder block supply oil at reduced pressure to the oil squirt jets (7) for piston cooling and gudgeon pin lubrication and via a restrictor (8) in the top of the cylinder block to the rear of the cylinder head. A full length drilling in the cylinder head directs oil to the camshaft journals (9) and tappets (10).
An oil pressure relief valve (11) is located in the oil pump body which also carries the oil filter adapter and the return union for the externally mounted oil cooler.

A thermostatic valve (12), comprising a valve, spring and diverter plug is located in the oil pump body.
The oil flow union to the oil cooler is screwed into the end of the diverter plug. The valve is closed during engine warm-up thereby preventing oil flow to the oil cooler. As the oil reaches a pre-determined temperature, the valve opens and allows oil to flow to the cooler.

Crankcase ventilation

A positive crankcase ventilation system is used to vent crankcase gases to the air induction system.

The gases are drawn from the camshaft cover, through a depression limiting valve and into the turbocharger intake.

As engine speed increases, the depression limiting valve progressively closes thereby limiting the depression in the crankcase.

Engine number location

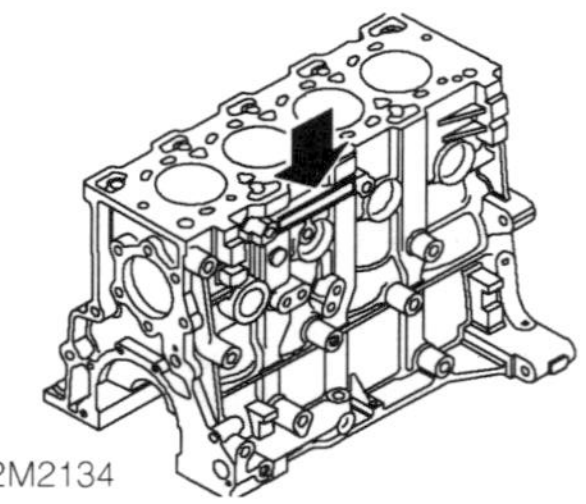

12M2134

The engine number is located on the side of the cylinder block adjacent to Number 2 cylinder.

CAMSHAFT TIMING BELT AND TENSIONER

Camshaft timing belt - remove

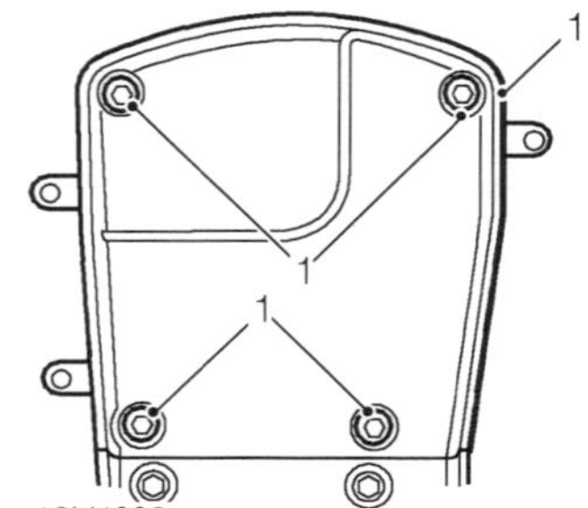

12M1880

1. Remove 4 screws securing camshaft timing belt upper front cover. Remove cover.

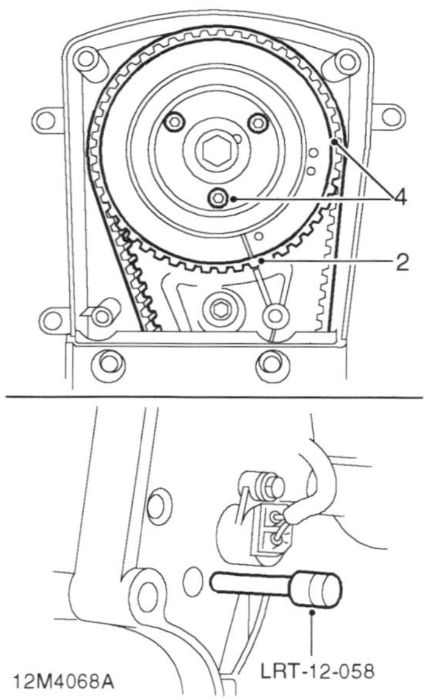

12M4068A

2. Using crankshaft pulley bolt, rotate crankshaft until the timing mark on camshaft gear damper is aligned with pointer on timing belt upper rear cover.

CAUTION: Do not use camshaft timing belt gear or fuel injection pump drive belt gear to rotate crankshaft.

3. Insert timing pin **LRT-12-058** into flywheel.
4. Remove and discard 3 bolts securing damper to camshaft gear. Remove damper

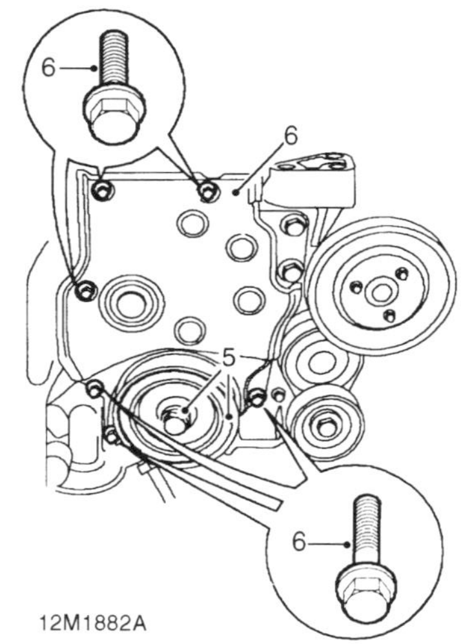

12M1882A

5. Remove crankshaft pulley bolt, withdraw pulley.
6. Noting fitted position of 3 longest screws, remove 6 screws securing camshaft timing belt lower front cover. Remove cover.

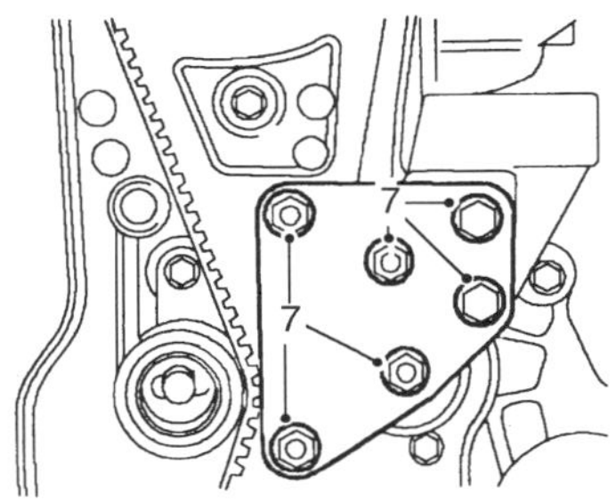

12M1883A

7. Remove 4 nuts and 2 bolts securing engine front mounting cover plate, remove plate.

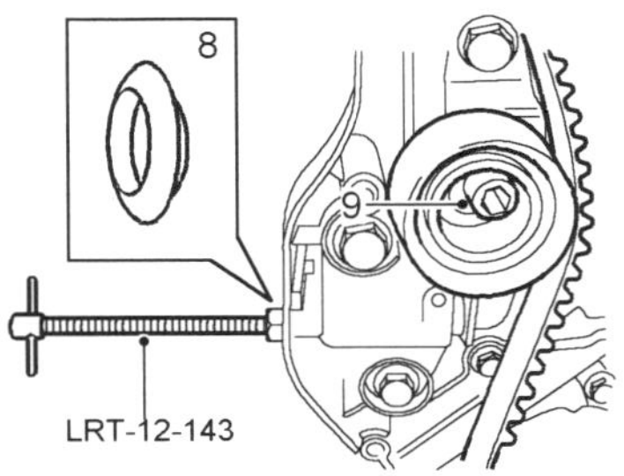

12M4069A

8. Remove access plug from camshaft timing belt lower rear cover.
9. Slacken but do not remove Allen screw securing timing belt tensioner pulley.
10. Screw timing belt tensioner retractor tool **LRT-12-143** into timing belt tensioner plunger.
11. Tighten nut on tool **LRT-12-143** until timing belt tension is released.

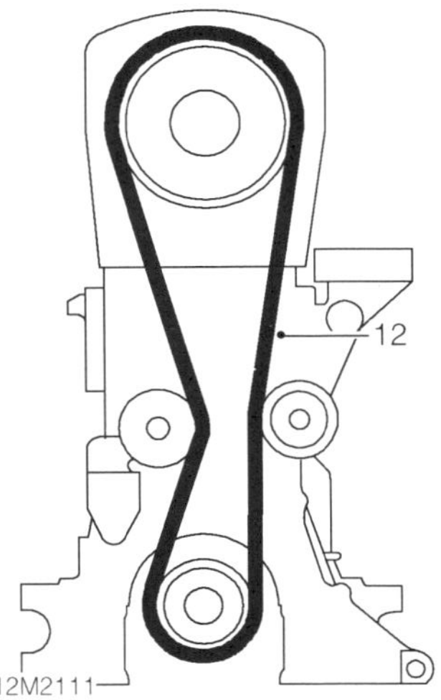

12M2111

12. Using the fingers only, ease timing belt from gears.
13. Remove tensioner retractor tool **LRT-12-143.**

CAUTION: Do not rotate camshaft or crankshaft with timing belt removed and cylinder head fitted.

Tensioner - remove

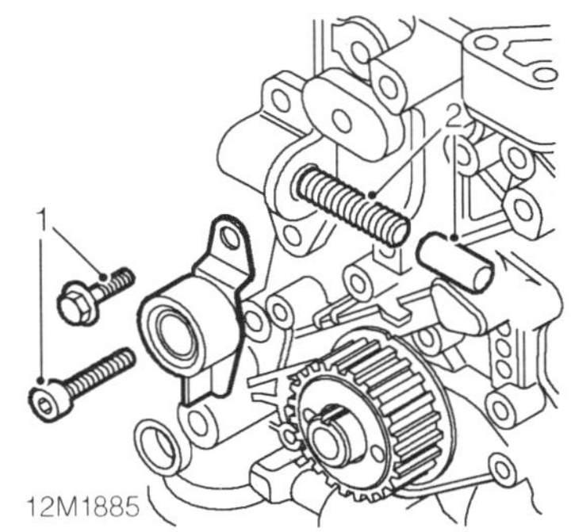

12M1885

1. Remove Allen screw and bolt securing timing belt tensioner. Remove tensioner.
2. Remove tensioner spring and plunger.

Camshaft timing belt and tensioner - inspection

1. Inspect timing belt for signs of splits at base of teeth, fraying, oil contamination or uneven wear. Renew timing belt if it fails inspection. The camshaft timing belt is replaced at 48 000 miles, 80 000 km.

CAUTION: If timing belt is contaminated with oil, cause of oil contamination must be rectified. Timing belts must be stored and handled with care. Always store a belt on its edge with a bend radius greater than 30 mm. Do not use a belt which has been bent double or twisted as this can fracture the reinforcing fibres. Do not use a belt that has been contaminated with oil.

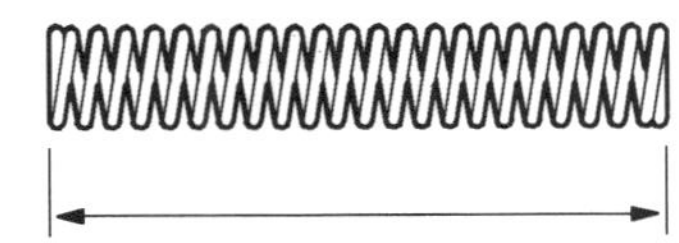
12M1886

2. Check tensioner spring for distortion, check spring free length:
   Free length = 65 mm.
3. Check tensioner plunger and bore of housing for wear and corrosion.

CAUTION: Do not attempt to remove corrosion by means of emery cloth, components must be replaced.

4. Check that tensioner and idler pulleys rotate smoothly and belt surfaces are smooth and clean.
5. Check that sealing strips in upper and lower covers are not split or damaged, replace as necessary.

Tensioner - refit

1. Ensure that bore of plunger housing is clean.

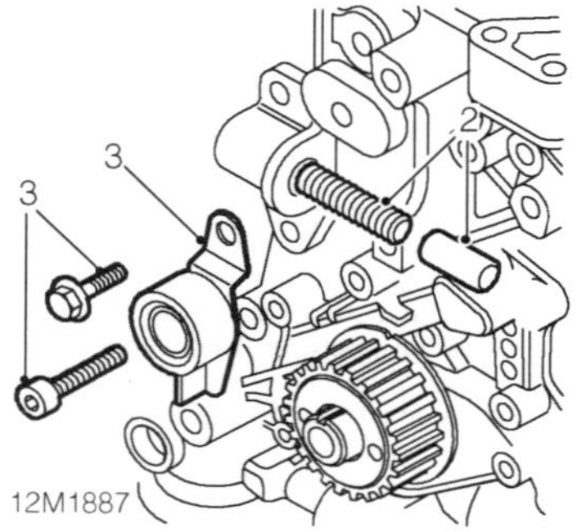

12M1887

2. Smear tensioner plunger with molybdenum disulphide based grease, locate spring and plunger in housing.
3. Position tensioner on cylinder block, fit and tighten bolt to 45 Nm, fit but do not fully tighten Allen screw.

Camshaft timing belt - refit and adjust

⚠ **CAUTION: It is important that a new timing belt is pre-tensioned before adjustment is carried out.**

1. Clean tensioner and idler pulleys and timing belt gears.
2. Check that camshaft timing belt upper and lower cover sealing strips are correctly located in covers.

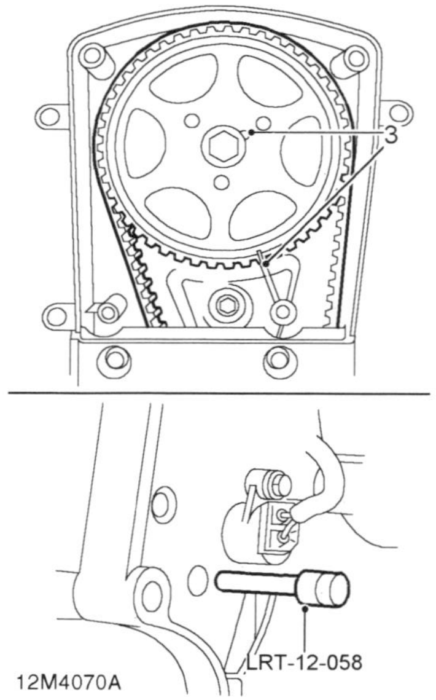

12M4070A

3. Ensure that timing pin **LRT-12-058** is inserted in flywheel, and camshaft gear timing mark is aligned exactly with pointer on timing belt upper rear cover.

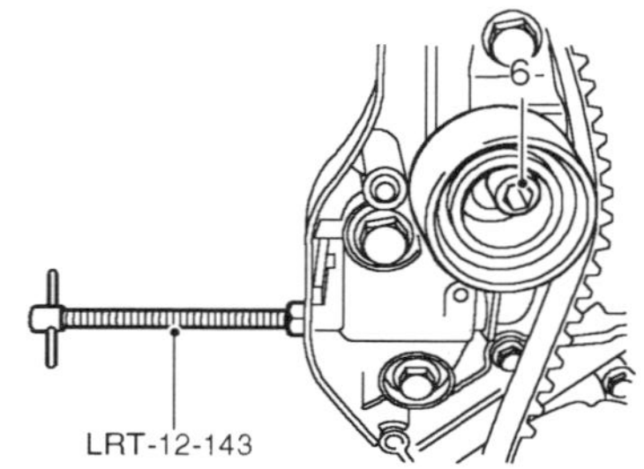

12M4071A

4. Screw timing belt tensioner retractor tool **LRT-12-143** into tensioner plunger until it is flush with the end of the plunger , tighten nut on tool to fully retract tensioner.
5. Using the fingers only, ease timing belt over crankshaft and camshaft gears keeping it as taut as possible on the idler pulley side.
6. Slacken Allen screw until tensioner pulley moves easily without tipping.
7. Turn centre spindle of **LRT-12-143** clockwise 14 complete turns to pre-tension timing belt. Tighten tensioner Allen screw to 55 Nm.
8. Fit crankshaft pulley and bolt, tighten bolt to 63 Nm. Do not tighten bolt further at this stage.
9. Remove timing pin **LRT-12-058**

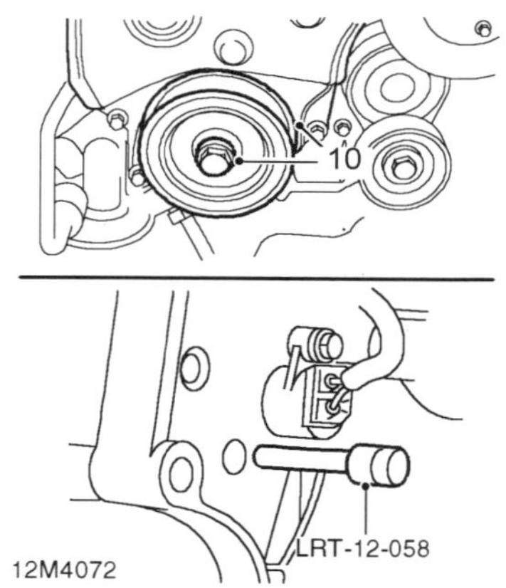

12M4072

10. Using crankshaft pulley bolt, rotate crankshaft clockwise 6 complete turns. Refit timing pin **LRT-12-058** into flywheel.

⚠ **CAUTION: Do not use camshaft timing belt gear or fuel injection pump drive belt gear to rotate crankshaft.**

11. Check that camshaft gear timing mark is aligned with pointer on timing belt upper rear cover.

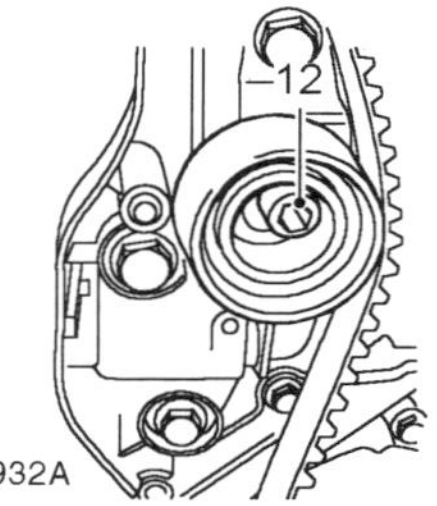

12M1932A

12. Loosen tensioner Allen screw. Remove tensioner tool LRT-12-143.
13. Tighten tensioner Allen screw to 55 Nm.
14. Insert access plug into lower rear cover.
15. Remove crankshaft pulley bolt and pulley.

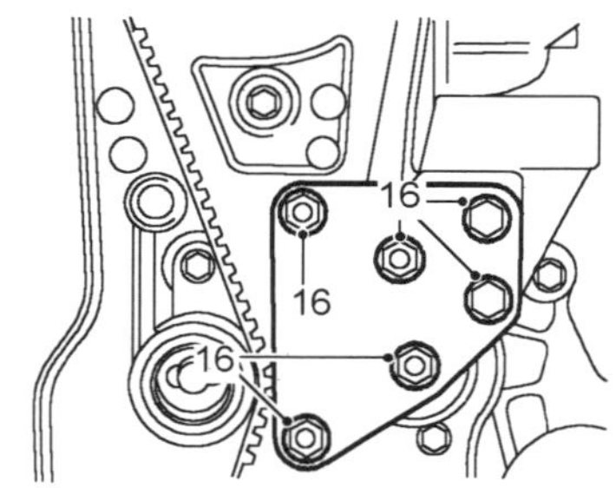

12m1930A

16. Fit engine front mounting plate, fit 4 nuts and 2 bolts and tighten bolts to 45 Nm and nuts to 35 Nm.

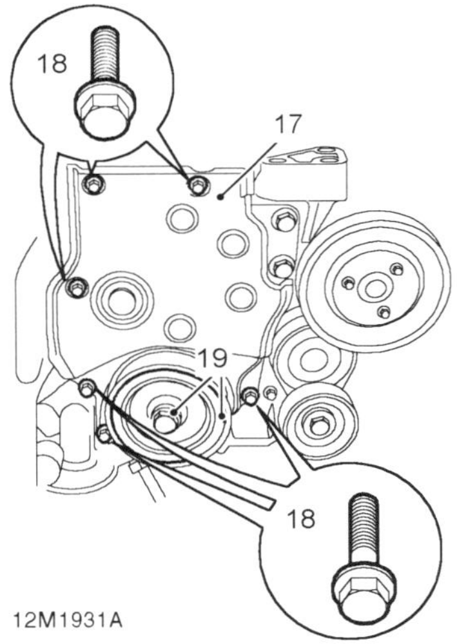

12M1931A

17. Position camshaft timing belt lower front cover to timing belt lower rear cover.
18. Fit lower front cover securing screws ensuring that 3 longest screws are in correct fitted position, tighten all screws to 5 Nm.
19. Fit crankshaft pulley and bolt, tighten bolt to 63 Nm then a further 90°.

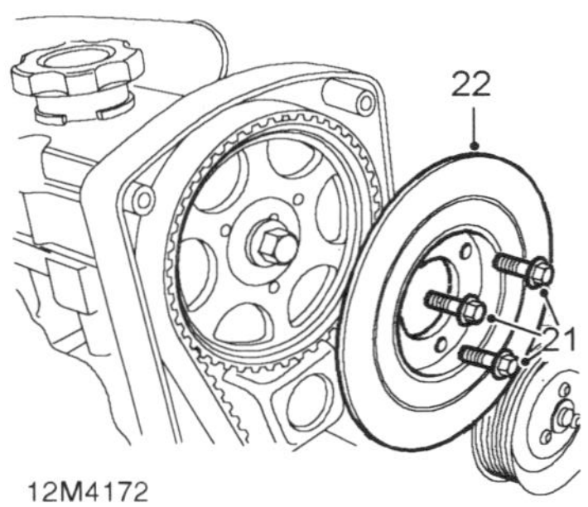

12M4172

20. Fit camshaft gear damper, ensuring that the timing mark on the damper is aligned to the timing mark on the camshaft gear.
21. Fit new 'Patchlok' torx screws and tighten to 10 Nm.
22. Remove timing pin **LRT-12-058** from flywheel.

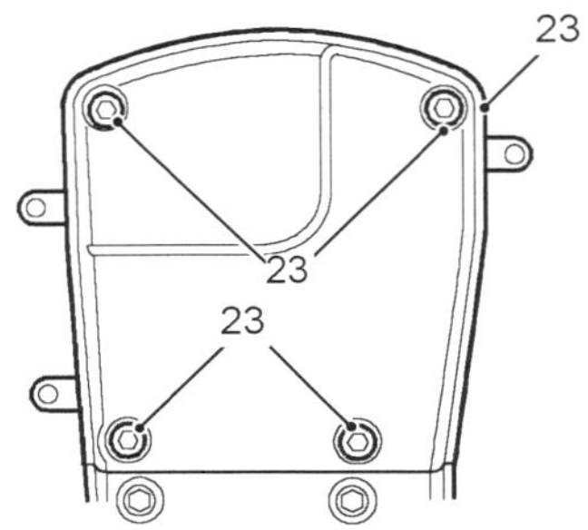

12M1933A

23. Position camshaft timing belt upper front cover to rear cover, fit and tighten screws to 5 Nm.

CYLINDER HEAD ASSEMBLY

Remove

1. Remove camshaft timing belt.

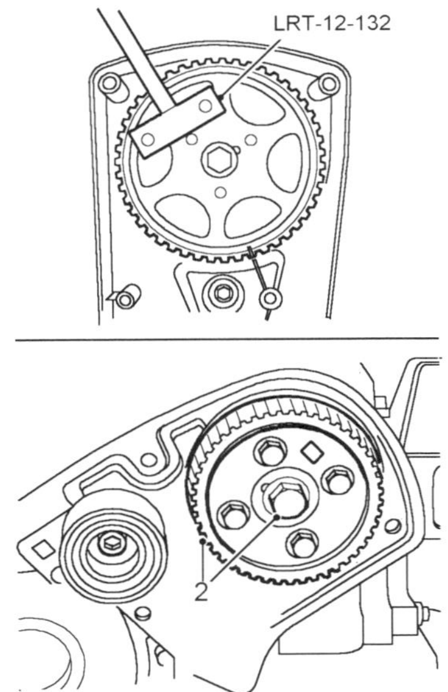

12M4073A

2. Restrain camshaft timing belt gear using tool **LRT-12-132** and remove bolt securing fuel injection pump drive belt gear to camshaft, remove gear, discard bolt.

CAUTION: Ensure camshaft does not rotate when removing bolt and do not rotate crankshaft or camshaft with timing belt removed and cylinder head fitted.

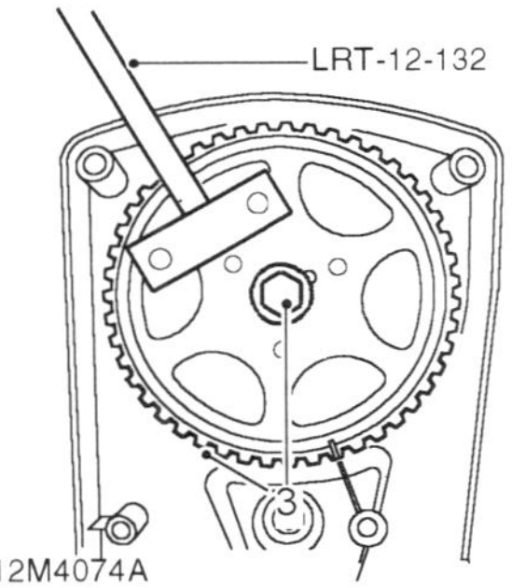

12M4074A

3. Restrain camshaft timing belt gear using tool **LRT-12-132** and remove bolt securing camshaft timing belt gear. Remove gear and discard bolt.

CAUTION: Ensure camshaft does not rotate when removing bolt and do not rotate crankshaft or camshaft with timing belt removed and cylinder head fitted.

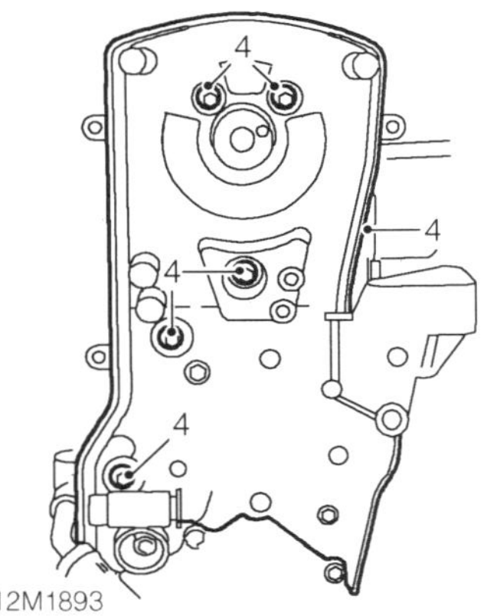

12M1893

4. Remove 5 screws securing camshaft timing belt upper rear cover, remove cover, recover sealing strip.

NOTE: Shortest screws are fitted in camshaft carrier.

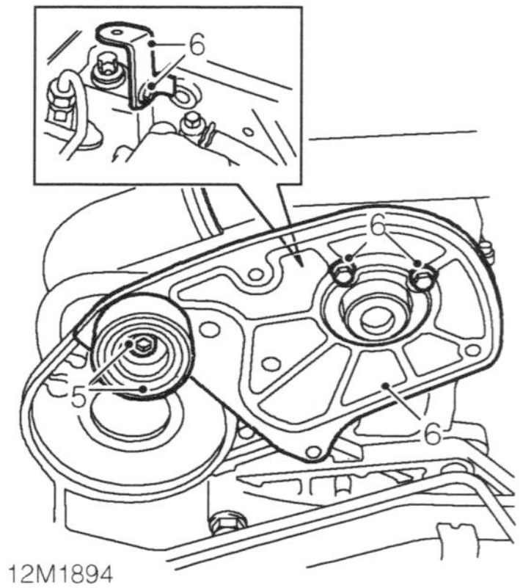

12M1894

5. Remove Allen screw securing fuel injection pump drive belt tensioner, remove tensioner.
6. Remove 3 screws securing fuel injection pump drive belt rear cover, remove cover and collect bracket.

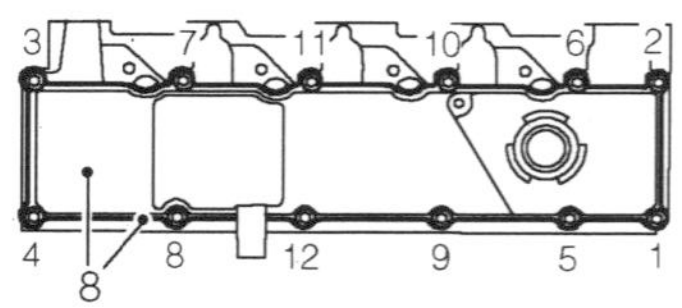

12M1895

7. Using sequence shown, progressively slacken then remove 12 bolts securing camshaft cover.
8. Remove camshaft cover and discard gasket.

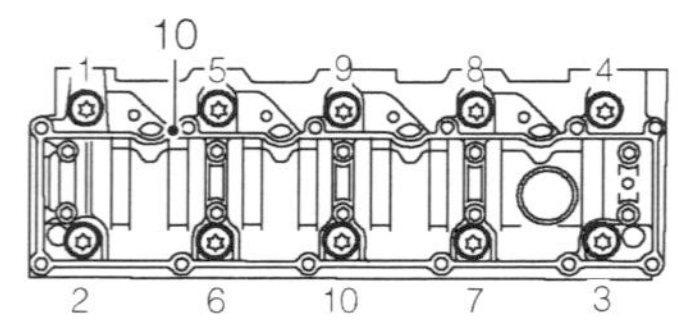

12M1896

9. Using sequence shown, progressively slacken then remove 10 head Torx bolts and washers.

CAUTION: Keep bolts in their fitted order, do not attempt to remove washers from bolts.

10. Using assistance, remove cylinder head assembly and support each end of cylinder head on blocks of wood to protect valves which, when open, protrude below face of cylinder head.

CAUTION: Cylinder head is dowel located, do not tap it sideways to free it from cylinder block.

11. Remove and discard cylinder head gasket.

Camshaft - check end-float

NOTE: Prior to removing the camshaft, check end-float.

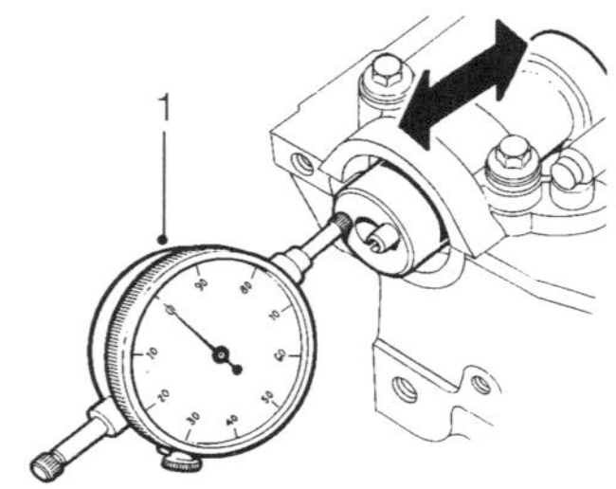

12M1897

1. Position a suitable DTI to front of camshaft. Move camshaft rearwards and zero DTI. Move camshaft forwards and measure end-float: End-float - maximum = 0.51 mm.

CAUTION: Camshaft end-float is controlled by the width of Number 1 bearing in the camshaft carrier. If end-float exceeds the above dimension, remove the camshaft and repeat the end-float check using a new camshaft. If end-float still exceeds the maximum, a new cylinder head and camshaft carrier asssembly must be fitted.

Camshaft - remove

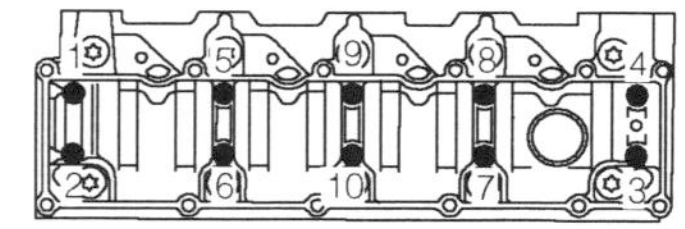

12M1898

1. Using sequence shown, slacken the 10 camshaft carrier retaining bolts 2 to 3 turns.

CAUTION: Do not fully remove bolts at this stage.

2. Gently tap the camshaft carrier upwards to break the sealant bond.

CAUTION: Camshaft carrier is dowel located, do not tap it sideways.

3. Using the same sequence, continue to progressively slacken the carrier retaining bolts until all loading is removed from the carrier.

CAUTION: If bolts are removed completely before loading is removed from the camshaft carrier, the carrier may be suddenly released and damage caused as a result.

4. Remove retaining bolts, remove camshaft carrier.

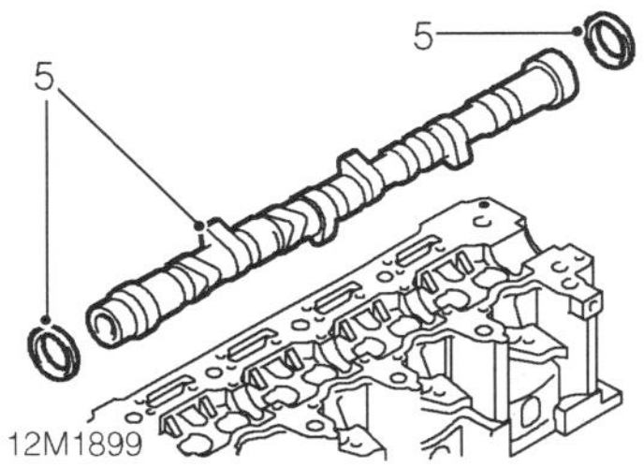

12M1899

5. Remove camshaft, remove and discard front and rear oil seals.

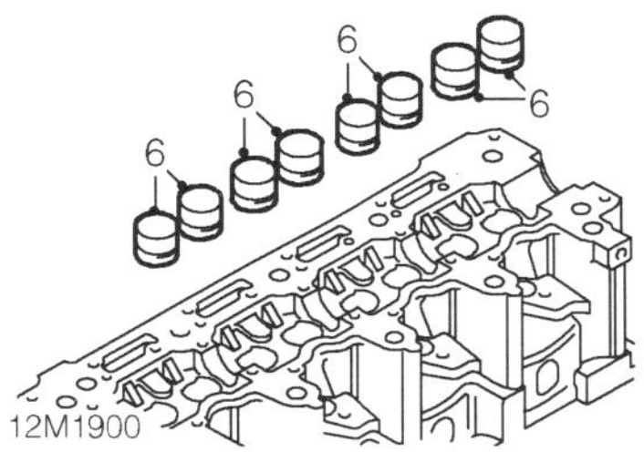

12M1900

6. Using a stick magnet, remove 8 tappets from the cylinder head.

CAUTION: Keep tappets in their fitted order and store inverted to prevent oil loss. Do not squeeze tappet chambers together.

Valves and springs - remove

1. Support cylinder head clear of valves, use a hollow drift and tap each spring cap to free collets.

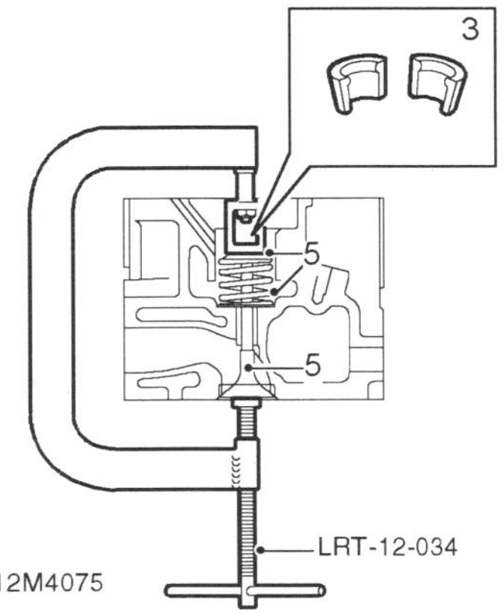

12M4075

2. Using tool **LRT-12-034**, compress valve spring.
3. Remove 2 collets from valve stem using a stick magnet.
4. Remove tool **LRT-12-034.**
5. Remove spring cap and valve spring, remove valve.

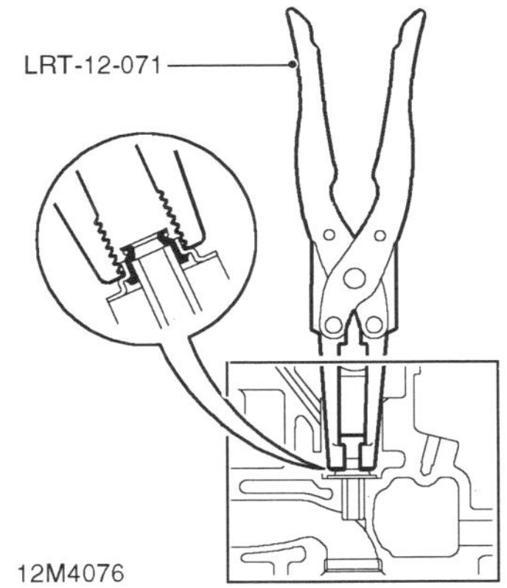

12M4076

6. Using tool **LRT-12-071**, remove valve stem oil seal; discard seal.
7. Repeat above operations to remove remaining valves.

CAUTION: Keep component parts of each valve assembly in their fitted order.

Cylinder head - inspection

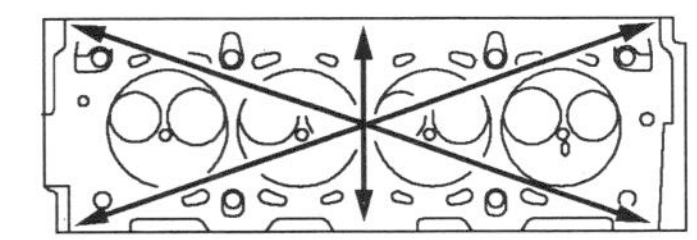
12M1903

1. Check cylinder head for warpage across centre and from corner to corner:
   Maximum warpage = 0.010 mm

CAUTION: Cylinder head may not be refaced. Replace head assembly if warpage exceeds figure given.

2. Check tappet bores for scoring and signs of wear or damage. Slight scoring or burring may be removed using fine emery cloth.

Tappets - inspection

1. Check tappets for signs of wear, scoring and overheating, replace as necessary.
2. Ensure oil hole in each tappet is clear.
3. Check outside diameter of each tappet: Diameter = 34.959 to 34.975 mm.

⚠ **CAUTION: Keep tappets in their fitted order and store inverted to prevent oil loss. Do not squeeze tappet chambers together.**

Camshaft and bearings - inspection

1. Check camshaft cams and bearing journals for signs of scoring and excessive wear.

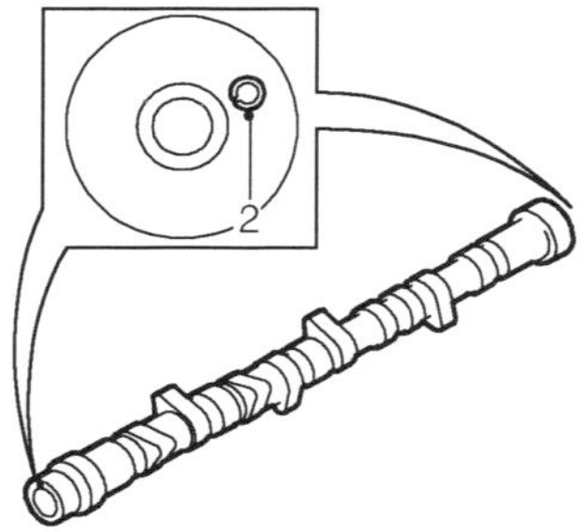

12M1904

2. Check camshaft timing belt gear and fuel injection pump drive belt gear drive pins for damage and wear, replace if necessary ensuring that split in pin faces towards centre of camshaft.
3. Check bearing journals in cylinder head and camshaft carrier for signs of scoring and excessive wear.

⚠ **CAUTION: Cylinder head and camshaft carrier are machined together as an assembly. If bearing journals in either component are found to be damaged, complete assembly must be replaced.**

Camshaft bearings - check clearance

1. Clean all traces of oil from camshaft, cylinder head and camshaft carrier.
2. Use a suitable cleaning solvent and plastic scraper to remove all traces of sealant from cylinder head and camshaft carrier.

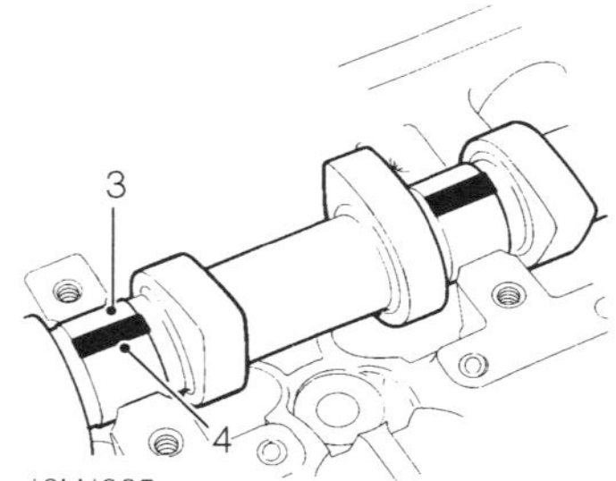

12M1905

3. Position camshaft in cylinder head.
4. Place a piece of Plastigage along the centre line of each camshaft journal.
5. Support each end of cylinder head on blocks of wood.

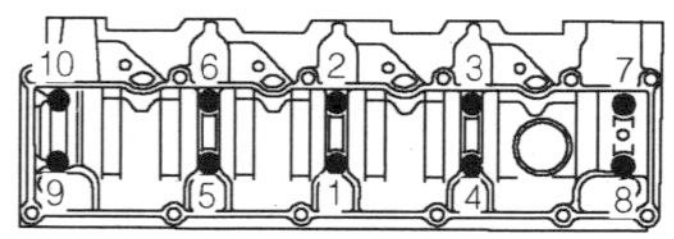

12M1906

6. Carefully fit the camshaft carrier, fit 10 retaining bolts and tighten in sequence shown to 11 Nm.

⚠ **CAUTION: Do not rotate camshaft.**

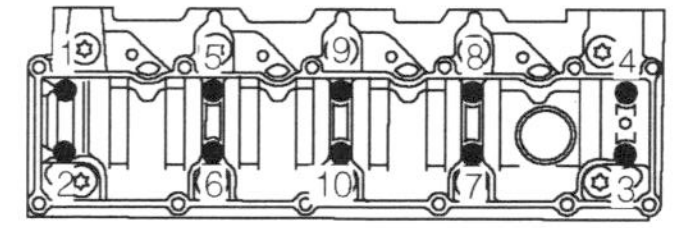

12M1898

7. Using sequence shown, progressively slacken, then remove 10 retaining bolts.
8. Carefully remove camshaft carrier.

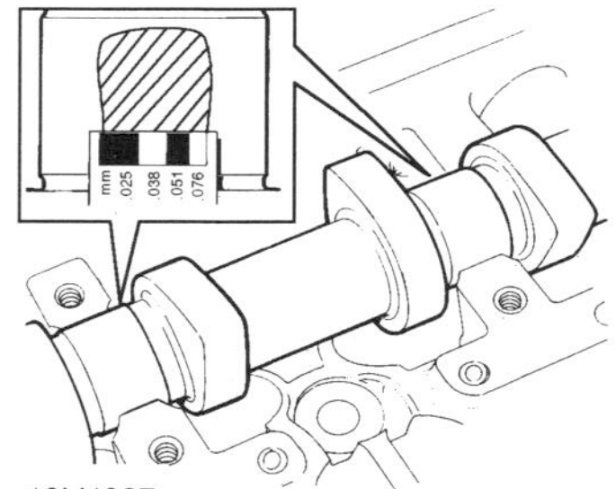

12M1907

9. Measure and record widest portion of Plastigage on each camshaft journal.
10. Compare figures obtained with camshaft bearing clearance: Bearing clearance = 0.043 to 0.094 mm
11. If any bearing clearance is found to be excessive, repeat the above procedure using a new camshaft.

⚠ **CAUTION: If, after repeating the bearing clearance check with a new camshaft the clearances are still excessive, a new cylinder head and camshaft carrier assembly must be fitted.**

12. Remove Plastigage using an oily cloth, do not use a scraper.

Valve springs - inspection

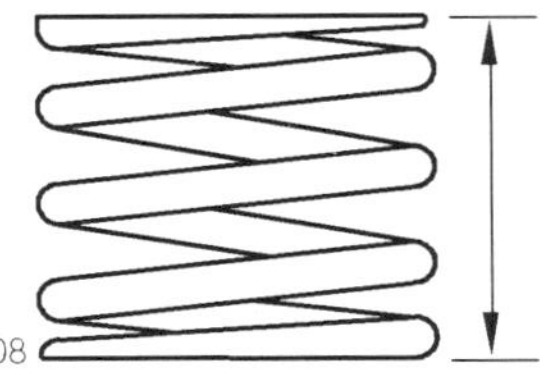

12M1908

1. Check valve springs free length:
   Free length = 37mm

CAUTION: Valve springs must be replaced as a set.

Valves and valve guides - inspection

1. Clean carbon from valves, check valves for burning, pitting or cracking; replace as necessary.

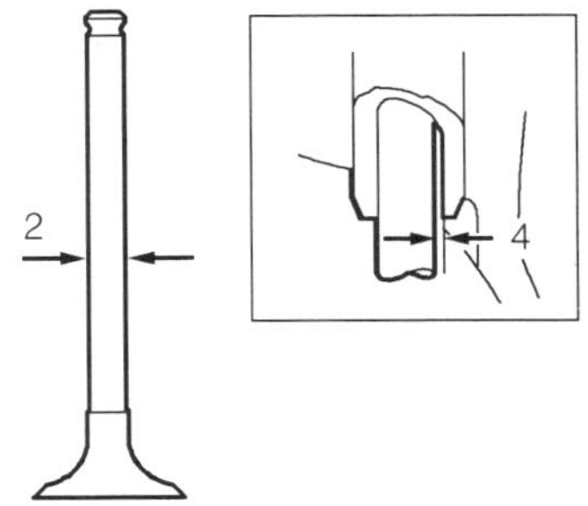

12M1909

2. Check and record diameter of each valve stem:
   Inlet = 6.907 to 6.923 mm.
   Exhaust = 6.897 to 6.913 mm.
3. Renew any valve if stem diameter is less than specified.
4. Insert each valve into its respective guide.
5. Extend valve out of seat by 10mm.
6. Position a DTi gauge against valve head, zero gauge, then rock valve head to check movement.

   Inlet valve = 0.056 mm.
   Exhaust valve = 0.066 mm.
7. Renew any guide and its associated valve if clearance is excessive.

Valve guides - renew

1. Check area on camshaft side of cylinder head around valve guide to be replaced for marks denoting previous valve guide replacement:
   \+ denotes 1st replacement
   \- denotes 2nd replacement

CAUTION: Valve guides may only be replaced twice.

2. Heat cylinder head uniformly to a temperature of 120°C.

WARNING: Take care when handling hot cylinder head.

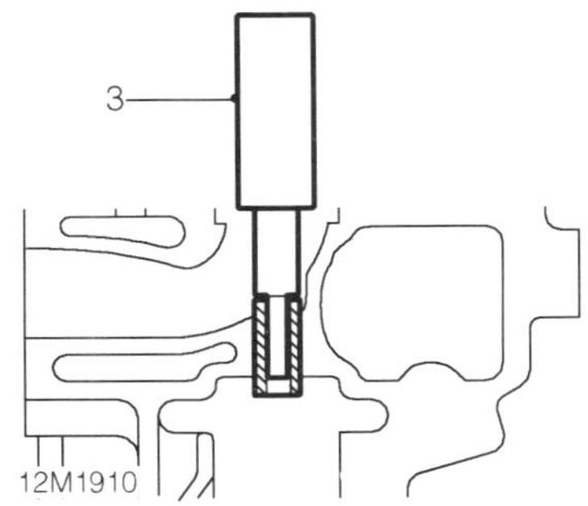

12M1910

3. Using a suitable pilotted mandrel, press valve guide out of cylinder head from combustion face side; discard guide.

NOTE: Only one size of replacement guide is available.

4. Reheat cylinder head to 120°C.

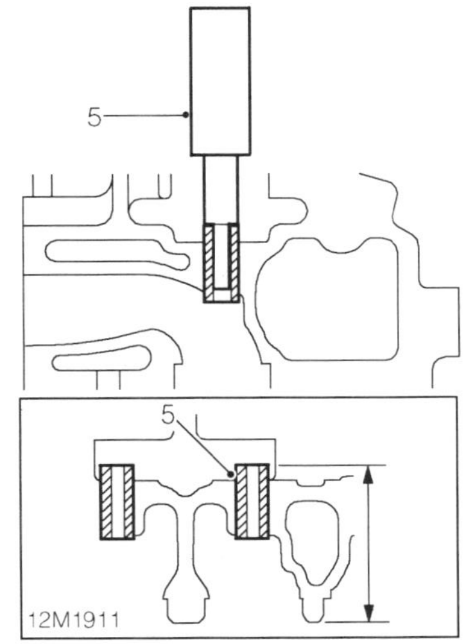

12M1911

5. Using the pilotted mandrel, press replacement valve guide into cylinder head from camshaft side of head until fitted height of guide from combustion face side of cylinder head to top of guide is 61.1 to 61.7 mm
6. Allow cylinder head to air cool.
7. Ream bores of replacement valve guide ensuring that reamer is kept perpendicular to and concentric with valve seat.
   Valve guide bore diameter = 6.950 to 6.963 mm

CAUTION: If valve seat insert has also been replaced, guide and insert must be machined together.

8. Suitably mark cylinder head on camshaft side of head to denote that guide has been replaced.
   1st replacement guide +
   2nd replacement valve guide -

CAUTION: A new valve must always be fitted whenever a guide is replaced.

Valve seat inserts and valves - refacing and lapping-in

Refacing valve seat inserts

1. Check valve seat inserts for pitting and burning, if necessary, valve seats may be refaced providing valve head stand down is within limits after refacing.

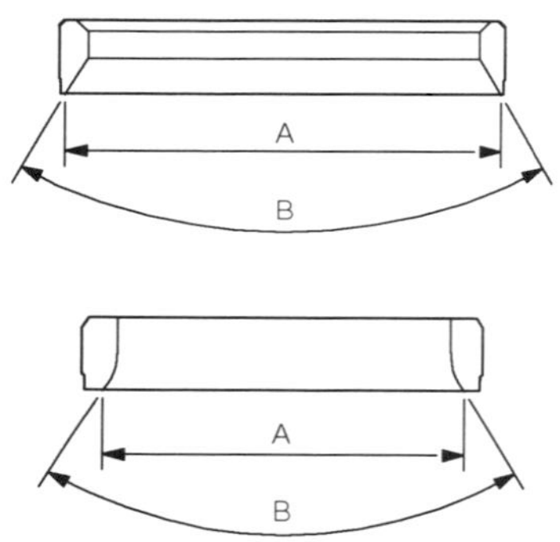

12M1912

2. Using a suitable pilotted cutter, cut valve seat insert to correct angle and width:

Inlet valve seat insert:
Seat width A = 35.697 mm
Seat angle B = 60°

Exhaust valve insert:
Seat width A = 31.05 to 31.55 mm
Seat angle B = 58°to 62°

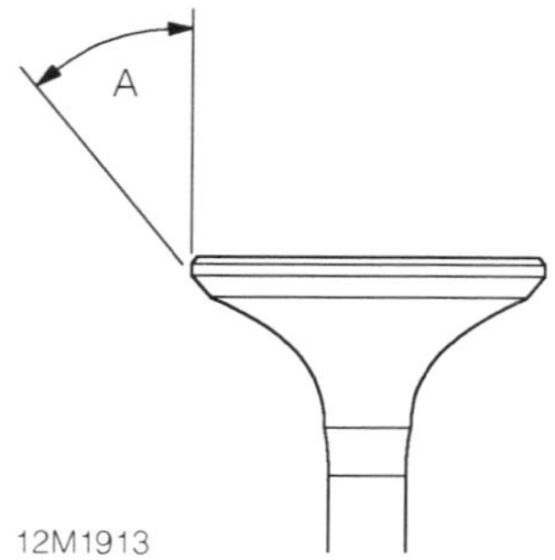

12M1913

3. Check face angle **A** of each valve, renew any valve with incorrect face angles, do not attempt to recut.
Valve face angle - Inlet and exhaust = 45°to 45°30'.

Lapping-in valves

1. Lap each valve to its seat using grinding paste.
2. Apply Prussian Blue to valve seat, insert valve into guide and press it firmly, without rotating, on to seat.

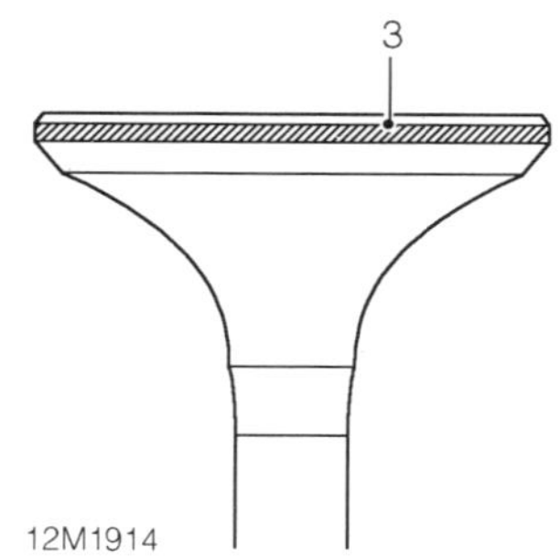

12M1914

3. Remove valve and check that a continuous, even line of Prussian Blue has been transferred on to valve face; continue lapping-in valve as necessary.

NOTE: Line does not have to be across whole width of valve face.

4. On completion of lapping-in, check valve head stand down. ***See this section***

Valve head stand down

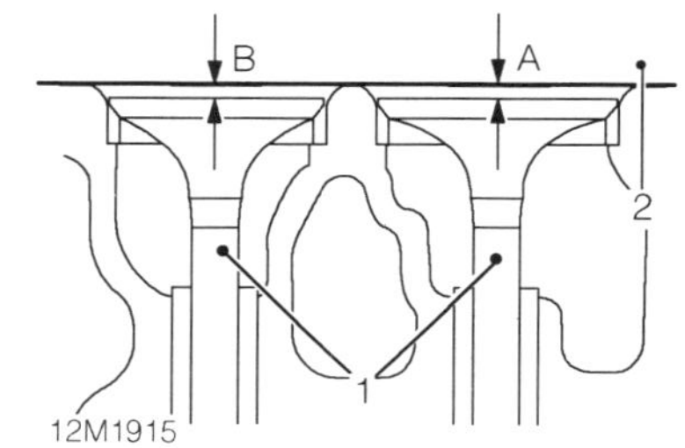

12M1915

1. Insert each valve into its respective guide.
2. Using a straight-edge and feeler gauges, check and record stand down of each valve head.
3. Compare figures obtained with figures given below. If any valve has a stand down greater than specified, valve seat insert and valve must be replaced:
Valve head stand down:
Inlet valve **A**= 1.45 mm.
Exhaust valve **B**= 1.35 mm.

Cylinder head bolts - inspection

1. Keeping bolts in their fitted order, clean bolts and washers, lightly oil threads.

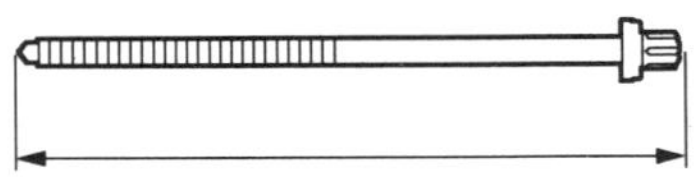

12M1916

2. Check bolt heads and threads for damage, replace individual bolts as necessary.
3. Check length of bolt from top of bolt head to end of bolt. If any bolt exceeds 243.41 mm in length, all 10 bolts and washers must be replaced.

CAUTION: Do not attempt to remove washers from bolts. Keep bolts in their original fitted order.

Cylinder head and camshaft carrier - cleaning

CAUTION: Use a suitable solvent to remove old sealant from cylinder head and camshaft carrier faces.

1. Clean mating surfaces of cylinder head and camshaft carrier, remove any deposits from camshaft oil seal recesses using a plastic scraper.
2. Clean gasket material from cylinder head and block using gasket removal spray and plastic scraper.

CAUTION: Do not use a metal scraper.

3. Clean all traces of carbon from combustion face areas.
4. Blow out all oilways and waterways.
5. Ensure threaded holes in cylinder block and camshaft carrier are clean and dry.
6. Check core plugs for corrosion and signs of leakage and replace if necessary; use Loctite 577 to seal replacement plugs.

Valves - assembling

1. Using tool **LRT-12-071,** fit new valve stem oil seals.
2. Lubricate valve stem oil seals, valve guides, valve stems, spring caps and springs with engine oil.
3. Assemble valves, springs and spring caps ensuring that they are in their correct fitted order.
4. Compress valve springs using tool **LRT-12-034,** fit collets, remove tool.
5. Using a wooden dowel and mallet, tap each spring cap lightly to seat collets.

Tappets and camshafts - assembling

1. Lubricate tappets and tappet bores with engine oil.
2. Fit tappets ensuring they are in their correct fitted order.
3. Lubricate cams and bearing journals on camshaft, cylinder head and camshaft carrier with engine oil.

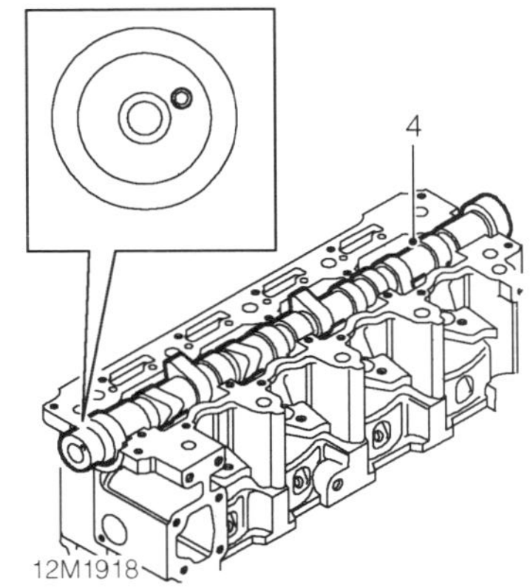

12M1918

4. Position camshaft in cylinder head with timing belt gear drive pin at approximately 2 o'clock position.
5. Support ends of cylinder head on blocks of wood.

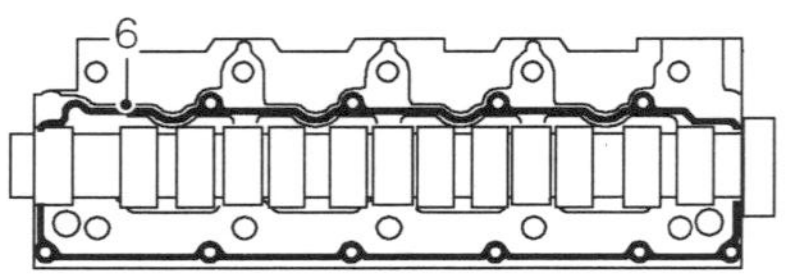

12M1919

6. Using sealant from kit, Part Number GUG 705548 GM, apply an even film of sealant to cylinder head; spread sealant to an even film using a brush or roller.

CAUTION: Ensure sealant does not block oilways or is spread on to bearing journals.

7. Fit camshaft carrier, fit and finger tighten bolts.

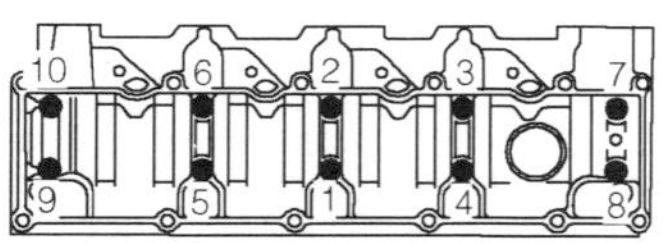

12M1906

CAUTION: With camshaft carrier bolted down, some valves will protrude below face of cylinder head; support each end of cylinder head on blocks of wood.

8. Using sequence shown, progressively tighten camshaft carrier bolts to 11 Nm.

CAUTION: Bolts must be tightened to correct torque within 20 minutes of applying sealant.

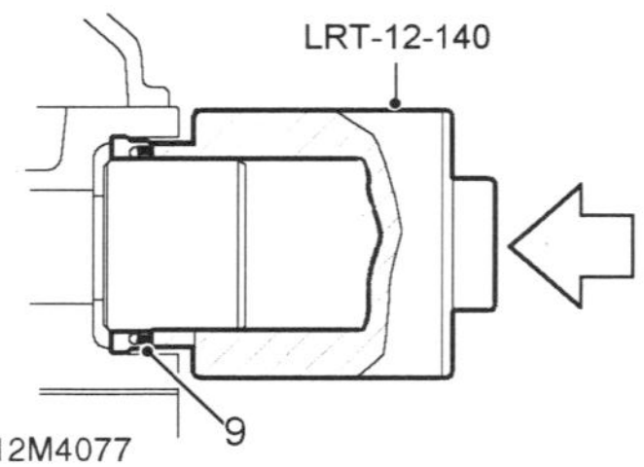

12M4077

9. Lubricate new camshaft front and rear oil seals with engine oil.
10. Fit oil seals using using tool **LRT-12-140**.

Cylinder head gasket selection

NOTE: There are three thicknesses of cylinder head gasket available and in order that the correct gasket is fitted, it is necessary to determine the stand proud (protrusion) of each piston above the top face of the cylinder block.

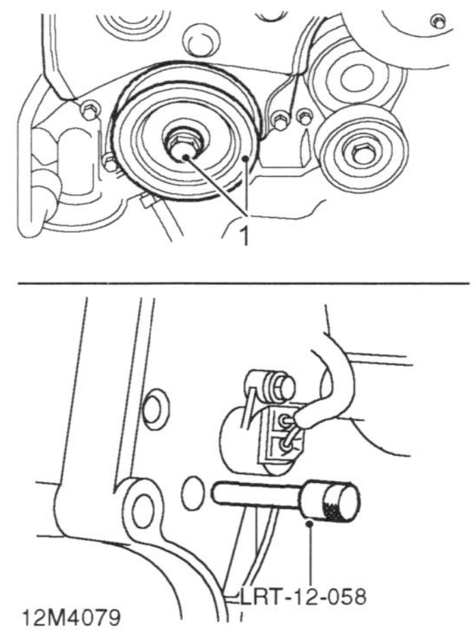

12M4079

NOTE: Gaskets have either 1, 2 or 3 identification holes and the following procedure must be followed in order that the correct gasket is selected.

1. Temporarily assemble pulley to crankshaft, fit and finger tighten bolt.
2. Remove timing pin **LRT-12-058** - if fitted.

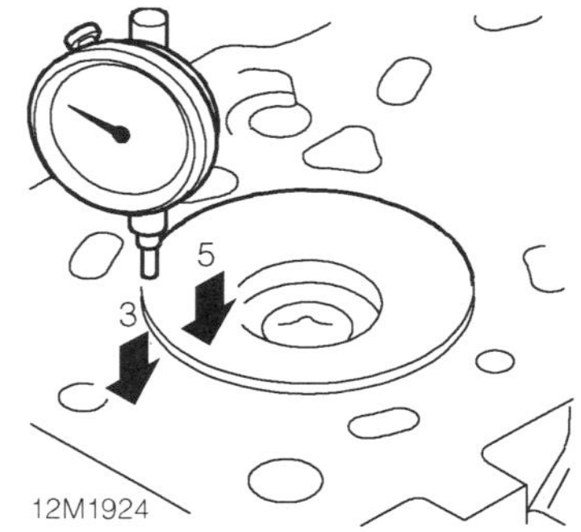

12M1924

3. Assemble a magnetic base DTI to cylinder block top face, zero DTI with stylus touching block top face.
4. Rotate crankshaft in a clockwise direction until Number 1 piston is at TDC.
5. Position stylus near edge of piston crown, measure and record Number 1 piston protrusion.

NOTE: Measurement must be taken at front and rear of piston.

6. Repeat above procedure for remaining pistons.

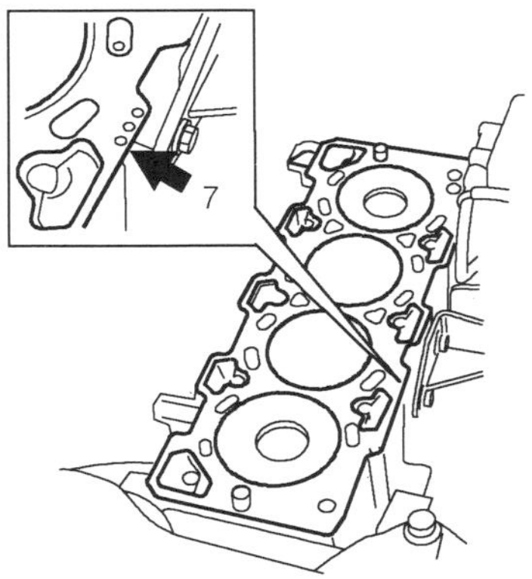

12M1923

7. From readings obtained, determine highest piston protrusion figure and select the appropriate cylinder head gasket:
Protrusion 0.10 to 0.25 mm - Select gasket with one identification hole.
Protrusion 0.25 to 0.40 mm - Select gasket with two identification holes.
Protrusion 0.40 to 0.55 mm - Select gasket with three identification holes.

Cylinder head - refit

1. Fit crankshaft pulley bolt and washer and tighten bolt to 63Nm. Do not tighten bolt further at this stage.
2. Remove timing pin **LRT-12-058.**
3. Ensure that cylinder block and head faces are clean and dry and that all traces of gasket material have been removed. Check that cylinder head location dowels are fitted in cylinder block.

12M1925

4. Check that oil feed restrictor in cylinder block is clear and that restrictor is below block face.
5. Ensure that cylinder head bolt holes in cylinder block are clean and dry.
6. Using crankshaft pulley bolt, rotate crankshaft anti-clockwise until Numbers 1 and 4 pistons are approximately 25 mm below cylinder block top face.
7. Position camshaft timing gear drive pin at 2 o'clock.
8. Position selected cylinder head gasket on cylinder block ensuring that it is correctly orientated.

CAUTION: Gasket must be fitted dry.

9. Using assistance, fit cylinder head ensuring that it is correctly located on dowels.
10. Lubricate cylinder head bolt threads and undersides of bolt heads with engine oil.

CAUTION: Do not oil undersides of washers.

11. Carefully enter cylinder head bolts in their fitted order. **DO NOT DROP BOLTS INTO CYLINDER BLOCK.**

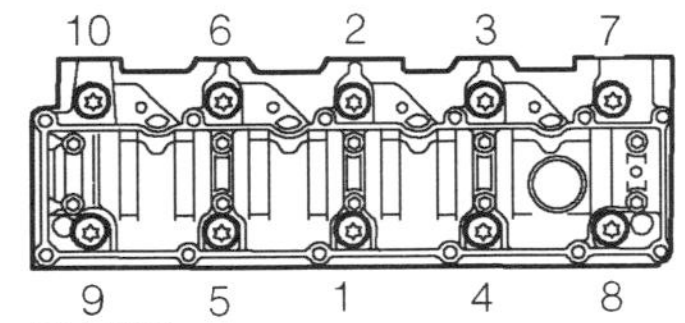

12M1920

12. Using sequence shown, tighten cylinder head bolts to:
Stage 1 - 30 Nm
Stage 2 - 65 Nm
Stage 3 - Further 90°
Stage 4 - Further 90°

CAUTION: Ensure that correct tightening sequence is followed for all four tightening stages.

13. Fit fuel injection pump drive belt rear cover and mounting bracket, fit 3 screws and tighten to 8 Nm.
14. Fit fuel injection pump drive belt tensioner, fit but do not fully tighten Allen screw.
15. Ensure sealing strip is correctly located on camshaft timing belt upper rear cover.
16. Fit upper rear cover ensuring that 2 shortest screws are fitted in camshaft carrier.
17. Tighten screws to 8 Nm.

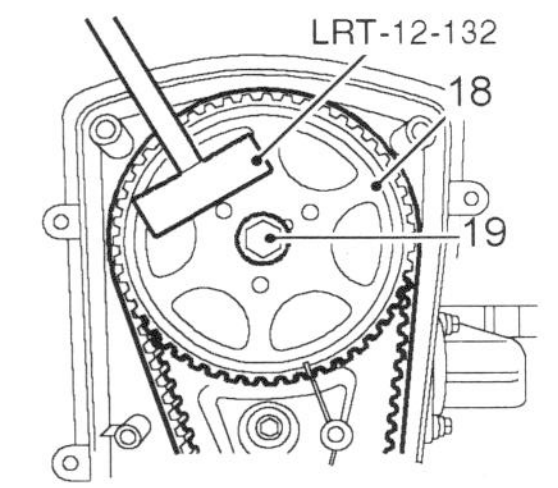

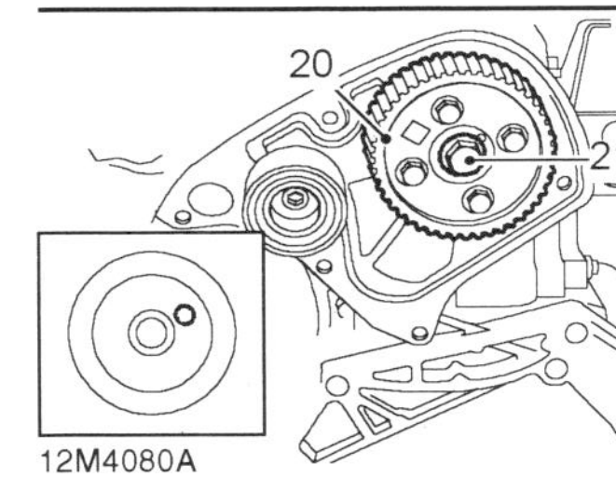

12M4080A

18. Fit camshaft timing belt gear, fit a new bolt.
19. Restrain camshaft timing belt gear using tool **LRT-12-132** and tighten bolt to 20 Nm then a further 90°.
20. Fit fuel pump drive belt gear to camshaft, use a new bolt.
21. Restrain camshaft timing belt gear using tool **LRT-12-132** and tighten fuel pump drive belt gear bolt to 20 Nm then a further 90°.

CAUTION: Ensure camshaft does not rotate as bolts are tightened.

22. Ensure that camshaft gear timing mark is aligned with pointer on timing belt upper rear cover.

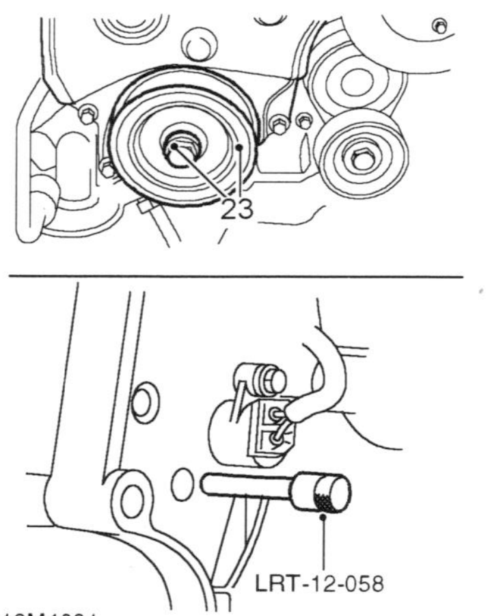

12M4081

23. Using crankshaft pulley bolt, carefully rotate crankshaft clockwise until timing pin **LRT-12-058** can be inserted in hole in flywheel.

CAUTION: Do not rotate crankshaft too far, pistons may contact the valves.

24. Remove crankshaft pulley bolt and washer.
25. Fit timing belt and adjust tension.

CAUTION: Ensure crankshaft pulley bolt is fully tightened.

26. Fit a new gasket to camshaft cover ensuring that raised holes in gasket are towards the cover and are located on the two spigots.

CAUTION: Gasket must be fitted dry.

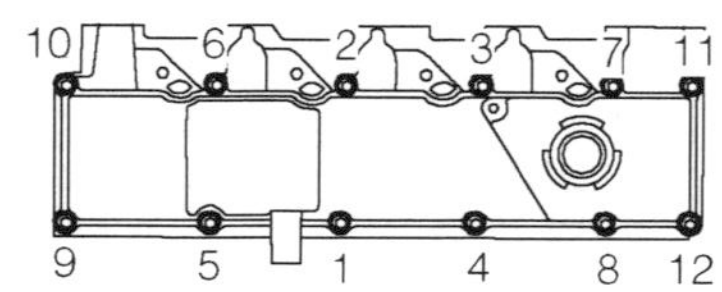

12M1928

27. Fit camshaft cover bolts and tighten in sequence shown to 12Nm.

FLYWHEEL AND STARTER RING GEAR

Flywheel - remove

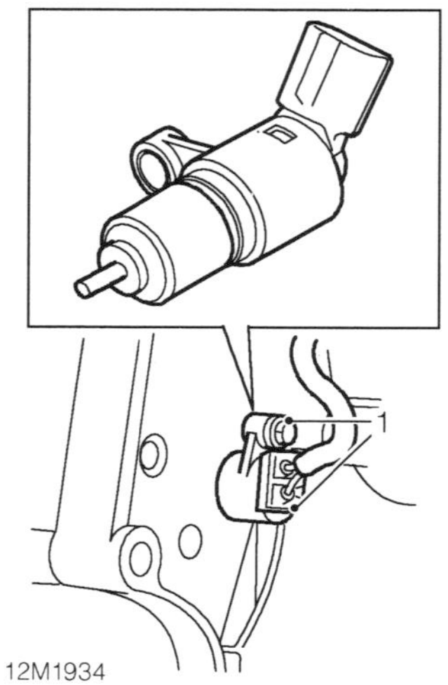

12M1934

1. Remove bolt securing crankshaft sensor to gearbox adaptor plate. Remove sensor.

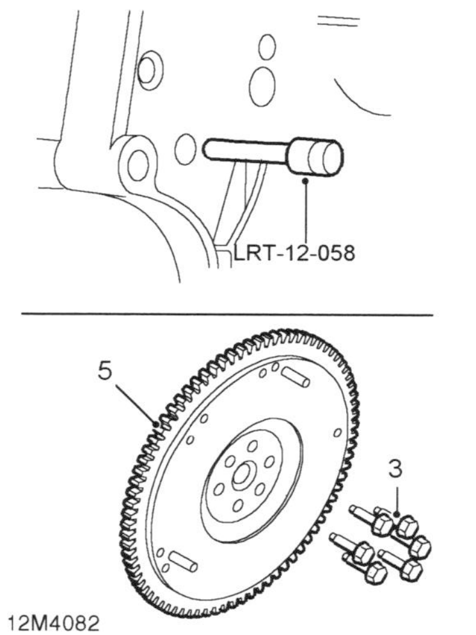

12M4082

2. Insert timing pin **LRT-12-058** into flywheel.
3. Remove and discard 6 bolts securing flywheel to crankshaft.
4. Remove timing pin **LRT-12-058.**
5. Using assistance, remove flywheel.

NOTE: Dowel located.

Starter ring gear - remove

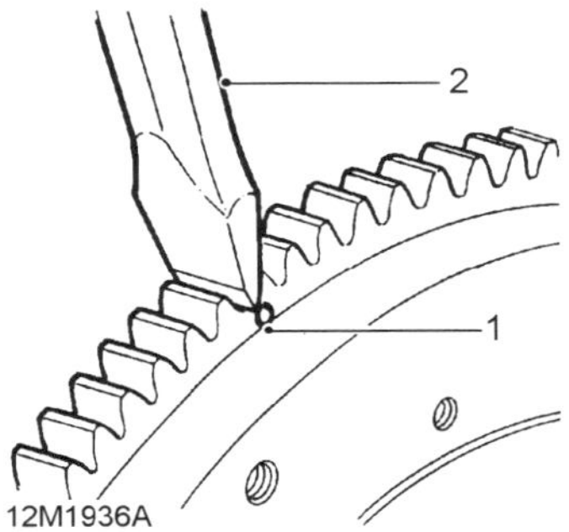

12M1936A

1. Drill a 3 mm diameter hole at the root of 2 teeth.
2. Apply a cold chisel to root of teeth, break ring gear and remove from flywheel.

WARNING: Suitable eye protection must be worn.

Starter ring gear - refit

1. Heat ring gear evenly to 350°C indicated by light blue colour. Locate ring gear on flywheel and press on to flange.

WARNING: Handle hot ring gear with care.

2. Allow ring gear to air cool.

Flywheel - refit

1. Clean threads in crankshaft using an old flywheel bolt having 2 saw cuts at 45°along thread of bolt.

CAUTION: Do not use a tap to clean threads.

2. Clean flywheel faces.
3. Using assistance, position flywheel on crankshaft, fit and finger tighten new Patchlok bolts.
4. Insert timing pin **LRt-12-058** into flywheel.
5. Tighten bolts to 15 Nm then a further 90°.
6. Position crankshaft sensor to gearbox adaptor plate, fit and tighten bolt to 8 Nm.

GEARBOX ADAPTOR PLATE

Remove

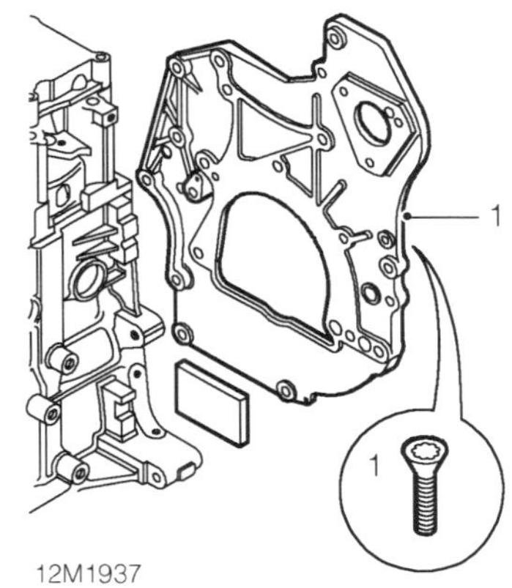

12M1937

1. Remove 4 Torx screws securing adaptor plate to cylinder block. Remove plate.

Refit

1. Check condition of foam rubber pad, replace if necessary.
2. Remove all traces of Loctite from Torx screws.
3. Ensure tapped holes in cylinder block are clean and dry.
4. Apply Loctite 275 to threads of Torx screws.
5. Position adaptor plate to cylinder block, fit and tighten Torx screws to 45 Nm.

SUMP AND OIL STRAINER

Sump - remove

1. Remove dipstick.
2. Remove oil pump.
3. Remove and discard crankshaft rear oil seal and housing.

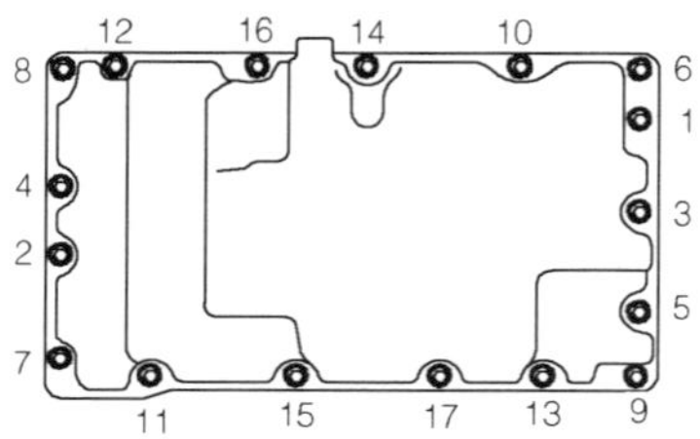

12M1938

4. Using sequence shown, remove 17 bolts securing sump to cylinder block.
5. Remove sump, remove and discard gasket.

Oil strainer - remove

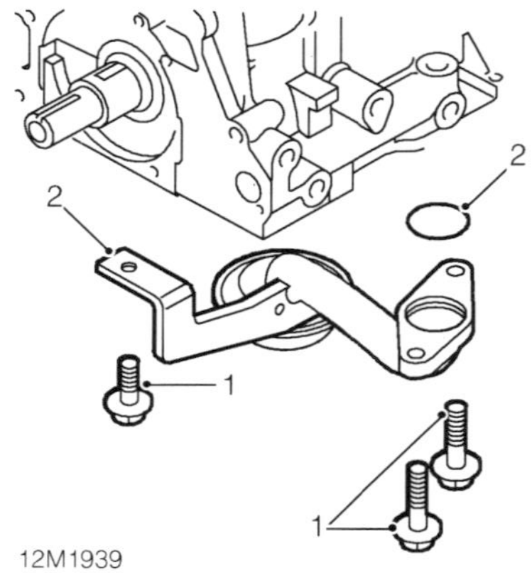

12M1939

1. Remove 3 bolts securing oil strainer to cylinder block and main bearing cap noting that shortest bolt is fitted in main bearing cap.
2. Remove oil strainer, remove and discard 'O' ring.

Oil strainer - refit

1. Clean strainer and pick-up pipe.
2. Ensure bolt holes in cylinder block and main bearing cap are clean and dry.

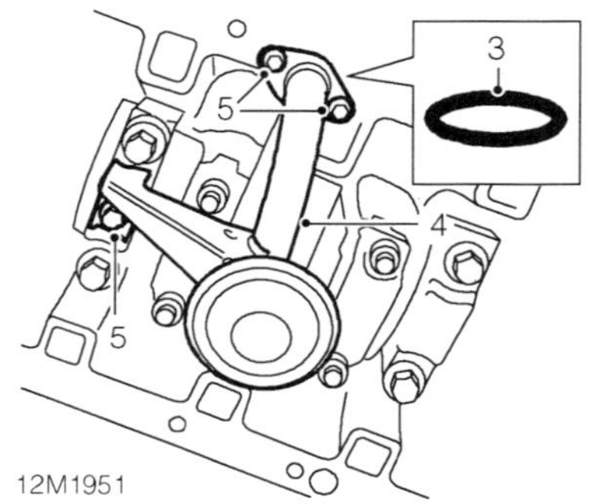

12M1951

3. Lubricate a new 'O' ring with engine oil and fit to pick-up pipe flange.
4. Position strainer to cylinder block and main bearing cap.
5. Fit 3 bolts noting that shortest bolt is fitted into main bearing cap. Tighten bolts to 8 Nm.

NOTE: Patchlok bolts may be re-used provided threads are undamaged.

Sump - refit

1. Clean sump flange and mating surfaces of cylinder block, ensure bolt holes in cylinder block and main bearing cap are clean and dry.

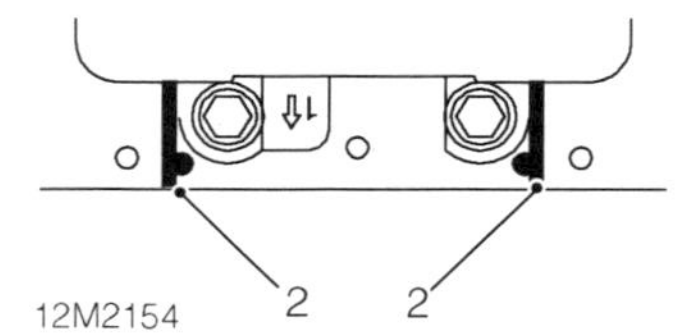

12M2154

2. Using sealant from kit, Part Number GUG 705548GM, fill grooves on each side of front - Number 1 main bearing cap and along joint lines of main bearing cap and cylinder block.

CAUTION: Do not apply sealant until immediately prior to fitting sump. Do not spread sealant bead.

3. Fit a new crankshaft rear oil seal and housing.

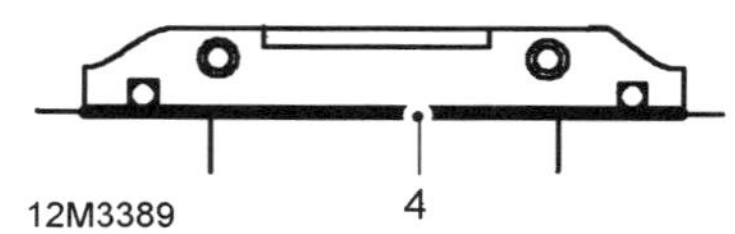

12M3389

4. Apply a 1 mm bead of sealant from kit to joint line of crankshaft rear oil seal housing, rear main bearing cap and cylinder block.

CAUTION: Do not apply sealant until immediately prior to fitting sump. Do not spread sealant bead.

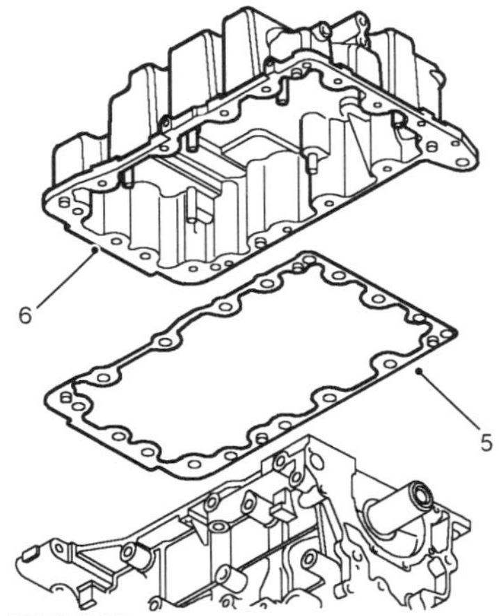

12M1943A

5. Position new gasket to sump ensuring that locating lugs are inserted in holes in sump.

NOTE: Gasket must be fitted dry.

6. Position sump to cylinder block ensuring that locating lugs are inserted in holes in block.

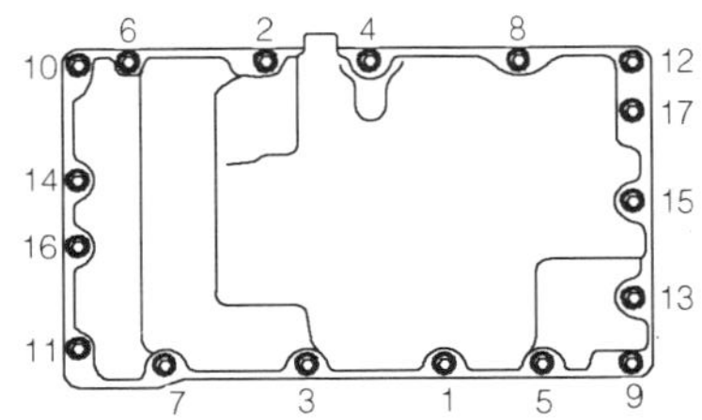

12M1944

7. Fit and finger tighten 17 bolts.
8. Using sequence shown, tighten bolts to 25 Nm.
9. Using the same sequence, re-check that all bolts are torqued to 25 Nm.
10. Fit dipstick.
11. Fit oil pump.

OIL PUMP

Remove

1. Remove camshaft timing belt.

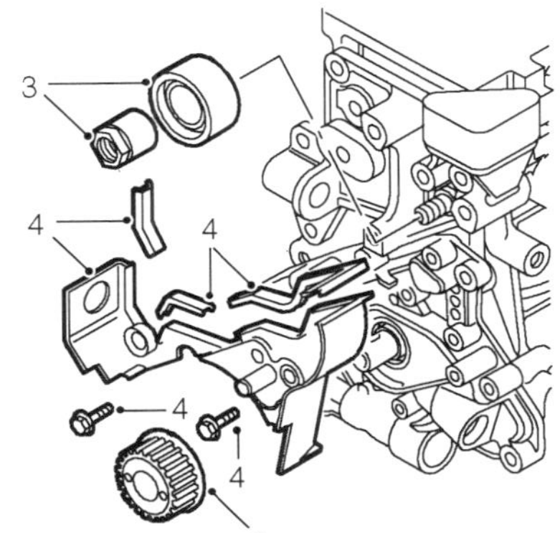

12M1945

2. Slide timing gear off crankshaft.

NOTE: The key is an integral part of the gear.

3. Remove nut securing camshaft timing belt idler pulley, remove pulley.

NOTE: Idler pulley mounting stud may be unscrewed as nut is removed.

4. Remove 2 bolts securing camshaft timing belt lower rear cover, remove cover and sealing strips.

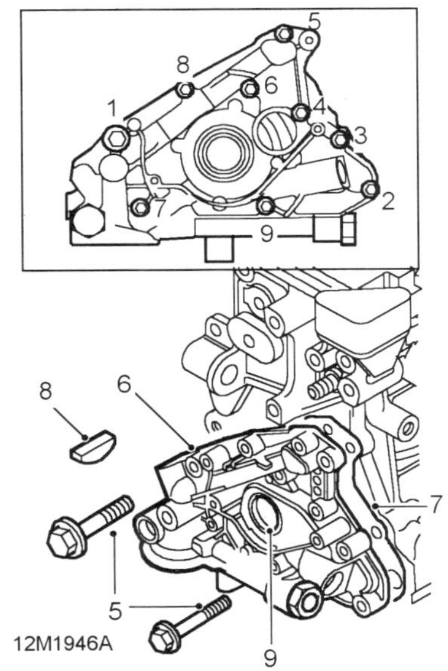

12M1946A

5. Using sequence shown, remove 1 M10 and 8 M6 bolts securing oil pump to cylinder block.

NOTE: Longest M6 bolt is fitted at position 9 (see inset).

6. Remove oil pump.
7. Remove and discard gasket.
8. Recover Woodruff key from crankshaft.
9. Remove and discard crankshaft front oil seal from oil pump body.

Oil pump - inspection

Oil pump

CAUTION: Overhaul procedures for the oil pump are limited to carrying out dimensional checks. In the event of wear or damage being found, a replacement pump must be fitted.

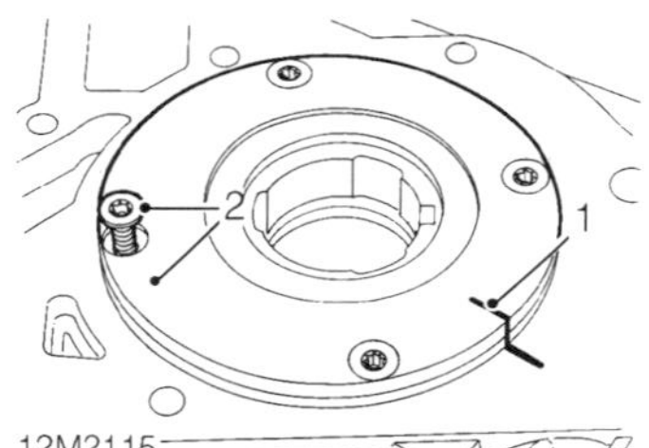

12M2115

1. Make suitable alignment mark between pump backplate and body.
2. Remove 4 Torx screws securing backplate to body, remove backplate.

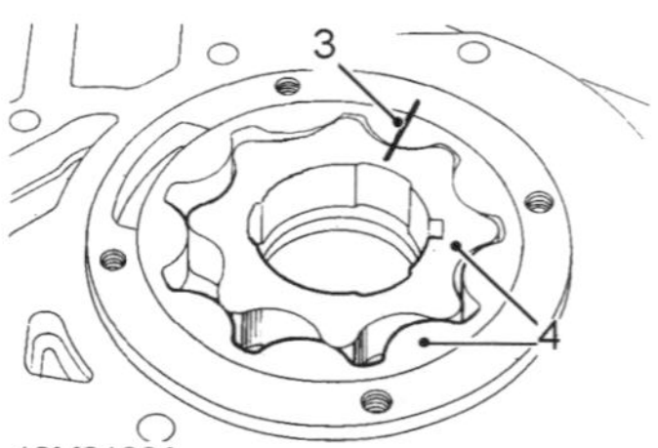

12M2120A

3. Using a felt tipped pen, make suitable alignment marks between inner and outer rotors and pump body.
4. Remove inner and outer rotors.
5. Check rotors and pump body for signs of scoring and wear.
6. Fit rotors ensuring that reference marks are aligned and chamfered side of outer rotor carrying a square identification mark is facing away from backplate side of pump body.

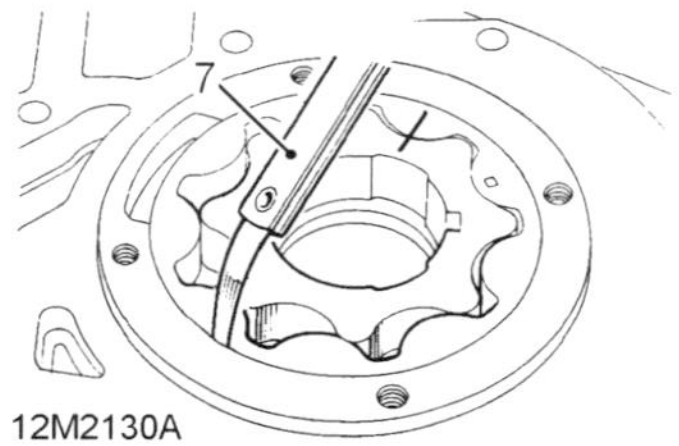

12M2130A

7. Using feeler gauges, check pump body to rotor clearance.
   Clearance = 0.05 to 0.10 mm.

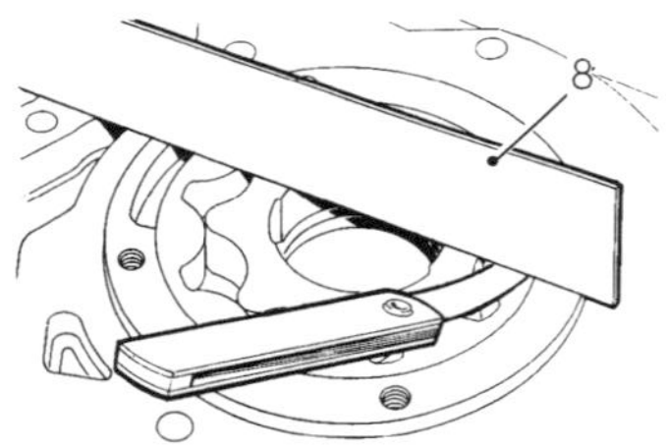

12M1953

8. Place a straight edge across pump body and using feeler gauges, measure end-float of outer rotor.
   End-float = 0.03 to 0.08 mm.

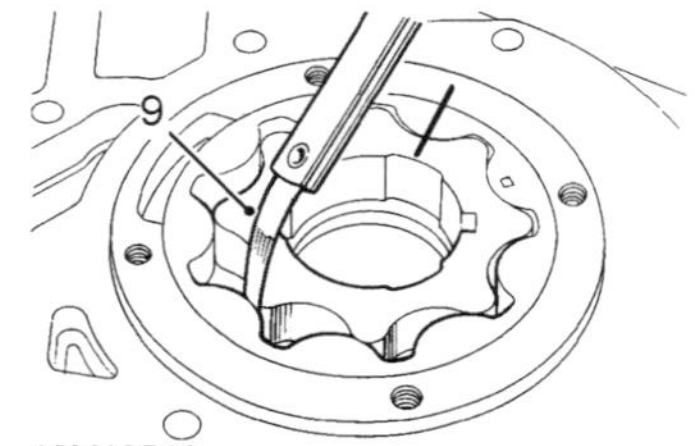

12M1954A

9. Using feeler gauges, check clearance between inner and outer rotor lobes.
   Clearance = 0.025 to 0.12 mm.
10. Renew oil pump assembly if excessive scoring exists or clearances exceed specified limits.

Oil pressure relief valve

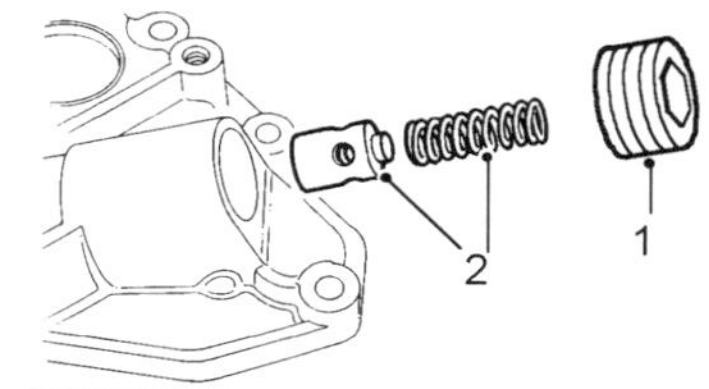

12M1955A

1. Remove and discard plug.
2. Remove spring and relief valve plunger.
3. Check plunger and bore for wear, corrosion and scoring.

NOTE: Light scoring may be removed using grade 600 emery cloth soaked in oil.

4. Check spring free length.
   Free length = 38.9 mm.
5. Renew relief valve as an assembly.
6. Remove all traces of sealant from plug threads in oil pump body.
7. Lubricate spring, relief valve plunger and bore with engine oil.
8. Fit plunger and spring, fit and tighten a new plug.

CAUTION: Do not attempt to re-seal and fit the original plug.

9. Check oil pressure switch - if fitted for damage, replace as necessary. Apply Loctite 577 to threads of replacement switch and tighten to 16 Nm.

Thermostatic valve

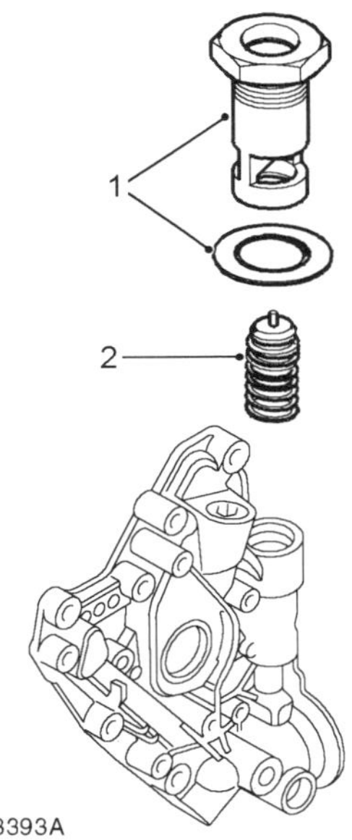

12M3393A

1. Remove diverter plug, remove and discard Dowty washer.
2. Withdraw spring and valve from oil pump body.

⚠ **CAUTION: Do not separate spring from valve.**

3. Check spring for distortion and corrosion.
4. Check valve for corrosion, seating faces of valve and diverter plug for damage and pitting; replace valve as an assembly.
5. Check valve bore for corrosion.

⚠ NOTE: Light corrosion may be removed from valve bore using grade 600 emery cloth soaked in oil.

6. Remove all traces of Loctite from threads of diverter valve plug and oil pump body.

⚠ **CAUTION: Do not remove blanking plug from oil gallery below thermostatic valve bore.**

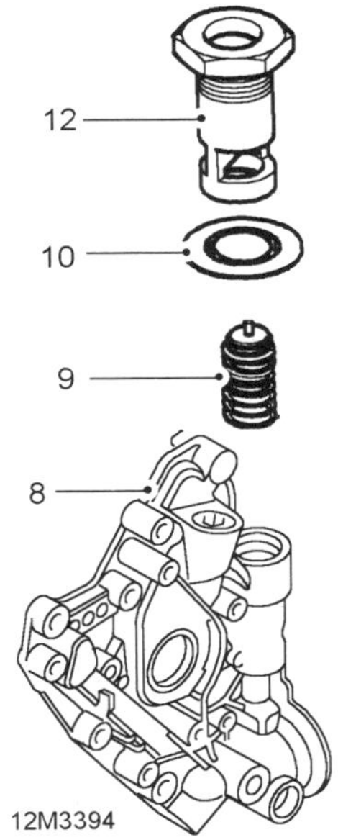

12M3394

7. Lubricate valve, spring and bore with engine oil.
8. Secure oil pump body in a soft-jawed vice with thermostatic valve bore facing upwards.

⚠ **CAUTION: Valve bore must be as near vertical as possible.**

9. Insert valve and spring in bore ensuring that it is positioned centrally in bore.

⚠ **CAUTION: Valve will not seat correctly in diverter plug if it is not positioned centrally.**

10. Fit a new Dowty washer to diverter plug.
11. Apply Loctite 577 to threads of diverter plug.
12. Fit diverter plug, carefully tighten plug by hand ensuring that valve is not diplaced as plug is tightened.
13. When diverter plug is screwed fully down, tighten to 35 Nm.

Oil pump - assembling

1. Using gasket removal spray and plastic scraper, remove all traces of gasket material from oil pump body.
2. Using solvent from kit, Part Number GUG 705548GM, remove all traces of sealant from oil pump body and backplate.
3. Remove all traces of Loctite from Torx screws and holes in oil pump body, ensure holes are clean and dry.

⚠ **CAUTION: Do not use a tap.**

4. Ensure all components are clean, lubricate rotors and housing with engine oil.
5. Fit rotors ensuring that reference marks are aligned and chamfered side of outer rotor carrying a square identification mark is facing away from backplate side of pump body.

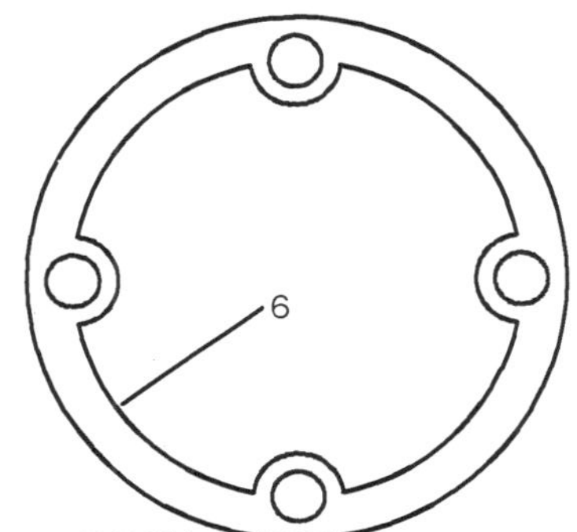

12M3391

6. Apply a 1 mm bead of Loctite 573 to pump backplate as shown.
7. Fit pump backplate ensuring reference marks on backplate and pump body are aligned.
8. Apply Loctite 222 to threads of Torx screws, fit and tighten screws.
9. Check that pump rotates freely.

Oil pump - refit

1. Using gasket removal spray and plastic scraper, remove all traces of gasket from cylinder block.
2. Using a suitable cleaning solvent, remove all traces of sealant from joint faces of front - Number 1 main bearing cap
3. Lubricate oil seal running surface on crankshaft with engine oil.
4. Fit Woodruff key to crankshaft.

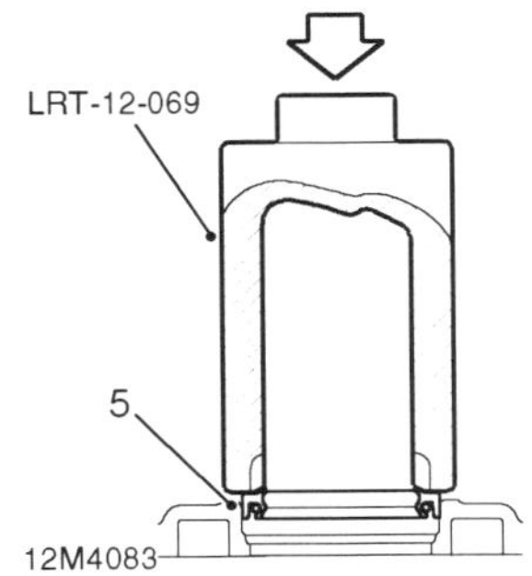

12M4083

5. Lubricate a new crankshaft front oil seal with engine oil.
6. Fit oil seal using tool **LRT-12-069.**

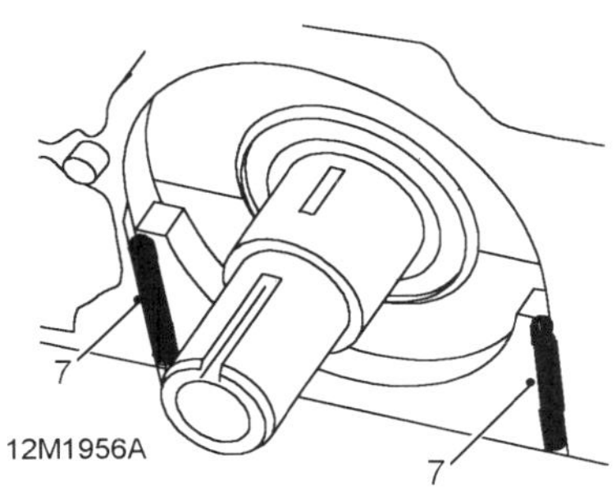

12M1956A

7. Using sealant from kit, apply a bead of sealant to joint line of front - Number 1 main bearing cap.

CAUTION: Do not fill grooves on either side of main bearing cap or apply sealant to sump mating flange of main cap until immediately before sump is fitted.

8. Position a new gasket to cylinder block.

NOTE: Gasket must be fitted dry.

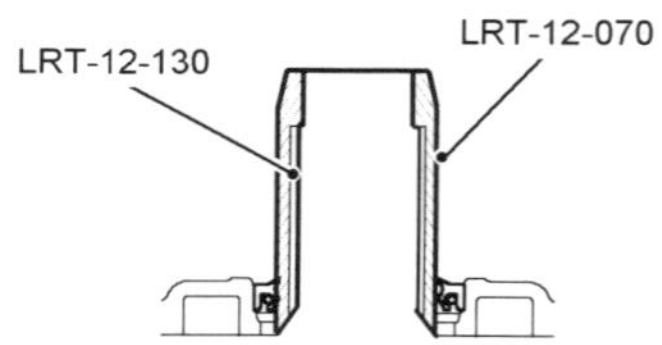

12M4084

9. Insert oil seal protector **LRT-12-070** and adaptor sleeve **LRT-12-130** into oil pump inner rotor.

NOTE: This will assist in locating oil pump inner rotor on Woodruff key.

10. Align Woodruff key slots in oil pump inner rotor with Woodruff key
11. Ensure bolt holes in cylinder block are clean and dry.

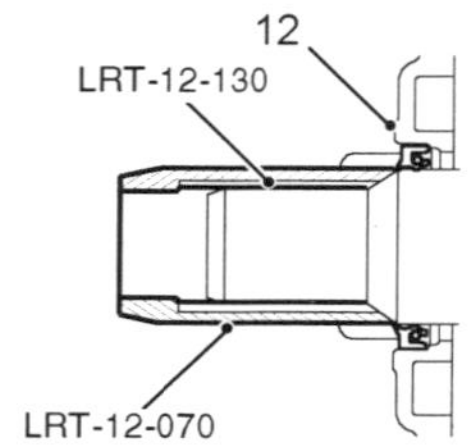

12M4090

12. Slide oil pump over crankshaft ensuring Woodruff key is located in keyway in inner rotor, locate oil pump on dowels.

NOTE: Tools LRT-12-070 and LRT-12-130 will be displaced as pump is fitted.

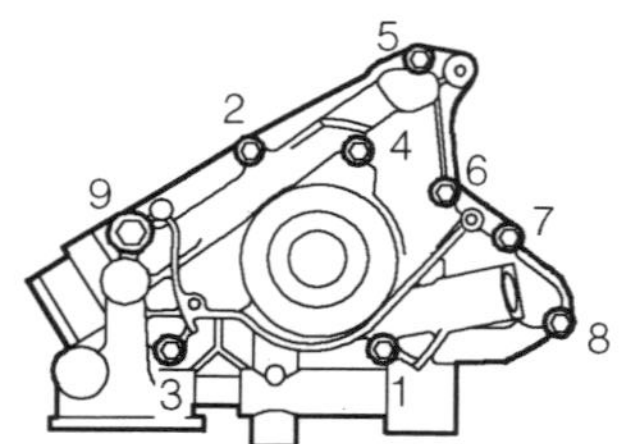

12M2695

13. Fit bolts ensuring that longest M6 bolt is fitted at position 1 and M10 bolt at position 9.
14. Tighten bolts in sequence shown to:
M10 bolt - 45 Nm
M6 bolts -8 Nm

NOTE: Patchlok bolts may be re-used provided threads are undamaged.

15. Ensure sealing strips are fitted to camshaft timing belt lower rear cover.
16. Fit lower rear cover, fit and tighten screws to 8 Nm.
17. Fit camshaft timing belt idler pulley ensuring that recessed side of centre boss faces away from engine.
18. Apply Loctite 275 to threads of idler pulley nut, fit and tighten nut to 45 Nm.
19. If stud was unscrewed during nut removal, clean old Loctite from threads of stud and ensure hole in cylinder block is clean and dry. Apply Loctite 275 to threads of stud and screw it into block, tighten stud to 12 Nm.
20. Slide timing gear on to crankshaft.
21. Fit camshaft timing belt and adjust tension.

CRANKSHAFT, MAIN AND BIG-END BEARINGS

Crankshaft rear oil seal - remove

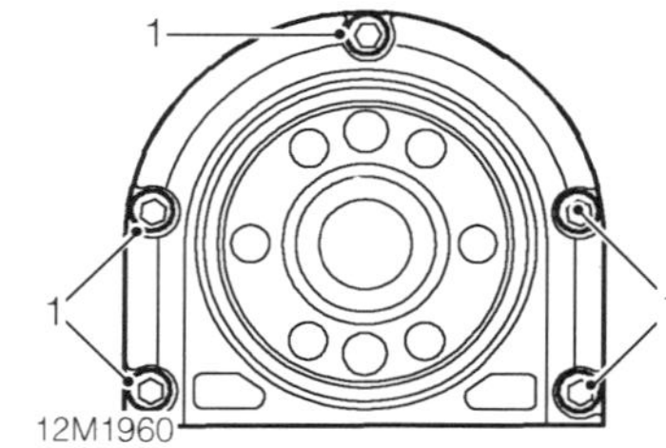

12M1960

1. Remove 5 bolts securing rear oil seal housing to cylinder block, remove and discard housing and oil seal.

Big-end bearings - remove

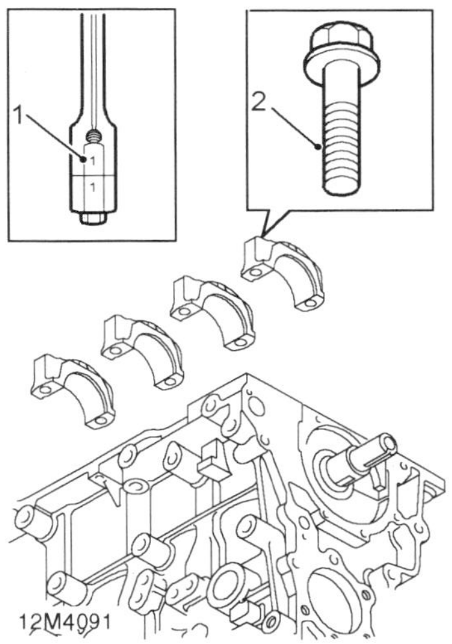

1. Suitably mark cylinder reference number on each big-end bearing cap and connecting rod.
2. Remove 2 bolts securing each big-end bearing cap, remove caps and recover big-end bearing shells.

NOTE: The big-end bearing shells do not have location tags for locating the bearings in the connecting rod and bearing cap. The big-end to connecting rod bolts are off-set 1mm to prevent incorrect fitment of the bearing cap to the connecting rod.

CAUTION: Keep bolts and bearing caps in their fitted order. Big-end bearing shells should always be replaced whenever crankshaft is removed.

3. Push each connecting rod up cylinder bore until connecting rod is clear of the crankshaft journals.

CAUTION: Ensure connecting rods do not contact oil squirt jets or cylinder bores.

Crankshaft end-float - check

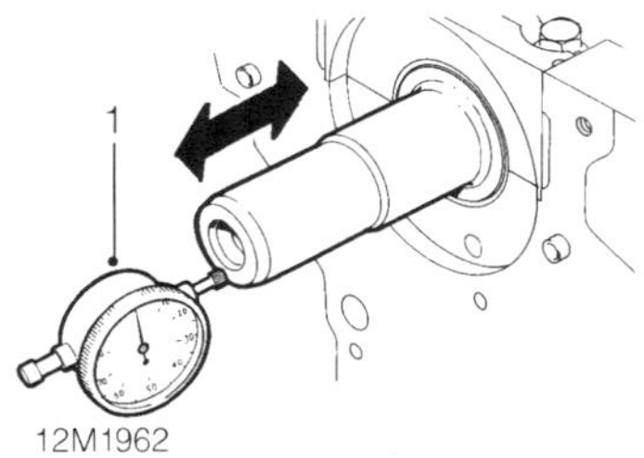

1. Attach a magnetic base Dial Test Indicator to front of cylinder block, move crankshaft rearwards, position stylus on end of crankshaft and zero DTI.
2. Move crankshaft forwards, measure and record end-float figure obtained:
End-float = 0.03 to 0.26 mm
3. If end-float exceeds above dimension, new thrust washers must be fitted:
Thrust washer thickness = 2.31 to 2.36 mm

Crankshaft - remove

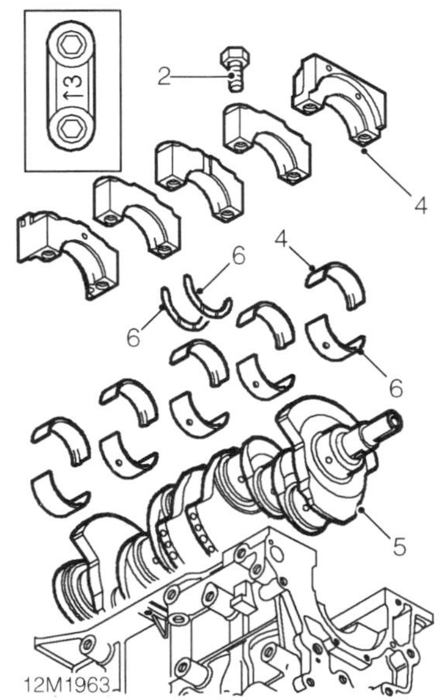

1. Check that identification marks, 1 to 5, and that the direction arrows face towards the front of the engine, are marked on each main bearing cap.

NOTE: The identification marks on number 2 main bearing cap are concealed by the oil strainer mounting bracket which is secured to the bearing cap.

2. Starting at centre main - Number 3 main bearing cap and working outwards, progressively slacken, then remove 2 bolts securing each cap.

CAUTION: Keep bolts in their fitted order.

3. Using fingers only, rock each main bearing cap until it is released from locating dowels.

CAUTION: Do not tap caps sideways.

4. Remove main bearing caps and plain bearing shells.
5. Using assistance, remove crankshaft.
6. Recover upper, grooved main bearing shells and 2 thrust washers.
7. Using a suitable cleaning solvent, remove sealant from front - Number 1 main bearing cap and cylinder block.

Crankshaft - inspection

1. Clean crankshaft, ensure all oilways are clear.

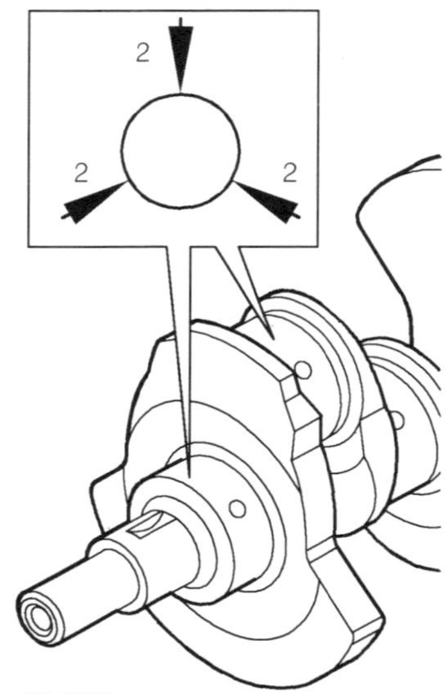

12M2127

2. Check crankshaft journals for wear and ovality, make three checks at 120°intervals in centre of journals.
   Crankshaft bearing journal diameters:
   Main bearings = 60.703 to 60.719 mm
   Big-end bearings = 57.683 to 57.696 mm
   Clearance in bearings = 0.005 mm

CAUTION: Crankshaft journals may not be reground undersize, if journals are worn, crankshaft must be replaced. Main and big-end bearings are only available in one size and should always be replaced whenever crankshaft has been removed.

3. Check thrust washers for wear and scoring, replace as necessary:
   Thrust washer thickness = 2.31 to 2.36 mm

Crankshaft - refit

CAUTION: If crankshaft end-float exceeded 0.26 mm, new thrust washers must be fitted.

1. Clean main bearing shell locations in cylinder block, clean main bearing caps.
2. Check that ring dowels are fitted in main bearing cap locations and that bolt holes are clean and dry.
3. Check threads of main bearing cap bolts for damage, renew bolts in pairs.
4. Lubricate new upper main bearing shells with engine oil and ensuring that they are centrally positioned, fit to their locations in cylinder block.

NOTE: These bearing shells are grooved.

5. Lubricate thrust washers with engine oil and fit, oil groove side outwards to each side of centre - (Number 3) main bearing in cylinder block.
6. Lubricate crankshaft journals with engine oil and using assistance, position crankshaft in cylinder block.

CAUTION: Ensure thrust washers are not displaced as crankshaft is fitted.

7. Lubricate new main bearing shells with engine oil and fit to main bearing caps.

NOTE: These bearing shells are plain.

8. Fit main bearing caps ensuring that they are correctly orientated and in their fitted order.

CAUTION: Do not apply sealant to grooves in front - (Number 1) main bearing cap until immediately before sump is fitted.

9. Lubricate threads of main bearing cap bolts with engine oil, fit and finger tighten bolts.
10. Starting from the centre - Number 3 main bearing cap and working outwards, tighten bolts to 112 Nm.
11. Check that crankshaft rotates smoothly.
12. Re-check crankshaft end-float. ***See this section***

CAUTION: If original thrust washers have been refitted and end-float exceeds 0.26 mm, crankshaft must be removed and new thrust washers fitted. If, with new thrust washers fitted, end-float is still excessive, crankshaft must be replaced.

Crankshaft rear oil seal - refit

CAUTION: Rear oil seal and housing must be fitted prior to fitting sump.

1. Ensure oil seal running surfaces on crankshaft and oil seal housing mating surface on cylinder block are clean and oil free and that bolt and dowel holes are clean and dry.

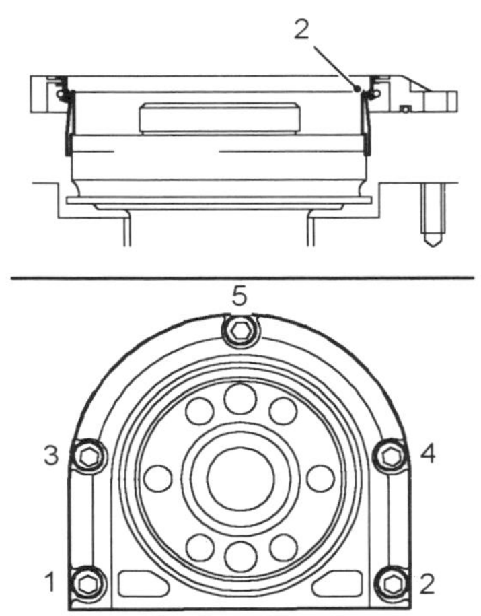

12M1964A

CAUTION: Do not lubricate oil seal or running surface on crankshaft. The oil seal is pre-lubricated at manufacture. Do not separate protector sleeve from oil seal and do not touch lip of seal. If seal is inadvertently handled it must not be fitted as the coating applied to the seal during manufacture will be destroyed and oil leakage can result.

2. Slide oil seal protector sleeve, oil seal and housing over end of crankshaft.
3. Position oil seal and housing on cylinder block.

NOTE: Oil seal protector will be displaced as seal and housing are fitted.

4. Fit bolts and working in sequence shown, tighten to 8 Nm.

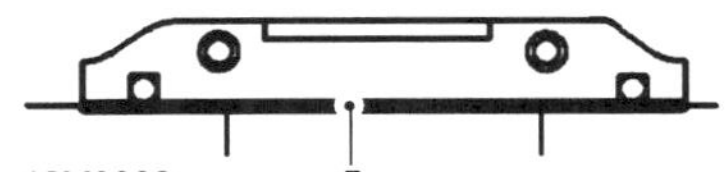

12M3390

5. Apply a 1 mm thick bead of sealant from kit, Part Number GUG 705548 GM along joint line of seal housing, rear main bearing cap and cylinder block.

Big-end bearings - refit

1. Rotate crankshaft until big-end bearing journals are correctly positioned.
2. Lubricate crankshaft big-end journals with engine oil.
3. Fit new big-end bearing shells to connecting rods, lubricate shells with engine oil.
4. Taking care not to damage oil squirt jets or to displace bearing shells, pull connecting rods on to crankshaft journals.
5. Check that new big-end bearing shells are correctly located on big-end bearing caps, lubricate shells with engine oil.
6. Fit big-end bearing caps ensuring that they are in their correct fitted order.
7. Lubricate threads of connecting rod bolts with engine oil. Fit bolts to their respective connecting rods and tighten to 20Nm then a further 85°.

PISTONS, CONNECTING RODS AND CYLINDER BORES

Pistons and connecting rods - remove

1. Remove crankshaft.

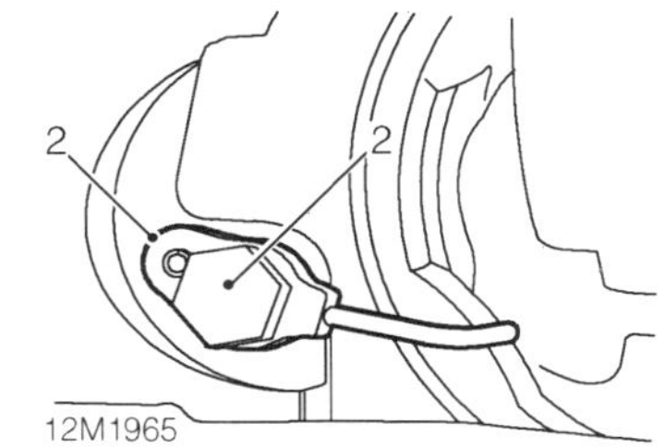

12M1965

2. Remove and discard banjo bolts securing oil squirt jets to cylinder block, remove jets.

NOTE: Each jet is located by means of a roll pin.

3. Suitably identify each piston and connecting rod assembly to its respective cylinder bore.
4. Using assistance, lay cylinder block on its side.
5. Push each piston and connecting rod up cylinder bore taking care to keep connecting rod clear of bore walls; remove pistons and connecting rods.
6. Recover big-end bearing shells from connecting rods.

CAUTION: Big-end bearing shells should always be replaced whenever pistons and connecting rods are removed.

Piston rings - remove

1. Using a suitable expander, remove and discard piston rings.
2. Use a squared off end of a broken piston ring to clean groove in piston.

CAUTION: Do not use a wire brush or emery cloth.

Piston ring gaps - checking

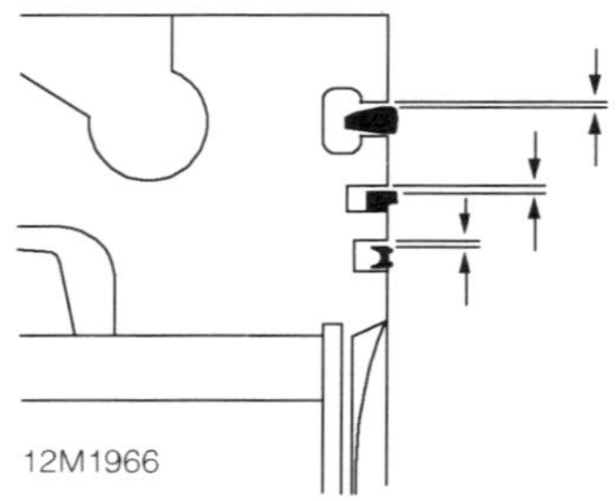

12M1966

1. Check new ring to groove clearance:
   Top compression = 0.115 to 0.135 mm.
   2nd compression = 0.050 to 0.082 mm.
   Oil control = 0.050 to 0.082 mm.

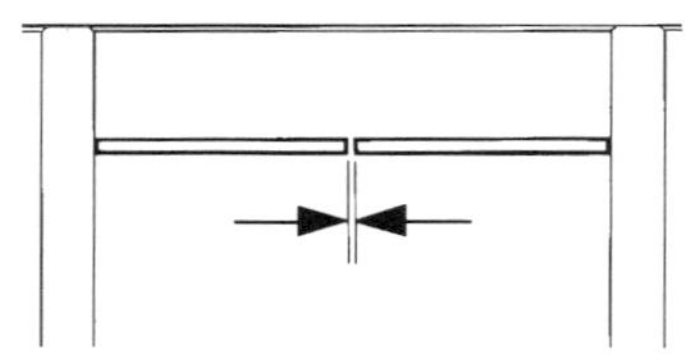

12M2108

2. Check new ring fitted gap 30 mm from top of cylinder bore, ensure rings are kept square to bore when checking gaps.
   Fitted gap:
   Top compression = 0.25 to 0.27 mm.
   2nd compression = 0.40 to 0.42 mm.
   Oil control rails = 0.30 to 0.32 mm.

Pistons - remove

1. Suitably identify each piston to its connecting rod, note position of cast boss on connecting rod relative to arrow on piston crown.

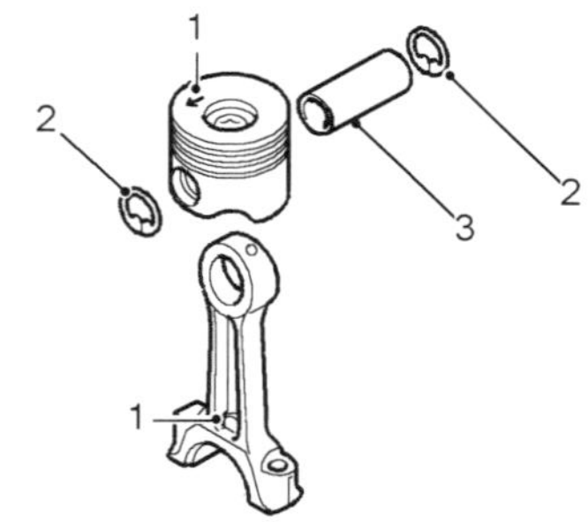

12M4092

2. Remove and discard circlips securing gudgeon pin.
3. Push gudgeon pin out of piston and connecting rod.

CAUTION: Keep gudgeon pins with their respective pistons and screw in bolts finger tight only to retain bearing caps to connecting rods.

Pistons and connecting rods - inspection

1. Clean carbon from pistons using fine emery cloth, do not use a wire brush or scraper.
2. Check pistons for cracks, distortion and damage.

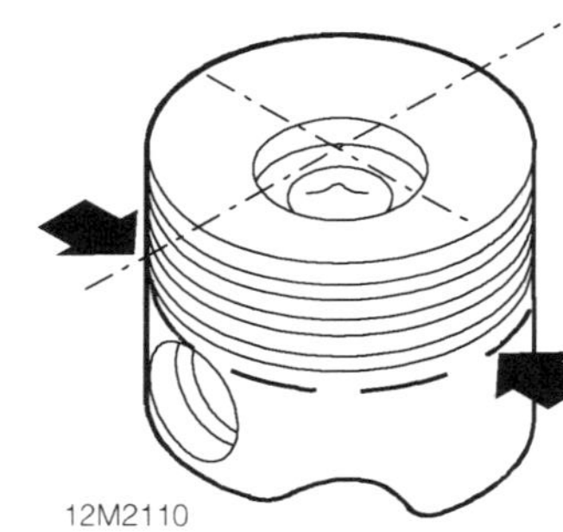

12M2110

3. Measure and record piston diameter at right angles to gudgeon pin hole and 44 mm from bottom of skirt:
   Diameter = 84.262 mm.

CAUTION: Measurement point must be on the ungraphited area of the piston.

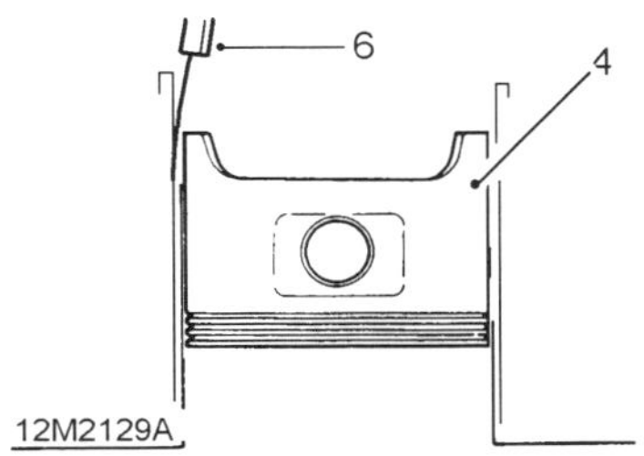

12M2129A

4. Starting with Number 1 piston, invert piston and with arrow on piston crown pointing towards REAR of cylinder block, insert piston into top of Number 1 cylinder bore.
5. Position piston with bottom of skirt 25 mm from top of cylinder bore.
6. Using feeler gauges, measure and record clearance between piston skirt and left hand side of cylinder bore 70 mm from top of bore (viewed from front of cylinder block).
   Piston to cylinder bore clearance = 0.18 to 0.2 mm.

7. Repeat procedures for remaining pistons.

CAUTION: Oversize pistons are not available, if clearances are excessive, measure diameter of cylinder bore before proceeding further. If, after inspection, cylinder bores are found to be the correct size, pistons must be replaced.

8. Check fit of each gudgeon pin in its respective piston, pin must be a tight, sliding fit with no perceptible side play.

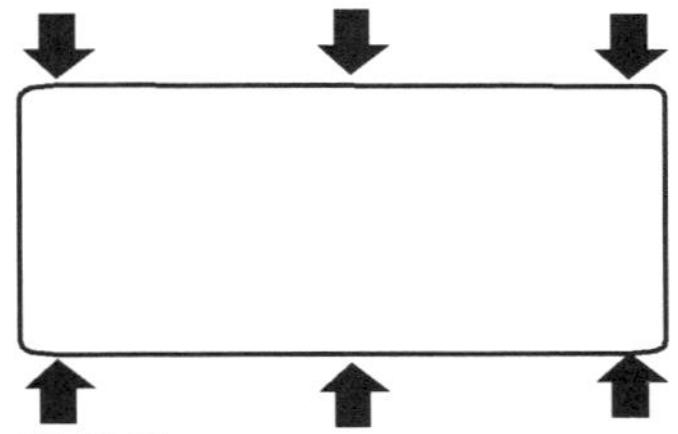
12M2112

9. Measure gudgeon pin diameter at each end and centre of pin:
   Diameter = 29.995 to 30.000 mm.
10. Renew gudgeon pins and pistons as an assembly if diameters are less than specified or if excessive pin to piston side play is evident.
11. Check connecting rods for alignment, reject any connecting rod which is bent.
12. Check small-end bushes for wear, check that gudgeon pin is a close\sliding fit in the bush, with no perceptible side play.

CAUTION: Small-end bushes may not be replaced, a new connecting rod must be fitted.

13. Using fingers only, check that each big-end bearing cap bolt runs freely in the threads of its respective thread in the connecting rod. If any bolt is tight, then the bolt must be replaced.

Pistons - refit

1. Lubricate gudgeon pin and small-end bush with engine oil.
2. Position piston to its respective connecting rod ensuring that bearing shell tag recess in connecting rod is to the left of the arrow on the piston crown when piston is viewed from the rear.
3. Fit gudgeon pin, fit new circlips ensuring they are fully seated in their grooves.
4. Repeat above procedures for remaining pistons.

Piston rings - refit

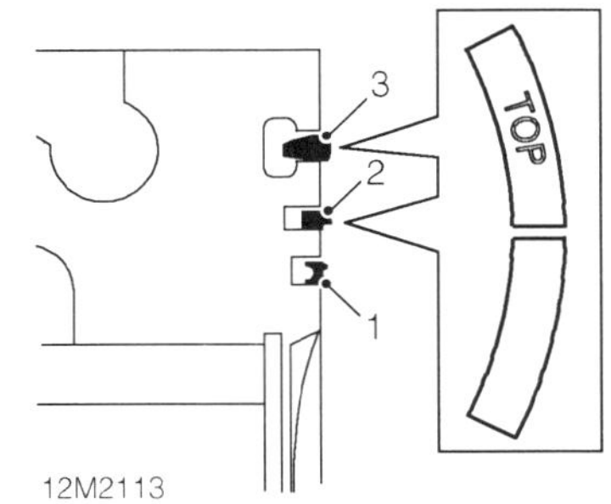

12M2113

1. Fit oil control rails and spring.
2. Fit 2nd compression ring with 'TOP' marking upwards.
3. Fit top compression ring with 'TOP' marking upwards.
4. Check that rings are free to rotate, position ring gaps at 120 °to each other and away from thrust side - left hand side of piston - viewed from front of piston.

Cylinder bores - inspection

1. Check cylinder bores for scoring.

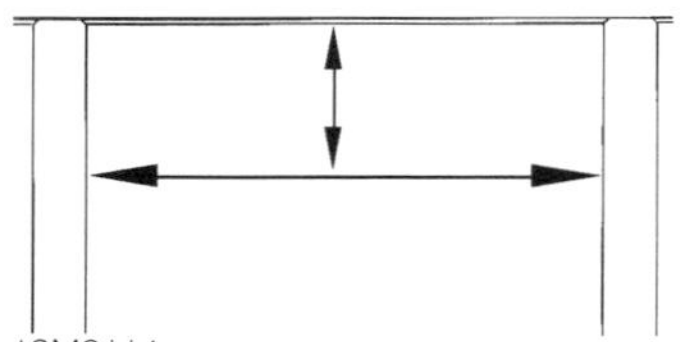

12M2114

2. Check cylinder bores for wear, measure and record diameter of each bore, 70 mm from top of bore.

CAUTION: Measurements must be taken from side to side and front to rear of bore.

Bore diameter = 84.442 to 84.460 mm.

CAUTION: No reboring, honing or glaze busting of cylinder bores is permissible; cylinder block must be replaced if out of specification.

Cylinder block

1. Check that all oilways are clear and that oil restrictor located in oilway to cylinder head is fitted below face of cylinder block.
2. Check that main bearing cap, crankshaft rear oil seal housing and cylinder head locating dowels are fitted.
3. Check core plugs for leakage and corrosion, replace as necessary.

NOTE: **Seal replacement core plugs and main oil gallery plug on rear of cylinder block with Loctite 577, tighten main oil gallery plug to 12 Nm.**

Pistons and connecting rods - refit

1. Lubricate cylinder bores, pistons, rings and crankshaft big-end journals with engine oil.
2. Lubricate new big-end bearing shells with engine oil and fit to connecting rods and bearing caps.
3. Check that piston ring gaps are positioned at 120°to each other and away from thrust - left hand side of piston - viewed from front of piston.

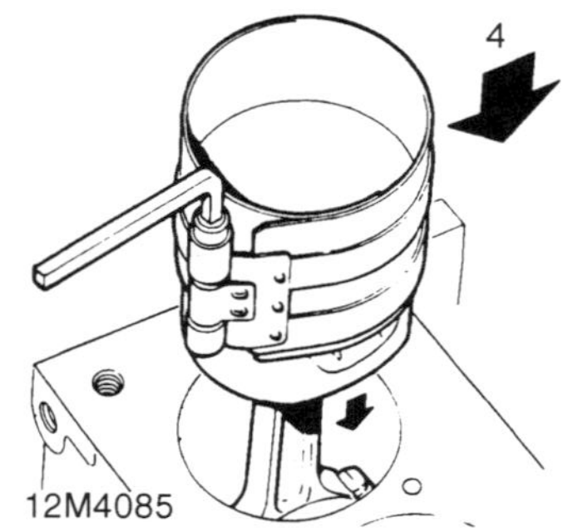

12M4085

4. Fit ring clamp to each piston in turn and ensuring that pistons are in their correct fitted order and that the arrow on piston crown and the cast boss above the big-end is facing towards front of cylinder block, push pistons into their respective cylinder bores.

CAUTION: Ensure that connecting rods do not contact cylinder bores.

5. Do not pull connecting rods fully down cylinder bores at this stage.
6. Check that cut-out in each piston skirt is positioned above oil squirt jet location.
7. Ensure oil squirt jets are clear and that roll pins are inserted in jet housings.
8. Position oil squirt jets in cylinder block ensuring that roll pins are inserted in locating holes.
9. Apply Loctite 275 to threads of new banjo bolts.

CAUTION: Do not allow Loctite to enter oil hole in banjo bolts.

10. Fit and tighten banjo bolts to 12 Nm.
11. Fit crankshaft and big-end bearings.

ENGINE DATA

Oil pump	
Outer rotor to body clearance	0.05 to 0.10 mm
Rotor lobe clearance	0.025 to 0.12 mm
Outer rotor end float	0.03 to 0.08 mm
Relief valve spring free length	38.9 mm
Camshaft	
Camshaft end-float	0.51 mm - max.
Camshaft bearing clearance	0.043 to 0.094 mm
Camshaft timing belt tensioner spring free length	65 mm
Tappets	
Tappet outside diameter	34.959 to 34.975 mm.
Cylinder head	
Cylinder head maximum warpage	0.010 mm
Cylinder head bolt length	243.41 mm
Valve springs	
Free length	37.0 mm
Valves	
Valve stem diameter:	
Inlet	6.907 to 6.923 mm
Exhaust	6.897 to 6.913 mm
Valve stem to guide clearance:	
Inlet	0.056 mm
Exhaust	0.066 mm
Valve face angle	45 °to 45 °30'
Valve head stand down:	
Inlet	1.45 mm
Exhaust	1.35 mm
Valve guides:	
Inside diameter after reaming	6.950 to 6.963 mm
Fitted length above cylinder head	61.1 to 61.7 mm
Valve seat inserts:	
Seat angle	
Inlet	60°
Exhaust	58 °to 62°
Insert diameter	
Inlet	35.697 mm
Exhaust	31.05 to 31.55 mm

Crankshaft

End-float	0.03 to 0.26 mm
Thrust washer halves thickness	2.31 to 2.36 mm
Main journal diameter	60.703 to 60.719 mm
Clearance in bearings	± 0.005 mm
Big-end journal diameter	57.683 to 57.696 mm
Clearance in bearings	± 0.005 mm

Piston rings

New ring to groove clearance:	
Top compression	0.115 to 0.135 mm
2nd compression	0.050 to 0.082 m m
Oil control	0.050 to 0.082 mm
Ring fitted gap 30 mm from top of cylinder bore:	
Top compression	0.25 to 0.27 mm
2nd compression	0.40 to 0.42 mm
Oil control rails	0.30 to 0.32 mm

Pistons

Piston diameter	84.262 mm
Clearance in bore	0.18 to 0.2 mm

Cylinder block

Cylinder bore	84.442 to 84.460 mm

TORQUE FIGURES

Camshaft timing belt upper front cover screws	5 Nm
Camshaft timing belt lower front cover screws	5 Nm
Camshaft timing belt upper rear cover screws	8 Nm
Camshaft timing belt lower rear cover screws	8 Nm
Camshaft timing belt tensioner bolt	45 Nm
Camshaft timing belt Allen screw	55 Nm
Camshaft timing belt idler pulley nut	45 Nm
Idler pulley stud	12 Nm
Engine front mounting cover plate nuts	35 Nm
Engine front mounting cover plate bolts	45 Nm
Crankshaft pulley bolt	63 Nm then further 90°
Oil pump bolts - Patchlok:	
M6	8 Nm
M10	45 Nm
Thermostatic valve diverter plug	35 Nm
Oil pressure switch	16 Nm
Oil pick-up pipe bolts - Patchlok	8 Nm
Fuel injection pump drive belt backplate screws	8 Nm
Camshaft timing belt gear bolt	20 Nm then further 90°
Camshaft gear damper torx screws	10 Nm
Fuel injection pump drive belt gear bolt	20 Nm then further 90°
Camshaft cover bolts	12 Nm
Camshaft carrier to cylinder head bolts	11 Nm
Cylinder head Torx bolts	
Stage 1	30 Nm
Stage 2	65 Nm
Stage 3	Further 90°
Stage 4	Then further 90°
Flywheel bolts - Patchlok	15 Nm then further 90°
Gearbox adaptor plate Torx screws	45 Nm
Crankshaft sensor to adaptor plate bolt	8 Nm
Oil sump bolts	25 Nm
Oil sump drain plug	25 Nm
Main bearing cap bolts	112 Nm
Connecting rod cap bolts	20 Nm then further 85°
Crankshaft rear oil seal housing screws	8 Nm
Oil squirt jet banjo bolts	12 Nm
Main oil gallery plug	12 Nm

TOOL NUMBERS

LRT-12-069	Replacer - Crankshaft Oil Seal
LRT-12-070	Oil Seal Protection Sleeve
LRT-12-130	Adaptor Sleeve
LRT-12-034	Valve Spring Compressor
LRT-12-132	Timing Gear Holding Tool
LRT-12-058	Timing Pin
LRT-12-071	Valve Stem Oil Seal Remover/replacer
LRT-12-140	Replacer - Camshaft Oil Seals
LRT-12-143	Camshaft Timing Belt Tensioner Retractor

'K' SERIES ENGINE

OVERHAUL MANUAL

This overhaul manual is applicable to the 1.8 'K' Series engine fitted to Land Rover 'Freelander'.

Publication Part No. LRL 0158 ENG
Published by Rover Technical Communication

'K' SERIES ENGINE OVERHAUL MANUAL

CONTENTS

Page

INTRODUCTION

How to use this manual

To assist in the use of this manual the section title is given at the top and the relevant sub-section is given at the bottom of each page.

This manual contains procedures for overhaul of the 'K' Series engine on the bench with the gearbox and clutch removed. For all other information regarding General Information, Adjustments, Removal of oil seals, engine units and ancillary equipment, consult the Repair Manual for the model concerned.

This manual is divided into 3 sections,

- Description and Operation,
- Overhaul and
- Data, Torque & Tools.
  To assist filing of revised information, each sub-section is numbered from page 1.

Individual items are to be overhauled in the sequence in which they appear in this Manual. Items numbered in the illustrations are referred to in the text.

Overhaul operations include reference to Service Tool numbers and the associated illustration depicts the tool. Where usage is not obvious the tool is shown in use. Operations also include reference to wear limits, relevant data, torque figures, and specialist information and useful assembly details.

WARNINGS, CAUTIONS and Notes have the following meanings:

WARNING: Procedures which must be followed precisely to avoid the possibility of injury.

CAUTION: Calls attention to procedures which must be followed to avoid damage to components.

NOTE: Gives helpful information.

References

With the engine and gearbox assembly removed, the crankshaft pulley end of the engine is referred to as the front.

Operations covered in this manual do not include reference to testing the vehicle after repair. It is essential that work is inspected and tested after completion and if necessary a road test of the vehicle is carried out particularly where safety related items are concerned.

Dimensions

The dimensions quoted are to design engineering specification with Service limits where applicable.

REPAIRS AND REPLACEMENTS

When replacement parts are required it is essential that only Land Rover recommended parts are used.

Attention is particularly drawn to the following points concerning repairs and the fitting of replacement parts and accessories.

Safety features and corrosion prevention treatments embodied in the car may be impaired if other than Land Rover recommended parts are fitted. In certain territories, legislation prohibits the fitting of parts not to the manufacturer's specification.

Torque wrench setting figures given in this Manual must be used. Locking devices, where specified, must be fitted. If the efficiency of a locking device is impaired during removal it must be renewed.

The Terms of the vehicle Warranty may be invalidated by the fitting of other than Land Rover recommended parts. All Land Rover recommended parts have the full backing of the vehicle Warranty.

Land Rover Dealers are obliged to supply only Rover recommended parts.

SPECIFICATION

Land Rover are constantly seeking to improve the specification, design and production of their vehicles and alterations take place accordingly. While every effort has been made to ensure the accuracy of this Manual, it should not be regarded as an infallible guide to current specifications of any particular component or vehicle.

This Manual does not constitute an offer for sale of any particular component or vehicle. Land Rover Dealers are not agents of the Company and have no authority to bind the manufacturer by any expressed or implied undertaking or representation.

CONTENTS

CONTENTS

This page is intentionally left blank

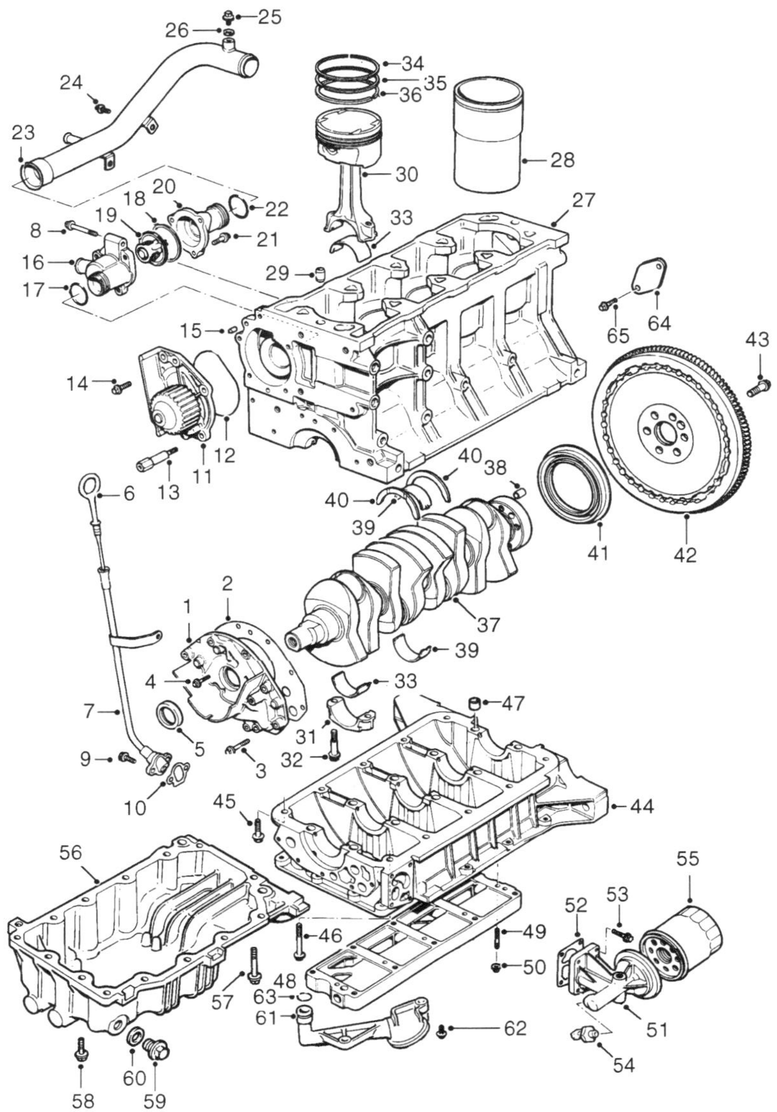

12M3938

CYLINDER BLOCK COMPONENTS

1. Oil pump assembly
2. Gasket - oil pump
3. Screw - M6 x 30 - oil pump
4. Screw M6 x 20 - oil pump
5. Crankshaft front oil seal
6. Dipstick
7. Dipstick tube
8. Screw - dipstick tube and thermostat housing
9. Screw - dipstick tube
10. Gasket
11. Coolant pump
12. 'O' ring - coolant pump
13. Pillar bolt
14. Bolt - coolant pump
15. Locating dowel
16. Thermostat housing - plastic
17. 'O' ring
18. Seal thermostat
19. Thermostat
20. Cover - plastic
21. Screw
22. 'O' ring
23. Coolant pipe
24. Screw - coolant pipe
25. Vent screw - if fitted
26. Sealing washer
27. Cylinder block
28. Cylinder liner
29. Ring dowel
30. Piston and connecting rod assembly
31. Big-end bearing cap
32. Connecting rod bolt
33. Big-end bearing shells
34. Top compression ring
35. 2nd compression ring
36. Oil control ring
37. Crankshaft
38. Ring dowel
39. Main bearing shells
    Plain in block Nos.1 and 5
    Grooved in block Nos. 2, 3 and 4
    Plain in bearing ladder
40. Thrust washers
41. Crankshaft rear oil seal
42. Flywheel assembly
43. Flywheel bolt - Patchlok
44. Bearing ladder
45. Bolt - bearing ladder
46. Bolt - oil rail
47. Ring dowel
48. Oil rail
49. Stud
50. Nut
51. Oil filter adapter
52. Gasket
53. Bolt
54. Oil pressure switch
55. Oil filter element
56. Alloy sump
57. Sump bolt - M8 x 20
58. Sump bolt - M8
59. Drain plug
60. Sealing washer
61. Oil pick-up pipe
62. Screw - pick-up pipe
63. 'O' ring
64. Blanking plate
65. Screw - blanking plate

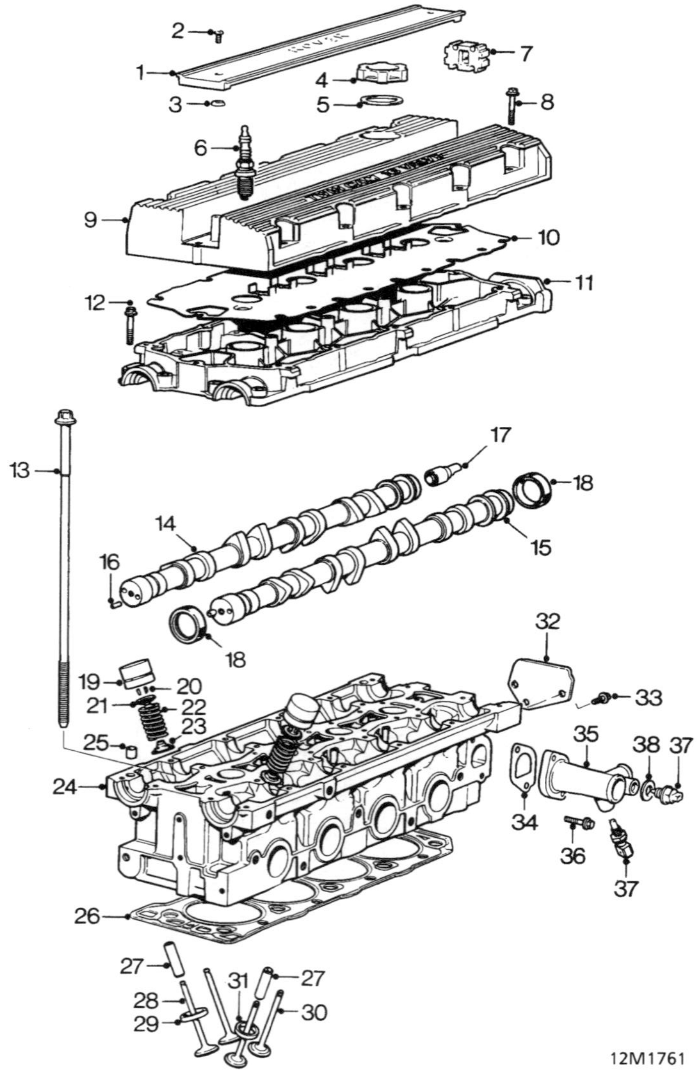

12M1761

CYLINDER HEAD COMPONENTS -

1. Spark plug cover
2. Screw M4 - cover
3. Screw retaining washer
4. Engine oil filler cap
5. Filler cap seal
6. Spark plug
7. Clip - HT leads
8. Bolt M6 - camshaft cover
9. Camshaft cover
10. Camshaft cover gasket
11. Camshaft carrier
12. Bolt M6 - camshaft carrier
13. Cylinder head bolt
14. Camshaft - inlet
15. Camshaft - exhaust
16. Drive pin - camshaft gear
17. Drive spindle - rotor arm
18. Camshaft oil seal
19. Hydraulic tappet
20. Collets - cap
21. Valve spring cap
22. Valve spring
23. Valve stem oil seal
24. Cylinder head
25. Ring dowel - cylinder head to camshaft carrier
26. Cylinder head gasket
27. Valve guide
28. Inlet valve
29. Valve seat insert - inlet
30. Exhaust valve
31. Valve seat insert - exhaust
32. Blanking plate
33. Screw M6
34. Gasket - coolant outlet elbow
35. Coolant outlet elbow
36. Screw M6 - coolant outlet elbow
37. Coolant temperature sensors
38. Sealing washer

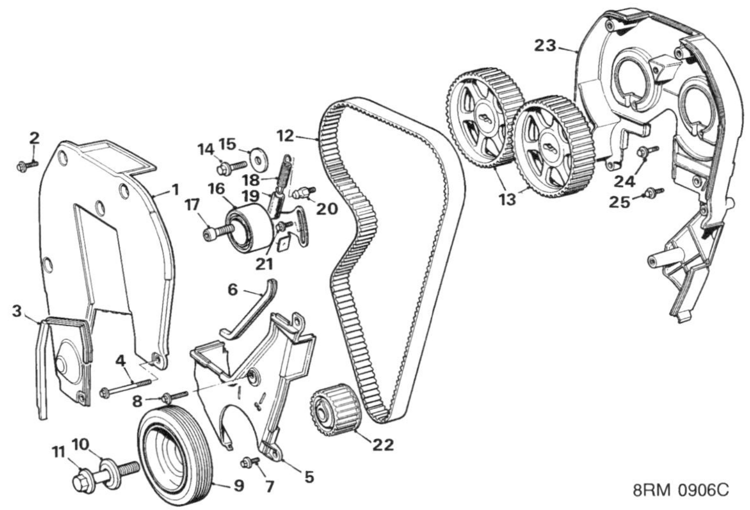

8RM 0906C

TIMING BELT COMPONENTS -

1. Upper front cover - timing belt
2. Screw M6 - upper cover
3. Seal - upper cover
4. Bolt M6 x 90 - upper and lower cover
5. Lower cover - timing belt
6. Seal - lower cover
7. Screw M6 - lower cover
8. Screw M6 x 16 - lower cover
9. Crankshaft pulley
10. Special washer - pulley bolt
11. Crankshaft pulley bolt
12. Camshaft timing belt
13. Camshaft timing gears
14. Camshaft gear bolt
15. Plain washer
16. Tensioner pulley and backplate
17. Allen screw - pulley
18. Tensioner spring
19. Sleeve - spring
20. Pillar bolt
21. Flange head screw - tensioner backplate
22. Crankshaft timing gear
23. Rear cover - timing belt
24. Screw - rear cover to cylinder head
25. Screw - rear cover to cylinder block

DESCRIPTION

The K Series engine is built up from aluminium castings bolted together. These consist of three major castings; the cylinder head, cylinder block and a bearing ladder which is line bored to provide the main bearing bores. Attached to these are three minor castings; above the cylinder head, the camshaft carrier and the camshaft cover. Below the bearing ladder is an oil rail.

Each of the ten cylinder head bolts passes through the cylinder head, cylinder block and bearing ladder to screw into the oil rail. This puts the cylinder head, cylinder block and bearing ladder into compression with all the tensile loads being carried by the cylinder head bolts. Additional fixings are used to retain the bearing ladder to the cylinder block, and the oil rail to the bearing ladder when the cylinder head bolts are removed;.

The cross flow cylinder head is based on a four valve, central spark plug, combustion chamber with the inlet ports designed to induce swirl and control the speed of the induction charge. This serves to improve combustion and hence fuel economy, performance and exhaust emissions. The camshafts are retained by the camshaft carrier, which is line bored with the cylinder head. Self adjusting hydraulic tappets are fitted on top of each valve and are operated directly by the camshafts. The valve stem oil seals are moulded onto a metal base which also acts as the valve spring seat on the cylinder head.

Carbon break type exhaust valves are fitted, which are identified by a machined profile on the valve stem. This removes any build up of carbon in the combustion chamber end of the valve guide, thereby preventing the valves from sticking.

The stainless steel cylinder head gasket has moulded seals around all coolant, breather and oil apertures and has steel cylinder bore eyelets. Compression of the gasket is controlled by limiters at each end of the gasket.

The cylinder block is fitted with 'damp' cylinder liners, the bottom, stepped half of the damp liner, being a sliding fit into the lower part of the cylinder block. The liners are sealed in the block with a bead of Hylomar sealant applied around the stepped portion of the liner. The seal at the cylinder head is effected by the cylinder head gasket with the liner top acting as a break between the combustion chamber and gasket. The aluminium alloy, thermal expansion pistons have a semi-floating gudgeon pin which is offset towards the thrust side and has an interference fit in the small end of the connecting rod. Pistons and cylinder liners are supplied in two grades. Big-end bearing diametric clearance is controlled by three grades of selective shell bearing.

The five bearing, eight balance weight crankshaft has its end-float controlled by thrust washer halves at the top of the central main bearing. Bearing diametric clearance is controlled by three grades of selective shell bearing. Oil grooves are provided in the upper halves of main bearings No. 2, 3 and 4 to supply oil, via drillings in the crankshaft, to the connecting rod big-end bearings.

K16 engine lubrication system

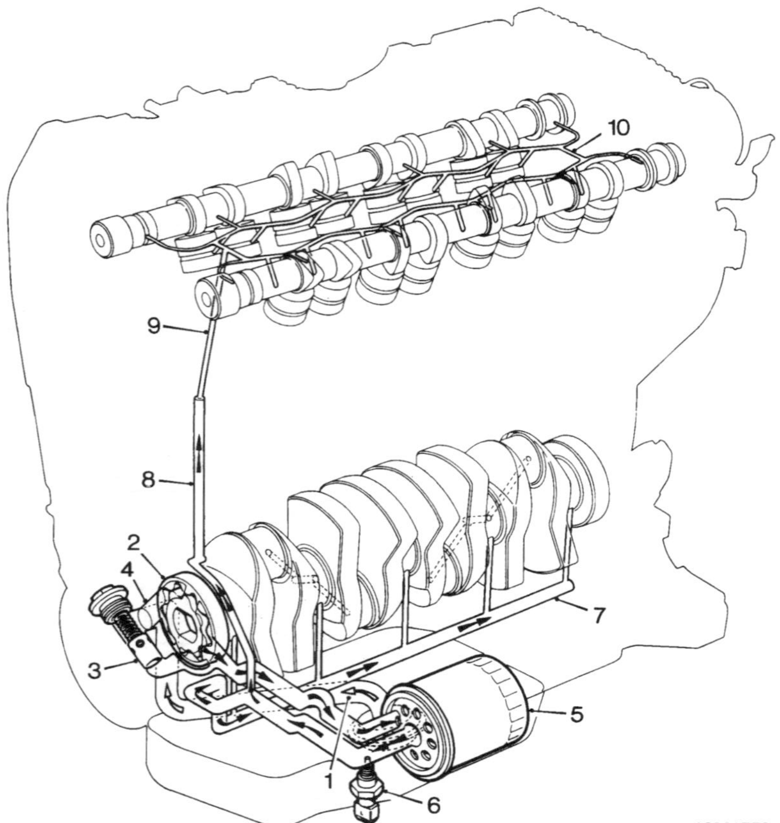

12M1758

Lubrication

The lubrication system is of the full-flow filtration, forced fed type. The oil sump is of alloy manufacture, sealed to the bearing ladder with a bead of sealant applied to the flange.

Oil is drawn, via a strainer and suction pipe (1) in the sump, into the crankshaft driven oil pump (2). The oil pump is of the trochoid type which has an integral pressure relief valve (3), excess oil is diverted into the intake (4) of the oil pump. Oil is pumped through the full-flow cartridge type oil filter (5), mounted on an adapter attached to the oil pump housing. The low oil pressure sensor (6) is also screwed into the adapter and registers the oil pressure in the main oil gallery on the outlet side of the filter.

The main oil gallery (7) is fed through the oil rail below the main bearing ladder in which drillings direct the oil to the main bearings. Cross drillings in the crankshaft from No. 2 and 4 main bearings carry the oil to the big-end bearings. A passage in the oil pump housing connects to a drilling (8) in the cylinder block to oilways (9) in the cylinder head.

Oil is fed through the cylinder head to twin full length oilways (10) in the camshaft carrier to supply oil to each hydraulic tappet and camshaft bearing.

Crankcase ventilation

A positive crankcase ventilation system is used to vent blow-by gas from the crankcase to the air intake system.

Crankcase gases are drawn through a gauze oil separator in the camshaft cover and passes via hoses into the throttle housing.

ENGINE NUMBER LOCATION

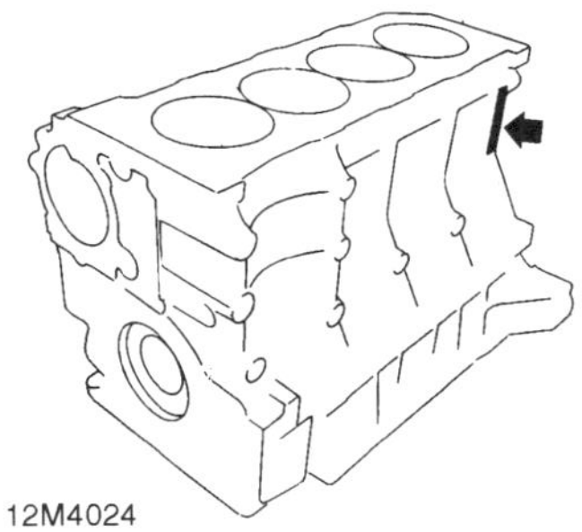

12M4024

The engine number can be found stamped on the rear LH side of the cylinder block.

CAMSHAFT TIMING BELT

Remove

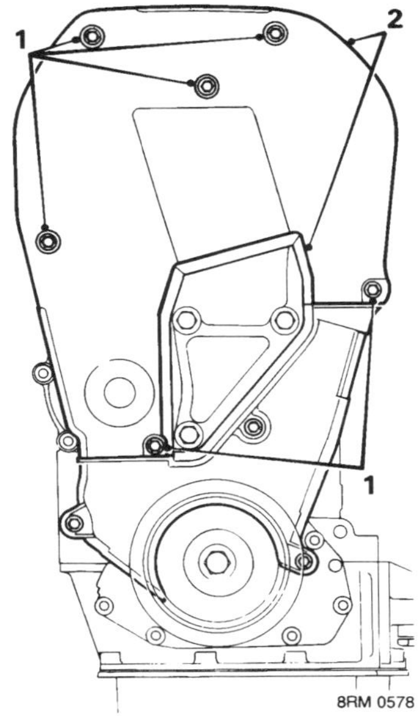

8RM 0578

1. Slacken bottom screw and remove 5 bolts securing timing belt upper front cover.

NOTE: Remove screw when cover is not slotted.

2. Remove timing belt upper front cover and seal.

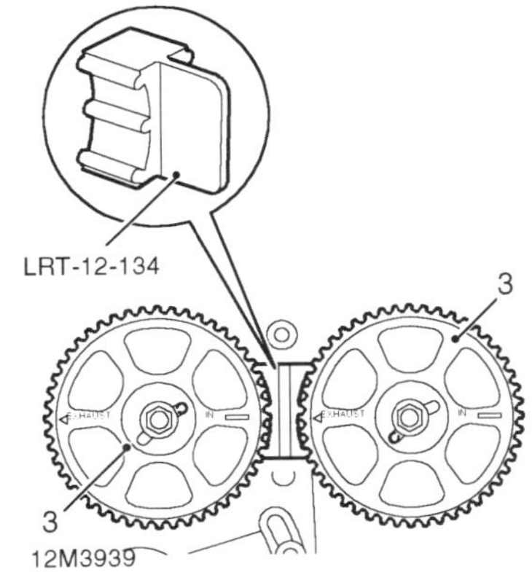

12M3939

3. Rotate crankshaft to align camshaft gear timing marks 90° BTDC.
4. Fit camshaft gear locking tool **LRT-12-134.**

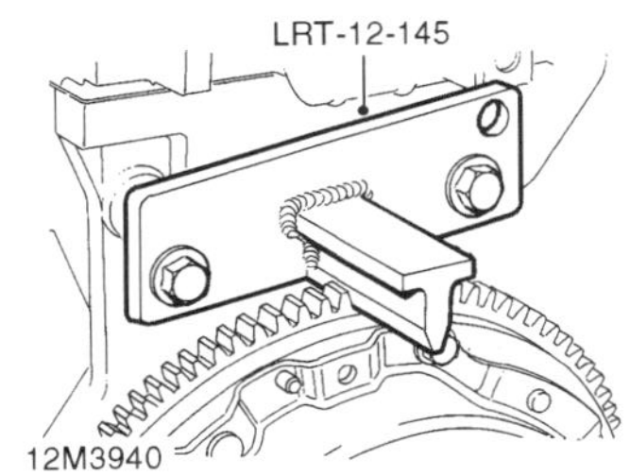

12M3940

5. Fit flywheel locking tool **LRT-12-145**
6. Secure with 2 bolts.

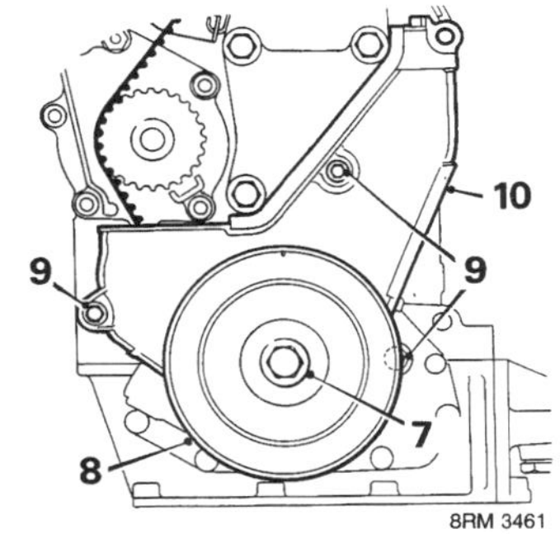

8RM 3461

7. Remove crankshaft pulley bolt and washer.
8. Remove crankshaft pulley.
9. Remove 3 bolts securing timing belt lower cover.
10. Remove lower cover and seals.

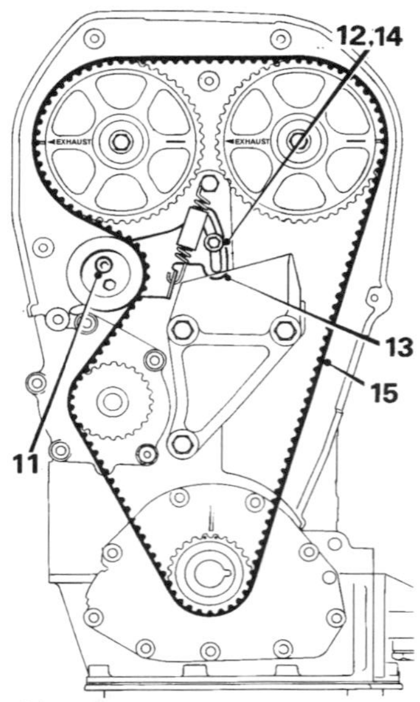

12M1763B

11. Slacken tensioner pulley Allen screw.
12. Slacken tensioner backplate screw.
13. Push tensioner pulley down to fully OFF position.
14. Tighten backplate screw to 10 Nm.
15. Ease timing belt from gears using the fingers only.
16. Discard timing belt.

CAUTION: Timing belt must always be replaced whenever it is removed. Do not rotate camshafts or crankshaft with timing belt removed and cylinder head fitted.

Refit

1. Clean timing gears and pulleys.

CAUTION: If the sintered gears have been subjected to prolonged oil contamination, they must be soaked in a solvent bath and then thoroughly washed in clean solvent before refitting. Because of the porous construction of sintered material, oil impregnated in the gears will emerge and contaminate the belt.

2. Check correct alignment of camshaft gear timing gear timing marks and crankshaft gear timing dots with flange on oil pump - 90° BTDC.
   Spring is fitted with a sleeve.

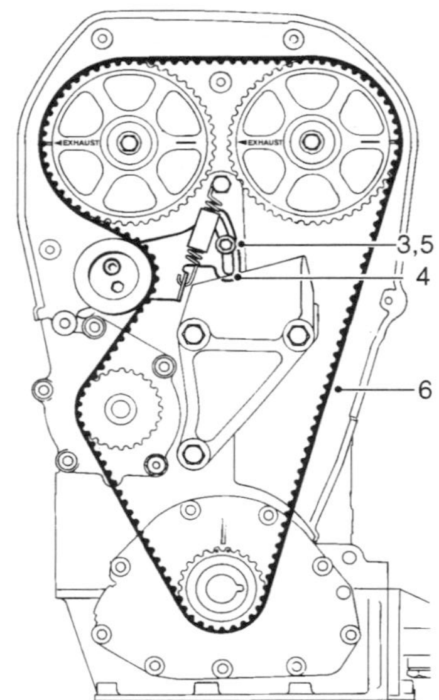

12M3922

3. Slacken tensioner backplate screw, ensure tensioner moves fully through its adjustment range and returns under spring tension.
4. Push tensioner down to fully OFF position.
5. Tighten tensioner backplate screw to 10 Nm.
6. Using the fingers only, fit a new timing belt over crankshaft timing gear and then over camshaft gears keeping belt taut between crankshaft timing gear and exhaust camshaft gear.

7. Ease timing belt over tensioner pulley and coolant pump drive gear ensuring belt is positioned centrally on gears and pulley.
8. Ensure inserts are fitted in timing belt lower cover.
9. Fit timing belt lower cover, ensuring correct position of seals, tighten screws to 5 Nm.

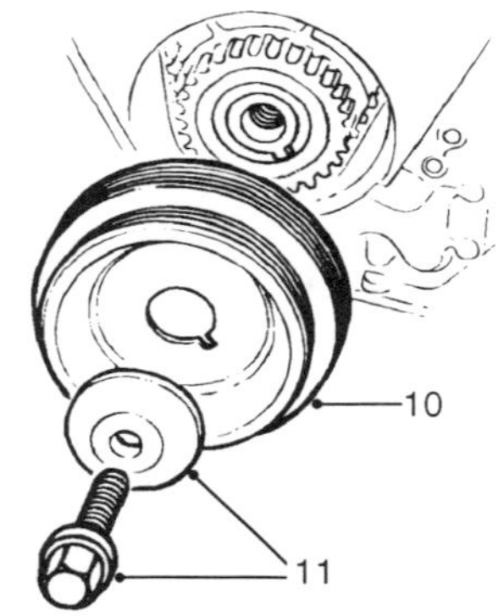

12M3923

10. Fit crankshaft pulley to crankshaft timing gear ensuring that indent on pulley locates over lug on gear.
11. Secure with crankshaft pulley bolt and washer, tighten to 205 Nm.
12. Remove camshaft and flywheel locking tools **LRT-12-134** and **LRT-12-145.**

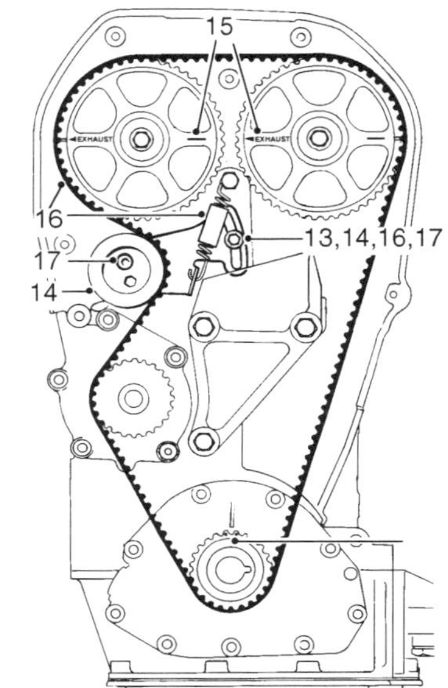

12M3924

13. Slacken tensioner backplate screw and tension timing belt by applying finger pressure to tensioner backplate.
14. With tensioner pulley against timing belt and backplate held in position, tighten backplate screw to 10 Nm.
15. Rotate crankshaft clockwise 2 complete revolutions and align camshaft gear timing marks.
16. Slacken tensioner backplate screw and check that belt is being tensioned by the tensioner spring.
17. Tighten tensioner backplate screw to 10 Nm and tensioner pulley Allen screw to 45 Nm.
18. Ensure inserts are fitted in timing belt front upper cover.
19. Fit timing belt upper front cover, ensuring correct position of seals, tighten screw and bolts to 5 Nm.

OIL PUMP

Remove

1. Remove and discard camshaft timing belt.
2. Remove crankshaft timing gear.

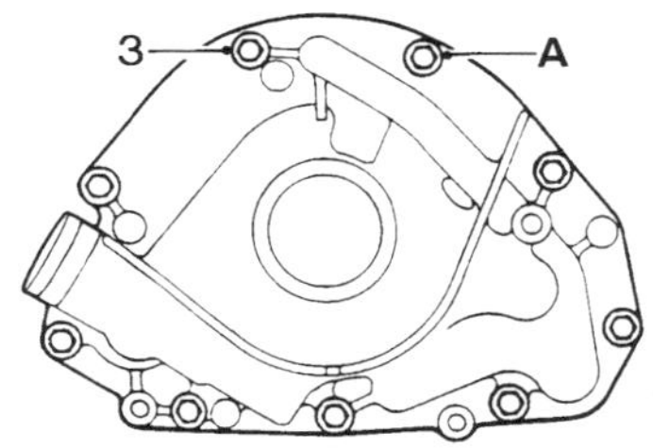

12M1765

3. Noting fitted position of M6 x 20 bolt 'A,' remove and discard 9 bolts securing oil pump to cylinder block.

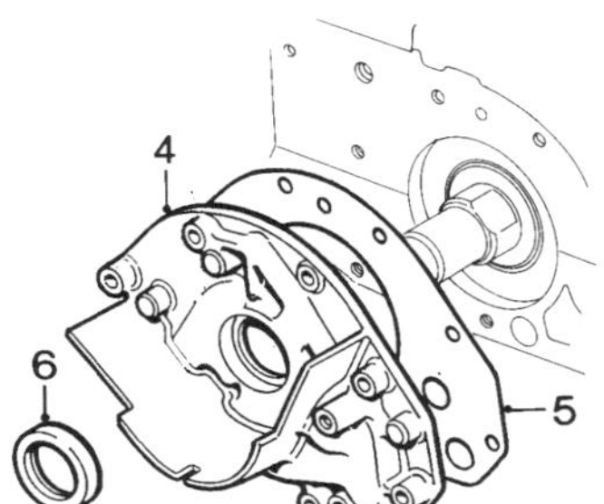

12M1766

4. Remove oil pump assembly.

NOTE: Dowel located.

5. Remove and discard oil pump gasket.
6. Remove and discard crankshaft front oil seal.

Inspection

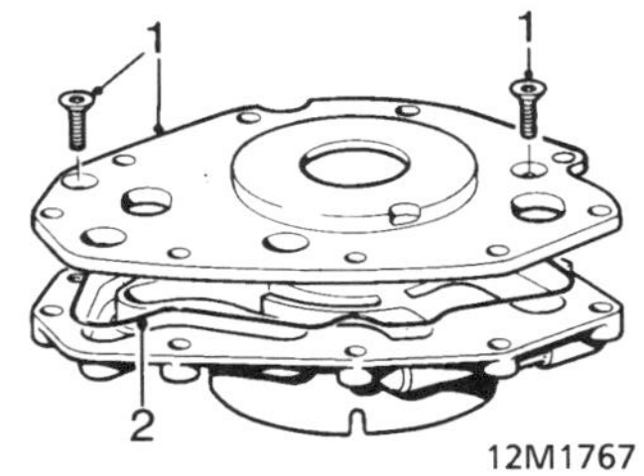

12M1767

1. Remove 2 screws and cover plate.
2. Remove and discard cover plate seal.

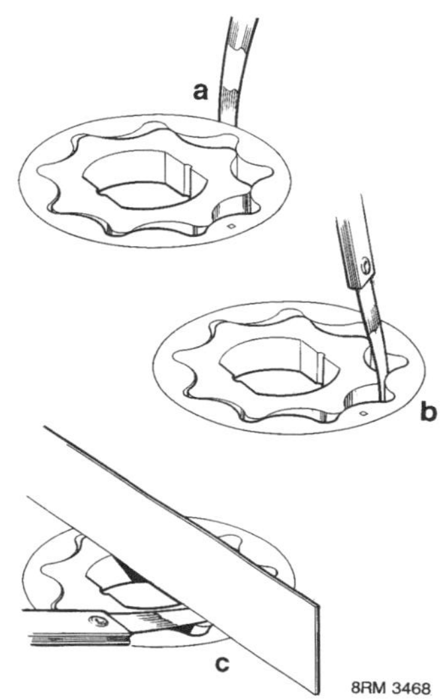

8RM 3468

3. Check rotor clearances:
   a. Outer rotor to housing = 0.28 - 0.36 mm
   b. Inner rotor tip = 0.05 - 0.13 mm
   c. Rotor end float = 0.02 - 0.06 mm
   Renew pump assembly if housing is scored or clearances are excessive.
4. Remove all traces of Loctite from cover plate securing screws and tapped holes in oil pump body; ensure screw holes are clean and dry.

Oil pressure relief valve

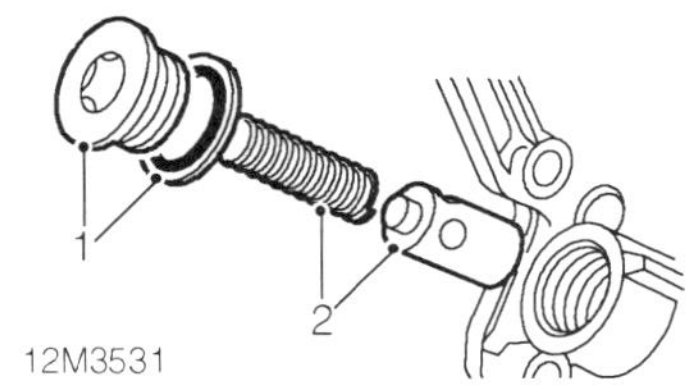

12M3531

1. Unscrew plug, discard sealing washer.
2. Remove spring and relief valve sleeve assembly.
3. Check that valve sleeve slides freely in bore and that bore and sleeve are free from scoring and corrosion.

NOTE: Light corrosion may be removed using grade 600 emery cloth soaked in engine oil.

4. Check free length of spring:
   Spring free length = 38.9 mm

   Replace relief valve as an assembly if scoring of plunger is evident or free length of spring is less than specified. Replace oil pump if relief valve bore is scored.
5. Remove all traces of Loctite from plug and threads in relief valve bore.

CAUTION: Do not use a tap.

6. Apply Loctite 577 to threads of plug.
7. Fit plug, use a new sealing washer.

Oil pump assembling

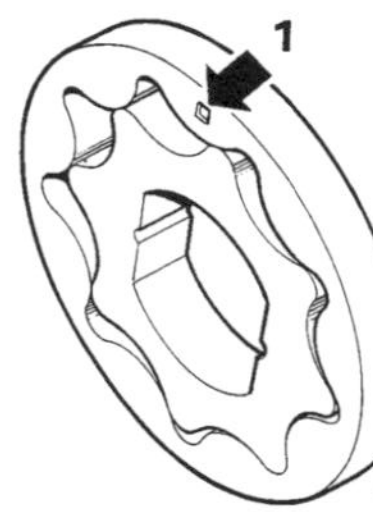

8RM 3469

1. Ensure outer rotor identification marking faces outward.
2. Lubricate pump rotors with engine oil.
3. Lubricate a new cover plate seal with engine oil.
4. Fit cover plate seal and cover plate.
5. Apply Loctite 222 to cover plate securing screws, fit and tighten screws.
6. Check that pump rotates freely.

Oil pump - refit

1. Clean oil pump.
2. Using gasket removal spray and a plastic scraper, remove all traces of gasket from oil pump.
3. Lubricate oil seal running surface on crankshaft with engine oil.
4. Fit a new, dry oil pump gasket.
5. Turn oil pump rotor to align drive with crankshaft
6. Fit oil seal protector sleeve, from seal kit, over crankshaft end.

NOTE: This will assist in locating oil pump inner rotor.

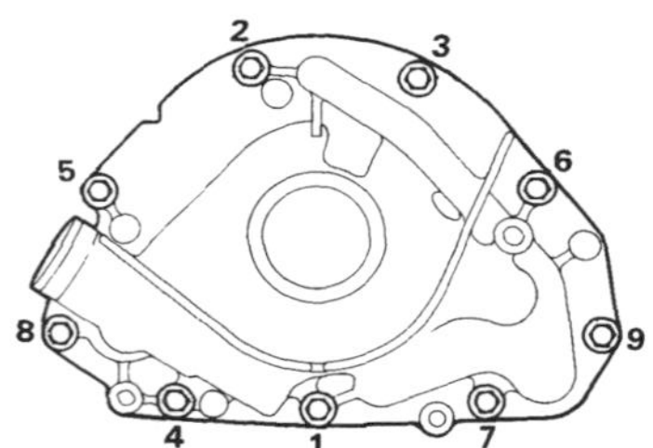

12M1769

7. Fit oil pump, fit new Patchlok bolts, M6 x 20 bolt at position 3. Tighten in sequence shown to 10 Nm.
8. Lubricate a new crankshaft front oil seal with engine oil.

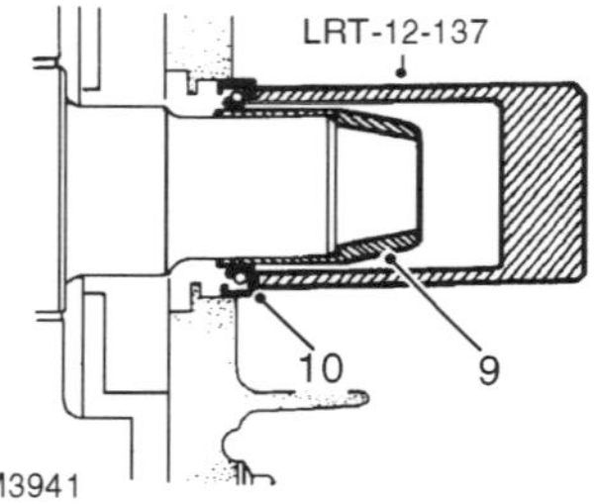

12M3941

9. Ensure oil seal protector sleeve is located over end of crankshaft.
10. Position new seal on crankshaft against oil pump housing. Drift seal into position using tool **LRT-12-137**
11. Remove tool **LRT-12-137** and oil seal protector sleeve.
12. Clean crankshaft timing gear.
13. Fit crankshaft timing gear.
14. Fit and adjust a new camshaft timing belt.

COOLANT PUMP

Remove

1. Remove and discard camshaft timing belt.

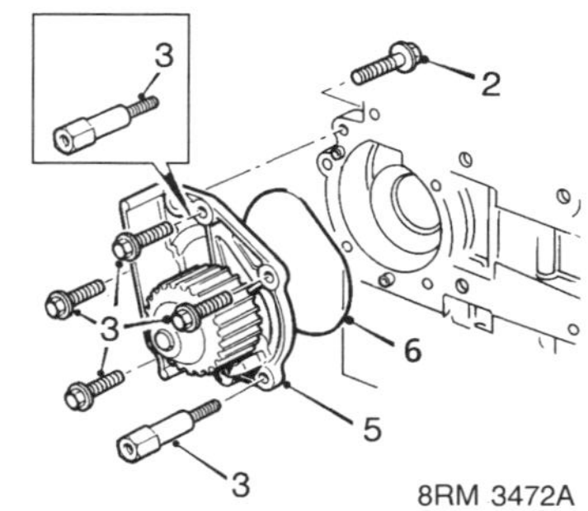

8RM 3472A

2. Remove bolt securing timing belt rear cover to coolant pump.
3. Remove 3 bolts and 2 pillar bolts securing coolant pump.
4. Release coolant pump from 2 dowels and rear cover.
5. Remove coolant pump.
6. Remove and discard 'O' ring from pump.

Inspection

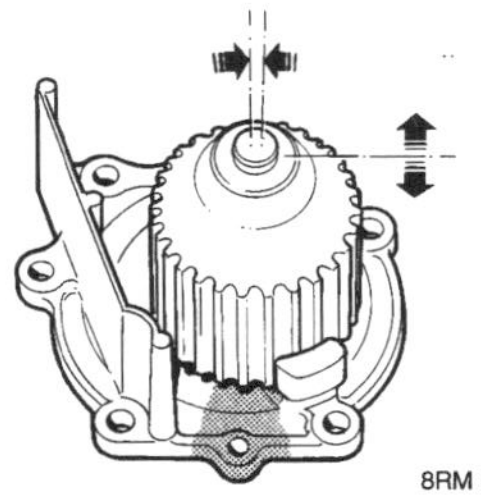

8RM 3473

1. Check for movement of pump spindle in bearing and for coolant leakage from seal.

Refit

1. Clean pump, mating face and dowels.
2. Fit new 'O' ring to coolant pump, use RTV sealant to retain 'O' ring.

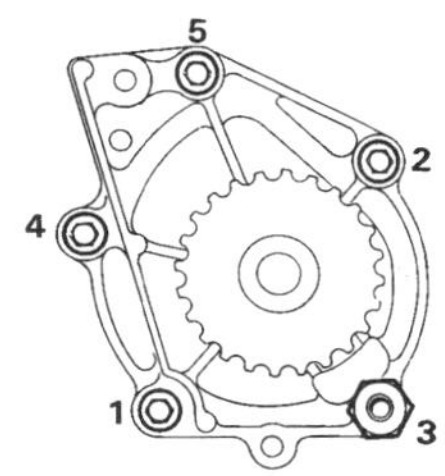

8RM 0055

3. Fit coolant pump to cylinder block, tighten bolts in sequence shown to 10 Nm.
4. Fit and adjust a new camshaft timing belt.

THERMOSTAT

Remove

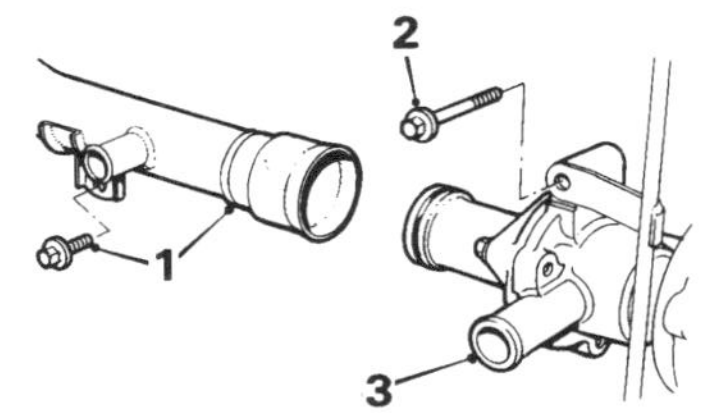

12M0558

1. Remove 2 bolts securing water rail to cylinder block, release rail from thermostat housing.
2. Remove bolt securing thermostat housing and dipstick tube to cylinder block.
3. Withdraw thermostat housing from coolant pump.

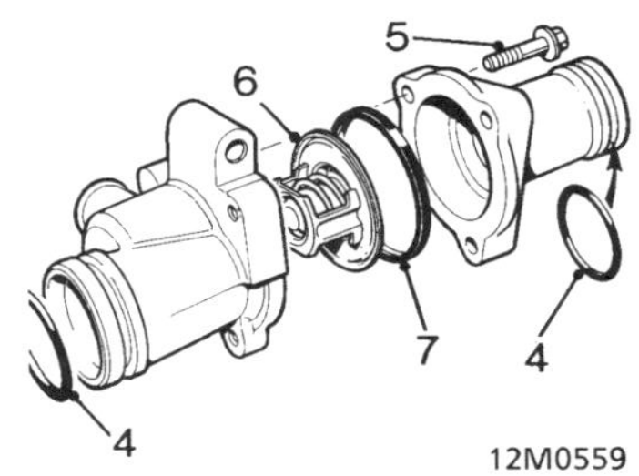

12M0559

4. Remove and discard 'O' rings from thermostat housing and cover.
5. Remove 3 bolts and remove cover from thermostat housing.
6. Withdraw thermostat from housing.
7. Remove and discard seal from thermostat.

Inspection

1. Test thermostat using thermostat test equipment, renew thermostat if necessary.
2. Thermostat open = 88° C
   Starts to open = 85° C

Refit

1. Clean thermostat housing, cover and sealing faces.
2. Lubricate new 'O' rings with silicone grease and fit to thermostat housing and cover.
3. Fit a new seal to thermostat.
4. Align and fit thermostat to shoulder in thermostat housing.
5. Fit cover to thermostat housing, fit and tighten bolts to 8 Nm.

CAUTION: Torque figure must not be exceeded.

6. Fit thermostat housing to coolant pump, align dipstick tube bracket, fit and tighten bolt to 10 Nm.
7. Connect water rail to thermostat cover.
8. Align water rail to cylinder block, fit and tighten bolts to 10 Nm.

FLYWHEEL AND STARTER RING GEAR

Flywheel - remove

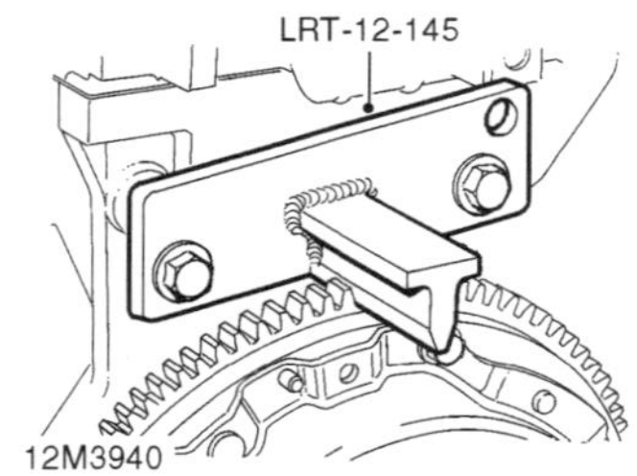

1. Fit flywheel locking tool **LRT-12-145** to cylinder block.

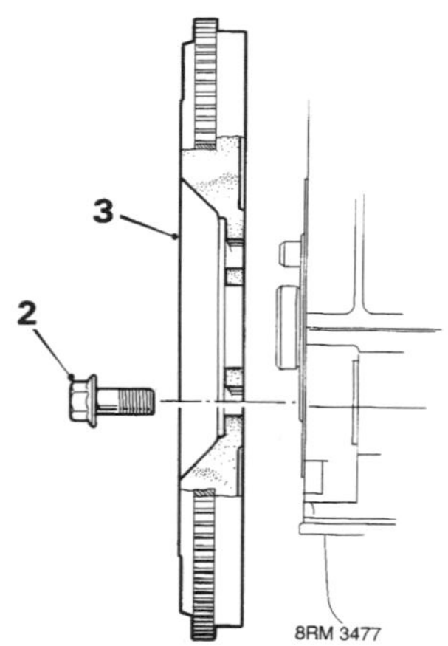

2. Remove and discard 6 bolts securing flywheel.
3. Using assistance, remove flywheel from crankshaft.

NOTE: Dowel located.

Starter ring gear - remove

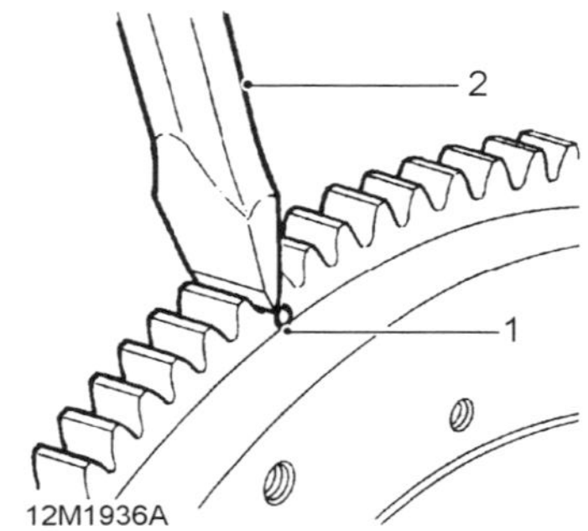

1. Drill a 3 mm diameter hole at root of 2 teeth.
2. Apply a cold chisel to root of teeth, break ring gear and remove from flywheel.

WARNING: Suitable eye protection must be worn.

Starter ring gear - refit

1. Heat ring gear evenly to 350°C, indicated by light BLUE colour. Locate ring gear on flywheel and press hard against flange.

WARNING: Handle hot ring gear with care.

2. Allow ring gear to air cool.

Flywheel - refit

CAUTION: The reluctor pattern machined into the flywheel has 4 missing teeth at unequally spaced intervals. If the flywheel is to be replaced, it is essential that the replacement is of the correct type.

1. Clean flywheel and crankshaft faces. Use a clean bolt with two saw cuts along threads and clean adhesive from threaded holes in crankshaft.
2. Using assistance, fit flywheel to crankshaft, fit and tighten new Patchlok bolts to 80 Nm.

Cylinder head - remove

CAUTION: If crankshaft is to be removed during overhaul it will be necessary to check and record crankshaft end-float prior to removing cylinder head.

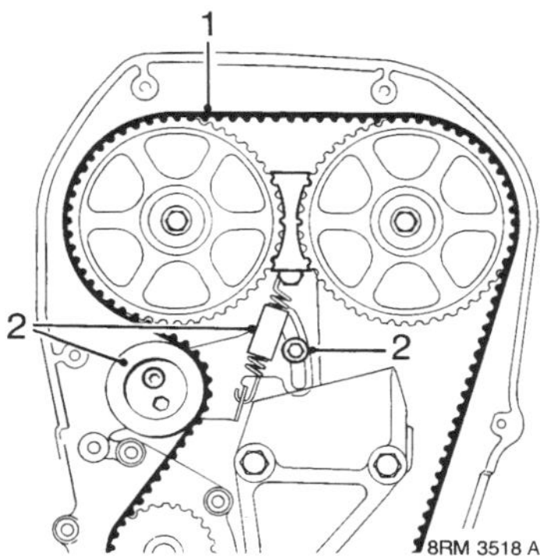

8RM 3518 A

1. Remove and discard camshaft timing belt.

CAUTION: Do not rotate crankshaft whilst timing belt is removed, pistons will contact the valves.

2. Disconnect tensioner spring, remove bolt, screw, tensioner and spring.

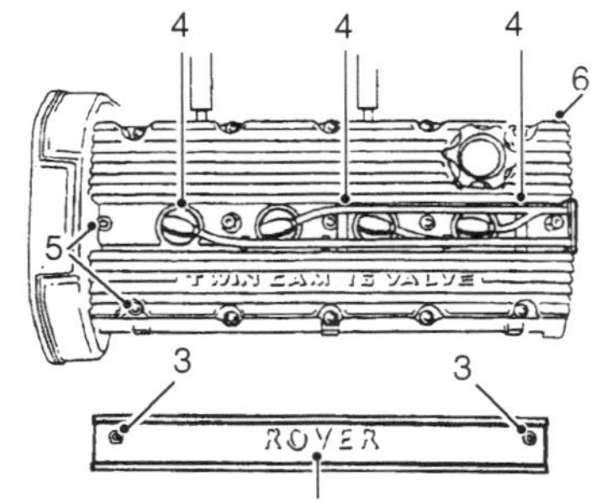

12M3928

3. Release 2 screws and remove spark plug cover.
4. Disconnect 4 plug tubes from spark plugs.
5. Progressively slacken then remove camshaft cover bolts
6. Remove camshaft cover assembly, remove and discard gasket.
7. Check and record crankshaft end-float. *See* ***Crankshaft end-float - checking.***

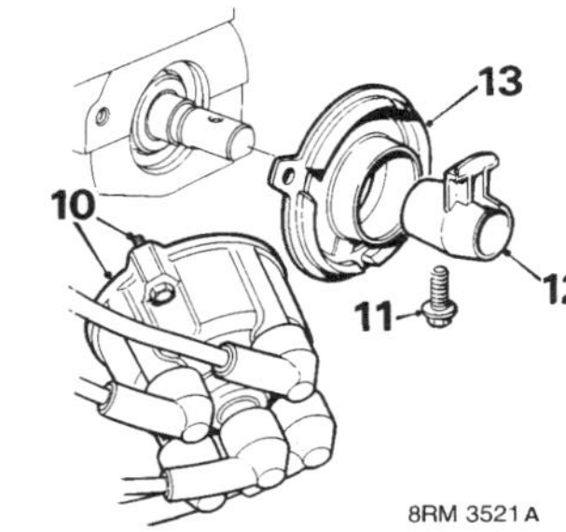

8RM 3521 A

8. Release 2 screws and remove distributor cap.
9. Remove and discard screw securing rotor arm.
10. Remove rotor arm.
11. Remove anti-flash shield.

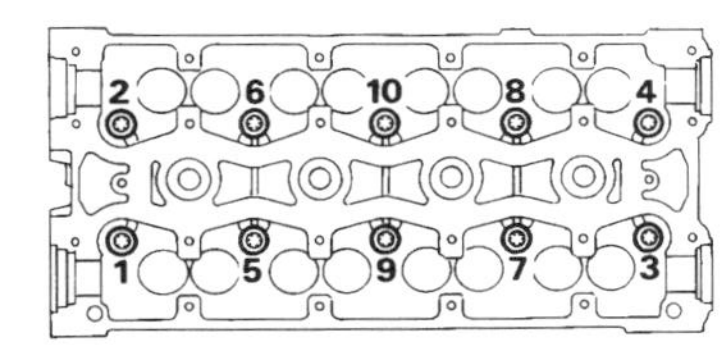

8RM 0740

12. Using sequence shown, progressively slacken 10 cylinder head to oil rail bolts. Remove bolts 1 to 8 and store in fitted order.

NOTE: It will be necessary to carry out the following operations in order to remove bolts 9 and 10.

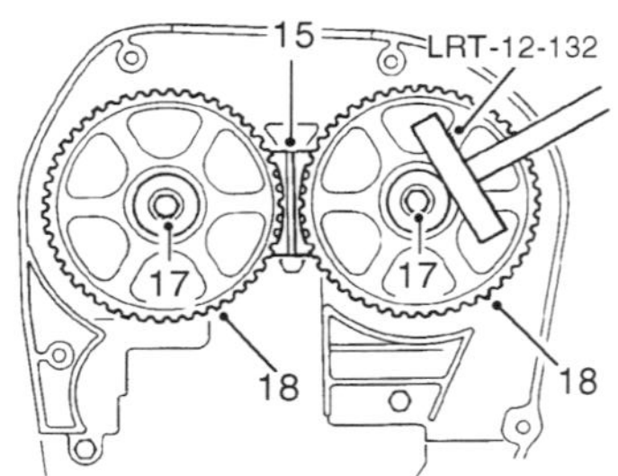

12M3942

13. Remove locking tool **LRT-12-134** from camshaft gears.
14. Using tool **LRT-12-132** turn both camshafts clockwise until camshaft location lugs clear bolt heads 9 and 10 and remove the bolts.

⚠ **CAUTION: Removal of cylinder head bolts results in a 'tightening-up' of crankshaft; rotation of crankshaft must, therefore, be kept to a minimum. Do not rotate crankshaft until cylinder liner retainer clamps are fitted.**

15. Suitably identify each camshaft gear to its respective camshaft and using tool **LRT-12-132** to hold camshaft gear against rotation, remove 2 bolts and plain washers from camshaft gears.
16. Remove camshaft gears.

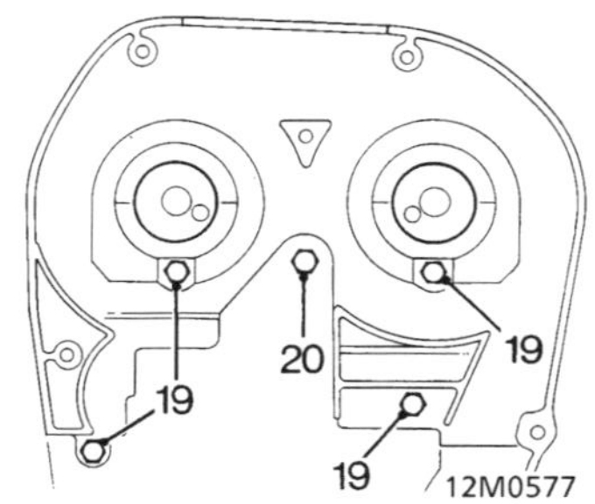

12M0577

17. Remove 4 bolts securing upper part of timing belt rear cover to cylinder head.
18. Remove timing belt tensioner spring pillar bolt.
19. Using assistance, remove cylinder head assembly from cylinder block.

⚠ **CAUTION: Cylinder head is dowel located, do not tap it sideways to free it from cylinder block. Place cylinder head assembly on blocks of wood to prevent damaging valves.**

20. Remove and discard cylinder head gasket.

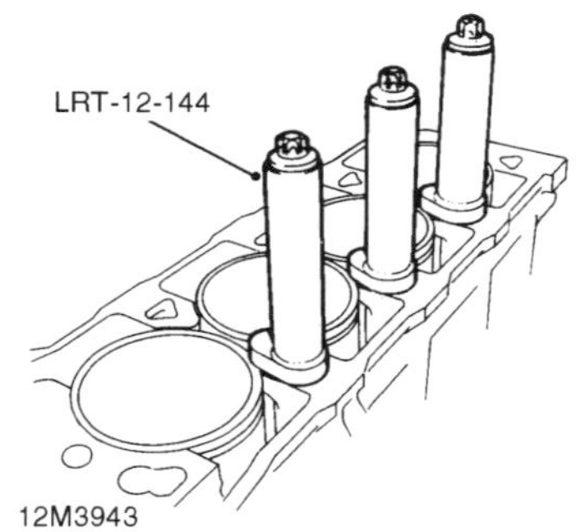

12M3943

21. Assemble cylinder liner retainer clamps **LRT-12-144** to cylinder head bolts. Position retainer clamps on cylinder liners ensuring clamps do not protrude over liner bores. Screw bolts finger tight into oil rail.

⚠ **CAUTION: Ensure that bolts used are those originally fitted in that location.**

Camshafts - check end-float

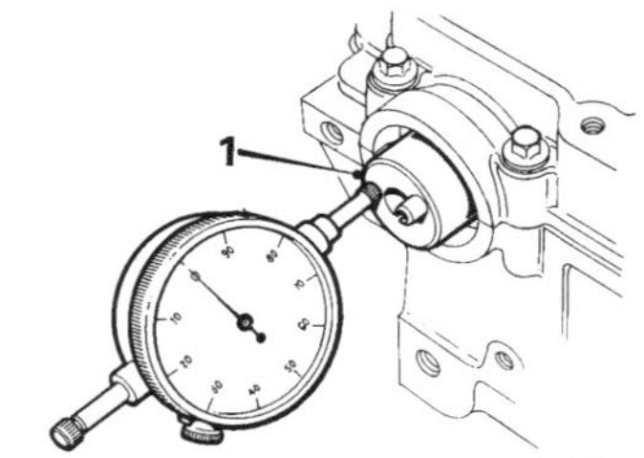

12M 0550

1. Check end-float of each camshaft using a DTI. Camshaft end-float = 0.06 to 0.19 mm Service limit = 0.3 mm
2. Renew components as necessary to achieve correct end-float.

Camshaft carrier and camshafts - remove

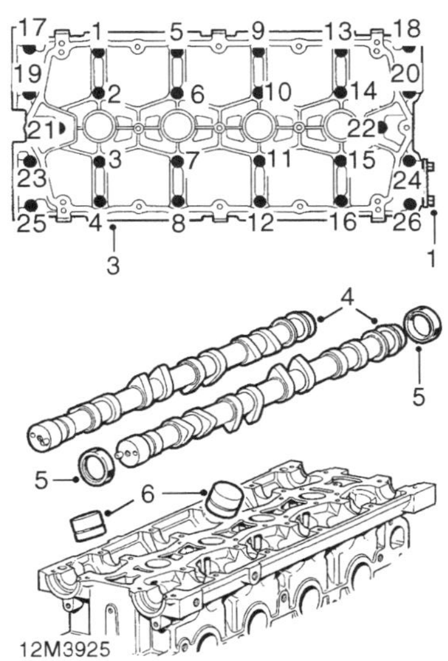

1. Remove 2 bolts securing blanking plate to rear of camshaft carrier, remove plate.
2. Using sequence shown,progressively slacken 26 bolts until valve spring pressure is released. Remove bolts.
3. Remove camshaft carrier.

NOTE: Dowel located.

4. Remove 2 camshafts.
5. Remove and discard 4 oil seals from camshafts.
6. Using a stick magnet, remove 16 tappets from cylinder head. Retain tappets in fitted order and invert to prevent oil loss.

Tappets - inspection

1. Check tappets for signs of wear, scoring and overheating.
2. Measure outside diameter of tappet, measurement must be taken half-way along tappet body.
   Tappet outside dia. = 32.959 to 32.975 mm.
3. Ensure oil hole in each tappet is clear.

NOTE: Retain tappets in their fitted order and keep them inverted to prevent oil loss.

Camshafts and timing gears - inspection

Camshafts

NOTE: Carry out camshaft inspection after removal of valves.

1. Clean camshafts, camshaft carrier and cylinder head bearing surfaces, use suitable solvent to remove sealant.
2. Inspect cams and bearing journals for wear, pitting and scoring; replace components as necessary.

Checking camshaft bearing clearance

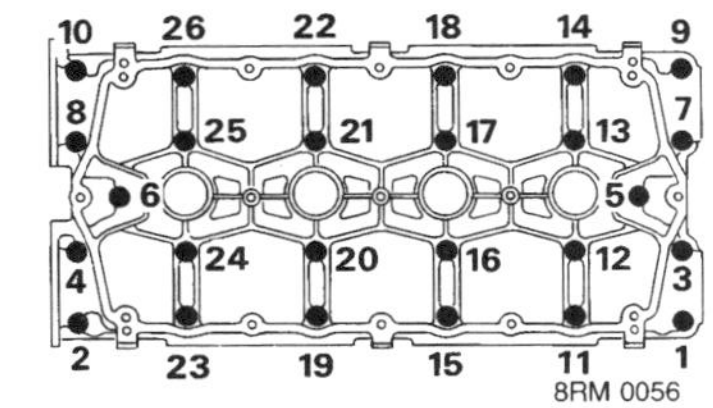

3. Position camshaft(s) in cylinder head and place Plastigage across each journal.
4. Fit camshaft carrier and tighten bolts in sequence shown to 10 Nm. Do not rotate camshaft(s).
5. Progressively slacken bolts and then remove camshaft carrier.

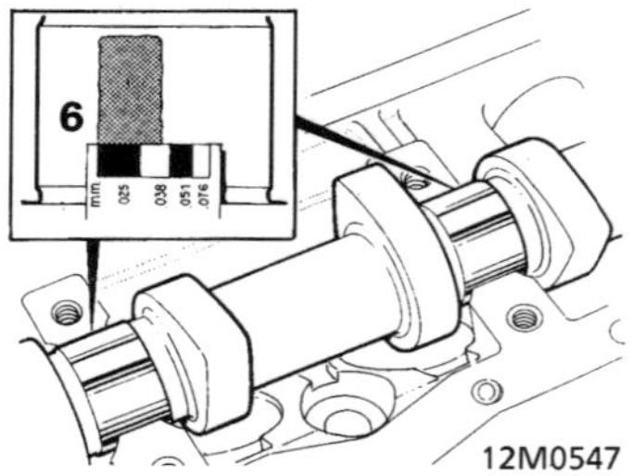

12M0547

6. Measure widest portion of Plastigage on each journal:
Camshaft bearing clearance = 0.060 to 0.094 mm
Service limit = 0.15 mm
If clearance is excessive, fit new camshaft(s) and repeat check. If clearances are still excessive, replace cylinder head and camshaft carrier assembly.

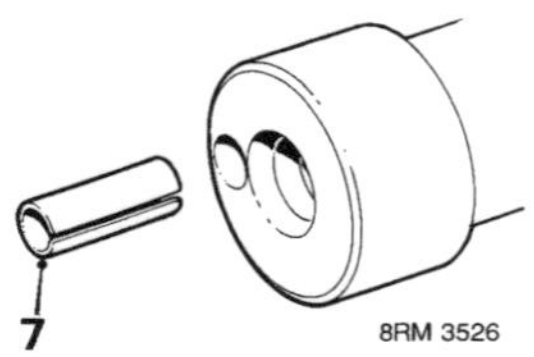

8RM 3526

7. Remove drive pin from old camshaft and fit to new with its split towards centre of camshaft.

Timing gears

1. Clean timing gears, check gear teeth for damage and drive pin slot for wear, replace gears as necessary.

CAUTION: If gears have been subjected to prolonged exposure to oil contamination, they must be soaked in a solvent bath and then thoroughly washed in clean solvent.

Valves and springs - remove

1. Support cylinder head clear of valves; use hollow drift and tap each spring cap to free collets.
2. Position cylinder head on its exhaust manifold face.

NOTE: : Remove inlet valves with cylinder head in this position.

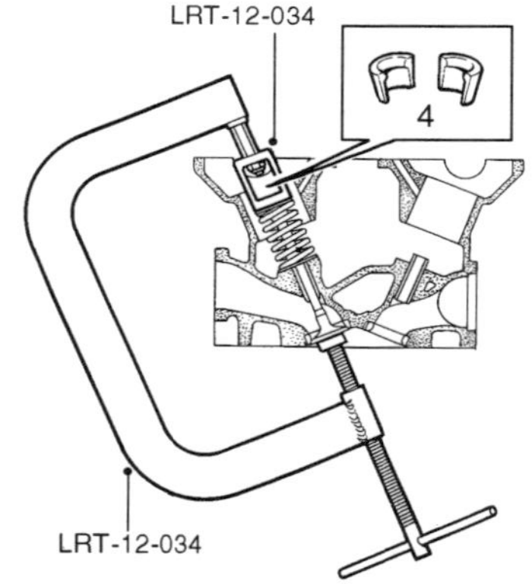

12M3944

3. Using tool **LRT-12-034** and adapter **LRT-12-034-1** compress valve spring.
4. Remove 2 collets from valve stem using a magnet.
5. Remove tool **LRT-12-034.**

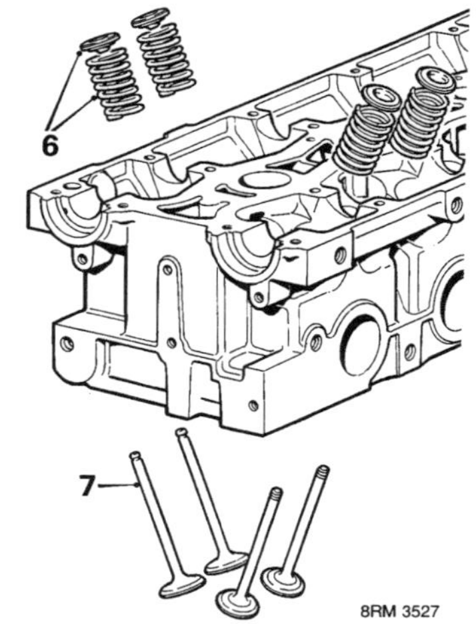

8RM 3527

6. Remove spring cap and valve spring
7. Remove valve.

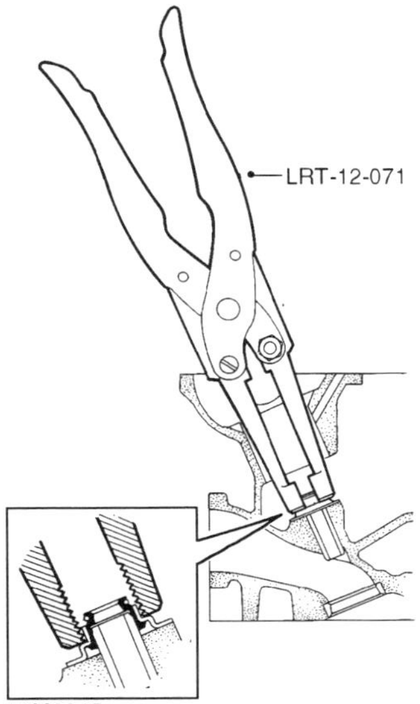

12M3945

8. Using **LRT-12-071,** remove valve stem seal.
9. Repeat operations to remove remaining inlet valves.

CAUTION: Retain valves and springs in fitted order.

10. Position cylinder head on its inlet manifold face.
11. Repeat operations to remove exhaust valves and valve stem seals.

CAUTION: Retain valves and springs in fitted order.

Cylinder head - cleaning

1. Clean sealing surfaces on cylinder head and camshaft carrier.
   Use foam action gasket remover and a plastic scraper - DO NOT USE A METAL SCRAPER ON SEALING SURFACES.
   Clean inlet and exhaust manifold joint faces.
   Blow out oilways and waterways. Ensure oil feed to camshaft carrier is clear.
2. De-carbonise combustion areas of cylinder head and valves as necessary.

CAUTION: With cylinder head removed, rotation of crankshaft must be kept to a minimum. Do not remove cylinder liner retainer clamps 18G 1736.

Cylinder head - inspection

1. Check cylinder head for damage, pay particular attention to gasket face of cylinder head.

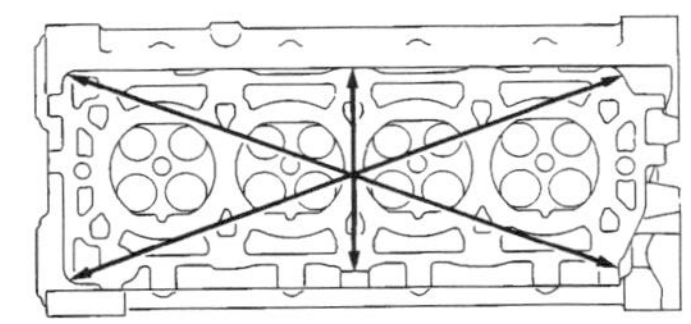
12M3926

2. Check cylinder head face for warping, across centre and from corner to corner:
   Cylinder head:
   Maximum warp = 0.05 mm
3. Check cylinder head height:
   New = 118.95 to 119.05 mm.

   Cylinder heads may be refaced:
   Reface limit = 0.20 mm

Valve springs - inspection

1. Check condition of valve springs:

Free length = 50.0 mm
Fitted length = 37.0 mm
Load - valve closed = 250 ± 12 N
Load - valve open = 450 ± 18 N

Valves and guides - inspection

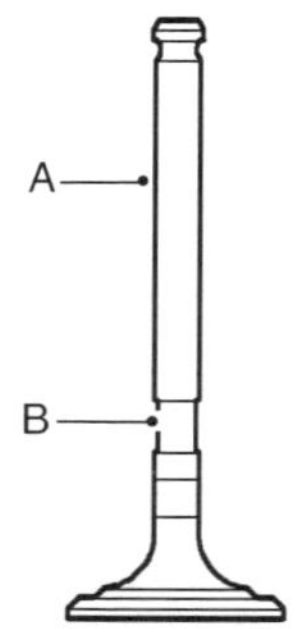

12M4025

NOTE: Carbon Break type exhaust valves are fitted, A in illustration, and are identified by the machined profile B on the valve stem. The machined profile is to prevent carbon build up on the valve stem and to prevent the exhaust valves from sticking.

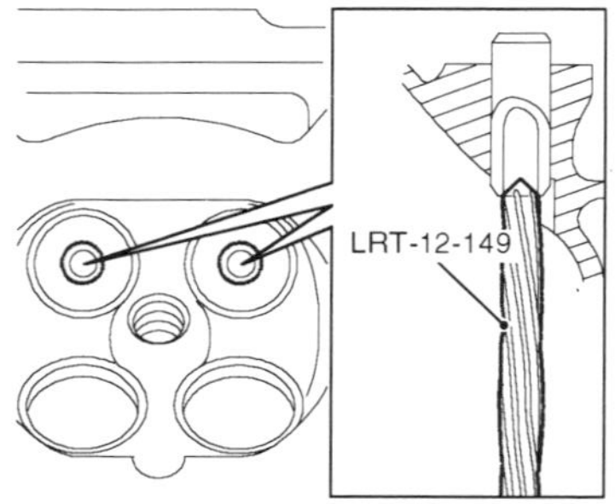

12M3946

1. Remove carbon deposits from exhaust valve guides using tool **LRT-12-149**.

CAUTION: Tool must be inserted into valve guide from combustion face side of cylinder head.

2. Remove carbon from inlet valve guides, inlet and exhaust valves and valve seat inserts. Remove all loose particles of carbon on completion.

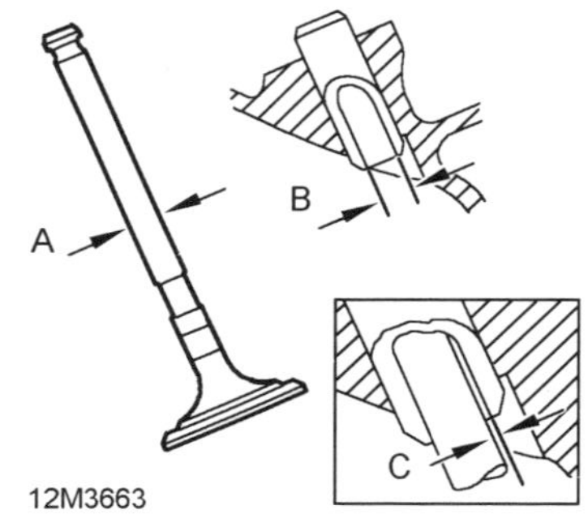

12M3663

3. Check existing valve stem diameters.
4. Check valve guide clearance using new valves.
5. Renew valves and guides as necessary:

Valve stem diameter **A:**
Inlet = 5.952 to 5.967 mm
Exhaust = 5.947 to 5.962 mm
Valve guides:
Inside diameter **B:**= 6.000 to 6.025 mm
Valve stem to guide clearance **C:**
Inlet = 0.033 to 0.063 mm
Service limit = 0.07 mm
Exhaust = 0.038 to 0.078 mm
Service limit = 0.11 mm

Valve guides - renew

1. Support cylinder head face down on wooden blocks.

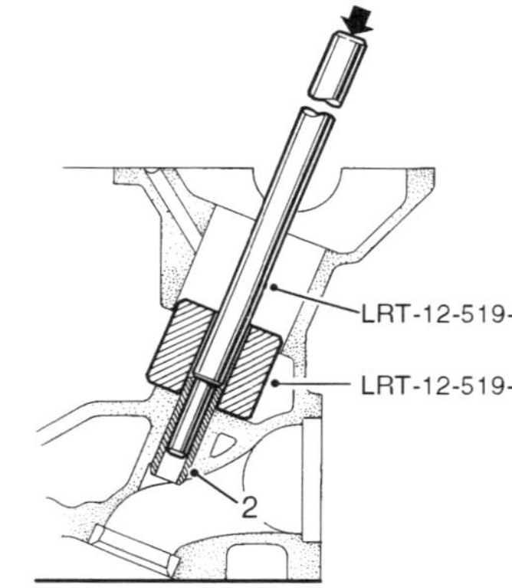

12M3947

2. Position tool guide **LRT-12-519-3** in tappet bore and drift out valve guide using tool drift **LRT-12-519-1.**

NOTE: Retain valve guides in their fitted order.

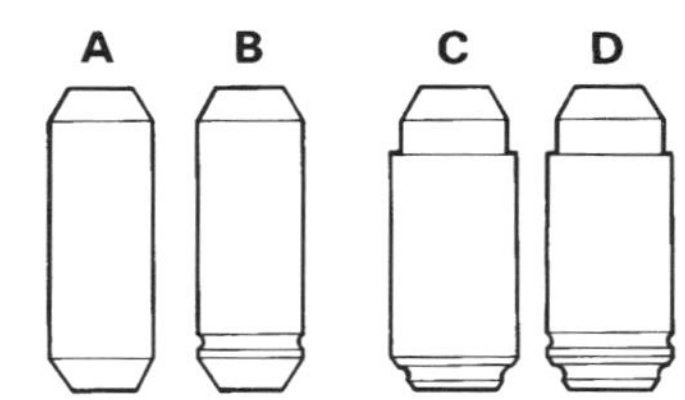

12M0007

3. Identify type of valve guide fitted:-
   A - Standard production
   C - Production oversize

NOTE: Two replacement sizes of valve guide are available, sizes B and D,replace original guide A with B and original guide C with D.

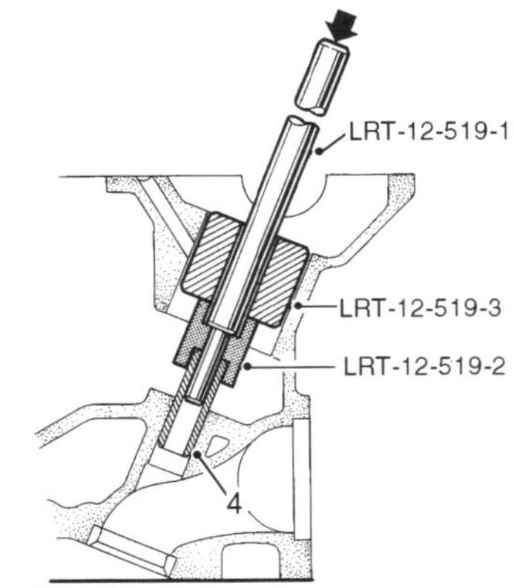

12M3948

⚠ NOTE: Cylinder head and valve guides must be at room temperature when fitting guides.

4. Locate valve guide in valve guide bore with identification groove(s)towards valve seat; position depth gauge:-
Use depth gauge **LRT-12-519-2.**
5. Position nylon guide **LRT-12-5196-3** in cylinder head, press guide into bore using driver **LRT-12-519-1** until depth gauge contacts top of valve guide bore.

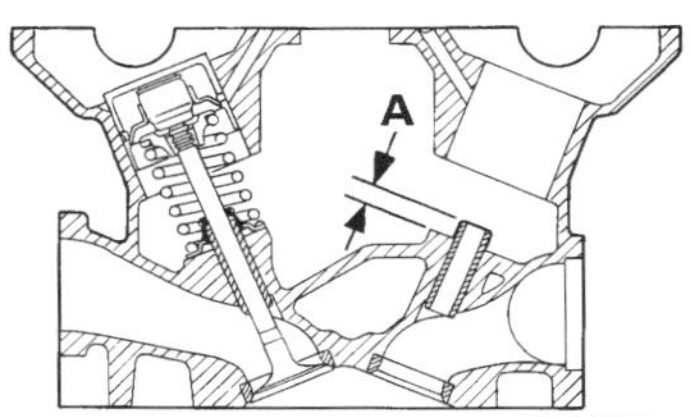

8RM 0052

6. Check fitted height **A** of valve guide = 6.0 mm

Valve seats - refacing

⚠ **CAUTION: Renew worn valve guides before refacing valves and seats.**

1. Check condition of valve seats and existing valves that are to be re-used.

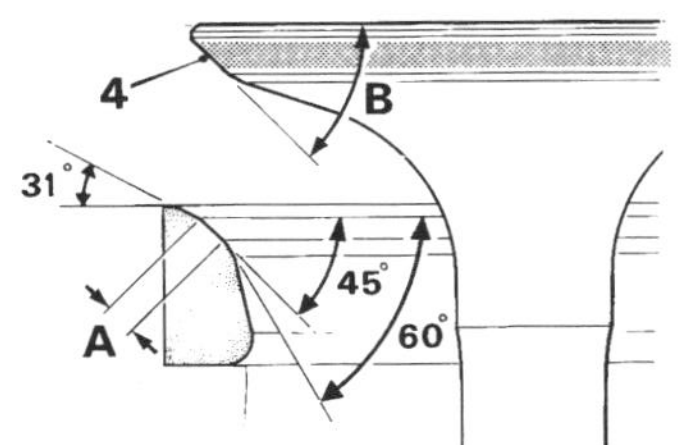

8RM 3530 A

2. Recut valve seats and use pilot **MS120-6** and **MS76-115** 31° cutter and **MS76-111** 60° cutter to narrow valve seats and obtain seat width. Make final cut with **MS76-122** 45° cutter to remove any burrs.

Valve seat:
Angle = 45°
Width **A** = 1.5 mm
Valve face angle **B**:
Inlet = 45°
Exhaust = 45°

3. Lap each valve to seat using fine grinding paste.
4. Apply Prussian Blue to valve seat, insert valve and press it into position several times without rotating. Remove and check valve for even and central seating:
Seating position shown by blue should be in centre of valve face:

a. High towards stem, increase 60° cut and restore seat width.

b. Low towards edge, increase 30° cut and restore seat width.
Lap and re-check valve seating.

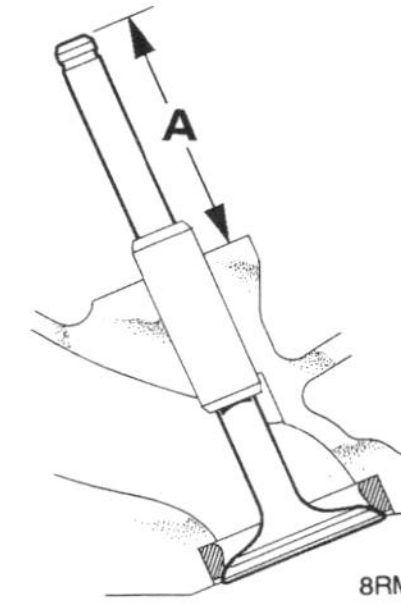

8RM 3531

5. Check valve stem fitted height A:

New = 38.93 to 39.84 mm
Service limit = 40.10 mm

If valve stem fitted height is above service limit, fit new valve and re-check, if still over limit, renew valve seat insert.

6. Remove all traces of grinding paste on completion.

Valve seat inserts - renew

1. Renew valve seat inserts as necessary.

⚠ **CAUTION: Do not damage counterbore when removing insert.**

2. Cut valve seat to correct angle and width.
3. Lap valve to seat.

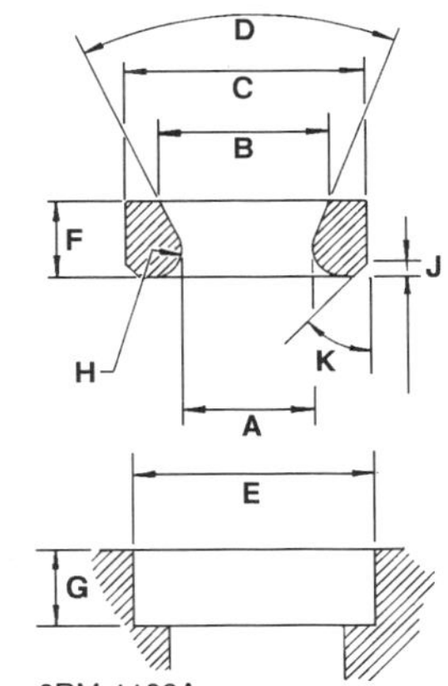

8RM 1102A

Inlet
A:= 22.98 to 23.13 mm
B:= 25.73 to 25.98 mm
C:= 29.560 to 29.573 mm
D:= 38°
E:= 29.475 to 29.500 mm
F:= 5.95 to 6.00 mm
G:= 6.53 to 6.69 mm
H:= 2.0 mm radius
J:= 0.75 to 1.25 mm
K:= 45°

Exhaust
A:= 19.58 to 19.73 mm
B:= 21.60 to 21.90 mm
C:= 25.960 to 25.973 mm
D:= 30°
E:= 25.888 to 25.913 mm
F:= 5.45 to 5.50 mm
G:= 5.75 to 6.41 mm
H:= 2.0 mm radius
J:= 0.75 to 1.25 mm
K:= 45°

Camshafts - refit

K16

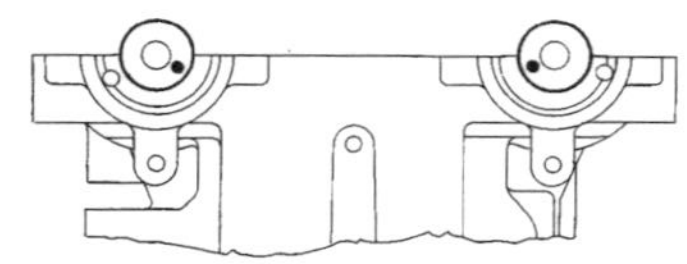

12M3927

1. Lubricate bearings and fit camshaft(s) and position drive pin for 90° BTDC as follows:
Inlet pin at 4 o'clock.
Exhaust pin at 8 o'clock.

Camshaft carrier and oil seals - refit

1. Ensure 2 locating dowels are fitted in camshaft carrier.

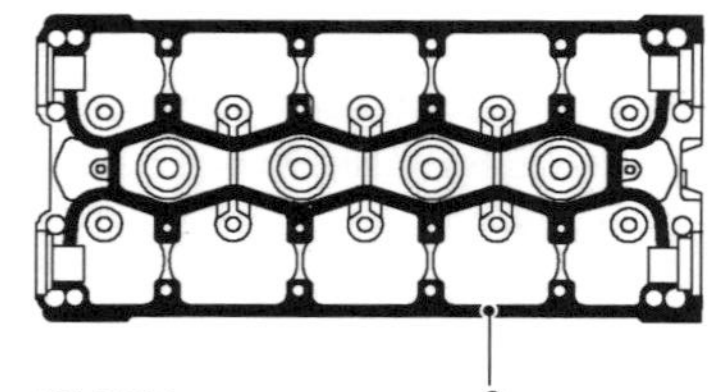

12M3523

2. Apply continuous, thin beads of sealant from kit, Part Number GUG 705548GM to paths on cylinder head as shown then spread to an even film using a brush or roller.

⚠ **CAUTION: Ensure sealant is kept clear of tappet oil feed holes and lubrication grooves in carrier and that assembly is completed within 20 minutes.**

3. Lubricate camshaft cams and journals with engine oil.

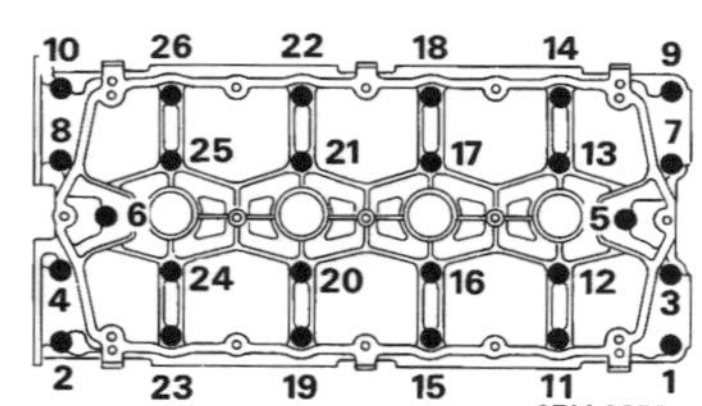

8RM 0056

4. Fit camshaft carrier and progressively tighten bolts, in sequence shown, to 10 Nm.

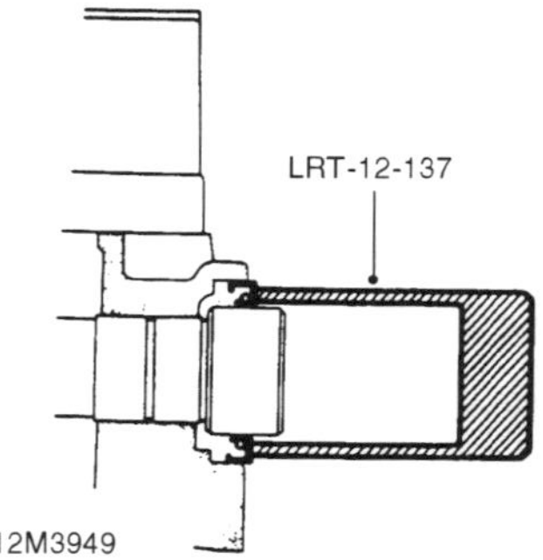

12M3949

5. Lubricate new camshaft oil seals with engine oil and using tool **LRT-12-137,** fit oil seals.
6. Fit blanking plate, fit and tighten bolts to 25 Nm.

Cylinder head - refit

CAUTION: If crankshaft has been rotated, check that timing mark on crankshaft timing gear is aligned with flange on oil pump and that tool LRT-12-145 is locking flywheel.

1. Check cylinder head bolts in oil rail. *See* ***Cylinder head bolt inspection.*** - Renew bolts as necessary.
2. Check that 2 locating ring dowels are fitted in cylinder block.

CAUTION: The type of ring dowel fitted must be maintained. A nylon ring dowel must not be used in place of a steel ring dowel.

3. Oil cylinder head bolts, under head and threads.
4. Remove cylinder liner retainer clamps **LRT-12-144.**

CAUTION: Do not rotate crankshaft until cylinder head bolts are fitted.

5. Fit new cylinder head gasket DRY, with identification markings facing upwards, on to cylinder block.

CAUTION: Take care not to damage sealing faces of gasket.

6. Using assistance, fit cylinder head on to cylinder block carefully locating ring dowels.
7. Carefully enter cylinder head bolts in their original fitted locations; DO NOT DROP. Finger tighten bolts.
8. Temporarily fit timing gears to camshafts, fit but do not fully tighten bolts.

NOTE: This will enable camshafts to be rotated in order to enable bolts 1 and 2 to be tightened.

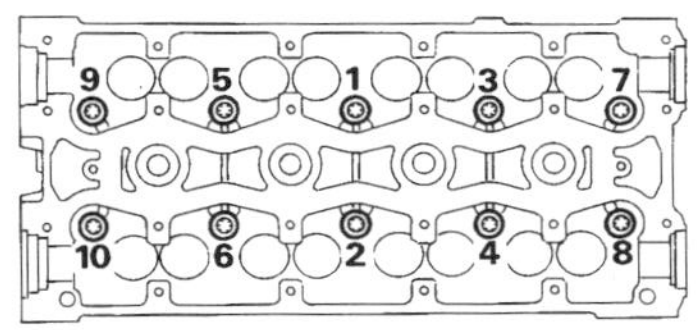

8RM 0057

9. Tighten cylinder head bolts progressively in sequence shown to 20 Nm.
   Use a felt tip pen to mark position of radial mark on each bolt head.
   Tighten all bolts in sequence shown through 180°
   Tighten all bolts in sequence shown through another 180° and align mark.

CAUTION: If any bolt is overtightened, back off 90° and re-align.

10. Upon completion of tightening sequence, position camshafts with inlet pin at 4 o'clock and exhaust pin at 8 o'clock; remove timing gears.
11. Fit new spark plugs, tighten to 25 Nm.
12. Fit camshaft cover and timing gears.

Camshaft cover and timing gears - refit

1. Clean mating surfaces and inside of camshaft cover.
   If necessary, wash oil separator elements in suitable solvent and blow dry.
2. Fit new camshaft cover gasket dry, to camshaft carrier, with either 'TOP' mark towards the inlet manifold or 'EXHAUST MAN SIDE' towards exhaust manifold.

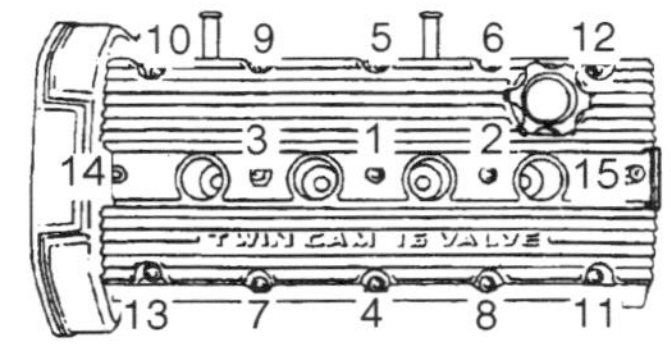

12M3929

3. Fit camshaft cover on to camshaft carrier, fit bolts and tighten in sequence shown to 10 Nm.
4. Locate HT leads in clips and press plug tubes on to spark plugs.
5. Fit spark plug cover to camshaft cover, tighten screws to 10 Nm.
6. Fit timing belt upper rear cover, fit and tighten bolts to 10 Nm.
7. Fit camshaft gears to their respective camshafts ensuring that the drive gear pins are located in correct slot in drive gears, hold gears using tool **LRT-12-132** and tighten bolts to:
   M10 bolts - 65 Nm

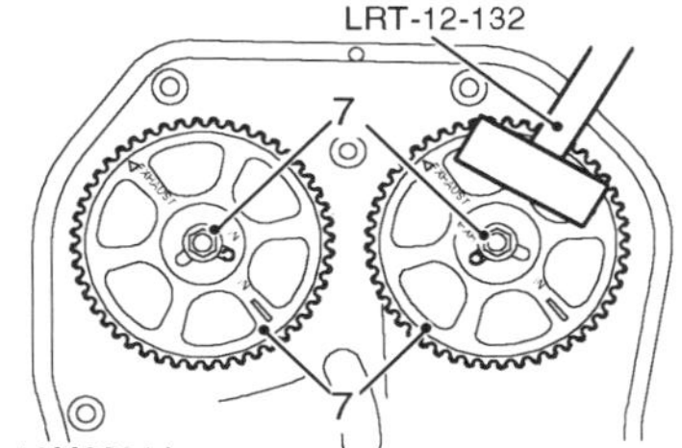

12M3931A

8. Using tool **LRT-12-132,** align camshaft gear timing marks and drive gear pins as shown.

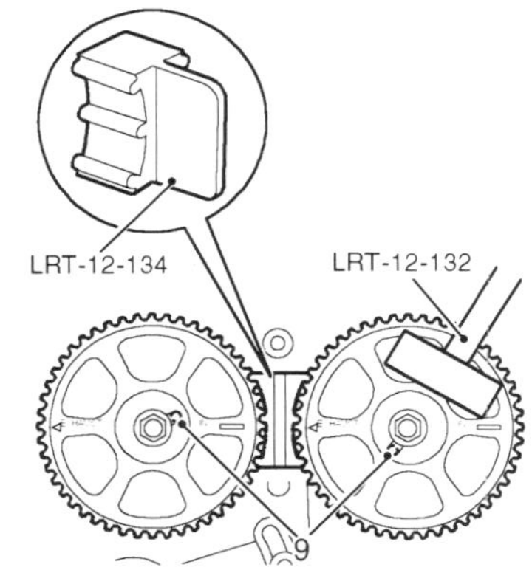

12M3930

9. Fit camshaft gear locking tool **LRT-12-134.**
10. Fit camshaft timing belt tensioner.

Camshaft timing belt tensioner - refit

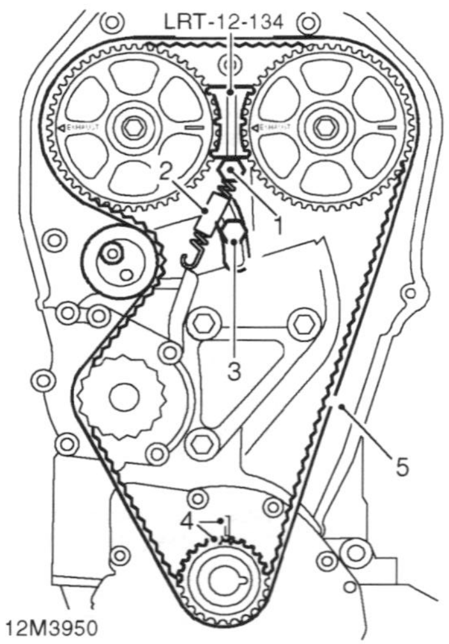

12M3950

1. Fit timing belt tensioner and pillar bolt.
2. Tighten tensioner backplate screw to 10 Nm to retain tensioner in released position.
3. Connect tensioner spring to tensioner and pillar bolt.
4. Check correct alignment of timing marks on crankshaft gear to mark on oil pump.
5. Fit and adjust a new camshaft timing belt.

Distributor - refit

1. Fit anti-flash shield and rotor arm. Use new rotor arm screw and tighten to 10 Nm.
2. Fit distributor cap assembly.
3. Place HT lead retaining plate and grommet in position, connect plug leads.
4. Fit HT lead cover, tighten screws to 5 Nm.

CYLINDER HEAD BOLTS INSPECTION

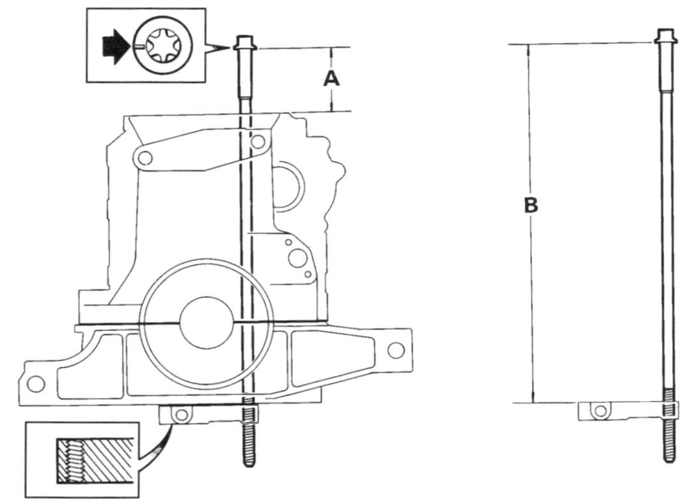

8RM 2463

1. Retain bolts in fitted order.
2. Wash all bolts, wipe dry and lightly oil threads.

Cylinder head bolts may be re-used provided they pass one of the following tests.

Test with cylinder head removed

1. Carefully enter cylinder head bolts in their original fitted location, DO NOT DROP. Screw each bolt into place until finger tight.

CAUTION: It will be necessary to temporarily remove cylinder liner retainer clamps LRT-12-144 in order to test the bolt used with the retainer clamp. Retainer clamps should only be removed one at a time and replaced immediately bolt test is completed. Take great care not to rotate crankshaft or disturb cylinder liners whilst clamps are removed.

2. Measure distance from cylinder block face to under bolt head 'A' in illustration:
   97 mm or less, bolt may be re-used.
   Over 97 mm, bolt must be discarded.

Test with oil rail removed

1. Screw each bolt into oil rail until finger tight.
2. If full length of thread is engaged, bolt may be re-used.
3. If full length of thread is not engaged, measure distance from top face of oil rail to under bolt head 'B' in illustration:
   378 mm or less, bolt may be re-used.
   Over 378 mm, bolt must be discarded

CAUTION: A new oil rail must be fitted if a thread is damaged. Thread inserts (Helicoil) are not acceptable.

CRANKSHAFT, MAIN & BIG-END BEARINGS

Crankshaft end-float - checking

⚠ **CAUTION: Crankshaft end-float must be checked and recorded prior to removing cylinder head.**

1. Check crankshaft end-float, using a DTI. Carefully lever against flywheel and press crankshaft away from DTI, zero DTI and push crankshaft towards DTI:
   Crankshaft end-float = 0.10 to 0.25 mm
   Service limit = 0.34 mm
2. Record end-float figure obtained.

Crankshaft, main and big-end bearings - remove

1. Remove flywheel.
2. Remove tool **LRT-12-145.**
3. Remove and discard camshaft timing belt.

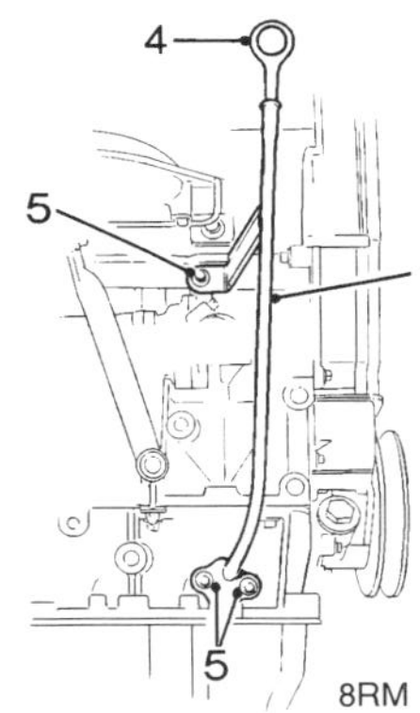

8RM 3480B

4. Withdraw dipstick
5. Remove 3 screws and dipstick tube, discard gasket.
6. Remove cylinder head assembly.

⚠ **CAUTION: Ensure cylinder liner retainer clamps LRT-12-144** are fitted.

7. Remove oil pump.
8. Using assistance, position cylinder block, cylinder head face down, on 2 wooden blocks.

⚠ **CAUTION: Ensure that wooden blocks are of sufficient thickness to prevent cylinder liner clamps contacting workbench.**

Alloy sump

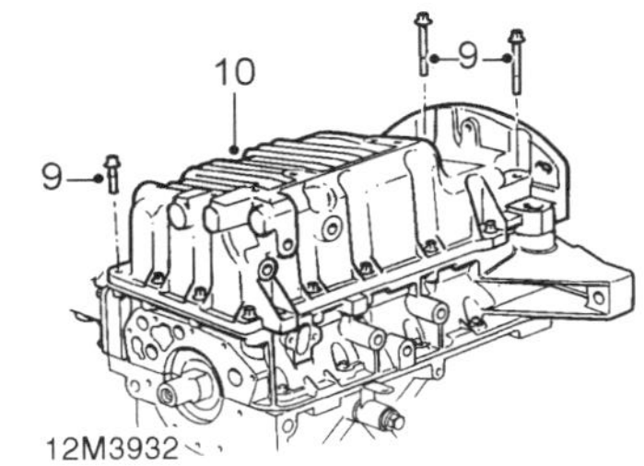

12M3932

9. Progressively slacken then remove 14 bolts securing sump to bearing ladder noting the fitted position of 2 M6 x 60 mm bolts.
10. Using a mallet, gently tap sump sideways to release sealant bond; remove sump.

⚠ **CAUTION: Do not lever between sump flange and bearing ladder.**

11. Temporarily remove cylinder retainer liner clamps **LRT-12-144.**

⚠ **CAUTION: Do not rotate crankshaft until retainer clamps are refitted.**

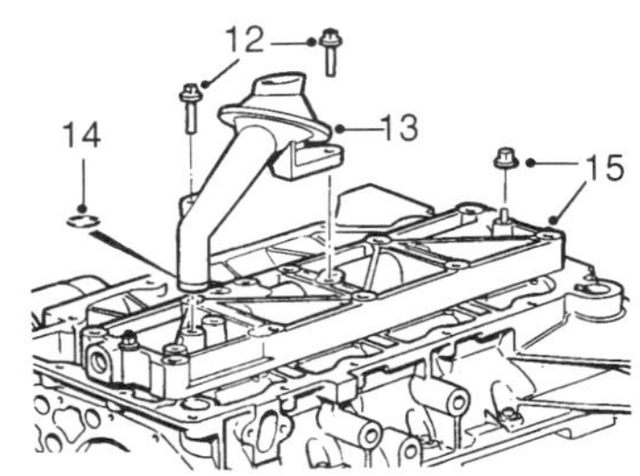

12M2933

12. Remove 2 screws, suction pipe to oil rail.
13. Remove suction pipe.
14. Discard 'O' ring.
15. Remove 2 nuts securing oil rail, remove rail.

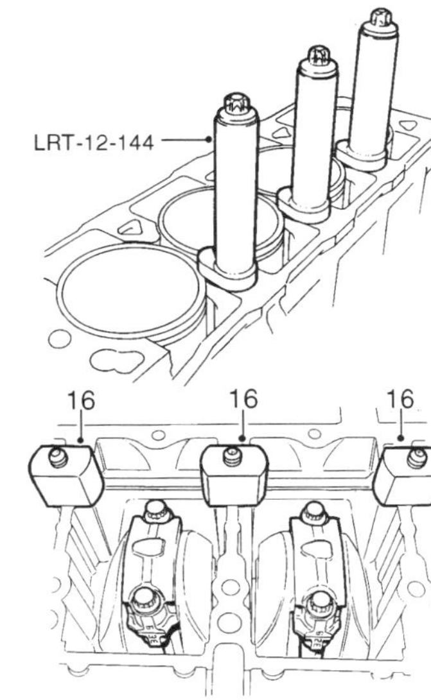

12M3934

16. Fit cylinder liner retainer clamps **LRT-12-144** using nylon nuts supplied to retain the clamps. Ensure that feet of clamps do not protrude over cylinder bores.

Big-end bearings - remove

1. Refit crankshaft timing gear and pulley.
2. Fit pulley bolt and washer, finger tighten bolt.
3. Ensure that cylinder liner retainer clamps **LRT-12-144** and nylon nuts are fitted and that feet of clamps do not protrude over cylinder liner bores.

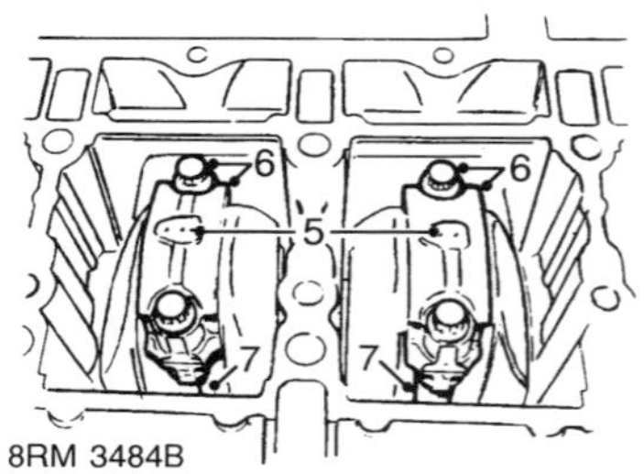

8RM 3484B

4. Rotate crankshaft to bring numbers 2 and 3 pistons to BDC.

CAUTION: Crankshaft will be tight, do not rotate crankshaft more than absolutely necessary.

5. Make cylinder number reference mark on big-end bearing caps.

NOTE: Number stamped below cap joint is bearing bore size code. Number stamped on connecting rod is cylinder number and letter is weight code.

6. Remove 4 dowel bolts and 2 big-end bearing caps from numbers 2 and 3 connecting rods, keep dowel bolts and caps in their fitted order. Remove and discard big-end bearing shells.
7. Release connecting rods from the crankshaft, carefully push pistons to top of their bores.
8. Rotate crankshaft 180°.
9. Remove numbers 1 and 4 big-end caps, remove and discard bearing shells. Push pistons to top of their bores.
10. Remove and discard 4 big-end bearing shells from connecting rods.

Crankshaft - remove

1. Remove big-end bearings, caps and bearing shells.
2. Remove pistons and cylinder liners.
3. Using assistance, position cylinder block, cylinder head face downwards on a smooth, clean wooden surface.

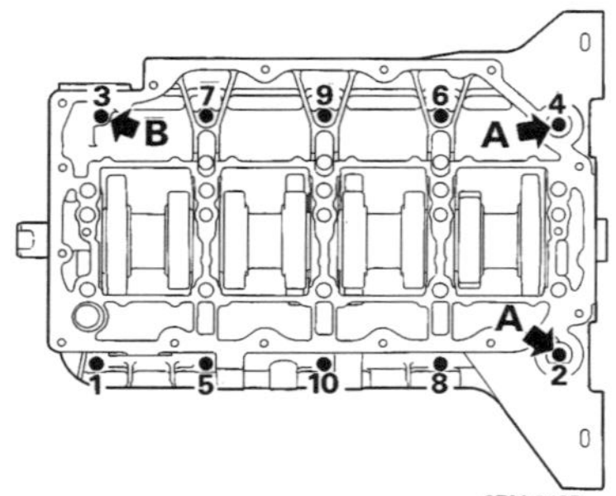

8RM 3485

4. Working in sequence shown, slacken then remove 10 bolts securing bearing ladder.

NOTE: 2 bolts 'A' are under the flanges of the rear mounting brackets. Also note position of flanged head longer bolt 'B' at front end of ladder.

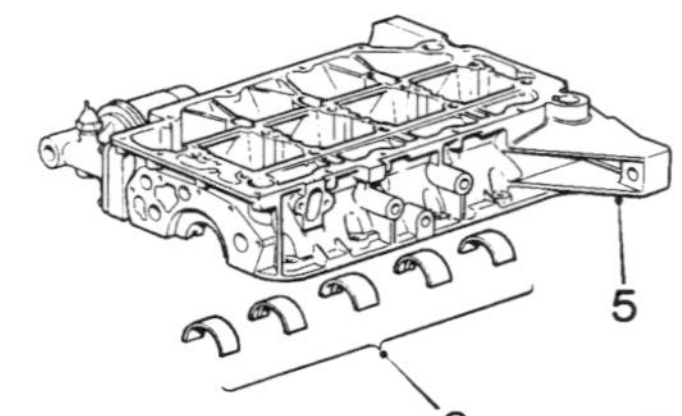

12M1777

5. Remove bearing ladder.
6. Remove and discard main bearing shells from bearing ladder.

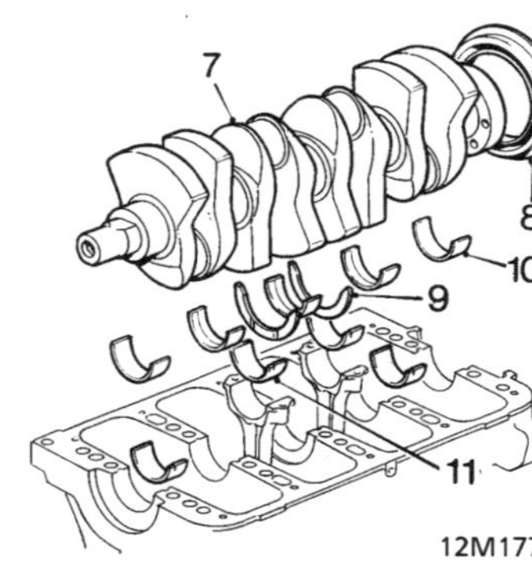

12M1778

7. Using assistance, lift crankshaft from cylinder block.
8. Remove and discard crankshaft rear oil seal.
9. Remove 2 thrust washer halves from number 3 bearing position.

CAUTION: Do not discard thrust washers at this stage.

10. Remove and discard main bearing shells from cylinder block.

Crankshaft - inspection

1. Clean joint surfaces on bearing ladder and cylinder block using suitable solvent.
   DO NOT USE A METAL SCRAPER ON SEALING SURFACES.
   Blow out crankshaft and bearing ladder oilways.
2. Measure total thickness of thrust washers removed and compare with new.
   Total thickness of new thrust washer halves = 5.22 to 5.30 mm.
3. Subtract total thickness of original thrust washers from total thickness of new thrust washers.
4. Add figure obtained to crankshaft end-float figure obtained.
5. If resultant figure will ensure crankshaft end-float is within limits specified, fit new thrust washers. If fitting new thrust washers will not bring end-float within limits, crankshaft must be replaced.
   Crankshaft end-float = 0.10 to 0.25 mm
   Service limit = 0.34 mm
6. Record main bearing code letters from bearing ladder.
   Record main bearing code numbers from crankshaft front web. First letter and number is Number 1 main bearing.
7. Check crankshaft main journal diameters:
   Main journal diameter = 47.979 to 48.000 mm
   Maximum out of round = 0.010 mm
   Crankshaft journal tolerance :
   Grade 1 = 47.993 to 48.000 mm
   Grade 2 = 47.986 to 47.993 mm
   Grade 3 = 47.979 to 47.986 mm
   Clearance in bearings = 0.02 to 0.05 mm
8. Replace crankshaft if outside tolerance.
9. Determine the appropriate bearing shells to be fitted from the main bearing size selection and type tables.

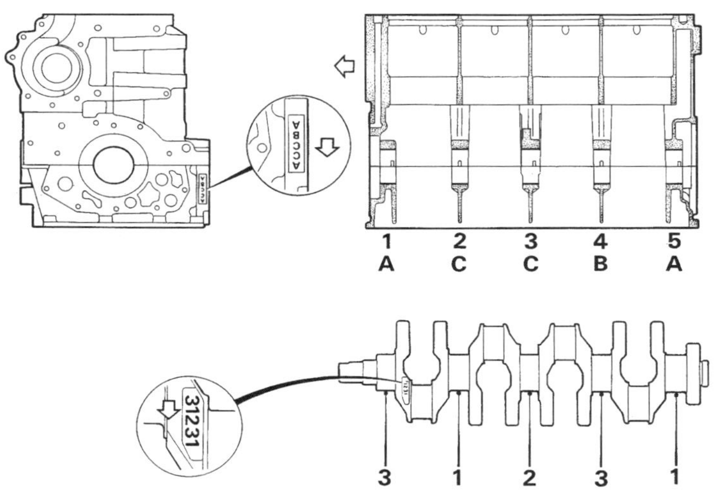

8RM 3489

Main bearings selection

Main bearings size

Bearing ladder	Crankshaft main journals		
	Grade 1	Grade 2	Grade 3
Grade A	BLUE - BLUE	RED - BLUE	RED - RED
Grade B	BLUE - GREEN	BLUE - BLUE	RED - BLUE
Grade C	GREEN - GREEN	BLUE - GREEN	BLUE - BLUE

Colour code on edge of bearing
Thickness progression:
GREEN - Thin
BLUE - Intermediate
RED - Thick

CAUTION: If two bearing colours are to be used, thicker bearing must be fitted to bearing ladder. When original crankshaft is to be refitted, bearing shells must be as selected from table, DO NOT FIT UNDERSIZE BEARINGS.

Main bearings type

	1	2	3	4	5
Block	Plain	Grooved	Grooved	Grooved	Plain
Ladder	Plain	Plain	Plain	Plain	Plain

Big-end bearings selection

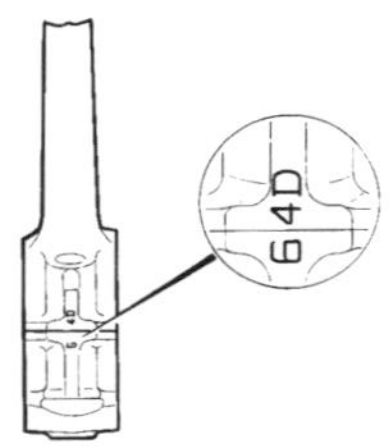

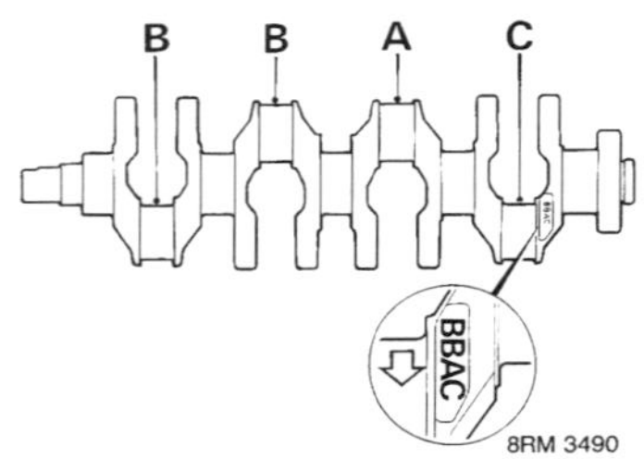

8RM 3490

1. Record big-end journal code letters from crankshaft rear web.
   First letter is number 1 big-end bearing.
   Record big-end bearing bore code numbers.
2. Check crankshaft big-end journal diameters:
   Big-end journal diameter = 47.986 to 48.007 mm
   Maximum out of round = 0.010 mm

Big-end journal tolerance:
Grade A = 48.000 to 48.007 mm
Grade B = 47.995 to 48.000 mm
Grade C = 47.986 to 47.993 mm
Clearance in bearings = 0.021 to 0.049 mm

3. Select the appropriate big-end bearing shells from the table.
4. Replace crankshaft if outside tolerance.

Big-end bearings size

Big-end bore	Crankshaft big-end journals		
	Grade A	Grade B	Grade C
Grade 5	BLUE - BLUE	RED - BLUE	RED - RED
Grade 6	BLUE - YELLOW	BLUE - BLUE	RED - BLUE
Grade 7	YELLOW - YELLOW	BLUE - YELLOW	BLUE - BLUE

Colour code on edge of bearing
Thickness progression:
YELLOW - Thin
BLUE - Intermediate
RED - Thick
If two bearing colours are to be used, thicker bearing must be fitted to big-end bearing cap.

Crankshaft, main and big-end bearings - refit

1. Clean all sealant surfaces on block, bearing ladder and oil rail.
   Use foam action gasket remover and a plastic scraper - DO NOT USE A METAL SCRAPER ON SEALING SURFACES.
   Ensure all oilways are clear.
   Examine shoulder location on each big end bolt, renew if damaged.
   Check that core plug at each end of oil rail is in good condition, renew as necessary.

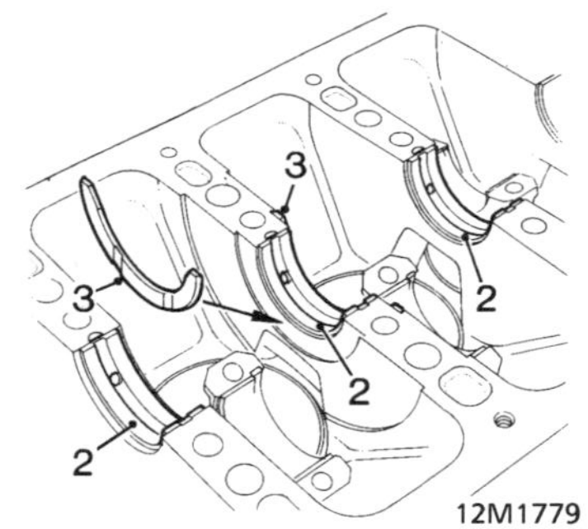

12M1779

2. Fit selected main bearing shells into cylinder block and bearing ladder as indicated in the table.
3. Fit thrust washers into block, each side of Number 3 main bearing with oil grooves facing outwards.
4. Lubricate crankshaft main journals with engine oil. Hold crankshaft with big-end journals horizontal and using assistance, lower crankshaft on to main bearings.
5. Clean sealing surfaces on cylinder block and bearing ladder using suitable solvent.

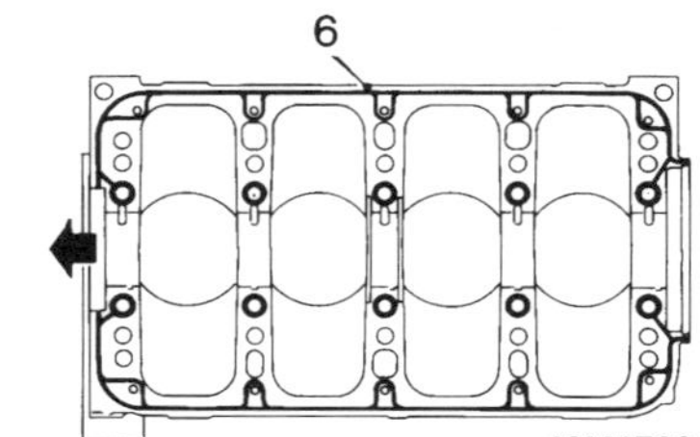

12M1780

6. Apply a continuous bead of sealant from kit, Part Number GUG 705548GM to paths shown on cylinder block then spread to an even film with brush or roller.

CAUTION: To avoid contamination, assembly should be completed immediately after application of sealant.

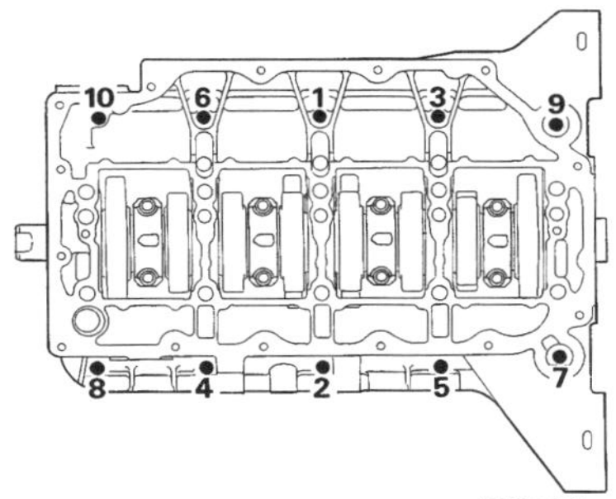

8RM 3492

7. Lubricate main journals with engine oil. Fit bearing ladder to block, fit bolts ensuring that flanged head bolt is fitted at position 10. Tighten bolts in sequence shown to 5 Nm then in same sequence to 15 Nm.

CAUTION: With bearing ladder fitted, crankshaft will be tight; do not rotate crankshaft more than absolutely necessary until cylinder head bolts are tightened to the correct torque.

8. Fit cylinder liners and pistons.

CAUTION: Ensure that cylinder liner retainer clamps LRT-12-144 and nylon nuts are fitted immediately cylinder liners are inserted into cylinder block.

9. Lubricate crankshaft big-end journals and bearing shells with engine oil. Carefully pull each connecting rod into place, fit big-end caps noting that featherways abut, fit and finger tighten dowel bolts in their original fitted order.
10. Tighten big-end dowel bolts in pairs to 20 Nm + 45°.

NOTE: Until the cylinder head is fitted, crankshaft will prove difficult to rotate once big-end bolts are tightened.

11. Wipe clean sealing surfaces on bearing ladder and oil rail using suitable solvent.

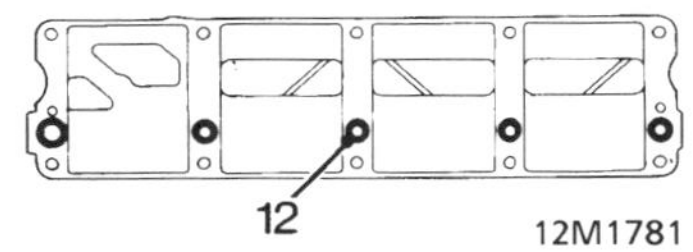

12M1781

12. Apply continuous beads of sealant from kit, Part Number GUG 705548GM to paths on oil rail as shown, then spread to an even film using a brush or roller.

CAUTION: To avoid contamination, assembly should be completed immediately after application of sealant.

13. Using assistance, position cylinder block on its side and temporarily remove cylinder liner retainer clamps **LRT-12-144.**

CAUTION: Take care not to disturb cylinder liners with retainer clamps removed

14. Fit oil rail to bearing ladder, tighten nuts to 5 Nm.

CAUTION: A new oil rail together with a plastic suction pipe must be fitted if a thread for cylinder head bolts is damaged. Thread inserts (Helicoil) are not acceptable.

15. Fit cylinder retainer clamps **LRT-12-144,** screw bolts finger-tight into oil rail.
16. Clean oil suction pipe and strainer.
17. Fit new 'O' ring and secure oil suction pipe, tighten screws to 10 Nm.

CAUTION: Screws used must be M6 x 20.

Alloy sump

18. Clean sealing surface on sump flange using suitable solvent.

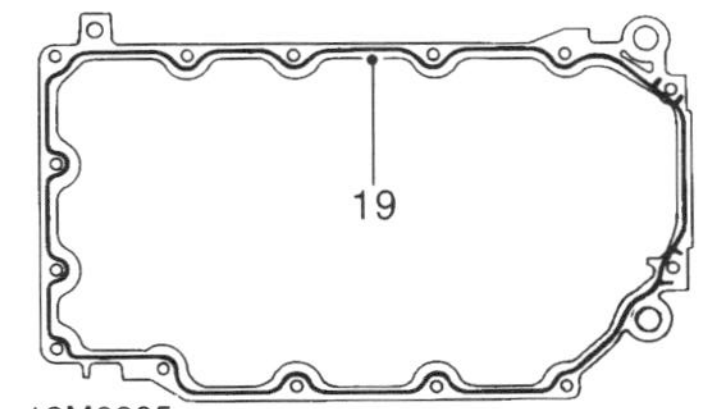

12M3935

19. Apply a 2 mm wide x 0.25 mm thick continuous bead of sealant from kit, Part Number GUG 705548 GM to sump flange as shown then spread to an even film using a brush or roller.

CAUTION: To avoid contamination, assembly should be completed immediately after application of sealant.

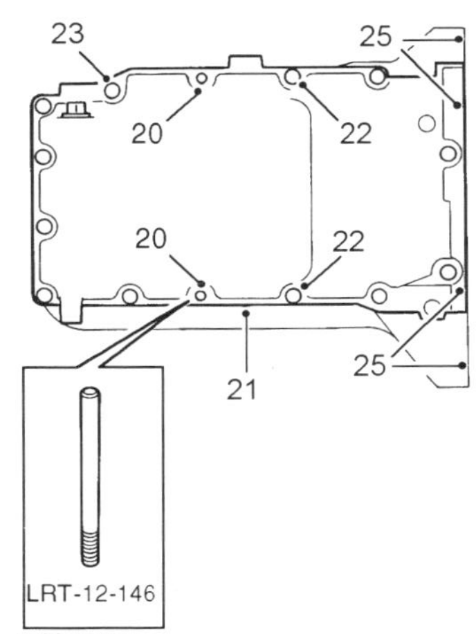

12M3936

20. Screw alignment pins **LRT-12-146** into holes shown.

21. Carefully lower sump over pins and on to bearing ladder.
22. Fit 2 bolts into holes shown, tighten to 4 Nm.
23. Fit 10 bolts into remaining holes, finger tighten all bolts.

CAUTION: Ensure M8 x 20 bolts are fitted in rearmost holes in sump.

24. Remove alignment pins **LRT-12-146,** fit and finger tighten remaining 2 bolts.
25. Using a straight edge, check that machined face of sump flange is level with rear face of cylinder block. Check in 3 positions and if necessary, tap sump gently to re-position.

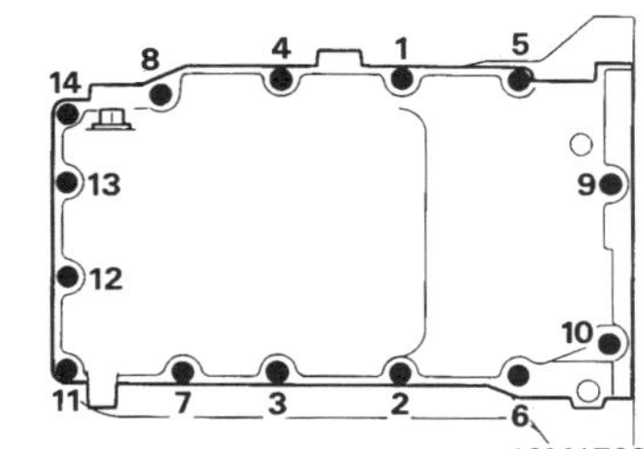

12M1783

26. Using sequence shown, tighten 14 bolts to 25 Nm.

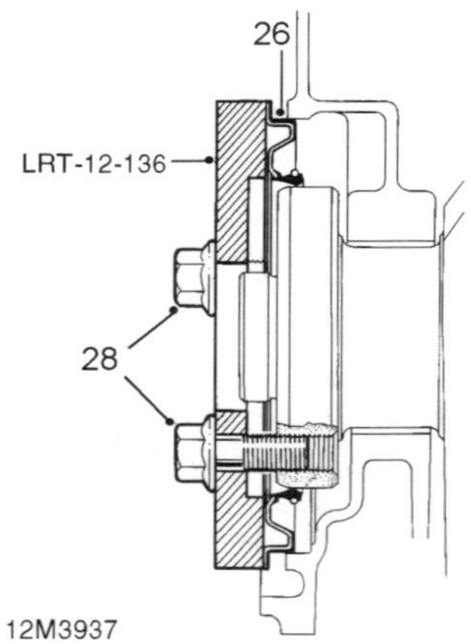

12M3937

27. Lubricate oil sealing surfaces with grease and position rear oil seal on crankshaft.
28. Fit oil seal replacer tool **LRT-12-136** to crankshaft.
29. Tighten replacer bolts to press oil seal into cylinder block.

NOTE: Do not remove replacer for 30 seconds to allow seal to relax.

30. Remove tool **LRT-12-136.**
31. Fit flywheel.
32. Fit oil pump and front oil seal.
33. Fit crankshaft timing gear.
34. Fit cylinder head assembly, do not fit spark plugs at this stage.
35. Fit a new camshaft timing belt.
36. Clean joint surfaces. Use new gasket and fit dipstick tube, tighten bolts to 10 Nm.

NOTE: Ensure bolts securing dipstick tube to bearing ladder are flanged head and do not exceed 12 mm in length.

37. Support engine and rotate crankshaft. Check that crankshaft can be rotated without undue binding, rotational torque should not exceed 31 Nm.
38. Fit spark plugs, tighten to 25 Nm.
39. After installation in vehicle, run engine at idle speed for 15 minutes before road testing.

PISTONS, RINGS & CYLINDER LINERS

Pistons and connecting rods - remove

1. Suitably identify each piston assembly with its respective cylinder liner.
2. Remove big-end bearings.
3. Using assistance, position cylinder block on its side.

CAUTION: Ensure that feet of cylinder liner retainer clamps LRT-12-144 do not protrude over cylinder bores.

4. Remove ridge of carbon from top of each cylinder liner bore.
5. Push pistons to top of their bores.
6. Carefully push out each piston assembly taking care that big-ends do not contact surface of cylinder liners.
7. Refit caps on to connecting rods, lightly tighten dowel bolts.

CAUTION: Removal of pistons will necessitate removal and re-sealing of cylinder liners.

Piston rings - checking

1. Using an expander, remove and discard old piston rings.
2. Use squared off end of broken piston ring and clean ring grooves.
3. Check new ring to groove clearance:

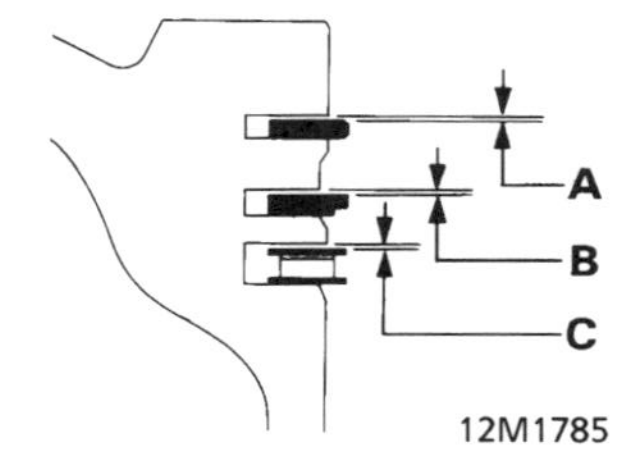

12M1785

Top compression **A** = 0.040 to 0.072 mm
2nd compression **B** = 0.030 to 0.062 mm
Oil control **C** = 0.010 to 0.180 mm

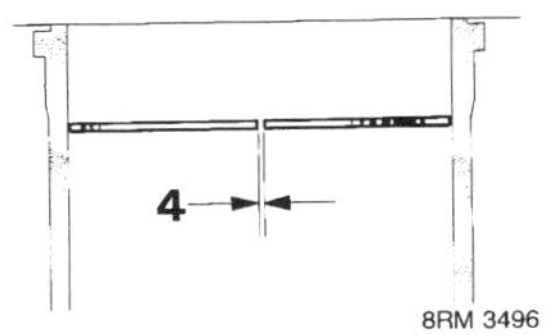

8RM 3496

4. Check new ring fitted gap 20 mm from top of cylinder liner bore:

⚠ **CAUTION: Ensure rings are kept square to liner bore and that they are suitably identified to the bore in which they are checked and fitted to the piston for that bore.**

Top compression = 0.20 to 0.35 mm
2nd compression = 0.28 to 0.48 mm
Oil control rails = 0.15 to 0.40 mm

Pistons - inspection

1. Check pistons for distortion and cracks.
2. Measure and record piston diameter at right angle to gudgeon pin and 8 mm from bottom of skirt.
3. Check piston diameter with figures given.
4. Measure and record piston diameter in line with gudgeon pin hole and 8 mm from bottom of skirt.
5. Check piston ovality with figures given.
6. Repeat above procedures for remaining pistons.

Grade A = 79.975 to 79.990 mm
Grade B = 79.991 to 80.005 mm
Maximum ovality = 0.3 mm
Service pistons are grade A and B

NOTE: Piston grades A or B are stamped on crown of piston.

Piston to cylinder liner bore clearance - checking

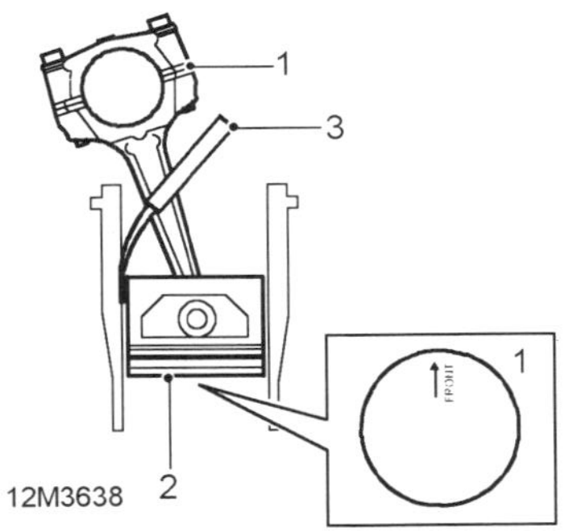

12M3638

1. Starting with number 1 piston, invert piston and connecting rod and with word FRONT or arrow on piston crown facing towards REAR of cylinder block, insert piston in cylinder liner.
2. Position piston with bottom of skirt 30 mm from top of cylinder block.
3. Using feeler gauges, measure and record clearance between piston and left hand side of cylinder liner - viewed from front of cylinder block.
4. Repeat above procedure for remaining pistons.

Clearance in cylinder bore = 0.01 to 0.04 mm

NOTE: **Pistons and connecting rods are only supplied as an assembly.**

Piston rings - refit

⚠ **CAUTION: Ensure that piston rings are fitted to piston for the cylinder bore in which they were checked.**

1. Fit oil control spring.
2. With 'TOP' or identification markings to top of piston, use an expander to fit piston rings in sequence; oil control, 2nd and top compression.

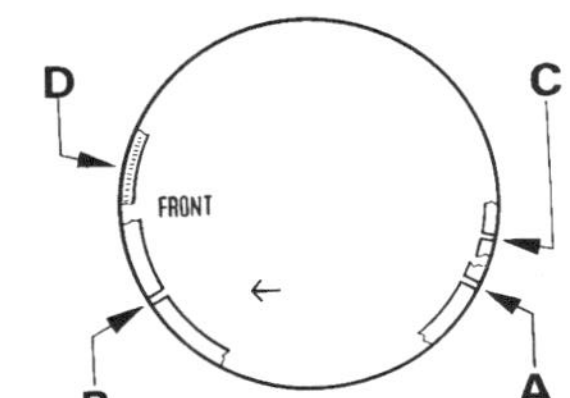

12M1811

3. Ensure rings are free to rotate, position compression ring gaps **A** and **B** at 120° to each other and away from thrust side - left hand side of piston when viewed from front. Position oil control ring gap **C** and spring gap **D** at 30° on opposite side of gudgeon pin axis.

Cylinder liners - inspection

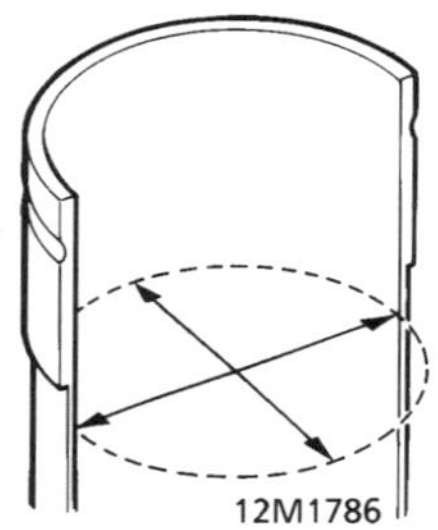

1. Measure wear and taper in two axes 65 mm from top of cylinder liner bore.
   RED grade A = 80.000 to 80.015 mm
   BLUE grade B = 80.016 to 80.030 mm
   Service liners are grade A and B.
   Cylinder liner grade will be found marked on outside diameter of liner.

CAUTION: Cylinder liners with excessively glazed, worn, scratched orscored bores must be replaced, do not attempt to hone or remove glazing from bore.

Cylinder liners - remove

1. Remove pistons.
2. Remove cylinder liner clamps **LRT-12-144.**
3. Using assistance, position cylinder block on its side.

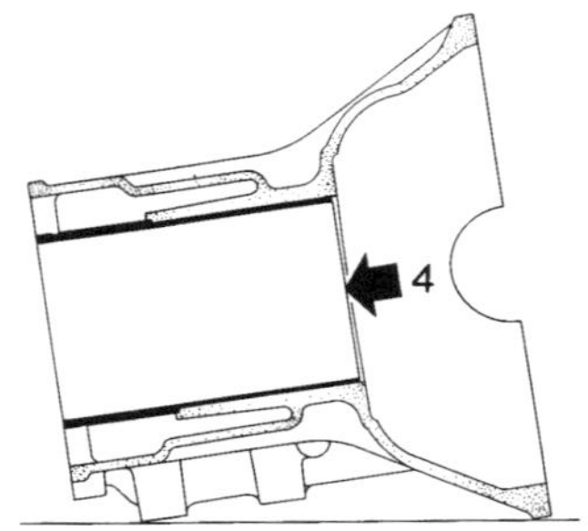

CAUTION: If original cylinder liners are to be refitted, use a felt tipped pen to make suitable alignment marks between liner and cylinder block. Do not etch or stamp liners.

4. Using hand pressure, push cylinder liners out towards cylinder head face of cylinder block; remove liners.

CAUTION: Keep cylinder liners in their fitted order.

Cylinder liners - refit

NOTE: To enable cylinder liner retainer clamps to be fitted when liners are inserted in cylinder block, crankshaft and bearing ladder must be fitted.

1. Fit crankshaft and bearing ladder.
2. Using assistance, support cylinder block on 2 wooden blocks.
3. Remove sealant from cylinder block and if original cylinder liners are to be refitted, from shoulder of liners.
4. Clean cylinder liners and wipe dry.

CAUTION: Ensure that if original cylinder liners are to be refitted, reference marks made during dismantling are not erased.

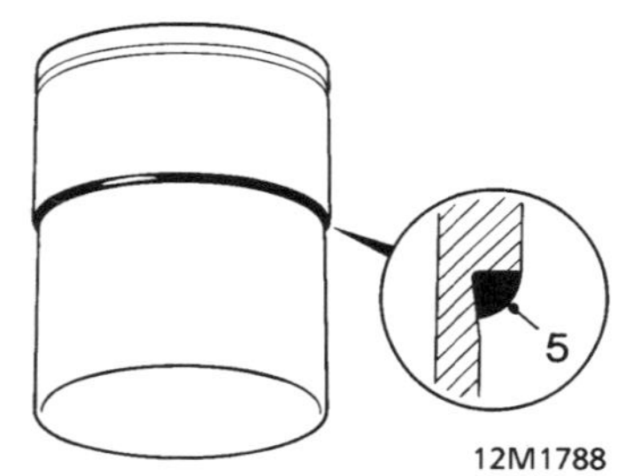

5. Apply a 2.0 mm thick continuous bead of Hylomar Universal Light Grade or Advanced Formulation Hylomar sealant around shoulder of cylinder liner.
6. Keeping cylinder liner 'square' to cylinder block, push liner fully down until shoulder of liner seats against cylinder block. Do not drop liners into position.

CAUTION: If original cylinder liners are to be refitted, align reference marks made during dismantling before liner is pushed fully down.

7. Fit cylinder liner retainer clamps **LRT-12-144.**
8. Fit pistons.

Pistons and connecting rods - refit

1. Using assistance, support base of cylinder block on 2 wooden blocks.
2. Ensure that cylinder liner retainer clamps **LRT-12-144** are fitted and that feet of clamps do not protrude over cylinder liner bores.
3. Lubricate cylinder bores, pistons and rings with engine oil, ensure ring gaps are correctly spaced.
4. Fit selected bearing shells into big-end bearing caps and connecting rods.
5. Fit a suitable piston ring clamp to each piston in turn and with **'FRONT'** mark on piston to engine front, push piston into bore until flush with top face of cylinder liner.
   Remove ring clamp.

CAUTION: If original pistons are to be fitted, ensure that each piston is inserted in its correct cylinder liner. Do not push pistons below top face of cylinder liner until big-end bearings and caps are to be fitted.

6. Fit big-end bearings.

DATA

Oil pump	
Outer rotor to housing clearance	0.28 to 0.36 mm
Inner rotor tip clearance	0.05 to 0.13 mm
Rotor end float	0.02 to 0.06 mm
Relief valve spring free length	38.9 mm
Cooling system	
Thermostat open	88°C
Nominal setting	85 to 91°C
Camshafts	
Camshaft end-float -	0.06 to 0.19 mm
Service limit	0.3 mm
Camshaft bearing clearance -	0.060 to 0.094 mm
Service limit	0.15 mm
Tappets	
Tappet outside diameter	32.959 to 32.975 mm.
Cylinder head	
Cylinder head maximum warp	0.05 mm
Cylinder head height:	
New	118.95 to 119.05 mm.
Reface limit	0.20 mm
Valve springs	
Free length	50.0 mm
Fitted length	37.0 mm
Load - valve closed	250 ± 12 N
Load - valve open	450 ± 18 N
Valve stem diameter:	
Inlet	5.952 to 5.967 mm
Exhaust	5.947 to 5.962 mm
Valve guides:	
Inside diameter	6.000 to 6.025 mm
Valve stem to guide clearance:	
Inlet	0.033 to 0.063 mm
Service limit	0.07 mm
Exhaust	0.038 to 0.078 mm
Service limit	0.11 mm
Valve stem fitted height:	
New	38.93 to 39.84 mm
Service limit	40.10 mm
Valve guides	
Fitted height:	6.0 mm
Valve seats	
Angle	45°
Width	1.5 mm
Valve face angle:	
Inlet	45°
Exhaust	45°

Crankshaft

Crankshaft end-float	0.10 to 0.25 mm
Service limit	0.34 mm
Thrust washer halves thickness	2.61 to 2.65 mm
Main journal diameter	47.979 to 48.000 mm
Maximum out of round	0.010 mm
Main journal tolerance:	
Grade 1	47.993 to 48.000 mm
Grade 2	47.986 to 47.993 mm
Grade 3	47.979 to 47.986 mm
Clearance in bearings	0.02 to 0.05 mm
Big-end journal diameter	47.986 to 48.007 mm
Maximum out of round	0.010 mm
Big end journal tolerance:	
Grade A	48.000 to 48.007 mm
Grade B	47.993 to 48.000 mm
Grade C	47.986 to 47.993 mm
Clearance in bearings	0.021 to 0.049 mm
Big-end end-float	0.10 to 0.25 mm

Piston rings

New ring to groove clearance:

Top compression	0.040 to 0.072 mm
2nd compression	0.030 to 0.062 mm
Oil control	0.010 to 0.180 mm

Ring fitted gap 20 mm from top of bore:

Top compression	0.20 to 0.35 mm
2nd compression	0.28 to 0.48 mm
Oil control	0.15 to 0.40 mm

Piston diameter

Grade A	79.975 to 79.990 mm
Grade B	79.991 to 80.005 mm
Clearance in bore	0.01 to 0.04 mm
Maximum ovality	0.3 mm

Cylinder block

Cylinder liner bore:

RED grade A	80.000 to 80.015 mm
BLUE grade B	80.016 to 80.030 mm

TORQUE FIGURES

Tensioner pulley backplate screw	10 Nm
Tensioner pulley screw	45 Nm
RH engine mounting bracket bolts	45 Nm
Crankshaft pulley bolt	205 Nm
Timing belt upper front cover screws	5 Nm
Timing belt lower cover screws	5 Nm
Timing belt rear cover screws	5 Nm
Oil pump bolts*	10 Nm
Coolant pump bolts*	10 Nm
Coolant pump cover bolts	10 Nm
Thermostat housing bolts	8 Nm
Thermostat housing to cylinder block bolt	10 Nm
Coolant rail to cylinder block bolts	10 Nm
Flywheel - new Patchlok bolts	85 Nm
Cylinder head bolts:*	
All bolts	20 Nm
Mark position of radial marks	
Turn all bolts through 180°	
Turn all bolts through another 180° align marks	
Spark plugs	25 Nm
Camshaft gear bolts	65 Nm
Camshaft carrier bolts*	10 Nm
Blanking plate to camshaft carrier bolts	10 Nm
Camshaft cover to carrier bolts*	10 Nm
Air cleaner support bracket bolts	10 Nm
Spark plug cover screws	10 Nm
Big-end bolts	20 Nm + 45°
Bearing ladder to block bolts*	15 Nm
Oil rail to bearing ladder bolts*	5 Nm
Alloy sump bolts*	25 Nm
HT lead brackets	10 Nm

* Tighten in sequence

SERVICE TOOLS

LRT-12-034	Valve Lifter Basic Tool
LRT-12-034/1	Valve Lifter Adaptor
LRT-12-132	Camshaft Holding Tool
LRT-12-134	Camshaft Locking Tool
LRT-12-145	Flywheel Locking Tool
LRT-12-136	Rear Oil Seal Replacer Tool
LRT-12-519/1	Valve Guide Remover/Replacer
LRT-12-519/2	Depth Gauge
LRT-12-519/3	Nylon Guide
LRT-12-071	Valve Stem Oil Seal Remover/Replacer
LRT-12-137	Front Oil Seal Replacer
LRT-12-144	Cylinder Liner Retainer Clamps
LRT-12-146	Sump Alignment Pins - 2 off
LRT-12-149	Valve Guide Reamer
MS 120-6	Valve Seat Cutter Pilot
MS 76-111	60° Valve Seat Cutter
MS 76-115	31° Valve Seat Cutter
MS 76-122	45° Valve Seat Cutter

PG1 MANUAL GEARBOX

OVERHAUL MANUAL

Publication Part No. LRL 0159 ENG
Published by Rover Technical Communication

PG1 MANUAL GEARBOX OVERHAUL MANUAL

CONTENTS

Page

INTRODUCTION

INTRODUCTION

How to use this manual

To assist in the use of this manual the section title is given at the top and the relevant sub-section is given at the bottom of each page.

This manual contains procedures for the overhaul of the gearbox on the bench with the gearbox removed from the engine. For all other information regarding General Information, Adjustments, Removal of oil seals, gearbox unit, consult the Repair Manual for the model concerned.

This manual is divided into 3 sections, Description and Operation, Overhaul and Data, Torque & Tools. To assist filing of revised information each sub-section is numbered from page 1.

The individual overhaul items are to be followed in the sequence in which they appear. Items numbered in the illustrations are referred to in the text.

Overhaul operations include reference to Service Tool numbers and the associated illustration depicts the tool. Where usage is not obvious the tool is shown in use. Operations also include reference to wear limits, relevant data, torque figures, specialist information and useful assembly details.

WARNINGS, CAUTIONS and Notes have the following meanings:

WARNING: Procedures which must be followed precisely to avoid the possibility of injury.

CAUTION: Calls attention to procedures which must be followed to avoid damage to components.

NOTE: Gives helpful information.

References

With the engine and gearbox assembly removed, the cranks pulley end of the engine is referred to as the front.

Operations covered in this manual do not include reference to testing the vehicle after repair. It is essential that work is inspected and tested after completion and if necessary a road test of the vehicle is carried out particularly where safety related items are concerned.

Dimensions

The dimensions quoted are to design engineering specification with Service limits where applicable.

REPAIRS AND REPLACEMENTS

When replacement parts are required it is essential that only Land Rover recommended parts are used.

Attention is particularly drawn to the following points concerning repairs and the fitting of replacement parts and accessories.

Safety features and corrosion prevention treatments embodied in the vehicle may be impaired if other than Land Rover recommended parts are fitted. In certain territories, legislation prohibits the fitting of parts not to the manufacturer's specification.

Torque wrench setting figures given in this Manual must be used. Locking devices, where specified, must be fitted. If the efficiency of a locking device is impaired during removal it must be renewed.

The Terms of the vehicle Warranty may be invalidated by the fitting of other than Land Rover recommended parts. All Land Rover recommended parts have the full backing of the vehicle Warranty.

Land Rover Dealers are obliged to supply only Land Rover recommended parts.

SPECIFICATION

Land Rover are constantly seeking to improve the specification, design and production of their vehicles and alterations take place accordingly. While every effort has been made to ensure the accuracy of this Manual, it should not be regarded as an infallible guide to current specifications of any particular component or vehicle.

This Manual does not constitute an offer for sale of any particular component or vehicle. Land Rover Dealers are not agents of Land Rover and have no authority to bind the manufacturer by any expressed or implied undertaking or representation.

Gearbox identification

This overhaul manual is applicable to PG1 gearboxes having the following Serial No. prefixes:

S4EM
S7EMU

CONTENTS

Page

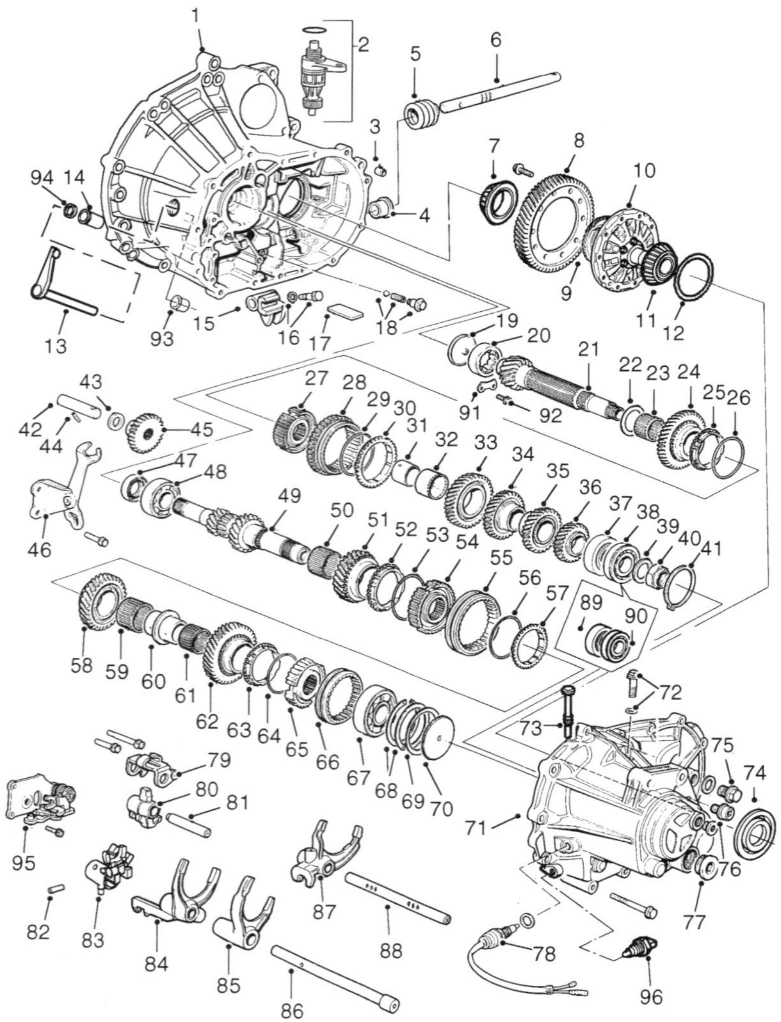

GEARBOX COMPONENTS

1. Clutch housing
2. Speedometer drive pinion and housing
3. Dowel
4. Oil seal - selector shaft
5. Boot
6. Selector shaft
7. Taper roller bearing
8. Final drive gear
9. Speedometer drive gear
10. Final drive carrier
11. Taper roller bearing
12. Non-selective shim
13. Clutch release shaft
14. Oil seal - clutch release shaft
15. Selector shaft guide
16. Dowel bolt and washer
17. Magnet
18. Detent cap bolt, ball and spring - selector shaft
19. Oil guide plate
20. Parallel roller bearing - output shaft
21. Output shaft
22. Selective thrust washer - 1st gear end-float
23. Needle roller bearing - 1st gear
24. 1st gear
25. Synchro ring - 1st gear
26. Synchro spring
27. Synchro hub - 1st/2nd gear
28. Synchro sleeve - 1st/2nd gear
29. Synchro spring
30. Synchro ring - 2nd gear
31. Selective collar - 2nd gear end-float
32. Needle roller bearing = 2nd gear
33. 2nd gear
34. 3rd gear
35. 4th gear
36. 5th gear
37. Ball bearing - output shaft*
38. Ball bearing - output shaft*
39. Tongued washer
40. Output shaft nut - L.H. thread
41. Circlip
42. Reverse idler shaft
43. Thrust washer - reverse idler gear
44. Roll pin - reverse idler shaft
45. Reverse idler gear
46. Reverse selector fork
47. Oil seal - input shaft
48. Ball bearing - input shaft
49. Input shaft
50. Needle roller bearing - 3rd gear
51. 3rd gear
52. Synchro ring - 3rd gear
53. Synchro spring
54. Synchro hub - 3rd/4th gears
55. Synchro sleeve - 3rd/4th gears
56. Synchro spring
57. Synchro ring - 4th gear
58. 4th gear
59. Needle roller bearing - 4th gear
60. Distance collar - 4th/5th gears
61. Needle bearing - 5th gear
62. 5th gear
63. Synchro ring - 5th gear
64. Synchro spring - 5th gear
65. Synchro hub - 5th gear
66. Synchro sleeve - 5th gear
67. Ball bearing - input shaft
68. Selective snap rings - input shaft end thrust
69. Belleville washer - input shaft end thrust
70. Oil guide plate
71. Gearbox casing
72. Reverse idler shaft bolt and washer
73. Breather pipe
74. Oil seal - gearbox casing
75. Filler/level plug
76. Drain plug
77. Access plug - output shaft bearing circlip
78. Reverse light switch
79. Gearshift holder
80. Gearshift arm guide
81. Shift shaft
82. Roll pin - 5th/reverse gear selector/reverse brake
83. Gear selector - 5th/reverse gears/reverse brake
84. Selector fork - 3rd/4th gears
85. Selector fork - 5th gear
86. Selector shaft - 5th/reverse gears
87. Selector fork - 1st/2nd gears
88. Selector shaft - 1st/2nd gears
89. Bearing - roller*
90. Bearing - ball*
91. Retainer plate - output shaft bearing**
92. Retainer plate bolts - Patchlok**
93. Clutch release shaft bush - inner
94. Clutch release shaft bush - outer
95. Interlock assembly
96. 1st gear switch

* Depending on application
** Fitted to gearboxes having the letter U in the gearbox serial number prefix

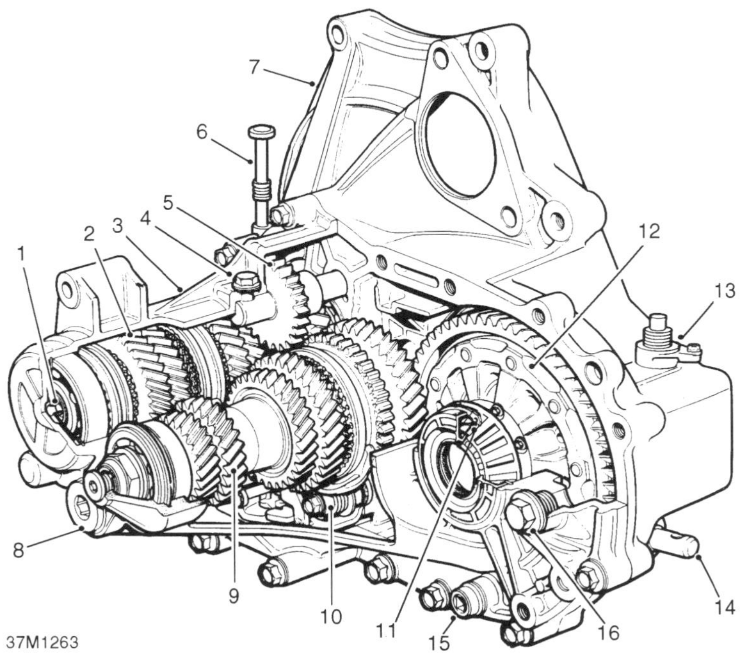

37M1263

SECTIONED VIEW OF GEARBOX

1. Oil guide plate
2. Input shaft assembly
3. Gear case
4. Reverse idler shaft bolt
5. Reverse idler gear
6. Breather pipe
7. Clutch housing
8. Access plug - output shaft bearing circlip
9. Output shaft assembly
10. Shift arm assembly and interlock
11. Taper roller bearing
12. Final drive gear carrier
13. Speedometer drive pinion housing
14. Selector shaft
15. Oil drain plug
16. Oil level/filler plug

DESCRIPTION

The 5 speed constant mesh gearbox employs single helical gears, running on two shafts, input and output. The input shaft incorporates 1st gear, reverse pinion and 2nd gear which are integral with the shaft, with 3rd, 4th and 5th gears rotating on caged needle roller bearings. The input shaft also incorporates the synchroniser hubs for 3rd/4th and 5th gears.

The input shaft is supported at each end by two ball races. Input shaft end float is controlled by selective circlips and a Belleville washer positioned in the bearing recess in the gear case. The short end of the input shaft eliminates the need for support in the engine crankshaft. The output shaft incorporates the output drive pinion, 1st and 2nd speed gears, which run on caged needle roller bearings, 1st and 2nd synchromesh hub, and 3rd, 4th and 5th gears, which are splined to the output shaft. The output shaft is supported in the clutch housing by a parallel roller bearing, and in the gear case by a single ball race and roller bearing on the uprated gearbox, and by a double ball race on the standard gearbox. The rear end of the output shaft is secured by a circlip which retains the bearings in the gear case.

The output shaft pinion drives the final drive gear which is mounted on the carrier, the carrier being supported on taper roller bearings in the gear case and clutch housing. There is no pre-load adjustment to the carrier bearings, this is controlled by the dimensional tolerances between the gear case and clutch housing bore depths. There are no differential gears in the carrier; a splined hub transmits drive to the Intermediate Reduction Drive, IRD unit, which controls the differential and drive to the front and rear axles.

Synchromesh is by spring rings and spline extensions in the inner faces of the synchro sleeves. Gear selection is by a gearshift holder assembly 'interlock', which transmits movement of the main selector shaft to the selector shafts and forks. The gearbox incorporates a 'Reverse Brake'; operated by the selector fork mechanism, which stops the input shaft from rotating prior to the engagement of reverse gear and provides quiet and smooth engagement of the reverse gear, providing the vehicle is stationary. Positioned below the reverse light switch in the gear case is the 1st gear switch. The 1st gear switch forms part of the Hill Decent Control (HDC) system, fitted to certain vehicles.

The transmission components are splash lubricated. An oil gutter located on the upperside of the gear case collects splashed oil from the final drive gear and directs the oil to an oil guide plate, which distributes oil to the hollow input shaft and lubricates 3rd, 4th and 5th gear needle roller bearings. Oil is also collected and distributed through a drilling in the clutch housing to an oil guide plate, positioned under the output shaft bearing in the clutch housing, which lubricates 1st and 2nd gear needle roller bearings on the output shaft.

Two different variants of the PG1 gearbox are available, standard or uprated. They are identified externally by the gearbox number prefix, S4EM prefix for standard gear box, and S7EMU for the uprated gearbox. With the difference in gearbox output drive ratios, the output shaft and final drive gears are not interchangeable.

OPERATION

With the exception of reverse, all gears are in constant mesh. Forward ratios are obtained by locking a gear to its shaft using its individual synchro hub and sleeve. Reverse gear is obtained by engaging the reverse idler gear with the reverse gears changing the direction of rotation of the output shaft. When a forward gear is selected the synchro sleeve presses the synchromesh female cone into contact with a corresponding male cone in the gear chosen. This synchronizes the speeds of the synchro hub and gear. The synchro sleeve incorporates three pairs of raised teeth, 120°apart, which contact a spring ring, and with the detents on the selector shaft, provides a positive detent as the gear is engaged or disengages.

The reverse brake utilizes the 3rd/4th synchro hub for its operation. The 5th/reverse shift piece, which is secured to the selector shaft by a roll pin, incorporates two guide lugs with two machined grooves that form a platform for a lock plate. The inner face of the lock plate is angled approximately at 45°, with two machined flanges either side of the lock plate which are positioned in machined grooves in the guide lugs. A return spring, which biases the lock plate against the stop surface, extends along the step at the front of the lock plate, with the two free ends of the spring held in position by two studs either side of the shift piece. A lug on the 3rd/4th selector fork has a machined face at an angle of 45°which acts as a ramp when in contact with the angled face of the lock plate. The 1st/2nd selector shaft has a machined abutment surface located below the detent grooves, the abutment surface being the area of contact for the lock plate.

In operation, when selecting reverse gear, the 5th/reverse shift piece (1) moves upwards, and the angled face of the lock plate (3) contacts the ramp on 3rd/4th selector fork (2). The upward movement carries the lock plate (3) outwards until it contacts the abutment (4) on 1st/2nd selector shaft. From this point, continued upward movement of the 5th/reverse shift piece (1) causes the lock plate (3) to move the 3rd/4th selector and synchro sleeve (5) towards 4th gear. The movement of the 3rd/4th synchro sleeve (5) is sufficient to restrain the input shaft (6), thus permitting smooth engagement of reverse gear.

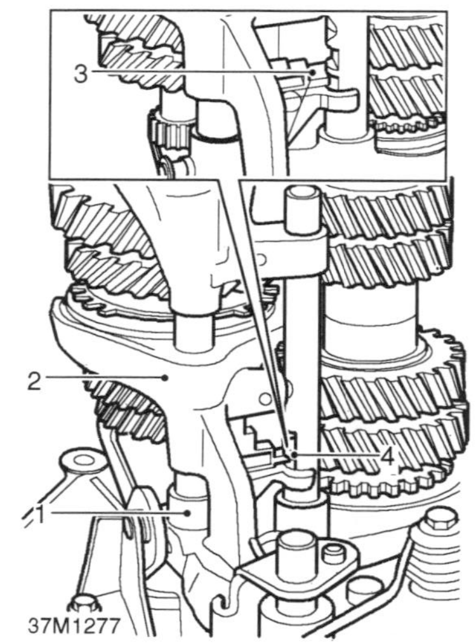

37M1277

To prevent any further movement of the 3rd/4th synchro sleeve (5) and engagement of 4th gear, the spring on the lock plate (3) moves the lock plate into the machined groove (7) above the abutment (4).

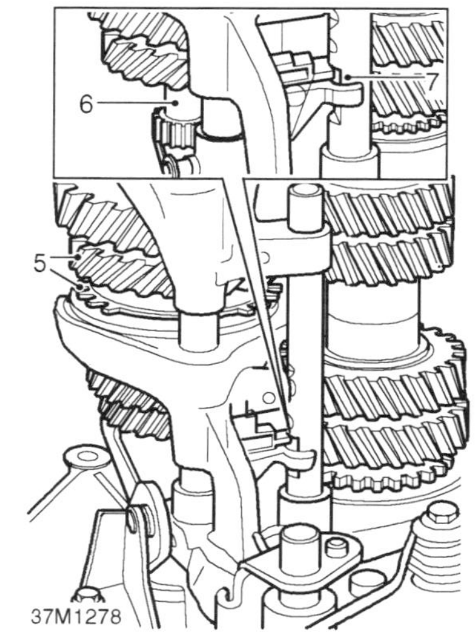

37M1278

Torque is transmitted from the input shaft through the selected gear to the output shaft,which transmits drive via the final drive carrier to the intermediate reduction drive unit, IRD, which transmits drive to the front and rear axles.

GEARBOX DISMANTLING

1. Thoroughly clean exterior of gearbox.

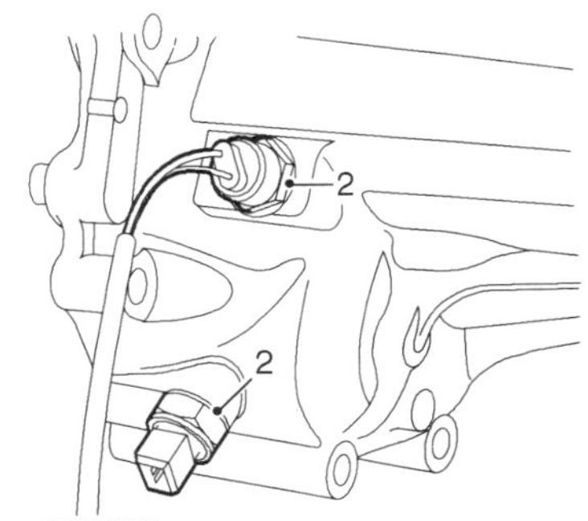

37M1265

2. Remove 1st gear and reverse light switches; discard sealing washer from reverse light switch.

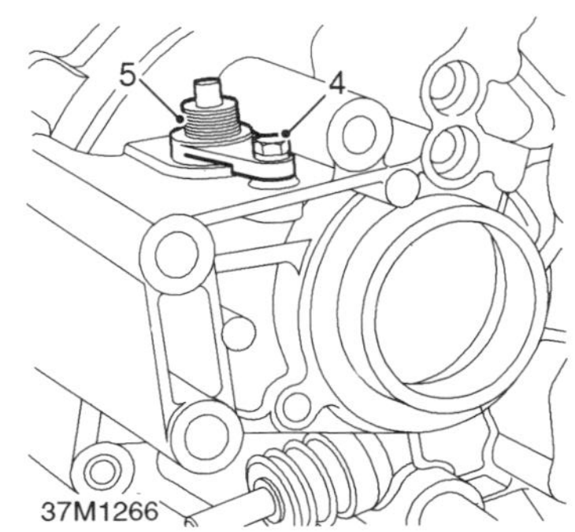

37M1266

3. Remove bolt and locating plate securing speedometer drive pinion and housing.
4. Remove speedometer drive pinion and housing, discard 'O'ring.

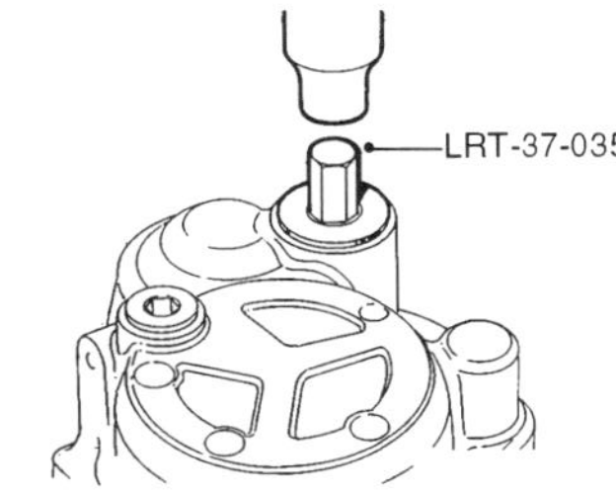

37M1250

5. Remove access plug using tool **LRT-37-035.**

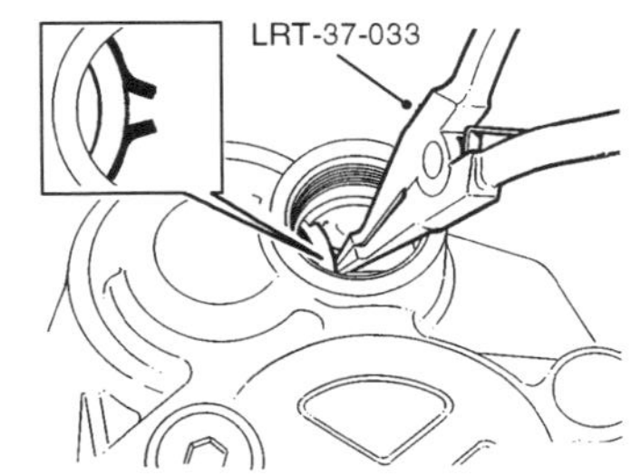

37M1251

6. Using tool **LRT-37-033,** release circlip retaining output shaft bearing.

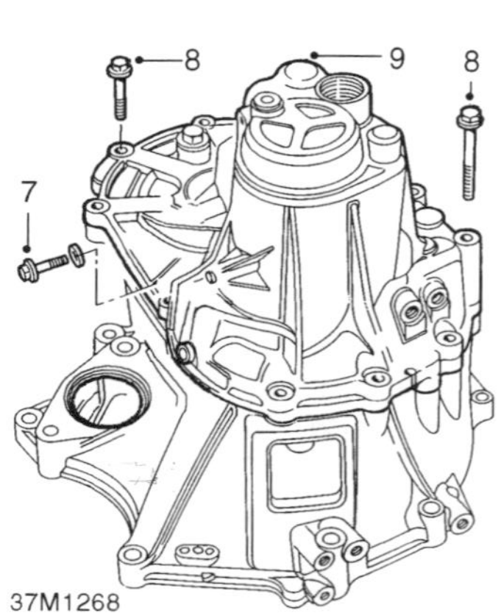

37M1268

7. Remove bolt retaining reverse idler shaft, discard washer.
8. Noting their fitted position, remove 14 bolts securing gear case to clutch housing.
9. Using a soft-faced mallet, release gear case from clutch housing; remove gear case.

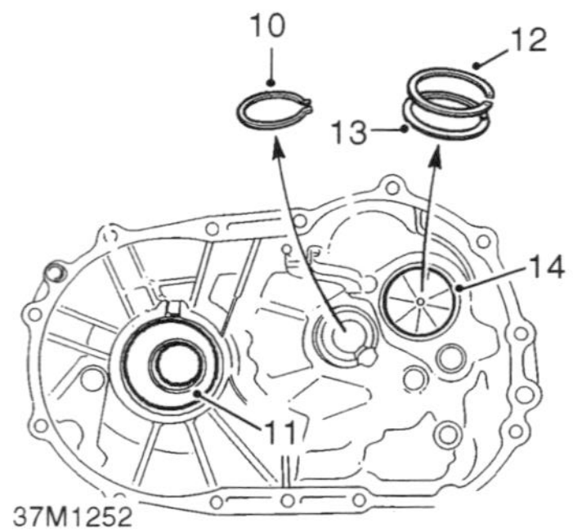

37M1252

10. Remove and discard output shaft bearing circlip from gear case.
11. Remove driveshaft oil seal from gear case.
12. Remove selective circlip(s) from input shaft bearing recess in gear case.
13. Remove and discard Belleville washer from gear case.
14. Remove input shaft oil guide plate from gear case.
15. Heat gear case to approximately 100°C, using a hot air gun, and remove and discard final drive carrier bearing track. Collect non-selective shim.

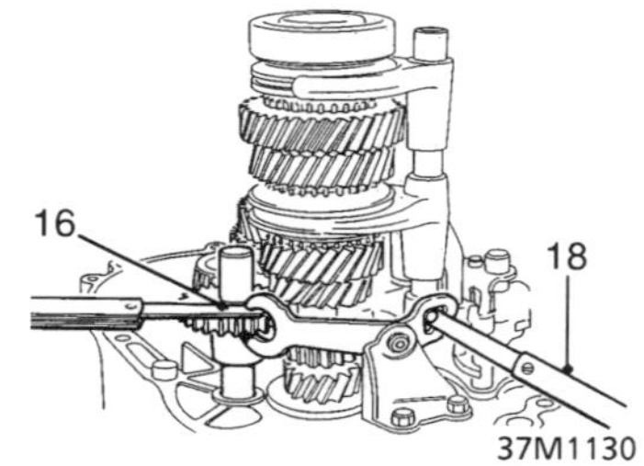

37M1130

16. Using feeler gauges, measure clearance between reverse idler gear and selector fork. Clearance = 0.5 to 1.1 mm
17. If clearance obtained exceeds above figure, measure width across prongs of selector fork. Prong width = 13.0 to 13.3 mm.
18. Using feeler gauges, measure clearance between pin and selector fork groove. Standard = 0.05 to 0.35 mm Service limit = 0.5 mm
19. If clearance obtained exceeds service limit, measure width of selector fork groove. Groove width = 7.05 to 7.25 mm

CAUTION: If dimensions obtained exceed figures given, selector fork must be replaced.

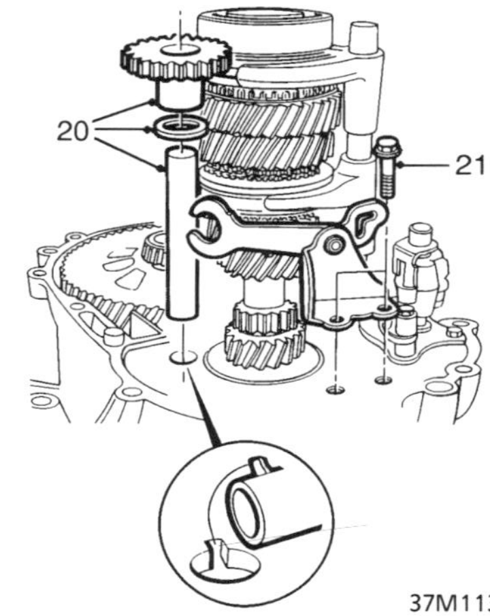

37M1131

20. Remove reverse idler gear, thrust washer and idler shaft.
21. Remove 2 bolts securing reverse selector fork bracket; remove bracket and fork.

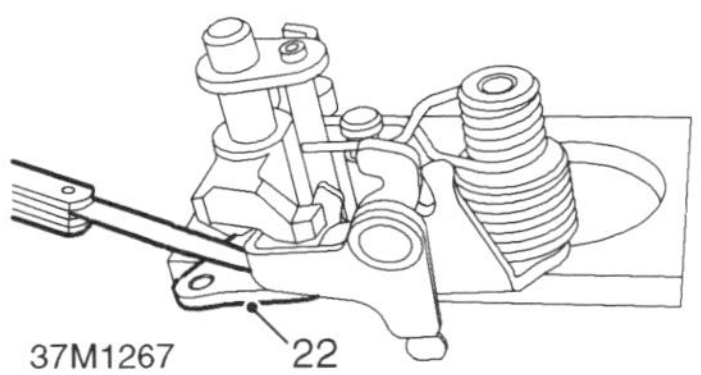

37M1267

22. Using feeler gauges, measure clearance between gearshift arm and guide.
Standard = 0.2 to 0.3 mm
Service limit = 0.55 mm

23. If clearance obtained exceeds service limit, measure width of groove in guide.
Groove width = 8.1 to 8.2 mm

⚠ **CAUTION: If dimensions obtained exceed figures given, interlock assembly must be replaced.**

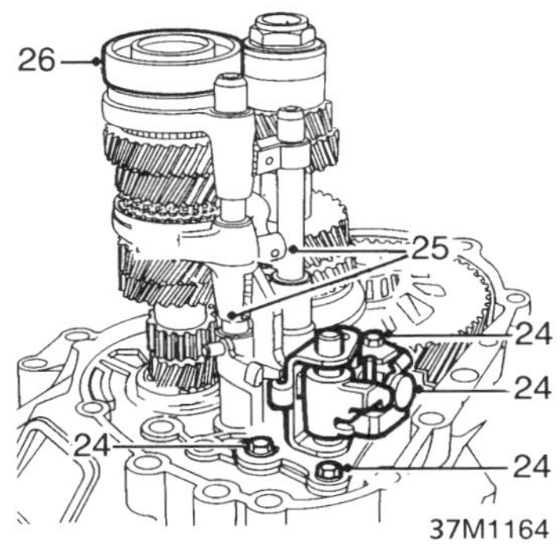

37M1164

24. Noting their fitted position, remove 3 bolts retaining interlock assembly; remove assembly.
25. Raise both input and output shafts slightly, remove selector forks and shafts.
26. Lift off, or use a suitable puller and remove input shaft bearing.

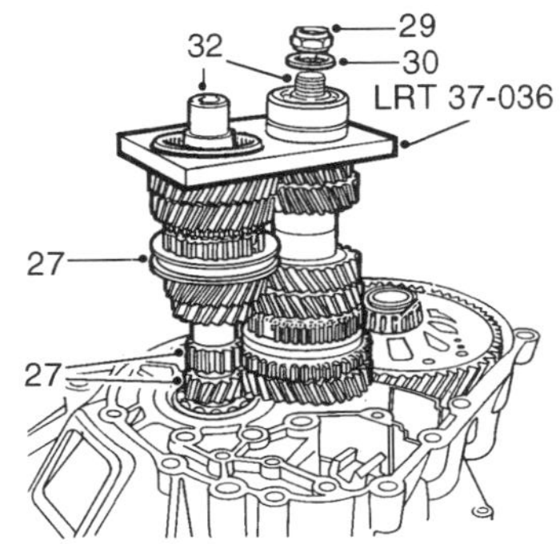

12M1253

27. Move synchro sleeves to engage 1st and 4th gears.

⚠ **CAUTION: Damage to components will result if gears other than 1st and 4th are engaged.**

28. Position tool **LRT-37-036** over 5th gear synchro on input shaft and around output shaft bearing.
29. Release staking, remove and discard stake nut from output shaft.

NOTE: Stake nut has a LH thread.

30. Remove and discard tongued washer.
31. Remove tool **LRT-37-036.**
32. Remove input and output shaft assemblies from clutch housing.

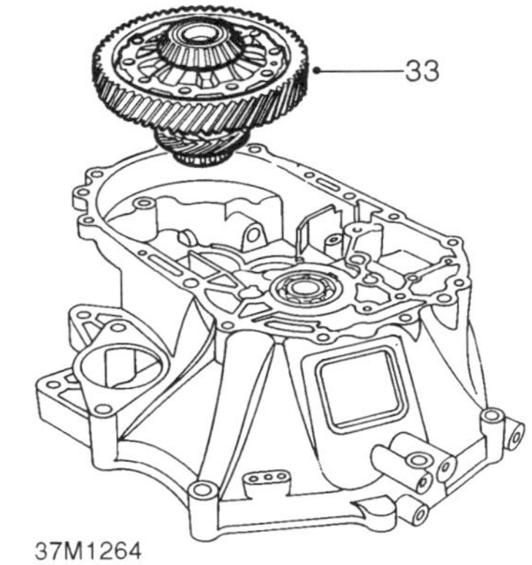

37M1264

33. Lift out final drive gear carrier assembly from clutch housing.

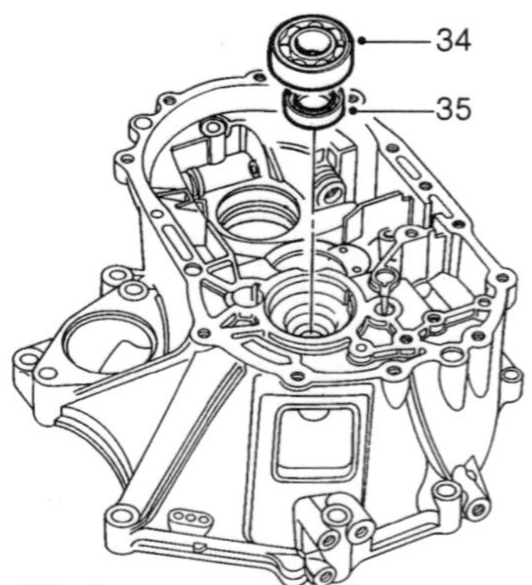

37M1274

34. Using a soft metal drift, carefully remove input shaft bearing from clutch housing; discard bearing.
35. Remove and discard input shaft oil seal.

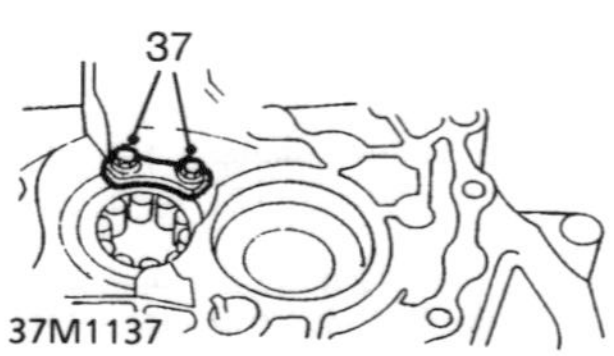

37M1137

36. Remove and discard 2 Patchlok bolts securing output shaft bearing retaining plate; remove plate, (S7EMU gearbox only).

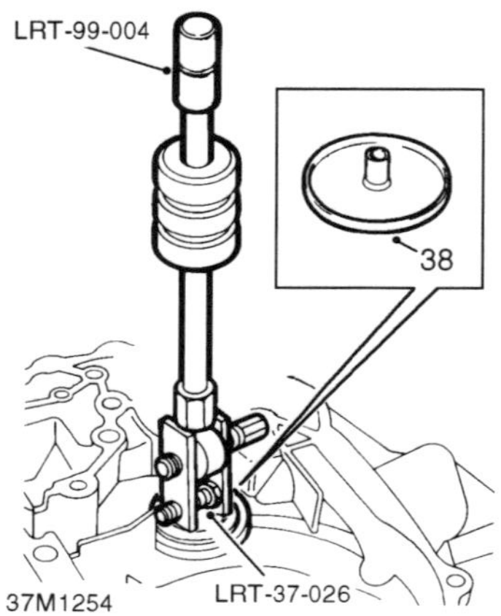

37M1254

37. Remove output shaft bearing using tools **LRT-99-004** and **LRT-37-026,** discard bearing.
38. Remove output shaft oil guide plate.

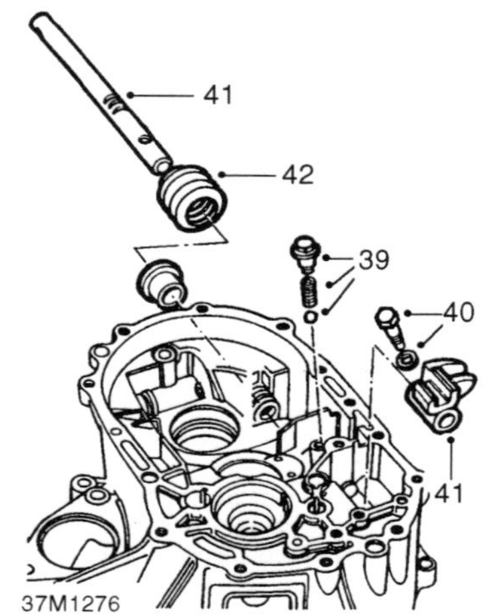

37M1276

39. Remove detent cap bolt and washer, recover detent spring and ball.

NOTE: Use a stick magnet to recover ball.

40. Remove bolt and washer securing selector shaft guide to shaft.
41. Withdraw selector shaft; remove selector shaft guide.
42. Remove gaiter from shaft.
43. Remove and discard selector shaft oil seal.

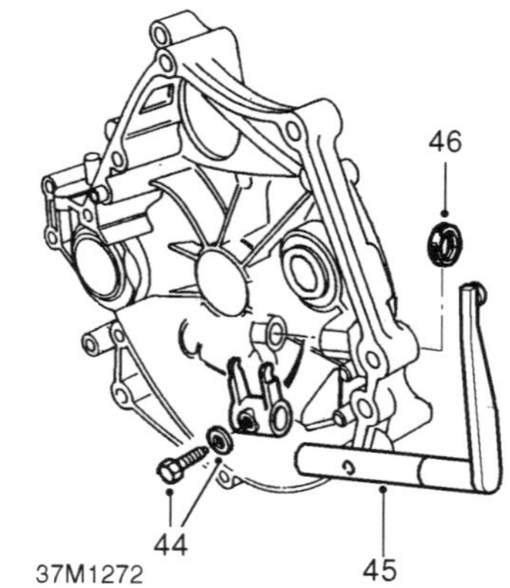

37M1272

44. Remove bolt and washer securing clutch release fork to release shaft.
45. Withdraw release shaft.
46. Remove and discard release shaft oil seal.
47. Heat the clutch housing using a hot air gun to approximately 100 ° C , remove and discard final drive carrier bearing track from housing.

COMPONENT DISMANTLING

Input Shaft

CAUTION: Keep component parts of each synchro assembly together.

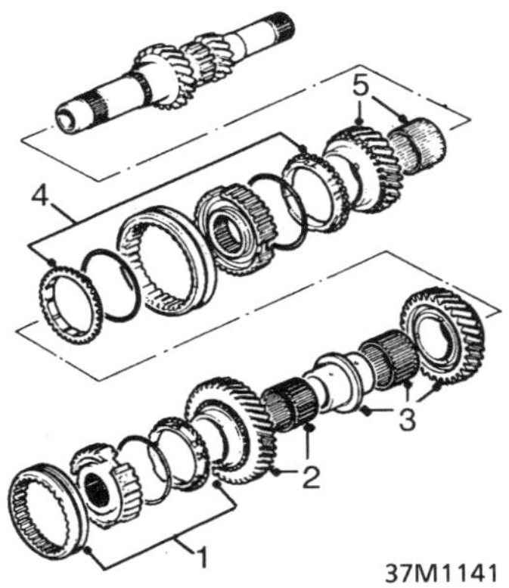

37M1141

1. Remove 5th gear synchro assembly.
2. Remove 5th gear and needle bearing.
3. Remove 4th gear together with collar and needle bearing.
4. Remove 3rd/4th synchro assembly.
5. Remove 3rd gear and needle bearing.

Output Shaft

NOTE: Gearboxes with the prefix number starting with S4EM have a double ball race fitted. Gearboxes with the prefix number starting with S7EMU have a single ball race and roller bearing fitted.

1. Remove double ball race or single ball race and roller bearing, discard bearings.

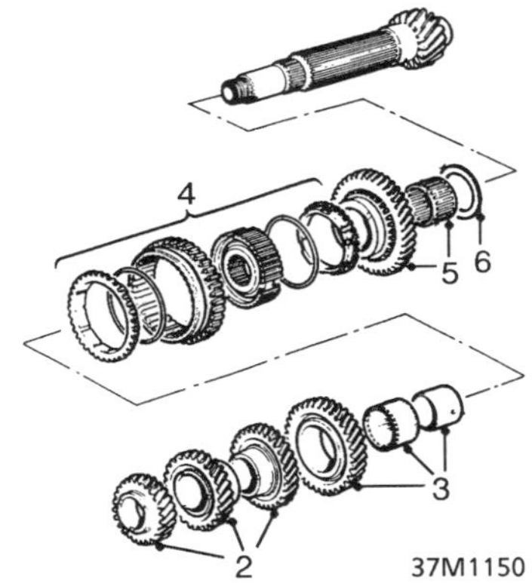

37M1150

2. Remove 5th, 4th and 3rd gears.
3. Remove 2nd gear, needle bearing and selective collar.

NOTE: The selective collar has a lubrication groove machined in its inner radius, which faces towards 1st/2nd synchro hub.

4. Remove 1st/2nd synchro assembly.

CAUTION: Keep component parts of synchro assembly together.

5. Remove 1st gear and needle bearing.
6. Remove and retain selective thrust washer.

Synchro assemblies

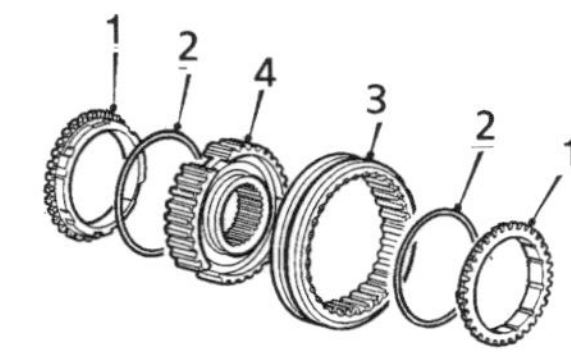

37M0148

Synchro Assembly Components

1. Synchro ring
2. Spring ring
3. Synchro sleeve
4. Synchro hub

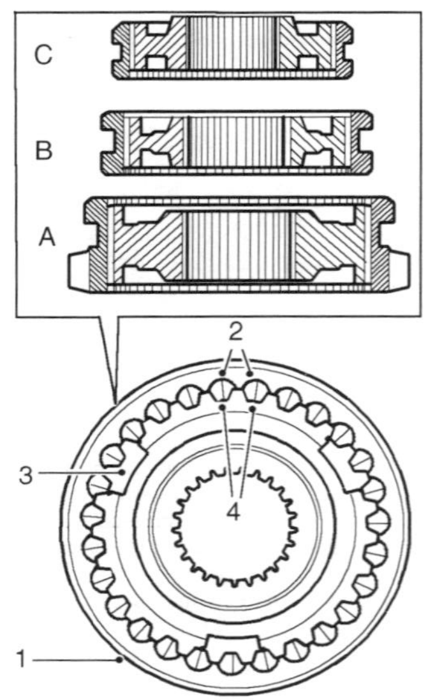

37M1271

Synchro Assembly Identification

A. 1st/2nd synchro
B. 3rd/4th synchro
C. 5th synchro

CAUTION: Keep component parts of each synchro assembly together.

1. Suitably mark relative position of each synchro hub to its respective sleeve.

NOTE: The synchro sleeve (1) incorporates 3 pairs of raised teeth (2) 120° apart. The synchro hub (3) incorporates 3 pairs of deeper grooves (4) 120° apart. The raised teeth on the synchro sleeve must always align with the deeper grooves in the synchro hub.

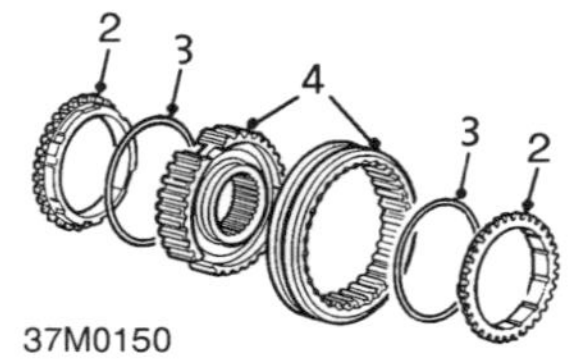

37M0150

2. Remove 2 synchro rings.
3. Remove 2 spring rings.

NOTE: Only one synchro ring and spring ring are fitted to 5th synchro.

4. Remove synchro hub from sleeve.

Selector shafts

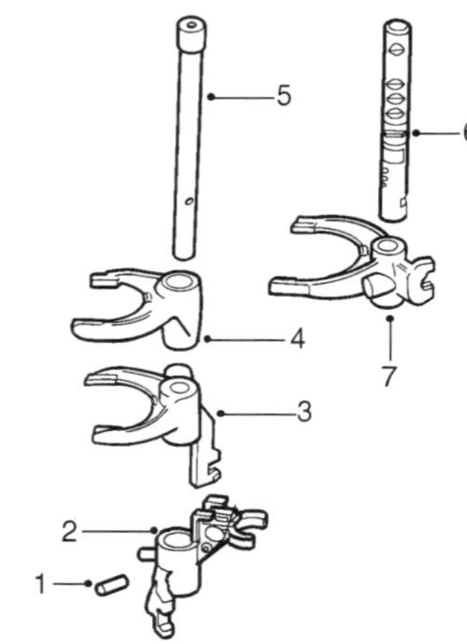

37M1261

Selector Shaft Components

1. Roll pin
2. 5th/reverse gear selector
3. 3rd/4th gear selector fork
4. 5th gear selector fork
5. 5th/reverse selector shaft
6. 1st/2nd gear selector shaft
7. 1st/2nd selector fork

1. Identify each selector fork and its fitted position to the relevant selector shaft. Slide 1st/2nd gear selector fork off 1st/2nd selector shaft.
2. Slide 1st/2nd selector shaft out of 5th gear selector fork and 5th/reverse gear selector.

3. Using a suitable pin punch, remove roll pin securing 5th/reverse gear selector; discard roll pin.
4. Slide 5th/reverse gear selector off 5th/reverse selector shaft.

NOTE: The 5th/reverse selector incorporates a lock plate, 2 screws and a return spring for reverse brake operation.

5. Slide 3rd/4th and 5th selector forks off 5th/reverse selector shaft.

5th/Reverse Selector

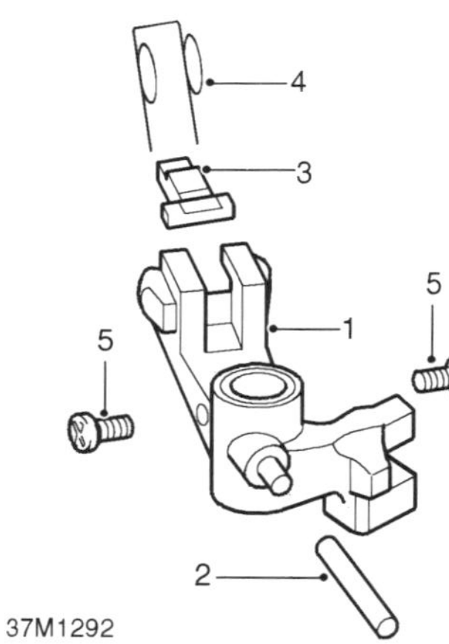

37M1292

The 5th/reversr selector (1) is secured to the 5th/reverse selector shaft by a roll pin (2). The selector incorporates the components for the reverse brake operation. This comprises of a lock plate (3) a retaining spring (4). The spring retains the lock plate in position, with the two ends of the spring located under two 'Taptite' screws (5) which are positioned either side of the 5th/reverse selector.

Interlock Assembly

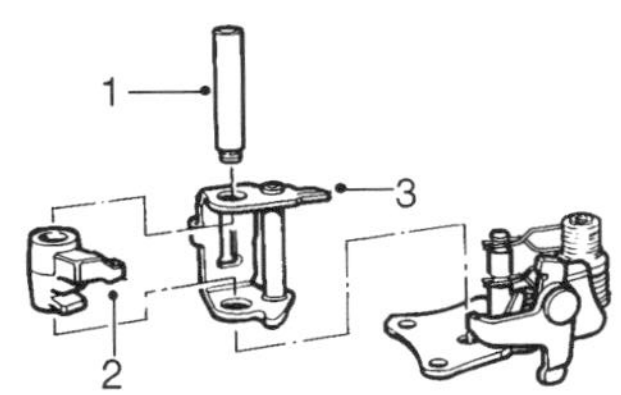

37M1273

1. Withdraw shift shaft from gearshift holder and arm guide.
2. Release lug on arm guide from slot in interlock.
3. Slide gearshift holder off arm guide.

Final Drive Gear and Carrier

1. Suitably mark fitted position of final drive gear to carrier.
2. Progressively slacken, then remove 10 bolts securing final drive gear to carrier, remove final drive gear.

NOTE: It is not necessary to remove the final drive gear from the carrier to remove the bearings.

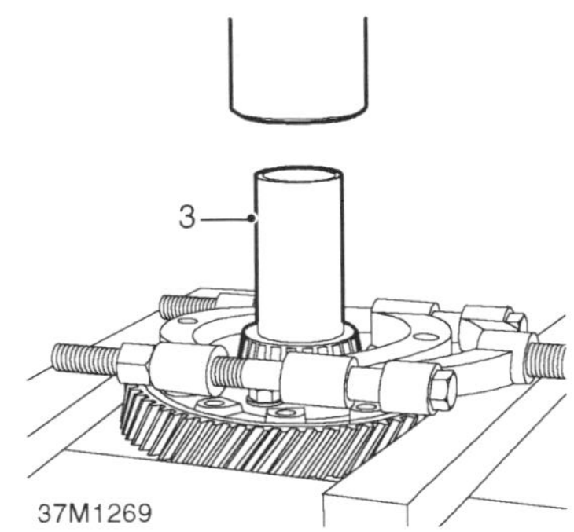

37M1269

3. Position bearing separator around bearing final drive gear side, position suitable adapter on splined inner hub and press from carrier, discard bearing.
4. Position bearing separator around carrier bearing, speedometer drive side, place assembly on press, position a suitable adapter on splined inner hub and press bearing from carrier, discard bearing.
5. Remove speedometer drive gear from carrier.

INSPECTING COMPONENTS

1. Clean all components ensuring all traces of RTV sealant are removed from gear case, clutch housing and access plug. Ensure oil drillings in input and output shafts and oil guide plates are clear. Ensure gearbox breather is unobstructed.

CAUTION: Do not clean plastic components with chlorinated solvent, e.g. tricloroethane.

2. Check speedometer drive for wear and pinion housing threads for damage.

Input and Output Shaft Assemblies

1. Check gears for worn or chipped teeth, cracks or uneven wear.
2. Check coning surfaces of gears for wear.
3. Check needle bearings for wear and overheating.

CAUTION: Where any of the above are evident, all gears and bearings on the shaft must be replaced.

4. Check shaft splines for wear and threads of output shaft for damage.
5. Check bearing collars for wear and damage.

Reverse Idler Shaft and Gear

1. Check idler shaft for wear.
2. Check gear for wear, chipping or cracking of teeth.
3. Check bearing bush for wear, replace idler gear as an assembly if wear is evident.

NOTE: The idler gear may have a bush or needle roller bearing fitted.

Synchro Assemblies

1. Check component parts of each synchro assembly for wear or damage, ensure teeth on hubs and sleeves are not chipped or rounded off.
2. Ensure teeth on synchro rings are not chipped or damaged, check inner surfaces of rings for wear.
3. Ensure each hub moves freely in its respective sleeve.
4. Place a synchro ring on its respective gear cone and rotate it until it grips (approximately 10 to 20°).

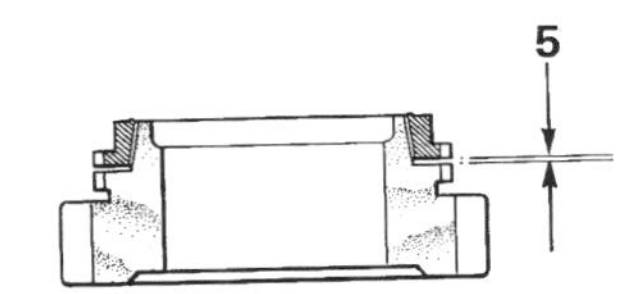

37M0155

5. Measure clearance between synchro ring and gear.
   Ring to gear clearance:
   Standard = 0.85 to 1.1 mm
   Service limit = 0.4 mm (minimum clearance)

6. Repeat for remaining rings and gears.

CAUTION: If any synchro ring to gear clearance is less than above service limit, fit a new synchro ring and recheck clearance.

Selector Shafts and Forks

1. Check shafts for wear and alignment.
2. Check selector forks for wear, cracks or damage.
3. Check the retained detent balls and springs, there must be no visible 'flats' on the balls and springs must keep balls in contact with the staked portion of the selector fork.

NOTE: It is not possible to replace balls or springs, selector fork must be replaced.

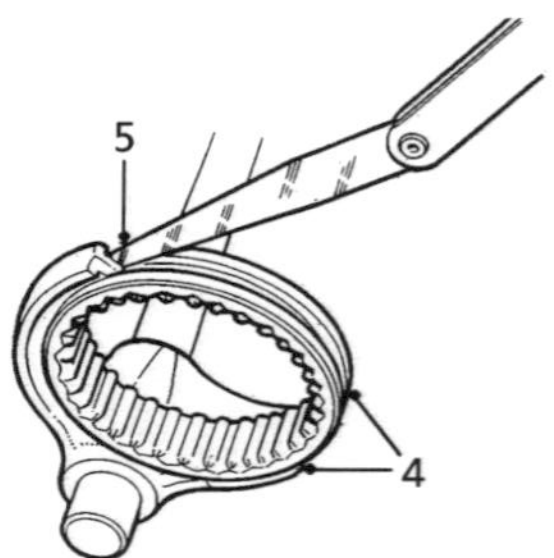

37M0156

4. Assemble each selector fork to its respective synchro sleeve.
5. Check clearance of selector fork in synchro sleeve groove.
   Selector fork to groove clearance:
   Standard = 0.45 to 0.65 mm
   Service limit = 1.0 mm

CAUTION: If clearance is found to exceed service limit, selector fork must be replaced.

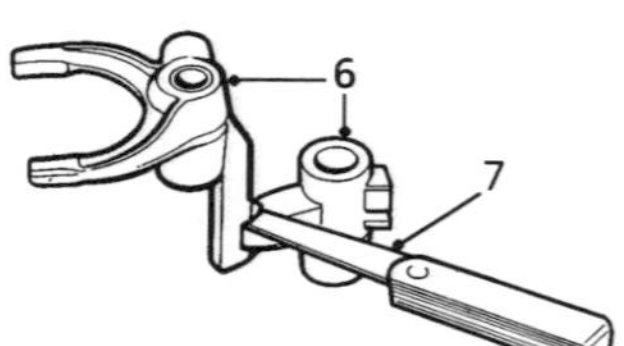

37M1156

6. Assemble gearshift arm guide to 3rd/4th selector fork.
7. Using feeler gauges, measure clearance between gearshift arm guide and fork.
   Standard = 0.2 to 0.5 mm
   Service limit = 0.8 mm
8. If clearance obtained exceeds service limit, measure width of tongue on gearshift arm guide.
   Standard = 11.9 to 12.0 mm

NOTE: If width of tongue is within limits, 3rd/4th selector fork must be replaced, if width of tongue is less than quoted, gearshift arm guide must be replaced.

9. Repeat above procedures for 1st/2nd selector fork.

Interlock Assembly

1. Check components for wear or damage, replace assembly if necessary.

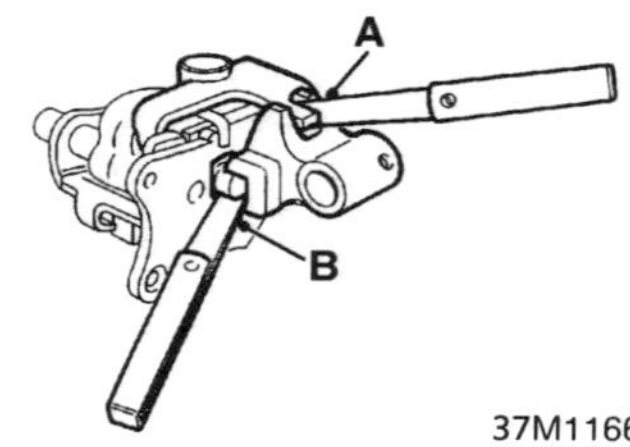

37M1166

2. Assemble gearshift arm guide to interlock assembly.
3. Using feeler gauges, measure clearance **A**.
   Clearance **A:**
   Standard = 0.02 to 0.3 mm
   Service limit = 0.55 mm
4. If clearance exceeds service limit, check width of groove in gearshift arm guide.
   Groove width = 13.05 to 13.25 mm

NOTE: If width of groove exceeds above dimension, gearshift arm guide must be replaced. If width of groove is within service limit, replace interlock assembly.

5. Using feeler gauges, measure clearance **B** between interlock ball and gearshift arm guide.
   Clearance **B:**
   Standard = 0.05 to 0.25 mm
   Service limit = 0.5 mm
6. If clearance exceeds service limit, measure outside diameter of interlock ball.
   Interlock ball outside diameter = 12.05 to 12.15 mm

CAUTION: If diameter of ball is within limits, replace gearshift arm guide, if diameter of ball is less than 12.05 mm, replace interlock assembly.

Final Drive Gear and Carrier Assembly

1. Check gear teeth on final drive gear for wear or chipping.
2. Check IRD and driveshaft output hub splines in bearing carrier for wear.
3. Check bearing rotation for smoothness and for excess movement.

CAUTION: It is not possible to overhaul the carrier. Replace complete assembly if splines or internal bearings are worn.

Clutch Housing

1. Check housing for damage, check and clean lubrication drilling for output shaft bearing, check that locating dowels are fitted; check clutch release shaft bushes for damage or wear and that shaft is free to turn, replace if necessary using the following procedure.

Remove

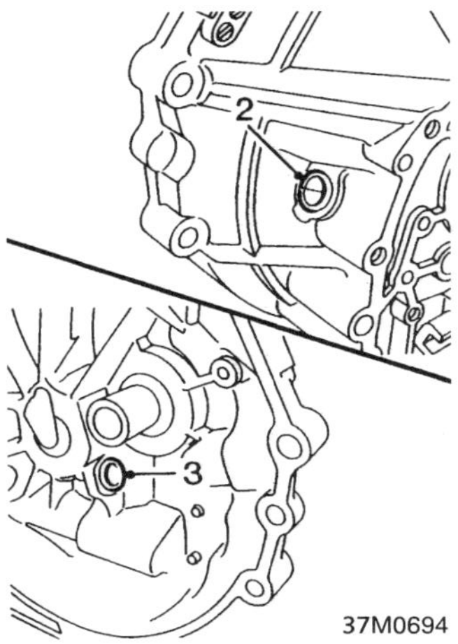

37M0694

2. *Outer bush:* Using a hacksaw blade, carefully cut a longitudinal slot opposite the split in the bush; prise bush out of clutch housing.
3. *Inner bush:* Carefully prise inner bush out of clutch housing.

Refit

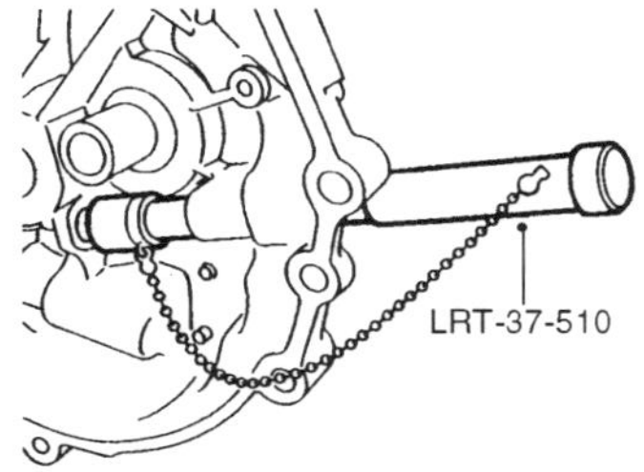

37M1255

4. *Inner bush:* Using tool **LRT-37-510,** drift inner bush into clutch housing.

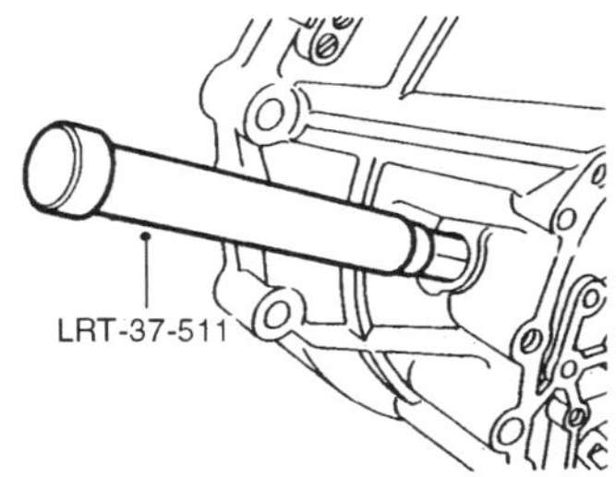

37M1256

5. *Outer bush:* Using tool **LRT-37-511,** drift outer bush into clutch housing.

CAUTION: Ensure end of tool LRT-37-511 is located in inner bush.

6. *Gearboxes fitted with output shaft bearing retainer plate:* Remove all traces of Patchlok compound from output shaft bearing retainer plate bolt holes using an M6 tap.

CAUTION: Ensure bolt holes are thoroughly cleaned.

7. Heat clutch housing to approximately to 100 °C using a hot air gun, and fit final drive carrier bearing track, making sure bearing track is fully seated in bearing recess.

Gear case

1. Fit non-selective shim in bearing recess.
2. Heat gear case to a approximately to 100°C using a hot air gun, and fit final drive carrier bearing track, making sure bearing track is fully seated against non-selective shim.

COMPONENT ASSEMBLING

Final Drive Gear and Carrier Assembly

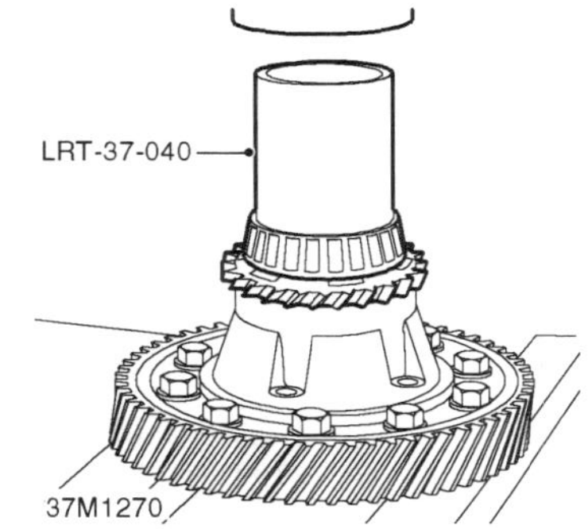

37M1270

1. Position speedometer drive onto carrier.
2. Position carrier assembly on press.
3. Press new bearings onto carrier using **LRT-37-040** adapter.
4. Align marks and fit final drive gear onto carrier.
5. Screw in and progressively tighten final drive gear retaining bolts to 110Nm.

Synchro Assemblies

1. Assemble each synchro hub to its respective sleeve ensuring that raised teeth on sleeve are aligned with the deeper grooves in hub.
2. Fit spring rings onto synchro rings.

NOTE: Only one spring ring is fitted on 5th speed synchro.

3. Assemble synchro rings to their respective synchro sleeves.

Selector Shafts

1. Slide 5th and 3rd/4th selector forks on to 5th/reverse selector shaft.

CAUTION: Ensure that longest portion of selector fork lugs face away from shoulder of shaft.

2. Ensure that the lock plate and return spring are correctly fitted, and slide 5th/reverse selector on to 5th/reverse selector shaft; secure selector with a new roll pin.
3. Slide 1st/2nd gear selector fork on to 1st/2nd selector shaft.
4. Locate 1st/2nd selector shaft in 5th/reverse gear selector and 5th gear selector fork.
5. Locate lug on shift arm guide in gearshift holder.
6. Position gearshift holder to interlock; fit shaft.

Reverse Idler Gear and Shaft

1. Fit a new thrust washer.
2. Lubricate idler gear bush with MTF94 gearbox oil.
3. Fit reverse idler gear to shaft.

NOTE: Boss on gear must face towards thrust washer.

Input Shaft

NOTE: Smear needle bearing rollers with petroleum jelly prior to assembly.

1. Fit needle bearing rollers in third gear.
2. Fit 3rd gear on shaft.
3. Fit 3rd/4th synchro assembly.
4. Fit needle bearing rollers in 4th gear, position gear on collar and fit assembly on shaft.
5. Fit needle bearing rollers in 5th gear, position gear on collar.

NOTE: Boss on 5th gear must face away from 4th gear.

6. Fit 5th synchro assembly.

NOTE: Machined groove in synchro hub must face towards 5th gear and large chamfer on synchro sleeve must face away from 5th gear, with the 3 pairs of raised teeth, 120°apart, in the coupling sleeve, aligned with the 3 pairs of deeper machined grooves, 120°apart, in the synchro hub.

CAUTION: It is possible to assemble the 5th gear synchro sleeve onto the hub with the 3 pairs of raised teeth aligned with the 3 machined cut-aways for the synchro ring lugs. This will prevent engagement of 5th gear when the gearbox is assembled.

7. Fit a new input shaft bearing.

Input Shaft Gear End-float - Check

1. Position input shaft on bed of a hand press with bearing located on a suitable socket.
2. Apply downward pressure to input shaft.

NOTE: Maintain pressure whilst checks are carried out.

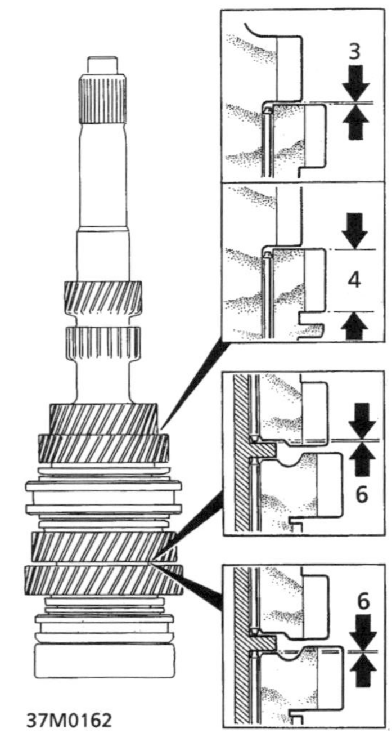

37M0162

3. Using feeler gauges, measure clearance between 2nd and 3rd gears.
3rd gear clearance:
Standard = 0.06 to 0.21 mm
Service limit = 0.3 mm
4. If clearance exceeds service limit, measure thickness of 3rd gear.
3rd gear thickness:
Standard = 35.42 to 35.47 mm
Service limit = 35.30 mm
5. If 3rd gear thickness is greater than service limit, replace 3rd gear synchro assembly; if thickness is less than service limit, replace 3rd gear.
6. Using feeler gauges, measure clearance between the spacer collar and 4th gear and spacer collar and 5th gear.
4th and 5th gear clearance:
Standard = 0.06 to 0.21 mm
Service limit = 0.3 mm

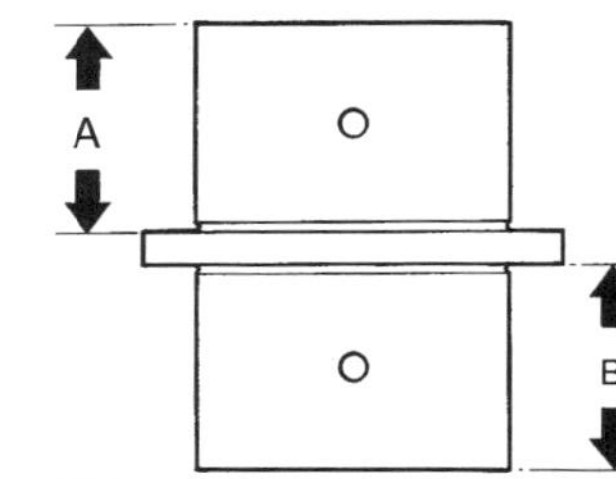

37M0163

7. If clearance of either gear exceeds service limit measure length of appropriate side of spacer collar **A** or **B**.
Length A = 4th gear side
Length B = 5th gear side
Spacer collar length **A** or **B**:
Standard = 26.03 to 26.08 mm
Service limit = 26.01 mm
8. If length **A** exceeds service limit, measure thickness of 4th gear.
4th gear thickness:
Standard = 30.92 to 30.97 mm
Service limit = 30.80 mm

9. If thickness of 4th gear exceeds service limit, replace 3rd/4th synchro assembly; if thickness of gear is less than service limit, replace gear.
10. If length **B** exceeds service limit, measure thickness of 5th gear.
    5th gear thickness:
    Standard = 30.42 to 30.47 mm
    Service limit = 30.30 mm

11. If thickness of 5th gear exceeds service limit, replace 5th synchro assembly; if thickness of gear is less than service limit, replace gear.

Output Shaft

NOTE: Smear needle bearing rollers with petroleum jelly prior to assembly.

1. Measure and record thickness of original thrust washer.
2. Fit original thrust washer on shaft.
3. Fit needle bearing rollers in 1st gear.
4. Fit 1st gear on shaft.
5. Fit 1st/2nd synchro assembly.

CAUTION: Ensure reverse gear on synchro sleeve is adjacent to 1st gear.

6. Measure and record length of 2nd gear collar.
7. Fit 2nd gear collar on shaft ensuring lubrication groove is towards 1st/2nd synchro assembly.
8. Fit needle bearing rollers in 2nd gear.
9. Fit 2nd gear on shaft.
10. Fit 3rd and 4th gears ensuring that bosses on gears are adjacent to each other.
11. Fit 5th gear ensuring that large boss on gear is towards threaded portion of shaft.
12. Fit new output shaft roller bearing and single ball race, (S7EMU gearbox) or double ball race (S4EM gearbox).
13. Fit a new tongued washer with dished side of washer towards bearing.
14. Secure output drive pinion of shaft in a soft-jawed vice.
15. Fit a new nut and tighten to 110 Nm.

NOTE: Nut has a LH thread; do not stake nut at this stage.

Output Shaft Gear End-float - Check

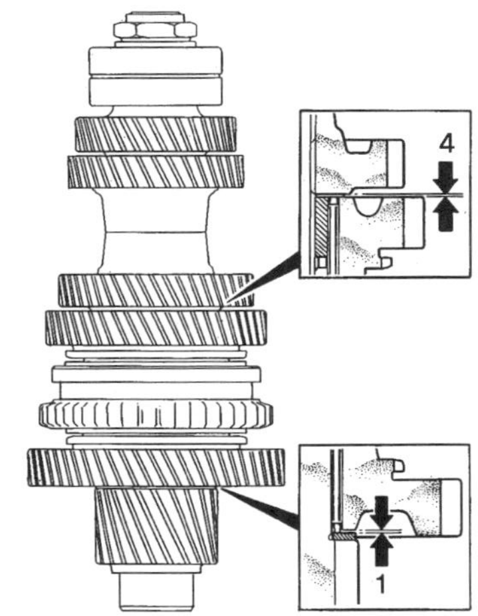

37M0164

1. Using feeler gauges measure clearance between 1st gear and thrust washer.
   Standard = 0.03 to 0.08 mm
   Service limit = 0.18 mm

2. From clearance obtained, calculate thickness of thrust washer required to give correct clearance. If clearance obtained exceeds service limit, fit a thicker thrust washer; if it is less than 0.03 mm, fit a thinner thrust washer.

NOTE: Thrust washers are available as follows:
1.96 to 2.08 mm thick in increments of 0.03 mm.

3. Select a thrust washer of the required thickness to bring end-float within limits.
4. Using feeler gauges measure clearance between 2nd and 3rd gears.
   2nd/3rd gear clearance = 0.03 to 0.10 mm

5. If clearance exceeds figure given, it will be necessary to fit a shorter 2nd gear collar; if clearance is less than figure given, it will be necessary to fit a longer collar.

6. Compare length of original collar and select a collar which will provide specified clearance. Collars are available in the following lengths: 28.99 mm and 29.04 mm

7. Having determined thickness of selective thrust washer and length of 2nd gear collar required, fit thrust washer and collar.
8. Secure output shaft nut by staking.

Input Shaft End thrust - Check and Adjust

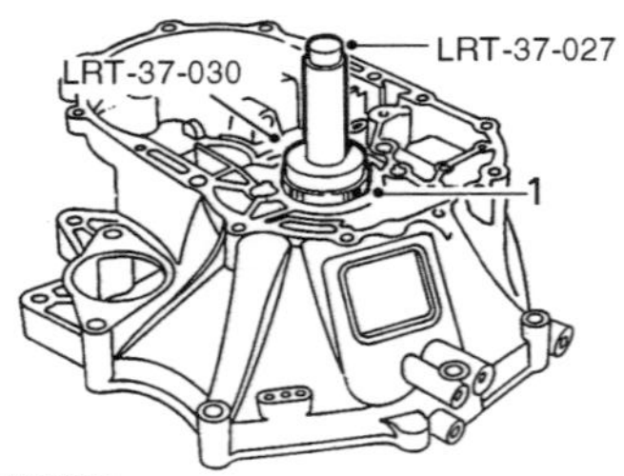

37M1257

1. Fit a new input shaft bearing in clutch housing using tools **LRT-37-027** and **LRT-37-030.**

CAUTION: Do not fit oil seal at this stage.

2. Position input shaft assembly in clutch housing ensuring it is fully inserted in bearing.

NOTE: Position housing so that end of shaft is clear of bench.

3. Fit gear case, fit and tighten bolts to 45 Nm.

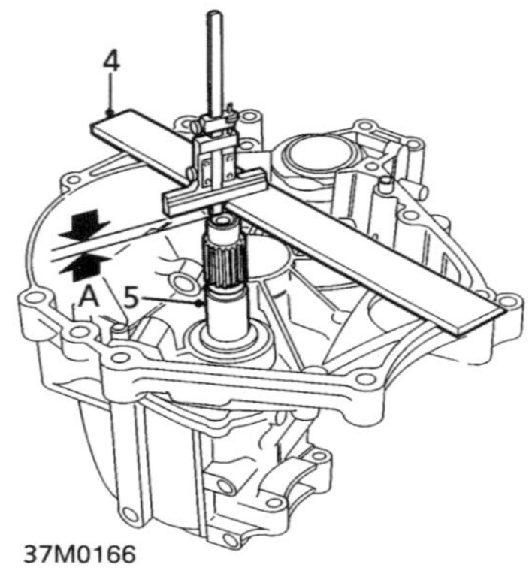

37M0166

4. Position a straight edge and depth gauge across face of clutch housing.
5. Pull input shaft into clutch housing and position end of depth gauge on end of shaft; record measurement shown on gauge.
6. Push input shaft towards gear case, record measurement shown on gauge.
7. Subtract first measurement from second measurement; record figure obtained. Call resultant measurement **A**.
8. Calculate thickness of circlip(s) required by subtracting 0.97 mm from dimension **A**.
   Input shaft end thrust = 0.14 to 0.21 mm

9. Select circlip(s) from sizes available which equal thickness required. Fourteen circlips are available ranging from 0.5 mm to 1.15 mm thick in increments of 0.05 mm.

NOTE: Two different outside diameter selective circlips are used, 75mm diameter for gearbox with S4EM prefix, and 78mm diameter for gearbox with S7EMU prefix. Ensure that the correct diameter circlips are used for each gearbox application.

CAUTION: No more than two circlips may be fitted. It is not always possible to select the exact thickness of circlips required; where this occurs, always fit a slightly thinner pack to avoid pre-loading bearings.

10. Remove bolts securing gear case; remove gear case.
11. Remove input shaft assembly.
12. Remove input shaft bearing from clutch housing.

GEARBOX ASSEMBLING

1. Lightly lubricate all components with MTF94 gearbox oil.

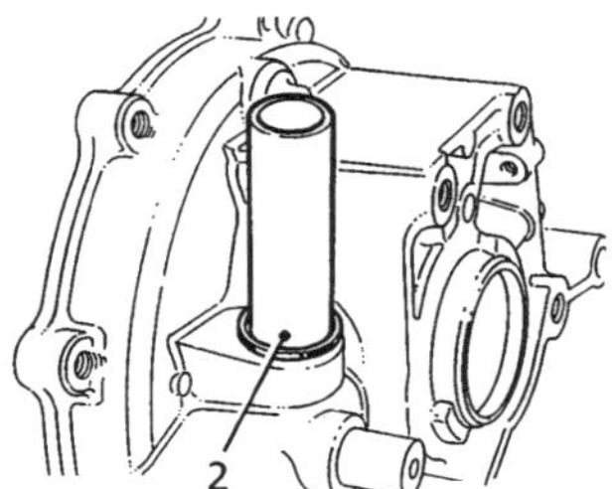

37M0174B

2. Using a suitable piece of tubing, fit a new selector shaft oil seal.
3. Fit output shaft oil guide plate in clutch housing.

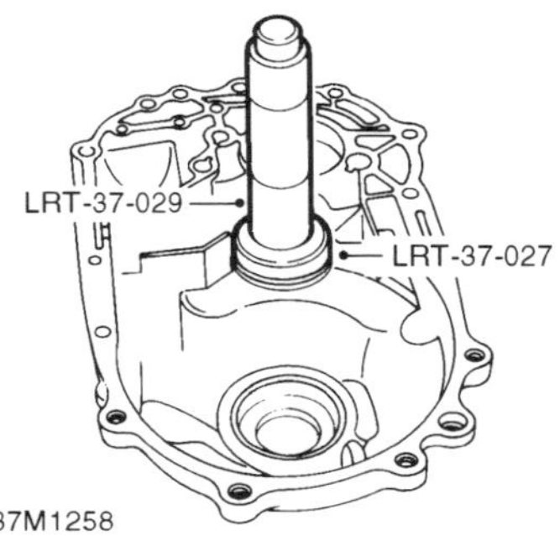

37M1258

4. Fit a new output shaft bearing in clutch housing using tools **LRT-37-027** and **LRT-37-029.**

NOTE: Depending on application, output shaft bearing may have oil holes drilled in bearing cage; these holes must face towards output shaft when fitting bearing. Bearings without the oil holes may be fitted either way round.

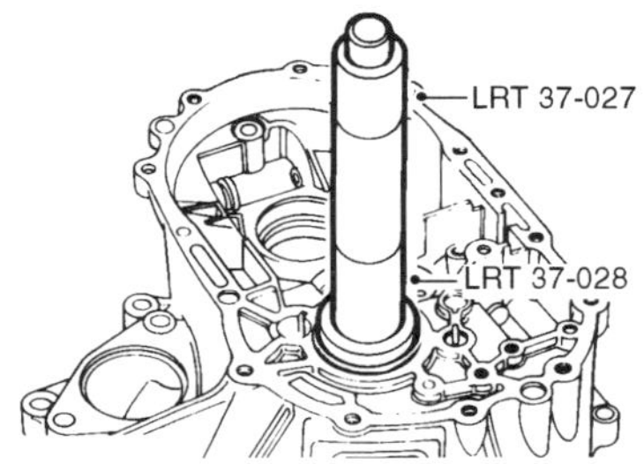

37M1259

5. Fit a new input shaft oil seal in clutch housing using tools **LRT-37-027** and **LRT-37-028.**

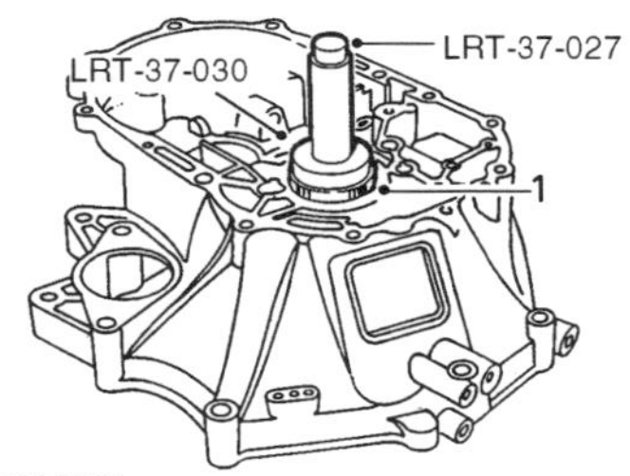

37M1257

6. Fit input shaft bearing into clutch housing using **LRT-37-027** and **LRT-37-030.**

7. Fit output shaft bearing retaining plate, (if fitted).

CAUTION: Ensure side marked TOP on retaining plate is facing towards output shaft.

8. Fit 2 new Patchlok bolts to secure bearing retaining plate; tighten bolts to 8 Nm.
9. Fit selector shaft and selector shaft guide.
10. Fit and tighten dowel bolt to 28 Nm.
11. Fit detent ball, spring and cap bolt, tighten bolt to 22 Nm.
12. Lubricate bearings with MTF94 gearbox oil and position final drive carrier assembly into clutch housing.
13. Wrap input shaft splines with masking tape to prevent damage to oil seal when fitting input shaft into clutch housing.
14. Place input and output shafts together and fit assembly in clutch housing.

NOTE: Position clutch housing so that the end of input shaft is clear of bench.

15. Remove masking tape from input shaft splines.
16. Ensure output shaft nut is staked.
17. Position gears in neutral.
18. Raise both shafts slightly and fit selector fork assembly, ensuring forks are located in each synchro sleeve groove.
19. Fit reverse idler gear, thrust washer and shaft.

NOTE: Large boss on idler gear faces towards clutch housing.

20. Fit reverse selector fork and bracket.
21. Fit and tighten retaining bolts.
22. Fit interlock assembly ensuring base of interlock locates in slot at lower end of 1st/2nd selector shaft.
23. Fit and tighten interlock retaining bolts.

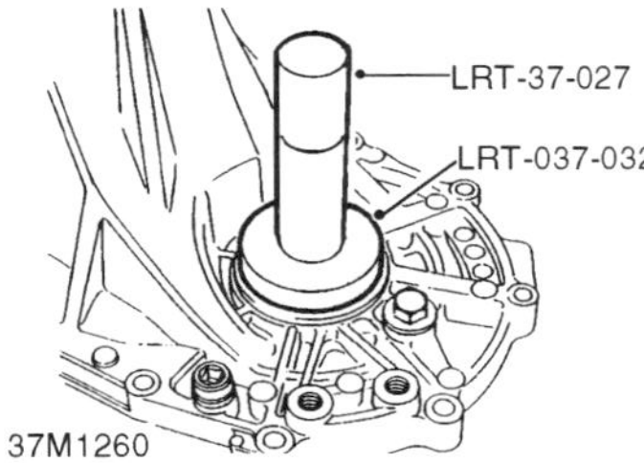

37M1260

24. Fit new oil seal in gear case using **LRT-37-027** and **LRT-37-032.**
25. Fit input shaft oil guide plate in gear case.
26. Fit a new Belleville washer.
27. Fit selected circlip(s).
28. Fit new output shaft circlip in gear case.
29. Apply a bead of RTV silicone sealant to mating face of gear case.

30. Position gear case over clutch housing keeping gear case square to clutch housing.
31. Lower gear case into position and at the same time, expand output shaft bearing circlip using tool **LRT-37-033.**
32. Push gear case fully down on to clutch housing, locating the dowels.
33. To ensure circlip is fully seated in groove in output shaft bearing, use a suitable lever and raise output shaft where a click will be heard as the circlip enters groove.
34. Fit and progressively tighten gear case bolts to 45 Nm.
35. Fit reverse idler shaft bolt with a new washer and tighten to 67Nm.
36. Apply thread sealant to access plug, fit and tighten plug using tool **LRT-37-035.**
37. Fit reverse light switch and new washer, tighten to 25 Nm.
38. Fit 1st gear switch, tighten to 25 Nm.
39. Fit speedometer drive pinion and housing, use a new 'O' ring; fit retaining plate, fit and tighten bolt to 5 Nm.
40. Fit new clutch release shaft oil seal.
41. Fit clutch release shaft and fork.
42. Fit release fork bolt and tighten to 29 Nm.

DATA

Reverse idler gear to selector fork clearance	0.5 to 1.1 mm
Selector fork prong width	13.0 to 13.3 mm
Selector fork groove to pin clearance:	
Standard	0.05 to 0.35 mm
Service limit	0.5 mm
Selector fork groove width	7.05 to 7.25 mm
Gearshift arm to guide clearance:	
Standard	0.2 to 0.3 mm
Service limit	0.55 mm
Interlock shift guide groove width	8.1 to 8.2 mm
Synchro ring to gear clearance:	
Standard	0.85 to 1.1 mm
Service limit (minimum clearance)	0.4 mm
Selector shaft forks in synchro sleeve grooves clearance:	
Standard	0.45 to 0.65 mm
Service limit	1.0 mm
Gearshift arm guide to selector fork clearance:	
Standard	0.2 to 0.5 mm
Service limit	0.8 mm
Gearshift arm guide tongue width	11.9 to 12.0 mm
Gearshift arm guide to interlock assembly clearance:	
Standard	0.05 to 0.35 mm
Service limit	0.6 mm
Gearshift arm guide groove width	13.05 to 13.25 mm
Interlock ball to gearshift arm guide clearance:	
Standard	0.05 to 0.25 mm
Service limit	0.5 mm
Interlock ball outside diameter	12.05 to 12.15 mm
2nd to 3rd gear clearance:	
Standard	0.06 to 0.21 mm
Service limit	0.3 mm
3rd gear thickness:	
Standard	35.42 to 35.47 mm
Service limit	35.30 mm
4th to 5th gear clearance:	
Standard	0.06 to 0.21 mm
Service limit	0.3 mm
Spacer collar length:	
Standard	26.03 to 26.08 mm
Service limit	26.01 mm
4th gear thickness:	
Standard	30.92 to 30.97 mm
Service limit	30.80 mm
5th gear thickness	
Standard	30.42 to 30.47 mm
Service limit	30.30 mm
1st gear to thrust washer clearance:	
Standard	0.03 to 0.08 mm
Service limit	0.18 mm
2nd to 3rd gear clearance	0.03 to 0.10 mm
Input shaft end thrust	0.14 to 0.21 mm

TORQUE SETTINGS

Output shaft nut - L.H. thread	110 Nm
Gear case to clutch housing bolts	45 Nm
Selector shaft guide to selector shaft bolt	28 Nm
Cap bolt - detent ball and spring	22 Nm
Reverse idler shaft bolt	67 Nm
Speedometer drive pinion retaining plate bolt	5 Nm
Reverse light switch	25 Nm
First gear switch	25 Nm
Clutch release shaft pivot bolt	29 Nm
Final drive gear to carrier bolts	110 Nm
Output shaft bearing retainer bolts - if fitted	8 Nm

TOOL NUMBERS

LRT-99-004	Slide hammer
LRT-37-026	Adapter - Slide hammer
LRT-37-027	Driver handle (main tool)
LRT-37-028	Input shaft oil seal replacer
LRT-37-029	Adapter - Bearing replacer
LRT-37-030	Adapter - Input shaft clutch housing bearing
LRT-37-032	Adapter - Gear case oil seal replacer
LRT-37-033	Circlip pliers
LRT-37-035	14 mm Hex key - access plug
LRT-37-036	Anti-spread plate
LRT-37-040	Adapter - Carrier bearing replacer
LRT-37-510	Clutch release shaft inner bush replacer
LRT-37-511	Clutch release shaft outer bush replacer

Distributed by Brooklands Books Ltd., PO Box 146, Cobham, Surrey, KT11 1LG, England Phone: 01932 865051 Fax: 01932 868803
E-mail: sales@brooklands-books.com

Part No. LRL 0144 ENG (5th Edition) plus LRL 0157, LRL 0158 and LRL 0159

ISBN 1 85520 6153 10/7Z2

Printed in England Ref: B-LRF1WH